Every Decker book is accompanied by a CD-ROM.

The disk appears in the front of each copy, in its own sealed jacket. Affixed to the front of the book will be a distinctive BcD sticker **"Book *cum* disk"**.

The disk contains the complete text and illustrations of the book, in fully searchable PDF files. As an added feature, an extended bibliography from the textbook is also included. The book and disk will be sold *only* as a package; neither will be available independently, and no prices will be available for the items individually.

B C Decker Inc is committed to providing high quality electronic publications that will compliment traditional information and learning methods.

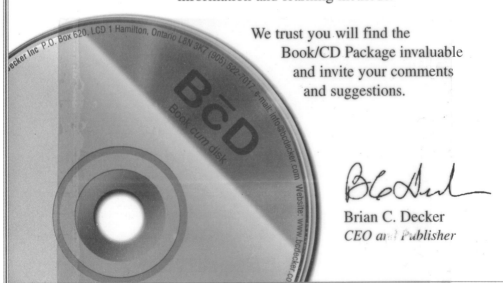

We trust you will find the Book/CD Package invaluable and invite your comments and suggestions.

Brian C. Decker
CEO and Publisher

Cutaneous Medicine

Cutaneous Manifestations of Systemic Disease

Cutaneous Medicine

Cutaneous Manifestations of Systemic Disease

THOMAS T. PROVOST, MD
Professor
Department of Dermatology
Johns Hopkins Medical Institutions
Baltimore, Maryland

JOHN A. FLYNN, MD
Associate Professor
Department of Medicine
Johns Hopkins Medical Institutions
Baltimore, Maryland

2001
BC Decker Inc.
Hamilton • London

B.C. Decker Inc.
20 Hughson Street South
P.O. Box 620, L.C.D. 1
Hamilton, Ontario L8N 3K7
Tel: 905-522-7017; 1-800-568-7281
Fax: 905-522-7839
E-mail: info@bcdecker.com
Website: www.bcdecker.com

00 01 / FP / 9 8 7 6 5 4 3 2 1

ISBN 1-55009-100-X
Printed in Canada

Sales and Distribution

United States
B.C. Decker Inc.
P.O. Box 785
Lewiston, NY 14092-0785
Tel: 905-522-7017 / 1-800-568-7281
Fax: 905-522-7839
E-mail: info@bcdecker.com
Website: www.bcdecker.com

Canada
B.C. Decker Inc.
20 Hughson Street South
P.O. Box 620, L.C.D. 1
Hamilton, Ontario L8N 3K7
Tel: 905-522-7017 / 1-800-568-7281
Fax: 905-522-7839
E-mail: info@bcdecker.com
Website: www.bcdecker.com

Foreign Rights
John Scott & Company
International Publishers' Agency
P.O. Box 878
Kimberton, PA 19442
Tel: 610-827-1640
Fax: 610-827-1671

U.K., Europe, Scandinavia, Middle East
Harcourt Publishers Limited
Customer Service Department
Foots Cray High Street
Sidcup, Kent
DA14 5HP, UK
Tel: 44 (0) 208 308 5760
Fax: 44 (0) 181 308 5702
E-mail: cservice@harcourt_brace.com

Australia, New Zealand
Harcourt Australia Pty. Limited
Customer Service Department
STM Division
Locked Bag 16
St. Peters, New South Wales, 2044
Australia
Tel: (02) 9517-8999
Fax: (02) 9517-2249
E-mail: stmp@harcourt.com.au
Website: www.harcourt.com.au

Japan
Igaku-Shoin Ltd.
Foreign Publications Department
3-24-17 Hongo
Bunkyo-ku,Tokyo, Japan 113-8719
Tel: 3 3817 5680
Fax: 3 3815 6776
E-mail: fd@igaku.shoin.co.jp

Singapore, Malaysia, Thailand, Philippines, Indonesia, Vietnam, Pacific Rim, Korea
Harcourt Asia Pte Limited
583 Orchard Road
#09/01, Forum
Singapore 238884
Tel: 65-737-3593
Fax: 65-753-2145

Dedication

This book is dedicated to Charles T. Provost, Richard S. Ross, Benjamin A. and William T. Peters.

Charles T. Provost, M.D., 1905 to 1977, a "good doc" and my intellectual rudder, encouraged me to form opinions, to express them honestly, to openly act upon them, and to accept responsibility for the consequences. His simplistic, honest, straight-forward code of morality lives on in the Federal Bureau of Investigation, the United States Department of Health and Human Services, and the legal profession through his grandchildren Charles "Chip"Provost, Christie Peters, and Tom "T" Provost.

Richard S. Ross, M.D., dean of the medical school, Johns Hopkins Medical Institutions, from 1975 to 1989, was a great leader with a strong intellect and moral courage, wise counselor, and friend of dermatology. His intact ego and dedication to academic excellence caused him to recruit vigorous, outspoken, highly accomplished basic and clinical departmental chiefs.

He once commented his chiefs couldn't agree on the time of day. Of course, he was wrong! We had complete trust that he or his friend Richard Johns, M.D., would alert us to institutional problems, allowing us to concentrate our efforts

on the development of our departments. He, more than anyone else, is responsible for putting in place the faculty that has gained The Johns Hopkins Hospital recognition as the leading hospital in the United States.

Benjamin A. and William T. Peters, two bright, energetic children, are the delight of their parents, uncles, and grandmother, Carol. I hope, in addition to the strong intellectual and moral guidance of their parents, Gene and Christie, their uncles, and grandmother Carol, that they know and work with men and women of the intellectual fervor and character of their great-grandfather C.T. Provost and Dean Richard S. Ross.

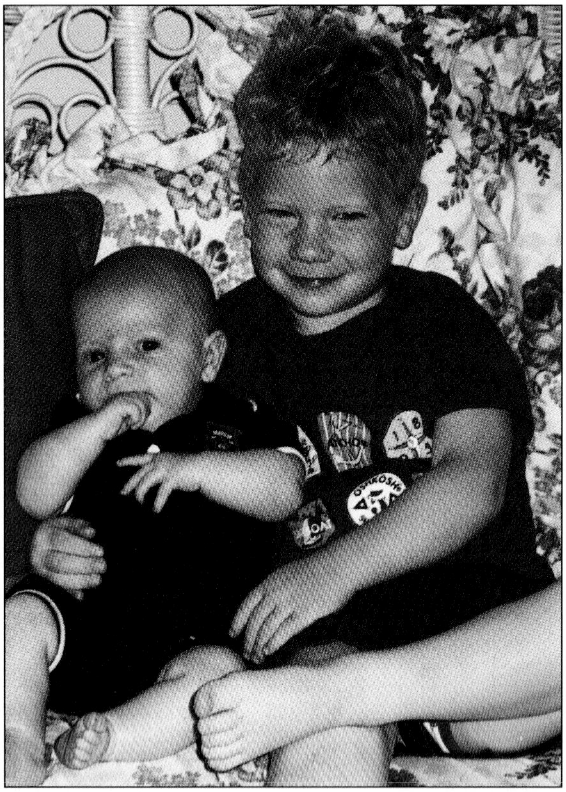

Contents

Foreword

As a first-year resident almost 50 years ago, I quickly learned that dermatology was defined as "the study of the skin *and* its contents." The dermatology resident was trained, or more properly, educated to be a consultant like the cardiologist or gastroenterologist, the only difference being the organ or system on which primary interest was focused. Major attention was given to the cutaneous manifestations of systemic diseases so that the consultant dermatologist had to be knowledgeable about internal medicine, psychiatry, opththalmology, obstetrics and gynecology, and virtually all other medical and surgical specialties. The obvious stimulus for this approach was that dermatologists were also syphilologists, and in the words of Sir William Osler, "To know syphilis is to know medicine." In those days, dermatology residents and faculty were indistinguishalbe from their medical colleagues. Dangling out of the pocket of the white coats were a reflex hammer, often an ophthalmoscope, and always a stethoscope. Incidentally, the pocket was generally the preferred "holster" for carrying the latter, rather than the current mode of having it dangle around the neck.

With the availability of penicillin and its almost universal ability to cure syphilis in all its stages, the incidence and prevalence of the disease rapidly declined, there by eliminating a significant percentage of many dermatologists' practice, as well as the incentive to devote up to one third of residency training to the disease. A concomitant effect was the loss of the need to emphasize training in the skin signs of systemic disease and in internal medicine. However, most training programs in the 1950s and 1960s still maintained large inpatient services, mostly for treating severe psoriasis or atopic dermatitis. Because residents were usually required to obtain a complete history and perform a complete physical examination of each of these patients on admission, and to care for their intercurrent illnesses while in the hospital, at least some experience in internal medicine remained part of their training.

Soon thereafter, two phenomena emerged that would drastically affect the scope and practice of dermatology. These were the development of more effective outpatient treatments for psoriasis, including both drugs and psoralen plus ultraviolet A; and the introduction of managed cared, first by Medicare in the

United States, and then by the private insurance sector. Within a few years, the inpatient dermatology services at academic medical centers withered and, in some cases, actually became extinct. Thus, what little exposure residents had to internal medicine was further diminished. With little knowledge, lack of interest naturally followed, so it is no wonder that rheumatologists rather than dermatologists quickly assumed responsibility for the total care of patients with lupus erythematosus, scleroderma, and dermatomyositis. It was not that these patients were "lost" to dermatologists, but rather that they were surrendered by the young dermatologists unprepared to deal with their many problems.

What would replace this patient population as the number of practicing dermatologists rapidly increased during this period? The introduction of fresh tissue Mohs' micrographic surgery, therapeutic and cosmetic modalities, the establishment of special surgical training requirements during residency by the American Board of Dermatology, and the institution of postgraduate training programs in dermatologic surgery — all contributed enormously to the decline of medical dermatology. Dermatology residents quickly learned that cognitive procedures were poorly and often slowly compensated, whereas even the most simple cosmetic procedures produced "cash on the barrel." The newly trained dermatologists faced with large educational debts, while having to support a young and growing family following 12 years of spartan existence. It is little wonder that many young dermatologists choose to pursue a practice emphasizing cosmetic procedures upon a wealthy, aging population committed to remaining youthful in appearance.

Still, the future of medical dermatology is bright. Although medical dermatologists like Tom Provost may be viewed as a "*vox clamantis in deserto*", he is not alone, as his multiauthored book clearly indicates. Why am I as optimistic about the future of dermatology as I am enamored of its past? The major reason is that nonsurgical cutaneous disease will continue to be prevalent, new diagnostic and therapeutic modalities will continue to be introduced, and advances in therapy in every field of medicine (e. g. cytokines, antibiotics, chemotherapy, immunosuppressives) will continue to produce unique and previously undescribed cutaneous reactions. This, combined with the ever-increasing aging population who are the heaviest consumers of health care and who demand the "latest and the best" therapy, will further the demand for services of the medical dermatologist. My prediction is that the well-trained medical dermatologist may occupy one of the few positions in medicine without competition regardless of the health care system that eventually emerges in the United States.

Richard L. Dobson, MD
Emeritus Professor and Chairman
Department of Dermatology
Medical College of South Carolina
Emeritus Editor
The Journal of the American Academy of Dermatology

Preface

In the summer of 1966, at the strong urging of my good friend Paul Porter, I began my dermatology career as a resident at Dartmouth. Otis Field Jillson, a gifted physician and the director, was planning to write a book. (This was the era prior to Rook and Fitzpatrick's landmark textbooks and Irwin Braverman's monumental personal treatise.)

Besides his acknowledged expertise as a clinical dermatologist, Otis had a keen interest in mycology and allergic diseases. He had no laboratory training but was a voracious reader of the medical literature and was conceptually very bright! He had made keen clinical observations on photoallergic contact dermatitis, the "persistent light reactor," and phytophotodermatitis. He had observed that ultraviolet light was capable of suppressing an allergic contact cutaneous reaction and that some mycosis fungoides patients, following a sunburn, experienced a transient resolution of their disease.

He was a master teacher interested in careers of his residents. He encouraged me to read everything I could about *Candida albicans* and thymoma in order to understand why a thymoma patient had developed a widespread *C. albicans* of her skin. He believed there was an immunologic relationship. He further commented that if I understood the relationship between candidiasis and a thymoma, I might discover a career for myself and, in doing so, help some patients. I have never received better advice!

Otis believed he could bring special insight to the discussion of a number of dermatologic diseases. I had expected to spend many hours during my residency in the library researching topics and learning to write a cogent English sentence.

In retrospect, for several reasons (none good) that book was never written. However, I continued to collect selected reprints and, as my interests grew, expanded my reprint files on internal medicine and dermatology to include immunology and molecular biology. As time passed, I decided that at the end of my academic career, I would write a book on cutaneous medicine to hopefully add a small amount of special insight to the discussion of several dermatologic diseases. Thus, in one sense, this is the book I had planned to write 30 years ago.

During my career, I have enjoyed immensely the explosion in our medical database as recorded in the various editions of the classic textbooks edited by the senior editors Rook and Fitzpatrick. They are truly scholarly efforts of the first magnitude.

After having spent the better part of 5 years organizing and writing this text, I am continually amazed at the intellectual prowess of Irwin Braverman that has allowed him to singlehandedly produce multiple editions of a highly factual, personal, authoritative treatise on *Cutaneous Signs of Systemic Diseases*.

During my academic career, I have become associated with many "good docs"—physicians who are or were masters of their speciality and took great pride in the practice of medicine. These physicians included Jack D. Myers (University of Pittsburgh), Alan Tisdale, Walter Fry, and John Milne (Dartmouth), Robert Kellum and Raymond Suskind (Oregon), Ray Partridge (who taught me a good deal of rheumatology), and Earl DeCoteau, Steve Hauptman, John Maize, Mike Apicella, Jim Allen, and Jim Nolan (Buffalo).

I am also indebted to scientists who have opened their laboratories to me: Gordon Caron (Oregon); Thomas B. Tomasi Jr. (Buffalo); and William Earnshaw (Johns Hopkins). I am especially indebted to Morris Reichlin for a long collaborative relationship and friendship in which we have experienced some heartaches and a modicum of success, but no matter our academic fortunes, we always took pride in and enjoyed our work.

Richard Dobson, a resident of Otis Jellson and Walter Lobitz at Dartmouth, taught me the meaning of being a good departmental chairman (Buffalo). Despite all the business aspects that now engulf a department chairman, "your most important job is to identify and recruit very smart residents and faculty (maintain and enhance the academic standards) and to push and promote their development. The accomplishments of the residents and faculty, not your own, propel[s] the department forward. In essence, you work for your faculty and residents—not the reverse."

During my 15-year tenure as chief of Dermatology at Johns Hopkins, in addition to developing a broad based department, I attempted to create and foster the development of a cadre of academic dermatologists with extensive training in both dermatology and internal medicine. At the Johns Hopkins Medical Institutions, we have a significant patient base to warrant such specialized people. My recruitment grounds for residents were the internal medicine services at Johns Hopkins. With the tacit, albeit grudging, approval of Victor McKusick and, later, John Stobo, each chairman of Internal Medicine, we enjoyed some success. In addition, the treatment of complex patients allowed our department faculty on a daily basis to form close working relationships with members of the Department of Internal Medicine. More recently, as medical director of a satellite, Johns Hopkins at Greenspring Station, I developed additional close ties with many part- and full-time Hopkins "good docs."

Based on these close ties, I was able to recruit physicians from other specialities, but especially internal medicine, to help me with this project.

In the final sense, this book, *Cutaneous Medicine*, is a signature book of the Johns Hopkins Department of Dermatology, at least during my tenure as chief.

We committed our most precious resource to develop this area of excellence—time. To paraphrase Barbara Streisand, "It was the way we were."

This book is designed to be a highly factual, readable text for dermatologic and internal medicine physicians. There are obviously subject matters that we have overlooked, treated too lightly, or overindulged. Our intent was to be as inclusive and balanced as possible, I, alone, however, as the senior editor, am responsible for these deficiencies.

In order to make the book more readable, we have employed an outline in the left-hand margin of the adjacent text, and encouraged our contributors to make liberal use of figures and tables. We have employed an annotated rather than authoritative bibliography to permit contributors to further emphasize points of interest and to permit ease of insertion of the latest data without disturbing large areas of text during the galley proof. An extended bibliography can be found on the CD-ROM accompanying this book.

As senior editor, I wish to thank all members of the Johns Hopkins faculty, past and present, for their contributions. I especially would like to thank Malcolm Greaves, who spent several months on sabbatical in our department and who was pressed into service (analogous to, but the reversal of, the situation that led to the War of 1812 with Great Britain).

I am especially indebted to John Flynn, director of the Division of General Internal Medicine, Department of Internal Medicine, Johns Hopkins Medical Institutions, for helping me organize the contributions of the many collaborators.

I also want to acknowledge the special role that Dr. Matthew Katz played in organizing a large collection of slides that residents at the Dartmouth affiliated hospitals, at the State University of Buffalo, and at Johns Hopkins had collected over the years. I also want to thank Dr. Rick Stearns (Tulsa, OK) for the many slides he has sent me over the years. Finally, I want to acknowledge the contributions of the late Dr. Raymond C. "Vale" Robinson. He had died the year before I came to Hopkins. His personal slide collection was in the bottom of a file cabinet. When I became departmental chairman, I learned of their existence but never had time to organize them until now.

A special thanks goes to Mary Daly, Joan McKew, Ellie Ziemba, and Linda Dovan for obtaining and copying additional references and for "guarding the files."

Patricia Lally provided technical competence, which proved invaluable to this computer illiterate. Her continued good humor allowed her to deal with my many requests. This is her third book in this department. However, none of her previous experiences prepared her for this undertaking!

I am also honored and touched that unsolicited patients, Constantine Dracopoulos, his son Andreas Dracopoulos, and Jon and Courtney Syzmanski, upon learning of this project, generously provided financial support.

Robert Jordon (chairman of Dermatology, University of Texas at Houston) once commented to me that our two academic careers were like riding a fast horse—the scenery was a blur. We didn't have time to enjoy developments outside of our own personal involvement. However, during the past 5 years, the writing of this book has provided me time to enjoy.

Contributors

Jihad M. Al Hariri, MD
Instructor, Dermatology
Johns Hopkins Medical Institutions
Baltimore, Maryland

Grant J. Anhalt, MD
Professor of Dermatology & Pathology
Johns Hopkins University School of Medicine
Baltimore, Maryland

Frank C. Arnett, MD
Professor of Internal Medicine and Director
Division of Rheumatology
University of Texas Medical School at Houston
Houston, Texas

Paul G. Auwaerter, MD
Assistant Professor of Medicine
Johns Hopkins University School of Medicine
Johns Hopkins Hospital

Lisa A. Beck, MD
Assistant Professor of Medicine and Dermatology
Johns Hopkins Asthma and Allergy Centre
Baltimore, Maryland

William R. Bell, MD, PhD
Professor of Medicine, Radiology, Oncology, Nuclear Medicine
Clinical Director
Division of Hematology
Department of Medicine
Johns Hopkins University School of Medicine
Baltimore, Maryland

Michael S. Boyne, MD, FRCPC
Lecturer in Endocrinology/Metabolism
University Hospital of the West Indies
Kingston, Jamaica

Michael R. Clark, MD, MPH
Associate Professor
Department of Psychiatry & Behavioral Sciences
Johns Hopkins Hospital
Baltimore, Maryland

Bernard A. Cohen, MD
Associate Professor of Pediatrics and Dermatology
Director Pediatric Dermatology
Johns Hopkins Childrens Center
Johns Hopkins Hospital
Baltimore, Maryland

Russell L. Corio, DDS, MSD, MA
Associate Professor in Dermatology, Pathology, Otolaryngology
Johns Hopkins Medical Institutions
Baltimore, Maryland

Adrian S. Dobs, MD
Johns Hopkins University School of Medicine
Baltimore, Maryland

Evan F. Farmer, MD
Norins Professor and Chairman
Department of Dermatology
Indiana University School of Medicine
University Hospital
Indianapolis, Indiana

John A. Flynn, MD
Associate Professor
Department of Medicine
Johns Hopkins Medical Institutions
Baltimore, Maryland

Rene Genadry, MD
Associate Professor, Gynecology and Obstetrics
Johns Hopkins School of Medicine
Baltimore, Maryland

Steve N. Georas, MD
Assistant Professor of Medicine
Division of Pulmonary and Critical Care
Johns Hopkins Asthma and Allergy Center
Johns Hopkins Hospital
Baltimore, Maryland

Adam S. Geyer, MD
St. Vincent's Hospital
New York, New York

Francis M Giardiello, MD
Johns Hopkins University School of Medicine
Baltimore, Maryland

Amy H. Gordon, MD
Instructor, Department of Medicine
Johns Hopkins Medical Institutions
Baltimore, Maryland

Malcolm W. Greaves, MD
Dean Ereritus
St. Johns Institute of Dermatology
St. Thomas Hospital
London, United Kingdom

Ginna V. Hanna, MD
Assistant Professor
Division of Maternal-Fetal Medicine
Department of Gynecology/Obstetrics
Johns Hopkins Hospital
Baltimore, Maryland

Mary L. Harris, MD
Associate Professor, Medicine
Johns Hopkins Medical Institutions
Baltimore, Maryland

David B. Hellmann, MD, FACP
Chairman, Department of Medicine
Physician in Chief
Johns Hopkins Bayview Medical Center
Mary Betty Stevens Professor of Medicine
Johns Hopkins University
Baltimore, Maryland

H. Franklin Herlong, MD
Associate Dean for Student Affairs
Associate Professor of Medicine
Johns Hopkins University School of Medicine
Baltimore, Maryland

Antoinette F. Hood, MD
Professor of Dermatology
Director of Dermatopathology
Indiana University School of Medicine
Indianapolis, Indiana

Thomas D. Horn, MD
Professor of Dermatology and Pathology
Chairman, Department of Dermatology
University of Arkansas for Medical Sciences
Little Rock, Arkinsas

Karen Huhn, MD
Associate Professor
Departments of Dermatology and Pathology
Johns Hopkins Medical Institutions
Baltimore, Maryland

Richard L. Humphrey
Associate Professor of Internal Medicine,
Oncology & Pathology
Johns Hopkins University School of Medicine
Associate Professor Health Policiy & Management
Johns Hopkins University School of Public Health

Susan E. Koch, MD
Adjunt Associate Professor of Dermatology
Oregon Health Sciences University
Portland, Oregon

Alan S. Krasner, MD
Associate Director
Department of Clinical Research
Pfizer Incorporated
Groton, Connecticut

Susan D. Laman, MD
Assistant Professor
Dermatology
Johns Hopkins University
Baltimore, Maryland

Julie R. Lange, MD
Assistant Professor of Surgery
Johns Hopkins Medical Institutions
Johns Hopkins Hospital, Department of Surgery
Baltimore, Maryland

Simeon Margolis, MD, PhD
Professor, Department of Medicine
Johns Hopkins Medical Institutions
Baltimore, Maryland

Don R. Martin, MD
Johns Hopkins University School of Medicine
Johns Hopkins Hospital
Baltimore, Maryland

Ciro R. Martins, MD
Assistant Professor
Department of Dermatology
Johns Hopkins Medical Institutions
Baltimore, Maryland

Stanley J. Miller, MD
Assistant Professor of Dermatology
Department of Dermatology
Johns Hopkins Medical Institutions
Baltimore, Maryland

David R. Moller, MD
Associate Professor
Department of Internal Medicine
Johns Hopkins Medical Institutions
Baltimore, Maryland

Warwick L. Morison, MD
Professor in Dermatology
Johns Hopkins Medical Institutions
Baltimore, Maryland

Andrew M. Munster, MD
Professor
Department of Surgery and Plastic Surgery
John Hopkins Medical Institutions
Baltimore, Maryland

Ken Nagamoto, MD
Minneapolis, Minnesota

Hossein C. Nousari, MD
Assistant Professor in Dermatology
and Medicine
Johns Hopkins University School of Medicine
Baltimore, Maryland

Kathryn O'Connell, MD, PhD
Assistant Professor
Department of Dermatology
Johns Hopkins Medical Institutions
Baltimore, Maryland

Michelle Petri, MD, MPH
Associate Professor
Department of Internal Medicine
Johns Hopkins Medical Institutions
Baltimore, Maryland

Thomas T. Provost, MD
Professor
Department of Dermatology
Johns Hopkins Medical Institutions
Baltimore, Maryland

Reed E. Pyeritz, MD
Allegheny General Hospital
Pittsburgh, Pennsylvania

Rachel Reitan, MD
Obstetrical Resident
Departments of Obstetrics and Gynecology
Louisiana State University
New Orleans, Louisiana

Noel R. Rose, MD, PhD
Professor in Pathology, and Molecular
Microbiology and Immunology
Johns Hopkins Medical Institutions
Baltimore, Maryland

David S. Rosenberg, MD
Plastic Surgery Resident
Northwestern University Medical School
Chicago, Illinois

Walter Royal III, MD
Associate Professor of Anatomy and Medicine
(Neurology)
Neuroscience Institute
Morehause School of Medicine
Atlanta, Georgia

George H. Sack Jr., MD, PhD
Associate Professor of Medicine, Pediatrics and
Biological Chemistry
The Johns Hopkins University School of Medicine
Baltimore, Maryland

Francisco A. Tausk, MD
Associate Professor of Dermatology
Johns Hopkins University
Baltimore, Maryland

Fredrich M. Wigley, MD
Department of Medicine
Director of Rheumatology
Johns Hopkins University School of Medicine
Baltimore, Maryland

Jerry A. Winkelstein, MD
Professor of Pediatrics, Medicine and Pathology
Johns Hopkins University School of Medicine
Baltimore, Maryland

CHAPTER 1

Pruritus as a Manifestation of Systemic Disease

Malcolm W. Greaves, M.D., Thomas T. Provost, M.D.

Itch is a sensation only of the skin and is defined as an unpleasant feeling which provokes scratching. Scratching theoretically removes noxious agents and provides transient relief from the sensation of itch.

Pain and itch are two separate modalities.

Unmyelinated C-fibers carry itch sensation.

The peripheral receptor for itch is most likely a C polymodal nociceptor. Previously, it had been proposed by Rothman that pain and itch are transmitted along the same nerve pathways. However, it is now believed that itch and pain are two separate modalities. This theory is based upon the following observations: (1) pain and itch are perceived as distinct entities, evoking different responses (ie, withdrawal and scratching), (2) morphine and its derivatives relieve pain and provoke itching, and (3) microneurography using microelectrodes has demonstrated separate subgroups of peripheral, nonmyelinated C-fibers, depending upon their conduction velocities. The majority transmit only pain; a small, identical minority transmit only itch.

The C-fiber primary neurons synapse with secondary neurons in the dorsal horn of the spinal cord and cross to the contralateral spinothalamic tract. This occurs one segment above the entrance of the C-fiber into the spinal cord. The C-fibers enter the thalamus and from there, the thalamocortical tracts relay the itch sensation to the cortex.

"Gate keeper" theory is plausible explanation for modulation of itch sensation by tactile and vibratory sensations.

Pruritus cannot be induced in areas of skin previously exposed to pain sensation.

Melzack and Wall have proposed the "gate keeper" theory to explain why mechanical stimulation in the form of scratching provides temporary relief from the itching sensation. This theory hypothesizes that signals in the C-fibers, upon reaching the spinal cord, are modulated by efferent impulses arriving via large myelinated A-fibers, transmitting touch and pressure. The large fibers activate inhibitory neuronal circuitry that close the gate for pain and itch impulses arriving via the unmyelinated C-fibers. This theory explains why mild, mechanical stimulation in the form scratching, temporarily relieves pruritus or how vibration or electrical stimulation to the skin (transcutaneous electrical nerve stimulation) and acupuncture may modify itch/pain sensation. Furthermore, it has been long known that pruritus cannot be induced in areas of the skin previously exposed to pain, known as "the antipruritic state." There is also evidence for brain activated descending inhibitory and excitatory circuitry acting on spinal cord dorsal horn interneurons, modulating itch and pain sensations.

The underlying neurophysiologic mechanism(s) responsible for itchy skin is (are) unknown. It is theorized that once itching has started, the surrounding skin has a heightened sensitivity to react to a minor or mild stimulus by itching. In other words, the itch threshold is reduced, being evoked by normally nonpruritogenic stimuli (allokenesis).

Pruritogenic Mediators

Histamine

H-1, but not H-2 receptors involved in histamine-induced pruritus

The injection of histamine into the skin at the dermal-epidermal junction will provoke an itch sensation. This itch is mediated by H-1 receptors in the skin. Antihistamines, acting as antagonists of histamine, block H-1 receptors. Histamine-2 receptors do not appear to be involved in the development of histamine-induced itch sensation.

Neuropeptides and Neurogenic Inflammation

Substance P induces itch sensation most likely via release of histamine

Substance P, synthesized by dorsal root ganglia and transmitted to sensory nerve endings of C-fibers, when injected intradermally, is capable of inducing inconsistent pruritogenic responses in humans. This may be due to increased local histamine release. Capsaicin, which is capable of depleting substance P, abolishes pain and itch sensations for several weeks after skin application. Vasoactive intestinal peptide and neurokinin are additional neuropeptides capable of inducing pruritus following intradermal injection. Recent evidence suggests a close link between activated dermal mast cells and C-fiber nerve endings. In this model, mast cell tryptase released from activated mast cells acts as a protein receptor substrate (PAR-2) located within C-fiber nerve terminals, resulting in liberation of intermediates which in turn causes release of substance P.

At the present time, the weight of evidence indicates that neuropeptides induce itch via release of histamine, and the pruritus induced by these neuropeptides is inhibited by antihistamines or previous depletion of histamine from skin mast cells.

Opioid Peptides

Opioid peptides modulate itch sensation, which may be relieved by the opioid antagonist naloxone.

Morphine and morphine-like analgesics provoke itching. Opioid receptors are distributed in the peripheral and central nervous systems. Evidence exists that the opioid peptides leucine enkephalin and methionine enkephalin may modulate the itch perception, especially in cholestatic jaundice and biliary cirrhosis. Naloxone, an opiate antagonist, is capable of relieving itch in some patients with cholestatic and possibly other causes of pruritus. Opioid peptides may work peripherally by causing an enhancement of histamine-induced pruritus. However, β-endorphin and metenkephalin analogues do not cause a release of histamine.

Proteinases

Proteinases are capable of inducing pruritus independent of histamine release.

Based on the work of Shelley and Arthur, it has been hypothesized that proteinases are potent pruritogens. These investigators demonstrated that the intradermal injection of spicules of cowage (*Mucuna pruriens*) produces local pruritus. Proteinases are capable of inducing pruritus independent of histamine releases and the pruritogenic effect is a consequence of the proteinase enzymatic activity.

Prostaglandins

Prostaglandin E_1 lowers the threshold of human skin to histamine-provoking pruritus.

Cytokines

IL-2 may induce pruritus. Cyclosporin A, which inhibits transcription of IL-2, is effective in treating pruritus in some patients.

Interleukin (IL)-2 may be involved in generating pruritus. For example, cyclosporine, a drug capable of inhibiting transcription of IL-2 genes, is an effective drug in rapid relief of pruritus in some patients with atopic eczema. In addition, patients given IL-2 in the treatment of their cancers, frequently develop erythema, pruritus, and eosinophilia shortly after initiation of this type of therapy. Human IL-2, given intradermally to patients with atopic eczema and healthy controls, produces pruritus after 6 to 48 hours. It is theorized that IL-2 may be an indirect pruritogenic agent acting via other mediators.

These studies collectively indicate that histamine, as well as unknown peptide mediators, play an important role in producing the pruritus associated with various inflammatory dermatoses. The evidence for various cytokines and prostaglandins is fragmentary at best but appears to indicate possible pathologic roles. Increasing amounts of data indicate that opioids and opioid receptors may play a significant role in modulating pruritus.

Pruritus as a Manifestation of Systemic Disease

Table 1–1 summarizes some of the systemic diseases associated with pruritus.

Renal Disease

Pruritus had been recognized as a complication of renal failure. Prior to renal dialysis, 10 to 20% of renal failure patients had prominent pruritus. With the advent of renal dialysis, pruritus has become an ever-increasing complication of renal failure. Today it is estimated that approximately 80% of patients on renal dialysis will develop recurrent significant pruritus. The pruritus is not related to the length of time on dialysis. The potential causes of the renal-associated pruritus are listed in Table 1–2.

Increased populations of mast cells have been detected in the skin of renal dialysis patients by some, but not all, investigators. Also, serum histamine levels are increased. In addition, these patients show an exaggerated response to histamine. Antihistamines, however, are generally ineffective.

Pruritus is very common in renal dialysis patients.

Pruritus in renal dialysis patients not related to length of time on dialysis and is not affected by antihistamines

The pruritus correlates poorly, if at all, with blood urea nitrogen or serum creatinine levels. Oral administration of cholestyramine anion exchange resin and perfusion of plasma through activated charcoal beads have been reported to improve the itch. Excessive xerosis of the skin is also commonly present in these patients, yet, emollients are generally unsuccessful in alleviating the pruritus.

Recent evidence suggests a role for endogenous opioids in the induction of uremic pruritus. The antiopioid naltrexone is capable of inhibiting uremic pruritus and reducing plasma histamine levels.

Secondary hyperparathyroidism, on unusual occasions, may be a cause of pruritus, responding to parathyroidectomy. In general, most cases of pruritus associated with renal dialysis respond to ultraviolet B (UVB) therapy, as little as

Increased levels of serum parathyroid hormone occur in renal dialysis patients.

TABLE 1–1 Systemic Diseases Associated with Pruritus

Uremia	Myeloproliferative disorders
Obstructive biliary disease	Polycythemia vera
Primary biliary cirrhosis	Myelodysplasia
Biliary duct carcinoma	Lymphomas
Drugs	Hodgkin's disease
Contraceptive drugs, chlorpromazine, testosterone	Multiple myeloma
Extrahepatic biliary obstruction	Solid tumors (anecdotal reports only)
Carcinoma of the head of the pancreas	Breast carcinoma
Carcinoma of ampulla of Vater	Gastric carcinoma
Intrahepatic cholestasis of pregnancy	Lung carcinoma
Infections hepatitis B and C	Neurologic disorders
Endocrine disease	Multiple sclerosis
Thyrotoxicosis	Brain abscess
Myxedema	Central nervous system infarct
	Mastocytosis

Adapted from: Denman ST. A review of pruritus. J Am Acad Dermatol 1986;14:375–392.

TABLE 1–2 Possible Pathophysiologic Mechanisms of Pruritus in Uremia

Xerosis
Increased serum vitamin A levels
Secondary hyperparathyroidism
Peripheral neuropathy
Increased histamine levels

UVB therapy is effective in treating the pruritus associated with dialysis.

a total of 6 to 10 treatments given three times a week. Furthermore, serum histamine and vitamin A levels decrease. The beneficial response is prolonged. Other studies indicate that UVB applied to one-half of the body is associated with a generalized improvement in the itch, suggesting a systemic effect.

Recently, we had one pruritic renal dialysis patient who failed to respond to UVB therapy. This is the only renal dialysis patient who in our hands has thus far failed to respond to UVL therapy. Investigations revealed the patient had secondary hyperparathyroidism with increased serum levels of parathyroid hormone and Ca^{++}, and decreased phosphorus. This patient's pruritus responded to a parathyroidectomy.

Hepatic Disease

Sudden onset of pruritus associated with increase in alkaline phosphatase should prompt investigation for malignancy of head of pancreas, common bile duct stone, or carcinoma of the ampulla of Vater.

A persistent pruritus generally accompanies the development of biliary obstruction. The sudden onset of this symptom, plus an elevated alkaline phosphatase, should prompt immediate investigation for an underlying malignancy occurring in the head of the pancreas or a common bile duct stone. In primary biliary cirrhosis, the onset of the pruritus is generally gradual, but the pruritus can be very intense and persistent. Liver biopsy and antimitochondrial antibodies help establish the diagnosis.

There does not appear to be any correlation between the serum concentration of bile salts and the degree of pruritus. However, the application of bile salts to a blister-base produces pruritus, and the use of such exchange resin drugs as cholestyramine may be effective in producing symptomatic improvement. Furthermore, plasma perfusion over charcoal-coated beads has been reported to be associated with an improvement in the pruritus. These latter observations suggest a nonbile salt byproduct of biliary occlusion may be responsible.

Pruritus associated with biliary cirrhosis may respond to UVB therapy or to naloxone.

Recent studies indicate a primary role for endogenous opioids in the pathogenesis of cholestatic- and biliary cirrhosis–induced pruritus. At least one group has postulated a central origin to pruritus in these conditions based on the facts that the pruritus and scratching are reduced or eliminated by the antiopioid naloxone and the presence of down regulation of μ-opioid receptors. Furthermore, the oral antiopioid nalmefene and, to a lesser extent, parenteral naloxone, induce a withdrawal state reminiscent of that seen in heroin drug addiction. We have found that the pruritus associated with chronic hepatitis and primary biliary cirrhosis is also responsive to UVB therapy.

Patients with generalized pruritus should be investigated for hepatitis B and C infection.

Hepatitis B and C may cause pruritus in the absence of clinical or biochemical evidence of liver disease, and evidence of infection should be sought in all cases of generalized pruritus.

Endocrine Disease

Thyrotoxicosis is frequently associated with a generalized pruritus. Furthermore, a small rise in skin temperature may evoke pruritus in these patients. Theoretically the increase in blood flow inducing increased warmth in the skin may decrease the itch threshold. In general, treatment of thyrotoxicosis is associated with symptomatic relief.

Pruritus is manifestation of hyperthyroidism

Hypothyroidism (myxedema) is also associated with pruritus due mainly to dryness. This symptomatology may be relieved by treatment of the xerotic skin with a variety of emollients.

Generalized pruritus has been said to be associated with diabetes mellitus. However, this statement is based on one report in the literature dating from 1927. It is true that localized pruritus can be associated with the neuropathy associated with diabetes, as well as the increased propensity to develop localized skin infection, but generalized pruritus in a diabetic, in our experience, is very unusual.

Generalized pruritus is probably not manifestation of diabetes mellitus

Postmenopausal women may also have a transient pruritus associated with flushing. Elevated pituitary luteinizing hormones and follicular-stimulating hormones help establish this diagnosis, and the pruritus should respond to hormone replacement therapy.

Iron Deficiency

Several reports have been published indicating that iron deficiency is a cause of pruritus. However, this statement has been challenged by a study of a large group of iatrogenically induced iron-deficient patients who failed to demonstrate pruritus.

Iron deficiency anemia is probably not associated with generalized pruritus.

Malignancies

Five to 10% of generalized pruritus patients have an associated malignancy (Table 1–3).

Anecdotal reports indicate solid tumors are infrequently associated with pruritus and suggest disappearance of pruritus with removal of solid tumors. Also, localized pruritus, such as intense nasal pruritus, has been associated with brain tumors.

Most cases of pruritus associated with malignancy occur, however, with lymphoreticular malignancy, including Hodgkin's disease. Approximately 30% of Hodgkin's patients have pruritus. Non-Hodgkin's lymphomas and lymphatic leukemia (~3%) may have associated pruritus. Many times, the onset is sudden and the pruritus persistent and recalcitrant to routine measures.

Hodgkin's and non-Hodgkin's lymphomas associated with pruritus

Aquagenic Pruritus

A pruritus has also been reported following exposure to water at all temperatures. There are no visible skin changes, and the pruritus can be very distressing. Although, usually idiopathic, some of these patients have underlying polycythemia rubra vera or myelodysplasia. Some are apparently healthy, elderly adults without evident underlying disease.

Pruritus without visible signs following water exposure seen in patients with polycythemia rubra vera or myelodysplasia may also be idiopathic.

We have seen three patients with aquagenic pruritus who demonstrated evidence of myelodysplasia. One patient demonstrated acute myelogenous leukemia on bone marrow aspirate; the second demonstrated atypical lymphocytes and

TABLE 1–3 Frequency of Malignancy in Unselected Patients Presenting with Generalized Recalcitrant Pruritus

	Total Number		
Source	Patients	Malignancies	%
Paul et al.*	125	8	6
Lyell	60	2	3
Beare	43	3	7
Kantor/Lookingbill**	44	5	11
TOTAL	272	18	~7

* 6-year follow-up.
** 6.5-year follow-up.

giant platelet forms; and the third patient demonstrated on bone marrow, myeloid proliferation with peripheral blood metamyelocytes suggestive of a preleukemic state. Aquagenic pruritus has also been reported to occur in patients with the hypereosinophil syndrome. It is important to follow up otherwise healthy individuals with aquagenic pruritus in case they subsequently develop polycythemia rubra vera or another bone marrow disorder.

A local release of histamine or acetylcholine may be responsible. Increased serum levels of histamine have been reported in patients with aquagenic pruritus and in patients with polycythemia rubra vera. However, these patients generally demonstrate a poor response to antihistamines. The preferred treatment is PUVA (8-methoxy-UVA photochemotherapy).

Pruritus of Atopic Dermatitis

See Chapter 18, "Atopic Dermatitis," for discussion.

Easily Missed Causes of Pruritus

Important causes of intractable pruritus often missed include pemphigoid nodularis, occult bullous pemphigoid, onchocerciasis, brachioradial pruritus, notalgia parestetica, and scabies.

Pemphigoid Nodularis

This entity presents as a nonspecific prurigo without obvious blistering. A biopsy of lesional skin may not show a subepidermal split, but direct immunofluorescence shows IgG (immunoglobulin) and C3 deposition along the basement membrane indicative of an antihemidesmosomal antibody characteristic of pemphigoid nodularis. Furthermore, occult bullous pemphigoid without prurigo may also be a cause of pruritus. We have seen 7 of approximately 43 chronic pruritic patients over the age of 50 years in whom the underlying cause turned out to be occult pemphigoid (ie, without blisters). Direct immunofluorescence demonstrate linear deposition of immunoreactants at the dermal epidermal junction.

Onchocerciasis

This should be suspected in any patient with persistent, widespread pruritus who has previously been a resident in an endemic area of Africa or Central or South America. It can present as a nondescript, persistent itch with an eosinophilia, and the diagnosis is confirmed by microscopic examination of a skin snip for filaria of *Onchocerca volvulus*. It responds to ivermectin.

Brachioradial Pruritus

This is a persistent, burning pruritus occurring on the outer surface of the elbows, forearms, and upper arms. It occurs in sun-damaged skin and is common in golfers, sailors, and tennis players. It may respond to topical capsaicin.

Notalgia Paresthetica

This fairly common, persistent itch is usually centered in the middle of the back and is associated histologically with an increased population density of sensory nerve fibers in the affected skin. It may respond to topical capsaicin.

Scabies

This disease continues to be a major cause of pruritus in the United States. Intense pruritus, which wakes a patient from a sound sleep, may be the only feature.

AIDS/HIV

See Chapter 64, "Human Immunodeficiency Virus," for discussion.

TABLE 1–4 Persistence of Pruritus: Follow-Up of Patients with Generalized Pruritus

	Follow-Up Period (N = 125)	
	3 Years	6 Years
Persistent pruritus	60	40
No pruritus	23	32
Questionnaire unanswered	14	26
Dead	14	26

Adapted from: Paul R, Paul R, Jansen CT. Itch and malignancy prognosis in generalized pruritus: a 6-year follow-up of 125 patients. J Am Acad Dermatol 1987;16:1179–1182.

Evaluation of Patients with Generalized Pruritus

Xerosis is the most common cause of pruritus in the elderly and responds well to emollients.

Generalized pruritus is a common dermatologic complaint. It is frequently seen in middle-aged or elderly individuals. In general, the most common cause of pruritus in the elderly is secondary to xerosis of the skin. In parellel with the extensive laboratory investigation of an elderly patient, hydration of the skin with emollients following showering or bathing should be done. Our experience indicates that many cases of pruritus in the elderly resolve with this simple technique.

Sudden onset of recalcitrant pruritus in a healthy individual is worrisome if simple causes such as scabies have been excluded.

The sharp onset of pruritus in an otherwise normal, healthy individual is a worrisome symptom. Simple causes such as scabies and papular urticaria due to insect bites need to be excluded. Complete history and physical examination as well as routine laboratory studies, such as a complete blood count, erythrocyte sedimentation rate, stool examination for parasites and occult blood, chest radiograph, routine blood chemistries, thyroid function studies, and direct immunofluorescence examination of normal skin are indicated. We reserve extensive imaging and endoscopic studies for those individuals with intractable pruritus.

Repeat follow-up examination of chronic pruritus patients is important in order to detect the emergence of evidence for systemic disease (Table 1–4). However, it should be recognized that as many as 50% of generalized pruritus patients will have persistence for at least 3 years without evidence of systemic disease.

Annotated Bibliography

Bickford RG. Experiments relating to itch sensation, its peripheral mechanism and central pathways. Clin Sci 1938;3:377–382.

Rothman S. Physiology of itching. Physiol Rev 1941;21:357–362.

Shelley WB, Arthur RP. Studies on cowhage (*Mucuna Pruriens*) and its pruritogenic proteinase mucunain. Arch Dermatol 1955;72:399–404.

Greaves MW, Wall PD. Pathophysiology of itching. Lancet 1996;348:939–940.

These are four highly quoted articles.

Tucker WF, Briggs C, Challoner T. Absence of pruritus and iron deficiency following venesection. Clin Exp Dermatol 1984;9:186–189.

Newton JA, Singh AK, Greaves MW, Spry CJ. Aquagenic pruritus associated with the idiopathic hypereosinophilic syndrome. Br J Dermatol 1990;122:103–106.

McGrath JA, Greaves MW. Aquagenic pruritus in the myelodysplastic syndrome. Br J Dermatol 1990;123:414–415.

Tötterman TH, Scheynius A, Killander A, et al. Treatment of therapy-resistant Sézary syndrome with Cyclosporin A: suppression of pruritus, leukemic T cell activation markers and tumor mass. Scand J Haematol 1985;34:196–203.

Fjellner B, Hägermark Ö. The influence of the opiate antagonist naloxone on experimental pruritus. Acta Derm Venereol 1984;64:73–75.

Gaspari AA, Lotze MT, Rosenberg SA, et al. Dermatologic changes associated with interleukin-2 administration. JAMA 1987;258:1624–1629.

Gilchrest BA, Rowe JW, Brown RS, et al. Ultraviolet phototherapy of uremic pruritus. Long-term results and possible mechanism of action. Ann Intern Med 1979;91:17–24.

This is a highly quoted paper.

Kantor GR, Lookingbill DP. Generalized pruritus and systemic disease. J Am Acad Dermatol 1983;9:375–382.

Lyell A. The itching patient. A review of the causes of pruritus. Scott Med J 1972;17(10):334–337.

Beare JM. Generalized pruritus. A study of 43 cases. Clin Exp Dermatol 1976;1:343–352.

Gilchrest BA. Pruritus: pathogenesis, therapy, and significance in systemic disease states. Arch Intern Med 1982;142;101–105.

These are four excellent review articles on pruritus.

Paul R, Paul R, Jansen CT. Itch and malignancy prognosis in generalized pruritus: a 6-year follow-up of 125 patients. J Am Acad Dermatol 1987;16:1179–1182.

Melzack R, Wall PD. Pain mechanisms: a new theory. Science 1965;150:971–979.

This is the classic article proposing a control system to modulate sensory input from the skin, prior to evoking pain perception and response.

Summerfield JA. Naloxone modulates the perception of itch in man. Br J Clin Pharmacol 1980;10:180–183.

Thornton JR, Losowsky MS. Opioid peptides and primary biliary cirrhosis. BMJ 1988; 297:1501–1504.

Jones EA, Bergasa NV. The pruritus of cholestasis and the opioid system. JAMA 1992; 268:3359–3362.

Bergasa NV, Alling DW, Talbot TL, et al. Effects of naloxone infusions in patients with the pruritus of cholestasis. A double-blind, randomized, controlled trial. Ann Intern Med 1995;123:161–167.

Peer G, Kivity S, Agami O, et al. Randomised crossover trial of naltrexone in uraemic pruritus. Lancet 1996;348:1552–1554.

These series of provocative articles provide evidence for the role of opioid peptides in the pathogenesis of the pruritus associated with primary biliary cirrhosis, cholestasis, and uremia.

Greaves MW. Anti-itch treatments: do they work? Skin Pharmacol 1997;10(5–6): 225–229.

An updated review of antipruritic therapies.

Provost TT, et al. Unusual subepidermal bullous diseases with immunologic features of bullous pemphigoid: variants of bullous pemphigoid. Arch Dermatol 1979;115: 156–160.

First description of prurigo bullous pemphigoid.

CHAPTER 2

Pigment Manifestations of Systemic Diseases

Thomas T. Provost, M.D.

Alteration in skin pigmentation occurs in a variety of systemic diseases. Most of the alterations are not specific (eg, hyperpigmentation associated with cachexia, malignancy). In other diseases, such as the Vogt-Koyanagi-Harada syndrome and tuberous sclerosis, the alterations in pigmentation are characterisitic.

Common feature of diseases

This chapter briefly discusses pigment alteration of various systemic diseases. For more complete discussions, see the appropriate sections as indicated and the two excellent references in the general bibliography at the end of the chapter.

Systemic Disorders Associated with Hyperpigmentation

Lentigines and Ephelides

Lentigines are macular, pigmented lesions characterized by an increased number of melanocytes. They are distinguishable from ephelides (freckles), which have normal melanocyte numbers but increased amounts of melanin.

Lentigine—increased melanocytes

Ephelides—increased melanin

LEOPARD Syndrome

LEOPARD syndrome, also known as multiple lentigines syndrome, is an autosomal dominant disease characterized by multiple lentigines associated with cardiac abnormalities.

LEOPARD syndrome characterized by multiple lentigines associated with cardiac abnormalities

The lentigines, which are detected in early infancy, occur over the entire body (Figures 2–1and 2–2). Arrythmias and cardiac conduction abnormalities are the most common associations. Pulmonary and subaortic stenosis have also been detected.

In addition, ocular hypertelorism and prognathism may occur. Sensorineural deafness and genital anomalies, including gonadal hypoplasia, hypospadias, are also frequent features. These features have been given the eponym "LEOPARD"— *l*entigines, *e*lectrocardiographic abnormalities, *o*cular hypertelorism, *p*ulmonic stenosis, *a*bnormalities of the genitalia, *r*etardation of growth, and *d*eafness. The lentigines histologically demonstrate an increased number of melanocytes with increased numbers of melanosomes including macromelanosomes.

Annotated Bibliography

Gorlin RJ, Anderson RC, Blaw M. Multiple lentigines syndrome. Am J Dis Child 1969; 117:652–662.

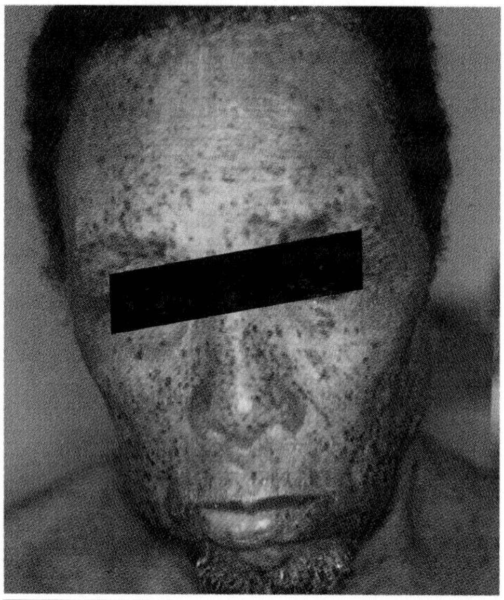

FIGURE 2–1 LEOPARD syndrome demonstrating multiple lentigines on face. (Courtesy of James Nordlund, M.D.) (Reproduced with permission from Nordlund JJ, Lerner AB, Braverman IM, McGuire JS. The multiple lentigines syndrome. Arch Dermatol 1973;107: 259–261.)

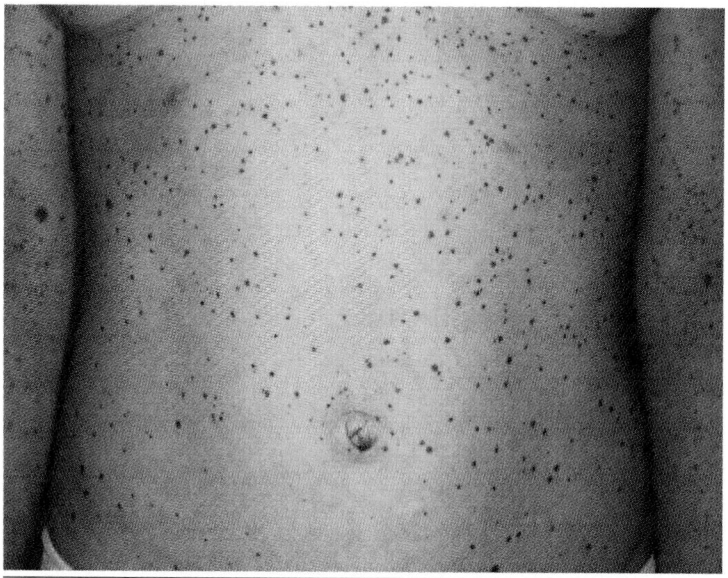

FIGURE 2–2 LEOPARD syndrome demonstrating multiple lentigines on trunk and abdomen. (Courtesy of James Nordlund, M.D.) (Reproduced with permission from Nordlund JJ, Lerner AB, Braverman IM, McGuire JS. The multiple lentigines syndrome. Arch Dermatol 1973;107: 259–261.)

Voron DA, Hatfield HH, Kalkhoff RK. Multiple lentigines syndrome. Case report and review of the literature. Am J Med 1976;60:447–456.

Nordlund JJ, Lerner AB, Braverman IM, McGuire JS. The multiple lentigines syndrome. Arch Dermatol 1973; 107:259–261.

Smith RF, Pulicicchio LU, Holmes AV. Generalized lentigo: electrocardiographic abnormalities, conduction disorders and arrhythmias in three cases. Am J Cardiol 1970;25:501–506.

These four excellent articles describe the cutaneous and systemic features of this syndrome. All are well written.

NAME Syndrome

NAME syndrome: multiple freckle-like lesions associated with atrial myxomas

In addition to the LEOPARD syndrome, there is another rare syndrome involving cutaneous hyperpigmentation associated with cardiac abnormalities. Hyperpigmentation, especially freckles, is seen associated with atrial and cutaneous myxomas. The designation "NAME" has been given to this syndrome because of the presence of *n*evi, *a*trial *m*yxoma, and *e*phelides. It has also been reported under the eponym of the "LAMB" syndrome (*l*entigines, *a*trial myxoma, *m*ucocutaneous myoxomas, and *b*lue nevi).

Annotated Bibliography

Reed OM, Mellette JR Jr, Fitzpatrick JE. Cutaneous lentiginosis with atrial myxomas. J Am Acad Dermatol 1986;15:398–402.

This well-written case report describes the presence of cerebral aneurysms in this syndrome.

Atherton DJ, Pitcher DW, Wells RS, MacDonald DM. A syndrome of various cutaneous pigmented lesions, myxoid neurofibromata and atrial myxoma: the NAME syndrome. Br J Dermatol 1980;103:421–429.

This article describes subcutaneous myxoid tumors.

Rhodes AR, Silverman RA, Harrist TJ, Perez-Atayde AR. Mucocutaneous lentigines, cardiomucocutaneous myxomas, and multiple blue nevi: the "LAMB" syndrome. J Am Acad Dermatol 1984;10:72–82.

Peutz-Jeghers Syndrome

This is an autosomal dominant disease characterized by development of perioral and oral lentigines in infancy or early childhood. The perioral lesions are dark, 1- to 2-mm macules, which may fade at puberty. The oral pigmentation is generally permanent. The etiology has been determined to be mutations of a serine threonine kinase enzyme localized to chromosome 19p13.3.

Perioral and oral lentigines

In recent years, multiple intestinal polyposis involving the small intestine has been recognized. In addition to malignant degeneration of the polyps, an increased frequency of pancreatic carcinoma has been observed. There is evidence for an increased frequency of ovarian, cervical, and breast malignancies. (For further information, see Chapter 30, "Hereditary Paraneoplastic Syndromes.")

Small-bowel polyps

Increased risk of malignancy

Annotated Bibliography

Jeghers H, McKusick VA, Katz KH. Generalized intestinal polyposis and melanin spots on the oral mucosa, lips and digits. N Engl J Med 1949;241:993–1005.

This is a classic, well-written description of the cutaneous manifestations of Peutz-Jeghers syndrome.

Giardiello FM, Welsh SB, Hamilton SR, et al. Increased risk of cancer in Peutz-Jeghers syndrome. N Engl J Med 1987;316:1511–1514.

This is a highly quoted reference demonstrating malignant degeneration of the hamartomatous polyps occurring in the small intestine. It also demonstrates that these patients have an 18-fold risk of developing cancer. There is a 100-fold risk of development of carcinoma of the pancreas.

Cronkhite-Canada Syndrome

This is a rare, adult-onset syndrome characterized by lentigines over the palms and dorsal surface of the hands. In addition, nail dystrophy and a patchy alopecia, which frequently becomes total, is seen.

Rare syndrome of macular hyperpigmentation of palms and fingers associated with a protein-losing enteropathy

Weight loss, presumably secondary to a malabsorption syndrome associated with a protein-losing enteropathy, occurs. Increased rugae of the stomach associated with dilated lymphatics and gastrointestinal polyposis have been detected. (For more information, see Chapter 29, "Paraneoplastic Dermatoses.")

Annotated Bibliography

Cronkhite LW, Canada W. Generalized gastrointestinal polyposis. N Engl J Med 1955; 252:1011–1015.

This is the classic description of the clinical features of this syndrome, including the cutaneous features.

Daniel ES, Ludwig SL, Lewin KJ, et al. The Cronkhite-Canada syndrome. Medicine (Baltimore) 1982;61:293–309.

This is a well-written review of a number of patients presenting with various features of the Cronkhite-Canada syndrome.

Incontinentia Pigmenti

Also known as Bloch-Sulzberger disease, this is an uncommon X chromosome–linked disease, usually lethal in males, characterized by the development in early infancy of vesicular, then verrucous (warty), and then pigmented, macular lesions. Two genetic types have been described. Sporadic cases are linked to translocation of X chromosome (Xp-1). Familial cases are linked to Xq28.

Slate gray, sometimes bizarre, linear, macular, hyperpigmented patches in females

May be preceded by bullous and verrucous phase

Generally lethal in males

The bullae, often linear, are subcorneal, associated with spongiosis. The inflammatory infiltrate contains numerous eosinophils. The verrucous lesions are characterized by acanthosis and macrophages laden with melanin pigmentation. The pigmented linear patches reveal large quantities of melanin in dermal melanophages. Clinically, the pigmented patches may be blue-gray or brown and have a bizarre pattern. They may occur alone or follow the bullous and verrucous phase of the disease.

Multiple structural abnormalities have been detected.

In addition to the prominent cutaneous features, dental and ocular defects (including blindness and microphthalmia), mental retardation, and skeletal abnormalities have been described.

Annotated Bibliography

Wiklund DA, Weston WL. Incontinentia pigmenti: a four-generation study. Arch Dermatol 1980;116:701–703.

Seven individuals spanning four generations are described.

Fanconi's Syndrome

Macular olive-brown hyperpigmentation associated with progressive anemia, neutropenia, and thrombocytopenia

This is an autosomal recessive disease process in which young children develop a generalized olive-brown pigmentation, most prominent on the lower trunk. Irregular pigmentation in the form of depigmented and pigmented macules are also detected.

A progressive pancytopenia occurs. In addition, these patients may demonstrate skeletal abnormalities (ie, rudimentary thumbs, aplasia of the radii, and microencephaly). Hypogonadism and mental retardation have also been detected.

These patients also have an increased frequency of neoplasias. Increased chromosomal breakage has been detected, and a deoxyribonucleic acid (DNA) repair defect is thought to be responsible.

Annotated Bibliography

Bloom GE, Warner S, Gerald PS, Diamond LK. Chromosome abnormalities in constitutional aplastic anemia. N Engl J Med 1966;274:8–11.

Albright's Syndrome

Macular light brown, hyperpigmented patches more extensive on one side associated with fibrous dysplasia and precocious puberty in females

This is a disease of unknown etiology characterized by light brown patches of hyperpigmentation occurring on the trunk, buttocks, and thighs. These lesions, generally more extensive on one side of the body, demonstrate irregular or serrated edges.

Fibrous dysplasia, characterized by bone pain and pathologic features, usually occurs during the first decade of life. Precocious puberty, generally before the age of 10, is characterized by enlargement of breasts and pubic hair growth. Biopsy may on occasion demonstrate giant melanosomes.

See Chapter 44, "Neurofibromatosis," for differentiation of Albright's syndrome from neurofibromatosis.

Annotated Bibliography

Benedict PH, Szabo G, Fitzpatrick TB, Sinesi SJ. Melanotic macules in Albright's syndrome and in neurofibromatosis. JAMA 1968;205:618–626.

Neurofibromatosis

More than six café-au-lait lesions 1.0 cm or greater and axillary freckling highly suggestive of neurofibromatosis

Café-au-lait lesions are seen in approximately 90% of neurofibromatosis patients. The presence of six or more of these lesions $\geq$ 1 cm carries a high probability of neurofibromatosis. This is especially true if axillary freckling is also detected. Biopsy of a café-au-lait macule will invariably demonstrate macromelanosomes. (See Chapter 44, "Neurofibromatosis," for additional details.)

Xeroderma Pigmentosum

Xeroderma pigmentosum patients frequently demonstrate the progressive development of freckle-like lesions on light-exposed areas of the body. These freckles begin in early childhood and are associated with the development of tumors (basal cell, squamous cell, and malignant melanomas). (For further information, see Chapter 30, "Hereditary Paraneoplastic Syndromes.")

Addisonian or Generalized Hyperpigmentation

Addisonian or generalized hyperpigmentation may be seen in various diseases.

Generalized or addisonian-like pigmentation associated with various disorders

Generalized hyperpigmentation most prominent in light-exposed areas is almost always found in patients with Addison's disease. The creases of the palms and soles are also hyperpigmented. Pigmentation of the buccal mucosa is almost always present, and the conjunctiva and vagina may also be involved.

Almost always present in Addison's disease

Palmar and plantar crease hyperpigmentation

Oral mucosa hyperpigmentation

The degree of hyperpigmentation in Addison's disease is variable. Not infrequently, the hyperpigmentation is first detected when the normal tan obtained during the summer months fails to disappear with the onset of fall. Vitiligo is also seen in these patients.

May begin as a suntan that fails to fade

Annotated Bibliography

Dunlop D. Eighty-six cases of Addison's disease. Br Med J 1963;ii:887–891.

Acromegaly

Addisonian hyperpigmentation may be seen in acromegalic patients, secondary to increased levels of melanocyte-stimulating hormone (MSH).

Cushing's Disease

An addisonian-like hyperpigmentation may be seen in patients with Cushing's disease and its presence suggests a pituitary tumor, secreting adrenocorticotropic hormone (ACTH) and/or β-lipotropin.

Generalized pigmentation in Cushing's disease associated with pituitary tumor

Nelson's Syndrome

Following adrenalectomy for Cushing's disease, a generalized addisonian hyperpigmentation may occur associated with the development of a pituitary tumor and very high plasma concentrations of ACTH and β-lipotropin.

Annotated Bibliography

Nelson DH, Meakin JW, Thorn GW. ACTH producing pituitary tumors following adrenalectomy for Cushing's syndrome. Ann Intern Med 1960;52:560–569.

Chronic Infections

Generalized hyperpigmentation is frequently detected in patients with chronic infections such as tuberculosis. The mechanism(s) is (are) unknown.

Neoplastic Diseases

An addisonian-like hyperpigmentation may be seen in patients with advanced neoplastic diseases. In some malignancies, such as oat cell carcinoma, an ectopic ACTH syndrome may be responsible.

Diffuse hyperpigmentation associated with ectopic ACTH-producing tumors

A diffuse addisonian-like hyperpigmentation may occur on unusual occasions with a melanoma. In addition, generalized hyperpigmentation may be seen in patients with lymphomas, especially Hodgkin's disease. The mechanism(s) is/are unknown.

Annotated Bibliography

Adrian RM, Murphy GF, Sato S, et al. Diffuse melanosis secondary to metastatic malignant melanoma. Light and electron microscope findings. J Am Acad Dermatol 1981;5:308–318.

Connective Tissue Diseases

An addisonian type of hyperpigmentation may uncommonly be detected in patients with scleroderma, dermatomyositis, and lupus erythematosus. The hyperpigmentation associated with scleroderma may demonstrate a peculiar localization around hair follicles or present as an isolated macular patch of hyper-

Generalized follicular and localized hyperpigmented lesions associated with scleroderma

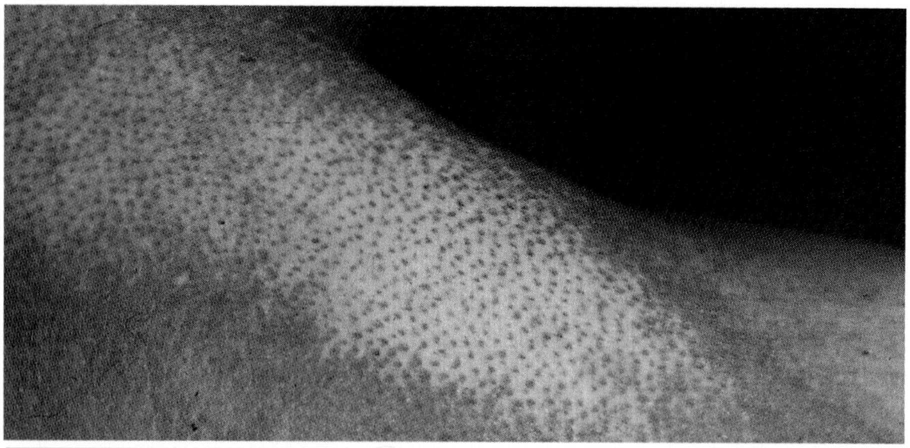

FIGURE 2–3 Patient with diffuse scleroderma demonstrating perifollicular hyperpigmentation in an "island" of scleroderma.

pigmentation. At times, a large patch of hyperpigmentation may be the only residuum of a previous scleroderma lesion (Figure 2–3).

In both dermatomyositis and lupus erythematosus, poikiloderma atrophicans vasculare characterized by hypo- and hyperpigmentation, atrophy, and telangiectasia may be present.

Chronic Renal Failure

A diffuse hyperpigmentation may be seen in patients with chronic renal failure. Elevated MSH may be present in the blood due to defective clearance by the kidney. Also, lipochromes and carotenoids may contribute to the hyperpigmentation.

Annotated Bibliography

Smith AG, Shuster S, Comaish JS, et al. Plasma immunoreactive beta-melanocyte-stimulating hormone and skin pigmentation in chronic renal failure. Br Med J 1975; 1:658–659.

This article explains that there is no correlation between severity of renal failure or the degree of pigmentation and plasma MSH level.

Hepatic Disease

Patients with chronic liver failure, especially primary biliary cirrhosis, may develop a generalized hyperpigmentation. The mechanisms are unknown.

Hemachromatosis

"Bronze diabetes": a term given to hemachromatosis

Hereditary and acquired forms

A diffuse, gray-brown pigmentation involving the face and other exposed areas occurs in patients with hemachromatosis, also known as "bronze diabetes." Hemachromatosis is an autosomal, recessive, inherited disease with a 10:1 male-to-female ratio, characterized by bronzing of the skin, diabetes mellitus, and cirrhosis of the liver. There is an increased frequency of the human leukocyte antigen (HLA)-A3 or HLA-B14 phenotypes. It is caused by increased iron deposition, the result of a defect in the control of iron absorption (see below).

An acquired form of hemachromatosis is seen with chronic iron intoxication (Bantu's drinking an iron-rich beer), alcoholic cirrhosis, and hemosiderosis in which anemic patients are given large quantities of iron in the form of transfusions. A similar rare condition also occurs with a congenital defect in the iron transport protein, transferrin.

Pigmentation due to melanin and iron deposits

The grayish-brown pigmentation may antedate other features of the disease process. This hyperpigmentation is due to an increase in melanin and dermal iron deposits around sweat glands.

Iron absorption in normal individuals occurs in the small intestine. It is controlled by upregulation of transferrin receptor expression. This leads to increased iron absorption. Following replenishment of iron, the ferritin stores in mucosa are increased, and the transferrin receptor expression is down regulated. In hereditary hemachromatosis, this regulatory mechanism is altered and transferrin receptor expression is continually high, resulting in excessive absorption of dietary iron.

Most common genetic disease affecting Caucasians in northern hemisphere

The iron deposition occurs predominantly in the hepatocytes and biliary epithelial cells. This leads to fibrosis, cirrhosis, liver failure, and an increased frequency of hepatocellular carcinoma. Iron deposition in the heart induces restrictive cardiomyopathy and congestive heart failure. Diabetes mellitus and joint disease are also the result of excessive iron deposition. In addition to hyperpigmentation, hair loss, generalized xerosis, testicular atrophy, and weight loss occur.

Defect in iron absorption regulation in the small intestine

The gene for hereditary hemachromatosis has been localized to the short arm of chromosome 6. A mutation in the gene, resulting in a cystine to tyrosine substitution in amino acid 282 of the gene (HFE) is responsible at least for some of the cases. A second gene defect substitution of histidine for aspartic acid at amino acid 63 has also been identified.

Gene defect localized to short arm of chromosome 6

Serum iron and total iron binding capacity are the diagnostic techniques. Fasting serum transferrin iron saturation ≥ 60% in men or ≥ 50% in women is a sensitive screening test for hereditary hemachromatosis. Liver biopsy is needed for staging the degree of fibrosis.

In first degree relatives, HLA typing is valuable. Those blood relatives sharing class 1 HLA-A and -B haplotypes are presumed to be homozygous and can be expected to develop iron overload. Transferrin saturation and serum ferritin levels should be employed to follow these high-risk patients.

Annotated Bibliography

Edwards CQ, Kushner JP. Screening for hemochromatosis. N Engl J Med 1993;328: 1616–1620.

A transferrin saturation of 50% in females and 60% in males is an excellent screening test. If serum ferritin levels are increased, perform liver biopsy and phlebotomies. If ferritin levels are normal, measure transferrin saturation and ferritin levels every 2 years. If ferritin levels become elevated, begin phlebotomies to maintain normal ferritin level.

Nierderau C, Fischer R, Sonnenberg A, et al. Survival and causes of death in cirrhotic and in noncirrhotic patients with primary hemochromatosis. N Engl J Med 1985; 313:1256–1262.

This article explains that liver cancer is 219 times more frequent in cirrhotic hemachromatosis patients than in normal controls.

Jazwinska EC, Lee SC, Webb SI, et al. Localization of the hemochromatosis gene close to D6S105. Am J Hum Genet 1993;53:347–352.

Chevrant-Breton J, Simon M, Bourel M, Ferrand B. Cutaneous manifestations of idiopathic hemachromatosis: study of 100 cases. Arch Dermatol 1977;113:161–165.

This is a highly quoted reference detailing the skin manifestations associated with idiopathic hemachromatosis. The study reports that abnormal skin and mucosal pigmentation was noted in 98% of patients. Buccal mucosal and diffuse, or perilimbic conjunctival pigmentation occurred in approximately 20% of patients. Skin atrophy, especially over the anterior surfaces of the lower leg, was noted in 42% of patients. Generalized xerosis was noted in 46% and ichthyosis vulgaris in 7%. Hair loss was detected in 62%. Twelve patients demonstrated total body loss of hair. Forty-nine of 100 patients demonstrated koilonychia, mainly of the thumb, index, and middle fingers. The degree of spooning was variable.

These authors found that the degree of pigmentation was altered by phlebotomies. They noted the amount of siderosis around eccrine sweat glands markedly decreased with phlebotomies, and the degree of pigmentation was related to the loss of iron and not to the degree of melanization. These authors believe that siderosis around eccrine sweat glands is a unique feature of hemachromatosis not detected in normal individuals.

Vitamin Deficiencies

Hyperpigmentation due to vitamin deficiencies is very unusual.

A generalized (or addisonian) type of hyperpigmentation has been reported in various vitamin deficiencies, including vitamins A and B_{12}, folate deficiency, scurvy, and pellagra. The pellagra hyperpigmentation is most commonly accentuated in light-exposed areas (around the neck; Casal's collar). A residuum of postinflammatory hyperpigmentation secondary to the phototoxic dermatitis may be the cause. Hyperpigmentation secondary to vitamin deficiencies is very unusual but may be seen in alcoholics and derelicts.

Malabsorption Syndrome

A diffuse, generalized hyperpigmentation may be seen in malabsorption syndromes of various etiologies (protein-losing enteropathy, adult celiac disease). The mechanism for this hyperpigmentation is not known.

POEMS Syndrome

POEMS has a diffuse addisonian-like hyperpigmentation.

This is a very rare disease, characterized by polyneuropathy, polyendocrinopathies, hepatosplenomegaly, lymphadenopathy, a monoclonal immunoglobulin, anasarca, and a diffuse addisonian-like pigmentation. The eponym "POEMS" is derived from *p*olyneuropathy, *o*rganomegaly, *e*ndocrinology, *M* protein, and *s*kin changes. The etiology of this disorder and the diffuse pigmentation is unknown. (For further information see discussion on POEMS syndrome in Chapter 24, "Leukemia, B-cell Lymphomas, and Multiple Myeloma.")

Drug Reactions

The diffuse, generalized hyperpigmentation associated with drugs is covered in Chapter 66, "Cutaneous Manifestations of Drug Reactions: Drug Eruptions."

Disorders Associated with Hypomelanosis

Generalized hypomelanosis, or hypopigmentation, as a cutaneous expression of a systemic illness is very uncommon.

Chédiak-Higashi Syndrome

Autosomal recessive rare disease in those with light skin, blond hair, and translucent irides

Repeated viral and bacterial infections

Increased risk of lymphoma

This is a rare autosomal, recessive disease characterized by partial albinism (light skin, blond hair, translucent irides) and increased susceptibility to viral and bacterial infections. Melanocytes contain giant pigmented granules. Large granules are also seen in white blood cells and platelets. The defective gene (Lyst) is localized to 1q42–43.

Most children with Chédiak-Higashi syndrome die with intractable respiratory infections. These children are also at increased risk for the development of lymphomas.

Annotated Bibliography

Blume RS, Wolff SM. The Chédiak-Higashi syndrome: studies in four patients and a review of the literature. Medicine (Baltimore) 1972;51:247–280.

This article provides a review of world literature at that time detailing clinical features. Recurrent febrile episodes, repeated bacterial infections, negligible granulocyte responses to infection, and an accelerated phase characterized by widespread tissue infiltrates of lymphoid and histiocytic cells are described.

Padgett GA, Reiquam CW, Gorham JR, Henson JB. Comparative studies of the Chédiak-Higashi syndrome. Am J Pathol 1967;51:553–571.

This article describes necropsy studies comparing human with mice and cattle Chédiak-Higashi syndrome. Unlike the human syndrome, the accelerated phase characterized by lymphohistiocytic infiltrates were not seen in mice or cattle.

Hermansky-Pudlak Syndrome

This rare disease is associated with oculocutaneous albinism and a bleeding tendency. Ceroid-like pigment deposits are detected in the reticuloendothelial system. In addition, these patients frequently develop colitis, pulmonary fibrosis, and systemic lupus erythematosus.

Annotated Bibliography

Bologna JL, Pawelek JM. Biology of hypopigmentation. J Am Acad Dermatol 1988;19: 217–255.

This very good review contains over 300 references.

Shanahan F, Randolf L, King R, et al. Hermansky-Pudlak syndrome: an immunologic assessment of 15 cases. Am J Med 1988;85:823–828.

According to this article, no defect in the immune system is detected. The Hermansky-Pudlak syndrome is more common in Puerto Ricans and is associated with increased frequencies of granulomatous colitis, interstitial lung disease, and possibly systemic lupus erythematosus.

Vogt-Koyanagi-Harada Syndrome

Rare disease has three phases:
- neurologic
- ocular
- skin and hair depigmentation

This very rare disease is characterized by a febrile illness associated with meningitis or encephalitis. The neurologic involvement is followed by bilateral uveitis and optic neuritis. Vitiligo and poliosis (acquired depigmentation of hair) occur in the majority of cases. In addition, halo nevi and alopecia areata may occur.

The poliosis may be limited or it may be extensive, involving all body hair. Blindness and deafness may occur infrequently.

The pathogenesis of this disease is unknown, although immunologic mediation is suspected. Cellular hypersensitivity has been detected to uveal pigment.

Annotated General Bibliography

Hammer H. Cellular hypersensitivity to uveal pigment confirmed by leukocyte migration tests in sympathetic ophthalmitis and the Vogt-Koyanagi-Harada syndrome. Br J Ophthalmol 1974;58:773–776.

Nordlund JJ, Albert D, Forget B, Lerner AB. Halo nevi and the Vogt-Koyanagi-Harada syndrome. Manifestations of vitiligo. Arch Dermatol 1980;116:690–692.

This is a provocative case report.

Sober AJ, Haynes HA. Uveitis, poliosis, hypomelanosis, and alopecia in a patient with malignant melanoma. Arch Dermatol 1978;114:439–441.

This article reports the possible immunologic mediated features of Vogt-Koyanagi-Harada syndrome detected in a melanoma patient with metastasis, clinically free of disease 8½ years later.

Vitiligo

Common disease

May be autoimmune disease

Associated with other autoimmune diseases

Vitiligo affects all races and occurs in approximately 0.5% of the world's population. The etiology is unknown, although evidence supports an autoimmune disease. This is based on the observation that there is a predominance of females; a family history in as many as one-third of patients; complement-fixing antibodies against melanocytes; and the association of vitiligo with various autoimmune diseases including hyperthyroidism, hypothyroidism, pernicious anemia, Addison's disease, diabetes mellitus, hypoparathyroidism, and myasthenia gravis.

Vitiligo can begin at any age and has a predilection for the face, axilla, and groin. The lesions are usually symmetrical. Damage to the skin such as that caused by friction or trauma may induce an isomorphic or Koebner's phenomena.

Annotated Bibliography

Betterle C, Peserico A, Bersani G. Vitiligo and autoimmune polyendocrine deficiencies with autoantibodies to melanin-producing cells. Arch Dermatol 1979;115:364.

Evidence for serum antimelanocyte antibodies in one of two patients with vitiligo detected with a complement-fixing, indirect fluorescent technique.

Bologna JL, Pawelek JM. Biology of hypopigmentation. J Am Acad Dermatol 1988; 19:217–255.

Cunliffe WJ, Hall R, Newell DJ, Stevenson CJ. Vitiligo, thyroid disease and autoimmunity. Br J Dermatol 1968;80:135–139.

Tuberous Sclerosis

Hypomelanotic macules and patches common in tuberous sclerosis

The hypomelanotic macules appearing as ovals (ash leaf), hypopigmented patches in a dermatomal distribution, confetti spots, and poliosis are the earliest signs of tuberous sclerosis. Careful examination of infants 1 year or less with a seizure disorder for these lesions are diagnostically important.

(See Chapter 43, "Tuberous Sclerosis," for further discussion.)

Annotated General Bibliography

Bleehen SS, Ebling FJG, Champion RH. Disorders of skin colour. In: Rook, Wilkinson, Ebling, eds. Textbook of Dermatology, Chapter 35. London: Blackwell Scientific, 1992; pp 1561–1622.

This is an excellent overview of pigment alterations associated with systemic diseases.

Mosher DB, Fitzpatrick TB, Ortonne JP, Hori Y. Normal skin color and general considerations of pigmentary disorders; hypomelanosis and hypermelanosis. In: Freedberg IM, Erson AZ, Wolff K, eds. Fitzpatrick's Dermatology in General Medicine, Chapters 88, 89. New York: McGraw-Hill, 1999, pp 936–1017.

These outstanding chapters provide authoritative data with excellent bibliographies.

CHAPTER 3

Human Leukocyte Antigen

Frank C. Arnett, M.D.

The immune system is known to play a prominent role in many diseases that affect frequently the skin. Many of these disorders are classified as autoimmune in origin because abnormal immune responses involving either innate immune effectors (complement defects) or acquired immune mechanisms (autoantibodies and/or autoreactive T cells) have been implicated in pathogenesis. Genetic contributions underlying these immunologic abnormalities also have been suspected because many of these diseases tend to recur in families, although not in classic mendelian patterns. Thus, it is not surprising that an important genetic region that controls the immune response, the major histocompatibility complex (MHC), has been associated with most of these immunologically mediated diseases in studies conducted over the last 25 years. Even though knowledge of the molecular structure and function of the MHC has evolved dramatically over the last decade and its associations with autoimmune diseases further solidified at the molecular level, the precise mechanisms by which it predisposes to certain diseases remain largely unknown. In addition, it is becoming clear that the MHC is not the sole genetic determinant of disease susceptibility. Rather, a large number of additional genetic loci are being linked or associated with autoimmunity, including those for cytokines and their receptors, apoptosis-related genes, and other loci yet to be identified. Thus, most of the autoimmune diseases are probably complex, polygenic traits that also are likely to be genetically heterogenous and require environmental contributions. Nonetheless, MHC associations remain important clues to disease pathogenesis and represent a challenging area of research and its translation to patient care. This chapter will first describe the molecular structure and function of the MHC and then review its currently known relationships with several important dermatological diseases.

Importance of MHC

The Major Histocompatibility Complex

The human MHC, or HLA (human leukocyte antigens) region, is located on the short arm of chromosome 6 and spans approximately 3.5 kb of DNA or 2 cM (recombinational units). Multiple gene loci are located within the MHC and are classified into three functionally distinct clusters: HLA-class I, II, and III (Figure 3–1). Human leukocyte antigen class I genes include HLA-A, B, C and other loci that encode glycoproteins co-expressed as dimers with β-2 microglobulin (class I molecules) on all nucleated cells. Class I molecules bind and present intracellularly processed antigens to T-cell antigen receptors on CD8-positive cytoxic T cells. The HLA-class II region includes HLA-DR, DQ, and DP genes, which

Class I molecules present antigen to CD8 T cells. Class II molecules present antigen to CD4 T cells.

encode the alpha and beta chains of class II heterodimeric molecules expressed on macrophages, dendritic cells, B lymphocytes, and activated T cells (ie, antigen-presenting cells). The class II molecules bind and present processed antigens to T-cell receptors on CD4-positive helper/inducer T lymphocytes. The class II region also encodes genes involved in intracellular antigen processing (proteosomes or LMP loci) and transport (TAP for class I and DM for class II), which for the sake of simplicity, are not depicted in Figure 3–1. The class III region, mapping between class I and II, includes genes for three complement proteins, C4A and C4B, which together comprise the fourth complement component (C4) and single genes each for C2 and factor B. The genes for tumor necrosis factor (TNF)–α and TNF-β (lymphotoxin) also reside in the HLA-class III region.

Polymorphism

HLA-DRB1 locus is most polymorphic
Alpha chain of DR locus is invariant

Striking polymorphism or variability in amino acid sequences characterizes most of the HLA-class I and II loci (see Figure 3–1). Human leukocyte antigen nomenclature was originally based on serologic typing of lymphocytes to define HLA specificities. Human leukocyte antigens were assigned a numerical designation prefixed by the letter of the locus from which they were encoded (ie, HLA-A3, HLA-B27, HLA-DR3, HLA-DQ2, etc). More recently, extensive cloning and DNA sequencing of the MHC has revealed additional HLA loci and even more extensive allelic polymorphism at the molecular level for each locus. For example, HLA-B27 has been found to have at least 20 molecular subtypes, which are now designated as HLA-B*2701, B*2702, etc. There are several HLA-DR loci (DRB1, DRB3, DRB4, and DRB5). The HLA-DRB1 locus is the most polymorphic (Figure 3–2), and multiple subtypes (alleles) of DR specificities can be defined using high resolution DNA typing. Thus, former HLA-DR4 specificities are now defined as HLA-DRB1*0401, *0402, *0403, etc. The DRA (alpha) chain is invariant and associates into a heterodimer with each of the encoded beta chains from the DRB loci. On the other hand, both alpha- and beta-chain loci of HLA-DQ (and also HLA-DP) are polymorphic and encode a large number of HLA-DQA1 (Figure 3–3) and DQB1 (Figure 3–4) alleles.

Linkage disequilibrium

The MHC, with its multiple loci and alleles, is inherited en bloc as a haplotype from each parent in a mendelian co-dominant fashion. There is, however, a 2% likelihood of a recombinational event occurring within the MHC region with each mating. Thus, given a long evolutionary period in a relatively outbred

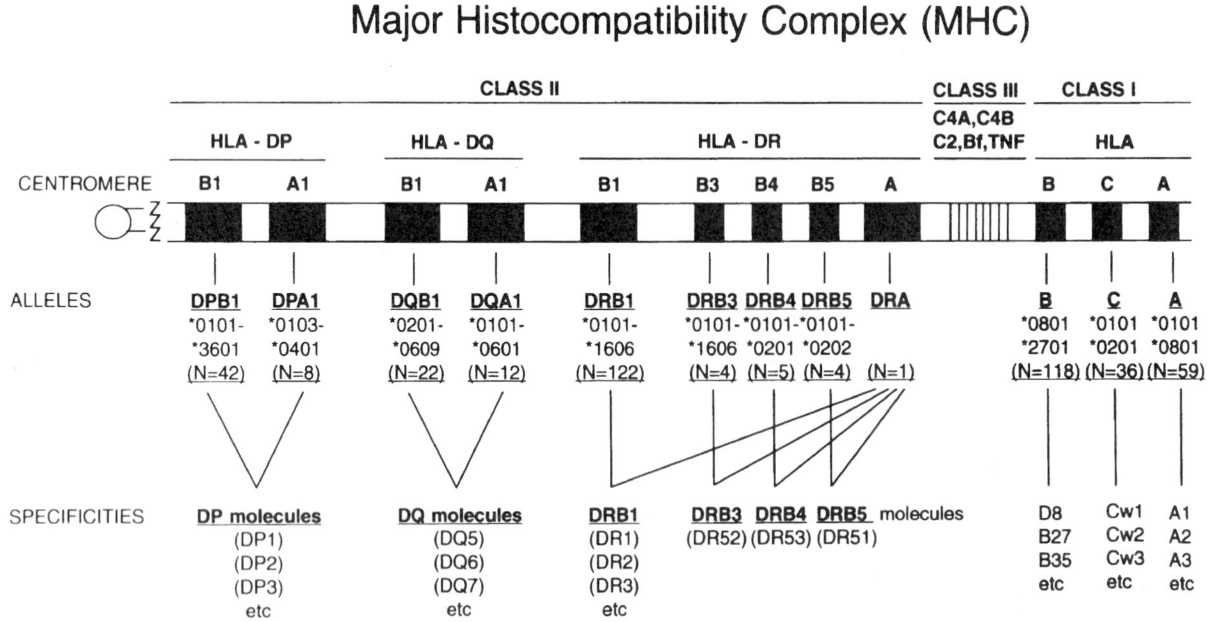

FIGURE 3–1 Map of the major histocompatibility complex (MHC) genes on human chromosome 6p. Class I and II loci encode specific alleles detectable by HLA DNA typing, which form heterodimers on cell surfaces (specificities) detectable by serologic HLA typing. All genes not shown and not drawn to scale.

human population, no specific HLA-A, B, C, DR or DQ alleles should occur together on the same haplotype more often than expected by chance alone. Such is not the case, however, because certain combinations of HLA alleles are observed to occur together more often than expected—a phenomenon referred to as linkage disequilibrium. Different extended haplotypes occur in different ethnic groups and populations and probably represent allelic combinations that have provided a selective advantage against certain endemic infections. One such haplotype in Caucasians of northwestern European descent is HLA-B8 (B*0801), DR3 (DRB1*0301), DQ2 (DQB1*0201; DQA1*0501), and there are many such examples in different populations.

Human Leukocyte Antigen Molecules

The three-dimensional structures of both HLA-class I and II molecules have been determined by x-ray crystallography. The most external domain of both HLA-class I and II molecules are configured as a floor of beta-pleated sheets surrounded on each side by alpha helices (Figure 3–5). This structure results in an antigen-binding groove or cleft which holds the peptides presented to T cells. Class I molecules can bind peptides 8 to 10 amino acids in length, whereas class II molecules bind larger peptides containing 18 to 25 amino acids. The allelic polymorphisms (see Figures 3–2 to 3–4), which make each HLA molecule distinct, line the antigen-binding cleft and confer to each a unique peptide-binding

HLA molecules: antigen-binding groove

Class I molecules bind peptides of 8–10 amino acids.

Class II molecules bind peptides of 18–25 amino acids.

```
                                    10        20        30        40        50        60        70        80        90
DRB1*0101          DR1 Dw1         RFLWQLKFECHFFNGTERVRLLERCIYNQEESVRFDSDVGEYRAVTELGRPDAEYWNSQKDLLEQRRAAVDTYCRHNYGVGESFTVQRR
DRB1*0102              Dw20        -------------------------------------------------------------------------------AV--------
DRB1*0103          DR Br           -------------------------------------------------------------I--DE-----------------------
DRB1*1501          DR2 Dw2         -----P-R------------F-D-YF---------------F-------------------I---A--------------V--------
DRB1*1502              Dw12        -----P-R------------F-D-YF---------------F-------------------I---A-----------------------
DRB1*1503                                 R------------F-D-HF---------------F-------------------I---A--------------V--------
DRB1*1601              Dw21        -----P-R------------F-D-YF-----------------------------------F--D------------------------
DRB1*1602              Dw22        -----P-R------------F-D-YF--------------------------------------D------------------------
DRB1*0301          DR3(DRw17)      ---EYSTS------------Y-D-YFH----N---------F-----------------------K-GR--N--------V--------
DRB1*0302             (DRw18)      ---EYSTS------------F---YFH----N---------------------------------K-GR--N-----------------
DRB1*0401          DR4 Dw4         ---E-V-H------------F-D-YF-H---Y---------------------------------K-----------------------
DRB1*0402              Dw10        ---E-V-H------------F-D-YF-H---Y-----------------------------I--DE--------------V--------
DRB1*0403              Dw13        ---E-V-H------------F-D-YF-H---Y------------------------------------E-----------V--------
DRB1*0404              Dw14        ---E-V-H------------F-D-YF-H---Y------------------------------------------------V--------
DRB1*0405              Dw15        ---E-V-H------------F-D-YF-H---Y-------------------S-------------------------------------
DRB1*0406              DKT2        ---E-V-H------------F-D-YF-H----------------------------------------E-----------V--------
DRB1*0407              Dw13        ---E-V-H------------F-D-YF-H---Y------------------------------------E--------------------
DRB1*0408              Dw14               H------------F-D-YF-H---Y---------------------------------------------------
DRB1*0409                                 H------------F-D-YF-H---Y-------------------S-------------K-----------------
DRB1*0410                                    ----------F-D-YF-H---Y-------------------S----------------------------V-
DRB1*0411                                    ----------F-D-YF-H---Y-------------------S----------------E-----------V-
DRB1*11011,11012 DR5(DRw11)        ---EYSTS------------F-D-YF-----Y---------F----------E--------F--D------------------------
DRB1*1102             (DRw11)      ---EYSTS------------F-D-YF-----Y---------F----------E--------I--DE--------------V--------
DRB1*1103             (DRw11)      ---EYSTS------------F-D-YF-----Y---------F----------E--------F--DE--------------V--------
DRB1*11041,11042      (DRw11)      ---EYSTS------------F-D-YF-----Y---------F----------E--------F--D---------------V--------
DRB1*1201             (DRw12)      ---EYSTG--Y-------------HFH----LL--------F---------V--S------I--D--------------AV--------
DRB1*1202             (DRw12b)     ---EYSTG--Y-------------HFH----LL--------F---------V--S------F--D--------------AV
DRB1*1301          DR6 (DRw13-Dw18)---EYSTS------------F-D-YFH----N---------F-------------------I--DE--------------V--------
DRB1*1302             (DRw13-Dw19) ---EYSTS------------F-D-YFH----N---------F-------------------I--DE-----------------------
DRB1*1303             (DRw13-DHAG) ---EYSTS------------F-D-YF-----Y-------------------S---------I--DK-----------------------
DRB1*1304             (DRw13)      ---EYSTS------------F-D-YF-----Y---------F---------S---------I--DE--------------V--------
DRB1*1305             (DRw13-PEV)  ---EYSTS------------F-D-YFH----N---------F-------------------F--D------------------------
DRB1*1306             (DRB1*13.MW) ---EYSTS------------F-D-YFH----N---------F-------------------I--D---------------V--------
DRB1*1401             (DRw14-Dw9)  ---EYSTS------------F-D-YFH----F-------------------A--H---------R---E-----------V--------
DRB1*1402             (DRw14-Dw16) ---EYSTS------------F---YFH----N---------------------------------------------------------
DRB1*1403             (JX6)        ---EYSTS------------F---YFH----N--------------------------------D---L--------------------
DRB1*1404             (DRw14)      ---EYSTG--Y---------F-D-YFH----F-------------------A--H---------R---E-----------V--------
DRB1*1405             (DRw14c)       -EYSTS--Q---------F-D-YFH----F--------------------------------R---E-----------V-
DRB1*1406                                TS------------F---YFH----N------------------------------------------------V-
DRB1*1407                                -EYSTS------------F-D-YFH----F-------------------A--H---------R---E--------------
DRB1*1408                                -EYSTS------------F-D-YFH----F----------------------H---------R---E-----------V-
DRB1*0701          DR7 Dw17        -----G-YK----------QF---LF-----F-------------------V--S------I--D--GQ---V----------------
DRB1*0702              DB1         -----G-YK----------QF---LF-----F-------------------V--S------I--D--GQ---V----------------
DRB1*0801          DRw8 Dw8.1      ---EYSTG--Y---------F-D-YF-----Y-------------------S---------F--D---L--------------------
DRB1*0802               Dw8.2      ---EYSTG--Y---------F-D-YF-----Y-----------------------------F--D---L--------------------
DRB1*0803               Dw8.3      ---EYSTG--Y---------F-D-YF-----Y-------------------S---------I--D---L--------------
DRB1*0804                          ---EYSTG--Y---------F-D-YF-----Y-----------------------------F--D---L-----------V
DRB1*0901          DR9             ---K-D--------------Y-H-G------N-------------------V--S------F--R---F---V--------
DRB1*1001          DRw10           ---EEV------------------RVH----YA-Y-----------------------------R------------------------
```

FIGURE 3–2 Polymorphic amino acid sequences of HLA-DRB1 alleles. Consensus sequence of DRB1*0101 is shown at the top followed by other DRB1 alleles. Letter designations for amino acids indicate positions where other alleles differ from DRB1*0101, whereas dashes (-) indicate identical residues. Note the polymorphic sequences cluster into three hypervariable regions.

HLA-DQA1 FIRST DOMAIN ALLELE SEQUENCES

```
D Q A               10        20        30        40        50        60        70        80
DQA1*0101 EDIVADHVASCGVNLYQFYGPSGQYTHEFDGDEEFYVDLERKETAWRWPEFSKFGGFDPQGALRNMAVAKHNLNIMIKRYNSTAATN
DQA1*0102 ---------------------------------Q-----------------------------------------------------
DQA1*0103 ------------------------F--------Q------K--------------------------------------
DQA1*0104 -G--------------------------------------------------------------------------------------
DQA1*0201 ----------Y------S------F-------------------V-KL-L-HRLR*----F--T-I--L------L---S-------
DQA1*0301 ----------Y------S-------S------------------V-QL-L-RR-RR----F--T-I--L------V---S-------
DQA1*0302 ----------Y------S-------S------------------V-QL-L-RR-RR----F--T-I--L------V---S-------
DQA1*0401 ----------Y------S---------------Q-----G----V-CL-VLRQ-R*----F--T-I--T------L---S-------
DQA1*0501 ----------Y------S---------------Q----------V-CL-VLRQ-R*----F--T-I--L-----SL---S-------
DQA1*0502 ----------Y------S---------------Q----------V-CL-VLRQ-R*--R-F--T-I--L-----SL---S-------
DQA1*0503 ----------Y------S---------------Q----------V-CL-VLRQ-R*----F--T-I--L-----SL---S-------
DQA1*0601 -----------------S------F--------Q-----G----V-CL-VLRQ-R*----F--T-I--T------L---S-------
```

FIGURE 3–3 Polymorphic amino acid sequences of HLA-DQA1 alleles. Consensus sequence of DQA1*0101 is shown at the top followed by other DQA1 alleles. Letter designations for amino acids indicate positions where other alleles differ from DQA1*0101, whereas dashes (-) indicate identical residues. Note the polymorphic sequences cluster into three hypervariable regions.

HLA-DQB1 FIRST DOMAIN SEQUENCES

```
D Q B1                10        20        30        40        50        60        70        80        90
DQB1*0501     RYSPEDFVYQFKGLCYFTNGTERVRGVTRHIYNREEYVRFDSDVGVYRAVTPQGRPVAEYWNSQKEVLEGARASVDRVCRHNYEVAYRGILQRR
DQB1*0502     --------------------------------------------------------------------------------------------------------------S-----------------------------------------------------------------------------
DQB1*05031,2  --------------------------------------------------------------------------------------------------------------D----------------------------------------------------------------------------
DQB1*0504     ----------------------------------------------------------Y------I------------------------------------------S-----------------DI------ED--------T----
DQB1*0601     ---------------L-----AM----------------------Y-----Y----------D--------------------------------------D----------------DI------RT---EL--T---------------------F------
DQB1*0602     ---------------F-------M----------------------L------Y-----------A-------------------------------------D---------------------------T---EL--T---------------------F------
DQB1*0603     ------------------------M---------------------L---------------------A-------------------------------------D---------------------------T---EL--T---------------------F-----
DQB1*0604     ------------------------M---------------------L---------------------A-----------------------------------------------------------------RT---EL--T--------------------G-------
DQB1*0605     -------------------------------------------------L--------Y-----------A-----------------------------------------------------------------RT---EL--T-------------------G------
DQB1*0606                                -------------------L-------Y-----------A-----------------------------------------------------------------RT---A-----
DQB1*0607                             ----------------------L--------------------A--------------------------------------D-------------------------RT---EL-T--------------
DQB1*0608     --------------------------------------------------L--------------------A-------------------------------------------------------------------T---EL-T-----------------
DQB1*0609     --------------------------------------------------L------Y-----------A-----------------------------------------------------------------RT---EL-T-------------------G------
DQB1*0201     ------------------------M----------------------L--S--S----------I--------------EF-------------LL--L--A---------------DI-----RK---A--------------------QLEL-TT----
DQB1*0202      -----------------------M----------------------L--S--S----------I--------------EF-------------LL--L--A---------------DI------RK---A-------------------QLEL-TT----
DQB1*0301     ----------------------AM----------------------Y------Y---------A--------E-----------------L--P--D--------------------------RT---EL-T--------------QLEL-TT----
DQB1*0302     --------------------------M---------------------L-------Y----------A-----------------------------L--P--A---------------------------RT---EL-T--------------QLEL-TT----
DQB1*03031,2  --------------------------M---------------------L-------Y----------A-----------------------------L--P--D---------------------------RT---EL-T--------------QLEL-TT----
DQB1*0304     ------------------------AM--------------------Y------Y----------A--------E-----------------L--P--A--------------------------RT---EL-T--------------QLEL-TT----
DQB1*0305     --------------------------M--------------------Y------Y----------A--------E-----------------L--P--D--------------------------RT---EL-T--------------QLEL-TT---
DQB1*0401     -----------------F-------M-----------------L----------Y----------A-----------------------------L---LD----------------DI-------ED------T--------------QLEL-TT-
DQB1*0402     -----------------F-------M-----------------------------Y----------A-----------------------------L---LD----------------DI-------ED------T--------------QLEL-TT---
```

FIGURE 3–4 Polymorphic amino acid sequences of HLA-DQB1 alleles. Consensus sequence of HLA-DQB1*0501 is shown at the top followed by other DQB1 alleles. Letter designations for amino acids indicate positions where other alleles differ from DQB1*0501, whereas dashes (-) indicate identical residues. Note the polymorphic sequences cluster into three hypervariable regions.

motif (see Figure 3–5). Only peptides comprised of amino acids having the appropriate sizes and charges can be bound by a specific HLA molecule.

Immune response genes

When an HLA molecule presents a peptide to a T cell that is recognized as nonself, a specific immune response occurs. Self-peptides, which also are continually being processed and presented by HLA molecules, should not elicit an immune response because autoreactive T cells recognizing self-peptides in the context of MHC have been deleted by the thymus during early development.

Thus, the multiple loci and alleles within the MHC should be viewed as specific immune response genes, which confer a unique repertoire to each individual and an extraordinarily diverse set of strategies for dealing with microbial challenges to the human population.

HLA and Diseases

Role of MHC in autoimmunity

The same polymorphisms in HLA alleles that determine specific immune responses also may confer susceptibility to disease. A large number of human disorders, especially those considered to be autoimmune in nature, have been associated with a variety of HLA alleles. Sequencing of several disease-associated HLA alleles has shown them not to be mutated or different from those found in normal individuals. Thus, other defects, whether genetic and/or environmental, leading to a breakdown of tolerance are more likely explanations for autoimmunity than structural changes within the MHC. On the other hand, the fact that genetic polymorphisms of HLA are associated with disease predisposition implies that the MHC plays some role. A likely possibility is that the MHC orchestrates autoimmune responses (ie, the binding and presentation of autoantigenic peptides to T cells) as effectively and specifically as it directs normal immune responses to foreign peptides.

MHC relationship with autoimmune diseases: a statistically significant increase or decrease in HLA frequency compared with controls suggests an association

Most HLA associations with diseases have been discovered using case-control studies. Such investigations are only valid when healthy, unrelated controls are well matched by ethnic background and locale to the unrelated disease cases. HLA allelic frequencies vary considerably among ethnic groups and in different locations. A large enough number of study subjects in each group to provide statistical power also is essential. A statistically significant increase or decrease of an HLA allele in the cases compared with the controls suggests an association.

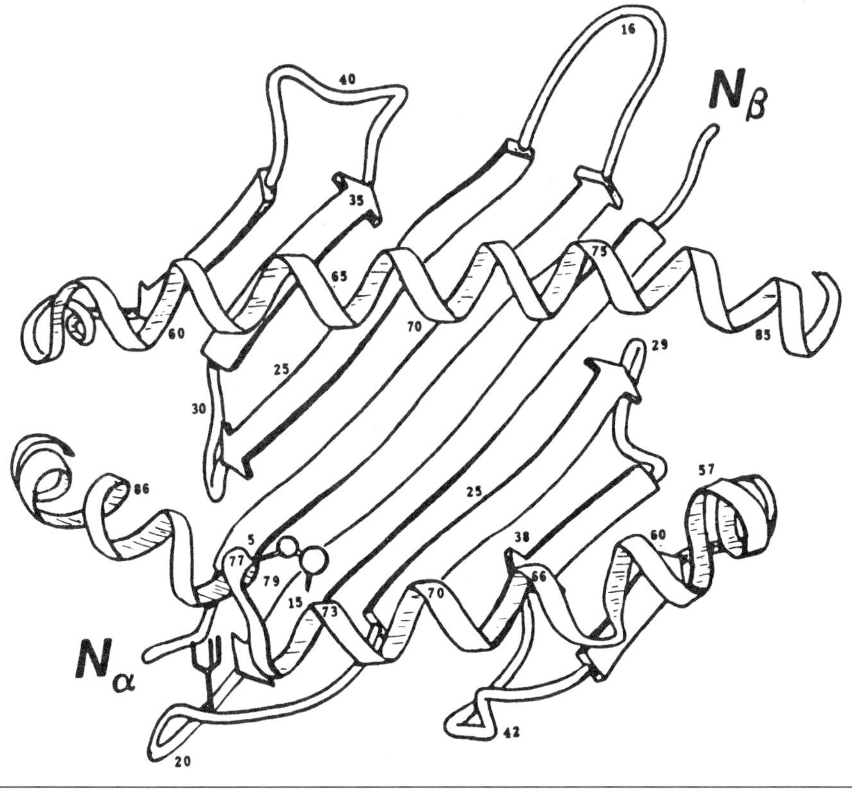

FIGURE 3–5 Schematic representation of the outermost domain of HLA-class II molecules shows configuration into an antigen-binding cleft. Numbers indicate the same amino acid positions as shown for the linear sequences of HLA-class II alleles (Figures 3–2 to 3–4).

When multiple comparisons are being made, however, there is a high probability that one or more alleles will be increased or decreased by chance alone. Therefore, a Bonferroni correction of multiplying the p value by the number of alleles compared is usually appropriate. If the same alleles have been found increased or decreased in an independent study, then this correction is not necessary. In addition to the p value, the strength of an association is also tested by determining an odds ratio (OR) or relative risk. With an OR of 1 showing no risk, higher or lower numbers give some indication of how much influence an HLA allele may have on disease risk. An OR of 2 indicates a twofold risk, whereas that of 100 has a 100-fold risk, the latter being more impressive. A negative OR implies that an HLA allele does not promote risk and is either neutral or protective. To be viewed as truly protective, an HLA allele should be consistently decreased from study to study and should prove to protect from the disease when inherited together with the allele that promotes the disease.

Importance of HLA associations across ethnic lines in evaluation of HLA associations with autoimmune diseases

At times, more than one HLA allele will be found to be associated with a disease. Often this is the case when different ethnic groups are studied. Such a finding could indicate that each of these alleles shares a common amino acid sequence that promotes the disease, the so-called "shared epitope hypothesis." Alternatively, it could be marking another nearby allele that is in linkage disequilibrium with each of the different associated alleles. The importance of comparing HLA associations across many ethnic lines cannot be overemphasized. In this way, the potential confounding effects of both shared allelic polymorphisms and linkage disequilibrium can be examined and a primary association established.

Several representative dermatologic diseases that have been associated with HLA and exemplify important concepts are discussed below.

Lupus Erythematosus

Lupus erythematosus (LE) is a multisystem autoimmune disease that may manifest a variety of cutaneous features, including the distinctive malar rash, discoid lesions, the annular and psoriasiform types of subacute cutaneous lupus erythematosus (SCLE), leukocytoclastic vasculitis, livedo reticularis, bullous lesions, and others. The clinical heterogeneity of LE is paralleled by a large number of circulating autoantibodies to both intracellular nuclear and cytoplasmic autoantigens, as well as some extracellular antigens. The many inflammatory lesions of LE are believed to result from these autoantibody responses, either in the form of immune complexes or directly from autoantibody-mediated injury, often in conjunction with complement activation.

SLE:
increased frequency in families
concordance of 25% in monozygotic versus 2% in dizygotic twins

Genetic factors clearly play important roles in both disease susceptibility and expression, but environmental contributions, probably ubiquitous in nature, also appear to be necessary. The disease tends to recur in families approximately 10% of the time, and the risk for first-degree relatives of a patient with lupus, especially females, is 2 to 3%. Other autoimmune diseases, circulating autoantibodies, and other markers of immune dysregulation also are found commonly in lupus families. No typical mendelian pattern of inheritance is apparent in such kindreds; however, concordance for LE in monozygotic twins (25%) versus dizygotic twins (2%) not only supports the importance of heredity but also demonstrates the need for environmental triggers.

Although MHC class I and, later, class II alleles were the first genetic markers to be associated with LE, and a large body of knowledge now exists about these correlations in many different ethnic groups, it appears likely that the effects of HLA genes on disease susceptibility are relatively modest. In fact, a variety of additional non-HLA genes recently has been shown to be associated with systemic lupus erythematosus (SLE), including certain cytokines (eg, TNF-α, interleukin [IL]-10, IL-6), immunoglobulin Fc cell-surface receptors, apoptosis genes (BCL-2), and others.

The most frequent HLA associations with lupus are the class II specificities, HLA-DR2 and HLA-DR3 (Figure 3–6). Each of these HLA types confers approximately a two- to threefold risk of developing lupus. The specific HLA-DR2 alleles that have been implicated are HLA-DRB1*1501 in Caucasians and Asians and HLA-DRB1*1503 in African Americans. These same alleles are in linkage disequilibrium with HLA-DQ6 (DQB1*0602, DQA1*0102) in each of these populations, so it is unclear which is the primary disease-conferring gene. Similarly, two different HLA-DR3 (DRB1*0301) and HLA-DQ2 (DQB1*0201, DQA1*0501) haplotypes associate with lupus in most Caucasian populations (see Figure 3–6). Recently, DR8 and DQ4 haplotypes have been found to associate with lupus in patients of Native American descent. Localization of the primary disease-conferring gene on the HLA-B8, DR3 haplotype is further confounded by the presence of a large deletion of the C4A gene in the class III region resulting in a partial deficiency of C4. Deficiency or null alleles of C4 occur on many other HLA haplotypes (but not typically on DR2 haplotypes) and appear to be independent risk factors for LE in many different populations. C4 null alleles show relative risks of approximately 3 in persons who are heterozygous but up to 20 in those who are homozygous. Total C2 deficiency, which is also linked to the MHC, predisposes to LE, typically an SCLE picture, and anti-Ro (SS-A) antibodies.

HLA-DR2 and HLA-DR3 associations with SLE

C4 null alleles are independent risk factors for SLE.

The major effect of HLA genes in lupus appears to be the promotion, if not the frank mediation, of many of the autoantibody responses that characterize the disease. Specific HLA alleles, as well as polymorphic amino acid sequences within the peptide-binding groove shared by certain alleles, show stronger correlations with certain autoantibodies than with the disease itself. In turn, auto antibodies are associated with and may cause some clinical features, including distinct dermatologic manifestations. Several examples of this pathway leading to cutaneous features of LE follow.

Association of HLA alleles with specific autoantibody responses in SLE

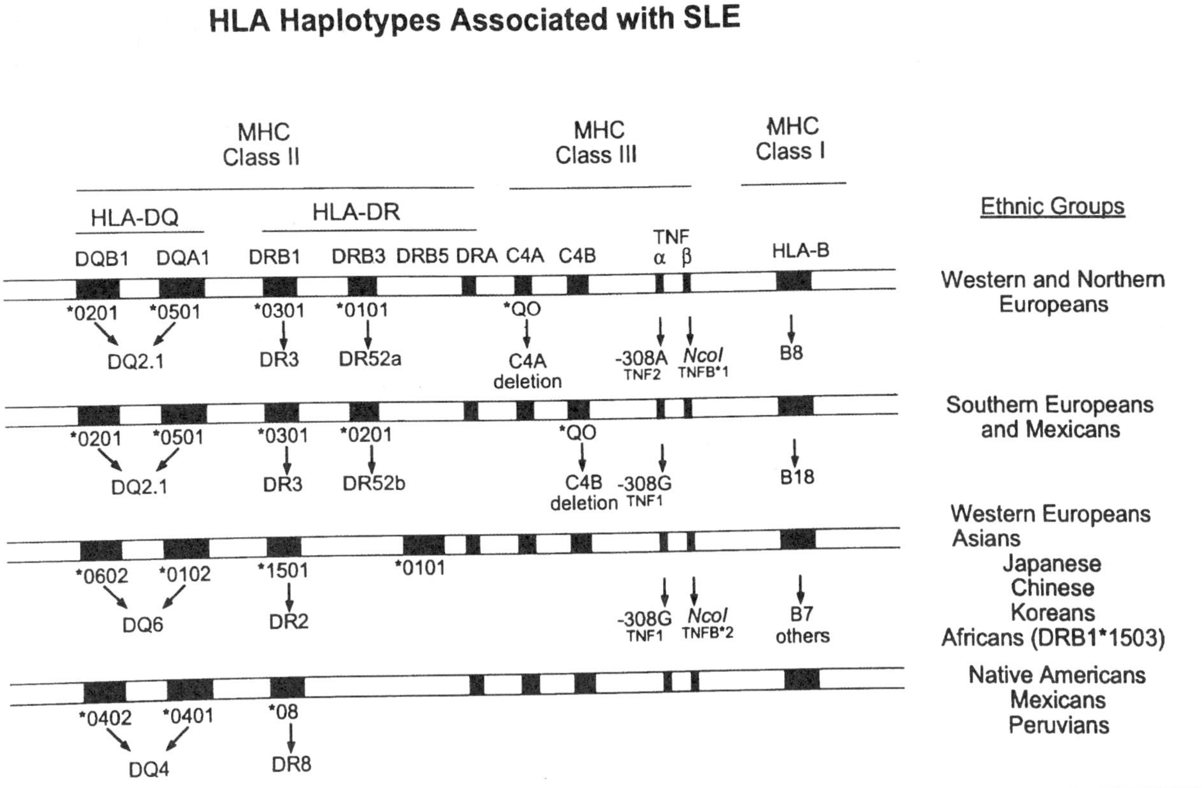

FIGURE 3–6 Human leukocyte antigen class II haplotypes associated with systemic lupus erythematosus in different ethnic populations. (Reproduced with permission from Tan FK, Arnett FC. The genetics of lupus. Curr Opin Rheumatol 1998;10:339–408.)

Anti-Ro (SS-A) and Anti-La (SS-B) Antibodies

The anti-Ro (SS-A) autoantibody, often accompanied by anti-La (SS-B), is strongly associated with photosensitive annular and papulosquamous skin lesions in lupus syndromes, such as SCLE, and with primary and most secondary forms of Sjögren's syndrome. Transplacental passage of maternal anti-Ro also is associated with a similar annular rash or congenital heart block in infants of anti-Ro–positive mothers. In fact, these cutaneous-autoantibody correlations are so strong as to suggest a cause-and-effect relationship.

Anti-Ro antibodies associated with both HLA-DR2 and HLA-DR3 phenotypes

Presence of leucine residue at position 26 of beta chain and glutamine residue at position 34 of alpha chain at DQ locus critical determinants

Anti-Ro, especially when accompanied by anti-La, is strongly associated with the HLA-DR3, DQ2 haplotype regardless of clinical disease setting, (ie, SLE vs Sjögren's syndrome vs SCLE vs neonatal LE). In anti-Ro–positive patients who are negative for HLA-DR3, DQ2, the HLA-DR2, DQ6 haplotype is found in the majority. Patients with the HLA-DR3 haplotype have been shown to produce higher antibody levels than those with other haplotypes; however, patients who are heterozygous for HLA-DQ2, DQ6 elaborate the very highest levels of anti-Ro and anti-La antibodies. Molecular studies have identified the specific HLA-DQB1 and DQA1 alleles that promote these autoantibody responses, and all of the promotive HLA-DQB1 alleles encode a leucine residue at position 26 of the DQ beta chain (see Figure 3–4), whereas all of the promotive HLA-DQA1 alleles encode glutamine at position 34 of the DQ alpha chain (see Figure 3–3). The most powerful MHC risk factor for anti-Ro in Caucasians and African Americans with SLE or Sjögren's syndrome is the presence of four such HLA-DQA1 and HLA-DQB1 alleles, and only rarely do patients have less than two such alleles bearing the appropriate amino acids. Because these associated amino acids are positioned within the peptide-binding cleft of HLA-DQ molecules (Figure 3–7), it appears likely that they play roles in binding an autoantigenic peptide that drives the anti-Ro/La autoimmune response.

Antiphospholipid Antibodies

Another important autoantibody system in LE is that directed to phospholipids. Antiphospholipid antibodies (aPL), as measured by anticardiolipin ELISA or lupus anticoagulant assays, occur in approximately 30% of SLE patients and, by

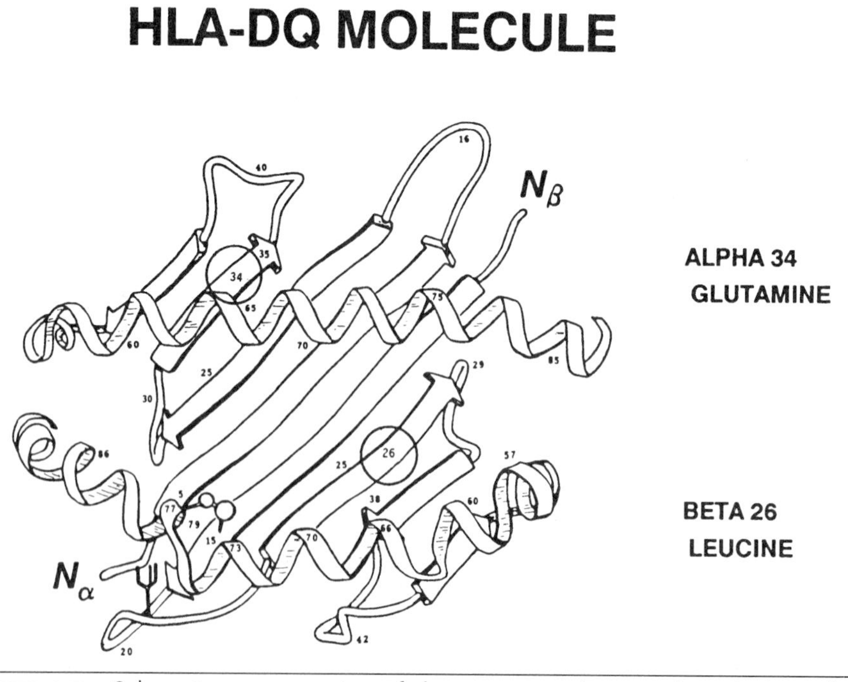

FIGURE 3–7 Schematic representation of the outermost domain of an HLA-DQ heterodimer. The critical polymorphic amino acids predisposing to the Ro (SS-A)/La (SS-B) autoantibody responses are shown within the antigen binding cleft.

definition, all patients with the primary antiphospholipid syndrome (APS). Although the autoantigenic targets of such antibodies are controversial, it seems clear that the serum factor β2-glycoprotein I (β2GPI) complexed to phospholipids represents at least one such important autoantigen. Clinically, patients with aPL show a heightened predisposition to spontaneous arterial and/or venous thrombotic events. Two dermatologic manifestations of aPL are livedo reticularis and chronic cutaneous ulcers, usually of the leg.

Antiphospholipid antibodies associated with specific amino acid sequence in DQ beta chain at positions 71–77

Human leukocyte antigen association studies with anticardiolipin antibodies have implicated HLA-DR4, DR7, and the DR53 specificity, which occurs on both DR4 and DR7 haplotypes. The HLA-DR4 association has been found primarily in Caucasians of Western European descent and the DR7 in those of Southern European descent. Similar studies of lupus anticoagulants have tended to implicate HLA-DQB1 alleles. A recent, large molecular HLA study in SLE patients of three ethnic groups with anti-β2GPI antibodies found the strongest associations to be HLA-DQB1*03 alleles (*0301, 0302, and 0303), especially in Mexican Americans and Caucasians, as well as the HLA-DRB*1302, DQB1*0604/*0605 haplotypes, especially in African Americans. The proposed sequence in the HLA-DQ chain, which may promote this aPL response, may be the amino acids TRAELDT spanning positions 71 to 77. It is perhaps notable that the HLA alleles associated with aPL antibodies in SLE, unlike those correlating with anti-Ro/La, are not those which have been associated with SLE itself. Most of the major autoantibody systems which occur in SLE have been associated with certain HLA alleles or haplotypes (Table 3–1).

Scleroderma

Scleroderma, or systemic sclerosis (SSc), is a multisystem disease of unknown etiology characterized by cutaneous and visceral fibrosis, as well as by obliterative arterial lesions. There is marked clinical heterogeneity to the expression of SSc both with respect to the amount of skin involvement and internal organ disease. Patients are typically classified into those having a limited cutaneous form, or the CREST (*c*alcinosis, *R*aynaud's phenomenon, *e*sophageal disease, *s*clerodactyly, *t*elangiectasia) syndrome, and those having the diffuse skin form in which vital organ involvement (ie, pulmonary, cardiac, renal) is more likely to occur. Similar to LE, a variety of circulating autoantibodies to nuclear and nucleolar compo-

TABLE 3–1 Lupus Autoantibodies: Clinical and HLA Associations

Autoantibodies Polymorphism	Associated Clinical Features	HLA Associations	Proposed Critical Polymorphism
Anti-Ro (SS-A) and anti-La (SS-B)	SCLE Neonatal LE Sjögren's syndrome Vasculitis	DQ2, DQ6, and DQ8	DQA1* glut 34 DQB1*leu 26
Antiphospholipids	Thromboses	DQ7, DQ8	DQB1*^{71}TRAELDT^{77}
Anti-β2GPI	Miscarriages Livedo reticularis Leg ulcers	DRB1*1302, DQB1*0604	
Anti-U1-RNP	Raynaud's phenomenon Myositis	DR4 haplotypes	Unknown
Anti-Sm	—	DR2 haplotypes	Unknown
Antiribosomal P	Cerebritis Hepatitis	DQ6 and DQ8	DQB1*leu 26-tyr 30
Anticollagen VII	Bullae	DR2 haplotypes	Unknown

nents have been discovered; however, individual patients tend to elaborate only one dominant autoantibody. Different autoantibodies tend to correlate with distinct clinical patterns and may be used prognostically (Table 3–2). For example, anticentromere antibodies are characteristically found in patients with limited SSc or the CREST variant, whereas anti-topoisomerase I (scleroderma-70) antibodies predict diffuse cutaneous involvement and pulmonary fibrosis.

Anticentromere antibodies associated with DQ5 alleles

Anti-topoisomerase I antibodies associated with DQ7 alleles

Also like LE, certain HLA associations with SSc itself (DR5, DR1, DR3) are weak, and molecular typing has shown more striking HLA allelic correlations with scleroderma autoantibodies. The anticentromere response is associated with HLA-DQ5 and specifically with other HLA-DQB1 alleles (*0301, 0402) possessing the polar-uncharged amino acids (glycine or tyrosine in position 26 of the DQ beta chain). Anti-topoisomerase I antibodies are associated with HLA-DQB1*0301 (DQ7), which is in linkage disequilibrium with HLA-DR5 in most ethnic groups, and with HLA-DQB1*0601, which is linked to HLA-DR2 in Asians. All of the associated HLA-DQB1 alleles possess a tyrosine residue in position 30. In addition, HLA-DPB1 alleles having glutamic acid in position 69, especially HLA-DPB1*1301, appear to predispose to the anti-topoisomerase I response. Finally, T-cell proliferative responses to topoisomerase I appear to be further restricted in SSc patients and normal controls to certain HLA-DR types, specifically DR5, DR2, and DR7. Each of the SSc autoimmune responses appears to show distinctive HLA correlations, some of which overlap (see Table 3–2).

Bullous Skin Diseases

Unlike the multisystem autoimmune diseases, lupus and scleroderma, the bullous skin disorders represent examples of organ-specific autoimmunity in which an autoantibody that is directed to a component of skin is directly pathogenic in each disease and the autoantigenic target is different, as is the predisposing HLA association (Table 3–3).

Pemphigus Vulgaris

DRB1 alleles displaying the combination of phenylalanine at position 26, leucine or isoleucine at position 67, valine at position 86, and hydrophilic residues at position 70 and 71 associated across ethnic lines with PV

Pemphigus vulgaris (PV) is a blistering disease caused by IgG (immunoglobulin G) antibodies to a 130 kD protein of the cadherin superfamily of adhesion molecules designated desmoglein III. Two distinct susceptibility HLA haplotypes show striking associations with the disease, as well as linkage in families to autoantibodies to desmoglein III, which occur frequently in asymptomatic relatives of PV patients. The HLA-DR4 (DRB1*0402), DQ8 (DQB1*0302) haplo-

TABLE 3–2 Scleroderma Autoantibodies: Clinical and HLA Associations

Autoantibodies	Associated Clinical Features	HLA Association	Proposed Critical Polymorphisms
Anticentromere	Limited skin disease (CREST syndrome)	DQ5 (DQB1*05), DQ7 (DQB1*0301), DQ4 (DQB1*0402)	DQB1* gly or tyr 26
Anti-topoisomerase I (SCL-70)	Diffuse skin disease Pulmonary fibrosis	DQ7 (DQB1*0301) DPB1*1301 DR5, DR2, DR7	DQB1* tyr 30 DPB1* glu 69 Unknown
Anti–PM-SCL	Overlap with myositis	DR3, DQ2	Unknown
Anti-U_1RNP	Overlap with myositis	DR4 haplotypes	Unknown
Anti-U_3RNP (fibrillarin)	Diffuse skin disease Cardiac and renal involvement	DRB1*1302, DQB1 0604 DQ8 (DQB1*0302)	Unknown

TABLE 3–3 Bullous Skin Diseases: Autoantigens and HLA Associations

Disease	Autoantigens	HLA Associations
Pemphigus vulgaris	Desmoglein III	DR4 (DRB1*0402), and DQ8 (DQB1*0302) DR14 (DRB1*1401), DQB1*0503
Pemphigus foliaceus	Desmoglein I	DR1 (DRB1*0101, 0102), DR4 (DRB1*0404), and DR14 DRB1*1402 (shared DRB1 sequence ^{67}LLEQRRAA^{74})
Epidermolysis bullosa acquista	Collagen type VII	DR2 haplotypes (DRB1*1501 and*1503)
Dermatitis herpetiformis	Unknown	DQ2 heterodimer (DQA1*0501 and DQB1*0201) and DQ8 (DQB1*0302)

type is almost universally found in Ashkenazi Jews and Iranians with PV, leading to speculation that these two groups arose from common central Asian origins. The HLA-DR6 (or DR14, DRB1*1401), DQ5 (DQB1*0503) haplotype predisposes to PV in non-Jewish persons, usually of Southern European descent, and in Pakistanis. In Japanese PV patients, HLA-DR4 (DRB1*0403 and *0406) and DR14 (DRB1*1401, *1405, and *1406) alleles also have been found. In comparisons of shared amino acid homologies of these disease-associated HLA-DRB1 alleles across ethnic lines, the combination of phenylalanine at position 26, leucine or isoleucine at position 67, valine at position 86, and hydrophilic residues at positions 70 and 71 have been proposed as the critical class II sequences predisposing to this autoimmune response.

Pemphigus Foliaceus

Pemphigus foliaceus association with DRB alleles with amino acid sequence homology in third hypervariable region positions 67–74

The endemic form of pemphigus foliaceus (PF), also known as fogo selvagem, is another organ-specific autoimmune skin disease in which IgG antibodies to desmoglein I appear to be causative. Epidemiologic evidence suggests that the disease is triggered by bites of the black fly in genetically susceptible people. Studies of HLA associations with endemic PF across several ethnic groups in Brazil have implicated HLA-DR1 (DRB1*0101, *0102), DR4 (DRB1*0404), and DR14 (DRB1*1402). Each of these associated alleles share amino acid sequence homology in their third hypervariable regions (^{67}LLEQRRAA^{74}), which may represent the disease-susceptibility factor.

Epidermolysis Bullosa Acquisita

EBA associated with HLA-DR2 phenotype

Epidermolysis bullosa acquisita (EBA) is caused by IgG autoantibodies to a component of type VII collagen. Predisposition to EBA is strongly associated with HLA-DR2 haplotypes in both Caucasians (DRB1*1501) and African Americans (DRB1*1503). Notably, some patients with lupus will develop bullae similar to those in EBA, and such patients have been found to have anti-type VII collagen antibodies and HLA-DR2.

Dermatitis Herpetiformis

DH associated with alleles at the DQ locus

Dermatitis herpetiformis (DH) is a blistering skin disease in which granular deposits of IgA are found by direct immunofluorescence at the dermal-epidermal junction. The nature of the autoantigen is currently unknown. Dermatitis herpetiformis frequently occurs concomitantly with celiac disease (gluten-sensitive enteropathy), and both diseases respond therapeutically to a gluten-free diet. Thus, DH and celiac disease are intimately linked pathogenetically and may actually represent different clinical expressions of the same disease. Genetically, DH and celiac disease also show the same HLA associations. Almost all patients

(85–90%) with DH possess the HLA-DR3, DQ2 haplotype. Among HLA–DR3-negative patients, an increased frequency of the HLA-DR7, DQ2 haplotype has been found and an excess of HLA-DR3/DR7 heterozygotes has been noted. The primary association appears to be with HLA-DQ2, specifically the HLA-DQ heterodimer composed of the HLA-DQB1*0201 and DQA1*0501 allelic products. The HLA-DR3 haplotype carries each of these alleles, whereas HLA-DR7 carries only the relevant HLA-DQB1 alleles. Both DQA1*0501 and DQB1*0201 alleles are necessary, but they can be inherited in either *cis* (as on DR3 haplotypes) or in *trans* positions (as in DR5/DR7 heterozygotes where DR5 carries DQA1*0501 and DR7 carries DQB1*0201). Only rare patients with DH are negative for the HLA-DQ2 heterodimer, but those found have been nearly universally positive for HLA-DQ8 (DQA1*03, DQB1*0302).

Psoriasis

Psoriasis more strongly associated with HLA class I alleles

Psoriasis vulgaris, a papulosquamous skin disease, is worthy of discussion because of its high prevalence in the population (2%) and because it is more strongly associated with HLA-class I rather than class II alleles. Also, it is not at all clear that psoriasis is an autoimmune disease. Nonetheless, multiple case-control studies over the last quarter century have demonstrated a variety of HLA associations, including HLA-B13, B17, and B37, especially in patients with young age of onset. Notably, each of these HLA-B alleles is in strong linkage disequilibrium with HLA-Cw6, and this C locus specificity is now believed to represent the strongest MHC association. In many populations, the extended haplotype HLA-B17, Cw6, DR7 correlates strongly with psoriasis. More recently, genetic studies in large numbers of families have definitely shown the strongest linkage of a psoriasis locus to HLA-B or C. It remains unclear whether there is another as yet unidentified gene in this region or whether the HLA-B or C loci themselves control susceptibility. In addition, it appears that a variety of non-MHC–linked genes also may be important in psoriasis. Several genome-wide scans in psoriasis families using microsatellite markers have suggested susceptibility loci on chromosomes 4q, 16q, 17q, and 20p, as well as on 6p (MHC). Psoriasis appears to be a genetically complex disease whose pathogenesis will only be understood after identification and study of the relevant predisposing genes.

Thus, it should be apparent from these examples that the MHC plays an important role in susceptibility to and expression of a variety of cutaneous disorders. Human leukocyte antigen associations provide important clues to underlying pathogenetic mechanisms and should help focus future investigative efforts.

Annotated Bibliography

Vyse TJ, Todd JA. Genetic analysis of autoimmune disease. Cell 1996;85:311–318.

This article gives an overview of emerging new concepts about the genetics of autoimmune diseases and how modern genetic analyses are revealing them to be genetically complex disorders.

Nepom BS, Nepom GT. Polyglot and polymorphism. Arthritis Rheum 1995;38:1715–1721.

A simplified but comprehensive discussion of HLA nomenclature and polymorphism is provided in this article.

Arnett FC Jr. The Genetics of Human Lupus. In: DJ Wallace, BH Hahn, eds. Dubois Lupus Erythematosus. Baltimore: Williams and Wilkens, 1997.

This article provides a comprehensive review of the genetics of lupus syndromes up to 1997, including a more in-depth discussion of HLA structure, function, and correlations of specific HLA alleles with autoimmune responses.

Tan FK, Arnett FC. The genetics of lupus. Curr Opin Rheumatol 1998;10:399–408.

This update examines newer genetic associations with lupus (since the previous reference), including non-MHC genes and chromosomal locations.

Reveille JD, Arnett FC. The immunogenetics of Sjögren's syndrome. Rheum Dis Clin North Am 1992;18:539–550.

This is a comprehensive review of what is known about the immunogenetics and HLA associations with Sjögren's syndrome, including the anti-Ro (SS-A) and anti-La (SS-B) autoantibodies.

Asherson RA, Khamashta MA, Ordi-Ros J, et al. The "primary" antiphospholipid syndrome: major clinical and serological features. Medicine (Baltimore) 1989; 68(6):366–374.

This article reviews the clinical manifestations of antiphospholipid antibodies and justification for the clinical recognition of primary antiphospholipid syndromes occurring in the absence of lupus.

Arnett FC. HLA and autoimmunity in scleroderma (systemic sclerosis). Int Rev Immunol 1995;12(2–4):107–128.

This article provides a comprehensive review of evidence for genetic factors in scleroderma, scleroderma-associated autoantibodies and their clinical correlations, and MHC allelic associations with scleroderma and its autoantibodies.

Hall RP, Rico MJ, Murray JC. Autoimmune skin disease. In: Rich R, ed. Clinical Immunology, Principles and Practice. St. Louis: Mosby Year Book, 1996, pp 1316–1342.

A comprehensive review of clinical and pathogenetic features of the auto immune bullous diseases is provided in this article.

Mobini N, Yunis EJ, Alper CA, et al. Identical MHC markers in non-Jewish, Iranian and Ashkenazi Jewish patients with pemphigus vulgaris: possible common central Asian ancestral origin. Hum Immunol 1997;57:62–67.

This provocative study investigates the major HLA haplotype predisposing to pemphigus vulgaris and how it may provide insight into the ancestral origins of Ashkenazi Jewish people. The study also reviews HLA and pemphigus vulgaris in other populations.

Moraes ME, Fernandez-Vina M, Lazaro A, et al. An epitope in the third hypervariable region of the DRB1 gene is involved in the susceptibility to endemic pemphigus foliaceus (fogo selvagem) in three different Brazilian populations. Tissue Antigens 1997;49:35–40.

This provocative research study provides data on HLA associations with pemphigus foliaceus in Brazilian populations.

Balas A, Vicario JL, Zambrano A, et al. Absolute linkage of celiac disease and dermatitis herpetiformis to HLA-DQ. Tissue Antigens 1997;50:52–56.

This article is a linkage study of celiac disease and dermatitis herpetiformis that confirms the previous HLA case-control studies showing the almost complete association of these diseases linked with HLA-DQ2.

Henseler T. Genetics of psoriasis. Arch Dermatol Res 1998;290:463–476.

A comprehensive review of the genetics of psoriasis is provided in this article, including the genetic associations of both MHC class I genes, as well as non-MHC genes localized to other chromosomes but not yet identified.

CHAPTER 4

Theories of Autoimmune Disease Mechanisms

Noel R. Rose, M.D., Ph.D.

Approximately 5% of US population has an autoimmune disease

The autoimmune diseases, in total, represent a major health problem in the United States. It has been estimated that approximately 5% of the US population suffers from a disease in which autoimmunity plays a significant role, and the total annual cost exceeds 83 billion in health care dollars. Many of the individual autoimmune diseases, however, are relatively rare and, therefore, are apt to escape the attention of both clinicians and investigators. Only when the problem is viewed collectively it is realized that autoimmune diseases deserve greater attention from the medical community.

Mechanisms of Self-Tolerance

Central and peripheral self-tolerance

The overall strategy of the immune system is to respond to the universe of foreign antigens while avoiding a harmful immune response to autologous (self) antigens. The mechanisms involved in self-tolerance can be divided into central and peripheral (Table 4–1).

Negative selection of T cells in thymus

Negative selection of B cells in the bone marrow

In the case of T cells, negative selection during the generation of T cells occurs in the thymus through an encounter with the self-antigen presented by a histocompatible thymic stromal cell. This leads to apoptosis and deletion of the precursor of a self-reactive clone. B cells undergo negative selection in the bone marrow, although the mechanism is less well understood. In addition to deletion of self-reactive clones directed to the most critical and plentiful antigens, B cells may undergo the process of receptor editing, allowing them to reformulate the B-cell receptor by reactivating the immunoglobulin recombination process.

Central tolerance is not 100% efficient

Self-reactive T and B cells are present in the periphery

Central tolerance must be regarded as a "leaky" device because many self-reactive B cells and T cells are present in the periphery. Self-reactive B cells are evident from their low-affinity IgM (immunoglobulin M) products, which form the population of natural autoantibodies found in all normal sera. The presence of self-reactive T cells in the periphery can now be shown directly by the use of peptide tetramers. Their function is attested to by the production of high-affinity IgG autoantibodies in patients' sera as well as in the relative ease of inducing examples of autoimmune disease in experimental animals.

Mechanisms to maintain self-tolerance in periphery are:

- *anergy*
- *suppression*
- *ignorance*
- *immune deviation*

A number of mechanisms are mobilized to maintain self-tolerance in the periphery or, at least, to avoid the harmful effects of autoimmunity. They include anergy, which is a state of unresponsiveness of T or B cells due to the absence of the required co-stimulatory ("second") signals in the presence of an antigen-specific stimulus; ignorance, which describes the absence of contact between a potentially self-reactive T-cell precursor and its autologous cognate antigen, even when both are present in the body; active suppression, which involves the production of regulatory cytokines, such as transforming growth factor-β or inter-

TABLE 4–1 Mechanisms of Self-Tolerance

Central-negative selection	
	Thymus (T cells)
	Bone marrow (B cells)
	Receptor editing
Peripheral	
	Anergy
	Ignorance
	Deviation
	Suppression

leukin-10; and immune deviation, which converts a potentially harmful type I (T_h1) cell response to a more benign type II (T_h2) cell response (as described below). These and other mechanisms, still to be elucidated, are involved in maintaining a delicate immunologic balance between self-reactivity and self-tolerance.

Immunopathogenesis of Autoimmune Disease

Like infectious diseases, autoimmune disease can affect any site and any organ system of the body. Therefore, the clinical manifestations vary greatly. Some general principles, however, underlie the immunopathogenesis of all the autoimmune diseases. A simplified scheme for envisioning the immunopathogenesis of auto immune disease is presented in Figure 4–1.

Self-reactive CD4 T–helper cells play a central role.

One factor common to virtually all autoimmune diseases is the critical role of the self-reactive CD4 T–helper cell. For that reason, many of the newer therapies for treating autoimmune disease are aimed at inactivating or eliminating the self-reactive T cell.

Inductive Mechanisms

With respect to induction, the five mechanisms given in Table 4–2 and Figure 4–1 are illustrative of a large number of possibilities.

Molecular mimicry

These days, one of the most popular ideas about the origin of autoimmune disease is molecular mimicry, suggesting that an encounter with a cross-reacting antigen from an invading microorganism initiates a response that affects a similar self-antigen. Appealing as this idea is, there are still no clear examples of molecular mimicry as a cause of human autoimmune disease. Even though it is well documented that streptococcal pharyngitis may precipitate rheumatic fever in susceptible individuals, we do not have an antigen of the streptococcus that can reproduce the typical pathogenic manifestations of the disease. An earlier idea to explain autoimmunity was that some tissues, such as the lens or the testis, are normally sequestered from the immune system. A newer version of this concept is that cryptic epitopes of large molecules are poorly presented by thymic stromal cells and, consequently, fail to induce self-tolerance at the central level. These cryptic epitopes, therefore, are the parts of an antigen most likely to induce an autoimmune response when they are later encountered in nature. (For further discussion of cryptic epitopes and autoimmunity, see Chapter 7, "Scleroderma.") As an alternative to molecular mimicry, infectious agents may instigate an autoimmune response if they bear superantigens that can bind and stimulate an entire family of T-cell receptors (TCR). Some of the receptors will be found on self-reactive T cells. In many instances, we can induce an autoimmune response experimentally by combining an autologous antigen with a potent adju-

Cryptic epitopes

Superantigens

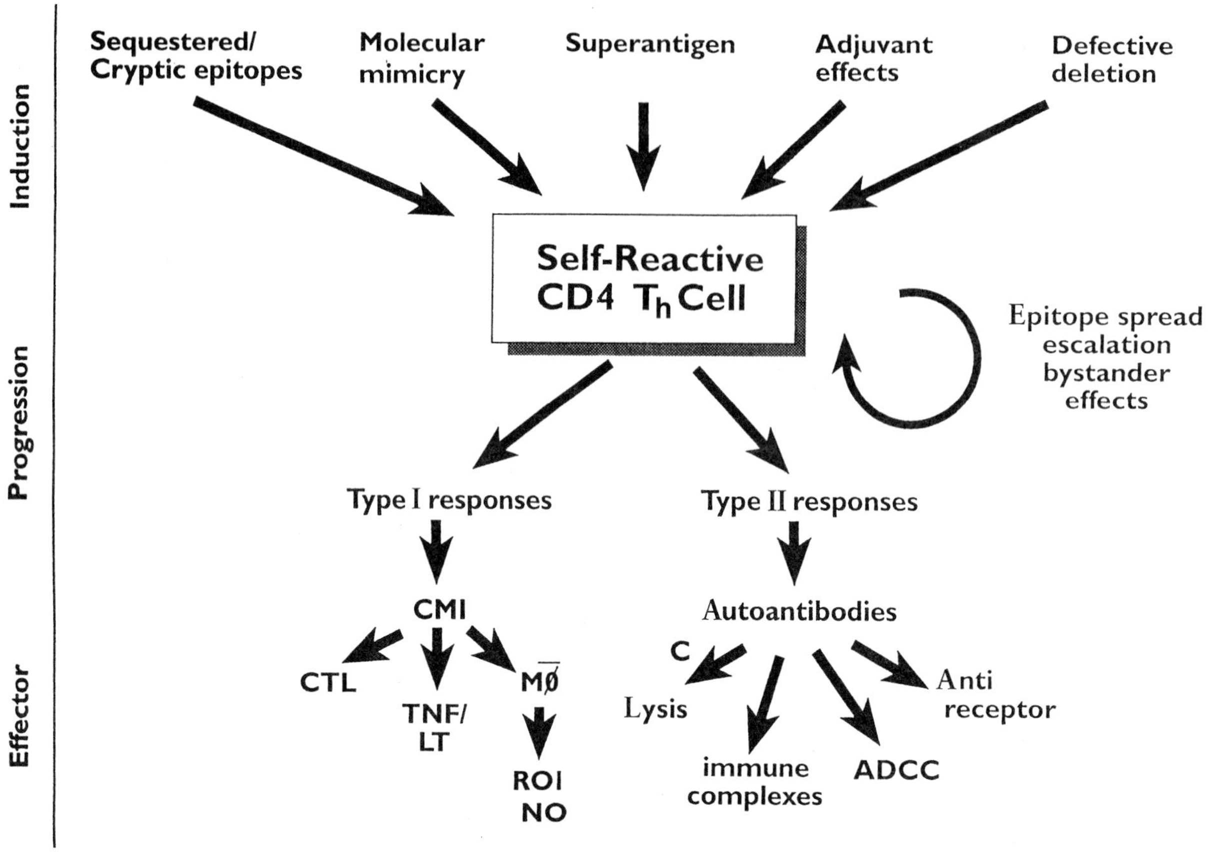

FIGURE 4–1 Simplified scheme of the immunopathogenesis of autoimmune disease. CMI = cell-mediated immunity; CTL = cytotoxic T lymphocyte; TNF = tumor necrosis factor; LT = lymphotoxin; M0 = activated macrophage; ROI NO = reactive oxygen intermediate; ADCC = antibody-dependent cell-mediated cytotoxicity; C = complement.

Adjuvant effect of infections

Fas-gene defect results in defective negative selection.

vant, such as complete Freund's adjuvant. We can speculate that some chronic infections exert an adjuvant effect.

The mechanisms described above are most likely to induce an organ-specific autoimmune response such as seen in Type I diabetes, chronic lymphocytic thyroiditis, or multiple sclerosis. An alternative mechanism by which autoimmunity may arise is a defect in negative selection and consequent clonal deletion of self-reactive T cells in the thymus. Such a defect in clonal deletion more likely results in multiple autoimmune responses and generalized or systemic autoimmune diseases. The MRL-*lpr/lpr* mouse, for example, carries a genetic defect in expression of *Fas* and, therefore, shows impaired intrathymic apoptosis so that negative selection is faulty. These animals characteristically produce lupus, one of the systemic autoimmune diseases.

TABLE 4–2 Induction of Autoimmunity

Sequestered/cryptic epitopes
Molecular mimicry
Superantigens
Adjuvant effects
Defective deletion

Effector Mechanisms

Effector mechanisms:
T_h1 versus T_h2 responses
cell mediated versus antibody mediated

The effector mechanisms responsible for the production of autoimmune disease are the same as those involved in the immune response to infectious microorganisms. The important factors determining the cytotoxic mechanism in any situation include the accessibility of the antigen as well as the nature of the autoimmune response itself. Some investigators distinguish T_h1 from T_h2 responses, although this dichotomy has never been clear cut in human autoimmune disease in which T_h1 and T_h2 responses are mixed. There may be great heuristic value in dealing separately with immune responses that are primarily cell mediated or antibody mediated (Table 4–3, see Figure 4–1).

Among the autoimmune diseases, a direct demonstration of pathogenic mechanisms is possible with the antibody-mediated disorders. Antibody, in general, acts upon antigens located at the cell surface. Antibody to blood cells is responsible for the hemolytic anemias and thrombocytopenias either through enhanced phagocytosis by reticuloendothelial cells, or by complement-mediated lysis. Antibody to receptors may block or simulate the normal ligand and produce the symptoms of myasthenia gravis and Graves' disease. Pemphigus vulgaris and bullous pemphigoid are associated with antibodies to intercellular antigens of the skin, inducing bullae. In lupus, the major nuclear antigens are found within living cells but are released when cells die so that the deposition of immune complexes in the brain, skin, kidneys, and other organs is the major pathogenic process. Antibodies can cooperate with killer lymphocytes to induce antibody-dependent, cell-mediated cytotoxicity.

Solid organ autoimmunity thought to be mediated by T cells

Most of the autoimmune diseases affecting solid organs are believed to be caused by cell-mediated effector mechanisms because T cells have greater access to these sites than do antibodies. Cytotoxic T lymphocytes have been implicated in multiple sclerosis and Type I diabetes through study of animal models. The cytokine products of T cells are probably mediators of cellular injury in such autoimmune diseases as rheumatoid arthritis, as evidenced by the recent demonstration that blocking the cytokine, tumor necrosis factor, can provide a useful therapeutic approach. T cells also activate macrophages to produce a long list of injurious products, such as reactive oxygen intermediates.

Progression

Amplification of helper T cell response:
- *epitope spreading*
- *immune escalation*
- *recruitment of bystander T cells*

The critical event in the progression from a harmless, benign autoimmune response to autoimmune disease is the activation of the self-reactive, CD4-positive helper T cells. This event requires presentation of the corresponding self-antigen by a histocompatible antigen-presenting cell, such as a macrophage, dendritic cell, or B cell. Once activated, the T-cell response rapidly amplifies the immune response. Epitope spread involves the participation of additional anti-

TABLE 4–3 Effector Mechanisms of Autoimmune Disease

Cell-mediated immune responses
Cytotoxic T lymphocytes
Cytotoxic cytokines (eg, tumor necrosis factor, lymphotoxin)
Reactive oxygen intermediates (eg, O_3^-, NO)
Antibody-mediated immune responses
Complement-mediated lysis or phagocytosis
Immune complex formation
Antibody-dependent, cell-mediated cytotoxicity
Antireceptor antibodies

genic determinants on the self-antigen, whereas immune escalation describes the extension of the autoimmune response to other antigenic molecules in the target organ. (For further discussion, see Chapter 5, "Lupus Erythematosus.") The local production by activated T cells of cytokines results in the recruitment of additional "bystander" T cells with differing specificities, causing further extension of the immune response.

Immunodiagnosis

Autoantibodies are easier to measure than T-cell–mediated immune responses.

As indicated in the previous section, some autoimmune diseases are mediated by autoantibodies. In many more instances, the presence of autoantibodies in a patient signifies the presence of an autoimmune response, but the pathologic changes are due primarily to T-cell–mediated immunity. The demonstration of autoantibodies, nevertheless, is the cornerstone of the diagnosis of autoimmune disease because there are no known human autoimmune diseases in which autoantibodies are not demonstrable. Tests for autoantibodies are relatively easy to perform compared with cellular methods, and the demonstration of autoantibodies is useful as an adjunct to the diagnosis of several infectious diseases in which autoimmunity is not known to play a pathologic role. For example, tests for antibodies to cardiolipin, a true autoantibody, are used in the diagnosis of syphilis, and cold hemagglutinins have been used to assist the diagnosis of mycoplasmal pneumonia. Testing for autoantibodies is now the major responsibility of the diagnostic immunology laboratory. It has even become difficult to establish the diagnosis of many diseases, such as systemic lupus erythematosus or thyroiditis, in the absence of the characteristic autoantibody response.

Yet it is important to keep in mind that autoantibodies are common in humans without autoimmune disease. If sufficiently sensitive methods are used, autoantibodies may well occur universally as a normal mechanism for purging the body of unwanted or effete cell products. Some naturally occurring autoantibodies may well be physiologic.

Caveat of autoantibody testing: autoantibodies can be detected in the absence of disease.

These considerations raise important caveats in the use of autoantibodies in clinical diagnosis. The first concern is that autoantibodies are commonly found in human serum in the absence of any discernible disease. In general, these autoantibodies are present in low titer, have relatively poor affinity for their corresponding antigen, and belong largely to the IgM isotype. Such is not always the case, however. Sometimes IgGs with reasonable binding affinities and elevated titers are present even in the absence of disease. (See Chapter 5, "Lupus Erythematosus," for further discussion.) The mere presence of high titers of autoantibodies without appropriate clinical evidence is rarely, if ever, a sound basis for diagnosis, but it may foreshadow some future problem. A second limitation in the use of autoantibodies for clinical diagnosis is based on the first one. Detection of autoantibodies requires some quantitative assessment so that they can be demonstrated above an empirically defined threshold value. Only if the titers of autoantibodies are well above this threshold can they be reliably considered in clinical diagnosis.

Some autoantibodies have value in classification of diseases and in assigning prognosis.

In addition to initial diagnosis, autoantibodies may be biomarkers of a particular pathologic process. Autoantibodies are proving to be valuable for discriminating subgroups of patients that differ in prognosis or response to therapy. Anti-neutrophil cytoplasmic antibody, for example, can be used to place patients in categories of vasculitides with differing clinical and pathologic features. (See Chapter 12, "Vasculitis," for further discussion.) In the connective tissue diseases, it is often the antibody profile, rather than a particular autoantibody, that gives the most valuable information about the expected course of the disease. (See Chapter 5, "Lupus Erythematosus," for further discussion.)

Pathologic autoantibodies may be directed at different epitopes than the autoantibodies from normal individuals.

Finally, progress is being made at the molecular level that holds promise of distinguishing the antibodies associated with disease from the autoantibodies present in clinically normal individuals. Patients with chronic thyroiditis, for example, generally produce a population of autoantibodies to antigenic determinants of thyroglobulin that differ from those targeted by autoantibodies from normal individuals. (See discussion in Chapter 9, "Antiphospholipid Syndrome," for another example of this phenomenon.)

New Approaches to Therapy

Treatment of autoimmune diseases:
- *treat altered function*
- *suppress immune response*

At present, there are two major approaches to the treatment of autoimmune diseases. If the disease is largely confined to a single organ, an attempt can be made to rectify the disturbed function. To treat the hypothyroidism of thyroiditis, thyroid hormone can be given. To replace the function of destroyed beta cells in Type I diabetes, we administer insulin. The overactive thyroid of Graves' disease can be removed surgically, reduced by radioactive iodine, or quieted with drugs. For treatment of more generalized autoimmune diseases, attempts can be made to reduce the inflammatory responses or, if necessary, to dampen the entire immune response. Clearly, a more promising strategy would be to turn off the pathogenic immune response without inducing global immunosuppression.

Figure 4–1 emphasizes the critical role of the self-reactive T cell in the progression of the autoimmune response. Early attempts to employ monoclonal antibodies to treat autoimmune disease by depleting the entire population of CD4-positive T cells produced very little in the way of beneficial clinical response and had the major drawback of producing general immunosuppression. More recent efforts have been directed at devising biologic approaches that specifically inactivate the pathogenic T cell, potentially leading to a cure.

Strategies now directed at the trimolecular complex to cure autoimmune diseases

A trimolecular complex, comprising the TCR, a peptide fragment of the antigen, and the class II major histocompatibility complex (MHC) molecule of the antigen-presenting cell, is required for the generation of an autoimmune response. This trimolecular complex, therefore, may be considered to be the optimal target for antigen-specific, highly selective therapies. Each component of the trimolecular complex can be attacked singly or in concert.

Immunize with specific portion of MHC allele involved in antigen binding.

Many autoimmune diseases are associated with particular MHC haplotypes, providing the rationale for therapies targeting disease-associated MHC gene products. Two approaches are being tried. In the first, antibody to a particular MHC allele product is being used. Such methods are successful in inbred mice, but humans are genetically heterogeneous so that one individual probably requires a panel of MHC reagents or an individualized panel for each patient. An even more elegant approach is to immunize with the portion of the MHC primarily involved in antigen binding, such as the peptides from the MHC class II beta-chain hypervariable region. Whether such a method will be useful for the heterogeneous response of human patients is still to be ascertained. Moreover, a single MHC binds a number of peptides so that the response to the MHC peptide may not be strictly specific for the pathogenic epitope.

Blocking peptides competing with antigen-binding sites on the MHC molecule

Once the autologous peptide responsible for the induction of an autoimmune disease has been identified, it is another logical target for immune intervention. One approach is to develop a blocking peptide that binds to the contact sites of the MHC but offers different amino acids to the TCR. Copolymer 1, a synthetic random polymer of L-alanine, L-glutamic acid, L-lysine, and L-tyrosine, has been used successfully for the treatment of relapsing-remitting multiple sclerosis. Copolymer 1 was originally believed to act by competing with myelin basic protein for binding to the MHC class II molecule expressed on antigen-presenting cells. As more of the characteristic binding pockets of the many MHC alleles are defined in the future, synthesis of blocking peptides will become more feasible. It is important, however, to determine that the blocking peptides act as antagonists rather than agonists of the pathogenic autoimmune response. They also must have great affinity for the MHC, so they will not be displaced by the natural self-peptide. In addition, the effect of such peptide analogs must be defined in terms of their effect on the various T-cell subpopulations. T-cell unresponsiveness may be temporary, requiring continued contact with the blocking peptide, or long lasting, due to elimination of corresponding T cells or generation of specific regulatory cells.

In applying this strategy to the treatment of human autoimmune disease, a major limitation is a lack of knowledge of the antigen initiating the pathogenic autoimmune response. The responsible antigen has been identified in relatively few human autoimmune diseases. It would be even better to know the particular epitope of the molecule responsible for initiation of the pathogenic autoimmune response if individuals at risk of developing an autoimmune disease can be identified.

Vaccination with the antigen-specific binding portion of the T-cell receptor

Another promising point of attack for an immune-based therapy for autoimmune disease is the TCR itself. The concept requires that the pathogenic immune response is associated with a restricted population of T-cell clones. That this is possible was shown by early experiments demonstrating the prevention of the induction of autoimmune disease in mice by a vaccination with suspensions of killed T cells. For human therapy, a more practical approach has been to isolate the antigen-specific TCR of self-reactive T cells rather than employing the whole cell. The hypervariable and most antigen-specific portion of the TCR is usually the third complementary determining region (CDR3) of the TCR. Therefore, in experimental studies, the CDR peptide has been isolated, combined with an appropriate adjuvant, and administered as a preventive or therapeutic vaccine. Although these methods have proved to be quite successful in experimental animals, they are not yet at a point at which they can be used for human therapy.

Autoimmunity as Cause or Consequence of Disease

Autoimmune disease may follow an infection.

As Figure 4–1 emphasizes, there are many reasons why a body may mount an autoimmune response. One of the most common causes of autoimmunity is infection and the accompanying inflammatory process. In contemplating antigen-specific therapies such as those described in the previous section, it is essential to distinguish autoimmunity as the cause of disease from autoimmunity as the harmless consequence. A prototype of a way in which this important question can be investigated comes from studies of myocarditis, heart muscle inflammation.

Myocarditis is an important cause of heart failure in younger individuals. It also appears to be the precursor of idiopathic dilated cardiomyopathy, a major indication for cardiac transplantation in this country. Myocarditis is frequently associated with a preceding viral infection, especially by picornaviruses such as Coxsackie virus B3 (CB3). A large proportion of patients suffering from Coxsackie-associated myocarditis develops autoantibodies to the heart muscle, demonstrable by fluorescence-tagged antibody. Thus, there is an autoimmune response to heart muscle, but it has been uncertain whether it contributes to pathology.

Autoimmune myocarditis associated with IgG rather than IgM antibodies reactive against heavy chain of myosin

The procedure followed in this investigation was to develop a mouse model using a cardiotropic strain of CB3. In most strains of mice, this virus produced an acute, self-limited myocarditis. In a few genetically inbred strains, however, a continuing form of myocarditis was found. During this latter phase of disease, no infectious virus could be isolated, but autoantibodies to heart were found resembling those demonstrated in many patients with myocarditis. Immunochemical studies showed that these autoantibodies in mice (as well as in human patients) are directed mainly to the heavy chain of myosin. Although autoantibodies to myosin are relatively common in normal human and normal mouse serum, the antibodies associated with myocarditis were distinguishable because they were typically IgG rather than IgM and reacted specifically with the cardiac isoform of myosin rather than with the skeletal isoform.

With the clue taken from the studies of antibody, the critical experiments were carried out. Mice were immunized with myosin incorporated in complete Freund's adjuvant. Two preparations of myosin were employed: cardiac myosin and skeletal myosin. Two different types of mice were immunized: strains that were susceptible to the ongoing form of myocarditis and strains that were resistant to it. The results showed that susceptible mice immunized with cardiac myosin developed typical histopathologic features of myocarditis. No heart lesions were found in animals immunized with skeletal myosin. Moreover, the cardiac pathology was seen only in the strains of mice genetically susceptible to the continuing form of myocarditis.

Genetically susceptible mice immunized with cardiac, but not skeletal, muscle myosin develop heart disease.

Myocarditis, like most organ-specific autoimmune diseases, cannot be readily transmitted by antibody. Therefore, the immunologist depends upon reproducing essential pathologic features of the disease in experimental animals to show that autoimmunity can be induced by the relevant antigen.

Conclusion

In this article, we have brought together some of the common threads that unite all of the autoimmune diseases. They resemble each other in their fundamental immunopathogenesis, especially the interaction between genetic and environmental (such as infectious) factors. All of the autoimmune diseases show a genetic predisposition and genes of the MHC are among the most prominent determinants. There is, moreover, a great deal of clustering of autoimmune diseases so that we may find several autoimmune diseases in members of the same family and even multiple autoimmune diseases in the same individual. (See discussions in Chapter 5, "Lupus Erythematosus," or Chapter 8, "Sjögren's Syndrome," for further discussion on autoimmune disease clustering.) As we discover more of the fundamental pathogenesis, opportunities for common approaches to treatment rise.

In autoimmunity, genetic plus environmental (eg, infectious) events appear to be important.

As with cancer, it is rational to think of the autoimmune diseases as a major category, although each disease may be relatively rare. In the aggregate, the autoimmune diseases are a major health problem and a major cause of health care dollar expenditure. This is true especially because these diseases, although often treatable, are not curable by the methods presently available to us.

In aggregate, autoimmunity is a major health problem in the USA

Annotated Bibliography

Adorini L, Sinigaglia F. Pathogenesis and immunotherapy of autoimmune disease. Immunol Today 1997;18(S):209–211.

Barnaba V, Sinigaglia F. Molecular mimicry and T cell-mediated autoimmune disease. J Exp Med 1997;185:1529–1531.

Falcone M, Sarvetnick N. The effect of local production of cytokines in the pathogenesis of insulin-dependent diabetes mellitus. Clin Immunol 1999;90:2–9.

Jacobson DL, Gange SJ, Rose NR, Graham NM. Epidemiology and estimated population burden of selected autoimmune diseases in the United States. Clin Immunol Immunopathol 1997;84:223–243.

Janeway CA Jr, Kupfer A, Viret C, et al. T-cell development, survival, and signalling. A new concept of the role of self-peptide: self-MHC complexes. The Immunologist 1998; 6:5–12.

Ji H, Korganow AS, Mangialaio S, et al. Different modes of pathogenesis in T-cell-dependent autoimmunity: clues from two TCR transgenic systems. Immunol Rev 1999;169:139–146.

Mondino A, Khoruts A, Jenkins MK. The anatomy of T-cell activation and tolerance. Proc Natl Acad Sci U S A 1996;93:2245–2252.

Oldstone MB. Molecular mimicry and immune-mediated diseases. FASEB J 1998;12: 1255–1265.

Rose NR. Autoimmune diseases: tracing the shared threads. Hosp Practice 1997;32(4): 147–154.

Rose NR. Fundamental concepts of autoimmunity and autoimmune disease. In: Krawitt EL, Wiesner R, Nishioka M, eds. Autoimmune Liver Diseases, 2nd ed. Amsterdam: Elsevier Science, 1998, pp 1–20.

Rose NR. Insights into mechanisms of autoimmune disease based on clinical findings. In: Paul S, ed. Contemporary Immunology: Autoimmune Reactions. Totowa, NJ: Humana, 1998, pp 5–17.

Tian J, Olcott A, Hanssen L et al. Antigen-based immunotherapy for autoimmune disease: from animal models to humans? Immunol Today 1999;20:190–195.

This group of up-to-date references provides excellent overviews of the theories of autoimmunity. Many of these review articles contain excellent bibliographies.

CHAPTER 5

Lupus Erythematosus

Thomas T. Provost, M.D., John A. Flynn, M.D.

Lupus erythematosus (LE) is a chronic inflammatory autoimmune disease demonstrating a variety of cutaneous and systemic manifestations. In its more benign form, the disease process is limited to the skin; in its more severe form, systemic disease with or without cutaneous features dominates the clinical picture. In this chapter, the abbreviation LE is used synonymously with SLE (systemic LE).

This chapter focuses on some of the dermatologic, epidemiologic, genetic, and serologic features of LE. (Those interested in more detailed treatises may consult the bibliography.)

Significant early contributors to our understanding of lupus erythematosus:

- *Hebra*
- *Kaposi*
- *Osler*
- *Friedberg*
- *O'Leary*
- *Klemperer*

Historically, there has been great progress in our knowledge of LE over the past century, with much of the progress having occurred in the past 30 years. The work of Hebra and Kaposi in the middle and latter part of the 1800s first drew attention to the facial dermatitis and related systemic manifestations of LE. At the turn of the century, the writings of Osler emphasized the multisystem involvement of LE. The classic description by Friedberg of SLE occurrence without cutaneous disease, the work by O'Leary to classify cutaneous manifestations of SLE, and the publication by Klemperer in 1941 of the pathologic features of SLE did much to advance our knowledge.

The description in the early 1960s by Rowell of erythema multiforme lesions in LE heralded the later work of Sontheimer and Gilliam in the 1970s describing the existence of a clinical subset of LE, termed "subacute cutaneous LE" (SCLE).

Spectrum of LE

Also in the 1960s, the work of the dermatologist Tuffanelli and the rheumatologist Dubois resulted in the publication of a classic paper describing the clinical features of 520 SLE patients. This work, as well as the later studies of Gilliam and our group, publicized the fact that LE should be viewed as a continuum of disease with cutaneous and systemic manifestations at opposite ends of the spectrum. (Other investigators believe discoid lupus erythematosus [DLE] and SLE are distinct entities.) For a discussion of this reasoning, see Annotated Bibliography.

Serologic testing:

- *1950s: "LE prep"*
- *1950s: Antinuclear antibody test*
- *1960s: Anti-dsDNA antibody test*

The landmark serologic studies of Hargraves and Haserick established the LE preparation (LE prep) as the first serologic test to evaluate lupus patients. In the late 1950s, Friou developed the antinuclear antibody (ANA) test, and Kunkel's group at the Rockefeller Institute, as well as later work by Schur in the 1960s, detailed the diagnostic specificity and the prognostic significance of anti-dsDNA antibodies in SLE patients.

Serologic testing:

- *1965: Sm (Tan)*
- *1969: Ro (Reichlin)*
- *1970: U1RNP (Sharp et al.and Reichlin et al.)*

The work of Tan and Reichlin's laboratories and, later, the work of Lerner and Steitz established the frequency and identity of anti-ribonucleoprotein (RNP) autoantibodies in LE patients. These anti-RNP autoantibody determinations have allowed for the early detection of atypical SLE patients prior to the development of classic features. Furthermore, the possible pathologic role of these antibodies in the genesis of the isolated congenital heart block and cutaneous features of the neonatal lupus syndrome has resulted from the initial observations of Weston's and our group.

Prognosis

Prognosis:
- *1940s: 50% 2-year survival*
- *1950s: 50% 4- to 5-year survival*
- *1960s: 70% 5-year survival*
- *1970s: 60% 10-year survival*
- *1980s: 75% 10-year survival*
- *1990s: > 90% 5-year survival*

The prognosis for SLE patients has improved dramatically during the past 50 years. In his 1941 paper, Klemperer indicated a 50% mortality 2 years after the onset of SLE. By 1955, the study by Merrel and Shulman detailing the Hopkins' experience indicated that the life expectancy in SLE had doubled over the previous 15 years. They reported a 50% mortality 4 to 5 years after the diagnosis of SLE. By the early 1960s, Kellum and Haserick reported a 69% 5-year survival and a 54% 10-year survival. In the 1970s, a 5-year survival of 77% and a 10-year survival of 59% was reported. In 1982, Ginzler et al. reported survival data on 1103 patients from nine centers. These data indicated a 5-year survival of 86% and a 10-year survival of 76%.

In the late 1980s and 1990s, 5-year survivals in excess of 90% are being reported. (For futher discussion, see Hochberg MC in the Annotated Bibliography.)

Causes of Death

Causes of death:
- *1940s: infection from active SLE*
- *1950s: infection, uremia, "lupus crisis"*
- *1960s: uremia, CNS disease*
- *1990s: active SLE infections, cardiovascular complications of long-term steroid therapy*

Another indicator substantiating the progress in the treatment of this disease can be found in an analysis of the causes of death. For example, in Klemperer's 1941 paper, 60% of the causes of death were attributed to infections. Five percent died of uremia and 25% died of central nervous system (CNS) complications. The study by Harvey et al. in the 1950s indicated that infections accounted for 30% of deaths, and that 24% died of uremia. In 39%, death was ascribed to SLE. (In this era, before our knowledge of aggressive steroid therapy had advanced, death from an acute exacerbation of the SLE process, many times precipitated by infection or inadvertent sun exposure, was not uncommon. This event was referred to as a "lupus crisis" and is quite rare today.)

Uremia and CNS complications continued to be a major cause of death until the 1970s. For example, Estes reported a frequency of 36%. At the present time, renal failure and CNS disease are infrequent causes of death. Active SLE, infections, and cardiovascular disease (the latter a complication of long-term steroid treatment) are now the common causes of death. Most recent data suggest as much as a ninefold increased risk of coronary artery disease among SLE patients. Among the risk factors identified by Petri et al. were longer duration of SLE and longer duration of prednisone therapy.

Deaths in SLE have a bimodal pattern. Deaths generally occurring within the first 2 years are a complication of active lupus or sepsis. Deaths occurring late in lupus are frequently due to cardiovascular disease. (For further discussion, see Hochberg MC in the Annotated Bibliography.)

Medical Advances and Diagnostic Criteria

Medical advances are responsible for the improved prognosis of lupus patients. These include:

1. Antibiotics
2. Aggressive use of steroids, including pulse techniques
3. Use of immunosuppressive drugs, such as steroid-sparing agents, including pulse cyclophosphamide therapy
4. Renal dialysis and transplantation
5. Increased recognition of LE at an earlier stage of onset

This last advancement has resulted from the establishment of acceptable diagnostic criteria for SLE by the American College of Rheumatology (ACR) (Table 5–1). The criteria recognize the specific and nonspecific cutaneous features of LE and the advances in serologic testing for LE, including the use of complement determinations to monitor renal disease activity.

The 1982 ACR revised criteria for the classification of SLE has done much to improve our ability to diagnose SLE patients, as will be seen in the next section

TABLE 5–1 1982 Revised Criteria of the American College of Rheumatology for the Diagnosis of SLE

1. Malar dermatitis
2. Discoid rash
3. Photosensitivity
4. Oral ulcers
5. Arthritis
6. Serositis
7. Renal disease
8. Neurologic disease
9. Hematologic disease
   - Leukopenia
   - Lymphopenia
   - Thrombocytopenia
   - Hemolytic anemia
10. Serologic abnormalities
    - Positive lupus erythematosus preparation
    - Anti-dsDNA antibodies
    - Anti-Sm antibodies
    - Biologic false-positive serologic test of syphilis
11. Antinuclear antibody

under "Cutaneous Manifestations." However, several caveats need acknowledgment when diagnosing SLE using these criteria. These involve SLE-specific antibodies, ANAs using human substrates, malar dermatitis, discoid lesions, mucous membrane ulcers, photosensitivity, and limitation of morphology.

SLE-Specific Antibodies

The diagnosis of SLE is based on a series of clinical and laboratory observations. Only anti-dsDNA and anti-Sm antibodies are diagnostically specific. These autoantibodies do not occur in any other condition.

Anti-Sm and dsDNA antibodies are specific for SLE. Occur in no other diseases

Antinuclear Antibodies Using Human Substrates

The employment of human tissue culture lines as a substrate for the antinuclear antibody determination has resulted in an increased sensitivity for the detection of ANA. Using human substrates, it is not unusual to see ANA titers of 2,560 or 5,120. It is important to emphasize that although one would think that such high-titer ANA are of great pathologic significance indicative of lupus disease process, this is not always true. In fact, several of our patients with elevated ANA titer and no evidence of connective tissue disease have been detected and followed up over a 2-year period and still failed to reveal any evidence for connective tissue disease. In addition, a number of these patients with very high ANA titers, using human substrates, demonstrated significantly lower ANA titers (ie, 160 to 640) when heterologous tissue (ie, mouse liver) was employed as an ANA substrate. It should also be noted that approximately 5 to 10% of the general population will at one time have a significant ANA titer. Thus, the magnitude of an ANA titer, although dramatic, may not necessarily signify the presence of a connective tissue disease. Finally, a diagnosis of SLE should never be based solely on a positive ANA determination.

ANA determinations using human substrates are very sensitive, resulting in high-titered ANAs.

High-titered ANAs occur occasionally in approximately 5–10% of normal individuals.

The diagnosis of SLE should never be based solely on a positive ANA.

Malar Dermatitis

Four of the 11 criteria for the diagnosis of SLE are dermatologic. Although it is true that patients with a malar dermatitis (acute cutaneous lupus erythematosus

Malar dermatitis may occasionally occur in LE patients who do not meet ACR criteria for SLE diagnosis.

[ACLE]) most commonly have an aggressive systemic disease process, the presence of a malar dermatitis does not invariably indicate the presence of systemic disease (see below).

Discoid Lesions

A morphologic descriptive term also, unfortunately, used to denote benign cutaneous LE

The term "discoid" in DLE means coin-shaped, scarring, atrophic, cutaneous lesions demonstrating hypo- or hyperpigmentation, telangiectasia, and follicular plugging. DLE is most commonly used to describe patients with benign cutaneous disease. However, approximately 15% of a well-characterized SLE patient population was found to have these lesions. Therefore, "discoid" should only be used as a morphologically descriptive term for a cutaneous LE lesion.

Mucous Membrane Ulcers

Oral ulcers seen in both cutaneous and systemic LE patients

Oral ulcers have pathology of cutaneous lupus, not vasculitis

Oral ulcerations have been used as a diagnostic criterion for SLE. Patients with benign cutaneous LE can also have oral ulcers. In fact, biopsy of oral ulcers demonstrate the pathologic features of cutaneous lupus and not a vasculitis.

Photosensitivity

Frequency of photosensitivity:
- *dependent on geographical location (much more frequent in southern climates)*
- *less frequent in African Americans, but some African Americans are exquisitely photosensitive*

Anti-Ro (SS-A) antibody patients have the most photosensitivity of all lupus subsets.

The frequency of photosensitivity appears to vary widely. It is undoubtedly due, in part, to the intensity of light exposure in the geographic area in which the LE cohort reporting originates. For example, Gilliam noted that almost all his lupus patients in Dallas, Texas, were photosensitive. This was not our experience in Buffalo, New York.

Most cutaneous lupus lesions, but not all, occur in light-exposed areas. Anti-Ro (SS-A) antibody–positive lupus patients appear to have a very high frequency of photosensitivity ranging between 60 and 90%. Other lupus patients (subsets) possessing other antibody systems do not appear to have such a high frequency. Although photosensitivity is reported to be unusual in African American patients, some of the most photosensitive anti-Ro (SS-A) antibody–positive patients that we have encountered have been African Americans.

The major manifestations of LE are presented in Tables 5–2 and 5–3.

Limitation of Morphology

DLE lesions occur in SLE patients, and malar (butterfly rash) lesions can occur in the abscence of systemic features.

By examining just cutaneous LE lesions, one cannot determine with certainty if patient has benign cutaneous or systemic disease.

Provost's experience indicates that one cannot, by examining the morphologic features of the cutaneous lupus lesion, ascribe with certainty to an LE patient a diagnosis of benign disease limited to the skin or SLE. This can only be achieved by performing history taking, physical examination, appropriate laboratory studies, and serologic testing.

TABLE 5–2 Major Manifestations of LE

	Study		
Manifestation	McGehee Harvey % (N = 105)	Dubois % (N = 520)	Hochberg % (N = 150)
Arthritis and arthralgia	90	92	76
Malar dermatitis	39	57	61
Oral-nasal ulcers	14	9	23
Photosensitivity	11	33	45
Raynaud's phenomenon	10	18	44
Nephritis	65	46	—
Nephrotic syndrome	—	23	13
Anemia	78	57	57
Leukopenia	—	43	41
Thrombocytopenia	26	7	30

TABLE 5–3 Clinical Manifestations of Anti-Ro (SS-A) Antibody–Positive Lupus Patients

Manifestation	Patients (N = 50)	(%)
Arthritis	41	(82)
Pulmonary disease	12	(24)
Serositis	10	(20)
Interstitial	4	(8)
Raynaud's phenomenon	23	(46)
Glomerulonephritis	18	(36)
Nervous system	18	(36)
Central	9	(18)
Peripheral	5	(10)
Myositis	2	(4)
Systemic vasculitis	2	(4)
Cutaneous disease	45	(90)
Malar dermatitis	29	(58)
Discoid lupus erythematosus	10	(20)
Subacute cutaneous lupus erythematosus	10	(20)
Vasculitis	3	(6)
Photosensitivity	30	(60)
Leukopenia	16	(32)
Thrombocytopenia	6	(12)
Anemia	8	(16)
Complement decrease	11	(22)
Rheumatoid factor	16 (of 27 tested)	(59)

Specific and Nonspecific Cutaneous Manifestations of Systemic Lupus Erythematosus

Investigations detailing the specific as well as the nonspecific manifestations of cutaneous LE have also done much to improve our diagnostic capabilities. The description by Gilliam and Sontheimer of subacute cutaneous lupus erythematosus (SCLE) and its characteristic cutaneous features is the best example of this advancement. The classification of the cutaneous manifestations associated with LE is presented in Table 5–4. This represents a modification of the classification initially proposed by Gilliam.

Studies of specific and nonspecific cutaneous LE lesions have played an important role in enhancing our ability to diagnose lupus patients.

Specific Lesions

Acute Cutaneous Lupus Erythematosus

ACLE is defined as the development of the classic malar (butterfly) dermatitis. In general, this cutaneous lesion is associated with the development of SLE; however, as noted earlier, this is not always true. For example, recent studies have indicated that the most common dermatitis seen in LE patients possessing anti-Ro (SS-A) antibodies is a malar dermatitis. Figures 5–1 and 5–2 provide two examples of patients with the classic butterfly or malar dermatitis who possess anti-Ro (SS-A) antibodies. Both these patients, although having significant ANA

The most common cutaneous lesion in anti-Ro (SS-A)–positive LE patients is a malar dermatitis (acute cutaneous LE lesion).

TABLE 5–4 Modification of Gilliam Classification of Specific and Nonspecific Lupus Erythematosus Skin Lesions

Histopathologically specific for LE
- Acute LE: malar dermatitis
- Subacute cutaneous LE
- Chronic cutaneous LE
  - Discoid LE
  - Hypertrophic LE
  - Lupus profundus panniculitis
  - Mucosal LE
  - Lupus tumidus
  - Chilblains LE
  - DLE/lichen planus overlap

Histopathologically Nonspecific for LE
- Vasculopathy
  - Vasculitis
  - Livedo reticularis with or without ulceration
  - Erythromyalgia
  - Raynaud's phenomenon
- Alopecia
  - Lupus hair
  - Telogen effluvium
- Sclerodactyly
- Rheumatoid-like arthritis and rheumatoid nodules
- Bullous lesions
  - Pemphigus erythematosus
  - Epidermolysis bullosa acquisita
  - Putative immune complex mediated (dermatitis herpetiformis–like bullous disease)
- Mucinosis
- Anectoderma

LE = lupus erythematosus.

titers and anti-Ro (SS-A) antibodies, failed to demonstrate clinical features of systemic disease. Thus, using the ACR diagnostic criteria, these patients would not be classified as having SLE. It should be emphasized, however, that the patients described here are the minority, and most patients having a malar dermatitis (butterfly dermatitis) do, indeed, have systemic features.

The frequency of a malar dermatitis in LE varies greatly. The experience at Johns Hopkins with patients evaluated in the late 1940s and 1950s indicated that 39% of LE patients had a malar dermatitis. A study conducted at the same institution in the mid-1980s indicated a frequency of 61% of malar dermatitis (see Tables 5–2 and 5–3).

Acne rosacea must be differentiated from LE malar dermatitis.

The lesions of malar dermatitis classically demonstrate erythema and edema involving the malar eminence (wings of the butterfly), with extension onto the bridge of the nose (the body of the butterfly). Characteristically, as Sontheimer has observed, the nasolabial fold and area beneath the nose are generally uninvolved. Differentiation of this malar dermatitis from acne rosacea at times is a diagnostic dilemma for colleagues not familiar with rosacea, especially if the acne rosacea begins as small, macular, papular lesions that evolve over a period of time into a confluent erythematous dermatitis. The lupus malar dermatitis may be very subtle, demonstrating only erythema with little or no edema. Hyperpigmentation, especially in African Americans, can be a prominent cosmetic problem.

Photosensitivity is usually a prominent feature of ACLE patients. Some patients unrecognized as having LE or who are undertreated, when exposed to excessive sunlight, may develop an explosive, diffuse, erythematous macular, papular dermatitis involving the face and other light-exposed areas. This form of generalized acute LE may demonstrates blister formation. On unusual occasions,

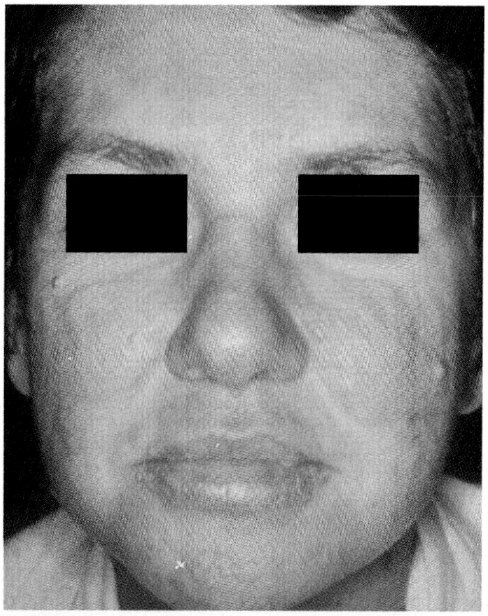

FIGURE 5–1 Classic butterfly dermatitis in an anti-Ro (SS-A) antibody–positive patient with no systemic disease.

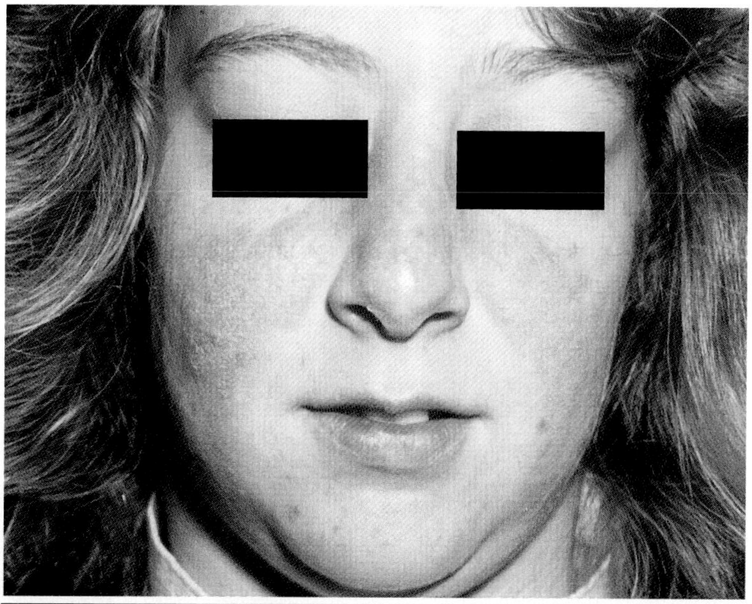

FIGURE 5–2 Classic butterfly dermatitis in an anti-Ro (SS-A) antibody–positive patient with no systemic disease.

some of these bullae may fill with leukocytes (sometimes, perhaps, secondary to injury to sweat ducts, producing a miliaria pustulosis-like event), giving the appearance of subcorneal pustulosis. The involved skin is generally very painful, and the patients usually demonstrate systemic toxicity (ie, fever, myalgia, arthralgias, fatigue). Wet dressings, together with mid-potency steroids, are effective when used in combination with parenteral steroids and/or immunosuppressive agents to treat the systemic disease.

Subacute Cutaneous Lupus Erythematosus

SCLE was described in 1979 by Sontheimer, Thomas, and Gilliam.

Strong positive relationship of SCLE with anti-Ro (SS-A) antibodies

Negative relationship of SCLE with anti-U_1RNP, -Sm, -dsDNA, and anticardiolipin antibodies

Two specific lesions have been associated with SCLE: annular polycyclic and papulosquamous (Figures 5–3 and 5–4). Photosensitivity is the dominant feature of these patients. In general, approximately 30 to 50% of these patients satisfy the minor criteria (ie, arthritis, anemia, leukopenia, but not renal or CNS disease) of the ACR for the diagnosis of SLE. Approximately 70% of these patients demonstrate the presence of anti-Ro (SS-A) antibodies. Furthermore, in addition to this positive, statistically significant association with the presence of anti-Ro (SS-A) antibodies, there are statistically significant, negative associations of SCLE with the presence of anti-U_1RNP, -Sm, -dsDNA, -ssDNA, and anticardiolipin antibodies.

SCLE is more frequent in women.

SCLE women have a higher frequency of anti-Ro (SS-A) antibody positivity than men.

Subacute cutaneous lupus erythematosus is most commonly found in women (female to male ratio 7:3). Women are more frequently anti-Ro (SS-A) antibody positive. In one study, female SCLE patients demonstrated an 85% frequency of anti-Ro (SS-A) antibodies; the men demonstrated a 30% frequency.

9–27% of total LE cohorts have SCLE

As many as 27% of a large cohort of lupus patients have been designated as having SCLE. In Sontheimer's experience, however, 9% of his total lupus cohort had SCLE. In a recent study, of 220 consecutive lupus patients seen and evaluated in the Johns Hopkins dermatology department, 15% were classified as SCLE. Approximately 60% of our SCLE patients were anti-Ro (SS-A) antibody positive—a frequency of positivity similar to what Sontheimer et al. had described in their original SCLE cohort.

SCLE lesions:

- *most common in sun-exposed areas*
- *unusual on face*
- *annular polycyclic*
- *psoriasiform*

The lesions of SCLE most commonly involve the V of the neck and the extensor surfaces of the arms (areas frequently sun exposed). Surprisingly, SCLE facial lesions are unusual. There is an approximately equal distribution of frequency of

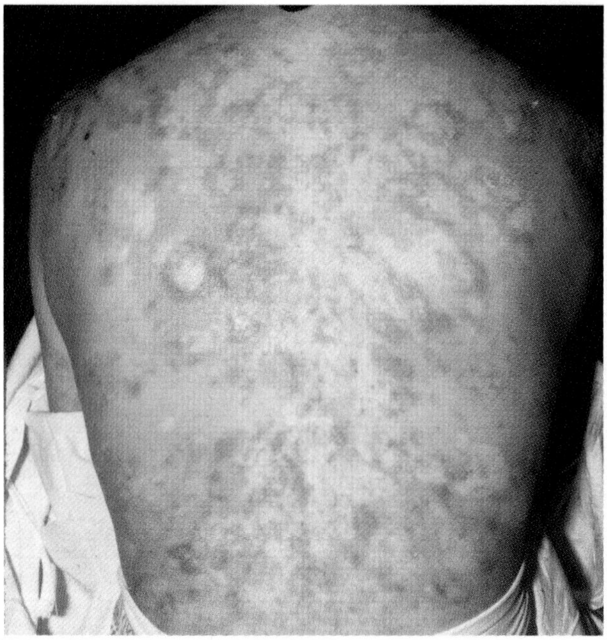

FIGURE 5–3 Classic annular, polycyclic SCLE lesions in an anti-Ro (SS-A) antibody–positive patient. Note extensive nature of lesions—patient burned through light cotton garment.

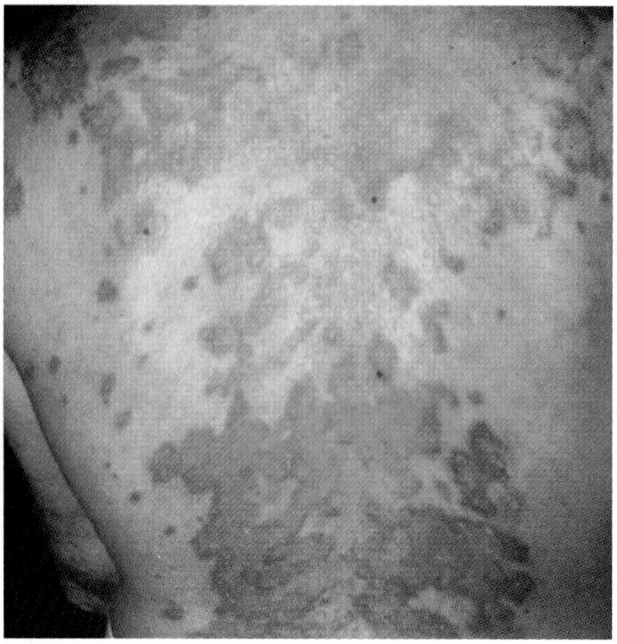

FIGURE 5–4 Psoriasiform lesion of SCLE. Note in upper right and left portions of back the presence of some annular lesions.

On occasion:
- *targetoid*
- *follicular*
- *exfoliative erythroderma-like*
- *toxic epidermal necrolysis-like*
- *pityriasis rosacea-like*

papulosquamous (psoriasiform) and annular polycyclic lesions of SCLE. On unusual occasions, targetoid lesions similar to those described by Rowell have been seen. Small vesicle/bullae at the periphery of SCLE lesions have been described; furthermore, some SCLE patients following heavy sun exposure may develop an exfoliated erythroderma-like LE (Figures 5–5 to 5–7). Others have been described as developing toxic epidermal necrolysis (lesions similar to pityriasis rosea or erythema annulare centrifugum, as well as follicular lesions, have also been detected.)

Post-inflammatory hypopigmentation may be prominent feature

Although scar formation is rare in SCLE patients, post-inflammatory hyperpigmentation and hypopigmentation can be a prominent cosmetic residual in African Americans.

In addition to the classic annular and psoriasiform lesions, SCLE patients may also demonstrate a malar dermatitis (ACLE) and/or chronic annular scarring DLE, and chronic cutaneous lupus erythematosus (CCLE) lesions (Figures 5–8 and 5–9).

20% of anti-Ro (SS-A) antibody–positive LE patients have SCLE or CCLE lesions; 60% have malar dermatitis.

Furthermore, one recent study examining lupus patients possessing anti-Ro (SS-A) antibodies, with or without other autoantibodies, determined that approximately 60% of these anti-Ro (SS-A) antibody–positive LE patients had a malar dermatitis (ACLE); 20% had SCLE and 20% had CCLE lesions. Thus, although the initial work detected the highly distinctive annular polycyclic and psoriasiform lesions associated with SCLE, it is now apparent that some of these SCLE patients will also concomitantly demonstrate the presence of classic malar (butterfly) dermatitis, and some will have coin-shaped DLE lesions.

Photosensitivity in SCLE patients:
- *dominant feature*
- *skin may burn from light*
- *passing through window glass may be activated by uncovered fluorescent bulbs or photocopier light*
- *UVB, UVB+UVA and UVA wavelengths alone can induce lupus lesions in SCLE patients*

Photosensitivity is a dominant feature of SCLE. The photosensitivity can be exquisite. Not infrequently, anti-Ro (SS-A) antibody–positive SCLE patients relate experiencing a persistent photosensitive dermatitis lasting weeks following exposure to sunlight that passes through window glass. Gradually, this phototoxic dermatitis may evolve into lesions of SCLE. In other words, long-wave, relatively low-energy ultraviolet A (UVA) light alone, which is not blocked by window glass, is capable of activating their disease, in addition to short-wave ultraviolet B (UVB) light. Several SCLE patients have indicated that uncovered fluorescent bulbs were responsible for activating their cutaneous LE. Recently, it was reported that the skin disease of an anti-Ro (SS-A) antibody–positive SCLE patient was activated by light from a photocopier.

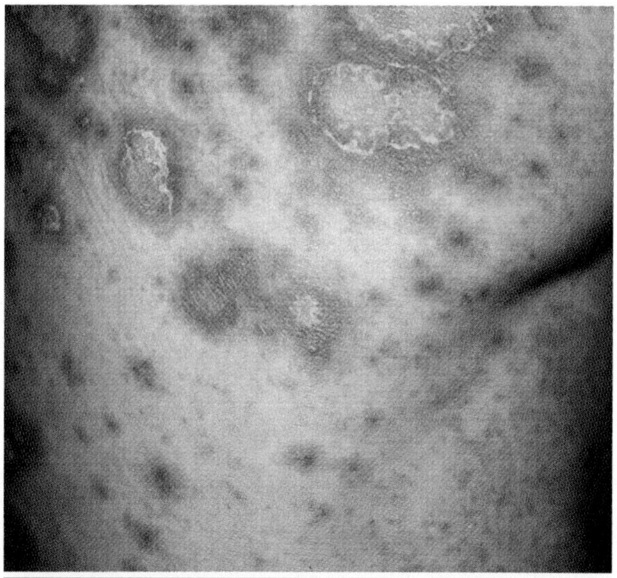

FIGURE 5–5 Pityriasis rosea–like eruption in an anti-Ro (SS-A) antibody–positive patient.

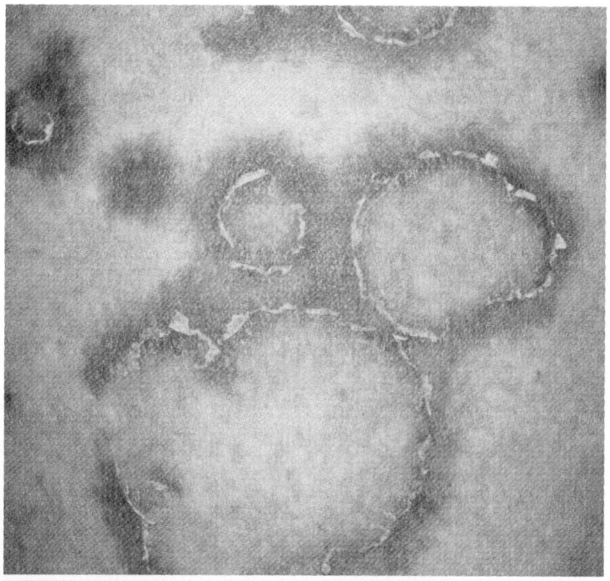

FIGURE 5–6 Erythema annulare centrifugum–like lesions in an anti-Ro (SS-A) antibody–positive patient.

Scientific data to support these clinical observations come from the studies of Kind et al. and Lehman et al. These investigators have reported that exposure to UVA (monochronometer) is capable of inducing in some SCLE patients a cutaneous lesion that clinically and histopathologically demonstrates features compatible with the diagnosis of LE. It is important to express a caveat at this point. Although there is a striking association between anti-Ro (SS-A) antibodies and photosensitivity in LE patients, it should be noted that anti-Ro (SS-A) antibody–positive Sjögren's syndrome patients are not photosensitive.

Anti-Ro (SS-A) antibody–positive Sjögren's syndrome patients NOT photosensitive

The prognosis of SCLE patients presenting to a dermatologist is an area of active interest. The work of Sontheimer, which involved evaluating approximately 50 SCLE patients over 10 years, indicates that ≥ 90% of these SCLE patients have a benign disease process. Only one of his patients succumbed to a lupus-related complication (pancreatic vasculitis).

SCLE patients presenting themselves to dermatologists generally have a good prognosis.

Chronic Cutaneous Lupus Erythematosus

The term "CCLE" encompasses a number of morphologically distinct cutaneous lesions, including the classic DLE, hypertrophic or verrucous LE, lupus panniculitis (profundus), mucosal LE, lupus tumidus, chilblain lupus, and a rare variant discoid lupus/lichen planus overlap. All these lesions have histopathologic features that are similar.

Chronic cutaneous LE includes:
- *DLE*
- *hypertrophic or verrucous LE*
- *lupus profundus/panniculitis*
- *mucosal lupus*
- *lupus tumidus*
- *chilblain lupus*
- *lupus/lichen planus overlap*

Unfortunately, "DLE," a morphologic term, has been usurped to indicate benign cutaneous disease. In this chapter, DLE is used as a morphologic term to mean coin-shaped, sharply demarcated, erythematous, scarring, atrophic lesions that heal with hypo- or hyperpigmentation. They are also associated with the presence of telangiectasia and follicular plugging.

DLE most commonly seen in LE patients who have benign cutaneous disease
Can also be seen in SLE patients

DLE lesions are prominent in the sun-exposed areas. Atrophy and scar formation are common and, in some patients, especially dark-skinned individuals (African Americans, Indians, and other Asians) postinflammatory hyperpigmentation is a common sequela. Other patients may demonstrate prominent hypopigmentation.

Involvement of the scalp frequently produces a scarring alopecia. At times this can be very extensive, necessitating the wearing of a wig (Figure 5–10). Discoid lupus erythematosus lesions may occur over the central portion of the face and, unlike the lesions of ACLE, produce scarring, potentially disfiguring lesions (especially in African Americans). On occasion, DLE may involve the eyelids, producing permanent loss of eyelashes (Figure 5–11). Rarely, a squamous cell carcinoma may arise in a chronic DLE lesion.

DLE:
- *sun-exposed areas*
- *scarring may be cosmetically significant*
- *scarring alopecia*
- *rarely, a squamous carcinoma can arise in chronic indolent DLE lesion*

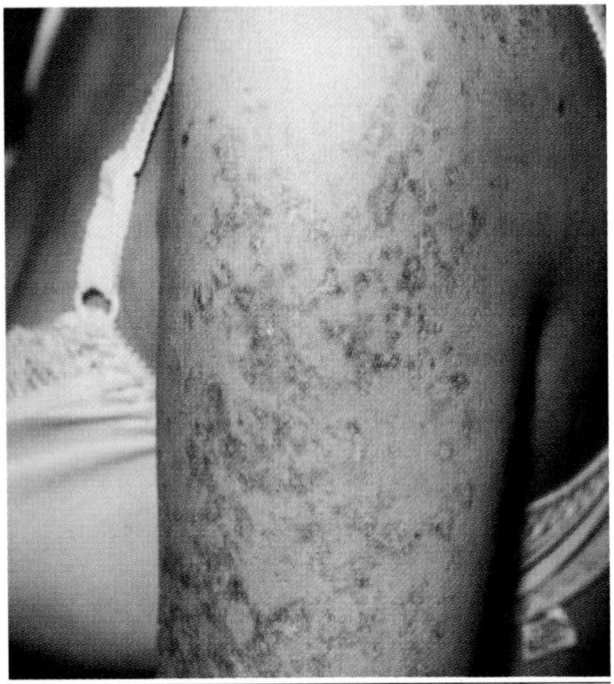

FIGURE 5-7 Follicular keratotic lesions in an anti-Ro (SS-A) antibody–patient of Asian extraction.

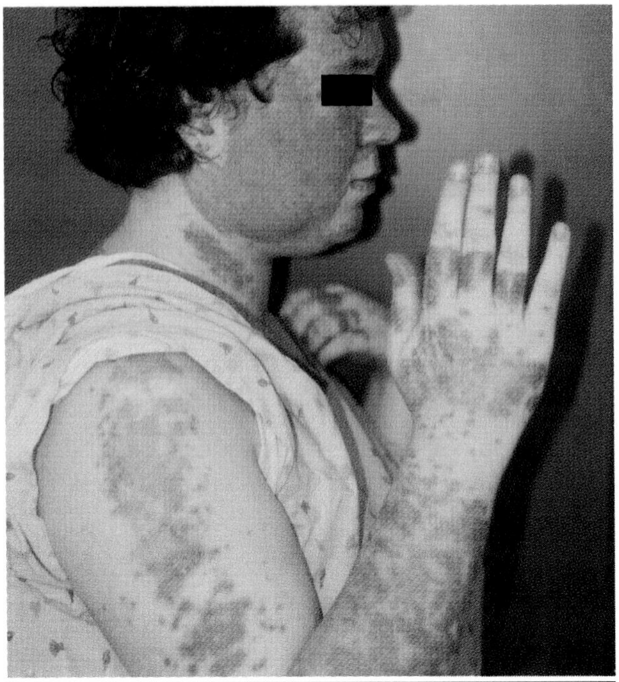

FIGURE 5-8 Anti-Ro (SS-A) antibody–positive exquisitely photosensitive patient demonstrating SCLE lesions on forearm and ACLE lesions (malar dermatitis) on face.

The V of the neck and the extensor surfaces of the arms are common sites for DLE lesions. DLE lesions involving the palms and soles can produce painful erosions, which cause significant morbidity and are very difficult to treat.

DLE lesions may arise at the sites of trauma.

A Koebner's phenomonen, an isomorphic response, may be responsible for the formation of DLE lesions. Several studies have noted the emergence of DLE lesions following trauma (ie, from radiographs, diathermy, chemical burns, sunlight exposure). It should be noted that although most of the DLE lesions occur

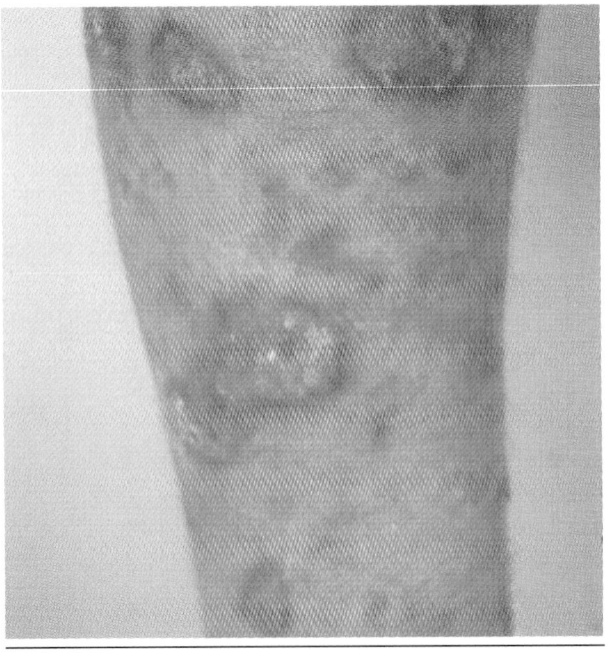

FIGURE 5-9 Annular scarring CCLE (DLE) in an anti-Ro (SS-A)–positive patient. (Reproduced with permission from Stephen Katz, M.D.)

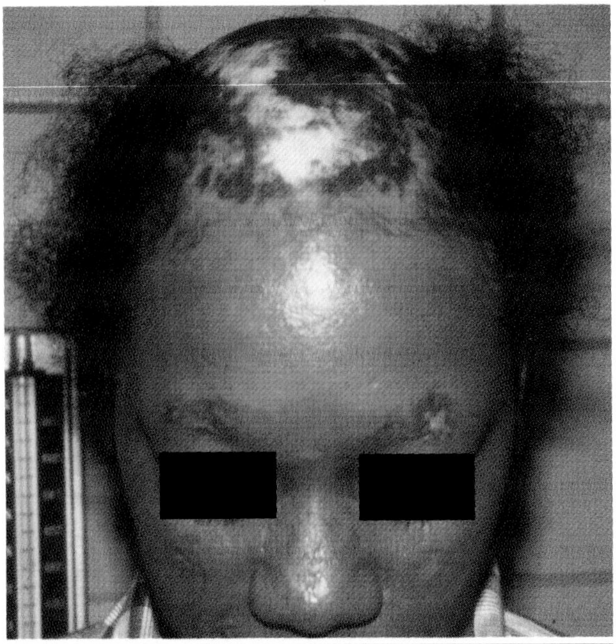

FIGURE 5-10 Severe scarring CCLE (DLE) lesions producing widespread alopecia. Severe scarring DLE lesions in African Americans are commonly detected.

in sun-exposed areas, a significant proportion do not appear to be related to sun exposure. For example, DLE lesions are frequently found in the external auditory canal, and some have been detected in the perineal region.

DLE lesions can occur in non–sun-exposed areas.

The work of Kind et al. and Lehman et al. have demonstrated that although DLE lesions can be induced with UV light, patients with these lesions do not appear to be as photosensitive as those having SCLE.

DLE lesions can be induced experimentally by UV exposure.

Approximately 25% of patients with CCLE demonstrate painless mucous membrane involvement. All mucous membranes can be involved, but these lesions occur most commonly on the oral mucous membranes. On rare occasions, these chronic lesions may also degenerate into squamous cell carcinoma.

It must be re-emphasized that mucous membrane lesions can occur both in benign cutaneous erythematosus as well as in SLE. Biopsies of these lesions demonstrate histopathologic features of DLE.

Other forms of CCLE have been recognized. One of these is lupus profundus. Approximately 50% of patients presenting with this disease process have classic DLE on the surface of the skin with very prominent induration extending to the subcutaneous area (Figure 5–12). This lesion may occur in the presence or absence of systemic features. It should be noted that the term "lupus profundus" is used interchangeably with "lupus panniculitis." The lesions are most commonly found on the face, upper arms, chest, buttocks, and thighs (see Figure 5–12). Severe involvement of the face can, on unusual occasions, produce features of lipodystrophy.

Lupus profundus/panniculitis can be seen in both cutaneous erythematosus and SLE.

The lesions of lupus profundus/panniculitis usually begin as firm, somewhat tender nodules deep in the skin. The overlying skin retracts producing a saucer-like deformity (Figure 5–13). These lesions may ulcerate, and dystophic calcification may occur infrequently.

Hypertrophic LE, also known as verrucous or hyperkeratotic LE, is an unusual variant of CCLE characterized by erythematous hyperkeratotic plaques (Figure 5–14). They are most commonly seen on the extensor surfaces of the arms, upper back, as well as the face. At times, overlapping features between this entity and lichen planus have been observed.

Chilblain (pernio) lupus is a very unusual form of LE, generally occurring acutely as pruritic, reddish-purplish macules and plaques on the periphery of the body, including ears, nose, toes, fingers, and lower legs. These lesions appear to be precipitated by cold, damp climates. They are very unusual in the United States and are more frequently seen in the United Kingdom. (Provost has seen only one chilblain patient in his entire career. This occurred during a cold and damp winter in Baltimore, MD.)

Chilblain LE:

- *rarely in the USA*
- *mostly reported from UK*
- *induced by cold, damp weather*

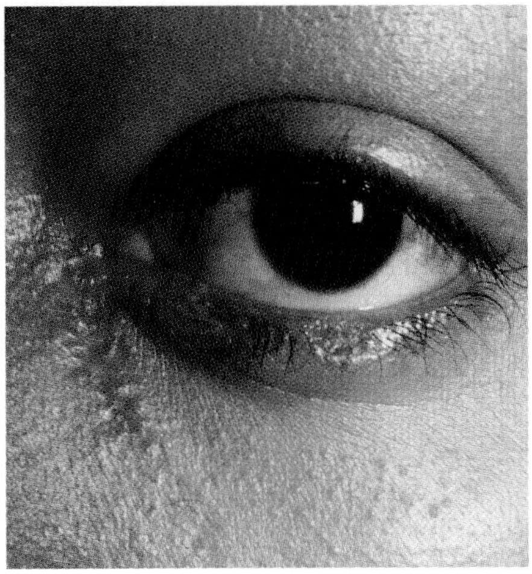

FIGURE 5-11 CCLE lesion involving loss of eye lashes on lower eyelid.

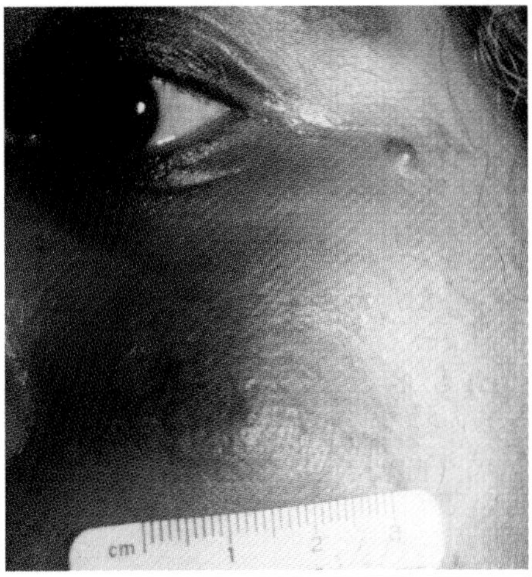

FIGURE 5-12 Lupus profundus in left cheek associated with DLE lesion on surface with prominent induration.

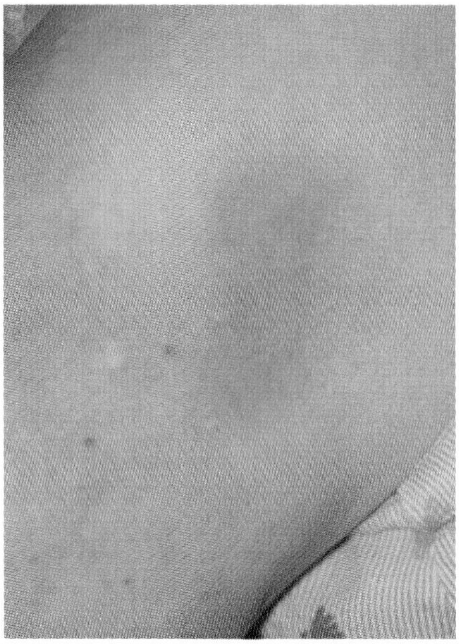

FIGURE 5–13 Lupus panniculitis lesion on posterior portion of left arm—mild postinflammatory hyperpigmentation resulting from inflammatory process in dermal subcutaneous regions.

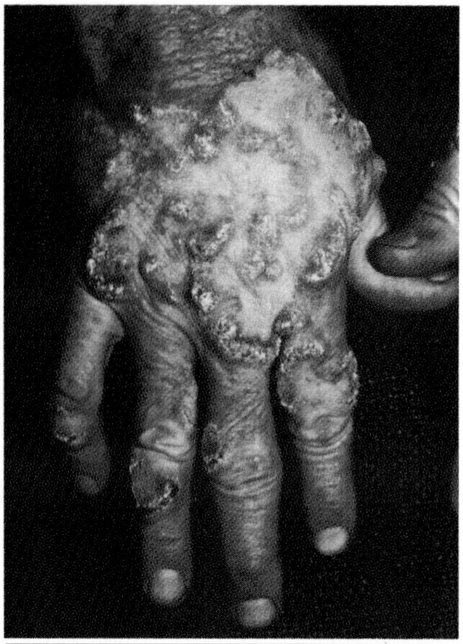

FIGURE 5–14 Hyperkeratotic scarring in CCLE. (Reproduced with permission from Rick Stearns, M.D.)

DLE lesions evolve
Systemic features occur in some patients.
Associated with anti Ro -(SS-A) antibodies

With time, these cold-induced lesions may evolve into classic DLE lesions suggesting that the wet, damp, cold environment acts as a Koebner's phenomenon. Some of these LE patients may subsequently develop features of SLE. Several recent reports indicate that chilblain may be associated with anti-Ro (SS-A) antibodies.

Lupus erythematosus tumidus is an unusual CCLE lesion characterized by succulent, erythematous, edematous plaques. These lesions contain excessive mucin, which may be responsible for the prominent edematous features. Photosensitivity also may be prominent in these patients.

The relationship between various forms of CCLE and the severity of the lupus disease process has been well studied. Most patients with CCLE have a benign disease process in which the lupus disease is localized only to the skin. However, a few patients with morphologically distinct DLE lesions may have prominent systemic features.

Conversion of CCLE patient to SLE is unusual, probably occurring at a frequency of 2% or less.

Prior to 1979, when SCLE was recognized as a distinct LE subset, it was estimated that 5 to 10% of CCLE patients (DLE), with time, would evolve into SLE. It is the opinion of Sontheimer and Provost that many of these patients were, in fact, SCLE patients. The frequency of conversion from benign cutaneous LE to SLE now appears to be approximately 2% or less. Provost has seen only two serologically negative CCLE patients, one with classic DLE lesions and the other with lupus profundus, who clinically and serologically over a 10-year period evolved into SLE (anti-U_1RNP and anti-Ro (SS-A) antibodies, respectively). The denominator for the patients with CCLE seen during this time was at least 100 DLE patients.

Other studies indicate that DLE patients possessing anti-ss-DNA antibodies are more likely, in comparison with DLE patients without these antibodies, to have systemic manifestations.

Pathogenesis of Specific Lesions

The exact pathophysiology of the ACLE disease process is unknown. The ACLE and SCLE lesions may be pathophysiologically closely related. This hypothesis is based on the following facts: (1) ACLE patients are generally photosensitive, (2) ACLE lesions (malar dermatitis) heal with little or no residual scar formation, (3) ACLE lesions are the most common lesions seen in anti-Ro (SS-A) antibody–positive LE patients, with or without other accompanying autoantibodies, and (4) patients described as having ANA-negative SLE possessing only anti-Ro (SS-A) antibodies are frequently detected to have ACLE lesions (Figures 5–15 and 5–16).

The ACLE and SCLE lesions may have a common pathophysiologic mechanism.

This hypothesis, however, is speculative, and no formal testing has been done to examine it. The data examining the pathogenesis of SCLE and CCLE lesions, however, are more substantial.

ACLE lesions, like SCLE lesions, are nonscarring and photosensitive.

Antigen-antibody reaction. The best evidence for the pathogenesis of SCLE lesions has come, in large part, from the study of the neonatal lupus erythematosus (NLE) syndrome (see below). In this syndrome, anti-Ro (SS-A) antibodies and, to a much lesser extent, anti-U$_1$RNP antibodies produced in the mother are passed via the placenta to the fetus. The infant may demonstrate at birth, or generally within the first 8 weeks, the presence of erythematous, macular lesions, many of which are reminiscent of the annular, polycyclic lesions of SCLE. Furthermore, many of these lesions are reported to develop following sun exposure or occasionally following exposure to bilirubin lights.

NLE syndrome provides best evidence for pathologic role of anti-Ro (SS-A) and, to a lesser extent, anti-U$_1$RNP antibodies in cutaneous lupus lesions

In vitro studies have indicated that keratinocytes cultured in the presence of nonlethal UV light or high doses of estrogen will express the Ro (SS-A) macromolecule on the plasma membrane (apoptosis). Thus, these normal autoantigens can be expressed on the plasma membrane where, theoretically, they are exposed to direct attack by cytotoxic T cells and/or antibodies. Furthermore, direct immunofluorescence examination of SCLE skin lesions demonstrates the deposition of the Ro macromolecule in a speckled distribution on the surface of keratinocytes similar to what has been demonstrated in vitro.

Serial antibody determinations in the infant indicate that the maternal anti-Ro (SS-A) antibody is catabolized during the first 6 months of life and is no longer detectable. This time frame corresponds with the disappearance of the cutaneous lesions.

Thus, there is a large body of evidence to suggest that antibodies (anti-Ro [SS-A] and anti-U$_1$RNP) produced in the mother and passed to the infant combine

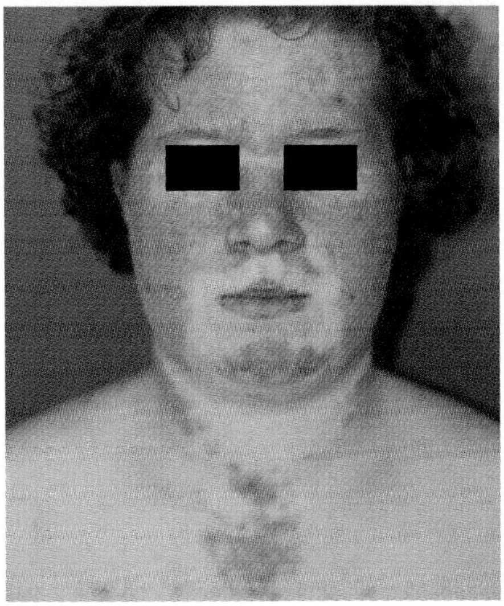

FIGURE 5–15 ACLE lesions in patient demonstrating only anti-Ro (SS-A) antibodies. The patient has no evidence of systemic disease.

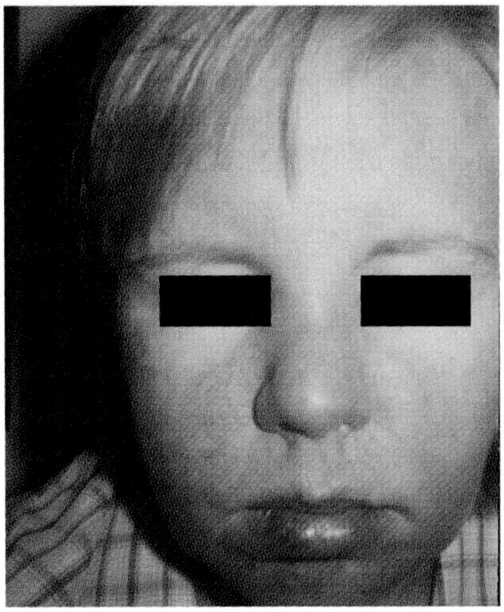

FIGURE 5–16 ACLE lesions in patient demonstrating only anti-Ro (SS-A) antibodies. The patient subsequently developed other autoantibodies, including anti-dsDNA antibodies, and died 18 months later of cerebral lupus.

with the RNPs expressed on the keratinocyte plasma membranes. It is hypothesized that this antigen–antibody reaction is being mediated by antibody-dependent cellular cytotoxicity in which the infant's own T cells are the effector cells.

In CCLE, the pathophysiologic mechanism appears to be different. Chronic, scarring DLE-like lesions are not the lesions that have been identified in the NLE. These lesions, unlike the lesions of SCLE and ACLE, produce scar formation.

Serologic studies in CCLE patients have generally demonstrated undetectable levels of autoantibodies. However, this statement must be tempered in view of the recent evidence indicating that a very sensitive enzyme-linked immunosorbent assay (ELISA) detected low-titer anti-Ro (SS-A) antibodies in patients with classic DLE.

In CCLE lesions, it is hypothesized that a T-cell–mediated cytotoxic mechanism induces the cutaneous lesions.

The inflammatory infiltrate in CCLE lesions is a mononuclear inflammatory infiltrate, and as demonstrated in Figure 5–17, the cellular infiltrate contains both CD4- and CD8-positive lymphocytes. In CCLE, it is hypothesized that a T-cell cytotoxic phenomenon is the effector mechanism resulting in the cutaneous lesions.

UV light induces or facilitates exposure of autoantigens to a sensitized immune system.

Photosensitivity. The role of UV light in the pathogenesis of cutaneous LE lesions has intrigued investigators. There is now a good deal of data indicating that with UV light exposure, putative autoantigens are generated or exposed to the sensitized host immune system resulting in various pathologic events that produce both cutaneous as well as systemic features of LE. It has long been recognized that UV light has been capable of generating the lesions of LE. Investigations designed to explore the components of the positive lupus band test (the deposition of immunoglobulin [Ig] and complement at the dermal–epidermal junction of nonlesional skin [Figure 5–18]) provided the initial observations. Deoxyribonuclease enzymatic digestion studies demonstrated the deposition of DNA in the lupus band. Further studies using UV light exposure of mice sensitized to UV-DNA coupled to methylated bovine serum albumin demonstrated

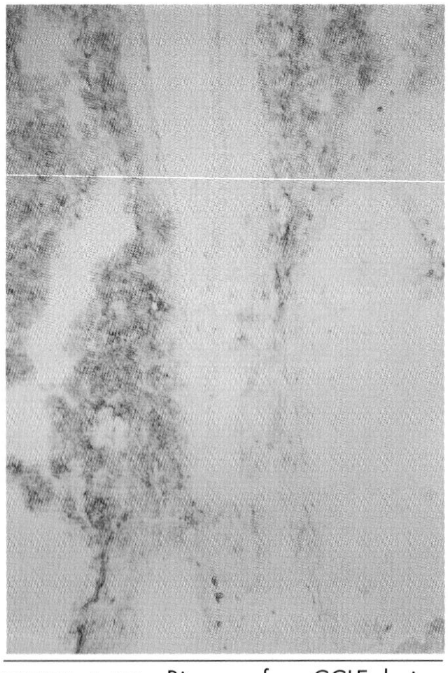

FIGURE 5–17 Biopsy of a CCLE lesion demonstrating a T-cell infiltrate surrounding a hair follicle. This is an immunoperoxidase staining technique using a mixture of CD4- and CD8-T-cell monoclonal antibodies.

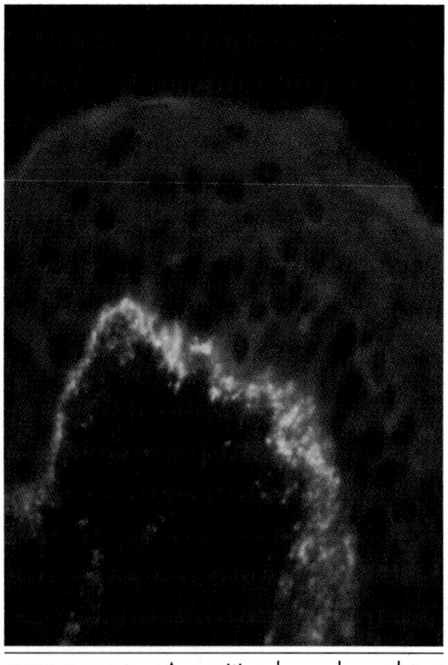

FIGURE 5–18 A positive lupus bound test demonstrating the depostion of Ig and complement in a granular pattern along the dermal–epidermal junction.

that following UV exposure, UV light–denatured DNA could be detected in epidermal nuclei. Surprisingly, with time, this UV light–denatured DNA passed across the basement membrane zone where it became part of the lupus band test. Other studies indicated that UV-denatured DNA could gain access into the systemic circulation and be found in the kidney.

More recent studies have indicated that following UV exposure, the UV–denatured DNA is excised from the normal DNA by endonucleases. Furthermore, this excised segment of UV–denatured DNA (thymidine dimers) contains all the epitopes reactive with anti-DNA antibodies.

Other intriguing studies by Kind et al. and Lehmann et al. have indicated variable degrees of photosensitivity among lupus patients. They have demonstrated that in some lupus patients, only relatively high-energy UVB is capable of inducing formation of LE lesions. In other patients, especially SCLE patients, relatively low-energy UVA is capable of producing LE lesions.

Thus, the data, although incomplete, strongly suggest that the role of UV light in the induction of photosensitivity is directed at creating or exposing autoantigens to the deleterious effect of the sensitized host immune system.

Lupus band test. One observation noted in these animal studies and in SLE patients with a positive lupus band test is the fact that the deposition of Ig and complement can occur in normal-appearing skin in the histologic absence of inflammatory cells (see Figure 5–18). Furthermore, continued observations of these SLE patients has failed to demonstrate the development of LE lesions. Some investigators believe that this is due to the fact that there may be a specific local inhibition of complement activation in the skin. For example, in positive lupus band tests occurring in lupus lesions, the complement attack membrane complex is present (C5b-C9). In the positive lupus band tests from uninvolved nonlesional skin, the complement attack membrane complex is not present.

A positive lupus band test from lesional skin contains the membrane attack complex C5b-C9.
This is not seen in a positive band test from noninvolved skin.

Today, the performance of a direct immunofluorescence examination of lesional and nonlesional skin of SLE patients for Ig and complement deposition has limited value. Although it is true that there is a positive correlation between the deposition of various Ig, especially IgG along the skin basement membrane in uninvolved SLE skin, and the presence of renal disease and anti-dsDNA antibodies, the performance of the lupus band test is labor intensive and costly, and its diagnostic value has been replaced by serologic testing. Today, the lupus band test is infrequently employed and generally used only to evaluate the most unusual cases.

Nonspecific Lesions

During the past 25 years, the study of nonspecific lesions associated with LE has been an active area of investigation. Although these lesions are not specific for LE, their presence in the context of LE may have prognostic significance.

Vasculitis

Perhaps the most commonly studied nonspecific lesion occurring in LE is vasculitis. The frequency of cutaneous vasculitic lesions varies. Several large studies report an approximate 20% frequency. Our data suggest a frequency of approximately 40% (Table 5–5).

The morphologic features of a cutaneous vasculitic lesion are dependent on the intensity of the inflammatory insult and the level of blood vessel involvement in the skin. Thus, vasculitic lesions in SLE vary from urticaria-like lesions to large ulcers. The site most frequently associated with vasculitic lesions is the lower extremities. There, the lesions may present as palpable or nonpalpable purpura with or without ulcer formation. Lesions on the acral portions of the body are also common and include Osler's nodes (the presence of tender, nodular, indurated lesions on the tips of the fingers), Janeway's lesions (erythematous, nontender lesions appearing on the hypothenar eminence of the hands), and capillary nailfold injection with or without infarction. The Osler's node–like lesions and the capillary nailfold injection may also occur on the toes. Rarely, the vasculitic disease process can involve vessels near the dermal–epidermal junction

Vasculitic lesions occurring in SLE include:
- *Osler's nodes*
- *Janeway's lesions*
- *capillary nailfold injection and infarction*
- *palpable and nonpalpable purpura*
- *urticaria-like lesions*
- *panniculitis (Weber-Christian disease)*

TABLE 5–5 Frequency of Cutaneous Vasculitic Lesions

Manifestations	Number N = 150	%
Cutaneous	132	(88)
Malar rash	91	(61)
Alopecia	68	(45)
Photosensitivity	68	(45)
Mucosal ulcers	35	(23)
Discoid rash	22	(15)
Nodules	18	(12)
Musculoskeletal	124	(83)
Arthritis	114	(76)
Ischemic necrosis	36	(24)
Myositis	7	(5)
Serositis	95	(63)
Pleurisy	85	(57)
Pericarditis	35	(23)
Peritonitis	12	(8)
Neuropsychiatric	83	(55)
Central nervous system	59	(39)
Peripheral neuropathy	32	(21)
Organic psychosis	24	(16)
Seizures	20	(13)
Raynaud's phenomenon	66	(44)
Vasculitis	65	(43)
Cutaneous	40	(27)
Mesenteric	19	(13)
Digital ulcers	14	(9)
Leg ulcer	9	(6)
Nephritis	46	(31)
Chronic renal failure	5	(3)
Cardiopulmonary	8	(5)

Adapted from:
Hochberg MC, Boyd RE, Ahearn JM, et al. Systemic lupus erythematosus: a review of clinico-laboratory features and immunogenetic markers in 150 patients with emphasis on demographic subsets. Medicine (Baltimore) 1985;64:285–295.

producing small blister formation. At times, the intensity of the inflammatory infiltrate can be great, resulting in a prominent leukocyte infiltration into the involved areas, which produces a pustular-like lesion. Finally, vasculitis can be deep, involving the small muscular arteries at the dermal-subcutaneous level. These polyarteritis nodosa–like lesions can produce tender nodular formation, and if the underlying subcutaneous tissue is involved, a significant painful panniculitis can occur. If the intensity of the inflammation is great, ulceration may ensue. Provost believes that one of the causes of febrile, relapsing, suppurative panniculitis (Weber-Christian disease), rarely reported today, may have represented an uncontrolled subcutaneous vasculitis in an SLE patient prior to the advent of corticosteroid therapy.

Pathophysiology most likely due to circulating immune complex formation

At the present time the best evidence for the pathophysiology of the majority of vasculitic lesions occurring in LE is circulating immune complex formation. The reason for the preponderance of vasculitic lesions in dependent areas, such as the back of bedridden patients or the lower extremities of upright patients, is probably due to the hydrostatic pressure of the vascular system as well as local constriction of blood vessels promoting eddying. Vasculitic lesions at the site of trauma (eg, following shaving of legs) or at sites of pressure or constriction, such as from a belt at the waist, are common.

Histopathologic examination of these lesions, in general, demonstrates the presence of a leukocytoclastic vasculitis characterized by fibrinoid necrosis, widespread fragmentation of polymorphonuclear leukocytes, and total disruption of the integrity of the blood vessel. Direct immunofluorescence examination most frequently will demonstrate the deposition of immunoglobulin and complement in the affected blood vessel walls.

On occasion, a predominantly lymphocytic inflammatory infiltrate may be seen. It is debatable whether this inflammatory infiltrate represents the end result of a classic leukocytoclastic angiitis or whether or not this is a true, lymphocytic vasculitis. (For a more complete discussion of these two types of vasculitis, please consult Chapter 8, "Sjögren's Syndrome," and Chapter 12, "Vasculitis.")

Urticaria-like vasculitis. Urticaria-like vasculitis has in recent years been recognized as a nonspecific cutaneous manifestation of active LE. These lesions are frequently characterized by the persistence of individual lesions for days (not the transient 4 to 6 hours of common urticaria), petechiae occurring in the urticaria, and a hyperpathia of the lesion to light touch. The frequency of urticaria-like vasculitic lesions in our SLE patient experience is approximately 8% (16 of 193 SLE patients). Furthermore, our and other investigators' experiences indicate that hypocomplementemia and renal disease are commonly found in this group of LE patients. In addition, anti-dsDNA as well as anti-U_1RNP, -Sm, and -Ro (SS-A) antibodies are frequently detected. In our experience, similar urticaria-like vasculitic lesions were not seen in a benign, cutaneous LE control cohort.

Urticaria-like vasculitis in SLE:
- *occurs in approximately 8% of patients*
- *guarded prognosis*
- *increased frequency of renal disease*
- *increased frequency of autoantibodies including anti-dsDNA antibodies*

Antiendothelial cell surface antibodies. In addition to immune complex–mediated vasculitis, other potential pathophysiologic mechanisms may be operative in the genesis of the SLE vasculitic lesions. It has been recognized that lupus patients make autoantibodies directed against endothelial cell surface molecules. Thus, it is conceivable that an autoantibody directed against an endothelial cell surface marker could activate the complement sequence producing an inflammatory destruction of the blood vessel that would mimic, in appearance, circinate immune complex–mediated vasculitis.

Pathophysiology of urticaria-like vasculitis lesions in SLE:
- *circulating immune complex formation*
- *anti-endothelial cell surface antibodies*
- *anti-C1q antibodies*
- *hypocomplementemic urticaria-like vasculitis immune complex–mediated*

Hypocomplementemic urticarial vasculitis. It has also been recognized that hypocomplementemic urticaria-like vasculitis is associated with the presence of autoantibodies directed against the collagen-like regions (CLR) of C1q. Furthermore, studies have demonstrated the presence of anti-C1q antibodies in the sera of some SLE patients. The exact mechanism whereby urticaria-like vasculitic lesions are generated and how the urticaria is related to anti-C1q antibodies are unknown. Conceivably, however, this could be immune complex–mediated.

Hypocomplementemic urticaria-like vasculitis feature:
- *anti-C1q antibodies*
- *urticaria-like vasculitis*
- *obstructive pulmonary disease*

Livedo Reticularis

In recent years, another form of vasculopathy has been recognized in LE patients. This form of vasculopathy associated with anticardiolipin antibodies (or the lupus anticoagulant) is characterized by the presence of livedo reticularis, frequently extending beyond the lower extremities to involve the upper extremities as well as the buttocks and back (Figure 5–19). Ulceration may or may not occur. Biopsies of the perilesional area of these ulcers demonstrate the presence of thrombi in multiple dermal blood vessels generally in the absence of inflammation. In addition to the presence of livedo reticularis, these LE patients frequently demonstrate thrombocytopenia, increased fetal wastage in the first trimester, and recurrent episodes of venous and arterial thromboses. Libman-Sacks endocarditis, myocardial dysfunction, myocardial infarction, and pulmonary hypertension also have been described. On unusual occasions, acral cyanosis, cutaneous infarction resembling Degos's disease, and small-vessel infarction occurring around the ankles (atrophie blanche–like lesions) have been detected. Recurrent central nervous system vascular thrombotic events in association with livedo reticularis (Sneddon's syndrome) occur. Many of these patients develop post-infarction dementia.

One report indicates that 11 of 66 SLE patients (17%) demonstrated livedo reticularis. Nine of these 11 (81%) were anticardiolipin antibody positive (see section in this chapter discussing antiphospholipid antibodies).

Features of anticardiolipin (phospholipid) syndrome in SLE:
- *recurrent arterial and venous thrombosis*
- *thrombocytopenia*
- *increased first trimester fetal wastage*
- *livedo reticularis with or without ulcers*
- *Libman-Sacks endocarditis*
- *ventricular dysfunction*
- *recurrent CNS thrombosis (Sneddon's syndrome)*

Raynaud's phenomenon:
- *most patients don't have a connective tissue disease*
- *striking increase in U_1RNP–positive patients*
- *mixed connective tissue syndrome*
- *frequent occurrence in SLE patients*
- *variation in frequency and severity, depending on region of country*

Raynaud's Phenomenon

Raynaud's phenomenon is a frequent occurrence in SLE ranging from 10 to 44%, with an average of approximately 30% (see Table 5–2). It is characterized by triphasic color changes involving the fingers and/or toes. A vasospastic initial component, characterized by blanching, is followed by a purplish, cyanotic discoloration. Finally, a reperfusion erythema occurs. The latter components of this phenomenon are commonly associated with pain.

Most patients with Raynaud's phenomenon do not have connective tissue disease. It has been estimated that only 2 to 10% of patients with Raynaud's phenomenon who are evaluated by a rheumatologist have SLE. The frequency of Raynaud's phenomenon varies among various serologic subsets of LE. For example, anti-U_1RNP antibody–positive lupus patients have a very high frequency of Raynaud's phenomenon ranging between 60 and 90% (Table 5–6). By contrast, a recent study examining 50 anti-Ro (SS-A) antibody–positive lupus patients has reported a 46% frequency of Raynaud's phenomenon (see Table 5–3).

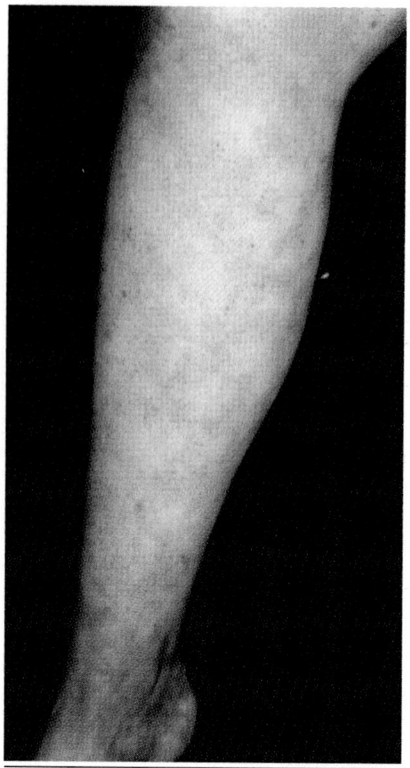

FIGURE 5–19 Livedo reticularis of the lower leg.

In addition to the variation in the frequency of Raynaud's phenomenon among different serologic subsets of LE, the frequency of Raynaud's phenomenon is dependent on environmental conditions. For example, a study of 520 SLE patients in southern California (Dubois) reported an 18% frequency, whereas a

TABLE 5–6 Comparison of Clinical Features of Anti-U_1RNP–Positive Patients

Clinical Feature	% SLE Patients N = 30	% SLE Patients N = 49	% MCTD Patients N = 55	% MCTD Patients N = 100
Arthritis	93	95	95	95
Cytopenia	67	55	36	—
Pleurisy/pericarditis	57	45	22	27
Malar rash	55	31	11	38
Raynaud's phenomenon	60	69	90	85
Myositis	10	—	49	63
Swollen hands	7	—	65	66
Sclerodermatous changes	3	—	—	33
Renal disease	13	2	2	10
Esophageal dysmotility	—	—	36	67*
Decreased pulmonary diffusion	—	—	—	67†

MCTD = mixed connective tissue disease; SLE = systemic lupus erythematosus.
*N = 75; †N = 43.

study of 150 SLE patients from Maryland (Hochberg) reported a 44% frequency (see Table 5–2).

Erythromelalgia

In addition to the vasospastic phenomena of Raynaud's phenomenon, on rare occasions, SLE patients have been reported to have erythromelalgia. This process is characterized by erythema, increased heat, and intolerable pain in the hands and/or feet following exposure to external heat. In addition, a burning sensation may also be noted. The most commonly associated conditions with erythromelalgia are myeloproliferative diseases, especially polycythemia vera, hypertension, and diabetes. However, in a large portion of patients, erythromelalgia occurs in the absence of other diseases.

Bullous Lesions

Extension of destruction of dermoepidermal junction. Bullae can occur in LE lesions. Most likely, this is caused by a direct extension of the liquefaction degeneration at the dermal–epidermal junction. Patients with anti-Ro (SS-A) antibodies who are exquisitely photosensitive may, on occasion, demonstrate blister formation at the periphery of the lesion. On rare occasions, with heavy sun exposure, these patients can develop a toxic epidermal necrolysis–like cutaneous lupus disease process.

Pathogenesis of bullous lupus lesions:

- *direct extension of liquefaction*
- *degeneration at the dermoepidermal junction*
- *immune complex–mediated anti-type VII collagen antibodies*

Putative immune complex–mediated vasculitis. A second cause of bullous lesions in LE, characterized by small blister formation on the sides of the neck reminiscent of dermatitis herpetiformis, has been reported. In these patients, biopsy demonstrates neutrophilic microabscess formation in the dermal papillae. They also have demonstrated a positive lupus band test in noninvolved skin, the presence of significant quantities of serum immune complexes, hypocomplementemia, and anti-dsDNA antibodies. Dapsone (diaminodiphenylsulfone) was therapeutically effective in all patients.

The best evidence at present indicates that this form of blister formation in LE is produced by immune complex–mediated vasculitis. It should be noted that dapsone has also been reported to be effective in the treatment of some non-SLE patients with putative immune complex–mediated vasculitis.

Immune complex–mediated bullous lesions:

- *suggests a result of vasculitis associated with guarded prognosis*
- *anti-dsDNA antibodies*
- *hypocomplementemia respond to dapsone*

Anti-type VII collagen antibodies. In addition to the blister formation caused by extension of the liquefaction degeneration at the dermal–epidermal junction and by putative immune complex vasculitis, lupus patients develop blister formation induced by autoantibodies directed against the noncollagenous portion of type VII collagen. This condition can occur in the presence or absence of erythema. By employing 1M NACL split skin, which produces cleavage through the lamina lucida, heavy deposition of IgG and complement is found on the dermal side of the blisters. Using Western blot analysis, autoantibodies have been found in some patients that are directed against a 290-kD polypeptide and a minor 145-kD polypeptide. Thus, these patients are similar to those patients with epidermolysis bullosa acquisita.

Anti-type VII collagen antibodies: similar disease process to epidermolysis bullosa acquisita

Other bullous disease associations. In addition to epidermolysis bullosa acquista, porphyria cutanea tarda (PCT) has also been found in association with LE. The occurrence of PCT with LE in the same patient is a very unusual event and appears to be frequently related to the employment of antimalarials to treat lupus skin lesions (unmasking PCT). Pemphigus erythematosus has also been described in association with LE (Snear-Usher syndrome). In Provost's experience, this too, is a very unusual occurrence.

Snear-Usher syndrome

Very uncommon

Alopecia

Three forms of alopecia exist in patients with LE: scarring, telogen effluvium, and lupus hair.

Alopecia has three clinically distinct forms:
- *scarring*
- *telogen effluvium*
- *lupus hair*

Scarring alopecia. As noted earlier, DLE lesions can produce a cosmetically objectionable scarring alopecia, which can be very extensive (see Figure 5–10).

Telogen effluvium. Lupus patients with chronic, active systemic disease may have hair loss (telogen effluvium). Chronic illness, especially associated with negative nitrogen balance, causes a number of the active growing hair (anagen) to enter a resting phase (telogen). This transition from an anagen to a telogen phase occurs over a 3-month period and produces a shedding of the hair (telogen effluvium). New hair growing in the same hair follicle replace has been the hair that are shed. This is a transient, nonscarring alopecia, and with control of the systemic disease process, normal hair growth will result.

Lupus hair. At times, with active disease, the patient may demonstrate a peculiar nonscarring alopecia characterized by unruly fragmented hairs. This wooly or lupus hair is another manifestation of chronic disease activity. In all probability, the catabolic effect of the chronic illness produces defective hair formation in which the diameter of the hair is unevenly narrower resulting in easy fragmentation. Again, with control of the systemic disease, normal hair growth resumes.

Arthritis

Rheumatoid-like arthritis in SLE:
- *non–HLA-DR4*
- *Jaccoud's-like deformity*
- *increased frequency of rheumatoid factor activity in anti-Ro (SS-A) antibody-positive patients*

Jaccoud's arthritis and anti-Ro (SS-A) antibodies. A nonerosive, symmetrical arthritis occurs in approximately 90% of SLE patients. A deforming, rheumatoid-like arthritis, however, is quite unusual. Recently, it has been recognized that a Jaccoud's type of arthritis characterized by a nonerosive, deforming arthritis with severe ulnar deviation occurs infrequently in anti-Ro (SS-A) lupus patients. This type of arthritis has also been described in SCLE patients. In addition, one study has detected that approximately 4% of a well-defined rheumatoid arthritis group had anti-Ro (SS-A) antibodies.

Thus, these collective studies indicate that although a deforming arthritis is unusual in SLE patients, there is a subset of anti-Ro (SS-A) antibody–positive lupus patients who develop a nonerosive, deforming type of arthritis, similar if not identical to Jaccoud's arthritis.

Rheumatoid nodules. Rheumatoid nodules are very unusual in LE. One study has reported six individuals, three of whom were biopsy proven. Rheumatoid factor activity was detected in 4 of these 6 patients. In a recent study of 50 anti-Ro (SS-A) antibody–positive lupus patients, two were detected to have rheumatoid nodules.

Rheumatoid factor. Rheumatoid factor activity occurs in approximately 25% of SLE patients. It is, however, detected in 70% of anti-Ro (SS-A) antibody–positive SLE patients. Anti-Ro (SS-A) antibodies cross-react with an epitope on the $F(ab')_2$ fragment of IgG.

Sclerodermatous Changes

Sclerodermatous features in SLE:
- *uncommon*
- *association with anti-U_1RNP patients*

Sclerodermatous changes are unusual in LE patients. However, anti-U_1RNP antibody–positive lupus patients in general have more sclerodermatous features than other serologic subsets of LE. For example, in one study of 100 anti-U_1RNP antibody–positive patients reported under the heading of mixed connective tissue disease, 66% had swollen hands. Furthermore, pulmonary diffusion abnormalities were detected in 67% of the 43 patients tested, and esophageal dysmotility was detected in 67% of 75 patients tested (see Table 5–6).

Serologic Testing in Diagnosis of Lupus Erythematosus

As noted earlier, during the last 30 years, significant progress has been made in the serologic evaluation of patients with LE. The relative frequency of these antibodies in our experience is depicted in Table 5–7.

Antinuclear antibody testing is a cost-effective screening examination for LE. Four immunofluorescent patterns are recognized: speckled, homogeneous, peripheral, and nucleolar. The speckled pattern is the most nonspecific but is also associated with anti-Ro (SS-A), -La (SS-B), and -U$_1$RNP antibodies; the homogeneous pattern is associated with antibodies directed against nucleoproteins (histones); the peripheral pattern is associated with anti-dsDNA antibodies (Figure 5–20); and the nucleolar pattern is not seen in LE but is found in some scleroderma patients.

Most important autoantibody determinations:
- *antinuclear*
- *anti-dsDNA*
- *anti-U$_1$RNP*
- *anti-Ro (SS-A)*
- *antiphospholipid*

Four antibody systems in addition to ANA are of particular value. These are anti-dsDNA, anti-U$_1$RNP, anti-Ro (SS-A), and antiphospholipid antibodies.

Other antibody systems, such as anti-ssDNA, anti-Sm, anti-La (SS-B), antiribosomal P, and antihistone antibodies, although important in evaluating some patients with LE, have not assumed the importance ascribed to these other antibody systems. For example, anti-ssDNA antibodies are found in approximately 70% of LE patients, and complement-fixing anti-ssDNA antibodies have been found in some patients with LE and glomerulonephritis who do not possess anti-dsDNA antibodies. However, anti-ssDNA antibodies have also been detected in other connective tissue diseases and, thus, are not specific for LE.

Anti-ssDNA antibodies: increased frequency in DLE patients at risk to develop systemic features
May be found in SLE patients with renal disease in absence of anti-dsDNA antibodies

Anti-Sm antibodies are specific for LE but, in general, are almost always found in the presence of anti-U$_1$RNP or other antibodies. Anti-La (SS-B) antibodies are found in approximately 15% of LE patients and almost always in the presence of anti-Ro (SS-A) antibodies. Antiribosomal P and antineuronal antibodies are found in LE patients with predominantly neurologic manifestations and will not be considered here further.

Antihistone antibodies are directed against cationic proteins of the nucleosome and are found in high titers in patients with the drug-induced LE associated with isoniazid, procainamide, and hydralazine therapy.

Antineuronal and antiribosomal P antibodies may be associated with increased frequency of neurologic manifestations.
Antihistone antibodies found in high titer in isoniazid, procainamide, and hydralazine drug-induced lupus

Anti-dsDNA Antibodies

Anti-dsDNA antibodies are specific for idiopathic LE and are not found in other rheumatic conditions. Anti-dsDNA antibodies are present in small quantities in the sera of patients with LE. They are generally detected employing radioimmunoassays using either a Farr test or a Millipore filter binding technique. These antibodies are also detected by an ELISA or an immunofluorescent test using *Crithidia lucillae* (Figure 5–21). There is good correlation between all anti-dsDNA antibody assays. The radioimmunoassay and ELISA techniques are very sensitive. Contamination of the assay reagents, however, with ssDNA can produce false-positive results.

Anti-dsDNA antibodies specific for SLE
correlate well with significant renal disease.

TABLE 5–7 Laboratory Features in SLE Patients

Features	Number (N = 150)	(%)
Anti-ssDNA antibodies	134	(89)
Anti-U$_1$RNP antibodies	51	(34)
Anti-Sm antibodies	26	(17)
Anti-dsDNA antibodies	42	(28)
Anti-Ro (SS-A) antibodies	48	(32)
Anti-La (SS-B) antibodies	18	(12)

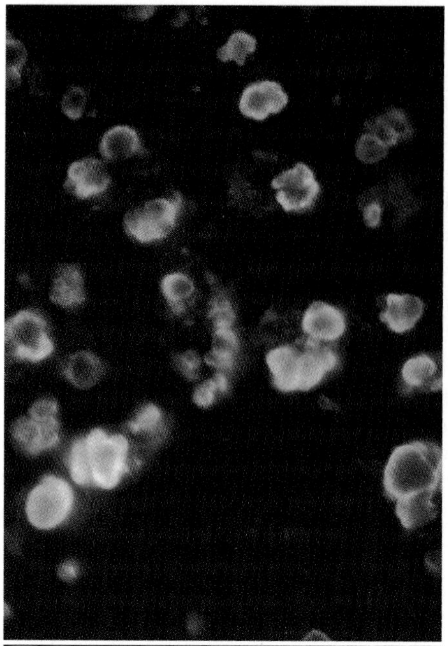

FIGURE 5–20 Indirect immunofluorescence demonstrating a peripheral staining pattern. Cells are from a spleen tissue imprint, and the serum contains anti-dsDNA antibodies.

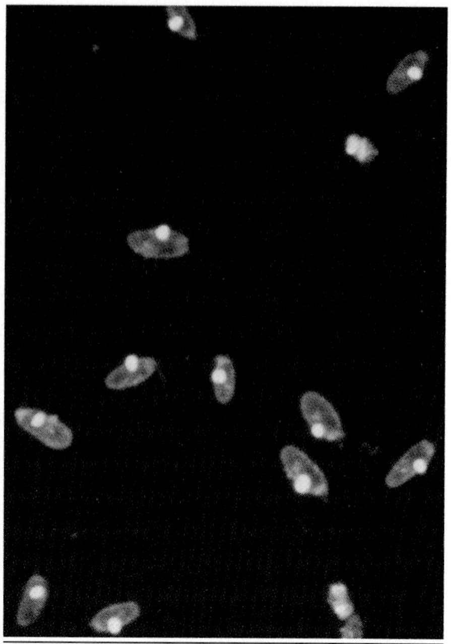

FIGURE 5–21 Indirect immunofluorescence using an anti-dsDNA patient's serum. Note staining of kinetoplast (containing circular DNA) near flagellum.

False-positive assays for anti-dsDNA antibodies due to presence of ssDNA contaminants in the dsDNA reagent or antihistone antibodies reacting with histones in Crithidia lucillae *kinetoplast*

The immunofluorescent test employs *C. lucillae*, a nonpathogenic hemoflagellate that contains near its flagellum a kinetoplast containing circular DNA. This circular DNA possesses all the epitopes reactive with anti-dsDNA antibodies. False-positive assays, however, can occur due to the presence in the patient's serum of antihistone antibodies, which, on occasion, can react with histone proteins present in the kinetoplast. Therefore, the practice in our laboratory is to confirm a positive *C. lucillae* assay with an ELISA using salmon testes dsDNA.

Value of detection of anti-dsDNA antibodies and hypocomplementemia in predicting flares of renal disease

Multiple studies also have demonstrated that the presence of anti-dsDNA antibodies generally has prognostic significance. The presence of anti-dsDNA antibodies in association with hypocomplementemia is generally predictive of a significant immunologic insult in the kidneys. Furthermore, the presence of anti-dsDNA antibodies and hypocomplementemia may antedate the development of hematuria and proteinuria. Additional studies have demonstrated that sharp drops in anti-dsDNA antibody titers and the development of hypocomplementemia herald the onset of a flare of lupus nephritis.

The correlation of anti-dsDNA antibodies and hypocomplementemia with active SLE appears to be limited to nephritis. Such alterations have generally not been detected in lupus patients suffering extrarenal flares, including CNS disease.

The exact reason for the relationship between anti-dsDNA antibodies and renal disease is unknown. However, there are two theoretic considerations: the development of pathologic, soluble, small- to intermediate-sized, circulating DNA/antiDNA immune complexes and in situ DNA/antiDNA immune complex formation in the kidney.

Circulating immune complexes: antigen excess

Because the quantity of anti-dsDNA antibodies in SLE patients is small, very sensitive techniques are needed for their detection. Their small quantity also makes it, in theory, relatively easy to form antigen–antibody complexes in antigen excess (small, soluble complexes that can escape clearance by the reticuloendothelial system). For example, the body contains 1.5 m^2 of skin, and the external layer of skin (epidermis) is generally 4- to 12-cells thick, depending on the region of the body. Excessive sun exposure producing sunburn can generate a great deal of UV light–denatured DNA, which contains epitopes reactive with anti-dsDNA antibodies. Furthermore, this UV light–denatured DNA can gain access to the systemic circulation, creating pathologic, small- and intermediate-sized, soluble antigen–antibody complexes in antigen excess.

In situ immune complex formation

In addition to the formation of circulating immune complexes, DNA is capable of binding to collagen along the glomerular basement membrane. There, theoretically, anti-dsDNA antibodies can bind to the DNA, activating the complement sequence that produces inflammation and results in the destruction of the glomeruli.

Thus, circulating immune complexes, as well as in situ immune complex formation, may explain the role of anti-dsDNA antibodies in the pathogenesis of lupus glomerulonephritis.

Complement Determination

CH_{50} (complement hemolytic activity 50%)
Serum must be tested within 1 to 2 hours of obtaining serum or frozen at –70°C until processed.

Complement determinations are an integral part of the laboratory evaluation of patients with LE. Hypocomplementemia correlates well with active renal disease. Complement is measured in a total hemolytic complement functional assay termed the "CH_{50}." This designation indicates complement hemolytic activity 50%. Sensitized sheep red blood cells (containing anti-sheep red blood cell antibodies) are incubated with serial dilutions of the patient's serum. The assay has been prearranged to detect spectrophotometrically the optical density associated with 50% hemolysis. The reciprocal of the dilution of the patient's plasma that will support 50% hemolysis of the sheep red blood cells is taken as the end point. In patients with active renal disease, the complement level may be as low as 20% of its normal quantity. If, however, the complement level is undetectable, then one should consider the possibility of homozygous complement deficiency associated with LE (eg, homozygous C1, C4, C2, or C5 deficiency).

A zero or unmeasurable CH_{50} determination found in homozygous deficiencies of components of the classic complement pathway

Single radioimmunodiffusion or rocket electrophoresis determinations of C3 and C4:
- *determines protein content*
- *can be sent through mail no special handling necessary*

In addition to a hemolytic complement assay, complement is measured by a single radioimmunodiffusion assay or rocket electrophoresis. The complement components measured by this technique are C4 and C3. This type of testing measures the complement component protein concentration and permits physicians in their office to send serum via the mail or courier for testing. Unlike the CH_{50} functional assay, which must be frozen at -70°C or processed within 1 to 2 hours of taking the blood sample, no such requirements are necessary for these determinations. Low C4 levels in the absence of low C3 levels may reflect the presence of a null C4 gene (ie, C4AQ0) the most common complement deficiency in SLE (see below).

Most common complement deficiency in SLE is a C4 null gene (C4AQ0)

Studies indicate that therapeutic regimens (immunosuppressive agents and/or corticosteroids) designed to normalize complement levels are superior therapeutic regimens than those designed to treat only symptomatic SLE flares. For example, long-term studies (ie, greater than 10 years) demonstrate that SLE patients treated in such a manner have a much better prognosis and have fewer complications.

Anti-Sm Antibodies

Anti-Sm antibodies are specific for SLE.

Anti-Sm antibodies are found in approximately 20 to 25% of SLE patients (gel double diffusion). The main value of the anti-Sm antibody determination in the evaluation of LE is that this antibody is specific for SLE. This antibody system rarely occurs alone and is most commonly associated with the presence of anti-U_1RNP antibodies. Anti-Sm antibodies are directed against the splicesome polypeptides of 29, 28, 16, and 13 kD. They are referred to as B, B', D, and E core polypeptides, respectively.

Anti-U_1RNP antibodies

Anti-U_1RNP antibodies recognize two polypeptides of the splicesome: A protein (33 kD) and C protein (22 kD). In addition, by Western blot analyses, anti-U_1RNP antibodies also recognize a 70-kD protein associated with the nuclear matrix.

Anti-U_1RNP antibodies are detected by gel double diffusion and ELISA technology. Using ELISAs, as many as 55% of SLE patients possess these antibodies. However, with gel double diffusion assays, the frequency is approximately 35%.

Anti-U_1RNP antibodies are found in:
- *35% of SLE patients*
- *10% of scleroderma patients*
- *10% of polymyositis patients*
- *100% of mixed connective tissue disease (MCTD) patients*
- *10% of cryptogenic fibrosing alveolitis patients*

These autoantibodies are found in a heterogeneous group of patients and, unlike anti-dsDNA and anti-Sm antibodies, are not specific for SLE. For example, in 1972, Sharp et al. reported a group of patients with overlapping features of progressive systemic sclerosis, SLE, and polymyositis. As determined by a hemagglutination assay, these patients had antibodies reactive against the soluble, extractable, ribonuclease (RNase)-sensitive nuclear protein U_1RNP. These patients demonstrated many sclerodermatous features. These features included Raynaud's phenomenon, sclerodactyly, esophageal dysmotility, and pulmonary abnormalities. As outlined in Table 5–7, these patients shared many features with LE, polymyositis, and scleroderma patients.

There is now evidence to indicate that this syndrome, termed the "mixed connective tissue disease" (MCTD) is generally, but not always, a transitory state and that many of these MCTD patients over time will either develop LE or scleroderma. For example, a 10-year follow-up of 22 of the original 25 patients reported by Sharp indicated that most had evolved into classic, systemic sclerosis. There is now evidence to indicate that the final transition of these MCTD patients is influenced by the genetic background of the patient (see Chapter 7, "Scleroderma," for further discussion).

In 1972, Reichlin and Mattioli published a series about patients with clinical features of SLE who possessed anti-U_1RNP antibodies. These patients, unlike anti-dsDNA antibody positive patients, had a very low frequency of renal disease. Like the patients described by Sharp et al., Raynaud's phenomenon was prominent.

It should also be noted that approximately 10% of scleroderma patients are anti-U_1RNP antibody–positive, and an equal frequency of patients with dermatomyositis/polymyositis also possess these antibodies.

Neonatal Lupus Erythematosus

Ten neonatal lupus infants have been born to anti-U_1RNP antibody–positive mothers. No isolated congenital heart block has been detected.

Recent data indicate that, on occasion, anti-U_1RNP antibodies can be associated with neonatal lupus syndrome. There are at least 10 NLE infants who have been reported to be born to anti-U_1RNP antibody–positive mothers. These infants develop a transient, erythematous, macular dermatitis during the first 8 weeks of life. In general, this dermatitis disappears by 6 months of age with no residua. On rare occasions, telangiectasia may be detected in these infants. Whether the telangiectasia is associated with a cutaneous lupus lesion is unknown (one infant developed telangiectasia of the vulva).

To date, no infant born to an anti-U_1RNP antibody–positive mother has been described to develop isolated congenital heart block.

Pulmonary Disease

Interstitial pulmonary disease is a common feature of anti-U_1RNP antibody–positive patients.

As noted in Table 5–6, more than 60% of anti-U_1RNP antibody–positive MCTD patients demonstrated pulmonary abnormalities. In a study of 122 patients with cryptogenic fibrosing alveolitis, 39 (32%) demonstrated a positive ANA titer. Anti-U_1RNP antibodies were detected in 15 patients (12%). The anti-U_1RNP antibody–positive patients with cryptogenic fibrosing alveolitis demonstrate arthritis, arthralgias, Raynaud's phenomenon, and sclerodactyly.

Raynaud's Phenomenon

A strong relationship exists between the presence of anti-U_1RNP antibodies and Raynaud's phenomenon. This is amply documented (see Table 5–7).

Renal Disease

Generally low frequency of renal disease in anti-U_1RNP antibody–positive compared with anti-dsDNA antibody–positive patients

Renal disease does occur in anti-U_1RNP antibody–positive SLE patients, but the frequency of renal disease is far less than that seen in anti-dsDNA antibody–positive SLE patients. Since lupus patients make milligram quantities of anti-U_1RNP antibodies (detected by the insensitive gel double diffusion assay), immune complex formation occurs in relative antibody excess. Thus, the immune complexes theoretically are larger, less soluble, and more easily cleared by the reticuloendothelial system. Also, unlike dsDNA, RNP macromolecules do not bind to collagen along the basement membrane zone. Thus, in situ immune complex formation probably is not a major immune mechanism in these patients.

Anti-Ro (SS-A) Antibodies

Anti-Ro (SS-A) antibodies are directed against human-specific epitopes located on a 60-kD polypeptide to which specific RNAs, ranging in size from 83 to 112 bases, bind. These RNAs are termed "hY-RNA$^{1-5}$." In addition, some anti-Ro (SS-A) antibodies by immunoblot analysis cross-react with a 52-kD polypeptide. This 52-kD polypeptide is structurally unrelated to the 60 kD polypeptide and it is controversial whether or not this 52-kD polypeptide is part of the Ro macromolecule. (See upcoming discussion on neonatal lupus erythematosus for further information [page 67].) There is also recent molecular evidence indicating intermolecular spread of the immune response from the 52-kD Ro and 60-kD Ro to calreticulin. These data suggest that at the very least, there is a transitory physical association of these molecules.

Anti-Ro (SS-A) antibodies directed against unique human epitopes on the 60-kD polypeptide

Some anti-60 kD Ro (SS-A) antibodies cross react with a denatured 52-kD polypeptide unrelated to the 60-kD polypeptide.

The exact function of the Ro (SS-A) RNP macromolecule is unknown. There is evidence that one of the Ro macromolecules (hY-^{5}) may be associated with the La (SS-B) macromolecule. Evidence indicates that the La (SS-B) macromolecule is a transcription and termination factor for all RNA polymerase III transcripts. There is, however, no direct evidence for the participation of the Ro (SS-A) macromolecule in transcription and termination of RNA polymerase III transcripts.

Harley's group has demonstrated that the 60-kD Ro shares sequence homology with a protein of the vesicular stomatitis virus. Furthermore, patients infected with this virus produce low anti-Ro titers. In addition, immunization with this viral protein produces an anti-Ro response in animals.

Equally intriguing are data showing that the IgM antibodies from anti-Ro and La-antibody–positive patients cross-react with dsDNA and denatured spliceosome proteins A(U_1RNP) and D(Sm). These and additional studies are examining the maturation of autoimmune responses. They suggest that a single peptide may be the initial immunogen (eg, D polypeptide of splicesome), and as the immune response matures, first we observe intramolecular antigenic determinant (epitope) spreading and then intermolecular epitope spreading. This is an area beyond the scope of this chapter but is highly intriguing.

Anti-Ro (SS-A) antibodies are detected most commonly by gel double diffusion or counter immunoelectrophoresis. They have also been detected by ELISA technology. Anti-Ro (SS-A) antibodies detected by gel double diffusion are found in approximately 35% of SLE patients. By ELISA technology, approximately 50% of SLE patients are positive.

Several distinctive photosensitive lupus patient populations possessing anti-Ro (SS-A) antibodies have been detected (Table 5–8).

Photosensitive cutaneous disease dominates the clinical picture of anti-Ro (SS-A) antibody–positive LE patients.

Antinuclear Antibody–Negative Systemic Lupus Erythematosus

Prior to the use of human antinuclear substrates, approximately 5 to 10% of SLE patients were found to have insignificant or negative ANA titers. The overwhelming majority of these patients possess anti-Ro (SS-A) antibodies. Subsequent studies have determined that the anti-Ro (SS-A) antibody is directed against unique human Ro (SS-A) 60-kD epitopes. These antibodies may or may not share cross-reactivity with heterologous (ie, mouse or rat) Ro (SS-A) macromolecules. Thus, if the patient produces ANAs that are dominantly anti-Ro in specificity, and if nonhuman substrates are employed as the ANA substrate, the patient may demonstrate an insignificant (or negative) ANA determination. With the use of human substrates as the ANA, the frequency of ANA-negative SLE has dramatically decreased. There is still an occasional anti-Ro (SS-A) antibody–positive patient who fails to demonstrate a significant ANA determination when human substrates are employed as the ANA substrate. Some of these ANA-negative SLE patients are also anti-ssDNA antibody positive. Single-strand DNA determinants are not exposed in tissues employed as ANA substrates.

Anti-Ro (SS-A) antibodies all directed against unique human epitopes expressed on the 60 kD polypeptide

Poor or no cross-reactivity with rodent Ro (SS-A) macromolecules

Photosensitive cutaneous disease, including a malar dermatitis, dominates the clinical picture. Renal disease does occur but is less frequent than in anti-dsDNA antibody–positive patients. Anti-Ro (SS-A) antibody–positive SLE patients in contrast to anti-Ro (SS-A) and anti-La (SS-B) SLE patients appear to be more at risk to develop renal disease.

Subacute Cutaneous Lupus Erythematosus

Subacute cutaneous lupus erythematosus patients have been described earlier in this chapter under the section Specific Lesions.

Homozygous Deficiencies

Patients with homozygous C2 and C4 complement deficiencies develop a lupus-like disease process characterized by prominent photosensitive skin disease (Figure 5–22), decreased frequency of renal disease, as well as a decreased frequency of anti-dsDNA antibodies. Approximately 50 to 75% of patients with a homozygous C2 or C4 deficiency possess anti-Ro (SS-A) antibodies. It is interesting to note that C2 is a protein encoded by two alleles on the short arm of chromosome 6 of the major histocompatibility complex. C4 proteins are encoded by two separate loci (4 alleles) in the major histocompatibility complex (MHC) class III region (C4A and C4B). The C4A-encoded proteins express the Rogers blood group antigens; the C4B-encoded proteins express the Chido antigens.

TABLE 5–8 Anti-Ro (SS-A) Antibody–Positive Patients

Diagnosis	Clinical and Central Nervous System Features	Comment
Antinuclear antibody-negative SLE	Photosensitive; malar dermatitis	Poor cross-reactivity of anti-Ro (SS-A) antibodies with nonhuman Ro (SS-A) macromolecules (see text)
SCLE	Photosensitive; make up 10 to 15% of total lupus population; Make up ~ 20% of all anti-Ro (SS-A) antibody–positive patients; annular and polycyclic lesions; good prognosis	~70% are anti-Ro (SS-A) antibody positive
Chilblain LE (pernio)	Purplish, violaceous lesions induced by cold, damp climate	In one study, ~90% of patients were anti-Ro (SS-A) antibody positive
Homozygous C2 or C4 complement deficient	Photosensitive skin disease; little systemic involvement	50–70% anti-Ro (SS-A) antibody–positive; low frequency of anti-dsDNA antibodies
Late onset LE	Photosensitive; increased frequency of Sjögren's syndrome; central nervous system and pulmonary manifestations	~90% anti-Ro (SS-A) antibody–positive
Sjögren's syndrome/LE	Similar features to late onset LE; increased frequency of vasculitis; guarded prognosis	—
Oriental lupus patient	Less photosensitivity and SCLE lesions than seen in anti-Ro (SS-A) antibody–positive American patients; "donut" cutaneous lesion	50–60% anti-Ro (SS-A) antibody–positive

SLE = systemic lupus erythematosus; SCLE = subacute cutaneous lupus erythematosus; LE = lupus erythematosus.

Late-Onset Lupus Erythematosus/Sjögren's Syndrome/Lupus Erythematosus Overlap Syndrome

Some patients developing lupus after the age of 55 years have a disease process characterized by the development of widespread photosensitive skin disease reminiscent of SCLE, an increased frequency of Sjögren's syndrome, CNS, and pulmonary manifestations. Renal disease is unusual.

In one study, a > 90% frequency of anti-Ro (SS-A) antibodies was detected. Other investigators have reported a closely related syndrome termed "Sjögren's syndrome/lupus erythematosus overlap syndrome," which may occur in a younger population. These patients also frequently manifest widespread SCLE photosensitive cutaneous disease, a decreased frequency of renal disease and Sjögren's syndrome, and an increased frequency of cutaneous vasculitis and pulmonary and CNS manifestations. Unlike patients seeing dermatologists with SCLE, the prognosis in late-onset as well as the Sjögren's syndrome/lupus erythematosus overlap syndrome appears to be more guarded.

Sjögren's syndrome/lupus erythematosus overlap syndrome patients have:
- *increased frequency of CNS manifestations*
- *increased frequency of pulmonary disease*
- *cutaneous vasculitis and photosensitive SCLE lesions*
- *possibly much more morbidity than SCLE patients*

Sjögren's Syndrome

It has been noted that patients both with primary and secondary Sjögren's syndrome may possess anti-Ro (SS-A) antibodies. It has been estimated that three to four million people in the United States have Sjögren's syndrome. Of this group, it is estimated that approximately 30% have anti-Ro (SS-A) antibodies (employing ELISA as well as gel double diffusion techniques). Some cohorts of Sjögren's syndrome, especially those reported from rheumatology groups, have demonstrated a frequency as high as 90% of anti-Ro (SS-A) antibodies (ELISA). Anti-Ro (SS-A) antibody–positive Sjögren's syndrome patients have a statistically significant increased frequency of extraglandular manifestations characterized by hypergammaglobulinemia, rheumatoid factor, cytopenias manifested by anemia, leukopenia, and thrombocytopenia, cutaneous vasculitis, and peripheral and central nervous system disease. (See below for a discussion of relationship between anti-Ro [SS-A] antibody–positive Sjögren's syndrome and anti-Ro [SS-A] antibody–positive SLE patients. Also, see Chapter 8, "Sjögren's Syndrome.")

Sjögren's syndrome patients possessing anti-Ro (SS-A) antibodies have increased frequency of extraglandular manifestations including:
- *cytopenias*
- *anemia*
- *leukopenia*
- *thrombocytopenia*
- *cutaneous vasculitis*
- *peripheral and CNS disease*

Neonatal Lupus Erythematosus

Approximately > 98% of infants born with the neonatal lupus syndrome are born to anti-Ro (SS-A) antibody–positive mothers. The exact pathophysiologic mechanism whereby the anti-Ro (SS-A) antibody is capable of inducing in the infant the cutaneous as well as the isolated congenital heart block features of this syndrome has been an active area of investigation. It is theorized that the mater-

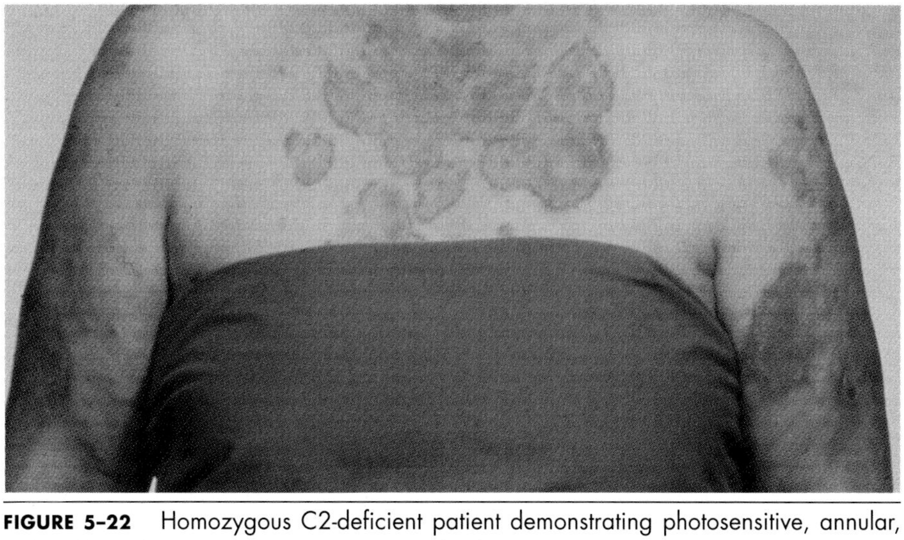

FIGURE 5-22 Homozygous C2-deficient patient demonstrating photosensitive, annular, polycyclic LE lesions and anti-Ro (SS-A) antibodies.

nal anti-Ro (SS-A) antibody passes across the placenta, binds to Ro (SS-A) macromolecules that are localized along the heart conduction system or the plasma membrane of keratinocytes. An antibody-dependent, cellular, cytotoxic immune mechanism involving the infant's T cells as effector cells is envisioned. One intriguing feature of these studies is the almost universal detection by immunoblotting of cross-reactivity of the anti-Ro (SS-A) antibody in the NLE mothers of isolated congenital heart block infants with the 52-kD polypeptide. Work by Buyon's group has demonstrated that the anti–52-kD Ro (SS-A) antibody binds L-type calcium (Ca++) channels in human fetal hearts. Furthermore, immunization of female mice with 52-kD constructs produces high-titer anti–52-kD antibodies. These immunized mice give birth to pups with varying degrees of heart block. Thus, it appears that the target antigen for the isolated congenital heart block is the L-type Ca++ channels in the neonatal heart, and anti–52-kD Ro (SS-A) antibodies cross-react with these calcium channels.

Anti-52 kD Ro (SS-A) antibody reactive against cardiac L-type Ca++ channel protein

The cutaneous manifestations of the neonatal lupus syndrome are characterized by widespread photosensitive erythematous, macular, at times annular and polycyclic lesions. Prominent periorbital involvement is characteristic (Figures 5–23 to 5–26). The skin lesions disappear in a time frame corresponding to the infant's catabolism of the maternal IgG anti-Ro (SS-A) antibodies (roughly 6 months). Little or no sequelae remain. Rarely, these infants may develop telangiectasia on previously normal skin and at sites of previous lupus lesions. Most recent data suggest that approxiamtely 5% of infants born to anti-Ro (SS-A) antibody–positive mothers develop isolated complete heart block. However, various heart blocks (first degree, 2:1 heart block) have also been described. Also asymptomatic infants of anti-Ro (SS-A) antibody–positive mothers frequently demonstrate prolonged QT intervals on electrocardiogram indicating subclinical cardiac involvement is probably common.

Significant neonatal mortality with isolated congenital heart block

Isolated congenital heart block is a very serious complication of the neonatal lupus syndrome. A 30% neonatal mortality has been reported, and approximately 60 to 70% of these infants require a pacemaker early in life.

In addition to the cutaneous and isolated congenital heart block features of the neonatal lupus syndrome, cholestasis, a mild hepatitis, and thrombocytopenia have also been reported. Isolated case reports of aplastic anemia and a neurologic hyperspasticity have also been reported, but these clinical features are exceedingly rare.

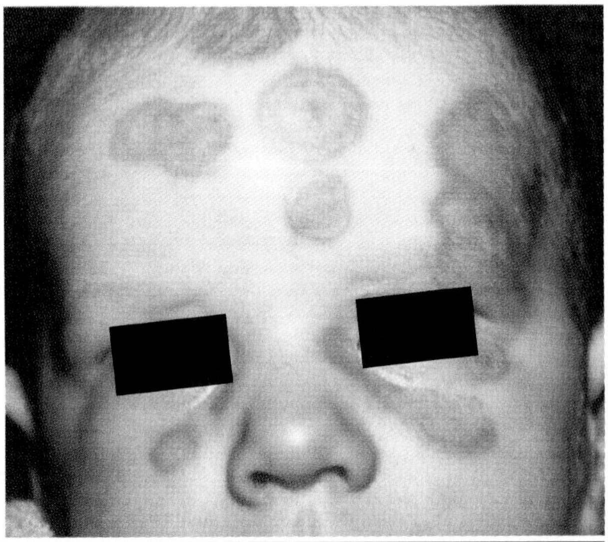

FIGURE 5–23 Annular erythematosus and targetoid lesions in an NLE infant born to an anti-Ro (SS-A) antibody–positive mother.

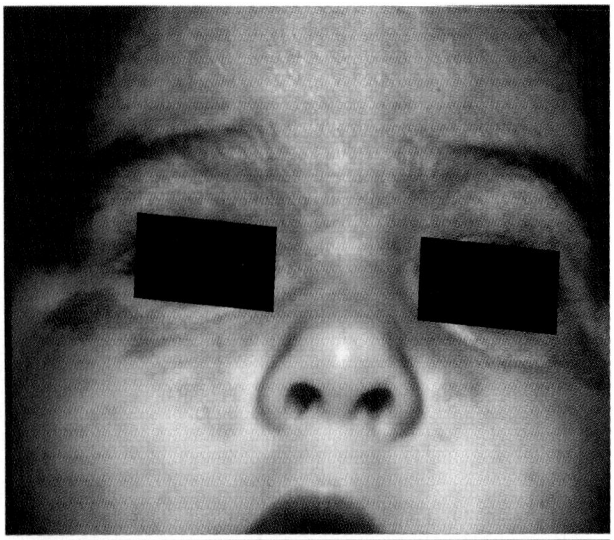

FIGURE 5–24 Erythematous, macular, periorbital lesions ("raccoon eyes") in NLE infant born to an anti-Ro (SS-A) antibody–positive mother.

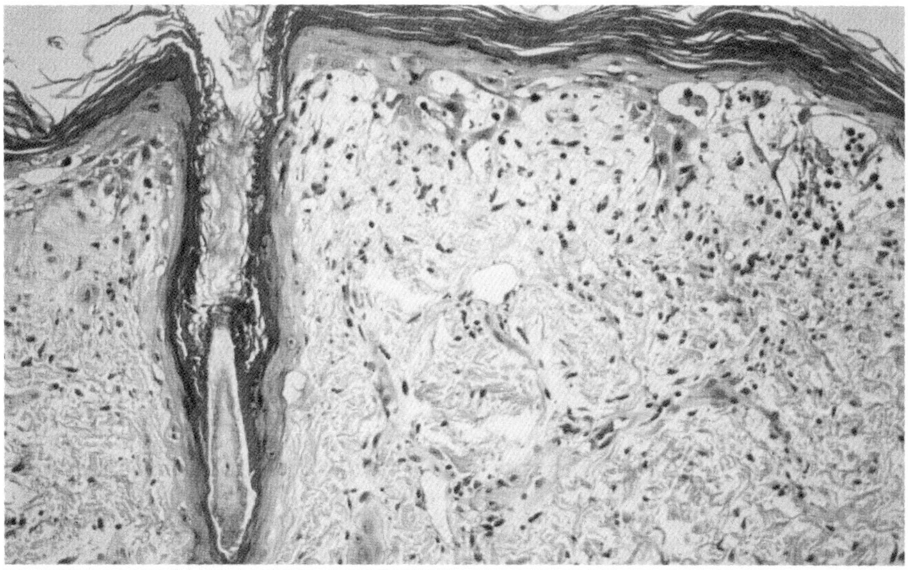

FIGURE 5–25 Biopsy of a neonatal lupus cutaneous lesion demonstrating a prominent interface dermatitis (liquefaction degeneration) and a sparse mononuclear infiltrate throughout papillary and reticular dermis.

Approximately 40% of NLE mothers asymptomatic at the time of birth of affected child

The anti-Ro (SS-A) antibody–positive mothers of these infants demonstrate features of a connective tissue disease, most commonly Sjögren's syndrome or lupus erythematosus approximately 60% of the time at the birth of their affected infant, The remaining 40% are asymptomatic, but recent evidence indicates that they too, generally within several years, will demonstrate features of a connective tissue disease. There are, however, examples of anti-Ro (SS-A) antibody–positive NLE

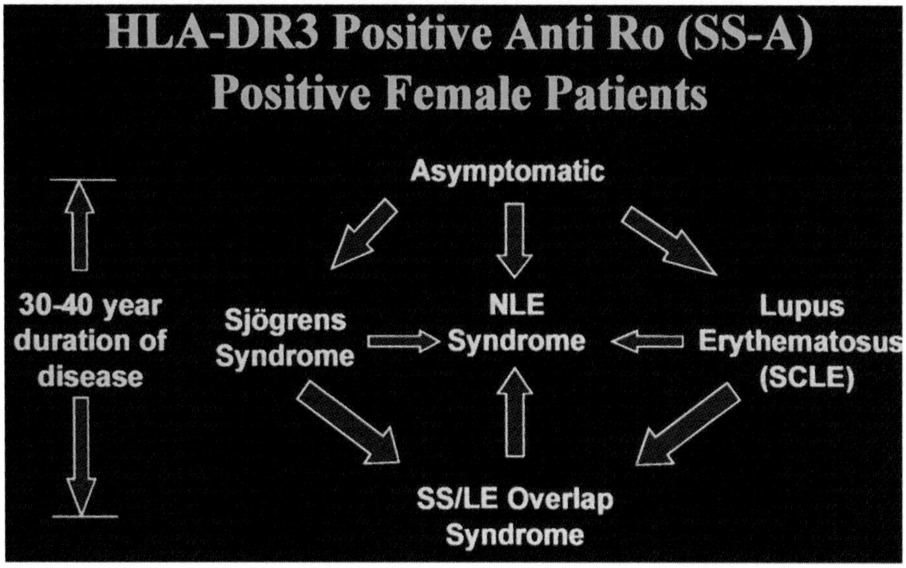

FIGURE 5–26 Diagram showing inter-relationships between clinically different, but immunogenetically similar, anti-Ro (SS-A) antibody–positive females. This indicates that (1) there is a closer relationship between anti-Ro (SS-A) antibody–positive Sjögren's syndrome and anti-Ro (SS-A) antibody–positive LE than has previously been recognized; (2) the phenotypic expression of these patients are heterogeneous and dynamic over time; (3) a chronic disease process is associated with low mortality and variable morbidity. The SCLE patients appear to have the most favorable prognosis; the Sjögren's syndrome/LE overlap patients have the most guarded; (4) all these phenotypically distinct females are at risk to give birth to an infant with the neonatal lupus syndrome.

mothers being asymptomatic for decades following the birth of an affected infant. The close inter-relationship of anti-Ro (SS-A) antibody–positive LE and Sjögren's syndrome patients is depicted in Figure 5–26.

Idiopathic Thrombocytopenic Purpura

Thrombocytopenia is a frequent finding in anti-Ro (SS-A) antibody–positive Sjögren's syndrome and LE patients (see Tables 50–2 and 5–3). In addition, thrombocytopenia may be a prominent feature of the neonatal lupus syndrome and may, on rare occasions, be the sole manifestation. In adults, idiopathic thrombocytopenic purpura (ITP) and anti-Ro (SS-A) antibodies may antedate by years the development of SLE. Our own experience indicates that 3 of 36 ITP patients (8%) were anti-Ro (SS-A) antibody positive.

Rheumatoid-Like Arthritis

It is now recognized that a small subset of rheumatoid arthritis patients demonstrating predominantly a Jaccoud's form of arthritis, characterized by nonerosive deforming arthritis in which ulnar deviation is prominent, is associated with the presence of anti-Ro (SS-A) antibodies. These patients, unlike classic rheumatoid arthritis patients, do not demonstrate an increased frequency of the human leukocyte antigen (HLA)-DR4 phenotype but, instead, have an increased frequency of HLA-DR3.

Asian Lupus Patients

Frequency of anti-Ro (SS-A) antibodies in Asian LE patients is almost two times greater than that seen in African American and Caucasian American patients.

In Korean, Chinese, and Japanese LE patients, the frequency of anti-Ro (SS-A) antibody positivity has been reported to be between 50 and 60% using gel double diffusion and counter immunoelectrophoresis techniques. This frequency of positivity is almost double that reported in African American and Caucasian American patients.

Antiphospholipid Antibodies

During the past 15 years, the importance of antiphospholipid antibodies in the pathogenesis of a thrombotic vasculopathy has been recognized. The antiphospholipid syndrome is classified as primary (ie, occurring in the absence of LE) or secondary (occurring in the presence of LE).

Anticardiolipin antibodies occur in 30 to 50% of SLE patients.

Antiphospholipid antibodies occur in 30 to 50% of SLE patients. In most instances, the titers are low. Evidence has been presented that this antibody system is found in a statistically significant association with the HLA-DQ7 phenotype. (The anti-Ro [SS-A] antibodies are associated with HLA-DQ1 and-DQ2 phenotypes, and thus this serologic subset of lupus has a relatively low frequency of antiphospholipid antibodies [approximately 10%].)

Biologic false-positive serologies (antiphospholipid antibodies) were detected in SLE patients in the 1950s. Conley and Hartman detected two SLE patients whose plasma from in vitro testing produced prolongation of the clotting time, which was not corrected by mixing with fresh plasma. This phenomenon was termed the "lupus anticoagulant." Later studies recognized that this in vitro anticoagulant activity was associated with a hypercoagulable state in the patient.

Great progress was made with the introduction of the anticardiolipin antibody ELISA test and, later, the development of functional assays to measure this hypercoagulable state. Today, anticardiolipin antibody determinations performed by ELISA and the Russell's viper venom test functional assay are commonly used to detect the presence of these antibodies. There is, however, a 25% approximate discordance between the antibody assay and the functional test. These data suggest the possible existence of other unknown autoantibodies capable of producing a hypercoagulable state.

Recent studies have indicated that pathologic antiphospholipid antibodies are directed against anionic phospholipids complexed with β_2-glycoprotein I. Anticardiolipin antibodies found in syphilis and chronic infections, such as leprosy, which are not associated with a hypercoagulable state, are directed against negatively charged phospholipids not complexed with β_2-microglobulin I. More recent studies have indicated that the antiphospholipid antibodies are directed at β2-glycoprotein I epitopes or epitopes formed by the complex of β2-glycoprotein I with the negatively charged phospholipid. Furthermore, most recent studies have suggested the possible roles of anti-annexin V and antiprothrombin antibodies in the antiphospholipid syndrome.

Pathologic anticardiolipin antibodies are directed against epitopes on β2-glycoprotein I or against epitopes formed by molecular complex of cardiolipin with β2-glycoprotein I.

The exact pathogenesis of these antibodies in the production of the hypercoagulable state is unknown. Conceivably, because of the heterogeneous nature of the autoantibodies as well as the fine specificity of some of the antibodies, multiple mechanisms may be operative. These include blockage of the anticoagulant activity of prostacyclin at the endothelial cell level inhibition of the anticoagulant activity of protein C and protein S, and direct binding to phospholipids on platelets inducing, for example, aggregation.

The anticardiolipin antibody ELISA is a sensitive technique. Thirty to 50% of SLE patients have anticardiolipin antibodies. One group with extensive experience with this assay believes that titers > 5 to 10 standard deviations above normal have great potential to be pathophysiologically significant, whereas titers <5 are generally not. The functional assay commonly employed to detect antiphospholipid antibodies is the Russell's viper venom test. The prothrombin time is insensitive and the activated partial thromboplastin time is not as sensitive as the Russell's viper venom test. The kaolin clotting time has been used by some investigators as a substitute for the Russell's viper venom test.

Clinical features of the antiphospholipid syndrome are the result of recurrent arterial and/or venous thrombosis. It should be noted that the clinical and laboratory features of this syndrome may be transient. (See earlier discussion in this chapter under Livedo Reticularis and Chapter 9, "Antiphospholipid Syndrome.")

Family Studies

Family studies of LE over the past 25 years have provided strong evidence for a genetic basis. It has long been recognized that SLE clusters in families, and noninvolved family members may demonstrate autoimmune phenomena. For example, in one study, 24 of 232 first-degree relatives had SLE. Twenty-seven had other autoimmune diseases, and 47 had serologic abnormalities. A mendelian dominant autoimmune, non–HLA-linked gene with a 91% penetrance dominance was postulated.

First-degree relatives of SLE patients have an increased frequency of SLE, other autoimmune diseases, and serologic abnormalities.

A non–HLA-linked autosomal dominant trait has been postulated.

In other studies, comparing the frequency of SLE among first-degree relatives of SLE patients with age-matched, nonrheumatic disease controls, a statistically significant increased frequency of SLE among first-degree relatives was demonstrated.

In a study of 12 identical twins and a review of the data on 17 other twin cases, an SLE concordance of 58% was reported. Another identical-twin study reported a 23% concordance for SLE. The controls for these two studies were 7% and 9% concordance for SLE among dizygotic twins.

There is a statistically significant increased concordance of SLE among monozygotic compared with dizygotic twins.

Complement Deficiencies and Systemic Lupus Erythematosus

The most striking evidence of a genetic basis for SLE has come from studies of complement deficiencies. It has been recognized that homozygous deficiencies of complement components 1, 2, 4, and, to a much lesser extent, 5 and 6 are associated with an increased frequency of LE. Furthermore, of all the complement deficiencies (C4A null alleles), C4AQ0 is the most common complement deficiency associated with SLE. This complement deficiency has been found in Caucasian American, African American, European, Chinese, Mexican, and Japanese SLE patients. In Caucasians, the C4AQ0 deficiency is seen in association with the HLA-B8, HLA-DR3 haplotype.

Homozygous complement deficiencies involving C1, C2, C4, and, to a lesser extent, C5 and C6 are associated with SLE.

C1 Deficiency

Homozygous C1 complement deficiency (C1s, C1r, and C1q) is associated with a strikingly increased frequency (> 90%) of a lupus-like disease process characterized by glomerulonephritis and cutaneous lesions.

C1INH deficiency has been associated with SLE.

C1 Inhibitor Deficiency

Deficiency in the C1 inhibitor (C1INH) has, in a few instances, been associated with the development of SLE. We have seen one patient with this combination of diseases. Interestingly, a synthetic androgen therapy to promote synthesis of C1INH was associated with the disappearance of the anti-dsDNA antibodies and a general improvement in the patient's SLE.

Late Complement Component Deficiencies

Homozygous deficiencies of late-acting (C5–C9) components of classic complement component pathway are associated with recurrent neisserial infections.

In sharp contrast to the increased frequency of LE among homozygous-deficient, early complement component patients, the frequency of LE among C3-, C5-, C6, C7-, C8-, and C9-deficiency patients is very low. Patients with homozygous complement deficiencies involving the late complement components have an increased frequency of neisserial infections (atypical meningococcemia and recurrent gonorrhea infections).

The reason(s) for the increased predisposition to develop SLE in patients with homozygous early complement component deficiencies (C1, C4, and C2) is/are unknown. It has been postulated that these early complement components stabilize immune complexes promoting their clearance from the systemic circulation. It is reasoned that defects in these early complement components, therefore, promote the development of circulating immune complexes.

CR1 Deficiency

The same reasoning has been employed to explain an increased frequency of SLE in patients with C3b receptor deficiency (CR1) on erythrocytes. However, the deficiency of the CR1 receptors in SLE is unclear (ie, whether it represents genetically determined deficiency or whether all the sites are occupied by immune complexes). Thus, the deficiency of the CR1 receptor, whatever the mechanism, would be associated with failure to bind immune complexes and the subsequent clearing of these complexes from the circulation.

The association of increased infections in patients with homozygous C3, C5, C6, C7, and C8 as well as C3b inactivator deficiencies appears to be related to defects in opsonization, chemotaxis, and phagocytosis.

Major Histocompatibility Complex Alleles and Systemic Lupus Erythematosus

Several investigators have reported the association of SLE in Caucasians with the presence of major histocompatibility complex (MHC) alleles HLA-DR2 and-DR3 phenotypes. In Asian SLE patients (Japanese and Chinese), an increased frequency of HLA-DR2 has been detected. Greek SLE patients have also demonstrated an increased frequency of the HLA-DR2 phenotype.

In addition, HLA-DR2 in some studies has been associated with an increased frequency of renal disease, compared with those patients without this HLA phenotype. Human leukocyte antigen–DQw1, which is found in linkage disequilibrium with HLA-DR2, was even more strongly associated with the presence of nephritis. The HLA-DR3 phenotype is significantly increased in late-onset LE. The HLA-DR2 phenotype is more commonly found in early-onset LE.

Western European SLE patients have increased frequency of HLA-DR2 and -DR3 phenotypes.

Asian and Greek SLE patients have increase of HLA-DR2.

When all these studies are taken together, it appears that HLA-DR2 and -DR3 phenotypes are increased in SLE Caucasian patients from Western Europe, and that HLA-DR2 phenotype is increased in Asian as well as Mediterranean SLE patients. Furthermore, there is evidence that DQw2.1, which is in linkage disequilibrium with HLA-DR3, is also increased in some Caucasian patients, whereas HLA-DQw1, which is in linkage disequilibrium with HLA-DR2, is increased in other SLE patient populations.

Association of Specific Autoantibody Responses

While performing serologic HLA studies, it became evident that if one subtracts the anti-Ro (SS-A) antibody SLE patients from the total SLE cohort, the statistically significant association of SLE with HLA-DR2 and-DR3 was markedly diminished, if not completely eliminated. This gave rise to the hypothesis that associations of SLE with various HLA phenotypes were not disease specific, but rather, these HLA associations were with the autoantibody response.

Anti-Ro (SS-A) and Anti-La (SS-B) Responses

Anti-Ro (SS-A) and anti-La (SS-B) responses associated with HLA-DR3

Anti-Ro (SS-A) and anti-La (SS-B) autoantibodies are found in a statistically significant association with the HLA-DR3 and HLA-DQw2 phenotypes. The anti-La (SS-B) antibodies, which almost never occur in the absence of anti-Ro (SS-A) antibodies, are also found in a statistically significant association with the HLA-DR3 and HLA-DQw2 phenotypes.

Anti-Ro (SS-A) antibody response without anti-La (SS-B) antibody associated with HLA-DR2

Highest titers of anti-Ro (SS-A) antibody associated with heterozygosity DQw1/DQw2

African American anti-Ro (SS-A) antibody–positive patients possess Caucasian and non-African HLA-DR3 DQw1 haplotype.

Other studies demonstrate that anti-Ro (SS-A) antibodies in the absence of anti-La (SS-B) antibodies are associated with the HLA-DR2 phenotype. Further studies emphasize the fact that late-onset LE, associated with anti-Ro (SS-A) antibodies as well as anti-La (SS-B) antibodies, is associated with the HLA-DR3 phenotype, whereas early-onset SLE (anti-Ro (SS-A) antibody–positive, anti-La (SS-B) antibody–negative) have an increased frequency of the HLA-DR2 phenotype. The presence of HLA-DR2 and HLA-DR3 phenotypes in the same patient correlates with high anti-Ro (SS-A) antibody titers. Subsequent investigations demonstrated that heterozygosity at the DQ locus (HLA-DQw1/DQw2) is associated with the highest anti-Ro (SS-A) and anti-La (SS-B) antibody titers.

Restriction fragment length polymorphism (RFLP) demonstrated that the HLA-DR3 (DRw17), DQw2.1 (Caucasian) haplotype is associated with the anti-Ro (SS-A) and anti-La (SS-B) antibody responses in both Caucasian and African Americans. The HLA-DR3 (DRw18), DQw4 haplotype (African) is not increased in African American anti-Ro (SS-A) and anti-La (SS-B) antibody–positive patients. Furthermore, the HLA-DQw2.1 allele demonstrated the most relevant specificity with this immune response.

Racial admixture over the centuries appeared to play the dominant role in determining the anti-Ro (SS-A) and anti-La (SS-B) antibody responses in African Americans, since the Caucasian HLA-DR3 (DRw17), -DQw2.1 haplotype and not the African American HLA-DR3 (HLA-DRw18) haplotype was present in these African American patients. Furthermore, heterozygosity at the HLA-DQ locus was present in approximately one-quarter of anti-Ro (SS-A) and anti-La (SS-B) antibody–positive African American patients. HLA-DQw6 (a subtype of HLA-DQw1) and HLA-DQw2.1 (a subtype of DQw2) was associated with the highest antibody responses.

All anti-Ro (SS-A) antibody–positive patients possess glutamine at position 34 of the DQ alpha-chain and a leucine at position 26 of the DQ beta-chain.

Thus, the anti-Ro (SS-A) and anti-La (SS-B) antibody responses appeared to be associated with a limited number of alleles present at the HLA-DQ locus. Furthermore, molecular studies have demonstrated that all the HLA-DQ alpha-chain alleles associated with the anti-Ro (SS-A) antibody responses have glutamine in position 34, whereas all the HLA-DQ beta-chain alleles possess a leucine at position 26.

On the basis of studies of the HLA alleles associated with the anti-Ro (SS-A) and anti-La (SS-B) antibody responses, it is not surprising that the HLA-B8, -DR3, and -DQ2 as well as the HLA-DR2 and -DQ1 alleles have been associated with SCLE patients. Furthermore, anti-Ro (SS-A) antibody–positive Sjögren's syndrome patients have an increased frequency of anti-La (SS-B) antibodies and a statistically significant increased frequency of HLA-DR3, DQ2 phenotypes.

The anti-Ro (SS-A) antibody–positive mothers of NLE infants have a statistically significant increased frequency of the HLA-B8, -DR3, and DQ2 phenotypes. In marked contrast, anti-Ro (SS-A) antibody–positive mothers giving birth to normal infants had a statistically significant increased frequency of HLA-DR2 and HLA-DQ1 phenotypes.

It should be noted that mothers of NLE infants may present with a phenotypic clinical picture of Sjögren's syndrome. Frequently, these anti-Ro (SS-A) antibody–positive patients also demonstrate the presence of anti-La (SS-B) antibodies and have a statistically significant increased frequency of HLA-DR3, -DQ2 alleles. The clustering of HLA-DR3, -DQ2–positive anti-Ro (SS-A) antibody–positive women giving birth to infants with NLE in marked contrast to relative absence of NLE infants in HLA-DR2 antibody–positive mothers has led to the hypothesis outlined in Figure 5–27. These collective studies indicate that the relationship between HLA-DR3, anti-Ro (SS-A) antibody–positive females with SCLE, Sjögren's syndrome, Sjögren's syndrome/lupus erythematosus overlap syndrome, and asymptomatic females is much closer than previously recognized. Although the clinical phenotypic expression of the mothers may be quite different, all are at risk to give birth to an infant with a neonatal lupus syndrome.

Anti-dsDNA Antibody Responses

Anti-dsDNA antibodies have been shown to have the strongest association with HLA-DQ beta-chain alleles. Ninety-six percent of SLE patients with anti-dsDNA antibodies have HLA-DQB1*0201 (linked to HLA-DR3 and HLA-DR7), HLA-DQB1*0602 (linked to HLA-DR2 and HLA-DRw6), and HLA-DQB1*0302 (linked to some HLA-DR4 haplotypes). These three HLA-DQ beta-chain alleles (*0201, *0602, and *0302) possess a methionine at position 14 and a leucine at position 26 of the HLA-DQ beta-chain.

Anti-U_1RNP and Anti-Sm Antibody Responses

HLA studies of the anti-U_1RNP and anti-Sm antibodies have failed to demonstrate associations based on serologic HLA typing. However, using RFLPs and oligonucleotide typing of African Americans and Caucasian Americans, evidence has been obtained indicating an association of these antibody responses with the HLA-DQw6 (HLA-DQA1*0102 and HLA-DQB1*0602). HLA-DQw5 is in linkage dysequilibrium with some HLA-DR2 and HLA-DRw6 haplotypes. Anti-U_1RNP antibodies in the absence of anti-Sm antibodies demonstrate an increased frequency of HLA-DQw5, -DQw8, and -DQw7.

Antiphospholipid Antibody Responses

Lupus anticoagulant associated with DQw7 allele

Recent studies have demonstrated an increased frequency of the HLA-DR5, HLA-DQw7 haplotypes in American patients with the lupus anticoagulant. Seventy percent of patients with the lupus anticoagulant have been found to have the HLA-DQB1*0301 allele. Those HLA-DQw7–negative patients possessed HLA-DQw8, -DQw9 and/or -DQw6 alleles. All these HLA-DQ beta-chain alleles have in positions 71 through 77, in the third hypervariable region, the same amino acid sequence.

Antiepidermolysis Bullosa Acquisita Antibody Responses

Antiepidermolysis bullosa acquisita antibodies have been demonstrated to occur in SLE patients. They have been detected to be associated with the HLA-DR2 phenotype in both Caucasian and African American SLE patients.

Anti-Ro Homozygous C2 Deficient Lupus Patients

In contrast to the presence of the HLA-DR3, -DQ2 phenotype associated with the neonatal lupus syndrome, anti-Ro (SS-A) antibody–positive lupus patients with a homozygous C2 deficiency are associated with a deficient gene located on the HLA-A10, -B18, -DR2, -DQw6 haplotype.

Racial Differences in Expression of Lupus Erythematosus

African Americans

African Americans have:
- *increased frequency of SLE*
- *increased mortality*
- *younger onset*

There is a three- to fourfold increase of SLE among African Americans, compared with Caucasian Americans. African American women are especially at risk. Furthermore, the onset of SLE and nephritis is at a much younger age in African American females than in Caucasian American females. Mortality is also greater among African Americans, especially African American females. Studies of morbidity and mortality in anti-Ro (SS-A) antibody–positive African American and Caucasian American patients has demonstrated that African American patients have a more severe disease process than their Caucasian counterparts. Additional serologic studies have demonstrated that African Americans demonstrate an increased frequency of both anti-Sm and anti-U_1RNP antibodies, compared with Caucasian SLE patients. For example, anti-Sm antibodies were detected by counterimmunoelectrophoresis or gel double diffusion in 15 (25%) of 60 African American SLE patients, compared with 11 (10%) of 106 Caucasian American SLE patients ($p < .02$). Using the same technology, anti-U_1RNP antibodies were detected in 24 (40%) of 60 African American SLE patients, compared with 24 (23%) of 106 Caucasian SLE patients. A more recent study has demonstrated in African American female lupus patients with renal disease a statistically significant increased frequency of anti-Ro (SS-A), anti-Sm, and anti-U_1RNP antibodies.

Serologic studies indicate African Americans have increased frequency of anti-U_1RNP and anti-Sm-antibodies.

African American females with renal disease have increased frequency of anti-Ro (SS-A), anti-Sm, and anti-U_1RNP antibodies.

Native Africans may not have the increased frequency of LE seen in African Americans.

The reasons for this increased mortality in African Americans are unknown. Environmental factors, access to medical care, and genetic predisposition are possibilities. Although the data are hard to obtain, the increased frequency of SLE among African Americans was not observed in native African patients by British physicians serving in West Africa in the 1960s (personal communication to Provost). Furthermore as noted above, the anti-Ro (SS-A) antibody response in African Americans is associated with the presence of the HLA-DR3 (DRw17) Caucasian haplotype and not the HLA-DR3 (DRWw18) African haplotype. Thus, it is conceivable that some African Americans who are a very heterogenous group through racial admixture over several generations may be genetically at risk to develop autoimmune diseases, especially SLE.

Asian Lupus Patients

In addition to the data indicating difference in the incidence, prevalence, morbidity, mortality, and serologic features in African American patients, there are data, albeit controversial, indicating that there may be an increased prevalence of SLE among Asians. In a highly quoted article examining the prevalence of SLE in Hawaii, Serdula and Rhoads reported, in 1975, a 5.8 prevalence rate per 100,000 among Caucasians, 24.1 among Chinese, 19.9 among Filipinos, and 18.2 among Japanese. A combined prevalence per 100,000 of SLE patients among Asians was 17.0.

Asians may have an increased frequency of SLE.
Area is controversial

In 1980, these studies were revised to indicate a prevalence of 10.3 among Caucasians; 33.5 among the Chinese; 44.0 among the Filipinos, and 27.5 among the Japanese. A total Asian prevalence rate of 25.8 was determined. In New Zealand, an age-adjusted prevalence of 50.6 has been determined for Polynesians versus 14.6 for Caucasians.

These results, however, have not been confirmed by studies examining Asian, especially Chinese, lupus patients living in the San Francisco area or by studies from China and Taiwan.

Studies, however, do indicate that Asian lupus patients, in sharp contrast to African American and Caucasian American SLE patients, have a much higher frequency of anti-Ro (SS-S) antibodies. Studies examining Korean, Japanese, and Chinese patients (Singapore) have demonstrated a 50 to 60% frequency of anti-Ro (SS-A) antibodies (gel double diffusion). Studies from China, as well as from Japan, suggest that the frequency of SCLE lesions (ie, annular polycyclic and psoriasiform) and photosensitivity are not as prevalent as seen in anti-Ro (SS-A) antibody–positive American SLE patients. Japanese patients develop an annular, erythematous plaque lesion with central clearing referred to as a "donut-like" lesion (Figure 5–27). Provost has, thus far, not observed this distinctive cutaneous lesion in African American or Caucasian American anti-Ro (SS-A) antibody–patients. Furthermore, recent data from Japan indicate only an 8% frequency of isolated congenital heart block among anti-Ro (SS-A) antibody–positive neonatal lupus infants, whereas there is at least a 50% frequency among a similar American patient population. Finally, the HLA-DR3 phenotype, which is found in the great majority of NLE mothers, is rare in Asian patients.

Asian compared with American lupus patients have:
- *increased frequency of anti-Ro (SS-A) antibodies*
- *less SCLE lesions*
- *less photosensitivity*
- *less isolated congenital heart block in anti-Ro (SS-A) antibody–positive lupus patients*
- *the presence of "donut" cutaneous lesions*

These studies collectively suggest different racial incidences of SLE, serologic abnormalities, morbidity, mortality, and clinical features. Obviously, this is an area in which additional observations are necessary before definitive statements can be made.

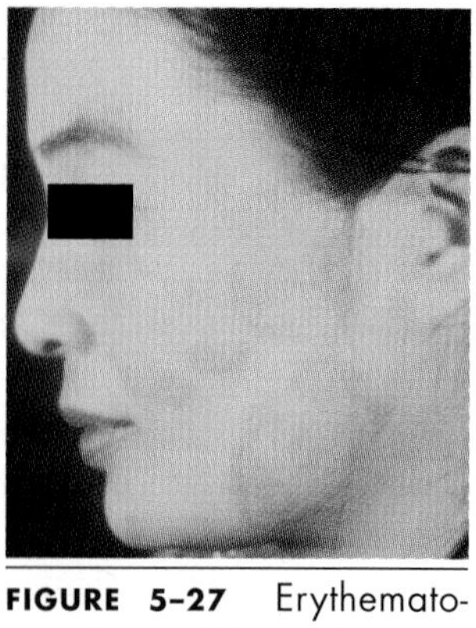

FIGURE 5-27 Erythematosus plaque "donut" lesion in an anti Ro (SS-A) antibody–positive Japanese female.

Role of Estrogens

NZB/W F_1 females have accelerated lupus disease. process characterized by death at approximately 12 months of age.
Males have protracted disease living > 20 months.
Castration and estrogen therapy of NZB/W F_1 males induces a female lupus temporal disease.

Systemic lupus erythematosus is a disease associated with the female gender (approximately 9:1 ratio). The possible role of estrogen in this disease process is very intriguing. Studies of the NZB/W F_1 hybrid mice, a murine model of SLE, indicate that estrogens can modulate the expression of SLE. Female mice, in contrast to male NZB/W F_1 progeny, develop a lupus disease process characterized by glomerulonephritis with demise at approximately 11 to 12 months. In contradistinction, the male F_1 progeny have a much more prolonged course with demise after 20 months. Castration of the male mice, followed by estrogen therapy, produces a temporal LE disease process similar to that seen in the female mice.

Klinefelter's syndrome patients (XXY karyotype) have an increased frequency of SLE.

Male and female SLE patients demonstrate altered metabolism of estrogens.

Other studies by Lahita et al. have shown that estrone is preferentially hydroxylated at the C16 position in both male and female SLE patients as well as in their first-degree relatives. In addition, Klinefelter's syndrome patients (XXY) appear to have an increased frequency of SLE. These patients also have an abnormal metabolism of estrogen, producing excessive quantities of 16α-hydroxyestearin and estral metabolites. It is thought that these metabolites produce a hyperestrogenic state. Furthermore, male SLE patients appear to have lower levels of testosterone as well as reduced levels of dehydroepiandrosterone (DHEA).

Whether androgen (DHEA) therapy will be effective in the treatment of patients with SLE remains for large clinical trials. Danazol and androgen preparations with slight masculinizing effects have been reported in isolated reports to have beneficial effects on the SLE disease process accompanying hereditary angioneurotic edema. We have also seen such an effect.

Drug-Induced Lupus Erythematosus

Procainamide, Hydralazine, and Isoniazid

Procainamide, isoniazid, and hydralazine–induced LE:
- *no skin or renal disease*
- *polyserositis*
- *antihistone antibodies*

It has long been recognized that procainamide, hydralazine, and isoniazid therapy is associated with a lupus-like disease process characterized by polyserositis and the presence of high-titer ANA. The fine specificity of the ANA indicates a predominance of antibodies against the H2A/H2B histone fragment. These patients, in general, do not have renal disease or skin disease and possess the HLA-DR4 phenotype.

D-Penicillamine

D-penicillamine induced LE:
- *renal and skin disease*
- *anti-dsDNA antibodies*

D-penicillamine therapy, on the other hand, is associated with a lupus-like disease process quite similar to idiopathic SLE. In addition, these patients develop inflammatory cutaneous lesions and glomerulonephritis. There appears to be an increased frequency of the HLA-DR3 phenotype.

Captopril

Captopril, an angiotensin-converting enzyme inhibitor, may also induce a lupus-like disease process associated with the presence of anti-dsDNA antibodies.

Hydrochlorothiazide

In recent years, hydrochlorothiazide has been implicated in inducing or aggravating the cutaneous manifestations of anti-Ro (SS-A) antibody–positive SCLE.

At least one of the five original patients became anti-Ro (SS-A) antibody negative 6 months following the discontinuation of hydrochlorothiazide. In all the patients, the dermatitis resolved 2 to 4 weeks after discontinuing the thiazides.

Hydrochlorothiazide and griseofulvin have been implicated in precipitating and/or aggravating expression of SCLE.

Griseofulvin

Additional evidence indicates that griseofulvin may aggravate SCLE. Discontinuation of the griseofulvin in two patients resulted in complete disappearance of the lupus dermatitis. Furthermore, the dermatitis reappeared upon re-challenging with griseofulvin.

Alfalfa-Induced Lupus Erythematosus

An intriguing report exists of an SLE-like syndrome in an adult who ingested, as part of his health diet, excessive amounts of alfalfa sprouts. Furthermore, the disease process completely disappeared with cessation of this diet.

The feeding of alfalfa sprouts to female adult monkeys induced an SLE-like syndrome. This was associated with the development of autoantibodies. The active ingredient in the alfalfa sprouts is a nonessential amino acid, L-canavanine.

Alfalfa sprouts fed to adult female monkeys were associated with a lupus-like disease syndrome.

Evaluation of Lupus Patients

Diagnosis: history, physical examination, and serologic studies

The purpose in detailing the data above is to emphasize to physicians the heterogeneous nature of LE. From a dermatologic point of view, many of the cutaneous features are diagnostic, and others, although nonspecific, have prognostic implications. However, it must be re-stated that one cannot examine the morphologic features of specific and nonspecific cutaneous lesions associated with LE and either make a definitive diagnosis of benign cutaneous erythematosus or SLE, or ascribe a definite prognosis. The evaluation of lupus patients is a clinical laboratory exercise involving a detailed history and physical examination with appropriate laboratory and serologic studies. The use of punch biopsies to examine the pathology of specific and nonspecific lesions associated with LE is invaluable. The routine evaluation of the lupus patient for anemia, leukopenia, or thrombocytopenia as well as the determination of erythrocyte sedimentation rate (ESR) has stood the test of time. It must be stated, however, that active SLE patients, may on occasion, have a normal ESR. A urinalysis or a 24-hour urine collection for protein has also proved invaluable as have renal biopsies.

Serologic studies, including antinuclear, anti-dsDNA, anti-Sm, anti-U_1RNP, anti-Ro (SS-A), and anticardiolipin antibodies, have been shown to be cost-effective serologic tests that help to identify, at the earliest possible moment, those patients with SLE and, in many instances, to predict a general prognosis for these patients. The Russell's viper venom test as an adjunct to anticardiolipin antibodies appears to be an excellent diagnostic tool to investigate for antiphospholipid antibodies.

Finally, the use of complement determinations (CH_{50}, C3, or C4) has shown their value in monitoring renal disease activity in SLE patients.

Treatment

Steroid treatment of LE lesions:
- *topical preparations*
- *steroid-impregnated tape*
- *burst of oral steroids*
- *pulse steroid therapy*

The treatment of the cutaneous lupus lesions has advanced greatly during the past 25 to 30 years. Topical steroids, ranging from 1 to 2.5% hydrocortisone to such potent steroids as betamethasone dipropionate, diflorasone diacetate, and clobetasol propionate, applied to the skin twice daily for a period of 2 weeks, have been shown to be efficacious in the treatment of most cutaneous lupus lesions. Steroid atrophy and telangiectasia occur with overuse of these preparations. Special care is necessary in the use of these agents on the face.

Steroid-impregnated tape

Fluocinonide-impregnated tape applied to the skin for 12 to 24 hours, then removed and repeated two to three times a week, is also an effective means of treating lupus lesions. This has been especially valuable in treating hyperkeratotic or verrucous cutaneous LE.

Lupus profundus/panniculitis also responds favorably to steroid-impregnated tape or the intralesional injection of triamcinolone 2.5 mg per mL. A local steroid atrophy, however, can at times occur even with this low-dose injection of steroids, and caution is advised.

Sun screens SPF15 or better

Sunscreens with a skin protection factor (SPF) ≥ 15, especially those containing Parsol 1789 (avobenzone) and titanium dioxide, which provide broad-spectrum protection from both UVB and UVA light waves, should be applied judiciously approximately 30 minutes before going outdoors. This should be done on a habitual basis whatever the weather.

Sun-protective clothing

Wide-brimmed hats and other protective clothing (ie, long-sleeve blouses) should be worn. As noted earlier, burning through light cotton clothing, especially in SCLE patients, is problematic. Sun-protective clothing has recently been marketed (Solumbra, Sun Precautions, 2815 Wetmore Ave., Everett, WA, 98201 USA; 1-800-822-7860).

Tinted windshields should be used in vehicles, and uncovered fluorescent lamps should be covered with Mylar-containing plastic to prevent deleterious UVA light exposure.

Antimalarials

Combination of quinacrine with either chloroquine or hydroxychloroquine is effective.

Antimalarials, such as hydroxychloroquine (200 mg once or twice a day), chloroquine (250 mg daily), or quinacrine (100 mg daily), have been shown to be effective in not only suppressing photosensitive cutaneous LE but also in treating myalgias and arthralgias associated with LE. The combination of either hydroxychloroquine or chloroquine together with quinacrine can be effective where either hydroxychloroquine or chloroquine alone has failed.

The antimalarials have been shown to interfere with antigen presentation and appear to be preferentially concentrated in the skin. Quinacrine will produce a yellowish tint to the skin, and the patient should be forewarned of this.

Both hydroxychloroquine and chloroquine in high doses are associated with retinal toxicity, but quinacrine is not. Six-monthly checkups by an ophthalmologist using an Amsler's marker is recommended. Neurotoxicity and muscular toxicity, as well as depigmentation of the hair, have been noted with these drugs.

Dapsone is effective in treating some recalcitrant SCLE patients.

The lesions of SCLE are generally responsive to the antimalarials. However, recalcitrant lesions occur frequently in some of these patients. Dapsone, 50 to 150 mg per day, has been shown by some investigators to be of benefit in treating recalcitrant SCLE. Dapsone has also been of benefit in treating some of the blistering lesions associated with LE, as well as other vasculitic lesions. A glucose-6 phosphate dehydrogenase determination should be performed. If this red blood cell enzyme is lacking, very severe homolysis may take place, and dapsone should not be given. In general, all patients who use dapsone develop a compensated hemolytic anemia, but the hemoglobin level generally does not fall below 11 g. Methemoglobinemia and sulfhemoglobinemia may develop producing an alarming-appearing, but generally asymptomatic, cyanotic picture in the patient. On unusual occasions, dapsone therapy may be associated with the development of aplastic anemia. A complete blood count is recommended every two to three weeks for at least the first 6 months of therapy to avoid this complication.

Burst of steroids or pulse steroids frequently effective

A "burst" of oral steroids, 30 to 40 mg per day completely tapered over a 1-month period, given in conjunction with the initiation of antimalarial therapy, has proven effective. On occasion, pulse steroids, 1 g of methylprednisolone given intravenously over a 4-hour period for 3 to 5 consecutive days, has been efficacious. If the patient is over the age of 50 years or has known cardiac disease, the patient should be monitored for arrhythmias while the infusion is being performed.

Oral vitamin A derivatives are effective in treating cutaneous LE lesions.

Oral vitamin A derivatives, such as isotretinoin and acitretin, and synthetic retinoids have been shown to be very effective in the treatment of recalcitrant cutaneous lupus lesions. Provost has had excellent results treating recalcitrant verrucous or hypertrophic cutaneous lupus lesions with these preparations.

Isotretinoin 40 mg per day is given for a 3- to 4-month period. Female patients during the childbearing years must practice maximum birth control while using this drug. In male and postmenopausal female lupus patients, acitretin 25 to 50 mg per day has been shown to be a very effective form of therapy.

Oral gold therapy (auranofin) or parenteral gold aurothiomalate or aurothioglucose has proven effective in the treatment of recalcitrant lupus lesions. Provost observed several anti-Ro (SS-A) antibody–positive SCLE patients who had been successfully treated during the 1940s with intramuscular gold.

Finally, European investigators have attested to the almost universal efficacy of oral thalidomide in the treatment of cutaneous LE lesions. This drug is now available in the United States. In addition to the well-known teratogenic effects, peripheral neuropathy is seen with these patients.

Thalidomide is effective therapy; now available in the US

It should be noted that if the systemic disease dictates the use of immunosuppressive agents, such as azathioprine or cyclophosphamide (oral or pulse), the immunosuppressive and anti-inflammatory effects of these drugs generally have a very beneficial effect on the cutaneous lupus lesion. We have successfully treated four long-time recalcitrant anti–Ro (SS-A) antibody–positive lupus patients with widespread photosensitive cutaneous disease with thalidomide 50 mg twice a day.

Annotated Bibliography

Lahita RG, ed. Systemic Lupus Erythematosus. New York: John Wiley and Sons, 1987.

This is an authoritative, multi-authored treatise on SLE that is generally well written with an excellent bibliography.

Wallace DJ, Hahn BH, eds. Dubois' Lupus Erythematosus, 4th ed. Philadelphia: Lea and Feibiger, 1993.

This heavily referenced scholastic treatise on LE by prominent investigators in the field provides an excellent bibliography and cross-references by author and subject.

Rowell NR, Goodfield RA. The connective tissue diseases. In: Champion RH, Burton JL, Ebling FJG, eds. Rook/Wilkinson/Ebling Textbook of Dermatology. London: Blackwell Scientific Publications, 1992, pp 2163–2225.

This excellent treatise on cutaneous LE by authors with different perspectives from their American counterparts has an excellent bibliography highlighting British and European papers.

Reichlin M. Antinuclear antibodies. In: Kelly W, Harris E, Ruddy S, Sledge M, eds. Textbook of Rheumatology, 3rd ed. Philadelphia: WB Saunders, 1989, pp 208–225.

Tan EM. Antinuclear antibodies diagnostic markers for autoimmune diseases and probes for cell biology. Adv Immunol 1989;44:93–151.

These are two excellent review articles on the value of serologic studies in SLE by two individuals whose laboratories have contributed much information to the field.

Hochberg MC. The epidemiology of systemic lupus erythematosus. In: Wallace DJ, Hahn BH, eds. Dubois' Lupus Erythematosus. Philadelphia: Lea and Febiger, 1993, pp 49–57.

This is an excellent, authoritative, well-referenced review of the epidemiology of LE by a recognized leader in the field.

Sontheimer RD, Provost TT. Cutaneous manifestations of lupus erythematosus. In: Cutaneous Manifestations of Rheumatic Diseases. Baltimore: Williams and Wilkins, 1996, pp 1–71.

This exhaustive description of the cutaneous manifestations of LE contains in excess of 450 references.

Sontheimer RD. Subacute cutaneous lupus erythematosus: a decade's perspective. Med Clin North Am 1989;73:1073–1090.

This is an excellent review of SCLE demonstrating, in general, a good prognosis over time.

Provost TT, Watson R, Simmons-O'Brien E. Significance of the anti Ro(SS-A) antibody in the evaluation of patients with cutaneous manifestations of a connective tissue disease. J Am Acad Dermatol 1996;35:147–169.

This summary of 25 years' experience with this antibody system contains unpublished as well as published data, as well as greater than 200 references.

Lehmann P, Holzle E, Kind P, et al. Experimental reproduction of skin lesions in lupus erythematosus by UVA and UVB radiation. J Am Acad Dermatol 1990;22;181–187.
Kind P, Lehmann P, Plewig G. Phototesting in lupus erythematosus. J Invest Dermatol 1993;100:53s–57s.

These two articles provide scientific documentation of the variability of frequency of photosensitivity among various clinical subsets of LE (ACLE, SCLE, and CCLE). Also they document that UVA without UVB is capable of inducing LE lesions in some patients.

Norris DA. Photomechanisms of photosensitive lupus erythematosus. J Invest Dermatol 1993;100:58s–68s.

This article is an excellent review of theories of photosensitivity in LE by an investigator who has made major contributions to this area.

Schur PH, Sandson J. Immunologic factors and clinical activity in systemic lupus erythematosus. N Engl J Med 1968;178:533–538.

This excellent article demonstrates the relationship of anti-dsDNA antibodies and hypocomplementemia with renal disease in SLE patients.

Maddison PJ, Mogavero H, Reichlin M. Patterns of clinical disease associated with antibodies to nuclear/ribonuclear protein. J Rheumatol 1978;5:407–411.
Ginsburg WW, Conn DL, Bunch TW, McDuffie FC. Comparison of clinical and serological markers in systemic lupus erythematosus and overlap syndrome: a review of 247 patients. J Rheumatol 1983;10:235–241.
Sharp GC, Irwin WS, May CM, et al. Association of antibodies to ribonucleoprotein and Sm antigens with mixed connective tissue disease, systemic lupus erythematosus and other rheumatic diseases. N Engl J Med 1976;295:1149–1154.

These three articles detail the clinical presentation of several hundred anti-U_1RNP–positive patients.

Kinoshita G, Keech CL, Sontheimer RD, et al. Spreading of the immune response from 52kDaRo and 60kDaRo to calreticulin in experimental autoimmunity. Lupus 1998; 7:7–11.

This study provides interesting information by suggesting that calreticulin is physically associated with Ro52 and/or Ro60. Immune sera from BALB/c and C3H/He mice immunized with recombinant Ro52 and Ro60 demonstrated that 5 of the 6 Ro52 immunized, C3H/HeJ mice and all 6 Ro60-immunized C3H/HeJ mice reacted with the calreticulin protein. In the BALB/c group, the response rate was lower (1 of 6 of the Ro52-immunized, and 1 of 5 of the Ro60-immunized mice demonstrated antibody spreading to the calreticulin).

None of either strain of mice immunized with La showed evidence of a recruited anticalreticulin antibody response. The authors believe that these studies suggest that a subpopulation of calreticulin or calreticulin-like molecules must be associated, under certain circumstances, with the Ro52 and Ro60 polypeptides.

James JA, Gross T, Scofield RH, Harley JB. Immunoglobulin epitope spreading and autoimmune disease after peptide immunization. J Exp Med 1995;181:453–461.

Topfer F, Gordon T, McClusky J. Intra and intermolecular spreading of autoimmunity involving the nuclear self-antigens La(SS-B) and Ro(SS-A). Proc Natl Acad Sci USA 1995;92:875–879.

Zhang W, Reichlikn M. IgM anti-A and anti D-SnRNP proteins and IgM anti dsDNA are closely associated in SLE sera. Clin Immunol Immunopathol 1995;74:70–76.

Lee LA. Neonatal lupus erythematosus. J Invest Dermatol 1993;100:9s–13s.

Buyon JP. Neonatal lupus erythematosus. Curr Opin Rheumatol 1994;6:523–529.

These are excellent reviews and commentaries of our state of knowledge and investigations into the pathogenesis of NLE. Both articles are well referenced.

Boutjdir M, Chen L, Zahng Z-H, et al. Arrhythmogenicity of IgG and anti-52kD SSA/Ro affinity purified antibodies from mothers with children with congenital heart block. Circ Res 1997;80:354–362.

This is an elegant series of studies demonstrating that anti-52-kD SS-A/Ro antibody affinity–purified sera of mothers whose children have congenital heart block induce complete atrioventricular block in the human fetal heart profused by the Langendorff technique. Further studies indicate L-type Ca++ currents at the whole-cell and single-channel level are inhibited. Immunization of BALB/c mice with recombinant 52-kD (SS-A/Ro) protein-generated, high-titer antibodies that crossed the placenta during pregnancy was associated with the development of varying degrees of atrioventricular conduction abnormalities in the pups.

These studies strongly suggest that anti–52 kD (SS-A/Ro) antibodies are of pathophysiologic significance in the development of isolated congenital heart block.

Roubey RAS. Immunology of the antiphospholipid syndrome. Arthritis Rheum 1996;39: 1444–1454.

Arnett FC. The genetic basis of lupus erythematosus. In: Wallace DJ, Holm BH, eds. Dubois' Lupus Erythematosus. Philadelphia: Lea and Febiger, 1993. pp 13–36.

This is a thoroughly well-written, clear, concise review of the genetic studies of LE by an individual who has contributed much to this field.

Lahita RG. Connective tissue diseases and the overall influence of gender. Int J Fertil 1996;41:156–165.

This is an excellent review of the influence of sex hormones on autoimmune diseases by an investigator who has a great deal of research experience with this field. It has 121 references cited.

Van Vollenhoven RF, Morabito LM, Engleman EG, McGuire JL. Treatment of systemic lupus erythematosus with dehydroepiandrosterone: 50 patients treated up to 12 months. J Rheum 1998;25:285–289.

This recent report suggests the benefit of DHEA in treating SLE patient. Mild acneiform dermatitis is the only side effect.

Franceschini F, Calvavara-Pinton P, Quinzanni M, et al. Chilblain lupus erythematosus is associated with antibodies to SSA/Ro. Lupus 1999;8:215–219.

This is the second paper indicating the association of Hutchinson's chilblain LE with the presence of anti-Ro (SS-A) antibodies. This is a thought-provoking paper because it indicates the association of a peculiar cutaneous lupus lesion associated with anti-Ro (SS-A) antibodies, possibly precipitated by physical factors (cold, damp weather).

Cimaz R, et al. QT interval prolongation in asymptomatic anti-SSA/Ro positive infants without congenital heart block. Arthritis Rheum 2000;43:1049–1053.

CHAPTER 6

Dermatomyositis

Thomas T. Provost, M.D., John A. Flynn, M.D.

Dermatomyositis is an inflammatory skin disease associated with myositis involving predominantly the pelvic and shoulder girdle muscles and producing varying degrees of weakness. This disease is distinguished from polymyositis by the presence of characteristic cutaneous and pathological muscle findings.

Great progress has been made during the past 25 years characterizing the clinical features of this disease. The classification initially proposed by Bohan and Peter (Table 6–1) in 1975, focusing upon muscle involvement, is the accepted standard.

Bohan and Peter classification

Additional works, initially by Krain in 1975 and more recently by Euwer and Sontheimer, Stonecipher et al., and Whitmore et al., have publicized that the cutaneous features of dermatomyositis may occur in the absence of clinical evidence of myositis. Furthermore, these patients with dermatomyositis sine myositis (amyopathic dermatomyositis) have been detected to develop an associated malignancy.

Paraneoplastic syndrome

Three recent Scandinavian national registry studies have confirmed the work of Callen et al. regarding the association of malignancy with dermatomyositis and, to a lesser extent, polymyositis. Thus, the detection of dermatomyositis with or without clinical muscle involvement in adults over the age of 40 has taken on increased importance because of the possibility of a paraneoplastic syndrome.

Serologic studies during the past 20 years have demonstrated the frequent presence of autoantibodies in dermatomyositis/polymyositis patients and have helped to classify some of these patients into specific subsets (ie, the antisynthetase syndrome).

A chronology of the events in the development of our knowledge regarding this disease over the past century is presented in Table 6–2.

TABLE 6–1 Classification of Polymyositis and Dermatomyositis*

I	Primary idiopathic polymyositis
II	Primary idiopathic dermatomyositis
III	Polymyositis or dermatomyositis with malignancy
IV	Juvenile dermatomyositis (or polymyositis)
V	Overlap syndrome of polymyositis or dermatomyositis with another connective tissue disease

*Bohan and Peter, 1975

Incidence and Prevalence

Dermatomyositis/polymyositis is uncommon. An annual incidence of 5 to 10 cases per million per year and a prevalence of 5 to 8 cases per 100,000 population have been reported. Females, especially African Americans, are at increased risk.

Pathogenesis

Both cell-mediated and humoral immune mechanisms may be involved in the pathogenesis.

In polymyositis, CD8 cytotoxic T cells may play a prominent pathologic role.

Cellular and humoral immune features are present in dermatomyositis/polymyositis. Until recently, these two entities were believed to be closely related pathologically; however, differences in immune responses and muscle pathologic features have been detected (Table 6–3).

Phenotypic examination of the lymphocytic infiltrate in inflamed muscles of both polymyositis and dermatomyositis indicate that activated (human leukocyte antigen [HLA]-DR–positive) lymphocytes are prominent. However, studies of dermatomyositis in comparison with polymyositis demonstrate a higher proportion of B lymphocytes and a lower proportion of CD8 (suppressor/cytotoxic) T lymphocytes. Furthermore, in polymyositis patients, CD8 T lymphocytes surround and invade muscle fibers. The presence of these CD8 T cells and HLA class I major histocompatibility complex (MHC) molecules on the cell surface of

TABLE 6–2 Dermatomyositis/Polymyositis Chronology of Development of Knowledge

1863	Wagner provides first description of dermatomyositis.
1930	Gottron provides extensive description of cutaneous manifestations.
1940	O'Leary and Waisman publish Mayo Clinic experience with 40 dermatomyositis patients.
1957	Everett and Curtis and later Banker and Victor, in 1966, emphasize differences between juvenile and adult dermatomyositis.
1959–62	Williams, Arundel, Wilkinson and Haserick, and Sky associate dermatomyositis with malignancy.
1960–70	Pearson publishes series of articles on polymyositis and dermatomyositis.
1975	Bohan and Peter classify polymyositis and dermatomyositis.
1975	Krain describes dermatomyositis sine myositis (amyopathic dermatomyositis).
1976–84	Reichlin, in collaboration with Mattioli, Nishikai, and Arnett, details the multiplicity of autoantibodies in dermatomyositis and polymyositis including recognition of anti–Mi-2 and anti–Jo-1 antibodies in a series of articles.
1980	Callen et al. demonstrate strong association of malignancy with dermatomyositis in contrast to a weak association with polymyositis.
1983	Matthews and Bernstein describe that anti–Jo-1 antibody inhibits histidyl-tRNA synthetase.
1984–90	Tan et al. characterize molecular and clinical features of polymyositis/scleroderma antigen and antibody.
1985–90	Targoff et al. detail specificity of additional autoantibodies in dermatomyositis and polymyositis in a series of articles.
1992–95	Swedish, Finnish, and Danish national registry studies establish that the malignant association is predominantly with dermatomyositis and, to a lesser extent, polymyositis, confirming Callen's 1980 observations.
1995	The occurrence of ovarian carcinoma in dermatomyositis sine myositis patients is demonstrated. Proposal made to modify Bohan and Peter's classification to reflect dominant association of malignancy with dermatomyositis, including dermatomyositis sine myositis.

TABLE 6–3 Comparison of Dermatomyositis and Polymyositis

	Dermatomyositis	Polymyositis
Dermatitis	100%	0%
Vasculopathy	Yes	No
Membrane attack complex	Yes	No
Myositis		
Perivascular and perifascicular infiltrate with perifascicular atrophy and muscle necrosis	Common	Unusual
Endomysial infiltrate with individual muscle fiber invasion by lymphocytes	Unusual	Common
Membrane attack complex	Common	Absent
CD8 T cells	Unusual	Common
B cells	Common	Unusual
Antisynthetase antibodies	Unusual	25–30%
Anti–Mi-2 antibodies	15–20%	Rare

Data from:

Emslie-Smith AM, Engel AG. Microvascular changes in early and advanced dermatomyositis: a quantitative study. Ann Neurol 1990;27:343–356.

Crowson AN, Magro CM. The role of microvascular injury in the pathogenesis of cutaneous lesions of dermatomyositis. Hum Pathol 1996;27:15–19.

Mascaro JM Jr, Hausmann G, Herrero C, et al. Membrane attack complex deposits in cutaneous lesions of dermatomyositis. Arch Dermatol 1995;131:1386–1392.

involved muscles suggests that a direct cytotoxic immune-mediated event plays a prominent role in the pathogenesis of polymyositis.

In dermatomyositis, humoral immune mechanisms have a prominent role.

Deposition of complement membrane attack complex in dermatomyositis skin and muscle blood vessels

In dermatomyositis, the intense B cell infiltrate, together with CD4 T cells in the muscle perivascular areas, suggests humoral immune mechanisms are important in the pathogenesis. Furthermore, in contradistinction to polymyositis, muscle vascular injury appears to be prominent. This vascular injury appears to be an early finding and may occur prior to the development of the inflammatory infiltrate and damage to the muscle fibers. Also, immunofluorescent studies of affected muscles demonstrate the deposition of the membrane attack complex of complement (C5b-C9) in the blood vessel walls. These findings are prominent in juvenile dermatomyositis but have also been detected in adult dermatomyositis. They are, however, absent in polymyositis.

Pathologic Muscle Features

In polymyositis, endomysial inflammation (around individual muscle fibers) and necrosis of individual muscle fibers occur (Figure 6–1). In dermatomyositis, the mononuclear inflammatory infiltrate is perivascular and perifascicular (around a muscle bundle). Muscle necrosis occurs at the periphery of the muscle bundle (Figure 6–2).

Pathologic Cutaneous Features

Skin pathology resembles cutaneous lupus erythematosus.

The histopathologic examination of dermatomyositis skin lesions demonstrates an interface dermatitis characterized by liquefaction degeneration at the dermal epidermal junction and a patchy mononuclear inflammatory infiltrate high in the reticular and papillary dermis. Mucin deposition is present. Blood vessel dilatation may be prominent. These features are very similar to those seen in lupus erythematosus and cannot be differentiated.

However, direct immunofluorescence examination demonstrates, in contrast to lupus lesions, the frequent deposition of the membrane attack complex of complement (C5b-C9) in dermal blood vessels in dermatomyositis.

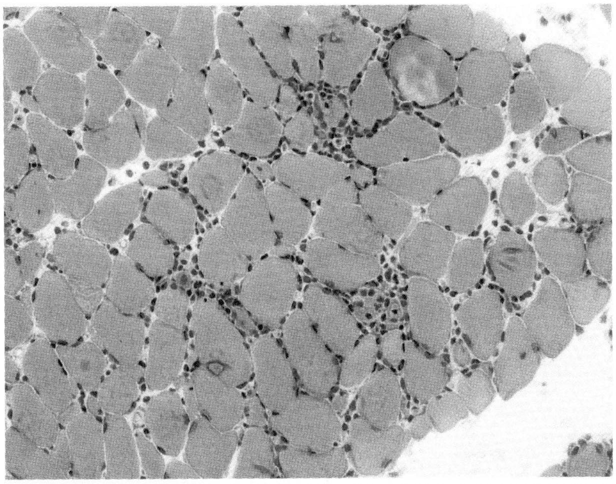

FIGURE 6–1 Polymyositis: H&E of skeletal muscle demonstrating primary endomysial inflammation, focal invasion of muscle fibers by mononuclear cells, and muscle fiber necrosis.

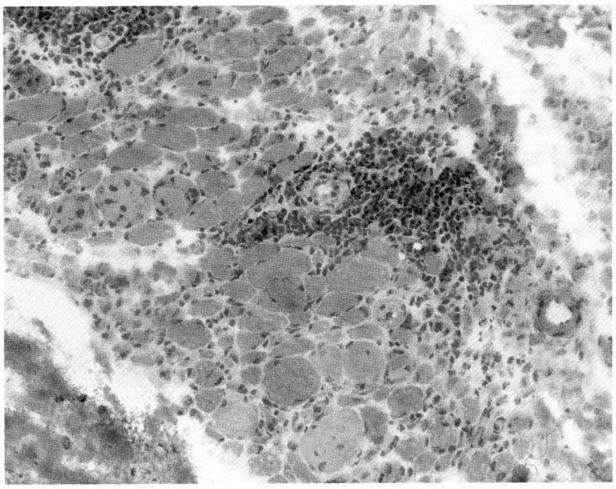

FIGURE 6–2 Dermatomyositis: H&E preparation of skeletal muscle biopsy demonstrating peri fascicular muscle fiber atrophy, perimysial and perifascicular inflammation.

Autoantibodies

Antinuclear antibodies are frequent in dermatomyositis.

Approximately 90% of dermatomyositis/polymyositis patients demonstrate significant antinuclear antibody titers.

Of dermatomyositis patients, approximately 15 to 20% possess anti–Mi-2 antibodies. ("Mi" denotes the first two initials of the surname of the patient Mitchell in whom the antibody was initially detected) (Table 6–4).

Anti–Mi-2 antibodies have high degree of specificity for dermatomyositis

These antibodies are reactive with a 240-kD nuclear antigen of unknown function. In addition, approximately 10% of juvenile dermatomyositis patients also possess this antibody. It has been estimated that 95% of patients with anti–Mi-2 autoantibodies have dermatomyositis. Thus, this is the only antibody system highly, but not absolutely, specific for dermatomyositis.

In addition to the anti–Mi-2 antibody, a number of other antibody systems have been described. These antibody systems predominantly occur in polymyositis but have also been detected in a small percentage of patients with dermatomyositis. These include five antibody systems directed against aminoacyl-tRNA synthetases. These antibodies are highly specific for dermatomyositis/polymyositis (Table 6–5). They do not occur in other connective tissue diseases. Each of these synthetases binds a specific amino acid to its cognate tRNAs. Furthermore, an individual polymyositis/dermatomyositis patient generally makes autoantibodies against only one of these synthetases. For example, an anti–Jo-1 (antihistidyl-tRNA synthetase) antibody–positive patient almost never makes antibodies against PL-7 (threonyl-tRNA synthetase), and vice versa.

Anti–Jo-1 antibodies found in 20% of polymyositis patients; A few dermatomyositis patients possess this antibody

The most common antisynthetase antibody detected in polymyositis/dermatomyositis patients is directed against histidyl-tRNA synthetase (anti–Jo-1). Approximately 20% of polymyositis patients, as well as a small percentage of dermatomyositis patients, possess this antibody. This antibody system almost never occurs in patients with the myositis associated with malignancy and has not been found in juvenile dermatomyositis. Interstitial lung disease is found in

TABLE 6–4 Dermatomyositis Specific Autoantibody

Antibody	Target	Frequency	Clinical Features
Anti–Mi-2	240 kD nuclear protein complex	20%	Adult or juvenile dermatomyositis

TABLE 6–5 Antisynthetase Autoantibodies in Dermatomyositis/Polymyositis

Antibody	Target	Frequency	Clinical Features
Anti–Jo-1	Histidyl-tRNA synthetase	~20%	Adult PM, DM, HLA-DR3, DRw52, DQA 1050, antisynthetase syndrome
Anti–PL-7	Threonyl-tRNA synthetase	~3%	Adult DM, PM, antisynthetase syndrome
Anti–PL-12	Alanyl-tRNA synthetase	~3%	Adult DM, PM, interstitial lung disease antisynthetase syndrome
Anti-OJ	Isoleucyl-tRNA synthetase	~1%	Adult DM, PM, interstitial lung disease antisynthetase syndrome
Anti-EJ	Glycyl-tRNA synthetase	~1%	Adult DM, PM, antisynthetase syndrome

PM = polymyositis; DM = dermatomyositis

50 to 70% of these patients. In fact, interstitial lung disease in association with anti–Jo-1 (antihistidyl-tRNA synthetase) antibodies may occur in patients with minimal or no evidence of myositis. A polyarthritis occurs in approximately 70% of these patients and Raynaud's phenomenon is common.

The other antisynthetase antibodies are directed against threonyl, alanyl, isoleucyl, and glycyl-tRNA synthetases. These tRNA synthetase antibodies compose approximately 10% of patients with polymyositis/dermatomyositis. All the antisynthetase antibody–positive patients have a clinical picture similar to patients with anti–Jo-1 (Table 6–6).

Antisynthetase syndrome

Myositis can be mild and the cutaneous manifestations of dermatomyositis may be more common in these antisynthetase patients than is seen in the anti–Jo-1 antibody positive patients. In addition, they may demonstrate cutaneous features of mechanic's hands (see below). The pulmonary interstitial disease, however, is very common and may be rapidly progressive. These antisynthetase dermatomyositis/polymyositis patients generally have recalcitrant disease with frequent relapses.

Anti–signal recognition particles and anti-KJ antibodies

In addition to the five antisynthetase antibodies, other antibody systems have been described in dermatomyositis polymyositis. Antibodies to the signal recognition particle (SRP) are found almost exclusively in adult polymyositis. On rare occasions, anti–KJ antibodies have been detected and patients with these appear to have a syndrome similar to the antisynthetase syndrome.

Myositis overlap syndrome associated with antibodies

A group of antibodies with distinct specificity have been detected in patients with a myositis-scleroderma overlap syndrome (Table 6–7). These include anti–polymyositis-scleroderma (PM-SCL), anti-Ku, anti-U_1RNP, and anti-U_2RNP. An overlap syndrome of myositis with Sjögren's syndrome or systemic lupus erythematosus (SLE) has been found to be associated with anti-Ro (SS-A) antibodies.

TABLE 6–6 Dermatomyositis/Polymyositis

Clinical Features of Antisynthetase Syndrome
Myositis
Interstitial lung disease
Arthritis
Raynaud's phenomenon
Recalcitrant disease with frequent relapses
Mechanic's hand

TABLE 6–7 Autoantibodies Associated with Scleroderma-Myositis Overlap Syndrome

Antibody	Target	Frequency	Clinical Features
Anti–PM-SCL	Nucleolar protein complex 11–16 proteins	~10%	Polymyositis-scleroderma, polymyositis, scleroderma, increased frequency HLA-DR2
Anti-U_1RNP	Splicesome U_1RNP particle	~10%	Mixed connective tissue syndrome; features of myositis, scleroderma and SLE
Anti-Ku	Unknown	~10%	Polymyositis and scleroderma overlap syndromes, SLE, scleroderma, more common in Japanese

PM-SCL = polymyositis-scleroderma; SLE = systemic lupus erythematosus.

Clinical Features

Dermatomyositis/polymyositis manifests itself in many ways, as summarized in Table 6–8.

Cutaneous Manifestations

Gottron's sign
Gottron's papules

The cutaneous manifestations of dermatomyositis are characteristic and frequently, diagnostic of the condition. These are characterized by an erythematous, violaceous, photosensitive dermatitis frequently with lesions over the extensor surfaces of the distal interphalangeal, proximal interphalangeal, and metacar-

TABLE 6–8 Summary of Clinical Manifestations of Dermatomyositis/Polymyositis

Cutaneous

- Photosensitive, erythematous macular dermatitis involving the upper eyelids (heliotrope); the extensor surface of the joints (Gottron's sign), the upper back (shawl sign) and the V of the neck; atrophy, telangiectasia, and hypo- and hyperpigmented macular patches (poikiloderma)
- Cuticle nailfold injection with or without microinfarcts
- Dystrophic calcification (most prominent in juvenile dermatomyositis)
- "Mechanic's hands" involving roughening and "dirty" hyperpigmentation of the dermaglyphics of the hands associated with xerosis and fissuring
- Raynaud's phenomenon

Musculoskeletal

- Arthralgia and arthritis
- Proximal muscle weakening of shoulder and pelvic girdles

Gastrointestinal

- Dysphagia with nasal regurgitation
- Perforation of gastrointestinal tract secondary to a vasculitis (juvenile dermatomyositis)

Pulmonary

- Decrease in ventilatory capability secondary to involvement of diaphragmatic and accessory muscles (intercostal, sternocleidomastoid, etc.)
- Aspiration pneumonia
- Infections as a complication of therapy
- Interstitial fibrosis

Cardiac

- Unusual to develop symptomatic myocarditis; associated with arrhythmias and congestive heart failure
- Cor pulmonale secondary to interstitial lung disease

pophalangeal joints of the hand, elbows, knees, and malleoli (Gottron's sign) (Figures 6–3 and 6–4). With time, edematous papules and plaques occur at these sites (Gottron's papules) (Figures 6–5 and 6–6). These lesions pathologically demonstrate an interface dermatitis and a superficial mononuclear inflammatory infiltrate and are clinically pathognomonic for dermatomyositis.

Heliotrope

Widespread erythematous, violaceous, macular lesions can involve the forehead and periorbital areas, associated at times with prominent edema. A lavender, erythematous dermatitis involving the upper eyelids (heliotrope) is characteristic. (Figures 6–7 to 6–9)

Shawl sign

Prominent erythematous, violaceous lesions in a photosensitive distribution may involve the V of the neck (V-sign). Furthermore, erythematous, violaceous, macular lesions can involve the posterior portion of the neck and the tops of the shoulders (shawl sign) (Figures 6–10 to 6–12). Widespread swaths of erythematous, violaceous, macular lesions in linear streaks (centripetal flagellate erythema) may be found over various areas of the body (suggesting that the trauma of scratching may have played a role in the pathogenesis [Koebner's phenomenon]) (Figure 6–13). On rare occasions an inflammatory lichenoid reaction may occur (Figure 6–14).

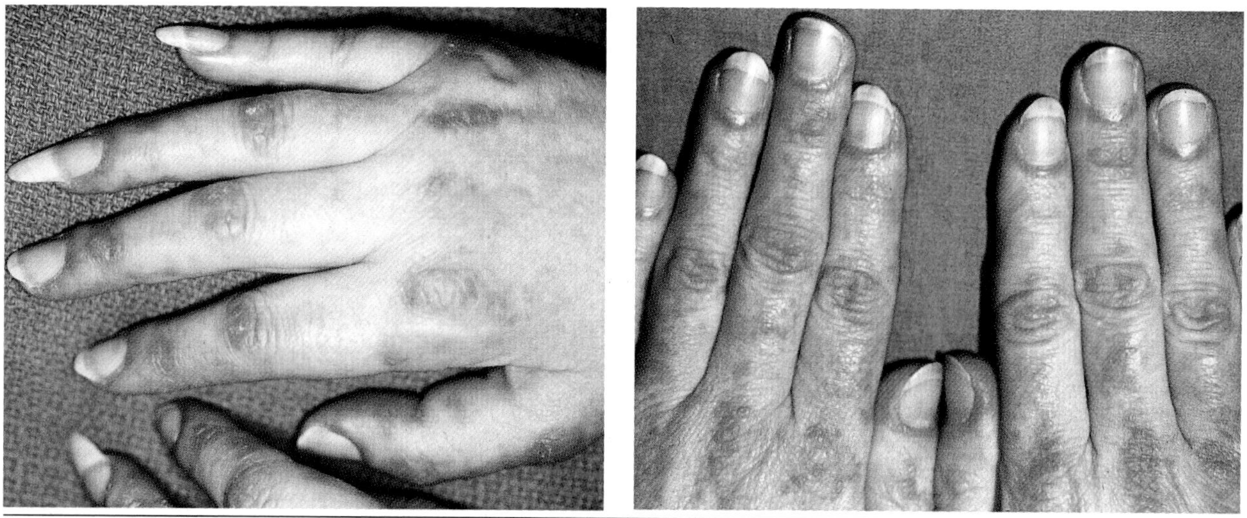

FIGURES 6–3 AND 6–4 Erythema over surface of distal interphalangeal (DIP), proximal interphalangeal (PIP), and metacarpophalangeal (MP) joints of hands (Gottron's sign) in dermatomyositis.

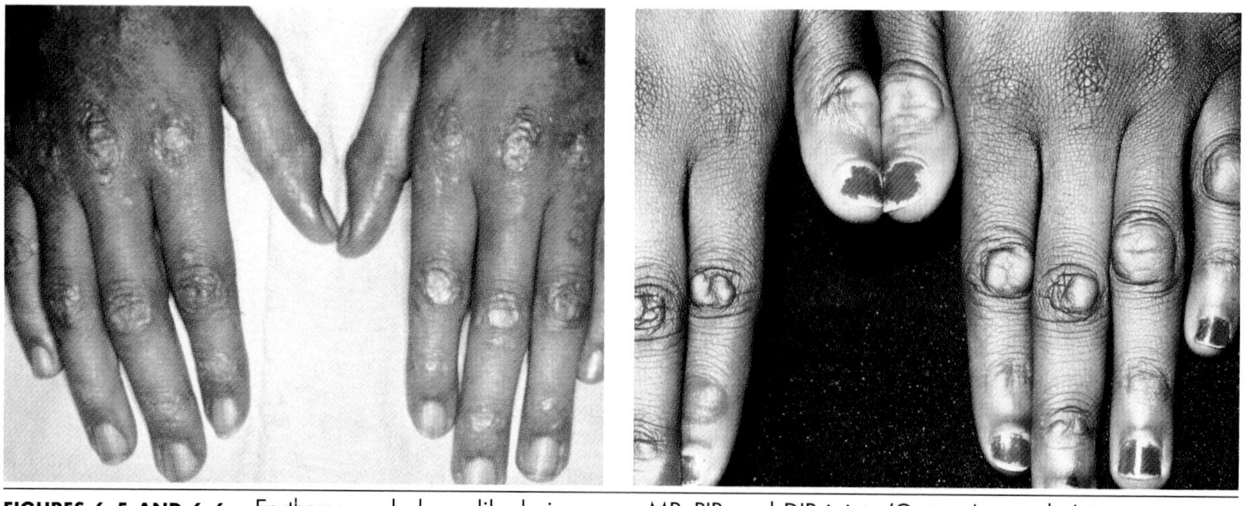

FIGURES 6–5 AND 6–6 Erythema and plaque-like lesions over MP, PIP, and DIP joints (Gottron's papules) in two patients with dermatomyositis.

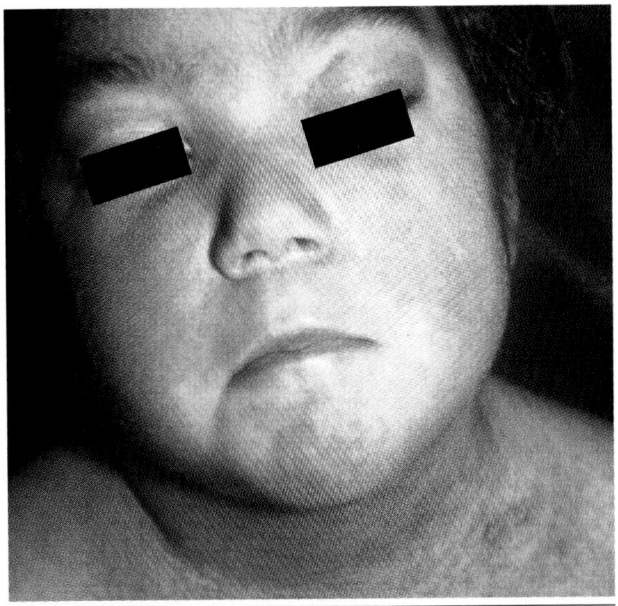

FIGURE 6–7 Child with dermatomyositis demonstrating prominent facial and eyelid edema. Patient had ptosis of eyelids due to muscle weakness. Also note violaceous erythema of upper eyelid (heliotrope).

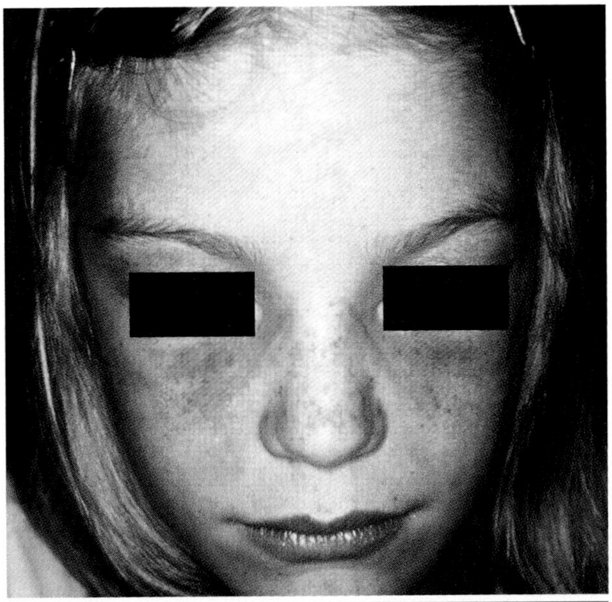

FIGURE 6–8 Child with dermatomyositis demonstrating erythematous violaceous dermatitis. Note heliotrope.

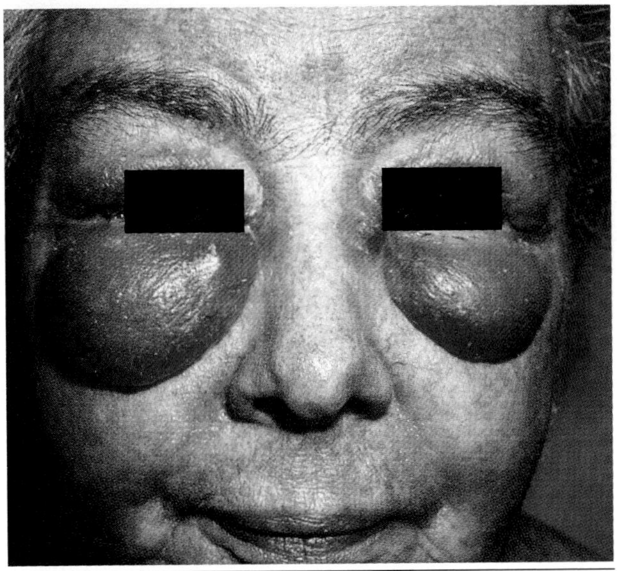

FIGURE 6–9 Severe periorbital involvement with prominent suborbital edema in a dermatomyositis patient without clinical or enzymatic evidence of muscle involvement. Patient succumbed to ovarian cancer.

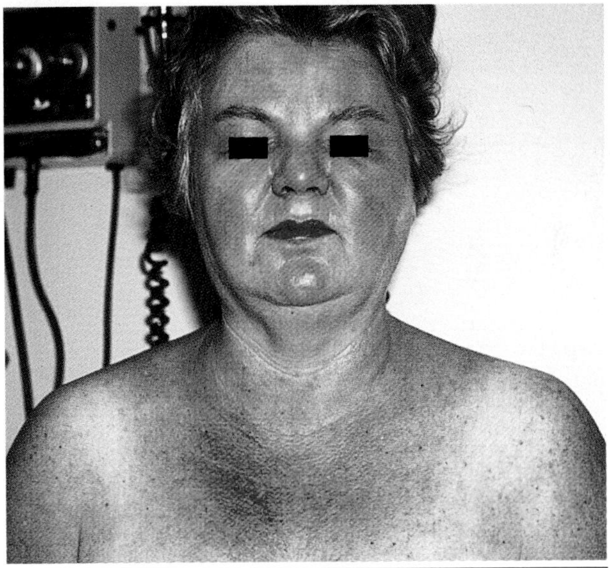

FIGURE 6–10 Adult female with explosive onset of dermatomyositis. Note photodistribution sparing skin in submental area and beneath bra strap.

Cuticle nailfold injection

Cuticle nailfolds frequently demonstrate the presence of periungual erythema and telangiectasia with or without infarction (Figure 6–15). A ragged irregular appearance is characteristic. Examination of the capillary loops of the cuticle nailfold using an ophthalmoscope or hand lens will frequently demonstrate the presence of giant capillary loops as well as the loss of capillaries.

Mechanic's hands

Additional cutaneous features involving the hands are seen predominantly, but not exclusively, in the antisynthetase syndrome. Hyperkeratosis with fissuring and hyperpigmentation of the normal skin markings produce the appearance of dirty hands, such as those seen in a mechanic. This has been dubbed "mechanic's hands" (Figure 6–16).

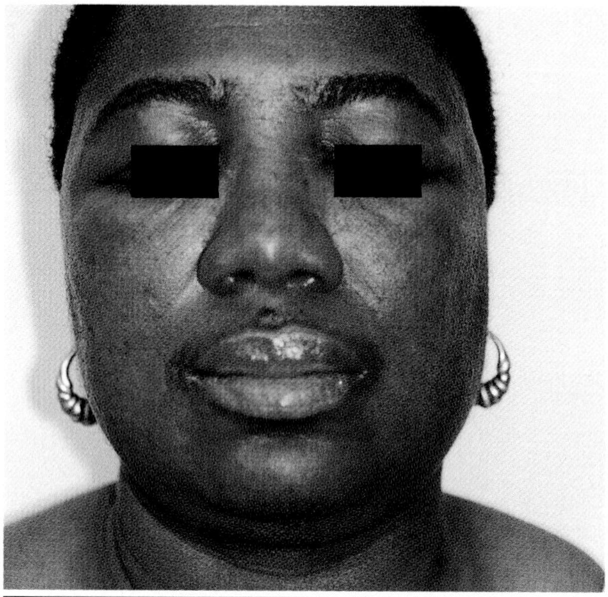

FIGURE 6-11 Subtle dermatitis around eyes with edema in an African American female with dermatomyositis.

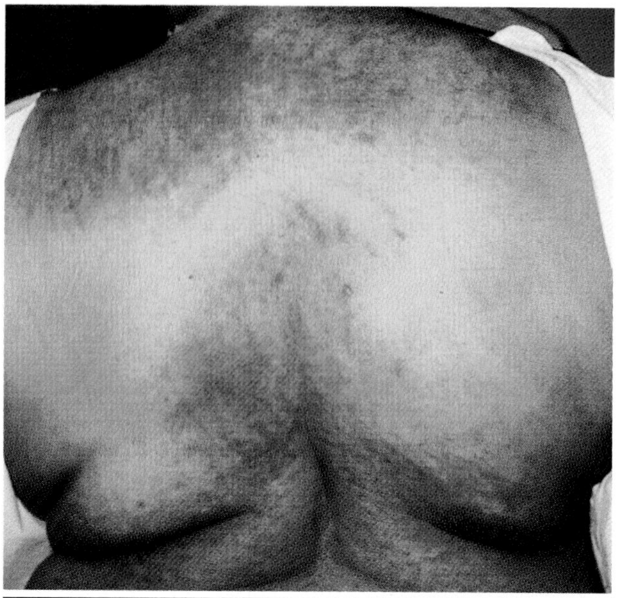

FIGURE 6–12 Shawl sign in a dermatomyositis patient.

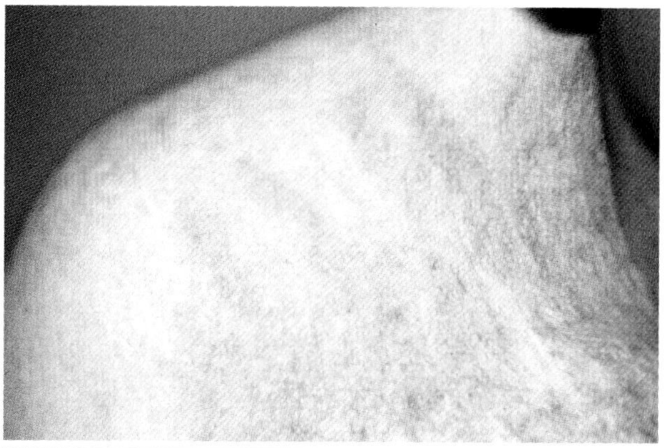

FIGURE 6–13 Centripetal flagellate erythema in a dermatomyositis patient.

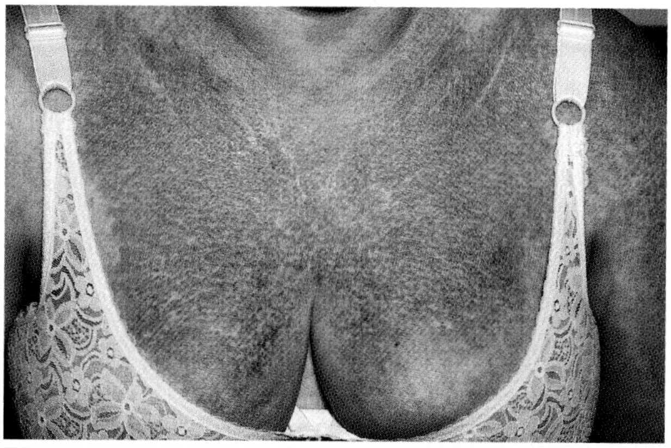

FIGURE 6-14 Lichenoid confluent erythematous photosensitive dermatitis in a dermatomyositis patient.

Calcinosis

Calcinosis is common and sometimes generalized in the juvenile form of dermatomyositis. However, we have observed that it can occur in adult dermatomyositis patients (Figure 6–17).

Poikiloderma

With time, the individual inflammatory lesions of dermatomyositis may develop features of hyper- and hypopigmentation, telangiectasia and atrophy. These lesions are termed "poikiloderma" (Figures 6–18 and 6–19). The pigmentary changes are a postinflammatory reaction. The atrophy may result in the development of superficial painful erosions and ulcers, which, if localized to the axillary and inguinal regions, can be debilitating (Figures 6–20 and 6–21).

Pruritus may be recalcitrant to therapy and may be debilitating.

The cutaneous lesions of dermatomyositis are very pruritic; in fact, pruritus is frequently so great as to be debilitating. In general, the pruritus is recalcitrant to standard topical steroids and antihistamines.

No relationship between skin disease and presence or severity of muscle disease

The cutaneous manifestations of dermatomyositis appear to bear no relationship to the presence or absence of myositis, and the severity of the cutaneous lesions does not appear to be related to the severity of the myositis. Furthermore, in many patients the myositic component is much more easily controlled with the use of corticosteroids and/or immunosuppressive agents than the skin disease. In fact, in a number of cases the cutaneous disease has continued to create severe debility in the patient long after the myositis has been controlled.

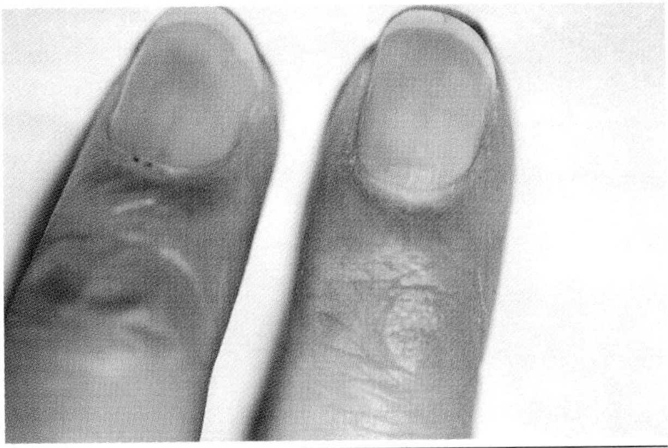

FIGURE 6–15 Periungual erythema with small microinfarcts in a patient with dermatomyositis.

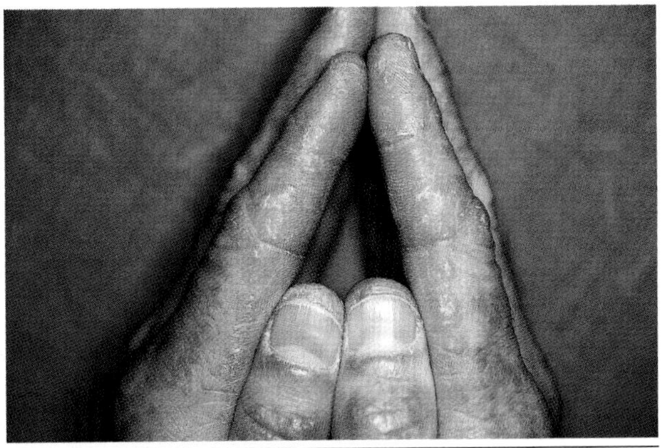

FIGURE 6–16 "Mechanic's hand" in a dermatomyositis patient.

In general, the cutaneous manifestations of dermatomyositis occur approximately 1 to 3 months before the onset of muscle weakness. However, there is an increasingly recognized group of dermatomyositis patients termed "amyopathic", or dermatomyositis sine myositis, who for prolonged periods of time (years) do not demonstrate or never demonstrate the clinical features of myositis. The cutaneous features of dermatomyositis may also occur simultaneously with the recognition of myositis. However, it is uncommon for the myositis to occur before the onset of the cutaneous manifestations.

Dermatomyositis Sine Myositis

Occurrence of dermatomyositis in absence of myositis

In 1975, Krain described in six patients the development of cutaneous features of dermatomyositis in the absence of evidence of muscle disease. All patients subsequently developed myositis. The time interval between the onset of cutaneous features of dermatomyositis and the development of clinical evidence for muscle disease ranged from 3 months to 10½ years. Furthermore, this distinctive variant of dermatomyositis occurred in children as well as adults. Two of the adult patients developed pulmonary fibrosis.

Euwer and Sontheimer subsequently reported six patients with dermatomyositis sine myositis. These patients did not develop clinical or laboratory evidence of myositis for at least 2 years after the onset of their skin manifestations. All six of these patients, like Krain's six patients, had classic cutaneous features of dermatomyositis.

Stonecipher et al. have suggested that all dermatomyositis sine myositis patients would demonstrate subtle, subclinical muscle disease if techniques such as needle biopsy or magnetic resonance imaging (MRI) were performed. We agree with this assessment but think that it is clinically irrelevant at the time of initial detection. It is also important to emphasize that some dermatomyositis sine myositis patients are at risk to develop an associated underlying malignancy. This latter fact was stressed by Whitmore et al. They detected 12 patients with dermatomyositis sine myositis. Two patients developed myositis after 18 and 28 months of observation, confirmed by muscle biopsies. Three women and one man developed carcinomas. The man developed adenocarcinoma of the lung 24 months after the diagnosis of dermatomyositis sine myositis. All three women developed stage II or stage III papillary serous ovarian carcinomas 8, 26, and 31 months after diagnosis. Furthermore, Euwer and Sontheimer noted that Braverman had previously reported a dermatomyositis sine myositis patient who had developed lung cancer, and Bohan et al. had reported the develop-

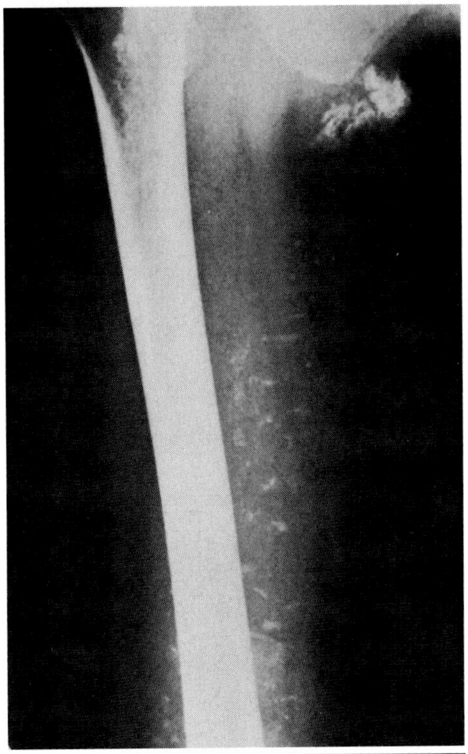

FIGURE 6–17 Widespread calcium deposition in a juvenile dermatomyositis patient.

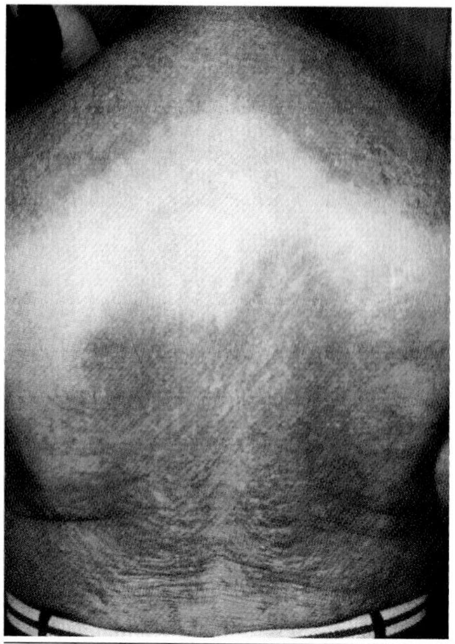
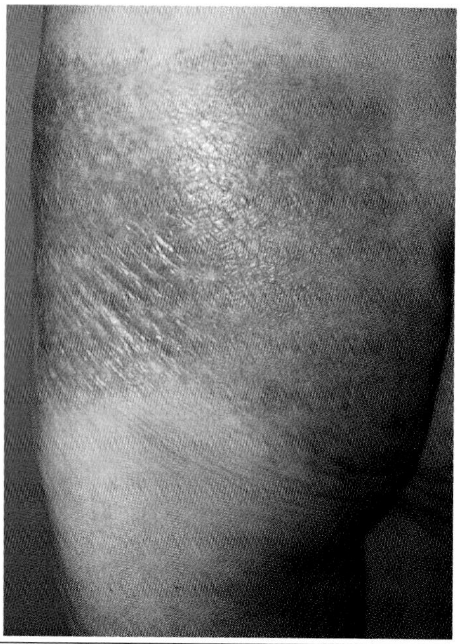

FIGURES 6–18 AND 6–19 Poikiloderma in two patients with dermatomyositis.

Occurrence of malignancies in dermatomyositis sine myositis patients

Modification of Bohan and Peter's classification of polymyositis/dermatomyositis

ment of carcinoma of the uterus in a patient with dermatomyositis who had no clinical evidence of myositis.

Thus, based on these observations, Whitmore et al. have proposed a modification to Bohan and Peter's classification of polymyositis and dermatomyositis (Table 6–9).

We have now seen 28 patients with dermatomyositis sine myositis. Seven (25%) have developed malignancy. The malignancies have included prostate, lung, breast, and ovary. One female patient has had her disease for 17 years without development of malignancy. Most patients without malignancy demonstrate a slow resolution of cutaneous lesions over a period of years, although there are notable exceptions.

Relationship of Dermatomyositis with Associated Malignancy

The possible relationship of dermatomyositis/polymyositis with malignancy has intrigued rheumatologists and dermatologists for the past 25 years. Although

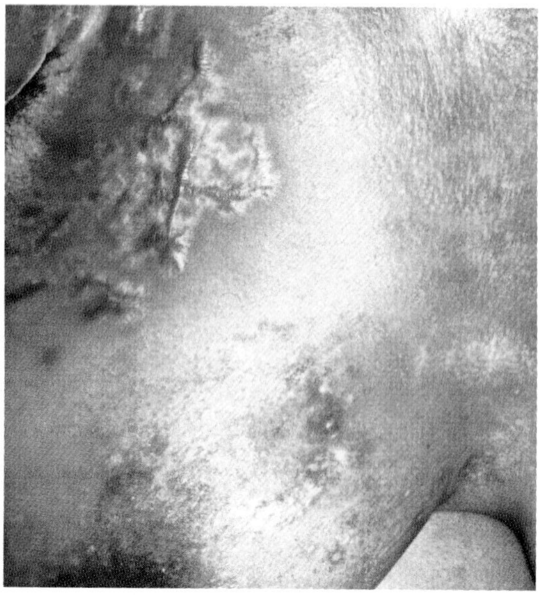
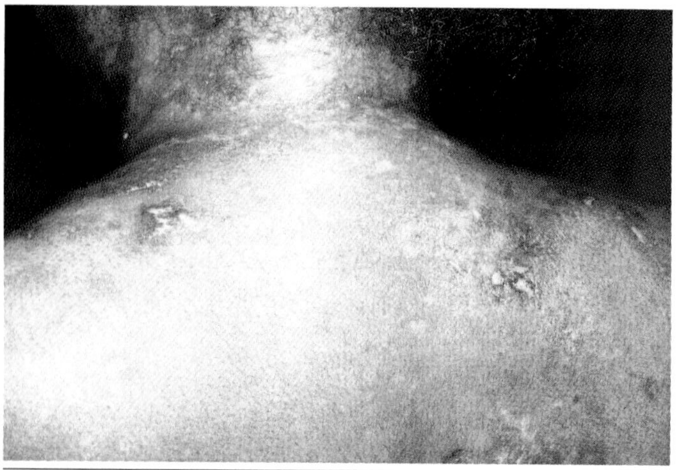

FIGURES 6–20 AND 6–21 Erosions and skin ulcerations in a dermatomyositis patient.

TABLE 6–9 Modification of Bohan and Peter's Classification of Polymyositis/ Dermatomyositis*

Typical polymyositis
Typical dermatomyositis or dermatomyositis sine myositis
Typical dermatomyositis, dermatomyositis sine myositis, or, less commonly, polymyositis associated with malignancy
Childhood dermatomyositis
Polymyositis or dermatomyositis connective tissue overlap syndromes

•Whitmore et al., 1995

reports of the association of dermatomyositis and polymyositis with malignancy are common, the relative frequency of the association has been addressed only recently. Callen, in 1980, reported a study on 58 patients with definite or probable dermatomyositis/ polymyositis (27 dermatomyositis; 31 polymyositis). He noted the incidence of malignancy amongst dermatomyositis patients was 25%. The incidence of malignancy in polymyositis was less than 3%.

Further documentation of the predominant association of malignancy with dermatomyositis recently has been provided by three Scandinavian national registry studies. Two of these studies' data are presented in Tables 6–10 and 6–11.

Predominant relationship of cancer with dermatomyositis and not polymyositis

These studies have indicated a strong association of malignancy with dermatomyositis and, to a lesser extent, polymyositis. Dermatomyositis occurring after the age of 40 has a high probability of being a paraneoplastic syndrome. Studies from various groups have indicated that dermatomyositis may precede the tumor by many years, is generally recalcitrant to therapy, may improve after the tumor is removed, and may or may not relapse with tumor reappearance.

Dermatomyositis is associated with common tumors (ie, breast, lung, etc). There is, however, a striking enrichment of ovarian carcinoma (relative risk 16–32), which has been noted by multiple investigators.

It also should be noted that the occurrence of malignancies in the myositis-associated connective tissue overlap syndromes (ie, scleroderma-polymyositis;

TABLE 6–10 Summary of Relationship between Malignancy and Dermatomyositis/Polymyositis (Swedish Study, 1992)

396 patients with polymyositis
1.8 relative risk of associated malignancy (male)
1.7 relative risk of associated malignancy (female)
Mortality ratio 0:90
392 patients with dermatomyositis
2.4 relative risk of associated malignancy (male)
3.4 relative risk of associated malignancy (female)
Mortality ratio 3:8
5 year-follow-up (polymyositis)
2.4 relative risk of associated malignancy (male)
1.8 relative risk of associated malignancy (female)
5.8 relative risk lung cancer (males)
5-year follow-up (dermatomyositis)
4.4 relative risk of associated malignancy (male)
4.8 relative risk of associated malignancy (female)
16.7 relative risk of ovarian carcinoma

Data from:
Sigurgeiersson B, Lindelöf B, Edhag O, Allander E. Risk of cancer in patients with dermatomyositis or polymyositis. A population-based study. N Engl J Med 1992;326:363–367.

TABLE 6–11 Summary of Relationship between Malignancy and Dermatomyositis/Polymyositis (Finnish Study, 1995)

Polymyositis (175 patients)	
	No increased risk for cancer
Dermatomyositis (71 patients)	
	SIR for cancer = 6.5
	Within first year of diagnosis SIR = 26
	Cancer of gastrointestinal tract SIR = 9
	Lung cancer SIR = 10
	Non melanoma skin cancer SIR = 29
	Ovarian cancer SIR = 32

SIR = standard incidence ratio

Data from:
Airio A, Pukkala E, Isomäki H. Elevated cancer incidence in patients with dermatomyositis: a population based study. J Rheumatol 1995;22:1300–1303.

polymyositis-Sjögren's syndrome/lupus erythematosus) and in dermatomyositis/polymyositis patients possessing autoantibodies is rare (Table 6–12).

Musculoskeletal Involvement

Polymyositis patients, especially with antisynthetase antibodies, frequently develop a nonerosive arthralgia/arthritis involving predominantly the small joints. Arthralgia and arthritis are not prominent features of dermatomyositis. Characteristically, dermatomyositis patients develop muscle weakness affecting the muscles around the shoulders and hips. In general, the onset is gradual, occurring over weeks to months. However, on occasions, onset can be acute with rapid development of weakness. Patients have difficulty walking up steps, arising from a sitting position, getting out of bed, or raising their heads from a pillow and may have difficulty with their gait. Patients may experience difficulty raising their arms and hands above their heads. Difficulty chewing food (masseter muscle involvement), and dysphagia (tongue and cricopharyngeal muscle involvement), although uncommon, can be potentially serious.

Gower's sign

In juvenile dermatomyositis, children have difficulty rising to a standing position, using their hands to push off their bodies to get to a standing position (Gower's sign).

In general, muscle tenderness upon palpation, though present, is not a prominent feature in adult dermatomyositis. In childhood dermatomyositis, however, muscle pain on palpation may be prominent.

Gastrointestinal Disease

Dysphagia occurs in approximately 25% of patients. In some patients, involvement of the muscles of the upper esophagus, the cricopharyngeal muscle, and other muscles in the hypopharynx may produce difficulty in swallowing and nasal speech and hoarseness. The sensation of food sticking in the back of the

TABLE 6–12 Risk Factors in Dermatomyositis for an Associated Malignancy

Dermatomyositis with or without clinical muscle involvement	
Greater than 40 years of age	
Poor response to therapy	
	Recalcitrant with relapses
Absence of features of other connective tissue diseases	
	Absence of polymyositis/scleroderma
	Absence of Raynaud's phenomenon
	Absence of autoantibodies

throat, esophageal reflux, and heartburn may become prominent. Aspiration, especially in those patients with compromised pulmonary functions, is potentially lethal. In patients with any of these symptoms, a swallowing study should be performed to evaluate for aspiration. If this is demonstrated, a gastric feeding tube should be passed to allow proper nutrition without risk of aspiration.

Pharyngeal dysfunction with aspiration can be life threatening.

In children, it is especially important to monitor handling of secretions during eating. Furthermore, children with dermatomyositis, much more so than adults, may develop a vascular insult along the gastrointestinal tract, which on occasions may produce perforation.

Pulmonary Manifestations

There are five major causes of pulmonary disease in patients with dermatomyositis:

1. Restrictive ventilatory defects—These defects develop from severe weakness of the diaphragm and the intercostal muscles. These occur in less than 10% of patients and may require patients to be intubated and have mechanical ventilation.

Pulmonary manifestations
Ventilatory defects

2. Pharyngeal dysfunction—Pharyngeal dysfunction may cause a problem with aspiration.

Aspiration

3. Interstitial lung disease—Although interstitial lung disease is most commonly seen in polymyositis patients possessing antisynthetase antibodies, it does occur in patients with dermatomyositis. In general, interstitial lung disease is an insidious process occurring over months. On occasions, however, a rapid onset of dyspnea, resulting in death, has been reported. Pathologic examination of the lungs demonstrates a mononuclear interstitial inflammatory infiltrate with variable amounts of fibrosis. Bronchiolitis obliterans has also been described. In addition, intimal thickening of small pulmonary arteries and arterials can be seen, resulting in pulmonary hypertension. The severity of the lung disease, like the skin disease, is unrelated to the severity of the muscle disease.

Interstitial lung disease
Severity of interstitial lung disease unrelated to severity of muscle disease

4. Methotrexate therapy—This therapy is commonly employed in the treatment of dermatomyositis and may cause some patients to develop a pneumonitis, characterized by dyspnea, cough, fever, and interstitial infiltrates.

Methotrexate-induced hypersensitivity pneumonitis

5. Infectious pneumonitis—Infectious pneumonitis can occur as a complication of high-dose steroid and/or immunosuppressive therapy.

Infectious pneumonitis

A summary of this information is provided in Table 6–13.

Cardiac Manifestations

Based on limited autopsy studies, cardiac involvement is probably common but, generally, clinically asymptomatic. Cardiac involvement may contribute to the morbidity and mortality in this disease. Conduction abnormalities are the most common features. Arrhythmias and myocarditis leading to congestive heart failure rarely occur. Autopsy material from our institution has demonstrated the presence of interstitial and perivascular mononuclear cell infiltrates similar to that seen in the skeletal muscle. Fibrosis may be extensive.

Generally clinically asymptomatic:
arrhythmias
Congestive heart failure

Renal Involvement

The kidneys are usually spared. However, in childhood dermatomyositis, severe muscle breakdown (rhabdomyolysis) producing myoglobinuria may induce renal failure.

Eye Involvement

Thrombosis of the vessels at the margin of the eyelid have been detected in juvenile dermatomyositis patients. Also, as a reflection of the vasculopathy that these children develop, transient "cotton wool" spots can be seen in the retina. Retinal artery inflammation can produce optic atrophy. In addition, vasculitis involving the conjunctival vessels can produce avascular areas and infarction.

Myositis Associated with Overlap Connective Tissue Syndromes

In general, myositis as a component of SLE will respond to steroids and/or immunosuppressive therapy. In addition, a myositis component has been recog-

TABLE 6–13 Pulmonary Disease in 42 Patients with Polymyositis/Dermatomyositis

Pulmonary Disease	% of Patients
Radiographic evidence of ILD	10
ILD by function testing	31
Ventilatory insufficiency	7
Aspiration pneumonia	14
Opportunistic infection	5
Pneumonia	10
More than one type of lung disease	10
Lung disease contributing to death	10

ILD = interstitial lung disease

Data from:
Dicky BF, Myers AR. Pulmonary disease in polymyositis/dermatomyositis. Semin Arthritis Rheum 1984;14:60–76.

nized in anti-Ro (SS-A) antibody–positive Sjögren's syndrome patients. These patients appear to have a perivascular mononuclear inflammatory infiltrate in the affected muscles. In scleroderma, an insidiously developing myositic component unresponsive to steroids is common.

Patients with myositis associated with connective tissue diseases may have prominent weakness. However, in contradistinction to dermatomyositis and polymyositis patients, muscle enzyme abnormalities are generally much less prominent.

Medical Evaluation of Dermatomyositis Patients

MRI plus needle muscle biopsy may be future techniques to evaluate muscle disease in patients suspected of having dermatomyositis.

Patients with the typical cutaneous involvement of dermatomyositis must be assessed for myositis and other organ involvement. The diagnosis of muscle involvement can be determined by physical examination demonstrating muscle weakness or loss of power, as well as by serum muscle enzyme studies [aspartate transaminase (AST), alanine transaminase (ALT), aldolase, and creatine phosphokinase and electromyography (EMG)]. Electromyographic studies detect evidence of muscle irritability and myopathy. A definitive diagnosis, however, should be established by muscle biopsy since other clinical conditions can produce muscle weakness and mimic an inflammatory muscle disease. It is our recommendation to obtain a muscle biopsy in all cases to establish a diagnosis of muscle involvement. Studies are appearing in the literature indicating that MRI studies detecting T-2–weighted images and phosphorus 31 MR spectroscopy may be sensitive techniques to detect muscle inflammation. These techniques, coupled with needle muscle biopsies, may become standards of practice in the near future, replacing EMG and open muscle biopsy techniques.

Upon determining the extent of muscle disease, it is essential to evaluate internal involvement. Generally this can be done by clinical evaluation. Pulmonary involvement can occur in the form of interstitial lung disease, which can be evaluated radiographically as well as with pulmonary function studies (spirometry and single-breath carbon monoxide diffusion studies). Patients can also develop esophageal dysmotility, which can lead to significant dysphagia or aspiration. If clinical symptoms are suggestive, then further evaluation with a cine-esophagram study is indicated.

The other issue of great importance is to determine if there is a coexisting malignancy. Numerous studies have demonstrated that dermatomyositis can be a paraneoplastic syndrome, especially after the age of 40. Our specific recommendations are to provide individualized and age-appropriate screening for evidence of lung, breast, colonic, and pelvic neoplasia. In our practice, patients are evaluated with a mammogram, urinalysis, chest radiograph, and screening for occult gastrointestinal blood loss. Female patients are also evaluated for possible ovarian or cervical tumors. We generally do not recommend any more extensive evaluation other than close follow-up for at least a 2-year period (time in which most malignancies are detected). However, our experience with dermatomyositis associated with ovarian carcinoma has caused us to modify our thinking. Because of the insidious nature of ovarian carcinoma and the fact that it has been reported to be detected as long as 6 years after the onset of dermatomyositis (unfortunately stage III), our female dermatomyositis patients receive a pelvic and intravaginal ultrasound examination at least once a year and a cancer antigen (CA) 125 examination twice a year (for at least 3 years). Although a CA 125 determination is not absolutely specific, our preliminary studies indicate that this assay would have detected 50% of our ovarian carcinoma dermatomyositis patients early in their disease.

Ovarian carcinoma evaluation is problematic.
CA 125 determinations twice yearly may be helpful for 3 years.

Treatment

Treatment of this condition should be aimed at bringing both the inflammatory skin and muscle diseases under control. To determine a course of treatment, it is important to assess the activity of the disease, remembering that the cutaneous activity may develop and respond separately from the inflammatory muscle manifestations.

Muscle Disease Therapy

In many instances, muscle disease of dermatomyositis is very easy to control. It is essential to provide recurrent assessment of muscle strength. This can be done with formal quantitative muscle testing as well as by assessing how patients are able to perform their activities of daily living.

Muscle enzyme studies can be followed on a serial basis; however, treatment decisions should not be based entirely on the level of muscle enzyme present. For example, in patients who maintain their strength despite elevated or increasing muscle enzyme levels, it is not always necessary to use higher doses of medication. It also should be noted that with treatment, clinical improvement in muscle strength may lag several weeks behind normalization of enzyme levels.

Prednisone is therapeutic mainstay

The cornerstone of therapy is immunosuppressive medication. The most commonly employed medication is corticosteroids. Patients who present with profound and progressive muscle weakness may require treatment with high-dose corticosteroids in a pulse fashion with methylprednisolone (1 g/day parenterally for 3–5 days). Thereafter, patients are generally treated with 1 mg per kg of prednisone orally per day. This dosage should be maintained until the patients have achieved and maintained disease stability for at least 4 to 8 weeks. The steroid dosage then can be tapered. This can typically be done by a 5 mg increment every 1 to 2 weeks until a dosage of 20 mg is reached. At that point, tapering is less rapid (ie, 1 mg/wk).

There are circumstances that may develop in which corticosteroid therapy is inadequate and further immunosuppressant medication is necessary. Specific instances where this may become necessary include intolerable side effects or the lack of response to high doses of corticosteroids. This is necessary in up to one-quarter of patients. Unfortunately, there are no double blind studies that compare different immunosuppressive regimens. The two most commonly employed medications are azathioprine and methotrexate. When azathioprine (1–2 mg/kg/day) in combination with prednisone has been compared with prednisone alone, the combination therapy has been shown to result in greater improvement with fewer side effects 1 year after initiating therapy. An example of this combination would be 1 mg per kg per day of prednisone and 50 to 100 mg per day of azathioprine.

With increased understanding of the use of methotrexate and its relative safety, this medication has been employed increasingly alone or in combination with prednisone (once weekly doses of 25–50 mg IM, 10–15 mg PO, or 2.5–5.0 mg q 12 hours × 3 once weekly).

Plasmapheresis and intravenous IgG are reserved only for the most refractory cases.

Calcification of soft tissue and muscle is problematic and difficult to treat. Aluminum hydroxide gel, diphosphonate, and recently the calcium channel blocker diltiazem have been proposed as therapy.

Cutaneous Disease Therapy

The cutaneous manifestations of dermatomyositis, in many instances, are recalcitrant to therapy. Topical fluorinated steroids are only marginally effective in suppressing the inflammatory condition. In many instances, immunosuppressive agents, and/or parenteral steroids in sufficient quantities to suppress the muscle disease, are ineffective in the treatment of the skin disease. Furthermore, as noted above, there is a general lack of correlation between the degree and severity of the skin disease and the muscle disease.

Commonly overlooked is the fact that the cutaneous manifestations of dermatomyositis are photosensitive. No studies have been reported indicating the wavelengths responsible for the development of photosensitivity in these patients. It is our practice to recommend the use of broad spectrum sunscreens with a skin protection factor rating of at least 15.

In addition, hydroxychloroquine, 200 mg twice daily, may have beneficial effect upon the photosensitive dermatitis of dermatomyositis. This is not a universal finding. Patients on long-term hydroxychloroquine therapy should be checked on a 6-month basis for the development of a retinopathy.

Severe involvement of the skin, although unusual, may be associated with superficial, painful erosions most commonly occurring in the axillary region and on the sides of the neck. In these patients, pulse steroid therapy (ie, 1 g of methylprednisolone) slowly infused over a 4-hour period, for 3 to 5 consecutive days, may be effective. As an alternative, pulse cyclophosphamide, 750 mg per square meter, may also be employed.

Cyclosporin A and mycophenolate appear to be reasonable alternatives in the treatment of the cutaneous features of dermatomyositis, especially in severe, recalcitrant disease. However, in our experience severe, recalcitrant dermatomyositis appears to be a worrisome feature. A number of patients with paraneoplastic dermatomyositis had such a course. The generalized pruritus associated with this condition is frequently very distressing to the patient. Unfortunately, in our experience, topical mid-potency steroids; steroid, phenol, and menthol in an emollient lotion preparation; and various antihistamines appear to offer only limited control of this very annoying symptom.

Despite no evidence for continuing muscle disease, we have seen many patients who persist in demonstrating active skin disease. The prominent resistance of this inflammatory dermatosis to various immunosuppressive agents, including steroids and thalidomide, is an unusual experience, generally not observed with other inflammatory dermatosis.

Therapies for Other Manifestations

Steroid treatment is also suitable for other manifestations. Opthalmologic occular complications arising from juvenile dermatomyositis respond well to steroids. In addition, acute respiratory failure from a complication of methotrexate therapy can be avoided by immediately instituting high-dose steroids after discontinuing methotrexate. In general, myositis as a component of SLE responds to steroids and/or immunosuppression drugs.

Prognosis

Prior to the availability of immunosuppressive therapy, the prognosis of patients with inflammatory muscle disease was poor. The 5-year mortality rates were greater than 50%. In the past 2 decades, there has been a dramatic decline in this mortality rate. In recent series where patients who have malignancy were excluded, the survival rate was greater than 90% at 5 years after the initial diagnosis. The factors that are associated with poor prognosis include cardiac involvement, pharyngeal dysfunction with aspiration pneumonia, and advanced age of patient.

Annotated Bibliography

Bohan A, Peter JB, Bowman RL, Pearson CM. A computer-assisted analysis of 153 patients with polymyositis and dermatomyositis. Medicine 1977;56;255–286.

Bohan A, Peter JB. Polymyositis and dermatomyositis (first of two parts). N Engl J Med 1975;292(7):344–347.

Bohan A, Peter JB. Polymyositis and dermatomyositis (second of two parts). N Engl J Med 1975;292(8):403–407.

These classic articles in the field detail the now accepted classification.

Krain L. Dermatomyositis in six patients without initial muscle involvement. Arch Dermatol 1975;11:241–245.

Euwer RL, Sontheimer RD. Amyopathic dermatomyositis (dermatomyositis sine myositis). Presentation of six new cases and review of the literature. J Am Acad Dermatol 1991;24:959–966.

Stonecipher MR, Jorrizo JL, White WL, et al. Cutaneous changes of dermatomyositis in patients with normal muscle enzymes: dermatomyositis sine myositis? J Am Acad Dermatol 1993;28:951–956.

Whitmore SE, Watson R, Rosenshein NB, Provost TT. Dermatomyositis sine myositis: association with malignancy. J Rheumatol 1996;23:101–105.

These four articles detail the existence of cutaneous manifestations of dermatomyositis without evidence for myositis for prolonged periods of time. Furthermore, these patients, on occasions have an associated malignancy, and preliminary data indicate that ovarian carcinoma is enriched in this group of patients. Because of the existence of dermatomyositis sine myositis and associated malignancies, an adjustment to the classification initially described by Bohan and Peter has been proposed.

Dawkins MA, Jorizzo JL, Walker FO, et al. Dermatomyositis: a dermatology-based case series. J Am Acad Dermatol 1998;38:397–404.

These authors report their findings on 65 patients with dermatomyositis in a dermatology-based setting. They observed 12 patients (18%) had dermatomyositis sine myositis. One of these patients had an adenocarcinoma of the breast. These authors also believe that dermatomyositis patients "without evidence of myositis should be evaluated for occult malignancy, in a manner similar to those with dermatomyositis."

Callen JP, et al. The relationship of dermatomyositis and polymyositis to internal malignancy. Arch Dermatol 1980;116:295–302.

Highly referenced paper demonstrating the strong relationship of dermatomyositis compared to polymyositis with internal malignancy.

Chow WH, Gridley G, Mellemkjaer L, et al. Cancer risk following polymyositis and dermatomyositis: a nationwide cohort study in Denmark. Cancer Causes Control 1995; 6:9–13.

Sigurgeirsson B, Lindelof B, Edhag O, Allander O. Risk of cancer in patients with dermatomyositis or polymyositis. A population-based study. N Engl J Med 1992;326;363–367.

Airio A, Pukkala E, Isomäki H. Elevated cancer incidence in patients with dermatomyositis: a population based study. J Rheumatol 1995;22:1300–1303.

These three articles, comprising national registries, document the paraneoplastic potential of dermatomyositis occurring after the age of 40 years.

Hochberg MC, Feldman D, Stevens MB. Adult onset polymyositis/dermatomyositis: an analysis of clinical and laboratory features and survival in 76 patients with a review of the literature. Semin Arthritis Rheum 1986;15:168–178.

This large study details the laboratory and clinical features of a group of patients seen and evaluated at our institution.

Miller FW. Myositis-specific autoantibodies. Touchstones for understanding the inflammatory myopathies. JAMA 1993;270:1846–1849.

Targoff IN. Humoral immunity in polymyositis/dermatomyositis. J Invest Dermatol 1993;100:116s–123s.

These excellent articles review autoantibodies associated with dermatomyositis/polymyositis.

O'Leary PA, Waisman M. Dermatomyositis: a study of 40 cases. Arch Dermatol Syphilol 1940;41;1001–1019.

This classic paper demonstrates the terrible prognosis of dermatomyositis in the pre-steroid era.

Emslie-Smith AM, Engel AG. Microvascular changes in early and advanced dermatomyositis: a quantitative study. Ann Neurol 1990;27:343–356.

This article demonstrates that capillaries are an early and specific target for the muscle disease process in dermatomyositis. This is in contradistinction to the lack of such involvement in inclusion body myositis and polymyositis.

Crowson AN, Magro CM. The role of microvascular injury in the pathogenesis of cutaneous lesions of dermatomyositis. Hum Pathol 1996;27:15–19.

This is a good article describing dermal blood vessel changes in skin lesions of dermatomyositis.

Mascaro JM Jr, Hausmann G, Herrero C, et al. Membrane attack complex deposits and cutaneous lesions of dermatomyositis. Arch Dermatol 1995;131:1386–1392.

This excellent paper demonstrates the deposition of the membrane attack complex of complement in the blood vessels of lesional biopsies of patients with dermatomyositis—a distinguishing characteristic.

Stahl NI, Klippel JH, Decker JL. A cutaneous lesion associated with myositis. Ann Intern Med 1979;91:577–579.

Features of "mechanic's hand" are detailed in this article.

Spencer-Green G, Crowe WE, Levinson JE. Nailfold capillary abnormalities and clinical outcome in childhood dermatomyositis. Arthritis Rheum 1982;25;954–958.

The article demonstrates frequency of occurrence of nailfold capillary abnormalities and its correlation with severity in childhood dermatomyositis; the presence of nailfold capillary abnormalities is correlated with the more severe forms of the disease (ulceration and chronic recalcitrant disease).

Hanno R, Callen JP. Histopathology of Gottron's papules. J Cutan Pathol 1985;12: 389–394.

Whitmore SE, Rosenshein NB, Provost TT. Ovarian cancer in patients with dermatomyositis. Medicine 1994;73:153–160.

Whitmore SE, Anhalt GJ, Provost TT, et al. Serum CA-125 screening for ovarian cancer in patients with dermatomyositis. Gynecol Oncol 1997;65:241–244.

These two articles detail the experience of our department as well as a review of the literature regarding the occurrence of ovarian carcinoma in patients with dermatomyositis. These articles document the extreme difficulty in making this diagnosis, despite compulsive gynecologic examination and pelvic and intrauterine ultrasound examination. Unfortunately, this diagnosis was not made until the tumors were stage III (peritoneal metastasis). Cancer antigen 125 studies, although very preliminary, indicate that this determination would have alerted us to the possibility of ovarian malignancy in approximately 50% of our patients.

Kagen LJ. Amyopathic dermatomyositis. Arch Dermatol 1995;131: 1458–1459.

This article reviews all the recent data of the significance of patients with dermatomyositis without evidence of myositis. It comes to the conclusion that "there is a need to distinguish the amyopathic patients from those with myositis insofar as treatment is concerned, but not to make a distinction when it comes to evaluation for a possible underlying, or occult, malignancy."

Pachman LM, Cooke N. Juvenile dermatomyositis: a clinical and immunologic study. J Pediatr 1980;96;226–234.

de Merieux P, Verity MA, Clements PJ, Paulus HE. Esophageal abnormalities and dysphagia in polymyositis and dermatomyositis. Arthritis Rheum 1983;26:961–968.

Dicky BF, Myers AR. Pulmonary disease in polymyositis/dermatomyositis. Semin Arthritis Rheum 1984;14:60–76.

Haupt HM, Hutchins GM. The heart and cardiac conduction system in polymyositis/dermatomyositis: a clinicopathologic study of 16 autopsied patients. Am J Cardiol 1982; 50:998–1006.

These articles are excellent references for the cardiac, pulmonary, and other clinical manifestations of dermatomyositis/polymyositis.

King LE Jr. Evaluation of muscles in a patient with suspected amyopathic dermatomyositis by magnetic resonance imaging and phosphorus-31-spectroscopy. J Am Acad Dermatol 1994;30:137–138.

Park JH, Vansant JP, Kumar NG, et al. Dermatomyositis: correlative MR imaging and P-31 MR spectroscopy for quantitative characterization of inflammatory disease. Radiology 1990;177:473–479.

These two articles demonstrate two new noninvasive techniques in the evaluation of inflammatory muscle disease. Conceivably, these two techniques may replace electromyographic techniques in the evaluation of dermatomyositis/polymyositis patients for suspected muscle involvement.

American College of Physicians. Screening for ovarian cancer: recommendations and rationale. Ann Intern Med 1994;121:141–142.

These recommendations, by the American College of physicians, indicate that in women at average risk, routine screening using CA 125 ultrasonography is not recommended because of low frequency of ovarian cancer and the relatively high false-positive rate of CA 125 results. Women who have a family history of ovarian cancer, but who are not members of a hereditary cancer syndrome kindred, have a threefold increased risk. The use of CA 125 testing in these women is also discouraged because it is estimated that annual screening with CA 125 results in approximately 9 false-positive results for every ovarian cancer detected.

Women who are members of a family with hereditary ovarian cancer have a lifetime risk of up to 50%. In this group of patients, prophylactic oophorectomy is one management strategy. Those women who wish to retain their ovaries are appropriate candidates for screening, using pelvic and intravaginal ultrasonography and CA 125 screening.

(Since the relative risk of women with dermatomyositis developing ovarian cancer, ranges between 16 and 32, we believe the recommendations for monitoring women from families with hereditary ovarian cancer syndrome who wish to retain their ovaries should be applied to this group of women for at least a 3-year period. It is conceivable that with more data, prophylactic oophorectomy, in the opinion of the authors, may be a legitimate consideration for selected patients with dermatomyositis.)

Pinto MM, Bernstein LH, Brogan DA, Criscuolo E. Immunoradiometric assay of CA 125 in effusions. Comparison with carcinoembryonic antigen. Cancer 1987;59:218–222.

This study demonstrates that the sensitivity of CA 125 antigen for detecting metastatic carcinoma in patients with carcinoma of the ovary and fallopian tube was 85%; specificity was 96%. The CA 125 assay has value in the detection of serous but not mucinous cystadenocarcinoma of the ovary.

Carlson TJ, Skates SJ, Singer DE. Screening for ovarian cancer. Ann Intern Med 1994; 121:124–132.

This study demonstrates that annual screening with CA 125 or ultrasonography in women older than 50 years without a family history of ovarian cancer would result in more than 30 false-positive results for every ovarian cancer detected. Thus, these data do not support either screening of pre- or post-menopausal women without evidence of a hereditary cancer syndrome.

Xu Y, Shen Z, Wiper DW, et al. Lysophosphatidic acid as a potential biomarker for ovarian and other gynecologic cancers. JAMA 1998;280:719–723.

Lysophosphatidic acid (LPA) is a normal product produced and released by activated platelets. It is a normal constituent of serum and is not detectable in whole blood or fresh platelet-poor plasma from healthy individuals. Ethylenediaminetetraacetic acid–collected plasma was obtained from 48 healthy control women, 48 women with various stages of ovarian cancer, and 36 women with other gynecological cancers.

Ovarian cancer group patients had significantly higher plasma LPA levels. Nine of 10 stage I ovarian cancer patients were positive, 24 of 24 with stage II, III, and IV ovarian cancers were positive, and 14 of 14 with recurrent ovarian cancers had elevated levels. By comparison, only 28 of 47 ovarian cancer patients had elevated CA 125 levels, including 2 of 9 patients with stage I disease.

These preliminary studies suggest that plasma LPA levels may be a valuable assay to detect dermatomyositis patients with early stage ovarian cancer.

Rubin SC, Benjamin I, Behbakht K, et al. Clinical and pathological features of ovarian cancer in women with germ-line mutations of BRCA1. N Engl J Med 1996;335: 1413–1416.

The breast ovarian cancer syndrome has been found to be linked to the BRCA locus on chromosome 17q21. The BRCA1 probably functions as a tumor-suppressor gene. In contradistinction to sporadic ovarian cancers, the cancers associated with the BRCA1 mutations have a significantly more favorable course.

Metzger AL, Bohan A, Golberg LS, et al. Polymyositis and dermatomyositis: combined methotrexate and corticosteroid therapy. Ann Intern Med 1974;81:182–189.

This excellent paper by physicians who have made significant contributions to the field demonstrates the efficacy of methotrexate as a therapeutic modality for the treatment of these patients and the corticosteroid-sparing effect of methotrexate.

Lang BA, Laxer RM, Murphy G, et al. Treatment of dermatomyositis with intravenous gammaglobulin. Am J Med 1991;91:169–172.

The article indicates the efficacy of intravenous gammaglobulin infusion in the treatment of five patients with juvenile dermatomyositis. Following the intravenous gammaglobulin therapy, prednisone could be discontinued or the dose of steroids dramatically reduced.

Palmieri GM, Sebes JI, Aelion JA, et al. Treatment of calcinosis with diltiazem. Arthritis Rheum 1995;38:1646–1654.

This article presents exciting new data suggesting that the benzothiazepine calcium channel blocker, diltiazem, which inhibits mitochondrial sodium-calcium exchange, may have a beneficial therapeutic effect in treating calcinosis. Neither the phenylalkylamine (verapamil) nor the 3,5 pyridinedicarboxylic acid (nifedipine) calcium channel blockers have this inhibiting effect on mitochondrial sodium-calcium exchange.

Gelber AC, Nousari HC, Wigley FM. Myophenolate mofetil in the treatment of severe skin manifestations of dermatomyositis: a series of four cases. J Rheumatol 2000;27: 1542–1545.

Vencovsky J, Jarosova K, Machacek S, et al. Cyclosporine A versus methotrexate in the treatment of polymyositis and dermatomyositis. Scand J Rheumatol 2000;29:95–102.

These two articles describe new therapies for the treatment of dermatomyositis.

CHAPTER 7

Scleroderma

Fredrick M. Wigley, M.D., Thomas T. Provost, M.D.

Scleroderma (systemic sclerosis) Chronic disease affecting skin, heart, lungs, kidneys, musculoskeletal system, and gastrointestinal tract
Rare disease

Systemic sclerosis, or scleroderma, is a chronic putative autoimmune disease that targets the skin, lungs, heart, gastrointestinal tract, kidneys, and musculoskeletal system. It is a unique vascular disease of small arteries, tissue fibrosis, and very specific autoimmune responses. In the diffuse cutaneous form, the most prominent clinical feature is hard skin, thus the term "scleroderma." It is a rare disease with an incidence rate of approximately 20 new cases per million per year. The United States is estimated to have 240 million cases. The average age of onset is between 35 to 50 years, and it is more common among females (3–7:1 female to male ratio). Scleroderma is rarely seen in more than one family member (< 2%), but it is fairly common to find other autoimmune diseases in these same family members. Scleroderma is found in all races but appears to be more severe among African Americans and Native Americans.

CREST syndrome, a limited variant of scleroderma more common in Caucasians

The limited variant of scleroderma, CREST syndrome, involves subcutaneous *c*alcinosis, *R*aynaud's phenomenon (RP), *e*sophageal disease, *s*clerodactyly or scleroderma of fingers, and *t*elangiectasia and is more common among Caucasians. Interstitial lung disease is a significant late complication occurring after the disease has been present for a decade or more.

Scleroderma may be associated with other autoimmune diseases. Overlap syndromes describe the presence of systemic sclerosis and features of another rheumatic disease. The most common overlap syndromes include polymyositis, rheumatoid-like polyarthritis, Sjögren's syndrome, and Hashimoto's thyroiditis. Mixed connective tissue disease (MCTD) is an overlap syndrome with features of scleroderma, systemic lupus erythematosus (SLE), polyarthritis, and polymyositis.

Localized scleroderma: generally involves only the skin.

Localized scleroderma is primarily a skin disease without evidence of systemic disease. It includes isolated morphea (Figure 7–1), multiple morphea lesions (generalized morphea), linear scleroderma (including the coup de sabre), (Figures 7–2 and 7–3) and, rarely, nodular or keloid sclerosis. Patients with systemic sclerosis may have localized scleroderma lesions (Figure 7–4); however, localized scleroderma patients rarely have systemic manifestations or scleroderma-specific autoantibodies (Table 7–1).

Prognosis worse for patients with diffuse cutaneous disease

The natural history of scleroderma varies among patients, but it is generally a chronic disease that evolves over many months or years. The degree of skin involvement (sclerosis of the skin) predicts the subsequent course of events. This concept has defined clinical subtypes of disease. Patients with diffuse cutaneous disease (arms, legs, and trunk) have a worse prognosis, compared with patients with limited (distal arms and legs only) skin involvement. Approximately 10% of patients with CREST syndrome develop isolated pulmonary hypertension without significant pulmonary fibrosis. These CREST syndrome patients have a poor prognosis. Fifty to 90% of patients with CREST syndrome have anticentromere antibody (Table 7–2) and the absence of antinucleolar antibodies.

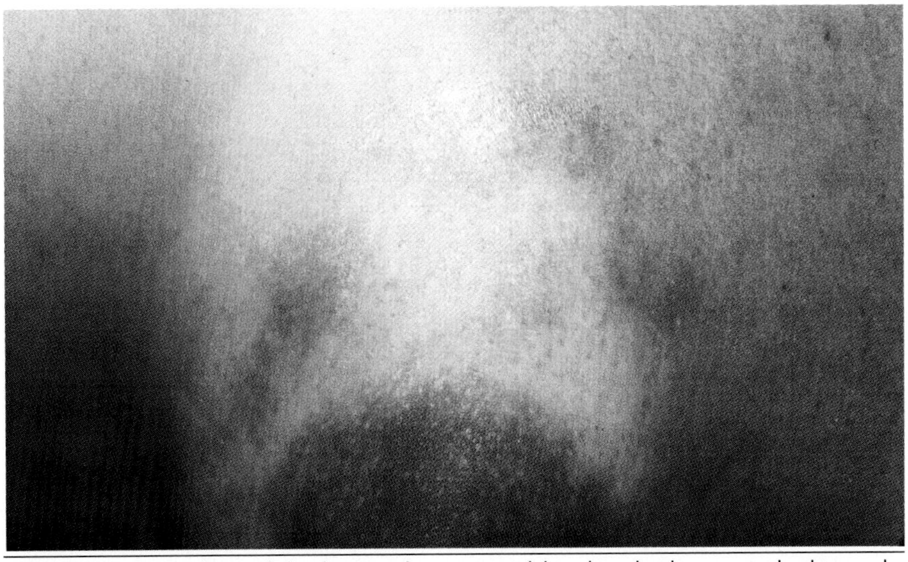

FIGURE 7-1 Morphea of the breast characterized by sharply demarcated white, sclerotic, indurated plaque. (Courtesy of Rick Stearns, M.D., Tulsa, OK)

In contrast to CREST syndrome, patients with diffuse scleroderma have a rapid progression of skin disease over several months to involve the fingers, hands, arms, trunk, and legs with thickened immobile skin. In concert with the skin disease, patients frequently develop signs of pulmonary, musculoskeletal, gastrointestinal, heart, and occasionally (10% of patients) kidney disease early in the course of their disease. Nailfold capillary dilatation and capillary dropout are common. These patients do not have anticentromere antibodies but do have a variety of antibodies that target the autoantigens located in the nucleolus of cells. Anti-topoisomerase I antibodies occur in approximately 30% of patients. The prognosis of diffuse scleroderma is improving, but approximately 25% of patients do not survive 5 years, with cardiopulmonary disease being the most common cause of death.

Diffuse scleroderma:
truncal and acral disease
renal and other systemic involvement
Anti-topoisomerase I antibodies

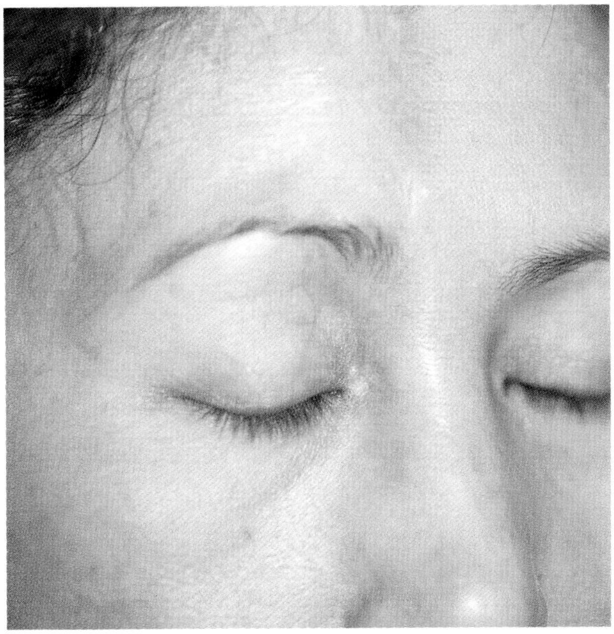

FIGURE 7-2 Linear morphea of the forehead, early coup de sabre lesion.

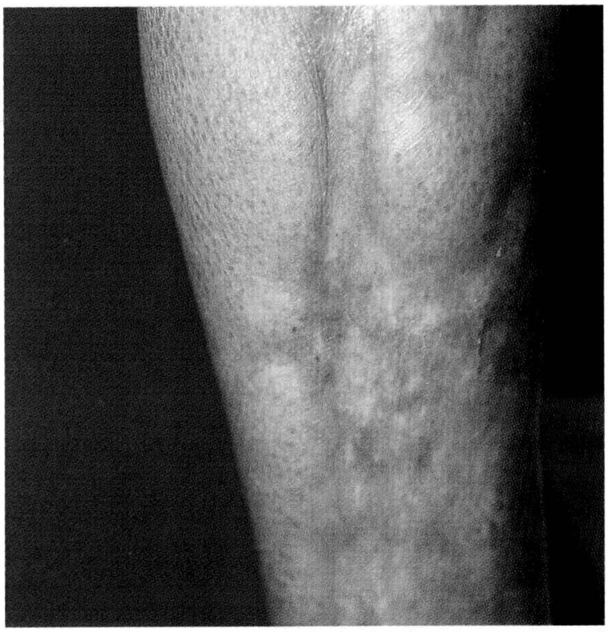

FIGURE 7-3 Linear scleroderma of the lower leg.

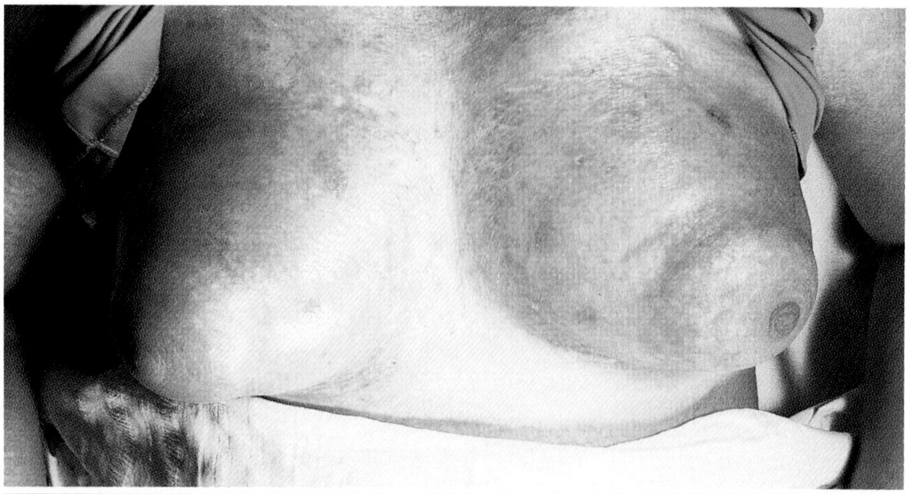

FIGURE 7–4 Young woman with generalized localized morphea involving chest.

A chronology of historic events in the development of our knowledge of scleroderma is presented in Table 7–3.

Etiology

The etiology of scleroderma is unknown. However, evidence accumulated during the past 20 years strongly implicates an autoimmune, genetically determined disease. Like other autoimmune diseases, the following features have been observed in scleroderma:

1. A familial clustering of scleroderma occurs rarely, but autoimmune disease is frequently present in other family members
2. Autoantibodies in systemic sclerosis patients and their first-degree relatives
3. Female predominance

Pathogenesis

The pathogenesis of scleroderma is unknown. Several features, however, must be explained. These are (1) autoantibody formation; (2) overproduction of collagen, fibronectin, and glycosaminoglycans by fibroblasts; (3) widespread vascular lesions (intimal and medial proliferation and vasospasm).

Autoantibodies

Autoantibodies are detected in approximately 90% of patients with systemic sclerosis (Table 7–4).

TABLE 7–1 Localized Scleroderma

Plaque morphea
Guttate morphea
Generalized morphea
Linear scleroderma
Coup de sabre
Nodular or keloid sclerosis

TABLE 7–2 Systemic Sclerosis: Limited and Diffuse

Sign or Symptom	Limited Cutaneous	Diffuse Cutaneous
Raynaud's phenomenon	May antedate by decades	Generally occurs within 1 year
Nailfold microscopy	Dilated capillary loops	Dilated loops with capillary dropout
Distribution of sclerosis	Acral	Acral and truncal
Visceral involvement*	Occurs late (> 10 years after onset)	Occurs early (within 5 years of onset)
Autoantibodies	Anticentromere antibodies	Anti-topoisomerase antibodies

* In general, limited cutaneous systemic sclerosis has no constitutional symptoms and minimal progression, with systemic involvement occurring after 10 years of disease. Diffuse cutaneous systemic sclerosis is generally characterized by rapid progression with visceral involvement during first 5 years of disease.

Anti–Scl-70 antibodies 70-kD degradation of 100-kD topoisomerase polypeptide

In addition to a positive antinuclear antibody determination, specific antinuclear and antinucleolar antibodies are frequently present. Anti–Scl-70, an antibody directed against a 70-kD degradation product of the 100-kD polypeptide, topoisomerase I, is very specific for patients with the diffuse form of systemic sclerosis. It is generally not seen in scleroderma patients with the limited cutaneous scleroderma.

Anticentromere antibodies directed against polypeptides of inner and outer kinetochore plates of centromere of chromosomes

The anticentromere antibody is directed against 17-, 80-, and 140-kD proteins located in the inner and outer kinetochore plates of the centromere of chromosomes. These antibodies are detected most commonly by indirect immunofluorescence of cells in metaphase (Figure 7–5). These antibodies are generally found in scleroderma patients with limited cutaneous scleroderma. Anticentromere antibodies are seen in less than 1% of patients with diffuse cutaneous scleroderma. In a percentage of patients with diffuse scleroderma, antinucleolar antibodies are found. For example, antibodies against RNA polymerase I associate with diffuse cutaneous scleroderma and cardiac involvement. Antifibrillarin (anti–U_3RNP protein) are less common but associate with diffuse cutaneous disease and severe lung involvement. Anti–PM-SCL antibodies are detected in a group of patients with features of scleroderma and myositis (see Table 7–4).

U_1RNP antibodies associated with MCTD

Anti-U_1RNP antibodies are detected most commonly in SLE patients but also in a small group of MCTD patients who have features of scleroderma, polymyositis, and lupus erythematosus. (See discussions on scleroderma overlap syndromes.)

TABLE 7–3 Glossary of Events in Development of Knowledge about Scleroderma

1753	Carlo Curzio, in Naples, Italy, first describes diffuse scleroderma, probably Buschke's scleredema.
1862	Maurice Raynaud describes syndrome that today bears his name.
1892	Osler reports pulmonary and renal causes of death in scleroderma.
1893	Hutchinson describes association of sclerosis and Raynaud's.
1910	Thibierge and Weissenbach describe acrosclerosis, vascular alterations, and calcium deposits.
1943	Weiss describes myocardial involvement.
1945	Goetz reports systemic involvement in scleroderma.
1964	Winterbauer describes CREST syndrome.
1975	Shulman describes eosinophilic fasciitis.
1980	Tan et al. describe anticentromere and anti–Scl-70 antibodies in systemic sclerosis.
1989	Description of eosinophil myalgia syndrome following L-tryptophan ingestion.

TABLE 7–4 Autoantibodies in Systemic Sclerosis

Antibody	Epitope	Comments
NUCLEAR ANTIBODIES		
Anti–Scl-70	Topoisomerase I	Found predominantly in diffuse scleroderma
Anticentromere	Kinetochore/centromere	Found predominantly in limited scleroderma
Anti-RNA polymerase III	RNA polymerase III complex	Diffuse cutaneous disease
Anti-U_1RNP	Splicesome	Overlap syndrome (MCTD)
NUCLEOLAR ANTIBODIES		
Antibody	**Epitope**	**Comments**
Anti-RNA polymerase I	RNA polymerase I complex	Diffuse cutaneous disease, increased organ involvement
Antifibrillarin	U_3RNP protein	Diffuse cutaneous disease
Anti–PM-Scl	Complex of 11 proteins	Limited cutaneous disease, myositis
Anti-NOR 90	Nucleolus organizer	N/A
Anti-To(Th)RNP	Proteined complex with 7-2 and 8-2 RNAs	Limited cutaneous disease

MCTD = mixed connective tissue disease; PM = polymyositis; Scl = scleroderma; NOR = nucleolus organizer region.

Almost every patient with scleroderma has evidence of an autoimmune reaction (an immune response directed against self-proteins or tissues) manifested by the presence of specific antibodies to autoantigens; T cells (CD4 and CD8) are found in abnormal numbers in their tissues (eg, skin, heart, lungs). These T cells can cause tissue damage (eg, perturb vascular endothelium) or, when activated, secrete chemicals (cytokines) that can then activate other cells (eg, fibroblast) or tissues. T cells can also directly kill cells by activating apoptosis, causing a cascade and/or amplifying loops of inflammatory events. Some think that these interacting inflammatory events feed each other and, in part, explain why scleroderma is a chronic disease. Despite the finding of an autoimmune process in scleroderma, the disease process does not appear to respond to immunosuppressive therapy (eg, corticosteroids).

One way to view the activation of the immune system is to find antibodies in the blood of patients that are very specific to scleroderma (Figure 7–5). These are usually IgG (immunoglobulin) of high titer, persistently present and directed against specific epitopes on the antigen. This finding supports the concept that the immune response is driven by the antigen itself and is T cell dependent. This suggests that the process that breaks tolerance to these self-antigens is occurring at unique and specific sites in the cells involved and is key to understanding scleroderma.

T-cell autoreactivity against cryptic antigens

Several studies have shown that the autoimmune response in scleroderma is driven by self-antigens and is T cell dependent. Accumulating data demonstrate that a potential for T-cell autoreactivity resides in the immunologic nonequivalency of different areas of self-molecules, since self-tolerance is only induced to efficiently presented dominant epitopes and not to the many cryptic ones. Therefore, autoreactive T cells that have not previously encountered cryptic self-epitopes are potentially present and available to react to newly exposed cryptic self-antigens. As determinant dominance is influenced by protein structure, circumstances that change the molecular context of epitopes (eg, molecule cleavage, altered conformation of tertiary structure) may permit the efficient presentation of previously cryptic determinants, thereby breaking tolerance. For exam-

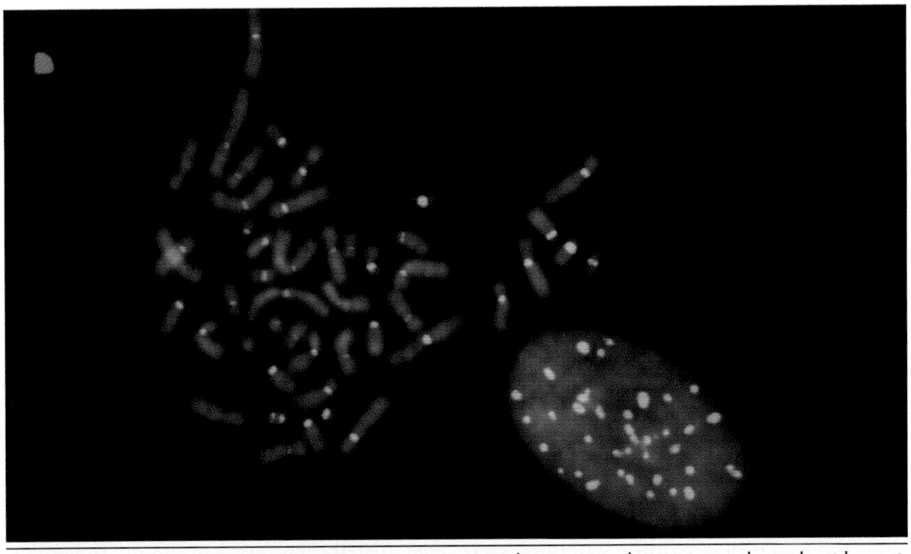

FIGURE 7–5 Chromosome preparation in metaphase as substrate incubated with anti-centromere antibodies from a CREST syndrome patient; developed with rhodamine conjugated anti–human IgG antisera.

ple, ultraviolet-induced apoptosis of keratinocytes causes lupus autoantigens to cluster and become concentrated in surface blebs of apoptotic cells where several of the molecules are specially cleaved by proteases of the caspase family. The fact that specific proteolytic cleavage unifies these lupus autoantigens has suggested that fragmentation might be one mechanism that defines molecules as autoantigens and has prompted the search for autoantigen fragmentation in other autoimmune diseases.

Reactive oxygen species

In scleroderma, one potential mechanism that might result in specific fragmentation of scleroderma autoantigens is suggested by the striking clinical problem of ischemia reperfusion (RP) that occurs in the tissues of these patients. Widespread vascular disease leads to dysfunction of the small arteries and arterioles of the extremities, skin, and internal organs of patients with scleroderma. There is a large body of knowledge which supports the notion that free radical species produce the tissue injury that follows reperfusion of ischemic tissues. The vascular disease in scleroderma has been implicated in the production of reactive oxygen species (ROS) in the tissues of patients with scleroderma. Studies in our laboratory (Rosen et al.) have underscored that several of the autoantigens targeted in diffuse scleroderma are unified by their susceptibility to modification by ROS. Thus, topoisomerase I, the large subunits of RNA polymerases I and II, the 90/100-kD nucleolus organizer region protein/upstream binding factor (NOR 90/UBF), and the 70-kD protein component of the U_1snRNP (U_1–70 kD) are all fragmented at highly specific sites on exposure to ROS. Interestingly, only scleroderma-specific or overlap antigens were susceptible to fragmentation by this mechanism. Although the scleroderma autoantigens are unified by their ability to bind metals and by their unique susceptibility to fragmentation by ROS, the circumstances under which such fragments might be produced in vivo are not yet known, and the immunogenicity of fragments, compared with intact autoantigens, has not yet been addressed. It is likely that the formation of ROS and the intranucleolar accumulation of metals play a pivotal role in the vascular injury, inflammation, and tissue fibrosis seen in scleroderma.

The role of T cells has also been studied by investigating the role of T-cell products in altering scleroderma antigens. Granzyme B, a serine protease, is released by T cells and can penetrate cells or act directly on cell surface molecules. Studies have shown that scleroderma autoantigens are susceptible to cleavage by granzyme B. Thus, granzyme B may unmask cryptic antigens by cleaving autoantigens into unique fragments.

Excess Collagen and Extracellular Matrix Production

Small number of fibroblasts are activated

Almost every patient with scleroderma develops a fibrotic reaction (scarring) in the tissues targeted in scleroderma (eg, skin, lungs, heart). It is now known that the fibrosis is caused by excess production of normal types of collagen and other extracellular molecules. Collagen is made by fibroblasts that can be provoked or activated to make more collagen. The excess collagen in tissue causes damage, decreased flexibility, and malfunction of the tissue or organ involved (Figure 7–6). A small proportion of the total number of skin fibroblasts appear to be activated in scleroderma, synthesizing increased quantities of collagen, fibronectin, and other extracellular matrix proteins. Increased amounts of mRNA for these matrix proteins have been detected indicating that the regulatory defect in these activated fibroblasts is at a pretranslational level.

Fibroblasts may be activated by cytokines, low oxygen, or oxygen radicals.

Although there is some evidence that there could be a defect in the fibroblasts themselves, most studies suggest that the fibroblasts are normal, innocent bystander, activated by molecules (eg, cytokines) made during other biologic events. It should be noted that biopsies of new scleroderma lesions will demonstrate, at the fascial and subcutaneous levels, a perivascular mononuclear cell inflammatory infiltrate, which theoretically could be the source of the cytokines inducing the dysregulation of normal collagen and matrix protein synthesis by fibroblasts. For example, cytokines made by activated T cells or other immune or inflammatory cells (eg, macrophages, mast cells, platelets) can activate fibroblasts. Some examples include platelet-derived growth factor released by activated platelets. Transforming growth factor beta and interleukin-1 are additional profibrotic cytokines made by a variety of cells, including macrophages and the fibroblasts themselves. Endothelin-1, produced by activated endothelium of blood vessels, can also activate fibroblasts, suggesting that injured blood vessels may release factors that activate tissue fibroblast to secrete excess collagen. Fibroblasts may also be activated by low oxygen or oxygen radicals produced during ischemic-reperfusion events associated with the vascular disease of scleroderma. Once activated, the fibroblasts may drive themselves by the production of cytokines that act through an autocrine mechanism. However, scleroderma fibroblasts are not transformed; in vitro studies demonstrate that the activated state disappears after several tissue culture passages.

Vascular Abnormalities

Raynaud's phenomenon: color changes
Vasospasm, followed by cyanosis and erythema

Almost every patient with scleroderma has RP (episodic color changes of the skin triggered by cold or emotional stress), associated with finger tissue damage caused by ischemic (low oxygen and nutritional state) events. Disease of the distal small arteries and arterioles of the vascular tree cause these ischemic events. This vascular disturbance can be viewed in the scleroderma patient by witnessing dramatic changes in skin color after cold exposure (RP).

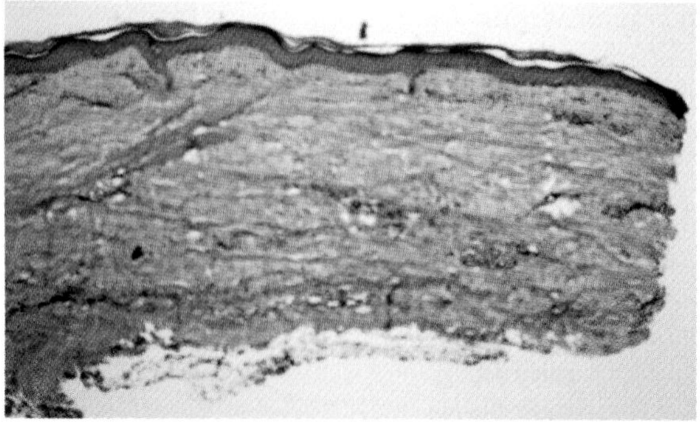

FIGURE 7–6 Biopsy of a patient with generalized, localized morphea. Note square shape of the 4-mm biopsy due to proliferation of collagen.

The vascular disease causes vasospasm, narrowing of the lumen secondary to fibrosis of the intimal layer, and occlusion secondary to either intravascular clotting or complete loss of the vessel lumen. This vessel disease causes low blood flow to the skin, loss of normal nutrition, and induces skin ulcerations or digital amputation. We now know that the low blood flow caused by the vascular disease can lead to tissue damage in much the same way that coronary vasospasm leads to a heart attack or that hardening of the arteries (arteriosclerosis) leads to a stroke in the brain. Damaged and malfunctioning blood vessels cause the production of oxygen radicals and cytokines that can cause tissue damage.

Raynaud's phenomenon occurs systemically.

Vascular endothelial cells may be targets in scleroderma.

The vascular disease is not limited to the skin but is also seen in all the organs targeted in scleroderma (eg, lungs, heart, kidneys, gastrointestinal tract). Vasospasm (RP) of the small arteries of the kidney can cause severe hypertension, kidney infarction, and, occasionally, renal failure. Episodic vasospasm and disease of the endomyocardial vessels of the heart cause contraction band necrosis and focal areas of fibrosis. Arrhythmia or cardiomyopathy results from this cardiac tissue damage. Disease of the pulmonary vessels can cause severe pulmonary hypertension and progressive right heart failure. Gastrointestinal dysfunction is also thought to be secondary to small artery disease in the vessels of the esophagus and gut.

Studies in scleroderma have shown that the small arteries and arterioles of the arterial tree are disturbed, activated, or injured, with a narrowed lumen that prevents normal blood flow to the skin or other organs. These small arteries lose normal control of vascular reactivity and thus undergo episodes of vasospasm (RP). Although the exact cause of this abnormality is unknown, the vessels are overly sensitive to cold temperature and other sympathetic stimuli. Perturbation of cutaneous vessels from scleroderma patients show a 300-fold increase in $alpha_2$ adrenergic smooth muscle receptors. This increase in adrenergic receptors likely causes the increased sensitivity to sympathetic stimuli.

Recent studies also indicate the frequent presence of antiendothelial antibodies in scleroderma patients suggesting that some immune injury to the blood vessel occurs. It is theorized that the primary injury may be to the endothelium that disturbs normal vessel function. The scleroderma vessels also have evidence of endothelial cell dysfunction. Normal endothelium function is key to normal vascular physiology. The endothelium is important in controlling coagulation and platelet activation, trafficking inflammatory cells, regulating local blood flow by secreting important constrictors (eg, endothelin-1) and vasodilators (eg, nitric oxide and prostacyclin), and producing mediators and regulators of inflammation (eg, oxygen radicals and cytokines). Disturbance of the endothelial cells of the blood vessel can produce many of the features of scleroderma vascular disease with a tendency to vasoconstriction, local tissue ischemia, and occlusive vascular events. It is conceivable that the endothelial cell of blood vessels is a target in systemic sclerosis. In addition to the possible direct toxic effects of specific autoantibodies directed against endothelial cell surface molecules, it is highly conceivable that cytokines released by inflammatory cells may target this organelle. In addition, endothelial cells may be perturbed to produce and release additional cytokines which could target fibroblasts or other endothelial cells.

Proliferation of intimal cells

Histologic studies demonstrate proliferation of cells in the intimal layer of the vessel and excessive collagen and other extracellular matrix narrowing the vessel lumen. It is thought that following vessel injury, the smooth muscle cell of the vessel is activated and migrates into the intimal cell, where it changes its phenotype from a contractile cell to a secretory fibroblast-like cell that produces excess collagen and fibrosis.

Understanding the cause of the blood vessel disturbance and disease in scleroderma is key to understanding the cause of scleroderma. Unproven theories in scleroderma suggest that the blood vessels are injured by the immune system (an autoimmune reaction), or by an infection, by an environmental toxin yet to be discovered. Some think there is a genetic defect in the control of the blood vessels and that repeated vasospasm causes the damage.

Abnormal neovascularization

There is also evidence of abnormal neovascularization in scleroderma. Telangiectasias appear as erythematous cutaneous spots that blanch on pressure and are a manifestation of abnormal capillary proliferation. Abnormalities in the nailfold capillaries can be viewed using microscopy after applying immersion oil to the skin surface. In early scleroderma, the nailfold capillaries appear enlarged; in the later stages of scleroderma, the nailfold capillaries are attenuated and bizarre in appearance (Figure 7–7). Although clinically silent, similar failed neovascularization is seen in other involved organs.

FIGURE 7–7 Cuticle nailfold telangiectasia in a scleroderma patient.

Clinical Features

Cutaneous Manifestations

Localized scleroderma generally located only to the skin

Although the localized forms of scleroderma (ie, morphea, linear scleroderma including coup de sabre and generalized morphea) generally are not associated with systemic manifestations, systemic involvement does occur on occasion. Hence, patients with systemic sclerosis sine scleroderma (ie, the presence of systemic sclerosis in the absence of cutaneous features) can have patches of cutaneous morphea. Likewise, some patients with systemic sclerosis will have localized scleroderma lesions. For example, a patient with generalized morphea was reported to have developed not only cutaneous bullous scleroderma but also gastrointestinal involvement producing lymphatic obstruction, which resulted in a protein-losing enteropathy. Furthermore, patients with linear scleroderma have been shown to frequently possess antibodies in their sera directed against single-stranded DNA (anti-ssDNA), and patients with morphea often have antihistone antibodies, suggesting a subtle but definite alteration in immune regulation.

Classically, cutaneous scleroderma is divided into three phases: the early edematous phase, classic sclerosis, and the late phase.

Early Edematous Phase

The earliest changes are limited to the development of swelling of the hands and feet, producing sclerosis of the fingers (sclerodactyly) (Figure 7–8). RP often antedates the development of tissue edema by years or occurs concomitantly with the onset. With the development of sclerodactyly, small painful ulcerations can occur at the tips of the fingers producing pitted scars. Repeated ischemic events in the progression of the disease causes digital sclerosis and resorption of the tissues of the fingerpad and, sometimes, distal bone (Figure 7–9). Subcutaneous calcinosis in small clusters is a frequent finding in CREST syndrome. Telangiectasia of hands and face also may occur (Figure 7–10).

As noted above, the limited form of systemic sclerosis is characterized by acral sclerosis and slow progression of the disease over many years. Tautness, fibrosing, and binding down of the skin over the dorsal portion of the hands is characteristic, together with the onset of facial involvement, producing an effacement of normal wrinkles. Tightness of the skin around the mouth and decreased oral aperature make it difficult for a dentist to perform operative procedures

(Figure 7–11). Facial and mucous membrane telangiectasia, (lips, tongue, or soft palate) are prominent in the limited form of scleroderma. In the diffuse form of the disease, the edema of the early inflammatory phase rapidly spreads to the forearms, upper arms, trunk, and legs. Vitiligo-like depigmentation and hyperpigmentation develop in the sclerotic areas of the skin, particularly of the dorsal hands, upper chest, upper back, forehead, and lower legs.

Classic Sclerotic Phase

Additional manifestations of scleroderma, generally occurring during the sclerotic phase, are coarseness and dryness of the skin, with decreased sweating and absence of hair growth. Prominent flexion contractures of the proximal interphalangeal joints of the fingers, wrist, or elbows and loss of hand function are the most disfiguring and disabling features of scleroderma. In the diffuse form of scleroderma, contractures of the wrists, elbows, shoulder girdles, knees, and ankles are severe complications associated with muscle atrophy and weakness.

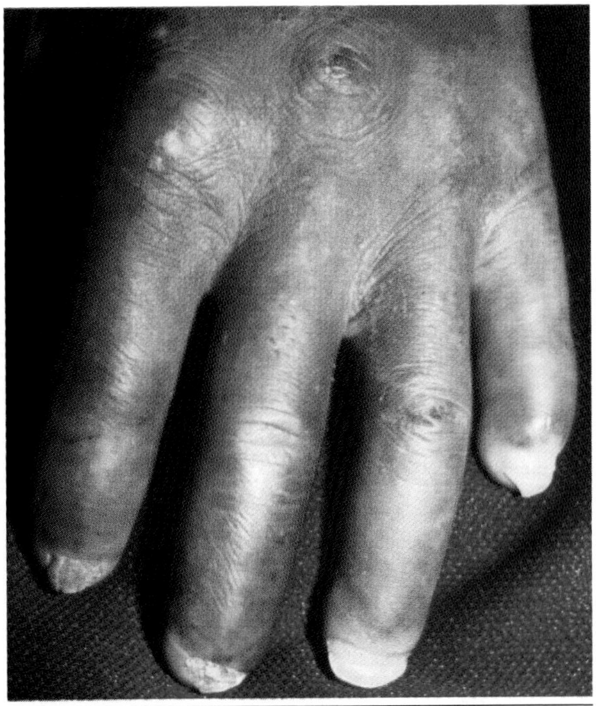

FIGURE 7–8 Swollen edematous fingers of patient with sclerodactyly.

Late Phase

Following the edematous and sclerotic forms of scleroderma, the late form, characterized by a generalized softening of the sclerotic skin of the trunk, arms, and legs occurs. However, the features of sclerodactyly generally persist. At times, the resolution of the cutaneous sclerosis can be striking, leaving only a residuum of hyperpigmentation. Mottled hypopigmentation with perifollicular hyperpigmentation can occur, producing a bizarre cutaneous pigmentation pattern. Ulceration of the skin is also a late complication.

At times, hyperpigmentation is only residuum of a scleroderma lesion

Raynaud's Phenomenon

RP is common, affecting 5 to 20% of adults. Most of these individuals are females who do not have any underlying disease process (primary RP). Less than 10% of patients with RP develop a connective tissue disease; scleroderma has the highest prevalence of RP among the rheumatic diseases. Abnormal vessel reac-

Only 10% of Raynaud's phenomena patients develop a connective tissue disease.

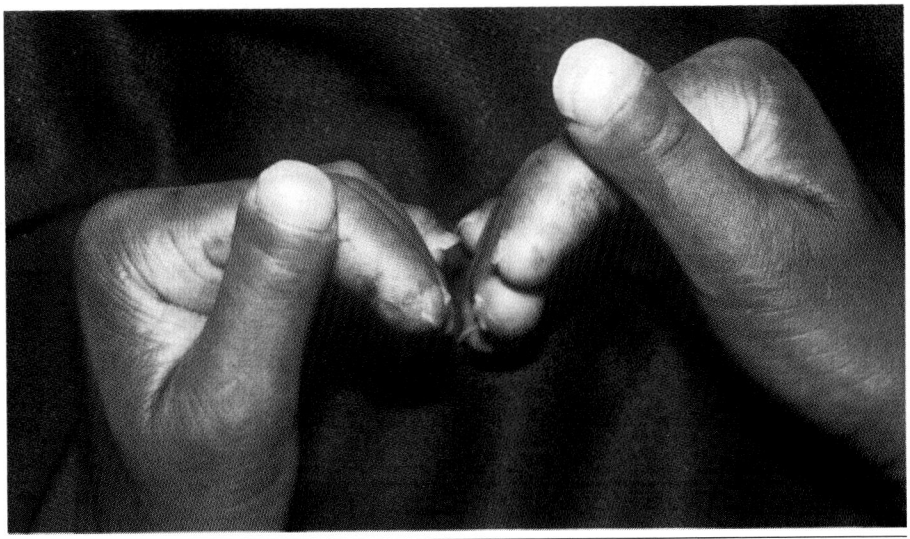

FIGURE 7–9 Lateral view of patient in Figure 7–8 showing resorption of terminal fat pads.

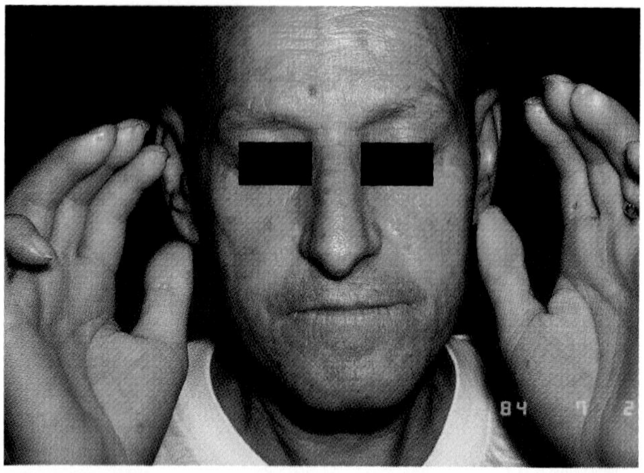

FIGURE 7–10 Patient with CREST syndrome demonstrating sclerodactyly facial involvement with perioral sclerosis and matted telangiectasia.

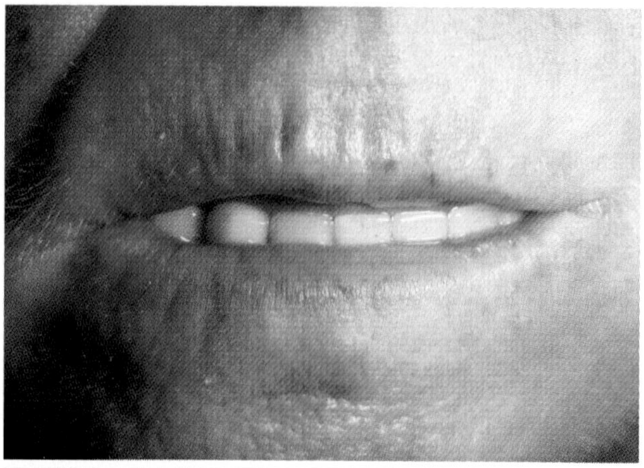

FIGURE 7–11 Radial perioral furrowing in a patient with limited scleroderma.

tivity to the environment affects the digits of the feet and hands and is initiated by cold exposure or emotional stress, resulting in the following:

1. The appearance of pallor of the digits (fingers, toes, nose, and rarely ears) is sharply demarcated involving the distal portion of the digits.
2. Cyanosis and numbness follow.
3. A diffuse erythema occurs with reperfusion and is generally associated with a "pins and needles" sensation or pain.

RP usually precedes onset of connective tissue disease

This phenomenon occurs in the digits of at least 90% of systemic sclerosis patients and is implicated in the vascular disease of esophageal, pulmonary, renal, and myocardial vasculature. RP usually precedes the development of sclerodermous features by weeks to years; rarely does sclerosis occur without RP. Patients with diffuse cutaneous systemic sclerosis have a short interval between the onset of RP and other manifestations of the disease (Table 7–5).

Avascular areas in cuticle nailfolds seen in connective tissue disease patients.

Nailfold investigations of the capillaries can be facilitated by the use of an ophthalmoscope or a hand lens. Normally, the capillaries are small, evenly spaced and orientated in a perpendicular manner to the nail. The capillary nailfold pattern in patients at risk of developing a connective tissue disease demonstrates irregular shapes and dilatation of the arterial, apical, and venular portions of the capillary loop. Furthermore, avascular areas, caused by the loss of capillaries (dropout), occur either diffusely or in areas adjacent to enlarged capillaries.

Gastrointestinal Involvement

Esophageal dysfunction

Loss of normal gastrointestinal function is present to some degree in almost every patient with scleroderma. Decreased flexibility of the face impairs normal movement and decreases the oral aperature, altering chewing in some patients. Pharyngeal dysfunction is an uncommon complication usually associated with polymyositis. Esophageal dysmotility occurs in approximately 90% of patients with systemic sclerosis and may antedate the development of cutaneous sclerosis. In the early phase of scleroderma, esophageal dysmotility may be asymptomatic, only detected by direct measurements of esophageal function. Over time,

TABLE 7–5 Raynaud's Phenomenon: Features Indicative of Increased Risk of a Connective Tissue Disease

Development of Raynaud's phenomenon after the age of 20 years
More severe Raynaud's phenomenon
Antinuclear antibodies
Abnormal nailfold microscopy

the patients will generally experience dysphagia of solids or liquids and retrosternal pain (heartburn) following meals or at night during sleep. Poor clearance of swallowed material and reflux of gastric acid into the distal esophagus causes esophagitis, mucosal ulceration, local blood loss, and stricture. Replacement of the squamous epithelium by columnar epithelium (Barrett's esophagus) predates stricture formation and rarely adenocarcinoma. Gastric contents and acid flow back into the distal esophagus because of abnormal gastric emptying (gastroparesis) and low pressure of the lower esophageal sphincter.

Small bowel involvement

Malabsorption

Small bowel involvement is manifested clinically by abdominal distension and changes in bowel habit. Hypomotility, secondary to microvascular disease, muscular wall atrophy, and fibrosis can lead to stasis, bacterial overgrowth, and malabsorption. Progressive weight loss despite reasonable caloric intake should make one think of malabsorption. Diarrhea usually presents with floating, foul-smelling stools indicative of steatorrhea and malabsorption. Severe involvement of the small bowel can also produce an adynamic ileus (pseudo-obstruction) manifested by abdominal pain and distension or leakage of gas into the bowel wall and peritoneal cavity (pneumatosis intestinalis).

Large bowel involvement

Wide-mouth diverticula

Involvement of the large bowel is generally asymptomatic. Wide-mouth diverticula form as the bowel wall becomes fibrotic and thinned. Severe hypomotility can cause pseudo-obstruction, toxic megacolon, bowel rupture, or volvulus. Constipation alternating with diarrhea is a common symptom of large bowel disease. Stool incontinence secondary to an inflexible bowel and involvement of the rectal sphincters are an unusual manifestation.

Myocardial Involvement

Myocardial fibrosis

Myocardial involvement is usually asymptomatic and is not appreciated until late complications occur. Reversible vasospasm of the myocardial vasculature has been demonstrated during cold-induced RP. Contraction-band necrosis and myocardial fibrosis are a consequence of repeated ischemia-reperfusion injury and microvascular disease. Diastolic dysfunction and cardiomyopathy are late manifestations of scleroderma heart disease. Conduction abnormalities or arrhythmias occur frequently. Pericardial effusions are often seen during echocardiographic studies of the heart. These are usually asymptomatic but can be associated with pericarditis or tamponade hemodynamics. Pulmonary hypertension or severe lung disease can lead to right-sided heart failure. Involvement of the heart has a guarded prognosis.

Pulmonary Involvement

Pulmonary fibrosis

In scleroderma, fibrosing alveolitis and pulmonary vascular disease involve the lungs. Pulmonary involvement is common, with dyspnea on exertion being the earliest symptom. Severe interstitial fibrosis of the lung is more likely to occur in diffuse scleroderma in African Americans and in patients with anti-topoisomerase antibodies. Pulmonary function testing is the most sensitive method to detect disease. A low-diffusing capacity and/or forced vital capacity often precede symptoms. Chest radiography demonstrates lower lobe interstitial fibrosis in more advanced disease. Fibrosis of the alveolar wall and pulmonary vessels causes a restrictive ventilatory defect with a decrease in normal gas exchange. On unusual occasions, patients develop pneumothorax, pleural involvement, or respiratory distress secondary to respiratory muscle involvement.

Pulmonary hypertension

Pulmonary hypertension, attributable to pulmonary vascular disease, is a serious and life-threatening complication. The vascular disease is typical of the vasculopathy of scleroderma, with marked intimal fibrosis, loss of vessel lumen, and some medial hyperplasia. Isolated pulmonary hypertension in the absence of significant lung fibrosis occurs in approximately 10% of patients with CREST syndrome. Studies have attempted to demonstrate that pulmonary vasoconstriction analogous to RP occurs in the lungs of these patients. Severe pulmonary hypertension in this setting has a very poor prognosis, with few patients surviving 3 years.

Renal Manifestations

Renal hypertension, a potentially lethal complication

Ischemic necrosis of the kidneys with uncontrollable hypertension is a dreaded complication of systemic sclerosis. Approximately 10% of patients with diffuse scleroderma have this complication, which generally occurs early in the course of the diffuse form of systemic sclerosis.

The characteristic feature of renal involvement is intimal proliferation of small and medium arteries. In a renal crisis, there is vasoconstriction (RP of renal vessels) of arcuate arteries and a reduction in renal blood flow. A microangiopathic process causes rapid anemia and thrombocytopenia. The process can produce a devastating renal cortical ischemia, loss of glomerular function, and tissue necrosis.

Musculoskeletal Involvement

Nonerosive polyarthropathy

A nonerosive polyarthropathy that is less likely to have significant synovial hypertrophy is typical in scleroderma. It usually involves the fingers, elbows, shoulders, and knees and is more common in patients with diffuse scleroderma. Fibrotic periarticular inflammation involving tendons and ligaments can produce the characteristic friction rubs and lead to flexion contractures. This process responds poorly to anti-inflammatory medication and is a major cause of disability in these patients.

Muscle fibrosis

Myopathy in scleroderma is a frequent complication and is often caused by more than one process. The fibrotic skin can immobilize movement and lead to disuse atrophy, malnutrition can cause muscle weakness, muscle fibrosis can be part of the scleroderma process, and polymyositis can directly involve striated muscle.

Treatment

There is no drug that has been proven safe and effective in the treatment of scleroderma. The course of the disease is highly variable and is different for patients with limited versus diffuse skin disease. Drugs used for scleroderma need to be tested in a placebo-controlled trial design to make sure that the patients are uniform in both subsets and disease activity. Most of the current treatment that has proven beneficial is directed at specific organ involvement. There are several disease-modifying drugs that are used and under study.

Cutaneous Disease

D-penicillamine has been the traditional drug used to treat patients with diffuse cutaneous scleroderma. However, a recent multicenter trial comparing high-dose D-penicillamine with low-dose D-penicillamine (125 mg every other day) found no difference in the clinical outcome of the skin score between the two treatment groups. This study suggests that D-penicillamine is not effective in scleroderma and has dampened the enthusiasm for use of this drug.

Colchicine, dimethyl sulfoxide, and para-aminobenzoate potassium are not recommended due to lack of efficacy in clinical trials. Studies with photopheresis demonstrate some mild reduction in skin score, but the study design was criticized, and the treatment is expensive.

Topical psoralen plus ultraviolet A (PUVA) therapy has been reported to be helpful for localized scleroderma and may reduce the pruritis of diffuse scleroderma. Provost and Morrison have treated several patients (generalized-localized morphea, morphea, and acral sclerotic form of scleroderma) with good success. Controlled studies with PUVA are needed. (See Chapter 71, "Phototherapy and Photochemotherapy," for more details.)

A recent, small (n = 6) unblinded series found that minocycline dramatically improved skin score. Most scleroderma experts are skeptical about this finding, and more studies will be needed.

Interferon therapy was initially reported helpful, but a new controlled trial reported no difference between placebo and interferon in patients with active diseases.

A number of immunosuppressive drugs have been studied (eg, chlorambucil, 5-fluorouracil, cyclophosphamide), but the evidence about their efficacy is not conclusive. Low-dose, weekly methotrexate was initially reported to improve the skin score in scleroderma; however, it now appears to be especially helpful for patients with active myositis or arthritis and of little benefit for the skin sclerosis or overall disease process.

Corticosteroids (pulse therapy or low doses) have been used and are helpful for myositis or active arthritis. Their role as a disease modifier is not proven. We believe that corticosteroids do not dampen the disease, and that the risk of precipitating a renal crisis is real.

Currently, there are a number of new agents being tested. Relaxin, a small peptide that rises during pregnancy and is known to downregulate collagen production, is now under study. An initial controlled trial found that relaxin decreased skin score of patients with diffuse scleroderma, compared with placebo. However, a new large multicenter study found no benefit of relaxin, compared with placebo.

Inhibition of profibrotic cytokines, such as endothelin-1 or transforming growth factor beta, could potentially help.

Recent studies suggest that patients with scleroderma are suffering from a type of chronic graft-versus-host disease because women with scleroderma are chronically engrafted with higher numbers of fetal cells than are controls. This finding and the concept that scleroderma is an autoimmune disease have inspired the treatment with autologous bone transplantation. Thus far, the reported results are too few to come to any conclusion, but clearly this type of therapy should be limited to a select group of patients with malignant diffuse disease.

Finally, there are a variety of other strategies being used for active diffuse disease, including high-dose cyclophosphamide, low-dose cyclophosphamide, mycophenolate, anti–tumor necrosis factor therapy, halofuginone, thalidomide, and oral tolerance to collagen.

When one reviews the long list of drugs used to control the scleroderma process, it becomes clear that no drug has been proven safe and effective. Therefore, it is recommended that patients with active diffuse scleroderma be treated in research centers specializing in developing new therapy. While the search continues for a disease-modifying drug, treatment for specific organ involvement needs to be aggressive.

No therapy, thus far, has been proven effective.

Raynaud's Phenomenon

Cold avoidance is the most potent therapy for all patients with RP. For example, patients with scleroderma have infrequent digital ischemic events and, therefore, much less intense RP during the summer months. Patients need to be educated about specific methods to avoid cold exposure including preheating the car in winter, using a space heater at work, and having someone else in the family shop in the cold areas of stores. Wearing layers of loose-fitting warm clothing during cold exposure is most important. The head should be covered, and gloves and warm stockings should be worn. Chemical heaters placed in gloves or pockets are very useful.

It may be difficult for patients to completely eliminate every attack; therefore, reasonable goals of therapy need to be established. Eliminating ischemic ulcerations and other more intense events can be accomplished. White attacks are characteristic of severe ischemia and loss of nutritional blood flow. Mottling with acrocyanosis is more common and usually is associated with closure of the highly temperature-sensitive thermoregulatory arteriovenous shunts in the skin. When this mottling of the skin is secondary only to vasospasm, it usually is not associated with cutaneous ulceration or gangrene (Figure 7–12). Vasodilators often can reduce white attacks, but it may be difficult to totally eliminate acrocyanosis.

Protective gloves and chemical heaters are effective.

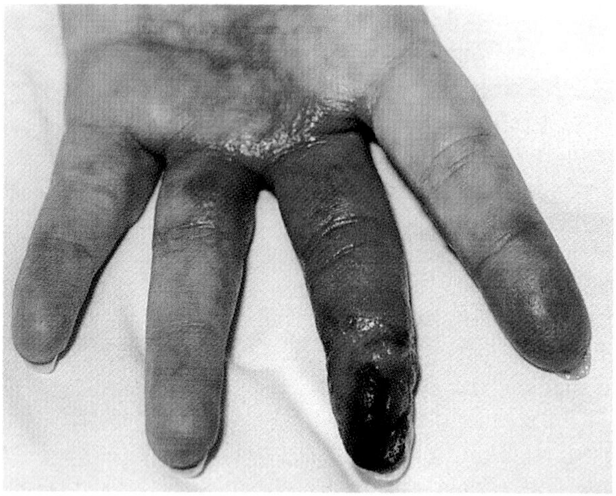

FIGURE 7–12 Raynaud's phenomenon in a scleroderma patient with gangrene.

Education is also important because it not only helps the patient understand what to do, it also decreases the severity and frequency of the RP attacks by reducing fear and tension. It is well known that emotional stress can trigger RP, and it can increase the cold sensitivity. In fact, creating a psychological stress can increase the likelihood that the patient will have an attack during cold exposure. Eliminating all aggravating factors is helpful. The most common problem is smoking because nicotine is a potent vasoconstrictor. A recent study showed that chronic smokers were more likely to have acute vasoconstriction following a smoke than a nonsmoker. This suggests that smoking can sensitize the vessels to cold-induced constriction. Several drugs have been implicated in aggravating or causing RP. These include unselected beta blockers, clonidine, interferon, chemotherapeutic drugs (eg, bleomycin), ergots, and over-the-counter cold preparations containing sympathomimetic agents.

Eliminate smoking

Behavioral therapy reportedly reduces RP attacks, but there is controversy as to which type of therapy is truly helpful. A recent, large multicenter study trial in primary RP comparing thermal biofeedback with nifedipine found that thermal biofeedback was no better than placebo or a control electromyogram procedure in scleroderma. The use of acupuncture or herbal medicine cannot be recommended because of the lack of adequate data and the fact that the placebo effect can reduce the attack rate of RP.

Calcium channel blockers

Patients with scleroderma should all be treated with vasodilators, if possible, because they are at risk for tissue ischemia and its complications, including digital ulcerations or digital amputations. It is also thought that vasodilator therapy may help other organs targeted by the vascular disease associated with scleroderma. Sympatholytic agents, adrenergic receptor inhibitors, adrenergic inhibitors, and direct vasodilators have been popular modes of treatment. However, calcium channel blockers (CCBs) continue to be the safest and most effective agents for the treatment of RP. The first agent to be tested was nifedipine, and it has remained one of the most popular. The published clinical trials used short-acting nifedipine at doses from 10 to 30 mg three times daily. However, most specialists now use the slow-release preparation of nifedipine in doses from 30 to 120 mg once daily. Currently, amlodipine is quite popular because, like nifedipine, it is a potent vasodilator but has less negative ionatropic effects on the heart. The CCBs are well tolerated, but dizziness, tachycardia, headache, constipation, and edema can occur in some patients.

An angiotensin-converting enzyme (ACE) inhibitor should be helpful in improving local blood flow by increasing kinins; however, their role in severe RP is not well studied. One uncontrolled study of captopril documented improvement in primary RP, but it was not helpful with scleroderma patients. Combinations of vasodilators are often used, but few studies are available to provide guidance. It is our experience that in the treatment of severe RP, combinations are not additive and often not tolerated.

Prostaglandins

Some prostaglandins are potent vasodilators, inhibit platelet aggregation, and have other biologic functions that may improve abnormal vascular reactivity. Treatment of severe refractory RP and ischemic digital ulcers has been reported with prostaglandin E_1 (PGE_1), prostacyclin (PGI_2), and Iloprost (a PGI_2 analogue). A large controlled trial of Iloprost given intravenously to patients with RP secondary to scleroderma found Iloprost effective for short-term palliation of severe RP. Iloprost can rapidly reverse an acute ischemic crisis. The clinical benefit of Iloprost appears to last approximately 8 to 10 weeks. However, one study suggests that CCBs were equally effective as intravenous Iloprost. Oral prostaglandins are now under study in Japan, Europe, and the United States.

A large multicenter study of oral Iloprost found that 50 μg given twice daily for 6 weeks was not better than placebo. Aerosol preparations of prostaglandins are being studied for the treatment of pulmonary hypertension. The exact role of oral prostaglandins in the management of severe RP will have to await more experience and more controlled studies.

Proximal sympathectomy

Controversy still remains as to the role of proximal sympathectomy in the management of RP because there have been no prospective controlled trials of cervical sympathectomy. Most reports are either individual cases or surveys that have included patients with various causes of RP or different types of peripheral vascular disease. A localized microsurgical digital sympathectomy as an alternative to proximal sympathectomy is now used. Because the exact role of digital sympathectomy has not been defined by good controlled investigations, the procedure should be limited to patients who have failed medical treatment. Patients with scleroderma with critical ischemia or active digital ulcers are likely to have some immediate improvement in blood flow following local sympathectomy, but the degree and duration of improvement is quite variable and may be only for a relatively short time. One practice is to only use surgical sympathectomy after temporary chemical sympathectomy demonstrates significant vasodilatation. There is some evidence that the sympathectomy procedure helps because it releases fibrous tissue encasing the digital vessel.

Patients with the CREST variant of scleroderma are more likely to have an ischemic crisis and that may lead to digital amputation. These patients will present with severe RP and critical ischemia that need urgent treatment. In these patients, there is almost always structural disease of the digital vessels and sometimes in the palmar arch, and radial or ulnar vessels. Irreversible obstruction of the vessel lumen may occur from fibrin deposition and platelet activation, aggregation, and clotting. As a result of total obstruction to blood flow, the patient will experience intense ischemic pain that often goes beyond the digit and extends into the hand or limb. Infarction of the skin or deeper tissues can occur suddenly in this setting. Therefore, patients with a demarcated ischemic digit should be hospitalized and given immediate attention. Medical therapy should include the following:

- Put the patient to rest in a warm ambient temperature. Eliminate stressful stimuli and provide adequate pain control, recognizing that narcotics are vasoconstrictors.
- Start vasodilator therapy immediately. Titrate CCBs to maximal tolerated dose. Intravenous prostaglandins (PGE_1, epoprostenol, Iloprost) can be very effective in reversing an acute reversible ischemic event. Phentolamine or nitroprusside infusion also can be helpful.
- Initiate antiplatelet therapy. Low-dose aspirin (81 mg daily) has been the traditional antiplatelet agent, but CCBs and prostaglandins also inhibit platelet function.
- Use temporary chemical digital sympathectomy aggressively. This provides non-narcotic pain relief and can be a potent vasodilator. If the chemical block provides relief, then repeated injections or moving to a surgical digital sympathectomy can be done. In the lower extremity, lumbar sympathectomy can be used.

Ischemic crisis

- Consider using anticoagulation or thrombolytic therapy during the acute phase of an ischemic event, recognizing that these treatments are best limited to embolic or vascular occlusive disease associated with new thrombosis. Anticoagulation with heparin may be used for short periods during a crisis. The use of chronic anticoagulation has not been studied and is generally not recommended. Patients with antiphospholipid antibodies with digital ischemia may require anticoagulation. Studies have suggested that thrombolytic therapy (eg, urokinase tissue plasminogen activator) may be helpful for patients with RP and scleroderma. However, controlled studies will need to be done before we know if this approach will reverse acute ischemia in severe RP.
- Often, the patients are seen in the later stages of ischemia, or they have severe structural disease without the capacity to vasodilate. In these patients, pain control and surgical amputation may be the only option.

Gastrointestinal Disease

Treatment of GERD: H_2-blockers proton pump inhibitors

Treatment of gastrointestinal disease in scleroderma should begin early with the appreciation that almost every patient has bowel disease. Diagnostic testing is dictated by the clinical symptoms. Patients who do not respond to therapy for gastroesophageal reflux disease (GERD) should have a barium swallow and endoscopy to evaluate the status of the distal esophagus. Standard treatment of GERD is used in scleroderma patients with neutralization of gastric acid with either an H_2-blocker or proton pump inhibitor. Most patients will require a proton pump inhibitor, and some will also benefit from a prokinetic drug (metoclopramide). Small frequent meals and care not to eat late at night are important. Small- or large-bowel hypomotility is treated with good hydration, diet, and prokinetic drugs (eg, octreotide). Malabsorption is treated in the standard manner with cyclic antibiotics and supplemental diet. Severe bowel involvement can be treated with bowel rest and total parenteral nutrition.

Myocardial Disease

The treatment of scleroderma heart disease follows standard management of heart failure and arrhythmias. Small asymptomatic pericardial effusions do not need treatment, but pericarditis will respond to anti-inflammatory drugs (eg, nonsteroidal anti-inflammatory or corticosteroids). Some advocate the use of calcium channel blocker to prevent myocardial vascular vasospasm.

Pulmonary Disease Therapy

Treatment of lung disease in scleroderma is an active area of current research. Patients with abnormal pulmonary function test should be evaluated for evidence of active alveolitis. A high-resolution computed tomography (HRCT) scan of the lung can detect active disease by demonstrating a ground-glass appearance of the lung. Performing a bronchoalveolar lavage (BAL) in those patients with declining lung function and/or abnormal lung CT scan confirms active disease. Studies suggest that a BAL that finds greater than 3% neutrophils in the alveolar fluid predicts progressive disease and warrants drug treatment. Treatment of patients with active alveolitis with the immunosuppressive drug cyclophosphamide has demonstrated stabilization of declining lung function. A multicenter trial of cyclophosphamide versus placebo in the treatment of scleroderma lung disease is underway.

Pulmonary hypertension without severe interstitial lung disease is treated with vasodilator therapy. Pulmonary vascular response to vasodilator (eg, CCB, prostacyclin) therapy is determined by direct measurement during right-heart catheterization. If pulmonary pressures decrease, then the patient is treated with diuretics, an oral vasodilator, and anticoagulation. A continuous intravenous infusion of epoprostenol (prostacyclin) is available for severe disease to decrease pulmonary pressure, increase cardiac output, and improve clinical status in scleroderma patients with isolated pulmonary hypertension. Lung transplantation is necessary to extend life in those patients with severe pulmonary hypertension.

Renal Disease

ACE inhibitors are effective therapy.

Treatment of scleroderma renal disease begins with early detection of any hypertension and, if present, the use of ACE inhibitors. Patients with diffuse scleroderma should purchase a blood pressure machine and do periodic home monitoring. Early recognition of diffuse scleroderma and aggressive treatment have reduced the frequency of renal failure. New anemia and rapidly progressive disease associate with renal disease, and the use of corticosteroids or cyclosporine have been associated with renal crisis. Patients with hypertension and evidence of renal disease should be hospitalized. If the creatinine rises above 3 mg per dL, the prognosis is poor. Captopril, an ACE inhibitor, should be used for rapid control of hypertension. Patients with renal failure can be treated with hemodialysis or peritoneal dialysis. Recovery after renal failure requiring dialysis has been reported. Renal transplantation also can be done. Cyclosporin and tacrolimus are being used because of their benefit in suppressing organ transplant rejection. Although there is some uncontrolled trial experience suggesting benefit, the toxicity (hypertension and renal failure) prohibits their use.

Annotated Bibliography

Salojin KV, Le Tonguese M, Saraux A, et al. Antiendothelial cell antibodies: useful markers of systemic sclerosis. Am J Med 1997;102:178–185.

These studies demonstrate the presence of antiendothelial cell antibodies in approximately 20% of RP, 44% of limited scleroderma, and 80% of diffuse scleroderma patients. The presence of these antibodies correlated with digital scars and ulcers, severe RP, lung involvement, and tortuosity of capillaries in the cuticle nailfold. The fine specificities of these antibodies are unknown.

Morison WL. Psoralen UVA therapy for linear and generalized morphea. J Am Acad Dermatol 1997;37:657–659.

Kerscher M, Volkenandt M, Meurer M, et al. Treatment of localised scleroderma with PUVA bath photochemotherapy. Lancet 1994;343:1233.

Scharffetter-Kochanek K, Goldermann R, Lehmann P, et al. PUVA therapy in disabling pansclerotic morphoea of children. Br J Dermatol 1995;132:830–831.

Moritz A, Sajakibarra S, Sajakibarra N, et al. Successful treatment of systemic sclerosis with topical PUVA. J Rheum 1995;22:2361–2365.

These four articles provide intriguing data suggesting that at least in some cases of scleroderma, PUVA therapy using topical as well as systemic psoralens may prove valuable. The mechanism of action is unknown. Theoretically, the ultraviolet light could be inhibiting the inflammatory infiltrate or downregulating fibroblasts, or it could be causing a combination of both effects.

Jablonska S. Scleroderma and Pseudoscleroderma, 2nd ed. Warsaw: Polish Medical Publishers, 1975.

Excellent treatise.

Black CM, Stephens C. Systemic sclerosis (scleroderma) and related disorders. In: Maddison PJ, Isinberg DA, Woo P, Glass DN, eds. Oxford Textbook of Rheumatology. Oxford: Oxford University Press, 1993, Ch. 5.8.1, pp 771–789.

Excellent, well-written chapter.

Carwile LeRoy E. Scleroderma (systemic sclerosis). Kelly W, Harris E, Ruddy S, Sledge C, eds. Textbook of Rheumatology, 2nd ed. Philadelphia: WB Saunders Co., 1985, Ch. 76, pp 1183–1205.

Excellent chapter.

Casciola-Rosen LA, Anhalt G, Rosen A. Autoantigens targeted in systemic lupus erythematosus are clustered in two populations of surface structures on apoptotic keratinocytes. J Exp Med 1994;179:1317–1330.

Mancini M, et al. Caspase-2 is localized at the golgi complex and cleaves golgin-160 during apoptosis. J Cell Biol 2000;149:603–612.

Casciola-Rosen LA, et al. Specific cleavage of the 70-kDa protein component of the U1 small nuclear ribonuclear protein is a characteristic biochemical feature of apoptotic cell death. J Biol Chem 1994;269:30757–30760.

Three articles from our institution detailing specific cleavage of autoantigens on the cell surface of apoptotic cells.

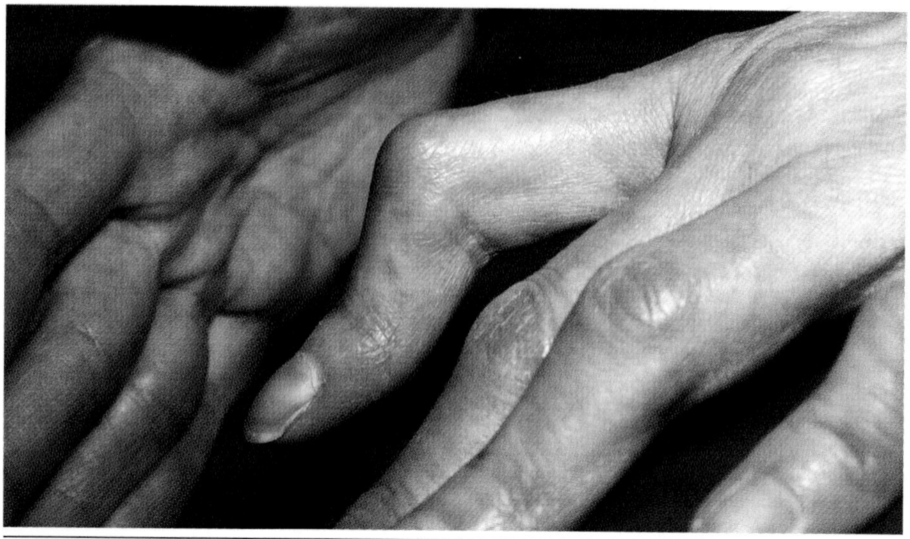

FIGURE 7–13 Hands of a patient with anti-U1RNP antibodies demonstrating sclerodactyly swan-neck deformities on the digits. Raynaud's phenomenon was prominent.

Scleroderma Overlap Syndromes

As noted previously, features of scleroderma may occur in association with manifestations of other connective tissue diseases and have been designated "overlap syndromes."

MCTD syndrome

In the early 1970s, Gordon Sharp et al., Stanford University, reported the existence of a group of patients with features of scleroderma, polymyositis, and lupus erythematosus. They designated these patients as having MCTD. These patients demonstrated RP, sclerodactyly, and other cutaneous features of scleroderma, myositis, and features of lupus erythematosus (Figures 7–13, 7–14, and 7–15). These patients possessed an antibody in their sera that was reactive against an RNase-sensitive, extractable nuclear antigen (ENA).

Subsequent work evaluating these original patients determined that over a 10-year period, many of these cases had evolved into a scleroderma clinical picture; others had developed SLE.

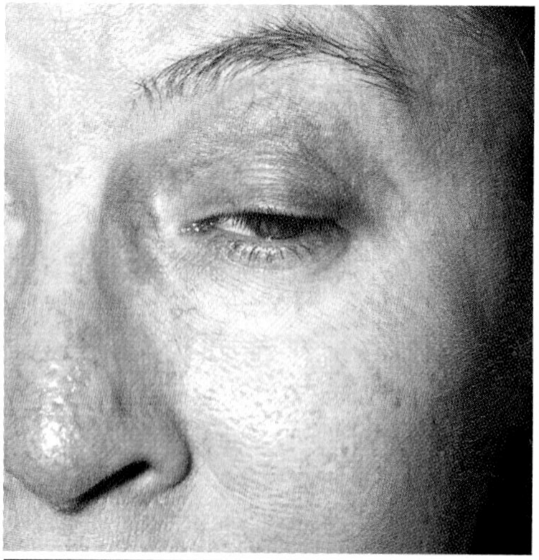

FIGURE 7–14 Ptosis of upper eyelid in patient from Figure 7–13. This ptosis is the result of plaque of morphea involving the upper eyelid.

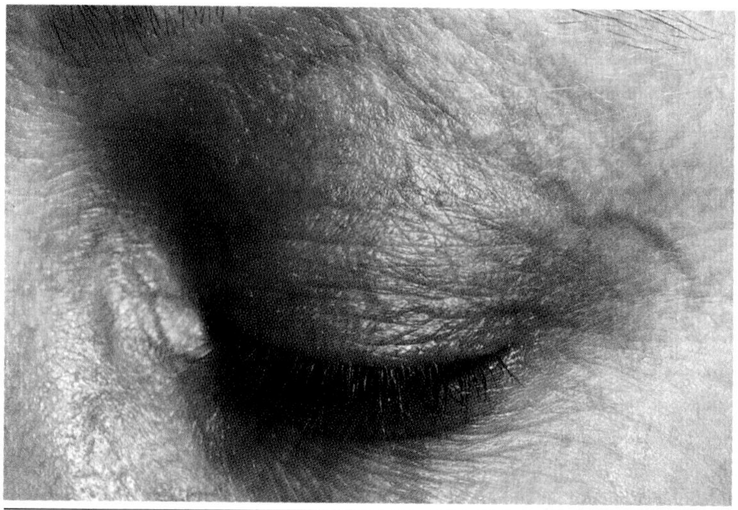

FIGURE 7–15 Close up of ptosis of upper eyelid showing morphea lesion.

Increased frequency of RP and interstitial fibrosis

Mattioli and Reichlin at the same time described a similar autoantibody system in patients satisfying the American Rheumatism Association criteria for the diagnosis of SLE. These patients were detected to have an increased frequency of RP and a low frequency of glomerulonephritis. Serologically, it is now recognized that anti-ENA antibodies directed against an RNase-sensitive protein are identical to anti-nRNA antibodies. These antibodies are now designated anti-U_1RNA antibodies. Systemic lupus erythematosus patients with these antibodies have an increased frequency of pulmonary interstitial disease. Furthermore, some pulmonary interstitial disease patients without clinical evidence of scleroderma or SLE possess anti-U_1RNP antibodies.

Recent studies indicate that MCTD is a transitory clinical state, and that the human leukocyte antigen (HLA) genetic background may determine, to a large extent, the final clinical designation. For instance, most MCTD patients possessing the HLA-DR3 phenotype generally evolve toward the clinical designation of SLE, whereas in those patients possessing the HLA-DR5 phenotype the MCTD evolves into a more classic scleroderma clinical picture (Table 7–6). Those MCTD patients possessing HLA-DR2 or -DR4 phenotypes remained undifferentiated.

These studies, performed in many laboratories over the last 25 years, have demonstrated the dynamic nature of the clinical disease associated with some anti-U_1RNP antibody–positive patients. As noted in Chapter 5, "Lupus Erythematosus," U_1RNP-positive patients generally have a more favorable prognosis with regard to the development of glomerulonephritis than anti-dsDNA antibody–positive patients. Furthermore, on unusual occasions, mothers with anti-U_1RNP–positive SLE may give birth to a child with the cutaneous features of the neonatal lupus syndrome. Other studies indicate that patients presenting with the clinical picture of polymyositis may have U_1RNP antibodies (approximately 5 to 10% of polymyositis patients). The data recounted above indicate that perhaps 5 to 10% of scleroderma patients possess anti-U_1RNP antibodies, and that on unusual occasions, in the absence of definable connective tissue diseases, the lung may be the only target.

In addition to MCTD associated with anti-U_1RNP antibodies, a scleroderma overlap syndrome has been seen in association with the presence of an antinucleolar antibody directed against 11 polypeptides and designated the anti-PM/SCL antibody. This is a rare syndrome; some of these patients have classic scleroderma, others have a combination of polymyositis and scleroderma, and still others have the clinical features of polymyositis.

Annotated Bibliography

Reichlin M, Mattioli M. Correlation of a precipitin reaction to a RNA protein antigen and a low prevalence of nephritis in patients with systemic lupus erythematosus. N Engl J Med 1972;286:908–911.

Sharp GC, et al. Mixed connective tissue disease: an apparent distinct rheumatic disease syndrome associated with a specific antibody to an extractable nuclear antigen (ENA). Am J Med 1972;52:148–159.

These two papers established the fact that lupus patients make autoantibodies against ribonuclear proteins in addition to dsDNA. Furthermore, this anti-

TABLE 7–6 Influence of HLA Background on Evolution of Anti-U_1RNP–Positive MCTD

HLA-DR3	Interstitial lung disease, Sjögren's syndrome, and a statistical trend toward SLE
HLA-DR5	systemic sclerosis

Data adapted from:
Gendi et al. HLA type as a predictor of mixed connective disease differentiation. Ten year clinical and immunogenic follow-up of 46 patients. Arthritis Rheum 1995;38:259–266.

nRNP antibody system was found in patients with many features of scleroderma (Raynaud's phenomenon and sclerodactily). Some patients with MCTD displayed features of lupus erythematosus, scleroderma, and myositis.

Atrophoderma of Pasini and Pierini

Variant of localized scleroderma

Atrophoderma appears to be a variant of localized scleroderma (morphea), characterized by sharply demarcated, depressed ("falling-off-a-cliff") lesions occurring in normal-appearing skin. The lesions, which most commonly occur on the back, are characterized by single or multiple oval, round, or irregular patches ranging in size from several to many centimeters in diameter. Characteristically, the skin around these lesions is absolutely normal. Sclerodermatous changes develop in the lesions, and the patients may demonstrate other features of localized scleroderma (morphea).

The etiology is unknown. Several reports indicate the occurrence in multiple family members. A dermal, perivascular infiltrate of macrophages and T lymphocytes is characteristic.

Annotated Bibliography

Kee CE, Brothers WS, New W. Idiopathic atrophoderma of Pasini and Pierini with coexistent morphea. A case report. Arch Dermatol 1960;82:154–157.

Facial Hemiatrophy

Facial hemiatrophy: progressive atrophy of skin, muscle, and perhaps bone
Generally unilateral; may be associated with cerebral cortex involvement

Facial hemiatrophy (Parry-Romberg syndrome) is a rare disorder that may or may not be related to localized scleroderma (morphea). The disease generally begins within the first two decades of life, involving predominantly the face. It may be heralded by muscle spasm or neuralgia and is quickly followed by irregular areas of pigmentation over the face and forehead. A progressive atrophy of the skin, muscle, and even bone ensues. The overlying skin is dry and atrophic. The area of involvement is usually unilateral but, on occasions, may be bilateral. The lesions may involve one area of the trigeminal nerve or can involve the entire side of the face. Although frequently occurring on the face, this atrophy may extend to the trunk and limbs.

Bony abnormalities may be detected, and on unusual occasions, there is evidence that the cerebral cortex may be involved. Although rare, focal epilepsy involving the contralateral side has been reported.

In contradistinction to the coup de sabre–type of atrophy seen in scleroderma, Parry-Romberg syndrome appears to be much more severe and involves the deeper structures in the skin.

Annotated Bibliography

Jablonska S. Scleroderma and Pseudoscleroderma, 2nd ed. Warsaw: Polish Medical Publishers, 1975.

Moscona R, Bergman R, Friedman-Birnbaum R. Multiple dermal grafts for hemifacial atrophy caused by lupus panniculitis. J Am Acad Dermatol 1986;14:840–843.

Other Conditions Associated with Scleroderma

During the past 20 years, three additional diseases characterized by sclerodermatous features have been described: eosinophilic fasciitis (Shulman's disease), toxic oil syndrome, and eosinophilic myalgia syndrome.

Eosinophilic Fasciitis

Eosinophilic fasciitis (Shulman's disease) was described by Laurence Shulman in 1974. This disease process is characterized by sclerodermatous features frequently precipitated by physical exertion. The skin becomes thickened and hardened and is associated with a very peculiar feature in which a blood vessel is fixed to underlying tissues. For example, when the arm is extended, a linear depression corresponding to the blood vessel is seen (most prominently on the inner aspect of the upper arm). This is the so-called "groove" sign (Figure 7–16). Unlike in classic scleroderma, RP, nailfold alterations, and autoantibodies are not seen.

Eosinophilic fasciitis: scleroderma-like disease, "groove sign"

Biopsy of the skin (elliptical incision) demonstrates an eosinophilic infiltration along the deep fascia in addition to dermal sclerosis. A peripheral eosinophilia, hypergammaglobulinemia, and a raised erythrocyte sedimentation rate are common. Hematologic abnormalities, such as thrombocytopenia, are occasionally detected, and several patients have developed aplastic anemia.

Aplastic anemia on rare occasions

Steroid therapy is effective in the edematous phase of this disease, but skin sclerosis may be progressive.

Annotated Bibliography

Naschitz JE, Boss JH, Misselevich I, et al. The fasciitis-panniculitis syndromes. Clinical and pathologic features. Medicine 1996;75:6–16.

These investigators report their experience with 32 consecutive patients who have fasciitis-panniculitis syndrome. Fourteen of these 32 patients had the eosinophilic fasciitis syndrome. Pathologically, the disorders were characterized by induration of the skin, secondary to chronic inflammation, and fibrosis of the subcutaneous septa and muscular fascia. In the remaining 18 cases, fasciitis-panniculitis syndrome was due to vascular disorders, infections, and neoplastic disorders.

These authors stress the diverse etiology resulting in a histologic picture similar to eosinophilic fasciitis that can be seen with morphea profunda, lupus panniculitis, circulatory disorders, toxic oil syndrome, a tryptophane-induced eosinophilic myalgia syndrome, graft-versus-host reaction, post-irradiation injury, infections, and cancer.

Toxic Oil Syndrome

Toxic oil syndrome was described in Spain, in May 1981. Its cause has been attributed to the ingestion of adulterated rapeseed oil. Patients developed a pro-

Caused by adulterated rapeseed oil

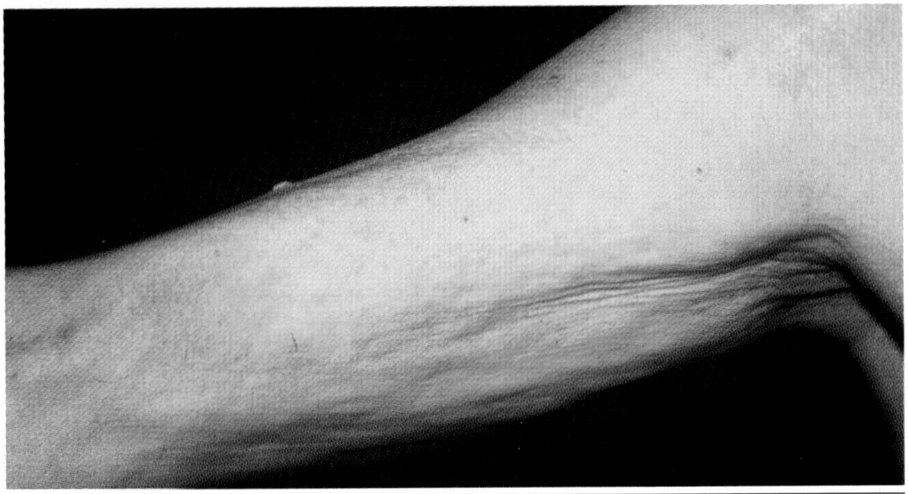

FIGURE 7–16 Groove sign in patient with eosinophilic fasciitis (Schulman's disease).

longed illness initially characterized by fever, chills, headache, dermatitis, lymphadenopathy, and chest pain with pulmonary infiltrates. Subsequently, several months after the onset of the initial phase, eosinophilia became prominent, accompanied by severe myalgia, fatigue, and progressive neuromyopathy.

This disease, which is quite similar to the eosinophilic myalgia syndrome, generally resolves within a 5-year period. High-dose prednisone therapy is indicated.

Eosinophilic Myalgia Syndrome

In 1989, eosinophilic myalgia syndrome was described. This disease process is characterized by severe myalgias and eosinophilia. The dermatitis is characterized as erythematous, edematous, sclerotic lesions quite similar to eosinophilic fasciitis (Figure 7–17). Although sclerotic skin changes, including the "groove sign," are common, RP, nailfold alterations, and autoantibodies associated with scleroderma are not found. Peripheral eosinophilia, at times in excess of 50% of the total count, has been detected.

Although the exact etiology is unknown, epidemiologic data suggest some contaminant of a particular batch of L-tryptophan was responsible. Like toxic oil syndrome, significant mortality occurs early in the disease. In those who do not succumb, a resolution of the disease occurs with time. However, cognitive dysfunction may be progressive.

Caused by a contaminant of L-tryptophan
Cognitive dysfunction may be progressive

Approximately 80% of these patients, during the acute phase of their disease, had a positive response to corticosteroids. There is, however, no evidence that corticosteroids are effective in long-term patient management.

Annotated Bibliography

Hertzman PA, Clauw DJ, Kaufman LD, et al. The eosinophilia-myalgia syndrome: status of 205 patients and results of treatments 2 years after onset. Ann Intern Med 1995;122:851–855.

These data, which are the experience of 15 physicians, comprise the largest yet collected on this syndrome. They document a triumph of modern and public health surveillance techniques in removing from society a putative, etiopathogenic factor responsible for this syndrome.

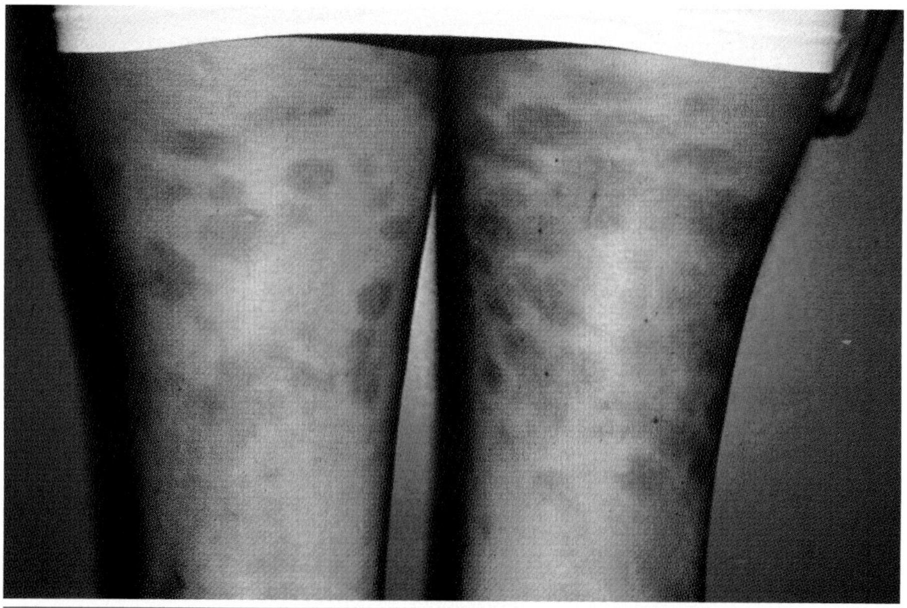

FIGURE 7–17 Patches of erythema in a patient with eosinophilic myalgia syndrome. The patient had been taking a preparation with L-tryptophan. Biopsy showed perivascular infiltrate with admixture of eosinophils and lymphocytes.

CHAPTER 8

Sjögren's Syndrome

Don R. Martin, M.D., Thomas T. Provost, M.D.

Sjögren's syndrome (SS) is an autoimmune disorder characterized by a lymphocytic infiltration of the lacrimal and salivary glands, most commonly manifested as dryness of the eyes (keratoconjunctivitis sicca) and mouth (xerostomia). Extraglandular manifestations are common, resulting from similar infiltration of various organs (Table 8–1).

Sjögren's syndrome:
- *autoimmune disorder of salivary glands*
- *extraglandular manifestations,*
- *primary versus secondary disease*

The presence of sicca (dryness) symptoms in the absence of another connective tissue disease is designated "primary Sjögren's syndrome," whereas their occurrence in association with another autoimmune process, such as rheumatoid arthritis, systemic lupus erythematosus, progressive systemic sclerosis, or polymyositis, is termed "secondary Sjögren's syndrome." This distinction may be challenging early in the course of the disease.

The constellation of clinical findings now termed "Sjögren's syndrome" was first reported over 100 years ago. In 1888, Mikulicz reported the case of a 42-year-old Prussian farmer who, likely in the setting of SS, developed a lymphoma. In 1933, Henrick Sjögren reported the association of keratoconjunctivitis sicca, xerostomia, and an inflammatory polyarthritis. In 1953, Morgan and Castleman's pathologic study of Mikulicz's disease and SS concluded that these diseases are identical. Subsequent studies by Bunim's group, at the National Institutes of Health, characterized the clinical features of SS and its association with other connective tissue diseases. Furthermore, their studies demonstrated the lymphoproliferative nature of the disease and noted that some patients with SS develop a lymphoma (Table 8–2).

TABLE 8–1 Extraglandular Manifestations of Sjögren's Syndrome

Cutaneous lesions, including vasculitis
Pulmonary disease
Gastrointestinal disease
Pancreatic disease
Liver disease
Endocrine disease
Musculoskeletal disease
Renal disease
Central and peripheral nervous system disease
Hematologic disease
Non-Hodgkin's lymphoma
Constitutional manifestations

TABLE 8–2 Sjögren's Syndrome Historical Events

1882	Leber describes filamentary keratitis.
1888	Mikulicz reports first case of a 42-year-old Prussian farmer (unusual Sjögren's patient in that he was a male and probably had lymphoma).
1888	Hadden reports SS occurring in a 65-year-old woman (classic case of Sjögren's syndrome).
1926	Gougerot describes mucous membrane dryness and atrophy involving the eyes, mouth, and vagina.
1927	Horuver describes keratitis and arthritis.
1933	Sjögren describes combination of dry eyes, dry mouth, and arthritis. He uses Rose Bengal dye to stain the cornea.
1953	Morgan and Castleman demonstrate that the histopathologic features of Mikulicz's disease and Sjögren's syndrome are identical.
1961	Anderson, Gray, Beck, and Kinnear describe two precipitating antibodies in Sjögren's syndrome patients: SjD and SjT.
1962	Bunim and Talal describe the association of lymphoma with Sjögren's syndrome.
1965	Bloch, Buchanan, Wohl, and Bunim publish the classic description of Sjögren's syndrome establishing the diagnostic triad of keratoconjunctivitis sicca, xerostomia, and rheumatoid arthritis.
1968–84	Chisholm and Mason; Tarpley, Anderson, and White; and Daniels emphasize pathologic features of the salivary gland as diagnostic criteria for Sjögren's syndrome.
1969	Clark, Reichlin, and Tomasi describe anti-Ro antibodies.
1974	Mattioli and Reichlin describe anti-La antibodies.
1975	Alspaugh and Tan describe anti–SS-A and anti–SS-B antibodies in Sjögren's syndrome.
1979	Alspaugh and Maddison demonstrate that anti-Ro and anti–SS-A antibodies and anti-La and anti–SS-B antibodies are identical.
1980's	Alexander et al. demonstrate the relationship between anti-Ro (SS-A) antibodies and the presence of extraglandular manifestations in Sjögren's syndrome, including cytopenias, serologic hyperreactivity, vasculitis, and central and peripheral nervous system disease.
	Arnett and Reveille demonstrate the human leukocyte antigens associations of the anti-Ro (SS-A) and anti-La (SS-B) antibody responses.

Epidemiology

Common disease
Women affected predominantly
More frequent in elderly

It has been estimated that SS affects 1:50 to 1:1000 people in the United States, with much of the difference likely due to referral bias at academic health centers and lack of agreement upon diagnostic criteria. Approximately 90% of patients are female. SS in men is generally a milder disease, with less extraglandular manifestations and a decreased frequency of anti-Ro (SS-A) antibodies. The disease develops most commonly in the fourth and fifth decades of life but has been reported in all ages. Elderly individuals have an increased frequency of both anti-Ro (SS-A) antibodies and SS.

Etiology

The etiology of SS remains an enigma. Detection of antinuclear antibodies and rheumatoid factor reflects the autoimmune nature of the process. Serologic studies have demonstrated the frequent occurrence of anti-Ro (SS-A) antibodies (40–90%) and, to a lesser extent, anti-La (SS-B) antibodies (15–60%) in Sjögren's patients. The frequency is dependent upon the cohort studied and the techniques employed (eg, gel diffusion or enzyme-linked immunosorbent assay

[ELISA]). It is now recognized that the anti-SjD antibody, reported by Anderson et al. in SS in 1961, is probably identical to both the anti-Ro antibody detected by Reichlin et al. and the anti–SS-A antibody detected by Alspaugh and Tan. Furthermore, the anti-SjT antibody, also reported by Anderson et al. is probably identical to both the anti-La antibody described by Mattioli and Reichlin and the anti–SS-B antibody described by Alspaugh and Tan. Studies indicate that the anti-Ro (SS-A) antibody response in SS is directed against 52-kD and 60-kD proteins, whereas the anti-Ro (SS-A) antibody response in systemic lupus erythematosus (SLE) is directed predominantly against the 60-kD protein. The anti-La (SS-B) antibody response is directed against a 48-kD protein. See Chapter 5, "Lupus Erythematosus," for further discussion.

Anti-Ro antibody identical to anti–SS-A and probably SjD antibody

Anti–La identical to anti–SS-B and probably anti–SjT antibodies

Immunogenetic studies have demonstrated the association of anti-Ro (SS-A) and anti-La (SS-B) antibody responses with the presence of the human leukocyte antigen (HLA)-B8, DR3, DQw2, and DRw52 phenotypes. Our studies indicate that at least 90% of anti-Ro (SS-A) antibody–positive patients possess the HLA-DR2 and/or HLA-DR3 phenotypes. Furthermore, all anti-Ro (SS-A) and anti-La (SS-B) antibody–positive patients have a glutamine residue at position 34 of the outer region of the HLA-DQ beta chain and/or a leucine residue at position 26 of the HLA-DQ alpha chain.

Studies have also demonstrated the association of anti-Ro (SS-A) antibodies and, to a lesser extent, anti-La (SS-B) antibodies with extraglandular manifestations of SS. These include serologic hyperreactivity (eg, hypergammaglobulinemia and rheumatoid factor–positivity), hypocomplementemia, cytopenias (eg, anemia, leukopenia, and thrombocytopenia), lymphadenopathy, and cutaneous vasculitis (Table 8–3).

Increased frequency of extraglandular manifestations in anti–Ro (SS-A) and anti-La (SS-B)–positive SS patients

Immunohistologic studies have shown that the lymphocytic infiltrate in affected tissues is comprised predominantly of CD4-positive T cells, primarily demonstrating the Th1-cytokine profile. The majority of these cells express alpha-beta rather than gamma-delta receptors. Unlike normal epithelium, the glandular epithelial cells express major histocompatibility complex class II antigens (HLA-DR, as well as the DP and DQ antigens) and B7 co-stimulatory molecules, allowing them to serve as antigen-presenting cells. The mechanism of tis-

T-cell inflammation infiltrate in tissues

TABLE 8–3 Clinical Features of Anti-Ro (SS-A)–Positive and Anti-Ro (SS-A)–Negative Sjögren's Syndrome Patients*

Feature	Anti-Ro (SS-A)+ (n = 33)	Anti-Ro (SS-A)– (n = 42)	*p* Value
Vasculitis	24	4	.0005
Lymphadenopathy	19	4	.0005
Purpura	12	1	.0005
Anemia	19	6	.0005
Leukopenia	14	3	.001
Thrombocytopenia	7	1	.025
Increased globulin	21	8	.0005
Rheumatoid factor	29	17	.0005
Antinuclear antibody	31	10	.0005
†Cryoglobulins	7/13	0/22	.001
Hypocomplementemia	11	2	.005

*Anti–Ro (SS-A) antibodies detected by gel double diffusion.
†Only 13 patients in the anti-Ro (SS-A)+ group and only 22 patients in the anti–Ro (SS-A)- group tested.

Data from:
Alexander EL, Arnett FC, Provost TT, Stevens MB. Sjögren's syndrome: association of anti-Ro (SS-A) antibodies with vasculitis, hematologic abnormalities, and serologic hyperreactivity. Ann Intern Med 1983;98:155–159.

sue destruction in SS is not clearly defined but likely involves the infiltrating CD4-positive T cells and associated serine proteases. Disruption of autonomic innervation may also play a role in disturbing exocrine glandular function.

Possible role for Epstein-Barr virus

A variety of genetic, immunologic, and environmental factors have been implicated in the development of sicca symptoms. For example, a diffuse infiltrative lymphadenopathy syndrome has been described in human immunodeficiency virus (HIV)–infected patients. Unlike SS, however, the infiltrating T lymphocytes are predominantly CD8-positive and the patients are generally ANA–negative. In contrast, impaired immune suppression of latent Epstein-Barr virus (EBV) infection has been implicated in the pathogenesis of primary SS. Primary infection with the ubiquitous EBV involves the salivary glands. Chronic, low-grade replication of the virus in the parotid epithelium is characteristic of the asymptomatic EBV carrier state. However, the salivary gland destruction characteristic of SS may be related to an inappropriate immune response to reactivated virus. For example, the salivary gland T cell infiltrates in SS are similar to those seen in nasopharyngeal carcinoma, a malignancy intimately associated with EBV. And anti-La (SS-B) antibody precipitates a ribonucleoprotein associated with EBV-encoded RNAs. As compared with normal controls, an increased number of salivary epithelial cells express EBV-associated antigens and DNA. Furthermore, impaired immune surveillance of EBV-infected B-lymphocytes may be related to the outgrowth of lymphomas in SS.

Clinical Features

Dry Eyes

Gritty or foreign-body sensation common symptoms of eye involvement

Dry eye (xerophthalmia) symptoms vary widely in severity. Lack of moisture renders the eyes more sensitive to both chemical and physical environmental irritants, producing a gritty sensation and conjunctival injection. The gritty or "foreign-body" sensation is perceived with blinking of the eyes, as the dry and inflamed palpebral and bulbar conjunctivae pass over each other, eventually producing defects on the ocular epithelial surface. Patients may experience an aching pain, which appears to be related to the lack of moisture, and is relieved by liberal application of artificial tears. These symptoms worsen as the day progresses. Blurred vision, secondary to drying and disruption of the cornea, is a common complaint. Photophobia is not generally reported, and its presence should raise the possibility of uveitis.

When there is a discrepancy between the symptoms and signs of ocular dryness, other etiologies must be considered. For example, the symptoms of blepharitis, with which SS may be confused, are worse in the morning after the products of the bacterial infection of the eyelid have accumulated overnight. They are reduced at the end of the day, when blinking and wiping of the eyes have removed most of the irritants. Blepharitis may, in fact, be exacerbated by preservatives in artificial tears and by more viscous ocular lubricants used at night for SS.

Examination of the eyes generally reveals prominent, dilated conjunctival blood vessels. The cornea, because of lack of moisture, loses its luster. Mucinous strings, resulting from the decreased quantity of tears diluting the mucin, can be detected. This process, termed "filamentary keratitis," may also give rise to the foreign-body sensation noted above.

Xerophthalmia can be objectively tested for with Rose Bengal staining of the cornea to detect superficial abrasions and with the Schirmer test to quantify tear production.

Dry Mouth

Increased dental caries may be an early sign of SS.

Dryness of the mouth (xerostomia) is a cardinal manifestation of SS. The dryness frequently presents as dysphagia, the inability to maintain a conversation without drinking fluids, the need to keep fluids at the bedside, alterations in the sense of taste and smell, problems in wearing dentures, and an increased frequency of dental caries. These symptoms generally develop gradually over a period of time.

Examination of the mouth frequently reveals a dry oral mucosa and a diminished or absent sublingual salivary pool. Patchy or diffuse erythema of the mucosal surfaces, papillary tongue atrophy, angular cheilitis, and extensive dental caries may be noted. The caries characteristically occur at the incisal edge and gingival margin of the tooth, making restoration difficult. Early onset of SS during the second decade of life frequently results in patients becoming edentulous by their third and fourth decades.

Salivary gland enlargement

Examination of the parotid and sublingual glands may demonstrate firm, diffuse, and nontender or minimally tender enlargement in approximately one-third of patients. The swelling may be transient and secondary to intermittent obstruction of the salivary gland ducts, or persistent and due to an inflammatory infiltrate. Massage of the parotid gland may reveal cloudy saliva expressed from Stensen's duct. Enlargement is usually bilateral but may be unilateral. Persistent asymmetry should raise the possibility of a neoplastic process.

Oral candidiasis and toxins released by the organism are frequently responsible for a generalized burning sensation of the mouth. Treatment with antibiotics and corticosteroids act as predisposing factors, and those patients who wear dentures are especially prone to develop the infection. Angular cheilitis (perlèche) may also result from candidiasis.

Oral candidiasis

Examination of the erythematous oral mucosa of symptomatic Sjögren's patients will frequently fail to reveal evidence of thrush. Yet treatment with oral antifungal agents (eg, nystatin suspension, or clotrimazole troches) will relieve most, if not all, of the burning sensation. Dentures also require treatment, best done by scouring the mucosal surface using a nystatin powder and a tooth brush.

Vaginal Dryness

Vaginal manifestations are frequently detected in SS. Patients complain of dryness, burning, pruritus, vaginal discharge, and dyspareunia. Dyspareunia may occur years prior to other sicca symptoms. These symptoms may have to be elicited by direct questioning.

Vaginal dryness commonly detected

Physical examination may demonstrate patchy or generalized erythema, as well as a mucoid discharge characteristic of a *Candida albicans* infection. However, mucous membrane atrophy and dryness may predominate.

In some SS patients, involvement of one mucous membrane may be predominant for years prior to involvement of other mucous membranes. Rarely are all mucous membranes symptomatic.

Cutaneous Manifestations

Xerosis

There is some evidence to indicate that patients with SS have impaired sweating. Biopsies have demonstrated lymphocytic periglandular sweat-gland infiltrates. Since the major source of lubrication of the skin is the sebaceous glands, cutaneous xerosis has also been attributed to infiltration of these glands, although there has been no formal histologic study to provide support for this. Pruritus and postinflammatory hyperpigmentation in areas of scratching are common.

Vasculitis

Cutaneous vasculitis may be seen in patients with SS, and its presence serves as a reminder of the systemic inflammatory nature of this disease. The most common lesions are palpable and nonpalpable purpuric lesions over the lower extremities (Figure 8–1). These lesions are indistinguishable from Waldenström's benign hypergammaglobulinemic purpura. Furthermore, it has been estimated that 20 to 30% of patients with benign hypergammaglobulinemic purpura develop SS. These patients are frequently rheumatoid factor-positive and have a type II, mixed cryoglobulinemia with monoclonal IgM-κ (immunoglobulin) rheumatoid factor. It is suspected that some patients described as having vasculitis and mixed cryoglobulins may actually have unrecognized SS.

Urticaria-like vasculitic lesions have been detected (Figure 8–2). In contrast to classic urticaria, which is transient, these lesions persist for days and even weeks. Frequently, they will demonstrate petechiae and the application of light touch will produce an annoying sensation (hyperpathia).

Digital ulceration, erythema multiforme, erythema perstans, erythema nodosum, and cutaneous nodules have also been detected in patients with SS. The pathophysiology of these latter lesions has not been elucidated.

Types of vasculitis: neutrophilic, lymphocytic

Histopathologic study of vasculitic lesions has detected two types of inflammatory vascular insults. A neutrophilic inflammatory process, indistinguishable from leukocytoclastic vasculitis, is the dominant finding. To a lesser extent, a mononuclear inflammatory process has been seen in which lymphocytes invade and destroy the integrity of the vessel wall. Both the palpable and nonpalpable purpuric lesions, as well as the urticaria-like lesions, demonstrate these two types of histopathologic changes. Furthermore, one cannot detect, by clinical examination of the individual vasculitic lesion, which inflammatory process is present.

Our studies employing multiple biopsies from individual Sjögren's patients failed to demonstrate a transition from the neutrophilic inflammatory vascular disease into the mononuclear inflammatory vascular disease. There are also consistent differences in the serologic profiles of these two processes. The neutrophilic process is generally seropositive with higher levels of circulating immune complexes, and the mononuclear process is seronegative with lower levels of circulating immune complexes. Based on these findings, we believe that the mononuclear inflammatory infiltrate does not represent the end result of a leukocytoclastic vasculitis.

The work of Nicholas Soter has also identified two histopathophysiologic forms of necrotizing vasculitis. In one of his studies that was performed on

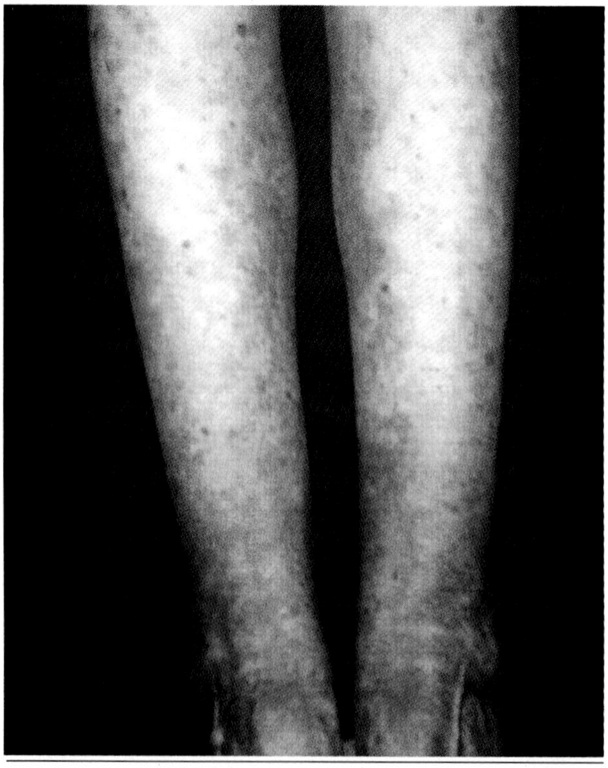

FIGURE 8–1 Palpable purpuric lesions over the lower extremities in an anti-Ro (SS-A) antibody-positive Sjögren's patient.

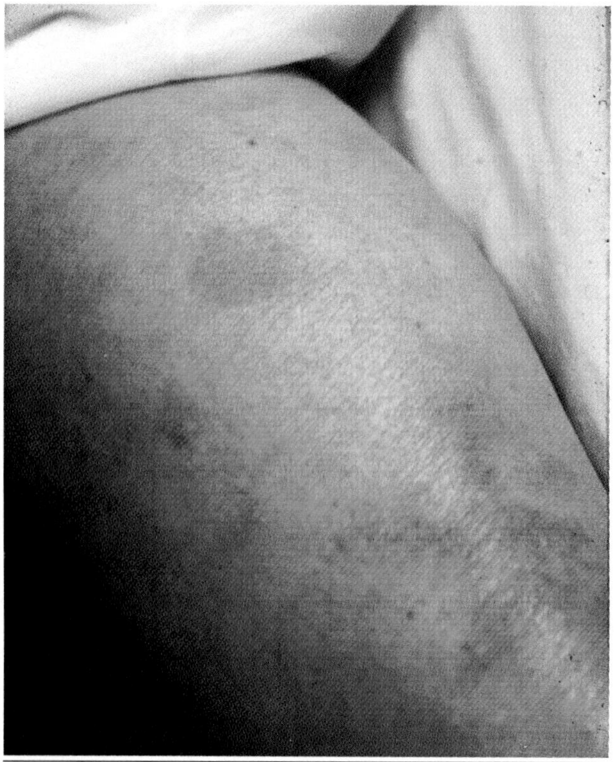

FIGURE 8–2 Urticaria-like lesion in an anti-Ro (SS-A) antibody-positive Sjögren's patient.

patients at a rheumatology inpatient service, Soter identified a leukocytoclastic angiitis associated with hypocomplementemia. The mononuclear vasculitic disease was associated with normal complement levels. He also was unable, on follow-up biopsies, to detect a transition from a neutrophilic to a mononuclear inflammatory infiltrate. Thus, his studies also suggest that mononuclear inflammatory vasculopathy is not the late stage of a leukocytoclastic angiitis. See Chapter 12, "Vasculitis," for further details.

Possible role of mononuclear cells in the pathogenesis of vasculitis is poorly understood

Studies by Lawley et al. are germane to this issue. They observed peculiar erythematous urticaria-like lesions over the lateral aspect of the feet in patients with aplastic anemia who had been given horse anti-human thymus antiserum in preparation for bone marrow transplantation. At a time when the patients lacked polymorphonuclear leukocytes, they developed an urticaria-like inflammatory vasculopathy, the result of a putative serum sickness (immune complex) reaction, and characterized by a mononuclear (lymphocytic) inflammatory infiltrate in and about the blood vessels.

Lawley's group also injected human volunteers with C5a. This activated complement component induced a brisk inflammatory response at the site of injection, characterized by a leukocytoclastic-like inflammatory infiltrate indistinguishable from necrotizing angiitis. However, within a 4 to 5 hour period, this inflammatory infiltrate and clinical evidence of inflammation had cleared.

These observations have led to speculation that the mononuclear inflammatory cell component of vasculitis in SS may be much more important than previously appreciated. The interrelationship between the different histopathologic types of vascular disease, and serologic hyperreactivity and hypocomplementemia in SS is depicted in Table 8–4.

Vasculitis may herald systemic vasculitis.

The presence of cutaneous necrotizing vasculitis in SS has also heralded the fact that these patients are at risk of developing a systemic vasculopathy with frequent involvement of the central and peripheral nervous systems.

"Donut-Like" Cutaneous Lesions

Donut-like lesion an erythematous plaque

Japanese workers have described an erythematous plaque, "donut-like" lesion in their Sjögren's patients (Figure 8–3). This lesion is described in Chapter 5, "Lupus Erythematosus."

Relationship between Anti-Ro (SS-A) Antibody–positive SLE and SS

Work in our department has described the relationship between anti-Ro (SS-A) antibody–positive lupus patients and anti-Ro (SS-A) antibody–positive Sjögren's patients. Patients exhibiting clinical features of both of these diseases have a high

TABLE 8–4 Serologic and Histopathologic Correlates in Inflammatory Vascular Disease in Sjögren's Syndrome

	Inflammatory Vascular Disease		
Serologic Feature	**Neutrophilic**	**Mononuclear**	***p* Value**
Antinuclear antibody	+	-	.02
Increased globulins	+	-	.01
Rheumatoid factor	+	-	.002
Anti–Ro (SS-A) antibody*	+	-	.00006
Anti–La (SS-B) antibody*	+	-	.036
Serum immune complexes	+	-	.04
Decreased complement levels	+	-	.03

*As determined by gel double diffusion

Data from:
Molina R, Provost TT, Alexander EL. Two types of inflammatory vascular disease in Sjögren's syndrome. Differential association with seroreactivity to rheumatoid factor and antibodies to Ro (SS-A) and with hypocomplementemia. Arthritis Rheum 1985;28:1251–1258.

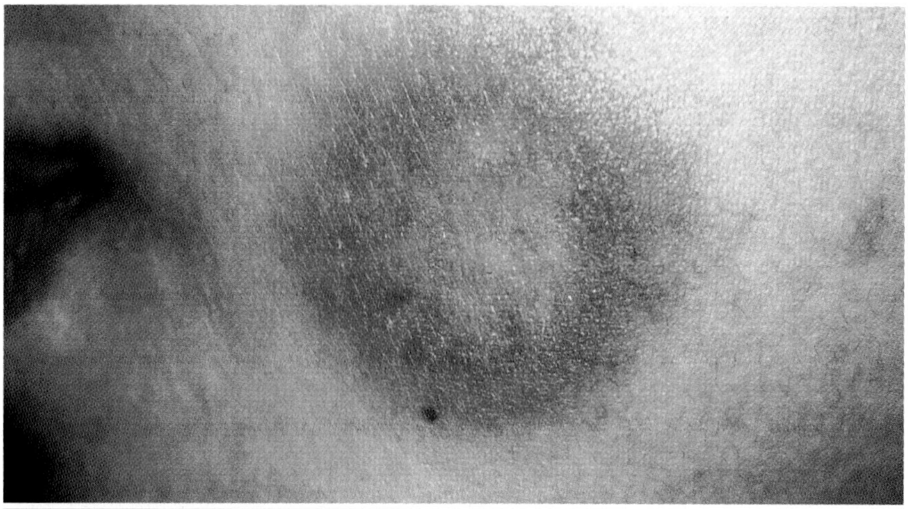

FIGURE 8–3 "Donut-like" cutaneous lesion in a Japanese anti-Ro (SS-A) antibody–positive Sjögren's patient.

frequency of cutaneous lupus, cutaneous vasculitis, and neurologic and pulmonary manifestations. A detailed description of these patients can also be found in Chapter 5, "Lupus Erythematosus."

Temperature-Sensitive Phenomenon

Raynaud's phenomenon a common manifestation

Raynaud's phenomenon is a common finding in SS, occurring in 20 to 40% of patients. Livedo reticularis may also be seen. Observation of one of these processes should raise the possibility of an associated vasculitis or cryoglobulinemia.

Pulmonary Manifestations

Upper airway xerosis is frequently complicated by recurrent upper respiratory infections including sinusitis. In the past, inspissated secretions causing tracheobronchitis and pneumonia were major causes of morbidity and death. More recently, the availability of antibiotics has minimized the pulmonary infectious complications in SS. However, these may still be seen as a peri-operative complication, promoted by the use of nonhumidified, supplemental oxygen and anticholinergic agents to minimize upper airway secretions.

Sjögren's patients may, less frequently, develop obstructive lung disease, and interstitial lung disease with impaired diffusion. In general, these pulmonary complications are asymptomatic, although on occasion cough and dyspnea may become a prominent feature of the extraglandular manifestations of SS. Progression to severe interstitial lung disease is uncommon.

Subclinical pulmonary disease is common

In recent years, bronchoalveolar lavage has revealed the frequent occurrence of alveolitis in SS. This is characterized by an increase in the number and proportion of various inflammatory cells. As many as 50% of asymptomatic primary SS patients will have evidence of a bronchoalveolitis.

Gastrointestinal Manifestations

Severe oral dryness may lead to dysphagia, with food sticking in the esophagus. This sensation is generally perceived in the upper portion of the throat, rather than in the substernal area as seen in progressive systemic sclerosis. Increased fluid intake with meals to ease the passage of food is common.

Esophagitis

Reflux esophagitis, presumed due to the lowered amount of neutralizing saliva, may be seen. Paradoxically, chronic atrophic gastritis has also been reported. The gastric mucosal inflammatory infiltrate, composed predominantly of activated CD4-positive T lymphocytes, is similar to that found in the minor salivary glands. A high incidence of antiparietal cell antibodies, hypochlorhydria, achlorhydria, and pernicious anemia have been reported in Sjögren's patients.

Pancreatic dysfunction

Pancreatic dysfunction, as measured by the secretin and pancreozymin tests, has been reported in SS. Hyperamylasemia of the pancreatic isotype has been detected, and acute pancreatitis has been reported. These findings collectively suggest that pancreatic disease, of a subclinical nature, may be common in SS, but only rarely is it clinically relevant.

Primary biliary cirrhosis

The relationship of SS to chronic liver disease has been more fully investigated. Approximately 10% of Sjögren's patients produce antimitochondrial and anti-smooth muscle antibodies. Mild elevations of hepatic enzymes may be seen. Furthermore, patients may demonstrate histopathologic liver abnormalities of primary biliary cirrhosis, chronic active hepatitis, and cryptogenic cirrhosis. The frequency of SS among primary biliary cirrhosis patients varies. In one study, 72% demonstrated evidence of SS and in another study, approximately 50%. Primary biliary cirrhosis patients with SS are purported to have an increased frequency of neuropsychiatric disease. Recent studies have indicated an increased frequency (approximately 20%) of anti-Ro (SS-A) antibodies and circulating immune complexes in primary biliary cirrhosis. It seems reasonable to conclude from these data that hepatic and salivary gland damage may be due to similar immunopathologic mechanisms.

Endocrine Manifestations

Thyroiditis is frequent

Serum antithyroglobulin and antithyroid microsomal antibodies occur in approximately 20% of Sjögren's patients. Clinical evidence of Hashimoto's thyroiditis has been detected in approximately 10 to 15% of patients. The onset of thyroiditis is most often subtle, although on occasion patients will complain of a persistent sore throat, and palpation of the thyroid gland will demonstrate tenderness.

Diabetes mellitus is no more common in SS than in the rest of the population.

Musculoskeletal Manifestations

Rheumatoid arthritis is the most common extraglandular manifestation of SS. It has been estimated that 30 to 60% of Sjögren's patients have an arthritis with clinical and laboratory features indistinguishable from adult-onset rheumatoid arthritis. Since the classic paper by Bloch, rheumatoid arthritis has been commonly recognized as part of the diagnostic triad of SS (ie, keratoconjunctivitis sicca, xerostomia, rheumatoid arthritis).

Rheumatoid factor-positivity

SS is also recognized as a complication of rheumatoid arthritis, occurring with varying frequency depending upon the cohort reported. Generally, manifestations of arthritis appear to antedate the diagnosis of SS by 5 to 10 years. Rheumatoid factor is frequently detected, especially in anti-Ro (SS-A) antibody–positive patients. The anti-Ro (SS-A) antibodies are commonly cross-reactive with an epitope on the $F(ab')_2$ fragment of IgG, providing one reason for the high frequency of rheumatoid factor-positivity in SS.

Polymyositis may be seen associated with SS. In the classic report of Bloch et al., 4 of 65 Sjögren's patients (6%) demonstrated myositis. Muscle enzymes are generally only mildly elevated. Biopsies demonstrate a perivascular mononuclear inflammatory infiltrate (Figure 8–4). This is similar to that seen in other organs of Sjögren's patients, suggesting a common immunopathogenesis.

Renal Manifestations

Renal tubular acidosis

Renal involvement in SS is most commonly in the form of distal tubular dysfunction causing renal tubular acidosis. This may be found in 20 to 40% of Sjögren's patients. Less frequently, more extensive tubular dysfunction may occur resulting in aminoaciduria; defects in the reabsorption of glucose, potassium, phosphate, and urate; and a diminished ability to concentrate their urine.

These defects in renal tubular function are thought to be the result of an interstitial inflammatory infiltrate composed of lymphocytes and plasma cells. Acute interstitial nephritis due to medications may exacerbate the problem. Electron microscopic studies have also demonstrated electron dense deposits along the peritubular basement membrane, suggesting that immune complexes are present.

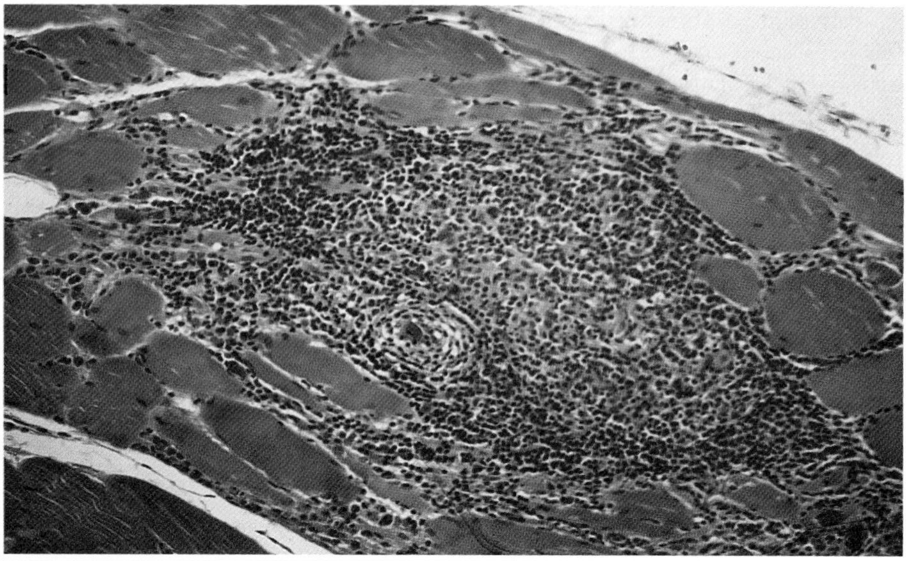

FIGURE 8–4 Histopathologic muscle section in Sjögren's patient with myositis. Note perivascular distribution.

Acute glomerulonephritis has been reported in SS but is unusual. It is conceivable, but remains unproven, that immune complexes may play a role in these cases. Proteinuria is an uncommon finding.

Central and Peripheral Nervous System Disease

Extensive studies by Alexander et al. using various techniques, including cerebrospinal fluid (CSF) analysis, histopathologic studies, psychiatric testing, neuroradiologic imaging, and electrophysiologic testing have emphasized the fact that Sjögren's patients may exhibit neurologic manifestations involving the entire neural axis (ie, brain, spinal cord, peripheral nerves) (Table 8–5).

Biopsy and autopsy material has demonstrated a mononuclear small vessel vasculopathy in the brain and a lymphocytic infiltrate involving the vasa nervorum of the sural nerve.

TABLE 8–5 Neurologic Abnormalities Reported in Sjögren's Syndrome Patients

Focal brain abnormalities
Motor and sensory nerve deficits
Movement disorder
Cerebellar focal lesions
Brain stem focal lesions
Seizures
Nonfocal brain abnormalities
Aseptic meningitis
Cognitive dysfunction
Dementia
Psychiatric disorders
Spinal cord disorders
Dorsal root ganglionitis
Subacute sensory neuronopathy
Transverse myelitis
Chronic progressive myelitis
Brown-Séquard's syndrome
Neurogenic bladder

Central Manifestations

CNS vasculopathy

A review of Johns Hopkins' autopsy data revealed that 5 of 9 Sjögren's patients had evidence of focal central nervous system (CNS) disease, characterized by a small vessel vasculopathy with hemorrhage and hemosiderin deposition. However, manifestations also may be nonfocal, as noted below.

Atypical cells (activated lymphocytes and/or macrophages) have been identified in the CSF as well as the parenchyma of the brain. Increased quantities of IgG, IgG oligoclonal bands, and complement activation, as detected by the presence of C5b-C9 (the membrane attack complex), have been observed in the CSF.

Using psychological profile testing (Minnesota Multiphasic Personality Inventory), affective psychiatric disturbances have been detected in Sjögren's patients (Table 8–6).

Psychologic abnormalities reflective of organic brain disease

Because symptoms may be multiple and vague, they may be considered "functional," and the patients hypochondriacal or neurotic. Formal cognitive function testing has revealed impairment of recent memory, concentration difficulties, and a decrease in the verbal intelligence quotient exceeding the reduction in performance intelligence quotient, providing evidence of a subcortical dementia. Neurologic involvement in SS is characterized by progressive deterioration over a prolonged period of time.

MRI studies demonstrate frequent presence of unidentified bright objects

Neuroradiologic studies have generally demonstrated that cerebral angiography is an inadequate technique to evaluate SS. We believe that this is due to the fact that the affected vessels are too small for detection by this technique. On the other hand, magnetic resonance imaging (MRI) has been demonstrated to be of benefit in the evaluation of a large group of Sjögren's patients. Eighty percent of Sjögren's patients with focal neurologic dysfunction demonstrated multiple areas of enhancement in the periventricular and subcortical white matter, on T-2–weighted images (Figure 8–5). Those Sjögren's patients with large (> 10 mm) areas of enhancement were frequently anti-Ro (SS-A) antibody–positive. In sharp contrast, those Sjögren's patients without evidence of CNS disease infrequently demonstrated these MRI findings.

Evoked response testing may be valuable

Electrophysiologic studies employing multimodality-evoked response testing (eg, visual-evoked responses, brain stem auditory-evoked responses, somatosensory-evoked responses, blink reflex, and electroencephalography) have demonstrated abnormalities indicative of a functional disruption of the involved neural pathways.

These studies detected multiple abnormalities in Sjögren's patients, including a multiple sclerosis (MS)–like picture but with immunogenetic features of SS and

TABLE 8–6 Minnesota Multiphasic Personality Inventory Abnormalities in Patients with Primary Sjögren's Syndrome

Clinical Feature	Number of Patients with Abnormality (N = 23)
Hypochondriasis	21
Depression	14
Hysteria	21
Psychopathic deviant	8
Paranoia	4
Psychasthenia	9
Schizophrenia	10
Hypomania	6
Social introversion	4

Data from:
Malinow KL, Molina R, Gordon B, et al. Neuropsychiatric dysfunction in primary Sjögren's syndrome. Ann Intern Med 1985;103:344–350.

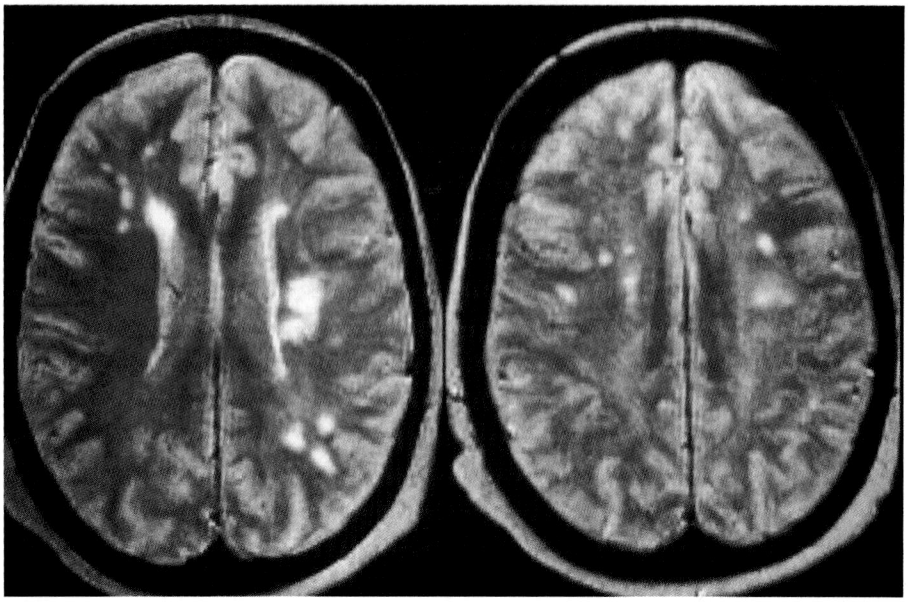

FIGURE 8–5 Focal white matter lesions on CNS MRI in Sjögren's patient.

not MS (ie, the presence of anti-Ro (SS-A) antibodies and the HLA-DR3 rather than the HLA-DR2 phenotype) (Table 8–7). However, in a 10-year follow-up of 100 anti-Ro (SS-A) antibody–positive patients from a rheumatology service, only one demonstrated features of MS. Thus, population selection bias is problematic in determining the frequency of an MS-like clinical picture.

Peripheral Manifestations

Peripheral neuropathy has long been recognized in SS and has been estimated to occur in as many as 16% of cases. Isolated trigeminal neuropathy appears to be the most common presentation. Table 8–8 details cases reported by Kaltrender and Talal demonstrating the chronicity of the SS, the biopsy evidence of a perivascular lymphocytic infiltrate, and the presence of trigeminal neuropathy.

Sensorineural deafness and peripheral neuropathy are frequent manifestations.

Recent studies reveal an increased frequency of sensorineural deafness in anti-Ro (SS-A) antibody–positive Sjögren's patients. Mononeuritis multiplex (associated with leukocytoclastic vasculitis) and small–fiber sensory neuropathy (associated with hypergammaglobulinemic purpura) may also be seen.

Hematologic Manifestations

Leukopenia has been reported in 6 to 33% of patients with SS. Anemia of chronic disease, hemolytic anemia, and thrombocytopenia may also be seen. Autoantibodies against all three hematopoietic cell lines have been detected.

TABLE 8–7 Evoked Sensory Response Testing in Sjögren's Syndrome Patients with CNS Disease Mimicking MS

Test	Positive (%)
Evoked potentials	15/18 (83)
Visual	10/17 (59)
Brain stem auditory	8/15 (53)
Somatosensory	5/11 (45)

Data from:
Alexander EL, Malinow K, Lejewski JE, et al. Primary Sjögren's syndrome with central nervous system disease mimicking multiple sclerosis. Ann Intern Med 1986;104:323–330.

TABLE 8–8 Peripheral Neuropathy in Sjögren's Syndrome

Patient Sicca Symptoms Duration	Neuropathy Duration	Cutaneous Purpura	Muscle Vasculitis
6 years	3 years	+	+
10 years	4 years	+	
5 years	3 years	+	+
14 years	10 years	-	+
8 years	3 years	+	+
12 years	4 years	-	
1 year	2 years	-	+
9 years	5 months	-	
13 years	6 months	+	+
7 years	4 months	+	+

Adapted from:
Kaltreider HB, Talal N. The neuropathy of Sjögren's syndrome. Trigeminal nerve involvement. Ann Intern Med 1969;70:751–762.

Type II mixed cryoglobulins

Paraproteins, including cryoglobulins, may be seen. Using sophisticated electrofocusing techniques, monoclonal immunoglobulins and light chains have been detected in the serum and urine of approximately 80% of Sjögren's patients with extraglandular manifestations. Furthermore, analysis of cryoglobulins in Sjögren's patients has demonstrated that the latter are often type II mixed cryoglobulins containing IgM-κ monoclonal rheumatoid factor, as is found in Waldenström's macroglobulinemia. These monoclonal rheumatoid factors also frequently demonstrate cross-reactive idiotypes that occur early in the disease and become more prominent with chronicity. Recent studies indicate that several idiotypes occur predominantly in Sjögren's patients with lymphoma. (See discussion on mixed cryoglobulinemic vasculitis in Chapter 33, "Hepatitis," for further discussion.)

Increased risk of non-Hodgkin's lymphomas

Non-Hodgkin's lymphomas, affecting particularly the cervical lymph nodes and salivary glands, occur with increased frequency in SS (relative risk 40). Sjögren's patients demonstrating extraglandular manifestations, including recurrent or persistent parotid swelling due to infiltration by non-neoplastic lymphocytes (pseudolymphoma), angioimmunoblastic lymphadenopathy, and splenomegaly appear to be at increased risk. The lymphomas, most commonly B-cell monocytoid lymphomas, are generally low grade. Studies strongly suggest that the development of lymphoma in SS is the result of somatic mutations, in particular translocation of the proto-oncogene *bcl*-2 t(14;18), occurring on a background of oligoclonal B-cell expansion stimulated by autoantigens and/or T cells.

Suspicious masses involving the parotid and submandibular salivary glands and the cervical lymph nodes are best evaluated by MRI and potentially biopsy. The distinction between pseudolymphoma and lymphoma may be challenging, but polymerase chain reaction may be helpful in identifying critical translocations.

Our experience with lymphoma occurring in SS has been surprisingly limited, considering the fact that we have seen and evaluated well over 100 anti-Ro (SS-A) antibody–positive Sjögren's patients during the past decade. One of our anti-Ro (SS-A) antibody–positive elderly Sjögren's patients developed a parotid lymphoma. The other Sjögren's patient who developed a lymphoma is a 46-year-old anti-Ro (SS-A) antibody–positive female with at least a 25-year history of SS. Her disease, characterized by generalized fatigue, rheumatoid factor-positivity, hypergammaglobulinemia, cutaneous vasculitis, arthralgias, and arthritis, has recently been complicated by the development of multiple dermal lesions. These lesions have demonstrated the various stages of a lymphomatous infiltrate, initially a banal perivascular lymphocytic infiltrate and more recently lymphoma cutis (marginal cell lymphoma). Nodular amyloidosis has also been detected in these dermal infiltrates. However, routine laboratory studies have detected no evidence of serum or urine paraproteins.

Constitutional Manifestations

Fatigue is commonly reported in SS. This may be a manifestation of the underlying inflammatory process and associated with inflammatory markers, such as an elevated erythrocyte sedimentation rate, C-reactive protein, or immunoglobulin levels. It may also be secondary to anemia, hypothyroidism, or an associated sleep disorder in the setting of depression, nocturnal polydipsia, or nocturnal myoclonus.

Diagnosis

The diagnosis of SS has been, and remains, problematic. Complaints of dry eyes and dry mouth are both common and nonspecific. Against this background, seven separate sets of diagnostic criteria have been proposed for SS during the past 35 years, distinguished primarily by the weight given to the different clinical and laboratory manifestations of the disease. The more stringent San Diego criteria for the diagnosis of SS were proposed in 1986 and are shown in Table 8–9.

The most recent classification criteria for SS, proposed by investigators in the European Economic Community (EEC) are a less stringent compromise, yielding a sensitivity and specificity of 93% each (Table 8–10).

However, proponents of the San Diego criteria argue that only 15% of the patients diagnosed with SS by the EEC criteria fulfill the San Diego criteria.

TABLE 8–9 San Diego Criteria for Diagnosis of Sjögren's Syndrome

Primary Sjögren's syndrome

Symptoms and objective signs of ocular dryness

1. Schirmer test less than 8 mm wetting per 5 minutes, and
2. Positive Rose Bengal staining of cornea or conjunctiva to demonstrate keratoconjunctivitis sicca

Symptoms and objective signs of dry mouth

1. Decreased parotid flow rate using Lashley cups or other methods, and
2. Abnormal findings from biopsy of minor salivary gland (focus score of ≥ 2 based on average of four evaluable lobules)

Serologic evidence of systemic autoimmunity

1. Elevated rheumatoid factor > 1:320, or
2. Elevated antinuclear antibody > 1:320, or
3. Presence of anti–SS-A (Ro) or anti–SS-B (La) antibodies

Secondary Sjögren's syndrome

Characteristic signs and symptoms of SS (described above) plus clinical features sufficient to allow a diagnosis of rheumatoid arthritis, systemic lupus erythematosus, polymyositis, scleroderma, or biliary cirrhosis

Exclusions

Sarcoidosis, pre-existent lymphoma, human immunodeficiency virus, hepatitis virus B or C, primary fibromyalgia, and other known causes of autonomic neuropathy, keratitis sicca, or salivary gland enlargement

"Definite" Sjögren's syndrome requires objective evidence of dryness of the eyes/mouth and autoimmunity, including a characteristic minor salivary gland biopsy (criteria IA, IB, and IC). "Probable" Sjögren's syndrome does not require a minor salivary gland biopsy but can be diagnosed by demonstrating decreased salivary function (criteria IA, IB-1, and IC).

Data from:
Fox RI, Robinson CA, Curd JG, et al. Sjögren's syndrome. Proposed criteria for classification. Arthritis Rheum 1986;29:577–585.

TABLE 8–10 EEC Criteria for Diagnosis of Sjögren's Syndrome

Ocular symptoms	
	Positive response to question of daily dry eyes for 3 months, or
	Sand or gravel feeling in eyes, or
	Need for tear substitutes more than 3 times a day
Oral symptoms	
	Positive response to question of daily dry mouth for 3 months, or
	Recurrent or persistent swollen glands
	Frequent drinking of fluids to aid swallowing of food
Ocular signs	
	Positive test results from either a Schirmer test (≤ 5 mm in 5 minutes) or a Rose Bengal score (≥ 4 according to van Bijsterveld scoring system)
Histopathology	
	A focus of ≥ 1 on a minor salivary biopsy (focus = aggregations of 50 or more mononuclear cells per 4 mm^2 of glandular tissue)
Objective evidence of salivary gland involvement	
	Positive test results by salivary scintigraphy, parotid stimulation, or unstimulated salivary flow (≤ 1.5 mL in 15 minutes)
Autoantibodies	
	Presence of anti-Ro (SS-A), anti-La (SS-B), or antinuclear antibodies, or rheumatoid factor
Sjögren's syndrome is diagnosed if four or more criteria are present.	

Data from:
Vitali C, Bombardieri S, Moutsopoulos HM, et al. Preliminary criteria for the classification of Sjögren's syndrome. Results of a prospective concerted action supported by the European Community. Arthritis Rheum 1993;36:340–347.

EEC criteria for SS is probably the best compromise.
San Diego criteria too stringent

These differences are significant in determining whether to seek other, nonautoimmune causes for sicca symptoms. They may have a very practical impact given the current concern over a patient being labeled with a pre-existing condition and the impact that this may have upon their eligibility for health insurance coverage. They are critical in performing and interpreting studies regarding the prevalence of clinical findings and the results of therapeutic trials. However, the experience of the senior author evaluating several hundred Sjögren's syndrome patients referred by obstetricians and gynecologists, allergists, rheumatologists, ophthalmologists, internists and dermatologists indicates the EEC provides the more practical criteria.

Subjectively decreased tear production can be objectively documented with the Schirmer test (Figure 8–6). A strip of filter paper is placed into the lower conjunctival sac and the degree of wetting is measured over a 5-minute period. Values of ≤ 8 mm are judged highly suspicious, and values of ≤ 2 mm are confirmatory of dry eyes. The Rose Bengal stain, which detects devitalized tissue, together with a slit lamp examination, is very useful in detecting Sjögren's patients whose ocular dryness is of sufficient severity to produce disruption in the integrity of the corneal and conjunctival epithelium (keratoconjunctivitis sicca).

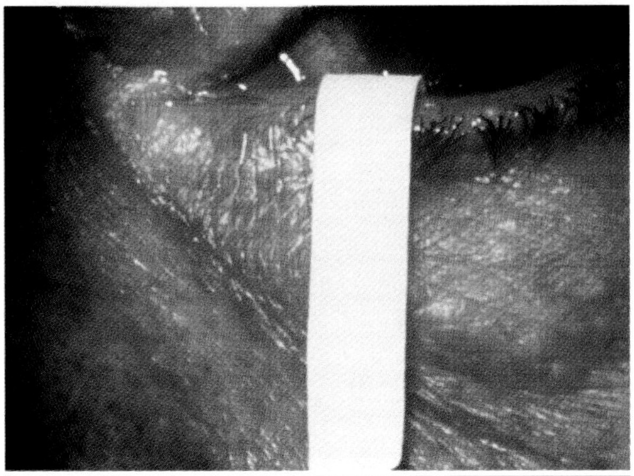

FIGURE 8–6 Performing Schirmer test in a Sjögren's patient. Note absence of tears on filter paper.

Testing for oral dryness is limited. Quantitation of saliva production may be accomplished using whole saliva sialometry or differential collection from Stensen's duct using Lashley cups. Salivary scintigraphy, performed on the parotid and submaxillary salivary glands after injection of sodium pertechnetate Tc 99m, assesses the function of these glands. Sjögren's patients demonstrate delayed uptake and delayed or absent secretion of labeled saliva, but the test lacks diagnostic specificity. Sialography, using intraductal injection of a water-based contrast agent (rather than the older and more complication-prone oil-based agents) will demonstrate tortuous, ectatic salivary gland ducts. Although useful in demonstrating the anatomy of the salivary glands, it is not frequently employed because of cost and a 15 to 20% false-positive rate.

Biopsy of the major salivary glands is not routinely indicated, but for approximately 25 years, a lip biopsy (Figure 8–7) demonstrating lymphocytic aggregates of 50 or more cells in the periductal region of minor salivary glands has been judged to be the "gold standard" for the diagnosis of SS (Figure 8–8). However, much as with the diagnostic criteria for SS itself, there are different systems for scoring minor salivary gland biopsies: Chisholm-Mason, Greenspan, Tarpley, and Daniels. Furthermore, this paradigm itself has recently been challenged by several articles demonstrating that a significant percentage of asymptomatic connective-tissue-disease patients, with normal lacrimal and salivary gland function, also possess these focal lymphocytic minor salivary gland aggregates. In one study, 15 of 80 (19%) asymptomatic patients had a focal score of ≥ 2 (2 lymphocytic aggregates of ≥ 50 cells/4 mm^2). However, none of these connective-tissue-disease patients developed clinical features of SS over a four-year period of observation. In another study, 8 of 18 (44%) asymptomatic rheumatoid arthritis patients demonstrated minor salivary gland biopsy evidence of grade IV changes. False-positive results may also be seen if the biopsy is obtained through inflamed, rather than normal, oral mucosa. Furthermore, SS must be differentiated from nonspecific chronic sialoadenitis, which is characterized by diffuse glandular epithelial atrophy and a scattered and generally nonfocal lymphocytic and plasma cell infiltrate.

Biopsy of minor salivary gland is problematic regarding establishment of SS diagnosis.

In addition to these studies, which question the specificity of the minor salivary gland biopsy in the diagnosis of SS, our own experience indicates that sample error in the performance of lip biopsies is problematic, yielding false-negative results. Examination of lip biopsies for minor salivary gland pathology will frequently demonstrate the very patchy nature of the inflammatory infiltrate. For example, one minor salivary gland may be totally free of the inflammatory process, but the next gland may be totally replaced by a lymphocytic infiltrate. On several occasions, symptomatic anti-Ro (SS-A) antibody–positive Sjögren's patients' initial lip biopsies failed to demonstrate the histopathologic findings of SS. However, upon repeat biopsy, the diagnostic features were detected.

The detection of rheumatoid factor and antinuclear antibodies, at a significant titer, supports the diagnosis of a systemic autoimmune process. Some investigators have employed the presence of the more specific anti-Ro (SS-A) and anti-La (SS-B) antibodies as diagnostic criteria for the presence of SS, although neither is disease-specific. Our studies indicate that this, too, is problematic. For example, serologic studies using gel double diffusion have demonstrated that only 40 to 45% of Sjögren's patients reported by rheumatologists may have anti-Ro (SS-A) antibodies. This same patient population has been reported to have a frequency of anti-Ro (SS-A) antibody–positivity approaching 90% when employing ELISA technology. Symptomatic Sjögren's patients, demonstrating grade III to IV minor salivary gland changes on biopsy and referred by internists, allergists, dermatologists, and gynecologists, have revealed only a 30% frequency of anti-Ro (SS-A) antibodies (detected by gel double diffusion and ELISA technology). Also, there is evidence that anti-Ro (SS-A) antibodies are directed against unique human Ro (SS-A) epitopes, which may or may not cross react with Ro (SS-A) macromolecules from non-human sources.

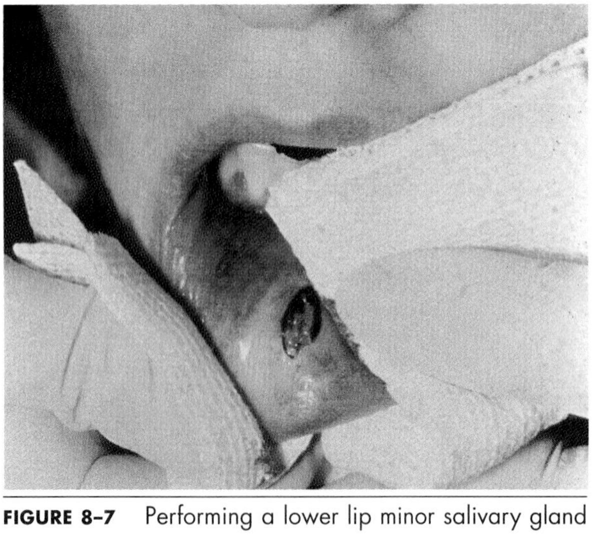

FIGURE 8–7 Performing a lower lip minor salivary gland biopsy in Sjögren's patient.

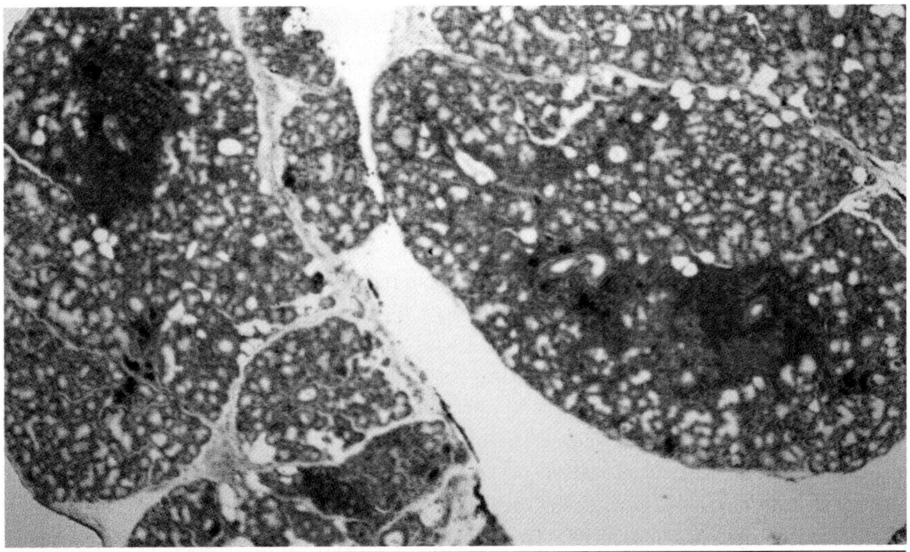

FIGURE 8-8 Histopathologic lip minor salivary gland section in Sjögren's patient. Note focal accumulation of mononuclear cells.

Because of the acquired immunodeficiency syndrome epidemic, human sources of Ro (SS-A) macromolecules are not used in testing. Thus, approximately 10% of Ro (SS-A) antibody–positive patients may fail to be detected. Proponents of the more strict diagnostic criteria would argue that the absence of autoantibodies in a patient with sicca symptoms suggests diagnoses other than Sjögren's syndrome, but this is difficult to support when the biopsy is diagnostic.

Selection patient bias is problematic

Selection bias is also a major problem in the evaluation of Sjögren's patients since it has been demonstrated that extraglandular manifestations, such as cytopenias, hypergammaglobulinemia, serologic hyperreactivity, and cutaneous vasculitis are more commonly detected in anti-Ro (SS-A) antibody–positive patients. These patients, because of their extraglandular manifestations, especially cutaneous vasculitis, are more frequently seen and evaluated by dermatologists and rheumatologists.

Drugs commonly create sicca symptoms.

The differential diagnosis of SS must exclude medications and other disorders that may cause sicca symptoms. Medications with significant anticholinergic side effects, that are given for a variety of indications including management of secretions (in upper respiratory infection [eg, antihistamines and decongestants] or perioperatively) or treatment of depression (eg, tricyclic antidepressants and monoamine oxidase–inhibitors), fibromyalgia, sleep disorders, blood pressure (eg, α- and β-blockers), cardiac dysrhythmias, gastrointestinal disorders (eg, metoclopramide), psychiatric disorders, or parkinsonism may cause or exacerbate symptoms. Disorders that may cause sicca symptoms, mimicking SS, include infiltrative processes (eg, amyloidosis, lymphoma, sarcoidosis, graft-versus-host disease), infectious processes (eg, hepatitis B and C, HIV and other retroviruses, syphilis, tuberculosis), autonomic and other neuropathies (eg, age-associated, and drug-induced neuropathies, MS), postradiation changes, fibromyalgia, and the normal decrease in tear and saliva production seen with aging.

Treatment

The goals of treatment are to provide symptomatic relief and reduce the risk of long-term damage. An assessment of the extent, activity, and aggressiveness of the disease process is the critical first step in determining the level of response.

Artificial tears, which vary in viscosity, are central to the management of keratoconjunctivitis sicca. Using preparations with higher concentrations of hydroxymethylcellulose will increase the viscosity and, therefore, the duration of action. If the duration of action is still insufficient, an ophthalmologist's assistance may be secured for punctal occlusion, first on a temporary basis (eg, with collagen or silicon plugs) to assess its efficacy and then permanently by electrocautery. Artificial tears containing older preservatives, such as benzalkonium chloride and thimerosal, could cause a burning sensation. Newer, less irritating preservatives, as well as preservative-free preparations, are now available. Patients also report relief by wearing swimming goggles, to which moistened soft cotton has been added, while sleeping.

Local application of agents to increase moisture

Production of saliva may be stimulated by a variety of local and systemic measures. Sugar-free candies and gum may be used, although they may contain other carbohydrates that can still promote dental caries. Chewing on an inert substance, such as paraffin, or sucking on a fruit pit, may also stimulate salivary flow. Sips of water are frequently sufficient to maintain oral moisture when symptoms are mild. However, artificial saliva preparations are available and are especially useful in perioperative patients who can take nothing by mouth.

Pilocarpine is effective. Side effects, including crampy abdominal pain, problematic

A number of systemic secretagogues have been evaluated, including bromhexine, anetholetrithione, cevimeline, and pilocarpine. Their effectiveness is dependent upon preservation of some residual glandular function. Both cevimeline and pilocarpine have been approved for use in the United States. They may increase both tear and salivary flow in some individuals, but their usefulness is limited by tolerance to the side effects such as flushing, sweating and crampy abdominal pain.

Given the dental risks in SS, special toothpastes have been developed for patients with xerostomia that generate low levels of peroxide to augment the antibacterial effects of saliva. Topical fluoride preparations are frequently indicated, particularly where the water supply is not fluoridated.

Saline nasal sprays provide symptomatic relief for nasopharyngeal dryness and noninfectious sinus symptoms.

Increasing ambient humidity in the home with a humidifier, as well as large leafy plants to create a "greenhouse" effect, is also very helpful.

Hydroxychloroquine may be helpful.

Constitutional and musculoskeletal manifestations are treated with acetaminophen, salicylates, and nonsteroidal anti-inflammatory drugs (NSAIDs). NSAIDs must be used with care, given their risk for both gastrointestinal and renal toxicity. Hydroxychloroquine has been useful in managing musculoskeletal manifestations and lymphadenopathy in some patients, although the results of controlled trials have been mixed. Corticosteroids are reserved for more serious or life-threatening major organ system involvement, such as vasculitis, central and peripheral nervous system involvement, hemolytic anemia, nephritis, and pneumonitis. Methotrexate, azathioprine, and cyclosporin A have been used for their corticosteroid-sparing effects. However, although there is frequently a reduction in the erythrocyte sedimentation rate and immunoglobulin levels, and the immunohistologic effects of immunosuppressive agents have also been demonstrated, the clinical effect upon sicca symptoms, arthralgias, and myalgias may be limited. Alkylating agents, such as chlorambucil and cyclophosphamide, should be used only with great caution, given the increased risk for the development of non-Hodgkin's lymphoma in these patients. For this reason, treatment with cyclophosphamide as monthly pulses is preferred to daily administration.

Prognosis

Sjögren's syndrome may range in severity from a mild annoyance, through significant ocular and oral involvement with the potential for blindness and carious dental loss, respectively, to major organ system involvement. Major organ system involvement, however, is rarely life-threatening.

Annotated Bibliography

Fox RI. Clinical features, pathogenesis, and treatment of Sjögren's syndrome. Curr Opin Rheumatol 1996;8:438–445.

Fox RI. Sjögren's syndrome. In: Kelley WN, Harris ED, Ruddy S, Sledge CB, eds. Textbook of Rheumatology, 5th ed. Philadelphia: WB Saunders, 1997, pp 955–966.

These are well-written reviews by one of the leading investigators in the field.

Daniels TE, Fox PC. Salivary and oral components of Sjögren's syndrome. Rheum Dis Clin North Am 1992;18:571–589.

This is a well-written review focusing on the oral manifestations of Sjögren's syndrome.

Simmons-O'Brien E, Chen S, Watson R, et al. One hundred anti-Ro (SS-A) antibody positive patients: a 10-year follow-up. Medicine 1995;74:109–130.

This paper reports the 10-year prospective follow-up of 100 anti-Ro (SS-A)–positive patients and their neurologic outcomes.

Fox RI, Chan EK, Kang HI. Laboratory evaluation of patients with Sjögren's syndrome. Clin Biochem 1992;25:213–222.

This is a detailed review of the histologic and serologic markers of Sjögren's syndrome.

Daniels TE. Labial salivary gland biopsy in Sjögren's syndrome. Assessment. as a diagnostic criterion in 362 suspected cases. Arthritis Rheum 1984;27:147–156.

This foundational study demonstrates that focal sialoadenitis, in an adequate labial salivary gland specimen, is the most disease-specific diagnostic criterion for the salivary component of SS.

Fox RI, Robinson CA, Curd JG, et al. Sjögren's syndrome. Proposed criteria for classification. Arthritis Rheum 1986;29:577–585.

This paper details the San Diego diagnostic criteria for Sjögren's syndrome.

Vitali C, Bombardieri S, Moutsopoulos HM, et al. Preliminary criteria for the classification of Sjögren's syndrome. Results of a prospective concerted action supported by the European Community. Arthritis Rheum 1993;36:340–347.

This paper details the EEC's diagnostic criteria for Sjögren's syndrome.

Fox RI, Saito I. Criteria for diagnosis of Sjögren's syndrome. Rheum Dis Clin North Am 1994;20:391–407.

This paper, written by a proponent of the San Diego criteria, reviews the differences between the various sets of proposed diagnostic criteria for Sjögren's syndrome and their implications.

Fox RI. Treatment of the patient with Sjögren's syndrome. Rheum Dis Clin North Am 1992;18:699–709.

This is an excellent review of the therapeutic options for treatment of patients with SS. Despite the absence of a cure for this disease, it details the many options for effective symptomatic management and preventive action.

This entire monograph, edited by R.J. Fox, gives an excellent overview of the diverse clinical features of Sjögren's syndrome.

Vivino FB, Al-Hashimi I, Khan Z, et al. Pilocarpine tablets for the treatment of dry mouth and dry eye symptoms in patients with Sjögren syndrome: a randomized, placebo-controlled, fixed dose, multicenter trial. P92-01 Study Group. Arch Int Med 1999;159: 174–181.

This paper reports symptomatic improvement in sicca symptoms in patients treated with oral pilocarpine.

Dalavanga YA, Detrick B, Hooks JJ, et al. Effect of cyclosporin A (CyA) on the immunopathological lesion of the labial minor salivary glands from patients with Sjögren's syndrome. Ann Rheum Dis 1987;46(2):89–92.

Fox RI, Chan E, Benton L, et al. Treatment of primary Sjögren's syndrome with hydroxychloroquine. Am J Med 1988;85(4A):62–67.

Kruize AA, Hene RJ, Kallenberg CG, et al. Hydroxychloroquine treatment for primary Sjögren's syndrome: a two year double blind crossover trial. Ann Rheum Dis 1993;52:360–364.

These studies demonstrate the serologic and immunohistologic impact of treatment with immunosuppressive agents. However, the clinical impact, although measurable, is often minimal.

Provost TT. Sjögren's syndrome. In: Freedberg IM, Eisen AZ, Wolff K, et al., eds. Fitzpatrick's Dermatology in General Medicine, 5th ed. New York: McGraw-Hill, 1999, pp 2067–2077.

This chapter provides an updated bibliography of various features of Sjögren's syndrome.

Alexander E. Central nervous system disease in Sjögren's syndrome. New insights in immunopathogenesis. Rheum Dis Clin North Am 1992;18:637–672.

This is a review of neurologic events detected in Sjögren's syndrome by an investigator who has made major contributions to this area of study.

For additional patient information, you may contact The National Sjögren's Syndrome Association; 3201 West Evans Drive; Phoenix, AZ 85023; Telephone (800) 395-6772, or The Sjögren's Syndrome Foundation, Inc.; 382 Main Street; Port Washington, NY 11050; Telephone (516) 767-2866.

CHAPTER 9

Antiphospholipid Syndrome

Michelle Petri, M.D., M.P.H., Thomas T. Provost, M.D.

The antiphospholipid syndrome is a recently recognized vasculopathy characterized by repeated venous and/or arterial thromboses, recurrent fetal wastage, and thrombocytopenia. The syndrome most frequently occurs in the presence of a connective tissue disease, most commonly systemic lupus erythematosus (SLE) (secondary antiphospholipid antibody syndrome). This syndrome, however, may also occur in the absence of a connective tissue disease (primary antiphospholipid antibody syndrome [PAPS]).

Syndrome characterized by recurrent venous and arterial thromboses

Most frequently seen with SLE (a secondary antiphospholipid syndrome)

Primary antiphospholipid syndrome seen in absence of a connective tissue disease

Many patients with PAPS and secondary antiphospholipid antibody syndrome demonstrate prominent cutaneous features (livedo reticularis with and without ulceration). The recognition by a dermatologist of this syndrome is of critical importance because early detection and aggressive anticoagulant therapy produce decreased morbidity and mortality.

Early recognition and aggressive anticoagulant therapy are the keys to successful management.

Historic Development

Our understanding of this syndrome is rapidly evolving (Table 9–1). Although the specificity of anticardiolipin antibodies for syphilis has been known since the beginning of this century and the nature of the antigen (anionic phospholipids, cardiolipin) elucidated by Mary Pangborn in the early 1940s, it was not until the observations by Conley and Hartmann, in 1952, that the in vitro features of this syndrome were recognized. They described two SLE patients with biologic false-positive serologic tests for syphilis (BFP-STS) whose plasma demonstrated an anticoagulant effect that could not be corrected by the classic hematologic investigative technique of mixing the affected plasma with fresh normal plasma. This anticoagulant, later termed the "lupus anticoagulant" (LA), was found to reside in the IgG and IgM (immunoglobulin) fractions of patients' sera.

Conley and Hartmann first describe in vitro anticoagulant effect of the blood of these patients.

Subsequent investigations by Bowie et al. determined that although these patients demonstrated in vitro an anticoagulant effect, thromboses were a prominent clinical feature. Further clinical observations revealed that SLE patients with this LA clotting abnormality sometimes demonstrated a BFP-STS and thrombocytopenia. Additional studies demonstrated that the lupus anticoagulant interfered with the prothrombin (PT) activator complex (factors Xa, Va, calcium, and phospholipid). Despite the presence of the LA activity in some BFP-STS–positive SLE patients, syphilitic patients failed to demonstrate either the clinical or in vitro anticoagulant features of the antiphospholipid syndrome.

Bowie et al. first describe in vivo thromboses of these patients.

In 1983, Nigel Harris, working in Graham Hughes' laboratory in the United Kingdom, devised a very sensitive solid-phase enzyme-linked immunosorbent assay (ELISA) technique for the detection of anticardiolipin antibodies. The aim

TABLE 9–1 Glossary of Events in Development of Knowledge of Antiphospholipid Antibody Syndrome

1907	Wasserman uses saline extract of livers from congenital syphilitic fetuses as antigen source to detect syphilitic antibody (reagin).
1924	Libman and Sacks describe sterile vegetations on heart valves of SLE patients.
1941	Mary Pangborn demonstrates syphilitic antigen is an anionic phospholipid and terms it "cardiolipin."
1951–52	Haserick and Long (1951) and Moore and Mohr (1952) describe the occurrence of SLE in patients with a preceding BFP-STS.
1952	Conley and Hartmann describe two SLE patients with BFP-STS reactions whose plasma demonstrated an in vitro inhibitor of coagulation.
1963	Bowie et al. report that four of eight SLE patients with the in vitro anticoagulant demonstrated in vivo thrombosis.
1966	Sneddon describes the association of livedo reticularis with recurrent cerebral vascular accidents.
1972	Feinstein and Rappaport term this inhibitor of in vitro coagulation the "lupus anticoagulant" (LA).
1974	Lechner reports the high frequency of BFP-STS, thrombosis, and thrombocytopenia in LA-positive SLE patients.
1983	Harris et al. develop a solid-phase immunoassay to detect anticardiolipin antibodies.
1983	Hughes describes association of venous and arterial thrombosis, recurrent fetal wastage, and thrombocytopenia with anticardiolipin antibodies in SLE patients.
1992	McNeil and Krilis detect that anticardiolipin antibodies are directed against anionic phospholipids complexed with β_2-glycoprotein I.
1990s	Multiple investigators present evidence for possible additional antibodies giving the phenotypic expression of the antiphospholipid syndrome (reviewed by Roubey)

SLE = systemic lupus erythematosus; BFP-STS = biologic false-positive serologic test for syphilis

1983 the development of a sensitive anticardiolipin ELISA assay
Anticardiolipin antibodies associated with syphilis do not have LA activity.

of this investigative group was to develop a sensitive assay to measure anticardiolipin antibodies, which were thought to play an important role in the development of LA activity. This assay, 200 to 400 times more sensitive than the venereal disease research laboratory (VDRL) test, quickly determined that patients demonstrating LA activity commonly possessed anticardiolipin antibodies. However, anticardiolipin antibody–positive syphilitic patients or patients with an infection (leprosy) or receiving drugs (chlorpromazine) who had developed an acute BFP-STS did not have LA activity.

Two tests for antiphospholipid antibodies
Anticardiolipin antibodies phospholipid-dependent coagulation test
May have 25% discordance

Subsequent studies using anticardiolipin antibodies and a functional phospholipid-dependent coagulation test (prothrombin [PT], the activated partial thromboplastin time, the kaolin clotting time, the Russell's viper venom time), generally demonstrated concordance between the serologic and functional assays. However, with further studies, especially in the evaluation of patients with the Sneddon's syndrome (livedo reticularis with recurrent central nervous system thromboses), a 25% discordance was detected.

Cardiolipin complexed with β_2 glycoprotein I contains epitopes of pathologic significance for anticardiolipin.
Anticardiolipin antibodies reactive against only cardiolipin not associated with LA activity

Also, it has now been demonstrated that cardiolipin complexed with β_2-glycoprotein I contains the epitopes reactive with anticardiolipin antibodies. In some studies, the epitope resides solely on the β_2-glycoprotein I. Anticardiolipin antibodies reactive against only cardiolipin (eg, syphilis, leprosy) are not associated with the LA.

Animal studies indicate that mice immunized with cardiolipin and β_2-glycoprotein I develop high titer anticardiolipin antibodies and LA activity, whereas cardiolipin in the absence of β_2-glycoprotein I is nonimmunogenic.

The triad of clinical features (thrombosis, thrombocytopenia, and recurrent fetal wastage) dominated the clinical picture of early investigations of this syndrome, and the recurrent nature of the disease process was emphasized. Furthermore, it was noted that thromboses generally involved the same structures (ie, arterial events following arterial events and venous events generally following venous events).

As experience was obtained, Graham Hughes' group noted that the same clinical events occurred in both PAPS and secondary antiphospholipid antibody syndrome patients. For example, in a large study of 70 PAPS patients, 54% had episodes of deep vein thrombosis; in 13 of these patients, the events were either multiple or bilateral; and in 18, pulmonary embolism occurred. In 31 patients (44%), arterial occlusions were observed; in 15, strokes or a transient ischemic attack; in 6, multi-infarct dementia; in 5, coronary artery occlusion; in 2, angina pectoris; and in 1, aortic occlusion. Recurrent fetal wastage (2 or more) was noted in 24 patients (34%). This large study revealed that livedo reticularis was present in 14 of these 70 PAPS patients, and in 6, it was associated with the presence of chorea, transient ischemic attacks, or a stroke.

In a study of 500 consecutive SLE patients by Mexican investigators, antiphospholipid antibodies were detected in 362 patients. Of these, 168 demonstrated titers that were 5 standard deviations above normal, which were considered by the investigators to be very significant. Forty-five of these patients had no clinical manifestations despite the presence of high titer anticardiolipin antibodies (> 5 standard deviations). Recurrent fetal wastage occurred in 36 patients (3 abortions or stillbirths). The odds ratio of having recurrent fetal wastage was 10.54 in patients with anticardiolipin antibodies titers equal to or greater than 5 standard deviations above normal. Fifty-two patients had thrombotic events. In 43, including 14 who had recurrent events, thrombophlebitis was present. Sixteen patients had arterial occlusions. These investigators also determined that 88 patients had thrombocytopenia, 25 patients had hemolytic anemia, and 15 patients had leg ulcers.

More recent studies indicate that over a 10-year period, 50% of asymptomatic anticardiolipin antibody–positive patients became symptomatic for the antiphospholipid antibody syndrome. Further studies have demonstrated additional antibodies (ie, anti-annexin V [lipomodulin] and anti-prothrombin antibodies), which clinically manifest as the antiphospholipid syndrome.

Antiannexin V and anti-PT antibodies are associated with an antiphospholipid-like clinical syndrome.

Asymptomatic anticardiolipin antibody positive patients frequently over time develop clinical features

Pathophysiology

Based on the data indicating the possibility of multiple antibodies occurring in patients with the antiphospholipid antibody syndrome, it is impossible, at the present time, to determine exactly the molecular level of interaction producing the thromboses. It is likely there are multiple sites of action. For example, these autoantibodies could inhibit anticoagulant activity and induce thromboses by blocking the anticoagulant action of annexin V, thrombomodulin, protein C, or protein S. It is also possible that these antibodies may interfere with endothelial cell anticoagulant activity in which β_2-glycoprotein I participates as a cell-surface receptor or ligand. It is also conceivable that these antibodies could produce a dysregulation of eicosanoids, resulting in the inhibition of endothelial cell prostacyclin production, or bind directly to platelets, promoting platelet activation and/or aggregation.

This is an area of active investigation at the present time. For an excellent review of this area of investigation see review article by Roubey (1996).

Multiple possible molecular sites of pathology may be present in this syndrome, dependent upon specificity of antibodies.

Clinical Features

Hemorrhagic Manifestations

Although the prolongation of clotting times of SLE patients with antiphospholipid antibodies first drew the attention of investigators, bleeding complications are rare and appear to occur only in association with thrombocytopenia or

Hemorrhagic tendencies in these patients uncommon

hypoprothrombinemia. For example, in one study of approximately 200 LA-positive patients, bleeding episodes were recorded in less than 10% of patients.

Thrombotic Manifestations

Multiple arterial and venous thromboses have been described.

Thrombosis involving both arterial and venous vessels is commonly detected in patients with PAPS and secondary antiphospholipid antibody syndrome. Cerebral artery involvement producing strokes or transient ischemic attacks, myocardial infarction, brachial artery thrombosis, and peripheral arterial and retinal artery occlusions have been detected. Trousseau's phenomenon (migratory superficial venous thrombosis), renal vein thrombosis, inferior vena cava, and hepatic vein thrombosis producing the Budd-Chiari syndrome and pulmonary hypertension produced either by multiple pulmonary emboli or intrapulmonary vascular thrombosis have also been reported.

Thrombocytopenia

Isolated thrombocytopenia may be a manifestation.

Thrombocytopenia (platelet counts < 100,000) have been shown to have a significant statistical association with the presence of IgG (immunoglobulin) anticardiolipin antibodies. Furthermore, studies have detected that approximately 10% of patients with autoimmune idiopathic thrombocytopenia purpura possess anticardiolipin antibodies.

Recurrent Fetal Wastage

Recurrent fetal wastage commonly detected in women with the antiphospholipid antibody syndrome

Recurrent fetal wastage and anticardiolipin antibodies have been detected in SLE. However, many patients with recurrent fetal wastage and antiphospholipid antibodies do not have SLE.

Cutaneous Manifestations

Leg Ulcers

Leg ulcers

A study of 110 chronic BFP-STS patients detected 7% with leg ulcers. The patients also possessed evidence of the LA. On rare occasions, leg ulcers associated with antiphospholipid antibody syndromes may resemble pyoderma gangrenosum.

Livedo Reticularis and Other Cutaneous Manifestations

Livedo reticularis with or without ulceration has been noted in patients with antiphospholipid antibody syndrome (Figure 9–1). It has also been seen in other conditions (Table 9–2). This cutaneous finding has been associated with the presence of recurrent arterial and venous thromboses, cardiac valvular abnormalities, and recurrent cerebrovascular thromboses (Sneddon's syndrome).

Livedo reticularis
Acral infarcts
Acrocyanosis
Atrophie blanche

Some patients with Degos's disease may have antiphospholipid syndrome.

Other cutaneous manifestations include acrocyanosis, acral infarcts with crusted ulcerations around the nail beds, peripheral gangrene, widespread hemorrhagic necrosis, recurrent deep vein thrombosis, necrotizing purpura, and atrophie blanche–like ulcerations about the ankles (Figure 9–2). On unusual occasions, Degos' disease (a multisystem vasculopathy characterized by wedge-shaped cutaneous ischemia and by cerebral and intestinal infarction) has been described in association with anticardiolipin antibodies and the LA (Figures 9–3 and 9–4).

"Bland thrombi"

Pathologic examination of the skin reveals multiple microthrombi, usually without an inflammatory infiltrate, involving multiple arteries and veins in the dermis. At times, the pathology ("bland" thrombi in multiple dermal blood vessels) may be the only evidence for the presence of the antiphospholipid antibody syndrome since anticardiolipin antibodies and the LA may be transient.

One such case involved a 65-year-old Caucasian female who, during the preceding 12 months, had developed transient amaurosis fugax in the left eye as well as a transient neurologic event of the brain stem producing ataxia. About 4 weeks prior, the patient developed painful, hemorrhagic erythematous ulcerating lesions on the lateral surface of her right calf.

Physical examination revealed a healthy-appearing female in no acute distress, with no residual evidence of her previous ataxia or amaurosis fugax.

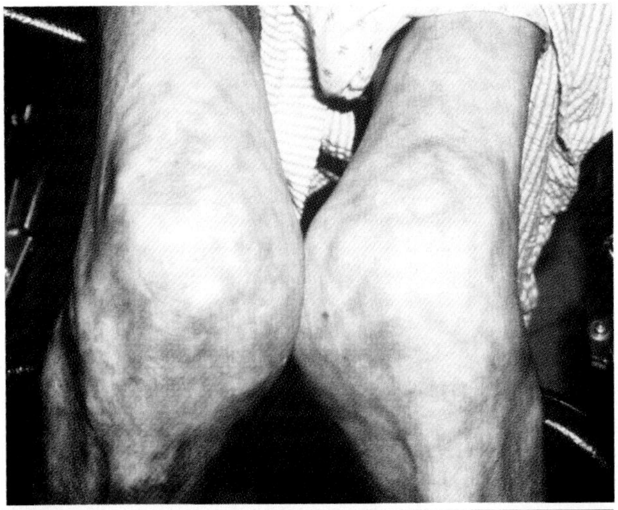

FIGURE 9–1 Prominent livedo reticularis over knees and thighs of an elderly woman with the antiphospholipid syndrome.

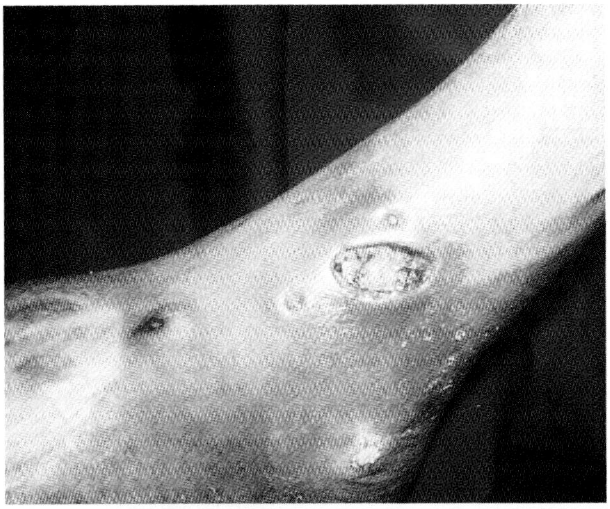

FIGURE 9–2 Ulceration and areas of atrophie blanche in a patient with the antiphospholipid syndrome.

Examination of both lower legs revealed extensive livedo reticularis with two ulcers on the lateral aspect of her right calf, which were painful to touch (Figure 9–5). The lesions were biopsied and demonstrated multiple microthrombi in multiple blood vessels throughout the dermis. Despite pathologic and clinical evidence of the antiphospholipid antibody syndrome, repeat determinations for anticardiolipin antibodies and an RVVT test were negative (Figure 9–6). However, anti-annexin V antibodies were detected. The patient was treated with high-intensity warfarin producing an international normalized ratio (INR) of 3. The ulcers quickly resolved and she remains asymptomatic 48 months later.

The bland arterial and venous thrombosis noted on biopsy must be differentiated from the bland thrombosis associated with warfarin necrosis. Warfarin can produce, on unusual occasions, a transient hypercoagulable state. Generally, this occurs within 10 days of initiation of anticoagulant therapy. Hemorrhagic necrosis of the skin, most commonly of the breast and thighs, occurs (Figures 9–7 and 9–8). Biopsies demonstrate thrombosis in venules and capillaries of the dermis and subcutaneous tissue. A transient deficiency of the warfarin-sensitive protein C anticoagulant occurs, generally in patients who are heterozygous-protein C deficient.

The very rare ulceration detected with heparin therapy is localized to sites of injection and represents a hypersensitivity reaction.

Atrophie Blanche

Atrophie blanche is characterized by smooth, white scarred areas, predominantly of the lower legs and feet, associated with telangiectasia and surrounding hyperpigmentation. Ulceration may be quite painful and is notoriously slow to heal.

Histopathology of some of these lesions has demonstrated thrombosis of small vessels. Also, fibrinoid changes have been detected. Recent evidence indi-

TABLE 9–2 Conditions Associated with Livedo Reticularis

I	Associated with connective tissue diseases, such as systemic lupus erythematosus, scleroderma, and rheumatoid arthritis
II	Associated with cryoglobulinemia
III	Associated with vasculitis, especially polyarteritis nodosa
IV	Antiphospholipid syndrome

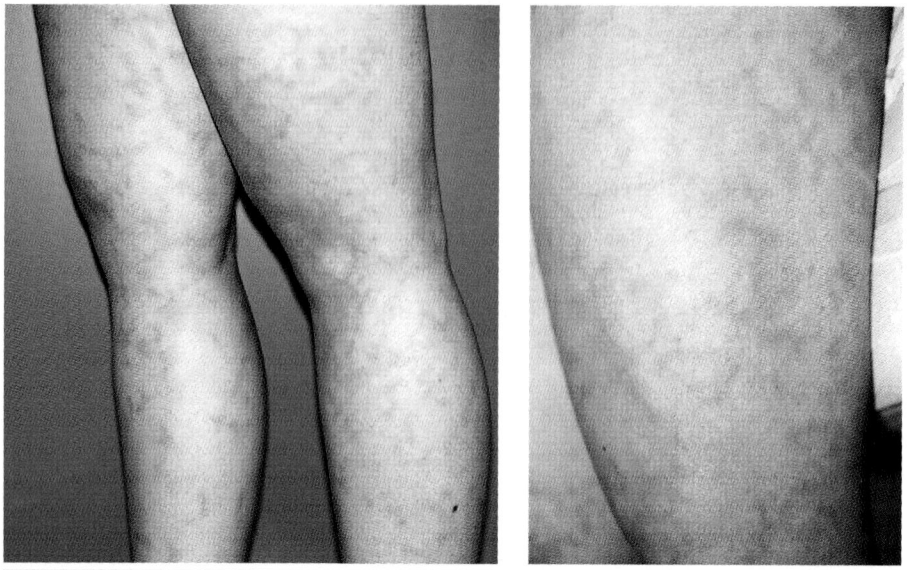

FIGURES 9-3 AND 9-4 Livedo reticularis of legs and a close-up of the thigh in a patient with the antiphospholipid syndrome.

cates that this type of ulceration, associated with livedo reticularis, may be seen in patients with antiphospholipid syndrome.

Myocardial Manifestations

Libman-Sacks endocarditis
Atrial and ventricular dysfunction

In recent years, it has been recognized that cardiac involvement is a common occurrence in patients with the antiphospholipid syndrome. The classic valvular involvement in SLE, Libman-Sacks endocarditis, is a bland, verrucous endo-

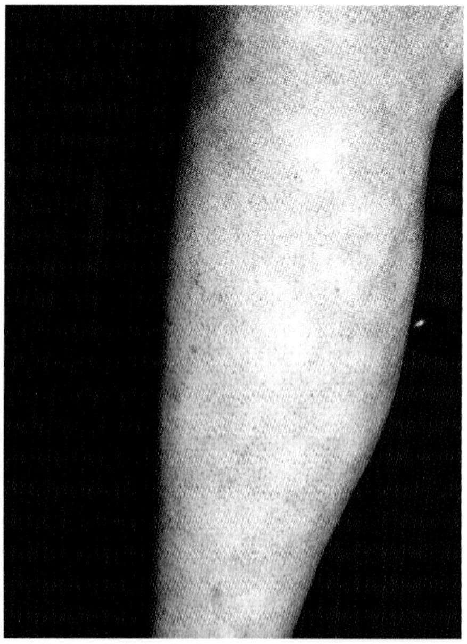

FIGURE 9-5 Livedo reticularis of leg in a middle-aged female who has had two transient neurologic events and atrophie blanche. Repeated anticardiolipin antibody and Russell's viper venom tests (RVVT) have been negative. Treated with pentoxifylline and a baby aspirin.

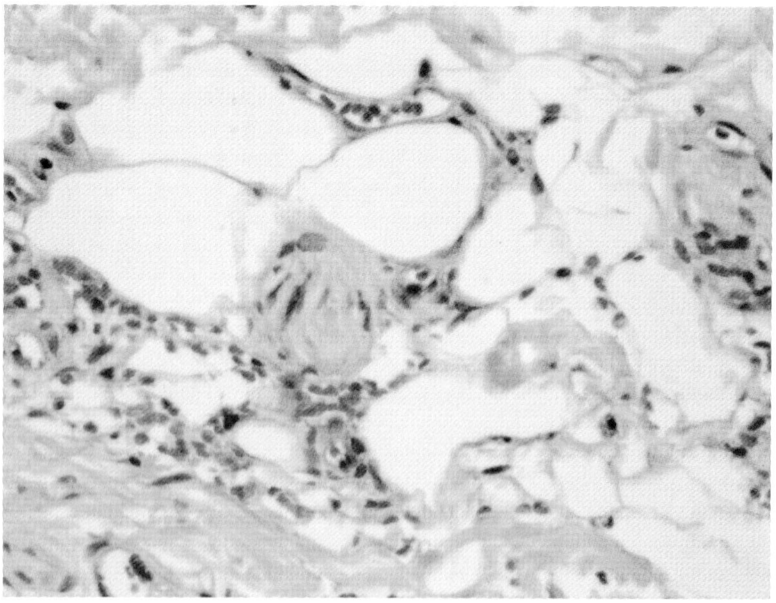

FIGURE 9-6 Multiple small vessel "bland" thrombi in a middle-aged Caucasian female with transient amaurosis fugax neurologic signs and ulceration right lower leg with livedo reticularis. Antiannexin V antibodies detected.

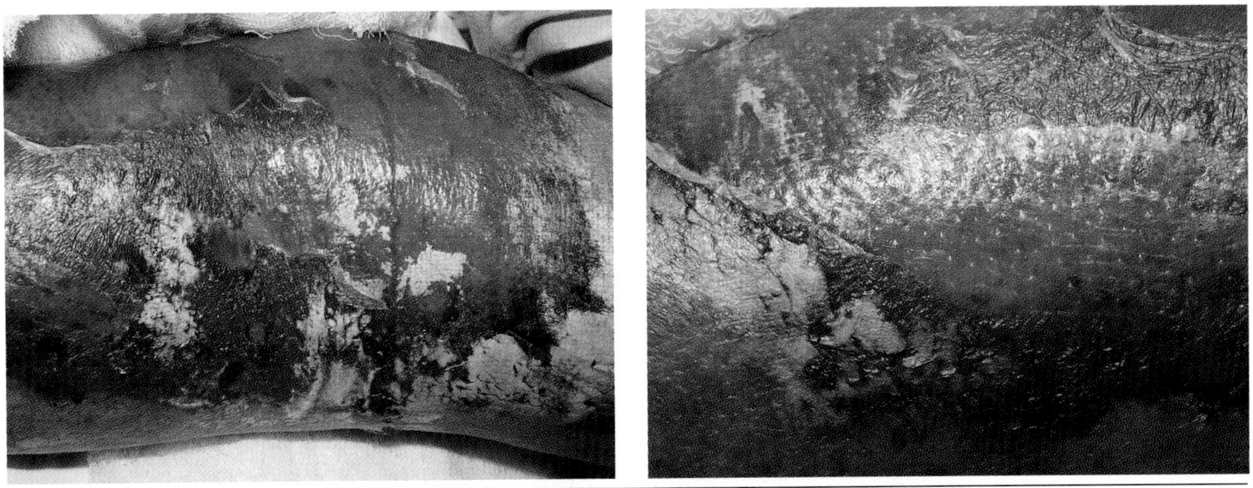

FIGURES 9–7 AND 9–8 Extensive hemorrhagic cutaneous necrosis of the flank in a patient treated with warfarin. White material is topical antibiotic sulfamylon.

carditis affecting atrioventricular valves of the heart. These vegetations are generally of limited hemodynamic significance. Recently, however, aortic valve involvement with aortic insufficiency and mitral valve involvement with mitral insufficiency have been reported. Atrial and ventricular dysfunction, multiple occlusive thrombi unaccompanied by vasculitis in intramyocardial arteries, and right atrial thrombosis mimicking an atrial myxoma have been reported in SLE patients with the antiphospholipid syndrome.

Cutaneous features may be prominent in antiphospholipid antibody patients with cardiac manifestations.

Cutaneous manifestations in these antiphospholipid patients with cardiac manifestations are common. For example, in one report, 60% of SLE patients with antiphospholipid-associated cardiac disease demonstrated cutaneous manifestations in the form of livedo reticularis and/or digital vasculitic lesions.

Young myocardial infarction patients may be at risk for antiphospholipid antibodies.

Perhaps the most important data regarding cardiac involvement with patients with antiphospholipid antibodies are the observations that antiphospholipid antibodies may play a role in the pathogenesis of acute myocardial infarction, especially in young (< 45 years of age) patients. Furthermore, studies indicate that approximately one-third of patients demonstrating late coronary artery graft occlusion, 12 months post–coronary artery bypass graft surgery, manifest antiphospholipid antibodies. In addition, approximately 60% of antiphospholipid antibody–positive, young, acute myocardial infarction patients experienced a recurrent thromboembolic event including cerebral infarctions, arterial occlusions of the lower extremities, and a second myocardial infarction.

Much information needs to be obtained regarding a possible role of antiphospholipid antibodies in the pathogenesis of acute myocardial infarction. However, the data recounted above suggest this may be a fruitful area of investigation.

Cerebral Manifestations

Sneddon's syndrome: most commonly defined neurologic manifestations of the antiphospholipid syndrome

In 1966, Sneddon described 6 patients with prominent livedo reticularis of at least 7-years duration associated with the presence of cerebral symptoms. Five of these 6 patients were females; 4 of 6 developed hemiplegia and 3 of 6 an associated aphasia. Hemiopsia was detected in 2, and a hemianesthesia was detected in 1. Subsequent investigations have indicated that Sneddon's syndrome is one of the most commonly defined neurologic syndromes associated with the antiphospholipid syndrome.

Our most dramatic experience with Sneddon's syndrome was a 59-year-old Caucasian male who, over a 6-month period, developed dementia. Physical examination revealed widespread livedo reticularis involving the lower legs, thighs, buttocks, and forearms. Magnetic resonance imaging of the brain demonstrated multiple enhanced T-2–weighted images throughout the brain indicative of multiple infarcts. The RVVT was positive and the cardiolipin ELISA was 69 standard deviations above normal. Anticoagulation was instituted. However, because of severe dementia, the patient was institutionalized for custodial care.

Young women who have strokes may have increased frequency of antiphospholipid antibodies.

In addition, it has been recognized that women who have no risk factors, are under the age of 45, and develop strokes have a high frequency of antiphospholipid antibodies. Furthermore, these vascular insults are repetitive, and over time, a number of these patients may develop postinfarct dementia. For example, one study, examining 46 unselected neurologic patients under the age of 50 for anticardiolipin antibodies and the LA, detected 21 stroke or transient ischemic attack patients. Multiple cerebral events were frequent. Concurrent diagnosis of SLE was found in most but not all cases.

Other Manifestations

Acute adrenal insufficiency

Acute adrenal insufficiency characterized by bilateral adrenal hemorrhage and/or infarction has been reported in both PAPS and secondary antiphospholipid syndrome. In addition, avascular necrosis has been reported in patients with PAPS and secondary antiphospholipid syndrome.

Anticardiolipin antibodies have also been detected in patients with temporal arteritis and in a patient with Takayasu's arteritis. Whether or not these anticardiolipin antibodies played a pathologic role in the development of the vasculitis is unknown.

Catastrophic Antiphospholipid Syndrome

Rapid onset of multiorgan thrombosis
Cutaneous manifestations may be prominent
High mortality rate

In addition to the classic manifestations of the antiphospholipid syndrome characterized by recurrent venous and arterial thromboses in multiple organs occurring over months to years, an acute form of the antiphospholipid syndrome exists. This syndrome, termed the "catastrophic antiphospholipid syndrome," is characterized by the rapid onset of multiple (at least three) organ involvement with renal failure, hypertension, central nervous system disease, and histopathologic evidence of multiple large- and small-vessel occlusions. Cutaneous features are prominent and include livedo reticularis, acrocyanosis, ischemic ulcers of the digits, and cutaneous necrosis. Central nervous system manifestations include hemiparesis, cerebral infarctions, confusion, emotional lability, status epilepticus, behavioral changes, a stuporous state, and unresponsiveness. In addition, adrenal and coronary artery vessel infarctions have been detected. Most of the patients have a lupus-like disease, but some have the PAPS. Renal disease is the primary or contributing cause of death.

The differential diagnosis of catastrophic antiphospholipid syndrome includes thrombotic thrombocytopenic purpura, disseminated intravascular coagulation, and vasculitis. The presence of schistocytes, a microangiopathic hemolytic anemia, and fibrinogen degradation products may help to differentiate these conditions from the catastrophic antiphospholipid syndrome.

Treatment

High-dose warfarin therapy INR ≥ 3 is effective in preventing recurrent episodes.
Risk of bleeding is problematic

Until recently, definitive data regarding the desired treatment regimen of these patients have been lacking. Recent studies have indicated that warfarin therapy at an INR level of 3 or greater is effective in preventing the recurrence of thrombosis in patients with antiphospholipid antibody syndrome. Thrombotic events often recur within 12 months of the initial event or within 1 year of cessation of warfarin therapy. In one study, patients given high-intensity warfarin therapy demonstrated an 8-year 100% survival without recurrence. In another large study of both PAPS and secondary antiphospholipid antibody syndrome patients, treatment with high-intensity warfarin, with or without low-dose aspirin, was effective in preventing further thrombotic events. This study demonstrated 90% effectiveness in preventing new thrombotic episodes over a 5-year period.

The complications of long-term, high-intensity anticoagulation therapy are problematic. It was noted, however, that the risk of bleeding compared favorably with the risk of bleeding associated with long-term warfarin therapy in other conditions. Overall, it has been concluded from these studies that benefits of warfarin therapy are much greater than the risks in the treatment of antiphospholipid antibody syndrome.

Annotated Bibliography

Kaburaki J, Kuwana M, Yamamoto M, et al. Clinical significance of anti-annexin V antibodies in patients with systemic lupus erythematosus. Am J Hematol 1997;54: 209–213.

This study demonstrates that 27 of 140 SLE patients (19%) possessed antiannexin V antibodies. These patients demonstrated a significantly higher frequency of arterial and venous thrombosis, intrauterine fetal loss and prolonged activated partial thromboplastin times compared with SLE patients without antiannexin V antibodies. Three SLE patients with thrombosis possessed antiannexin V antibodies in the absence of anticardiolipin antibodies. These studies indicate that antiannexin V antibodies may also be capable of participating in a syndrome that is now broadly known as antiphospholipid syndrome.

Nalbandian RM, Mader IJ, Barrett JL, et al. Petechiae, ecchymosis and necrosis of skin induced by Coumadin congeners on rare, occasionally lethal complications of anticoagulant therapy. JAMA 1965;192:107–111.

Broekmans AW, Bertina RM, Loeliger EA, et al. Protein C and the development of skin necrosis during anticoagulant therapy. Throm Haemost 1983;49:251–255.

These two articles describe clinical features of Coumadin-associated necrosis and relationship to protein C levels.

Tuneu A, Moreno A, de Moragas JM. Cutaneous reactions secondary to heparin injections. J Am Acad Dermatol 1985;12:1072–1075.

This article describes a rare occurrence of hypersensitivity reaction to heparin.

Englert HJ, Hawkes CH, Boey ML, et al. Degos's disease: association with anticardiolipin antibodies and the lupus anticoagulant. Br Med J 1984;289:576.

Assier H, Chosidow O, Piette JC, et al. Absence of antiphospholipid and anti-endothelial cell antibodies in malignant atrophic papulosis: a study of 15 cases. J Am Acad Dermatol 1995;33:831–833.

These two articles indicate that only rarely is Degos's disease associated with anticardiolipin antibodies.

Khamashta MA, Cuadrado MJ, Mujic F, et al. The management of thrombosis in the antiphospholipid-antibody syndrome. N Engl J Med 1995;332:993–997.

This is an excellent article demonstrating the effectiveness of warfarin therapy (INR = 3) in preventing recurrent thrombosis in the antiphospholipid antibody syndrome. Although spontaneous hemorrhage can occur with an INR = 3, the authors feel that the risk/benefit ratio, because of the recurrent nature of the thrombosis, favors intense warfarin therapy.

Shah N, Khamashta NA, Atsumi T, Hughes GR. Outcome of patients with anticardiolipin antibodies: a 10 year follow-up of 52 patients. Lupus 1998;7:3–6.

This study, from the leading investigators of this syndrome, demonstrates that 52 anticardiolipin antibody–positive patients were seen and evaluated in 1986. Thirty-one patients had the antiphospholipid antibody syndrome. Sub-

sequently, 9 of these 31 (29%) had further thrombotic events during the follow-up period. Of the 21 anticardiolipin antibody–positive patients who were without clinical manifestations, the 10-year follow-up demonstrated that 11 (52%) developed the syndrome. Five patients (10%) died during the 10-year follow-up. The authors believe that close monitoring of all patients with anticardiolipin antibodies is indicated because the development of clinical features of the the antiphospholipid syndrome is high.

Lakasing L, Poston L. Adverse pregnancy outcome in the antiphospholipid syndrome: focus for future research. Lupus 1997;6:681–684.

This is an excellent editorial summarizing the complex pathogenic role of antiphospholipid antibodies in producing recurrent fetal loss, pre-eclampsia, interuterine growth restriction, and placental abruption. The areas of research efforts to explain these various complications are outlined. The article contains 56 references, the majority of which were published within the last 5 years.

Roubey RA. Immunology of the antiphospholipid antibody syndrome. Arthritis Rheum 1996;39:1444–1454.

This is an excellent review that discusses specificities of the antiphospholipid antibodies. Using the anticardiolipin ELISAs, anticardiolipin anti–β_2 glycoprotein I are detected. The lupus anticoagulant assays will detect antiprothrombin, antifactor V, antifactor X, and anti–β_2 glycoprotein 1.

It is also apparent that patients may have features of the antiphospholipid syndrome and have antibodies not detectable by standard antiphospholipid assays. These antibodies include antibodies to components of the protein C pathway, antivascular heparin sulfate proteoglycan, antiannexin V, antikininogens, and anti-CD36. It is also speculated that antiphospholipid antibodies may be directed against a phospholipase A_2-phospholipid complex. This review article cites 116 references.

Rand JH, Wu XX, Andree HA, et al. Pregnancy loss in the antiphospholipid-antibody syndrome—a possible thrombogenic mechanism. N Engl J Med 1997;337:154–160.

This study demonstrates that antiphospholipid antibodies may reduce levels of annexin V. Annexin V is a phospholipid-binding protein with potent anticoagulant activity. This in vitro study demonstrated a marked reduction of annexin V on trophoblast and endothelial cells exposed to antiphospholipid IgG antibody. Compared with controls, loss of annexin V was associated with accelerated plasma coagulation times. These studies suggest that the reduction of annexin V levels on vascular cells may be an important mechanism of thrombosis and pregnancy loss in the antiphospholipid antibody syndrome.

Wilson WA, et al. International consensus statement on preliminary classification criteria for definite antiphospholipid syndrome: report of an international workshop. Arthritis Rheum 1999;43:1309–1311.

These authors have proposed the following preliminary criteria for the classification of the antiphospholipid syndrome:

Clinical Criteria

(1) Vascular thrombosis
One or more clinical episodes of arterial, venous, or small vessel thrombosis in any tissue or organ. Thrombosis must be confirmed by imaging or Doppler studies, or histopathology with the exception of superficial venous thrombosis. For histologic confirmation, thrombosis should be present without significant evidence of inflammation in the vessel wall.

(2) *Pregnancy morbidity*
a) One or more unexplained deaths or morphologically normal fetus at or beyond the 10th week of gestation with normal fetal morphology documented by ultrasound or by direct examination of the fetus, or b) One or more premature births of a morphologically normal neonate at or before the 34th week of gestation because of severe pre-eclampsia or eclampsia, or severe placental insufficiency, or c) Three or more unexplained consecutive spontaneous abortions before the 10th week of gestation with maternal anatomic or hormonal abnormalities, and paternal and maternal chromosomal causes excluded.

Laboratory Criteria

(1) *Anticardiolipin antibody of IgG and/or IgM isotype in blood, present in medium or high titer on two or more occasions at least 6 weeks apart, measured by a standard enzyme link immunoabsorbent assay for β_2-glycoprotein I-dependent anticardiolipin antibodies.*

(2) *Lupus anticoagulant present in plasma on two or more occasions at least 6 weeks apart, detected according to the guidelines of the International Society of Thrombosis and Hemostasis, in the following steps: a) prolonged phospholipid-dependent coagulation demonstrated on a screen test (eg, activated partial thromboplastin time, kaolin clotting time, dilute Russell's viper venom time, dilute prothrombin time, Textarin time); b) failure to correct the prolonged coagulation time on the screening test by mixing with normal platelet poor plasma; c) shortening or correction of the prolonged coagulation time on the screening test by the addition of excess phospholipid; and d) exclusion of other coagulopathies (eg, factor VIII inhibitor or heparin as appropriate).*

Definite antiphospholipid antibody syndrome is considered to be present if at least one of the clinical criteria and one of the laboratory criteria are met.

(Reproduced with permission)

CHAPTER 10

Relapsing Polychondritis

Thomas T. Provost, M.D., John A. Flynn, M.D.

Systemic disease characterized by recurrent inflammation of organs containing glycosaminoglycans, elastic tissue, and cartilage matrix

Relapsing polychondritis is an inflammatory cartilage disease producing widespread clinical features (Table 10–1). It is characterized by recurrent, painful, violaceous, erythematous swellings of one or both external ears. Two-thirds of patients develop nasal chondritis producing, with repeated insults, a saddle-nose deformity. A mono- or oligo-nondeforming arthritis involving large and small joints frequently occurs. In addition, parasternal joints (costochondral, sternoclavicular) are commonly involved. Laryngotracheal bronchial involvement can produce collapse of the tracheal bronchial tree, suffocation, and death. Ocular inflammation, characterized by conjunctivitis, scleritis, and iritis, occurs in approximately 60% of patients.

Cardiovascular involvement occurs in approximately 25% of patients and may lead to death. This cardiovascular involvement is especially due to inflammation of the aorta with aortic root dilatations leading to valvular destruction and insufficiency. Additionally, the thoracic and abdominal aorta may become involved with aneurysmal dilatation.

Skin manifestations occur in approximately 20% of patients. They are most commonly a leukocytoclastic vasculitis. Systemic vasculitis involving medium and large vessels has also been detected.

This inflammatory cartilage disease may occur alone or in the presence of other connective tissue diseases (eg, systemic lupus erythematosus, Sjögrens syndrome, Graves' disease, hypothyroidism, Hashimoto's thyroiditis). We have detected two relapsing polychondritis patients in association with connective tissue diseases. One had anti-Ro (SS-A) antibody–positive SCLE; the other anti-Ro (SS-A) antibody–positive Sjögrens syndrome.

May also be associated with myelodysplastic and myeloproliferative disorders (paraneoplastic disorder)

Most recent studies indicate that relapsing polychondritis may on occasions be a paraneoplastic disease process occurring in the presence of myelodysplasia and lymphomas.

TABLE 10–1 Organ Involvement in Relapsing Polychondritis in Order of Descending Frequency

External ears
Joints
Nose
Eyes
Tracheobronchial tree
Skin
Kidney
Heart
Aorta (vessels)

Pathology

A perichondral inflammatory infiltrate composed of polymorphonuclear leukocytes, lymphocytes, and plasma cells is characteristic. Focal or diffuse cartilage matrix loss of basophilic staining, the result of glycosaminoglycan depletion, is present. With recurrent attacks, the cartilage is replaced by granulation and fibrous tissue producing ear deformity, tracheal bronchial narrowing, and collapse.

Pathologic examination of the aorta reveals an inflammatory infiltrate in the media, collagen, and glycosaminoglycan dissolution, and fragmentation of the elastic fibers. Intimal and adventitial fibrosis and aneurysmal dilatation occurs.

Examination of the joint synovium demonstrates a chronic inflammatory infiltrate with an increase in synovial lining type A cells.

Fragmentation of the elastic tissue at the scleroconjunctival angle and the presence of plasma cells and lymphocytes around episcleral vessels are noted on pathologic examination of the eye. Furthermore, edematous necrotic changes in the corneal stroma associated with an inflammatory cell infiltrate composed of lymphocytes and plasma cells occurs.

It is also theorized that the ubiquitous nature of elastic tissue, glycosaminoglycans, and collagenous matrix may explain the diffuse clinical features of this disease.

Mixed inflammatory pericartilagenous infiltrate resulting in dissolution of cartilate
Replacement of glycosaminoglycans by fibrosis

Etiology

The etiology is unknown, although a great deal of evidence suggests immunologic mechanisms. The injection of papain into the ears of rabbits produces a chondrolysis similar to that observed in relapsing polychondritis patients. This observation has led to the hypothesis that proteolytic enzymes, released by the inflammatory infiltrate, are responsible for the pathologic features.

Etiology is not known
Evidence of autoimmune disease in which constituents of cartilage are epitopes.
Actual destruction of cartilage mediated by inflammatory cell proteolytic enzymes

Relapsing polychondritis has been associated with the presence of anti–type II collagen antibodies and the presence of the human leukocyte antigens HLA-DR4 phenotype (as many as 60% of patients are HLA-DR4–positive). The presence of this disease process in association with other connective tissue diseases (ie, vasculitis, rheumatoid arthritis, Sjögren's syndrome, systemic lupus erythematosus) also suggests an autoimmune mechanism. Placental transfer of this disease from an affected mother to her unborn infant may have occurred on at least one occasion suggesting placental transfer of causative factors (eg, antibody). The infant developed tender, red, swollen knees and a saddle-nose deformity. During the pregnancy the mother had developed tender, swollen, red-to-bluish black discoloration of the ears, nose, and digits. The costochondral junctions were very tender. Subsequently, she developed a mild bilateral episcleritis and a saddle-nose deformity. Biopsy of her ears and trachea demonstrated the characteristic features of relapsing polychondritis with loss of the normal basophilic cartilage matrix. The mother required a tracheostomy to treat respiratory distress, which occurred secondary to collapse of the tracheal and laryngeal cartilage.

Antibodies against type II collagen

Placental transfer of disease suggested

Clinical Features

This disease occurs predominantly in Caucasians and affects both sexes equally. The diagnostic criteria are listed in Table 10–2.

Although the onset has been reported at birth and as late as the ninth decade of life, the majority of cases occur between the fifth and seventh decades of life.

External Ear Involvement

The most common site of involvement is the external ear, which occurs in approximately 90% of patients and is the initial sign in approximately one-third of patients. An acute inflammatory episode lasting a few days to a few weeks,

TABLE 10–2 Diagnostic Criteria for Relapsing Polychondritis*

Recurrent external ear involvement
Nonerosive, nondeforming arthritis
Nasal involvement
Ocular inflammation
Laryngeal tracheal involvement
Cochlear and/or vestibular involvement

*Three or more of above criteria or one criterion plus histologic confirmation of chondritis in two separate locations with a response to treatment are required.

Data from:
McAdam LP, O'Hanlan MA, Bluestone R, Pearson CM. Relapsing polychondritis: prospective review of 23 patients and a review of the literature. Medicine (Baltimore) 1976;55:193–215; Damiani JM, Levine HL. Relapsing polychondritis—report of 10 cases. Laryngoscope 1979;89:929–944.

External ear involvement most common clinical manifestation

before spontaneously subsiding, is characteristic. The helix and antihelix become swollen with a violaceous erythematous hue and tenderness is generally prominent. Obliteration of the normal contours of the ears occurs, but the lobe of the ear is characteristically spared (Figures 10–1 to 10–4). Repeated attacks result in a droopy appearance of the pinna, producing "cauliflower ears." Closure of the external auditory meatus may occur, associated with a clear, serous-like discharge. A conduction-hearing defect is noted in approximately one-third of patients. A serous otitis media, secondary to inflammation of the cartilaginous portion of the eustachian tube, may occur. In addition, inflammation of the middle ear may produce a neurosensory hearing loss. Finally, vestibular dysfunction may occur secondary to arteritis.

MAGIC syndrome

The MAGIC syndrome (*m*outh *a*nd *g*enital ulcers with *i*nflamed *c*artilage) is the occurrence of polychondritis in association with Behçet's syndrome.

Nasal Involvement

Approximately 30% of patients will initially present with involvement of the cartilaginous portion of the nose (Figure 10–5). Another 10% of patients may initially experience involvement of the laryngotracheal bronchial tree. With time, approximately 40 to 50% of patients will be so affected. Hoarseness is a fre-

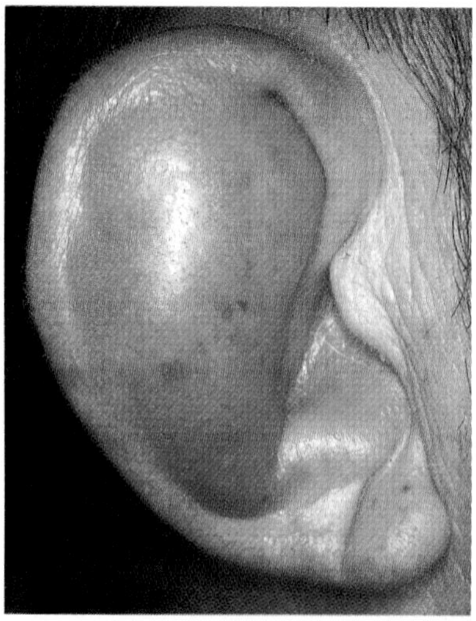

FIGURE 10–1 Acute and chronic painful swelling of ear in relapsing polychondritis. Note sparing of ear lobe.

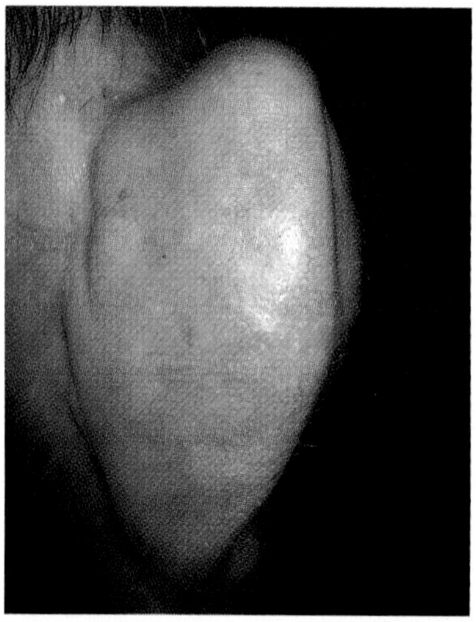

FIGURE 10–2 Posterior picture of the same ear as in Figure 10–1. Note loss of normal contours.

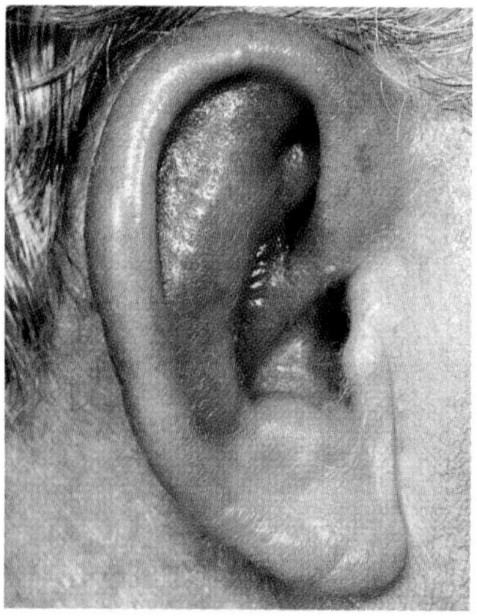

FIGURE 10–3 Acute early inflammation of ear in relapsing polychondritis. Note normal ear lobe.

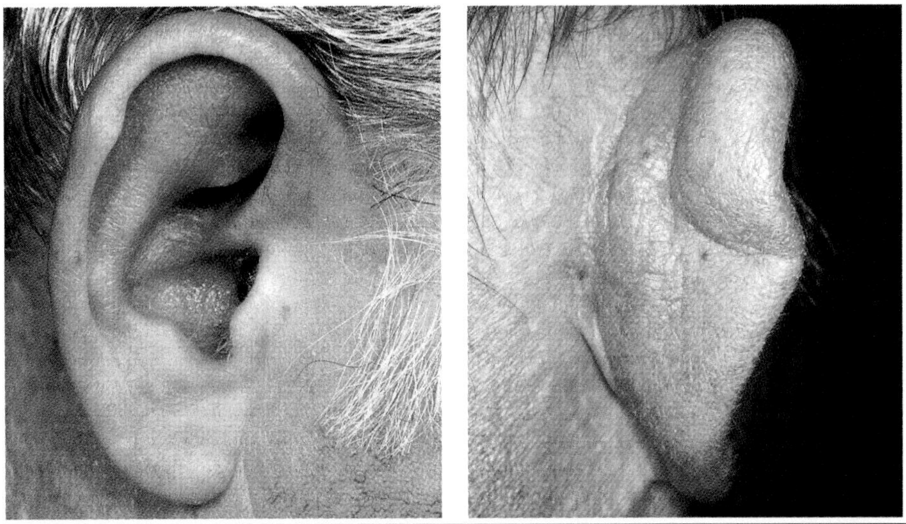

FIGURE 10–4 Other ear of same patient showing milder involvement. Again, note normal ear lobe.

quent symptom of this involvement. In the pre-steroid era, life-threatening bronchial tree collapse was a great concern.

Tracheobronchial collapse potentially fatal

Articular Manifestations

A nonerosive, nondeforming arthritis occurs in approximately one-third of patients initially and can develop in up to two-thirds of patients over time. Chronic back pain may result from chondritis involving the thoracic and lumbar spine.

Ocular Manifestations

Approximately 15% of patients will develop evidence of an episcleritis, conjunctivitis, iritis, or keratitis as the initial manifestation of their disease. With time, approximately one-half of patients develop ocular involvement.

Cutaneous Manifestations

Approximately 20% of relapsing polychondritis patients may demonstrate cutaneous features. Livedo reticularis, erythema nodosum, panniculitis, and a leukocytoclastic vasculitis have been described (Figure 10–6).

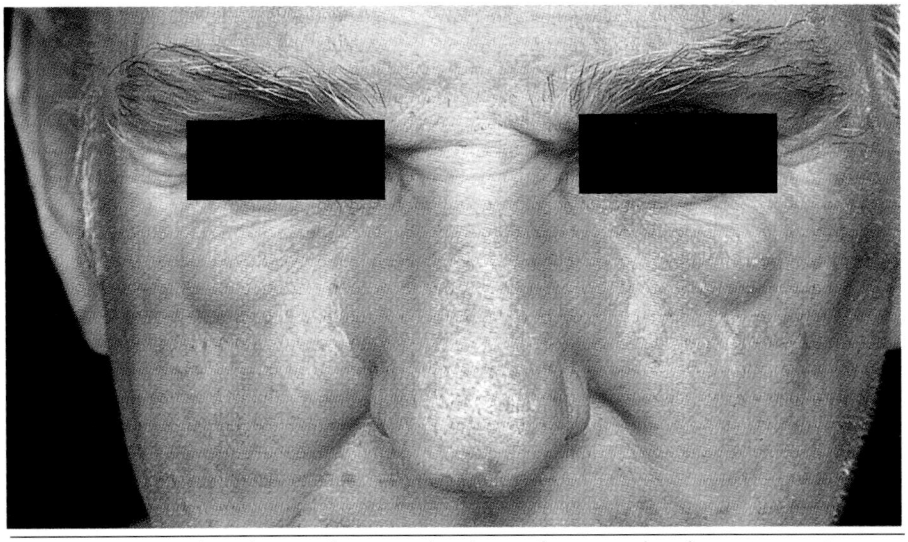

FIGURE 10–5 Red tender tip of nose with edema of nose and malar eminence in acute onset polychondritis.

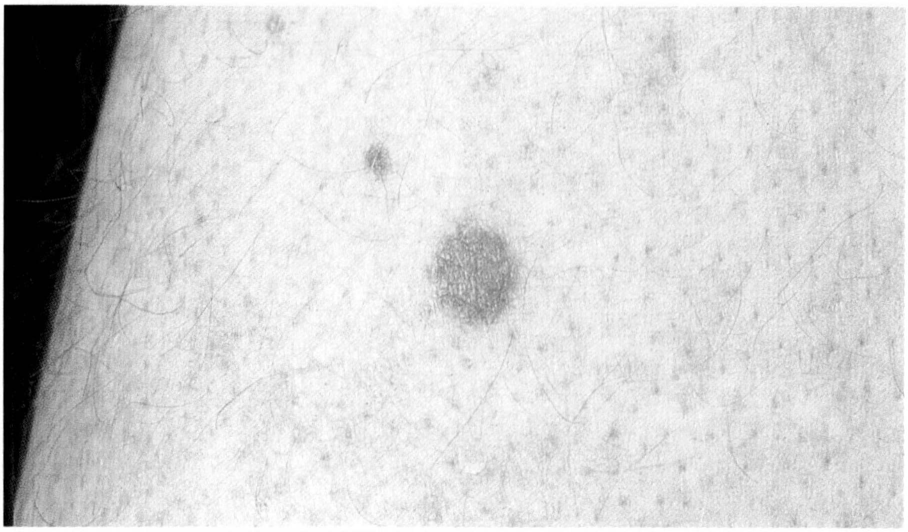

FIGURE 10-6 Sharply demarcated persistent urticaria lesion. Low grade leukocytoclastic vasculitis on biopsy.

Cardiovascular Manifestations

Aortic valve and mitral valve insufficiency in addition to aneurysms of the ascending aorta have been reported in relapsing polychondritis. On occasion, valvular replacement is necessary. Additionally cardiac inflammation can lead to conduction abnormalities including complete heart block.

Vasculitic Manifestations

Aneurysm of ascending aorta

Systemic vasculitis involving the subclavian, intercerebral, hepatic, superior mesenteric, and peripheral arteries has been reported. In addition, temporal arteritis and Takayasu's disease have been described. Whether vasculitis is part of the relapsing polychondritis disease process or represents an associated condition is unknown at the present time.

Renal Disease

Approximately one-fifth of patients develop cutaneous and/or systemic evidence of vasculitis.

Renal disease may occur in 20% of patients. Mesangial, segmental, and proliferating necrotizing glomerulonephritis occurs. Patients with renal involvement frequently have extrarenal vasculitis and they have the worst prognosis. Immune complex formation is thought to be the pathophysiologic mechanism.

Paraneoplastic Relapsing Polychondritis

Approximately 10% of relapsing polychondritis patients may have an associated myelodysplastic syndrome.

Recent evidence indicates that relapsing polychondritis occurs with increased frequency in patients with a myelodysplastic syndrome. Myelodysplastic syndrome is defined by ineffective clonal stem-cell maturation leading to leukopenia, lymphopenia, or thrombocytopenia and a high risk of progression to acute myelogenous leukemia. In three studies totalling 179 relapsing polychondritis patients, 15 (8%) demonstrated a concurrent myelodysplastic or myeloproliferative syndrome. Another study has reported that 5 myelodysplastic patients had an associated relapsing polychondritis. These 5 myelodysplastic syndrome patients with associated relapsing polychondritis composed 28% of the 18 relapsing polychondritis patients diagnosed at the same institution during the same time frame. This has also been reported in association with lymphoma.

Treatment

Once a diagnosis has been established for mild relapsing polychondritis with simple chondritis or arthritis, treatment can be initiated with nonsteroidal anti-inflammatory medications. This can be augmented with low-dose corticosteroids if there is no response. For more severe manifestations, such as inflammatory eye disease, vasculitis, aortitis, or severe involvement of the trachea, high-dose corticosteroids are indicated. These patients can receive parenteral solumedrol at 500 to 1000 mg per day for 3 days followed by initiation of an oral regimen of prednisone (1 mg/kg/day).

In this rare condition the number of patients that develop recurrences or refractory disease is small, such that suggested therapy is based on anecdotal evidence. This includes the use of colchicine or dapsone as well as immunosuppressive medications including azathioprine, cyclophosphamide, or cyclosporine A. It is important that medical therapy be tailored to the individual. In severe cases, especially with airway involvement, surgical intervention may be necessary for placement of tracheal stents or for correction of postinflammatory subglottic stenosis. Ideally, these interventions are performed once the inflammation has been suppressed.

Annotated Bibliography

Diebold J, Rauh G, Jager K, Lohrs U. Bone marrow pathology in relapsing polychondritis: high frequency of myelodysplastic syndromes. Br J Hematol 1995;89:820–830.

Hebbar M, Brouillard N, Wattel E, et al. Association of myelodysplastic syndrome and relapsing polychondritis: further evidence. Leukemia 1995;9:731–733.

These two articles record the heterogeneous nature of relapsing polychondritis and indicate that it may be a paraneoplastic phenomenon of an underlying myelodysplastic disorder.

Balsa A, Espinosa A, Cuesta M, et al. Joint symptoms in relapsing polychondritis. Clin Exp Rheumatol 1995;13:425–430.

This article describes articular disease in relapsing polychondritis.

Ridgway HB, Hansotia PL, Schorr WF. Relapsing polychondritis: unusual neurological findings and therapeutic efficacy of dapsone. Arch Dermatol 1979;115;43–45.

Barranco VP. Inhibition of lysosomal enzymes by dapsone. Arch Dermatol 1974;110: 563–566.

Martin J, Roenigk HH, Lynch W, Tingwald FR. Relapsing polychondritis treated with dapsone. Arch Dermatol 1976;112:1272–1274.

These three articles demonstrate therapeutic benefit of dapsone.

Massry GG, Chung SM, Selhorst JB. Optic neuropathy, headache, and diplopia with MRI suggestive of cerebral arteritis in relapsing polychondritis. J Neurolophthalmol 1995; 15:171–175.

This article provides a description of cerebral arteritis in relapsing polychondritis.

Arundell FW, Haserick JR. Familial chronic atrophic polychondritis. Arch Dermatol 1960;82:439–440.

This is a case description of possible placental transfer of polychondritis to fetus.

Foidart JM, Abe S, Martin G, et al. Antibodies to type II collagen in relapsing polychondritis. N Engl J Med 1978;299:1203–1206.

Cremer MA, Pitcock JA, Stuart JM, et al. Auricular chondritis in rats. An experimental model of relapsing polychondritis induced with type II collagen. J Exp Med 1981;154: 535–542.

These two articles present relevant data pertaining to possible pathogenesis of relapsing polychondritis.

Herman JH. Polychondritis. In: Kelly WN, Harris ED, Ruddy S, Sledge CB, eds. Textbook of Rheumatology, 2nd ed. Philadelphia: WB Saunders, 1985, pp 1458–1468.

This is a well-written review of the disease.

Miller SB, Donlon CJ, Roth SB. Hodgkin's disease presenting as relapsing polychondritis. A previously undescribed association. Arthritis Rheum 1974;17:598–602.

Fransen HR, et al. Chondrosarcoma in a patient with relapsing polychondritis. Skeletal Radiol 1995;24:477–480.

Provocative paper!

Damiani JM, Levine HL. Relapsing polychondritis—report of 10 cases. Laryngoscope 1979;89:929–944.

McAdam LP, O'Hanlan MA, Bluestone R, Pearson CM. Relapsing polychondritis: prospective review of 23 patients and a review of the literature. Medicine (Baltimore) 1976;55:193–215.

CHAPTER 11

Behçet's Disease

Don R. Martin, M.D., Thomas T. Provost, M.D.

Behçet's disease is an inflammatory multisystem disease that may have been first described by Hippocrates approximately 400 B.C. However, it is Hulusi Behçet, a Turkish dermatologist, who is credited with first describing, in 1937, the classic diagnostic triad of oral and genital ulcers with uveitis, which bears his name.

Probably known in ancient times

Epidemiology

Behçet's disease usually develops in the third or fourth decades of life. Occurrence in childhood or beyond middle age is uncommon. It is more common in Middle Eastern and Asian (Japan) populations, where the male to female ratio is 2:1, than in North America, where the disease is uncommon and the gender distribution more even. It is generally agreed that Middle Eastern and Asian patients have more severe disease than North Americans and that men have more severe involvement than women.

Highest frequency of occurrence in Asia (Japan) and Middle East

Etiology

The etiology of Behçet's disease remains unknown. Despite a wealth of information detailing a variety of immunologic aberrations, no unifying theory has been proven. Behçet's disease is thought to have originated in the Far East and may have spread to the Mediterranean region via the "Silk Route."

Histologically, polymorphonuclear neutrophil leukocyte (PMN), T lymphocyte, and plasma cell infiltrates may be seen in the cutaneous lesions. Deposition of immunoglobulins IgM and IgG, and complement may be detected. Antibodies to endothelium and oral mucosa, circulating immune complexes (seen in up to half of patients), lymphocytotoxic activity to oral epithelium, a reduction in the number and function of CD4 lymphocytes (but only in the "pre-active" phase, returning to normal in active or inactive disease), and increased levels of soluble interleukin-2 receptors have been described. Streptococci (*S. sanguis* and *S. pyogenes*) and herpes viruses have been proposed as etiologic agents, and the identification of increased numbers of CD8 lymphocytes expressing gamma-delta receptors suggests a microbial etiology.

Variety of immunologic abnormalities

Human leukocyte antigen HLA-B5 (HLA-B51 split) occurs with increased frequency in Middle Eastern and Japanese Behçet's patients. In one study, a frequency of 80% was noted. Familial clustering is reported, but uncommon. No consistent HLA associations have been identified in Northern European, North American, or East Indian patients with Behçet's disease.

Increased frequency of HLA-B5 (HLA-B51 split)

Clinical Features

Oral Ulcers

Universally present

Recurrent major or minor aphthous, or herpetiform oral ulcers are universally present and frequently the first feature of the disease (Figures 11–1 to 11–3). At times they may herald the onset of Behçet's disease by many years. The painful, rounded ulcers may be present 50 to 100% of the time and may affect any part of the oral mucosal surface: labia, bucca, gingiva, tongue, or pharynx. They reflect inflammation and separation at the dermo-epidermal junction and heal spontaneously over a period of days to weeks. Scarring is rare.

Genital Ulcers

Genital ulcers may produce scar formation.

Genital ulcers are detected in as many as 80% of patients (Figure 11–4). Involvement of the scrotum is frequent, involvement of the shaft and glans of the penis less common, and epididymitis and orchitis rare. Vulvar, vaginal, and cervical ulcers are common in affected women. Intractable pain may occur, but some genital ulcers may be asymptomatic. Scar formation is almost universally present.

Ocular Inflammation

Ocular involvement can lead to eventual blindness.

The third component of the triad described by Behçet is ocular inflammation, which occurs in 60 to 70% of patients (Figures 11–5 and 11–6). Though this manifestation may occur early in the course of disease, it is generally preceded by several years of recurrent aphthous ulcers. Anterior uveitis may, in its most extreme form, be associated with a hypopyon (inflammatory cells layered inferiorly in the anterior chamber), although this is less common today. Posterior uveitis, vitreous cellular infiltrates, macular and disc edema, and retinal vasculitis and perivasculitis may also be seen and may be manifest as painless blurring of the vision. Scleritis and conjunctivitis may be demonstrated but are not considered characteristic of the process. Ocular involvement tends to become chronic and bilateral (approximately 90%) and may lead to blindness. This is more prevalent in male patients. Recurrent flares (especially following eye surgery) produce scarring.

Vascular Manifestations

The common theme in the histologic lesions of Behçet's disease is vasculitis (Figure 11–7). It is unique among the vasculitides in that it may affect vessels of all types and sizes: aorta to arterioles and venules to vena cava.

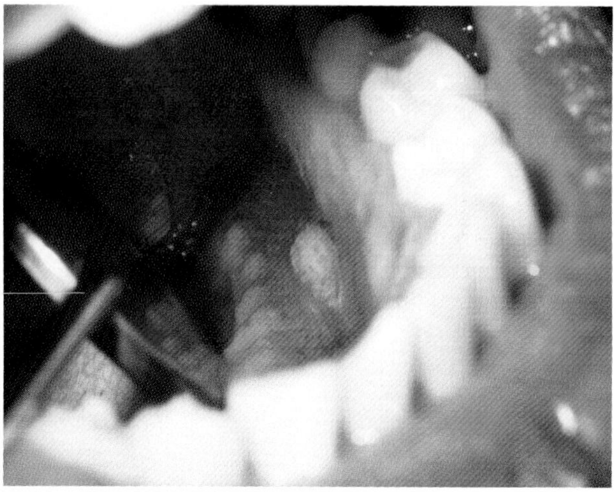

FIGURE 11–1 Aphthous ulcer on the lower jaw in Behçet's patient.

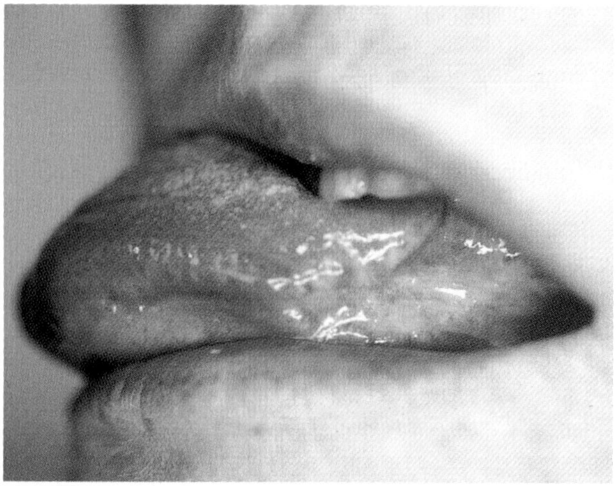

FIGURE 11–2 Aphthous ulcer on the lateral lingual surface in Behçet's patient.

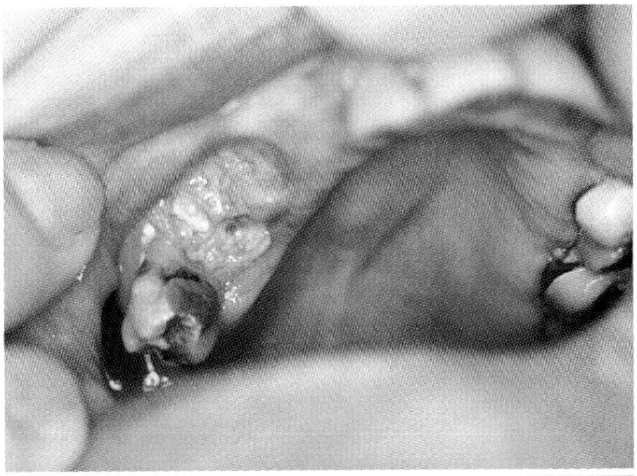

FIGURE 11-3 Necrotic ulcer on upper gingival surface in Behçet's patient.

FIGURE 11-4 Scrotal scars in Behçet's patient at sites of previous ulcers.

Vasculopathy involves arteries and veins

Approximately 25% of Behçet's patients develop deep venous thrombophlebitis. Although the calf is most commonly involved, thrombosis can occur in other sites, including the iliac veins, inferior or superior vena cavae, or the hepatic vein producing a potentially lethal Budd-Chiari syndrome. Pulmonary emboli rarely occur. Superficial phlebitis may be manifested clinically as palpable nodules on the extremities. Venous thrombosis has been described after venipuncture.

Aneurysms

Panarteritis of large blood vessels can produce aneurysms and pseudo aneurysms of the abdominal aorta as well as smaller vessels including the carotid, iliac, femoral, and popliteal arteries. Bronchopulmonary artery fistulae may present as life-threatening hemoptysis. They are best diagnosed by high-resolution computed tomography scanning, given concerns about possible pathergy and subsequent thrombosis or aneurysm formation at the site of vascular puncture sites for angiographic procedures. Peripheral arterial involvement and aneurysm formation may be detectable as a pulsatile mass.

Cutaneous Manifestations

Although not part of the original triad described by Behçet, cutaneous manifestations may be prominent (Figures 11–8 and 11–9). Papular and pustular lesions are common. Though pseudofollicular and acneiform lesions are frequently seen, they are considered by some to be too nonspecific to be diagnostically relevant. Leukocytoclastic vasculitis and pustular erythema nodosum-like lesions may be seen.

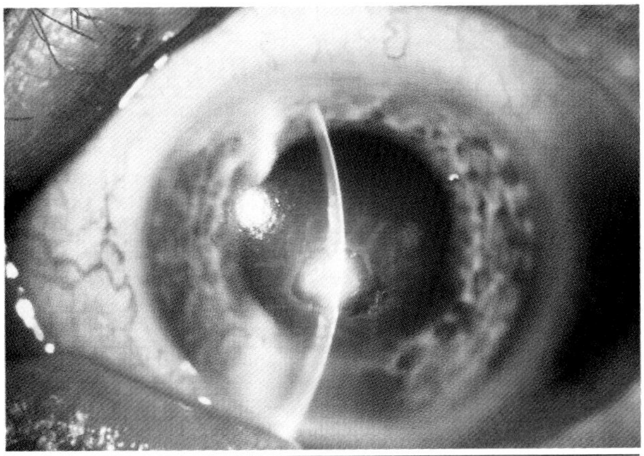

FIGURE 11-5 Hypopyon in Behçet's patient. Collection of leukocytes at inferior pole of anterior chamber of the eye.

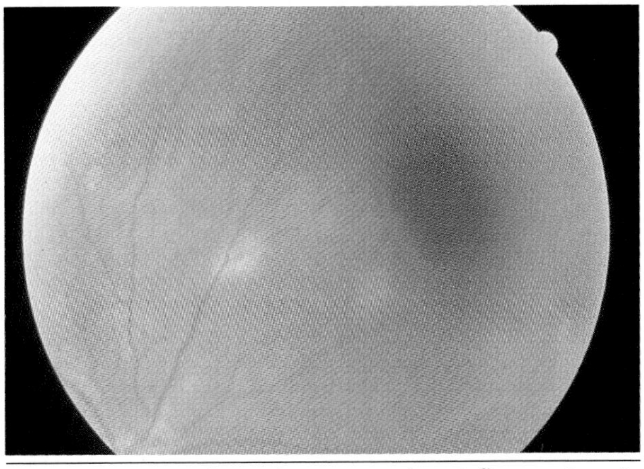

FIGURE 11-6 Retinal perivascular inflammation in Behçet's patient.

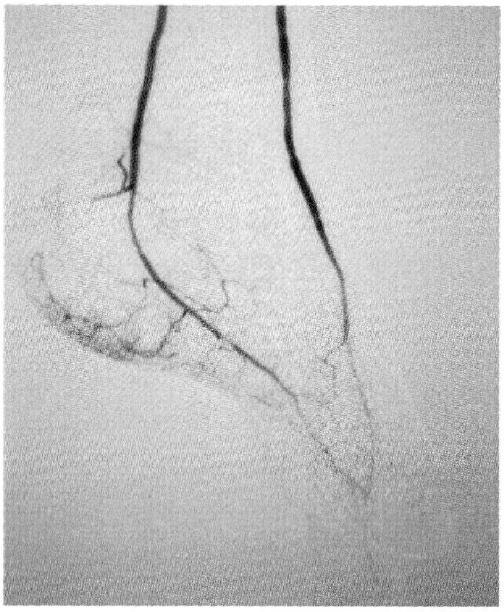

FIGURE 11-7 Anterior tibial artery beading in Behçet's patient with vasculitic toe lesions.

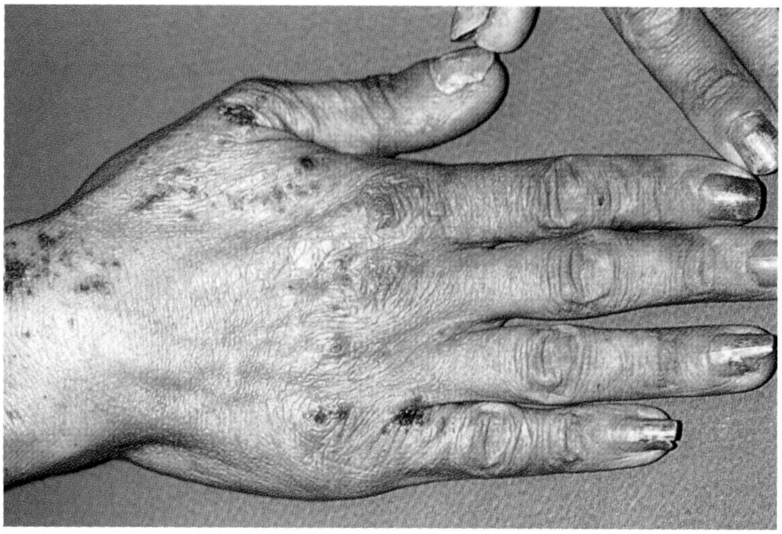

FIGURE 11-8 Cutaneous eruption on the dorsum of the hand in Behçet's patient.

Pathergy

Pathergy, a neutrophilic dermatosis, is manifested as an erythematous papule or sterile pustule arising 24 to 48 hours after a needle prick. This finding is reported frequently in Middle Eastern patients, but is less common in North America. However, in those patients in whom it is found, it may prove highly specific. An Israeli study demonstrated that 45 of 46 Jewish and Arab-Israeli Behçet's patients exhibited a positive response, whereas 46 of 46 patients with other connective tissue and vasculitic diseases were nonreactive. Agreement upon a standard methodology for performing this test has proven difficult but involves pricking the skin of the forearm obliquely with a 20 to 25 gauge needle to a depth of 5 to 10 mm. A papule or pustule forms within 24 to 48 hours at the site of needle prick. Similar neutrophil reactions can occur with angiographic procedures or other surgical trauma and are especially problematic with eye surgery. Pathergy may be associated with more severe disease.

Neurologic Manifestations

Multiple neurologic events

Among the most serious complications of Behçet's disease is neurologic involvement. This occurred in up to 28% of patients in the Mayo Clinic experience, where all patients presented with headache and fever. It may manifest as aseptic meningitis, meningoencephalitis, cranial nerve lesions (eg, ocular and vestibulo-auditory), cerebellar ataxia, pseudobulbar palsy, corticospinal tract lesions, peripheral neuropathy, or stroke. Dementia is rare. Venous sinus thrombosis can produce severe headache and papilledema, with cerebrospinal fluid (CSF) pressures of 400 to 500 mm of H_2O. Early brain lesions demonstrate perivascular inflammation or frank vasculitis, whereas later lesions may demonstrate demyelination or gliosis.

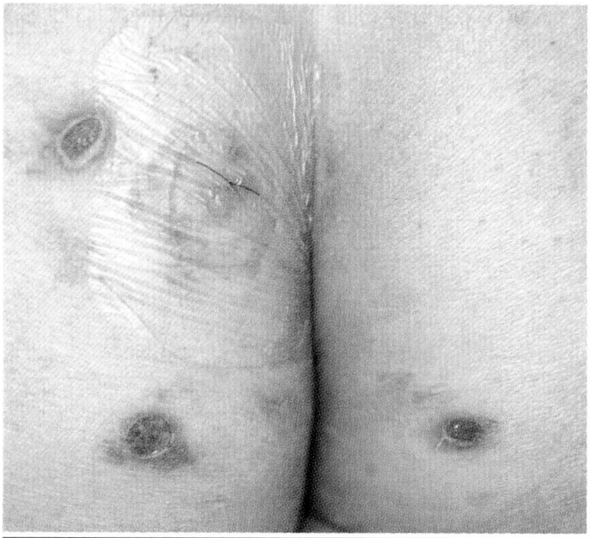

FIGURE 11-9 Buttock ulceration in Behçet's patient.

The CSF is modestly inflammatory, with 5 to 100 white blood cells per cubic millimeter. Initially, PMNs predominate, but these are later replaced by mononuclear cells. The CSF protein may be elevated, and specific (eg, oligoclonal bands) or nonspecific increases in immunoglobulins (eg, IgM, IgA, IgG) may be identified. Only the IgM index appears to fall with resolution of disease activity.

Magnetic resonance imaging may reveal increased signal intensity in the periventricular white matter, basal ganglia, or brain stem. Cerebral angiography is seldom useful because the vessels involved are generally too small to be evaluated radiographically.

Gastrointestinal Manifestations

Japanese patients frequently develop gastrointestinal perforation

Abdominal pain and hemorrhage characterize the gastrointestinal involvement of Behçet's disease. Mucosal ulceration in the terminal ileum, cecum, and ascending colon are described most frequently, although any portion of the gastrointestinal tract, from mouth to anus, may be affected. Pancreatic involvement has been reported. Perforation, especially of ileocecal ulcers, is reported to occur in up to 25% of patients. The Japanese, in particular, have reported recurrence at the site of previous bowel resection and re-anastomosis, but immunosuppresive therapy may lower this risk.

Musculoskeletal Manifestations

Turkish investigators dispute sacroiliitis in Behçet's disease

Approximately 50% of patients exhibit a nonerosive synovitis involving large or small joints (eg, knees, ankles, wrists, elbows, hands, feet in decreasing order of frequency). The arthritis may be symmetrical, leading to confusion with rheumatoid arthritis. However, the arthritis is usually mono- or oligoarticular in distribution. In the past, Behçet's disease has also been grouped by some investigators (British) with the seronegative spondyloarthropathies, given the reported observation of mild erosive sacroiliitis and calcaneal spurs. However, it is not associated with an increased frequency of HLA-B27, and Turkish investigators dispute the association. As a vasculitis, Behçet's disease may occasionally be associated with osteonecrosis unrelated to corticosteroid therapy. Synovial fluid is inflammatory, with 5,000 to 25,000 white blood cells per cubic millimeter. These are predominantly PMNs. Synovial biopsies are nonspecific and may show PMNs or mononuclear cells.

A patchy myositis can occur but is not generally associated with enzyme elevation.

Miscellaneous Manifestations

Myocarditis, endocarditis, cardiovalvular disease, IgA nephropathy, glomerulonephritis, and secondary amyloidosis (AA protein) have been reported in Behçet's patients.

Diagnosis

Diagnosis is problematic.

The diagnosis of Behçet's disease is frequently problematic as there are no specific clinical, histologic, or serologic findings. Further confounding the diagnostic process is the fact that the clinical findings are episodic: they rarely all occur simultaneously but more likely occur over several years' time. See Table 11–1 for an explanation of recently proposed international diagnostic criteria. The presence of recurrent aphthous oral ulcers is mandatory, and two of the other four criteria must also be found: aphthous genital ulcers, ocular inflammation, cutaneous inflammation, and pathergy. However, because pathergy is uncommon in Northern European and North American patients, cerebral vasculitis, arterial aneurysms, or phlebitis may be substituted for it.

It must be remembered that aphthous mucosal oral ulcers occur in 20% of the normal population. Behçet's disease must also be differentiated from herpes simplex viral eruptions (excluded with Tzanck cell test and/or viral culture), Stevens-Johnson syndrome, cicatricial pemphigoid, lichen planus, hypereosinophilic syndrome, myelodysplastic syndromes, acquired immunodeficiency syndrome, inflammatory bowel disease, and Reiter's syndrome. In the case of bowel involvement, endoscopic biopsies and surgically resected specimens are free of granulomata, and the associated presence of genital ulcers may further support the diagnosis of Behçet's disease. An entity characterized as pseudo-Behcet's syndrome has been described in young women presenting with subjective symptoms without clinical findings or factitious mucosal lesions.

TABLE 11–1 Proposed International Criteria for Behçet's Disease

Criteria	Prevalence	Comment
Aphthous oral ulcers	100%	Recur at least three times in a year
Aphthous genital ulcers	80%	Scrotal, penile, vulvar, vaginal, or cervical lesions or scarring
Ocular inflammation	60–70%	Anterior or posterior uveitis or retinal vasculitis
Cutaneous inflammation	60–80%	Papulopustular or erythema nodosum-like lesions
Pathergy	Variable	May substitute cerebral vasculitis, arterial aneurysms, or phlebitis

Diagnosis of Behçet's disease: Aphthous oral ulcers plus 2 other features. Jorrizo JL, Rogers RL. Behçet's disease. J Acad Dermatol 1990;23:738–741.

MAGIC syndrome association of relapsing polychondritis and Behçet's disease

An overlap with relapsing polychondritis, termed the MAGIC syndrome (*m*outh *a*nd *g*enital ulcers with *i*nflamed *c*artilage) has been described.

Treatment

Corticosteroids are effective when applied topically to mucosal ulcers (in Orabase) and when administered systemically (eg, orally or intravenously) for more severe manifestations (eg, neurologic or vascular). However, they are only palliative and the disease generally flares when they are tapered. Tetracycline may be effective for palliation of oral mucosal ulcers. Cyclosporin A (5 mg/kg/day) has been demonstrated to suppress disease activity but fails to induce a remission. Colchicine (0.6–1.2 mg/day), thalidomide (50–200 mg/day), dapsone, levamisole, and interferon-α may also provide palliation of symptoms.

Cytotoxic agents are effective.

Only cytotoxic agents, such as chlorambucil (0.1 mg/kg/day), cyclophosphamide (pulse therapy), and azathioprine (2.5 mg/kg/day), have been demonstrated to induce remission of disease activity, allowing tapering and eventual discontinuation of the medication over a period of 1 to 3 years. Some investigators suggest that azathioprine may be less effective. The possibility of ovarian and testicular failure with cyclophosphamide should be considered in choosing these medications.

Interestingly, early reports noted improvement in some patients after blood transfusion, although the mechanism remains unexplained and the finding did not consistently hold up in prospective studies.

Gastrointestinal, ophthalmologic, and vascular surgery may give rise to local pathergy and recurrence of disease, necessitating adjunctive pharmacologic therapy.

Prognosis

Eye prognosis is especially problematic.

Behçets's disease is characterized as an indolent, chronic disease and morbidity may be significant. According to Benezra and Cohen, 74% of Israeli patients progress to blindness in 6 to 10 years, despite treatment with corticosteroids and cytotoxic agents. A 40% mortality is quoted, which is usually attributable to central nervous system disease, bowel perforation, or vascular disease, or as a complication of immunosuppressive therapy itself.

Annotated Bibliography

Arbesfeld SJ, Kurban AK. Behçet's disease. New perspectives on an enigmatic syndrome. J Am Acad Dermatol 1988;19:767–779.

This is a well-written review by a dermatologist with extensive experience in the Middle East, which details the clinical features and therapeutic choices in this disease.

Yazici H. Behcet's syndrome. In: Maddison PJ, Isenberg DA, Woo P, Glass DN, eds. Oxford Textbook of Rheumatology. Oxford, United Kingdom: Oxford Medical Publications, 1993, pp 884–889.

This is a well-written review by an investigator who has participated in the care of more than 3000 patients with Behçet's disease.

O'Duffy JD, Carney JA, Deodhar S. Behçet's disease. Report of 10 cases, 3 with new manifestations. Ann Intern Med 1971;75:561–570.

Chajek T, Fainaru M. Behçet's disease. Report of 41 cases and a review of the literature. Medicine 1975;54:179–196.

O'Duffy JD, Goldstein NP. Neurologic involvement in seven patients with Behçet's disease. Am J Med 1976;61:170–178.

These are three highly quoted articles detailing the multisystem involvement in patients with Behçet's disease.

Lehner T. Oral ulceration and Behçet's syndrome. Gut 1977;18:491–511.

This is a detailed review of the differential diagnosis, pathophysiology, and treatment of oral ulcers, including Behçet's syndrome.

Colvard DM, Robertson DM, O'Duffy JD. The ocular manifestations of Behçet's disease. Arch Ophthalmol 1977;95:1813–1817.

This paper details the extent of ocular involvement and the clinical course of 21 patients with Behçet's disease and uveitis.

Benezra D, Cohen E. Treatment and visual prognosis in Behçet's disease. Br J Ophthalmol 1986;70:589–592.

This paper, which emphasizes the potentially devastating nature of ocular complications in Behçet's disease, reviews the experience of 49 patients, 74% of whom lost useful visual acuity in 6 to 10 years despite treatment with corticosteroids and cytotoxic agents.

Jorrizo JL, Solomon AR, Zanolli MD, Leshin B. Neutrophilic vascular reactions. J Am Acad Dermatol 1988;19:983–1005.

This provocative article draws analogies between Behçet's disease, leukocytoclastic vasculitis, Sweet's syndrome, bowel bypass syndrome, erythema nodosum, and pyoderma gangrenosum. All have clinical commonalities as well as a putative immune complex-mediated pathogenesis.

O'Duffy JD. Vasculitis in Behçet's disease. Rheum Dis Clin North Am 1990;16:423–431.

This is a review of the evidence that vasculitis is a key feature of Behçet's disease by one of the leading North American investigators in the field.

Koc Y, Gullu I, Akpek G, et al. Vascular involvement in Behçet's disease. J Rheumatol 1992;19:402–410.

This study from Turkey demonstrates that Behçet's disease is a multisystem disorder that may present with primarily vascular manifestations rather than the classic triad of oral and genital ulcers and ocular inflammation.

Friedman-Birnbaum R, Bergman R, Aizen E. Sensitivity and specificity of pathergy test results in Israeli patients with Behçet's disease. Cutis 1990;45:261–264.

This report documents the high sensitivity and specificity of the pathergy test in a Middle Eastern population.

Yurdakul S, Yazici H, Tuzun Y, et al. The arthritis of Behçet's disease: a prospective study. Ann Rheum Dis 1983;42:505–515.

This prospective study details the articular manifestations and clinical course in 47 patients with Behçet's disease.

International Study Group for Behçet's Disease. Criteria for diagnosis of Behçet's disease. Lancet 1990;335:1078–1080.

Jorrizo JL, Rogers RS III. Behçet's disease: an update based on the international conference held in Rochester, Minnesota, Sept. 14 and 15, 1989. J Am Acad Dermatol 1990; 23:738–741.

The first report contains the consensus diagnostic criteria for the diagnosis of Behçet's disease, and the second a critical review of the criteria and important data on the efficacy of various immunosuppressive agents in treatment.

O'Duffy JD, Robertson DM, Goldstein NP. Chlorambucil in the treatment of uveitis and meningoencephalitis of Behçet's disease. Am J Med 1984; 76:75–84.

Tessler HH, Jennings T. High-dose short-term chlorambucil for intractable sympathetic ophthalmia and Behçet's disease. Br J Ophthalmol 1990;74: 353–357.

These two reports demonstrate the efficacy of chlorambucil in inducing a sustained remission in Behçet's disease.

Yazici H, Pazarli H, Barnes CG, et al. A controlled trial of azathioprine in Behçet's syndrome. N Engl J Med 1990;322:281–285.

This study demonstrates that azathioprine is effective in controlling the progression of Behçet's syndrome, especially one of its most serious manifestations, eye disease.

For additional patient information, you may contact The American Behçet's Disease Association; P.O. Box 27494; Tempe, AZ 85285-7494; Telephone (800) 7BEHCETS.

CHAPTER 12

Vasculitis

David B. Hellmann, M.D., Thomas T. Provost, M.D.

Vasculitis is defined as an inflammatory destruction of the integrity of blood vessel walls. A history of events in our understanding of vasculitis is presented in Table 12–1.

There are many vasculitis classifications that have been proposed over the years. In general, classification is based on the size of the involved vessels, and the pathology and clinical features of the disease. The American College of Rheumatology has recently proposed a series of classifications for individual types of vasculitis. They are presented in this chapter in table form.

In this chapter, we will use a vasculitis classification based on the size of the blood vessels involved (ie, small, medium, or large). A classification based on size, however, is flawed because the organ from which the biopsy is taken has a selection bias for the size of blood vessel sampled (eg, skin, small blood vessels; kidneys, medium-sized blood vessels). It should be realized that the classification indicates the size of the blood vessel predominantly involved. It does not imply that blood vessels of one size are involved to the exclusion of other-sized blood vessels.

Classifications of vasculitis based on clinical and pathologic features, as well as size of involved blood vessels

Small-Vessel Vasculitis

Small vessel vasculitis is the most common form of vasculitis, characterized by inflammation involving predominantly the postcapillary venules. In general, but not always, biopsy of these lesions demonstrates the presence of a leukocytoclastic vasculitis characterized by an infiltration of polymorphonuclear neutrophils, some of which demonstrate fragmentation (karyohexis). Fibrinoid necrosis of the blood vessel walls is also characteristic.

Small-vessel vasculitis most common form of vasculitis

Leukocytoclastic vasculitis most common pathologic form of vasculitis

The pathologic process is dynamic; the neutrophilic infiltrate may evolve into a mononuclear infiltrate as the vasculitic lesion matures. (There are instances, however, in which repeated biopsy of vasculitic lesions will consistently demonstrate the presence of a predominantly mononuclear cell infiltrate with no evidence of an early neutrophilic infiltrate. [See Chapter 8, "Sjögren's Syndrome."]) An extravasation of red blood cells into the surrounding tissue may occur as well as formation of intraluminal fibrin thrombi. Small-vessel vasculitis may present in clinically distinct forms. These are listed in Tables 12–2, 12–3, and 12–4.

Paradigm is that leukocytoclastic phase is followed by a mononuclear cell infiltrate.

Pathogenesis

Immunologic studies performed in the late 1950s and 1960s by Germuth and Dixon et al., employing animal models, delineated many of the features in this putative immune complex–mediated vasculitis. For example, the injection of bovine serum albumin into rabbits results in the development of an immune

TABLE 12–1 Glossary of Events in Our Understanding of Vasculitis

1837 and 1874	Schönlein and Henoch, respectively, describe the vasculitic entity that bears their names "Henoch-Schönlein purpura."
1866	Kussmaul and Maier describe polyarteritis nodosa.
1911	Von Pirquet and Schick describe serum sickness in humans treated with equine antidiphtheria serum.
1932	Horton, Magath, and Brown describe temporal vasculitis.
1936	Wegner describes triad of signs consisting of upper and lower airway disease, systemic vasculitis, and glomerulonephritis.
1943	Waldenström describes longstanding lower extremity vasculitis and hypergammaglobulinemia.
1951	Churg and Strauss describe association of systemic vasculitis with asthma, transient pulmonary infiltrates, hypereosinophilia, and glomerulonephritis.
1952	Zeek provides classification of necrotizing vasculitis and description of hypersensitivity angiitis.
1953–1961	Germuth, Dixon, Feldman, and Vasquez describe experimental animal models for serum sickness and immune complex–mediated arthritis.
1967	Frobnet and Sheps discover association of hepatitis B with polyarteritis nodosa.
1971 and 1973	Novack and Pearson and Fauci and Wolff describe dramatic improvement in the survivability of Wegener's granulomatous patients treated with steroids and cyclophosphamide.
1971	Cochrane discovers role of platelet clumping and vasoactive amines in tissue deposition of immune complexes.
1973	McDuffie et al. describe urticaria as a manifestation of a necrotizing angiitis.
1975	Myels recognizes association of temporal arteritis with polymyalgia rheumatica.
	Braverman and Yen demonstrate role of histamine in the tissue deposition phase of immune complex–mediated vasculitis.
1977	Katz et al. demonstrate that erythema elevatum diutinum is a low-grade small-vessel vasculitis.
1982, 1984, and 1985	Davis et al., Hall et al., and von der Woude et al. respectively, determine value of cANCA in evaluation of microscopic polyarteritis and Wegner's granulomatous.
1984	Lawley et al. perform prospective study of the development of serum sickness–like features, circulating immune complexes, and urticaria-like vasculitis lesions in aplastic humans treated with equine antithymic sera prior to bone marrow transplantation. Study provides strong evidence for a role for mononuclear cells in vascular injury associated with immune complex disease.

Germuth and Dixon et al. pioneered the development of laboratory data regarding pathogenesis of immune complex–mediated vasculitis.

Immune complexes in antigen excess are pathologic.

response characterized by the rapid disappearance of the bovine serum albumin from the rabbit's circulation on days 5 to 7. This time frame corresponds with the development of rabbit antibovine serum albumin antibodies. During this phase of the immune response, immune complexes are formed in antigen excess (small- and intermediate-sized soluble complexes). These pathologic circulating immune complexes escape clearance by the reticuloendothelial system, producing arthritis and renal disease, manifested by proteinuria. Immunofluorescent studies demonstrate the deposition of immunoglobulin and complement in the diseased tissue. Furthermore, these immune complexes induce circulating basophils to release platelet-activating factor. This causes platelets to clump, releasing vasoactive amines. These vasoactive amines induce enhanced permeability of the blood vessel, facilitating the egression of circulating immune complexes into the tissue.

Complement activation releasing neutrophil chemotactic factors is important.

Complement-mediated release of mast cell vasoactive amines also important

Activation of complement occurs, confirmed by direct immunofluorescence examination, demonstrating the presence of C3 as well as the terminal components of complement (C5b-C9) in the affected blood vessel walls. Adhesion molecules on the vascular endothelium are upregulated. Subsequent to the activation of complement, chemotactic factors (C3a and C5a) are released. These chemotactic factors stimulate the migration of neutrophils into the involved area. In

TABLE 12–2 Small Vessel Vasculitis

Hypersensitivity angiitis
50% idiopathic
May be associated with infections, connective tissue disease, and drug reactions
Clinical presentation of palpable and nonpalpable purpura of lower legs
Cryoglobulins (cryoglobulinemic vasculitis)
Waldenström's benign hyperglobulinemic purpura

addition, C3a induces degranulation of mast cells with the further release of vasoactive amines and eosinophilic chemotactic factor.

This acute phase is followed by an influx of mononuclear cells and macrophages. The inflammatory cells release lysosomal enzymes (eg, elastase, collagenase), free radicals, and cytokines, which modulate the inflammation and subsequent cellular constituents.

Proteolytic enzymes and other products released by inflammatory cells mediate inflammation.

Intracutaneous injection of antigen into sensitized animals produces a local Arthus phenomena (vasculitis), characterized by an antigen-antibody reaction occurring in antigen excess. Immune complex formation, complement activation, a neutrophilic infiltrate, and inflammation sequentially occur.

Arthus phenomenon resembles small vessel vasculitis.

Studies suggest that histamine plays a prominent role in the pathogenesis of the tissue deposition phase of immune complex–mediated vasculitis. For example, the injection of histamine into the skin of patients with circulating immune complexes induces vasculitis in clinically normal-appearing skin. Furthermore, other studies indicate that the putative release of histamine following local trauma to the skin (eg, shaving of the hair on the lower extremities, a venesection needle stick) will induce immune complex tissue deposition, producing vasculitis. Additional studies indicate antihistamines interfere with immune complex deposition. (See below in serum sickness section.)

Blood flow and hydrostatic pressure also play a role in determining the sites of vasculitis. Eddying of blood in blood vessels in areas of constriction (eg, tight clothing, belt along waistline) or at a bifurcation of a blood vessel is associated with an increased propensity to develop vasculitic lesions. Also, an increase in hydrostatic pressure plays a pathologic role in producing vasculitic lesions on the lower extremities and in dependent areas, such as the back in patients confined to bed.

Histamine may play crucial role in the tissue deposition phase of immune complexes.

The morphology of the individual vasculitis lesion is determined by the severity of the inflammatory insult and depth of blood vessel involvement vasculitis high in the reticular portion of the dermis produces nonpalpable purpuric lesions; with deeper involvement nonpalpable purpura or plaques occur. Minor inflammatory insults produce urticaria-like lesions; intense inflammation produces hemorrhagic, necrotic, or ulcerative lesions.

Allergic Vasculitis

Allergic vasculitis (hypersensitivity angiitis, leukocytoclastic angiitis) is a small-vessel vasculitis and the most common form of cutaneous vasculitis. Palpable and nonpalpable lesions are generally found over the lower legs but can be pre-

TABLE 12–3 Small Vessel Vasculitis

Other clinically distinct forms of small vessel vasculitis
Serum sickness
Henoch-Schönlein purpura
Urticaria-like vasculitis
Erythema elevatum diutinum
Pustular vasculitis

Palpable and nonpalpable purpura most common clinical features of hypersensitivity vasculitis

sent on the buttocks, trunk, as well as upper extremities (Figure 12–1). The lesions may be erythematous, purpuric macules, vesicles, bullae, urticarial plaques, pustules, hemorrhagic bullae, or ulcers (Figure 12–2). Arthralgia and arthritis occur in as many as 50% of patients. Much less common is the presence of abdominal pain, melena, fever, malaise, and microscopic hematuria. Pulmonary and neurologic manifestations are even rarer. (Also, see Table–2.)

Mild to moderate anemia may be present. Hypocomplementemia uncommon

In general, these patients may demonstrate a mild to moderate anemia and an elevated erythrocyte sedimentation rate. Hypocomplementemia is uncommon and is usually associated with a significant renal insult. Persistent hematuria and proteinuria may occur, and a renal biopsy will demonstrate immunologic and histologic features of a glomerulonephritis.

Self-limited disease

In most cases, this is a self-limited disease process and may not require therapy. However, on occasions, renal disease and gastrointestinal hemorrhage and perforation may occur. It must be emphasized that although cutaneous features are prominent, allergic hypersensitivity vasculitis (leukocytoclastic angiitis) must be viewed as a systemic disease (Figure 12–3). In most instances, systemic involvement is silent but, on occasions, may be very significant and even life-threatening.

Etiology

Unknown etiology may be associated with chronic infection, drugs, and autoimmune diseases.

Drugs and infections. In over 50% of cases, the etiology of the hypersensitivity vasculitis is unknown. However, allergic vasculitis can be precipitated by drugs, especially sulfonamides, penicillins, and thiazides. Also, infections, such as hepatitis A, B, and C, may be associated with this type of vasculitis. Various bacterial infections, including β-hemolytic streptococcus, may also be of etiologic significance.

Autoimmune diseases. In addition to chronic infections, autoimmune diseases, such as rheumatoid arthritis, Sjögren's syndrome, systemic lupus erythematosus (SLE), ulcerative colitis, and Crohn's disease, may also be etiologically important. Some of these patients will demonstrate rheumatoid factor activity as well as hypergammaglobulinemia. These patients have been described under the

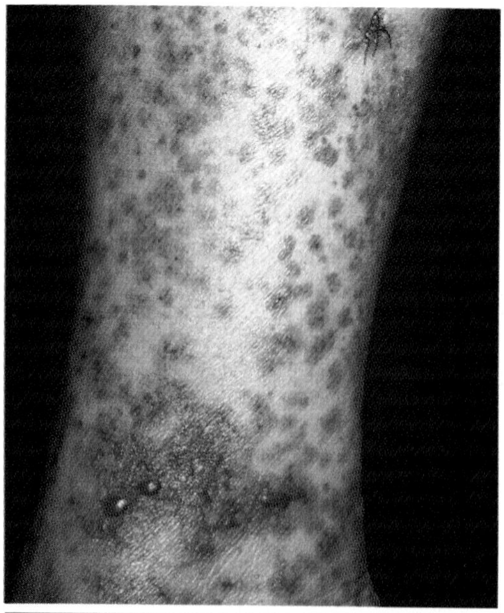

FIGURE 12–1 Palpable and nonpalpable purpura of the lower extremity induced by a leukocytoclastic angiitis. Note areas of infarction around ankle.

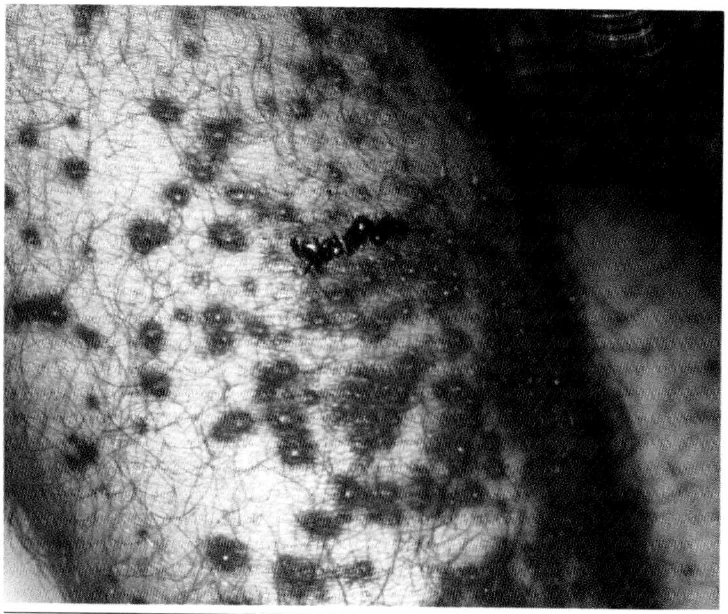

FIGURE 12–2 Palpable purpura of lower extremities. Note small sterile pustules reflective of intense inflammatory infiltrate.

TABLE 12–4 Classification Features of Hypersensitivity Angiitis

Age of onset > 16 years
Medication at disease onset (may be of etiologic significance)
Palpable purpura
Maculopapular rash
Biopsy of artery and venules showing polymorphonuclear leukocytes
Hypersensitivity angiitis is diagnosed if 3 of 5 features present. Three of five features demonstrate a 71.0% sensitivity and an 83.9% specificity.

Data from:
Calabrese LH, Michel BA, Bloch DA, et al. The American College of Rheumatology 1990 criteria for the classification of hypersensitivity angiitis. Arthritis Rheum 1990;33:1108–1113.

rubric of Waldenström's benign hypergammaglobulinemic purpura. For example, as many as 30% of Waldenström's patients have Sjögren's syndrome.

Frequently associated with rheumatoid factor Waldenström's benign hypergammaglobulinemia purpura

Mixed cryoglobulins (predominantly type II composed of monoclonal IgM [immunoglobulin] rheumatoid factor and polyclonal IgG) have been detected in some of these patients (Figure 12–4). Hence, the designation of cryoglobulinemic vasculitis attached to some of these patients. (The cryoglobulins are immune complexes that precipitate when the serum is refrigerated at 4°C.) In reality, both Waldenström's benign hypergammaglobulinemic purpura and cryoglobulinemic vasculitis are hypersensitivity small vessel vasculitic disease processes in which specific laboratory features have been emphasized (Figure 12–5).

Malignancies. Myelogenous and lymphocytic malignancies, especially hairy cell leukemia, have been associated with vasculitis. In one study, 10 of 13 patients exhibited vasculitis prior to the detection of the malignancy (Table 12–5). Hodgkin's disease, especially following treatment with high-voltage irradiation has been personally witnessed by Provost to result in widespread vasculitis.

Vasculitic lesions associated with internal malignancy can present as purpura, urticaria-like lesions, superficial ulcerations, or gangrene. The vasculitis can be associated with arthralgias, arthritis, and renal involvement as well as hepatic abnormalities. These lesions are the manifestations of a putative immune complex disease process.

Frequently, cryoglobulins are detected in the serum of these vasculitic patients. Most commonly, these are type II cryoglobulins.

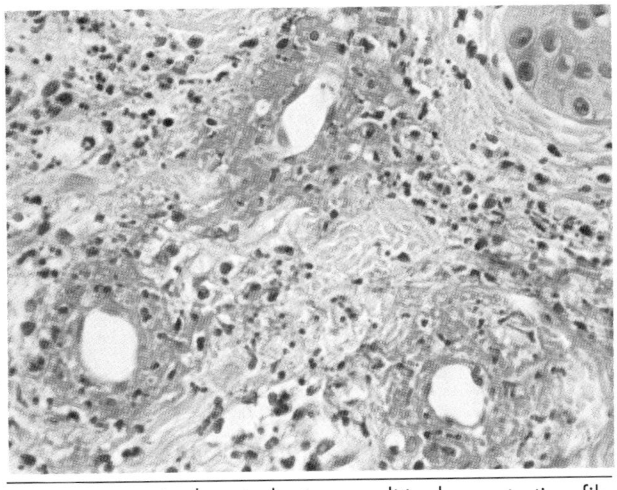

FIGURE 12-3 Leukocytoclastic vasculitis demonstrating fibrinoid necrosis around involved blood vessels.

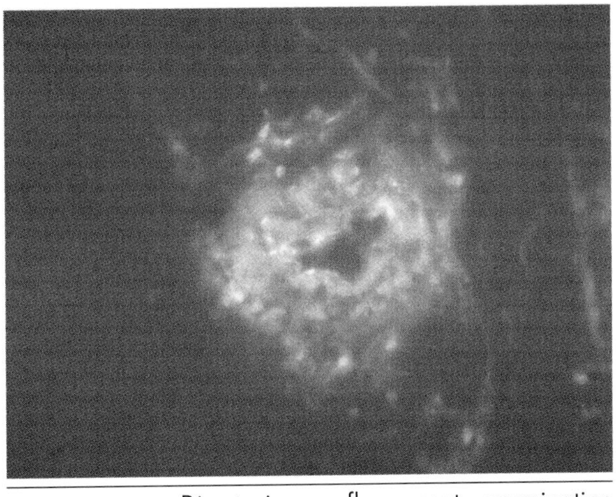

FIGURE 12-4 Direct immunofluorescent examination demonstrating IgG blood vessel deposition in the papillary portion of the dermis.

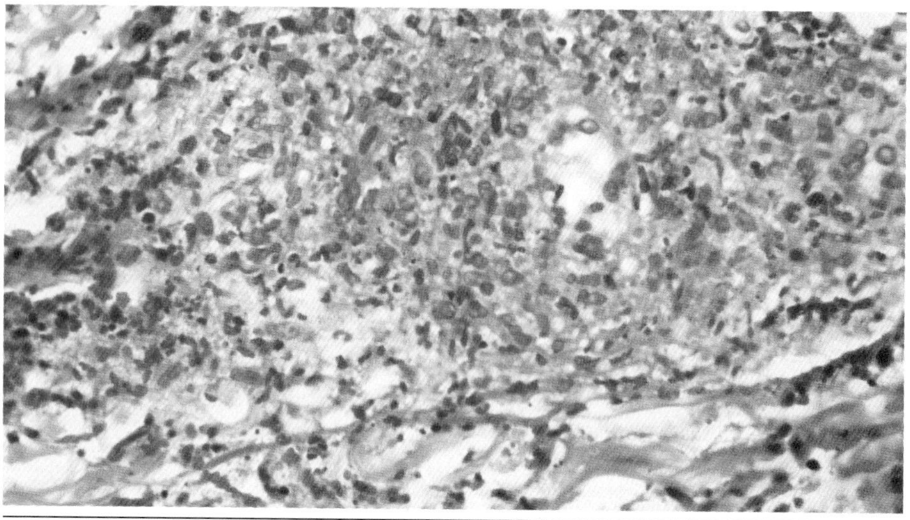

FIGURE 12–5 Histology of a leukocytoclastic vasculitis demonstrating intense polymorphonuclear infiltrate into blood vessel wall. Note fragmentation of leukocytes (leukocytoclasis).

Lesions generally occur in presence of low titered-antibody responses to corresponding antigen.

It is theorized that chronic antigen stimulation related to the malignancy produces an immune response in which relatively low-titer antibodies are formed. These are favorable conditions for the development of pathologic immune complexes (relative antigen excess). Also, supervoltage radiation or drug therapy can destroy a large tumor mass flooding the circulation with large quantities of antigen (producing relative antigen excess).

It must be re-emphasized, however, that despite thorough investigations for evidence of chronic antigemia resulting from infections—such as chronic sinusitis; apical dental abscess; and hepatitis A, B, and C; and exhaustive searches for autoimmune and malignant diseases at least 50% of these small vessel vasculitis patients fail to demonstrate an underlying etiology.

Annotated Bibliography

Winkelmann RK, Ditto WB. Cutaneous and visceral syndromes of necrotizing or "allergic" angiitis: a study of 38 cases. Medicine 1964;43:59–70.

This is an excellent review article.

Greer JM, Longley S, Edwards NL, et al. Vasculitis associated with malignancy. Experience with 13 patients and literature review. Medicine (Baltimore) 1988;67:220–230.

This excellent article demonstrates the strong association of vasculitis with hematologic, rather than solid tumor, malignancies.

TABLE 12–5 Vasculitis Associated with Malignancy

Type	Total Patients (N=66)
Lymphoma	6
Leukemia	22
Hairy cell leukemia	19
Myeloma	6
Sarcoma	2
Malignant histiocytosis	1
Solid tumors	9

Data from:
Greer JM, Longley S, Edwards NL, et al. Vasculitis associated with malignancy. Experience with 13 patients and literature review. Medicine (Baltimore) 1988;67:220–230.

Agnello V, Chung RT, Kaplan LM. A role for hepatitis C virus infection in type II cryoglobulinemia. N Engl J Med 1992;327:1490–1495.

The article demonstrates that the majority of patients diagnosed with essential mixed cryoglobulinemia actually have hepatitis C infection. Successful treatment with interferon eliminates the cryoglobulin and the signs and symptoms of vasculitis, indicating that the vasculitis syndrome and the cryoglobulinemia are caused by hepatitis C.

Serum Sickness

A serum sickness–like reaction (ie, fever, arthralgias, arthritis, renal disease, urticaria-like vasculitis) secondary to an allergic drug reaction may occur. This, too, is a manifestation of circulating immune complexes and was initially reported in patients receiving horse antidiphtheria sera and, later, horse antipneumococcal sera. On unusual occasions, such drugs as penicillin and sulfonamides can produce a similar reaction.

Prophylactic treatment with antihistamines (H-1 blockers) has been shown to inhibit the frequency of serum sickness in 300 children given horse antidiphtheria serum. There was a progressive decrease in the frequency of serum sickness, compared with controls with the use of two, compared with one, antihistamines.

Lawley et al. have described prospectively the development of a very peculiar serpiginous, erythematous, hemorrhagic lesion on the sides of feet and hands in aplastic patients treated with horse antithymus sera in preparation for an allogenic bone marrow transplantation. This cutaneous feature appears to be a unique feature of serum sickness (Figures 12–6 and 12–7).

Annotated Bibliography

Von Pirquet C, Schick B. Serum sickness. Baltimore: Williams & Wilkins, 1991.

Germuth FC Jr. A comparative histologic and immunologic study in rabbits of induced hypersensitivity of the serum sickness type. J Exp Med 1953;97:257–282.

Dixon FJ, Feldman JD, Vazquez JJ. Experimental glomerulonephritis: the pathogenesis of a laboratory model resembling the spectrum of human glomerulonephritis. J Exp Med 1961;113: 899–920.

Lawley TJ, Bielory L, Gascon P, et al. A prospective clinical and immunologic analysis of patients with serum sickness. N Engl J Med 1984;311:1407–1413.

These four articles, spanning medical and experimental experience over three-quarters of a century, document the pathogenesis of immune complex–mediated serum sickness in both humans and animals. Cutaneous vascular insult was a prominent feature of serum sickness.

The article by Lawley et al. is most interesting because a severe vascular insult occurred in aplastic anemia patients treated with horse antithymus sera when there was a paucity of cellular elements in the blood, and those cellular elements that were present were predominantly mononuclear. This tantalizing investigation suggests that mononuclear cells may play a much more prominent role in the vasculopathy of immune complex–mediated vasculitis than has been previously recognized. (All patients who were biopsied demonstrated neutropenia and thrombocytopenia at the time of biopsy. Furthermore, the biopsies revealed low-grade perivascular accumulation of lymphocytes and histiocytes with only rare polymorphonuclear neutrophils.)

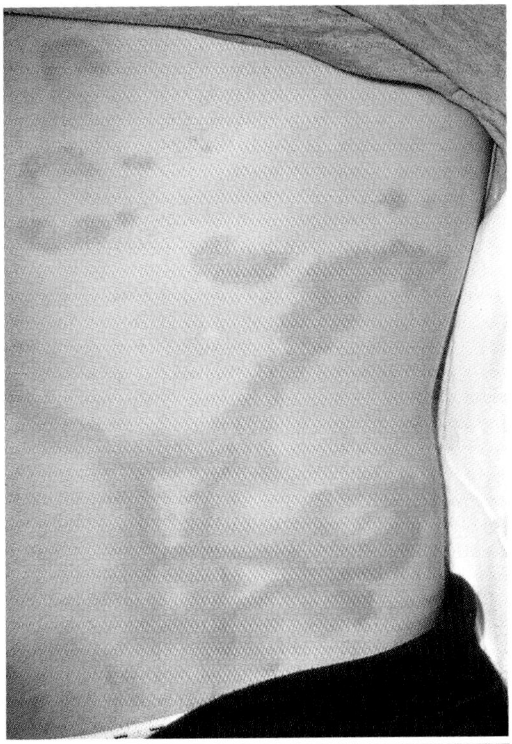

FIGURE 12–6 Serum sickness in an aplastic patient treated with horse antithymic sera in preparation for allogeneic bone marrow transplantation (Courtesy of Thomas Lawley, M.D.). (Lawley TJ, Bielory L, Gascon P, et al. A prospective clinical and immunologic analysis of patients with serum sickness. N Engl J Med 1984;311:1407–1413.

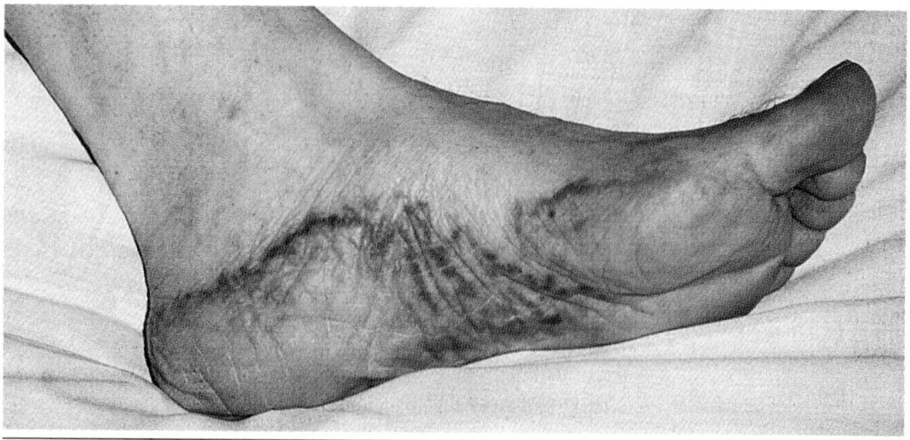

FIGURE 12–7 Distinctive urticaria hemorrhagic reaction on the medial aspect of foot of a patient with a serum sickness reaction induced by horse antithymic sera (Courtesy of Thomas Lawley, M.D.). (Lawley TJ, Bielory L, Gascon P, et al. A prospective clinical and immunologic analysis of patients with serum sickness. N Engl J Med 1984;311:1407–1413.)

Henoch-Schönlein Purpura Syndrome

This form of small vessel, cutaneous vasculitis occurs most frequently in children but can and frequently does occur in adults. See Table 12–6 for classification features of this syndrome.

Henoch-Schönlein purpura is seen in both adults and children.

Presence of IgA deposition in affected blood vessels is characteristic.

In children, the classic presentation is palpable and nonpalpable purpura involving predominantly the extensor surfaces of the knees, hands, and elbows, as well as the buttocks (Figure 12–8). Arthritis, gastrointestinal symptomatology (cramping abdominal pain and melena), and glomerulonephritis also commonly occur. In at least 30 to 40% of cases, especially in children, the disease process is preceded by an upper respiratory infection. Direct immunofluorescence of the skin lesions demonstrates immunoglobulin deposition in and about affected blood vessels. All immunoglobulin classes may be present, but IgA is always present. Many times, it is the only immunoglobulin detected.

Clinical Features

Skin lesions indistinguishable from hypersensitivity vasculitis

Cutaneous manifestations. The skin lesions are generally indistinguishable from those of allergic vasculitis.

May be related to IgA nephropathy (Berger's disease)

Renal disease. In general, the focal glomerulonephritis of Henoch-Schönlein purpura, characterized by microscopic hematuria, remits. Approximately 10% of patients, however, may develop slowly progressive renal failure. The relationship between this vasculitic disease and IgA glomerulonephritis (Berger's IgA nephropathy), the most prevalent form of glomerulonephritis, is unknown. It is conceivable that Henoch-Schönlein purpura and Berger's disease represent different parts of the spectrum of the same disease process.

Associated with no permanent deformities

Arthritis. Joint involvement occurs in as many as 60 to 90% of Henoch-Schönlein purpura patients. The knees, ankles, wrists, and elbows, are most commonly involved. However, pelvic and shoulder girdle involvement also occur. The arthritis is transient and nondeforming.

Intussusception and bowel perforation are uncommon complications.

Gastrointestinal disease. In children, gastrointestinal disease is a common symptom and occurring in as many as 50 to 70% of patients. It is characterized by colicky pain associated with bloody diarrhea or melena. Intussusception and, rarely, bowel perforation may occur.

Frequently, gastrointestinal symptomatology presents as an acute abdomen, and the patients are explored for a possible appendicitis. Examination of the serosal surface of the gastrointestinal tract will demonstrate vasculitic lesions, characterized by sharply demarcated, erythematous, macular lesions.

TABLE 12–6 Classification Features of Henoch-Schönlein Purpura Syndrome

Palpable purpura
Age ≤ 20 at onset
Bowel angina
Wall granulocytes on biopsy specimen (polymorphonuclear leukocytes in walls of arterioles or venules)
Henoch-Schönlein purpura is diagnosed if 2 of 4 features are present. The presence of any two features is associated with an 87.1% sensitivity and an 87.7% specificity.

Data from:
Mills JA, Michel BA, Bloch DA, et al. The American College of Rheumatology 1990 criteria for the classification of Henoch Schönlein purpura. Arthritis Rheum 1990;33:1114–1121.

It should be noted that the full-blown disease process of Henoch-Schönlein purpura (ie, simultaneous skin, joint, gastrointestinal, and renal manifestations) is unusual. Most patients will demonstrate the sequential development of one feature followed by another (eg, skin disease followed by joint, gastrointestinal, or kidney disease).

Prognosis

Henoch-Schönlein purpura is generally an acute disease process, occurring most frequently in the winter. An upper respiratory infection, especially in children, is commonly detected in one-third. Although as many as 10% of patients may develop evidence of renal failure, the disease generally subsides without sequelae.

Occurs more commonly in winter. One-third follow an upper respiratory infection.

Adult Henoch-Schönlein purpura patients tend to have a more severe disease with a greater frequency of renal involvement.

Pathogenesis

From a conceptional point of view, it is attractive to hypothesize that the antigenic stimulation inducing the immune response in these patients is presented to the host via the respiratory or gastrointestinal mucosa (secretory immune system). However, although some patients demonstrate increased serum IgA levels, the subclass of IgA is IgA_1 (the type of IgA secreted by the systemic and not the IgA_2 secreted by the secretory immune system).

Treatment

Parenteral steroids are given for severe cases involving the gastrointestinal tract and kidneys. Dapsone (diaminodiphenylsulfone) also has been reported to be beneficial.

Annotated Bibliography

Allen DM, Diamond LK, Howell DA. Anaphylactoid purpura in children (Schönlein-Henoch syndrome). Am J Dis Child 1960;99:833–840.

This article provides a classic description of this entity in children.

Saulsbury FT. Henoch-Shönlein purpura in children: report of 100 patients and review of the literature. Medicine 1999;78:395–409.

Classic description of this entity in children.

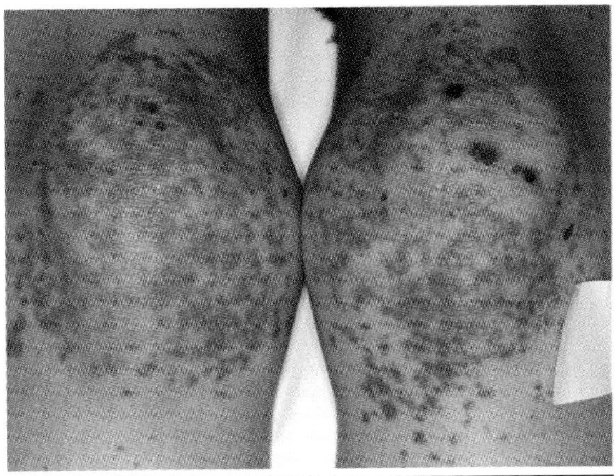

FIGURE 12–8 Small-vessel vasculitis in a 10-year-old boy with Henoch-Schönlein purpura.

Urticaria-Like Vasculitis

During the past 25 years, it has been recognized that urticaria-like lesions may be the cutaneous expression of a small-vessel vasculitis. From a conceptional point of

Low-grade vasculitis found as a prodrome of hepatitis and associated with systemic erythematosus and Sjögren's syndrome.

view, it is visualized that the urticaria-like vasculitis represents predominantly, but not solely, a low-grade leukocytoclastic vasculitis, which is the result of a putative immune complex disease process. (Some patients demonstrate a lymphocytic vasculitis. For further discussion, see Chapter 8, "Sjögren's Syndrome.") These urticaria-like vasculitic lesions, in contradistinction to common urticaria, are persistent for greater than 24 hours, may be associated with a burning-type pruritus, may have petechiae in the urticarial lesion, and may be associated with a hyperpathia to the application of light touch (Figure 12–9). Urticaria-like vasculitis lesions have been detected as a prodromal sign of hepatitis B, occurring with arthralgias and arthritis prior to the onset of jaundice; as a paraneoplastic vasculitis; and in association with connective tissue diseases (SLE and Sjögren's syndrome).

Urticaria-like vasculitis found in approximately 10% of SLE and Sjögren's syndrome patients.

In SLE, urticaria-like lesions have been detected in approximately 10% of untreated patients. They are not a feature of patients with benign cutaneous lupus erythematosus. Furthermore, urticaria-like vasculitic lesions in SLE are frequently associated with renal disease and the presence of anti-Ro (SS-A) and anti-dsDNA antibodies. In Sjögren's syndrome, urticaria-like vasculitic lesions are seen in anti-Ro (SS-A) antibody–positive patients with an increased frequency of extraglandular features. For further discussion, see Chapter 8, "Sjögren's Syndrome."

Laboratory studies may be unremarkable. An elevated erythrocyte sedimentation rate has been reported to be present in approximately one-third of patients. In addition, these patients may demonstrate hypocomplementemia. According to Provost, it appears that the presence of hypocomplementemia and urticaria-like vasculitic lesions in SLE patients generally is associated with the presence of active renal disease.

Hypocomplementemic urticarial vasculitis is associated with C1q antibodies.
Some of these patients have developed SLE, and approximately 20 to 25% develop obstructive pulmonary disease.

In addition to the form of urticaria-like vasculitis described above, a group of patients has been described under the rubric of hypocomplementemic urticarial vasculitis syndrome (HUVS). These patients clinically, however, are indistinguishable from the urticaria-like vasculitic patients described above, although they demonstrate the presence of an IgG autoantibody directed against the collagenous portion of C1q. In addition to urticaria-like vasculitis, these patients frequently demonstrate angioedema, arthritis, and glomerulonephritis and approximately 20 to 25% of these patients develop an obstructive lung disease.

The anti-C1q antibody was initially detected as a C1q precipitin in low–ionic strength agar gels. Although initially thought to be a protein-protein interaction involving the Fc portion of IgG and C1q, it has now been conclusively shown by Wisnieski's and Mannik's groups that this interaction is a true antigen–antibody interaction involving the $F(ab')_2$ fragment of IgG. The relationship between anti-C1q antibodies and the vasculitic disease process associated with this syndrome is unknown. Additional studies have shown the presence of 7S (IgG) as well as 19S (IgM) C1q precipitins in SLE sera. Furthermore, anti-C1q antibodies have been detected in SLE sera, and several hypocomplementemic urticaria-like vasculitic patients have subsequently developed SLE. Thus, it appears that the hypocomplementemic urticarial vasculitis syndrome may be closely related to SLE.

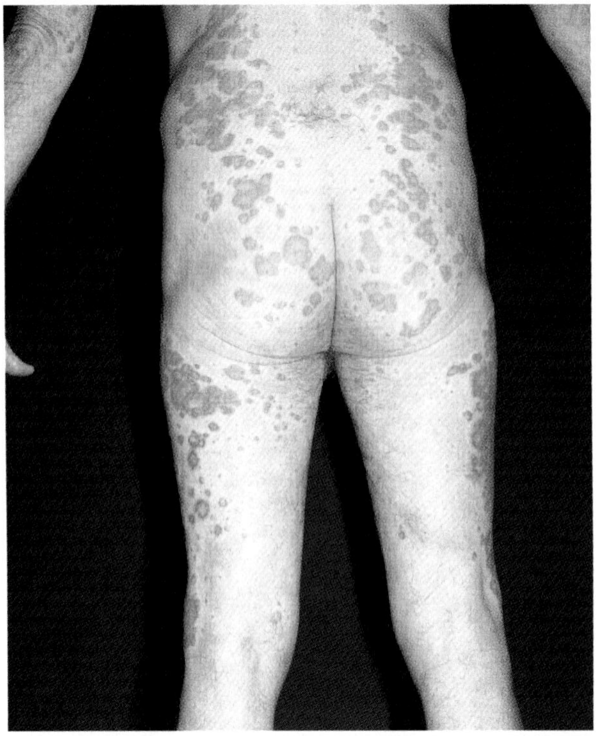

FIGURE 12–9 Widespread urticaria-like vasculitic lesions.

Annotated Bibliography

Soter NA, Austen F, Gigli I. Urticaria and arthralgias as manifestations of necrotizing angiitis (vasculitis). J Invest Dermatol 1974;63:485–490.

This is a classic article demonstrating the association or urticaria-like lesions with an underlying vasculitis.

Alexander E, et al. Sjögren's syndrome: association of anti-Ro (SS-A) antibodies with vasculitis, hematological abnormalities, and serological hyperreactivity. Am Intern Med 1983;98:155–159.

Provost TT, et al. Unusual cutaneous manifestations of SLE: urticaria-like lesions, correlation with clinical and serologic abnormalities. J Invest Dermatol 1980;75:495–499.

Two articles from our own institution detailing urticaria-like vasculitis lesions in systemic lupus erythematosus and Sjögren's syndrome patients.

McDuffie FC, Sams WM, Maldonado JE, et al. Hypocomplementemia with cutaneous vasculitis and arthritis. Possible immune complex syndrome. Mayo Clin Proc 1973; 48:340–348.

Schwartz HR, McDuffie FC, Black LF, et al. Hypocomplementemic urticarial vasculitis: association with chronic obstructive pulmonary disease. Mayo Clin Proc 1982;57: 231–238.

Agnello V, Koffler D, Eisenberg JW, et al. C1q precipitins in the sera of patients with systemic lupus erythematosus and other hypocomplementemic states: characterization of high and low molecular weight types. J Exp Med 1971;134:228s–241s.

Uwatoko S, Mannik M. Low-molecular weight C1q-binding immunoglobulin G in patients with systemic lupus erythematosus consists of autoantibodies to the collagen-like region of C1q. J Clin Invest 1988;82:816–824.

Wisnieski JJ, Naff GB. Serum IgG antibodies to C1q in hypocomplementemic urticarial vasculitis syndrome. Arthritis Rheum 1989;32:1119–1127.

The preceding five references detail the development of knowledge of HUVS. This syndrome, characterized by the presence of IgG autoantibodies directed against the collagen-like region of C1q, is associated with angioedema, urticarial vasculitis. On biopsy, the involved organ demonstrates a leukocytoclastic angiitis and the presence of chronic obstructive lung disease in approximately 20 to 25% of patients. Most recent data indicate that some of these patients may progress to develop lupus erythematosus suggesting a relationship between this syndrome and SLE—the exact nature of which is currently being explored.

Erythema Elevatum Diutinum

Erythema elevatum diutinum is a chronic form of a low-grade small-vessel vasculitis.

Erythema elevatum diutinum is a rare, chronic, inflammatory small vessel vasculitis, characterized by red, purple, and yellowish papules, plaques, and nodules that occur over the extensor surfaces of the joints of the hand, knees, and buttocks. These lesions demonstrate in the early phase a leukocytoclastic angiitis and a fibrotic replacement of blood vessels in the late phase (Figure 12–10). The cause of erythema elevatum diutinum is unknown, but the inflammatory lesions are thought to result from a putative immune complex disease process. Many of these patients demonstrate an exaggerated 4- to 6-hour (Arthus) and a 48-hour delayed hypersensitivity reaction to the intracutaneous injection of streptokinase and streptodornase. Recurrent upper respiratory infections involving β-hemolytic *Streptococcus* have been noted in some patients. In other patients, an IgA gammopathy has been associated with the development of these lesions. Some patients describe recurrent infections, fevers, arthralgias, and arthritis, as well as recurrent crops of painful skin lesions. Systemic features, however, are generally lacking.

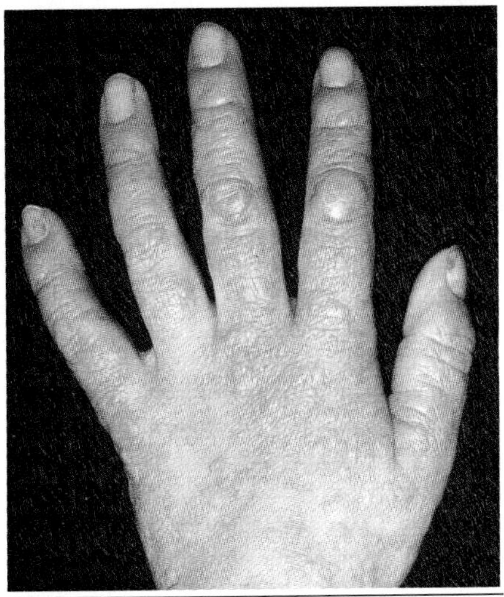

FIGURE 12-10 Plaque lesions on the dorsal surface of the hand of a patient with erythema elevatum diutinum (Courtesy of Stephen I Katz, M.D.)

On occasion, the epidermis may erode, producing ulcerations as well as vesicles and pustules. Histologically, the inflammatory infiltrate involves small blood vessels in the upper and middle dermis. Fibrinoid necrosis, as well as fragmentation of polymorphonuclear leukocytes are detected. Eosinophils may also be present. The older lesions demonstrate fibrosis in the dermis accompanied by capillary proliferation. There may be large amounts of extracellular cholesterol deposits.

In addition, other studies have demonstrated circulating immune complexes. Furthermore, the exacerbation of this disease with streptococcal infections and the Arthus-like histology implies that at least some of these patients may develop a chronic vasculitis as a consequence of repeated streptococcal infections.

Dapsone is an effective form of therapy.

Diaminodiphenylsulfone (dapsone) is capable of suppressing the inflammatory response in this form of vasculitis.

Annotated Bibliography

Katz SI, Gallen JI, Hertz KC, et al. Erythema elevatum diutinum: skin and systemic manifestations, immunologic studies, and successful treatment with dapsone. Medicine (Baltimore) 1977;56:443–455.

This is a classic paper on this area.

Pustular Vasculitis

Pustular vasculitis is a morphologic form of vasculitis in which an intense leukocyte response is the dominant pathologic feature.

On rare occasions, pustular lesions may be the cutaneous expression of a small-vessel vasculopathy. Some of these patients have a definite leukocytoclastic angiitis. In others, the neutrophilic inflammatory infiltrate is seen without definite evidence of a vasculitis. Some of these lesions have been seen in association with bowel bypass syndrome, blind loop syndromes, inflammatory bowel disease, and Behçet's disease. Fever, myalgias, and polyarthritis commonly accompany these lesions. Similar cutaneous manifestations may be seen in patients with acute febrile neutrophilic dermatosis (Sweet's syndrome) and pyoderma gangrenosa. In addition, patients with gonococcal arthritis syndrome frequently develop vasculitic lesions characterized by erythematous, painful macules and papules, some of which are surmounted by pustules. These lesions usually appear distal to the elbows and knees and number approximately 10 or less (Figure 12–11). Biopsies of the lesions reveal a neutrophilic inflammatory infiltrate with some evidence for vasculitis. Gonococcal organisms are rarely cultured from these lesions.

From a conceptual basis, the entities described above are thought to result from a putative immune complex disease in which the vasculitic insult is associated with a pronounced neutrophilic inflammatory infiltrate. The release of lysosomal products from the leukocytes produces a severe inflammatory, painful lesion. Recurrent crops of these lesions and pain disproportional to the size of the lesion are characteristic.

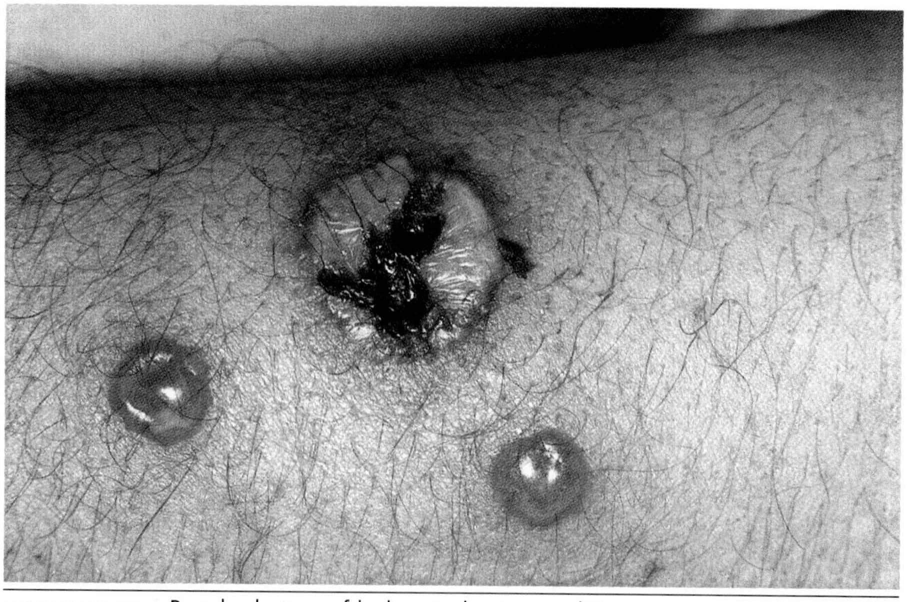

FIGURE 12–11 Postular lesions of leukocytoclastic vasculitis.

Annotated Bibliography

Diaz LA, Provost TT, Tomasi TB Jr. Pustular necrotizing angiitis. Arch Dermatol 1973;108:114–118.

This is the first paper for Diaz, who has subsequently become famous for his work in bullous diseases.

Medium Vessel Vasculitis

Polyarteritis nodosa, Churg-Strauss syndrome, (allergic granulomatosis, allergic angiitis), and Wegner's granulomatosus are classified as medium-sized vessel vasculitis. These inflammatory vasculopathies, however, can also involve small blood vessels and have cutaneous presentations similar to those seen with hypersensitivity angiitis.

Polyarteritis Nodosa

Polyarteritis nodosa is a systemic disease associated with significant morbidity and mortality. It is more frequent in men and occurs commonly in the fourth and fifth decades of life. See Table 12–7 for the classification of this disease.

The multiorgan involvement in classic polyarteritis nodosa is presented in Table 12–8. The disease process characteristically spares the pulmonary vasculature.

Clinical Features

Cutaneous manifestations. Cutaneous manifestations occur in approximately 40 to 50% of patients (Figures 12–12 and 12–13). Nodules, ulcers, and livedo reticularis are common. Small vessel disease, characterized by palpable purpura and urticaria-like vasculitis, can also be seen, but these are unusual. Biopsies generally reveal a necrotizing vasculitis of subcutaneous (muscular) arteries (Figure 12–14 and Figure 12-15).

Nodules and ulcers characterize the cutaneous lesions of polyarteritis nodosa.

A limited form of polyarteritis nodosa that is confined only to the skin has been reported. Tender and nontender nodules with or without an accompanying livedo reticularis have been described. Several reports exist demonstrating a failure for systemic manifestations to develop.

One patient with this entity developed nodular vasculitic lesions on the right foot with livedo reticularis. A biopsy was reported to show polyarteritis nodosa. An extra-articular ankylosing fibrosis of the right ankle occurred. Repeated sys-

TABLE 12–7 Classification Features of Polyarteritis Nodosa

Weight loss ≥ 4 kg
Livedo reticularis
Testicular pain or tenderness
Myalgias, weakness, or leg tenderness
Mononeuropathy or polyneuropathy
Diastolic blood pressure > 90 mm Hg
Elevated blood urea nitrogen or creatinine
Hepatitis B virus
Arteriographic abnormality
Biopsy of small- or medium-size artery containing polymorphonuclear leukocytes

Polyarteritis nodosa is diagnosed if 3 of 10 features are satisfied.
Three or more criteria demonstrate an 82.2% sensitivity and an 86.6% specificity.

Data from:
Lightfoot RW Jr, Michel BA, Bloch DA, et al. The American College of Rheumatology 1990 criteria for the classification of polyarteritis nodosa. Arthritis Rheum 1990;33:1088–1093.

TABLE 12–8 Clinical Features Detected in Polyarteritis Nodosa Patients

Area Affected	% of Involvement
Kidney	70
Peripheral neuropathy	51
Gastrointestinal tract	44
Skin	43
Cardiac	36
Central nervous system	23

Adapted from:
Cupps TR, Fanci AS. The Vasculitides. Philadelphia: WB Saunders, 1981, p 29.

temic evaluations were negative. The disease process was stabilized with oral cyclophosphamide. Discontinuance of cyclophosphamide after 1 year of therapy was followed by a complete remission for 5 years (the duration of her life).

Hypertension is a common feature.

Renal manifestations. Renal involvement is common and is due to medium-size vessel vasculitis, producing ischemia and renal vascular hypertension. Glomerulonephritis is seen infrequently, uncontrolled hypertension is thought to be responsible for the development of chronic renal failure. Angiography frequently reveals aneurysms of the renal, hepatic, and visceral vasculature.

A second limited form of polyarteritis has been described. This form of the disease, involving capillaries and arterioles (not the medium-size arteries of classic polyarteritis), most frequently causes glomerulonephritis with or without pulmonary capillaritis and is associated with the prescence of anti P-ANCA antibodies.

Affect 50% of patients
Rupture of micro-aneurysms can cause hemorrhage.

Gastrointestinal manifestations. Gastrointestinal manifestations occur in approximately 50% of patients. Abdominal pain, nausea, vomiting, and diarrhea, as well as pancreatitis, occur. Ischemic necrosis can occur throughout the gastrointestinal tract. Rupture of microaneurysms in mesenteric arteries can produce catastrophic intra-abdominal and gastrointestinal hemorrhage.

Cardiac manifestations. Cardiac disease occurs in approximately one-third of patients. Congestive heart failure, secondary to coronary artery vasculitis, and

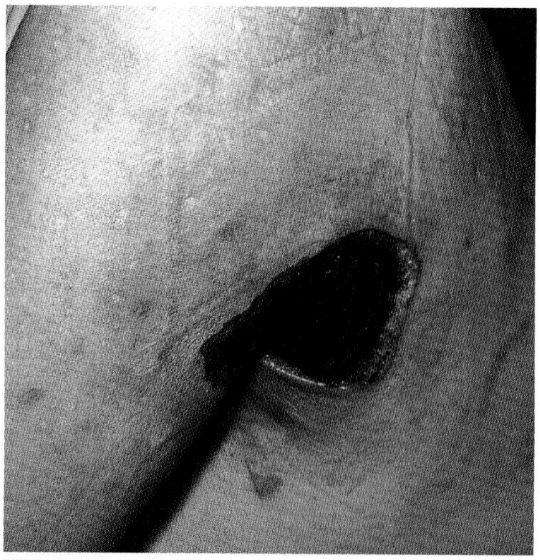

FIGURE 12–12 Large infarction of skin in posterior axillary region of a patient with polyarteritis nodosa.

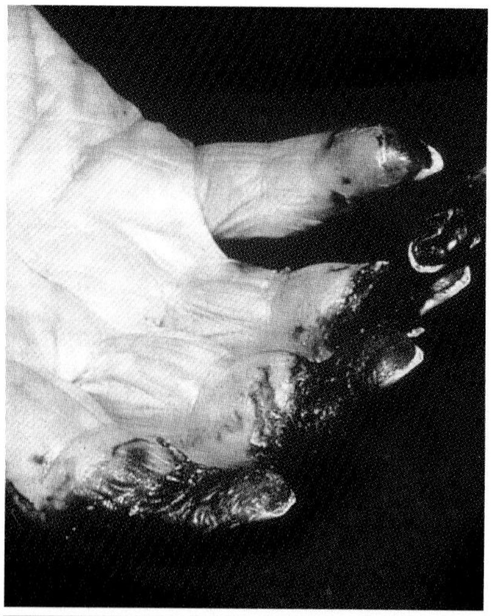

FIGURE 12–13 Gangrene of the fingers in a patient with polyarteritis (Courtesy of Matthew Katz, M.D.).

FIGURE 12-14 Vasculitis involving muscular artery at the dermal–subcutaneous junction in a patient with polyarteritis nodosa (Courtesy of Matthew Katz, M.D.).

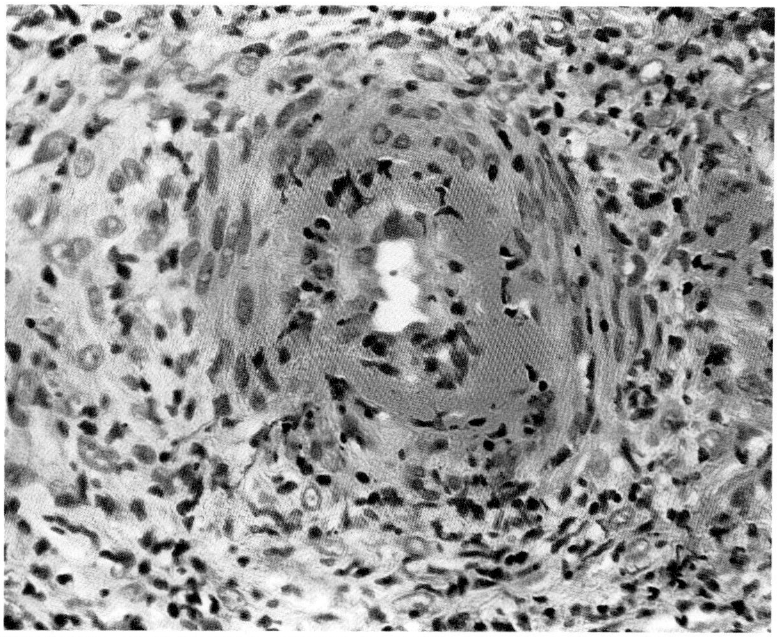

FIGURE 12-15 Vasculitis involving muscular artery at the dermal–subcutaneous junction in a polyarteritis nodosa patient. Note fibrinoid necrosis and invasion of blood vessel wall (Courtesy of Matthew Katz, M.D.).

hypertensive cardiovascular disease are most common presentations. However, pericarditis and vasculitic involvement of the conduction system can also occur.

Peripheral neuropathy. Peripheral nerve involvement, producing mononeuritis multiplex and sensory and motor polyneuropathy, is common. Cerebral vascular accidents, seizures, and altered mental status also occur.

Peripheral neurologic manifestations are commonly detected.

Pathogenesis

In the majority of cases of polyarteritis nodosa, the etiology is unknown. In the 20 to 30% of patients with polyarteritis who have either hepatitis B or C, the vasculitis is caused by deposition of circulating immune complexes composed of viral antigen and antibodies. When antiviral therapy clears the hepatitis infection, the symptoms and signs of polyarteritis resolve. The higher incidence of polyarteritis nodosa in intravenous drug abusers is probably related to their high rates of infection with hepatitis B or C.

Immune complex–mediated disease

Prognosis

The combined use of corticosteroids and cyclophosphamide has achieved an approximate 5-year survivability of 80%.

Annotated Bibliography

Diaz-Perez JL, Winkelmann RK. Cutaneous periarteritis nodosa. Arch Dermatol 1974;110:407–414.

This highly quoted paper describes this dermatologic entity.

Guillevin L, Lhote F, Sauvaget F, et al. Treatment of polyarteritis nodosa related to hepatitis B virus with interferon-alpha and plasma exchanges. Ann Rheum Dis 1994;53: 334–337.

This article demonstrates the success of treating hepatitis B–associated polyarteritis nodosa with 2 weeks of prednisone, followed by plasmapheresis and antiviral therapy.

Guillevin L, Lhote F, Gayraud M, et al. Prognostic factors in polyarteritis nodosa and Churg-Strauss syndrome. A prospective study in 342 patients. Medicine (Baltimore) 1996;75:17–28.

The risk factors for mortality are proteinuria > 1 g/dL or renal insufficiency with serum creatinine > 1 g mg per dL.

Churg-Strauss Syndrome

Churg-Strauss syndrome, also known as allergic granulomatosis or granulomatous vasculitis, is a medium-sized vasculitis characterized by hypereosinophilia, asthma, and glomerulonephritis. Transient pulmonary infiltrates and a mono- or polyneuropathy are frequently detected. The peripheral neuropathy, involving both sensory and motor fibers, can be profound. Tissue biopsies demonstrate, in sites of involvement, infiltrates of eosinophils. Peripheral blood eosinophilia may exceed 10%. Table 12-9 provides the classification of features of Churg-Strauss syndrome.

Churg-Strauss syndrome is a rare form of vasculitis. It is approximately one-third as common as polyarteritis nodosa. A 2:1 male/female ratio has been reported. This vasculitis most commonly occurs during the fifth decade of life but may be seen in all ages.

Rare form of vasculitis characterized by systemic vasculitis associated with pulmonary manifestations and hypereosinophilia.

Churg-Strauss syndrome involves the muscular arteries affecting the heart, spleen, kidney, gut, pancreas, gallbladder, and liver. Pulmonary involvement is generally the initial clinical presentation. The asthmatic phase may antedate the development of cutaneous vasculitis by months or years. In general, the asthma is associated with hypereosinophilia and fever.

The cutaneous manifestations include tender nodules occurring on all parts of the body, including the scalp. Other lesions are macular or papular and associated with purpura. Ulceration may occur, and livedo reticularis may be present.

Skin biopsies frequently demonstrate extravascular granulomas that contain eosinophils. The blood vessels involved are muscular arteries in the dermis and subcutaneous tissue. However, necrotizing vasculitis of small vessels in the papillary and middle portions of the reticular dermis is also seen. Gastrointestinal involvement, characterized by crampy abdominal pain and at times bloody diarrhea, is commonly detected. Also, hypertension is frequently noted.

Pathogenesis

Etiology unknown but evidence suggests immune complex–mediated.

The exact pathogenesis of this form of vasculitis is unknown, although deposition of immunoglobulins and complement has been demonstrated in involved blood vessel walls.

Eosinophils are prominent in the inflammatory infiltrate.
Vascular involvement at all stages

Vascular involvement is present in all stages of the disease process. Fibrinoid necrosis may be seen, associated with a leukocytoclastic vasculitis in which eosinophils predominate. There is, however, also an admixture of polymorphonuclear leukocytes and lymphocytes.

TABLE 12–9 Classification Features of Churg-Strauss Syndrome

Asthma
Eosinophilia
Mononeuropathy or polyneuropathy
Pulmonary infiltrates (migratory or transient)
Paranasal sinus abnormalities
Extravascular eosinophils (biopsy demonstration)

Churg-Strauss syndrome is diagnosed if 4 of 6 features are present. The demonstration of any 4 features demonstrates an 85% sensitivity and a 99.7% specificity.

Data from:
Masi T, Hunder GG, Lie T, et al. The American College of Rheumatology 1990 criteria for the classification of Churg-Strauss syndrome (allergic granulomatosis and angiitis). Arthritis Rheum 1990;33:1094–1100.

In the chronic stage, giant cell formation predominates. Endothelial proliferation and fibrotic narrowing of the blood vessel lumen characterize the chronic phase. Aneurysms and thrombosis may occur. Macrophage and giant cell formations around necrotic areas of arterial involvement are common.

Clinical Features

Pulmonary manifestations. Asthma frequently antedates the development of vasculitis by many years. Fever and weight loss and the presence of transient, parenchymal pulmonary lesions are almost always detected on radiographic examination.

Asthma and/or pulmonary infiltrates invariably present

Cutaneous manifestations. Approximately 50% of patients demonstrate cutaneous features, which include petechiae, purpura, nodules, and ulcerations.

Cardiac manifestations. Cardiac involvement is often characterized by epicardium granulomas. In addition, eosinophilic infiltrations associated with scattered fibrosis are commonly detected in the myocardium.

Other clinical features. Peripheral neuropathy (mononeuritis multiplex) is commonly detected. Abdominal pain, secondary to granulomatous vasculitis of blood vessels (abdominal angina) in the large and small bowels, may occur. Polyarthralgias and arthritis are uncommon. Hematuria is a common finding indicative of renal involvement. A focal glomerulonephritis associated with eosinophilic infiltrates and granuloma formation is often detected. However, renal failure is unusual.

Laboratory features indicate an eosinophilia. In some cases, it has been as high as 60,000 per mm^3. An elevated erythrocyte sedimentation rate is commonly detected. Rheumatoid factor may be positive. P-ANCA's are present in 40 to 60% of patients.

Eosinophilia can be extremely high.
Elevated erythrocyte sedimentation rate common

Recently, a 49-year-old law enforcement officer demonstrated many of the classic features of Churg-Strauss type of vasculitis. The patient had been treated for asthma for many years. He had been hospitalized on several occasions for pulmonary infiltrates and fever. He had a 15% eosinophilia. Although pneumonia was suspected, no pathogens were detected, and the infiltrates cleared.

Approximately 10 days prior to hospitalization, the patient developed urticaria and was treated with a short course of oral steroids. Subsequent to the tapering of the steroids, the patient noted the onset of tingling and numbness in his left lower leg followed by similar symptoms in both hands (Figure 12–17). Sharp, crampy abdominal pain followed, and the patient was hospitalized.

Skin examination revealed urticaria lesions on his arms and back. Biopsy revealed small vessel vasculitis with prominent eosinophilia. Biopsy of the sural nerve revealed a vasculitis of the vaso nervorum. P-ANCA determination was positive.

Neurologic examination revealed evidence of a motor and sensory mononeuritis multiplex involving ulnar and peroneal nerves.

Intravenous methylprednisolone 1 g for 3 days resulted in the rapid clearance of symptoms. Currently, the patient is slowly recovering on 60 mg of prednisone and 150 mg of cyclophosphamide.

This case report emphasizes that these patients may have an upper respiratory disease process or asthma for years prior to the onset of vasculitis. In this patient's case, the cutaneous manifestation was an urticaria-like vasculitis. The rapid onset of neurologic disease was dramatic and the residual neurologic sequelae problematic.

Diagnosis

The history of asthma in a middle-aged patient associated with nodular skin disease, noncavitary pulmonary infiltrates, cardiac failure, and an eosinophilia suggest the diagnosis. Biopsy of the skin, lung, or other involved areas reveals the characteristic eosinophilic, necrotizing vasculitis and associated extravascular granulomas.

Prominent eosinophilia in blood and tissue associated with necrotizing vasculitis and granuloma diagnostic

Treatment

Responds to oral steroids

The Churg-Strauss type of vasculitis responds to 40 to 60 mg per day of prednisone. The combination of immunosuppressive agents (eg, azathioprine, cyclophosphamide) with prednisone may produce even better results.

Annotated Bibliography

Crotty CP, DeRemee RA, Winkelmann RK. Cutaneous clinical pathologic correlation of allergic granulomatosis. J Am Acad Dermatol 1981;5:571–581.

This article provides a good description of cutaneous features associated with Churg-Strauss vasculitis.

Guillevin L, et al. Churg-syndrome: clinical study and long term follow up of 96 patients. Medicine 1999;78:26–37.

Excellent review with 30 references.

Wegener's Granulomatosis

In 1936, Wegener described three patients with upper and lower respiratory tract necrotizing granulomas, systemic vasculitis, and glomerulonephritis. During the early granulomatous phase, he believed that the disease process may be restricted to the upper and lower respiratory tracts. After a period of months to years, vasculitis and glomerulonephritis may occur. Clinical experience over the years has promoted the concept that the disease usually progresses from involvement of the ears, nose, throat, and sinuses to involvement of the lungs and, finally, the kidneys. Cases exist in which isolated pulmonary and renal involvement (limited Wegener's) exist. The disease process appears to affect men and women equally. Table 12–10 summarizes the classification features for Wegner's granulamatosis.

Classic triad of respiratory involvement, systemic vasculitis, and glomerulonephritis described by Wegener in 1936.
Isolated pulmonary and renal disease (limited Wegener's) has been reported.

The disease usually occurs during the fifth decade. All races appear to be involved, but the predominance is in Caucasians.

At least 50% of Wegener's granulomatosis patients have mucocutaneous manifestations. These include granulomas of the nasomucosa and middle ear and ulcerations of the buccal mucosa, tongue, and lips. Alveolar bone loss is common.

Cutaneous features may be the initial presentation. They include petechiae, purpura, ecchymosis, papules, and nodules, which may or may not be tender, occurring on all areas of the body. Ulceration of papules and nodules may occur. Livedo reticularis may also be noted.

In approximately 50% of patients, ocular manifestations including episcleritis, uveiitis, retinal artery thrombosis, and proptosis may be detected. The proptosis results from a granulomatous inflammation occurring in the retro-orbital space.

Limited Wegener's granulomatosis in which pulmonary lesions dominate with few cutaneous features has been reported.

Antineutrophilic antibodies are detected in 80 to 95% of patients with active Wegener's granulomatosis. Cytoplasmic staining for (C-)ANCA (caused by anti-

TABLE 12–10 Classification of Features of Wegener's Granulomatosis

Nasal or oral inflammation
Abnormal chest radiograph
Hematuria or red blood cell casts
Granulomatous inflammation on biopsy

Wegener's granulomatosis is present if 2 of 4 criteria are satisfied.
The presence of any 2 of these features demonstrates an 88.2% sensitivity and a 92.0% specificity.

Data from:
Leavitt RY, Fanci AS, Bloch DA, et al. The American College of Rheumatology 1990 criteria for the classification of Wegener's granulomatosis. Arthritis Rheum 1990;33:1101–1107.

bodies to serine proteinase-3) is much more specific for Wegener's than is P-ANCA (caused by antibodies to myeloperoxidase). Of the Wegener's patients with a positive ANCA, approximately 80% have C-ANCA and 20% have P-ANCA. ANCA is not detected in classic polyarteritis nodosa.

Clinical Features

Severe destructive necrotizing disease of central portion of face with nasal and/or oral involvement.

Involvement of the ears, nose, sinuses, and upper airway is a common early feature of Wegener's granulomatosis. Rhinitis, nasal stuffiness, epistaxis, sinusitis, and erosion of the nasal septum with destruction of the nasal cartilage producing a saddle-nose deformity are common (Figure 12–16). Furthermore, eustachian tube involvement leads to a serous otitis media. Granulomatous involvement of the middle ear, producing a chronic otitis media, recurring infections, and mastoiditis may occur. Cochlear vasculitis produces a sensorineural deafness.

Pulmonic involvement includes hoarseness, stridor, and bronchial stenosis.

Hoarseness, dyspnea, and stridor are the early symptoms of upper airway involvement. Granulomatous involvement may produce subglottic stenosis. Transient, recurrent, solitary, or multiple nodules are commonly detected in the lungs. These lesions may cavitate. Pulmonary hemorrhage and bronchial stenosis may also occur. Pleural effusions may be found. However, hilar adenopathy is unusual.

Proptosis is common.

Eye involvement. Proptosis, conjunctivitis, scleritis, and uveitis are common ocular features.

Renal disease. Hematuria and proteinuria are common, and renal failure may develop rapidly.

Cutaneous manifestations range from palpable purpura to nodular, ulcerating lesions.

Cutaneous manifestations. Approximately 40 to 50% of patients develop significant skin disease, characterized most commonly by palpable purpura over the lower extremities (see Figure 12–16). Nodular, ulcerating lesions may also be seen. These manifestations indicate both small- and medium-size vessel involvement

Arthritis/arthralgias. Approximately 70% of patients may develop significant joint manifestations. In a few patients, a nondeforming, arthritis involving lower extremity joints has been detected (Figure 12–17).

Neurologic involvement. Approximately 20% of patients develop evidence of nervous system disease, which may include the cranial nerves II, V, VII, VIII, IX, and XIII. Involvement of the pituitary may produce diabetes insipidus, and a polyneuropathy, and mononeuritis multiplex has been described when the peripheral nervous system has been affected.

Diagnosis

Presence of nasomucosal ulcerations, pulmonary infiltrates and proteinuria highly suggestive
Biopsy is confirmatory.

Development in a middle-aged patient of protracted upper respiratory symptoms associated with nasomucosal ulcers, proptosis, pulmonary infiltrates with or without cavitation, and proteinuria is suggestive. A positive C-ANCA also strongly supports the diagnosis of Wegener's granulomatosis. Biopsy of tissue from the upper respiratory tract, lungs, or kidneys is confirmatory.

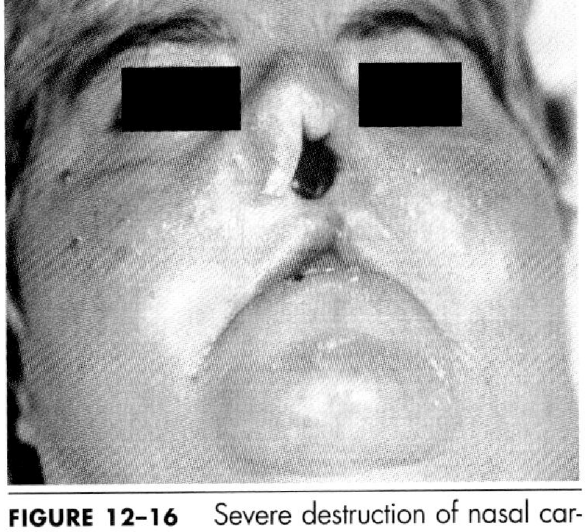

FIGURE 12-16 Severe destruction of nasal cartilage in a Wegener's granulomatous patient (Courtesy of Matthew Katz, M.D.).

Pathogenesis. The pathogenesis of Wegener's granulomatosis is unknown. Subepithelial deposits on electron microscopy examination of the glomeruli suggest possible immune complex disease.

Pathology. There are three pathologic hallmarks in Wegener's granulomatosis: (1) granulomatous inflammation, (2) necrosis

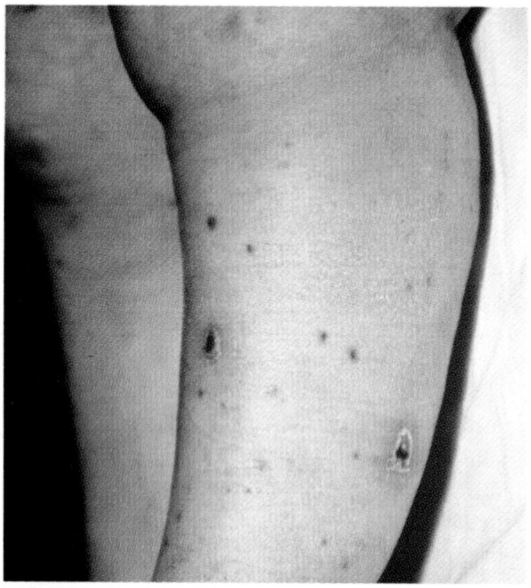

FIGURE 12–17 Vasculitis lesions occurring on lower legs of a patient with Wegener's granulomatosis (Courtesy of Matthew Katz, M.D.).

(often in large areas, designated as necrobiosis), and (3) vasculitis. Unfortunately, most biopsy specimens do not show all three changes. Indeed, only large (open) lung biopsies are likely to show the entire range of histopathology.

Necrotizing small vessel vasculitis, associated with fibrinoid necrosis and a mononuclear cell inflammatory infiltrate adjacent to a granuloma, is common. The blood vessel walls of medium-size vessels are thickened, with focal destruction of elastic lamina. Obliteration and narrowing of the lumen of blood vessels is common. Granuloma formation with scattered giant cells (foreign body and Langerhans'-type) is also common.

Granulomatous vasculitis may occur in all organs. The skin lesions may demonstrate nonspecific, acute, or chronic inflammation, or a necrotizing granulomatous vasculitis. Granulomatous involvement of the vasa nervorum is responsible for the mononeuritis multiplex. Granulomatous vasculitis can occur along the tracheal bronchial tree as well as in the heart, where pericardial, myocardial, and coronary arteries may be involved.

Proliferating glomerulonephritis with crescent formation is characteristic.

The glomerulonephritis ranges from diffuse, proliferative glomerulonephritis and interstitial nephritis to sclerosis of the glomeruli with crescent formation. Small renal arteries may be involved, with a necrotizing vasculitis that is associated with granulomatous formation. Immunofluorescent studies of kidney biopsies are usually negative.

Treatment

Wegener's granulomatosis, prior to the introduction of steroids and, later, cyclophosphamide, was universally fatal. Renal failure was the major cause of death.

Combination of steroids and cyclophosphamide associated with major improvement in survivability

Subsequent to the work at The National Institutes of Health by Fauci et al., treatment with a combination of oral cyclophosphamide in a dose of 2 mg per kg per day and corticosteroids has produced a 90% 5-year survivability of these patients. However, morbidity secondary to the disease as well as complications of the therapy (especially infection, hemorrhagic cystitis, and increased risk of malignancy) occurs in a significant number of these patients.

Co-trimoxazole may be effective in preventing relapses

In patients who do not have immediately life-threatening disease, the combination of methotrexate and prednisone is usually effective. Whether co-trimoxazole (trimethoprim/sulfamethoxazole) is effective in treating limited Wegener's granulamatosis is not clear. However, studies have demonstrated that for patients with Wegener's granulamatosis in remission, this treatment reduces the chance of subsequent flare-up. Whether the co-trimoxazole is exerting a specific effect on the pathogenesis of the Wegener's granulomatosis or whether other antibiotics capable of suppressing upper respiratory bacteria, especially *Staphylococcus aureus*, would also be effective in preventing relapses is unknown at the present time.

Annotated Bibliography

Fauci AS, Wolff SM. Wegener's granulomatosis: studies in eighteen patients and a review of the literature. Medicine (Baltimore) 1973;52:535–561.

This is a classic paper in this area.

Hoffman GS, Kerr GS, Leavitt RY, et al. Wegener granulomatosis: an analysis of 158 patients. Ann Intern Med 1992;116:488–498.

Thorough review of the National Institutes of Health experience.

Reinhold-Keller, et al. An interdisciplinary approach to the care of patients with Wegener's granulomatosis: long term outcome in 155 patients. Arthritis Rheum 2000; 43:1021–1032.

This study reports a median survival of > 21 years. It documents that cyclophosphamide is essential in the treatment of Wegener's granulomatosis. However, if not closely administered for as briefly as possible, serious complications, such as cystitis and myelodysphastic syndromes, can occur. The report indicates that a dose of 100 g or more of cyclophosphamide produces increased morbidity compared with lower cyclophosphamide doses.

Antineutrophil Cytoplasmic Antibodies

Antineutrophil cytoplasmic antibodies, initially detected in patients with segmental necrotizing glomerulonephritis and later in patients with Wegener's granulomatosis, has been a significant diagnostic advancement.

Two staining patterns of the cytoplasm are noted. The ethanol-fixed neutrophils demonstrate diffuse cytoplasmic staining (C-ANCA) with the sera of patients with Wegener's granulomatosis. The antigen to which the antibodies are directed is a neutrophil serine proteinase-3. The C-ANCA titers tend to correlate with Wegener's granulomatosis activity (ie, relapse and remission). However, the correlation is not so tight that treatment can be dictated by the titer. Measurement of C-reactive protein and factor VIII levels together with C-ANCA titers may be of more value in monitoring Wegener's granulomatous patients.

C-ANCA is a very important diagnostic test in Wegener's granulomatosis.
May fluxate in titer with relapse and remission

A second pattern of perinuclear staining is usually caused by antibodies to myeloperoxidase. This P-ANCA pattern is very nonspecific, as it can be found in some patients with Wegener's granulomatosis and also in patients with microscopic polyangiitis, Churg-Strauss syndrome, or Kawasaki syndrome. Atypical P-ANCA, usually caused by antibodies to lactoferrin or other antigens, can be seen in patients with SLE, rheumatoid arthritis, and inflammatory bowel disease.

Antiendothelial Cell Antibodies

Intriguing studies have demonstrated in patients with vasculitis the presence of antiendothelial cell antibodies. Whether these antibodies are of pathologic significance is unknown. However, from a conceptual point of view, complement-fixing antiendothelial cell antibodies could theoretically induce a type II immunologic reaction, characterized by complement activation and the migration of neutrophils into the site of the antigen–antibody reaction. The resulting inflammation could closely resemble an immune complex–mediated vasculitis. The best evidence suggesting a pathologic role for these antibodies is Kawasaki syndrome.

Antiendothelial antibodies are commonly detected in vasculitis patients.
Significance currently unknown

Kawasaki Syndrome

Kawasaki syndrome is an inflammatory disease process originally described in Japanese children. It is characterized by fever, conjunctivitis, mucous membrane erythema, and an erythematous, macular, papular dermatitis of the trunk. Diffuse erythema involving the palms and soles, edema, and desquamation are characteristic. Cervical lymphadenopathy is prominent. These features are reminiscent of scarlet fever and staphylococcal toxic shock syndrome.

Autoantibodies (IgM) are directed against endothelial cells. The antigenic determinants to which the autoantibodies are directed are induced by interleukin (IL)-1, tumor necrosing factor-α or interferon-γ. From a conceptual point of view, it is hypothesized that during a viral infection, or perhaps by superantigen activation induced by group A β-hemolytic streptococci and coagulase-positive *S. aureus* infections, T-cell derived cytokines induce endothelial cell neoantigen upregulation, and subsequently, antibodies are produced. These antibodies, on reaction with the antigen, induce coronary arteritis and aneurysm formation. Other arteries are also involved, including the iliac, hepatic, brachial, and mesenteric arteries. Characteristically, death may occur suddenly from coronary occlusion and thrombosis 4 to 5 weeks after onset of the disease.

Kawasaki syndrome is most likely the result of a viral infection or "superantigen" T cell activation by β-streptococci and staphylococcal aureus toxins.

Autoantibodies against endothelial cell neoantigens occur
Coronary arteritis aneurysms and myocardial infarction may occur

Although the condition was originally described in Japan, it is now recognized in the United States and Europe. There is a male predominance. African, Caribbean, and Oriental patients appear to be at increased risk. In the United

States, the incidence appears to be approximately 10 per 100,000, whereas in Japan the incidence is approximately 150 per 100,000 children.

Pericarditis, myocardial infarction, ventricular aneurysm as well as mitral and aortic valve incompetence may be seen in approximately one-third of patients. An aneurysm of the coronary arteries occurs in about one-quarter of patients. Mortality from cardiovascular complications is on the magnitude of 1 to 2%.

Laboratory studies indicate the presence of immune complexes and ANCA, which demonstrate diffuse cytoplasmic staining. Antiendothelial cell antibodies are diagnostic.

Aspirin, as well as high-dose intravenous gammaglobulin (IVGG), has been effective. In addition, dipyridamole has also been recommended. Corticosteroids are employed to treat patients failing to respond to aspirin and IVGG therapy.

Annotated Bibliography

Leung DY, Giorno RC, Kazemi LV, et al. Evidence for superantigen involvement in cardiovascular injury due to Kawasaki syndrome. J Immunol 1995;155:5018–5021.

Leung DY, Meissner HC, Fulton DR, et al. Toxic shock syndrome toxin-secreting *Staphylococcus aureus* in Kawasaki syndrome. Lancet 1993;342:1385–1388.

These are two excellent articles regarding the possible role of the superantigen hypothesis in the pathogenesis of Kawasaki syndrome.

Large Vessel Vasculitis

Temporal Arteritis

Temporal arteritis (giant cell arteritis) was first described by Jonathan Hutchinson in 1890. In 1932, Horton described the granulomatous pathologic features of the disease. The vasculitis preferentially involves the extracranial branches of the carotid artery, although other vessels including the aorta and the subclavian and the axillary arteries may be involved. Temporal arteritis is a disease of the elderly, with the average age of onset being 72 years. The annual incidence is less than 2 per 100,000 in the United States. However, in Northern European studies, an incidence of 28 per 100,000 in Sweden and 76 per 100,000 in Denmark has been reported. The disease process is more common in Caucasians. Table 12–11 provides the criteria for the diagnosis of temporal (giant cell) arteritis.

Clinical Features

The most common presenting symptoms are headache, polymyalgia rheumatica, jaw claudication, and visual disturbances. Fever, malaise, and weight loss are also common. Large artery involvement commonly produces Raynaud's phenomenon or upper extremity claudication.

Characterized by sudden onset of unilateral headaches, temporal area pain on palpation, and generally an elevated erythrocyte sedimentation rate in a patient over the age of 50 years

Headache (unilateral) is the most common feature, present in 90% of patients. Headache may be associated with tenderness of the scalp such that the patient will notice discomfort while combing or brushing hair. Polymyalgia rheumatica is pain and stiffness localized to the shoulders and pelvic region. The pain and stiffness are worse in the morning. Jaw claudication consists of pain over the masseter or muscle that occurs with prolonged chewing. The pain results from ischemia of the masseter and temporalis muscles and is a pathognomic feature. Visual symptoms include diplopia, ptosis, and visual loss. Visual loss is almost always permanent. Blindness results from arteritis of the posterior cilliary artery, which is the branch of the ophthalmic artery supplying the optic nerve head. Fortunately, blindness is usually not the initial manifestation of the disease but develops in untreated patients several months after disease onset.

Necrosis of the tongue or temporal area of the scalp a rare finding

Examination of the temporal arteries may be normal or demonstrate tenderness, swelling, and nodularity. Although rare, necrosis of the tongue or scalp as well as neurologic defects may be present.

TABLE 12–11 American College of Rheumatology Criteria for Diagnosis of Giant Cell Arteritis

Age at disease onset ≥ 50 years
New headache
Temporal arteritis tenderness or decreased pulsation
Elevation of erythrocyte sedimentation rate ≥ 50 mm/hr
Abnormal artery biopsies showing necrotizing arteritis with mononuclear infiltrate or granulomatous inflammation, usually with multinucleated giant cells.
Diagnosis of giant cell arteritis can be made if 3 of 5 criteria are present.

Data from:
Hunder GG, et al. The American College of Rheumatology 1990 criteria for the classification of giant cell arteritis. Arthritis Rheum 1990;33:1114–1121.

Temporal arteritis frequently associated with polymyalgia rheumatica

The relationship of temporal arteritis to polymyalgia rheumatica has gained a great deal of attention in recent years. Polymyalgia rheumatica may occur in the absence of temporal arteritis. Polymyalgia rheumatica is two to three times more common than temporal arteritis. Approximately 50% of patients with temporal arteritis also have polymyalgia rheumatica.

Laboratory Features

A high sedimentation rate, often > 100 mm per hr, is common. Normal sedimentation rates can be seen early in the course of the disease and in patients who have received corticosteroids. A normochromic, normocytic anemia occurs in the majority of patients. A slightly elevated alkaline phosphatase (derived from liver rather than bone) develops in 20 to 30% of patients.

Pathology

Sample area is problematic Vasculitic lesions may be patchy, tending to skip areas of the artery

Biopsy of the temporal arteries may demonstrate a granulomatous inflammation with destruction of the internal elastic lamina of the temporal artery. Skip lesions are characteristic, and sample error when biopsying is problematic. Recent evidence indicates that polymyalgia rheumatica patients with recent onset of headache, jaw claudication, abnormal temporal arteries on examination, and 70 years of age or older at onset have the best set of clinical predictors for a positive temporal artery biopsy. A mixed cellular inflammatory infiltrate composed of mononuclear neutrophils and eosinophils, with or without giant cells, may be detected.

Pathogenesis

Immune complex–mediated disease

The cause of temporal arteritis is unknown. Circulating immune complexes have been detected, and both humoral and cell-mediated immunities have been implicated in the pathogenesis. Direct immunofluorescence examination of temporal artery biopsies have shown immunoglobulin and C3 deposition. Other studies have indicated that circulating lymphocytes are cytotoxic for cultured endothelial cells. High levels of IL-6 have been found in untreated patients.

More recent studies have detected *Chlamydia* pneumonia in temporal artery specimens, suggesting a possible role in the pathogenesis.

A 57-year-old Caucasian female presented with ulceration on her right thumb. A biopsy of this ulcerated lesion revealed the presence of a necrotizing leukocytoclastic angiitis. A complete history and physical examination at that time, with the exception of an elevated erythrocyte sedimentation rate of 88, failed to reveal any evidence for systemic disease. The patient was successfully treated with oral prednisone over a 2- to 3-month period. However, with discontinuance of the oral steroids, the patient noted the onset of right-sided headaches as well as pain and tenderness in the scalp. She consulted a neurologist who suspected temporal arteritis, but a biopsy of the temporal artery failed to reveal any evidence of vasculitis.

Subsequently, the erythrocyte sedimentation rate was >100 mm per hr and because of the patient's age, the onset of unilateral headaches, temporal artery and scalp tenderness, and the history of previous vasculitis, she was treated over an 18-month period with tapering doses of prednisone beginning at 80 mg for suspected temporal arteritis. This therapy resulted in a resolution of all the signs and symptoms and a return of the erythrocyte sedimentation rate to normal levels. The patient is alive and well without symptoms 5 years after cessation of therapy.

Treatment

Temporal arteritis requires prednisone initiated at 40 to 60 mg per day. Patients who have experienced visual loss should be treated with even higher doses. This initial dose of prednisone is continued for 1 month and then tapered gradually. Recent studies indicate serial determination of IL-6 plasma levels are superior to determination of the erythrocyte sedimentation rate to monitor disease activity.

Annotated Bibliography

Gur H, Rapman E, Ehrenfeld M, Sidi Y. Clinical manifestations of temporal arteritis: a report from Israel. J Rheumatol 1996;23:1927–1931.

This study indicated that headache occurred in 87%, fever in 64%, visual abnormalities in 41%, polymyalgia rheumatica in 20%, and weight loss in 20%. An elevated erythrocyte sedimentation rate ≥ 50 mm per hour was present in all patients. The average value was 91 mm per hour.

This report indicates that 13% of patients had pulmonary disease, and 38% had abnormal liver function tests.

Hunder GG. Giant cell arteritis and polymyalgia rheumatica. Med Clin North Am 1997;81:195–219.

Weyand CM, et al. Treatment of giant cell arteritis: interleukin as a biological marker of disease activity. Arthritis Rheum 2000;43:1041–1048.

This article demonstrates plasma IL-6 is more sensitive than the erythrocyte sedimentation rate detecting disease activity in giant cell arteritis patients. Furthermore, the study indicates that systemic steroids may only partially suppress the vascular inflammation. Plasma IL-6 levels continue to reflect ongoing vasculitis. In 89% of clinical flares, IL-6 levels were above the normal range, making this the more sensitive marker to detect relapse, compared with erythrocyte sedimentation rate (p = 0.03).

Wagner AD, et al. Detection of *Chlamydia pneumoniae* in giant cell arteritis and correlation with the topographic arrangement of tissue infiltrating dendritic cells. Orthoped Rheum 2000;43:1543–1551.

Thought provoking article!

Takayasu's Arteritis

Rare form of large vessel vasculitis

This is a chronic granulomatous arteritis, affecting large, elastic arteries, such as the aorta and its major branches. This is a rare form of arteritis initially described in Japan. It also occurs in the United States and Europe. The incidence is one to two cases per million per year. Women below the age of 40 appear to be at increased risk.

Granulomatous disease process involving aorta and major branches

A transmural inflammation with patchy destruction of the medial elastic lamina, associated with a lymphocytic, plasma cell infiltrate and variable numbers of giant cells are seen. Healing occurs with fibrotic scarring of the intima and adventitia of the blood vessel. The diagnostic criteria for Takayasu's arteritis are listed in Table 12–12.

Clinical Features

Approximately one-third of patients present with nonspecific signs of inflammation, such as fever, myalgia, arthralgia, anemia, and weight loss and two-

Table 12–12 American College of Rheumatology Criteria for Diagnosis of Takayasu's Arteritis

Age at onset ≤ 40 years
Claudication of extremities
Decreased brachial artery pulse
Blood pressure differences > 10 mm Hg between arms
Bruit over subclavian arteries or aorta
Arteriogram abnormalities (narrowing or nonarteriosclerotic occlusion of aorta or large blood vessels)

Takayasu's disease diagnosed if 3 of 6 criteria present. The presence of 3 or more criteria 90.5% sensitivity; 97.8% specificity.

Arend P, et al. The American College of Rheumatology 1990 criteria for classification fo Takayasu's arteritis. Arthritis Rheum 1990;33:1129–1135.

thirds present with evidence of large artery involvement. Loss of a pulse, unequal blood pressures in the arms, hypertension (from renal artery stenosis), diastolic murmurs (from aortic regurgitation), and lower extremity claudication are the most common symptoms and signs. Stroke, myocardial infarction, visual loss, and glomerulonephritis can also occur. Takayasu's is one of the few forms of vasculitis that affect the pulmonary arteries and can lead to breathlessness and right heart failure.

On unusual occasions, erythema nodosum–like and pyoderma gangrenosum–like lesions have been reported.

The diagnosis of Takayasu's arteritis is usually confirmed by angiography showing areas of stenosis and dilatation involving the aorta and its major branches. These changes can also be demonstrated by magnetic resonance imaging (MRI).

The prognosis of Takayasu's arteritis is guarded, although a 5-year 90% survival on treatment has been reported. Myocardial infarction, heart failure, cerebral vascular accidents, and renal disease as well as rupture of an aneurysm are potentially lethal complications.

Pathogenesis

It is hypothesized that granulomatous arteritis is an autoimmune disease. Circulating immune complexes, as well as antiendothelial cell antibodies, have been described. Increased numbers of CD8 T cells have been detected, both in the affected blood vessel as well as in the circulation.

We have detected this form of vasculitis occurring in two anti–Ro (SS-A) antibody–positive connective tissue disease patients.

Suspected immune complex disease

Has been seen in anti-Ro (SS-A) antibody–positive connective tissue diseases

Despite these fragmentary reports, no clear evidence has emerged establishing the etiology of this disease.

Treatment

High-dose corticosteroids, with or without immunosuppressive agents (cyclophosphamide or methotrexate), appear to be efficacious.

Annotated Bibliography

Frances C, Boisnic S, Bletry O, et al. Cutaneous manifestations of Takayasu arteritis. A retrospective study of 80 cases. Dermatologica 1990; 181(4)266–272.

Ten of 80 cases of Takayasu's arteritis demonstrated cutaneous manifestations (12.5%). The most common manifestation occurring in 5 patients was erythema nodosum–like lesions on the lower legs. Two patients had ulcerated nodules on the lower legs, and 1 had pyoderma gangrenosum. In addition, 1 patient had urticarial lesions with livedo reticularis, and one had lupus-like malar rash. In biopsies, 4 patients demonstrated granulomatous vasculitis in the subcutaneous tissue.

Perniciaro CV, Winkelmann RK, Hunder GG. Cutaneous manifestations of Takayasu's arteritis. A clinicopathologic correlation. J Am Acad Dermatol 1987;17:998–1005.

This excellent article reviews the Mayo Clinic experience with this entity.

Kerr GS, Hallahan CW, Giordano J, et al. Takayasu arteritis. Ann Intern Med 1994; 120:919–929.

Degos's Disease

This is a rare, distinctive vasculopathy, characterized by deep, dermal blood vessel lymphocytic inflammation, proliferation, and thickening with the deposition of para-aminosalicylic acid (PAS)-positive material, and thrombosis. The adjacent connective tissue disease is replaced by fibrosis.

Individual lesions slowly develop. They may involve all areas of the body but generally spare the palms, soles, and face. Erythematous, dome-shaped papules, measuring 2 to 15 mm in size, initially appear. Many of the lesions rapidly develop central areas of necrosis. The epidermis, initially ulcerated, is replaced by a thin, atrophic epidermis with a porcelain-white center. A surrounding erythematous, edematous ring is characteristic.

The lesions tend to occur in crops and may continue for years. More commonly, however, these lesions are rapidly followed by the development of abdominal and other systemic manifestations. Cramping abdominal pain and vomiting are common manifestations. Intestinal perforation, with hemorrhage and peritonitis, frequently occurs with significant mortality.

In addition to abdominal blood vessels, there is evidence to indicate that the cerebral and renal blood vessels are also involved.

Pathogenesis

The exact pathogenesis of this condition is unknown. Immune complexes have not been demonstrated. Abnormalities of coagulation are thought to play a role, and indeed, antiphospholipid antibodies been demonstrated in several patients with Degos's syndrome. However, an additional study of 15 Degos's patients failed to document an association.

The best evidence indicates a lymphocytic-mediated vasculopathy with thrombosis, ischemia, and infarction.

Degos's syndrome: best evidence indicates a lymphocytic vasculopathy with thrombosis

Treatment

The treatment of Degos' s syndrome is difficult. Steroids are ineffective. Anticoagulation appears to be of some benefit but is not universally successful.

Annotated Bibliography

Winkelmann RK, Howard FM, Perry HO, et al. Malignant papulosis of skin cerebrum. Arch Dermatol 1963;87:54–62.

This is a report of two cases of Degos's syndrome involving the central nervous system. On autopsy, the brain showed multiple old and recent infarcts in the white matter. Old recanalized thrombus and a recent thrombus were detected in one of the larger arteries. Infarcts were also seen microscopically in the posterior columns of the spinal cord.

The other case demonstrated thrombosis of many small cortical arteries and veins.

Degos R. Malignant atrophic of papulosis. Br J Dermatol 1979;100:21–35.

This is a summary based on the literature as well as personal experience of Dr. Degos regarding the syndrome named in his honor. He describes the cutaneous lesions as not being painful. However, pruritus has been noted. He also notes that classic lesions have been found on the genital as well as buccal mucous membranes. He stresses that the intestinal involvement carries a very grave prognosis and is of the opinion that intestinal lesions will appear sooner or later in the majority, if not all, of the cases. Perforation of the bowel, however, at laparoscopy may not be detected. Avascular patches are usually found throughout the intestine and peritoneum. He further notes that postmortems have usually demonstrated infarcts and necrosis, as well as vascular thrombosis in many organs (eg, heart, kidneys, bladder, lungs, pleura, liver, pancreas). However, these are generally clinically silent.

Skin biopsies reveal endothelial proliferation with thrombus formation. In general, there are only a few lymphoid cells surrounding the necrotic tissue. Other authors have remarked on the presence of inflammatory elements. He believes that the absence or sparsity of signs of histologic inflammation remains a distinctive characteristic of malignant atrophic papulosis.

The prognosis in these patients is grim. He quotes a French article from 1977 that detected 38 deaths in 70 patients. In the 32 survivors, however, the onset of disease had not been longer than 2 years. From his personal experience, he rationalizes that the death rate may be even higher as the patients are followed up for a prolonged period of time.

Soter NA, Murphy GF, Mihm MC Jr. Lymphocytes and necrosis of the cutaneous microvasculature in malignant atrophic papulosis: a refined light microscope study. J Am Acad Dermatol 1982;7:620–630.

This is a careful study demonstrating lymphocyte vasculitis in the early lesions of Degos's syndrome. These authors, using 1-µm epon-embedded skin biopsies, have documented the presence of activated lymphocytes in and about diseased blood vessels. They feel that the lesions of malignant atrophic papulosis in the skin most likely represents a lymphocytic-mediated injury to the small vessels of the superficial plexus and deep plexus. They reason that thrombosis may be a secondary event following endothelial cell injury.

Englert HJ, Hawkes CH, Boey ML, et al. Degos' disease: association with anticardiolipin antibodies and the lupus anticoagulant. Br Med J 1984;289:576.

This article details the presence of anticardiolipin and lupus anticoagulant in a patient with classic malignant atrophic papulosis disease. Although this area of investigation is still in its infancy, it appears that vasculopathy associated with Degos's syndrome may be heterogeneous in etiology. Some of these patients may indeed have antiphospholipid syndrome, but others may have, as Soter et al. have suggested, a low-grade lymphocytic–mediated vasculopathy.

General References

Conn DL, Hunder GG. Necrotizing Vasculitis. In: Kelly WN, Harris ED, Ruddy S, Sledge C, eds. Textbook of Rheumatology, 2nd edition. Philadelphia: WB Saunders Co. 1983, pp 1137-1165.

Collin JP, Kallenberg CGM. The vasculitides of relationship of cutaneous vasculitis to systemic disease. In: Kater L, de la Faille HB, eds. Multi-Systemic Autoimmune Diseases. Amsterdam: Elsevier Science 1995, pp 267-298.

Kater L, Provost TT. Classification criteria, disease activity criteria and chronicity criteria. In: Kater L, de la Faille HB, eds. Chapter 3 in Multi-Systemic Autoimmune Diseases. Amsterdam: Elsevier Science 1995, pp 43-60.

Adu D, Lugmani RA, Bacon PA. Polyarteritis, Wegners granulomatosis and Churg–Strause Syndromes. In: Maddison PJ, Isenberg DU, Woo P, and Glass DN, eds. Oxford Textbook of Rheumatological Diseases. Oxford U.K.: Oxford Medical Publications 1993, pp 846-859.

CHAPTER 13

Rheumatoid Arthritis

John A. Flynn, M.D., Thomas T. Provost, M.D.

Probably most common autoimmune connective tissue disease

Rheumatoid arthritis is an inflammatory systemic disease with an annual incidence as high as 20 per 10,000. Its prevalence in the United States ranges between 0.5 and 1.5%. Generally, it is considered to be the most common autoimmune connective tissue disease occurring in a frequency equal to or greater than Sjögren's syndrome.

Decreased life expectancy

Rheumatoid arthritis is associated with a reduced life expectancy. In general, the increased mortality is related to arthritis disease severity. Infections, renal and respiratory disease also contribute to the increased mortality.

The diagnostic criteria for rheumatoid arthritis are presented in Table 13–1.

Clinical Features

The physical manifestations of rheumatoid arthritis are listed in Table 13–2.

Joint Manifestations

Arthritis

In general, the onset of arthritis is insidious, with pain and stiffness occurring in small joints. Symmetrical synovitis involving the small joints of the hands, spar-

TABLE 13–1 American College of Rheumatology Diagnostic Criteria for Rheumatoid Arthritis

(1)	Morning stiffness lasts for a period of 1 hour and has occurred for > 6 weeks.
(2)	Arthritis involves at least three areas characterized by soft-tissue swelling or induration lasting > 6 weeks. The areas of involvement are generally the proximal interphalangeal joints, metacarpal phalangeal joints, wrists, elbows, knees, ankles, and metatarsal phalangeal joints.
(3)	Arthritis of the hands is characterized by involvement of the wrists and metacarpal, phalangeal, or proximal interphalangeal joints lasting > 6 weeks.
(4)	Symmetrical arthritis lasts for > 6 weeks.
(5)	Rheumatoid nodules are demonstrated and confirmed by a physician.
(6)	Serum rheumatoid factor is determined by a method in which < 5% of control subjects are positive.
(7)	Radiographic changes characteristic for rheumatoid arthritis are detected in the wrists and hands.

Data from:
Arnett FC, Edworthy SM, Bloch DA, et al. The American Rheumatism Association 1987 revised criteria for the classification of rheumatoid arthritis. Arthritis Rheum 1988; 31:315–324.

TABLE 13–2 Cutaneous Features Associated with Rheumatoid Arthritis

Joint deformities
Rheumatoid nodules
Vasculitis lesions
Rarely pyoderma gangrenosum
Rarely Sweet's syndrome
Rarely rheumatoid bands

ing the distal interphalangeal joints, is characteristic. The main joints involved are the wrists and the metacarpal-phalangeal and proximal interphalangeal finger joints (Figure 13–1). The ankles, metatarsal phalangeal joints, elbows, knees, shoulders, and hips are also frequently involved.

Metacarpal-phalangeal and PIP joint involvement characteristic

Examination of the hands frequently demonstrates tender fusiform swelling of the proximal interphalangeal and metacarpal-phalangeal joints. With time, ulnar deviation of the fingers, caused by volar subluxation of the metacarpal-phalangeal joints, occurs. In addition, a swan-neck (or boutonnière) deformity of the fingers may occur, and the functionality of the hand is compromised. The patients cannot make a fist or pinch objects, and they lose their strength of grip. These characteristic alterations are the result of bone and cartilage destruction as well as the weakening and rupture of tendons.

Jaccoud's Arthritis

Jaccoud's arthritis

In addition to these characteristic interarticular destructive features of the hand, approximately 5% of patients with rheumatoid arthritis will demonstrate a peculiar extra-articular joint deformity in the absence of interarticular erosive disease. These patients have severe ulnar deviation, but unlike patients with classic arthritis, pressing of the hand against a flat surface will correct the ulnar deviation. This form of arthritis, termed "Jaccoud's arthritis," has also been described in patients with rheumatic fever and systemic lupus erythematosus. Jaccoud's patients, unlike those with classic rheumatoid arthritis, do not have an increased frequency of the human leukocyte antigen HLA-DR4 phenotype and frequently possess anti-Ro (SS-A) antibodies.

Rheumatoid Nodules

In addition to the articular deformities associated with rheumatoid arthritis, approximately 25 to 50% of patients develop rheumatoid nodules. These are

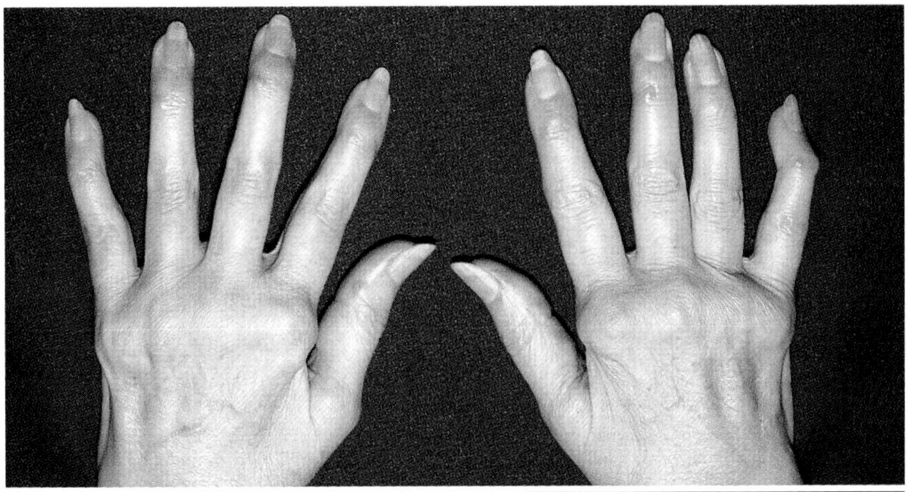

FIGURE 13–1 Rheumatoid arthritis demonstrating prominent swelling of metacarpal phalangeal joints.

Occurs in approximately 25% of patients
Generally associated with more severe disease

firm, round nodules measuring approximately 0.5 cm in diameter that occur most commonly on the extensor surfaces of the forearm as well as on other areas where direct pressure is applied (Figures 13–2 and 13–3). Individuals confined to bed commonly develop rheumatoid nodules on the occipital region of the skull and the sacral region. You can also find them on the antihelix of the ear where they must be distinguished from tophaceous gout and chondrodermatitis nodularis chronica helicis. On rare occasions, rheumatoid nodules of the conjunctiva can occur (scleromalacia).

In general, the presence of rheumatoid nodules indicates a more severe form of rheumatoid arthritis, although there are exceptions. Rarely do rheumatoid nodules precede the development of joint disease. Accelerated nodulosis has been reported with methotrexate therapy

Subcutaneous bands

Elongated subcutaneous bands (3 to 5 mm wide and as long as 10 cm) have been detected in rheumatoid arthritis patients with rheumatoid nodules.

Palisading granuloma

The rheumatoid nodules demonstrate fibrinoid necrosis in the dermis with fibroblast and histiocytes in a "palisading" fashion surrounding the areas of necrosis. Similar histopathologic features are found in the subcutaneous bands.

Vasculitis

A systemic vasculitis may also produce a sensory or motor neuropathy secondary to involvement of the vaso nervorum. In addition, rheumatoid nodules may ulcerate, as an indication of a low-grade vasculitis. This may also present as ulceration and hemorrhagic bullae with palpable and nonpalpable purpura of the lower legs. On rare occasions, the vasculitis may present as a painful, red eye secondary to scleritis. Pyoderma gangrenosum has also been reported.

Rheumatoid arthritis patients may demonstrate evidence of small-vessel vasculitis, characterized by cuticle nailfold infarctions as well as splinter hemorrhages beneath the nails (Bywaters' lesions) (Figures 13–4 and 13–5).

Generally associated with high-titer rheumatoid factor

In general, those rheumatoid arthritis patients with cutaneous vasculitis usually have high-titer rheumatoid factor. Many of these patients will have had, preceding the development of vasculitis, changes in their steroid dosage. It is hypothesized that these cutaneous vasculitic lesions are the result of immune complex deposition in the tissue.

On unusual occasions, Sweet's syndrome has been observed in rheumatoid arthritis. See Acute Febrile Neutrophilic Dermatosis in Chapter 29, "Paraneoplastic Dermatoses," for discussion on Sweet's syndrome.

Felty's Syndrome

Felty's syndrome is the development of splenomegaly and leukopenia in rheumatoid arthritis. Typically, patients have had long-standing seropositive, nodular

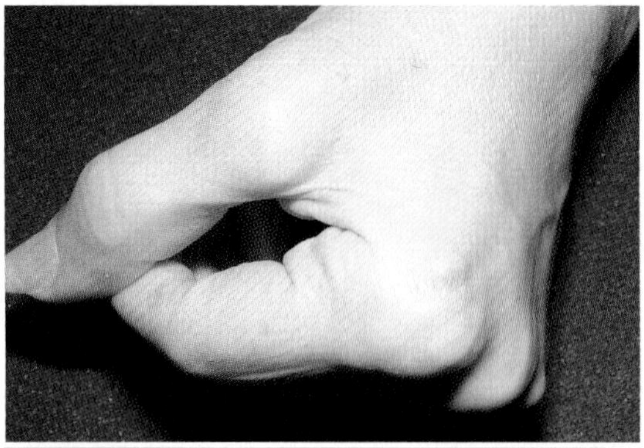

FIGURE 13–2 Lateral review of metacarpal phalangeal joints of a rheumatoid arthritis patient. Prominent metacarpal-phalangeal swelling and rheumatoid nodules.

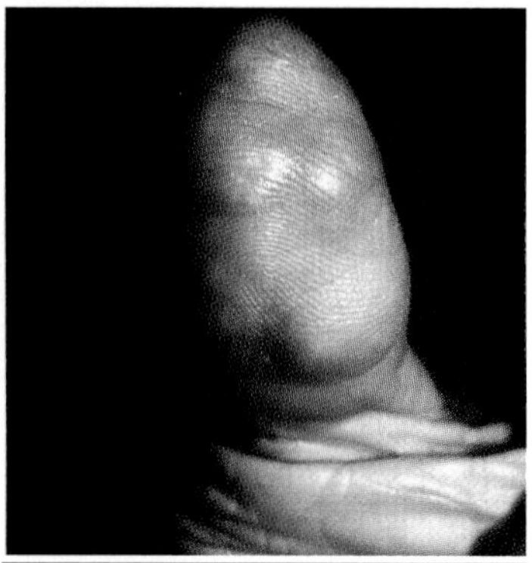

FIGURE 13–3 Rheumatoid nodules of the thumb.

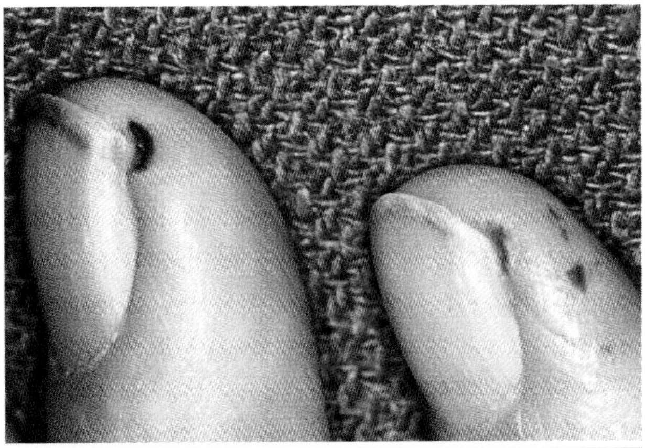

FIGURE 13-4 Vasculitic lesions on tips of fingers in rheumatoid arthritis patient.

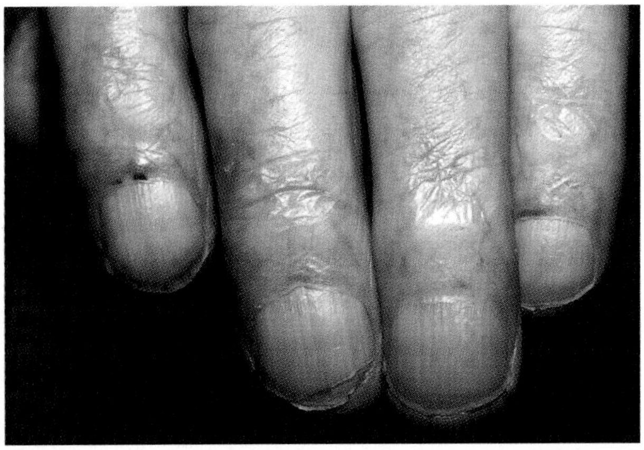

FIGURE 13-5 Cuticle nail-fold injection with small infarcts in a patient with rheumatoid arthritis.

disease when this syndrome develops. The cutaneous manifestations include lower extremity ulcers and hyperpigmentation. There can be a cutaneous vasculitis associated with these ulcerations. These patients are also more susceptible to bacterial infections, especially when there is a significant leukopenia. Thrombocytopenia is also seen. An increased incidence of non-Hodgkin's lymphoma has been reported in men with Felty's syndrome.

Management requires treatment of the underlying rheumatoid disease with standard therapy. Vasculitis may require therapy with immunosuppressive regimens. In cases of severe neutropenia, neutrophil-stimulating factors have been used.

Juvenile Rheumatoid Arthritis

In children with rheumatoid arthritis, a transient erythematous, urticaria-like dermatitis, also known as Still's disease, occurs predominantly on the trunk. These lesions are reminiscent to erythema marginatum.

Adult Still's disease is a febrile illness in which arthritis and rash can develop. The typical rash is salmon-pink in color with macular or maculopapular features. This rash will frequently come and go and generally occurs in the presence of a fever spike. More typically, it is seen in the trunk and proximal extremities.

Treatment

General principles in treating rheumatoid arthritis are to relieve pain and reduce inflammation. It is hoped by doing this functional capacity can be preserved. Nonsteroidal anti-inflammatory agents are typically used initially to suppress the inflammation. This may be done in conjunction with low-dose corticosteroids for a limited period. Second-line agents, including disease-modifying antirheumatic drugs (eg, methotrexate, sulfasalazine, Entanercept) are generally being used more frequently and earlier in the course of the disease than in the past. Treatment requires an individualized approach with regular monitoring to determine if inflammation has been suppressed and to avoid toxicity of the medications chosen.

Annotated Bibliography

Jorizzo JL, Daniels JC. Dermatologic conditions reported in patients with rheumatoid arthritis. J Am Acad Dermatol 1983;8:439–459.

This gives an excellent review of cutaneous manifestations associated with rheumatoid arthritis.

Stolman LP, Rosenthal D, Yaworsky R, et al. Pyoderma Gangrenosum and rheumatoid arthritis. Arch Dermatol 1975;111:1020–1203.

Dykman D, Galens GJ, Good AE. Linear subcutaneous bands in rheumatoid arthritis. Ann Intern Med 1965;63:134–140.

These two articles describe unusual cutaneous features in rheumatoid arthritis.

Bywaters EGL. Peripheral vascular occlusion in rheumatoid arthritis and its relationship to other vascular lesions. Ann Rheum Dis 1957;16:84–103

Kemper JW, Baggenstoss AH, Slocumb CH. The relationship of therapy with cortisone and the incidence of vascular lesions in rheumatoid arthritis. Ann Intern Med 1957; 46:831–851.

These two articles describe vasculitis lesions in rheumatoid arthritis. Both are highly quoted.

Harary AM. Sweet's syndrome with rheumatoid arthritis. Arch Intern Med 1983;143: 1993–1995.

Long D, Thiboutot DM, Majeski JT, et al. Interstitial granulomatous dermatitis with arthritis. J Am Acad Dermatol 1996;34:957–961.

This is an interesting study and review of the literature of a linear granuloma, annularlike, histologic lesion clinically presenting as asymptomatic truncal bands in three patients with arthritis. The etiology of the condition is unknown, but the patients demonstrated a positive rheumatoid factor, a positive antinuclear antibody determination, and an elevated erythrocyte sedimentation rate. Is this a forme fruste of linear cutaneous bands described in rheumatoid arthritis?

Arnett FC, Edworthy SM, Bloch DA, et al. The American Rheumatism Association 1987 revised criteria for the classification of rheumatoid arthritis. Arthritis Rheum 1988; 31:315–324.

Kerstens PJ, Boerbooms AM, Jeurissen ME, et al. Accelerated nodulosis during long term methotrexate therapy for rheumatoid arthritis: an analysis of ten cases. J Rheumatol 1992;19:867–871.

Gridley G, Klippel JH, Hoover RN, et al. Incidence of cancer among men with Felty's syndrome. Ann Intern Med 1994;120:35–39.

CHAPTER 14

Rheumatic Fever

John A. Flynn, M.D., Thomas T. Provost, M.D.

Rheumatic fever is an inflammatory complication occurring 2 to 3 weeks after a pharyngeal infection with group A β-hemolytic streptococcus. It is characterized by migratory arthritis predominantly involving large joints; myocarditis, pericarditis, and valvulitis; and by central nervous system involvement (Sydenham's chorea). In general, rheumatic fever rapidly resolves, but the valvulitis may produce severe functional impairment.

Complication of streptococcal pharyngitis

Valvular heart disease is problematic

With the exception of underdeveloped countries, this is an unusual disease with an annual incidence of less than 2 per 100,000. Over 10 million new cases per year occur in developing countries. In times prior to antibiotics, the incidence was much higher. However, for unknown reasons, the incidence decreased even before the introduction of antibiotics.

Uncommon disease in developed countries

Streptococcal infections of specific M sera types (types 5, 14, 18, 24) are associated with rheumatic fever. Rheumatic fever is associated only with streptococcal pharyngitis and almost never occurs after outbreaks of impetigo. The reason for this striking clinical finding is unknown.

There is some evidence to suggest that genetic susceptibility to rheumatic fever exists. However, the exact etiology of rheumatic fever is unknown. The best evidence suggests that the streptococcal infection induces the production of cross-reactive antibodies capable of reacting with various structures in the heart. Also, autoantibodies have been found in acute rheumatic disease patients that react against cells of the caudate nucleus (possibly of pathophysiologic significance in Sydenham's chorea). There is also evidence that the heart in patients with acute rheumatic fever contains reactive CD4-positive lymphocytes.

Best evidence is autoantibody formation reacting with cardiac and central nervous system autoantigens.

Clinical Features

Arthritis

The classic presentation of articular disease in rheumatic fever is a migratory polyarthritis that begins several weeks after the antecedent streptococcal infection. Large joints are more commonly involved, in particular, the ankles and knees. When these joints become inflamed, the pain associated with the arthritis is frequently out of proportion to the degree of inflammation present on physical examination. This pain and swelling will typically resolve over several days, at which point another joint may become involved and follow the same pattern.

Carditis

The carditis of acute rheumatic fever may affect the myocardium, valvular structures, and the pericardium. Clinically, this may be demonstrated by a new or changing heart murmur, pericardial friction rub or effusion, an enlarged heart, or congestive heart failure. The most common chronic result is scarring of the heart valves with subsequent valvular stenosis.

Chorea (Syndenham's chorea, St. Vitus dance)

This neurologic disorder is most commonly detected in children and is characterized by an insidious onset of purposeless involuntary movements which may be predominantly unilateral, disappearing during sleep.

In addition, muscle weakness, including dysphagia and dysarthria, occurs. Characteristically, examination of the patient's handgrip demonstrates continuous increases and decreases in the handgrip strength and may be accompanied by involuntary associated movements of the face, trunk, and extremeties.

Facial grimaces and neurologic involvement characterized by inappropriate behavior, including emotional outbursts and rarely psychosis are detected.

Chorea rarely occurs in the absence of other post-strepococcal features. More commonly chorea occurs weeks following the onset of arthritis and clinical examination of the heart generally detects murmurs.

Rarely chorea results in death. Much more commonly the chorea resolves completely over several months.

Treatment is symptomatic. Phenobarbitol and tranquilizers such as chloropromazine and diazepam are beneficial.

Cutaneous Lesions

Small subcutaneous, asymptomatic nodules most commonly found on elbows

In addition to arthritis, carditis, and chorea, subcutaneous nodules, as well as a transient, evanescent, nonpruritic skin rash termed "erythema marginatum" occur. The subcutaneous nodules of rheumatic fever are round, firm lesions measuring from a few millimeters to 1 to 2 cm. They are asymptomatic, few in number, and tend to occur over bony prominences (ie, elbows). These nodules usually occur during the first weeks of illness and generally disappear within 1 month.

Transient urticaria-like eruption on trunk

The dermatitis of erythema marginatum is characterized by a faint, red, sharply demarcated urticaria-like lesion most commonly detected on the trunk. These annular or ring-like lesions usually disappear within hours and, like the subcutaneous nodules of rheumatic fever, occur during the first weeks of disease. These lesions may persist, however, after resolution of rheumatic fever. These lesions and the nodules are generally associated with rheumatic carditis.

The Jones revised criteria for the diagnosis of rheumatic fever is presented in Table 14–1.

Management

In the acute phase, management consists of appropriate treatment for group A β-hemolytic streptococcal infection and symptomatic treatment of the acute inflammatory manifestations of the condition and its sequelae. If streptococcal pharyngitis is present at the time of diagnosis, antibiotics are required. Oral therapy with penicillin for a 10 to 14 day duration should be adequate. If compliance is an issue, then intramuscular therapy can be given. Erythromycin is appropriate for patients with penicillin allergy. Additionally, the inflammation needs to be suppressed with anti-inflammatory medications. Traditionally, salicylates have been the medication used. However, other nonsteroidal anti-inflammatory agents may be just as efficacious. Corticosteroids are generally reserved for the treatment of carditis, although there is no evidence in controlled studies to suggest their benefit. Rarely is surgical intervention required in the acute setting. The patient's cardiac status must be carefully monitored. In general, the inflammatory phase of this condition responds to therapy and generally the anti-inflammatory agents can be tapered and discontinued within 3 months.

It is essential to prevent recurrent infection from group A β-hemolytic streptococcus by using continuous prophylactic antibiotics. This can be given with monthly intramuscular injections of benzothene penicillin or the daily adminis-

TABLE 14–1 Jones Revised Criteria for Diagnosis of Rheumatic Fever

Major Manifestations

- Carditis
- Polyarthritis
- Chorea
- Erythema marginatum
- Subcutaneous nodules

Minor Manifestations

- Fever
- Arthralgia
- Previous history of rheumatic fever or rheumatic heart disease

Additional Data

Supporting evidence for a preceding streptococcal infection:

- Increased antistreptolysin O and other streptococcal antibodies
- Positive throat culture for group A β-hemolytic streptococci
- Recent history of scarlet fever

Data from:
Stollerman GH, Markowitz M, Tartanta A, et al. Jones criteria (revised) for guidance in the diagnosis of rheumatic fever. Circ 1965;32:664–668.

tration of oral penicillin. The appropriate length of prophylaxis is unknown. All patients who have had rheumatic fever do require continued medical follow-up with special attention being paid to the possibility of the development of valvular disease. This may require surgical intervention with valve replacement at some point.

Annotated Bibliography

Gibofsky A, Wetzler LM, Zabriske JB. Rheumatic fever. In: Maddison PJ, Isenberg DA, Woo P, Glass DN, eds. Oxford Textbook of Rheumatology. Oxford United Kingdom: Oxford University Press, 1993, pp 613–620.

This is an excellent, well-written authoritative review from one of the leading laboratories.

Veasy LG, Wiedmeier SE, Orsmond GS, et al. Resurgence of acute rheumatic fever in the intermountain area of the United States. N Engl J Med, 1987; 316: 421–427.

Article demonstrating that rheumatic fever is still a problem in developed countries.

Stollerman GH, Markowitz M, Tartana A, et al. Jones criteria (revised) for guidance in the diagnosis of rheumatic fever. Circ 1965; 32: 664–668.

CHAPTER 15

Autoimmune Bullous Diseases

Hossein C. Nousari, M.D., Grant J. Anhalt, M.D.

Autoimmune Blistering Mucocutaneous Diseases

Intraepidermal bullae caused by destruction of normal epidermal cell-cell adhesion

Subepidermal bullae caused by disruption of normal epidermal-dermal adhesion

The autoimmune bullous mucocutaneous diseases are generally classified in two broad categories: intraepithelial and subepithelial diseases. Numerous adhesion molecules, synthesized by keratinocytes and fibroblasts, are critical in anchoring the keratin cytoskeleton of one cell to another (keratinocyte-keratinocyte adhesion) and, additionally, to the underlying dermis (keratinocyte-basement membrane adhesion), enabling the epithelium to resist mechanical trauma. Many of these adhesion molecules become targets of autoantibodies in acquired blistering skin diseases. A list of the molecules recognized by autoantibodies in these diseases is shown in Table 15–1. New concepts of immunologic and molecular mechanisms of blister formation of these autoimmune diseases provide a rational diagnostic and therapeutic approach to affected patients.

Keratinocyte-keratinocyte Interactions

Desmosomal proteins targets in pemphigus autoimmune diseases

Envoplakin and periplakin are autoantigens targeted in paraneoplastic pemphigus

Two categories of cellular junctions that participate in the adhesion between individual keratinocytes are recognized: adherens junctions and desmosomes (Figure 15–1). Both junctions consist of transmembrane proteins that bind opposing junctional proteins, and interact intracellularly with cytoplasmic protein plaques into which cytoskeletal filaments insert. Although adherens junctions have not been shown to be involved in any of the blistering diseases, desmosomal proteins are known to be targeted by autoantibodies in all forms of blistering intraepidermal disease. Desmosomes are disk-like structures at which the plasma membranes of two adjacent cells are attached, separated only by a glycoprotein-filled space known as the desmoglea. These junctions have a dense cytoplasmic attachment plaque into which keratin intermediate filaments of the cytoskeleton insert. The major desmosomal plaque proteins belong to the plakin family of proteins. Desmoplakin-I, the most abundant plakin protein of the plaque, is present in all epithelial desmosomes as well as other structures such as the intercalated disks of myocardium. Desmoplakin-II is a product of alternate splicing of the desmoplakin-I gene and has a more limited tissue expression. Plakoglobin is another well characterized plaque protein. Two new desmosomal plakin proteins have been identified: envoplakin and periplakin. Envoplakin

TABLE 15–1 Known Antigens Recognized by Autoantibodies in Autoimmune Skin Diseases

Disease	Autoantigen
Pemphigus vulgaris (mucosal)	Desmoglein-III
Pemphigus vulgaris (mucocutaneous)	Desmoglein-III and desmoglein-I
Pemphigus foliaceous (idiopathic, endemic, and drug induced)	Desmoglein-I
Paraneoplastic pemphigus	Desmoplakin-I, desmoplakin-II, bullous pemphigoid antigen I, envoplakin, periplakin, plectin, desmoglein-III, desmoglein-I, 170-kD antigen-unknown
IgA pemphigus	Desmocollin-I, desmocollin-II, desmoglein-III, desmoglein-I
Bullous pemphigoid	Bullous pemphigoid antigen I, bullous pemphigoid antigen II
Gestational pemphigoid	Bullous pemphigoid antigen II
Cicatricial pemphigoid	Bullous pemphigoid antigen I, bullous pemphigoid antigen II, laminin V, laminin VI, type VII collagen, 45 kD keratin, $\alpha\beta4$ integrin
IgA pemphigoid (linear IgA bullous disease)	Bullous pemphigoid antigen II (collagenous ectodomain)
Epidermolysis bullosa acquisita	Type VII collagen

plays an important role in the development of the cornified cell envelope. Both envoplakin and periplakin are autoantigens in paraneoplastic pemphigus.

Extending from the desmosomal plaque, through the plasma membrane and into the desmoglea, are transmembrane glycoproteins known as desmogleins and desmocollins. These glycoproteins are members of the cadherin supergene family (Ca++-dependent cell adhesion molecules) and mediate adhesion by homophilic interaction with opposing desmosomal cadherins. Among the desmogleins, desmogleins I and III share approximately 60% primary structural homology. The desmogleins have complex interactions with the various plaque proteins, including covalent bonding with plakoglobin.

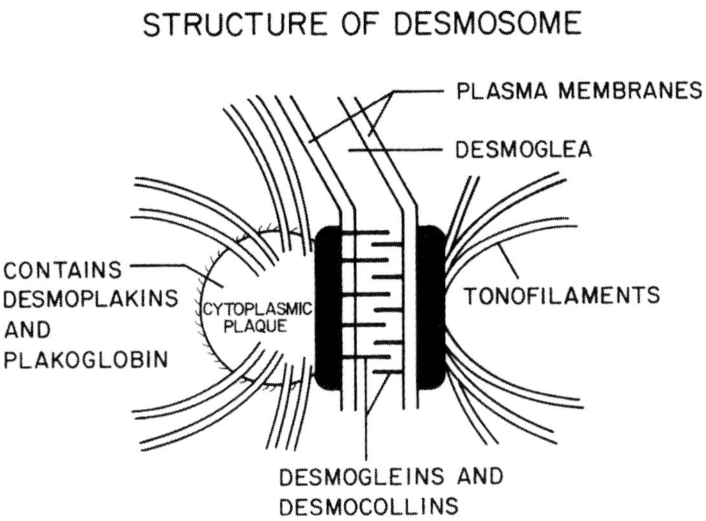

FIGURE 15–1 Dramatic sketch of organelles responsible for keratinocyte-keratinocyte adhesion.

Autoimmune Intraepithelial Blistering Diseases: Pemphigus Spectrum

Acantholysis

The autoimmune intraepithelial blistering diseases are collectively known as pemphigus, of which there are three subsets: pemphigus vulgaris (PV), pemphigus foliaceous (PF), and paraneoplastic pemphigus (PNP). All of these subsets are characterized by a loss of normal epidermal cell-cell adhesion (acantholysis) and by the presence of pathogenic IgG (immunoglobulin) autoantibodies directed against desmogleins, but each possesses distinct clinical, histologic, and immunologic features. Another form of pemphigus, called IgA pemphigus, has been recently reported. The inclusion of this form of pemphigus in the category of pemphigus is controversial.

Pemphigus Vulgaris (Figures 15–2 to 15–10)

Oral erosions common presentation of disease

PV is the most common form of pemphigus in North America and Europe, affecting both sexes equally and occurring most often during the fourth and fifth decades of life. It is a chronic disorder characterized by blister formation on the skin and mucous membranes. Virtually all patients with PV first present with painful oral ulcerations or develop oral lesions early in the course of the disease. These oral ulcers have ill-defined borders, and they favor the posterior buccal mucosae and gingivae. Any mucous membrane covered by stratified squamous epithelium can be affected. In many patients, lesions occur only on mucous membranes throughout the course of the disease. When skin lesions do appear, they occur as fragile vesiculobullous lesions that favor the head and neck. On unusual occasions isolated scalp pyoderma in an elderly patient may be the first sign. Extension to the trunk and flexural area next develops, and generalized involvement of the skin can occur in severe cases. Periumbilical involvement is common.

Pemphigus vegetans refers to PV lesions that are characterized by exophytic lesions. These lesions favor the mucosal surfaces and intertriginous areas. The pathogenesis of pemphigus vegetans is thought to be partially treated lesions and/or lesions that are subject to irritation by trauma, humidity or infection.

Pemphigus vegetans and pemphigus herpetiformis are clinical variants.

Pemphigus herpetiformis is just a clinical phenotype of either PV or pemphigus foliaceous that is characterized by herpes-like grouped vesicles.

The natural history of PV is one of relentless progression, with death, usually from sepsis, within 5 years of onset. Histologic examination of mucocutaneous lesions shows the distinctive intraepithelial blistering that defines pemphigus. There is loss of cell-cell attachment with rounding of individual epithelial cells

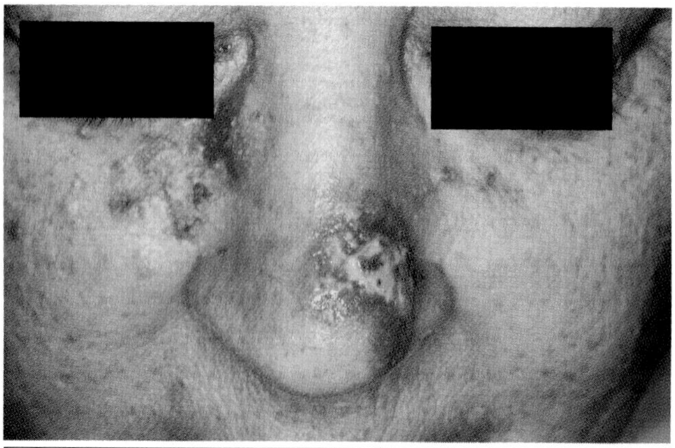

FIGURE 15–2 Pemphigus vulgaris showing typical ruptured bullae in the mid face.

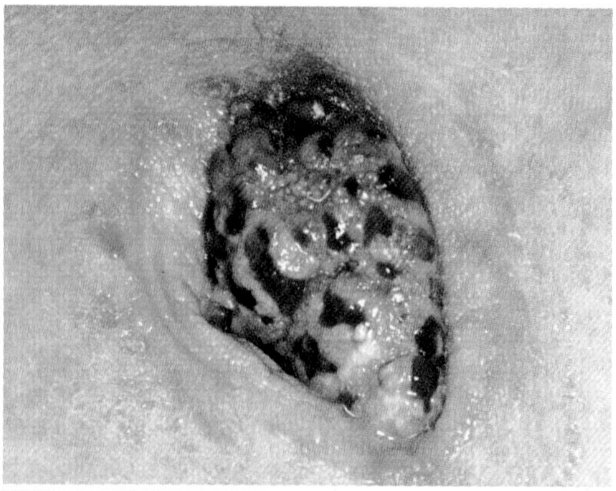

FIGURE 15–3 Pemphigus vulgaris/vegetans involving the umbilicus.

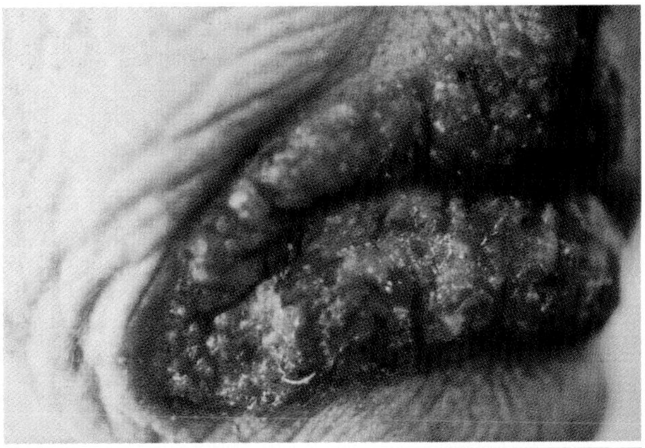

FIGURE 15-4 Pemphigus vegetans involving the lips of a partially treated patient.

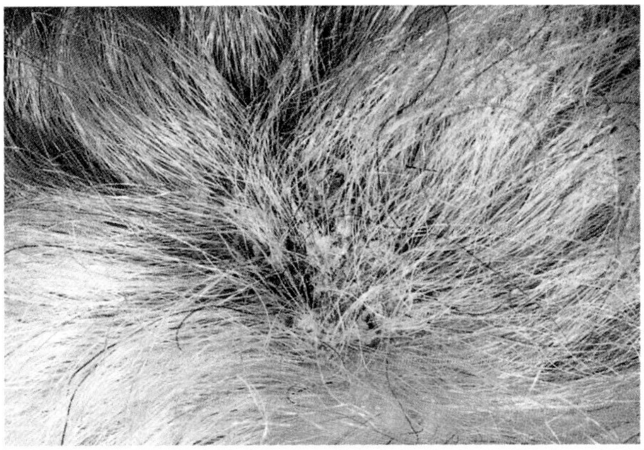

FIGURE 15-5 Pemphigus vulgaris and scalp pyoderma as a manifestation of disease in an elderly male.

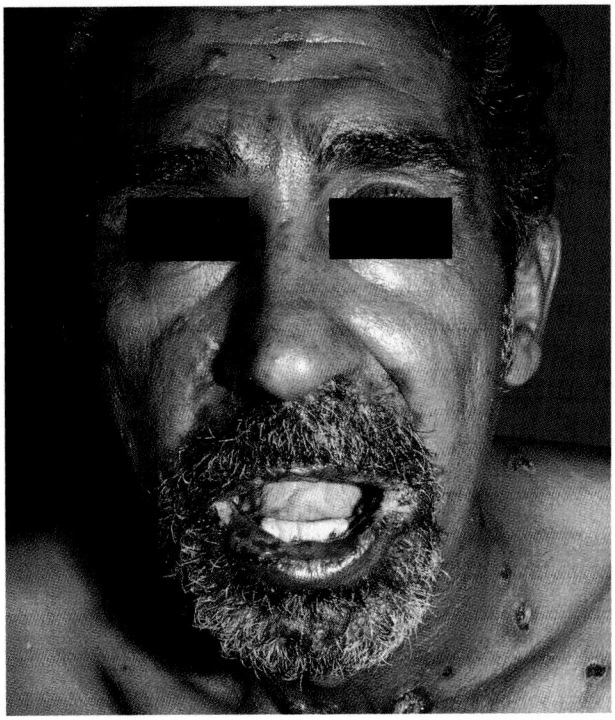

FIGURE 15-6 Pemphigus vulgaris lesions involving the lips.

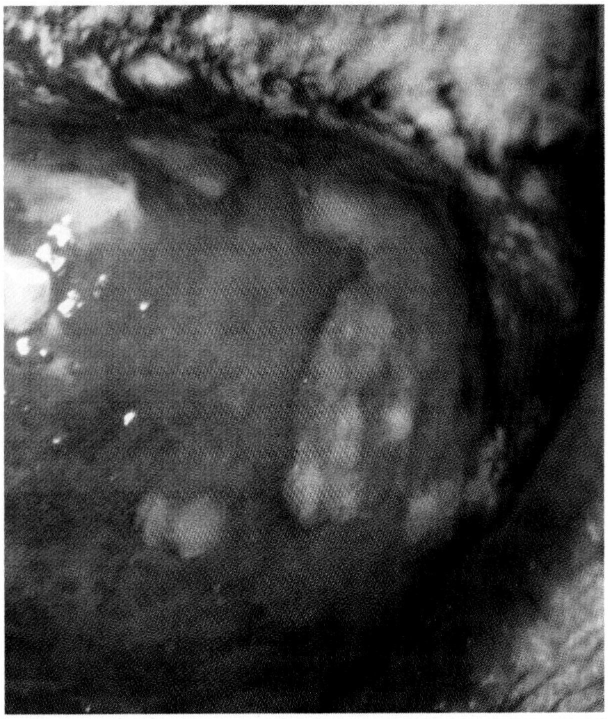

FIGURE 15-7 Pemphigus vulgaris showing severe erosions of the tongue. Condition also complicated by oral candidiasis, a frequent complication of oral pemphigus, especially if the patient is treated with steroids and/or immunosuppressive agents.

(acantholysis). There is no disruption of attachment of basal cells to the underlying basement membrane. The result is a fragile intraepithelial blister. Inflammatory cellular infiltration is minimal or absent. Direct immunofluorescence of affected skin or mucosa shows consistent IgG and variable C3 deposition on the epithelial cell surfaces without deposition along the basement membrane zone. Indirect immunofluorescence of serum demonstrates circulating IgG autoantibodies that specifically bind to stratified squamous epithelium in virtually all patients with active disease. These IgG autoantibodies in PV patients are directed against desmoglein-III, the 130 kD PV antigen.

However, recent studies have shown that there are autoantibodies in PV patients' sera that also recognize desmoglein-I, the pemphigus foliaceous antigen.

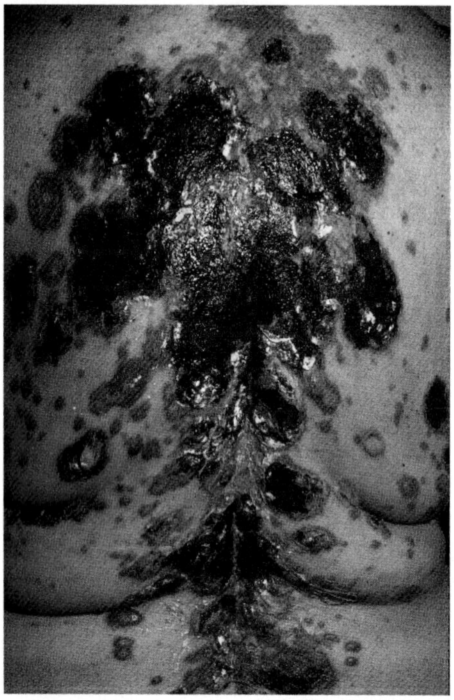

FIGURE 15–8 Pemphigus vulgaris demonstrating widespread erosive lesions on the back.

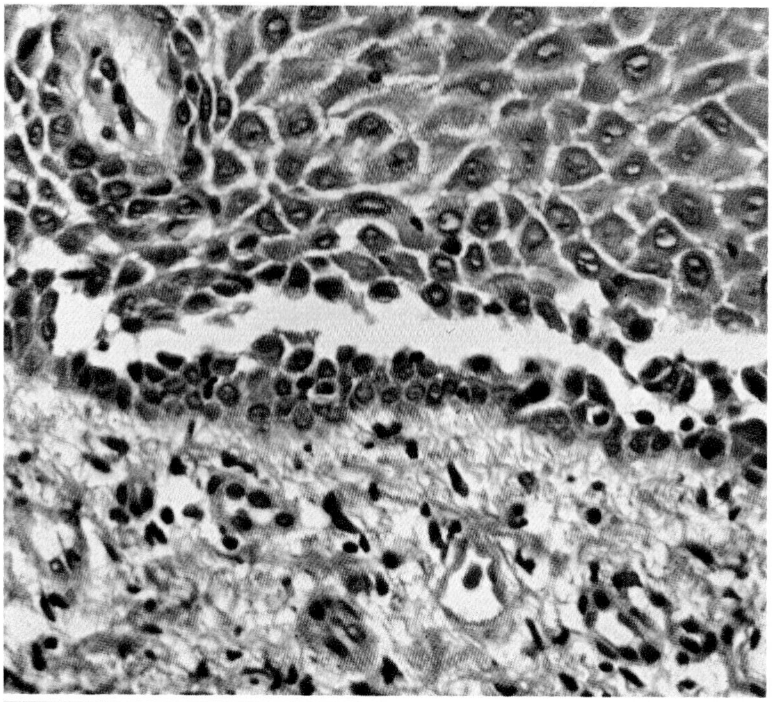

FIGURE 15–9 Pemphigus vulgaris demonstrating classic suprabasilar cell cleft formation. Acantholytic cells in the cleft. Basal cells beginning to take on the appearance of a row of tombstones.

Anti–desmoglein-III antibodies seen in mucous membrane pemphigus patients
Anti–desmoglein-I antibodies detected in pemphigus patients with mucous membrane and cutaneous blisters

All forms of pemphigus can be passively transferred to mice neonatal pups
Complement is not essential

PV patients with oral disease have almost exclusively anti–desmoglein-III antibodies; however, these patients develop anti–desmoglein-I antibodies as they evolve and develop skin disease. The pathogenic epitopes are located in the ectodomain of desmogleins.

The development of a very sensitive and specific enzyme-linked immunosorbent assay (ELISA) using recombinant desmoglein baculoproteins has allowed the identification of antidesmoglein antibodies in pemphigus patients' sera in whom traditional techniques were incapable of detecting these autoantibodies. In all forms of pemphigus, passive transfer of human autoantibodies into neonatal mice pups reproduce the disease. Complement activation can amplify the tissue injury produced by autoantibodies; however, it is not an essential component for acantholysis.

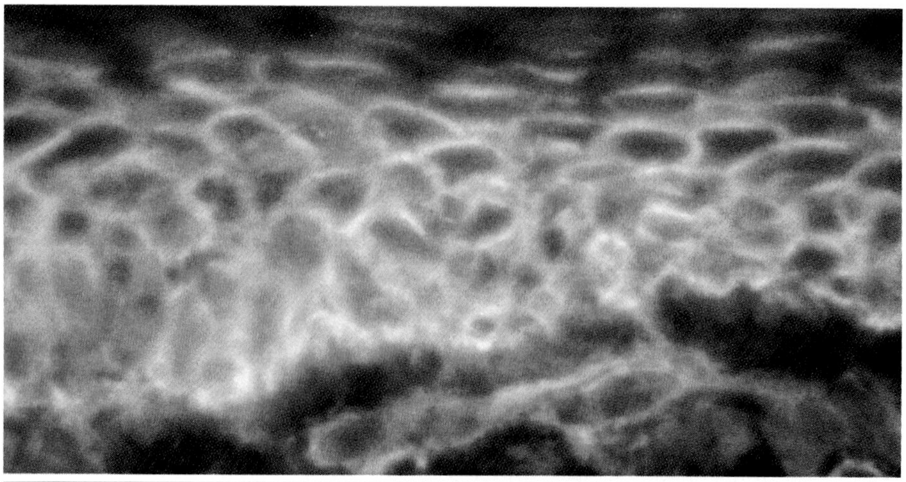

FIGURE 15–10 Pemphigus vulgaris demonstrating, by direct immunofluorescence examination of perilesional area, the presence of IgG in the intercellular spaces of the epidermis.

The exact pathophysiologic mechanism by which IgG autoantibodies induce acantholysis in PV is not completely clear. It is conceivable that the autoantibodies induce allosteric changes in desmoglein-III upon binding, impairing its ability to participate in homophilic binding with other cells and resulting in acantholysis. Although studies have shown plasminogen is not involved, the activation of other proteolytic enzymes necessary for transmigration of epidermal cells to the stratum corneum could be involved in the pathogenesis.

The critical role of desmoglein-III in adhesion, at least within oral epithelium, was demonstrated by the development of desmoglein-III knock-out mice. Genetically engineered mice with a targeted disruption of the desmoglein-III gene (DSG 3 -/-) were apparently normal at birth, but soon after they became grossly runted. Oropharyngeal biopsies of these mice have shown typical histologic and ultrastructural findings of PV.

*Genetic alterations in beta-1 chain of HLA class II may confer susceptibility HLA-DRB1*0402*

*PV also linked to DQB1*0503 valine to aspartic acid substitution at DQβ57*

Little is known about the mechanisms that induce autoantibody formation, but an immunogenetic predisposition has been reported. Specific alterations in the hypervariable region of the beta-1 chain of HLA class II genes may confer susceptibility to PV. This susceptibility has been linked to a rare subtype of HLA-DR4 (DRB1*0402, one of the 22 known DR4 subtypes). This rare subtype differs from a rheumatoid arthritis-associated DR4 subtype, DRB1*0404 at only three residues, DRβ67, -70, and -71. Among Ashkenazi Jews, more than 90% of PV patients carry the DRB1*0402 haplotype, which is rare in the general population. In other ethnic groups including non-Ashkenazi Jews, Caucasians, and Japanese, susceptibility for PV is linked to DQ1 allele (DQB1*0503). This allele differs from a common DQB1 allele (DQB1*0501) only by a valine to aspartic acid substitution at DQβ57. DQβ57 is important in the diabetes-linked DQ genes. In contrast to PV-linked DQ genes where Asp-57 confers susceptibility, in diabetes suceptibility is linked to alleles that do not carry a negative charge at DQβ57. Although the genetic predisposition genes are known, the rarity of the disease, even in susceptible populations, as well as the low frequency of familial cases, suggests that a "second hit" during an individual's life may be necessary to induce autoantibody production, but the nature of this event is unknown. Based on the DRB1*0402 binding motif, some candidate peptides from desmoglein-III were synthesized and were capable of stimulating specific T-cell clones. These desmoglein-III–specific autoreactive T cells were capable of secreting high levels of interleukin (IL)-4 and -10, thus exhibiting a T_h2 cytokine profile, which is crucial for autoantibody synthesis. A negatively charged residue of the P4 pocket in the DRB1*0402 binding site (DRβ70 and -71) appears to be a critical determinant of major histocompatibility (MHC)–linked susceptibility to PV. Similar studies have shown that desmoglein-III specific T-cell clones could be developed using three immunoreactive segments of the ectodomain of desmoglein-III. These autoreactive T cells were shown to express a CD4-positive memory T-cell phenotype and to be restricted to HLA-DR and not -DQ and -DP.

Viral infections, especially those related to herpesviruses, have been implicated in triggering certain autoimmune diseases. However, recent studies have found no role for human herpesvirus 8 in the pathogenesis of any form of pemphigus. PV is one of the prototypes of humoral-mediated, organ-specific autoimmune disease, thus being a dominant T_h2 profile-mediated autoimmune disease. Keratinocytes can act as antigen-presenting cells since they express MHC class II molecules upon cytokine stimulation. Thus, keratinocytes could present desmoglein-III peptides to T cells, and keratinocytes are known to influence T-cell responses toward a T_h2 cytokine profile (IL-4 and IL-10) due to failure to synthesize significant levels of IL-12. Langerhans' cells may also be involved in the presentation of desmoglein-III peptides to T cells.

Current mortality rate is 5% secondary to complications of therapy.

The goal in the therapy of pemphigus patients is the reduction of synthesis of autoantibodies, and this is accomplished with the use of systemic corticosteroids alone or in conjunction with other immunosuppressive drugs. Before the development of oral corticosteroids in the 1950s, PV had a 50% mortality after 2 years and almost a 100% mortality at 5 years. Currently, the mortality rate for

Azathioprine generally not effective in inhibiting synthesis of antibodies unless given in relatively high doses.
Low levels of enzyme thiopurine methyl transferase may result in leukopenia.

PV remains about 5% at 10 years. Complications due to the use of very high doses of corticosteroids are almost always responsible for the current mortality rate in PV. Prednisone in doses higher than 1 mg per kg per day (maximum 80 mg per day) are risky, and early use of effective immunosuppressive drugs as steroid sparing agents is advised. In PV, azathioprine should be used at an initial dose of 4 mg per kg per day, since lower doses tend to be ineffective in inhibiting the synthesis of autoantibodies. The efficacy of this drug, as well as the predisposition for severe side effects appears to be genetically mediated by the activity of the enzyme thiopurine methyl transferase. Lower activity of TPMT produces higher effective levels of azathioprine with the risk of severe cytopenias, whereas individuals with higher activity of this enzyme may require higher doses of azathioprine to reach the therapeutic window. Mycophenolate mofetil, an inhibitor of the inosine monophosphate dehydrogenase, which is an enzyme for the de novo synthesis of purines, has been tried in moderate cases of pemphigus patients with promising results.

Ablative therapy with cyclophosphamide is promising.

Stem cells protected by relatively high concentrations compared with lymphocytes of aldehyde dehydrogenase IgG4 autoantibodies directed against desmoglein

Alkylating agents including cyclophosphamide and chlorambucil with or without plasma exchange are very effective; however, because of their toxicity, they are reserved for refractory cases. Immunization with modified desmoglein-III peptides appears to be a logical future therapeutic approach. Autologous and allogeneic bone marrow transplantations have been considered as an alternative for refractory autoimmune diseases including pemphigus. Ablative doses of cyclophosphamide without bone marrow transplant may also become a promising alternative for the therapy of autoimmune diseases. (See Cyclophosphamide Chapter 72, "Immunosuppressive Therapy," for further discussion.) Stem cells are particularly refractory to high doses of cyclophosphamide as compared with the autoreactive lymphocytes, which would be ablated with this therapy, thus allowing the stem cells to repopulate with normal lymphocytes. The morbidity, mortality, and cost of this therapy for autoimmune diseases are lower than those of bone marrow transplantation.

Annotated Bibliography

Anhalt GJ, Labib RS, Vorhees JJ, et al. Induction of pemphigus in neonatal mice by passive transfer of IgG from patients with the disease. N Engl J Med 1982;306: 1189–1196.

This pivotal article demonstrated that the circulating autoantibodies in pemphigus vulgaris are pathogenic. After injecting IgG from patients with pemphigus vulgaris, mouse pups developed clinical and immunopathologic features of pemphigus vulgaris.

Amagai M, Klaus-Kovtum V, Stanley JR. Autoantibodies against a novel cadherin in pemphigus vulgaris. Cell 1991;67:869–877.

The authors in this article identified desmoglein 3, a novel epithelial desmosomal adhesion molecule as the autoantigen for pemphigus vulgaris.

Ding X, Aoki V, Mascaro JM, et al. Mucosal and mucocutaneous (generalized) pemphigus vulgaris show distinct autoantibody profiles. J Invest Dermatol 1997;109: 592–596.

In this article, the authors demonstrated that pemphigus vulgaris patients with mucosal disease have antibodies only against desmoglein 3. The development of cutaneous disease in pemphigus vulgaris patients presenting wtih mucosal disease is associated with the development of antibodies against demoglein 1.

Ahmed AR, Yunis EJ, Khatri K, et al. Major histocompatibility complex haplotype studies in Ashkenazi Jewish patients with pemphigus vulgaris. Proc Natl Acad Sci U S A 1990;87:7658–7662.

This article established one of the strongest associations between a certain HLA haplotype and susceptibility for disease. The authors demonstrated that more than 90% of Ashkenazi Jewish patients with pemphigus vulgaris possess an unusual MHC class II DR4 haplotype (DRBI 0402).

Sinha AA, Brautbar C, Szafer F, et al. A newly characterized HLA DQ beta allele associated with pemphigus vulgaris. Science 1988;139:10026–10029.

This article established a strong association between a certain class II MHC DQ0503 and non Ashkenazi Jewish, Caucasian, and Oriental patients with pemphigus vulgaris.

Koch PJ, Mahoney MG, Ishikawa H, et al. Targeted disruption of the pemphigus vulgaris antigen (desmoglein 3) gene in mice causes loss of keratinocyte cell adhesion with a phenotype similar to pemphigus vulgaris. J Cell Biol 1997;137:1091–1102.

This article defined the crucial role of desmoglein 3 in cellular adhesion of mucous membranes. Mice genetically disrupted for the desmoglein 3 gene developed similar clinical and pathologic features of pemphigus vulgaris in mucous membranes.

Pemphigus Foliaceus (Figures 15–11 to 15–14)

PF can be divided into four subsets: idiopathic, endemic, pemphigus erythematosus, and drug-induced. Each has similar clinical and immunopathologic features, but they arise in unique circumstances. The primary lesion common to all is a superficial vesiculopustule, which ruptures, leading to formation of a scaly crust. Mucosal involvement does not occur. Exacerbation or triggering of pemphigus foliaceus has been reported in association with pregnancy.

Idiopathic PF is a rare and sporadic disease that is seen predominantly in the elderly, and there are no known predisposing factors. IgG autoantibodies bind to epidermal cell surfaces in vivo, and circulating autoantibodies are detected in all patients. The autoantigen in this disease is desmoglein-I, a 160 kD polypeptide. Pathogenic autoantibodies are directed against the calcium-dependent ectodomain of this desmosomal cadherin. Purified IgG4 from patients with PF induces acantholysis in skin-organ culture and in the neonatal mouse model. This induced acantholysis occurs through the granular cell layer of the epidermis, identical to the level of cleavage observed in the human disease. PV and PF are characterized by transplacental crossing of autoantibodies, occasionally

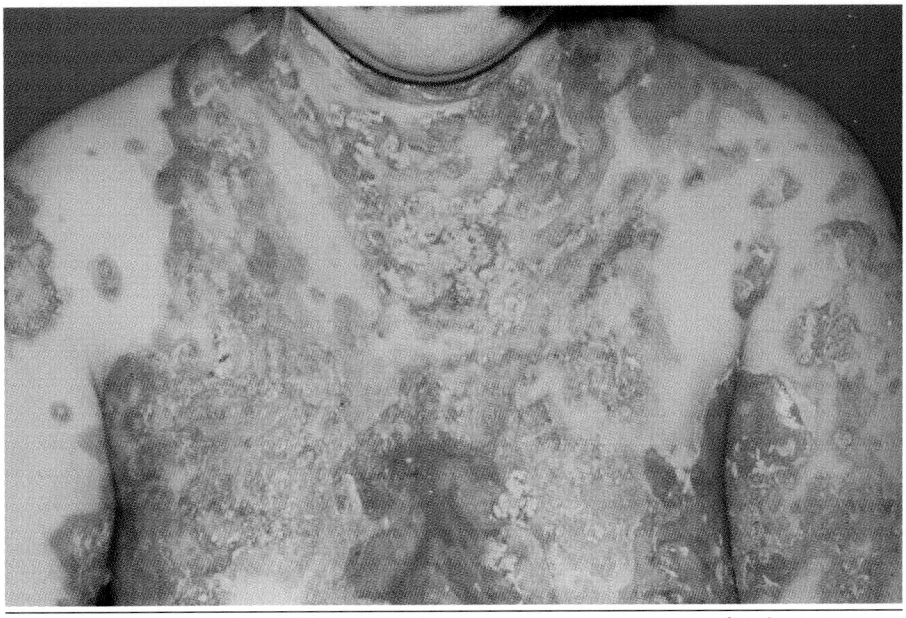

FIGURE 15–11 Pemphigus foliaceous demonstrating extensive superficial erosions on anterior chest.

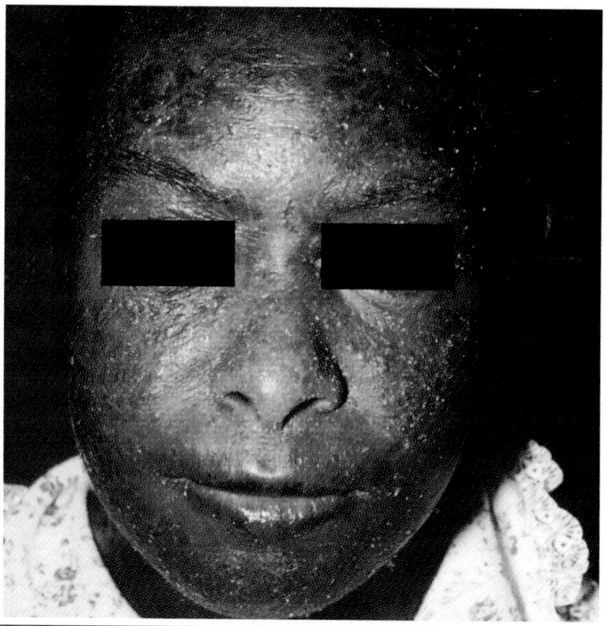

FIGURE 15-12 Pemphigus foliaceous demonstrating extensive scaling lesions on face.

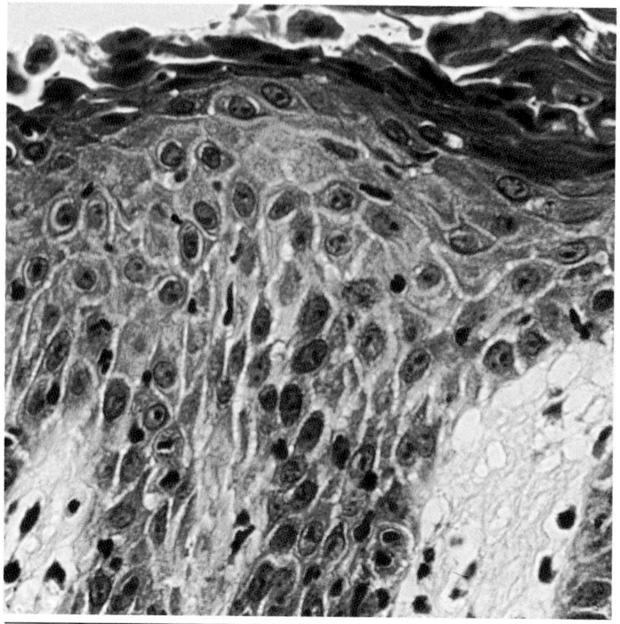

FIGURE 15-13 Pemphigus foliaceous demonstrating characteristic pathology of interepidermal cleft formation at the level of the stratum granulosum.

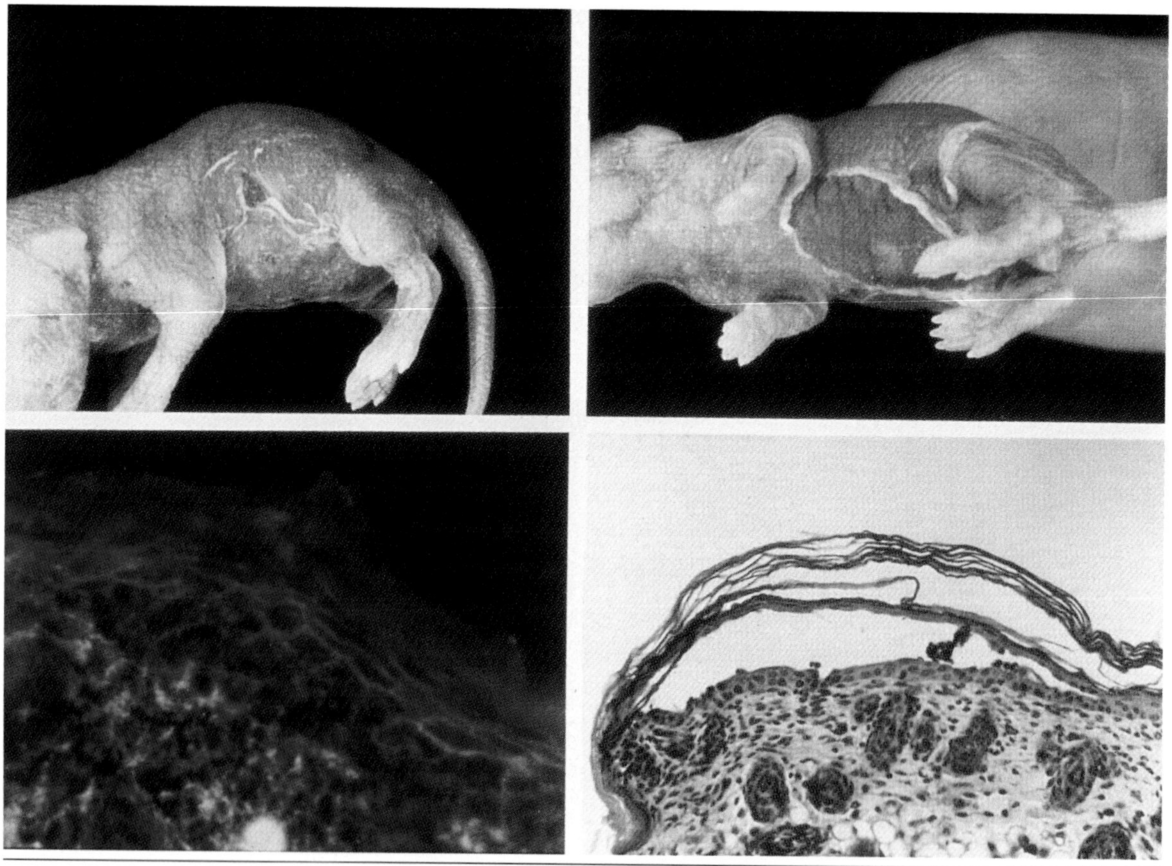

FIGURE 15-14 Pemphigus foliaceous demonstrating the neonatal mouse experiment confirming the pathogenicity of the IgG epidermal anti-intercellular antibody. Upper panels demonstrate superficial in mouse pups injected intraperitoneally with pemphigus foliaceous IgG. In the lower left panel, human IgG is deposited in mouse epidermal intercellular spaces. In the lower right panel, superficial interepidermal cleft formation is demonstrated. All forms of pemphigus produce similar experimental results in the mouse pup model, providing excellent evidence for the pathologic role of these antibodies.

causing neonatal blistering in PV. Neonatal blistering disease almost never occurs in PF. See annotated bibliography for details.

The absence of mucosal lesions in PF patients can be explained by two factors: (1) desmoglein-I in adult human mucosa is not abundant and (2) in mucosal surfaces, desmoglein-III is coexpressed and this redundancy of adhesion molecules compensates for the potential desmosomal disruption caused by the binding of autoantibodies to the less abundant mucosal desmoglein-I.

Absence of mucous lesions in PF

In cornified epithelium (skin), the blister formation in PF occurs superficially because the most differentiated layer of the epidermis is the only area in which desmoglein-I is present without the coexpression of desmoglein-III, and thus, lacks the protective redundancy of desmoglein-III to maintain an intact desmosome.

Superficial bullae

Fogo Selvagem

The immunohistologic features and immunopathogenic mechanisms of fogo selvagem are identical to those of idiopathic PF. The endemic variant differs, however, in its epidemiologic characteristics. This entity is seen in all age groups and is found primarily in southwestern and central Brazil. There is an increased frequency of four specific HLA-DRB1 haplotypes, DRB1*0404, -1402, -1406 or -1401, and all four share an identical amino acid sequence at positions 67–74 on the third hypervariable region of the DRB1 gene. There is also evidence that the HLA-DR7, DQw2 haplotype may confer resistance to the development of endemic PF in Brazil. Unlike all other forms of pemphigus, it is not unusual to see the disease in two or more related family members. An infectious etiology is suspect but not proven to be the environmental "second hit": *Simulium prunosum*, a black fly, is a suspected vector. T cells of endemic PF patients react to multiple epitopes of the ectodomain of desmoglein-I.

Fogo selvagem found in related family members

Pemphigus Erythematosus

Pemphigus erythematosus (Senear-Usher syndrome) is a rare disease and it represents a clinical and immunopathologic overlap of PF and cutaneous lupus erythematosus. Many patients have serologic and clinical features of systemic lupus erythematosus. An association with thymoma with or without myasthenia gravis has been reported. Ultraviolet light increases desmoglein-I and decreases desmoglein-III expressions in neoplastic squamous cells. This could explain the association of lupus and the sporadic reports of cutaneous flare in PF patients upon sun or ultraviolet light exposure.

Pemphigus erythematosus Combination of cutaneous lupus erythematosus and pemphigus foliaceous

Drug-induced Pemphigus Foliaceous

Drug-induced PF appears in the context of the administration of certain drugs, and almost all patients follow a course similar to the idiopathic disease once the autoimmune process is initiated. The most commonly implicated drugs are compounds such as D-penicillamine and captopril that have a highly reactive sulfhydryl group that is suspect in haptenating desmoglein-I. Patients with this disorder usually have autoantibodies directed against desmoglein-I and, less frequently, desmoglein-III. Some patients lack evidence of circulating autoantibodies and generally develop a mild and transient disease that resolves shortly after discontinuation of the drug. This may be due to a direct chemical acantholysis by which the drug inserts into the disulfide bonds between desmoglein-I and plakoglobin, splitting the two and impairing desmosomal adhesion.

D-penicillamine and captopril can induce PF

Therapy of PF does not differ substantially from that of PV, except that treatment can be less aggressive as the mortality rate of untreated disease is much lower than that of PV.

Annotated Bibliography

Ward SJP, et al. The prevalence of antibodies against desmoglein-1 in endemic pemphigus foliaceous in Brazil. N Engl J Med 2000:343;23–30.

This article demonstrates that antibodies against desmoglein-1 are commonly found among normal subjects living in areas where fogo selvagem is endemic.

Furthermore, the onset of the disease is preceded by a sustained antibody response. These findings strongly support the concept that fogo selvagem is an autoimmune disease, induced by an environmental exposure, the nature of which is unknown.

Wu H, et al. Protection against pemphigus foliaceous by desmoglein-3 in neonates. N Engl J Med 2000:343;31–35.

This article demonstrates the presence of desmoglein-3 in the superficial epidermis of neonates. This explains why there is no transmission of pemphigus foliaceous to neonates. The presence of desmoglein-3 compensates, maintaining the integrity of the epidermis, despite an assault by anti desmoglein-1 autoantibodies.

Diaz LA, Sampaio SAP, Rivitti EA, et al. Endemic pemphigus foliaceous (fogo selvagem): current and historic epidemiologic studies. J Invest Dermatol 1989;92:4–12.

This article is a complete description of the clinical and immunopathologic features of this unique variant of pemphigus foliaceous. This article discusses the geographic, familial, and biological aspects of this fascinating disease.

Paraneoplastic Pemphigus (Figures 15–15 and 15–16)

Paraneoplastic pemphigus associated with:
non-Hodgkin's lymphoma
chronic lymphocytic leukemia
Castleman's disease
thymoma
Walderström's macroglobulinemia
spindle cell sarcomas

PNP almost always fatal
If tumor is benign (thymoma or Castleman's tumor) and removed, the disease will slowly remit

PNP is a recently described blistering disorder that arises exclusively in the context of known or occult neoplasms, such as non-Hodgkin's lymphoma, chronic lymphocytic leukemia, Castleman's disease, thymoma, Waldenström's macroglobulinemia, and spindle cell sarcomas. Patients develop prominent mucous membrane ulcerations, intraepidermal acantholytic blisters, and lichenoid cutaneous lesions. Virtually all patients with PNP first present with oral ulcerations. Involvement of the vermilion borders of the lips is quite common.

The disease course is progressive and almost always fatal within 2 years when associated with a malignant neoplasm. When it is associated with a benign neoplasm, such as a benign thymoma or Castleman's tumor, and the tumor is completely excised, the autoimmune disease will slowly enter into a remission.

Autoantibodies against desmosomal and hemidesmosomal components are present and target a complex group of proteins including (a) plakin proteins desmoplakins-I and -II, the bullous pemphigoid antigen I, envoplakin, periplakin, and plectin; (b) desmogleins-III and -I; and (c) a still uncharacterized 170 kD protein. The presence of antiplakin antibodies are the basis for differentiation of this form of pemphigus from PV and PF by indirect immunofluorescence or immunochemical techniques. However, the evaluation of such sera is somewhat complex. The presence of antidesmoplakin autoantibodies alone do

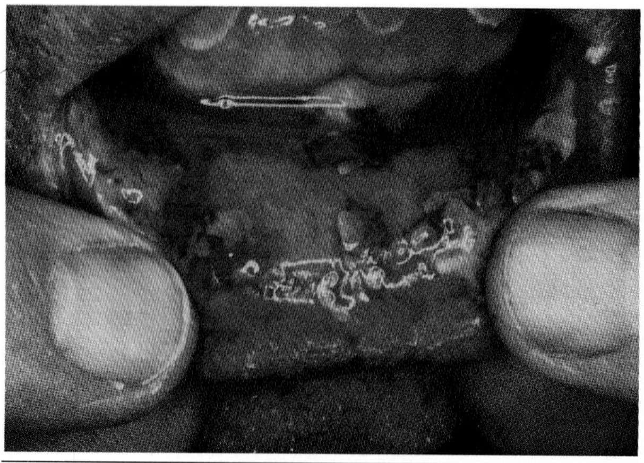

FIGURE 15–15 Paraneoplastic pemphigus demonstrating ulcerations on the lower labial mucosa.

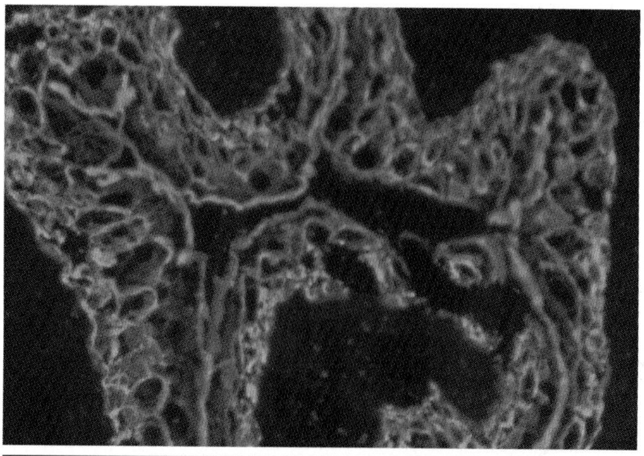

FIGURE 15–16 Paraneoplastic pemphigus demonstrating IgG intercellular staining (antiplakin IgG antibodies) binding the mouse bladder epithelium.

not indicate PNP with certainty for they are present in some patients with erythema multiforme major, bullous pemphigoid, and even PV patients. Furthermore, antidesmoplakin antibodies are absent in some PNP patients, and antibodies against envoplakin and periplakin may be more specific for PNP. To properly evaluate the multiple antigens, immunoprecipitation is currently the "gold standard" for diagnosis.

In PNP, antibodies against envoplakin and periplakin may be more specific.

PNP is thought to be the result of a humoral and cellular immune response to tumor antigens that cross-react with normal mucocutaneous proteins, but other more complex interactions between tumor cells and the immune system have also been proposed as possible mechanisms. High levels of IL-6 in the serum of these patients have been reported. It has been suggested that IL-6 may play a crucial role in the pathogenesis of certain autoimmune diseases. There is evidence that interferon alpha, a potent enhancer of IL-6 expression has been associated with triggering PNP. This suggests that enhanced production of this cytokine by the associated tumors may have a key role in inducing PNP. The role of IL-6 in autoimmune diseases, including PNP, is intriguing. However, further studies are necessary to determine if this cytokine originates from the associated neoplasms or from anti tumor-reactive lymphocytes in PNP.

Possible pathologic role of IL-6

Cell injury from autoimmune or inflammatory processes could induce a new autoimmune process or expand an already present autoimmune mechanism to a normally sequestered antigen or epitope. This hypothesis is known as epitope spreading. The diversity of autoantigens in PNP, including transmembrane and intracellular antigens could be explained by this epitope-spreading mechanism, in which antidesmoglein antibodies could be one group of the initial triggering mechanisms with subsequent exposure of the intracellular antigens and development of antiplakin antibodies.

Epitope-spreading phenomenon

The clinical course of PNP is independent of the activity and severity of the underlying neoplasm, but the presence of PNP invariably worsens the prognosis of these oncologic patients. However, the prognosis for cases of resectable benign neoplasms (thymoma and the hyaline-vascular type of Castleman's disease) is much more favorable. Progressive respiratory failure due to respiratory involvement in PNP has been described. Systemic corticosteroids and a myriad of other immunosuppressive agents have been tried without consistent efficacy. Cyclosporine and cyclophosphamide appear to be superior to other conventional treatments in efficacy. Ablative therapy using intravenous cyclophosphamide without bone marrow transplantation has been successfully performed in one patient.

Clinical course of PNP characterized by progressive respiratory failure.

Annotated Bibliography

Anhalt GJ, Kim S-C, Stanley JR, et al. Paraneoplastic pemphigus. An autoimmune mucocutaneous disease associated with neoplasia. N Engl J Med 1990;323:1729–1735.

This is a seminal article that defined the association between certain neoplasms and a unique and severe form of pemphigus.

Nousari HC, Deterding R, Wojtczack HA, et al. The mechanism of respiratory failure in paraneoplastic pemphigus. N Engl J Med 1999;340:1406–1410.

This article defined one of the lethal and unique complications of paraneoplastic pemphigus. Patients with paraneoplastic pemphigus can develop a sloughing of bronchial epithelium and also bronchiolar involvement that resembles bronchiolitis obliterans. This respiratory complication is the terminal event in the course of the disease. This article also demonstrates that the well-known autoantigens for paraneoplastic pemphigus, plakin proteins, are also present in the respiratory epithelium.

IgA Pemphigus (Figure 15–17)

IgA pemphigus
Some patients have IgA autoantibodies against desmocollin-I, some against desmoglein-III
In majority of patients autoantigens not defined

IgA pemphigus is an uncommon intraepidermal vesicopustular disease that may clinically and histologically mimic subcorneal pustular dermatosis (Sneddon-Wilkinson disease), PF, and even PV. All of these patients have IgA antibodies

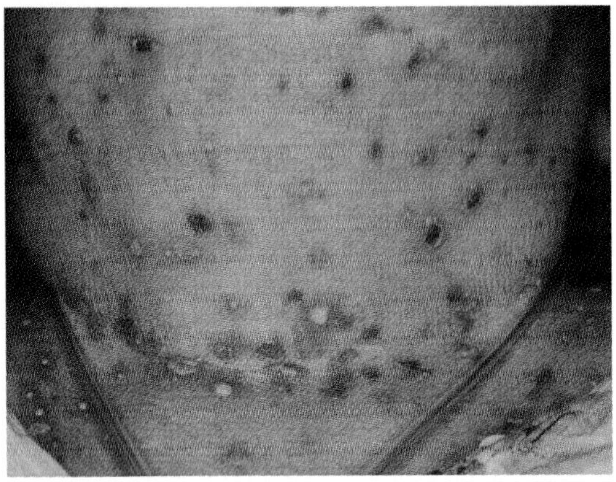

FIGURE 15-17 IgA pemphigus showing pus-filled vesicles on anterior neck.

bound to the epidermal cell surfaces and about half of these patients have circulating anti-epidermal IgA antibodies detected by indirect immunofluorescence. IgA pemphigus serum induced acantholysis in skin explant culture conditions, but there have been no studies demonstrating the pathogenicity in vivo of these IgA autoantibodies. Autoantibodies directed against desmocollin-I have been described in a subset of patients with the subcorneal pustular dermatosis variant of IgA pemphigus, and anti–desmoglein-III antibodies have been reported in the intraepidermal variant. However, in the majority of the cases, the antigens remain unidentified. An association with monoclonal gammopathies has been recently reported. IgA pemphigus patients usually respond to dapsone, retinoids, or prednisone in combination. However, a severe and refractory case requiring plasmapheresis and cyclophosphamide for control has been reported.

Dermal-Epidermal Interactions

Hemidesmosome composed of:
- *BPAG1*
- *BPAG2*
- *α6β4 integrin*

The basement membrane is a complex layer of structural proteins, which mediate the attachment of epidermal cells to the dermis most significantly through an anchoring junction known as the hemidesmosome. Located at the basal pole of the basal cell layer of epithelia, hemidesmosomes (Figure 15–18) have a structure similar to desmosomes but do not possess an opposing hemiorganelle attachment site in the basement membrane. Proteins that are known to form the hemidesmosome include the bullous pemphigoid antigens BPAG1 and BPAG2, and the α6β4 integrin. BPAG1 is an intracellular hemidesmosomal plaque protein with 30% homology to the desmosomal plaque protein desmoplakin-I. BPAG2 is an unrelated unique transmembrane protein with multiple collagenous domains in the extracellular portion of the molecule. The subcellular distribution of the BPAG2 is regulated by the β4 integrin subunit. The α6β4 integrin is presumed to mediate adhesion with its ligand in the underlying basement membrane, laminin V (also called epiligrin).

Laminin V also called epiligrin, kalinin, nicein, and BM600.

The area just beneath the basal cell layer of the epidermis is an electron lucent zone known as the lamina lucida. Anchoring filaments extend from the hemidesmosomes, transverse the lamina lucida, and insert into an electron-dense region which is rich in type IV collagen, known as the lamina densa. The anchor-

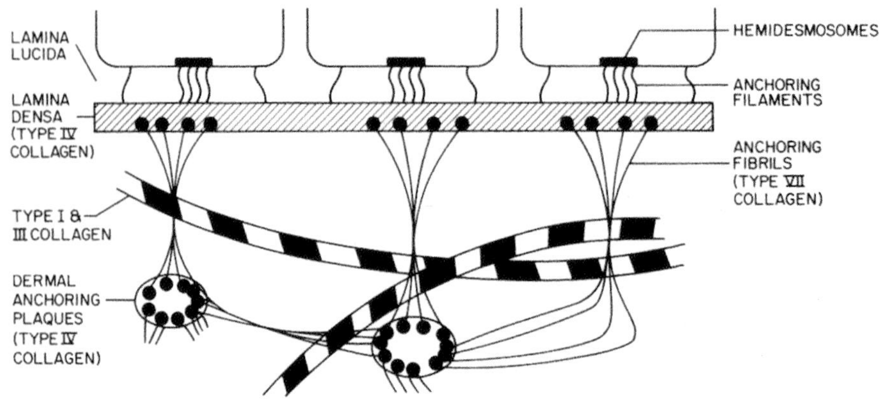

FIGURE 15-18 Schematic sketch showing organelles responsible for epidermal-dermal adhesion.

ing filaments are associated with laminin V, a trimeric protein that originally had been called epiligrin, kalinin, nicein, or BM600 before a consensus on its nosology was achieved. Laminin V is the ligand for basal cell adhesion via both the hemidesmosomal integrin $\alpha 6\beta 4$ and an $\alpha 3\beta 1$ integrin belonging to a less well-studied junctional complex, the focal adhesion. Laminin V interacts with laminin VI ($\alpha 3\beta 1\gamma 1$), another laminin that in turn interacts with collagen IV in the lamina densa via nidogen.

Laminin V chains are proteolytic processed in vitro and in vivo. An enzyme called bone morphogenic protein-1 is involved in this processing in vivo, cleaving the gamma-2 chain, and this cleavage appears to be crucial in the assembling of the basement membrane.

Anchoring fibrils composed of type VII collagen

Extending from the lamina densa into the upper dermis are anchoring fibrils, some of which loop and reconnect with the lamina densa, while others insert into dermal anchoring plaques. This forms a loose basket-weave structure in this area. The anchoring fibrils are composed of type VII collagen, a protein composed of three identical chains, each consisting of an N-terminal noncollagenous (NC1) domain and a C-terminal collagenous domain. The NC1 domain primarily consists of sequential fibronectin type III-like repeats and an area homologous to the A-2 domain of von Willebrand's factor. These epitopes are relevant for the interaction with other components of the complex extracellular matrix.

Autoimmune Subepithelial Blistering Diseases: Pemphigoid Spectrum and Epidermolysis Bullosa Acquisita

Bullous Pemphigoid (Figures 15–19 to 15–21)

Subepidermal blistering disease of the elderly
Linear deposition of IgG and other Ig along basement membrane zone

Bullous pemphigoid (BP) is the most frequent of the subepidermal blistering diseases, occurring most often in elderly patients. Tense blisters, most prominent in intertriginous areas, and the general absence of mucous membrane lesions characterize this disease. Histologic examination of the lesions shows a subepidermal blister with intense eosinophilic and neutrophilic infiltrates. Direct immunofluorescence of the skin reveals linear IgG and C3 deposition along the basement membrane zone. Indirect immunofluorescence evaluation of the patients' sera using human salt split skin as a substrate reveals circulating IgG autoantibodies that bind the epidermal (roof) side of the induced blister.

These patients possess IgG autoantibodies reactive against BPAG1 and BPAG2. A recent epitope mapping study revealed that BP and gestational pemphigoid autoantibodies recognize an immunodominant epitope within the noncollagenous portion of the human BPAG2 ectodomain that lies adjacent to the plasma membrane in the lamina lucida. This critical epitope is structurally quite different in the murine BPAG2 ectodomain, precluding the use of murine models for testing the pathogenicity of human anti-BPAG2 autoantibodies. However, rabbit polyclonal antibodies against the murine epitope of the BPAG2 have been produced, and passive transfer into mice reproduces characteristic inflammatory subepidermal blisters in mice. The production of blisters requires antibody binding to the BPAG2, complement activation, and polymorphonuclear cell infiltration. Further studies have reinforced the crucial role of neutrophils in the

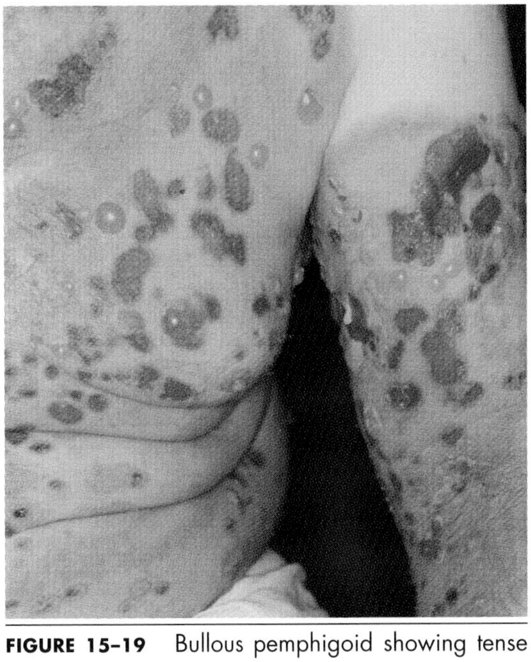

FIGURE 15–19 Bullous pemphigoid showing tense blister formation anterior chest and left arm.

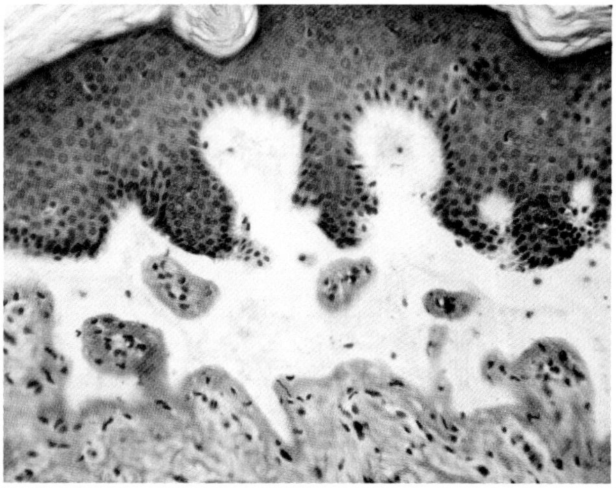

FIGURE 15-20 Bullous pemphigoid demonstration of subepidermal blister formation.

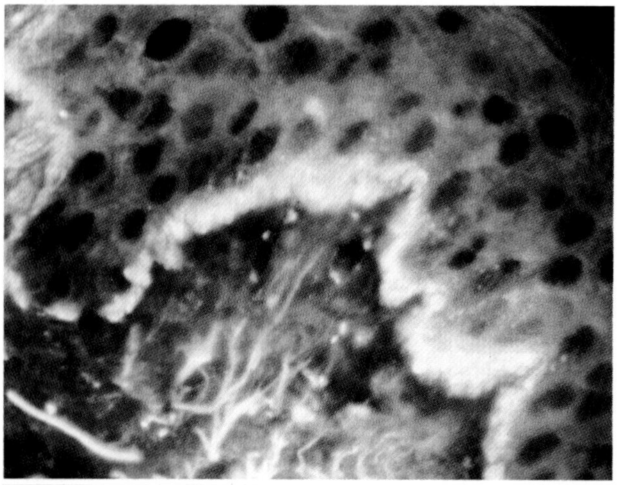

FIGURE 15-21 Bullous pemphigoid demonstrating, by direct immunofluorescence examination, the linear deposition of IgG along the basement membrane zone.

Epitope on BPAG2 adjacent to plasma membrane

Complement-dependent AgAb reaction

Proteolytic enzymes of neutrophils are important pathogenically.

pathogenesis of BP demonstrating that neutrophils recruited to the skin via C5a-dependent pathways are critical in the development of BP. Gelatinase-B–deficient mice were resistant to the blistering effect of passive transfer antibodies against murine BP 180 antigen. When these gelatinase-deficient mice were reconstituted with neutrophils from normal mice, they developed blistering in response to antimurine BP 180 antibodies. Elastase, another neutrophil enzyme, has been shown to be important in the blistering formation of BP. A highly sensitive ELISA or the detection of circulating anti-BP 180 autoantibodies using the NC16A epitope has been recently developed. Another very specific ELISA, but not as sensitive as the previously mentioned ELISA, has also been developed using the ectodomain of BP 180.

Pro-inflammatory cytokines secreted by mast cells, such as IL-1 and tumor necrosis factor, upregulate the keratinocyte expression of eotaxin, an eosinophil-specific chemoattractant in BP lesions.

Other clinical variants of bullous pemphigoid exist including lichen planus pemphigoides.

An overlap of BP with lichen planus is known as lichen planus pemphigoides. Autoantibodies against uncharacterized 105 kD and 200 kD proteins found in the lower lamina lucida recently have been recognized in patients with a blistering disease resembling pemphigoid. These BP-like diseases are characterized by dermal staining on human salt split skin indirect immunofluorescence, an excellent response to conventional therapy, and the presence of mild mucosal lesions. More immunologic and clinical data are required to characterize these diseases as unique subepidermal blistering disorders.

BP, unlike PV, is an inflammatory-mediated disease Relatively low-dose steroids and immunosuppressive agents are effective.

The clinical variants of BP are listed in Table 15-2.

Therapy of BP includes both anti-inflammatory–reducing and antibody-reducing immunosuppressive therapy. As opposed to pemphigus where the autoantibodies are almost exclusively responsible in the pathogenesis, in BP a combination of the autoantibodies, complement activation, and a cascade of inflammatory events are crucial to blister formation. Immunosuppressive therapy that is similar to that of pemphigus but at lower dosages, with or without the addition to anti-inflammatory drugs including dapsone, are logical therapeutic approaches.

Annotated Bibliography

Liu Z, Giudice GJ, Swartz SJ, et al. The role of complement in experimental bullous pemphigoid. J Clin Invest 1995;95:1539–1544.

This article presented the first animal model for bullous pemphigoid, thus helping to define the role of inflammatory events in bullous pemphigoid.

TABLE 15-2 Clinical Variants of Bullous Pemphigoid

Bullous pemphigoid
Gestational pemphigoid (herpes gestationis)
Cicatricial pemphigoid
Brunsting Perry, associated with scalp and face bullae
Solitary lesion
Hyperkeratotic or prurigo-like lesions
IgA bullous pemphigoid
Occult bullous pemphigoid
Associated with pruritus in absence of inflammatory urticaria or bullae
Lichen planus pemphigoides
Others
Poorly described, demonstrating antibodies against uncharacterized dermal-epidermal structures

Giudice GJ, Emery DJ, Zelickson BD, et al. Bullous pemphigoid and herpes gestationis autoantibodies recognize a common noncollagenous site on the BP180 ectodomain. J Immunol 1993;151:5742–5750.

This article demonstrated that patients with bullous pemphigoid and herpes gestationis recognize the same autoantigen, the BP180 antigen, and thus established that these two diseases have the same immunopathologic features, but subtle clinical differences.

Gestational Pemphigoid (Figures 15–22, 15–23)

Gestational pemphigoid, more commonly known as herpes gestationis (HG), is a blistering disease immunologically similar to BP. However, it occurs during the late second or third trimester of pregnancy and is highly pruritic. Urticarial and vesicular lesions may resolve after delivery. Commonly mild exacerbations occur with resumption of menses. The disease is mediated by an avid complement-fix-

Highly pruritic bullous disease may be recurrent with subsequent pregnancies.

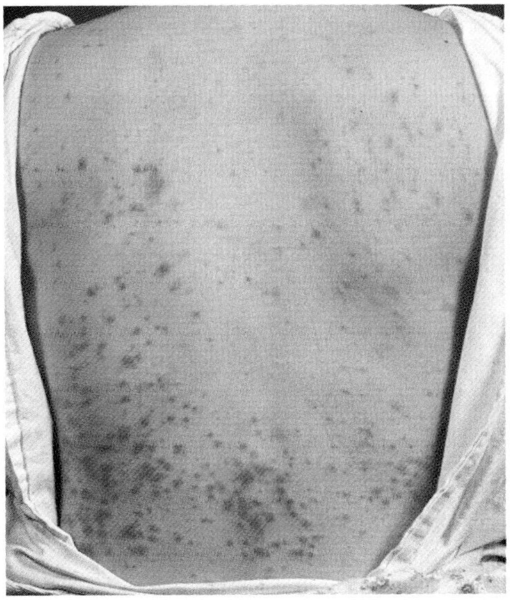

FIGURE 15–22 Gestationis pemphigoid (herpes gestationis) demonstrating urticaria-like, highly pruritic lesions over back.

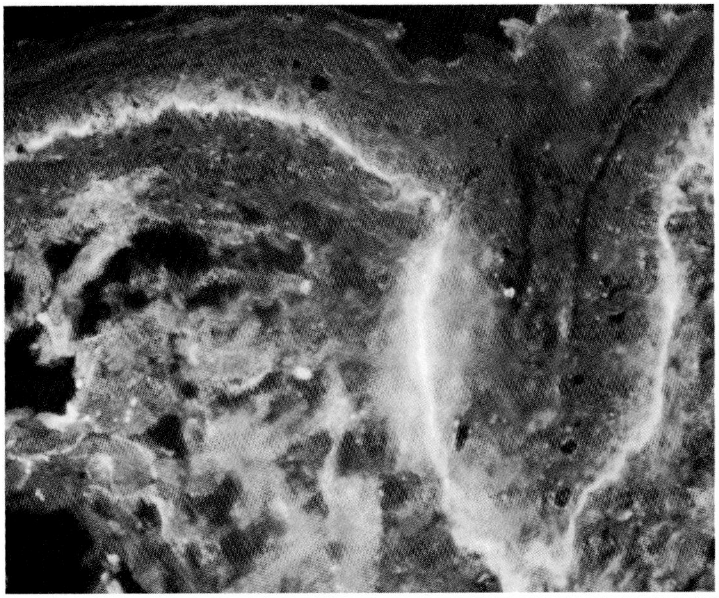

FIGURE 15–23 Gestationis pemphigoid demonstrating, by direct immunofluorescence, the linear deposition of C3 along the basement membrane zone.

ing, anti-basement membrane IgG_1 autoantibody. This autoantibody was originally detected by an in vitro complement fixation immunofluorescence assay, and was thought not to be an immunoglobulin, hence it was called the HG factor. In HG, the autoantibodies (HG factor) are directed almost exclusively against the NC16A epitope of the BPAG2 and only occasionally recognize epitopes of the BPAG1. This disease is of interest because the autoantibody can be induced by pregnancy, molar pregnancies, ovarian tumors, and challenge with oral estrogens. The mechanisms of this induction are unexplored. Prednisone is the main therapy for this disease.

Cicatricial Pemphigoid (Figures 15–24 to 15–27)

Mucous membrane subepidermal bullous disease

CP is defined by the presence of subepidermal blistering that almost exclusively involves mucous membranes. This blistering leads to scarring and dysfunction of the organs affected, and there are autoantibodies against the basement membrane zone of the affected epithelium. The immunohistologic features of CP, though similar to those of BP, are distinguished by two characteristics: (1) only a minority of patients have circulating autoantibodies directed against the base-

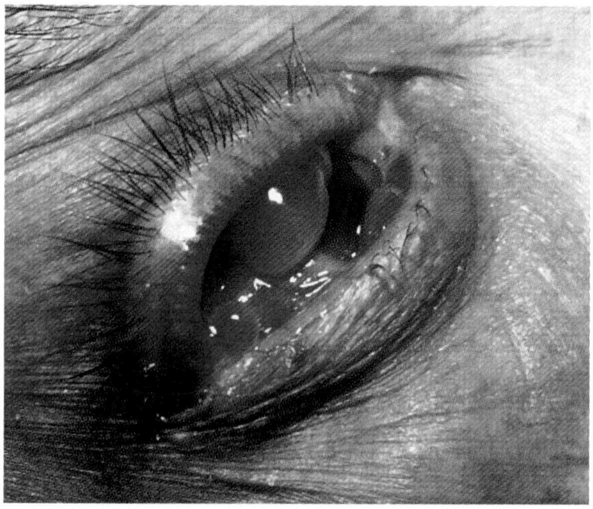

FIGURE 15-24 Cicatricial pemphigoid bullae of the upper lid conjunctiva.

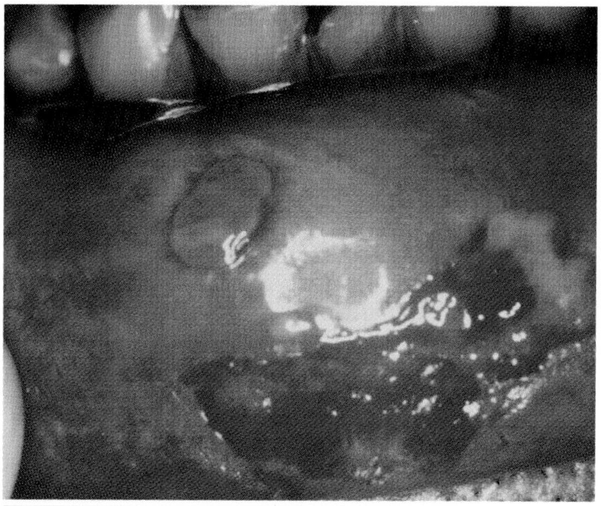

FIGURE 15-25 Cicatricial pemphigoid showing well-demarcated erosions on the lower labial mucosa.

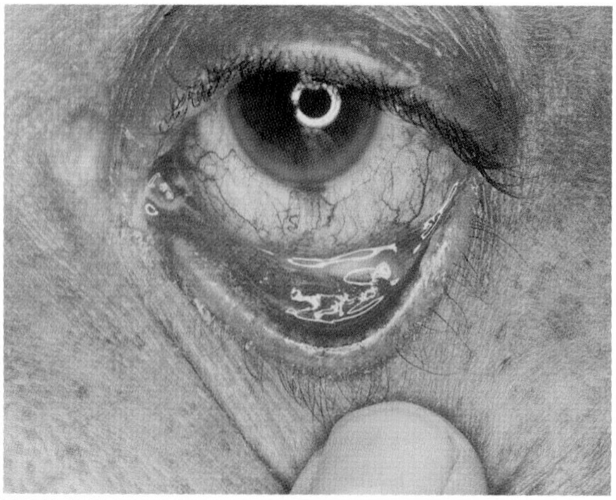

FIGURE 15-26 Cicatricial pemphigoid showing anti-epiligrin antibody–positive patient with significant scarring conjunctivitis with obliteration of the fornices.

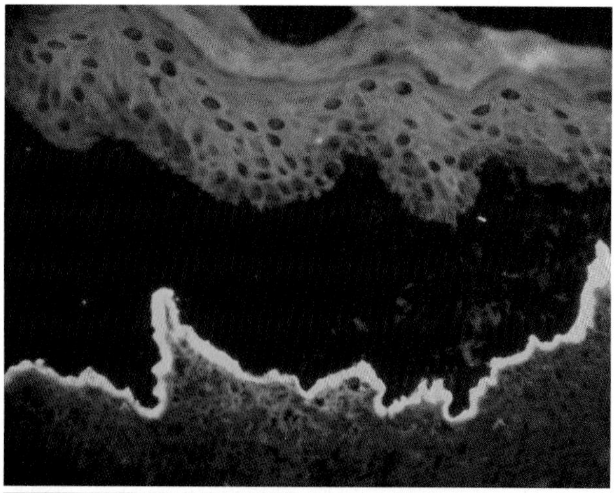

FIGURE 15-27 Cicatricial pemphigoid demonstrating, by indirect immunofluorescence examination, the presence of circulating IgG autoantibodies (anti-laminin V IgG) binding the dermal side of a human split skin substrate.

ment membrane and (2) the predominance of scarring mucosal lesions. Those who have autoantibodies display activity against a wide variety of basement membrane components including, but not limited to, BPAG1 and BPAG2, laminin V, α6β4 integrin, type VII collagen, and 45 kD keratin.

The BP 180 epitopes recognized by autoantibodies in CP patients appear to be located at the carboxy terminus of the ectodomain (the membrane's most distal ectodomain), explaining the scarring nature of the disease, as opposed to BP where the pathogenic antibodies are directed against the NC16A epitope, the membrane's most proximal ectodomain. However, antibodies against epitopes located in the NC16A domain (BP noncollagenous ectodomain) are also present in CP patients.

Antibodies against epitopes in carboxy terminal of 180 kD BPAG2

Antibodies against laminin V

The differences in the clinical presentation of CP patients, however, cannot be explained by reactivity with specific BP antigens. A minority of patients with CP have autoantibodies that are specific for epiligrin (laminin V), and this disease has been called anti-epiligrin CP. Indirect immunofluorescence evaluation of the patients' sera using human salt split skin as a substrate reveals circulating IgG autoantibodies that bind the dermal (floor) side of the induced blister.

This lamina lucida protein, laminin V, has been shown to be absent in patients with junctional epidermolysis bullosa, a hereditary scarring bullous disease. In antiepiligrin CP, antibodies against the α3 subunit of laminin V are almost invariably present. These anti-α3 laminin V antibodies have cross-reactivity with the α3 chain of laminin VI, another anchoring protein of the basement membrane. Antibodies against the β3 and γ2 chains of laminin V have also recently been reported. Previous studies using a murine model have failed to demonstrate the pathogenicity of these antilaminin V antibodies since the murine laminin V molecule differs from the human protein. These antilaminin V antibodies have demonstrated to be pathogenic using a very interesting animal model. This animal model consisted of severe combined immunodeficient mice grafted with human skin that were perfused with antilaminin V antibodies. These antibodies were capable of inducing subepidermal blisters only at the site of the human grafted skin. These autoantibodies in anti-epiligrin CP are predominantly IgG_4 and do not fix complement.

Antiepiligrin antibodies have been shown in a murine model to be pathogenic

Topical and systemic corticosteroids, azathioprine, and dapsone are proven to be effective for mild to moderate involvement of oral, nasal, anogenital, and cutaneous disease. However, for severe, refractory, life-threatening cases, or lesions involving the conjunctiva, and the pharyngoesophageal and tracheobronchial mucosae, preferred therapy should be cyclophosphamide in conjunction with prednisone.

Annotated Bibliography

Domloge-Hultsch N, Anhalt GJ, Gammon WR, et al. antiepiligrin cicatricial pemphigoid. A subepithelial bullous disorder. Arch Dermatol 1994;130:1521–1529.

Cicatricial pemphigoid, or better known as mucous membrane pemphigoid, is a clinical phenotype term that includes several autoimmune subepithelial blistering diseases with well-defined immunopathologic features.

IgA Pemphigoid (Figures 15–28 and 15–29)

This vesicobullous disease, also known as linear IgA bullous disease or chronic bullous disease of childhood, is characterized by pruritic lesions distributed over the trunk, with or without mucosal involvement, predominantly affecting preschool children and adults. A transient drug-induced variant was recently reported in association with vancomycin and a small number of other drugs.

Immunofluorescence evaluation shows linear deposition of IgA along the basement membrane, with circulating autoantibodies present in a minority of patients. This bullous disease may represent several different conditions mediated by a single Ig isotype. One of the most common autoantigens is the 120 kD lamina lucida antigen called LAD-1, formerly identified as a 97 kD antigen by

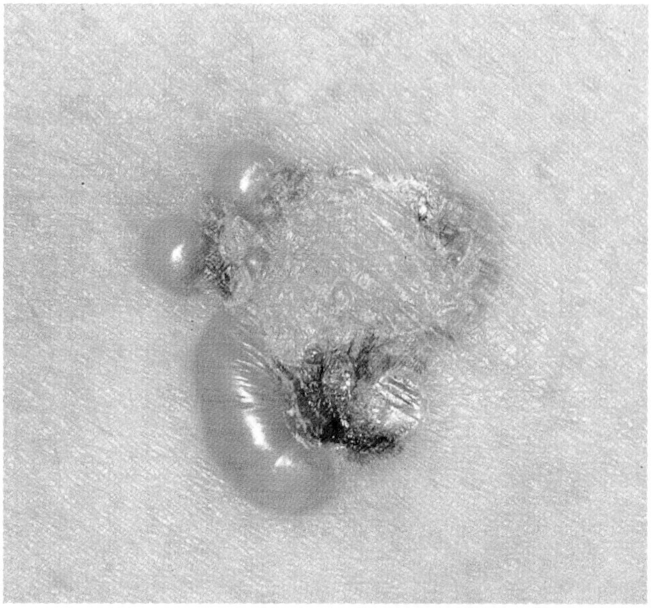

FIGURE 15-28 IgA bullous pemphigoid demonstrating small, tense vesicle bullae.

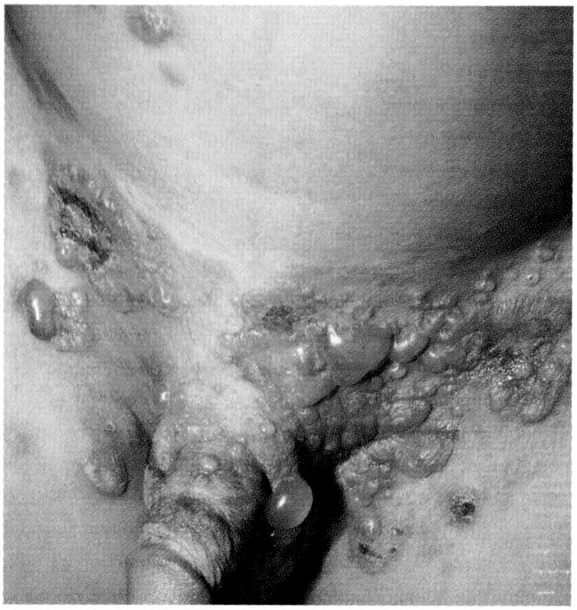

FIGURE 15-29 Chronic bullous disease of childhood (linear IgA dermatosis) demonstrating tense bullae in the groin of child. This disease is closely related, if not identical, to IgA bullous pemphigoid.

Small subepidermal blisters
IgA deposition along basement membrane zone
Also components of alternative complement pathway

immunoblotting. Recent studies have shown that the 120 kD lamina lucida antigen shares complete homology with a portion of the collagenous ectodomain of the BP 180 antigen. Prednisone alone or in conjunction with dapsone has shown to be very effective in the management of these patients.

Epidermolysis Bullosa Acquisita (Figures 15–30 and 15–31)

Epidermolysis bullosa acquisita (EBA) is an uncommon blistering disorder characterized by scarring lesions located predominantly in areas of trauma, with blisters occurring beneath the lamina densa in the upper dermis. Indirect immunofluorescence evaluation of the patients' sera using human salt split skin as a substrate reveals circulating IgG autoantibodies that bind the dermal (floor)

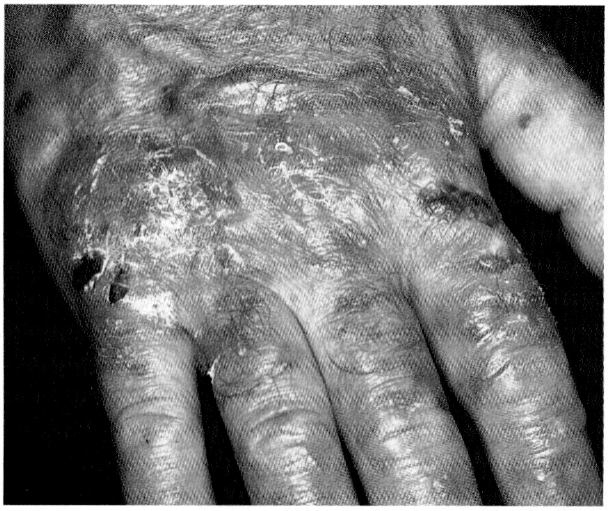

FIGURE 15-30 Epidermolysis bullosa acquisita demonstrating subepidermal blister formation on dorsal surface of hands. Fragile skin and blister formation on dorsal surface hands and fingers is reminiscent of porphyria cutanea tarda.

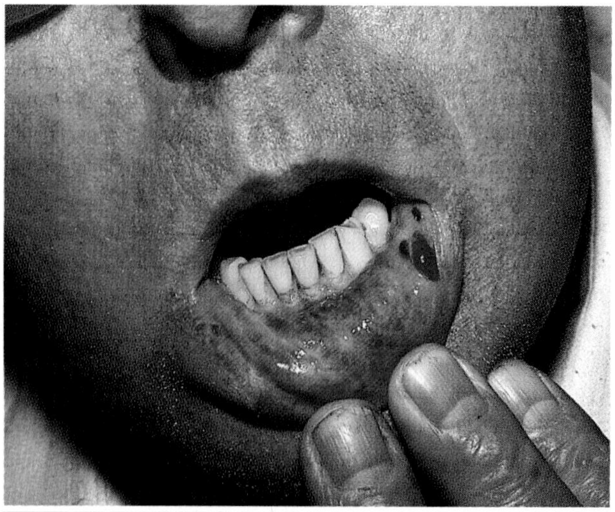

FIGURE 15-31 Epidermolysis bullosa acquisita demonstrating subepidermal blister on lower labial mucosa.

side of the induced blister. This immunofluorescent finding is similar to that of anti-epiligrin CP.

Antibodies against NC1 domain of type VII collagen

Passive transfer experiments in mice

Association with HLA-DR2 phenotype

Immunologic studies indicate that these patients have IgG autoantibodies reactive against various epitopes within the NC1 domain of the anchoring fibrils, which are composed of type VII collagen, and the most dominant epitopes are found in fibronectin-like repeats within the molecule. These fibronectin-like repeats bind the β3 chain of laminin V, so perturbation of the NC1–laminin V interaction may contribute to the pathogenesis of EBA. However, antibodies reacting against the triple helical domain of the type VII collagen also have been recently described. Passive transfer of autoantibodies to mice induced immunohistologic changes in the murine skin that are similar to those seen in human patients, although spontaneous blistering has not been reliably reproduced. There is a strong association with the HLA- DR 2 haplotype.

EBA seen in association with systemic lupus erythematosus and Crohn's disease.

Recalcitrant to therapy

In unusual circumstances, patients with systemic lupus erythematosus can develop subepidermal blisters, and one of the mechanisms whereby this occurs is through the development of autoantibodies against type VII collagen (Figure 15–32). This condition is known as bullous systemic lupus erythematosus (BSLE) and represents the presence of anti-type VII collagen antibodies in the context of co-existent systemic lupus erythematosus. Both BSLE and EBA share similar immunopathologic and genetic characteristics, but they differ in some histologic and therapeutic features. The exact pathophysiologic mechanisms responsible for these diseases remains a subject of research, and the relationship between the two is still unclear. Inflammatory bowel disease is the most common disease associated with EBA. A significant number of patients with Crohn's disease have circulating antibodies against the NC1 domain of the type VII collagen. EBA is probably the most refractory of the subepidermal autoimmune bullous diseases. Prednisone, azathioprine, and cyclosporine appear to be the most effective drugs. Anecdotal reports of the use of other anti-inflammatory medications and plasmapheresis also exist.

Dermatitis Herpetiformis (Figures 15–33 to 15–36)

IgA granular deposition at the dermal-epidermal junction

Association with gluten-sensitive enteropathy

Dermatitis herpetiformis (DH) is an uncommon IgA-mediated bullous disease with a mean age of onset in the fourth decade. DH is not an autoimmune skin disease since the detection of antibodies directed against a cutaneous antigen has been unsuccessful. Primary lesions consist of pruritic papulovesicles on extensor surfaces. Although almost all patients have histologic evidence of a gluten-sensitive enteropathy (GSE), only about 10% are symptomatic. Gliadin is the most relevant gluten-containing protein. Intestinal lymphoma has been reported in DH patients, even in the absence of demonstrated GSE.

Although several hypotheses are currently being investigated, the pathophysiology of this disorder and its association with GSE remain unclear. DH may be familial, and first-degree relatives can be affected both with DH and celiac disease. This feature could be explained by the strong genetic association observed with the HLA haplotypes DQ9 (α1*0501, β1*02) and DQ α1*03, β1*0302. Immunoelectronmicroscopy shows IgA deposition around fibrillin, the most important component of microfibrils in elastic fibers of the papillary (upper) dermis. Direct immunofluorescence reveals granular IgA deposits at the basement membrane zone and at the tips of the dermal papillae. Despite these findings, IgA autoantibodies against skin components are notably absent. Cutaneous IgA deposition in DH

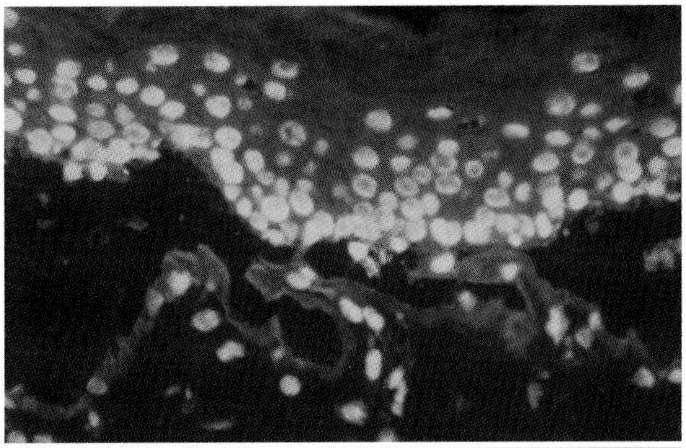

FIGURE 15-32 Bullous systemic lupus erythematosus demonstrating, by indirect immunofluorescence, the presence of circulating IgG autoantibodies (anticollagen VII IgG antibodies) binding the dermal side of a human split skin substrate. There is also striking nuclear staining of the keratinocytes and dermal cells (in vivo antinuclear antibodies).

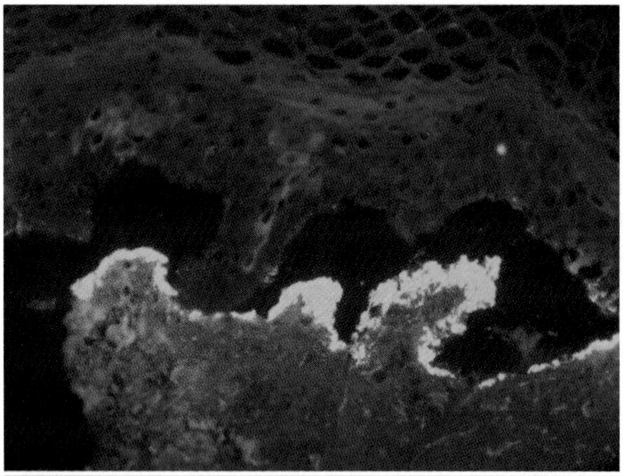

FIGURE 15–33 Dermatitis herpetiformis demonstrating, by direct immunofluorescence, intense granular IgA staining in dermal papillae beneath cleft formation.

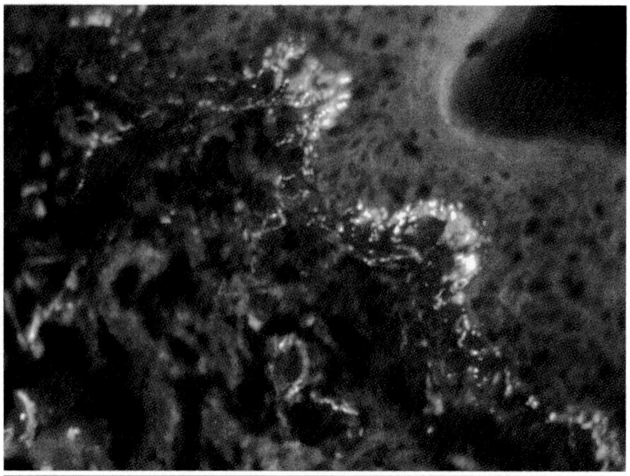

FIGURE 15–34 Dermatitis herpetiformis showing granular deposition of IgA along dermal epidermal junction.

Dermatitis herpetiformis and celiac disease occur in same families.

Antiendomysial antibodies are specific and are directed against tissue transglutaminase enzyme.

patients is not uniformly distributed throughout the skin. The best yield in the direct immunofluorescence evaluation of DH lesions is obtained from a normal-appearing skin that is adjacent to an active lesion. However, IgA immune complexes and antireticulin, antigliadin, and anti-endomysial IgA are commonly found in patients. Anti-endomysial antibodies are the most specific and sensitive antibodies found in DH and GSE. Recent studies have shown that the antigen of the anti-endomysial antibodies is the tissue transglutaminase (TGase). TGase is a calcium-dependent enzyme that catalyzes the transamidation of specific bound glutamine residues.

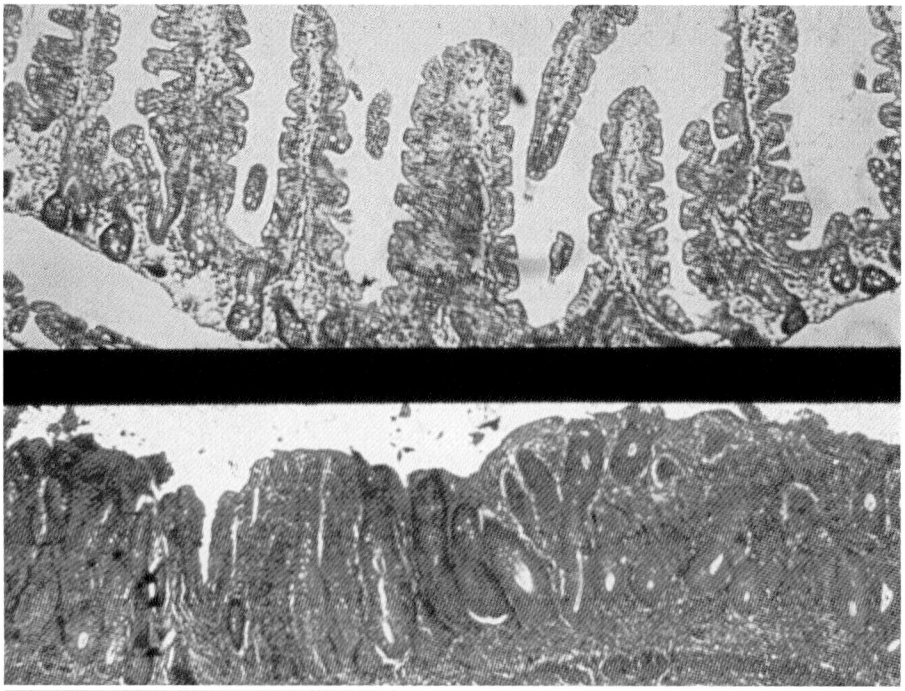

FIGURE 15–35 Dermatitis herpetiformis showing on bottom small intestinal biopsy of an area of patchy atrophy. Note edema, inflammatory cells, and flattening of normal villi. Compare with normal jejunal biopsy on top. (Reproduced with permission from John Zone, M.D.).

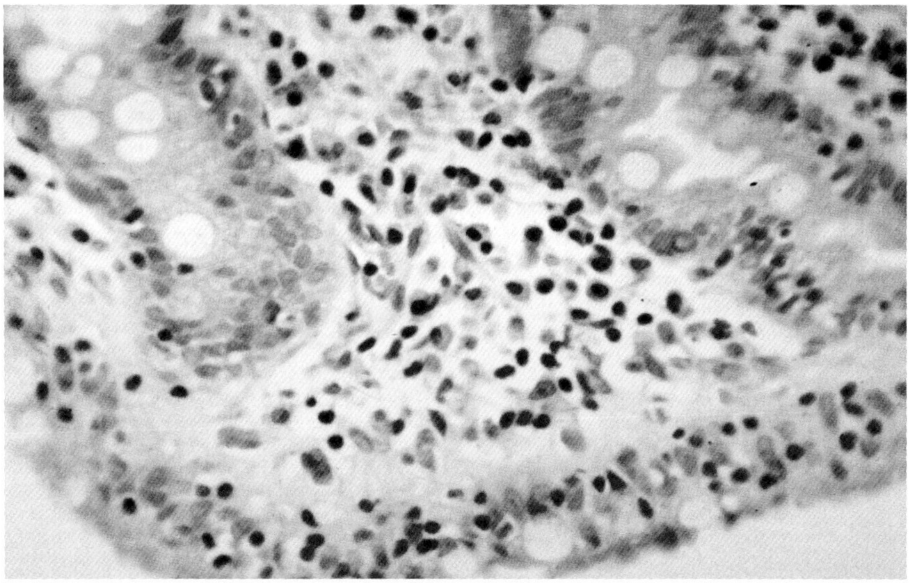

FIGURE 15–36 Dermatitis herpetiformis showing jejunal biopsy. Note flattening of normal villi edema and mononuclear cell infiltrate. (Reproduced with permission from John Zone, M.D.).

An increase in the TGase activity has been observed in jejunal biopsies. TGase selectively deamidates gluten peptides, which in turn results in a strongly enhanced T-cell stimulatory activity leading to amplification of the gluten-specific T-cell responses. This deamidation creates an epitope in gliadin that binds efficiently to DQ2, and this is recognized by gut-derived T cells. This generation of epitopes by enzymatic modification is a new mechanism that may be relevant for breaking tolerance and initiation of the gastrointestinal disease.

An increased density of gamma/delta T-cell receptor intraepithelial lymphocytes in the jejunum of patients with celiac disease and DH is very characteristic, which is not normalized on a gluten-free diet, and the density of the lymphocytes seems to have a positive correlation with age.

Urokinase plasminogen activator is expressed early in lesional skin of DH patients. Subsequent participation of interstitial collagenase and stromelysin-1 may contribute to the degradation of the basement membrane in DH lesions. The recruitment of neutrophils and eosinophils in DH is induced by IL-8, granulocyte-macrophage colony–stimulating factor, and T_h2 cytokines including IL-5 and IL-4.

A strict gluten-free diet produces a clearance of IgA cutaneous deposits.

Restriction of gluten and administration of sulphones, (dapsone and sulphapyridine), are the mainstays of therapy. Gluten is found in wheat, rye, barley, and oats. However, a recent study has shown that low-to-moderate quantities of oats could be safe in DH patients. The nontoxic nature of oats may be due to a low percentage of oat prolamin; however, these patients may have an exquisite sensitivity even to this low amount of prolamins. Moreover, oats are usually contaminated with gluten during harvesting and milling. Thus, from a practical point of view, patients should be advised to avoid oats. The cutaneous IgA immune complexes in DH patients can clear only after adhering to a strict gluten-free diet for 6 months or longer. An additional potential benefit of observing a gluten-free diet is the potential reduction of the risk for the development of intestinal lymphoma, as shown in a retrospective study; however, further studies are necessary to confirm these results.

Annotated Bibliography

Dieterich W, Ehnis T, Bauer M, et al. Identification of tissue transglutaminase as the autoantigen of celiac disease. Nat Med 1997;3:725–726.

Although a few patients with dermatitis herpetiformis have clinical symptoms of gluten sensitive enteropathy, all dermatitis herpetiformis patients have immunohistologic features of gluten sensitive enteropathy in intestinal biopsies. Among the group of autoantibodies that these patients have, the anti-endomysial antibodies are the most sensitive and specific markers of active disease. This article identified the antigen of these anti-endomysial antibodies, the tissue transglutaminase.

CHAPTER 16

T_h1 versus T_h2 Responses

Steve N. Georas, M.D.

Classification of Adaptive Immune Responses

Immune responses can be grouped into two general categories: *innate,* in which first-line defense mechanisms, such as the complement cascade, are nonspecifically induced upon encountering foreign antigen; and *adaptive,* in which T and B lymphocytes regulate the outcome of a given immune response by secreting soluble mediators, such as cytokines and immunoglobulins, that interact with and activate effector cells.

In recent years, it has become clear that CD4-positive T helper (T_h) cells can be classified into two distinct phenotypes characterized by differences in cytokine production (Figure 16–1).

Upon encounter with antigen, T_h1 cells secrete primary interferon gamma (IFN-γ) and interleukin (IL)-2, whereas T_h2 cells secrete IL-4 and IL-5. T_h1- and T_h2-driven immune responses are qualitatively different. T_h1 cytokines are efficient at inducing cell-mediated immunity, and T_h1-responses are characterized by activated T cells (IL-2) and monocytes/macrophages (IFN-γ). In contrast, IL-4 efficiently activates B cells, induces humoral immune immunity, and tends to downregulate cellular (especially monocyte) responses (Table 16–1).

Additionally, IL-4 is the major factor inducing the expression of IgE (immunoglobulin) in B cells, and IL-5 is the major cytokine driving eosinophilopoiesis. It was, therefore, conceptually appealing when diseases known to be characterized by elevated IgE levels and eosinophilia (eg, atopic dermatitis, allergic asthma, idiopathic hypereosinophil syndrome) were found to be associated with the expansion of T_h2 cells.

In summary, the outcome of many immune responses is currently thought to depend on the balance between the pro-inflammatory effects of IL-4 and T_h2 cytokines with their ability to downregulate cellular immunity. Consequently, a growing number of human diseases are now thought to arise due to dysregulation of T_h-cytokine production.

Regulation of T_h1 and T_h2 Differentiation

The functional dichotomy of CD4-positive T cells into T_h1 and T_h2 cells was originally described in the mouse, and in general, the phenotype of murine T_h cells is quite distinct. Although human CD4-positive T-cell responses are more

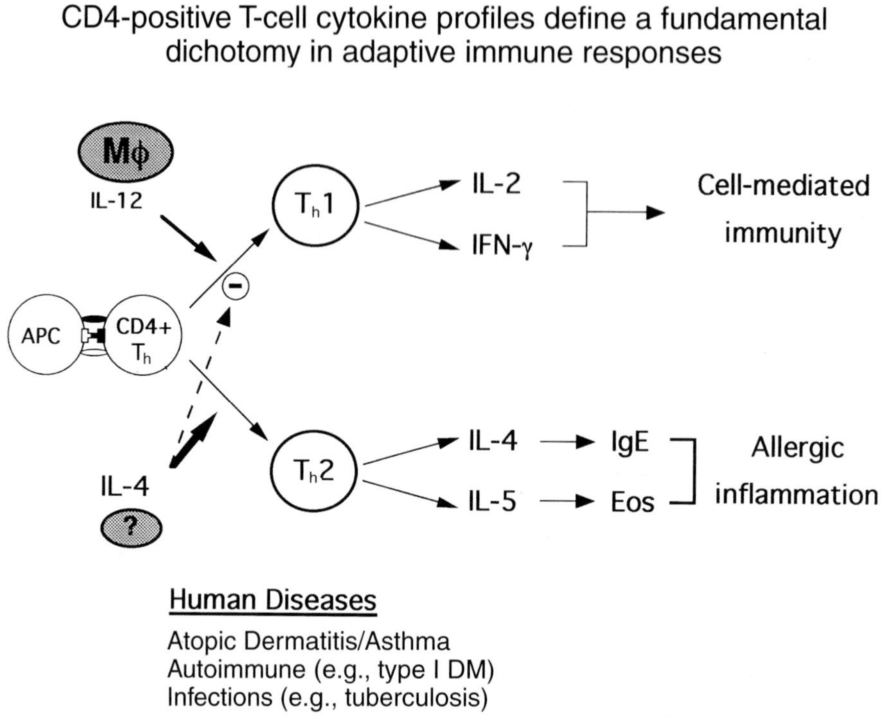

FIGURE 16–1 Schematic diagram of the CD4-positive T_h cell differentiation. Upon encountering antigen (and other signals) displayed by an antigen-presenting cell (APC), a naive CD4-positive T cell will differentiate into T_h1 or T_h2 cells. T_h differentiation is controlled largely by locally produced cytokines: IL-4 induces T_h2 differentiation, whereas IL-12 (produced by macrophages, Mϕ) induces T_h1 differentiation. Not indicated on this figure are overlapping patterns of cytokine production that are often detectable in disease states or other determinants of T_h differentiation. APC = antigen-presenting cell; Mϕ = macrophages; IL = interleukin; IFNγ = interferon-gamma; IgE = immunoglobin E; Eos = eosinophils; DM = Diabetes Mellitus.

IL-4 plays key role in development of a T_h2 response

heterogeneous (ie, overlapping patterns of cytokine production are usually detected), polarization of T_h-cell cytokine production is currently thought to underlie many allergic, inflammatory, and autoimmune diseases. It is now clear that T_h subsets differentiate from naive precursor CD4-positive T cells largely under the influence of locally secreted cytokines. IL-4 is the critical factor that induces T_h2 differentiation and inhibits T_h1 cells, whereas IL-12 and IFN-γ induce T_h1 differentiation. Thus, these phenotypes tend to be self-reinforcing and mutually exclusive (see Figure 16–1).

TABLE 16–1 Pro-inflammatory Effects of IL-4 Relevant to Skin Diseases*

Target Cell	Effect
B cells	Proliferation and activation, IgE immunoglobulin expression
T cells	Proliferation, T_h2 differentiation
Keratinocytes	Proliferation, enhanced antigen presentation
Dermal fibroblasts	Collagen synthesis, chemokine expression
Dendritic cells	Differentiation and growth
Endothelial cells	Vascular cell adhesion molecule-1 expression
Eosinophils	Chemotaxis
Monocytes	Inhibition and apoptosis

*Note: IL-4 shares many of these effects with its close congener IL-13.

The initial source of IL-4 responsible for T_h2 differentiation is currently not known, and it is becoming clear that other signals besides cytokines can also influence this process. Whether a given encounter with antigen will induce a T_h1 or T_h2 response will likely depend on still poorly characterized host factors, antigen affinity, co-stimulatory signals, and the nature of the antigen presenting cell itself. Interestingly, it has been suggested that early childhood exposure to some antigens might induce long-lasting deviation of T_h responses in a given individual. According to this theory, exposure to strong T_h1-inducing antigens (such as bacille Calmette-Guérin and mycobacteria) would serve to inhibit T_h2-driven processes and atopic diseases. In support of this notion, Shirakawa et al. found an inverse association between tuberculin reactivity and atopy in a Japanese population.

Vaccinations producing cell-mediated responses may be associated with decreased atopy.

The molecular basis for differential cytokine gene expression in T_h subsets is under intense investigation and will likely be elucidated within the next decade. Regulation of the T_h2 cytokine gene expression occurs at the level of gene transcription, and it is likely that modulation of chromatin structure at the T_h2 cytokine gene locus (containing the genes for IL-4, IL-5, and IL-13 and located on chromosome 5q31–33) plays an important role in this process. Interestingly, Chan et al. found that T cells from patients with atopic dermatitis preferentially expressed a unique pattern of IL-4 gene-specific transcription factors. This important study suggested that dysregulation of IL-4 gene transcriptional activation was a fundamental defect in atopic dermatitis.

Molecular basis unknown, but dysregulation of gene transcription may be important

Cutaneous Diseases and T_h1/T_h2 Paradigm

At present, there is no surface marker that reliably distinguishes differentiated T_h1 and T_h2 cells, although CD30 and certain chemokine receptors are preferentially expressed on some T_h2 cells. Classification of T cells as T_h1 or T_h2 currently relies on the detection of polarized cytokine mRNA (ribonucleic acid) and/or protein expression. Several cutaneous diseases are now thought to be characterized by T_h2 responses based on increased expression of IL-4 with reduced IFN-γ in tissue biopsies, circulating T cells, or patient-derived T-cell clones. These include the idiopathic hypereosinophilic syndrome, bullous pemphigoid, Sézary syndrome, and (lepromatous) multibacillary leprosy. As in most allergic diseases, increased expression of T_h2-cytokines is also a feature of atopic dermatitis (AD) and helps explain the elevations in serum IgE and tissue eosinophilia characteristic of this disease. AD also illustrates some of the difficulty with the current paradigm, however, in that IFN-γ is frequently detected in the lesional skin of patients with chronic disease. An attractive hypothesis is that there is a switch from T_h2-dominant acute phase to T_h1-driven chronic phase in AD, which is currently under active investigation in several laboratories.

Classification of T_h1 versus T_h2 response is determined by cytokine profiles:

- *IL-2 and INF-γ (T_h1)*
- *IL-4 and IL-5 (T_h2)*

T_h2 driven diseases:

- *atopic dermatitis*
- *bullous pemphigoid*
- *idiopathic hypereosinophili syndrome*
- *Sézary syndrome*
- *multi bacillary (lepromatous) leprosy*

Other skin diseases are now thought to be predominantly T_h1-driven, such as herpes gestationis and psoriasis. Although the role of specific antigens in the pathogenesis of psoriasis is currently unclear, growing evidence points to the importance of dysregulated IFN-γ (but not IL-4) expression in this disease. Because T-cell clones from patients with psoriasis co-express IFN-γ and IL-5 (without IL-4), it may be more appropriate to refer to this disease as IFN-γ dependent and T_h1 like. Additionally, the observation that some novel antipsoriatic therapies enhance T_h2-cytokine production supports a model in which an imbalance of T_h1:T_h2 responses is a fundamental component of this disease.

T_h1 driven diseases include psoriasis and herpes gestationis.

In summary, our knowledge of and the ability to characterize T_h-dependent immune responses is rapidly growing. This is already translating into a better understanding of disease pathophysiology and will hopefully lead to more specific and effective therapies.

Annotated Bibliography

Medzhitov R, Janeway CA Jr. Innate immunity: impact on the adaptive immune response. Curr Opin Immunol 1997;9:4–9.

This concise summary provides functional links between adaptive and innate immune responses from a leading immunologist.

Mosmann TR, Coffman RL. TH1 and TH2 cells: different patterns of lymphokine secretion lead to different functional properties. Ann Rev Immunol 1989;7:145–173.

Although somewhat dated, this thorough review from the two investigators who originally defined the T_h1/T_h2 dichotomy in mice provides a solid foundation for this paradigm.

Abbas A, Murphy K, Sher A. Functional diversity of helper T lymphocytes. Nature 1996;383:787–793.

This is a recent summary of the factors regulating T_h differentiation, and the importance of T_h subsets in disease states.

Kay AB, Sun Ying, Varney V, et al. Messenger RNA expression of the cytokine gene cluster, interleukin 3 (IL-3), IL-4, IL-5, and granulocyte/macrophage colony-stimulating factor, in allergen-induced late-phase cutaneous reactions in atopic subjects. J Exp Med 1991;173:775–778.

This is an important early paper establishing a T_h2-phenotype in allergen-challenged subjects with atopic dermatitis.

Robinson DS, Hamid Q, Ying S, et al. Predominant TH2-like bronchoalveolar T-lymphocyte population in atopic asthma. N Engl J Med 1992;326:298–304.

Using in situ hybridization, these investigators discovered that lung lymphocytes recovered from subjects with allergic asthma expressed IL-4 and IL-5 with little IFN-γ mRNA, a T_h2 phenotype.

Casolaro V, Georas S, Song Z et al. Biology and genetics of atopic disease. Curr Opin Immunol 1996;8:796–803.

This is a recent review of the molecular factors regulating IL-4 gene expression and possible genetic factors predisposing to T_h2-dependent responses in atopy.

Romagnani S. Lymphokine production by human T cells in disease states. Annu Rev Immunol 1994;12:227–257.

A concise summary of recent evidence that CD4-positive T_h cell–derived cytokines contribute to some human diseases.

O'Garra A. Cytokines induce the development of functionally heterogeneous T helper cell subsets. Immunity 1998;8:275–283.

This is a comprehensive, recent analysis of the role of cytokines in the induction of T_h differentiation.

Rissoan MC, Soumelis V, Kadowaki N, et al. Reciprocal control of T helper cell and dendritic cell differentiation [see comments]. Science 1999;283:1183–1186.

This important paper in the emerging area of dendritic cell heterogeneity shows that subsets of dendritic cells can differentially regulate T_h-cell differentiation.

Constant SL, Bottomly K. Induction of Th1 and Th2 CD4+ T cell responses: the alternative approaches. Annu Rev Immunol 1997;15:297–322.

This is a concise and thoughtful review that summarizes recent evidence that the mechanisms by which T cells encounter antigen (and possibly antigens themselves) can influence T_h differentiation.

Shirakawa T, Enomoto T, Shimazu S, et al. The inverse association between tuberculin responses and atopic disorder. Science 1997;275:77–79.

This interesting paper reports an inverse association between tuberculin reactivity and atopy in a Japanese population. It suggests that early exposure to T_h1-dominant antigens, such as bacille Calmette-Guérin and tuberculosis might induce long-lasting protection from T_h2-driven atopic diseases. This paper has also inspired a number of ongoing studies investigating the efficacy of administering bacille Calmette-Guérin and related compounds in atopic disorders.

Brown MA, Hural J. Functions of IL-4 and control of its expression. Crit Rev Immunol 1997;17:1–32.

Chan SC, Brown MA, Willcox TM, et al. Abnormal IL-4 gene expression by atopic dermatitis T lymphocytes is reflected in altered nuclear protein interactions with IL-4 transcriptional regulatory element. J Invest Dermatol 1996;106:1131–1136.

This paper shows that nuclear proteins extracted from T cells from subjects with atopic dermatitis expressed a unique pattern of transcription factors that interacted with an IL-4 promoter element. It suggests that abnormalities in transcriptional regulation of cytokine genes are a fundamental component of atopy.

Sallusto F, Lenig D, Mackay CR, et al. Flexible programs of chemokine receptor expression on human polarized T helper 1 and 2 lymphocytes. J Exp Med 1998;187: 875–883.

This is one of several studies showing that T_h1 and T_h2 cells can be distinguished by their expression of chemokine receptors. This might help explain the preferential recruitment of T_h2 cells to sites of allergic inflammation at which specific chemokines are often expressed.

Budinger L, Borradori L, Yee C, et al. Identification and characterization of autoreactive T cell responses to bullous pemphigoid antigen 2 in patients and healthy controls. J Clin Invest 1998;102:2082–2090.

This is an important investigation of the cytokines produced by autoreactive T-cell clones from controls and subjects with bullous pemphigoid. The observation that bullous pemphigoid antigen 2-specific clones from patients produced both T_h1 and T_h2 cytokines, whereas clones from control subjects produced IFN-γ only, suggests that T_h2 responses contribute to the pathogenesis of this disease.

Cogan E, Schandene L, Crusiaux A, et al. Brief report: clonal proliferation of type 2 helper T cells in a man with the hypereosinophilic syndrome. N Engl J Med 1994;330: 535–538.

Salgame P, Abrams JS, Clayberger C, et al. Differing lymphokine profiles of functional subsets of human CD4 and CD8 T cell clones. Science 1991;254: 279–282.

This is one of the first demonstrations that differing patterns of T-cell cytokine production correlates with a human disease. These investigators studied T-cell clones from human subjects with leprosy and found that individuals with strong cell-mediated responses produced mostly IFN-γ (T_h1), whereas immunologically unresponsive subjects produced IL-4 (T_h2).

Vowels BR, Cassin M, Vonderheid EC, et al. Aberrant cytokine production by Sezary syndrome patients: cytokine secretion pattern resembles murine T_h2 cells. J Invest Dermatol 1992;99:90–94.

Vowels BR, Lessin SR, Cassin M, et al. Th2 cytokine mRNA expression in skin in cutaneous T-cell lymphoma. J Invest Dermatol 1994;103:669–673.

These publications demonstrate a predominant T_h2 pattern of cytokine production in patients with the Sézary syndrome. This pattern is most apparent in skin biopsies of subjects with tumor-stage skin lesions.

Yamamura M, Uyemura K, Deans RJ, et al. Defining protective responses to pathogens: cytokine profiles in leprosy lesions. Science 1991;254:277–279.

Thepen T, Langeveld-Wildschut EG, Bihari IC, et al. Biphasic response against aeroallergen in atopic dermatitis showing a switch from an initial TH2 response to a TH1 response in situ: an immunocytochemical study. J Allergy Clin Immunol 1996;97: 828–837.

These investigators propose that early inflammatory responses in atopic dermatitis are primarily T_h2-driven, whereas the chronic phase is characterized by activation of IFN-γ producing T_h1 cells.

Lin M, Gharia MA, Swartz SJ, et al. Identification and characterization of epitopes recognized by T lymphocytes and autoantibodies from patients with herpes gestationis. J Immunol 1999;162:4991–4997.

In this analysis of T cell–dependent responses to the hemidesmosomal protein BP180 (the major target of autoantibodies in herpes gestationis), T-cell clones derived from patients with this disease produced IL-2 and IFN-γ, but no IL-4, and were thus classified as T_h1.

Szabo SK, Hammerberg C, Yoshida Y, et al. Identification and quantitation of interferon-gamma producing T cells in psoriatic lesions: localization to both CD4+ and CD8+ subsets. J Invest Dermatol 1998;111: 1072–1078.

This important paper establishes the following: (1) there was a large increase in IFN-γ secreting CD3-positive T cells in psoriatic lesional skin (compared with normal controls); (2) these T cells were both CD4-positive and CD8-positive; and (3) no IL-4 production was detectable under similar conditions. T cell–derived IFN-γ is likely critical for keratinocyte proliferation in this disease.

Vollmer S, Menssen A, Trommler P, et al. T lymphocytes derived from skin lesions of patients with psoriasis vulgaris express a novel cytokine pattern that is distinct from that of T helper type 1 and T helper type 2 cells. Eur J Immunol 1994;24:2377–2382.

These investigators analyzed T-cell clones from patients with psoriasis and found an intermediate pattern of cytokine production: cells produced both IFN-γ and IL-5, with little IL-4. Thus, these cells do not easily fit into the classical T_h1/T_h2 paradigm.

de Jong R, Bezemer AC, Zomerdijk TP, et al. Selective stimulation of T helper 2 cytokine responses by the anti-psoriasis agent monomethylfumarate. Eur J Immunol 1996;26: 2067–2074.

By studying the most active metabolite of the novel antipsoriatic drug Fumaderm, these investigators found that this agent selectively enhanced IL-4 and IL-5 production (without affecting IFN-γ) in peripheral blood T cells. This suggests that a T_h1/T_h2 imbalance plays an important role in the pathogenesis of psoriasis.

CHAPTER 17

Idiopathic Hypereosinophilic Syndrome

Thomas T. Provost, M.D.

The idiopathic hypereosinophilic syndrome is a multisystemic disease characterized by sustained peripheral eosinophilia and damage to organs, including the peripheral and central nervous systems, lungs, heart, and skin.

Multisystemic disease
Internal organ involvement
Sustained eosinophilia

The disease was initially described by Hardy and Anderson in 1968. Subsequent studies at the National Institutes of Health established the diagnostic criteria. The diagnosis is established by demonstrating the following: (1) sustained peripheral eosinophilia for at least 6 months as well as the detection of organ involvement; (2) elimination of other etiologies associated with eosinophilia such as parasitic infections, allergic disease, L–tryptophan–associated eosinophilic myalgia syndrome, eosinophilic fasciitis, and eosinophilic pneumonia.

The exact role of eosinophilia in the pathophysiology of organ disease has intrigued investigators. For example, the cardiac manifestations are not unique to the idiopathic hypereosinophil syndrome. They may develop with eosinophilia that is associated with other diseases. However, perplexing is the observation that not all patients with hypereosinophilia develop organ involvement.

Syndrome associated with:
T-cell dysregulation
eosinophilic leukemia

It now appears that the idiopathic hypereosinophil syndrome is not one entity but may be associated most commonly with several lymphocyte disorders. These range from clonal and nonclonal proliferation of T_h2 lymphocytes to lymphomatoid papulosis and T-cell lymphoma (Sézary syndrome). Also, some patients with this syndrome have eosinophilic leukemia.

The idiopathic hypereosinophil syndrome occurs predominantly between the ages of 20 and 50. Men are affected in greater numbers than women (9:1 ratio). A few children have been reported.

Clinical Features

Cutaneous Manifestations

Approximately 50% of patients with the idiopathic hypereosinophil syndrome have prominent cutaneous features. Those patients with angioedema and urticaria (also termed "angioedema and eosinophilia") have a benign disease. Another benign condition, hypereosinophilic dermatitis characterized by prominent blood and tissue eosinophilia, has also been described. Systemic organ involvement is unusual. Thus, these two entities (ie, angioedema and eosinophilia and hypereosinophilic dermatitis), although similar to the idiopathic hypereosinophilic syndrome, are probably distinct, readily respond to therapy, and have a much better prognosis.

Erythematous, pruritic papules and nodules
Vasculitis, vesiculobullous lesions
Mucocutaneous lesions

Erythematous, pruritic papules and nodules are seen in patients with the idiopathic hypereosinophil syndrome. Vasculitis, vesiculobullous lesions, erythema annulare centrifugum, generalized erythema (erythrodermia), aquagenic pruritus, and digital necrosis occur. Mucocutaneous involvement of the mouth, nose, pharynx, penis, esophagus, stomach, and anus have also been reported (Figures 17–1 to 17–3).

Hematologic Manifestations

Hypereosinophilia as high as 50,000 per μL

Sustained eosinophilia is a diagnostic feature. In general, eosinophil counts range between 6,000 and 20,000 μL. However, very high counts in excess of 50,000 eosinophils per μL have been reported. In general, those patients with extremely high eosinophil counts have the worst prognosis.

Examination of eosinophils generally demonstrates mature forms, but occasionally eosinophil myeloid precursors are detected. Cytoplasmic vacuolization, nuclear hypersegmentation, and small cytoplasmic granules may also be seen.

Anemia and thrombocytopenia may be present

The neutrophil count may also be elevated and the platelets can either be increased or decreased. Anemia is seen in approximately 50% of patients. Evidence of extramedullary hematopoiesis, characterized by nucleated red blood cells and teardrop-shaped red blood cells, is frequently found. Splenomegaly may also contribute to the thrombocytopenia and anemia. A bone marrow aspirant will demonstrate prominent eosinophilia (30–60%).

Cardiac Manifestations

Cardiac disease a prominent feature
Endocarditis
Mural thrombi
Endomyocardial scarring

Cardiac involvement is a major cause of morbidity and mortality. Three distinct phases of cardiac disease are noted in the idiopathic hypereosinophil syndrome: (1) a generally subclinical, eosinophilic endomyocarditis characterized by eosinophil microabscess formation in the myocardium; (2) thrombi formation on damaged endocardium, which may produce valvular dysfunction or occlusion of myocardial vessels, leading to congestive heart failure, or which may also embolize to other organs; (3) fibrotic organization of the mural thrombi and endomyocardial scarring, which produces a restrictive cardiomyopathy and valvular scarring.

It is important to note that the risk of developing cardiac disease is not related to the degree of eosinophilia or the duration of the idiopathic eosinophilic syndrome. Those patients appearing at risk to develop cardiac manifestations have an increased frequency of the human leukocyte antigen (HLA)-

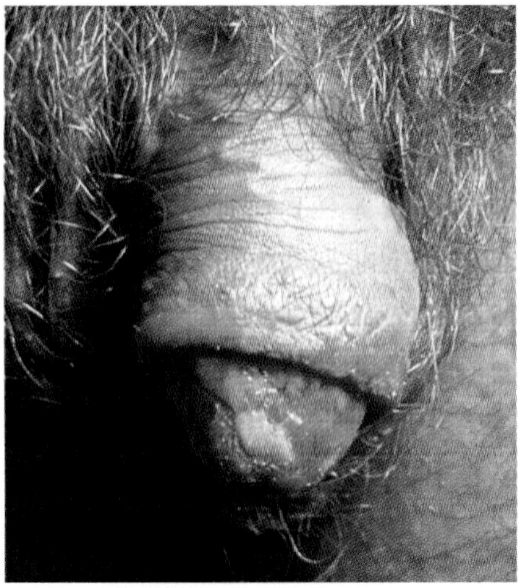

FIGURE 17–1 Penile ulcer in a patient with the hypereosinophilic syndrome. (Reproduced with permission from K. M. Leiferman, MD; Rochester, MN)

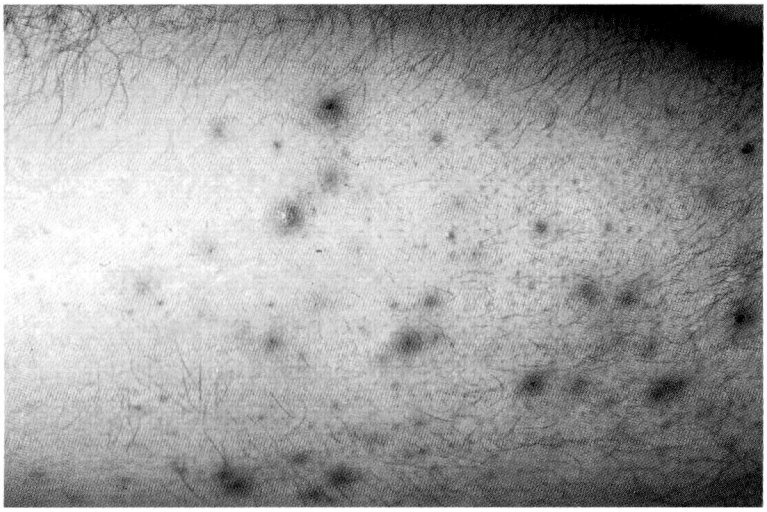

FIGURE 17–2 Perifollicular leg abscess in patient with the hypereosinophil syndrome. (Reproduced with permission from K. M. Leiferman, MD; Rochester, MN)

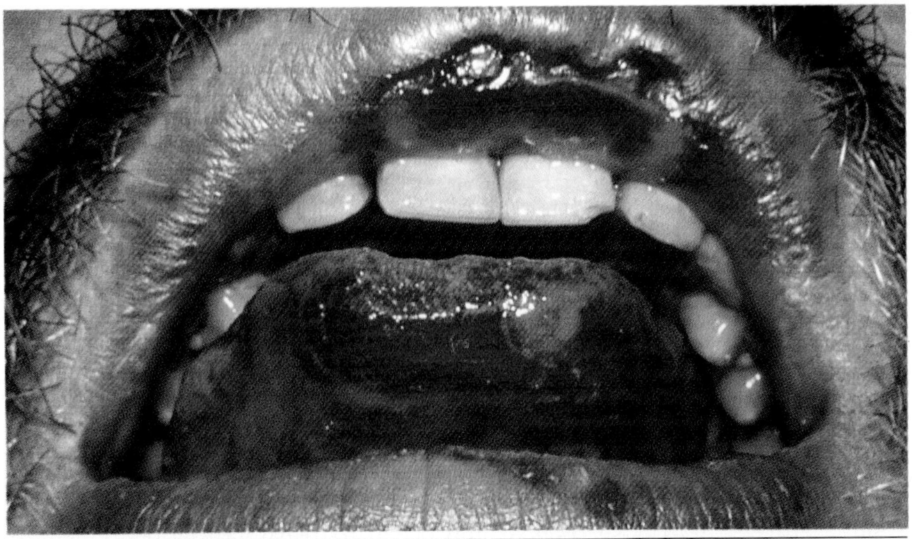

FIGURE 17–3 Oral ulcerations (lip and tongue) in a patient with the hypereosinophil syndrome. (Reproduced with permission from K. M. Leiferman, MN; Rochester, MN)

Bw44 phenotype, splenomegaly, thrombocytopenia, elevated vitamin B_{12} levels, and abnormal eosinophils in the peripheral blood.

Risk of cardiac disease not related to extent or duration of eosinophilia

Neurologic Manifestations

Neurologic manifestations include:
focal neurologic signs
diffuse encephalopathy
motor and sensory neuropathies

Three types of neurologic manifestations have been recognized in patients with the idiopathic hypereosinophil syndrome: (1) transient ischemic attacks or focal neurologic signs, which are the result of thromboembolic phenomena, or possibly intravascular thrombosis of cerebral vessels; (2) diffuse toxic effects producing an encephalopathy associated with behavioral changes, ataxia, memory loss, and confusion, and sometimes significant cognitive dysfunction, psychoses, dementia, and seizure activity; and (3) peripheral neuropathies, both sensory and motor.

Pulmonary Manifestations

Eosinophil infiltrates in lungs

Diffuse or focal infiltrates may be detected in any region of the lungs. These infiltrates are composed of eosinophils. Pulmonary fibrosis may result.

Pulmonary emboli

In addition, pulmonary manifestations secondary to the development of congestive heart failure may occur. Pulmonary emboli originating from thrombi in the right ventricle or secondary to intravascular pulmonary thrombi may also be found.

Ocular Manifestations

Ocular symptomatology, most commonly blurring of vision, has been frequently noted. It is thought to result from microemboli or possible focal thrombosis of small retinal blood vessels.

Rheumatologic Manifestations

Raynaud's phenomenon may occur on occasion in these patients. Myalgias and arthralgias are common. Synovial fluid eosinophilia has been reported.

Etiology

Eosinophilic leukemia

Only a small number of patients with the idiopathic hypereosinophil syndrome have eosinophilic leukemia. In those patients with eosinophilic leukemia, chromosomal abnormalities described in other acute nonlymphocytic leukemias have been detected.

Lymphomas

Sézary syndrome, T-cell lymphoblastic lymphoma and adult T-cell leukemia/lymphoma have been associated with the hypereosinophil syndrome. These lymphomas are thought to produce the eosinophilopoietic cytokines (interleukin[IL]-5, IL-3 and granulocyte-macrophage colony–stimulating factor [GM-CSF]).

IL-5 likely candidate for pathogenesis of the hypereosinophilic syndrome

In a majority of patients with the idiopathic hypereosinophilic syndrome, however, a dysregulation of T-cell function associated with IL-5 secretion appears to be involved. For example, although IL-3 and GM-CSF may have a substantial role in the proliferation of eosinophils, they also act on other marrow-derived cells. In general, the hypereosinophilic syndrome is unassociated with hyperproliferation of other marrow-derived cells. On the contrary, IL-5 is an eosinophilopoietic cytokine without evidence of other major bone marrow or B-cell stimulatory activity. Thus, overproduction of IL-5 appears to be a likely candidate for the pathogenesis of the hypereosinophilic syndrome.

The discovery in mice of the existence of two types of T helper cell responses, one (T_h1) associated with the IL-2, interferon alpha (INF-α) cytokine profile, the other (T_h2) associated with the IL-3, IL-4, and IL-5 cytokine profile, lead to the discovery of a similar compartmentalization of the T helper response in humans. In some idiopathic hypereosinophilic syndrome patients, cloned CD4-positive, CD8-negative T cells have been demonstrated to release eosinophilopoietins, especially IL-5. Furthermore, IL-5 transgenic mice, although asymptomatic and without evidence of organ damage, develop lifelong, striking eosinophilia.

Our experience with this unusual syndrome has been limited to a 75-year-old male with a T-cell lymphoma. His only cutaneous manifestations were highly pruritic, erythematous, nodular eosinophilic infiltrates in the skin.

Pathogenesis

Eosinophil capable of releasing various phlogistic cationic proteins

The eosinophil is thought to play a central role in the pathogenesis of the organ dysfunction. Various cationic proteins are present in the granules of eosinophils, including eosinophil peroxidase, eosinophil-derived neurotoxin, eosinophil cationic protein, and eosinophil major basic protein. Eosinophils are also capable of elaborating transforming growth factors alpha and beta, tumor necrosis factor alpha, IL-1α, IL-6, and IL-8 as well as the eosinophilopoietic cytokines IL-5, IL-3, and GM-CSF. The exact mechanisms whereby these cytokines produce injury is not known. One intriguing observation as noted above, is that not all patients with hypereosinophilia develop organ dysfunction.

Differential Diagnosis

Differentiate from eosinophilic pneumonia, eosinophilic gastroenteritis

The hypereosinophil syndrome must be differentiated from eosinophilic syndromes limited to isolated organs, such as eosinophilic pneumonia or eosinophilic gastroenteritis. The lack of multiplicity of organ involvement differentiates these entities from the hypereosinophilic syndrome.

Churg-Strauss vasculitis must be differentiated from the hypereosinophilic syndrome. Biopsies will demonstrate necrotizing vasculitis and asthma (two features not seen in the hypereosinophilic syndrome).

Eosinophilic fasciitis

Kimura's disease (angiolymphoid hyperplasia with eosinophilia), Wells' syndrome (eosinophilic cellulitis), eosinophilic pustular folliculitis, eosinophilic fasciitis, L-tryptophan–induced eosinophilia-myalgia syndrome are differentiated by the pathology and clinical presentation.

Angioedema and eosinophilia

Angioedema and eosinophilia can be differentiated from the idiopathic hypereosinophilic syndrome by the absence of cardiac and pulmonary involvement.

Parasitic diseases

Finally, the eosinophilia associated with parasitic or protozoan infection must be eliminated by appropriate stool cultures. Strongyloidiasis may be problematic because patients may be asymptomatic. Furthermore, steroid therapy in these patients may result in a disseminated fatal strongyloidiasis disease (hyperinfection syndrome).

Treatment

Prednisone

In hypereosinophilic patients, prednisone in a dosage of 1 mg per kg per day is usually the initial therapy in the treatment of patients with organ involvement. Approximately 70% of patients respond well or partially to prednisone therapy. It has been noted that those patients who have angioedema and urticaria or who experience a prolonged eosinopenic response following a single dose of prednisone respond well to prednisone therapy. Those hypereosinophilic patients with neurologic or cardiac disease generally have a less favorable response.

Prednisone effect in approximately two-thirds of patients

Interferon-α

Most recent studies have successfully employed INF-α. This drug has been shown to inhibit IL-5 cytokine production. The growing number of isolated case reports and small series of hypereosinophilic patients treated with this drug indicate that it has great possibilities.

Interferon-α inhibits IL-5 production

Other Drugs

Hydroxyurea has been employed to manage steroid-unresponsive hypereosinophilic patients. The drug interferes with DNA synthesis inhibiting all marrow-derived cells. Anemia and/thrombocytopenia are common, especially with chronic therapy. Vincristine, which spares the bone marrow, has been beneficial in some patients. Neurologic complications, including paresthesia, limit its usefulness. Chlorambucil and cyclosporin have been effective in hypereosinophilic patients who are resistant to other therapies.

Hydroxyurea, chlorambucil and cyclosporin are effective alternatives in prednisone-resistant cases

Annotated Bibliography

Weller PF, Bubley GJ. The idiopathic hypereosinophil syndrome. Blood 1994;83: 2759–2779.

This is an excellent review!

Hardy WR, Anderson RE. The hypereosinophil syndrome. Ann Intern Med 1968;68:1220–1229.

This original article describes the syndrome.

Chusid NJ, Dale DC, West BC, et al. The hypereosinophil syndrome: analysis of 14 cases with review of the literature. Med (Baltimore) 1975;54:1–27..

This article provides a good review of clinical manifestations.

Gleich GJ, Schroeter AL, Marcoux JP, et al. Episodic angioedema associated with eosinophilia. New Engl J Med 1984;310:1621–1626.

This article presents the rather benign variant of hypereosinophil syndrome.

Uwe-Simon H, Yousefi S, Dommann-Scherrer CC, et al. Expansion of cytokine producing CD4-CD8 T cell associated with abnormal FAS suppression and hypereosinophilia. J Exp Med 1996;183:1071–1082.

Brigaudeau C, Liozon B, Bernard P, et al. Deletion of chromosome 20q associated with hypereosinophil syndrome. Cancer Genet Cytogenet 1996;87:82–84.

Malbrain MLNG, Vandenbergh H, Zachee P. Further evidence for clonal nature of the idiopathic hypereosinophil syndrome: complete hematological and cytogenetic remission induced by interferon-α in a case with a unique chromosomal abnormality. Br J Haematol 1996;92:176–183.

These are three interesting articles indicating the diverse nature of this syndrome.

Leiferman KM. Hypereosinophil syndrome. Sem Dermatol 1995; 14:122–128.

This is a good review.

Schandene L, Del Prete GFF, Cogan E, et al. Interferon-alpha selectively inhibits the production of interleukin-5 by human CD4+ T cells. J Clin Invest 1996;97:309–315.

Brugnoni D, Airo P, Rossi G, et al. A case of hypereosinophil syndrome is associated with the expansion of CD3- CD4+ T-cell population able to secrete large amounts of interleukin-5. Blood 1996;87:1416–1422.

These two articles indicate the central role of interleukin-5.

Aractingi S, Janin A, Zini JM, et al. Specific mucosal erosions in the hypereosinophil syndrome. Arch Dermatol 1996;132:535–541.

This article provides a description of a clinical manifestation of this syndrome.

Papo T, Piette JC, Hermine O. Treatment of the hypereosinophil syndrome with interferon-α. Ann Intern Med 1995;123:155–156.

This is a good article indicating the role of interferon-α as a therapeutic agent.

Means-Markwell M, et al. Eosinophilia with abnormal T cells and elevated serum levels of interleukin-2 and interleukin-15. N Engl J Med 2000;342:1568–1571.

In this study, like other studies on the hypereosinophil syndrome, abnormal T cells were detected. In this patient, all circulating T cells expressed the activation marker CD25. They also expressed CD16, CD56, typical of natural killer cells.

Interleukin-3, interleukin-5, and granulocyte macrophage stimulating factor, the primary eosinophilopoetic cytokines were normal. However, elevated interleukin-2 and interleukin-15 were detected. It is reasoned that interleukin-2, a product of activated T cells stimulates production of interleukin-5 by T cells resulting in eosinophilia. Furthermore, the exogenous use of interleukin-2 to treat AIDS patients frequently produces eosinophilia.

Interleukin-15 may also induce production of interleukin-5 by T cells independent of interleukin-2. Furthermore the production of interleukin-5 can be blocked by monoclonal antibodies against the interleukin-5 receptor.

This article llustrates the complex cytokine interactions, which may induce eosinophilia and highlights the fact that the hypereosinophil syndrome has a heterogenous etiology.

CHAPTER 18

Atopic Dermatitis and the Hyper-IgE Syndrome

Thomas T. Provost, M.D.

In addition to the idiopathic hypereosinophilic syndrome in which a putative T helper cell (T_h2) response is thought to contribute to hypereosinophilia, T_h2 responses are thought to play a role in atopic dermatitis and the closely related hyper-IgE (immunoglobulin E) syndrome.

Atopic dermatitis and the hyper- IgE syndrome: T_h2 responses are thought to be important

The discussion on atopic dermatitis will be limited to the infectious complications and pruritus, which theoretically may be, at least in part, secondary to the T_h2, CD4 Tcell response.

Atopic Dermatitis

Atopic dermatitis is a chronic, hereditable (autosomal dominant), distinctive pruritic form of eczema commonly associated with asthma, hayfever, and cutaneous autonomic dysfunctions and affecting approximately 5% of the general population. Xerosis is also a common feature. The role, if any, of IgE in the development of eczema in atopic individuals has not been proven, although it is an area of controversy at the present time. It should be noted that approximately 80% of atopic dermatitis patients have elevated IgE levels.

Atopic dermatitis: inherited disease associated with xerosis, asthma, and hayfever

Pruritus

Pruritus is a dominant feature of atopic dermatitis. It is a clinical fact that if the pruritus in atopic dermatitis is not controlled, the dermatitis persists. Many of the cutaneous features associated with atopic dermatitis are secondary to scratching, induced by this pruritus. These features include lichenification, Dennie's sign, increased markings of the palmar surfaces, hyperpigmentation around the eyes, and the so-called "allergic nasal crease," which is the result of rubbing the tip of the nose producing a crease across the nose at the junction of the cartilage and bony portion of the nose (Figures 18–1, 18–2, and 18–3). Atopic dermatitis patients appear to respond to lower threshold pruritogenic stimuli with prolonged scratching than nonatopic dermatitis individuals (eg, wool). White line dermographism and vasoconstriction upon injection of methacholine are also distinctive (Figure 18–4).

Pruritus is a dominant clinical feature.

Dennie's sign

Many clinical features are the result of scratching and rubbing.

Elevated IgE Levels

Although elevated serum and tissue IgE levels are detected in 80% of atopic eczema individuals, 20% of atopic eczema patients have normal levels. Despite the fact that there are statements in the literature that there is a direct relationship between disease activity and the quantity of serum IgE levels, this has not been our experience. Instead, there is evidence to indicate that the IgE quantification appears to correlate with the presence or absence of allergic rhinitis.

IgE levels: 80% of patients have elevated levels
No direct relationship to cutaneous disease
May be more closely related to allergic rhinitis

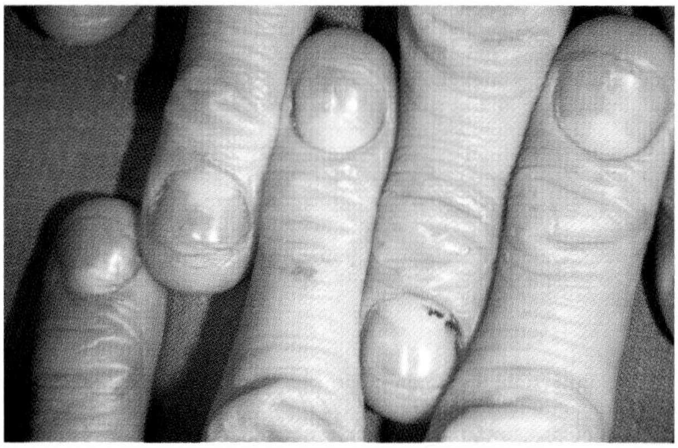

FIGURE 18–1 Buffed nails caused by repeated rubbing of the skin by an atopic dermatitis patient. (Reproduced with permission from James Rasmussen, M.D., Ann Arbor, MI)

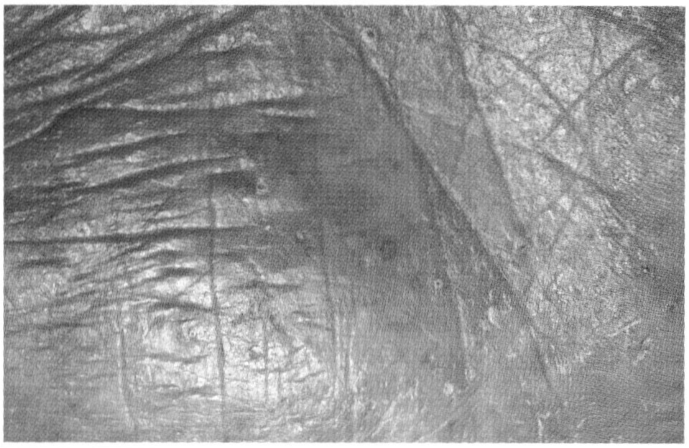

FIGURE 18–2 Increased palmar markings in an atopic dermatitis patient. (Reproduced with permission from James Rasmussen, M.D., Ann Arbor, MI)

In recent years, it has been recognized that atopic individuals have increased quantities of cutaneous lymphocyte antigen (CLA) $CD4^+$, CD45 RO^+ T cells in skin lesions and peripheral blood, which exhibit, upon stimulation, a T_h2 lymphokine profile associated with the elaboration of interleukin (IL)-4 and IL-5 in preference to interferon gamma (INF-γ) and tumor necrosis factor alpha (TNF-α) (Table 18–1). Interleukin-4 is necessary for immunoglobulin isotype switching to IgE. IL-5 promotes the maturation, differentiation, activation, and survival of eosinophils. Acute exzema demonstrates prominent IL-9 expression; chronic eczema, prominent IL-5. This cytokine profile in chronic atopic eczema resembles the IgE mediated late phase reaction.

Evidence indicates that T_h2 response of atopic dermatitis lymphocytes is inherited.

Most recent studies suggest that this lymphokine profile in atopic individuals may be inherited. For example, cloned T cells from umbilical cord blood of infants born of atopic parents demonstrate a T_h2 lymphokine profile, whereas similar experiments from infants of nonatopic individuals exhibited a T_h1 profile. Furthermore, it has been recently shown that the atopic trait (IgE reactivity) is linked to chromosome 11q. Other studies suggest linkage to chromosome 7. In addition, bone marrow derived cells of atopic infants demonstrate abnormal IgE responses.

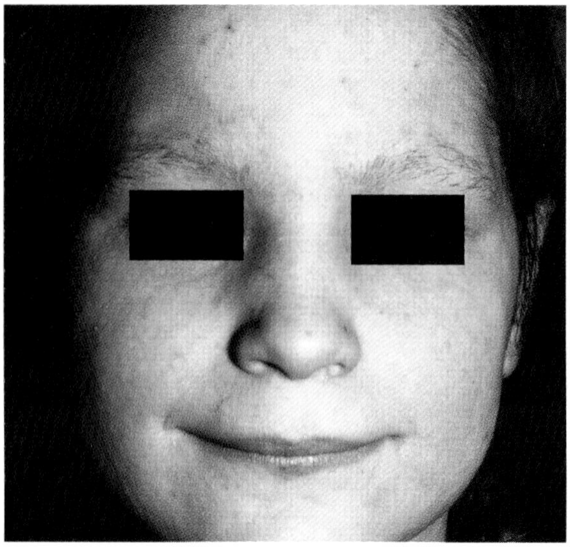

FIGURE 18–3 Increased periorbital hyperpigmentation in an atopic dermatitis patient produced by rubbing of the eyes. (Reproduced with permission from James Rasmussen, M.D., Ann Arbor, MI)

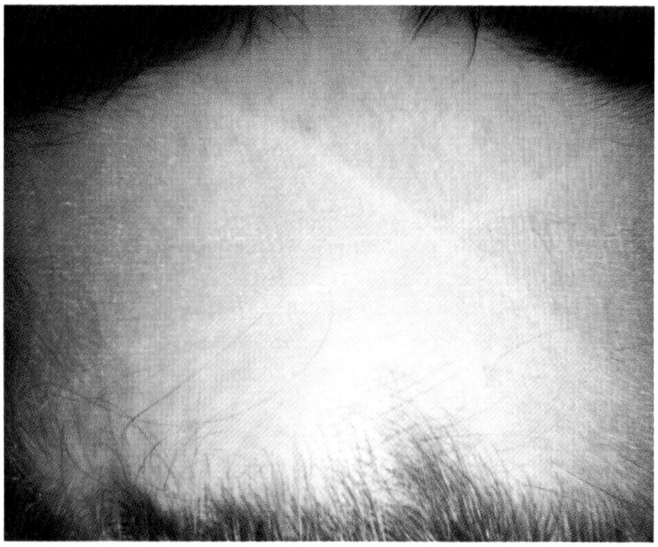

FIGURE 18–4 White line dermographism in an atopic dermatitis patient. (Reproduced with permission from James Rasmussen, M.D., Ann Arbor, MI)

TABLE 18–1 Atopic Dermatitis

Atopic individuals produce IL-4, IL-5 even in response to bacterial antigens such as purified protein derivative and streptokinase.
T cells preferentially respond to antigenic stimulation with relatively lower INF-γ and TNF-α responses (may explain relative defects in cell-mediated immune responses).
Cloned T-cells from umbilical cord blood of atopic infants born of atopic parents demonstrate a T_h2 profile.

Atopic dermatitis may result from dysregulation of T-cell response in which T_h2 cytokine profile is dominant.

The initiation of the atypical T_h2 response in atopic individuals is an area of active interest. Extensive studies have examined and continue to examine individual components of the recognition triad (antigen-presenting cell, the structure of the antigen, and the type of CD4 T cell involved (T_h0, T_h1, or T_h2). IL-4 promotes the T_h2 response. The local source of this IL-4 may be the mast cell or basophil cell. Hanifin, on the other hand, has postulated that a hyperreactive isoform of phosphodiesterase activity resulting in increased quantities of prostaglandin E_2 (PGE_2) produced by antigen-reactive cells may be responsible for shifting, or stimulating, the T_h2 response resulting in increased quantities of IgE and eosinophils.

Defective Cell-Mediated Immunity

Defective cell-mediated immunity results in decreased ability to mount primary immune response to dinitrochlorobenzene and Rhus antigens.

It long has been recognized that atopic dermatitis patients have relative defects in cell-mediated immunity, characterized by the decreased frequency of positive patch tests, the decreased frequency of positive 48-hour delayed responses to the purified protein derivative, and the decreased ability to be sensitized to dinitrochlorobenzine and to pentadecacolamine (the immunogen associated with the Rhus family). In the late 1960s and early 1970s it was demonstrated that atopic individuals have a significant relative decreased frequency of sensitization to the Rhus antigen compared to nonatopic individuals. Other studies have indicated that the quantity of CD4 lymphocytes in atopic individuals is low and the ability of lymphocytes to respond to specific and nonspecific mitogens, compared with nonatopics, is defective but not absent.

This difficulty in mounting a cell-mediated immune response could also be secondary to the relative decreased quantities of INF-γ and TNF-α that atopic CD4-positive T cells produce in response to antigenic stimulation compared with normal CD4 T cells.

Increased Susceptibility to Viral and Fungal Infections

Decreased cell-mediated immunity may predispose to topical viral and fungal infections.

This relative deficiency in cell-mediated immunity may be responsible for the suspected increased frequency of a variety of intracellular pathogens, including human papilloma virus (warts), pox virus (molluscum) and herpes simplex (eczema herpeticum; Kaposi's varicelliform eruption) (Figure 18–5). In addition, it may be responsible for the increased frequency of *Trichophyton rubrum* infections (Figures 18–6 and 18–7).

Perhaps the best illustration of the cell-mediated immune defect in these patients are the clinical studies of smallpox vaccinations in atopic eczema patients. Soon after the end of the World War II, smallpox cases were detected in New York City and London, England. A massive vaccination campaign was begun (approximately 5.5 million vaccinations were given), 185 complications were detected (disseminated vaccinia, local progressive vaccinia). In 148 of the 185 patients, a personal history of atopic dermatitis was obtained. Accidental inoculation of these individuals was very common, and approximately two-thirds of these patients, when they contracted the vaccinia, were clinically free of cutaneous disease. The most frequent and serious complications occurred in atopic dermatitis children under the age of 5 years.

This study is very important because it demonstrates an intrinsic defect in the immune system, rather than cutaneous disease (defective barrier function), was responsible for the increased frequency of vaccinia amongst atopic eczema individuals.

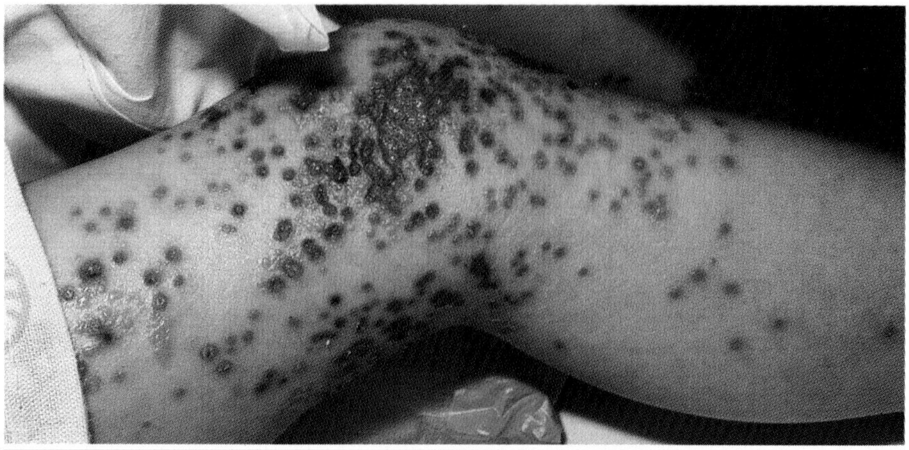

FIGURE 18-5 Eczema herpeticum in a young atopic dermatitis patient. Note groups of ulcerated vesicles over lower thigh and knee.

Defective Chemotaxis

Defective neutrophil chemotaxis is associated with recurrent cutaneous abscess formation.

In addition to defective T-cell functions in atopic individuals, atopic dermatitis patients may have transient defects in neutrophil chemotaxis as well as monocyte chemotaxis. This defect in neutrophil chemotaxis has been associated with the development of recurrent *Staphylococcus aureus* cutaneous abscess formation in patients with atopic eczema. Random migration, as well as phagocytosis, appears to be normal.

Both in vitro and in vivo studies suggest that increased quantities of histamine may be responsible for the neutrophil chemotactic defect. For example, neutrophils cultured in the presence of increased quantities of histamine demonstrate decreased migration across a Millepore membrane in response to a chemotactic gradient compared with controls. In vivo studies examining neutrophil chemotaxis in a patient developing cold urticaria (associated with increased release of histamine) demonstrated, prior to the start of the experiment, normal chemotaxis. Within a short period of time of a cold challenge, chemotactic defects were detected in neutrophils removed by venisection on the ipsilateral side of the cold challenge. Finally, with the passage of time, neutrophils removed from the contralateral side demonstrated defective chemotaxis.

The defective chemotaxis may be induced by histamine.

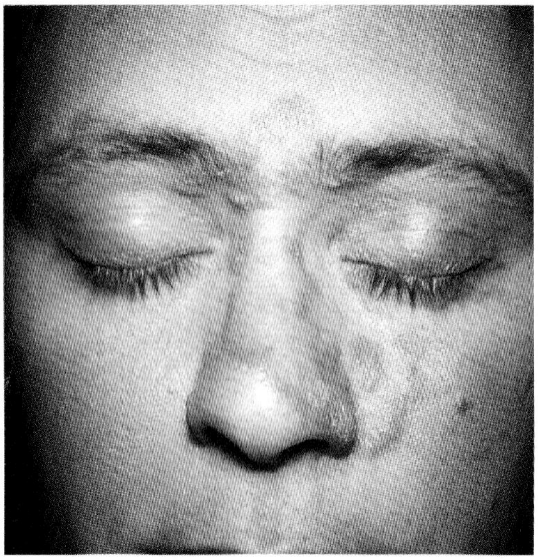

FIGURE 18-6 Widespread *T. rubrum* infection in an atopic dermatitis patient. Note involvement in the central portion of face.

Annotated Bibliography

Leung DYM. Pathogenesis of atopic dermatitis. J Allergy Clin Immunol 1999;104:S99–S108.

Excellent review!

Hanifin JM, Chan S. Biochemical and immunologic mechanisms in atopic dermatitis: new targets for emerging therapies. J Am Acad Dermatol 1999;41:72–77.

This is a very good review article of the senior author's hypothesis that the central defect in atopy is genetically defined isoforms of phosphodiesterase (PDE). Under normal circumstances, adenyl cyclase stimulatory agents such as histamine and prostaglandin E_2 *generate cAMP production which activates protein kinase A (PKA). PKA inhibits protein kinase C (PKC), reducing mediator release. It is theorized that the isoform of PDE in atopic individuals is increased, causing increased release of various mediators and cytokines.*

Hanifin believes that this theory explains the dominant nonimmunologic characteristics of atopic dermatitis as well as some of the immunologic abnormalities.

Robert C, Kupper TS. Inflammatory skin diseases, T cells and immune surveillance. N Engl J Med 1999;341:1817–1827.

This is an outstanding review article demonstrating how T cells, possessing the cell surface marker CLA, are recruited to the skin during inflammation. Nonspecific as well as specific insults to the skin generate primary cytokines (interleukin-1 and tumor necrosis factor). These cytokines, after binding to their cognate receptors on keratinocytes, activate cellular signalling pathways including nuclear factor-κB (NF-κB) pathway. Subsequent to this activation genes for E-selectin chemokines and cytokines, intracellular adhesion molecule-1, and vascular cell adhesion molecule-1 in the keratinocytes, are upregulated.

In addition, Toll-like receptors, which serve as ligands for gram-bacteria lipopolysaccharides as well as gram positive bacteria lipoteichoic acid are present in the skin. Binding to these receptors results in the translocation of NF-kB to the nucleus, and the transcriptions of genes noted above.

It has long been noted that the skin of patients with atopic eczema can easily be induced to develop a prolonged scratching to minor insults. It is theorized that this scratching traumatizes keratinocytes, inducing interleukin-1α, β, and tumor necrosis factor-α production. In addition, microbial products from Staphylococcus aureus, *which are known to be present in increased quantities on the skin of patients with atopic eczema, and perhaps the house dust mite* Dermatophagoides pteronyssinus *bind Toll-like receptors inducing upregulation of various endothelial cell adhesion molecules which recruit CLA-positive T cells into the epidermis. Furthermore, cutaneous mast cells containing specific IgE antibodies, directed against various products of* Staphylococcus aureus *upon binding with the antigen could theoretically release histamine initiating pruritus.*

Thus, the time-honored clinical adage first proposed by Jacquet over 100 years ago (atopic eczema is the itch that erupts) now has a theoretical molecular basis.

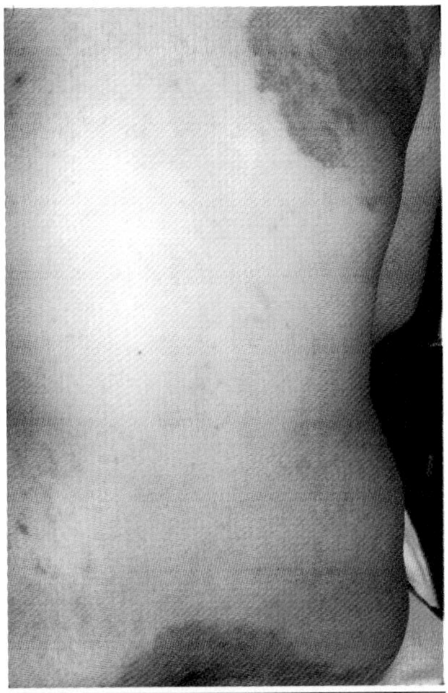

FIGURE 18-7 Same individual as in Figure 18–2 demonstrating involvement of right upper back and buttocks.

Hyper-IgE Syndrome

Perhaps the most exaggerated Th2 immunologic responses, as well as infectious complications, can be seen in patients with the hyper-IgE syndrome. These patients may or may not have a personal or family history of atopic dermatitis and have been described under the heading of Job's syndrome (recurrent *S. aureus* abscess formation in blond or redhead females) or the Buckley syndrome (recurrent *S. aureus* abscess formation occurring in nonatopic individuals with coarse facial features, and association with mucocutaneous candidiasis).

Recurrent *Staphylococcus aureus* Infections

Recurrent staphylococcal abscess formation and osteomyelitis mucocutaneous candidiasis

Subsequent studies indicate these patients may have severe atopic dermatitis with the onset in early childhood of recurrent pyogenic infections of the skin, due almost solely to *S. aureus* infections, including cutaneous abscess formation and osteomyelitis. These patients may develop staphylococcal pneumonia and also frequently demonstrate mucocutaneous candidiasis.

Elevated IgE Serum Levels

Very elevated IgE levels Directed against Staphylococcus aureus *and* *Candida albicans epitopes*

Laboratory studies have indicated that these patients have extremely high serum IgE levels (ie, 20,000–40,000 IU compared with a normal level of < 400 IU). These IgE antibodies are directed predominantly against *S. aureus* and *Candida albicans*. In addition, circulating immune complexes containing IgE combined with autoantibodies to IgE have been detected. A low-grade blood eosinophilia is common. Defects in delayed type cutaneous hypersensitivity, lymphocyte proliferation to recall antigens, deficient T-cell suppressor activity, and defects in neutrophil and monocyte chemotaxis have been described.

Other studies have demonstrated that circulating T cells from patients with a hyper-IgE syndrome produce reduced quantities of INF-γ in response to specific and nonspecific mitogen challenges (Table 18–2). These patients also have lower proportions of peripheral T cells capable of producing INF-γ and TNF-α compared with controls. In vitro studies of peripheral B cells from hyper-IgE patients indicate that both INF-γ and INF-α are capable of suppressing synthesis of IgE. In vivo experiments indicate a similar response.

Aberrant IgE Antibody Response

Aberrant or ineffective antibody response

Difficulty with *S. aureus* infections in the hyper-IgE syndrome and, to a lesser extent, atopic dermatitis is a significant clinical problem. The aberrant IgE response directed at *S. aureus* epitopes (including cytotoxins) is problematic for two theoretical reasons: (1) binding of the IgE to the *S. aureus* organism may inhibit the binding of IgG antibodies (stearic hindrance); and (2) IgE is a noncomplement-fixing immunoglobulin and, with the exception of mast cells and basophils, is not associated with receptors on phagocytic cells. Thus, antibody-mediated cytotoxic activity as well as opsonization are defective. Recent studies indicate IgE on Langerhan's cells, suggesting a possible role in antigen presentation.

In addition, from a theoretical point of view, this aberrant IgE response against the *S. aureus* bacteria releasing histamine may also, in part, play an indirect role in defective chemotaxis and the genesis of pruritus; the latter dominates the clinical picture of atopic dermatitis.

Theoretical Relationship between *Staphylococcus aureus*, IgE Response, and Histamine Release

For many years, it has been known that many patients with atopic dermatitis have heavy colonization of their skin with *S. aureus* organisms. It is conceivable that antigenic determinants elaborated by these organisms on the skin, diffuse across the epidermis and come in contact with specific IgE bound via Fcε R1 receptors on mast cells. Following an immune reaction, histamine is released by the mast cell. As noted above, histamine may induce defective neutrophil chemotaxis, and increased levels of histamine may induce pruritus.

It should be noted that in the past, dermatologists commonly employed topical systemic antistaphylococcal therapy in the treatment of atopic dermatitis. Indeed, hyposensitization using *S. aureus* extracts were practiced by both dermatologists and allergists. Although some success with this approach was reported, this type of therapy has fallen into disfavor.

Possible role of increased S. aureus skin colonization and pathogenesis of dermatitis

We recently saw lifelong atopic eczema patients whose response to antistaphylococcal therapy suggested that in some atopic dermatitis patients colonization of the skin with *S. aureus* may play a very significant etiologic role in the pruritus.

A 43-year-old Caucasian female with lifelong atopic dermatitis, characterized by widespread, highly pruritic, eczematous lesions that were poorly controlled with a variety of topical steroids and antihistamines, developed breast cancer and an IgE of 8,000 IU (normal < 400 IU). Following a lumpectomy, the patient developed a *S. aureus* abscess and was treated with dicloxacillin by her surgeon. Following a 3-week course of antibiotic therapy, the abscess disappeared and the patient noted that, for the first time in many years, she was free of pruritus and

TABLE 18–2 Hyper-IgE Syndrome: Lymphocyte Activity

Lymphocytes produce decreased quantities of INF-γ in response to specific and nonspecific nitrogen stimulation.
T cells produce markedly lower INF-γ and TNF-α.
Studies in vitro and in vivo suggest that INF-γ and INF-α are capable of inhibiting IgE production.

had no evidence for eczematous disease. Within several weeks, however, the pruritus and eczematous disease recurred, only to disappear with a short course of dicloxacillin. Over the past 18 months, daily low-dose dicloxicillin has been associated with almost a complete disappearance of her disease. Several attempts to discontinue the dicloxacillin has resulted in a reemergence of her disease within a 2- to 3-week period.

A 65-year-old judge with lifelong, highly pruritic atopic dermatitis, allergic rhinitis, and asthma and an IgE level of 5,000 IU has had the same response. Instead of dicloxacillin, erythromycin 250 mg per day has been associated with dramatic improvement in not only the patient's eczema but also his pulmonary disease. Topical steroids over the years had failed to control his dermatitis and had induced and accelerated atrophy of his skin. Antihistamines were only partially effective in suppressing the pruritus.

A similar response has been seen in additional, but not all, atopic dermatitis patients. These studies, together with the studies delineating the T_h2 CD4 T lymphocyte response suggest the need for new therapies, and reevaluation of old therapies in the treatment of patients with atopic eczema and the hyper-IgE syndrome.

Annotated Bibliography

Romangnani S. Lymphokine production by human T cells in disease states. Ann Rev Immunol 1994;12:227–257.

This is an excellent review published in 1994 by a leading investigator in this area of research. This article details the possible role of the aberrant T_h2 immunologic response in various diseases, including the hyper-IgE syndrome, atopic eczema, and acquired immune deficiency syndrome. An excellent bibliography of 178 references is supplied.

King CL, Gallin JI, Malech HL, et al. Regulation of immunoglobulin production in hyperimmunoglobulin E recurrent infections syndrome by interferon-γ. Proc Natl Acad Sci 1989;86:10085–10089.

This article demonstrates the regulatory capabilities of INF-γ in reducing both in vitro and in vivo quantity of IgE synthesized by B cells in the hyper-IgE syndrome. A similar study, using INF-α by Souillet et al. has been published (Lancet 1989;2:1384–1385).

Del Prete G, Tiri A, Maggi E, et al. Defective in vitro production of γ-interferon and tumor necrosis factor-α by circulating T cells from patients with the hyperimmunoglobulin E syndrome. J Clin Invest 1989;84:1830–1835.

This article demonstrates, by clonal analysis, that patients with the hyper-IgE syndrome produce markedly lower proportions of circulating T cells capable of producing IFN-γ and TNF-α when challenged with phytohemagglutinin than controls. These investigators postulate that this relative defect in the synthesis of IFN-γ and TNF-α may be responsible for detective cell-mediated immune response and undue susceptibility to infections seen in patients with the hyper-IgE syndrome.

Grimbacher B, Holland S, Gallin JI, et al. Hyper-IgE syndrome with recurrent infections—an autosomal dominant multisystem disorder. N Engl J Med 1999;340:692–702.

This excellent article describes immunologic abnormalities in addition to multiple skeletal abnormalities.

CHAPTER 19

Urticaria

Lisa A. Beck, M.D., Thomas T. Provost, M.D.

Common problem
Transient evanescent disease; individual lesions lasting less than 24 hours

Urticaria occurs in approximately 20% of the population at least once in their lifetime and is detected in 0.1% of all physical examinations. Urticarial lesions are typically circumscribed, raised, erythematous areas that range in size from several millimeters to 30 cm in diameter (Figures 19–1 and 19–2). These lesions are evanescent and typically last less than 24 hours. Some patients develop indurated plaques, referred to as angioedema, involving the lips, tongue, and hands. One-half of all patients referred to dermatology clinics for urticaria will have lesions of both urticaria and angioedema, whereas 40% will have urticaria only and 10% angioedema only.

Urticaria occurs in all age groups but is more common in women. Although most patients complain primarily of itch, burn, or even pain, at least 10% will also experience associated headaches, gastrointestinal symptoms, dyspnea, or even heartburn.

Acute urticaria lasting less than 6 weeks in adults
Chronic urticaria persistent for greater than 6 weeks

40% of chronic urticaria patients with persistence for 6 months have urticaria 10 years later.

Acute urticaria is defined as urticaria lasting less than 6 weeks in adults or less than 12 weeks in children. Acute urticaria is probably due to IgE (immunoglobulin)-induced or direct mast cell degranulation. Chronic urticaria, which accounts for up to 70% of all urticaria seen by dermatologists, persists for longer than 6 weeks in adults and longer than 12 weeks in children (Table 19–1). A minority of chronic cases can be characterized as physical urticaria, which is defined by the whealing stimulus (ie, heat, solar light, cold, pressure, and vibratory, aquagenic, cholinergic), but the majority of cases are idiopathic. Some patients with chronic idiopathic urticaria (CIU) will also have a physical

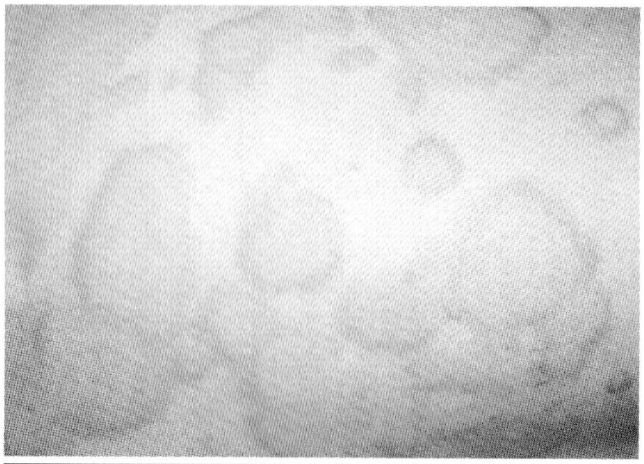

FIGURE 19–1 Large edematous plaque lesions of acute urticaria.

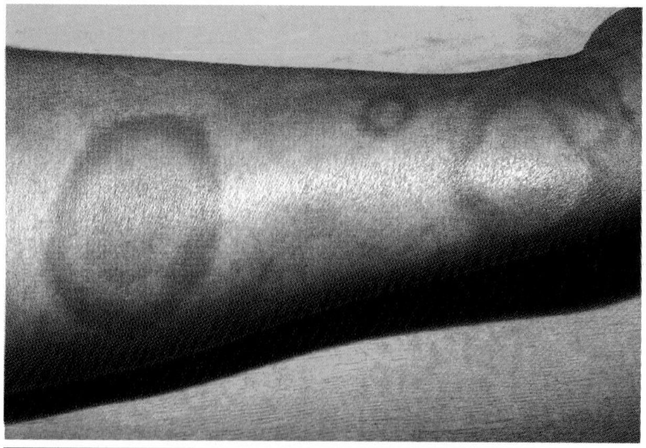

FIGURE 19–2 Large annular urticarial lesions with prominent erythema.

urticaria, and at least 40% of patients with CIU for more than 6 months persist in having urticaria 10 years later.

Chronic Urticaria

The following is a discussion of factors that may play a role in chronic urticaria.

Role of Mast Cell

Mast cell plays a critical role in urticaria.

Central role for histamine, but other mediators and inflammatory cells may be important

Many seemingly related and unrelated laboratory abnormalities have been identified in the skin and blood of patients with CIU. There is compelling evidence that the mast cell is a critical pro-inflammatory cell in the pathophysiology of urticaria. Not only are mast cell numbers increased in the skin of patients with urticaria, but also mast cell-derived mediators, such as histamine, tryptase, and PGD_2 (a prostaglandin), can be found in blisters experimentally produced over urticarial lesions. Further evidence suggests that these mast cells are more sensitive to degranulating agents, such as compound 48/80. Some investigators have suggested that neuropeptides, such as substance P, may provide the initial stimulus for mast cell degranulation. This is an appealing hypothesis that may help explain the exacerbation of urticaria with stress. Other investigators have indicated that approximately 50% of CIU patients have an autoantibody directed against either IgE or the alpha chain of the high affinity IgE receptor. Although histamine is thought to be critical for the development of urticarial lesions, it alone may not be sufficient to produce chronic lesions since intradermal injection with histamine produces a wheal and flare that lasts no longer than 6 hours. Recent evidence indicates that other pro-inflammatory mediators (ie, arachidonic acid metabolites, platelet activating factor, cytokines, neuropeptides) may also play a role.

Histology

Increased mast cells in lesional skin

Activated CD4-positive T cells present

Eosinophils may play a role in chronic urticaria.

Biopsies of urticaria demonstrate dermal edema with a relatively nonspecific, mild perivascular infiltrate. In angioedema, the edema extends into the deep dermis or subcutaneous tissue. Biopsies are essentially nondiagnostic and are usually performed to rule out an underlying vasculitis. Phenotyping of the infiltrate has revealed a fourfold increase in mononuclear cells and a 10-fold increase in mast cells, compared with control sites. Immunophenotyping has determined that the majority (> 90%) of the mononuclear cells are T lymphocytes (predominantly CD4 cells). In addition, over one-half of these cells are human leukocyte antigen (HLA)-DR–positive (indicative of activation). Another study of a smaller number of CIU patients found a mixed infiltrate consisting of monocytes/macrophages, neutrophils, T lymphocytes, and eosinophils. A retrospective review of 265 pathologic specimens found that 9% of cases showed a predominance of neutrophils and eosinophils. Although intact eosinophils are not commonly seen in CIU, staining for one of the eosinophil granule proteins, major basic protein has been found in approximately 50% of patients. This observation suggests that eosinophils had degranulated, and since eosinophil granule proteins are pro-inflammatory, they likely play a role in CIU. It has been proposed that early urticarial lesions are characterized by a predominance of neutrophils and eosinophils, and as the lesion ages, more mononuclear cells infiltrate. This same pattern can be seen in experimentally induced delayed pressure urticaria.

The cellular infiltrate in some chronic urticaria lesions resembles the IgE late phase reaction.

The late phase reaction, seen after intradermal challenge with a relevant allergen in atopic subjects, also resembles that seen in CIU. This suggests that some of the same inflammatory cascades initiated by allergen IgE interactions with consequent mast cell degranulation may also occur in chronic urticaria. Further phenotyping of the infiltrate in chronic urticaria at different time points needs to be done to understand the relative importance of various leukocyte cell types. Despite this confusion regarding the relative importance of various cell types, it seems clear that most chronic urticaria is characterized by the recruitment of

TABLE 19–1 Classification of Urticaria and Angioedema

- Presumed IgE-mediated, specific antigen sensitivity
  - Food
    - Shellfish
    - Nuts
    - Chocolate
    - Strawberries
  - Therapeutic agents
    - Penicillin
    - Sulfa
  - Airborne allergens (most commonly seen in atopic individuals)
    - Animal dander
    - Dust mite
    - Grasses
  - Arthropod
    - Hymenoptera venom
  - Allergic contact urticaria
    - Seminal vesicle fluid
    - Bacitracin
- Non-IgE mechanisms for mast cell degranulation
  - Codeine and opiates
  - Radiocontrast media
  - Curare
  - Polymyxin
  - Sea nettles
  - Food additives (eg, benzoates, tartrazine)
  - Acetysalicylic acid/nonsteroidal anti-inflammatory drugs
- Physical urticarials
  - Delayed pressure (constant pressure)
  - Dermatographism (stroking)
  - Cholinergic (generalized heat, sweating)
  - Solar (ultraviolet light)
  - Cold (local cooling or generalized cooling)
  - Localized heat (unrelated to sweating)
  - Aquagenic stimuli (water)
  - Vibratory stimuli (vibration)
- Urticarial vasculitis (immune complex–mediated) (See Chapter 12, "Vasculitis," for discussion)
  - Sjögren's syndrome
  - Systemic lupus erythematosus
  - Serum sickness
  - Hepatitis B infection
  - Idiopathic
- Angioedema
  - C_1 esterase inhibitor abnormalities (See chapter on inherited complement deficiencies for discussion)
    - Inherited
      - Type 1: deficiency of C_1 esterase inhibitor
      - Type 2: dysfunctional C_1 esterase inhibitor
- Acquired (secondary to lymphoproliferative or autoimmune disease) (See chapter on acquired complement deficiencies for discussion)
  - Normal C1 esterase inhibitor
    - Idiopathic (with or without chronic idiopathic urticaria)
    - Physical urticarias
    - Angiotensin-converting enzymes (eg, captopril, enalapril)
    - Episodic angioedema with eosinophilia

monocytes, T lymphocytes, and eosinophils, which may serve to potentiate the edema that is initially the result of mast cell histamine release.

Endothelial Adhesion Molecules

It is now known that both endothelial cells and circulating leukocytes regulate the characteristics of tissue infiltrates via the expression of adhesion molecules. Adhesion molecules can be divided into a number of distinct families based on similarities in their structure.

The immunoglobulin supergene family is so named because they possess one or more globular domains that resemble those found in immunoglobulins. Representative members of this family found on endothelium include intercellular adhesion molecule 1 (ICAM-1) and vascular cell adhesion molecule 1 (VCAM-1). ICAM-1 is constitutively expressed by endothelium, whereas VCAM-1 is not. Expression of both ICAM-1 and VCAM-1 can be upregulated by cytokines, such as interleukin-1 alpha (IL-1α), tumor necrosing factor (TNF), or lipopolysaccaride.

Another adhesion molecule family, known as the integrins, consists of two noncovalently bounded polypeptides termed alpha and beta. Subfamilies of integrins are based on a common beta chain of which there are at least eight characterized. The β_1 integrins are important in cell adhesion to extracellular matrix proteins, whereas β_2 integrins are involved in leukocyte adhesion to endothelium or to other immune cells. One exception is the β_1 integrin very late activation antigen (VLA)-4 ($\alpha_4\beta_1$), which can bind to VCAM-1 present on endothelium in addition to the extracellular matrix protein fibronectin. Two members of the β_2 integrin family, leukocyte function–associated antigen (LFA)-1, which is found on all circulating leukocytes, and Mac-1, present on all leukocytes, except lymphocytes, are capable of binding to ICAM-1 expressed by endothelium.

A more recently defined family of adhesion molecules, the selectin family share structural homology including an N-terminal lectin domain. This lectin domain allows selectins to recognize complex carbohydrate moieties, such as sialylated Lewis X antigen. All circulating cells have sLe^x on their surface, although some differences in both the quantity and type of glycoprotein have been found between eosinophils and neutrophils. These differences may ultimately be shown to confer some selectivity for cell type. One of the members of the selectin family found on endothelium is E-selectin (endothelium leukocyte adhesion molecule 1).

Possible role for E-selectins in facilitating granulocyte influx in urticaria

Only one study has investigated the kinetics of endothelial adhesion molecule expression in urticaria. Thirteen subjects with delayed pressure urticaria (DPU) underwent biopsies at various time points after pressure stimulation to clinically nonaffected skin. There was a moderate-to-marked increase in the intensity of endothelial E-selectin staining by 6 hours that was maintained for 24 hours and diminished by 48 hours. Vascular cell adhesion molecule 1 expression was only noted on perivascular cells, not on endothelium, and did not differ significantly from that seen in the six control subjects. No differences were seen in endothelial ICAM-1 staining between DPU and control subjects, either in unchallenged or pressure challenged skin. Four CIU patients without associated DPU underwent biopsies of unchallenged, spontaneous wheals and demonstrated a moderate increase in endothelial E-selectin. Interestingly, these four CIU patients also had a significant proportion of neutrophils (33%) in their tissues. These preliminary results suggest that endothelial E-selectin expression contribute to the neutrophil influx seen early in urticaria and agree with studies of perennial allergic rhinitis and intradermal endotoxin injection, which demonstrate that E-selectin expression parallels neutrophil numbers.

Although not yet studied, other adhesion molecules expressed by activated endothelial cells undoubtedly contribute to the influx of other cell types in chronic urticaria. Since infiltrating cells may contribute to the pathophysiology of urticaria, adhesion molecule antagonists may ultimately prove useful in the treatment of this disease.

Mast Cell and Basophil Inflammatory Mediators

Two types of mast cells

A variety of potent vasoactive and pro-inflammatory mediators are produced by mast cells. These include histamine, PGD_2, neutral proteases, leukotriene C_4 platelet-activating factor (LTC_4 PAF), proteoglycans, several cytokines, including TNF-α, interleukins IL-4, IL-5, IL-13, and several chemokines. Recent evidence suggests the presence of two types of human mast cells: (1) the connective tissue type found in skin, peritoneal cavity, and intestinal submucosa; and (2) the mucosal type, found primarily in the gastrointestinal mucosa and peripheral airways.

Connective tissue mast cells contain tryptase and chymase Mucosal mast cells contain tryptase.

Both mast cell types respond to IgE, but they differ in their response to various histamine-releasing agents, such as codeine, compound 48/80, and substance P. In general, connective tissue type mast cells are more responsive to these stimuli. They also differ with regard to size, lifespan, ultrastructural characteristics, mediator release, and their proteolytic enzyme composition. For example, the connective tissue mast cells contain both tryptase and chymase (M_{TC}), whereas the mucosal mast cells contain only tryptase (M_T).

As noted above, there is considerable evidence that the cutaneous mast cell plays a critical role in the development of urticaria. Mast cell numbers are increased and some appear degranulated in the lesional skin of CIU as compared with normal skin. Typically, almost 90% of mast cells in the skin are M_{TC}, but in the nonlesional skin of CIU patients, there are increased numbers of M_T or mucosal-type mast cells, suggesting selective recruitment or local production of these cells. The significance of this finding is unclear.

Histamine actions

Histamine levels are increased in areas of urticaria.

Histamine is a preformed mediator present in large amounts in all mast cells and in smaller amounts in basophils. Its primary effects are mediated through H_1 and H_2 histamine receptors, and include vasodilatation, pruritus, and vascular permeability. Histamine injected into the skin of healthy controls produces a wheal-and-flare reaction that clinically mimics an urticarial lesion, with the possible exception that it lasts approximately 2 to 3 hours as opposed to urticarial lesions, which typically last from 6 to 12 hours. Histamine injected intradermally in CIU patients demonstrates a prolonged wheal and flare, compared with healthy controls. This may be explained by impaired histamine metabolism or enhanced release of other vasoactive mediators in CIU patients. Several investigators have documented elevations in plasma histamine after induction of lesions with the appropriate physical stimuli of cold, solar light, and heat and in certain patients with cholinergic urticaria. However, patients with CIU have normal plasma histamine levels during active disease. Plasma histamine is not a very sensitive measure of mast cell degranulation in the skin, since it is metabolized rapidly. Therefore, many investigators have measured tissue fluid histamine levels and found them to be elevated over challenged sites, compared with baseline measurements in cold and solar light and delayed pressure urticaria.

In chronic urticaria, mast cells in noninvolved areas appear to have increased sensitivity to nonspecific mast cell degranulators.

The nonaffected skin of CIU patients is more sensitive to the nonspecific mast cell degranulators, codeine sulfate and compound 48/80 than that of normal control subjects. This enhanced mast cell releasability returns to control levels when CIU patients are in remission. Possible explanations for this enhanced releasibility may include increase in cutaneous mast cell density, increase in histamine content per mast cell, or priming of the mast cells for mediator release by cytokines, such as IL-3 or granulocyte-macrophage colony–stimulating factor (GM-CSF).

Finally, antihistamines, to a great extent, alleviate not only the pruritus but also some of the swelling associated with urticaria and angioedema. These findings collectively implicate the mast cell histamine–releasing factors and mast cell–derived mediators in the pathogenesis of urticarial lesions.

Role of basophils

In addition to mast cells, basophils are a main source of histamine and have also been implicated in the pathogenesis of urticaria. Greaves et al. first documented that the maximum histamine release from urticarial patients' basophils treated with anti-IgE (reverse anaphylaxis) was reduced, compared with controls. There were no differences in spontaneous and compound 48/80–induced histamine release between the two groups. Other investigators have confirmed this finding of decreased basophil histamine releasibility and have suggested that this may be due to desensitization of the basophil as a result of in vivo stimulation. These results were not thought to be due to quantitative or qualitative differences in basophil-bound IgE, or differences in serum IgE, or in mechanisms of histamine release between the two groups. Interestingly, with clinical improvement, basophil histamine release dramatically increases.

In conclusion, these findings highlight important differences between CIU and normals and suggest that IgE-mediated basophil stimulation with consequent histamine release is occurring in vivo during periods of disease activity.

Arachidonic Acid Metabolites and Platelet-Activating Factor

LTD_4 and LTE_4 act synergistically with histamine to produce vasodilatation.

Prostaglandins and leukotrienes (LTs) are metabolites of arachidonic acid that are produced by most circulating leukocytes, as well as resident tissue cells, such as mast cells and endothelial cells. Prostaglandins are the product of the cyclooxygenase pathway, and leukotrienes are 5-lipoxygenase products. M_{TC} predominantly produce PGD_2, whereas M_T and eosinophils preferentially synthesize LTC_4. Leukotriene C_4 and its metabolites, LTD_4 and LTE_4, act synergistically with histamine to increase vascular permeability and together compose what was previously known as the slow-reacting substance of anaphylaxis. LTB_4 is a potent neutrophil chemoattractant both in vitro and in vivo. Nanomolar amounts of LTB_4, LTC_4, LTD_4, and LTE_4 injected intracutaneously produce vasodilatation and edema formation lasting as long as 6 hours.

Platelet-activating factor (PAF) is a phospholipid that derived its name from its effects on platelet aggregation and activation. In addition to these effects, it is also a potent chemotactic agent, induces enzyme secretion by neutrophils, stimulates monocytes, and increases vascular permeability. It is produced by circulating leukocytes, platelets, and endothelial and mast cells.

Little is known about the role of arachidonic acid metabolites and PAF in CIU, although several studies have been published on physical urticarials. CIU patients have been shown to respond similarly to normal subjects with regard to wheal and flare sizes following intradermal injection with LTC_4, LTD_4, and LTE_4. Thus, there appears to be no enhanced end-organ sensitivity to these mediators, as opposed to the increased sensitivity to histamine-releasing agents seen in CIU.

In cold urticaria subjects, the venous blood draining challenged sites demonstrated elevated levels of LTE_4 and PGD_2. In delayed pressure urticaria, no differences in tissue levels of LTB_4, LTC_4, LTD_4, LTE_4, PGE_2, and hydroxy-eicosatetraenoic acid (HETE)-12 were noted between lesional and nonlesional skin.

The injection of PAF into the skin induced an immediate blanching, burning, and pruritus, which subsided within 60 minutes. A PAF-like lipid was isolated from the venous blood-draining, cold-challenged sites and seemed to correlate with the severity of the reaction. Therefore, by virtue of their in vivo effects and their presence in at least cold urticaria, prostaglandins, leukotrienes, and PAF may induce or enhance the development of hives.

Neuropeptides

Neuropeptides may facilitate vasodilatation and leukocyte infiltration.

Over 100 years ago, it was observed that antidromic stimulation of sensory neurons produced cutaneous vasodilatation, plasma extravasation, and leukocyte infiltration, collectively referred to as neurogenic inflammation. Studies performed over the last several decades have shown that a group of small, biologically active peptides, called neuropeptides (NPs), are critical mediators of these processes. Substance P, vasoactive intestinal protein (VIP), somatostatin neurotensin, and calcitonin gene-related peptide (CGRP) are a few of the members of this nonadrenergic, noncholinergic system. At least 17 different NPs have been co-localized with classic neurotransmitters in both the sensory afferent and autonomic efferent nerves of the skin and other organs.

Neuropeptides released from afferent C-fibers

Recently, some of these NPs have also been found in leukocytes and mast cells. Following nociceptive stimulation and pain and temperature and chemical irritants, NPs are released from cutaneous afferent C fibers. The biologic effects of NPs are varied and include effects on vascular tone, vascular permeability, cellular proliferation, immunoglobulin production, cytokine production and secretion, phagocytosis, mediator release, chemotaxis, and endothelial adhesion molecule expression. The nature of their release and their biologic effects would suggest that NPs may be involved in a wide variety of skin diseases, including infection, injury, eczema, bullous pemphigoid, wound healing, and urticaria/angioedema.

It has long been accepted that a secondary neural reflex can generate urticarial lesions (eg, cholinergic urticaria). Cholinergic urticaria develops after an increase in core body and skin temperature that often follows a warm shower or

Cholinergic urticaria can be induced by injection with methacholine chloride.

Substance P stimulates connective tissue mast cell release of histamine.

exercise and consists of 1- to 2-mm pruritic wheals. In approximately one-third of patients, these lesions can be elicited by intracutaneous injection of cholinergic agents, such as methacholine chloride.

Neuropeptides were first thought to play a role in urticaria when it was discovered that substance P and other NPs could stimulate M_{TC} to release histamine. This histamine release is thought to be a non–IgE-dependent process, as it occurs more quickly than IgE-dependent histamine release (maximum release within 10 seconds versus 10 minutes) and does not require extracellular calcium. Injection of as little as 40 pmol of substance P into human skin produces a wheal-and-flare response, upregulation of the endothelial adhesion molecule E-selectin, and a cellular infiltrate consisting of neutrophils and eosinophils.

Substance P has been shown to be critical in the development of the axon reflex or flare that is seen following injection with histamine or PAF but, interestingly, has no effect on the flare following intradermal allergen challenge.

Calcitonin gene-related peptide produces a delayed onset, long-lasting erythema in human skin that is more prominent than the erythema induced with histamine, PGE_2, PGI_2, substance P, or VIP. Like substance P, CGRP injection sites also develop a predominantly neutrophilic infiltration with upregulation of the endothelial adhesion molecule, E-selectin.

When CIU subjects were injected with VIP, they demonstrated increased sensitivity to this NP as demonstrated by an increase in mean wheal size and prolonged wheal duration, compared with healthy controls. This was not seen with compound 48/80, CGRP, substance P, and neurokinin A.

The only direct measurements of NP in urticaria have been in cold urticaria, where the blister fluid over a cold-challenged site was found to have increased levels of substance P and VIP.

These results suggest that NPs may be of primary importance in urticaria, since they are released following mast cell stimulation and may prolong and enhance the histamine-induced wheal and flare. Additionally, they may be secondarily released as a consequence of stress, heat, or physical stimulus and thereby provide one explanation for the mechanisms of exacerbations of urticaria. It is also possible that the release of NPs may, in part, explain the cellular recruitment seen in CIU. Finally, the enhanced sensitivity seen with injection of VIP would suggest that urticaria patients' skin is "primed" to respond when given the appropriate stimulus.

Cytokines

Cytokines may prime mast cells and basophils for histamine release.

Cytokines are proteins that instruct cells bearing the respective receptor to alter their proliferation, differentiation, activation, migration, or secretion of other inflammatory mediators. Initially referred to as monokines or lymphokines, named for the cells that produced them, cytokines are now known to be produced by essentially all cell types, including keratinocytes and mast cells. It is conceivable that cytokines could be responsible for many of the biologic features of CIU, such as "priming" the mast cell or basophil for histamine release, histamine release itself, endothelial activation, chemotaxis, cellular activation, and immunoglobulin production. For example, in vitro treatment of human basophils or mast cells with either IL-3 or GM-CSF "primes" them to release histamine after stimulation with cytokines that previously would not have caused release. These same cytokines and some members of the chemokine family (monocyte chemotactic proteins-1, -2, -3) have been shown at physiologic concentrations to have histamine-releasing activity. Several cytokines are capable of inducing or enhancing the expression of endothelial adhesion molecules, including IL-1, IL-4, IL-13, interferon gamma (IFN-γ) and tumor necros factor alpha (TNF-α).

Chemokines are a newly recognized class of low-molecular-weight proteins that are characterized by their potent in vitro chemotactic activity, as their name would imply (*chemo*tactic + cyto*kines*). This family is subdivided into alpha and beta subfamilies on the basis of the presence of (C-X-C) or absence of (C-C) of an intervening amino acid between the first two of four conserved cysteine residues.

Probably the best characterized C-X-C chemokine is IL-8, which, like other members of this subfamily, is known for its effects on neutrophil chemotaxis and granule release with no effects on monocytes. Not all members of this subfamily are neutrophil selective. For example, platelet factor-4 (PF4) and β-thromboglobulin (βTG) are more selective for T cells and fibroblasts. Members of the beta subfamily or C-C chemokines are known for their chemotactic activity for mononuclear cells (monocytes and lymphocytes) and, in some cases, eosinophils and possibly mast cells, although immunoglobulin production is a complex event which requires several cytokines, including IL-1, IL-4, IL-6, and interferons.

Chemokines affect neutrophil chemotaxis.

Although earlier studies documented the presence of chemotactic factors in the tissue fluid, serum, and plasma of subjects with urticaria, the first identifiable chemotactic factor was PF4, which was detected in the plasma of cold urticaria patients after challenge. Since PF4 is a platelet-specific protein that is released after platelet stimulation, it was assumed that urticaria, like asthma, resulted in platelet activation. A subsequent study by a different group of investigators found no increase in plasma PF4 or βTG levels in cold urticaria subjects followed up for up to 20 minutes after cold challenge, compared with healthy controls. The difference between these two groups may be explained by the indwelling catheter used in the first study, which can activate platelets and may have indirectly elevated levels of both PF4 and βTG.

The identification of macrophage migration inhibitory factor (MIF) on the endothelium and perivascular dendritic cells of acute and chronic urticaria patients was made using immunohistochemical techniques. Migration inhibiting factor was not found in the skin of normal control or pressure urticaria subjects. Migration inhibiting factor is thought to play a role in delayed-type hypersensitivity (DTH) reactions, as demonstrated by complete blockade of this reaction in animals pretreated with anti-MIF antibody. For this reason, several authors have suggested that chronic urticaria is similar to a DTH response.

Lastly, IL-6, but not IL-1, was significantly elevated in the blister fluid over an induced lesion of delayed pressure urticaria, compared with that measured in an unaffected site. IL-6 may be acting as a lymphocyte chemoattractant, B-cell activator, and stimulator of immunoglobulin production. Further work needs to be done to identify other cytokines produced in urticarial lesions with special attention paid to their time course (with relationship to the clinical lesion) and cell source, remembering that structural cells and mast cells may also release cytokines.

Chronic urticaria can be classified into four etiologic categories: autoimmune urticaria, the physical urticarials, urticarial vasculitis, and idiopathic urticaria.

Autoimmune Urticaria

The first indication of a histamine-releasing factor in the serum of CIU was by Grattan et al. in 1986, who documented that approximately one-half of CIU patients developed a wheal-and-flare response following injection of autologous serum that persisted for 8 hours. This response was present during disease activity but not during disease remission. The histology of this cutaneous reaction consisted of an early neutrophil predominance, followed by a more sustained infiltrate of CD4-positive T lymphocytes and eosinophils. There was a decreased mast cell density and ultrastructural evidence of mast degranulation. (This histology is similar to that seen in the IgE-mediated late-phase reaction.)

50% of chronic urticaria patients develop hives following the intracutaneous injection of their sera.

The wheal-and-flare response could be suppressed by antihistamines, and 60% of the sera elicited histamine release from basophils of healthy donors, suggesting that a histamine-releasing factor was responsible for this finding. Further characterization of this protein demonstrated that wheal formation and in vitro basophil activity were confined to ultrafiltered serum fractions >100 kD. In most cases, the histamine-releasing factor was IgG (rarely IgM) as demonstrated by affinity chromatography. This autoantibody was largely directed against IgE, as determined by

Antibodies against IgE

three different experiments: (1) basophils desensitized to anti-IgE by incubation with anti-IgE in calcium-depleted media no longer respond to CIU serum but could still respond to calcium ionophore A23187; (2) the effects of CIU sera could be significantly depleted by incubation with monoclonal IgE, but not with polyclonal IgG; and (3) lactic acid stripping of donor basophils, which selectively removes IgE, results in reduced histamine release when incubated with CIU sera.

Naturally occurring anti-IgE autoantibodies have also been detected in patients with atopic diseases and in healthy, nonallergic children and adults. Although the significance of these autoantibodies in healthy and atopic subjects have not been well studied, investigators have found that some are functional.

Antibodies against high-affinity IgE receptor

More recently, it was noted that the sera from some CIU subjects were able to induce histamine release from the low-IgE donor basophils, which were otherwise unresponsive to anti-IgE. This histamine-releasing activity could be blocked by passively sensitizing low-IgE basophils with IgE and restored by removing it, suggesting direct binding to the high-affinity IgE receptor (FcεR1). This unique autoantibody was thought to be directed against the alpha chain of the FcεR1 because the histamine-releasing activity of CIU sera could be neutralized by incubation with the soluble extracellular domain of the alpha subunit. The relative significance of this autoantibody as opposed to anti-IgE in CIU is still unclear.

Most recent studies by Kaplan's group indicate that approximately 60% of chronic urticaria patients have IgG antibodies directed against the alpha subunit of the IgE receptor on mast cells and basophils. The IgG antibodies directed against high affinity IgE receptor, activates the complement system, and C5a is most likely responsible for the mast cell degranulation. It had been previously thought that mast degranulation was a result of cross-linking the FcεR1 receptor by IgG antibody. Ten percent have IgG anti-IgE antibodies.

There is a third group whose sera demonstrate in vitro histamine release in which no autoantibodies have thus far been detected.

In addition to histamine-releasing factor autoantibodies, CIU patients have also been shown to have thyroid-associated autoantibodies. Two separate studies demonstrated that between 13 and 14% of CIU have either antimicrosomal or antithyroglobulin antibodies, but less than one-half have clinically significant thyroid disease. Both studies can be criticized for the lack of a control group, but published expected figures for the general population are < 6%.

Although this work provides some of the most promising ideas about the pathogenesis of CIU, it remains somewhat puzzling and unsatisfying. For example, there are inconsistencies regarding the percentage of CIU patients who demonstrate the wheal-and-flare reaction of their own serum. Why do some patients have anti-IgE and anti-FcεR1 alpha autoantibodies and no urticaria? Why would patients with anti-IgE or anti-FcεR1-α not develop anaphylaxis or widespread urticarial lesions? Since preliminary trials with humanized anti-IgE for allergic diseases have resulted in a decrease in total IgE, why do urticaria patients have normal or elevated total IgE levels?

Annotated Bibliography

Tong LJ, Balakrishnan G, Kochan JP, et al. Assessment of autoimmunity in patients with chronic urticaria. J Allerg Clin Immunol 1997;4:461–465.

This is an excellent article!

Greaves MW. Chronic urticaria. N Engl J Med 1995;332:1767–1772.

This is an excellent, well-written, well-referenced article on chronic urticaria by an individual who has made significant contributions in this field.

Ferrar M, Kinet JP, Kaplan AP. Comparative studies of functional and binding assays for IgG anti-Fe (epsilon) RI alpha (alpha-subunit) in chronic urticaria. J Allergy Clin Immunol 1998;101(5):672–676. Published erratum appears in J Allergy Clin Immunol 1998;102(1):156.

Grattan CE, Wallington TB, Warin RP, et al. A serological mediator in chronic idiopathic urticaria—a clinical immunological and histological evaluation. Br J Dermatol 1986;114(5):583–590.

Physical Urticarias

These are a group of urticarias in which physical factors play a role in their pathogenesis. The physical urticarias include dermographism, delayed dermographism, and pressure, solar, cold, aquagenic, and cholinergic urticaria. The physical urticarias have a tendency to be chronic.

Physical urticarias induced by physical factors

Dermographism

This is a common form of physical urticaria, characterized by a wheal-and-flare reaction to the stroking of the skin. It is commonly elicited in normal individuals. However, as many as 5% have an exaggerated response. This response (triple response of Lewis) consists of the immediate development of erythema following stroking of the skin. This is quickly followed by the development of edema and a surrounding flare, the result of axon reflex blood vessel dilatation. Passive transfer (Prausnitz-Küstner [PK] reaction) is positive in some patients, indicating that IgE may be involved in the pathogenesis. Histamine appears to be the main mediator.

Histamine appears to be mediator of dermographism

Dermographism may be associated with other forms of urticaria. It may occur spontaneously or in individuals who have had an infection or drug reaction. The patients generally report of whealing and pruritus following rubbing or inadvertent trauma to the skin.

Antihistamines are effective

Antihistamines are generally effective.

Delayed Dermographism

Delayed dermographism is characterized by whealing 4 to 6 hours after trauma. Recurrence of the lesion, which may persist for 1 to 2 days, is commonly observed.

Delayed dermographism whealing delayed 4 to 6 hours after physical challenge

Pressure Urticaria

Pressure urticaria is a form of delayed urticaria, usually occurring on the feet following walking or on the buttocks following sitting. Characteristically, the urticaria occurs 3 to 6 hours following the insult and may last several days. It may be associated with arthralgias, leukocytes, and an elevated erythrocyte sedimentation rate.

The mediators responsible are unknown, and histamine does not appear to play a central role. Evidence suggests that the kinins or prostaglandins may be involved.

Histamine probably does not play a central role.

Systemic steroids are effective in controlling these lesions.

Responds to systemic steroids

Cholinergic Urticaria

This is an unusual form of urticaria, characterized by sudden onset following exertion or emotional disturbances. Increased body heat is thought to play a primary role.

Cholinergic urticaria: increased core body temperature

The whealing is characteristically small (1 to 3 mm in diameter), generally associated with a diffuse, erythematous flare. Pruritus is prominent. Wheezing and shortness of breath may occur. Indeed, experimental exercise challenge and acetylcholine inhalation in these patients produce alterations in pulmonary function. The individual flares may persist for a few minutes to 1 hour.

Characteristic whealing
Wheezing and asthma may occur
Histamine appears to be mediator

Histamine appears to be the mediator. Characteristically, following an attack, there is a refractory phase, lasting as long as several days, in which repeat exposures to the exciting event fails to produce the urticaria.

Cholinergic urticaria may be seen in the spring of the year, with the resumption of increased exercise. With repeated conditioning, the frequency and severity of attacks generally fade.

The diagnosis may be made by stroking the skin and observing an immediate flare characterized by the development of 1- to 2-mm papules along the stroke line.

The lesions can also be frequently duplicated by intradermal injection of methacholine chloride, acetylcholine, or nicotine.

Partial relief is frequently obtained with hydroxyzine.

Annotated Bibliography

Soter NA, Wasserman S, Austen KF, et al. Release of mast cell mediators and alteration in lung function in patients with cholinergic urticaria. N Engl J Med 1980;302: 604–608.

This article demonstrates pulmonary alterations occurring in cholinergic urticaria.

Baughman RD, Jillson OF. Seven specific types of urticaria with special references to delayed persistent dermographism. Ann Allergy 1963;21:248–255.

Commens CA, Greaves MW. Test to establish the diagnosis in cholinergic urticaria. Br J Dermatol 1972;98:47–51.

Gorevic PD, Kaplan AP. The physical urticarials. Int J Dermatol 1980;19:417–435.

Greaves MW, Sneddon IB, Smith BJ, et al. Heat urticaria. Br J Dermatol 1974;90: 289–292.

Wong RC, Fairley JA, Ellis CN. Dermographism: a review. J Am Acad Dermatol 1984;11: 643–652.

Kaplan AP, Beaven MA. In vivo studies of the pathogenesis of cold urticaria, cholinergic urticaria, and vibration induced swelling. J Invest Dermatol 1976;67:327–332.

This is an excellent article!

Barlow RJ, Warburten F, Watson K, et al. Diagnosis and incidence on delayed pressure urticaria in patients with chronic urticaria. J Am Acad Dermatol 1993;29:954–958.

Gruber BL, Baeza ML, Marchese MJ, et al. Prevalence and functional role of anti IgE autoantibodies in urticarial syndromes. J Invest Dermatol 1988;90:213–217.

Dover JS, Black AK, Ward AM, et al. Delayed pressure urticaria: clinical features and laboratory investigation. The response to therapy in 44 patients. J Am Acad Dermatol 1988;18:1289–1298.

Cold Urticaria

Cold urticaria is defined as the induction of whealing on exposure to cold. On unusual occasions, it can be acquired and detected in association with cryoglobulins, cryofibrinogen, or cold agglutinins (infectious mononucleosis patients). Passive transfer has been demonstrated in some of these acquired cases.

More commonly, cold urticaria is seen as a rare, familial disease, inherited as an autosomal dominant. Histamine appears to be an important mediator, although leukotrienes may also be important.

In familial cold urticaria, the disease onset occurs very early in life and is lifelong. Whealing on exposure to cold may be associated with arthralgias, myalgias, fever, headache, and a leukocytosis.

The acquired cold urticaria may come on at any time. It may be preceded by an infection. The onset is generally sudden. At times, the symptomatology is minimal but may be alarming. Shock-like symptomatology, including loss of consciousness and even death, has been reported following bathing or swimming in cold water.

Diagnostically, patients generally respond to an ice cube challenge where the ice cube is placed on the forearm for 5 to 10 minutes. Following removal of the ice cube challenge, an urticarial wheal develops at the challenge site.

In general, the symptoms are suppressed with antihistamines. Cyproheptadine is especially effective.

Annotated Bibliography

Houser DD, Arbesman CE, Ito K, et al. Cold urticaria: immunologic studies. Am J Med 1970;49:23–33.

Kaplan AP, Garofaro J, Sigler R, et al. Idiopathic cold urticaria: in vitro demonstration of histamine release upon challenge of skin biopsies. N Engl J Med 1981;305:1074–1077.

Tindall JP, Beeker SK, Rosse WF. Familial cold urticaria: generalized reaction involving leukocytosis. Arch Intern Med 1969;124:129–134.

Solar Urticaria

This is a rare disorder induced by ultraviolet light exposure. Solar urticaria can be induced by all forms of ultraviolet light, but most commonly by ultraviolet B. In addition, visible ultraviolet light may on occasions be causative.

Some patients with solar urticaria have an allergic reaction in which circulating antibodies, presumably IgE, are causative. Passive transfer experiments (PK reaction) may be positive. Other forms of solar urticaria are not related to the presence of circulating IgE antibodies.

In the allergic form of solar urticaria, histamine, major basic protein released from tissue eosinophils, and eosinophilic and neutrophilic chemotactic factors may be important mediators.

Solar urticaria is characterized by whealing within 5 to 10 minutes of exposure to ultraviolet light sources. The patient may note an irritating burning sensation of the skin, followed by erythema and whealing. The face and back of hands are most commonly involved, but any exposed area may be the site of involvement. On rare occasions, headache, bronchospasm, and syncopal episodes have been reported.

Solar urticaria, on occasions, may be associated with polymorphic light eruption, or anti-Ro (SS-A) antibodies. In addition, it may also be associated with an erythropoietic protoporphyria.

Antihistamines (H_1, but generally not H_2) may be effective. Also, hydroxychloroquine or chloroquine may also be beneficial in some cases. Desensitization with low-dose psoralen plus ultraviolet A therapy has been reportedly effective in some patients.

Annotated Bibliography

Hasei K, Icihihashi M. Solar urticaria: determinations of action and inhibition spectra. Arch Dermatol 1982;118:346.

Hawk JLM, Eady RAJ, Challoner AVJ, et al. Elevated blood histamine levels and mast cell degranulation in solar urticaria. Br J Clin Pharmacol 1979;9:182–186.

Horio T, Fujigaki K. Augmentation spectrum in solar urticaria. J Am Acad Dermatol 1988;18:1189–1193.

Horio T, Minami K. Solar urticaria: photoallergen in a patient's serum. Arch Dermatol 1977;113:157–160.

Leiferman KM, Norris PG, Murphy GM, et al. Evidence for eosinophil degranulation with deposition of granule major basic protein in solar urticaria. J Am Acad Dermatol 1989;21:75–80.

Norris PG, Murphy GM, Hawk JLM, et al. The histological study of the evolution of solar urticaria. Arch Dermatol 1988;124:80–83.

Parrish JA, Jaenicke KF, Morison WL, et al. Solar urticaria: treatment with PUVA and mediator inhibitors. Br J Dermatol 1982;106:575–580.

Soter NA, Wasserman SI, Pathak MA. Solar urticaria: release of mast cell mediators into the circulation after experimental challenge. J Invest Dermatol 1979;72:282–285.

Aquagenic Urticaria

Aquagenic urticaria is very rare and is characterized by the development of pruritus and small 1- to 2-mm papules. It is induced by water at all temperatures. It is seen in elderly patients with xerotic skin. On unusual occasions, it is seen with myeloproliferative and myelodysplastic disorders.

Vasculitis Manifesting as Chronic Urticaria

One of the significant advancements in our understanding of chronic urticaria has been the demonstration that chronic urticaria may be a manifestation of vasculitis (see Chapter 12, "Vasculitis," for discussion).

Annotated Bibliography

Soter NA. Chronic urticaria as a manifestation of necrotizing vasculitis. N Engl J Med 1977;296:1440–1442.

Classic paper demonstrating that urticaria may be a manifestation of low-grade leukocytoclastic vasculitis.

Idiopathic Chronic Urticaria

At least 50% of chronic urticaria patients fail to demonstrate urticarial vasculitis or anti-IgE receptor antibodies or anti-IgE antibodies and are designated as idiopathic. As noted above, the pathogenesis of these lesions is presently unclear.

CHAPTER 20

Cutaneous Manifestations of Primary Immunodeficiency Diseases

Francisco A. Tausk, M.D., Jerry A. Winkelstein, M.D.

The primary immunodeficiency diseases are a heterogeneous group of disorders characterized by intrinsic defects in one or more of the components of the immune system. An increased susceptibility to infection is a prominent clinical finding in most patients with a primary immunodeficiency disease, but autoimmune diseases and a variety of inflammatory disorders can also occur. As a result of a number of different pathophysiologic processes, cutaneous disorders are relatively common in patients with primary immunodeficiency diseases. The purpose of this chapter will be to provide an overview of the primary immunodeficiency diseases, discuss the pathophysiologic mechanisms that lead to cutaneous disease in these patients, and describe the specific dermatologic diseases that can occur in each of the disorders.

Primary immunodeficiency diseases are commonly associated with:

- *increased susceptibility to infections*
- *autoimmune diseases*
- *inflammatory disorders*

Clinical Manifestations of Primary Immunodeficiency Diseases

The primary immunodeficiency diseases affect virtually every component of the immune system. There are disorders that primarily affect B-cell function (eg, X-linked agammaglobulinemia [XLA]), some that primarily affect T-cell function (eg, purine nucleoside phosphorylase deficiency), some that affect both B- and T-cell function (eg, severe combined immunodeficiency disease [SCID]), others that affect the complement system (eg, C2 deficiency), and still others that affect phagocytic cells (eg, chronic granulomatous disease [CGD]). Although most of the disorders are genetically determined and inherited as single-gene defects, the etiologies of some, such as common variable immunodeficiency (CVID) and selective IgA deficiency, remain unknown.

Primary immunodeficiency diseases include:

- *T-cell defects*
- *B-cell defects*
- *complement component deficiencies*
- *phagocyte defects*

Because many of the primary immunodeficiency diseases were first described in infants and children, these disorders were initially viewed as diseases that were characteristic of, if not largely confined to, infancy and early childhood. It has become apparent, however, that these disorders are just as common in older children and adults as they are in infancy. For example, some of the primary immunodeficiency diseases can present at any age and commonly have their initial presentation in adult life. In addition, for many of the disorders that characteristically present in infancy, there are some patients who have a mild enough clinical phenotype to allow initial clinical presentation in later childhood and adult life. And finally, with improvements in supportive care and specific therapy, most infants and children with primary immunodeficiency diseases survive into adult life.

Primary immunodeficiencies frequently detected in adulthood

Increased susceptibility to infection most common presentation

The most common clinical presentation of patients with a primary immunodeficiency disease is an increased susceptibility to infection. The infections may either be caused by common pathogens that usually cause infections in "normal" hosts or by opportunistic organisms that more commonly cause infections in "immunodeficient" hosts. Most patients present with recurrent or chronic respiratory infections, although infectious diarrhea and blood-borne infections are also seen more commonly in these patients than in normal hosts. In addition to their increased susceptibility to infection, patients with primary immunodeficiency diseases can also present with a variety of other clinical features, such as autoimmune and inflammatory disorders. In some instances, the autoimmune or inflammatory disorder may affect a single organ or tissue, such as occurs in immune thrombocytopenic purpura (ITP), autoimmune hemolytic anemia, or myasthenia gravis. In other instances, the manifestations of the autoimmune or inflammatory disorder may be more global and affect a number of different target organs or tissues, such as occurs in systemic lupus erythematosus (SLE), rheumatoid arthritis, and sarcoidosis. Finally, some patients with primary immunodeficiency diseases may not present with an increased susceptibility to infection, autoimmune diseases, or inflammatory disorders. Rather, their immunodeficiency may occur in the context of a recognized syndrome, such as Wiskott-Aldrich syndrome (WAS) or DiGeorge syndrome, and their initial clinical presentation relates to a clinical feature of the syndrome other than to the immunodeficiency per se. For example, the typical infant with DiGeorge syndrome presents initially with hypocalcemia and/or cardiac disease rather than with an increased susceptibility to infection, even though the infant may have deficient T-cell function and ultimately demonstrate an increased susceptibility to infection. Thus, although an increased susceptibility to infection remains the hallmark of a primary immunodeficiency disease, these patients may present initially with a variety of other problems.

Pathophysiology of Cutaneous Disease

There are a number of different pathophysiologic mechanisms by which cutaneous disease can arise in patients with primary immunodeficiency diseases.

Infection

T-cell defects may present with recalcitrant cutaneous infections caused by:
- *viruses*
- *fungi*

B-cell defects may present with cutaneous bacterial infections:
- *pyoderma*
- *furunculosis*
- *cellulitis*
- *abscesses*

Most of the primary immunodeficiency diseases are characterized by an increased susceptibility to infection, and in many, cutaneous infections are prominent clinical features. In general, the kind of cutaneous infection reflects to some degree the role of the deficient component in host defense. For example, patients with T-cell defects (eg, severe combined immunodeficiency, ataxia telangiectasia [AT]) can present with mucocutaneous candidiasis (*Candida albicans*), herpes simplex of the skin and mucous membranes, severe varicella-zoster infections of the skin, warts, and/or molluscum contagiosum, since T cells are important in the host's defense against fungal and viral infections. In contrast, patients with B-cell defects or phagocytic defects usually manifest cutaneous infections, such as pyoderma, furunculosis, cellulitis, or subcutaneous abscesses caused by pyogenic bacteria (eg, staphylococci and streptococci), since antibody-mediated opsonization and phagocytosis are critical in the host's defense against these kinds of bacteria. Finally, patients with complement deficiencies, particularly deficiencies of the terminal components, are unduly susceptible to systemic neisserial infections, such as meningococcemia, and thereby can develop the petechiae and/or purpura characteristic of this infection.

Autoimmune and Rheumatic Diseases

Patients with primary immunodeficiency diseases can also develop cutaneous diseases as manifestations of autoimmune or rheumatic disorders. The most common setting in which autoimmune diseases occur are in those patients who have defects in T-cell function, with or without concurrent defects in B-cell function. Paradoxically, even those patients with some degree of hypogammaglobulinemia can produce autoantibodies and develop a variety of autoimmune diseases. Some of these autoimmune diseases may have cutaneous features directly related to the autoimmune disease, such as vitiligo, discoid lupus erythematosus (DLE), or SLE. However, they may also develop cutaneous manifestations indirectly related to the autoimmune disease, such as purpura and petechiae secondary to thrombocytopenia.

Not all rheumatic diseases occur in patients with primary immunodeficiency diseases who have defects in lymphocyte function. Patients with complement deficiencies, especially those with deficiencies of C1, C4, C2, or C3, often develop a lupus-like syndrome that has prominent cutaneous manifestations (Figures 20–1 and 20–2). Although the precise pathogenic mechanism by which complement-deficient patients develop the lupus-like syndrome is unclear, current evidence suggests that it relates to the role of C3 and the components of the classic pathway that activate C3 (ie, C1, C4, and C2) in the clearance and processing of circulating immune complexes.

Female carriers of chronic granulomatous disease have increased frequency of lupus-like disease.

Patients with either the autosomal recessive or X chromosome-linked forms of chronic granulomatous disease (CGD) may also develop DLE or SLE. Interestingly, discoid lupus is also relatively common in the female carriers of the X-linked recessive form of CGD. In fact, it is more common in female carriers than it is in affected males. The pathogenic mechanism by which these lupus syndromes occur in either the patients with CGD or carrier females of the X-linked form of the disease is unknown.

Finally, in rare instances, an infection in an immunodeficient host can masquerade as a rheumatic disorder. Such is the case in XLA in which chronic enteroviral infections can cause a syndrome resembling dermatomyositis.

Angioedema

C1INH inhibitor deficiency

In one specific instance, the underlying immunodeficiency can produce angioedema of the skin and mucus membranes (Figure 20–3). A deficiency of C1 esterase inhibitor (C1INH) causes the clinical syndrome of hereditary angioedema (HAE). The exact pathogenic mechanism by which the edema is caused is unclear. C1INH not only inhibits the activation of C4 and C2 of the classic pathway by C1, but it also inhibits other serine proteases, including Hage-

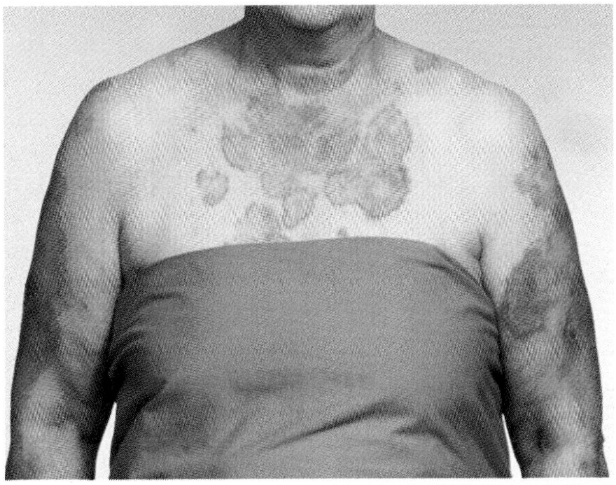

FIGURE 20–1 Widespread annular, polycyclic, erythematous lesions of subacute cutaneous lupus erythematosus in an anti-Ro (SS-A) antibody–positive homozygous C2-deficient patient. Approximately 75% of these patients are anti-Ro (SS-A) antibody positive.

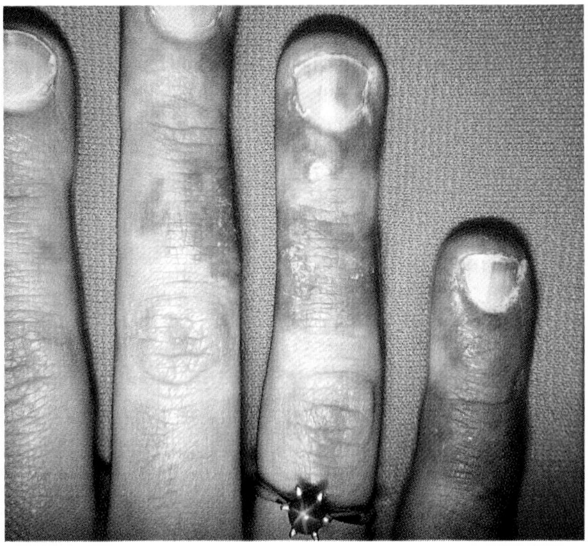

FIGURE 20–2 Photosensitive lupus lesions on hand of an anti-Ro (SS-A) antibody–positive homozygous C2-deficient patient.

man factor, plasma thromboplastin antecedent, plasma kallikrein, and the fibrinolytic enzyme plasmin. The relative contribution of these different proteases in generating the angioedema is unknown.

Miscellaneous

A variety of other cutaneous diseases occur in patients with primary immunodeficiency diseases, but in some, their pathogenesis is unclear.

Elevated IgE levels in Wiskott-Aldrich syndrome and hyper-IgE syndrome

Two of the primary immunodeficiency diseases in which IgE (immunoglobulin E) levels are high are WAS and hyper-IgE syndrome (Figure 20–4). There is no direct evidence that the elevated IgE levels are the cause of the eczema. However, at least in the case of WAS, the eczema is clearly related to the underlying immunodeficiency, since it resolves after bone marrow transplantation.

Ataxia telangiectasia:
- *cerebellar dysfunction*
- *immunodeficiency*
- *telangiectasia*

Patients with ataxia telangiectasia present with a number of clinical features, including progressive central nervous system degeneration, immunodeficiency, and telangiectasia of the bulbar conjunctiva and skin. Although the underlying molecular defect has been defined, the pathogenic mechanism responsible for these disparate clinical features, including the telangiectasia, has not been identified.

Specific Primary Immunodeficiency Diseases

There are over 80 different primary immunodeficiency diseases. The following disorders have been selected for discussion, either because cutaneous lesions occur relatively frequently or, if they occur rarely, because they are especially prominent.

X-Linked Agammaglobulinemia

X-linked agammaglobulinemia mutations in BTK gene

X-linked agammaglobulinemia (XLA) is an X-linked recessive defect in B-cell function. The disease results from mutations in *BTK*, a gene encoding an intracellular tyrosine kinase that is necessary for the maturation of pre–B cells to B cells and ultimately to immunoglobulin-producing plasma cells. Affected boys have marked hypogammaglobulinemia and a marked increased susceptibility to bacterial and systemic enteroviral infections.

Dermatomyositis-like syndrome with echovirus

All of the cutaneous manifestations of XLA relate to their increased susceptibility to infection. These patients have an increased susceptibility of the skin and underlying subcutaneous tissues to pyogenic infections, such as impetigo, cellulitis, and subcutaneous abscesses caused by staphylococci or streptococci. In

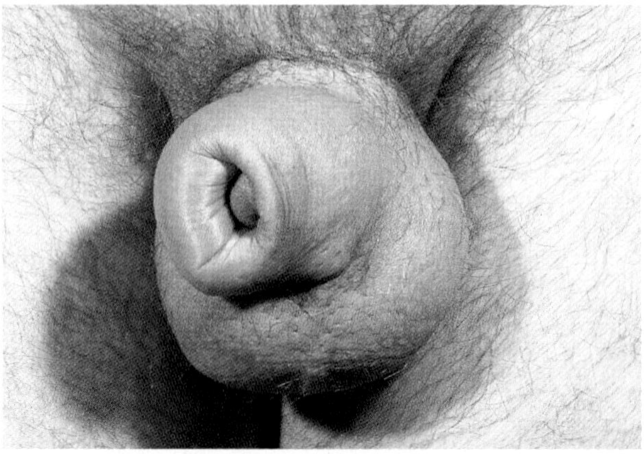

FIGURE 20–3 Severe genital edema following intercourse in a patient with hereditary angioneurotic edema.

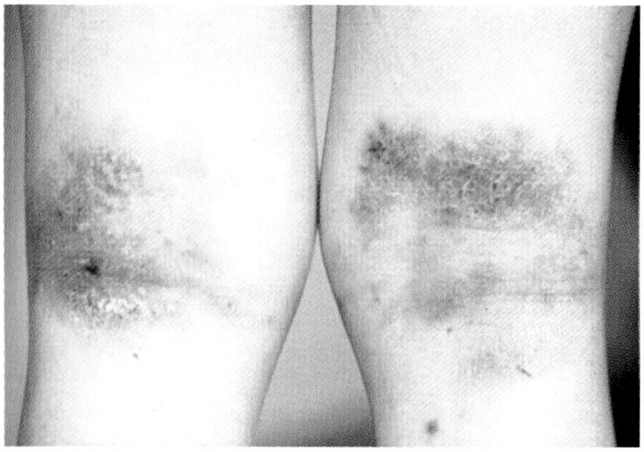

FIGURE 20–4 Popliteal eczema with petechiae in a Wiskott-Aldrich patient (Reproduced with permission from James Rasmussen, M.D., Ann Arbor, MI)

addition, they have a particular susceptibility to chronic disseminated infections with *e*nteric *c*ytopathic *h*uman *o*rphan virus (echovirus), one manifestation of which can be a syndrome resembling dermatomyositis (Figure 20–5). Patients with XLA who develop echovirus-related dermatomyositis demonstrate the typical violaceous erythema over the eyelids, extensor surfaces of joints, and occasionally the entire extensor surfaces of the limbs, accompanied by subcutaneous edema. In addition, they manifest the proximal muscle weakness, muscle pain and/or tenderness, and muscle atrophy that ultimately are part of the syndrome in children with dermatomyositis who do not have XLA.

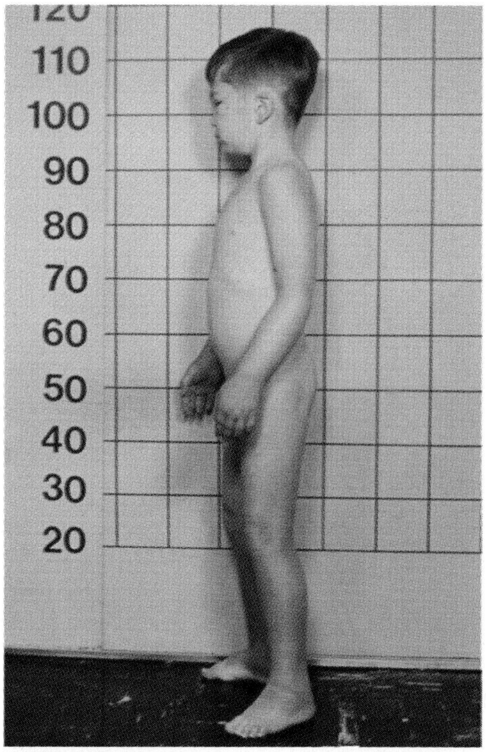

FIGURE 20–5 A 7-year-old boy with X-linked agammaglobulinemia and a dermatomyositis-like syndrome demonstrating flexion contractures of his upper and lower extremities and edema of his lower extremities.

X-linked Hyper-IgM Syndrome

The X-linked hyper-IgM syndrome is an X-linked recessive defect in the expression of a T-cell surface molecule, CD40 ligand. This cell surface molecule, when engaged with its complementary protein on the surface of B-cells, CD40, provides the signal for B cells to switch from IgM production to IgG, IgA, and IgE production. Thus, males with this disorder have normal to elevated levels of serum IgM but markedly decreased levels of IgG and IgA. In addition to its role in providing T-cell help to B cells, the interaction of CD40 on the surface of B cells and other antigen presenting cells provides a signal in the other direction, which facilitates antigen-driven T-cell responses. Because of their low levels of IgG and IgA, patients with this disorder have an increased susceptibility to infection with some of the same bacteria to which patients with XLA are susceptible. However, because of their T-cell defect, they are also susceptible to a number of viruses, fungi, and opportunistic organisms, such as *Pneumocystis carinii*.

The cutaneous diseases found in patients with the X-linked hyper-IgM syndrome are the result of increased susceptibility to infection. Like the patients with XLA, they too can have cutaneous infections, such as impetigo, cellulitis, and subcutaneous abscesses. However, because of their defect in T-cell function, they can also present with thrush and other candidal infections.

X-linked hyper-IgM syndrome: defect in expression of T-cell CD40 ligand
Lack of T-cell help to B cells to switch to IgA and IgG production

Selective IgA Deficiency

Selective IgA deficiency is a relatively common primary immunodeficiency, occurring in as many as 1 in 500 individuals. The etiology of this disorder is unknown. Affected individuals have serum levels of IgA that are less than 5 mg per dL, normal levels of IgG and IgM, and intact T-cell function—thus the designation of selective IgA deficiency. However, in spite of its designation, in some patients, there is a concurrent decrease in IgG_2 levels. Although many individuals with selective IgA deficiency have few, if any, symptoms referable to their immunodeficiency, many others have prominent clinical symptoms, such as an increased susceptibility to respiratory infections, chronic diarrhea and/or malabsorption, and a variety of autoimmune diseases.

Selective IgA deficiency:
- *common*
- *sinopulmonary infections*
- *autoimmune diseases*

The major cutaneous manifestations of selective IgA deficiency relate to its association with a variety of autoimmune diseases. Thus, patients with selective IgA deficiency may develop vitiligo or the cutaneous lesions of SLE, DLE, or juvenile rheumatoid arthritis (JRA).

Common Variable Immunodeficiency

Common variable immunodeficiency (CVID) is a relatively common primary immunodeficiency disease of unknown etiology characterized by hypogammaglobulinemia. In some patients, a variable and partial T-cell deficiency also is present. Although most patients have reduced levels of IgG, the other components of the immune system that are affected and the degree to which they are involved vary

May initially present in childhood or adulthood

from individual to individual. Because of the variable immunologic findings from patient to patient, the disorder(s) has been given the designation CVID. The initial clinical presentation can occur in either childhood or adulthood. The most common clinical symptoms relate to an increased susceptibility to infection, diarrhea and/or malabsorption, and a variety of inflammatory and autoimmune diseases.

Autoimmune diseases
Inflammatory bowel disease
Sarcoidosis

The cutaneous manifestations of CVID are varied and relate to a number of different pathogenic mechanisms. Although cutaneous infections are not as common as sinopulmonary infections in CVID, they do occur. More commonly, because these patients have a propensity to develop autoimmune diseases, such as lupus, scleroderma, or vitiligo, they can present with the cutaneous manifestations of these disorders as well. Finally, patients with CVID can develop inflammatory disorders, such as inflammatory bowel disease or sarcoidosis, and therefore, they can manifest the cutaneous lesions of these diseases.

Ataxia Telangiectasia

Mutations of ATM gene
Ataxia initial presentation

Ataxia telangiectasia is an autosomal recessive disorder characterized by progressive ataxia, ocular and cutaneous telangiectasia, immunodeficiency, and an increased incidence of malignancies. Recently, the molecular genetic basis for the disease has been identified as residing in mutations of the *ATM* gene, although the exact mechanism by which the genetic defect leads to the multisystem clinical phenotype has not been elucidated. Affected patients usually present with ataxia soon after they begin to walk and develop progressive cerebellar signs including dysarthria. The immunodeficiency is variable from patient to patient and progressive, but the most common findings are IgA deficiency, IgG_2 subclass deficiency, and lymphopenia. The patients are susceptible to recurrent infections caused by a variety of bacteria and viruses, most prominently recurrent sinopulmonary infections. Finally, there is a relatively high incidence of malignancies, most commonly leukemia and lymphoma.

Verruca vulgaris
Molluscum contagiosum

The most characteristic cutaneous manifestations of AT are the telangiectasia. Telangiectasia are most prominent on the bulbar conjunctiva (Figure 20–6) but also occur in areas of sun exposure, such as the ear and malar eminence. The telangiectasia are usually not present in the first year of birth but do develop in the majority of patients by 5 years of age. Thus, they are not available as a useful diagnostic clue either in infancy or in the preschool years. In addition to telangiectasia, patients with AT also may have chronic and severe warts (verruca vulgaris). In some patients, the warts can be so severe as to interfere with walking, an additional difficulty for these patients. Finally, molluscum contagiosum also occurs more commonly in these patients.

Wiskott-Aldrich Syndrome

Wiskott-Aldrich syndrome is an X-linked recessive disorder characterized, in its classic form, by the clinical triad of immunodeficiency, thrombocytopenia, and eczema (see Figure 20–4). However, the recent identification of the *WASP* gene has allowed more precise delineation of atypical cases, and a substantial number of patients with the disorder may have only one or two of the three clinical features. For example, the disorder X-linked thrombocytopenia is also due to mutations in the *WASP* gene. The immunodeficiency is variable from patient to patient but most commonly includes mild to moderate deficiencies in serum IgM, poor antibody responses to polysaccharide antigens, and abnormal T-cell function. As a result of their B-cell and T-cell immunodeficiencies, patients with WAS have an increased susceptibility to infection with a wide variety of microorganisms, including bacteria, viruses, and fungi. The thrombocytopenia is chronic in nature, characterized by small platelets, and may lead to life-threatening bleeding episodes into the gastrointestinal

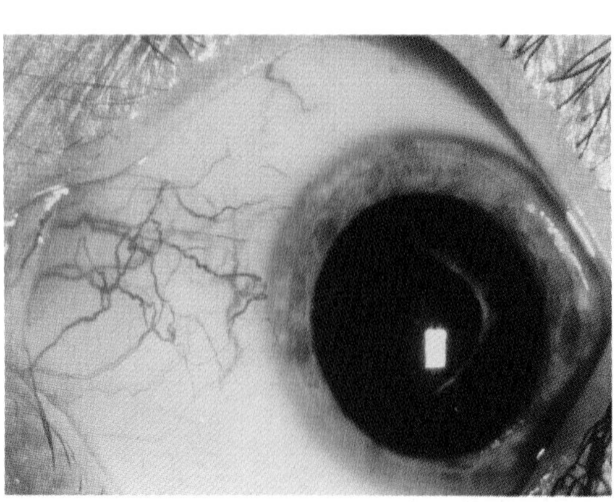

FIGURE 20–6 Ocular telangiectasia in a 12-year-old girl with ataxia telangiectasia.

tract or central nervous system. The eczema develops within the first year of life and is likely related to the immunodeficiency, since correction of the immunodeficiency by bone marrow transplantation also corrects the eczema.

The most common cutaneous manifestations of WAS are related to the thrombocytopenia and/or eczema. Petechiae, especially in eczematous lesions, and purpura are common in affected males and often are the first clinical clue to thrombocytopenia and, thus, the underlying disorder. The eczema may be difficult to treat and, on occasion, may have associated bleeding.

Severe Combined Immunodeficiency Disease

Deficiency of both B and T cells

Severe combined immunodeficiency disease describes a clinical syndrome in which there is a severe deficiency of both B-cell and T-cell functions. There are a variety of molecular genetic causes of SCID. The X-linked recessive form is caused by mutations in the gene for the gamma chain of the T-cell antigen receptor. The autosomal recessive forms of the disease are caused by deficiencies of an enzyme of the purine salvage pathway in T cells (adenosine deaminase [ADA] deficiency), intracellular signaling molecules (ZAP-70 or JAK-3) or nucleic acid recombinases (RAG-1, 2). Although there are some differences in the immunologic characteristics between the different forms of SCID, all the forms have significant deficiencies in T-cell number and function and significant hypogammaglobulinemia. Most patients present clinically within the first year of life and many before 6 months of life, reflecting the severe nature of their immunodeficiency. Patients usually demonstrate a marked increased susceptibility to infections, the most common being pneumonia, otitis, infectious diarrhea, bacteremia, and meningitis. A wide variety of microorganisms are responsible for their infections, including common pathogens, such as the pneumococcus, *Haemophilus influenzae* type B, the herpesviruses, influenza virus, and *Candida* spp. However, they also have problems with opportunistic infections, such as *P. carinii* and a variety of fungi. Definitive treatment depends on bone marrow transplantation from either a human leukocyte antigen (HLA)–identical sibling, an HLA-matched but unrelated donor or an HLA-haploidentical parent. In addition, in ADA deficiency, enzyme replacement therapy and/or gene therapy have also proven effective.

Adenosine deaminase deficiency

Treatment: bone marrow transplantation

Graft-versus-host disease

The cutaneous manifestations of SCID are protean. Many of the cutaneous manifestations are direct consequences of infections. For example, candidal infections of the mouth or skin, specifically thrush and monilial diaper dermatitis, are especially common in SCID patients. Similarly, cutaneous infections with herpesviruses, such as varicella-zoster, can be life threatening. In fact, in the era of routine vaccinia virus immunization, gangrenous vaccinia cutaneous infections and disseminated vaccinia infections were often prominent clinical presentations of SCID (Figure 20–7). In addition to these dramatic cutaneous infections, other more common infections, such as impetigo, cellulitis, and subcutaneous abscesses, can occur as well. Finally, because of their T-cell deficiency, these patients are unable to reject the transplanted lymphoid tissue and, therefore, are at risk to develop graft-versus-host disease. This might occur naturally from their mother before or during delivery or as a consequence of a whole blood or red cell transfusion or a bone marrow transplantation to treat the disorder. Thus, these patients are prone to develop graft-versus-host disease and the cutaneous manifestations of that phenomenon.

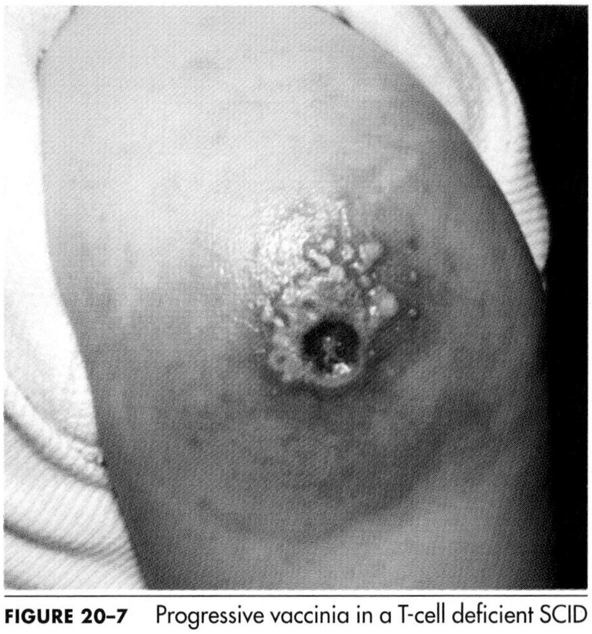

FIGURE 20–7 Progressive vaccinia in a T-cell deficient SCID patient.

Hyper-IgE Syndrome

The hyper-IgE syndrome is a primary immunodeficiency disease of unknown etiology. In its classic form, the disorder is characterized by markedly elevated serum IgE levels (from which it derives its name); marked eosinophilia, which may approach 50%; poor primary and secondary antibody responses; and depressed T-cell function in vitro and in vivo (eg, cutaneous delayed hypersensitivity anergy). Its clinical features include an increased susceptibility to cutaneous, pulmonary, and upper respiratory infections, as well as severe atopic dermatitis (Figure 20–8). In addition, many patients will have additional nonimmunologic features, including delayed shedding of primary teeth, hyperextensible joints, and scoliosis. Both the cutaneous and pulmonary infections are most commonly caused by *Staphylococcus aureus*; but *Candida* spp., *H. influenzae*, pneumococci, and *Aspergillus* spp. have also been seen. Recent evidence would suggest that it is a genetically determined disorder with variable penetrance and expressivity, leading to different clinical phenotypes and different degrees of clinical severity, even within the same family.

Eczema

Staphylococcus aureus cutaneous infections

The cutaneous features can be the most prominent clinical manifestations of the disorder. Nearly all patients present with pruritic dermatitis at the time of diagnosis. The cutaneous lesions resemble eczema with lichenified skin. Cutaneous infections are also quite prominent and occur in virtually all patients and include impetigo, furunculosis and cellulitis, all of which are usually caused by *S. aureus*. For further discussion, see Chapter 18, "Atopic Dermatitis and the Hyper-IgE Syndrome."

Chronic Mucocutaneous Candidiasis

Various defects in T-cell immunity

Chronic mucocutaneous candidiasis is a clinical disorder characterized by chronic candidal infections of mucous membranes and the skin and nails. In some patients, the disorder occurs as part of a well-recognized, underlying immunodeficiency disease, such as SCID, whereas in other patients the underlying immunodeficiency is less well defined and not clearly a manifestation of a defined primary immunodeficiency disease. Most patients in the latter category have deficiencies in T-cell number and/or function of unknown etiology. However, in some patients, the only demonstrable immunologic defect is to *Candida* spp., characterized by absence of cutaneous delayed hypersensitivity to candidal antigen in vivo and markedly reduced, if not absent, T-cell proliferative responses to candidal antigen in vitro. Although the name given to this immunodeficiency disease implies a limited clinical spectrum, many patients have associated autoimmune diseases and endocrinopathy. Thus, many of the patients will have hypothyroidism, Addison's disease, hypoparathyroidism, autoimmune hemolytic anemia, and/or ITP in addition to their mucocutaneous candidal infections. Similarly, their increased susceptibility to infection may not be limited to candidal infections. Many patients also have an increased susceptibility to a wide variety of bacterial, viral, and other fungal infections, such as herpesviruses, histoplasmosis, and atypical mycobacteria, suggesting a more global defect in T-cell function.

Their candidal infections of the mucous membranes, skin and nails are dramatic and most often involve the oral mucosa, esophagus, and nail beds (Figures 20–9A to 20–12). They are chronic in nature, and although they respond to systemic antifungal therapy, they usually recur in a matter of weeks after therapy has been discontinued.

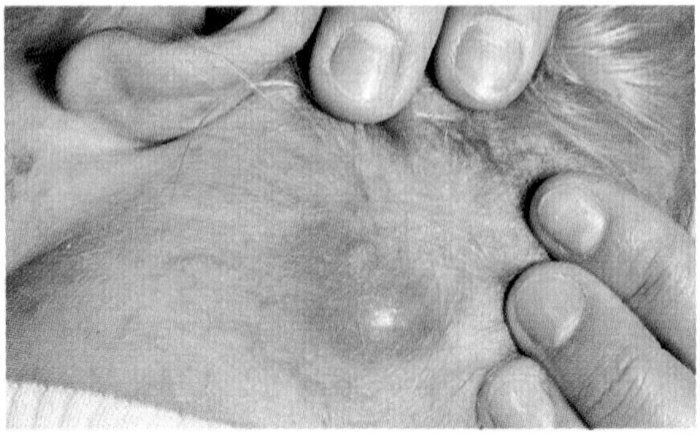

FIGURE 20–8 *Staphylococcus aureus* skin infection in a hyper-IgE syndrome patient.

Chronic Granulomatous Disease

Chronic granulomatous disease (CGD) is characterized by a relative inability of the patient's phagocytic cells to kill certain bacteria and fungi after ingesting them. The underlying defect is an inability of their phagocytic cells to reduce molecular oxygen and create the reactive oxygen metabolites that are needed for efficient intracellular microbicidal activity. Their increased susceptibility to infection is limited to a specific class of microorganisms. Bacteria and fungi that

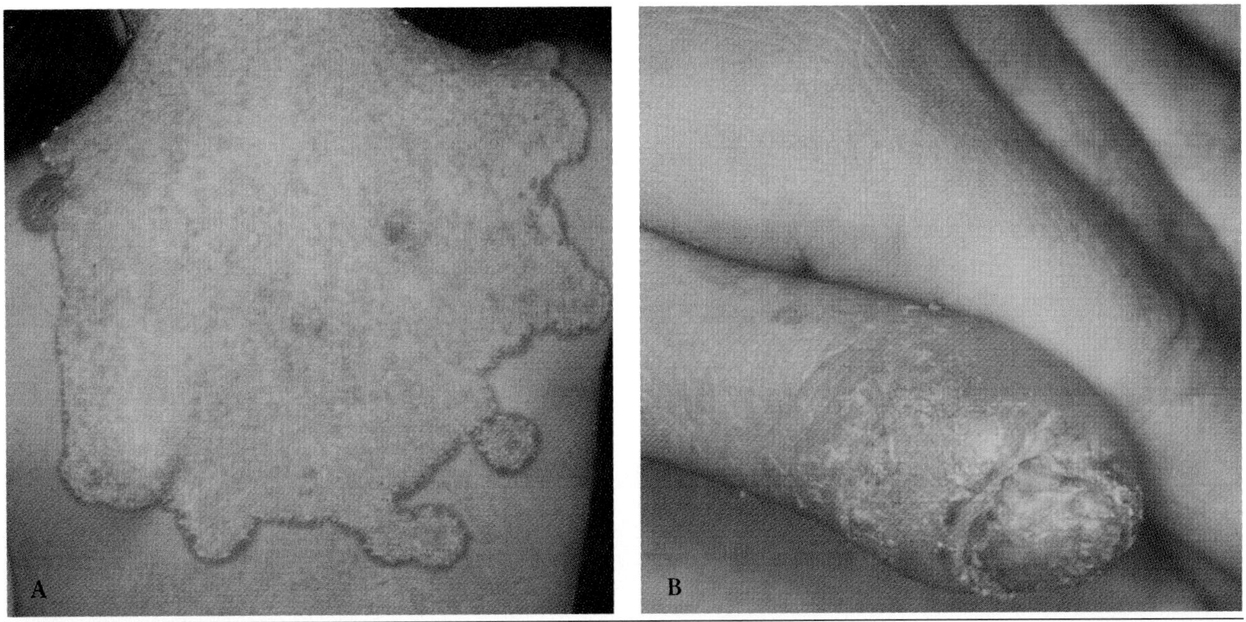

FIGURE 20–9A AND 20–9B Cutaneous candidal lesions (*A*) and nail candidal lesions (*B*) in an 8-year-old girl with chronic mucocutaneous candidiasis.

are catalase positive and do not themselves have a net production of reduced oxygen metabolites, such as hydrogen peroxide, are not killed efficiently by the phagocytic cells of patients with CGD and are responsible for the overwhelming majority of serious infections in these patients. In contrast, microorganisms that are catalase negative and do have a net production of hydrogen peroxide supply the missing reactive oxygen metabolites when they are ingested and correct the metabolic defect, thereby contributing to their own death; thus, they are infrequent causes of infection in these patients. Although there are a number of different metabolic defects that can cause CGD, they all affect one or another component of the NADPH oxidase of the phagocytic cell. The most common form of the disease is due to an X-linked recessive defect in gp91-phox, an integral membrane protein of the NADPH oxidase. At least three other forms of the disease are due to autosomal recessive defects in other components of the oxidase, p22-phox, p47-phox, and p67-phox, each of which are encoded on different autosomal chromosomes. Their most prominent clinical presentation is an increased susceptibility to infection characterized by recurrent pneumonias, pul-

Catalase-positive organisms resistant to killing by phagocytic cells from CGD patients

Catalase-negative organisms are killed by phagocytic cells from CGD patients.

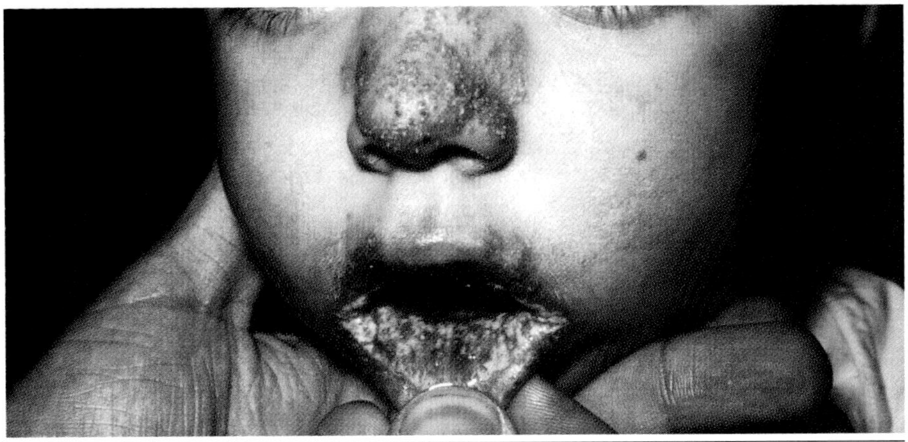

FIGURE 20–10 Granulomatous *C. albicans* infection involving nose and mouth in a child with a severe T-cell deficiency. Patient later succumbed to varicella pneumonia.

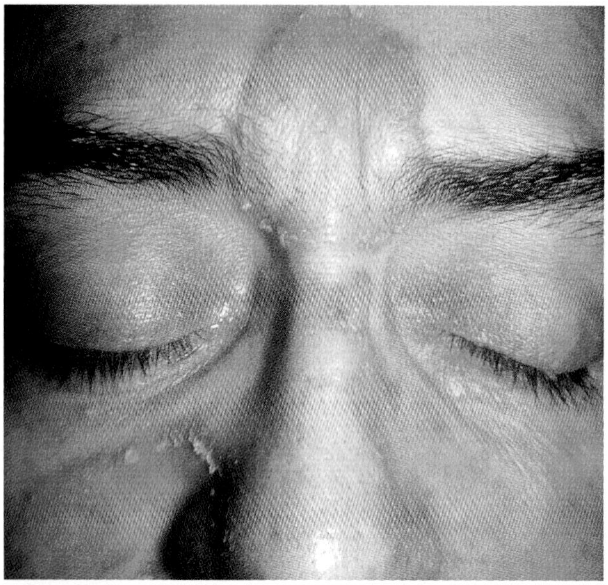

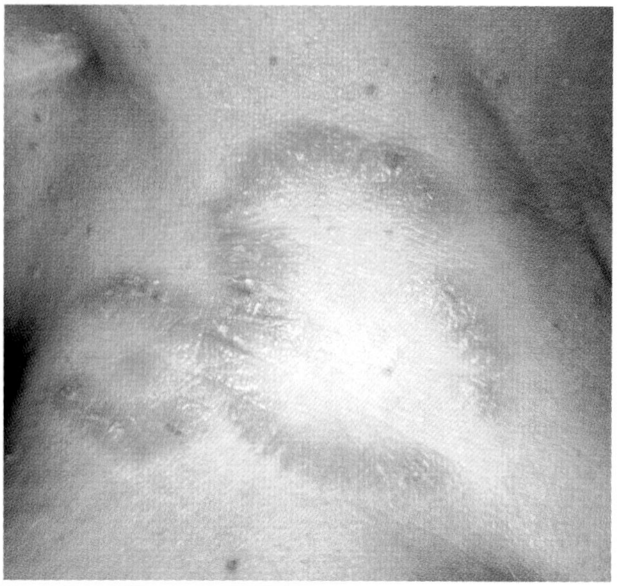

FIGURE 20–11 AND 20–12 Cutaneous *C. albicans* infections of face and shoulder in a T-cell deficient patient with a thymoma. (Reproduced with permission from Richard Baughman, M.D., Hanover, NH)

monary and visceral abscesses, osteomyelitis, and sepsis. In addition to their increased susceptibility to infection, patients with CGD also are prone to develop a variety of inflammatory and/or rheumatic diseases, such as inflammatory bowel disease and a lupus-like syndrome.

Suppurative adenitis

Lupus common in female carriers of X-linked form of disorder

The cutaneous manifestations of CGD primarily relate to patients' increased susceptibility to infection and include a relatively high prevalence of subcutaneous abscesses, cellulitis, and suppurative adenitis. In addition, on rare occasions, the patients may develop a lupus-like syndrome that has characteristic features of DLE. Interestingly, although the patients themselves may develop a lupus syndrome with its accompanying cutaneous manifestations, lupus is much more common among the female carriers of the X-linked recessive form of the disorder, the basis of which is unknown.

Leukocyte Adhesion Deficiency

Defective beta subunit of CD18

Neutrophilia

Leukocyte adhesion defect (LAD) is an autosomal recessive disorder in which the common beta subunit (CD18) of the leukocyte-specific heterodimers CD11a/CD18 (LFA-1), CD11b/CD18 (CR3), and CD11c/CD18 (p150,95) is defective. This leads to inadequate expression of the heterodimer on the leukocyte surface and a resultant defect in the ability of the cells to adhere to the endothelium, epithelium, and target cells. As a result, mobile phagocytic cells are unable to adhere to the vascular endothelium, extravasate from the vascular space, move toward chemotactic stimuli, or accumulate at sites of infection. Neutrophilia is usually present, even when the patient is not infected (> 15,000/ mm^3). This is due to the fact that the cells are unable to adhere to the vascular endothelium and marginate, thereby enriching the number of neutrophils in the circulation. Patients with LAD have a marked increased susceptibility to infection. Their infections include surface infections of the skin, mucous membranes, and/or intestinal tract. In addition, pneumonia, sinusitis, otitis, deep abscesses (especially perirectal), and septicemia are not infrequent. Later in childhood, gingivitis and peridontitis are common. The most common organisms isolated are staphylococci, *Pseudomonas* spp., *Enterobacter* spp., and *Candida* spp.

Cutaneous infections are relatively common in patients with LAD. The infections may appear early as superficial ulcers with sharply demarcated borders and progress to necrotic lesions (Figure 20–13). Cellulitis may also occur. The lesions are characterized by a relative paucity of pus-producing cells due to the lack of accumulation of mobile phagocytic cells at the site of infection.

Hereditary Angioedema

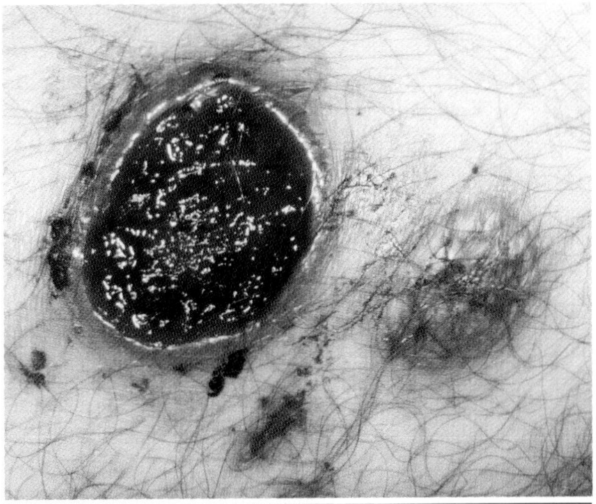

FIGURE 20–13 Infected skin lesion in a 16-year-old patient with leukocyte adhesion syndrome.

A genetically determined deficiency of an inhibitor of the first component of complement, the C1 esterase inhibitor (C1INH), is responsible for the clinical disorder HAE. C1INH deficiency is inherited in an autosomal dominant fashion. There are at least two forms of C1INH deficiency. In the most common form (type I), which accounts for about 85% of patients, the serum of affected individuals is deficient in both C1INH protein (5 to 30% of normal) and C1INH activity. In the less common form (type II), a dysfunctional protein is present in normal or elevated concentrations, but its functional activity is markedly reduced. The pathophysiologic mechanisms by which the absence of C1INH activity leads to the angioedema characteristic of the disorder are still incompletely understood. Neither the mediators responsible for producing the edema nor the mechanisms initiating their production have been clearly identified, although evidence implicates both the complement system and the kinin system in the pathogenesis of the edema. The clinical symptoms of HAE are the result of submucosal or subcutaneous edema. The lesions are characterized by noninflammatory edema associated with capillary and venule dilatation. The three most prominent areas of involvement are the skin, respiratory tract, and gastrointestinal tract.

Noninflammatory edema

Laryngeal edema

Gastrointestinal symptoms

Attacks involving the upper respiratory tract represent a serious threat to the patient with HAE. Pharyngeal edema occurs at least once in nearly two-thirds of the patients. The patients may initially experience a tightness in the throat, and swelling of the tongue, buccal mucosa, and oropharynx follows. In some instances, laryngeal edema, accompanied by hoarseness and stridor, progresses to respiratory obstruction and represents a life-threatening emergency. The gastrointestinal tract can also be affected by HAE. Symptoms are secondary to edema of the bowel wall and may include anorexia, dull aching of the abdomen, vomiting, and crampy abdominal pain. Abdominal symptoms can occur in the absence of concurrent cutaneous or pharyngeal involvement. The onset of symptoms referable to HAE occurs in more than half the patients before adolescence, but in some patients, symptoms do not occur until adulthood. Even though trauma, anxiety, and stress are frequently cited as events that initiate attacks, more than half the patients cannot clearly identify an event that initiated an attack. Dental extractions and tonsillectomy can initiate edema of the upper airway, and cutaneous edema may follow trauma to an extremity.

Onset generally before adolescence but may be delayed until adulthood

Precipitated by minor trauma

Attacks involving the skin are very common in patients with HAE. They may involve an extremity, the face, or genitalia (see Figure 20–3). The edema may vary in size from a few centimeters to involvement of a whole extremity. The lesions are pale rather than red, usually not warm, and characteristically nonpruritic. There may be a feeling of tightness in the skin caused by accumulation of subcutaneous fluid. Attacks usually progress for 1 to 2 days and resolve over an additional 2 to 3 days.

Deficiencies of C3 and Components Which Activate C3

Cleavage products of the third component of complement (C3) are responsible for generating complement-mediated serum opsonizing activity (C3b) and anaphylatoxic activity (C3a). They also play an important role in the clearance and processing of soluble immune complexes and in the generation of a normal humoral immune response. However, in order to subserve its biologic functions, C3 must first be activated by cleavage via the classic and/or alternative pathways. Therefore, genetically determined deficiencies of C3, or the components of the classic pathway (C1q, C1r/s, C4, and C2) or the alternative pathway (factor H, factor I, and factor P) necessary for its activation, share certain clinical fea-

Increased frequency of infections by encapsulated pyogenic bacteria

tures. Patients with deficiencies of C3 or one of its activating components demonstrate both an increased susceptibility to infection and an increased propensity to develop rheumatic disorders. Blood-borne infections, such as bacteremia/sepsis, meningitis, and osteomyelitis, are very common, although these patients may also be susceptible to recurrent respiratory tract infections, such as pneumonia. Their infections are most commonly caused by encapsulated pyogenic bacteria, such as the pneumococcal, streptococcal, meningococcal, and *H. influenzae,* organisms for which C3b-dependent opsonization plays a critical role in host defense. These patients can also develop a variety of rheumatic disorders, such as SLE and DLE, anaphylactoid purpura, and membranoproliferative glomerulonephritis.

Their dermatologic manifestations most commonly reflect the underlying rheumatic condition. For example, the cutaneous lesions of SLE or DLE can be quite prominent in patients with C1q, C4, C2, or C3 deficiency (Figure 20–14) (see also Figures 20–1 and 20–2). In fact, the cutaneous lesions may be the most prominent of the clinical signs of lupus in these patients; visceral and central nervous system involvement occurs less commonly than in patients with lupus who do not have inherited complement deficiencies. Recurrent anaphylactoid purpura has also been described in patients with C2 deficiency. Finally, since patients with deficiencies of C3, or one of the components responsible for activating C3, are susceptible to sepsis caused by *Meningococcus* and *Pneumococcus,* the petechiae and purpura that may accompany these blood-borne infections may also occur.

Deficiencies of Terminal Components of Complement

The terminal complement components, C5, C6, C7, C8, and C9, assemble after activation of the complement system to form a multimolecular complex termed the membrane attack complex. The membrane attack complex is responsible for the cytolytic actions of complement, including bactericidal and bacteriolytic activities. Patients with genetically determined deficiencies of one of the terminal components are uniquely susceptible to blood-borne neisserial infections, such as meningococcal sepsis, meningitis, and extragenital gonococcal infections.

The dermatologic manifestations of deficiencies of one of the terminal components are directly related to their susceptibility to systemic neisserial infections and include the petechiae and purpura that accompany these infections (Figure 20–15).

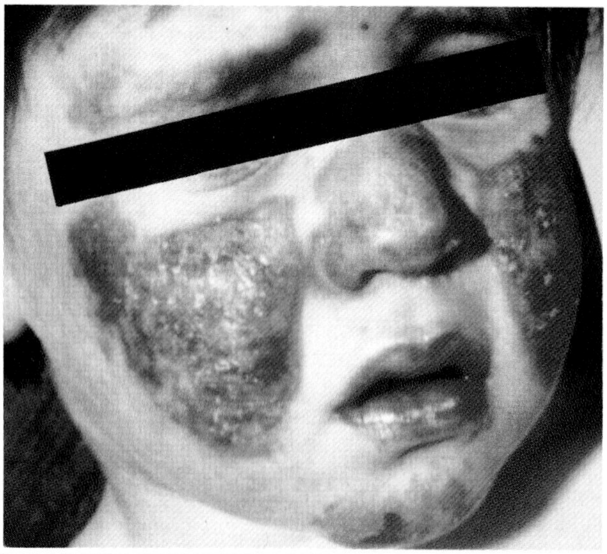

FIGURE 20–14 Cutaneous lupus lesions in a 4-year-old boy who is homozygous C4 deficient. Approximately 50% of these patients are anti-Ro (SS-A) antibody positive.

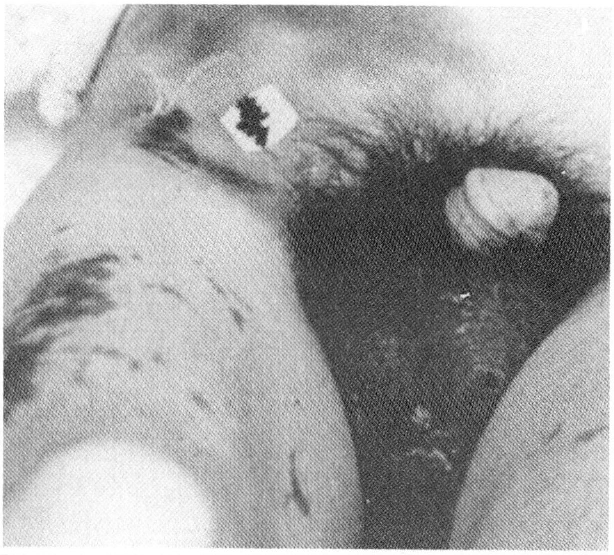

FIGURE 20–15 Purpura fulminans in an adult with homozygous C8 deficiency and meningococcal sepsis.

Annotated Bibliography

Buckley RH, Schiff RI, Schiff SE, et al. Human severe combined immunodeficiency disease: genetic, phenotypic, and functional diversity in one hundred and eight infants. J Pediatr 1997;130:378–387.

Curnutte JT. Chronic granulomatous disease: the solving of a clinical riddle at the molecular level. Clin Immunol Immunopathol 1993;67:S2–S15.

Grimbacher B, Holland SM, Gallin JI, et al. Hyper IgE syndrome with recurrent infections—an autosomal dominant multisystem disorder. N Engl J Med 1999;340:692–701.

Lederman HM, Winkelstein JA. X-linked agammaglobulinemia: an analysis of 96 patients. Medicine 1985;64:145–157.

Levy J, Espanol-Boren T, Thomas C, et al. Clinical spectrum of X-linked hyper-IgM syndrome. J Pediatr 1997;131:47–54.

Report of a WHO Scientific Group. Primary immunodeficiency diseases. Clin Exp Immunol 1997;109:S28.

Saurat JH, Woodley D, Helfer N. Cutaneous symptoms in primary immunodeficiencies. Curr Probl Dermatol 1985;13:50–91.

Sneller MC, Strober W, Eisentein E, et al. New insights into common variable immunodeficiency. Ann Intern Med 1993;119:720–730.

Sullivan KE, Mullen CA, Blaese RM, et al. A multi-institutional survey of the Wiskott-Aldrich Syndrome. J Pediatr 1994;125:876–885.

Sullivan K, Winkelstein JA. Genetically determined deficiencies of the complement system. In: Ochs HD, Smith CIE, Puck J, eds. Primary Immunodeficiency Diseases: A Molecular and Genetic Approach. Oxford, United Kingdom: Oxford University Press, 1998.

These are the ten latest articles discussing these entities. Each article provides an excellent bibliography.

Delves PJ, Roitt IM. Advances in immunology. The immune system. N Engl J Med 2000;343:37–49;108–117.

Excellent up-to-date review of the immune system.

CHAPTER 21

Nonimmunologic and Reactive Arthritides

Thomas T. Provost, M.D., John A. Flynn, M.D.

Psoriatic Arthritis

For the past 30 to 35 years, the inflammatory arthropathy associated with psoriasis has been recognized as a distinct entity. Prior to that time, psoriatic arthritis was considered to be part of rheumatoid arthritis. Although the arthritis associated with psoriasis is generally rheumatoid factor-negative, it must be remembered that as many as 10 to 15% of the general population, especially over the age of 60, are rheumatoid factor-positive. Furthermore, since most studies indicate an incidence between 0.5% and 1% of rheumatoid arthritis and an incidence of 1 to 3% of psoriasis in the general population, the association of psoriasis with rheumatoid arthritis may sometimes be fortuitous. In addition, osteoarthritis, which is also common, may also occur in patients with psoriasis.

Approximately 5% frequency of arthritis in psoriatic patients

In general, approximately 5% of psoriatic patients have psoriatic arthritis. Psoriatic arthritis generally occurs in the third to fourth decade of life and has an equal sex distribution. The arthritis commonly involves the distal interphalangeal joints, but may affect any peripheral joint (both small and large), producing an inflammatory, destructive, oligoarthropathy associated with pain and stiffness. The stiffness generally improves with activity. Axial skeletal and sacroiliac joint involvement frequently occurs. However, the sacroiliitis of psoriatic spondyloarthropathy is frequently asymptomatic, and patients generally have a full range of back motion.

Dactylitis and enthesopathy

The features differentiating psoriasis from rheumatoid arthritis are presented in Table 21–1. The clinical patterns of psoriatic arthritis are presented in Table 21–2.

Two characteristic features of psoriatic arthritis are dactylitis and enthesopathy. Dactylitis is characterized by diffuse swelling of the whole digit of the finger or toes, such that the digit resembles a sausage (Figures 21–1 and 21–2).

Psoriatic arthritis distinguished from rheumatoid arthritis by:
- *clinical features*
- *rheumatoid factor negativity*
- *radiologic features*

Enthesopathy is characterized by inflammation at sites of tendons (eg, the Achilles' tendon or plantar fascia, both causing heel pain) or ligamentous insertions (eg, ligamentous insertion around the pelvic bones). This is an extra-articular manifestation in psoriatic arthropathy, which is commonly detected. Plantar fasciitis patients will have pain on the bottoms of the feet when they walk. Achilles' inflammation patients may have swollen tendons, which are painful on palpation.

In addition to the clinical features and lack of rheumatoid factor activity, radiologic features may readily distinguish psoriatic arthritis from rheumatoid arthritis (Figure 21–3) (Table 21–3).

Cutaneous Manifestations

Classic features of psoriasis occur in the majority of patients with psoriatic arthritis, these being erythematous plaques with discrete borders and silvery,

TABLE 21–1 Differentiation of Psoriatic Arthritis from Rheumatoid Arthritis

Feature	Psoriatic Arthritis	Rheumatoid Arthritis
Rheumatoid factor	± (~10%)	+ (90%)
Nail involvement	+ (~80%)	-
Skin disease	+	-
Symmetric arthritis	-	+
DIP joint involvement	+	-
Spondyloarthropathy	+	-
Human leukocyte antigens	Multiple alleles	DR4

DIP = distal interphalangeal.

TABLE 21–2 Clinical Patterns of Psoriatic Arthritis

Peripheral arthritis
DIP joint involvement
Asymmetric oligoarthritis of small- or medium-sized peripheral joints
Symmetrical arthritis indistinguishable from rheumatoid arthritis
Arthritis mutilans
Spondyloarthropathy (may be asymptomatic)

DIP = distal interphalangeal.

flaking scales. Psoriatic arthritis may also occur in association with pustular psoriasis and generalized psoriatic erythroderma. However, the extent of cutaneous psoriasis does not correlate with the severity of the arthritis. The arthritis may antedate, by 10 to 15 years, the discovery of cutaneous manifestations of psoriasis, or it may occur concomitantly. On the other hand, patients may have cutaneous psoriasis for years (decades) prior to the onset of arthritis. The psoriasis may be subtle, involving a small patch on the elbows, knees, or scalp. "Pinking" of the postauricular areas or the gluteal cleft may be the only cutaneous features of psoriasis.

Cutaneous psoriasis may be present a variable period of time before onset of arthritis. Cutaneous psoriasis may not be prominent.

The most unusual cases of psoriatic arthritis that we have encountered are those associated with "Tulipans or rupioid" cutaneous psoriasis lesions. These lesions, most frequently encountered on the lower extremities, have a prominent eczematous component. Indeed, biopsies of these lesions are frequently reported as "psoriasiform dermatitis." The arthritis in these patients had a prominent enthesopathy of the heel and ankles making walking very difficult.

We have also seen one case of arthritis mutilans in which osteolysis produced shrunken, functionless fingers associated with prominent redundant folds of skin. Nail changes and a sacral patch of psoriasis were the only cutaneous features.

The most common cutaneous finding seen in association with psoriatic arthritis is nail involvement. On occasion, nail involvement (pitting) is the only manifestation of psoriasis detected in a patient with psoriatic arthritis. The clinical features of nail involvement in psoriasis are depicted in Table 21–4.

Nail lesions are found in approximately 80% of psoriatic arthritis patients and in approximately 25 to 30% of a general psoriatic patient population.

Nail involvement commonly associated with arthritis.

Thus, there are no distinctive patterns of cutaneous psoriasis associated with the presence of psoriatic arthritis. All forms of psoriasis, from very small patches to the widespread exfoliative erythroderma, have been observed. Some investigators have commented how frequently patients with psoriatic arthritis are unaware that they have psoriasis, and how often the subtle features of psoriasis are missed. In these cases, nail involvement and/or a family history of psoriasis is/are helpful. Rheumatologists have also commented on the fact that the psori-

No distinctive clinical feature of psoriasis associated with arthritis.

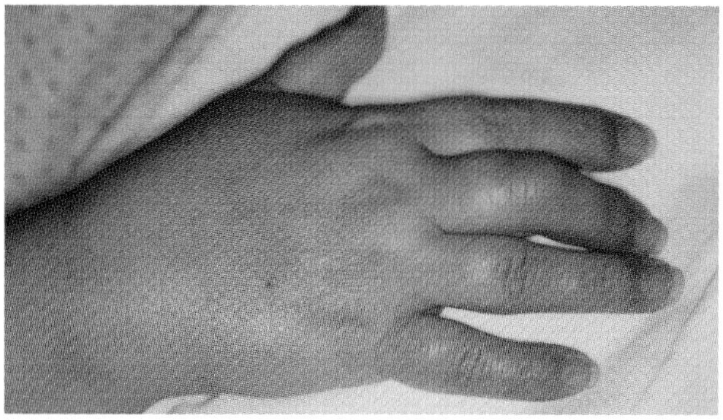

FIGURE 21–1 Psoriatc dactilytis involving fingers of right hand of a psoriatic patient. Note psoriatic arthritis involving PIP joints.

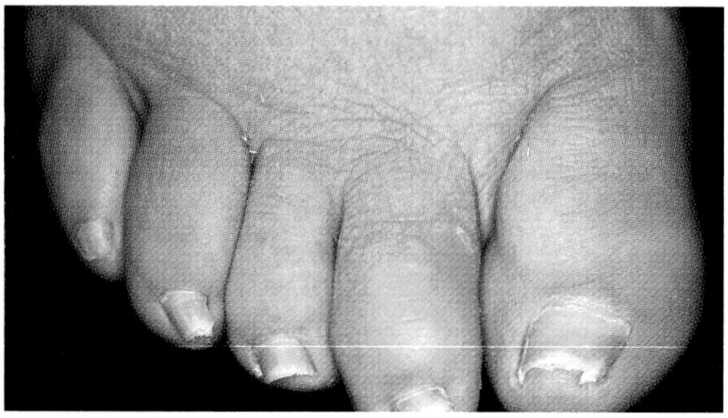

FIGURE 21–2 Dactilytis and arthritis involving toes of a psoriatic patient.

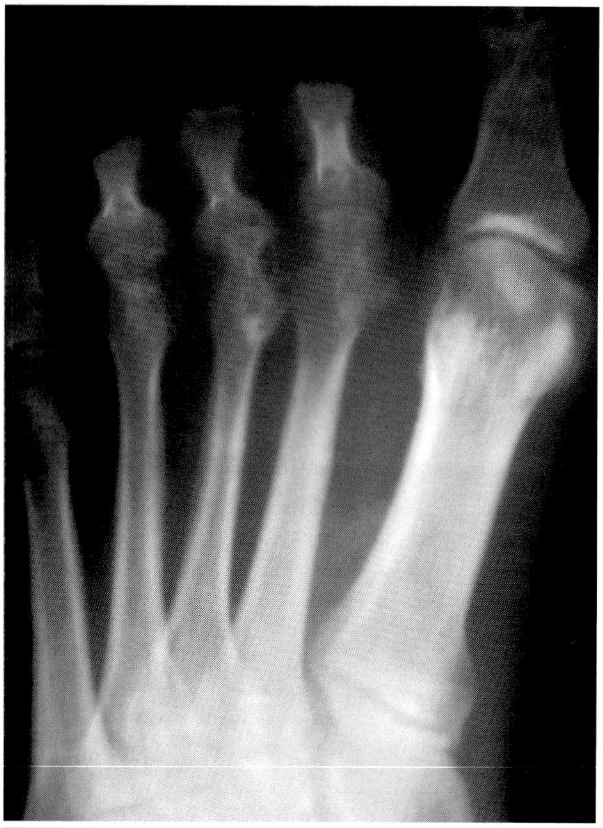

FIGURE 21–3 Radiograph of the foot of a psoriatic patient demonstrating severe destructive arthritis of the metatarsal phalangeal joints. Note osteolysis, especially of the great toe.

atic arthritis may be initiated by trauma (analogous to the skin in Koebner's phenomenon). For example, they have noted the onset of arthritis of the knee following trauma.

In the past, anecdotal reports indicated that psoriatic arthritis would improve with ultraviolet light–clearing of the cutaneous lesions. In general, this is probably not true, but occasionally, patients will demonstrate this association.

Increased uric acid levels correlated with extent of skin disease.

Elevated uric acid levels have been detected in psoriasis patients. Elevation in uric acid reflects increased purine metabolism in the skin and is correlated with the extent of cutaneous psoriasis. For example, minimal psoriasis is generally associated with normal serum uric acid levels. Patients with extensive psoriasis and elevated uric levels may be at increased risk for developing gout.

TABLE 21–3 **Radiologic Features of Psoriatic Arthritis**

Juxta-articular osteoporosis
Osteolysis ("whittling") of terminal phalanges
"Pencil-in-cup" appearance
Asymmetric disease
Gross destruction of involved joints
Ankylosis
Periostitis
Spondylitis

TABLE 21–4 Clinical Features of Psoriatic Nail Involvement

Pitting
Onycholysis
Subungual keratosis
Yellowish "oil drop" discoloration of the nail (due to psoriatic lesion of nail bed)

Etiology

In recent years, it has become clear that genetic factors are of prime importance in the etiology of uncomplicated psoriasis, as well as psoriatic arthritis. For example, in a study of over 100 families of patients with psoriasis and arthritis, Moll detected that first-degree relatives of psoriatic arthritis probans demonstrated at least a 50-fold increased frequency of psoriatic arthritis. The prevalence of arthritis in first-degree relatives, compared with spouse controls, was highly significant, implicating genetic rather than environmental factors.

Fiftyfold increase of psoriatic arthritis amongst first-degree relatives of psoriatic patients.

Other classic studies by Baker have shown that psoriasis is more prevalent among patients with arthritis, and conversely, arthritis is found more frequently in psoriatic subjects.

These epidemiologic findings have been augmented by human leukocyte antigen (HLA) studies, which suggest that psoriasis is a multifactorial autosomal dominant disease demonstrating increased frequencies of HLA-B13, -B17, -B37, -Cw6, and -DR7. In psoriatic arthritis, HLA-B13, -B17, -B27, -B38, -B39, -DR4, and -DR7 appear to be increased. The presence of HLA-B27 is associated with an increased frequency of spondylitis, whereas HLA-DR4 may be associated more with the development of peripheral arthritis.

HLA studies indicate inheritance pattern is autosomal dominant. HLA associated with spondylitis form of psoriatic arthritis.

Treatment

Nonsteroidal anti-inflammatory drugs are of benefit in the treatment of mild cases of arthritis. For severe cases, which alter quality of life, methotrexate, with usual doses from 7.5 to 15 mg per week, has proven effective. In general this can be effective for both the skin and the joints. Provost, however, has seen several patients with psoriatic arthritis treated with once weekly doses of methotrexate to control the arthritis in whom significant cutaneous psoriasis persisted. The same amount of methotrexate divided into 3 doses and administered 12 hours apart, cleared the skin disease and suppressed the arthritis. The use of antimalarials for any reason in a psoriatic patient may be problematic, exacerbating cutaneous psoriasis.

Antimalarials may produce a flare of cutaneous psoriasis.

Annotated Bibliography

Luzar MJ. Hydroxychloroquine in psoriatic arthropathy: exacerbations of psoriatic skin lessions. J. Rheumatol 1982;9:462–464.

Slagel GA, James WD. Plaquenil-induced erythroderma. J Am Acad Dermatol 1985;12: 857–862.

These two articles document that plaquenil, on occasions, can exacerbate cutaneous psoriasis.

Shuster S. Metabolic and hemodynamic effects of skin disease. Ann Clin Res 1971;3:135–142.

This excellent article documents severe metabolic alterations induced by exfoliative erythroderma.

Wright V, Moll JMH. Psoriatic arthritis. Bull Rheum Dis 1971;21:627–632.

Cohen GL. Psoriatic arthritis. Prog Dermatol 1976;10:5–8.

Moll JMH, Wright V. Psoriatic arthritis. Semin Arthritis Rheum 1973;3:55–78.

Lambert JR, Ansell BM, Stephenson E, et al. Psoriatic arthritis in childhood. Clin Rheum Dis 1976;2:339–352.

These four articles describe clinical features of psoriatic arthritis. All are highly quoted.

Green FA. Distal interphalangeal joint disease and nail abnormalities. Ann Rheum Dis 1968;27:55–59.

This article details the relationship of pitting of nails to psoriatic arthritis.

Baker H, Golding DN, Thompson M. Psoriasis and arthritis. Ann Intern Med 1963;58:909–913.

Baker H. Epidemiologic aspects of psoriasis and arthritis. Br J Dermatol 1966;78:249–261.

These two articles detail epidemiologic aspects. Both are highly quoted.

Aandorfi N, Freundlich B. Psoriatic and seronegative inflammatory arthropathy associated with a traumatic onset: 4 cases and a review of the literature. J Rheumatol 1997;1:187–192.

Describes onset of psoriatic arthritis after trauma in 3 patients.

Cuellar ML, Espinoza LR. Methotrexate use in psoriasis and psoriatic arthritis. Rheum Dis Clin North Am 1997;23:797–809.

Useful review of effectiveness of methotrexate in the treatment of psoriatic arthritis.

Seronegative Spondyloarthropathies

Seronegative spondyloarthropathies
Reiter's syndrome
Arthritides of ulcerative colitis and Crohn's disease
Psoriasis
SAPHO syndrome

The seronegative spondyloarthropathies include Reiter's syndrome; psoriasis associated with spondyloarthropathy; the arthritides associated with ulcerative colitis and Crohn's disease; and the SAPHO syndrome (an acute sternocleido or sternomanubrium arthritis associated with palmoplantar pustulosis lesions and multifocal aseptic osteomyelitis).

The exact pathogenesis of the seronegative spondyloarthropathies is unknown. Much attention has been given to an infectious disease process occurring on a specific genetic background (high association with the HLA-B27 allele).

In 1990, Taurog et al. described the spontaneous inflammatory disease in transgenic rats who had HLA-B27 and human β2-microglobulin genes introduced into their cell lines. Rats from the transgenic lines LEW 21-4H and 33-3 would spontaneously develop inflammatory lesions in the gastrointestinal tract, axial and peripheral joints, and the urethral tract. This evidence supports further genetic susceptibility to the initiation and subsequent proliferation of these inflammatory lesions. Interestingly, they could not duplicate these findings in mice.

The seronegative spondyloarthropathies have four distinct phases that vary in severity: (1) peripheral arthritis phase, (2) enthesopathic phase, (3) pelviaxial phase, and the (4) extramusculoskeletal phase.

The peripheral arthritis phase of the seronegative spondyloarthropathies is characterized by the acute onset of a mono-, oligo-, or polyarthritis. Diffuse swelling of fingers or toes may occur. Heel pain is the most frequently recognized enthesopathic symptom. Low back pain or pain in the buttocks are very characteristic features of seronegative spondyloarthropathies of the pelviaxial phase (Figures 21–4 and 21–5). Uveitis is a characteristic extramusculoskeletal finding.

Reiter's Syndrome

Reiter's syndrome
Balanitis circinata

In Reiter's syndrome, balanitis circinata, a painless, papulosquamous inflammatory lesion of the glans penis, frequently occurs. Similar lesions may involve the

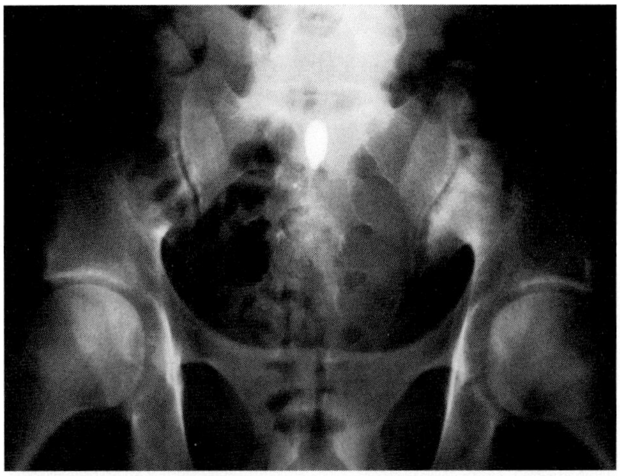

FIGURE 21–4 Reiter's syndrome demonstrating spondylitis involving the sacroiliac joints. Note prominent sclerosis in the left sacroiliac joint.

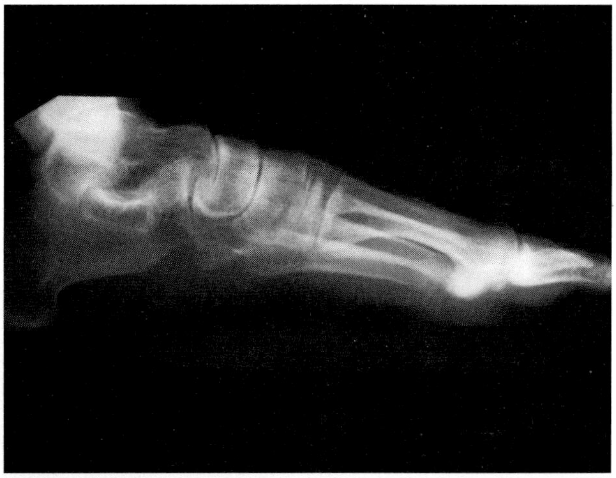

FIGURE 21–5 Reiter's syndrome demonstrating involvement of calcaneus. Note osteolysis.

Keratoderma blennorrhagicum

Relationship of Reiter's syndrome to psoriasis

oral mucosa. Keratoderma blennorrhagicum, as well as subungual hyperkeratosis of the nails, may also occur. Together with classic psoriatic lesions, these are all arguably the cutaneous manifestations of psoriasis occurring in a patient with Reiter's syndrome (Figures 21–6 to 21–8). Indeed, Provost, in caring for a Veterans' Administration population, detected a number of psoriatic patients who had been discharged from the military service for Reiter's syndrome. Careful questioning of these people indicated that the initial onset of their psoriatic disease process occurred with the development of Reiter's syndrome.

Patients with Reiter's syndrome may develop conjunctivitis, uveitis with acute iritis, and, subsequently, chronic iridocyclitis, producing impaired vision. On unusual occasions, granulomatous involvement of the aortic root producing aortic and mitral valve incompetence occurs. Varying degrees of heart block may also occur.

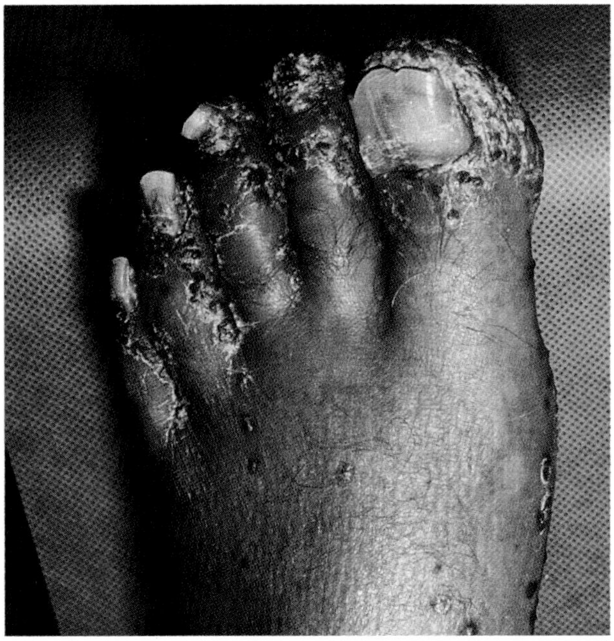

FIGURE 21–6 Reiter's syndrome demonstrating severe involvement of the toes.

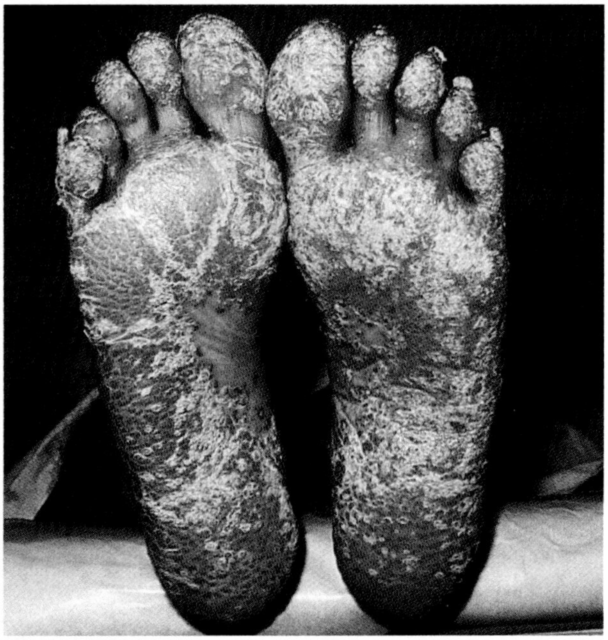

FIGURE 21–7 Reiter's syndrome demonstrating keratoderma blennorrhagia of the soles of the feet. Patient is human immunodeficiency virus-positive.

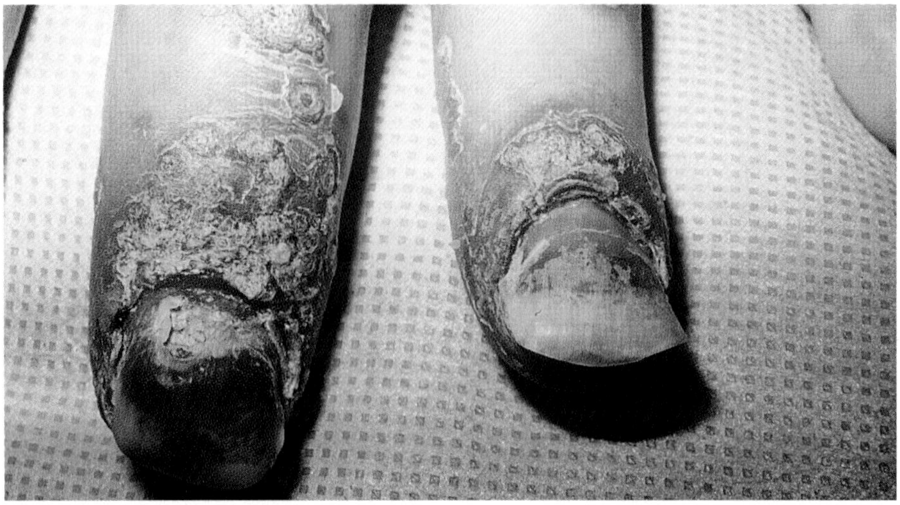

FIGURE 21–8 Reiter's syndrome demonstrating involvement of the fingers with prominent onycholysis and periungual involvement.

Two types of Reiter's syndrome are recognized: one is endemic and associated with diarrhea; the other is venereal.

Reiter's syndrome
May be heralded by diarrhea

Classic Reiter's syndrome may be heralded by the development of acute diarrhea 4 to 6 weeks prior to the onset of joint disease. At times, the diarrhea may be mild and totally overlooked by the patient. Various bacterial species have been associated with the development of Reiter's syndrome, including those from the genera *Shigella*, *Salmonella*, and *Yersinia*.

May be associated with urethritis

Since the original description of the syndrome by Reiter, nonspecific urethritis has been associated with the development of seronegative spondyloarthropathies. Many times the urethritis is mild and asymptomatic. On occasions, however, it may be severe and associated with prostatitis. The urethral infections associated with the development of seronegative spondyloarthropathies are unknown, although *Chlamydia trachomatis* is the organism most frequently isolated.

The exact pathogenesis of Reiter's syndrome is unknown. The fact that this syndrome occurs with increased severity among acquired immunodeficiency syndrome (AIDS) patients suggests a role for CD8 T cells. In addition, there is a high frequency of the HLA-B27 phenotype or HLA-B27 cross-reacting antigens (CREGs) in Reiter's syndrome patients. These CREGs share structural and antigenic similarities with HLA-B27 and include HLA-B7, -BW22, -BW40, and -BW42.

These facts have lead to the speculation that the key immunologic reaction in Reiter's syndrome involves recognition of a peptide (most likely derived from a bacterial product) presented by a class I HLA molecule (B27 or a cross-reacting antigen) to a CD8 T cell.

Arthritides Associated with Bowel Disease

It is increasingly recognized that inflammatory bowel disease on uncommon occasions (< 5%) may be associated with the features of spondyloarthropathies. These inflammatory bowel conditions include ulcerative colitis and Crohn's disease. These patients also demonstrate an increased frequency of HLA-B27.

Annotated Bibliography

Moll JMH, Haslock I, Mac Rae IF, et al. Associations between ankylosing spondylitis, psoriatic arthritis, Reiter's disease, the intestinal arthropathies, and Behçet's syndrome. Medicine 1974;53:343–364.

This article describes diseases associated with spondyloarthropathies. Turkish investigators dispute inclusion of Behçet's disease.

The SAPHO Syndrome

The SAPHO syndrome Prominent cutaneous pustular diseases

The SAPHO (synovitis-*a*cne-*p*ustulosis-*h*yperostosis-*o*steomyelitis) syndrome is of special interest to dermatologists. This syndrome is characterized by osteosclerotic swelling and pain of the proximal clavicle, sternum, and first ribs. On occasions, there may be manubriosternal arthritis and spondylitis, which can mimic a septic arthritis. This reactive arthritis is seen in association with palmoplantar pustulosis, acne conglobata, acne fulminans, hidradenitis suppurativa, and recurrent osteomyelitis (Figure 21–9).

The HLA-B27 alleles are slightly increased in these patients, consistent with the theory that SAPHO is part of the spondyloarthropathies.

May be seen with acne vulgaris and hidradenitis suppurativa

Bacterial cultures have generally been negative except for one notable study that demonstrated, via open articular and periarticular biopsy, the presence of *Propionibacterium acnes* in 7 of 15 cases.

There is obviously a great deal of overlap between the classic features of psoriasis, Reiter's syndrome, and spondyloarthropathies, which, although difficult to explain clinically, may be explainable by the genetic makeup of the patient (ie, the presence of HLA-B27 and other unknown alleles).

Annotated Bibliography

Hammer RE, Malka SD, Richardson JA, et al. Spontaneous inflammatory disease in transgenic rats ecpressing HLA-B27 and human β_2-microgolbulin: an animal model of HLA-B27 associated human disorders. Cell 1990;63:109–112.

This is the original description of the transgenic model for reactive arthritis in which these genetically altered rats developed colitis, urethritis, peripheral, and axial arthritis.

Bradensen RE, Dekel S, Yaron M, et al. SAPHO syndrome. Dermatology 1993;186: 176–180.

Benhamou CL, Chamot AM, Kahn MF. Synovitis-acne-pustulosis-hyperostosis-osteomyelitis syndrome (Sapho): a new syndrome among spondyloarthropathies? Clin Exp Rheumatol 1988;6:109–112.

Edlund E, Johansson U, Lidgren L, et al. Palmoplantar pustulosis and sternocostoclavicular arthro-osteitis. Ann Rheum Dis 1988;47:809–815.

Bookbinder SA, Fenske NA, Clement GB, et al. Clavicular hyperostosis and acne arthritis. Ann Intern Med 1982;97:615–618.

These articles draw attention to a recently described reactive arthritis (spondyloarthropathy) associated with palmoplantar pustulosis, acne conglobata, acne fulminans, and hidradenitis suppurativa.

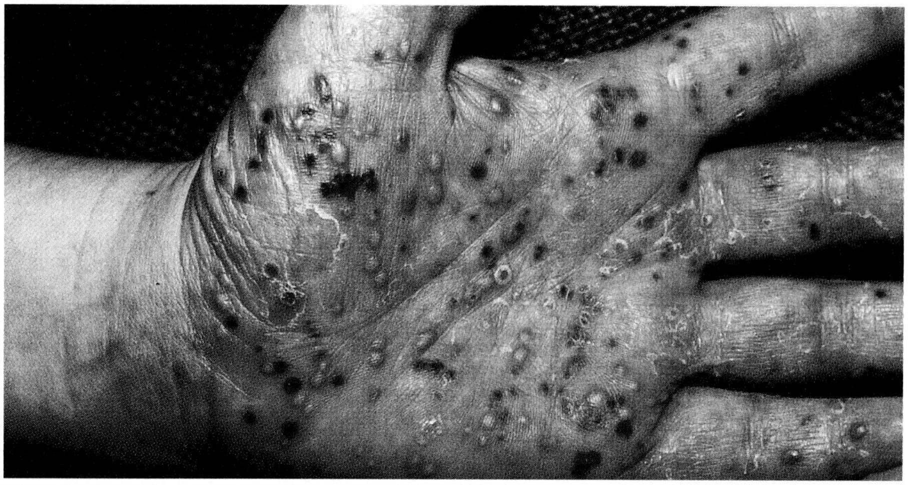

FIGURE 21–9 Pustular involvement of hands. This type of lesion may be associated with the SAPHO syndrome. (Reproduced with permission from Rick Stearns, M.D., Tulsa, OK.)

Amor BA, Toubert AA. Reactive arthropathy Reiter's syndrome and enteric arthropathy in adults. In: Maddison PJ, Isenberg DA, Woo R, Gloss DN, eds. Oxford Textbook of Rheumatology. New York: Oxford University Press 1993, pp 699–709.

This is a well written, excellent discussion with a good bibliography.

Reactive Arthritides

There is a group of reactive arthropathies associated with infections that possess a good deal of clinical similarities to the seronegative spondyloarthropathies. Among these conditions are the cutaneous arthritis syndrome associated with *Neisseria gonorrhoeae* infections, the cutaneous arthritis syndromes associated with a bowel bypass and blind loop operative procedures, and the arthritides associated with chronic cutaneous infections of acne conglobata, acne fulminans, and hidradenitis suppurativa.

Reactive arthritidis
? Immune-complex mediated

Current theory postulates that because of the general lack of culture evidence of infection, the joint and cutaneous manifestations of these diseases and syndromes are immune-complex related. It is theorized that products of infection, including nonviable bacterial products, gain access to the systemic circulation and an immune response is induced. As additional products of infection enter the circulation, pathologic immune complexes (antigen excess) form. These circulating immune complexes induce, in the skin and joints, the signs and symptoms associated with these diseases and syndromes. The clinical hallmark of this group of diseases is chronic infection, and with the exception of some gonococcal patients with purulent arthritis, bacterial cultures are negative.

Gonococcal Cutaneous Arthritis Syndrome

Gonococcal cutaneous arthritis syndrome
A few painful distal pustules

This is an uncommon syndrome generally occurring in women. The gonococcal infection is generally asymptomatic, characterized by the development of painful, erythematous, macular lesions, which rapidly become vesicular, pustular, and hemorrhagic (Figure 21–10). Necrosis of lesions is common. The lesions are acral (distal to the elbow and knees), few in number (10 to 20), and are frequently detected around the small joints of the hands and feet. Onset generally occurs during menses and pregnancy and with childbirth.

Migratory arthritis
tenosynovitis

A migratory arthritis is characteristic, associated with effusion, pain, and at times, a marked limitation of movement. A tenosynovitis, involving the wrists and hands, is common. Headache, fever, and myalgia are commonly present.

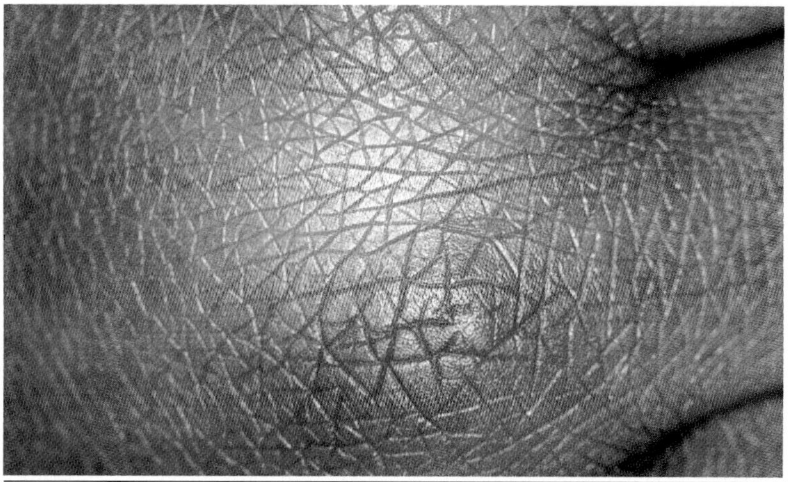

FIGURE 21–10 Gonococcal arthritis syndrome. Small pustule over the fourth metacarpal phalangeal joint. Very tender.

Bacterial culture of joints, skin, and blood are positive in only 20% of cases. The gonococcal organism is difficult to culture. Culture on chocolate and Thayer-Martin agar under carbon dioxide conditions must be rapidly carried out. Delay in sending culture swabs to the laboratory generally produces false-negative results.

Cultures of joints, skin, and blood infrequently positive
Neisseria gonorrhoeae *organism difficult to culture*

Although routine culture of joints, blood, and skin lesions are generally negative, immunofluorescent studies of cutaneous biopsies, using anti-gonococcal antisera have been reported to demonstrate in a high percentage of cases bacterial products in diseased blood vessels. Despite the relatively infrequent ability to culture gonococcus from blood and peripheral tissue, one should culture the cervix, pharynx, and rectum in attempt to demonstrate the organism.

Direct immunofluorescence of lesion biopsy using anti-gonococcal antisera may be valuable.
Cervical and rectal cultures may be helpful.

An arthrocentesis of a purulent joint with a white count > 50,000/mm^3 and low glucose levels will generally demonstrate the organism.

Recurrent gonococcal infections should promote a search for a homozygous complement deficiency involving the terminal complement components (C5 to C9).

As noted above, it is thought that most of the arthritides associated with a gonococcal infection are sterile, secondary to an immune complex-mediated disease process involving nonviable bacterial products. Nevertheless, because *Neisseria gonorrhoeae* is capable of destroying heart valves and joints within a short period of time, hospitalization and aggressive antibiotic therapy are indicated. The Centers for Disease Control recommends the following:

Neisseria gonorrhoeae *organism quickly destroys joints and heart valves*
Need for aggressive antibiotic therapy

- ceftriaxone 1 g IM or IV every 24 hours, or
- cefotaxime 1 g IV every 8 hours, or
- ceftizoxime 1 g IV every 8 hours

These drug regimens should be continued 24 to 48 hours after improvement begins. Therapy is then switched to oral medications to complete a full week of antibiotic therapy:

- cefixime 400 mg PO bid, or
- ciprofloxacin 500 mg PO bid

For those individuals allergic to penicillin and penicillin derivatives, spectinomycin 2 g IM every 12 hours is recommended.

Bowel Bypass– and Blind Loop–Associated Cutaneous Arthritis Syndromes

Bacterial overgrowth occurring as complications of jejunoileal bypass and blind loops due to Billroth II and Roux-en-Y operative procedures may induce recurrent episodes of a cutaneous arthritis syndrome. This syndrome is frequently characterized by showers of erythematous, painful, macular lesions that rapidly become pustular (Figure 21–11). Fever, myalgias, arthralgias, and an inflammatory polyarthritis occur.

Bacterial overgrowth in blind loop
Showers of painful, macular, papular, pustular lesions
Pain disproportionate to size of lesion

Biopsy of the skin lesions demonstrates a prominent neutrophilic inflammatory infiltrate similar to Sweet's syndrome.

Anti-inflammatory therapy (ie, prednisone) is very effective in treating acute episodes. However, chronic therapy designed to suppress and eliminate bacterial overgrowth (tetracycline, metronidazole) is recommended. On unusual occasions, corrective surgery to remove the blind loop must be performed.

Acute attacks controlled with oral steroids
Prophylactic antibiotics control bacterial overgrowth

We have evaluated one patient with this syndrome who presented with a history of jejunoileal bypass surgery 25 years ago for obesity. Soon after surgery, she was diagnosed with acne rosacea and was treated with tetracycline once daily. The tetracycline was continued for at least 22 years. Due to the death of her dermatologist, her prescription ran out and the patient began to experience recurrent episodes of pustular cutaneous lesions occurring on an erythematous base. She also had fever, myalgia, and a polyarthritis. Reinstitution of daily tetracycline therapy suppressed her disease process.

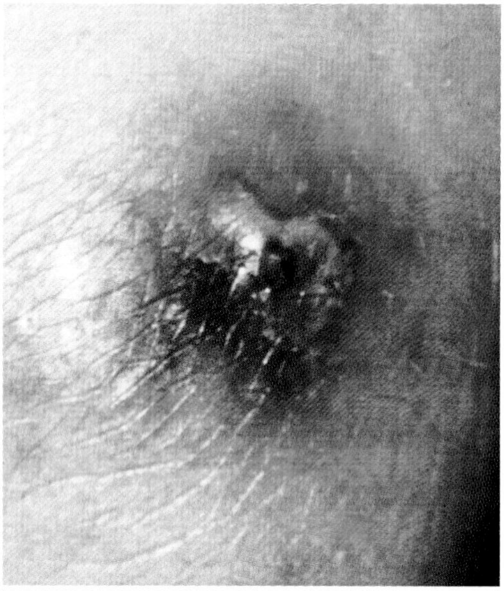

FIGURE 21-11 Bowel bypass syndrome pustular lesion on erythematous base of the mid lower leg. Recurrent "crops" of these painful lesions disappeared with tetracycline therapy.

Arthritides Associated with Acne Conglobata, Acne Fulminans, and Hidradenitis Suppurativa

On unusual occasions a generalized polyarthropathy, fever, and myalgias have been described in association with severe acne (acne conglobata, acne fulminans) and, less often, with hidradenitis suppurativa. Anti-inflammatory drugs, including oral steroids, may be necessary. Since the introduction of isotretinoin, this complication is even more rare, although on occasions, the use of this drug may initiate this complication. Antibiotics have also been used in this condition to suppress the primary infection and the secondary manifestations.

As noted above, these conditions have been associated with the SAPHO syndrome.

Annotated Bibliography

Jorrizo JL, Schmalstieg FC, Dinehart SM, et al. Bowel-associated dermatosis-arthritis syndrome: immune complex mediated vessel damage and increased neutrophil migration. Arch Intern Med 1984;144:738–740.

Dickin CH. Bowel-associated dermatosis-arthritis syndrome: bowel bypass without bowel by-pass. Mayo Clin Proc 1984;49:43–46.

These two highly quoted articles describe this unusual syndrome.

Hughes RA. Arthritis precipitated by isotretinoin treatment for acne vulgaris. J Rheumatol 1993;20:1241–1242.

Hellman DB. Spondyloarthropathy with hidradenitis suppurativa. J Am Med Assoc 1992;267:2363–2365.

These two articles detail the unusual occurrence of reactive arthritis with dermatologic diseases.

Goldenberg DL. Post infectious arthritis: new look at an old concept with particular attention to disseminated gonococcal infection. Ann J Med 1983;74:925–928.

Keiser H, Ruben KL, Wolensky E, et al. Clinical forms of gonococcal arthritis. N Engl J Med 1968;279:234–240.

These excellent articles describe gonococcal-mediated arthritis cutaneous syndrome.

CHAPTER 22

Inherited Connective Tissue Diseases

Reed E. Pyeritz, M.D., Ph.D., Thomas T. Provost, M.D.

Pseudoxanthoma Elasticum

Pseudoxanthoma elasticum (PXE) is an inherited disorder characterized by fragmentation of elastic tissue (elastorrhexis); collagen and ground substance may also be abnormal. Prominent cutaneous blood vessel and eye lesions occur. Progressive calcification of elastic fibers, related to total calcium ingestion, is commonly detected.

Inherited disorder of elastic tissue

Collagen and ground substance may also be abnormal.

The inheritance pattern is complex, involving two autosomal dominant and three autosomal recessive types of the disease. The autosomal recessive forms are, by far, the most common. The extreme variability in expression has suggested genetic subtypes, but all forms of PXE show linkage to the same locus on human chromosome 16p13.1.

Complex inheritance pattern
All forms show linkage to chromosome 16p13.1

Clinical Features

"Chicken-plucked skin"

The cutaneous manifestations of PXE include yellowish macules and papules, most prominent in the folds of the skin, producing a characteristic "chicken-plucked skin" appearance. The neck, clavicles, axilla, groin, and perineum are common sites of involvement (Figures 22–1 and 22–2). With time, the skin becomes lax and wrinkled, producing folds. The disease may uncommonly be generalized.

Mucous membrane involvement of the mouth, rectum, and vagina may occur. On occasions, elastosis perforans serpiginosa occurs, most commonly on the sides of the neck.

The vascular pathology is an arteriolar sclerosis, affecting the medium-sized muscular arteries and arterioles. The internal elastic laminae become calcified, stiff, and fragile. When the arteriole ruptures, the calcified media cannot constrict and stop the bleeding.

Arteriolar sclerosis is often associated with hypertension, coronary artery disease, and intermittent claudication. Angiomatous malformations, aneurysmal dilatation, cerebral hemorrhage, and gastrointestinal hemorrhage may develop.

Vascular involvement
Accelerated arteriolar sclerosis
Intermittent claudication, angina pectoris, and abdominal angina

Angina pectoris and abdominal angina may be severe. Myocardial infarction is the most common cause of death.

The cardiovascular abnormalities have been reported to produce increased risk to mothers during pregnancy. This is controversial as other studies have found no serious complications. (See Annotated Bibliography.)

In general, pregnancy is uneventful, but catastrophic hemorrhage has been described.

Involvement of the elastic tissue in the eye (Bruch's membrane) produces characteristic angioid streaks. These are slate gray, radiating, linear streaks from the optic disc (Figure 22–3). They usually appear in the third and fourth decades of life, are bilateral, and generally do not impair vision. Vision is impaired, how-

Angioid streaks

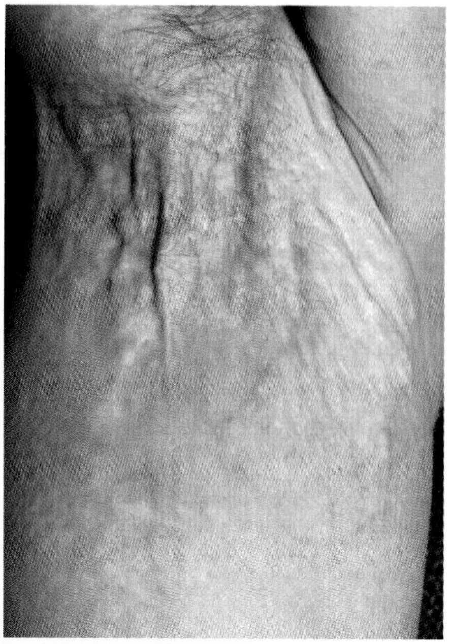

FIGURE 22–1 Pseudoxanthoma elasticum involvement in the axilla. Note folds of skin. (Reproduced with permission from Rick Stearns, M.D.)

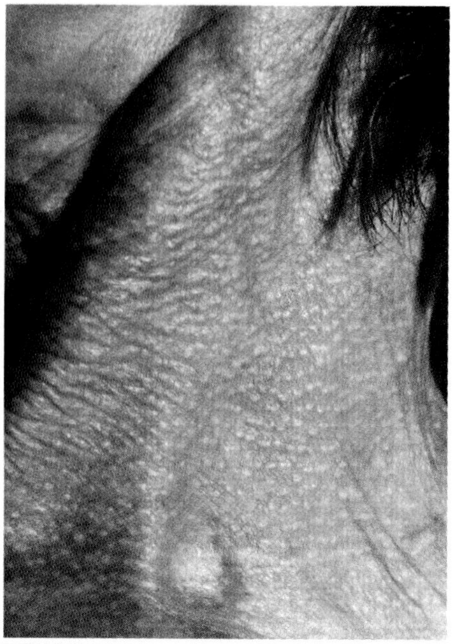

FIGURE 22–2 Pseudoxanthoma elasticum involvement of the side of the neck. "Chicken plucked" skin. (Reproduced with permission from Rick Stearns, M.D.)

ever, by rupture of retinal blood vessels producing hemorrhage, with subsequent retina detachment.

Pathology

Swollen, fragmented elastic tissue
Calcium deposition

Routine hematoxylin and eosin examination demonstrates degenerative, fragmented, swollen elastic fibers in the middle portion of the dermis. A von Kossa stain demonstrates calcium deposition on the elastic fibers (Figure 22–4). There is also evidence that the collagen may be abnormal because of the presence of small, collagenous fibers.

In addition to calcium deposition on damaged elastic fibers, electron microscopic studies demonstrate the deposition of amorphous deposits of glycosaminoglycans and fibrinogen on elastic fibers.

Pathophysiologic mechanism is unknown

One theory suggests underlying defect is production of abnormal glycosaminoglycans.

The underlying pathophysiologic mechanism responsible for the fragmentation of elastin is unknown. Defects in glycosaminoglycan metabolism have been proposed to be significant. (In areas of elastic fiber calcification, increased quantities of glycosaminoglycans are detected.) It has been theorized that these abnormal glycosaminoglycans, produced by fibroblasts, are deposited on the surface of elastic fibers and, in an unknown manner, facilitate or initiate the fragmentation and calcification noted in these fibers.

The elastic fibers in the media and intima of blood vessels of the skin, heart, and Bruch's membrane of the eye show these pathologic features.

As noted above, recent linkage analysis studies in families showing autosomal recessive or consistent autosomal dominant pattern inheritance indicates a locus at band 16p13.1 contains the causative gene. The gene has recently been identified as *ABCC6* (also called *MRP6*), which encodes a transmembrane protein that binds ATP. The function of this gene and how malfunction results in the pathology of PXE remains unclear.

Subtypes

Five genetic types: two autosomal dominant, three autosomal recessive

The two dominant types of PXE include a severe form, type I, and a milder form, type II. Type I is characterized by "chicken-plucked skin," severe accelerated arteriolar sclerosis, degenerative retinopathy, and blindness.

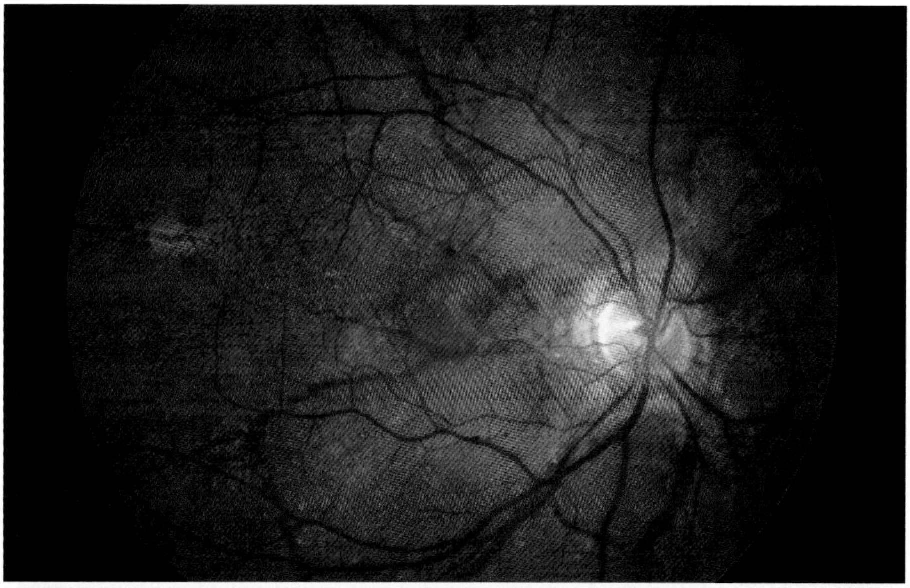

FIGURE 22–3 Slate gray angioid streaks radiating in linear fashion from optic disc. Similar lesions are detected in sickle cell anemia and Paget's disease.

Type II is characterized by minimal vascular and mild retinal changes. These patients may have a yellow macular dermatitis or no rash at all. Some may also have mitral valve prolapse, a high, arched palate, and myopia. The skin may demonstrate increased extensibility.

Three recessive forms of PXE have been described. In the recessive type I, the vascular and retinal changes are similar to but milder than in the dominant type I. The other two recessive types of PXE are rare. In the type II variant, skin laxity without systemic complication has been detected. In the type III group, severe visual impairment, occurring after the third decade of life, is noted. These patients may also demonstrate mild-to-moderate skin and cardiovascular disease.

Annotated Bibliography

Walker ER, Fredrickson RG, Mayes MD, et al. The demineralization of elastic fibers and alterations of extracellular matrix in pseudoxanthoma elasticum. Ultrastructure, immunochemistry of x-ray analysis. Arch Dermatol 1989;125:70–76.

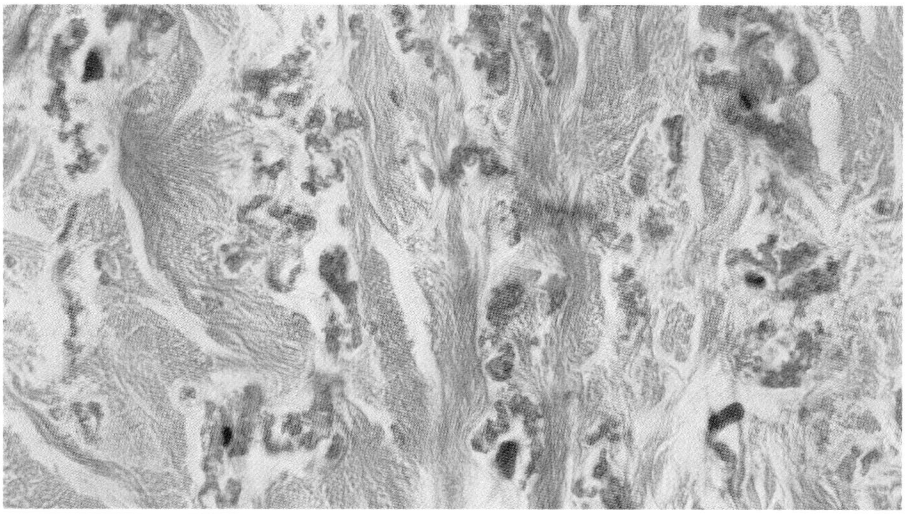

FIGURE 22–4 Pseudoxanthoma elasticum biopsy demonstrating fragmented and clumped elastic fibers in the middle dermis.

Huang SN, Steele HD, Kumar G, Parker J. Ultrastructural changes of elastic fibers in pseudoxanthoma elasticum. A study of histogenesis. Arch Pathol 1967;83:108–113.

Eddy DD, Farber EM. Pseudoxanthoma elasticum: internal manifestations: case reports and a review of the literature. Arch Dermatol 1962;86:729–740.

This classic paper describes the systemic manifestations of this disease.

Viljoen DL, Beatty S, Beighton P. The obstetric and gynecological implications of pseudoxanthoma elasticum. Br J Obstet Gynaecol 1987;94:884–888.

Elejalda BR, de Elejalda MM, Samter E. Manifestations of pseudoxanthoma elasticum during pregnancy: a case report and review of the literature. Am J Med Genet 1984;18:755–762.

These two articles indicate most women with PXE have uneventful pregnancies.

Berde C, Willis DC, Sandberg EC. Pregnancy in women with pseudoxanthoma elasticum. Obstet Gynecol Surg 1983;38:339–344.

These authors review seven cases of pregnancies in women with PXE. Five of these women suffered serious gastrointestinal bleeding; one had epistaxis, and the other had cardiac failure. Most patients had not bled prior to pregnancy. The patient with severe congestive failure died 2 weeks later of an arrhythmia.

The differences in experiences with catastrophic bleeding during pregnancy may be reflective of different subtypes of PXE.

Pyeritz RE, Weiss JL, Rennie W, Fine SL. Pseudoxanthoma elasticum and mitral valve prolapse. N Engl J Med 1982;3307:1451–1452.

Lebwohl MG, Distefano D, Prileau PG, et al. Pseudoxanthoma elasticum and mitral valve prolapse. N Engl J Med 1982;307:228–231.

These two papers (one a letter to the editor) suggest that mitral valve prolapse is a common finding of the autosomal dominant type II PXE. These patients have mild typical skin and ocular changes with joint hyperextensibility. They also may have a thoracic cage deformity or a highly arched palate.

Renie WA, Pyeritz RE, Combs J, et al. Pseudoxanthoma elasticum: high calcium intake in early life correlates with severity. Am J Med Genet 1984;19:235–244.

This article explains that the more calcium consumed (generally as dairy products) early in life, the earlier and more severe are the systemic manifestations.

Sturk B, Nelder KH, Rao VS, et al. Mapping of both autosomal recessive and dominant variants of pseudoxanthoma elasticum to chromosome 16p13.1. Hum Mol Genet 1997;6:1823.

This is the first report of localizing the gene for PXE by linkage analysis.

Ringpfeil, Lebwohl MG, Christiano AM, Uitto J. Pseudoxanthoma elasticum: mutations in the *MRP6* gene encoding a transmembrane ATP-binding cassette (ABC) transporter. Proc Natl Acad Sci U S A 2000;97:6001–6006.

This article describes identification of the gene for both autosomal recessive and dominant forms of PXE.

Cunningham JR, Lippman SM, Renie WA, et al. Pseudoxanthoma elasticum: treatment of gastrointestinal hemorrhage by arterial embolization and observations of autosomal dominant inheritance. Johns Hopkins Med J 1980;147:168–173.

This article describes the progressive ocular features and one approach to intractable gastrointestinal bleeding.

Cutis Laxa

Cutis laxa is a skin disease process characterized by a loss of elastic tissue. It may be inherited (autosomal dominant, autosomal recessive, or X-linked recessive) or acquired. The acquired form has been associated with drug hypersensitivity reactions, multiple myeloma, amyloidosis, systemic lupus erythematosus, and complement deficiencies and has also been reported in infants born of mothers taking D-penicillamine.

Cutis laxa: inherited or acquired disease of elastic tissue

Pathology

The exact biochemical defect is unknown. There is in vitro evidence, however, that skin fibroblasts from some patients with cutis laxa demonstrate decreased production of elastin. There is evidence for a reduced level of messenger ribonucleic acid (mRNA), indicating a pretranslational defect. (There is little support for this with regard to decreased elastin production. For example, in Williams syndrome, the basic defect is a deletion of part of chromosome 7 that invariably involves the *ELN* locus. Everyone with Williams syndrome has only one tropoelastin allele. However, they have none of the features of cutis laxa and, indeed, develop a progressive arterial occlusive process reminiscent of PXE but without the calcification. In some tissues, the remaining allele overcompensates, and too much tropoelastin is synthesized.)

Unsure that decreased fibroblast production of elastin is cause

Histopathologic investigation and electron microscopic studies demonstrate sparse, short, fragmented, clumped elastic fibers. These elastic fiber abnormalities are detected in the epidermis, lungs, and aorta.

Skin, lungs, and aorta may be involved.

Clinical Features

Inherited Cutis Laxa

The autosomal dominant form of the disease is generally characterized by the development of hanging folds of skin, giving a "bloodhound" appearance to the face. In general, no internal organ abnormalities are detected, and the patients have a normal life expectancy.

However, those individuals who develop cutaneous features of cutis laxa in infancy may have systemic features, including pulmonary emphysema, due to the loss of elastic tissue in the lungs.

Clinical features: bloodhound appearance; those without systemic features, normal life expectancy; pulmonary emphysema

The autosomal recessive form of cutis laxa is rare, severe, and evident in infancy. Hernias and diverticula of multiple sites, pulmonary emphysema, joint laxity, pulmonary stenosis, and a characteristic facies resembling that of a bloodhound are typical features. Some affected children have developmental delay, and few survive to age 5 years.

The systemic manifestations of this autosomal recessive form of cutis laxa are identical to those seen in infants with the maternal D-penicillamine syndrome. These latter children may improve with age as new connective tissue is synthesized.

Maternal penicillamine syndrome

The X-linked recessive form was formally classified as type IX Ehlers-Danlos syndrome and is associated with defective copper metabolism. Lysyl oxidase, a key enzyme in type I collagen cross-linking, is copper dependent.

X-linked recessive form of cutis laxa formally classified as type IX Ehlers-Danlos syndrome

Annotated Bibliography

Agha A, Sakati NO, Higginbottom MC, et al. Two forms of cutis laxa presenting in the newborn period. Acta Paediatr Scand 1978;67:775–780.

These investigators describe two recessive inheritance patterns of cutis laxa. One is associated with a generalized disorder of elastic tissue characterized by infantile emphysema and diaphragmatic, gastrointestinal, and urinary tract involvement. This form of the disease is usually lethal within the first year.

The second form of congenital cutis laxa (recessive inheritance) is characterized by a widely patent anterior fontanel, growth retardation, and development of various malformations.

Patton MA, Tolmie J, Ruthnum P, et al. Congenital cutis laxa with retardation of growth and development. J Med Genet 1987;24:556–561.

This is a description of seven patients with the autosomal recessive form of congenital cutis laxa associated with a widely patent anterior fontanel and growth retardation.

Fitzsimmons JS, Fitzsimmons EM, Guibert TR, et al. Variable clinical presentation of cutis laxa. Clin Genet 1985;28:284–295.

This is another article demonstrating the heterogeneity of congenital cutis laxa.

Brown FR III, Holbrook KA, Byers PH, et al. Cutis laxa. Johns Hopkins Med J 1982;150:148–153.

This article provides examples of the distinct conditions associated with autosomal dominant and recessive inheritance and the maternal D-penicillamine syndrome.

Acquired Cutis Laxa

This rare condition, also known as "post-inflammatory elastolysis," has been seen in association with extensive inflammatory conditions involving the skin, such as urticaria, angioedema, systemic lupus erythematosus, erythema multiforme, and allergic reactions.

Generalized elastolysis may occur in these conditions, and fibrous nodules may be detected. Cutaneous purpura and ecchymosis, following trauma, have been reported. Emphysema and tracheobronchomegaly, secondary to loss of elastic tissue in the lungs and upper airways, respectively, have also been reported.

Annotated Bibliography

Winkelmann RK, Peters MS, Venencie PY. Amyloid elastosis: a new cutaneous and systemic pattern of amyloidosis. Arch Dermatol 1985;121:498–502.

Scott MA, Kauh YC, Luscombe HA. Acquired cutis laxa associated with multiple myelomatosis. Arch Dermatol 1976;112:853–855.

Harpey JP, Jaudon MC, Clavel JP, et al. Cutis laxa and low serum zinc after antenatal exposure to penicillamine. Lancet 1983;2:858.

Lewis PG, Hood AF, Barnett NK, Holbrook KA. Postinflammatory elastolysis and cutis laxa: a case report. J Am Acad Dermatol 1990;22:40–48.

This is a description from our institution of a case of post-inflammatory elastolysis and cutis laxa characterized by a prodrome of fever, then the development of urticaria-like lesions associated with atrophy. Histologically, there was a destruction of elastic fibers.

Wanderer AA, Ellis EF, Goltz RW, Cotton EK. Tracheobronchiomegaly and acquired cutis laxa in a child. Pysiologic and immunologic studies. Pediatrics 1969;44:709–715.

This is an interesting case report demonstrating the association between cutaneous cutis laxa and tracheobronchiomegaly. An association between these pulmonary features and acquired cutis laxa is suggested.

Randle HW, Muller S. Generalized elastolysis associated with systemic lupus erythematosus. J Am Acad Dermatol 1983;8:869–873.

This is an excellent article describing acquired generalized elastolysis in a systemic lupus erythematosus patient. The authors provide an excellent discussion of the heterogeneity of elastolysis.

Marfan Syndrome

Marfan syndrome is a relatively common (2–3/10,000) autosomal dominant condition of the connective tissue due to a heterogeneous collection of mutations at the *FBN1* gene that encodes the glycoprotein fibrillin-1 (chromosome 15q21.1). Marfan syndrome involves most organ systems, especially the eye, the cardiovascular, and musculoskeletal systems, the lungs, and the skin.

Autosomal dominant disease
Lack of fibrillin
Genetic defect localized to chromosome 15q.21.1

Clinical Features

Although specific cutaneous features are absent, the general habitus of the patient may be important in establishing the diagnosis. Affected people are exceptionally tall, with disproportionately long limbs and digits (arachnodactyly); high, arched palates; hyperflexible joints; deformities of the spine, including kyphoscoliosis, and anterior chest. Other characteristics include mitral valve prolapse, dilatation of the aortic root (which leads to aortic dissection and premature death), displacement of the ocular lens (ectopia lentis), spontaneous pneumothorax, and hernias. In addition, these patients may have hypotonic, underdeveloped muscles.

Patients may have underdeveloped muscles. Kyphoscoliosis may be prominent.

Cardiovascular complications
Dissecting aneurysm of aorta

Around puberty, many people with Marfan syndrome develop striae at points of flexural stress, such as at the anterior shoulders, breasts, back, buttocks, and thighs (Figure 22–5). These typically are violaceous for the first year or two and gradually take on the appearance of depigmented, widened scars. They do not disappear after puberty. Striae gravidarum can be very prominent.

Major surgical procedures are prone to the development of incisional hernias; however, healing of skin is generally not disturbed.

Pathology

Fragmented elastic fibers, as well as mucinous material, are detected in the media of the aorta. These changes occur in early life and lead to dilatation and dissection of the aorta, most frequently in the fourth decade.

Fragmented elastic fibers

Diagnosis and Therapy

Early recognition is a key to the ultimate prognosis of these patients, and a dermatologist recognizing clinical features may play an important role. Even though the basic genetic defect has been discovered, mutations in the *FBN1* gene also cause conditions related to Marfan syndrome, and mutations are very expensive and difficult to define. Thus, the diagnosis is generally based on clinical features, and diagnostic criteria have been defined. The diagnosis, however, is problematic if all the clinical features are not present.

Early recognition is key to successful therapy

Diagnostic features have been divided into major and minor categories. The major features are mitral and aortic valve incompetence, dilated ascending aorta, dissecting aneurysm of the aorta, dislocation of the lens, as well as a trembling iris.

The minor features are asthenic build, joint laxity (especially of the ankles), scoliosis, flat feet, arachnodactyly, high, arched palate, pectus excavatum, severe myopia, a floppy mitral valve without incompetence, and a history of spontaneous pneumothorax.

Management of these patients involves the combined efforts of ophthalmology, orthopedic surgery, cardiology, and cardiac surgery.

Early treatment with β-adrenergic blocking agents, such as atenolol, retards the rate of aortic dilatation. Prophylactic repair of the ascending aorta has greatly extended life expectancy.

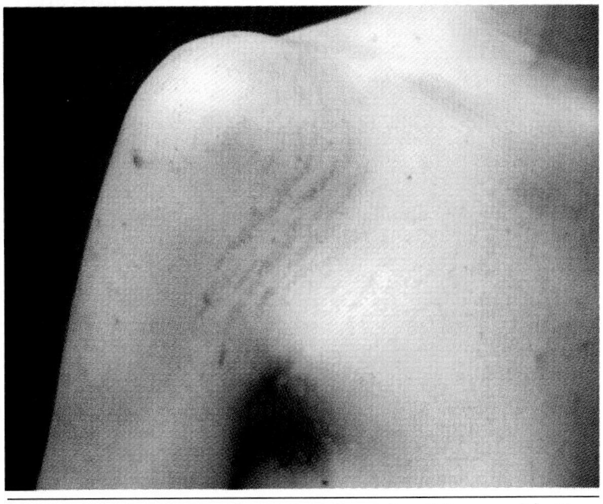

FIGURE 22–5 Marfan syndrome in 21-year-old Caucasian male, demonstrating extensive atrophic striae over his shoulder.

Annotated Bibliography

DePaepe A, Deitz HC, Devereux RB, et al. Revised diagnostic criteria for the Marfan syndrome. Am J Med Genet 1996;62: 417–426.

This article provides the set of rules to follow when deciding at the bedside if someone warrants a diagnosis of Marfan syndrome.

Dietz HC, Pyeritz RE. Mutations in the human gene for fibrillin-1 (FBN1) in the Marfan syndrome and related disorders. Hum Mol Genet 1995;4:1799–1809.

This is a recent review of the different types of mutations found in the microfibrillar protein, fibrillin-1 gene and the indications for searching in any given patient.

Gott VL, Greene PS, Alejo DE, et al. Surgery for ascending aortic disease in Marfan patients: a multi-center study. N Engl J Med 1999;340: 1307–1313.

This article is a follow-up of nearly 700 people with Marfan syndrome who have had replacement of the ascending aorta. For those repaired prophylactically, life expectancy is nearly normal.

Grahame R, Pyeritz RE. Marfan syndrome: joint and skin manifestations are prevalent and correlated. Br J Rheumatol 1995;34:126–131.

Although ocular, cardiovascular, and skeletal features are highly variable and uncorrelated, thick skin and joint problems, such as arthritis and hypermobility, do tract together.

Pyeritz RE. Marfan syndrome and other disorders of fibrillin. In: Rimoin DL, Connor JM, Pyeritz RE, eds. Principles and Practice of Medical Genetics, 3rd ed. New York: Churchill Livingstone, 1997, pp 1027–1066.

This review covers all aspects of Marfan syndrome and related conditions.

Ehlers-Danlos Syndrome

Ehlers-Danlos syndrome is characterized by skin and blood vessel fragility, hyperelasticity of the skin, and joint hyperextensibility (Figure 22–6). There are at least six major phenotypically different conditions composing Ehlers-Danlos syndrome (Table 22–1). Those elucidated thus far are caused by hereditary defects in the synthesis or processing of collagen.

Ehlers-Danlos syndrome: hereditary defects in type I and type III, skin and blood vessel fragility, hyperextensibility of skin, at least six different phenotypes

By light microscopy, qualitative and quantative alterations of collagen are present. By electron microscopy, abnormal periodicity of striations of collagen fibers have been detected, but the changes are nonspecific. A compensatory or relative increase in elastic fibers is often present. Defects in small artery adventitia have been described, which likely predispose to the abnormal bleeding tendencies. Mitral valve prolapse and aortic dilatation also have been found in some Ehlers-Danlos syndrome patients.

Although Ehlers-Danlos syndrome has been subdivided into multiple types, some patients demonstrate overlapping features and cannot be classified into one type. The following is a brief discussion of the various types (Figures 22–6 to 22–8).

The classic type is inherited as an autosomal dominant trait. It is characterized by hyperextensible fragile skin and joints. Trauma to the skin produces gaping wounds with broad, atrophic, "cigarette paper" scars (Figure 22–9). Pseudotumor formation, secondary to accumulations of connective tissue, is common. Joint extensibility may be severe but subluxation surprisingly is rare. Kyphoscoliosis and genu recurvatum are common (Figure 22–10). Life expectancy is normal.

TABLE 22–1 Classification of Ehlers-Danlos Syndrome

Type	Former Name	Clinical Features*	Inheritance	OMIM Number†	Molecular Defect
Classic	EDS I & II	Joint hypermobility; skin hyperextensibility; skin atrophic	AD	130000	Structure of type V collagen
Hypermobility	EDS III	Joint hypermobility; some skin hyperextensibility ± smooth and velvety	AD	130010	Believed to be *COL5A1*, *COL5A2*
Vascular	EDS IV	Thin skin; easy bruising; pinched nose; acrogeria; rupture of large and medium caliber arteries, uterus, and large bowel	AD	130050 (225350) (225360)	Deficient type III collagen
Kyphoscoliotic	EDS VI	Joint hypermobility; congenital progressive scoliosis; scleral fragility with globe rupture; tissue fragility; aortic dilatation; mitral valve prolapse	AR	225400	Lysyl hydroxylase deficiency
Arthrochalasis	EDS VII and B	Joint hypermobility severe with subluxations; congenital hip skin hyperextensibility; tissue fragility	AD	130060	No cleavage of *N*-terminus of type I procollagen dislocation; due to mutations in *COL1A1* or *COL1A2*
Dermatosparaxis	EDS VIIC	Severe skin fragility; decreased skin elasticity; easy bruising; hernias; premature rupture of fetal membranes	AR	225410	No cleavage of N-terminus of type I procollagen due to deficiency of peptidase
Unclassified	EDS V	Classic features	XL	305200	Unknown
	EDS VIII	Classic features and periodontal disease	AD	130080	Unknown
	EDS X	Mild classic features, mitral valve prolapse	Unknown	225310	Unknown
	EDS XI	Joint instability	AD	147900	Unknown
	EDS IX	Classic features; occipital horns	XL	309400	Allelic to Menkes syndrome

AD = autosomal dominant; AR = autosomal recessive; XL = X-linked; EDS = Ehlers-Danlos syndrome.

*Listed in order of diagnostic importance.

†Entries in Online Mendelian Inheritance in Man (www.ncbi.nlm.nihigov/omim).

The hypermobility form of Ehlers-Danlos syndrome is also inherited as an autosomal dominant trait. This form is characterized by prominent hyperextensible joints with minimal skin involvement.

The vascular form of Ehlers-Danlos syndrome is generally a very severe autosomal dominant disease characterized by deficient synthesis of type III collagen and blood vessel abnormalities. Although true aneurysms are rare, large- and medium-caliber arteries spontaneously rupture and cause life-threatening surgical emergencies. Maternal mortality, secondary to a ruptured artery, may occur in 25%. The disease is also characterized by a predisposition to ecchymosis, pneumothorax, rupture of the large arteries, and perforation of the gastrointestinal tract.

This is the most serious form of Ehlers-Danlos syndrome. Deficient synthesis of type III collagen
Vascular complications, catastrophic hemorrhage during pregnancy

The kyphoscoliotic form of Ehlers-Danlos syndrome is an autosomal recessive disease, associated with lysyl hydroxylase deficiency. This deficiency results in type I and type III collagens failing to be hydroxylated, and the hydroxylysine-containing cross-links are not formed.

These patients have a tendency to develop keratoconus as well as intraocular hemorrhage. Lysyl hydroxylase activity can be measured in amniotic fluid. Thus, prenatal diagnosis is now possible. Kyphoscoliotic patients may respond to vitamin C therapy.

Two forms of Ehlers-Danlos syndrome are due to an inability to cleave the *N*-propeptide from type I procollagen. This recessive disorder, termed "der-

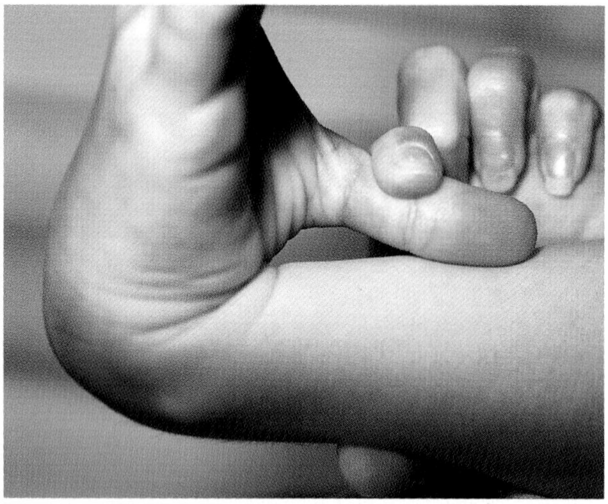

FIGURE 22–6 Hyperextensibility in Ehlers-Danlos syndrome patient.

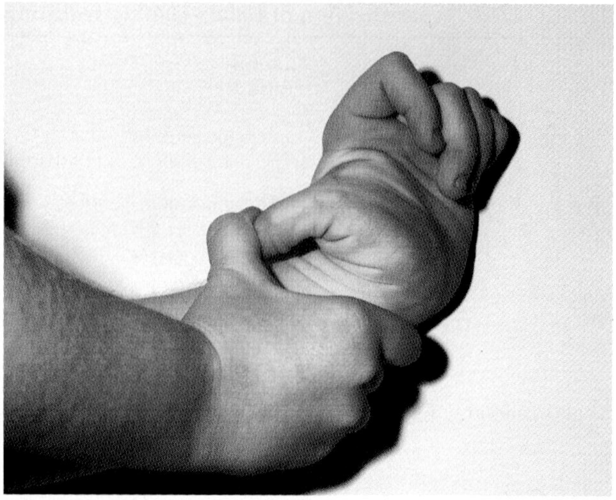

FIGURE 22–7 Hyperextensibility in Ehlers-Danlos syndrome patient.

matosparaxis," is secondary to a defective peptidase enzyme. Skin fragility is very severe and out of proportion to joint laxity.

The dominant form of this type of Ehlers-Danlos syndrome is termed "arthrochalasis" and is caused by structural abnormality in or near the cleavage site of some pro-alpha chains. This defect results in the accumulation of partially processed collagen molecules that interfere with normal collagen function. Clinically, these patients have extreme hyperextensibility of large and small joints and congenital hip dislocation.

Rare forms of Ehlers-Danlos syndrome may exist as unique entities, but their causes are not known.

Annotated Bibliography

Rudd NL, Holbrook KA, Nimrod C, et al. Pregnancy complication in type IV Ehlers-Danlos syndrome. Lancet 1983;1:50–53.

This is a report of a study of 15 families containing 20 women with Ehlers-Danlos syndrome type IV. In vitro measurement of type III collagen production by dermal fibroblast was used to confirm the diagnoses in all patients. Each patient showed defective synthesis of type III collagen. Ten women had been pregnant, and 5 had died from pregnancy-related complications. These complications included rupture of the bowel, aorta, vena cava, uterus, vaginal laceration, and postpartum uterine hemorrhage. The overall risk of death in each pregnancy was 25%. The periods of greatest risk to women are labor, delivery, and the postpartum period. Extensive perineal tears, avulsion of the bladder, and prolapse of the bladder and uterus have been described.

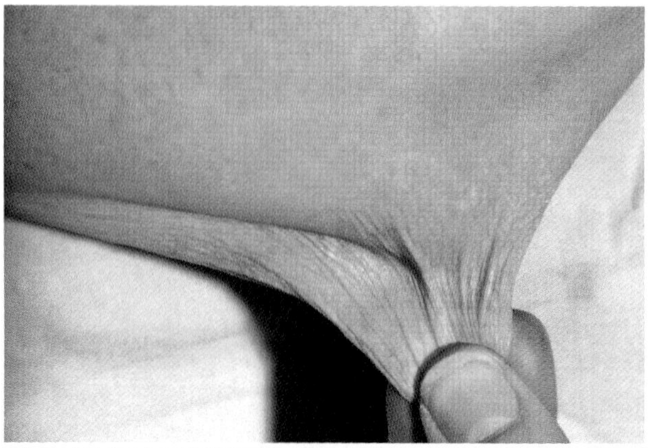

FIGURE 22–8 Ehlers-Danlos type VI in 46-year-old female with the kyphoscoliotic form. Elbow shows extensive scarring and skin hyperextensibility.

Pope FM, Narcisi P, Nicholls AC, et al. Clinical presentations of Ehlers-Danlos syndrome type IV. Arch Dis Child 1988;63:1016–1025.

This is a highly quoted article describing acrogeric Ehlers-Danlos syndrome type IV. These patients have broad foreheads, large eyes, pinched noses, and premature aging of the hands (acrogeria). In addition, these patients demonstrate a joint hypermobility.

Radiolabeled studies demonstrate, by polyacrylamide gel electrophoresis, deficient type III collagen.

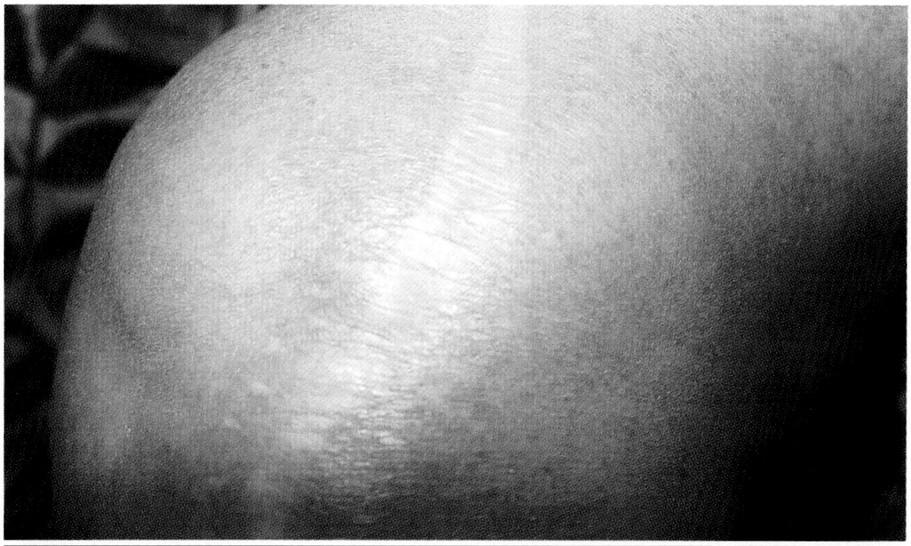

FIGURE 22-9 Weak, thin, atrophic, wide scar in an Ehlers-Danlos syndrome patient.

Beighton P, DePaepe A, Steinmann B, et al. Ehlers-Danlos syndromes: revised nosology. Villefranche, 1997. Am J Med Genet 1998;77:31–37.

Major revision of the classification scheme and diagnostic criteria.

Byers PH. The Ehlers-Danlos syndromes. In: Rimoin DL, Connor JM, Pyeritz RE, eds. Principles and Practice of Medical Genetics, 3rd ed. New York: Churchill Livingstone, 1997, pp 1067.

This book provides a review of the clinical and biochemical features of Ehlers-Danlos syndrome.

Steinmann B, Royce PS, Superti-Furga A. The Ehlers-Danlos syndrome. In: Royce PM, Steinmann E, eds. Connective Tissue and Its Heritable Disorders: Molecular, Genetic, and Medical Aspects. New York: Wiley-Liss 1993, p 351.

This book provides an excellent review chapter, based on the old classification scheme for Ehlers-Danlos syndrome.

Perforating Serpiginosa Elastosis

Approximately 40% of elastosis perforans serpiginosa patients have pseudoxanthoma elasticum, Ehlers-Danlos syndrome, or Marfan syndrome. It has also been reported in Down syndrome and in individuals taking D-penicillamine. These lesions can also occur in healthy individuals.

The disease is characterized by annular or polycyclic lesions composed of small, hyperkeratotic papules, occurring on the back or sides of the neck. These lesions generally persist for months, then heal leaving atrophic scars.

Biopsy of the papules demonstrates epidermal hyperplasia and an epidermal channel, containing elastic tissue, communicating directly with the dermis. Foreign body giant cells may be detected in the dermis.

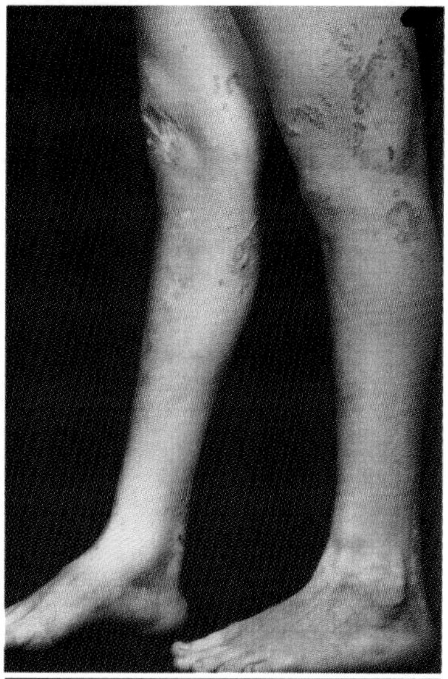

FIGURE 22-10 Ehlers-Danlos type IV in 11½-year-old Caucasian with the vascular form of Ehlers-Danlos syndrome. Legs show genu recurvatum, atrophic scarring, and elastosis perforans serpiginosa.

Annotated Bibliography

Whyte HJ, Winkelmann RK. Elastosis perforans—the association and anomalies and salient facts in histology. J Invest Dermatol 1960;35:113–122.

This is a classic description of this entity.

CHAPTER 23

Cutaneous T-cell Lymphoma

Thomas D. Horn, M.D., Thomas T. Provost, M.D.

Mycosis Fungoides and Sézary Syndrome

Thomas D. Horn, M.D.

Cutaneous T-cell lymphoma:
- *mycosis fungoides*
- *Sézary syndrome*
- *lymphomatoid papulosis*

Mycosis fungoides represents a neoplastic proliferation of T lymphocytes that begins in the skin. It may remain limited to the skin throughout its course, or it may disseminate to the lymph nodes, blood, and rarely viscera. The diagnosis of mycosis fungoides and Sézary syndrome falls under the more comprehensive heading of cutaneous T-cell lymphoma (CTCL) and is generally used to identify a commonly indolent lymphoma presenting with erythematous patches, plaques, and/or nodules. Sézary syndrome is a distinctive erythrodermic leukemic phase of mycosis fungoides. The nosology of lymphomatoid papulosis is less clear. Some authors consider this disease to represent a benign inflammatory condition of the skin, with characteristically malignant-appearing histologic features and an associated incidence of transformation to lymphoma, whereas others place lymphomatoid papulosis in the category of cutaneous lymphoma at the outset with only certain cases extending beyond the skin. This distinction may be more a matter of philosophy than fact.

Clinical Features

Macules, patches, plaques, and tumors typify mycosis fungoides.

The most common presentation of mycosis fungoides consists of erythematous, pruritic patches with scales in any distribution but commonly involving the skin of the pelvic girdle (Figure 23–1). These patches are typically well defined and tend not to trouble the patient overly, except for their persistence. Some clearing centrally may occur. Patches may progress to plaques and then to nodules or tumors (Figure 23–2). Plaques may be round, arcuate, or reniform, or they may assume bizarre shapes. Alternatively, mycosis fungoides may first present with plaques or tumors or may proceed from patch-stage disease directly to tumor-stage disease. Indolent disease may transform into an aggressive phenotype in which nodules and tumors arise rapidly with subsequent lymph node involvement. The trigger for this transformation is unclear but, presumably, corresponds to a subsequent alteration of the tumor's genome, which imparts more rapid proliferation and the ability to extend to lymph nodes, peripheral blood, and viscera.

Clinically, mycosis fungoides is fairly distinct. The patches and plaques are usually several centimeters in size and lack scales or have minimal surface change. These features help distinguish the disease from psoriasis and dermatophyte infec-

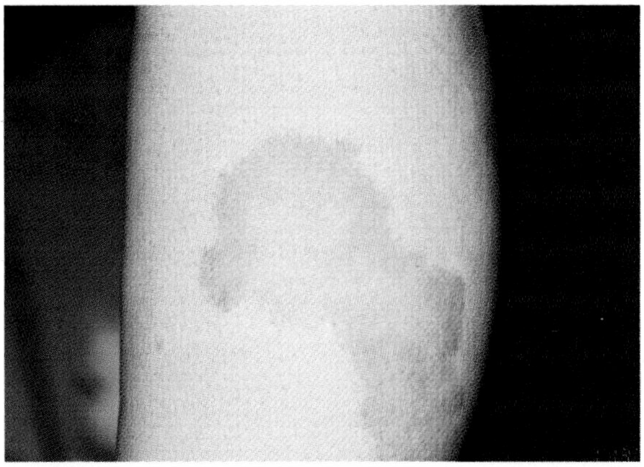

FIGURE 23–1 Patch-stage mycosis fungoides presenting with a well-demarcated, erythematous patch on the arm.

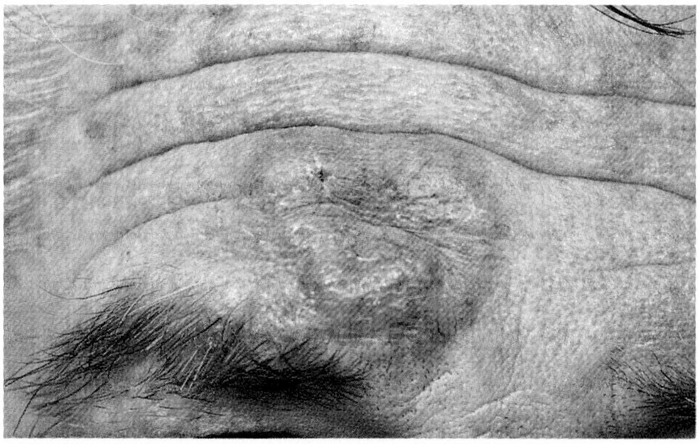

FIGURE 23–2 Tumor-stage mycosis fungoides. Tumors may arise at the onset or evolve from the patch and plaque stages of mycosis fungoides.

tion. Granuloma annulare consists of erythematous papules and plaques that may reach several centimeters in diameter and lack surface change. The plaques of granuloma annulare are generally more uniform and are distinctly more annular, compared with those of mycosis fungoides. The concept of large plaque parapsoriasis and parapsoriasis in general is poorly defined. Although large plaque parapsoriasis was historically viewed as a precursor to mycosis fungoides, it is best considered to be mycosis fungoides without diagnostic findings in skin samples (see below).

Erythroderma is characteristic of Sézary syndrome.

Erythroderma with or without an identifiable leukemic phase is a rare but ominous manifestation of mycosis fungoides. The association of erythroderma with an appreciable number of atypical lymphocytes in the peripheral circulation is known as Sézary syndrome (Figure 23–3). The erythroderma of Sézary syndrome is associated with scales in most patients but is generally not clinically specific. A clue to the diagnosis is its resistance to standard therapies directed to other causes of erythroderma.

Clinical variants exist.

Uncommon variant clinical presentations include a poikilodermatous form, a follicular mucinosis form, a hypopigmented form, a disease resembling pigmented purpuric eruption, a psoriasiform-like disease characterized by plaques of limited distribution (Worringer-Kallop disease or pagetoid reticulosis), a verrucous form, a form in which bullous lesions occur, and a type in which prominent elastolysis and granulomatous changes occur (termed “granulomatous slack skin”).

Lymphadenopathy may arise in association with mycosis fungoides. Not all clinically abnormal lymph nodes will contain identifiable lymphoma on sampling (see below), but the presence of lymphadenopathy has prognostic significance as can be seen in the staging system outlined in Table 23–1.

The incidence of mycosis fungoides is age dependent, ranging from 0.5 individuals per 100,000 per year below age 40 to 1.28 individuals per 100,000 per year in the eighth decade of life.

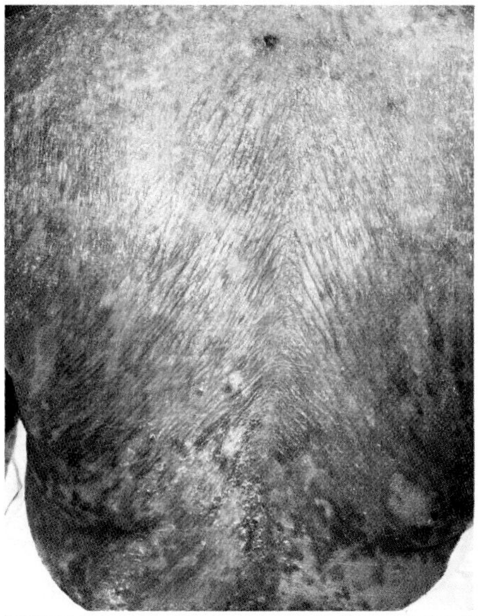

FIGURE 23–3 Patient with Sézary syndrome displays erythroderma as well as some features of poikiloderma.

Histopathology

The diagnosis of mycosis fungoides rests on the identification of malignant lymphocytes within the dermis and extending and clustering in the epidermis (epidermotropism) to form Pautrier’s microabscesses (Figure 23–4). Similar clustering may occur in follicular and/or eccrine epithelium. Recognizing these features proves more difficult in practice than in theory, and several biopsies may be required until the diagnosis is confirmed histologically. The malignant lymphocyte possesses a nucleus with an irregular out-

TABLE 23–1 TNM Classification of Mycosis Fungoides

Classification	Description
T:SKIN	
T_0	Clinically and/or histopathologically suspicious lesions
T_1	Limited plaques, papules, or patches covering 10% or less of the skin surface
T_2	Generalized plaques, papules, or patches covering 10% or more of the skin surface
T_3	Tumors, one or more
T_4	Generalized erythroderma
N:LYMPH NODES	
N_0	No clinically or palpably abnormal peripheral lymph nodes; pathology negative for mycosis fungoides
N_1	Clinically abnormal peripheral lymph nodes; pathology negative for mycosis fungoides
N_2	No clinically abnormal peripheral lymph nodes; pathology positive for mycosis fungoides
N_3	Clinically abnormal peripheral lymph nodes positive for mycosis fungoides
B:PERIPHERAL BLOOD	
B_0	Atypical circulating cells not present or less than 5%
B_1	Atypical circulating cells present in 5% or more of total blood lymphocytes
M:VISCERAL ORGANS	
M_0	No involvement of visceral organs
M_1	Visceral involvement (must have confirmation of pathology, and organ involved should be specified)

TNM = primary tumor, regional nodes, metastasis

Adapted from:
Heald P, Shapiro P, Madison J, et al. Cutaneous T-cell lymphoma. In: Arndt KA, Leboit PE, Robinson JK, Wintroub BU, eds. Cutaneous Medicine and Surgery, Vol 2. Philadelphia: W.B. Saunders, 1996, p 1650.

line, imparting a cleaved or crenated appearance (Figure 23–5). These nuclei display hyperchromatism. Overall, the malignant cells are small and often not readily recognized, even by the trained observer. However, the cells have a propensity to enter the epidermis and reside in clear lacunae, singly or in small aggregates. The malignant lymphocytes are accompanied by a larger number of reactive inflammatory cells, especially in earlier stages of the disease, whereas at later stages, the number of malignant lymphocytes increases, as does the degree of

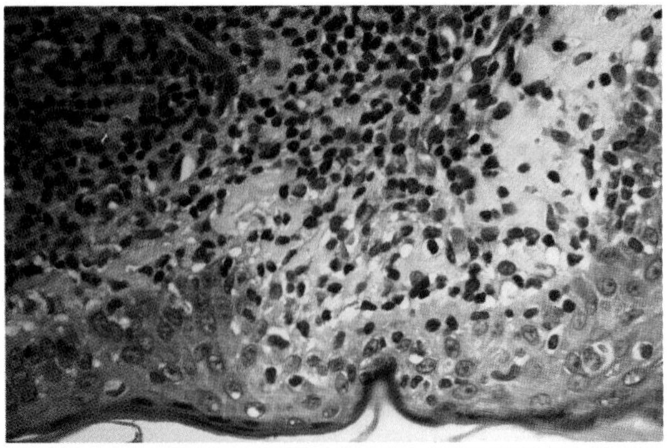

FIGURE 23–4 In mycosis fungoides, lymphocytes infiltrate the papillary dermis and extend into the epidermis without associated intercellular edema. A small collection of lymphocytes is termed a Pautrier's microabscess (x40 original magnification, hematoxylin and eosin stain).

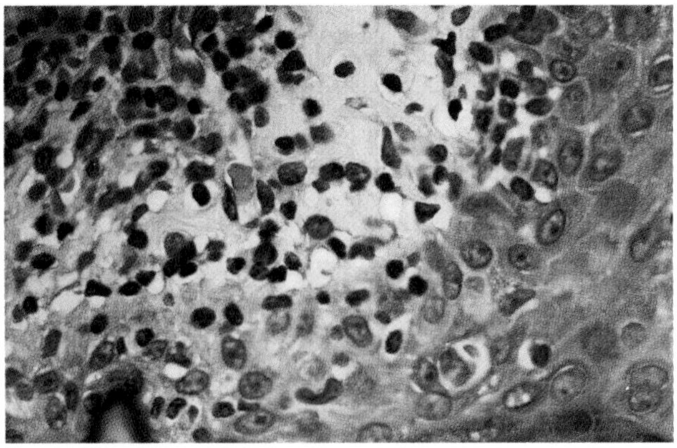

FIGURE 23–5 At higher magnification, the lymphocyte nuclei are seen to be irregular and angulated, as is typical of mycosis fungoides (×100 original magnification).

nuclear atypia. In pagetoid reticulosis, a disproportionate number of lymphocytes enter the epidermis in relation to the total mononuclear infiltrate. Aggregation of large numbers of atypical lymphocytes in the dermis produce nodules and tumors. Fibroplasia of the papillary dermis (a secondary feature) aids in the diagnosis.

Malignant lymphocytes extend into the epidermis.

Pautrier's microabscess formation

Immunophenotypic analysis reveals a predominant CD3-positive, CD4-positive infiltrate with admixture of smaller amounts of CD8-positive lymphocytes as well as scattered B lymphocytes (Table 23–2).

The ratio of CD4-positive cells to CD8-positive cells increases as the disease progresses. The malignant cell is a memory (CD45Ro-positive), CD4-positive T lymphocyte, with rare cases arising from a CD8-positive clone. Most patients possess cells with an alpha/beta receptor, but in rare cases, the tumor is composed of T lymphocytes with a gamma/delta receptor. Loss of certain cell surface markers may provide diagnostic information. Loss of CD7 characterizes the malignant lymphocytes of Sézary syndrome, and estimation of this loss in conjunction with an increased CD4/CD8 ratio in peripheral blood provides useful diagnostic data as well as quantitative measures of response to therapy. The usefulness of estimating CD7 loss in T-lymphocyte populations within the skin remains less clear. When the diagnosis of mycosis fungoides proves difficult in routine sections, immunophenotypic analysis of the infiltrate to discern relative decrease of CD7 expression will rarely add valuable information.

A typical immunophenotypic pattern is present.

The cutaneous histopathology of Sézary syndrome resembles patch stage mycosis fungoides. Often, the degree of nuclear atypia is more pronounced in infiltrates of Sézary syndrome, whereas the degree of epidermotropism is less. CD30 (Ki-1–, Reed-Sternberg–associated antigen) expression may evolve with transformation of patch- or plaque-stage mycosis fungoides to a more aggressive phenotype or when disease manifests with tumors at the outset. Nuclear irregularity and hyperchromatism become more striking, typical of all anaplastic Ki-1–positive lymphomas.

The histopathology of Sézary syndrome resembles mycosis fungoides.

Genotypic analysis of skin and peripheral blood for T-cell receptor gene rearrangement has value diagnostically when the measures noted above fail to provide resolution. Results of determination of clonality must be placed in the context of the clinical and histopathologic findings in a given patient, as pitfalls exist in the interpretation of this technology, that is, some benign diseases may occasionally display clonal populations, and the reliability of a negative finding is not clearly established.

Genotypic analysis

Pathogenesis

The causes of mycosis fungoides and the factors that explain the varied progression of disease among individuals defy explanation. A process of aberrant exten-

TABLE 23–2 Selected Immunophenotypic Markers Useful in the Analysis of Cutaneous Lymphoid Infiltrates

Classification	Description
CD2	Pan T-cell marker
CD3	T-cell receptor–related antigen
CD4	Helper/inducer subset
CD5	Pan T-cell marker
CD7	Pan T- and B-cell marker lost in Sézary syndrome
CD8	Cytotoxic/suppressor subset
CD20/22	Pan B-cell marker
CD45	Common leukocyte antigen
CD56	NK cells
Kappa and lambda light chains	Plasma cells (to determine monoclonality)

Malignant cells produce a T_h2 cytokine profile.

sion of T lymphocytes into the epidermis is postulated with subsequent genetic alterations leading to clonal expansion and neoplasia. As noted above, the malignant lymphocyte is a CD4-positive T cell with a memory phenotype (CD45 Ro-positive). The malignant cells generally produce a cytokine profile typical of T_h2 cells. Weakened host immunity and tumor surveillance referable to reduced number and function of CD8 and CD4 T cells likely contribute to disease progression. Speculation that a retrovirus plays a role in the etiology of mycosis fungoides lacks confirmation to date.

Therapy

Various therapies produce remission.

Controversy exists regarding optimal therapy for the various stages of mycosis fungoides. It is unclear whether treatment results in cure or even significant prolongation of life for some stages of the disease, but disease-free remissions are achieved by using various modalities alone and in combination. The most frequently encountered forms of the disease, namely, patch and plaque stages, generally respond to photochemotherapy (psoralen plus ultraviolet A light [PUVA]), topical application of nitrogen mustard, or total skin electron beam radiation. (For further discussion of the use of ultraviolet light in the treatment of mycosis fungoides, see Chapter 71, "Phototherapy and Photochemotherapy of Skin Disease.") Extracorporeal photophoresis is the treatment of choice in erythrodermic forms of the disease, especially with the leukemic phase. In tumor stage disease or with other disease progression, systemic administration of interferon alpha or interferon gamma, beginning at a dose of 3 million units three times weekly may provide a beneficial response. Table 23–3 lists therapies employed in treating mycosis fungoides.

Prognosis

Prognosis parallels extent of disease

Prognosis is best for patients with limited extent (10% of body surface or less) patch- or plaque-stage disease, approaching a 10- to 12-year survival. The advent of tumors, erythroderma, palpable lymph nodes (whether microscopically involved or not), and visceral involvement all portend a worse prognosis with a 2- to 3-year survival being average.

Annotated Bibliography

Heald P, Yan SL, Latkowski J, et al. Profound deficiency in normal circulating T-cells in erythrodermic cutaneous T-cell lymphoma. Arch Dermatol 1994;130:198–204.

This article discusses the role of host immunity in the progression of cutaneous T-cell lymphoma.

TABLE 23–3 Mycosis Fungoides: Selected Therapies

PUVA
Nitrogen mustard
Total skin radiotherapy
Extracorporeal photophoresis
Spot radiotherapy
Topical carmustine (BCNU)
Interferon
DAB-interleukin-2 toxin
Methotrexate
Etoposide
Fludarabine

Adapted from:
Heald P, Shapiro P, Madison J, et al. Cutaneous T-cell lymphoma. In: Arndt KA, Leboit PE, Robinson JK, Wintroub BU, eds. Cutaneous Medicine and Surgery, Vol. 2, Philadelphia: W.B. Saunders, 1996, p 1651.

Lamberg SI, Bunn PA Jr. Proceedings of the workshop on cutaneous T-cell lymphomas (mycosis fungoides and Sézary syndrome). Cancer Treat Rep 1979;63:561–572.

This article provides a clinical review of a large series of patients with mycosis fungoides.

Lessin SR, Roo AH, Rovera G. Molecular diagnosis of cutaneous T-cell lymphoma: polymerase chain reaction amplification of T-cell antigen receptor beta-chain gene rearrangements. J Invest Dermatol 1991; 96: 299–302.

The polymerase chain reaction has value in the identification of clonality for diagnostic purposes.

Mostow EN, Neckel SL, Oberhelman L, et al. Complete remissions in psoralen and UVA (PUVA)-refractory mycosis fungoides-type cutaneous T-cell lymphoma with combined interferon alfa and PUVA. Arch Dermatol 1993;129:747–762.

The article explains the value of PUVA as a mainstay in the therapy of mycosis fungoides.

Spapiro PE, Pinto F. The histologic spectrum of mycosis fungoides/Sézary syndrome (cutaneous T-cell lymphoma): a review of 222 biopsies, including newly-described patterns and the earliest pathologic changes. Am J Surg Pathol 1994;18:654–667.

This is a large review of histopathologic changes in mycosis fungoides.

Wood GS, Bahler DW, Hoppe RT. Transformation of mycosis fungoides: T-cell receptor beta gene analysis demonstrates a common clonal origin for plaque-type mycosis fungoides and CD 30 large cell lymphoma. J Am Acad Dermatol 1987;17:40–52.

Lymphomatoid Papulosis

Thomas D. Horn, M.D.

Rare disease

Lymphomatoid papulosis is a rare disease with a prevalence of 1.2 to 1.9 individuals per million population per year. Men and women are affected in roughly equal proportion. Peak incidence is in the fourth to fifth decades of life, although children and the elderly also develop the disease.

Relationship with Hodgkin's disease and mycosis fungoides

An association exists between lymphomatoid papulosis and Hodgkin's disease, mycosis fungoides, and anaplastic (CD30-positive) large cell lymphoma. The frequency of this association is unclear but ranges between 10 and 20% of cases. The diagnosis of lymphoma may precede, be concomitant with, or follow the diagnosis of lymphomatoid papulosis. Men are more likely to have an associated lymphoma.

Clinical Features

Dynamic disease
New lesions are occurring at same time others are regressing.

Lymphomatoid papulosis consists of erythematous papules and nodules with erosion and ulceration distributed widely on any skin surface but mostly on the trunk. Individual lesions resolve spontaneously with new lesions forming at other sites resulting in the continual presence of the disease in a dynamic state of evolution and regression (Figure 23–6). Papules heal with hyperpigmentation. Because the disease is photosensitive (see below), the face is often spared. Mucous membranes are not involved. Clinically, lymphomatoid papulosis may resemble pityriasis lichenoides et varioliformis acuta (PLEVA) and arthropod bite reactions. A skin biopsy specimen is required to establish the diagnosis.

Histopathology

Malignant cell is CD30 positive.

Lymphomatoid papulosis displays two histopathologic variants. The more common (type A) consists of a polymorphous dermal infiltrate composed of small

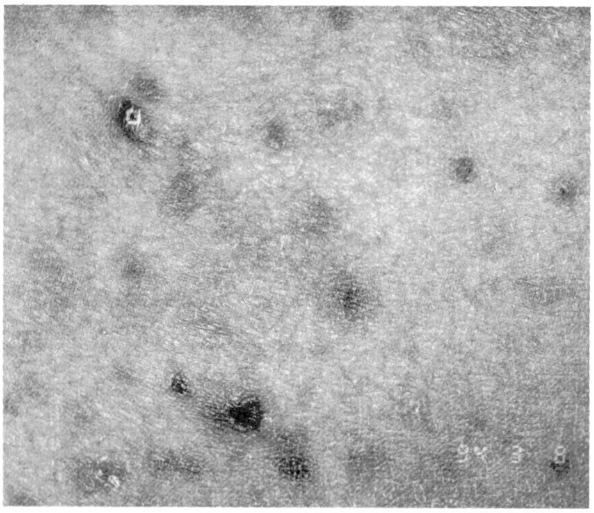

FIGURE 23–6 Lymphomatoid papulosis—erythematous papules in various stages of evolution are present.

lymphocytes, eosinophils, histiocytes, and overtly malignant lymphocytes (CD30-positive) with abundant cytoplasm bearing highly irregular hyperchromatic nuclei (Figure 23–7). Mitotic figures are common and frequently atypical. The infiltrate assumes a wedge or inverted triangle configuration. Epidermal erosion and ulceration occur commonly. The less common form (type B) resembles mycosis fungoides so strongly as to be indistinguishable on histopathologic criteria.

In type A, the number of CD30-positive cells varies greatly in proportion to the total infiltrate but should comprise 15 to 20% at a minimum. Sheets of large atypical CD30-positive cells occur more commonly in CD30-positive anaplastic large cell lymphoma, and this finding should only be interpreted as lymphomatoid papulosis with caution.

Differential diagnosis includes PLEVA.

Pityriasis lichenoides et varioliformis acuta may be distinguished from lymphomatoid papulosis by the absence of an atypical mononuclear cell population. Further, the infiltrate of PLEVA is composed almost solely of lymphocytes, lacking the prominent eosinophils of lymphomatoid papulosis. The distinction of lymphomatoid papulosis from an arthropod bite may be more problematic in that samples from the latter disorder may display mononuclear cells with large and irregular contours, some of which will express CD30. Although overlay may exist, the proportion of CD30-positive cells in an arthropod bite reaction will generally be less than in lymphomatoid papulosis.

Loss of CD7

As noted, a significant population of CD30-positive lymphocytes characterizes the immunopathology of lymphomatoid papulosis. The cells lack CD15 expression, typical of Hodgkin's disease. The neoplastic cell is a CD4-positive T lymphocyte with aberrant pan–T-cell marker expression, including loss of CD7 among others.

Pathogenesis

Lymphomatoid papulosis is a clonal or oligoclonal proliferation of T lymphocytes. The same clone may be identified in lesions of lymphomatoid papulosis as in an associated lymphoma, when present. Aneuploidy and polyploidy are reported. The cause of the disease remains unknown. Whether lymphomatoid

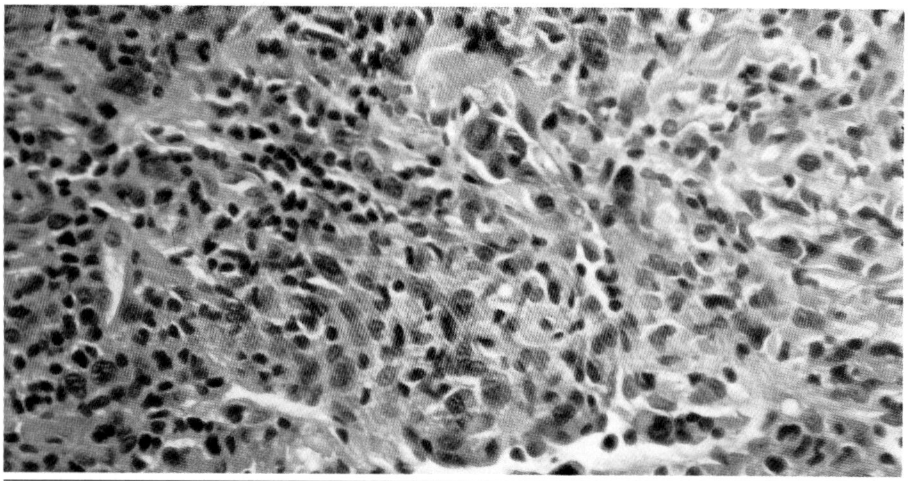

FIGURE 23–7 Lymphomatoid papulosis—a polymorphous infiltrate is seen. Large cells possessing prominent irregular and hyperchromatic nuclei represent the CD30-positive population. (×100 original magnification)

papulosis is a benign disease that is associated with lymphoma or whether lymphomatoid papulosis is a lymphoma that from the outset remains localized to the skin in the majority of cases is controversial.

Therapy

Therapy of lymphomatoid papulosis is directed toward control of the disease rather than cure. Ultraviolet light B or psoralen plus ultraviolet A, alone or in combination with erythromycin or tetracycline is beneficial. Failing this regimen, topical nitrogen mustard or orally/parenterally administered methotrexate may be employed. Methotrexate is given in a regimen similar to that for psoriasis. There is no evidence that treatment of lymphomatoid papulosis prevents progression to systemic lymphoma.

Ultraviolet light is very effective.

Topical nitrogen mustard
Methotrexate

Prognosis

In the absence of the development of systemic lymphoma, lymphomatoid papulosis follows a benign course with a variable number of lesions over long periods of time. The prognosis of the disease in the presence of systemic lymphoma is related directly to the course of the systemic malignant neoplasm.

Annotated Bibliography

Beljaards R, Willemze R. The prognosis of patients with lymphomatoid papulosis associated with malignant lymphoma. Br J Dermatol 1992;126:596–602.

Davis T, Morton C, Miller-Cassman R, et al. Hodgkin's disease, lymphomatoid papulosis and cutaneouse T-cell lymphoma derived from a common T-cell clone. N Engl J Med 1992;326:1115–1122.

These articles describe the relationship of lymphomatoid papulosis with Hodgkin's disease.

Kadin M, Nasu K, Sako D, et al. Lymphomatoid papulosis: a cutaneous proliferation of activated helper T-cells expressing Hodgkin's disease-associated antigens. Am J Pathol 1985;119:315–325.

Kadin M, Vonderheid E, Sako D, et al. Clonal composition of T-cells in lymphomatoid papulosis. Am J Pathol 1987;126:13–17.

Macaulay W. Lymphomatoid papulosis: a continuing, self-healing eruption, clinically benign-histologically malignant. Arch Dermatol 1968;97:23–30.

Sanchez N, Pittelkow M, Muller S, et al. The clinicopathologic spectrum of lymphomatoid papulosis: study of 31 cases. J Am Acad Dermatol 1983;8:81–94.

Smoller B, Longacre T, Warnke R. Ki-1 (CD30) expression and differentiation of lymphomatoid papulosis from arthropod bite reactions. Mod Pathol 1992;5:492–496.

Vonderheid EC, Sajjadian A, Kadin ME. Methotrexate for lymphomatoid papulosis and other primary cutaneous CD30-positive lymphoproliferative disorders. J Am Acad Dermatol 1996;34:470–481.

Weiss L, Wood G, Trela M, et al. Clonal T-cell population in lymphomatoid papulosis: evidence of a lymphoproliferative origin for a clinically benign disease. N Engl J Med 1986;315:475–479.

This series of articles details various aspects of lymphomatoid papulosis.

Adult T-cell Leukemia/Lymphoma

Thomas T. Provost, M.D.

This is an aggressive, rare form of T-cell leukemia, induced by the human T-cell lymphotrophic virus type I (HTLV-1). The disease is endemic in the southern part of Japan, the southeastern United States, the Caribbean, and in sub-Saharan Africa.

Caused by retrovirus

The HTLV-1 virus infects CD4-positive T lymphocytes. The virus, via reverse transcriptase, inserts its genome randomly into the host cell DNA. Malignant degeneration, however, occurs in only a few patients.

The most common way of transmission is from mother to child via breast milk. The disease can also be transmitted by sexual contact and transfusion (leukocytes).

Clinical Features

Prominent skin involvement

Recalcitrant hypercalcemia is characteristic

This may be a rapidly progressive and fatal disease (survival measured in months) whose skin manifestations include erythematous nodules and a generalized erythematous, exfoliative, hyperpigmented dermatitis involving large areas of the body. Approximately 5% of patients with adult T-cell lymphoma have smoldering disease, with a survival frequently exceeding 4 years. Recalcitrant hypercalcemia is a characteristic frequent feature, as are lytic bone lesions. The best evidence indicates that the hypercalcemia is induced by the tumor secretion of tumor necrosis factor alpha and beta, and a parathyroid-like peptide.

This is a multiorgan disease characterized by generalized lymphadenopathy, hepatosplenomegaly, and central nervous system involvement, in addition to skin involvement.

Pathology

"Flower cell"
CD4-positive, CD25-positive T-cell

Pautrier's microabscess formation is present, and the disease must be differentiated from Sézary syndrome and mycosis fungoides. In the peripheral blood, the atypical lymphocytes have a multilobular nucleus ("flower cell"). The malignant cells are CD4 positive, CD25 positive. The presence of CD25 (interleukin-2 receptor) distinguishes this disease from Sézary syndrome. The presence of anti-HTLV-1 antibodies and the clonal presence of HTLV-1 DNA also help to establish the diagnosis.

Annotated Bibliography

Kim JH, Durack DT. Manifestations of HTLV-1 infection. Am J Med 1988;84:919–928.

This is a good article reviewing clinical features.

Angiocentric T-cell Lymphomas

Thomas T. Provost, M.D.

Angiocentric T-cell lymphoma is a systemic disease that frequently involves the skin and is part of the spectrum of diseases termed "angiocentric immunoproliferative lesions." These lesions include lethal midline granuloma (polymorphic reticulosis), lymphomatoid granulomatosus, and angiocentric lymphoma.

Angiocentric localization of malignant T-cells

The skin lesions of these systemic lymphomas are variable, ranging from violaceous papules to nodules or ulcers frequently involving the nose and central portion of face. In contradistinction to the epitropism of mycosis fungoides and lipotropism of subcutaneous T-cell lymphoma, these lesions are clearly angiocentric and angiodestructive. A perivascular infiltrate of atypical T lymphocytes (CD3-positive, CD4-positive) is detected. However, at times both angiocentric and subcutaneous T-cell lymphomas have been associated with a fatal outcome and a hemophagocytic syndrome. In addition, at least one patient has been reported to have demonstrated both an angiocentric and subcutaneous T-cell lymphoma. Thus, There may be some overlap between these two syndromes.

Epstein-Barr virus has been detected in these cutaneous T-cell lymphomas.

Annotated Bibliography

Jaffe ES, et al. Lymphomatoid granulomatosis and angiocentric lymphoma: a spectrum of post-thymic-T cell proliferation. Semin Respir Med 1989;10:167–180.

Su IJ, Tsai TF, Cheng, AL, Chen CC. Cutaneous manifestations of Epstein-Barr virus-associated T cell lymphoma. J Am Acad Dermatol 1993;29:685–690.

These are two good articles!

Medeiros LJ, Peiper SC, Elwood L, et al. Angiocentric immunoproliferative lesions: a molecular analysis of eight cases. Hum Pathol 1991;22:1150–1157.

Subcutaneous T-cell Lymphoma

Thomas T. Provost, M.D.

It is only within the past 8 to 10 years that this distinct clinicopathologic entity has been recognized as a specific subset of T-cell lymphomas. Prior to that time, immunohistologic staining techniques were unavailable and the true nature of the lesion unrecognized. It is highly likely that many cases previously described as fatal Weber-Christian disease and cutaneous malignant histiocytosis included this entity.

Previously described as part of spectrum of malignant histiocytosis or Weber-Christian disease

Clinical Features

In contradistinction to the epitropism associated with mycosis fungoides and Sézary syndrome, subcutaneous T-cell lymphomas demonstrate lipotropism. In general, these patients develop subcutaneous nodular lesions involving all areas of the body, with a predilection for the lower extremities, mimicking a panniculitis. Frequently, the malignant nature of the disease process is not recognized. A benign, acute, or chronic panniculitis or lobular panniculitis is frequently diagnosed. Fever, chills, malaise, and a sore throat may accompany these lesions. The nodules may demonstrate erythema and increased warmth and can range in size from 1 to 10 cm. Ulceration frequently occurs.

Histology

Histologically, the lesions demonstrate a moderate-to-dense lymphocytic infiltrate in the subcutaneous fat. Early lesions may demonstrate only atypical lymphocytes. In addition to the subcutaneous localization, the deep reticular dermis may also be involved with atypical lymphocytes. Karyorrhexis, necrosis, and erythrophagocytosis by histiocytic-appearing cells is characteristic.

Immunophenotypic findings, using both paraffin and frozen section immunoperoxidase techniques, have demonstrated that the subcutaneous infiltrate is composed of T lymphocytes and histiocytes. Furthermore, the T cells have a mature phenotype (CD1-negative, CD2-positive, and CD3-positive). Most T cells express the CD4 antigen. The CD8 antigen has also been infrequently detected. In some patients, a pan–T-cell antigen loss (CD5-negative) and (CD7-negative) has also been detected. CD5 antigen loss has only been found in association with malignancy. A CD7 antigen loss is suggestive of malignancy but may occur in some benign cutaneous lesions. T-cell receptor gene rearrangement of the beta chain has also been demonstrated.

Immunotypic studies have established true nature of the disease: a malignant T-cell lymphoma

Prognosis and Therapy

Subcutaneous T-cell lymphoma commonly develops into a hemophagocytic syndrome, characterized by fever, hemorrhage, cytopenia, and evidence of erythrophagocytosis in sites outside the subcutaneous tissue. It is associated with a high mortality rate. For example, in the series reported by Jaffe's group, The National Institutes of Health, five of eight patients with subcutaneous T-cell lymphoma died, and despite aggressive chemotherapy, all at the time of death demonstrated a hemophagocytic syndrome. In general, this syndrome is associated with a rapid demise, although some patients have been successfully treated with a combination of cyclophosphamide, doxorubicin, vincristine, and prednisone and have

Hemophagocytic syndrome is associated with a high mortality rate.

Two clinical types most common
A rapidly fatal disease
A chronic, indolent cutaneous disease

remained in prolonged remission, free of evidence of lymphoma (see reference by Gonzalez for further information). Although, classically, subcutaneous T-cell lymphoma has a rapid progressive fatal course, there is some evidence to suggest the existence of a more benign chronic variant characterized by recurrent, self-healing subcutaneous nodules occurring over a 5- to 10-year period.

The author has personally seen two cases of subcutaneous T-cell lymphoma and both had a rapidly progressive fatal outcome. One was a 29-year-old laboratory technician who developed chronic erythematous nodules on her arms and legs, some of which demonstrated central necrosis with a discharge of yellowish serosanguinous material. Repeated biopsies revealed an atypical lymphocytic infiltrate. The duration of the disease process until the onset of a fatal hemophagocytic syndrome was 14 months. This occurred despite aggressive chemotherapy.

The other patient was a 38-year-old Caucasian male who had widespread cutaneous necrotic lesions, which on biopsy were felt to represent a form of Weber-Christian disease. The true nature of his lymphomatous disease process was not recognized antemortem.

Annotated Bibliography

Wick MR, Sanchez AG, Crotty CP, et al. Cutaneous malignant histiocytosis—a clinical and histopathologic study of eight cases with immunohistochemical analysis. J Am Acad Dermatol 1983;8:50–62.

This article is a classic, early description of this entity.

Gonzalez CL, et al. T cell lymphoma involving subcutaneous tissue: clinical pathologic entity commonly associated with hemophagocytic syndrome. Am J Surg Pathol 1991; 15:17–27.

Perniciaro C, et al. Subcutaneous T cell lymphoma. A report of two additional cases and further observations. Arch Dermatol 1993;129:1171–1176.

These two articles detail the immunophenotypic profile of the invading cells.

CHAPTER 24

Leukemia, B-cell Lymphomas, and Multiple Myeloma and Paraproteins

Karen Huhn, M.D., Thomas T. Provost, M.D., Richard L. Humphrey, M.D.

Leukemia

Karen Huhn, M.D., Thomas T. Provost, M.D.

Cutaneous manifestations are common in all forms of leukemia. Most of the cutaneous manifestations in acute leukemia, with present treatment regimens, however, are not related to the disease process but are secondary to drug reactions, graft-versus-host disease, or bacterial or fungal infections. For example, in one study that examined biopsies of skin lesions from 71 acute myelogenous leukemia (AML) patients, 30% demonstrated leukemia cutis, 17% demonstrated graft-versus-host disease, and 32% demonstrated drug reactions. Eight fungal and 3 bacterial folliculitis lesions were detected. Six biopsies of leukocytoclastic vasculitis (8%) and 4 biopsies (6%) of intraepidermal blistering disorders were seen (2 Grover's disease, 1 Hailey-Hailey disease, and 1 patient with an unspecified intraepidermal acantholytic blister).

In acute leukemia, most cutaneous manifestations not related to leukemic process
Drug reactions and graft-versus-host reactions more prominent

In chronic myelogenous leukemia (CML) and chronic lymphocytic leukemia (CLL), leukemia cutis may occur in as many as 20% of patients (Figure 24–1). On occasion, Sweet's syndrome is seen, most commonly in AML. Sweet's syndrome can also be rarely detected in patients with CLL (For further discussion on Sweet's syndrome, see Chapter 29, "Paraneoplastic Syndromes.")

In chronic myelogeneous leukemia and chronic lymphocytic leukemia, infiltrates are frequent.

Clinical Features

The cutaneous infiltrates of leukemia may be pink, red, brown, or violaceous papules, plaques, arciform lesions, nodules, or tumors, which occur on all areas of the body. In CLL, a leonine facies may be present. Purpura, reflective of thrombocytopenia, may be present. Ulceration of lesions is most frequent in monocytic leukemias. Rarely, subcutaneous nodules simulating erythema nodosum may occur. (We have recently evaluated a 43-year-old African American female with erythematous nodular lesions around the ankles, simulating erythema nodosum. Blood studies revealed AML.)

Violaceous nodules and plaques are characteristic.

Oral lesions occur in all forms of leukemia but are especially prominent in acute monocytic leukemia where gingival hyperplasia is characteristic. (For further discussion, see Chapter 73, "Oral Manifestations of Systemic Disease.")

Oral lesions found in all forms of leukemia
Gingival hyperplasia prominent in monocytic leukemia

Acute myelogenous leukemia is also associated with chloroma or granulocytic sarcoma, an uncommon tumor produced by an infiltration of myeloblasts into the periosteum of orbital or cranial bones or other sites, including the skin. The

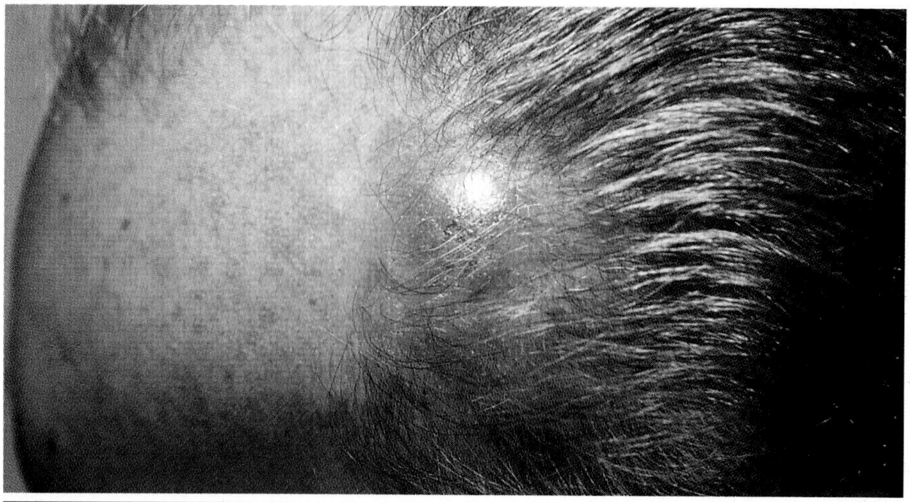

FIGURE 24–1 Leukemic nodule, left side of the scalp, in a patient with chronic myelogenous leukemia.

name "chloroma" is derived from the greenish color of air-exposed specimens due to the high cellular concentration of myeloperoxidase. Chloromas may occur as harbingers of AML, several years before other signs and symptoms develop; in CML, a chloroma is indicative of blast transformation.

Clinical Course

Leukemia cutis is most frequently seen several months after the diagnosis of leukemia. The prognosis of patients with CML or AML and leukemia cutis is grave. Most patients die within 2 months of the histologic diagnosis of leukemia cutis. (For example, in one study of 134 patients, none of the leukemia cutis patients survived greater than 7 months.) Patients with CLL have a longer survival period; the mean interval between diagnosis and death is 16 months.

Histology

The histopathology of leukemia cutis includes a diffuse monomorphous infiltrate of leukemic cells in the dermis and subcutaneous tissue, often infiltrating between collagen bundles. The morphology of infiltrating cells is predominantly small mature lymphocytes in CLL, lymphoblasts in acute lymphoblastic leukemia, immature granulocytes in AML, mature granulocytes in CML, and monocytes in acute myelomonocytic leukemia.

Cytochemical and cytomorphologic studies of the bone marrow and peripheral blood smears are reliable for determining the type of leukemia.

Annotated Bibliography

Desch JK, Smoller BR. The spectrum of cutaneous disease in leukemias. J Cutan Pathol 1993;20: 407–410.

This article provides a good summary!

Ratnam KV, Su WPD, Ziesmer SC, et al. Value of immunohistochemistry in the diagnosis of leukemia cutis: study of 54 cases using paraffin-section markers. J Cutan Pathol 1992;19:193–200.

These authors provide data on the efficacy of the use of the following immunohistochemical stains for leukemia cutis: lymphocytes—CD45 (leukocyte common antigen)-positive; T-cells—CD45Ro (UCHL-1)–positive, but only scattered; B-cells—CD20 (L-26)-positive and CD43 (Leu-22) usually negative; granulocytes—lysosome-positive in well- and poorly differentiated granulocytes; chloroacetate esterase–positive in well-differentiated granulocytes, CD68 (KP-1) usually negative in all granulocytes; and monocytes-lysosome–positive in well- and poorly differentiated monocytes; CD68 (KP-1)–positive in well-differentiated monocytes; and chloroacetate esterase usually negative.

SuWPD. Clinical, histopathologic, and immunochemical correlations in leukemia cutis. Semin Dermatol 1994;13:223–230.

This excellent review includes a very good bibliography.

Baer MR. Management of unusual presentations of acute leukemia. Hematol Oncol Clin North Am 1993;7:275–290.

This article provides a good review of cutaneous manifestations.

B-cell Lymphomas

Karen Huhn, M.D., Thomas T. Provost, M.D.

A variety of cutaneous B-cell lymphomas, presenting as nodules and tumors, have been described (Figures 24–2 to 24–5). In this chapter, the European Organization for Research and Treatment of Cancer (EORTC) classification is employed.

Immunohistochemical markers employed for the analysis of cutaneous lymphomas on routine formalin-fixed, paraffin-embedded tissue are listed in Table 24–1.

Follicle Center Cell Lymphoma

Follicle lymphoma: good prognosis

This is a low-grade cutaneous lymphoma characterized by solitary or grouped erythematous papules, plaques, or tumors, usually involving predominantly the scalp and forehead. Ulceration is rare. Biopsies demonstrate nodular or diffuse pandermal infiltrates extending into the subcutaneous fat composed of small- and large-cleaved follicle center cells (centrocytes) and large follicle center cells with prominent nucleoli (centroblasts). Follicle formation is almost never seen. In addition, accompanying reactive (human leukocyte antigen–positive HLA+) small lymphocytes and histiocytes/macrophages are present.

The neoplastic B-cells express Ig, CD19, CD20, CD22, and CD79a; staining for bcl-2 is negative in contrast to nodal follicle lymphoma. Monoclonal rearrangement of the JH immunoglobin gene is detected in the majority of cases. No specific chromosome alteration has been identified. Treatment involves radiotherapy, excision of single lesions, and systemic steroids. A 95% 5-year survivability has been reported.

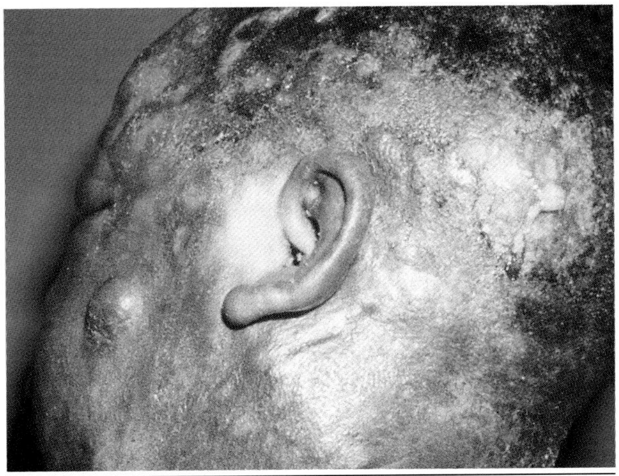

FIGURE 24–2 Nodular tumor lesions of a B-cell lymphoma. Note ulcerating tumor on the scalp.

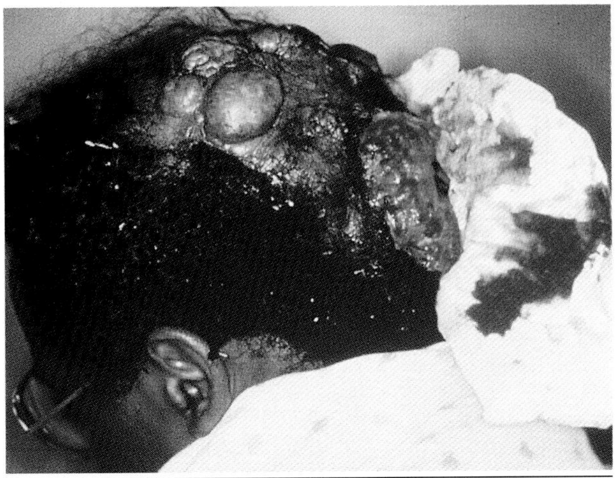

FIGURE 24–3 Multiple nodules and tumors of a B-cell lymphoma of the scalp. Note ulceration.

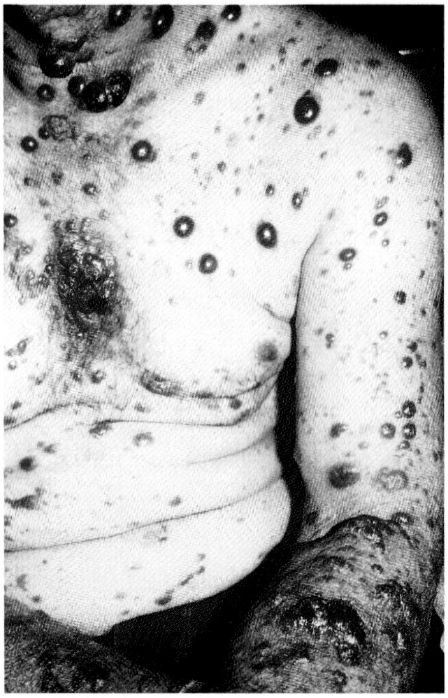

FIGURE 24–4 Lymphoma of acute onset producing widespread erythematous nodules and tumors.

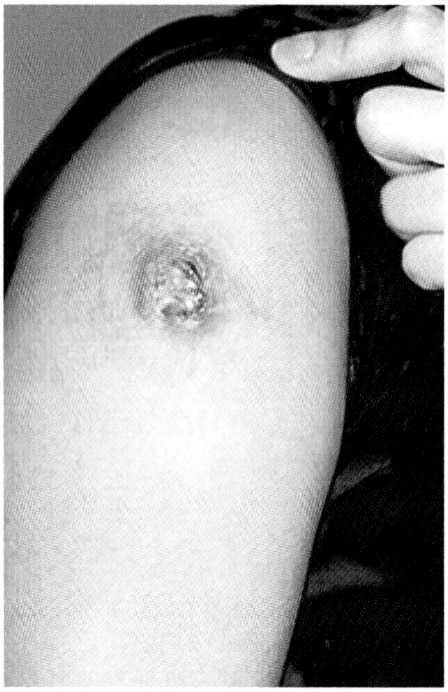

FIGURE 24–5 Solitary nodular lesion of a lymphoma.

Immunocytoma

These lesions present as a solitary nodule or as multiple subcutaneous nodules generally located on the lower extremities. Immunocytoma is a proliferation of plasma cells, lymphoplasmacytoid cells, and small lymphocytes. Primary cutaneous immunocytoma differs from nodal immunocytoma, in that patients do not show features of Waldenström's macroglobulinemia. The prognosis of immunocytoma is excellent, though skin relapses are common.

The term immunocytoma was based on the terminology of the Kiel classification. In the REAL and WHO (World Health Organization) classification, extranodal immunocytomas were included in the group of extranodal marginal B-cell lymphomas. The EORTC group recognized the overlapping features between cases and included a category of immunocytoma/marginal zone B-cell lymphoma.

Marginal Zone B-cell Lymphoma

Marginal zone B-cell lymphoma: good prognosis

Marginal zone B-cell lymphoma is a low-grade lymphoma characterized by recurrent, solitary red to reddish-brown papules and nodules, localized predominantly on the upper extremities and face. Biopsy reveals a patchy, nodular, or diffuse dermal infiltrate of plasma, dendritic, T, and B-cells. The nodular aggregate is composed of a germinal center with mantle zone surrounded by marginal zone cells. The malignant clonal proliferation is confined to the marginal zone (hence, the origin of the name). The malignant cells express CD20, CD79a, and bcl-2. CD5 is not detected. Most cases demonstrate monotypic immunoglobin light chain expression with clonal rearrangement of the J_H gene. No specific genetic alteration has been identified. These patients usually respond to local radiotherapy. Prognosis is excellent.

At the present time, we are following up a 43-year-old African American female with a 10-year history of this type of lesion. Initially, the lesion involved the forehead and scalp and was treated with local radiation therapy. The patient was in complete clinical remission for at least 7 years before developing a biopsy-proven solitary recurrent lesion over her right eyebrow. Intralesional steroid injection caused the disappearance of the lesion.

TABLE 24–1 Immunohistochemical Markers Useful in Typing Lymphomas

CD Number	Interpretation
CD1a	Langerhans' cell marker
CD2	T lymphocyte marker
CD3	Pan T-cell marker (mature thymocytes, peripheral T lymphocytes)
CD4	T helper/inducer cell marker
CD5	T lymphocyte marker
CD7	
CD8	T suppressor, natural killer cell marker
CD15	Hodgkin's cell marker
CD19	B-cell marker
CD20	B-cell marker
CD21	Dendritic reticulin cell marker
CD22	B-cell marker
CD30	(also termed "Ki -1") Hodgkin's cell marker, anaplastic large cell lymphoma, plasma cells
CD43	B-cell marker
CD45Ro	T-cell marker
CD56	Natural killer cell marker
CD68	Macrophage marker
CD79a	B-cell marker
Kappa/lambda	Light chain marker
KI-67	Proliferation marker
LCA	Leukocyte common antigen present on all white blood cells
TIA-1	Cytotoxic T-cell marker
Bcl-2	Protein inhibits apoptotic cell death

TIA-1 = T-cell intracellular antigen-1.

Large B-cell Lymphoma of the Leg

Large B-cell lymphoma: guarded prognosis

This cutaneous lymphoma is characterized by reddish-blue nodules and tumors occurring almost always on distal lower extremities of elderly patients, usually female. The lesions often ulcerate. Biopsy demonstrates a dense, diffuse pandermal, subcutaneous infiltrate of large B-cells, centroblasts, and immunoblasts. Mitoses are frequent. Small reactive lymphocytes are sparse. The cell-surface marker bcl-2 is present, and monotypic surface or cytoplasmic immunoglobulin and light chains are detected. There is monoclonal rearrangement of the J_H gene. Specific chromosomal alterations are not detected. Treatment for solitary lesions is radiotherapy and surgical excision. Relapse after treatment for multiple lesions is common. Systemic spread may occur years after treatment. This tumor has a 50% survivability at 5 years.

Intravascular Cutaneous B-cell Lymphoma

Intravascular cutaneous B-cell lymphoma: poor prognosis

The disease process of intravascular cutaneous B-cell lymphoma (formerly malignant angioendotheliomatosis) is characterized by violaceous plaques and patches on the trunk and thighs. Biopsy demonstrates large lymphoid cells within dilated dermal and subcutaneous blood vessels expressing CD19, CD20, CD22, and CD79a markers. Monotypic cell surface immunoglobulins are detected. There is monoclonal rearrangement of the J_H gene. No specific chromosomal alteration has been detected. Treatment is systemic chemotherapy. Prognosis is poor.

Annotated Bibliography

Küppers R, Klein U, Hansmann ML, et al. Cellular origin of human B-cell lymphomas. N Engl J Med 1999;341:1520-1529.

This is an informative review of the origins of B-cell lymphomas.

Willemze R, Kerl M, Sterry W, et al. EORTC classification for primary cutaneous lymphomas: a proposal from the Cutaneous Lymphma Group of European Organization for Research and Treatment of Cancer. Blood 1997;90:354–371.

Kerl M, Cerroni L. Primary B-cell lymphomas of the skin. Ann Oncol 1997;8(Suppl2): 529–532.

Good review!

Multiple Myeloma and Paraproteins

Richard L. Humphrey, M.D., Thomas T. Provost, M.D.

Cutaneous manifestations associated with multiple myeloma and paraproteins are uncommon. These manifestations include plasmacytomas or cutaneous features induced by the paraprotein (eg, cryoglobulins, amyloid) and are listed in Table 24–2.

Plasmacytomas

Plasmacytoma: associated with increased tumor burden
Late event
Poor prognosis

Extramedullary plasmacytomas are metastatic lesions of plasma cells. The plasmacytomas may appear as solitary, reddish, violaceous, nontender dermal or subcutaneous nodules. In general, this is a late manifestation of multiple myeloma generally associated with a poor prognosis. However, on unusual occasions, extramedullary plasmacytomas may antedate (by months) the onset of multiple myeloma.

Biopsy demonstrates sheets of plasma cells. Monoclonal cytoplasmic immunoglobulin is demonstrated. The cells are CD38 positive and CD20 negative.

TABLE 24–2 Cutaneous Manifestations Associated with Multiple Myeloma and Paraproteins

Cutaneous plasmacytomas
Primary (or immunoglobulin-related) amyloidosis
Type I cryoglobulinemia
POEMS syndrome
Xanthomas
Scleredema adultorum
Subcorneal pustular dermatosis (Sneddon-Wilkinson disease)
Pyoderma gangrenosum
Necrobiotic xanthogranuloma
Acquired cutis laxa
Lichen myxedematosus (scleromyxedema)
Schnitzler's syndrome

POEMS = *p*olyneuropathy, *o*rganomegaly, *e*ndocrinopathy, *M* protein (serum and/or urine monoclonal immunoglobulin proteins), *s*kin changes.

Annotated Bibliography

Kois JM, Sexton M, Lookingbill DP. Cutaneous manifestations of multiple myeloma. Arch Dermatol 1997;127:69–74.

This review of 115 multiple myeloma patients demonstrates that cutaneous features are very unusual.

Daoud MS, Lust J, Kyle RA, et al. Monoclonal gammopathies and associated skin disorders. J Am Acad Dermatol 1999;40:507–535.

This is an excellent article from the Mayo Clinic, documenting many of the cutaneous features associated with monoclonal gammopathies, including multiple myeloma. These features include plasmacytomas, amyloidosis, type I cryoglobulins, osteosclerotic myeloma (POEMS or Crow-Fukase syndrome), scleromyxedema, scleroderma, necrobiotic xanthogranuloma, plane xanthoma, Schnitzler's syndrome, vasculitis, pyoderma gangrenosum, subcorneal pustular dermatosis, and Sweet's syndrome.

Much work in this area has been performed by Dr. Richard K. Winkelman.

The review articles contain excellent bibliographies.

Primary Amyloidosis

Primary amyloidosis is a form of amyloid deposition in which the amyloid fibril is composed of an immunoglobulin light chain or variable V_L region light chain fragment. Approximately 30 to 40% of primary amyloidosis patients have cutaneous features. By light microscopy, amorphous material is shown to accumulate in the heart, tongue, gastrointestinal tract, kidneys, liver, nerves, and blood vessels.

Characteristically, amyloidosis patients with cutaneous involvement demonstrate persistent bleeding at venisection sites and the development of ecchymosis and purpura following the application of shearing pressure to the skin (Barth's sign), also known as "pinch purpura" (Figures 24–6 and 24–7). Increased pressure in the blood vessels around the eyes, induced by the Valsalva's maneuver, vomiting, or proctoscopy, will also produce dramatic ecchymoses (Figure 24–8). Repeated episodes of tiny ecchymoses at the margins of the eyelids produces hyperpigmentation and violaceous coloration. Rarely, bullous lesions have been detected.

Eyelid ecchymosis

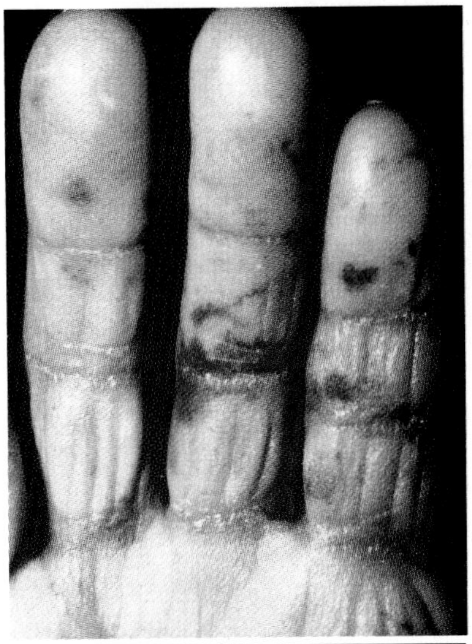

FIGURE 24–6 Hemorrhage into the skin of fingers, following shearing pressure, in a patient with primary amyloidosis.

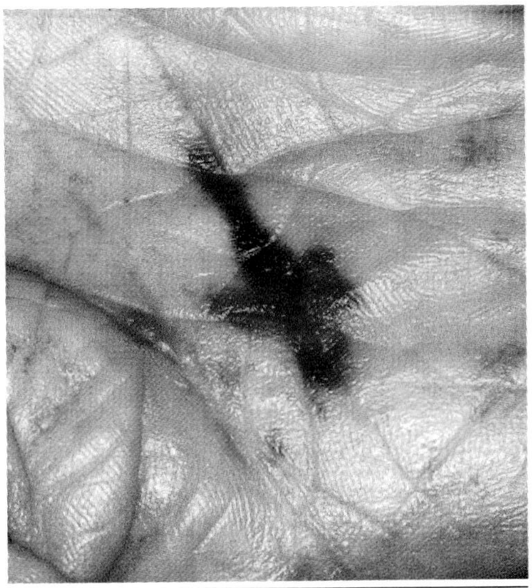

FIGURE 24–7 Palmar lesion of hemorrhage into the skin of a patient with amyloidosis and an IgA myeloma.

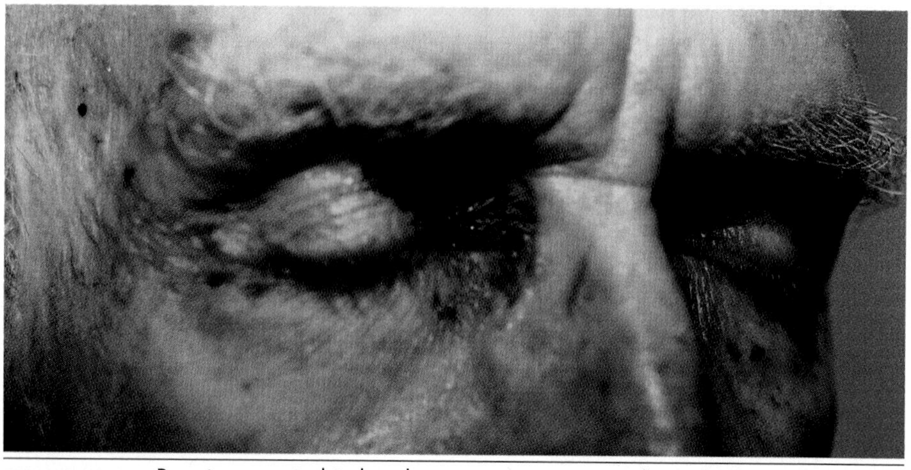

FIGURE 24–8 Prominent periorbital ecchymosis in a patient with amyloidosis. The patient also had significant amyloid deposition in his heart and died shortly thereafter of an arrhythmia.

Purpuric halos around Campbell de Morgan spots

Yellowish, waxy, nontender papules and plaques with surrounding ecchymosis are commonly seen on the face and eyelids. In some patients, purpuric halos have been detected around Campbell de Morgan spots.

Macroglossia

Swelling of the tongue (macroglossia) with indentation from the teeth on the sides, as well as areas of ecchymosis, occurs in approximately 10% of patients (Figures 24–9 and 24–10). Hoarseness due to laryngeal involvement occurs and may progress to interfere with swallowing and the handling of saliva.

Carpal tunnel syndrome

A sclerodermatous-like tightening of facial skin causing difficulty in opening the mouth may occur. Paresthesia of the first, second, and third fingers of the hands, due to carpal tunnel syndrome, and hepatosplenomegaly are commonly seen.

Amyloid deposition in blood vessels

Biopsy of the skin will frequently demonstrate a "signet ring" deposition of amyloid surrounding dermal blood vessels. Furthermore, this material will stain purple with crystal violet and reddish (brick) with congo red, and it will demonstrate apple-green birefringence with polarized light (Figures 24–11 to 24–13). Although a rectal biopsy is generally recommended for diagnosis (approximately a 70% yield), noninvolved skin (50% yield) and cutaneous lesions (100% yield) will demonstrate the characteristic amyloid deposits.

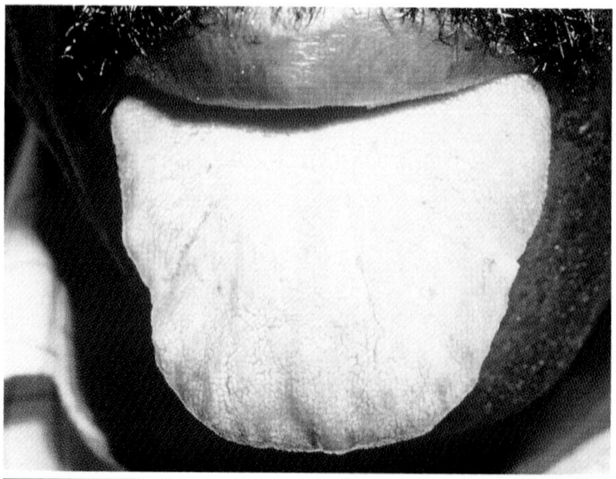

FIGURE 24–9 Amyloidosis of the tongue. Note indentations from teeth on lateral edges. Many times, ecchymosis occurs in and about these indentations.

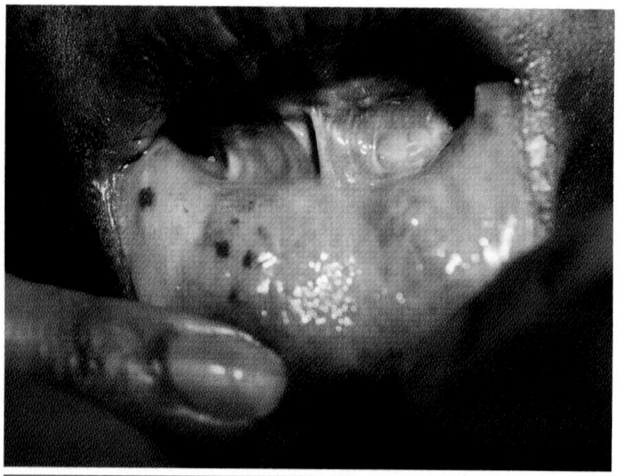

FIGURE 24–10 Ecchymotic areas on the oral mucous membranes in a patient with amyloidosis.

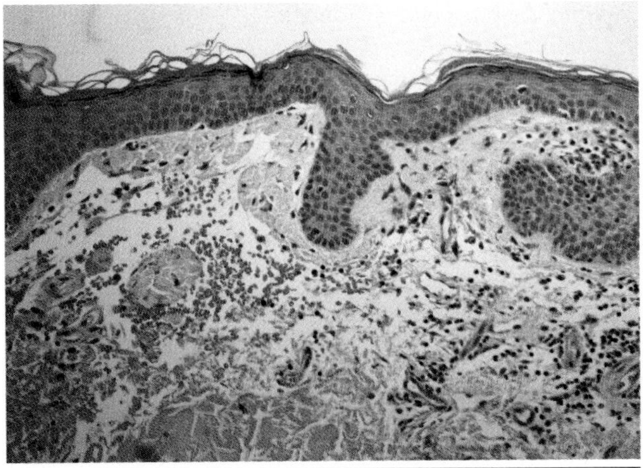

FIGURE 24–11 Biopsy demonstrating deposition of amorphous material in the skin of a patient with amyloidosis. Note hemorrhage in the dermis. (×20 original magnification)

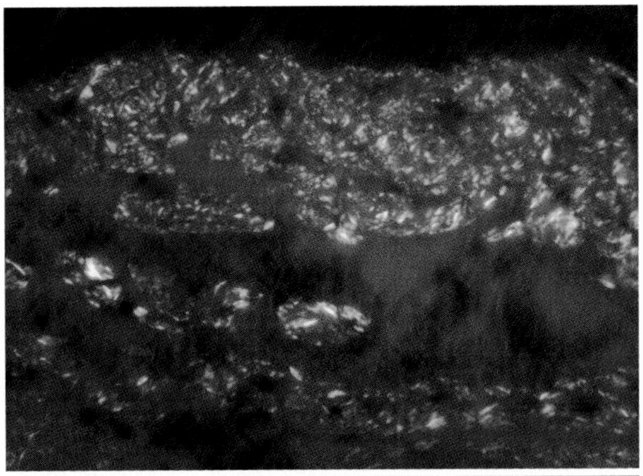

FIGURE 24–12 Congo red stain. Note apple-green birefringence of amyloid deposits after examination with polarized light in the papillary portion of the dermis. (×40 original magnification)

In primary amyloidosis, protein electrophoresis and immunofixation electrophoresis will frequently demonstrate a monoclonal gammopathy and often a decreased quantity of the noninvolved immunoglobulins. Often, in the amyloidosis associated with multiple myeloma, only a monoclonal light chain is produced by the myeloma cells. Unless the light chains aggregate, they will pass through the kidney and can be detected only by a concentrated 24-hour urine specimen (Bence Jones protein, light chain disease). Serum electrophoretic studies will fail to detect the light chains. The erythrocyte sedimentation rate is characteristically elevated. Hypercalcemia and renal or hepatic insufficiency may be detected. Prognosis is guarded and is determined by the organs involved. (For example, cardiac involvement prognosis is measured in months.)

Primary amyloid fibrils composed of light chains or the N-terminal fragment of light chains

As noted above, the fibrils in primary amyloidosis associated with the monoclonal gammopathies (including multiple myeloma) are composed of intact light chain and/or the *N*-terminal fragment of the light chain. Lambda light chains are more commonly detected than kappa light chains. Light chains appear to vary from patient to patient in their propensity to form amyloid.

The amyloid fibril in secondary amyloidosis, occurring with chronic infections (eg, tuberculosis, osteomyelitis), familial Mediterranean fever, and a syndrome characterized by urticaria, deafness, and nephropathy (Muckle-Wells syndrome) is a proteolytic cleavage product of the acute phase reactant protein SAA.

The rarer forms of hereditary amyloidosis are associated with other proteins. (For a more complete discussion, see Hashimoto K. Amyloidosis. In: Arndt K, LeBoit PE, Robinson JK, Wintroub BU, eds. Cutaneous Medicine and Surgery. Philadelphia: W.B. Saunders, 1996 [177], pp 1818–1826.)

Finally, it should be mentioned that lichen amyloidosis, a chronic, intensely pruritic lichenoid dermatosis of predominantly the anterior shins, appears to be a disease process resulting from local amyloid deposition (derived from keratin) following persistent rubbing and scratching of the skin.

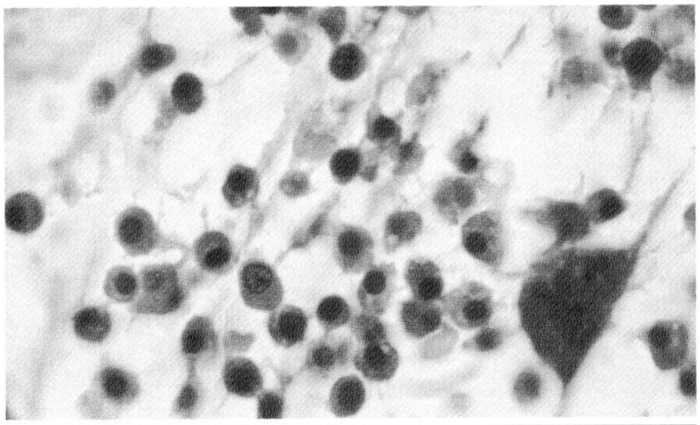

FIGURE 24–13 Bone marrow aspirate showing sheet of plasma cells in a patient with an IgA myeloma and amyloidosis. (×60 original magnification)

Annotated Bibliography

Kyle RA. "Benign" monoclonal gammopathy: after 20 to 35 years of follow up. Mayo Clin Proc 1993;68:26-36.

This is a valuable article! Of 241 patients with a monoclonal gammopathy of undetermined significance, long-term follow-up determined that approximately 20% were alive with a benign monoclonal gammopathy; 10% had a serum monoclonal gammopathy greater than 3 g per dL requiring no therapy; 50% were dead from unrelated causes; and 25% had developed multiple myeloma amyloidosis, macroglobulinemia, or a lymphoproliferative disorder.

Kyle RA, Bayrd ED. Amyloidosis: review of 236 cases. Medicine (Baltimore) 1975; 54:271-299.

Of 236 cases of amyloidosis, primary amyloidosis without evidence of coexisting disease occurred in 132 cases (56%), and amyloidosis associated with multiple myeloma occurred in 61 patients (26%).

Rubinow A, Cohen AS. Skin involvement and generalized amyloidosis: a study of clinically involved and uninvolved skin in 50 patients with primary and secondary amyloidosis. Ann Intern Med 1978;88:781–786.

This is a good article explaining the value of biopsy of uninvolved skin.

Furie B, Voo L, McAdam KPWJ, et al. Mechanism of factor X deficiency in systemic amyloidosis. N Engl J Med 1981;304:827–831.

This interesting article indicates that the acquired factor X deficiency may be related to the binding of factor X to amyloid fibrils. This fact may contribute to the hemorrhagic features of the amyloid deposits.

Type I Cryoglobulinemia

Type I cryoglobulins are monoclonal immunoglobulins. Precipitate commonly above 30°C; occur in acral areas; ischemic insults are produced

There are three types of cryoglobulinemia. Type I cryoglobulinemia is composed of monoclonal immunoglobulin, most commonly IgM or IgG (immunoglobulins). Type I cryoglobulinemia is commonly associated with Waldenström's macroglobulinemia and multiple myeloma but also may occur with benign monoclonal gammopathies of undetermined significance (MGUS). Monoclonal immunoglobulin cryoglobulins may precipitate at temperatures above 30°C (Figure 24–14). The cryoprecipitates may induce a hyperviscosity syndrome producing obstruction of the capillaries, and small- and medium-sized arteries, inducing ischemia necrosis. The cooler parts of the body (hands, feet, and ears) are most commonly involved (Figure 24–15). Cyanosis, Raynaud's phenomenon, bleeding gums, and epistaxis may also be seen. Biopsy of the periphery of lesions will often demonstrate the presence of eosinophilic material in multiple small blood vessels (Figures 24–16 and 24–17). Presumably, this is the monoclonal cryoprecipitate.

The most striking example of type I cryoglobulinemia that we have seen was an elderly African American female with an IgG myeloma. The patient developed gangrene of her feet, secondary to ischemic infarction induced by the monoclonal

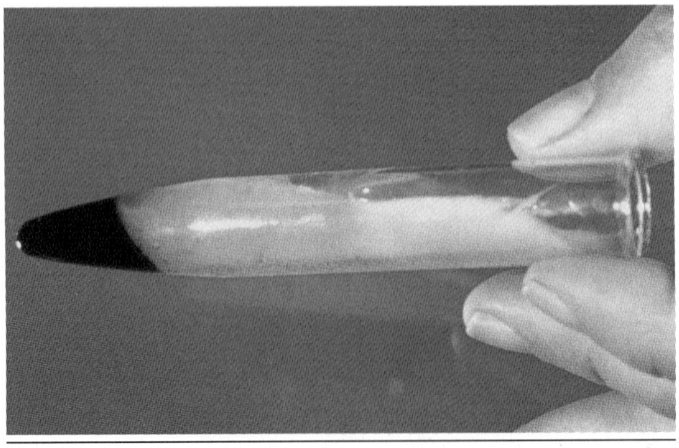

FIGURE 24–14 Monoclonal IgG precipitate at 30°C. This patient had an IgG myeloma and developed infarctions of both feet.

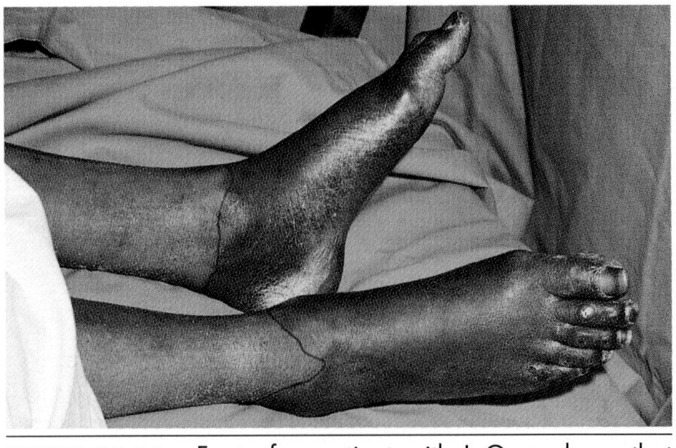

FIGURE 24–15 Feet of a patient with IgG myeloma that cryoprecipitated at 30°C resulting in infarction of both feet.

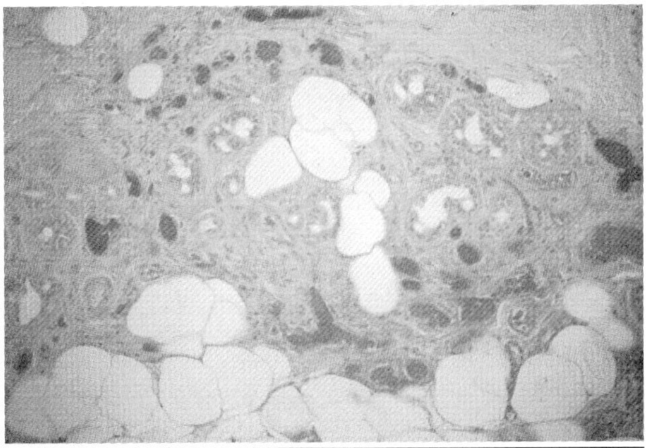

FIGURE 24–16 Biopsy demonstrating cryoprecipitates in tissue of a patient with type I cryoglobulin (IgG myeloma). (×60 original magnification)

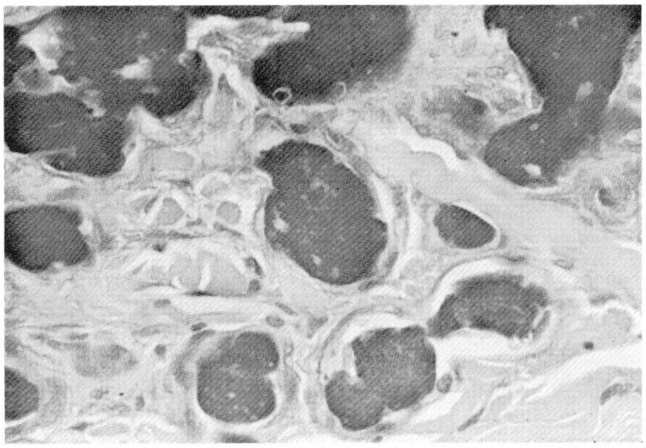

FIGURE 24–17 Close-up of the precipitates in dermal blood vessels. PAS stain. Precipitated material presumably IgG cryoglobulin. (×100 original magnification)

cryoglobulin, necessitating amputation. An infarction developed on the tip of her tongue after she had been inadvertently given some ice chips. This patient's serum, obtained at 37°C, was carried by a technician in his axilla across the street to the laboratory. Initially, no cryoprecipitate was detected because the cryoprecipitate began to form at 30°C.

To avoid missing a cryoglobulin, the needle and test tube should be heated to 37°C before use, and the blood kept at 37°C until it clots. The serum is then placed in a Wintrobe hematocrit tube and refrigerated at 4°C for 24 to 48 hours. The hematocrit tube is then centrifuged and the quantity of cryoglobulin expressed as a cryocrit (analogous to a hematocrit). Characteristically, type I cryoglobulins precipitate above 25°C, whereas types II and III precipitate at much lower temperatures (ie, 4°C overnight).

Must preheat syringe and test tube to 37°C to avoid missing a type I cryoglobulin

Types II and type III cryoglobulins (mixed cryoglobulins) are seen generally in association with chronic infections, such as hepatitis, leukemia, lymphomas, and connective tissue diseases, and are associated with vasculitis (Figure 24–18). The type II cryoglobulins are composed of a monoclonal IgM directed against polyclonal IgG. Type III cryoglobulinemias contain mixed polyclonal immunoglobulins with rheumatoid factor activity. Nonimmunoglobulins, such

Types II and III cryoglobulins are seen with immune complex diseases.

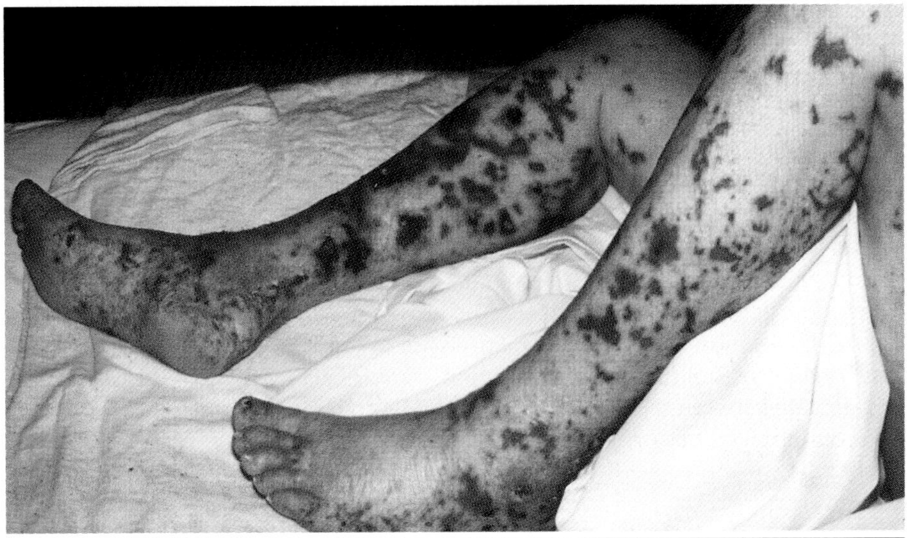

FIGURE 24–18 Cryoglobulinemic vasculitis associated with types II and III mixed cryoglobulins. This patient has hepatitis C.

as C1q, may also be detected. (For discussion of the essential mixed cryoglobulinemia, see Chapter 33, "Hepatitis," subsection on hepatitis C.)

Annotated Bibliography

Block KJ, Franklin E. Plasma cell dyscrasias and cryoglobulins. JAMA 1982;248: 2670–2676.

This is a good review!

POEMS Syndrome

POEMS syndrome
Sclerodermatous-like skin changes

Patients with POEMS (*p*olyneuropathy, *o*rganomegaly, *e*ndocrinopathy, *M* protein [serum and/or urine-monoclonal immunoglobulin], *s*kin changes) syndrome demonstrate diffuse sclerodermatous hyperpigmented skin, anasarca, hypertrichosis, and a progressive sensory and motor polyneuropathy. Hepatosplenomegaly and generalized lymphadenopathy are common. Gynecomastia and impotence are also common in men. Capillary hemangiomas, presenting as 2- to 3-cm reddish-purple papules, and nodules are frequently detected.

Osteolytic lesions uncommon

Radiologically, these patients demonstrate solitary or multiple osteosclerotic bone lesions composed of plasmacytomas. Unlike multiple myeloma, lytic lesions are uncommon. Nerve biopsy demonstrates demyelination and axonal degeneration.

The skin of patients with POEMS syndrome has sclerodermatous features, which can be distinguished from scleroderma by biopsy.

Annotated Bibliography

Kanitakis J, Roger H, Soubrier M, et al. Cutaneous angiomas in POEMS syndrome. Arch Dermatol 1988;124:695–698.

Approximately 25% of patients have cutaneous angiomas.

Bardwick PA, Zvaifler NJ, Gill GN, et al. Plasma cell dyscrasia with polyneuropathy, organomegaly, endocrinopathy, M protein and skin changes: the POEMS syndrome. Report of two cases and review of the literature. Medicine 1980;59:311–322.

This is an excellent review of the literature.

Shelly WB, Shelly ED. The skin changes in Crow-Fukas (POEMS) syndrome. Arch Dermatol 1987;123:85–87.

This article explains the sclerodermatous-like changes but indicates that the skin is not bound down, and that biopsies fail to demonstrate evidence of scleroderma.

Association of Myelomas with Xanthomas

Multiple myeloma may be associated with xanthomas, with or without evidence of lipid abnormalities.

We reported an 87-year-old Caucasian female who developed xanthoma disseminatum, characterized by firm, waxy, yellowish-brown nodules and plaques with a faint erythematous halo involving the inguinal creases, inframammary regions, axilla, buttocks, and perineum. The patient also had bilateral xanthelasma. The patient had mild diabetes mellitus, a normal lipid profile, and an IgG kappa (IgG-κ monoclonal gammopathy with a kappa Bence Jones protein. Diffuse osteoporosis of the bones was demonstrated. There were no lytic lesions. No complexing between the paraprotein and lipids could be demonstrated on immunoelectrophoresis performed in agar and stained for lipid.

Because of the vigor of the patient and lack of symptomatology, no therapy was given.

Myeloma proteins may interfere with lipid metabolism, producing xanthomas.

It is theorized that the xanthoma resulted from the M protein interference with normal catabolism of lipids, either by a protein/lipid interaction or, perhaps, by a blockage of a lipid-binding receptor.

Annotated Bibliography

Maize JC, Ahmed AR, Provost TT. Xanthoma disseminatum and multiple myeloma. Arch Dermatol 1974;110:758–761.

Lynch PJ, Winkelmann RK. Generalized plain xanthoma and systemic disease. Arch Dermatol 1966;93:639–646.

Cortese C, Lewis B, Miller NE, et al. Myelomatosis with type III hyperlipoproteinemia: clinical and metabolic studies. N Engl J Med 1982;307–379.

These three articles describe the association of xanthomas with the presence of paraproteins.

Scleredema

On rare occasions seen with myeloma

This disease process is most commonly associated with children who have a preceding upper respiratory infection and with adults with the onset of diabetes mellitus. It is characterized by the deposition of mucin in the dermis. Recently, it has been associated with several patients who had multiple myeloma. There is also evidence that the sera of some of these patients were capable of stimulating normal fibroblasts to produce collagen.

Annotated Bibliography

Oikarinen A, Ala-Kokko L, Palatai R, et al. Scleredema and paraproteinemia enhanced collagen production and elevated type I procollagen messenger RNA in fibroblasts grown from cultures from the fibrotic skin of a patient. Arch Dermatol 1987;123: 126–129.

Ohta A, Uitto J, Oikarinen A, et al. Paraproteinemia in patients with scleredema: clinical findings and serum effects on skin fibroblasts in vitro. J Am Acad Dermatol 1987;16: 96–107.

These are two very thought-provoking articles!

Pyoderma Gangrenosum and Subcorneal Pustulosis

It also should be noted that IgA myelomas have been associated with pyoderma gangrenosum and subcorneal pustular dermatosis (Sneddon-Wilkinson disease).

Annotated Bibliography

Powell FC, Schroeter Al, Su, WPD, et al. Pyoderma gangrenosum and monoclonal gammopathy. Arch Dematol 1983;119:468–472.

Kasha EE, Epinette WW. Subcorneal pustular dermatosis (Sneddon-Wilkinson's disease) associated with a monoclonal IgA gammopathy. A report and review of literature. J Am Acad Dermatol 1988;19:854–858.

These two articles describe these unusual associations.

Necrobiotic Xanthogranuloma

Necrobiotic xanthogranuloma generally associated with paraprotein

Another cutaneous manifestation of paraproteinemia has been described in recent years—necrobiotic xanthogranuloma. Patients demonstrate papular, nodular, plaque-like lesions, violaceous to reddish-orange in color. Periorbital involvement occurs in over 90% of patients. Central atrophy, telangiectasia, and ulceration are common. A paraproteinemia has been described in approximately 90% of patients. An IgG gammopathy is most frequently detected. A few of the patients have developed multiple myeloma.

Histologically, these lesions demonstrate sheets of epithelioid histiocytes, and Teuton-type and foreign body giant cells.

Annotated Bibliography

Finan MC, Winkelmann RK. Necrobiotic xanthogranuloma with paraproteinemia: a review of 22 cases. Medicine 1986;65:376–388.

This is a highly quoted article.

Cutis Laxa

On rare occasions, acquired cutis laxa may be associated with multiple myeloma. It is postulated that the binding of the monoclonal immunoglobulin with elastic tissue disrupts the normal function of elastic tissue.

Annotated Bibliography

Ting HC, Foo MH, Wang F. Acquired cutis laxa and multiple myeloma. Br J Dermatol 1984;366:363–366.

This article demonstrates an interesting association.

Macroglobulinemia and Heavy Chain Disease

Macroglobulinemia IgM myeloma

Macroglobulinemia, also termed "lymphoplasmacytic lymphoma," is a monoclonal gammopathy in which the plasma cells secrete increased quantities of IgM. Oral bleeding and epistaxis commonly occur, as well as weakness, fatigue, and neurologic symptomatology. These signs and symptoms are related to increased blood viscosity produced by the increased quantities of IgM.

Heavy chain disease is a lymphoma-like disease in which the M component is a fragment of the heavy chain (Fc component) of IgG. Several cases of heavy chain disease involving IgA and IgM have also been described.

Heavy chain disease presents as a lymphoma-like disease. Elderly patients

Characteristically, these patients are in the seventh and eighth decades of life and may present with soft tissue nodules and tumors as well as swelling of the mucous membranes. Prominent lymphadenopathy, which may fluctuate, is common. The diagnosis is made by the demonstration of a heavy chain fragment in the serum and urine and the presence of atypical plasma cells in the bone marrow.

Annotated Bibliography

Frangione B, Franklin EC. Heavy chain disease: clinical features and molecular significance of the disordered immunoglobulin structure. Semin Hematol 1973;10:53–73.

This is a classic description by two of the leading investigators in the area.

Scleromyxedema

Waxy, papular lesions over hands, arms, neck, face, and upper trunk

Scleromyxedema is a rare disease characterized by waxy or slightly red papules over the hands, arms, face, neck, and upper trunk. The disease may, however, be generalized, producing thickness and rigidity of the skin. Papular and nodular involvement of the face may produce a leonine facies (Figures 24–19 to 24–21).

A mucinous variety (papular mucinosis) is characterized by widespread papular lesions in the absence of sclerosis. In general, scleromyxedema/papular mucinosis is not associated with systemic manifestations. However, individual case reports indicate, on occasion, the presence of neurologic disorders, most commonly, acute psychosis. Furthermore, cardiovascular disorders, characterized predominantly by atherosclerosis, hypertension, and myocardial infarction have also been described.

The most common systemic feature detected in these patients is the presence of a slowly migrating monoclonal gammopathy usually characterized by the presence of a lambda IgG (IgG-λ) paraprotein. On unusual occasions, the paraprotein is IgA. The presence of lambda light chains in at least 75% of these patients is unusual when one considers that the usual ratio of kappa light chains to lambda light chains is 2:1.

Although the paraprotein is characterized as an MGUS, scleromyxedema also has been detected in several patients with multiple myeloma.

Pathology

The pathology of this disease is characterized by the deposition of mucinous material in the upper portion of the dermis. These mucinous deposits are a heterogeneous mixture of acid mucopolysaccharides. Similar deposits may occur in

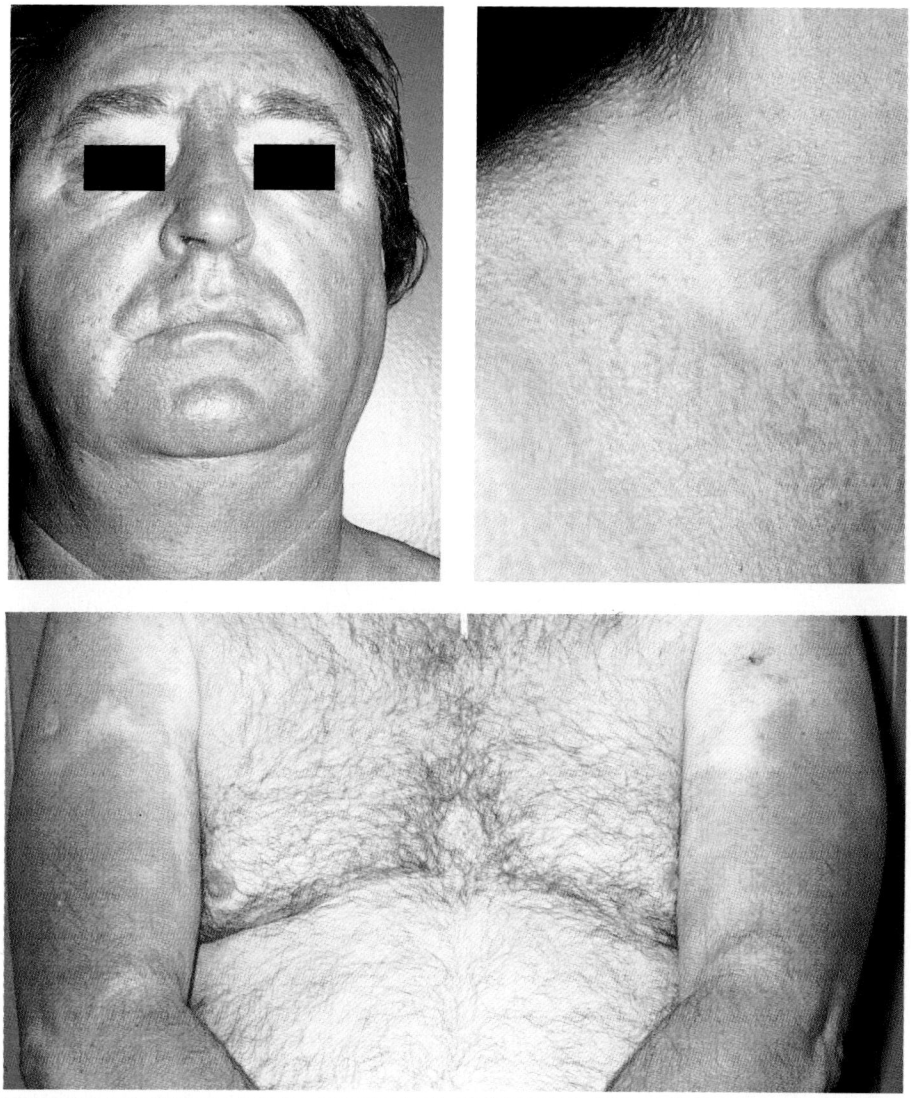

FIGURES 24–19 TO 24–21 Patient with scleromyxedema demonstrating reddish papular lesions over the face, arms, and neck.

Mixture of acid mucopolysaccharides in dermis

the media and adventitia of blood vessels. The myocardium, as well as the skeletal muscles, may be involved with similar infiltrates.

Large, stellate fibroblasts are present within the mucinous material. In the sclerotic variant, thick collagen bundles with increased numbers of fibroblasts in the papillary and reticular dermis are seen.

The mucinous material stains positively with colloidal iron, Alcian blue, and toluidine blue. The positive staining may be abolished by predigestion with hyaluronidase.

Cutaneous Manifestations

Flexion contracture of fingers may occur

In general, the disease process occurs in middle-aged adults. The patients generally demonstrate a tan-colored, waxy, lichenoid eruption over the entire body with accentuation on the hands, face, and neck. Diffuse thickening of the skin may produce flexion contractures of the fingers. Unlike scleroderma, there is no evidence for Raynaud's phenomenon. A linear array of waxy or slightly erythematous papules on a thickened, indurated background is a characteristic feature.

Serologic Studies

On electrophoresis, IgG paraprotein associated with lichen myxedema migrates into the far cathodal area of the gamma region. There is no depression of the

A IgG cationic paraprotein generally present

normal quantity of other immunoglobulins, nor is there any evidence for skeletal involvement, although bone marrow studies may demonstrate a mild increase in plasma cells. Unlike the normal 160 kD molecular weight of IgG, this paraprotein has an approximate molecular weight of 110 kD. Furthermore, immunochemical studies indicate that this paraprotein is an incomplete IgG molecule, missing a significant portion of the Fd fragment.

Serum factor capable of stimulating proliferation of cultured fibroblasts

The relationship between this very unique paraprotein and the cutaneous features of this disease is unknown. However, one piece of intriguing investigation indicates that the serum from a patient with scleromyxedema, devoid of the IgG paraprotein, was capable of inducing proliferation of cultured fibroblasts.

Diagnosis

The diagnosis is made by the detection of the typical clinical features, skin biopsy, and the presence of the typical IgG-λ monoclonal gammopathy.

Treatment

The treatment is generally unsatisfactory. Melphalan has been recommended to treat the paraprotein, but there is no evidence that reduction of the paraprotein results in improvement of the skin disease.

Psoralen plus ultraviolet A therapy, in our experience, has been partially successful in the treatment of the skin disease.

Annotated Bibliography

Kantor GR, Bergfeld WF, Katzin WE, et al. Scleromyxedema associated with scleroderma, renal disease, and acute psychosis. J Am Acad Dermatol 1986;14:879–888.

This is a case report with an excellent review of the literature detailing that, on occasion, scleromyxedema may be associated with systemic features, especially neurologic and cardiac manifestations.

Harper RA, Rispler J. Lichen myxedematous serum stimulating human skin fibroblast proliferation. Science 1978;199:545–547.

This provocative paper indicates that the serum of lichen myxedematous patients contains a factor capable of stimulating fibroblasts.

Kitamura W, Matsouka Y, Miyagawa S, et al. Immunochemical analysis of the monoclonal protein in scleromyxedema. J Invest Dermatol 1978;70:306–308.

This article provides chemical analysis of a monoclonal paraprotein in a patient with scleromyxedema, demonstrating the deletion of a major portion of the Fc fragment. These studies indicate that this paraprotein abnormality is similar to the heavy chain disease described in IgG.

It is interesting to observe that the paraprotein in POEMS syndrome can induce mucin deposition in the skin, the paraprotein in papular mucinosis is associated with either mucin deposition in the skin, the paraprotein in papular mucinosis is associated with either mucin depostition in the skin and/or sclerosis, and the paraproteins associated with sclerodema are associated with mucin deposition. Furthermore, a plasma factor, probably not the paraprotein in scleromyxedema, in vitro, can induce fibroblast proliferation, and there is evidence that the paraprotein in sclerodema is capable of stimulating collagen production by normal fibroblasts associated with an increase in messenger RNA for type I procollagen. These data suggest that the paraprotein and, perhaps, other plasma factors associated with the monoclonal gammopathy are capable of inducing altered metabolic fibroblast activity, the result of which are cutaneous manifestations that are prominent clinical features of the respective diseases.

Also, data suggest that paraproteins may, on unusual occasions, interfere with the normal metabolism of lipids and the function of histiocytes. These alterations of lipid metabolism and histiocyte function can also produce prominent cutaneous manifestations.

Finally, paraproteins may alter the normal function of elastic fibers, inducing acquired cutis laxa.

Schnitzler's Syndrome

Associated with IgM-κ paraproteins

Schnitzler's syndrome is a chronic neutrophilic urticaria most commonly, but not always, associated with a monoclonal IgM-κ gammopathy. Bone pain and hyperostosis are also commonly detected. Fever and lymphadenopathy are also commonly present. Biopsy of the urticarial lesions demonstrates a perivascular infiltrate composed predominantly of neutrophils. On occasion, a frank leukocytoclastic vasculitis may be present. IgM and C3 are frequently detected in the affected blood vessels. IgM-κ is the most common monoclonal gammopathy detected in Schnitzler's syndrome. (Approximately 10 to 15% of Schnitzler's syndrome patients develop a lymphoplasmacytic lymphoma.)

Annotated Bibliography

Janier M, et al. Chronic urticaria and macroglobulinemia (Schnitzler's syndrome): report of two cases. J Am Acad Dermatol 1989;20:206–211.

This article provides a good review of the clinical features.

Detection of a Monoclonal Gammopathy

Richard L. Humphrey, M.D., Thomas T. Provost, M.D.

Restricted migration on electrophoresis

The testing for a monoclonal immunoglobulin takes advantage of the fact that the monoclonal protein is the product of a proliferation of a clone of lymphoplasmacytic cells and will demonstrate restricted migration on electrophoresis. These proteins are generally composed of excessive quantities of normal immunoglobulins but, as detailed above, may consist of fragments of heavy chains or intact light chains.

Monoclonal peak

On electrophoresis, a monoclonal band demonstrated by a sharp "church spire" peak is present. In contradistinction, a polyclonal gammopathy is detected as a broad-based peak. The monoclonal peak is the product of the clonal proliferation of one cell. Thus, only a single heavy chain and a single light chain (kappa or lambda) will be represented.

Urine and protein electrophoresis

The testing for a monoclonal gammopathy often begins with a clinical suspicion; however, many times it is the result of an abnormality detected on a routine multichannel chemistry panel by screening urinalysis. When suspected, confirmation begins by ordering a serum and urine protein electrophoresis. Some of the common protein electrophoretic patterns are illustrated in Figure 24–22.

Immunofixation

Immunofixation electrophoresis is the next step in the analysis of a putative monoclonal spike. This technique, using electrophoresis and immunostaining, determines whether the protein has restricted mobility and whether the protein is limited to one heavy chain class (ie, gamma, alpha, mu, delta, episilon) and one light chain class (ie, kappa, lambda).

Very sensitive technique

The immunofixation electrophoresis technique should always be performed when a monoclonal gammopathy is suspected, even if serum and/or urine protein electrophoresis are normal. The immunofixation electrophoresis technique is very sensitive and will detect low concentrations of a monoclonal gammopathy hidden by other proteins in the serum or urine electrophoretic patterns.

Also, if a monoclonal gammopathy is suspected, both the serum and urine should be studied. If the serum is studied and a monoclonal gammopathy is excluded, the absence of a plasma cell disorder is only 75% confirmed. If both urine and serum are studied, a plasma cell disorder can be excluded to about a 98% confidence, leaving only the possibility of a nonsecretory myeloma or a very low protein burden to be excluded.

When a serum and/or a urine monoclonal gammopathy is discovered, the next task is to determine if it has clinical significance or whether it is an MGUS.

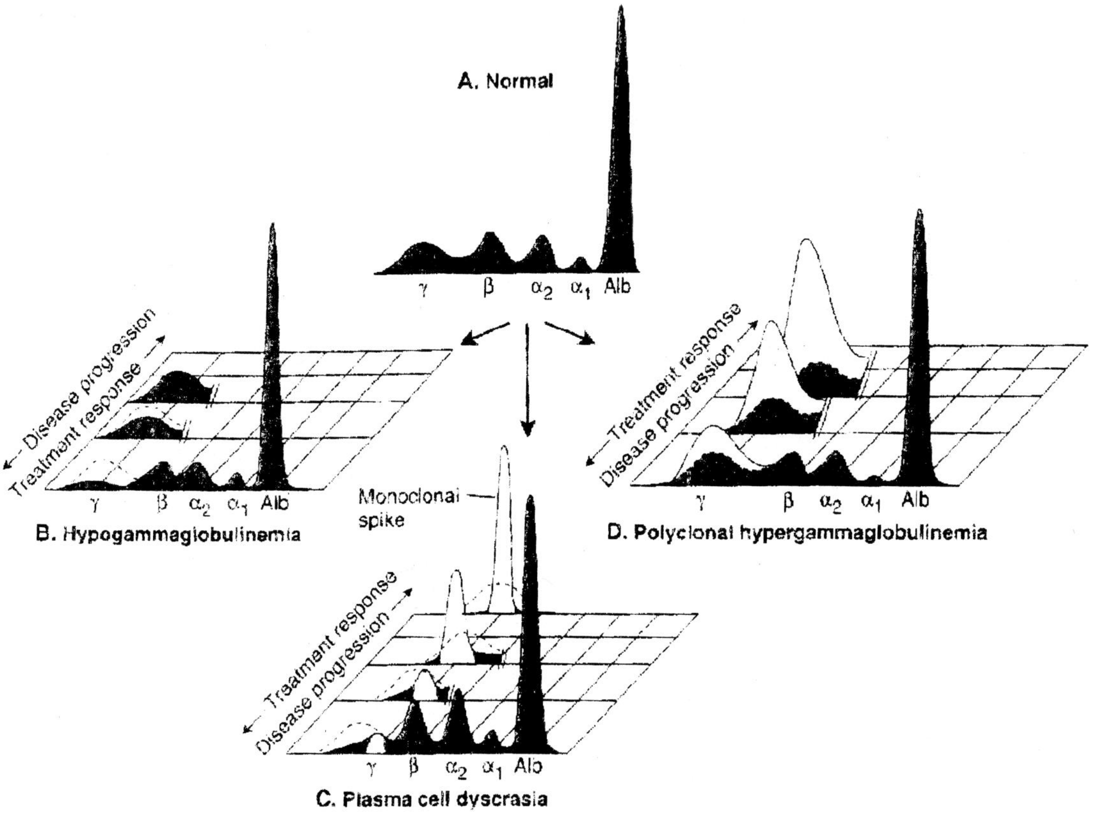

FIGURE 24–22 Common serum protein electrophoretic patterns. A: Normal pattern. B: Hypogammaglobulinemia. The dotted line shows progressive loss of the gamma region as disease worsens. C: Plasma cell dyscrasia. Normal immunoglobulins are suppressed. With disease progression, the "spike" generally increases; with effective treatment, it decreases. D: Polyclonal hypergammaglobulinemia (polyclonal gammopathy). (Reproduced with permission from: Humphrey RL. Plasma cell dyscrasia. In: Stobo JD, Hellmann DB, Ladenson PW, Petty BG, Traill TA, eds. The Principles and Practice of Medicine, 23rd ed. Stamford, CT: Appleton and Lange, 1997, pp 802–812.)

CHAPTER 25

Cutaneous Sarcomas

Kathryn O'Connell, M.D., Ph.D., Thomas T. Provost, M.D.

Kaposi's Sarcoma

Kathryn O'Connell, M.D., Ph.D.

Overview and Historical Perspective

Kaposi's sarcoma (KS) is a disease with features of a neoplastic process, an infectious process, and an inflammatory process. KS has been studied with great interest for over 100 years, but it remains a puzzle despite many recent advances (Table 25–1).

Currently, four distinct clinical presentations of KS are recognized (Table 25–2).

Classic Kaposi's Sarcoma

Elderly Eastern European males at increased risk

In 1872, Kaposi, a professor of dermatology at the University of Vienna, described the first form of KS, multiple idiopathic hemorrhagic sarcoma, now called "classic KS." This form is rare, with the highest incidence in older men of Eastern European or Mediterranean descent. It is most commonly diagnosed on the lower extremities, and the clinical course tends to be relatively benign. An immune deficit has not been defined in classic KS, but these patients have a higher incidence of lymphoma.

African Endemic Kaposi's Sarcoma

African endemic Kaposi's sarcoma is more common in males.

An immune deficit has not been defined in African endemic KS, and this form also shares a male predominance, about 15:1. It accounts for approximately 10% of diagnosed tumors in equatorial Africa and affects a younger population than does classic KS. In adults, it can resemble the indolent classic form but also occurs as a locally aggressive or widely disseminated disease. In African children, it is often a fulminant disease clinically similar to lymphoma. When opportunities exist for management, the adult form is usually amenable to therapy.

Iatrogenic Kaposi's Sarcoma

It was not until the appearance of the disease among recipients of organ transplants that the contribution of immune deficiency became evident. This form of KS, sometimes referred to as iatrogenic KS, occurs most frequently in immunosuppressed organ transplant recipients but has also been reported in other iatrogenically immunosuppressed patients. The incidence in renal transplant recipients is approximately 0.4% in Western countries but is higher in Mediterranean countries. KS is the most common tumor in immunosuppressed renal transplant

TABLE 25–1 Historical Perspective on Kaposi's Sarcoma

1872	Moritz Kaposi identifies classic KS: multiple idiopathic hemorrhagic sarcoma.
1891	Koebner suggests name "Kaposi's sarcoma."
1902	Phillippson hypothesizes viral infection with capillary and spindle cell proliferation.
1932	Dörffel hypothesizes reticuloendothelial cell hyperplasia.
1957	Bluefarb publishes classic monograph on KS.
1962	Oettle reviews 1950s recognition of African endemic KS.
1970s	Multiple studies describe KS in the iatrogenically immunosuppressed.
1980s	Multiple studies find KS is epidemic in homosexual men.
1990	Beral et al. and others find epidemiologic evidence for involvement of a sexually transmitted infection in acquired immunodeficiency syndrome (AIDS)–associated KS.
1994	Chang et al. discover human herpes virus–8 sequences by representational difference analysis of KS tissue.
1997	Introduction of highly active antiretroviral therapy and increasing understanding of pathogenesis hold therapeutic promise.

KS = Kaposi's sarcoma.

Immunosuppressed renal transplant patients at increased risk

recipients in Saudi Arabia. This form of KS is more common in males but does not share the striking male predominance seen in the classic and African endemic forms. Most cases of iatrogenic KS regress on cessation of immunosuppression, but the disease can progress and is sometimes fatal with widespread visceral involvement.

AIDS-Associated Kaposi's Sarcoma

Harbinger of AIDS epidemic in United States

The sudden appearance of KS in the early 1980s among young homosexual males underscored the apparent importance of immune deficiency, as this presentation was a harbinger of the AIDS epidemic in the United States. Subsequent to the recognition that human immunodeficiency virus (HIV) destroys T-cells, it became widely accepted that the responsible deficit is one of T-cell immunity. Accordingly, it has been suggested that the relatively benign course of classic and endemic KS might reflect a mild, as yet undetected, T-cell defect. It has also been noted, however, that KS is not a complication of congenital T-cell deficiency syndromes, and that immune dysfunction due to immunosuppressive drugs or HIV infection is not confined to the T lymphocyte.

Pathogenesis

AIDS-Associated Kaposi's Sarcoma

Long before the occurrence of AIDS or organ transplantation, it had been hypothesized that KS is a disease of the reticuloendothelial system, initiated by an infectious agent (see Table 25–1). The epidemiologic features of AIDS-associated KS support this early infectious disease hypothesis and suggest that the agent can be sexually transmitted. For example, the risk for AIDS-associated KS in the United States is greatest in homosexual men, especially those whose partners resided in areas with the highest incidence of KS, New York and California. AIDS-related KS is associated with male sexual practices involving fecal-oral contact, and the risk in women is greater if HIV is acquired from a male partner who is bisexual rather than an intravenous drug user.

Human Herpesvirus-8

Early in the AIDS epidemic, cytomegalovirus was a strong candidate as the infectious agent associated with KS, but this theory was eventually abandoned. In 1994, Chang et al. discovered DNA sequences of a new human herpesvirus (HHV) in KS tissue from an AIDS patient; this virus is now known as HHV-8. HHV-8 transforms endothelial cells in vitro and encodes chemokine-like proteins

TABLE 25–2 Currently Recognized Clinical Forms of KS

	Known to be Immuno-deficient	Marked Male Predominance	HIV +	HHV-8 +
Classic KS	no	yes	no	yes
Endemic KS	no	yes	no	yes
Iatrogenic KS	yes	no	no	yes
AIDS-KS	yes	yes	yes	yes

KS = Kaposi's sarcoma; HIV = human immunodeficiency virus; HHV = human herpesvirus; AIDS = acquired immunodeficiency syndrome.

that have angiogenic activity. HHV-8 is found in all forms of KS. It has been reported that renal allograft recipients are at increased risk of developing KS if the kidney donor is seropositive for HHV-8. Reports of detection in a wide variety of other diseases have not been consistently confirmed, but HHV-8 is likely involved in the pathogenesis of primary effusion lymphoma and multicentric Castleman's disease, both of which are associated with immunosuppression. The current serologic, molecular, and epidemiologic evidence strongly supports the hypothesis that HHV-8 is an infectious cofactor in all four forms of KS.

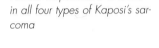

Human herpesvirus-8 is found in all four types of Kaposi's sarcoma

It has been debated for over a century whether KS is a true malignancy or a reactive inflammatory process. There continues to be debate about whether KS is a disseminated clonal cancer or a multicentric proliferative disease. It has recently been demonstrated that in vitro HHV-8–induced transformation of primary human endothelial cells involves paracrine factors that immortalize cells that are not HHV-8 infected, a majority population. This observation demonstrates that HHV-8 can promote the growth of the main proliferating cells in KS, the endothelial cells. It is likely that the answers to this long debate about KS will broaden our understanding of cancer and its relationship to infection and immunity.

Histopathologic Features of Kaposi's Sarcoma

The histopathologic features of KS vary with the clinical stage of the lesion (Figure 25–1). Clues to the diagnosis of KS include hemosiderin deposits, a mononuclear cell infiltrate, and spindle cell formations with narrow slits containing erythrocytes. The histopathologic differential diagnosis of KS is extensive and has been reviewed elsewhere (see Friedman-Kien, Annotated Bibliography).

Clinical Features

The individual cutaneous lesions of KS do not differ markedly in appearance among the four clinical presentations if viewed in the same stage of development. The lesions include patches, papules, plaques, nodules, and tumors and can mimic a number of widely disparate diseases (Figures 25–2 to 25–4). Biopsy confirmation is important, since a number of diseases in the differential diagnosis are benign, easily amenable to available therapy, or require emergent attention. The cutaneous differential diagnosis includes bacillary angiomatosis, secondary syphilis, malignant melanoma, hemangiomas, cutaneous lymphoma, pyogenic granuloma, purpura, sarcoidosis, and a variety of other skin lesions. The clinical/radiographic presentations of visceral KS lesions can be found in texts specific to the organ system of interest. A definitive diagnosis is of additional importance because KS is often the presenting sign of AIDS, and current evidence supports the benefit of antiretrovi-

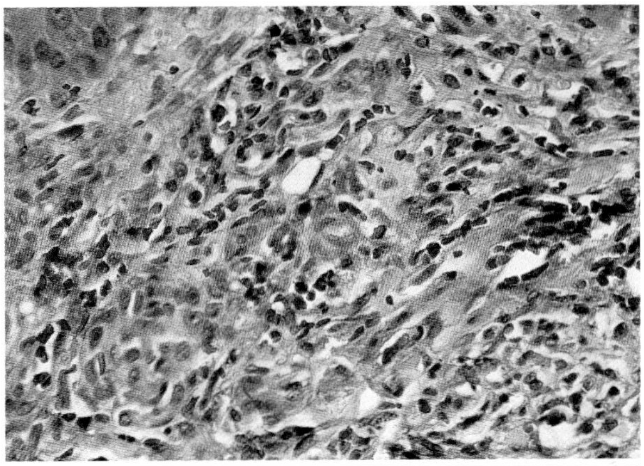

FIGURE 25–1 Patch-stage Kaposi's sarcoma histopathology demonstrating slit-like vascular channels extravasation of red blood cells and neoangiogenesis. (original magnification ×40)

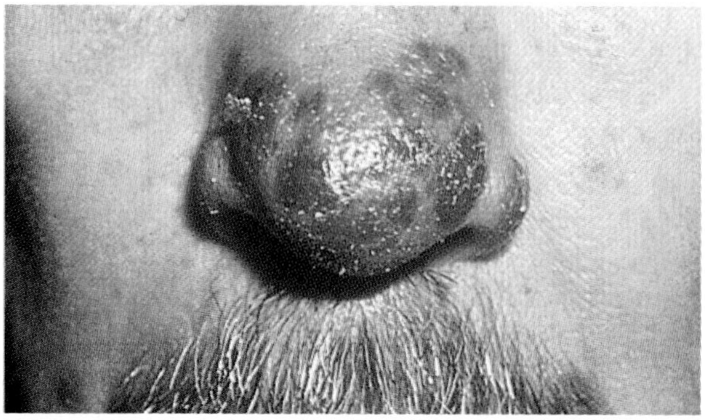

FIGURE 25–2 Kaposi's sarcoma involving nose of an AIDS patient.

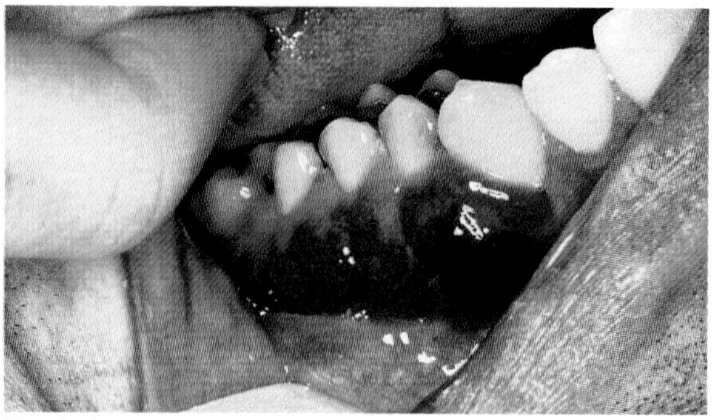

FIGURE 25–3 Kaposi's sarcoma involving gingiva of an AIDS patient.

The differential diagnosis is broad, and definitive diagnosis is important.

ral therapy for HIV infection. All patients diagnosed with KS should be encouraged to undergo testing for HIV infection.

Classic KS often remains confined to the lower extremities but may involve the regional lymphatics. It is sometimes accompanied by edema, may ulcerate and cause significant pain, but is seldom the cause of death. Non-HIV–associated endemic KS in African adults can resemble classic KS or follow a fulminant course with widespread visceral involvement. Endemic KS in children often presents as a disease that clinically resembles lymphoma. It bears a grim prognosis. Iatrogenic KS usually remains localized but can be systemic, with involvement that includes the lungs and gastrointestinal tract. Most cases resolve with discontinuation of immunosuppressive drugs, but some cases are fatal despite chemotherapy for nonremitting disease. AIDS-associated KS is often distinguished by the simultaneous occurrence of multiple patches on the trunk. Oral and genital sites are common, as is involvement of the gastrointestinal tract, lungs, and lymphatics. In some cases, visceral lesions occur in the absence of clinically detectable cutaneous disease.

Treatment

Management decisions depend on many factors.

The discovery of HHV-8 may alter the management of all forms of KS, and the most recent therapeutic guidelines should be consulted. At the present time, there is no known curative therapy for KS. Traditionally, the most commonly employed treatment options are local surgery or cryotherapy, intralesional vinblastine, interferon alpha, radiotherapy, and systemic chemotherapy including liposomal preparations of doxorubicin or daunorubicin. In some cases, only close observation is indicated. Management decisions depend on many factors. These include the patient's underlying condition and wishes; number, extent, duration, and symptoms of cutaneous lesions; the rate of new lesion appearance; visceral involvement; and the toxicities of available treatment options. Indications for referral to an oncologist include the presence of visceral lesions, lymphedema, ulceration, extensive mucocutaneous disease, and significant pain. Oral lesions require specialized care because treatment can be accompanied by debilitating ulceration. For patients with iatrogenic KS, discontinuation of immunosuppressive drugs is often sufficient, but this form of KS may require aggressive systemic treatment. Cases involving organ transplant recipients should be managed by specialists in transplantation-related complications.

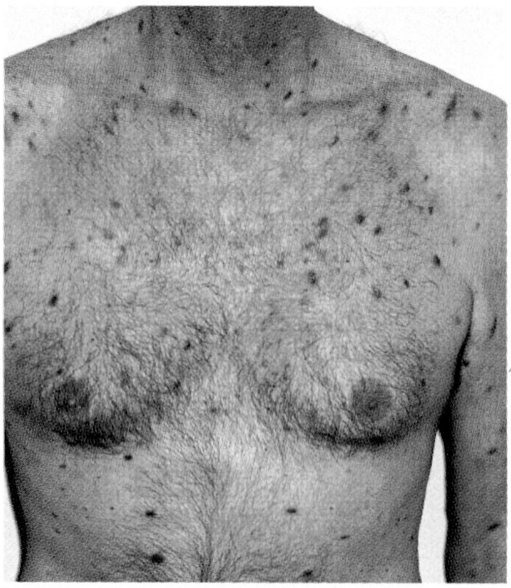

FIGURE 25–4 Widespread Kaposi's lesions over the chest and abdomen of an AIDS patient.

The use of highly active antiretroviral therapy (HAART) for HIV infection may offer benefit in the management of AIDS-associated KS, since this therapy has been shown to have positive effects on the immune system. Currently, no prospective study has been published documenting the effects of HAART on KS, but published reports are generally optimistic. It has been noted, however, that mucosal lesions require monitoring in this setting, since a restored inflammatory response to the tumor may compromise vital functions. The most current recommendations should be consulted by those treating AIDS-associated KS, since treatment of the underlying condition is in evolution.

The most current guidelines for treatment should be consulted.

In addition to possible antiviral approaches for treating KS, a number of other experimental therapies are under study. Many target the autocrine and paracrine processes that are likely involved in the pathophysiology of KS. It is important to note that some experimental treatments have worsened KS. An improved understanding of the pathophysiology of KS is critical to identifying new approaches most likely to confer clinical benefit.

Annotated Bibliography

Beral V, Peterman T, Berkelman R, et al. Kaposi's sarcoma among persons with AIDS: a sexually transmitted infection? Lancet 1990;335:123–128.

This is an excellent article.

Bluefarb SM. Kaposi's sarcoma. In: Curtis AC, ed. Springfield: Charles C. Thomas, 1957.

This is an classic reference in the field on Kaposi's sarcoma.

Friedman-Kien AE. In: Tucker T, ed. Color Atlas of AIDS. Philadelphia: W.B. Saunders, 1989.

Gallo RC. The enigmas of Kaposi's sarcoma. Science1998;282:1837–1839.

Greenblatt RM. Kaposi's sarcoma and human herpesvirus-8. Infect Dis Clin North Am1998;12:63–82.

Moore PS, Chang Y. Kaposi's sarcoma, KS-associated herpesvirus, and the criteria for causality in the age of molecular biology. Am J Epidemiol 1998;147:217–221.

Regamy N, Tamm M, Wernli M, et al. Transmission of HHV-8 infection from renal transplant donors to recipients. N Engl J Med 1998;339:1358–1363.

Flore O, Rafii S, Ely S, et al. Transformation of primary human endothelial cells by Kaposi's sarcoma-associated herpesvirus. Nature 1998;394:588–592.

Dermatofibrosarcoma Protuberans

Thomas T. Provost, M.D.

Clinical Features

This is a very uncommon malignant tumor arising in the dermis. It is composed of fibroblasts. The tumor most commonly detected on the trunk (back) is locally aggressive; metastases to regional and distant lymph nodes are very unusual (Figure 25–5). It appears to be more common in men, and some evidence indicates it may be more common in African Americans.

Local aggressive disease

Prognosis and Treatment

Treatment is wide local excision. The prognosis is generally good. We have seen two African American males in their 40s who presented with slowly growing nodular lesions of dermatofibrosarcoma on the back. The lesions were successfully eradicated by a wide local excision.

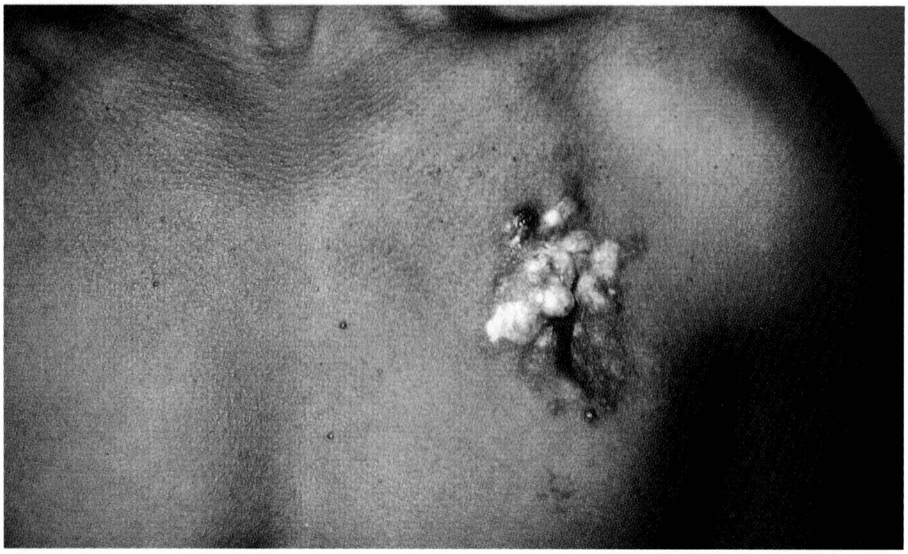

FIGURE 25–5 Nodular tumors of dermatofibrosarcoma protuberans on the chest of an African American male. The lesion was eradicated by a wide local excision.

Annotated Bibliography

Taylor HB, Hedwig EG. Dermatofibromasarcoma protuberans. A study of 115 cases. Cancer 1962;15:717–725.

This is a classic article!

Hemangioendothelioma

Thomas T. Provost, M.D.

Hemangioendothelioma (hemangiosarcoma) is a rare, malignant vascular tumor. Histologically, there are two types: (1) a hemangioendothelioma, and (2) hemangiopericytoma.

Clinical Features

Angiosarcoma in the elderly is generally a very aggressive disease.

Two clinical variants are recognized: one occurring mainly on the face and scalp of elderly patients and the other as an isolated nodular lesion in children. The angiosarcoma of the scalp in elderly patients presents with a dusky red, sharply demarcated, edematous lesion resembling erysipelas (Figure 25–6). Unfortunately, distant metastases occur rapidly.

Prognosis and Treatment

Poor prognosis

Wide surgical excision is the treatment of choice.The prognosis of this tumor, however, is grim. We have observed two of these patients, who, within 8 months of diagnosis, succumbed to widespread metastases.

Annotated Bibliography

Girard C, Johnson WC, Graham JH. Cutaneous angiosarcoma. Cancer 1970;26:868–883.

Holden, CA, Spittle, MF, Wilson-Jones E. Angiosarcoma of the face and scalp. Prognosis and treatment. Cancer 1987;48:1907–1921.

These two articles highlight the grim prognosis in elderly patients with hemangioendotheliomas.

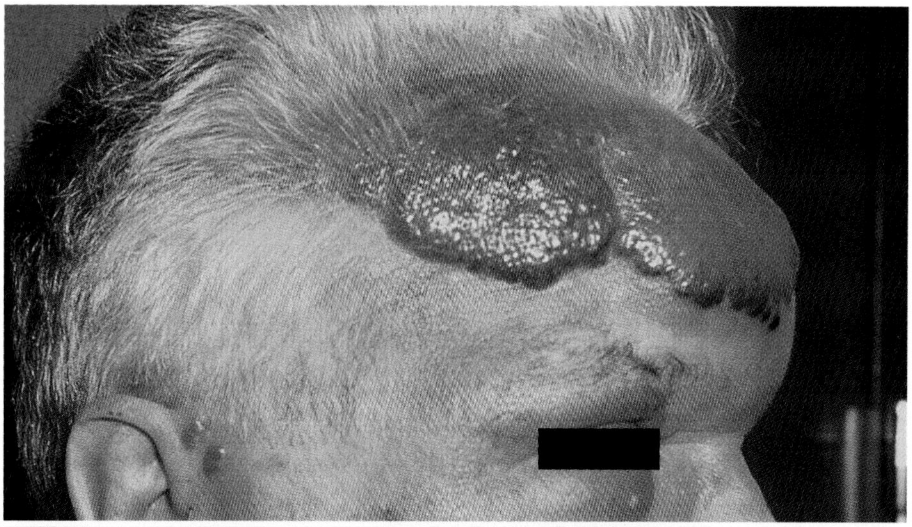

FIGURE 25–6 Hemangiosarcoma in a 70-year-old male—rapid onset and demise within 6 months. Fifty years previously, he had received scalp radiography for tinea capitis, which may or may not have been etiologically significant.

Lymphangiosarcoma

Thomas T. Provost, M.D.

Occurrance in edematous upper extremity

In 1948, Stewart and Treves published a description of six patients who developed lymphangiosarcoma in edematous upper extremities. In five cases, the edema occurred on the ipsilateral side following radical mastectomy for carcinoma of the breast. In the sixth case, a radical mastectomy was performed, but a careful pathologic study failed to reveal a breast carcinoma. In five cases, the edema occurred in the postoperative period. In one case, the massive edema occurred 1 year following radical mastectomy.

Occurs, on average, a decade after radical mastectomy

Their observations indicated that this complication occurred without evidence of axillary metastasis of the breast cancer in individuals with or without postoperative irradiation and in sites where no radiation had been administered. The onset of the lymphangiosarcoma occurred, on average, 12.5 years after the breast operation (range of 6 to 24 years).

Their studies indicated that following radical mastectomy, fat necrosis occurs at the upper angle of the mastectomy scar. The entire fat layer is replaced by fibrosis, which ultimately compresses the nerve, artery, vein, and lymphatics in the area.

Anecdotal case reports indicate the occurrence of lymphangiosarcoma in chronic edematous limbs not associated with malignancy.

Clinical Features

Lymphangiosarcoma, also known as Stewart-Treves syndrome, begins insidiously with the development of purplish-red, subcutaneous nodules on an upper chronic, edematous extremity. The lesions initially may be solitary or associated with similar satellite lesions, which may become confluent (Figure 25–7). Larger lesions may develop papillomatous growths; others may ulcerate and discharge a serosanguinous material.

Prognosis and Treatment

Prognosis is guarded.

The prognosis of lymphangiosarcoma is very guarded. Disarticulation amputation at the shoulder is the surgical treatment of choice. However, metastatic disease to the lung is frequent, and the mortality rate is high.

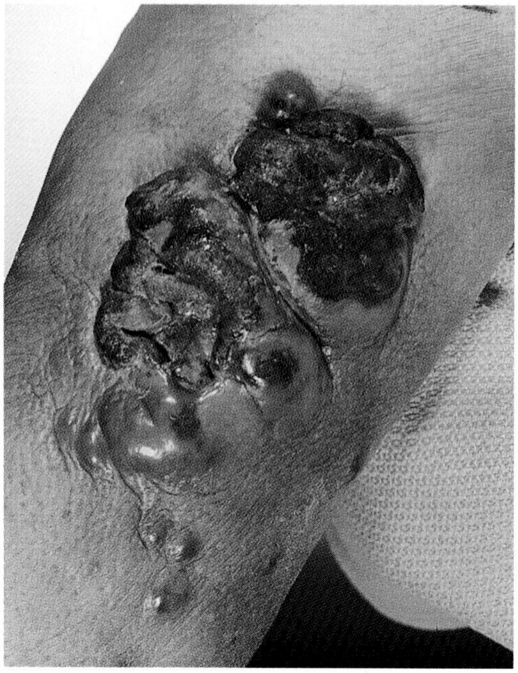

FIGURE 25–7 Development of ulcerative nodules and tumors of lymphangiosarcoma in a patient with chronic edema of the ipsilateral limb, following radical mastectomy a decade ago.

Annotated Bibliography

Scott RB, Nydick I, Conway H. Lymphangiosarcoma arising in lymphedema. Am J Med 1960;28:1008–1012.

MacKenzie DH. Lymphangiosarcoma arising in chronic congenital and idiopathic lymphedema. J Clin Pathol 1971;24:524–529.

These two case reports and literature reviews describe the unusual occurrence of lymphangiosarcoma arising in association with chronic lymphedema. It is interesting to note that in the article by Scott et al., mention is made that lymphedema secondary to chronic infection producing classic elephantiasis is almost never associated with the development of a malignant tumor.

CHAPTER 26

Basal Cell and Squamous Cell Carcinomas

Stanley J. Miller, M.D., Rachel Reitan, M.D.

Basal cell carcinoma (BCC) and squamous cell carcinoma (SCC) of the skin are the most common human cancers. Although rarely metastatic, they are capable of great local destruction and disfigurement. Because of their high incidence rates, they impose a significant economic burden on the health care system. Collectively, these entities are referred to as nonmelanoma skin cancers (NMSCs).

Nonmelanoma skin cancers are very common.

Incidence and Prevalence

More than one million NMSCs will be diagnosed in the United States in 2000. BCCs develop more frequently than SCCs, with a typical BCC:SCC ratio of 4:1. Nonmelanoma skin cancers develop much more frequently in skin types I and II (fair-skinned Caucasians who sunburn) and much less commonly in skin types V and VI (brown and black-skinned individuals). The incidence is also higher in males, in climates with more sunlight, and with increasing proximity to the equator. Mortality is generally quite low, although a 3 to 4% mortality due to cutaneous SCC has been reported in transplantation patients.

More than one million cases in the United States per year

Etiology/Pathogenesis

Genetics

Although BCC and SCC are lumped together under the title of NMSC, important differences exist. Different genes appear to play a role in each tumor's development. The types of ultraviolet (UV) light exposure that appear to produce BCC and SCC and the body sites on which they occur are subtly different. Only SCC develops through a clinical stage of dysplasia, termed an "actinic keratosis," that has the potential to either resolve or develop into fully invasive carcinoma. By contrast, there is no known precancerous phase for BCC. Finally, the metastatic risk of these two entities, although relatively low compared with many internal cancers, is significantly greater in SCC than in BCC.

Different genes are involved in BCC and SCC development.

Several syndromes predispose to NMSC development (Table 26–1), although at this time, only two have known genetic etiologies.

Nevoid Basal Cell Carcinoma Syndrome

The human *PTCH* gene, initially identified as a developmental gene in the fruit fly and in mice, has recently been shown in humans to be a tumor suppressor gene. Homozygous allelic loss in *PTCH* has been detected in the nevoid basal cell carcinoma syndrome, a rare condition with myriad potential clinical features,

Human PTCH tumor suppressor gene

TABLE 26–1 Etiologic Factors in NMSC Formation

Syndromes
Nevoid basal cell carcinoma syndrome
Xeroderma pigmentosum
Epidermodysplasia verruciformis
Ferguson Smith epithelioma
Bazex's syndrome
Oculocutaneous albinism
Vitiligo
Settings
Chronic diseases (discoid lupus erythematosus, lichen sclerosus et atrophicus)
Chronic wounds (irradiation, burns, chronic osteomyelitis)
Dermatofibroma
Nevus sebaceus
Linear unilateral basal cell nevus
Porokeratosis
Environmental carcinogens
Ultraviolet light
Ionizing radiation
Chemicals (arsenic, hydrocarbons)
Human papilloma virus
Immunosuppression (transplant recipients, others)

including short fourth metacarpal bones, jaw cysts, bifid ribs, calcification of the falx, palmar pits, central nervous system tumors, and multiple BCCs. Patients with this condition often develop hundreds of BCCs during their lifetime (Figures 26–1 to 26–3). Tumor development typically begins or increases at puberty, and it is markedly accelerated by radiation therapy, which should be avoided in these individuals. Mutations in the *PTCH* gene have also been observed in over one-third of all sporadic BCCs that develop in the nonsyndrome population.

Mutations in PTCH genes are found in all types of BCC.

The *PTCH* gene (9q22.3) encodes a transmembrane protein, which in the fruit fly *Drosophila melanogaster* controls patterning and growth in numerous tissues. In addition to its role in the development of basal cell carcinomas in humans, it is also postulated that this gene plays a role in the development of the associated bone abnormalities and nervous system tumors in the nevoid basal cell carcinoma syndrome.

Xeroderma Pigmentosum

Defect in excisional repair

Xeroderma pigmentosum is a collection of closely related syndromes in which affected individuals have significant impairment of their UV light–induced, unscheduled DNA repair (eg, excisional repair). If these persons are exposed to sunlight, they will develop great numbers of NMSCs and melanoma, beginning at an early age. The genetics of this syndrome have been well worked out. There also appears to be a form of mildly impaired excisional repair, similar to xeroderma pigmentosum but much less dramatic, that has been observed in families who develop multiple BCCs and/or BCCs at an early age.

P53 *Gene*

Sun-exposed skin frequently contains mutations in the *P53* gene that have characteristic UV-induced C–T and CC–TT dipyrimidine dimers. The effect that these *P53* mutations have on NMSC development is unclear, but any role is probably an early event in the carcinogenic process. *P53* mutations are found in approximately 50% of BCCs and in the majority of SCCs. They are also present in many actinic keratoses, which are dysplastic precursors to SCCs. Mutations in *ras* and *fos* oncogenes are present in only a minority of NMSCs.

Other Predisposing Syndromes and Settings

Epidermodysplasia Verruciformis

Epidermodysplasia verruciformis is a rare, inherited disease characterized by multiple warts on the hands, feet, face, neck, and back (usually beginning in childhood) induced by the human papilloma virus (HPV) types 5, 8, 9, 12, 14, 15, 17, 19–25, 28, and 29. A family history usually demonstrates vertical penetrance, indicative of an autodominant inheritance; some patients have an X-linked inheritance. Other cases are sporadic. Development of SCC from these lesions can occur in light-exposed areas. Defective T-cell immunity has been demonstrated. In nonsyndrome individuals, HPV does not appear to have any etiologic role in BCC development, but it is associated with the occurrence of some SCCs, primarily those developing in the genital and digital regions. HPVs may also play a role in the development of SCCs in immunosuppressed transplant recipients. HPV subtypes with carcinogenic potential have sections of their DNA (viral oncogenes) that interfere with the normal functioning of the human RB and P53 proteins.

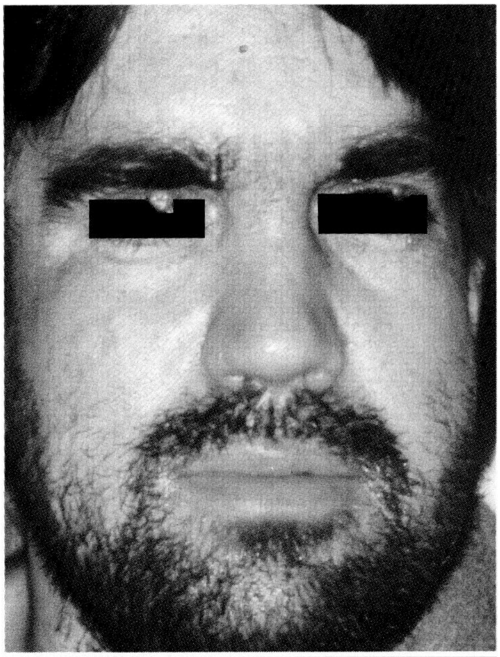

FIGURE 26–1 Young male with nevoid basal cell carcinoma syndrome, note BCC, lesion on upper eye. Also note coarse skeletal features.

Ferguson Smith Epithelioma

Ferguson Smith epithelioma is an uncommon disorder in which multiple keratoacanthomas develop. These lesions, although in many cases self-healing, may represent a form of SCC.

Epidermodysplasia verruciformis, human papilloma virus, Ferguson Smith epithelioma, Bazex's syndrome, oculocutaeous albinism, vitiligo, irradiation, burns and chronic osteomyelitis, dermatofibroma, nevus sebaceus, linear unilateral basal cell nevus, and porokeratosis

Bazex's Syndrome

Bazex's syndrome is a rare condition characterized by ice-pick–like scars on the dorsum of the hands and feet, varying amounts of anhidrosis and hypotrichosis, and multiple BCCs.

Albinism, Vitiligo

Settings in which melanin, one of the skin's important defenses against UV light exposure, is absent can predispose to skin cancer development. These conditions include oculocutaneous albinism and vitiligo.

Chronic Inflammation

Chronic inflammation, such as discoid lupus erythematosus and lichen sclerosus et atrophicus, uncommonly undergo malignant degeneration.

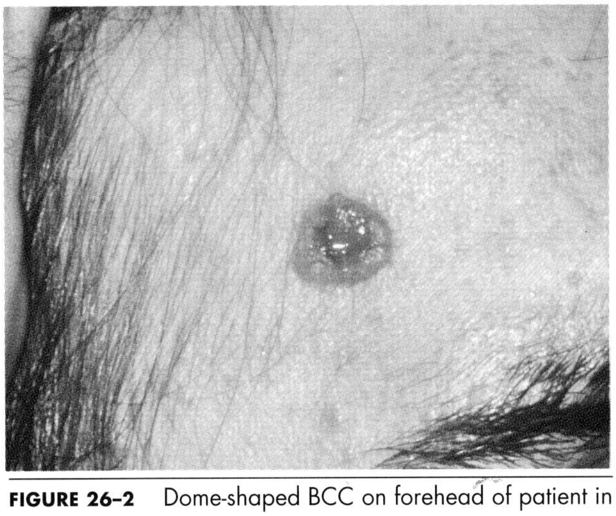

FIGURE 26–2 Dome-shaped BCC on forehead of patient in Figure 26–1.

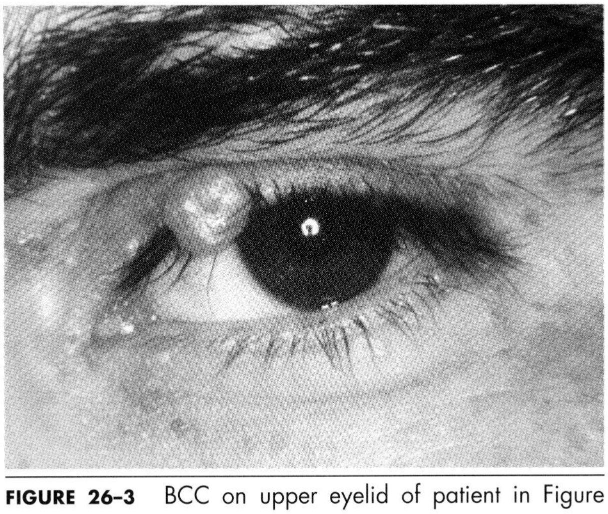

FIGURE 26–3 BCC on upper eyelid of patient in Figure 26–1.

Irradiation, Burns, Chronic Osteomyelitis

Chronic wounds, such as those caused by excessive irradiation, burns, chronic heat applications, and chronic osteomyelitis, can produce both BCCs and SCCs, typically after a 15- to 20-year time period. SCCs that develop in these settings carry a significant (30%) risk of metastasis. BCCs that develop in sites of prior irradiation are often more locally invasive as well.

Several clinical settings exist in which cytokine signaling in the dermis is thought to play a role in stimulating overlying epidermal BCC development. These include smallpox vaccination sites, dermatofibroma, nevus sebaceus, and linear unilateral basal cell nevus.

Finally, some forms of porokeratosis may predispose to SCC development.

Environmental Carcinogens

UV light, ionizing radiation, arsenic, immunosuppression

Ultraviolet Light

UV light plays a major etiologic role in the development of many NMSCs. Its effects on SCC and BCC formation appear to be slightly different. SCC development appears to result from a person's total UV dose accumulated over a lifetime, as well as any recent UV exposure. BCC incidence appears to rise with increasing total lifetime UV light exposure. A threshold appears to be reached, however, beyond which additional exposure adds only small amounts of additional risk. Episodic overexposure and exposure at a younger age, both of which are risk factors for melanoma development, may represent important forms of UV light exposure that lead to BCC formation. The carcinogenic mechanisms of UV light have been studied most extensively in animal models of SCC development, where it appears to function as an initiator, a promoter, and an immunosuppressant.

Ionizing Radiation

Ionizing radiation can produce both BCCs and SCCs typically after a period of 15 to 30 years. Radiation appears to act as both a complete carcinogen, an initiator, and a tumor converter. Risk increases with total accumulated dose, although whether a minimal threshold dose exists is unclear.

Arsenic

Arsenic is a chemical carcinogen that was common in well water and Fowler's medical solution several decades ago. It leads to both BCC and SCC development.

Immunosuppressive Agents

Certain types of immunosuppression predispose to primarily SCC development. The most extensively studied group of immunosuppressed individuals are the kidney and heart transplant recipients. In these patients with a history of UV light exposure, SCC incidence rates can be up to 25 times the normal. Whether individual tumors are also more likely to metastasize is unclear, but one large study of renal transplant recipients with skin cancers found that 3 to 4% died from their SCCs. Basal cell carcinoma development in these groups is also slightly elevated (2 to 5 times the normal).

Psoralen Plus Ultraviolet A Treatments

Patients who have undergone significant numbers of psoralen plus UVA treatments, which are known to be immunosuppressive and consist of oral psoralen ingestion combined with topical UVA exposure, have an increased risk of developing SCC and, to a lesser extent, BCC and melanoma as well.

Human Immunodeficiency Virus

Human immunodeficiency virus–positive patients appear to have only a slightly increased risk of NMSC development.

Clinical Features

Basal Cell Carcinoma

BCCs are often subclassified, on the basis of their clinical and histologic features, into macronodular, superficial spreading, aggressive, and basosquamous types. Table 26–2 provides the TNM (primary tumor, regional nodes, metastasis) staging system for NMSCs.

BCC subtypes include macronodular, superficial spreading, aggressive and basosquamous

Macronodular

Macronodular BCC

Macronodular BCCs are the classic BCCs (Figures 26–4 and 26–5). They present as solitary, well-demarcated papules or plaques, which are pearly or reddish in color and shiny surfaced, often with overlying telangiectasias. As a lesion slowly enlarges, its center may become depressed and sometimes crusted, leaving behind

TABLE 26–2 TNM Staging System for Carcinoma of the Skin*

Primary Tumor	
TX	Primary tumor cannot be assessed
T0	No evidence of primary tumor
Tis	Carcinoma in situ
T1	Tumor ≤ 2 cm in greatest dimension
T2	Tumor > 2 cm but < 5 cm in greatest dimension
T3	Tumor of > 5 cm in greatest dimension
T4	Tumor invades deep extradermal structures (eg, cartilage, skeletal muscle, bone)
Regional Lymph Nodes	
NX	Regional nodes cannot be assessed
N0	No regional node metastasis
N1	Regional node metastasis
Distant Metastasis	
MX	Presence of distant metastasis cannot be assessed
M0	No distant metastasis
M1	Distant metastasis
Histopathologic Grade	
GX	Grade cannot be assessed
G1	Well differentiated
G2	Moderately well differentiated
G3	Poorly differentiated
G4	Undifferentiated

Staging

Stage	Tumor	Nodes	Metastasis
0	Tis	N0	M0
I	T1	N0	M0
II	T2	N0	M0
	T3	N0	M0
III	T4	N0	M0
	T any	N1	M0
IV	T any	N any	M1

*Excluding eyelid, vulva, and penis.

Adapted from:
American Joint Committee on Cancer (AJCC) Staging and End Results Reporting and the International Union Against Cancer (UICC). In: Beahrs OH, Henson DE, Hutter RVP, Kennedy BJ. Manual for Staging of Cancer, 4th ed. Philadelphia: JB Lippincott, 1992, pp 137–139.

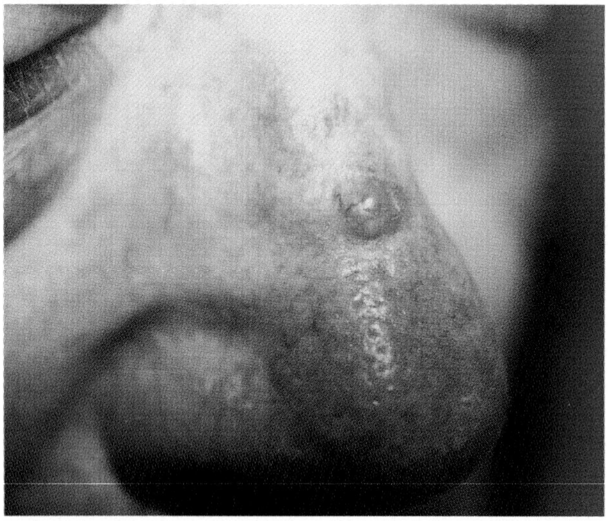

FIGURE 26–4 A well-circumscribed macronodular BCC located on the nose.

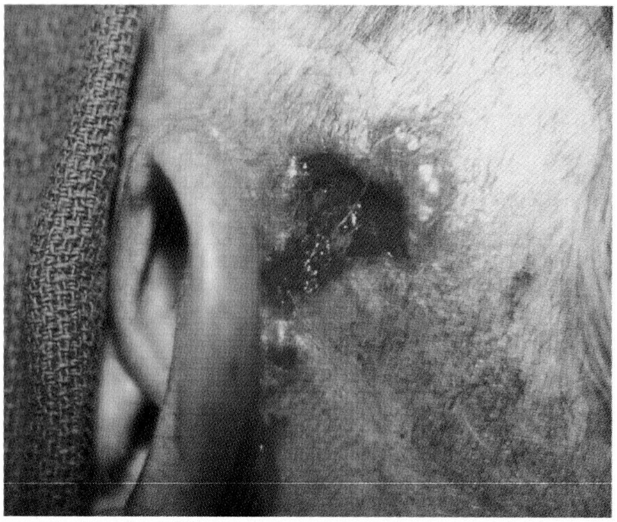

FIGURE 26–5 A larger, centrally ulcerated macronodular BCC located on the mastoid neck extending into the postauricular sulcus of the ear.

a still elevated, smooth and rolled pearly border. Macronodular BCCs may also be pigmented, a common presentation in darker-skinned individuals (Figure 26–6).

Superficial

Superficial BCC

Superficial spreading BCC presents as an erythematous, slightly scaly, irregularly shaped, flat papule or plaque. Sometimes, there will be a thread-like, pearly rolled border and an atrophic center. As with most BCCs, this border may be accentuated by stretching the skin surrounding the plaque. Superficial spreading BCC develops most commonly on the neck, trunk, and extremities. The lesions may be clinically confused with eczema, psoriasis, and tinea.

Aggressive

Morpheaform/sclerosing BCC

Aggressive BCCs consists of the micronodular, infiltrative, and morpheaform/sclerosing histologic subtypes. There are no clinical features that can distinguish a micronodular from a macronodular BCC (Figure 26–7). Infiltrative BCCs are typically more ill-defined than macronodular tumors (Figure 26–8). Morpheaform/sclerosing BCCs are uncommon and usually present as an ill-defined,

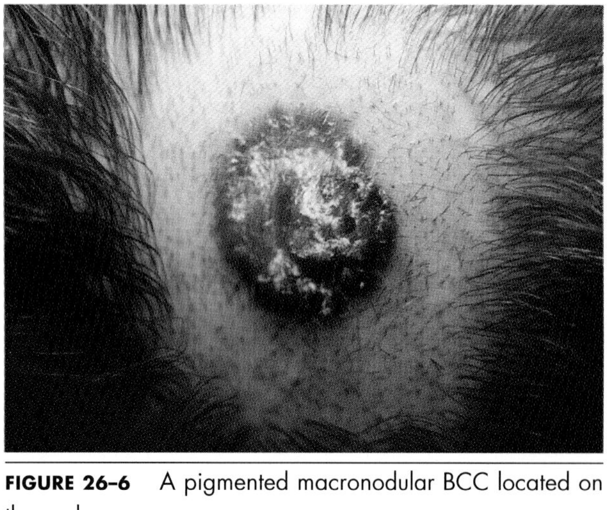

FIGURE 26–6 A pigmented macronodular BCC located on the scalp.

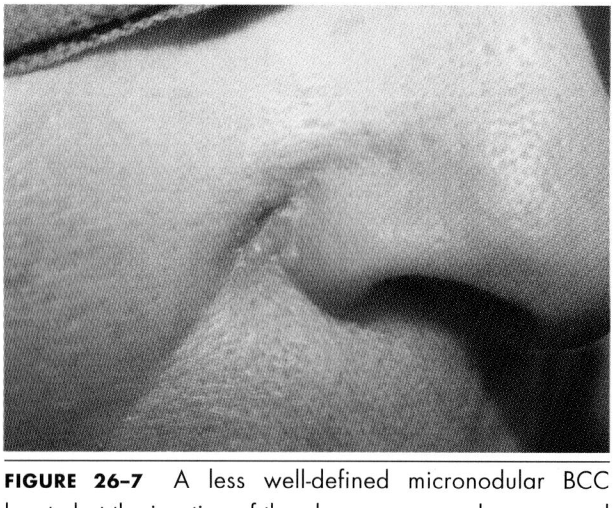

FIGURE 26–7 A less well-defined micronodular BCC located at the junction of the alar crease, nasal crease, and meliolabial fold.

indurated area of whiteness, like a scar, secondary to the tumor's desmoplastic fibrous stroma. Ulceration rarely occurs.

Basosquamous

Basosquamous carcinoma, also called metatypical BCC, is a somewhat controversial entity. Some basosquamous carcinomas may represent a collision of two separate tumors, some may represent irritated BCCs that have developed squamoid change superficially, and some may represent true carcinomas that contain histologic features of both BCC and SCC. The diagnosis is made histologically, and its importance may be prognostic. Several studies have suggested that the metastatic rate of basosquamous carcinoma is more like that of SCC than BCC.

Basosquamous BCC
May have increased metastasis

Actinic Keratosis

Solar or actinic keratoses (AKs) are precancerous growths that develop on chronically sun-exposed body sites. Common locations include the face, scalp, arms, ears, and dorsum of hands. Only a small percentage (1 to 5%) of the growths will develop into frankly invasive SCC. Lesions may be singular or multiple and typically present as flat, irregularly shaped keratotic papules, often with a surrounding reddish hue (Figure 26–9). Some may be quite hyperkeratotic. Squamous cell carcinomas may also develop within other forms of epidermal dysplasia, such as thermal keratoses, chronic radiation keratoses, cicatricial keratoses, cutaneous horns, and arsenical keratoses.

Actinic keratoses are precancerous dysplastic growths.

Squamous Cell Carcinoma In Situ

Bowen's Disease

Squamous cell carcinomas that are confined to the full thickness of the epidermal layer are termed "SCC in situ." Morphologic forms include Bowen's disease and erythroplasia of Queyrat. Bowen's disease develops on both sun-exposed and non–sun-exposed skin surfaces. It appears as a sharply demarcated, flat, scaly, often fiery red papule or plaque. There is sometimes scale or crust on the top of the lesion. As with the superficial spreading form of BCC, Bowen's disease may be clinically confused with eczema, psoriasis, and tinea.

Morphologic forms of SCC in situ include Bowen's disease and erythroplasia of Queyrat

Erythroplasia of Queyrat

Erythroplasia of Queyrat refers to SCC in situ located on the glans penis (Figure 26–10). It develops more commonly in uncircumcised males. Clinically and histologically, the lesion appears similar to Bowen's disease, although there is often less scaling. Progression to an invasive SCC has been observed in up to 30% of cases.

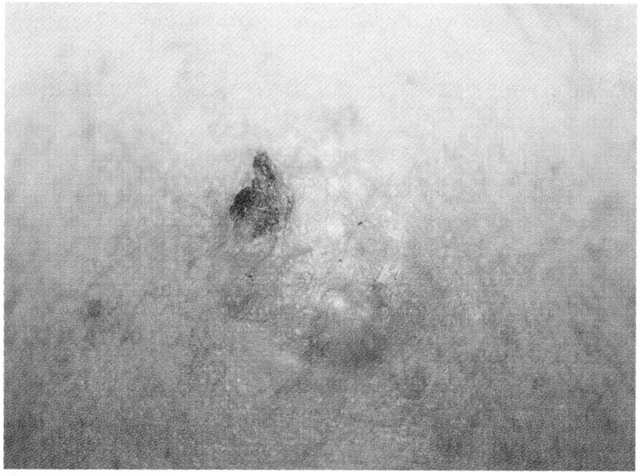

FIGURE 26–8 An ill-defined infiltrative BCC on the forehead.

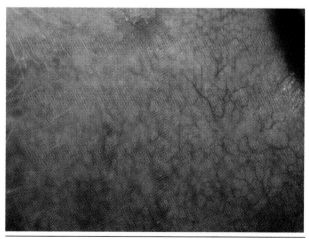

FIGURE 26–9 An angular, keratotic papule located on the lateral neck that is an AK. These lesions frequently can be more easily felt than visualized.

Invasive Squamous Cell Carcinoma

Wounds that do not heal

Invasive SCC commonly arises on the sun-exposed fair skin of fair complexioned, elderly individuals. Squamous cell carcinomas often present as areas of friable, granulation-like tissue that frequently bleed and may be thought of as wounds that do not heal (Figures 26–11 and 26–12). They often have an overlying hemorrhagic crust and sometimes show evidence of secondary infection. Their growth rate may occasionally be quite rapid. The lesions are usually located on sun-exposed areas, such as the face, scalp, ears, dorsum of hands, legs, and chest. Cutaneous SCCs do have the capacity to metastasize, most commonly to the regional lymph nodes. If metastasis occurs, there will be regional lymphadenopathy.

Keratoacanthoma

Rapid growth

Many involute; others continue to enlarge and are SCC

Cannot differentiate with certainty

Keratoacanthoma (KA) may represent a subtype of SCC. It typically presents as a volcano-like, dome-shaped, red to skin-colored, firm nodule with a central keratinous crater surrounded by a cup-like border of epithelium (Figure 26–13). KAs develop most commonly on sun-exposed skin, such as the dorsum of hands, nose, neck, ears, and face. They are thought to arise from hair follicles. The lesions characteristically enlarge rapidly over a period of weeks to months, followed by a period of stability, and then many will regress completely over a period of months, leaving behind only a puckered or pitted scar. However, some will not involute but continue to enlarge and grow as frank SCC. It is unknown whether KA biologically represents an SCC that, in many instances, has the capacity to involute or, instead, is a wastebasket term encompassing both benign involuting tumors and true SCC that we are unable to differentiate on the basis of clinical or histologic features.

Verrucous Carcinoma

Verrucous carcinoma may be locally aggressive but rarely metastasizes.

Verrucous carcinoma is another form of low-grade SCC. It presents as a cauliflower-like, verrucous-surfaced papule or plaque, often located on the weight-bearing surfaces. It may initially appear as a plantar wart. Sometimes there are several openings from which a malodorous material may be expressed. The lesions enlarge slowly. They may also develop on the mucosal surfaces in the mouth, larynx, perianal region, cervix, and penis. Verrucous carcinoma can be locally aggressive, but it rarely metastasizes.

Features Associated with Recurrences and Metastasis

A number of well-defined risk factors exist for NMSC recurrence and metastasis.

A number of clinical and histologic features are associated with an increased risk of local recurrence by BCC and SCC and an increased risk of regional or distant metastasis by SCC (Table 26–3).

Basal cell carcinoma very rarely metastasizes, and there are no defined clinical or histologic features to predict this event.

Development of BCC or SCC in the mask areas of the face and in sites of prior irradiation and development of SCC on the digits and genitalia increase the likelihood of local recurrence. SCCs that develop on the ear, lip, mucosal surfaces of the genitalia, or in chronic nonhealing wounds, as well as those that enlarge rapidly, are at increased risk for metastasis. Prior treatment (ie, recurrence) and a diameter greater than 2 cm increase the risk of both BCC and SCC recurrence and of SCC metastasis. Infiltrative histologic features in a BCC (ie, micronodular, infiltrative, morpheaform/sclerosing subtypes) portend a greater risk of recurrence. Infiltrative features, poor differentiation, adenosquamous and spindle cell subtypes, evidence of parotid gland involvement, perineural invasion, and greater depth of invasion all increase the risk of SCC recurrence and metastasis. Organ trans-

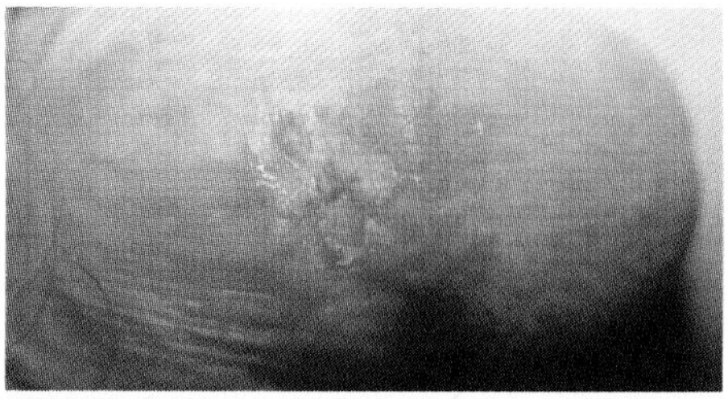

FIGURE 26–10 Erythroplasia of Queyrat, which is an SCC in situ of the dorsal penis.

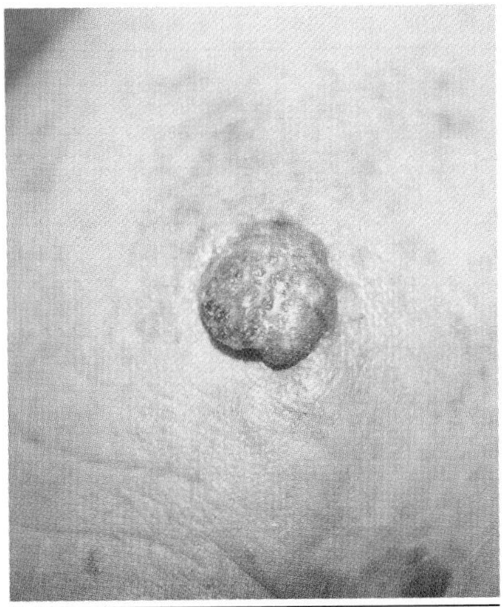

FIGURE 26–11 A well-circumscribed, friable SCC of the forehead.

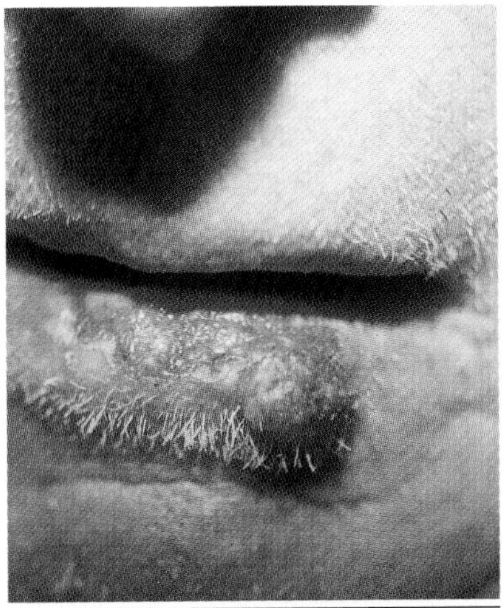

FIGURE 26–12 A large and somewhat ill-defined SCC of the lower lip.

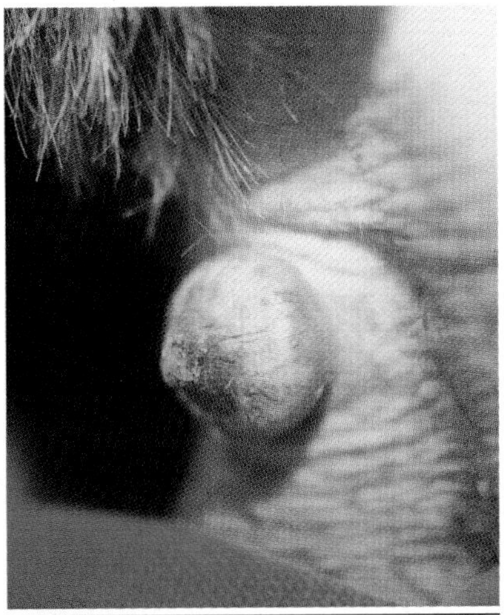

FIGURE 26–13 A pedunculated KA of the lateral neck. These lesions appear and then grow rapidly, typically developing within a period of weeks to months.

plantation and certain other settings of immunosuppression significantly increase SCC incidence and possibly the risk of recurrence and metastasis as well.

Treatment

Therapy is chosen based on the clinical and histologic features of a tumor as well as the needs of the patient.

The goal of treatment of any cutaneous malignancy or premalignancy is to remove all the malignant cells without impairing function, while achieving a good cosmetic result. The selection of a treatment modality depends on the clinical and histologic features of the tumor, as discussed above, as well as the patient's desires.

A skin biopsy is first obtained to verify the clinical diagnosis and to gather prognostic histologic information about the tumor. Shave excisions are often performed on tumors that are small or shallow. With larger or deeper lesions, a punch biopsy is preferred to obtain a histologic assessment of the tumor's deep advancing border.

Liquid Nitrogen and Topical Chemotherapy

Liquid nitrogen

Liquid nitrogen and topical chemotherapy are often used to treat precancerous lesions (AKs). Liquid nitrogen is −195°C and is applied to individual skin lesions by spray or by a cotton-tipped applicator. A sufficient freezing will lead to crusting and, occasionally, blister formation that resolves in about a week. Any growths that remain following cryotherapy probably require a biopsy to rule out invasive disease.

5-fluorouracil

The most common topical agent used to treat AKs is 5-fluorouracil cream. Application is made twice daily to an entire body region for 2 to 6 weeks. Common side effects during the treatment period include redness, crusting, pain, and weeping that can resemble a severe sunburn. Benefits include resolution of subclinical dysplasia as well as obvious lesions in the treated region.

Curettage and Electrodesiccation

Curettage and desiccation
Simple office procedure
High cure rate

Curettage and electrodesiccation (C+E) can be used to treat shallow, low-risk NMSCs, that are typically less than 1 cm in diameter and located on the trunk or extremities. The success of the C+E procedure is highly operator dependent. Healed C+E scars are typically flat and hypopigmented. Advantages of C+E are a high cure rate when properly selected tumors are treated by experienced clini-

TABLE 26–3 NMSC Features Associated with Recurrence and Metastasis

Clinical
Location
Size
Previous treatment (recurrence)
Prior irradiation
Development in chronic nonhealing wounds or ulcers (SCC)
Patient immunosuppression (SCC)
Growth rate (SCC)
Histologic
Infiltrative histology
Poorly differentiated, spindle cell, adenosquamous, verrucous, acantholytic histology (SCC)
Depth of invasion
Perineural infiltration

cians in a simple office procedure. Potential disadvantages include the lack of tissue with which to examine surgical margins, and the necessity for secondary intention healing.

Surgical Excision

Surgical excision is the treatment of choice for many NMSCs: surgical margins may be sampled to insure clearance of the malignant cells, the healing time is shorter than with secondary intention healing, and the final scar can be cosmetically elegant.

Mohs' Micrographic Surgery

Mohs' surgery

Mohs' micrographic surgery (MMS) is the treatment of choice for all high-risk NMSCs. Virtually 100% of the surgical margins are examined for malignant cells, resulting in the highest cure rates. MMS is also tissue sparing because only tissues containing tumor are removed. MMS consists of removing the lesion with a scalpel at a 45° angle so that the excised piece is bowl shaped. The tissue is subdivided into sections that are numbered, and a corresponding map is created. Each cut edge is colored with different colored dyes for orientation. Horizontal frozen sections are made in a cryostat to visualize the complete undersurface and outer periphery of the excised surgical specimen. If residual tumor is noted under the microscope, another surgical layer is obtained. This is continued until surgical margins are completely free of malignancy. A variety of reconstructive approaches to repair the defect may then be considered.

Mohs' micrographic surgery is not required for the majority of NMSCs. However, it is the treatment of choice for clinically ill-defined tumors, locally or histologically aggressive tumors, recurrent tumors, and tumors that are located in high-risk locations (Table 26–4).

Cryosurgery

Cryosurgery

Cryosurgery involves freezing malignant cells in a controlled fashion with liquid nitrogen. The underlying stroma that remains provides a structural framework for healing. Cryosurgery can be used to treat high-risk surgical candidates, pregnant women, and people with pacemakers or coagulopathies. It can be used to debulk inoperable tumors and relieve pain. It is effective over cartilaginous areas, such as the nose and ear, because cartilage is relatively resistant to freezing damage so the architecture of the structure is preserved. Contraindications to cryotherapy include people with cold intolerance, cold urticaria, cryoglobulinemia, and cryofibrinogenemia.

Radiation Therapy

Radiation

Radiation therapy is indicated for the treatment of tumors located in the head and neck region. It can help to minimize cosmetic or functional deficits. Like cryosurgery, it can be useful where surgery is contraindicated or for palliative treatment of large and inoperable cancers. Radiation therapy may also be used as an adjunct to surgery to treat residual tumor at a primary site or to treat regional metastatic disease.

Prevention

Individuals who develop BCC have a 30 to 50% chance of developing another over the next 5 years.

Follow-up is crucial for patients with a history of NMSC, both to monitor for recurrences as well as to detect new cancers. Individuals who have had one BCC have a 30 to 50% chance of developing another one in the next 5 years, usually at another sun-exposed site. The vast majority of SCCs that recur or metastasize regionally will do so within 2 years of initial therapy. Therefore, examination of

TABLE 26–4 Indications for MMS

- Located in the so-called "mask area" of the face
  - Central face, eyelids, eyebrows, periorbita, nose, lips (cutaneous and vermillion), chin, mandible, preauricular skin/sulcus, postauricular skin/sulcus, temple, entire ear (including ear canal)
- Other locations
  - Genitalia
  - Hands and feet
  - Nail unit/periungual area
- Recurrent
  - Aggressive histology (infiltrative, micronodular, sclerotic, fibrosing, morpheaform, keratotic, spikey-shaped cell groups, superficial multicentric, desmoplastic, perineural or perivascular invasion, nuclear pleomorphism, high mitotic activity)
  - Adenoid SCC, verrucous carcinoma
  - Rapid growth in an SCC
  - Longstanding duration in an SCC
  - Large size
    - ≥ 1 cm in middle-risk areas (cheek, forehead, scalp)
    - ≥ 2 cm in low-risk areas (trunk, neck, extremities)
  - Positive margins on recent excision
  - Poorly defined borders
  - In the very young (< 40 yr of age)
  - Radiation induced
  - In patients with proven difficulty with skin cancers or who are immunocompromised
  - Nevoid basal cell carcinoma syndrome
  - In an old scar (eg, a Marjolin's ulcer)
  - Associated with xeroderma pigmentosum
  - Deeply infiltrating lesion or with a depth that is difficult to estimate
  - Perineural invasion on biopsy or clinical suspicion of same

Adapted from:
The HCFA Guidelines for Mohs' Micrographic Surgery, Medicare Part B Newsletter No. 023, February 6, 1998.

Recurrences are problematic

Value of annual examinations

both the primary tumor site and the draining regional lymph nodes at 3 to 6 month intervals during this 2-year period is recommended. All patients with an NMSC probably need annual skin examinations for the remainder of their lives. Patients also need to be taught how to do their own skin self-examination, which should be performed at home on a monthly basis.

Encourage individuals with NMSC to minimize their sun exposure.

Sun avoidance should be encouraged. Outdoor activities should be minimized during the midday hours (10:00 am to 3:00 pm) when UV rays are strongest. Protective clothing, such as hats with a 4-inch wide brim, long-sleeved shirts, and full-length pants, should be worn while in the sun. For other exposed skin sites, broad spectrum UVB/UVA sunscreens with a skin protection factor of at least 15 should be used routinely. Application should be made 30 minutes prior to sun exposure and then repeated every 2 to 3 hours while individuals are in the sun.

Low doses of oral retinoids, although still experimental, may provide useful chemopreventive effects in certain high-risk individuals.

Treatment of precancerous AKs in at-risk individuals with topical 5-fluorouracil, chemical peels, dermabrasion, or laser resurfacing should be considered. Chemoprevention with low-dose oral retinoids may prove useful in high-risk individuals, such as transplant recipients.

Conclusion

Nonmelanoma skin cancers are the most common human cancers. An awareness of developmental risk factors can help to optimize detection and prevention in at-risk individuals. Preventative behaviors include regular skin examinations, treatment of precancers, and sun avoidance. A knowledge of the clinical and histologic features that predispose to recurrence and metastasis guides the clinician's choice of therapy for individual tumors. By optimizing the care of at-risk patients, morbidity and mortality associated with NMSC can be minimized.

Annotated Bibliography

Preston DS, Stern RS. Nonmelanoma cancers of the skin. N Engl J Med 1992;327: 1649–1662.

Miller SJ. Biology of basal cell carcinoma. Part I. J Am Acad Dermatol 1991;24:1–13.

Miller SJ. Biology of basal cell carcinoma. Part II. J Am Acad Dermatol 1991;24: 161–175.

Kwa RE, Campana K, Moy RL. Biology of cutaneous squamous cell carcinoma. J Am Acad Dermatol 1992;26:1–26.

These are four good general reviews of NMSC. The first is more clinical, whereas the last three focus on the biology of the tumors.

Miller DL, Weinstock MA. Nonmelanoma skin cancer in the United States: incidence. J Am Acad Dermatol 1994;30:774–778.

Weinstock MA. Nonmelanoma skin cancer mortality in the United States, 1969 through 1988. Arch Dermatol 1993;129:1286–1290.

These are two good epidemiologic studies of incidence and mortality rates for NMSC in the United States.

Penn I. Skin disorders in organ transplant recipients [editorial]. Arch Dermatol 1997;133: 221–223.

This review of a large cohort of transplant recipients with skin cancer points out that 5% die of their skin cancers, and most of these are from SCC.

Gallagher RP, Hill GB, Bajdik CD, et al. Sunlight exposure, pigmentary factors, and risk of nonmelanocytic skin cancer. I. Basal cell carcinoma. Arch Dermatol 1995;131: 157–163.

Gallagher RP, Hill GB, Bajdik CD, et al. Sunlight exposure, pigmentation factors, and risk of nonmelanocytic skin cancer. II. Squamous cell carcinoma. Arch Dermatol 1995; 131:164–169.

These are two good epidemiologic studies of how sunlight exposure appears to have different effects on BCC and SCC development.

Gailani MR, Bale AE. Developmental genes and cancer: role of patched in basal cell carcinoma of the skin J Natl Cancer Inst 1997;89:1103–1109.

This is a good review of the PTCH gene–BCC story.

Gorlin RJ. Nevoid basal-cell carcinoma syndrome. Medicine (Baltimore) 1987;66:98–113.

This provides a comprehensive review of the clinical features of the nevoid basal cell carcinoma syndrome.

Kraemer KH, Lee MM, Scotto J. Xeroderma pigmentosum. Cutaneous, ocular, and neurologic abnormalities in 830 published cases. Arch Dermatol 1987;123:241–250.

This article provides a good review of xeroderma pigmentosum.

Ziegler A, Jonason AS, Leffell DJ, et al. Sunburn and p53 in the onset of skin cancer. Nature 1994;372:773–776.

van der Riet P, Karp D, Farmer E, et al. Progression of basal cell carcinoma through loss of chromosome 9q and inactivation of a single p53 allele. Cancer Res 1994;54:25–27.

These two articles discuss the ways in which several tumor suppressor genes and oncogenes may or may not play roles in NMSC development.

Miller SJ. Etiology and pathogenesis of basal cell carcinoma. In: Moy R, Telfer N, ed. Clinics in Dermatology. New York: Elsevier, 1995, pp 527–536.

This article provides a good review of risk factors for BCC development.

Johnson TM, Rowe DE, Nelson BR, Swanson NA. Squamous cell carcinoma of the skin (excluding lip and oral mucosa). J Am Acad Dermatol 1992;26:467–484.

This article provides a good review of risk factors for SCC development.

Lowe L, Rapini RP. Newer variants and simulants of basal cell carcinoma. J Dermatol Surg Oncol 1991;17:641–648.

This article discusses a practical way to think of BCC subtypes.

Marks R, Rennie G, Selwood T. The relationship of basal cell carcinomas and squamous cell carcinomas to solar keratoses. Arch Dermatol 1988;124:1039–1042.

The key point of this study is that AKs are precursors to SCC, but not BCC.

Schwartz RA. Keratocanthoma. J Am Acad Dermatol 1994;30:1–19.

Schwartz RA. Verrucous carcinoma of the skin and mucosa. J Am Acad Dermatol 1995; 32:1–21.

These articles provide comprehensive reviews of two SCC subtypes.

Swanson NA. Mohs' surgery. Technique, indications, applications, and the future. Arch Dermatol 1983;119:761–773.

This article discusses risk factors for BCC recurrence and elaborates on Mohs' micrographic surgical technique.

Rowe DE, Carroll RJ, Day CL. Prognostic factors for local recurrence, metastasis, and survival rates in squamous cell carcinoma of the skin, ear, and lip. J Am Acad Dermatol 1992;26:976–990.

This article is a meta-analysis of many earlier studies of SCC. It discusses risk factors for recurrence and metastasis, as well as rates of recurrence, using different therapeutic modalities.

Rowe DE, Carroll RJ, Day CL Jr. Long-term recurrence rates in previously untreated (primary) cell carcinoma: implications for patient follow-up. J Dermatol Surg Oncol 1989;15:315–328.

Rowe DE, Carroll RJ, Day CL Jr. Mohs surgery is the treatment of choice for recurrent (previously treated) basal cell carcinoma. J Dermatol Surg Oncol 1989;15:424–431.

Two exhaustive meta-analyses that review rates of recurrence for BCC using different therapeutic modalities.

Robinson JK. Risk of developing another basal cell carcinoma. A 5-year prospective study. Cancer 1987;60:118–120.

Karagas MR. Occurrence of cutaneous basal cell and squamous cell malignancies among those with a prior history of skin cancer. J Invest Dermatol 1994;102:10s–13s.

These two articles discuss the significant risk that a skin cancer patient has of developing additional primary tumors (30 to 50%) over the coming years.

CHAPTER 27

Melanoma

Susan E. Koch, M.D., Julie R. Lange, M.D.

Melanoma represents a cancer of the pigment-producing cells of the skin, eyes, and mucosa. In a recent large hospital–based cancer registry, the distribution of melanoma cases in the United States is as follows: cutaneous 91.7%, ocular (conjunctival and uveal) 5.1%, metastatic disease with no known primary 2%, and mucous membrane 1.2%. The vast majority of tumors in all locations occur in Caucasians.

Most melanomas cutaneous in origin

Incidence

In contrast to ocular and mucosal melanoma, which have remained constant, the incidence of cutaneous melanoma has been steadily rising between 4 and 6% per year since the early 1970s. In 2000 in the United States, it is estimated that 47,700 new cases of invasive melanoma of the skin will occur, and there will be 7,700 deaths from the disease. Malignant melanoma of the skin accounts for the majority of deaths due to skin cancer.

Significant clinical problem

Risk Factors

Multiple risk factors have been identified for cutaneous melanoma. A prior history of basal cell carcinoma, squamous cell carcinoma, or melanoma is a risk factor for melanoma. Nonmelanoma skin cancer is associated with a relative risk of 4, and a prior history of melanoma has a relative risk of 8.5. Other risk factors include fair complexion, blond or red hair, freckling, a history of sunburns, and a family history of melanoma. Recent studies implicate long-term therapeutic psoralen plus ultraviolet A light treatment with an increased risk of melanoma.

Excessive sun exposure in fair-skinned individuals

Nevus Phenotype

One group of individuals at risk for developing melanoma are those who have atypical (dysplastic) nevi. There is no pathognomonic clinical feature of atypical nevi. They are often larger than 5 mm in diameter and may reach 10 mm or more in size. The borders are ill defined ("smudgy"), and their outline is often irregular. Given the large diameter of the nevi, their overall profile is flat though skin markings are often accentuated. Some atypical nevi have a central papule that may be darker or lighter in color, compared with the macular periphery. Color variation is common, but hypertrichosis, a feature of congenital nevi, is absent. Atypical nevi share some clinical characteristics with melanoma. Itching or bleeding is not a fea-

Dysplastic nevi

ture of atypical nevi. Most patients with atypical nevi have numerous common nevi as well. Clusters of nevi in such patients show a dramatic heterogeneity, a feature highlighted in the original description of the syndrome (Figure 27–1).

Patients with dysplastic nevi with a personal or family history of melanoma are at increased risk.

Atypical nevi usually appear in late childhood or early adolescence and may first appear in the scalp. They may occur on any part of the skin surface but are most common on the trunk and upper arms. The number of atypical nevi in a given individual varies from a solitary lesion to more than 100. The risk of melanoma in those with atypical nevi is greater than for those without this nevus phenotype. Among those with atypical nevi, the relative risk of melanoma is dependent on the family and personal history. Those at highest risk are from melanoma kindred in which two or more family members have melanoma and/or have a personal history of melanoma. Those with the lowest risk have neither personal nor family history of melanoma. Clarification of many aspects of this clinical syndrome is problematic due to the lack of a uniformly accepted clinical definition.

Follow-up examinations every 3 to 6 months recommended for patient with prior melanoma or a family history of melanoma.

The management of patients with the atypical nevus phenotype includes dermatologic examinations at least annually. Patients with a history of prior melanoma and those from melanoma kindred should be followed up every 3 to 6 months. Patients should be taught to do monthly skin self-examinations as prospective studies employing such instruction have shown that a significant number of melanomas are self-discovered. Clinical photography is a useful tool in identifying melanoma and minimizing excision of stable, presumably benign lesions. The clinician should be aware that early melanoma in this group of individuals can be clinically subtle, can arise from a pre-existing nevus or de novo, and may be difficult to find in the array of pigmented lesions.

Patients with multiple nevi may have a two- to fourfold increased risk to develop a melanoma

Another nevus phenotype associated with an increased risk of melanoma is the finding of numerous (> 25) common nevi. Early literature suggested that such individuals have a greatly elevated risk of melanoma. These studies have been criticized because they have included patients with atypical nevi as well. In a recent multicenter study designed to carefully exclude those with atypical nevi, the relative risk of melanoma in patients with increased numbers of nondysplastic nevi is two to four times that of a control population. Further studies are needed to clarify this issue.

Clinical Features

ABCDE rule for diagnosis

Cutaneous melanoma can develop on any skin surface. The appearance of melanoma is highlighted by the ABCDE rule (Table 27–1).

These tumors are often asymmetric and irregular in outline. Various color combinations of brown, tan, black, red, and white may be present within the same lesion. Even though the tumor diameter is often larger than 6 mm, a smaller lesion with an enlarging diameter by history or objective measurement is highly suspicious. A lesion that becomes more raised from the surface is also suspect.

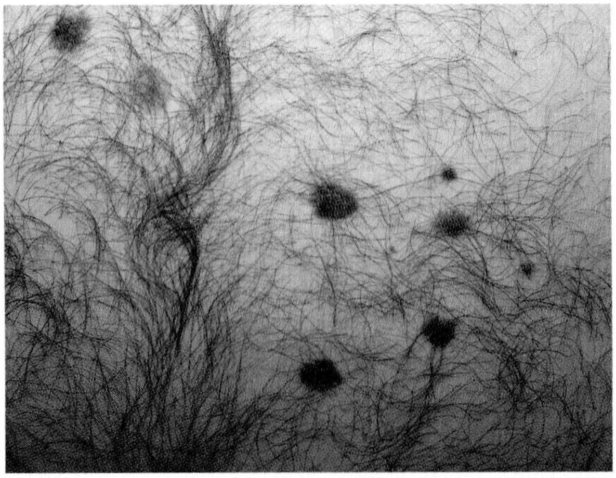

FIGURE 27–1 A cluster of atypical nevi showing heterogeneity.

Major Subtypes

There are four major subtypes of cutaneous melanoma, although not all tumors can be classified into these subtypes.

Superficial Spreading Melanoma

The most common is superficial spreading melanoma, which may arise from a pre-existing nevus or de novo. A typical tumor is a variably raised, asymmetric plaque

TABLE 27–1 Clinical Features of Melanoma: ABCDE Criteria

Asymmetry of the lesion
Border or outline is irregular
Color is variable within the tumor
Diameter enlarging
Elevation or change of a lesion

Superficial spreading type

lacking uniform color. The perimeter of the tumor is typically irregular and may be notched (Figure 27–2). The most common location for this tumor in males is the back and in females the lower extremity. Superficial spreading melanoma is initially confined to the epidermis and, as such, has a flat profile. A nodule within the tumor is evidence for dermal invasion, although invasion may occur in tumors lacking a discrete nodule. Ulceration is more common with thicker tumors. White areas represent areas of tumor regression. The differential diagnosis of superficial spreading melanoma includes the following: atypical nevus, pigmented basal cell carcinoma, Bowen's disease, junctional nevus, and congenital nevus. Keratotic tumors may mimic seborrheic keratoses or verruca.

Nodular Melanoma

Nodular or polypoid type

Nodular melanoma is the second most common subtype notable for its rapid growth and often the absence of the clinical characteristics listed in Table 27–1. These nodular or polypoid tumors can be black, dark brown, or gray with a smooth outline. Tumor ulceration is common. The differential diagnosis includes epidermal inclusion cyst, blue nevus, angiokeratoma, metastatic melanoma, and pyogenic granuloma.

Lentigo Maligna/Lentigo Maligna Melanoma

Lentigo maligna type

Lentigo maligna and lentigo maligna melanoma arise primarily on the sun-exposed skin of the head and neck region in the elderly. Lentigo maligna, the in situ stage, exhibits as a large, unevenly pigmented macule with an irregular contour. This form of in situ melanoma may remain confined to the epidermis for years. Invasion is difficult to discern using clinical criteria alone. The presence of a nodule or palpable induration within the lesion is characteristic but not necessarily present. The differential diagnosis includes solar lentigo, pigmented actinic keratosis, and pigmented basal cell carcinoma.

Acral Lentiginous Melanoma

Acral lentiginous type

Subungual melanoma

Hutchinson's sign

Acral lentiginous melanoma occurs on the volar aspect of the hand or foot or beneath the nail (subungual). The sole of the foot is the most common location (Figure 27–3). Although the incidence of this subtype is approximately the same among races, these tumors constitute the majority of melanomas occurring in African Americans and Asians. On the sole and palm, invasive tumors may be deceptively flat in profile. Color variegation and an irregular outline are frequent. At the time of diagnosis, tumors are often very large and have an average diameter of 3 cm. The differential diagnosis includes Kaposi's sarcoma, subcorneal hemorrhage, melanocytic nevus, and tinea nigra. Subungual melanoma may occur in any nail but is most common on the thumb and great toenail. The tumor originates in the nail matrix and presents as a variably broad pigmented band with or without associated nail plate deformity. Hutchinson's sign, pigmentation of the adjacent periungual skin, is present in some tumors and is a poor prognostic sign.

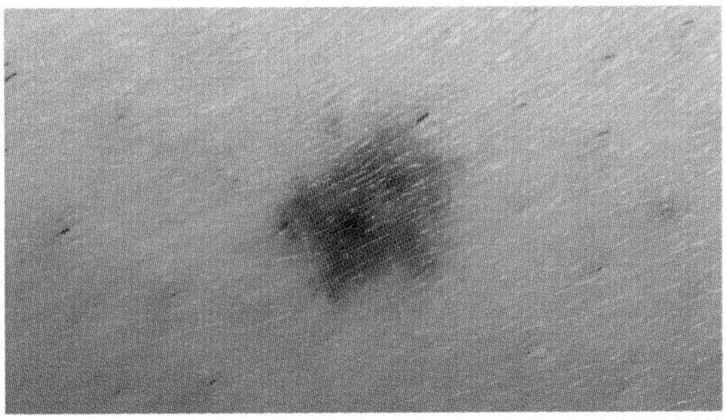

FIGURE 27–2 In situ superficial spreading melanoma showing asymmetry, color variation, and an irregular outline.

Amelanotic melanoma

Amelanotic melanoma, a tumor lacking pigmentation, may occur as any of the above mentioned subtypes and constitutes 1 to 8% of tumors (Figure 27–4). Both primary and metastatic melanoma can be amelanotic. Since the characteristic pigmentation is absent, these tumors may imitate a variety of benign and malignant lesions. A clinical clue of an amelanotic primary tumor is the presence of macular pigmentation in the adjacent skin. The lack of telangectasia distinguishes amelanotic melanoma from basal cell carcinoma. Desmoplastic melanoma, a rare variant characterized by its association with a dense collagenous stroma, lacks pigmentation in more than half the cases. This form of melanoma occurs on sun-exposed skin in the elderly as an indurated plaque sometimes associated with lentigo maligna. One-quarter of subungual melanomas are amelanotic leading to diagnostic confusion with a variety of conditions. The prognosis of amelanotic melanoma is no different from its pigmented counterpart. These tumors often present at a thicker stage than pigmented tumors due to a delay in diagnosis.

A change in mole warrants a biopsy

Pruritus important symptom

The current emphasis to improve the survival of patients with melanoma relies on early diagnosis. This is a challenge for the dermatologist because early melanoma is often clinically subtle. The physician should maintain a high index of suspicion in those with known risk factors, such as those with atypical nevi. Cutaneous melanomas, even when small in diameter, are often "out of character" when compared with other pigmented lesions on the patient's skin. Patients who seek consultation because a lesion is changing should be carefully evaluated, even if the lesion in question lacks the characteristic features listed in Table 27–1. Itching is present in 20% of thin melanomas and 50% of thick tumors. This complaint may be a valuable clue to the clinician. Epiluminescent microscopy in experienced hands may also increase diagnostic accuracy.

Metastatic melanoma with no known primary may present as localized nodal disease (43%) or as distant metastases (57%). Careful examination of the skin and mucous membranes may reveal an undiagnosed primary tumor. A pigmented lesion removed in the past may be diagnosed as melanoma on re-examination. In a significant number of cases, no primary tumor is identified.

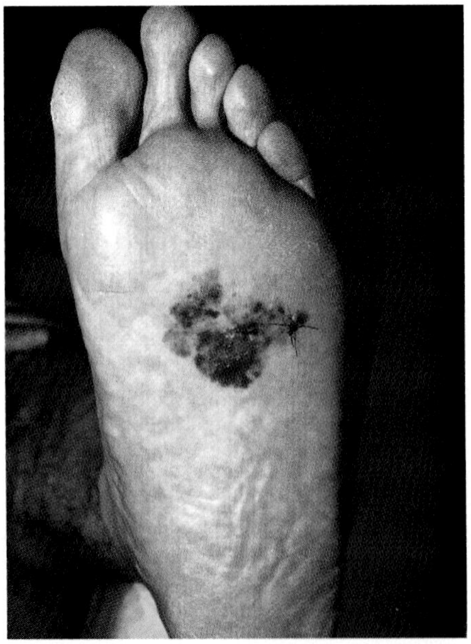

FIGURE 27–3 Acral lentiginous melanoma with a tumor thickness of 1.5 mm, Clark's level IV. This patient presented with a localized disease but developed regional disease 1 year later.

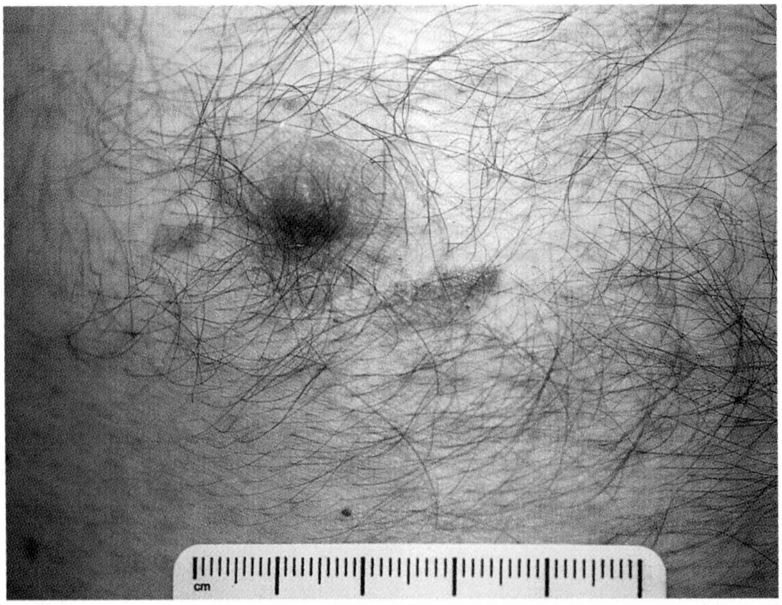

FIGURE 27–4 Amelanotic melanoma masquerading as a superficial basal cell carcinoma.

Biopsy of Suspicious Lesions

Since the staging, treatment, and prognosis for melanoma rely on the tumor thickness, every attempt should be made to obtain this information from the surgical biopsy specimen. In addition, the ease with which the dermatopathologist is able to render a diagnosis is dependent on the tissue sample submitted. For these reasons, the optimal biopsy is one that includes the entire lesion with a margin of uninvolved tissue at the lateral and deep margins. This is best accomplished by an elliptical excision including a 2- to 3-mm lateral margin and superficial subcutaneous fat oriented along the lines of lymphatic drainage. In small lesions, a punch excision may be adequate. A deep shave excision or saucerization may be used in selected flat lesions in which the differential diagnosis includes atypical nevus and where no clinical evidence of regression is present. This technique, as outlined by Geisse, is best accomplished by using a pliable surgical blade. Large lesions may preclude excisional biopsy. In these instances, one or more incisional punch biopsies or an elliptical incisional biospsy is appropriate. The biopsy should include the most elevated portion of the tumor, or in a flat lesion, the most darkly pigmented portion.

Evaluation

Approximately 5% of individuals with a melanoma develop multiple melanomas.

Dysplastic nevi occur frequently in patients with multiple primary melanomas.

Any patient with histologically confirmed melanoma should have a complete cutaneous examination. This examination should characterize the mole phenotype and screen the patient for the presence of a second primary melanoma, nonmelanoma skin cancer, and cutaneous metastases. Approximately 5% of individuals with melanoma develop multiple primary tumors. Dysplastic nevus syndrome is present in 38 to 46% of patients with multiple primaries. Subsequent tumors may occur in different body regions, and one-third are diagnosed within 1 month of the initial melanoma.

The skin, subcutaneous tissue, and draining lymph node basin are common sites for metastatic foci. Cutaneous or subcutaneous metastases appear as pigmented or amelanotic nodules on or under the skin. They may be located between the primary tumor and the regional nodal basin as "in-transit" metastases, or they may occur in a distant location on the skin. Large metastatic nodules may ulcerate.

Other common areas for metastatic disease include the lungs, liver, and lymph nodes. The physical examination should include careful palpation of the lymph node groups. The clinician should be aware that melanoma of the trunk, head and neck, and proximal extremities may have ambiguous drainage and/or multiple draining nodal basins, and it is, therefore, important to examine all node groups. A careful review of systems is helpful in identifying systemic involvement and will help direct imaging studies. Chest radiography and liver function studies are routinely performed in patients with invasive tumors. Other studies such as computed tomography and bone scans are performed in the presence of clinical signs and symptoms or if the screening studies are abnormal.

Staging

AJCC staging

The American Joint Committee on Cancer (AJCC) staging system used for cutaneous melanoma, outlined in Table 27–2, relies on the tumor thickness and Clark's level, and the presence or absence of regional or distant disease. The sentinel lymph node biopsy allows for more precise staging of patients with invasive tumors and should be performed before or at the time of the wide local excision. This staging system will undergo substantial revision in the near future to better incorporate prognostic features and includes the results of the sentinel node biopsy.

TABLE 27–2 Staging of Melanoma

Disease	Stage	Description/Level
Localized disease	0	In situ
	IA	< 0.75 mm; Clark's level II
	IB	> 0.75 mm – 1.5 mm; Clark's level III
	IIA	> 1.5 mm – 4.0 mm; Clark's level IV
	IIB	> 4.0 mm; Clark's level V
Regional disease	III	Regional lymph node disease/in-transit metastasis
Systemic disease	IV	Systemic metastasis

Adapted from:
The AJCC Manual

Melanoma lesions less than 1 mm in depth have less than a 10% risk of identifiable nodal metastasis.

The regional nodal basin is the most common site of metastatic disease for patients with newly diagnosed primary melanoma. The risk of finding occult identifiable nodal disease at the time of diagnosis is associated with the depth of the primary lesion. Patients with a primary tumor less than 1 mm in depth have a less than 10% risk of having identifiable nodal metastasis. For patients with intermediate thickness lesions, the risk of nodal metastasis is approximately 20 to 25%. The status of the regional nodes is of tremendous prognostic and clinical significance; it is the single most important prognostic factor for patients with newly diagnosed melanoma without distant disease.

The option of elective lymph node dissection has been largely supplanted by sentinel lymph node biopsy. The concept is that melanoma travels through specific lymphatic channels to one or two specific and identifiable lymph nodes as the first site of spread. If that sentinel node lacks tumor, then the remainder of the nodes will be disease-free. Clinical studies using completion lymphadenectomy following the identification of the sentinel node have documented the accuracy of this technique.

Technique of sentinel node biopsy

The first technique developed for sentinel node biopsy used isosulfan blue dye as a tracer; now the accuracy of the technique has been improved with the addition of technetium sulfur colloid as an additional tracer. An intradermal injection of tracer around the primary tumor site travels through lymphatics to the sentinel node. A lymphoscintigraphy documents the node basin that contains the sentinel node and gives a first approximation of the location of that node. Intraoperatively, a gamma probe is used to detect the radioactive material in the sentinel node allowing for its recovery via a very small incision. The sentinel node is step-sectioned and examined using permanent sections and immunohistochemistry. Patients with a positive sentinel lymph node return to the operating room to receive a therapeutic complete lymphadenectomy of that nodal basin and are considered for systemic adjuvant treatment. It is important to remember that the accuracy of the technique has only been documented in patients who have not yet undergone a wide local excision.

The sentinel lymph node biopsy provides accurate staging information and has low morbidity. Although the majority of patients will have a negative sentinel node, the few who do have a positive sentinel node will have the opportunity for early treatment of their high-risk disease.

Treatment

The diagnosis and management of patients with melanoma lend themselves to a combined multidisciplinary approach. A cooperative effort ensures comprehensive care. All patients with newly diagnosed melanoma require wide local excision for local control of the disease. Fortunately, most patients today present with thin melanomas. For patients with a thin melanoma and negative regional lymph nodes, wide local excision is the only recommended treatment.

The primary goal of wide local excision in newly diagnosed melanoma is local control. Decades ago, the standard surgical treatment for melanoma was wide local excision with 5-cm margins. It is now well accepted that less radical surgery is necessary. A number of clinical trials have documented that 1- to 2-cm margins are appropriate for most patients with invasive tumors. This results in lower morbidity and a much less frequent need for skin grafting.

Recommendations for wide local excisions

The World Health Organization Melanoma Group randomized patients who had melanoma less than 2 mm in thickness to wide local excision using 1-cm versus 3-cm margins. Only four patients had a local recurrence as the first site of melanoma recurrence. All these had a melanoma between 1 and 2 mm in thickness and had received a 1-cm excision. This study demonstrated that a 1-cm margin of excision is safe for melanomas less than 1 mm in thickness. The Intergroup Trial for intermediate thickness melanoma was a large prospective study that randomized patients with primary melanomas 1 to 4 mm in depth to excision margins of 2 cm versus 4 cm. At a median follow-up of 6 years, the local recurrence rates and overall survival rates were equivalent in the two groups. Patients whose melanomas were excised using a 2-cm margin were much less likely to require skin grafting and had shorter hospital stays.

Current recommendations for wide local excision are summarized as follows:

- in situ tumors—0.5 cm
- invasive tumors ≤ 1 mm in thickness—1 cm
- invasive tumors 1 to 4 mm in thickness—2 cm
- invasive tumors > 4 mm in thickness—≥ 2 cm

Adherence to these guidelines should result in a less than 5% risk of local recurrence. Excision margins for melanomas greater than 4 mm in depth have not been subjected to prospective studies. Two to 3-cm margins are considered acceptable for most thick primary melanomas.

Prognosis

Prognosis is largely dependent on depth of melanoma

In the absence of metastatic disease, the prognosis for invasive melanoma is most closely related to the Breslow tumor thickness. Clark's level of invasion is a useful but less accurate predictor than tumor thickness. Unfavorable prognostic factors include tumor ulceration; tumor location on the head, neck, and trunk; patient age greater than 60 years; and male gender. The overall 10-year survival for stage I patients is approximately 85%. Regional lymph node metastasis has a less favorable prognosis and depends, in part, on the number of involved nodes. The 10-year survival for patients with one involved node is 40%, two to four nodes is 26%, and five or more nodes is 15% and is no different for the patients with known versus unknown primaries. Patients with stage IV disease have a poor prognosis, with a median survival of 6 months.

Annotated Bibliography

Chang AE, Karnell LH, Menck HR. The National Cancer Data Base report on cutaneous and noncutaneous melanoma. Cancer 1998;83:1664–1678.

This article details the epidemic faced by dermatologists.

Barnhill RL, Fitzpatrick TB, Fandrey K, et al. In: Color Atlas and Synopsis of Pigmented Lesions. New York: McGraw-Hill, 1995.

This is a good clinical reference.

Tucker MA, Halpern A, Holly EA, et al. Clinically recognized dysplastic nevi. A central risk factor for cutaneous melanoma. JAMA 1997;277:1439–1444.

Halpern AC, Guerry D, Elder DE, et al. A cohort study of melanoma in patients with dysplastic nevi. J Invest Dermatol 1993;100:346S–349S.

These two articles detail risk factors of dysplastic nevi.

Koch SE, Henneberry JM. Clinically subtle primary cutaneous melanoma. J Am Acad Dermatol 1999;40:252–254.

This is a sobering article about subtle melanomas.

Geisse JK. Biopsy techniques for pigmented lesions of the skin. In: LeBoit PE, ed. Malignant Melanoma and Melanocytic Neoplasms. Philadelphia: Handley & Belfus, 1994, pp 181–193.

Balch CM, Houghton AN, Sober AJ, Soong S, eds. In: Cutaneous Melanoma, 3rd ed. St Louis: Quality Medical, 1998.

This is an excellent general reference.

Johnson TM, Hamilton T, Lowe L. Multiple primary melanoma. J Am Acad Dermatol 1998;39:422–427.

Schuchter L, Schultz DJ, Synnestvedt M, et al. A prognostic model for predicting 10-year survival in patients with primary melanoma. Ann Intern Med 1996;125:369–375.

This is a good reference.

Kirkwood JM, Strawderman MH, Ernstoff MS, et al. Interferon alfa 2b adjuvant therapy of high-risk resected cutaneous melanoma: the Eastern Cooperative Oncology Group Trial EST 1684. J Clin Oncol 1996;14:7–17.

This article describes a new technique for treatment of advanced cutaneous melanoma.

Morton DL, Wen D, Wong JH, et al. Technical details of intraoperative lymphatic mapping for early stage melanoma. Arch Surg 1992;127:392–399.

Alex JK, Weaver DL, Fairbank JT, et al. Gamma probe-guided lymph node localization in malignant melanoma. Surg Oncol 1993;3:303–308.

This article describes the newer technique for sentinel node biopsy.

Balch CM, Soong S, Bartolucci AA, et al. Efficacy of an elective regional lymph node dissection of 1 to 4 mm thick melanomas for patients 60 years of age and younger. Ann Surg 1996;224:255–266.

Balch CM, Urist MM, Karakousis CP, et al. Efficacy of 2-cm surgical margins for intermediate-thickness melanomas (1 to 4 mm): results of a multi-institutional randomized surgical trial. Ann Surg 1993;218:262–267.

Krag DN, Meijer SJ, Weaver DL. Minimal-access surgery for staging of malignant melanoma. Arch Surg 1995;130:654–658.

Veronesi U, Cascinelli N. Narrow excision (1-cm margin): a safe procedure for thin cutaneous melanoma. Arch Surg 1991;126:438–441.

These four articles detail surgical studies in the treatment of melanoma.

Gilcrest BA, Eller MS, Geller AC, et al. The pathogenesis of melanoma induced by ultraviolet radiation. N Engl J Med 1999;17:1341–1348.

This is an excellent, well-written paper reviewing the epidemiology of melanoma, which indicates that the number of sunburns over the years, not the cumulative ultraviolet light exposure, is of prime etiologic significance. The authors propose that the high content of antiapoptotic proteins, such as bcl-2 in melanocytes, may play a role in the pathogenesis of melanoma. They reason that following sunburn, keratinocytes at risk for incomplete DNA repair and subsequent mutations are destroyed by apoptosis. By contrast, melanocytes with relatively high concentrations of bcl-2 proteins are relatively resistant to apoptosis, allowing the subsequent mutations of ultraviolet-damaged DNA.

CHAPTER 28

Cutaneous Metastasis

Thomas T. Provost, M.D.

Molecular Basis of Metastasis

The biologic sequence of steps producing metastases is complex. However, in recent years, a great deal of progress has been made in deciphering the molecular steps required to produce metastases. This is now an exciting area of research with potential therapeutic implications.

Biologic steps in metastasis are complex

Six distinct phases of metastases have been proposed (Table 28–1).

Detachment of cells

The first phase, detachment of cells from the primary tumor, is poorly understood. However, it is assumed that tumor cells are easily separable from one another, and functional autonomy is present. This latter fact allows the tumor cell to survive separated from the tumor mass.

Invasion of tissue
receptors for matrix components
Hydrolytic enzymes

Phase two, invasion of tissue and intravasation of blood vessels, involves a complex set of events, in which malignant cells via specific receptors attach to matrix components of tissue (eg, fibronectin, laminin). Following attachment, the tumor cells release various hydrolytic enzymes (eg, collagenase, elastase) digesting the extracellular matrix structures. The malignant cells move into the damaged matrix area. This is accomplished by chemotactic substances produced by the malignant cell (autocrine) or by a chemotactic gradient produced by degradation of extracellular matrix components.

Intravasation of lymphatics and blood vessels

Phase three, intravasation of lymphatics and blood vessels, occurs via the above three mechanisms (ie, attachment to blood basement membrane, hydrolytic enzyme release disrupting the integrity of the blood vessel, followed by movement of malignant cells into the circulation). The ability to disrupt basement membrane is a key event in metastasis. The presence of increased concentrations of type IV collagenase activity is characteristic of the metastatic phenotype.

Phase four involves survival in the circulation, which is problematic due to mechanical and immunologic host defense mechanisms. The overwhelming

TABLE 28–1 Metastatic Sequence of Events

(1)	Detachment from primary tumor
(2)	Invasion of cells into a vessel (intravasation)
(3)	Passage through blood or lymphatic vessels
(4)	Stasis in a vessel at recipient site
(5)	Extravasation through vessel wall
(6)	Proliferation of cells at this site

Homotypic and heterotypic aggregation in circulation

majority of malignant cells do not survive. Two mechanisms, allowing malignant cells to escape destruction, are homotypic and heterotypic aggregation. In the former, the cells self-aggregate, producing small multicellular microemboli. In heterotypic aggregation, some malignant cells protect themselves by activating and coating themselves with fibrin. Another escape mechanism is the loss of human leukocyte antigen (HLA) on malignant cells. This, in effect, blunts the immune system's capacity to destroy the cells.

Extravasation into tissue
Growth factors

Phase five, extravasation of the malignant cells into tissue, employs the same mechanisms as noted above. Specific growth factors secreted by the host tissue are obviously important and probably to a great extent explain why some metastatic tumors' growth is better than the primary tumor's (eg, metastatic prostate cancer in the vertebrae). In addition, autocrine-produced growth factors secreted by the malignant cells are important.

Angiogenesis

Finally, phase six is angiogenesis, resulting in neovascularization of malignant cells, which is also critical in sustaining tumor growth. Metastatic tumor cells are also capable of secreting factors to promote angiogenesis.

Angiostatin, a cleavage product of plasminogen that inhibits angiogenesis, produces shrinkage of metastatic tumors. Furthermore, primary tumors frequently produce inhibitors of angiogenesis. This, in all probability, may explain, at least in part, why removal of a primary tumor is frequently associated with the rapid growth of metastatic lesions.

Animal models have confirmed the critical nature of these complex biologic sequences of events in metastasis. For example, blockade of fibronectin and laminin receptors on malignant cells prevents metastasis. Inhibition of homotypic and heterotypic aggregation can also prevent tumor metastases.

Annotated Bibliography

Stracke ML, Liotta LA. Molecular mechanisms of tumor cell metastasis. In: Mendelsohn J, Howley PM, Israel MA, Liotta LA, eds. The Molecular Basis of Cancer. Philadelphia: W.B. Saunders, 1995, pp 233–247.

Folkman J. Tumor angiogenesis. In: Mendelsohn J, Howley PM, Israel MA, Liotta LA, eds. The Molecular Basis of Cancer. Philadelphia: W.B. Saunders, 1995, pp 206–224.

These are two excellent reviews of molecular mechanisms of metastases, including exhaustive bibliographies.

Clinical Features

Firm and rubbery or hard nodules

Most cutaneous metastases are discrete, round-to-oval, firm, rubbery-to-stone-hard masses. They may vary from several millimeters to many centimeters in diameter. They are generally painless and freely mobile. Ulceration is uncommon. The skin overlying the metastatic deposit is generally normal in color but occasionally may assume varying shades of red, blue, purple, brown, or black. Scalp metastasis may be confused for a pilar cyst. Alopecia may be present. Cutaneous metastasis may appear as a zosteriform lesion. Metastases are most often multiple but can occur as a solitary lesion. Most metastases tend to occur on cutaneous surfaces near the site of the primary tumor.

Metastasis to sites of trauma

Invasive diagnostic as well as therapeutic maneuvers on rare occasions can result in localization of cutaneous metastases. For example, placement of a chest tube or drain can facilitate the occurrence of metastatic skin nodules along the tract of thoracentesis or a paracentesis needle.

New nodules in old scars should be examined to rule out the possibility of metastatic disease. Carcinomas of the breast, ovary, colon, lung, kidney, and endometrium may metastasize to surgical or traumatic scar sites. These nodules may be mistaken for a foreign body reaction, hypertrophic scar, granulation tissue, or calcification within a scar.

Annotated Bibliography

Rosen T. Cutaneous metastasis. Med Clin North Am 1980;64:885–900.

This is a well-written review of cutaneous metastasis, with an interesting discussion on iatrogenically induced metastasis in operative sites.

Frequency of Cutaneous Metastases

Frequency of cutaneous metastases 1–9%

The frequency of cutaneous metastases from internal malignancies ranges from 0.6 to approximately 9%. Table 28–2 presents the data on a retrospective clinical study of 7,000 patients, as well as an autopsy study of a similar number of patients from Roswell Park Memorial Institute in Buffalo, NY. The considerably higher frequency reported in this latter study may be reflective of a selection bias due to the fact that patients with well-advanced (terminal) cancer are referred to that institution for new and advanced therapies.

Approximately 0.5 to 1% of cancer patients will present with cutaneous metastases as the initial manifestation of their malignancy.

In Table 28–3, the frequency of primary malignancies with cutaneous manifestations are presented. In men, lung cancer, colon cancer, and squamous cell carcinoma of the oral cavity are the most frequent tumors metastasizing to the skin; in women, it is breast cancer. In Table 28–4 the frequency of skin metastasis in hematologic malignancies are presented.

TABLE 28–2 Cutaneous Metastasis of Internal Malignancies

	Retrospective Clinical Study (N = 7,316)		Autopsy Study (N = 7,518)
Organ	**Skin Metastasis (%)**	**Presenting with Skin Involvement(%)**	**Total (%)**
Breast	23.9	6.3	26.5
Oral cavity	5.3	1.0	17.3
Lung	1.7	0.3	5.9
Colon/rectum	2.3	0.5	6.0
Ovary	3.0	0.6	5.1
Larynx	3.9	0.0	17.7
Bladder	2.2	0.0	5.6
Upper digestive	1.1	0.4	5.4
Nasal sinuses	10.0	2.5	16.6
Endometrium	0.6	0.2	2.7
Uterine cervix	0.3	0.0	0.0
Prostate	0.0	0.0	1.6
Kidney	2.6	0.0	6.0
Stomach	0.0.	0.0	4.5
Total	5.0	1.3	9.0

Data from:
Lookingbill DP, Spangler N, Sexton FN. Skin involvement as the presenting sign of internal carcinoma. J Am Acad Dermatol 1990;22:19–26.
Spencer PS, Helm TN. Skin metastases in cancer patients. Cutis 1987;39:119–121.

TABLE 28–3 Frequency of Primary Malignancy in Cutaneous Metastases

Patients (N = 724)	Primary Cancer (%)
Men (n = 482)	
Lung	24
Intestine	19
Melanoma	13
Squamous cell carcinoma of oral cavity	12
Kidney	6
Stomach	6
Women (n = 242)	
Breast	60
Intestine	9
Melanoma	5
Ovary	4
Lung	4

Data from:
Brownstein MH, Helwig EB. Patterns of cutaneous metastases. Arch Dermatol 1972;105:862–868.

Metastases to skin generally occur late.
Bad prognosis

In general, cutaneous metastases are a late event, and their presence is associated with a bad prognosis (a life expectancy of approximately 4 months, although isolated reports indicate individual patients living for years).

Annotated Bibliography

Schwartz RA. Cutaneous metastatic disease. J Am Acad Dermatol 1995;33:161–182.

This is a very scholarly review of the clinical features of cutaneous metastases from various organs by a dermatologist who has had a great deal of experience in this area. It is well written and contains 382 references.

Brownstein NH, Helwig EB. Patterns of cutaneous metastasis. Arch Dermatol 1972; 105:862–868.

This is a classic, highly referenced paper discussing the cutaneous metastatic patterns of 724 patients in whom there was histopathologic confirmation of both primary and secondary deposition in the skin. The most frequent primary tumors of cutaneous manifestations in men were cancers of the lung (24%) and colon (19%), melanoma (13%), and squamous cell carcinoma of the oral cavity (12%).

TABLE 28–4 Frequency of Skin Metastases of Hematologic Malignancies

Disease	Number of Patients with Skin Metastases	%
Non–Hodgkin's lymphoma (N = 674)	61	9.1
Chronic lymphocytic leukemia (N = 71)	5	7.0
Acute myelocytic leukemia (N = 444)	26	5.9
Acute lymphocytic leukemia (N = 142)	8	5.6
Hodgkin's disease (N = 205)	6	2.9

Data from:
Spencer PS, Helm TN.Skin metastases in cancer patients. Cutis 1987;39:119–121.

In women, the most common malignancies metastasizing to the skin were breast cancer (69%), colon cancer (9%), melanoma (5%), and ovarian cancer (4%).

Spencer PS, Helm TN. Skin metastasis in cancer patients. Cutis 1987;39:119–121.

This is an analysis of 7,518 patients with internal cancer, seen at a prestigious cancer institute in Buffalo, NY. A 9% frequency of skin metastasis is reported.

Lookingbill DP, Spangler N, Sexton FM. Skin and bone as the presenting sign of internal carcinoma. J Am Acad Dermatol 1990;22:19–26.

These authors detected 367 cases of skin metastasis from a tumor registry of 7,316 cancer patients (5%). Of these, 92 patients (1.3%) had cutaneous metastasis at the time of presentation.

Lookingbill DP, Spangler N, Helm KF. Cutaneous metastasis in patients with metastatic carcinoma: a restrospective study of 4020 patients. J Am Acad Dermatol 1993;29: 228–236.

This study reports 420 of 4,020 patients with a cutaneous metastasis (10%).

Patterns of Cutaneous Metastases

Regional variations in the frequency of metastases of the skin exist. In a study of 724 patients with biopsy confirmation of both the primary tumor and skin metastases, 75% of men demonstrated metastatic lesions localized to the head, neck, and anterior parts of the chest and abdomen. This comprises one-quarter of the body surface area.

75% of metastatic lesions in men located on head, neck, chest, and abdomen

In women, metastatic lesions were found in three-quarters of patients localized to the skin of the anterior part of the chest and abdomen. This comprises less than one-fifth of the body total surface area.

75% of metastases in women detected on chest and abdomen

Scalp Metastases

Scalp metastases in men are most commonly associated with pulmonary or renal carcinoma. Furthermore, in contradistinction to cutaneous metastases in general, these metastases appear to occur early in the disease process. In women, breast carcinoma is the most frequent primary malignancy to metastasize to the scalp. It is a late event.

Face

Facial metastases occur in approximately 6% of patients and are most commonly due to squamous cell carcinomas of the oral cavity, followed by carcinoma of the lung and kidney.

In women, carcinoma of the breast is the most frequent primary site of tumor metastasizing to the face. Eyelid metastasis from a primary breast carcinoma is a rare site of metastases.

Neck

In men, the most common primary site of malignancy with cutaneous metastases to the neck is squamous cell carcinoma of the oral cavity followed by carcinoma of the lung. In women, carcinoma of the breast is the most common primary site.

Upper Extremities

This is an uncommon site of metastases and usually occurs late in the disease process. Carcinomas of the lung, kidney, and large intestine are the most frequent primary malignancies to metastasize to the upper extremities in men, whereas breast carcinoma is the most common primary tumor to metastasize to these sites in women.

Lower Extremities

Rare site for cutaneous metastases

This is a relatively rare site for cutaneous metastases. The lower extremities constitute about 36% of the total body surface, yet only 4% of cutaneous metastatic lesions are found in this region. The primary tumors to metastasize to this region are those of the lung and kidney in men.

Anterior Portion of the Chest

This is the most common site of cutaneous metastases in women with breast cancer (nearly always the source of primary tumor) (Figure 28–1).

In men, carcinoma of the lung is the most frequent cause.

Abdomen

The abdomen is the most common area for metastatic disease presenting as the initial manifestation of internal cancer. This is the site of most frequent metastases in men. The most common primary tumor is that of the large intestine, followed by tumors of the lung and stomach.

In women, the primary tumor metastasizing to the abdomen is carcinoma of the large intestine, followed by those of ovary and breast.

Umbilical metastasis; in general, poor prognosis

Of special note are umbilical metastases, referred to as "Sister Joseph's nodule," named for an early Mayo Clinic nurse superintendent who noted its significance. Many embryologic vascular connections persist in or near the umbilicus. This probably explains the peculiar susceptibility of this area for metastatic lesions. About one-third of the metastatic lesions to the umbilical skin represent the first indication of internal neoplasia. Gastric, ovarian, and pancreatic adenocarcinomas are the most frequent sources of tumor. Uterine, kidney, and breast metastases, however, have also been detected in the umbilical area. In general, this is a poor prognostic sign, with death occurring within months.

Back and Flank

This is a relatively uncommon site of metastases. Despite accounting for 20% of the body surface area, only 8% of patients demonstrate metastatic lesions in this area. In men, carcinoma of the lung is the most common tumor; in women, it is carcinoma of the breast (Figure 28–2).

Pelvic Region

Eight percent of patients with metastatic lesions demonstrate metastasis in the pelvic region. Carcinoma of the large intestine is the primary tumor is both men and women.

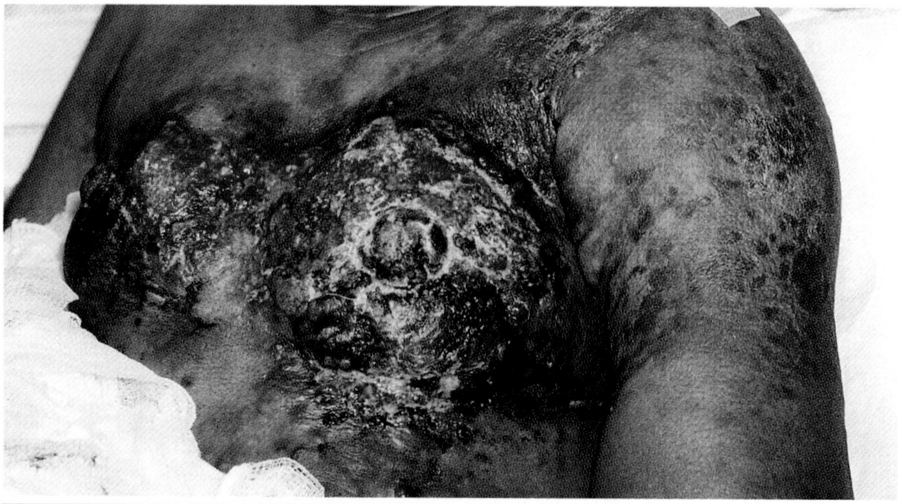

FIGURE 28–1 Extensive metastatic cutaneous lesions to anterior chest in woman with primary carcinoma of breast.

Extramammary Paget's disease is a rare, ductal, adenocarcinoma almost always occurring in the vulvar, groin, and perianal regions. This disease may arise from (1) an intraepidermal duct adenocarcinoma (most common), (2) the cutaneous extension of an adnexal adenocarcinoma, or (3) an underlying internal malignancy (? paraneoplastic sign).

The association with an underlying internal malignancy (putative paraneoplastic sign) is unclear. Concurrent malignancy studies (defined as a malignancy occurring either within 1 year before or after diagnosis of Paget's disease) of 135 extramammary Paget's disease patients, about whom data were available in the literature, demonstrated a concurrent malignancy in 18 patients (13%) and a nonconcurrent malignancy in 26 (19%). A concurrent plus nonconcurrent malignancy was demonstrated in 44 (33%) patients.

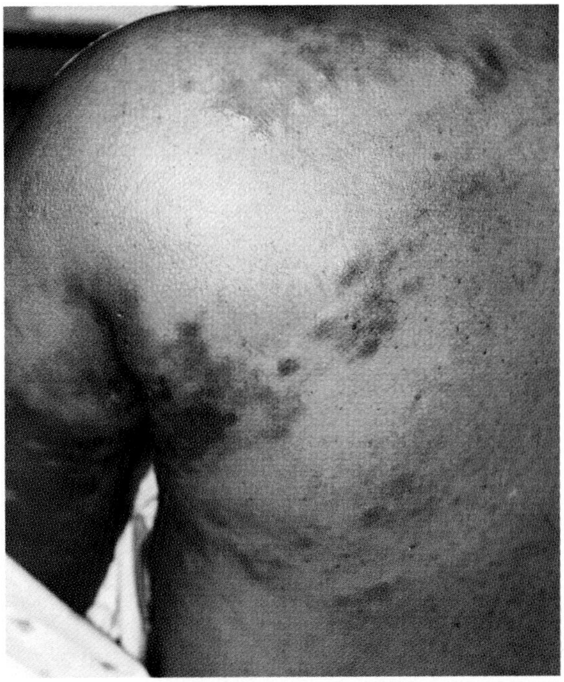

FIGURE 28-2 Uncommon site of metastasis is on the back and flank. Primary breast carcinoma.

The mortality associated with extramammary Paget's disease is significant. For example, in one study, the overall mortality was 26% in treated patients. Of 46 patients with an underlying cutaneous adnexal carcinoma, 21 (46%) died of metastatic carcinoma. Nineteen of these patients succumbed to metastatic extramammary Paget's disease. In two individuals, death occurred secondary to metastasis of the associated adnexal malignancy. In the same study, 18% (27 of 148) of patients with extramammary Paget's disease, without underlying adnexal carcinoma or associated internal malignancy, died of metastatic disease or internal malignancy.

Guarded prognosis

Chandra, after reviewing the literature of 197 patients with extramammary Paget's disease, makes a strong case for extramammary Paget's disease being a paraneoplastic event. He points out that all the internal malignancies (2 concurrent, 2 nonconcurrent) detected with extramammary Paget's disease of the penis, scrotum, or groin occurred in the genitourinary tract (1 bladder, 1 hypernephroma, 2 prostatic carcinomas). Furthermore, he indicates that 8 of 9 internal malignancies (6 concurrent, 3 nonconcurrent) associated with perianal extramammary Paget's, occurred in the digestive system (6 rectal adenocarcinomas, 2 anaplastic small cell, cloacogenic rectal carcinomas).

It is his conclusion that the frequency of Paget's disease and concurrent internal malignancy (12%) is a conservative estimate because a thorough investigation for an underlying carcinoma was missing in many of the case reports. In addition, he believes that the association between the anatomic site of extramammary Paget's disease and the anatomic location of internal malignancy is strongly suggestive.

On the basis of these observations, it is his conclusion that for perianal Paget's disease, a directed internal malignancy search of the gastrointestinal tract should be performed. For male inguinal extramammary Paget's disease, the internal malignancy search should be directed at the male genitourinary tract.

After a review of the literature, it appears to this author, there is evidence that Paget's disease arises from an intraepidermal duct carcinoma, the epidermal metastasis of adnexal duct carcinoma, and the epidermal metastasis of, for example, bladder and colon cancers whose metastatic cells are able to exist in a symbiosis with epidermal keratinocytes. I believe epidermal metastasis, rather than a paraneoplasic event, best explains Paget's disease.

Extramammary Paget's disease arises from:
- *intraepidermal*
- *adenocarcinoma*
- *adnexal metastasis to the epidermis*
- *distant metastasis from internal malignancy to epidermis*

Approximately 68 to 80% of patients reported with extramammary Paget's disease are women. Most of the cases occur in the seventh decade of life. The disease generally presents as an insidious onset of an erythematous, oozing, sharply demarcated lesion involving the vulvar, perianal, or inguinal region. Ulceration, pruritus, tenderness, and pain may occur. In one series, 90% of patients com-

Pruritus common component

Must differentiate from:
- *Bowen's disease*
- *melanoma*
- *erythroplasia of Queyrat*

plained of pruritus. The disease clinically must be differentiated from eczema and Bowen's disease.

A biopsy of the Paget lesion may be confused with carcinoma in situ. However, the use of mucicarmine or a periodic acid Schiff's reagent will demonstrate the presence of mucin in the pagetoid cells that histologically can be confused with melanoma or squamous cell carcinoma. Other pathologists believe that the aldehyde fuchsin stain is the most reliable histologic stain, differentiating Paget's disease from melanoma, Bowen's disease, or erythroplasia of Queyrat.

Annotated Bibliography

Chandra JJ. Extramammary Paget's disease: prognosis and relationship to internal malignancy. J Am Acad Dermatol 1985;13:1053–1065.

This is an excellent, well-written review!

Histopathologic Patterns of Cutaneous Metastases

Adenomatous Carcinoma

In general, cutaneous metastases from carcinoma of the kidney preserve their characteristic adenomatous architecture. In those men with adenomatous metastatic disease that does not histologically suggest carcinoma of the kidney, bronchogenic carcinoma is the most common primary source. Moderately differentiated adenocarcinoma is most likely from the gastrointestinal tract. Poorly differentiated or anaplastic adenocarcinomas are most frequently from the lung.

Squamous Cell Carcinoma

Metastatic squamous cell carcinoma most often is seen with primary carcinoma of the lung or oral cavity. Anaplastic squamous cell carcinomas are most commonly from the lung.

Area of Skin Metastases

It is important to note that the area of localization of metastases in the skin is of limited value in uncovering the site of primary tumor. For example, among 72 men presenting with cutaneous metastases from the lung, the sites of metastases included the chest wall (20), abdominal wall (12), neck (10), back or flank (12), scalp (6), and other areas (12).

Underlying Primary Malignancy

Breast Cancer

Breast carcinoma is a common cancer metastasizing to the skin. In one study, skin involvement was detected in approximately 6% of patients at the time of diagnosis. In 3.5%, it was the presenting sign.

Several distinct patterns of cutaneous metastasis from breast cancer exist: (1) inflammatory breast cancer, (2) carcinoma en cuirasse, (3) telangiectatic metastatic breast cancer, (4) metastatic nodular breast carcinoma, (5) alopecia, (6) Paget's disease, and (7) inframammary crease.

Inflammatory Breast Cancer

Inflammatory breast cancer resembles erysipelas.

This is a form of metastatic disease characterized by erythematous patches or plaques with an indurated border, resembling erysipelas. Dermal edema, characterized by a peau d'orange appearance of the skin, is characteristic. In contradistinction to bacterial erysipelas, systemic toxic features are absent. This peculiar form of metastasis appears to be caused by capillary congestion and is not restricted to breast carcinoma. It also has been detected, rarely, in association with carcinomas of the pancreas, parotid, tonsils, colon, stomach, ovary, uterus, prostate, and lung.

Carcinoma En Cuirasse

Sclerotic metastases

A morphea-like skin lesion can be seen in patients with carcinoma of the breast. Red-blue, papular metastatic lesions coalesce to form sclerotic plaques not associated with inflammation. However, such lesions can also be seen, rarely, in gastrointestinal, kidney, and lung metastases.

Telangiectatic Metastatic Breast Cancer

This metastatic lesion is characterized by violaceous, vesicular lesions resembling lymphangioma. Dilated vascular channels filled with blood are responsible for the violaceous hue.

Metastatic Nodular Breast Carcinoma

This form of metastatic disease appears as papular, nodular lesions, which may be solitary or multiple. Ulceration and bullous formation are rare.

Alopecia

Rarely produces nodular alopecic scalp metastases

Alopecia, as a manifestation of metastatic breast carcinoma, is a rare form of scalp metastasis, characterized by painless, nonpruritic, nodular plaques. These plaques can resemble lichen planopilaris, pseudopelade, morphea, or chronic discoid lupus erythematosus.

Paget's Disease

Paget's disease of breast

A sharply demarcated, eczematous plaque or patch with erythema and scaling on the nipple and areola is almost always associated with an underlying ductal carcinoma of the breast (Figures 28–3 and 28–4). In general, the lesion is unilateral but, on occasions, may be bilateral. The differential diagnosis includes eczema, but unlike eczema, the cutaneous lesions of Paget's do not respond to the frequent application of a mid-potency steroid. Therefore, all nipple or areola lesions not responding to a 7- to 10-day course of topical steroids should be biopsied.

Inframammary Crease

On unusual occasions, the cutaneous metastatic lesions from a breast carcinoma may present as a cutaneous exophytic nodule in the inframammary crease. This lesion may resemble a callus or basal cell or squamous cell carcinoma.

Colon Carcinoma

Carcinomas of the colon and rectum are the second most common metastatic cutaneous tumors. Metastases are most commonly found on the abdomen and perineal

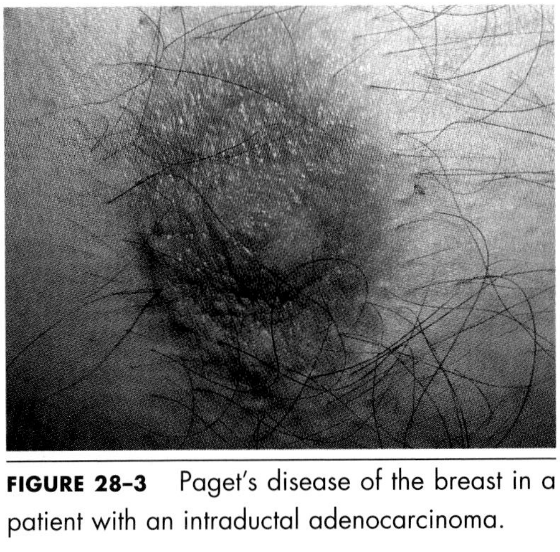

FIGURE 28-3 Paget's disease of the breast in a patient with an intraductal adenocarcinoma.

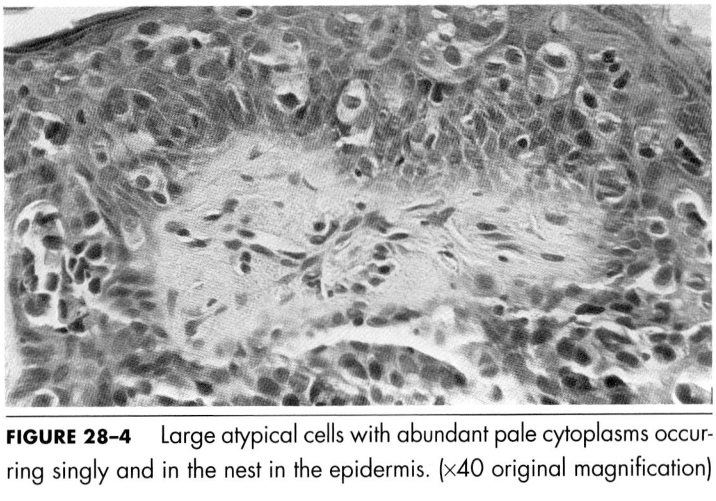

FIGURE 28-4 Large atypical cells with abundant pale cytoplasms occurring singly and in the nest in the epidermis. (×40 original magnification)

regions. They are generally detected after the primary tumor has been discovered. On unusual occasions, metastatic lesions may occur on the scalp and face.

Hypernephroma Carcinoma of the Lung

These tumors metastasize most commonly to the head and neck, appearing as well-circumscribed cutaneous nodules. Vascularity may be prominent. Scalp metastases may be mistaken for a cylindroma or inclusion cyst.

Metastatic lung cancer is much more common in men than in women. Cutaneous metastasis may occur on any area of the body; however, the most common site is the anterior chest wall and abdomen. Metastasis may occur along the needle aspiration tract, a thoracotomy site, or other scars.

Gastric Carcinoma

Metastatic adenocarcinoma from the stomach generally occurs as a solitary lesion or as multiple lesions involving the head, neck, chest, and abdominal regions.

Oral Cavity Cancer

Squamous cell carcinomas of the oral cavity most commonly metastasize to the head and neck. They may be solitary or multiple nodules.

Ovarian Carcinoma

Ovarian carcinomas may metastasize to the abdomen and umbilical areas (Figure 28–5).

Carcinoma of the Cervix

The most common cutaneous sites of cervical cancer metastasis are the abdominal wall and vulva.

Uterine Endometrial Cancer

Uterine endometrial cancer metastasizes to the skin. The tumor may present as a nodule in a laparotomy scar or appear as a solitary nodule or as multiple subcutaneous nodules on the scalp, trunk, and legs.

Carcinoma of the Bladder

This may appear as a zosteriform, inflammatory metastatic carcinoma on the lower abdomen, but it very rarely metastasizes to the skin.

Pancreatic Cancer

Pancreatic cancer produces: nodular fat necrosis, recurrent superficial thrombophlebitis

Pancreatic tumors usually metastasize to the abdominal wall, especially the umbilical area. They may be associated with (1) nodular fat necrosis; (2) recurrent superficial migratory thrombophlebitis, or (3) in the case of the alpha cell secreting glucagonoma, migratory epidermal necrolysis.

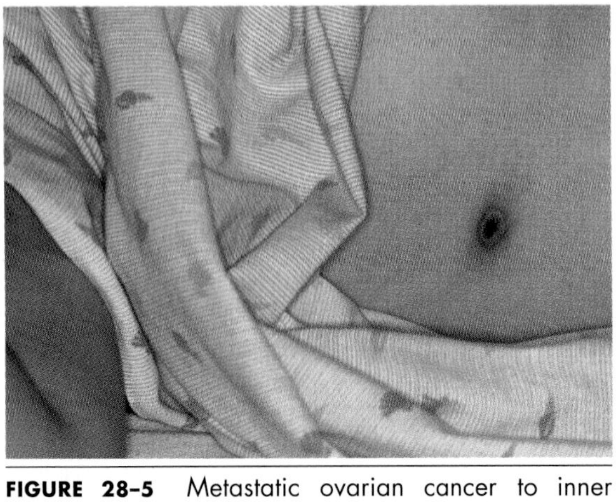

FIGURE 28–5 Metastatic ovarian cancer to inner aspect of thigh.

Prostate Cancer

Prostate cancer rarely metastasizes to the skin. Cutaneous metastases are usually in the inguinal region and lower abdominal wall.

Other Malignancies

Metastatic liver disease may be associated with liver failure, producing jaundice, palmar erythema, and spider nevi. The rapid onset of painless jaundice and pruritus suggests common duct involvement, with a gallstone, carcinoma of the ampule of Vater, or carcinoma of the head of the pancreas.

Mediastinal tumors may produce a superior vena cava syndrome, with prominent venous patterns over the chest, neck, and upper extremities, as well as edema of the face, conjunctiva, and neck.

CHAPTER 29

Paraneoplastic Dermatoses

Thomas T. Provost, M.D., Susan D. Laman, M.D., William R. Bell, M.D.

The paraneoplastic dermatoses are listed in Table 29–1.

Digital Clubbing

Clubbing of the digits occurs when the normal 15- to 20-degree angle (unguophalangeal, Lovibond's angle) between the cuticle nailfold and the downward curve of the nail is lost (Figure 29–1). The increased convexity of the nail and the enlargement of the distal phalanges are produced by local connective tissue proliferation, edema, and a lymphocytic infiltrate. In addition to the characteristic clinical appearance, the nail gives the perception of floating on the nail bed.

Associated with bronchogenic carcinomas and mesotheliomas

The etiology of the clubbing is unknown, although humoral factor(s) released from tumors may be involved. Bronchogenic carcinomas and mesotheliomas are the most common tumors associated with adult-onset clubbing. The clubbing may occur prior to, simultaneously, or following the diagnosis of the carcinoma. Clubbing has also been seen in association with bronchiectasis and lung abscesses. It has been seen in patients with cyanotic heart disease, bacterial endocarditis, inflammatory bowel disease, and cirrhosis as well.

TABLE 29–1 Paraneoplastic Dermatoses

Papulosquamous dermatoses	Erythema annulare centrifugum
Tripe palms	Urticaria
Palmar hyperkeratosis	Sweet's syndrome
Bazex's syndrome	Exfoliative erythroderma
Sign of Leser-Trélat	Autoimmune dermatoses
Florid cutaneous papillomatosis	Dermatomyositis
Vascular dermatoses	Paraneoplastic pemphigus
Trousseau's syndrome	Hormonal dermatoses
Vasculitis	Cushing's syndrome
Pyoderma gangrenosum	Carcinoid syndrome
Erythromelalgia	Necrolytic migratory erythema
Musculoskeletal dermatoses	Miscellaneous dermatoses
Digital clubbing	Acanthosis nigricans
Hypertrophic osteoarthropathy	Extramammary Paget's disease
Multicentric reticulohistiocytosis	Acquired ichthyosis
Inflammatory dermatoses	Amyloidosis
Erythema gyratum repens	Hypertrichosis lanuginosa acquisita

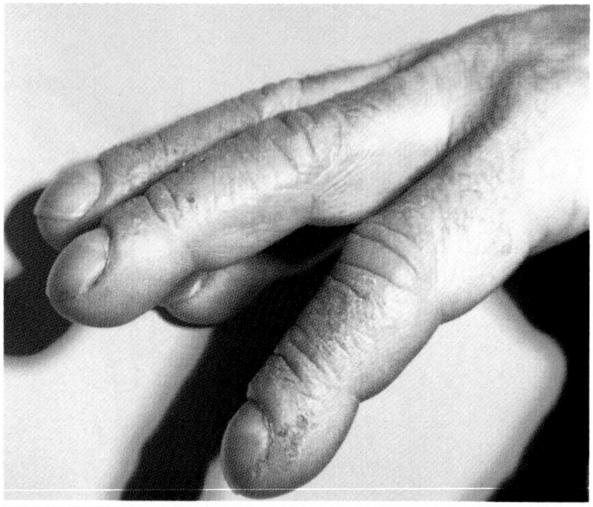

FIGURE 29–1 Clubbed fingers. Note loss of normal unguophalangeal angle.

Annotated Bibliography

Knowles JH, Smith LH. Extrapulmonary manifestations of bronchogenic carcinoma. N Engl J Med 1960;262: 505–510.

This classic article examines two large studies indicating that between 5.2 and 12% of bronchogenic carcinoma patients had clubbing.

Hypertrophic Osteoarthropathy

Hypertrophic osteoarthropathy, also known as "pachydermoperiostosis," is characterized by new periosteal bone formation along the shafts of the radius, phalanges, and tibia. It is associated with pain and may occur with clubbing. In addition, thickening of the forearms and legs, hyperkeratosis of the palms and soles, and coarsening of the facial features may occur. Cutis verticis gyrata also may be present. Hypertrophic osteoarthropathy is generally symmetric and may be associated with swelling, tenderness, and increased warmth of the affected joints (Figure 29–2). Approximately 10 to 20% of patients demonstrating clubbing have this complication.

Pathologic examination of the tissues reveal subperiosteal edema. The periosteum is lifted, and new bone formation may appear.

Hypertrophic osteoarthropathy may be inherited.

Strong relationship of adult onset with lung cancer

The exact pathogenesis is unknown, but neurogenic and humoral factors associated with a tumor may be involved. The role of the vagus nerve is unknown, but reversal of the syndrome following vagotomy suggests an etiologic role. As with clubbing, the most common associated tumor is carcinoma of the lung. Rarely, it may be associated with liver disease, chronic lung disease, and congenital heart disease. A familial form exists.

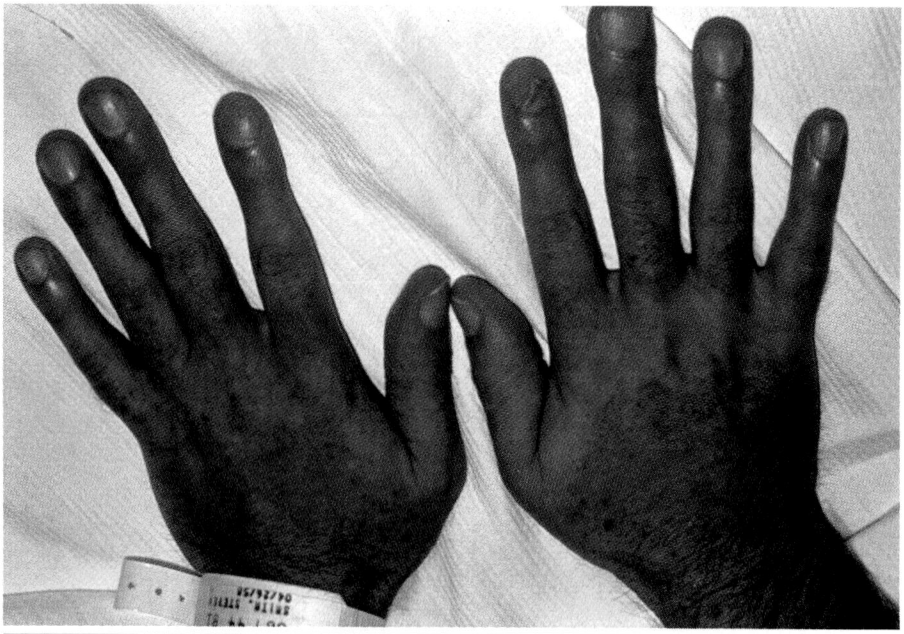

FIGURE 29–2 Hypertrophic osteoarthropathy (pachydermoperiostosis). Note swelling tips of the fingers. Patient had tenderness of the wrists and fingers.

Annotated Bibliography

Hambrick GW, Carter M. Pachydermoperiostosis. Touraine Solente-Golé syndrome. Arch Dermatol 1966;94:594–608.

This is a good review of this syndrome.

Gynecomastia

Gynecomastia, especially painful gynecomastia, has been described in association with bronchogenic carcinomas. (Hypertrophic osteoarthropathy is generally present.) Increased gonadotropin activity has been demonstrated in patients' plasma as well as in the tumor.

Elevated levels of gonadotropins can be produced by carcinomas of the pancreas, stomach, and colon. Teratomas and embryonal cell choriocarcinomas also may be associated with elevated levels of urinary gonastrotropins and gynecomastia. The presence of hypertrophic osteoarthropathy, however, suggests carcinoma of the lung.

May be associated with lung malignancy

In addition to carcinomas, there are a number of non-neoplastic causes of adult gynecomastia that must be considered in the differential diagnosis. The drugs reserpine, chlorpromazine, spironolactone, digitalis, and cimetidine are all capable of producing gynecomastia. Gynecomastia also may be seen in chronic liver disease and malnutrition.

We recently saw a 47-year-old male who had pemphigus vulgaris for 10 years, which was successfully controlled on a combination of azathioprine (50 mg/day) and prednisone (10 mg/day). Gynecomastia (slightly tender) developed. Laboratory investigations revealed markedly elevated levels of 17-ketosteroids, dehydrandrosterone and estradiol, and a low testosterone level. Prolactin, progesterone, and human chorionic gonadotropin levels were normal. Computer axial tomography scans of the testes were normal but demonstrated a 10-cm by 9-cm by 9.5-cm left adrenal mass. This mass was surgically excised. Pathologic examination revealed an adenocarcinoma.

Multicentric Reticulohistiocytosis

Multicentric reticulohistiocytosis, characterized histologically by the presence of multinucleated giant cells with a ground-glass cytoplasmic appearance, occurs as reddish-brown papules and nodules involving, predominantly, the face and hands (Figure 29–3). The facial involvement may produce a leonine facies. A severe destructive arthritis involving the hands, knees, shoulders, wrists, hips, ankles, elbows, feet, and spine may occur. (Arthritis mutilans may occur in as many as 50% of patients.)

A review of the literature indicates that approximately one-quarter of patients with this condition develop malignancies. In general, multicentric reticulohistiocytosis precedes the cancer. However, no predominance of one tumor has been detected, and its acceptance as a paraneoplastic event is questionable. It also appears that 25% of the patients have thyroid abnormalities (either hyper- or hypothyroidism).

Not definitely established as a paraneoplastic event

Annotated Bibliography

Nunnink JC, Krusinski PA, Yates JW. Multicentric reticulohistiocytosis and cancer: a case report and review of the literature. Med Pediatr Oncol 1985;13:273–279.

These investigators reviewed 82 cases reported in the literature. A documented 28% had an associated neoplasm; however, no one type of neoplasm predominated.

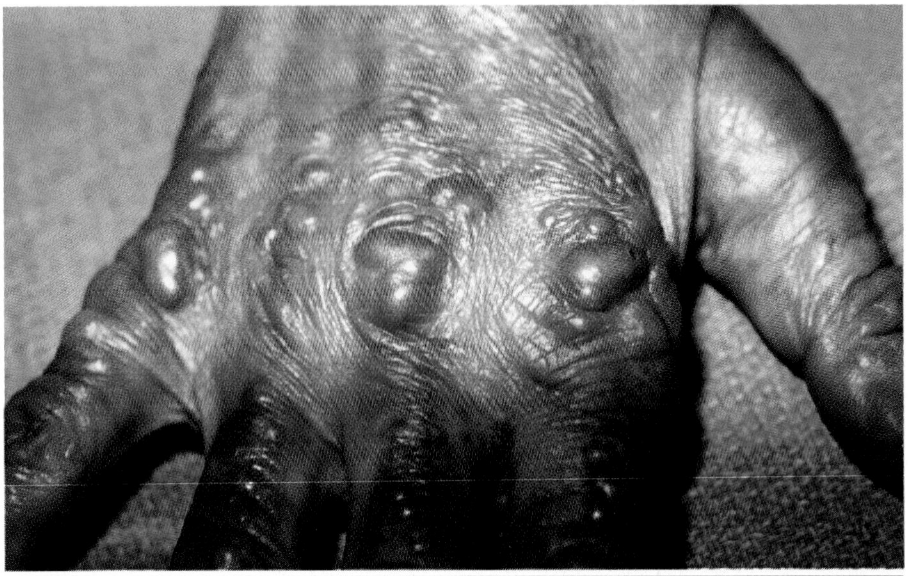

FIGURE 29–3 Nodular lesions on the dorsal surface of the hand in a patient with reticulohistiocytosis.

Barrow MV, Holubar K. Multicentric reticulohistiocytosis: a review of 33 patients. Medicine 1969;48:287–305.

This is an excellent review of the clinical manifestations and histology of this entity.

Reactive Erythemas

Several inflammatory conditions, notably erythema gyratum repens, erythema annulare centrifugum, and urticaria have been associated with an underlying malignancy.

Erythema Gyratum Repens

Erythema gyratum repens is a very unusual, cutaneous inflammatory reaction pattern, characterized by erythematous lesions forming concentric rings and producing a "wood grain" appearance. Hyperkeratosis of the palms and soles may occur, and pruritus may be severe. A perivascular lymphohistiocytic infiltrate is detected. Carcinoma of the lung is the most commonly associated tumor, although other malignancies, such as those of the esophagus and breast, have been reported. The cutaneous change may precede, occur concomitantly, or postdate development of the associated malignancy.

Annotated Bibliography

Kawakami T, Saito R. Erythema gyratum repens unassociated with underlying malignancy. J Dermatol 1995;22:587–589.

This review of the world literature indicates that 60 cases of erythema gyratum repens have been detected, and 46 (77%) have been associated with malignancies. (Their review indicated that the interval between the discovery of the cancer and the onset of the dermatitis was usually 7 months or less.)

Erythema Annulare Centrifugum

Erythema annulare centrifugum is a condition characterized by erythematous, annular rings with a trailing scale and central clearing. Pathologic examination reveals a nonspecific lymphohistiocytic perivascular infiltrate. This condition is much more commonly associated with chronic fungal infection. It has rarely been reported in association with underlying malignancies. No one tumor has predominated.

Urticarial Lesions

On rare occasions, urticarial lesions, generally persisting for prolonged periods of time and not the transient 3- to 5-hour classic urticarial reaction, have been reported in association with underlying malignancies, especially ovarian carcinoma (Figure 29–4).

We have seen one female, 35 years of age, with a 1-year history of recurrent, erythematous, edematous, plaque-like lesions, especially on the chin, who at laparotomy for an acute appendicitis was diagnosed to have an ovarian carcinoma. Pathology of the urticarial lesion revealed a perivascular lymphocytic infiltrate with many eosinophils. No vasculitis was detected. Removal of the ovarian carcinoma was associated with a marked decrease, but not a total disappearance, of the urticarial lesions. Following surgery, the marked decrease in the number of the urticarial lesions had been viewed as evidence to indicate that the urticaria was associated with the malignancy. The persistence of low-grade activity is of concern because of the possibility of persistence of tumor.

Bazex's Syndrome

Malignancies of the upper aerodigestive tracts

Bazex's syndrome is a relatively new syndrome, initially described in 1965. The disease process is generally characterized by an asymptomatic nail dystrophy associated with erythematous-to-violaceous psoriasiform lesions over the dorsal surface of digits, the bridge of the nose, and the helix of the ears. Involvement of the entire central portion of the face, the external ears and the hands and feet may occur. In general, a squamous cell carcinoma of the upper aerodigestive tract has been found. Metastatic head and neck lymph node involvement, in the absence of a recognized primary lesion, has also been associated with this condition.

The disease process is generally progressive. However, treatment of the primary malignancy may produce a remission.

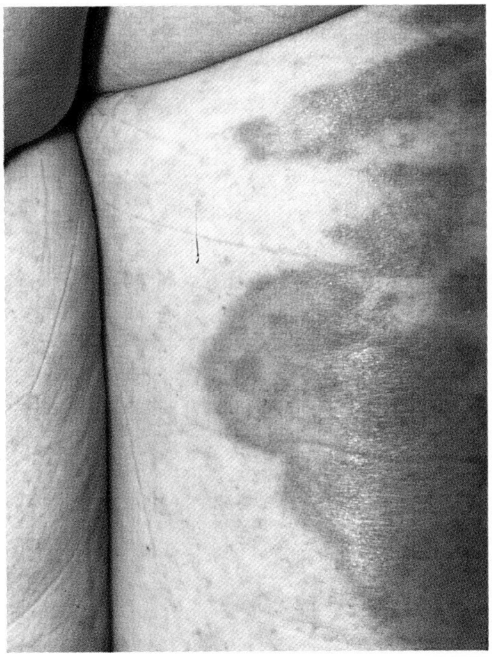

FIGURE 29–4 Urticaria-like lesion (erythema perstans) on the thigh.

Annotated Bibliography

Pecora AL, Landsman L, Imgrund SP, et al. Acrokeratosis paraneoplastica (Bazex's syndrome): report of a case and review of the literature. Arch Dermatol 1983;119:820–826.

These investigators highlight the fact that there are three distinct stages of this syndrome, something that other investigators also acknowledge. The initial phase is characterized by vesicles and periungual and subungual hyperkeratosis. These psoriasiform changes involve the fingers, toes, outer margin of the helix, and the nose. If the tumor is not treated, a secondary stage of Bazex's syndrome is noted, characterized by progressive hyperkeratosis and violaceous color changes of the palms and soles.

The third stage, which occurs if the tumor is not diagnosed and treated, is characterized by a progression of the psoriasiform disease to involve the arms, elbows, knees, legs, trunk, axilla, and hips.

Richard M, Giroux JM. Acrokeratosis paraneoplastica (Bazex's syndrome). J Am Acad Dermatol 1987;16:178–183.

A case report with an excellent review of the literature. There are 42 reference citations.

Hypertrichosis Lanuginosa

Generally occurs with other paraneoplastic features

Hypertrichosis lanuginosa is characterized by the sudden appearance of silky hair on the face, which is termed "malignant down." This hairy appearance has been associated with the development of all types of tumors, but especially those of the colon and lung. Other skin changes, such as acanthosis nigricans, pruritus, and glossitis, may be present. The hypertrichosis can gradually extend to involve all areas of the body, except the palms and soles. Unfortunately, at the time of discovery, the internal malignancy is generally widespread. However, hypertrichosis may disappear with successful treatment of the internal malignancy.

Annotated Bibliography

Jemec GBE. Hypertrichosis lanuginosa acquisita: report of a case and review of the literature. Arch Dermatol 1986;122:805–808.

This article provides an excellent review of this rare paraneoplastic event. Multiple tumors, including lymphomas, have been associated.

Tripe Palms and Tylosis

Associated with lung and stomach carcinomas

Tripe palms, also known as "pachydermatoglyphy," a soft acanthosis of the palms, is characterized by prominent epithelial thickening and hyperkeratosis producing an accentuation of normal skin markings of the palms and fingers. Pruritus may also be present. This condition appears to be a marker of internal malignancies, especially carcinomas of the lung and stomach.

Tylosis is a keratoderma of the palms and soles that may or may not be associated with carcinoma of the esophagus. The carcinoma has been described to occur up to 15 years after the onset of the keratoderma.

Associated with carcinoma of esophagus

The Howell-Evans syndrome is a hereditary variant of tylosis, first described in the United Kingdom in 1958. There is a striking increased frequency of carcinoma of the esophagus in tylotic kindred members.

Annotated Bibliography

Cohen PR, Grossman ME, Almeida L, et al. Tripe palms and malignancy. J Clin Oncol 1989;7:669–678.

This is a well-written article, which reviews 77 patients with idiopathic and malignancy-associated tripe palms. Ninety-four percent occurred in patients with malignancy; 77% of the cases were seen in association with acanthosis nigricans. Carcinoma of the lung was most frequently found in patients presenting only with tripe palms. In those patients with tripe palms and acanthosis nigricans, there is an increased frequency of gastric carcinomas. In 40% of the cases, tripe palms was the presenting feature.

Harper PS, Harper RMJ, Howell-Evans AW. Carcinoma of the oesophagus with tylosis. QJ Med 1970;39:317–333.

This is a follow-up study of the original family reported in 1958 with this condition. At the time of writing, 14 members of the family had died. Deaths from carcinoma of the esophagus were confined to the tylotic individuals. Six of the 8 deaths of the tylotic members of this family were from carcinoma of the esophagus.

Shine I, Allison PR. Carcinoma of the oesophagus with tylosis (keratosis palmaris et plantaris). Lancet 1988;1:951–953.

This is an interesting report of a family with tylosis who probably had esophageal abnormalities manifesting as dysphagia. One individual has developed carcinoma of the esophagus. Another individual was detected to have a gastric mucosa at the lower end of the esophagus (Barrett's esophagus).

Sign of Leser-Trélat

Eruptive keratotic lesions

This rare sign is characterized by the sudden appearance and explosive growth of pre-existing seborrheic keratosis over the entire body. It is associated with acanthosis nigricans in approximately one-third of cases. It is frequently accompanied by pruritus. Adenocarcinoma of the stomach as well as hematopoietic, breast, and lung neoplasms have been associated. Unfortunately, the internal malignancies are generally very aggressive. It is thought that growth factors produced by the malignancy are responsible for the rapid proliferation of new and pre-existing seborrheic keratosis.

Annotated Bibliography

Schwartz RA, Burgess GH. Florid cutaneous papillomatosis. Arch Dermatol 1978; 114:1803–1806.

This paper contains an excellent discussion on the relationship of the sign of Leser-Trélat with acanthosis nigricans and the development of cutaneous wart-like lesions. Schwartz, over the years, has established himself as an authority on the cutaneous manifestations of malignancy.

Venencie PY, Perry HO. Sign of Leser-Trélat: report of two cases and review of the literature. J Am Acad Dermatol 1984;10:83–88.

This is an excellent review of this disorder.

Ichthyosis

Most frequently associated with Hodgkin's disease

This sign most commonly resembles ichthyosis vulgaris and is characterized by a scaly eruption, most prominent over the arms and legs (Figure 29–5). Palmar, plantar, as well as flexural areas of the skin are frequently involved. On occasions, mild erythema in the affected areas can be detected. Hodgkin's disease is the most frequently implicated associated malignancy, but other lymphoreticu-

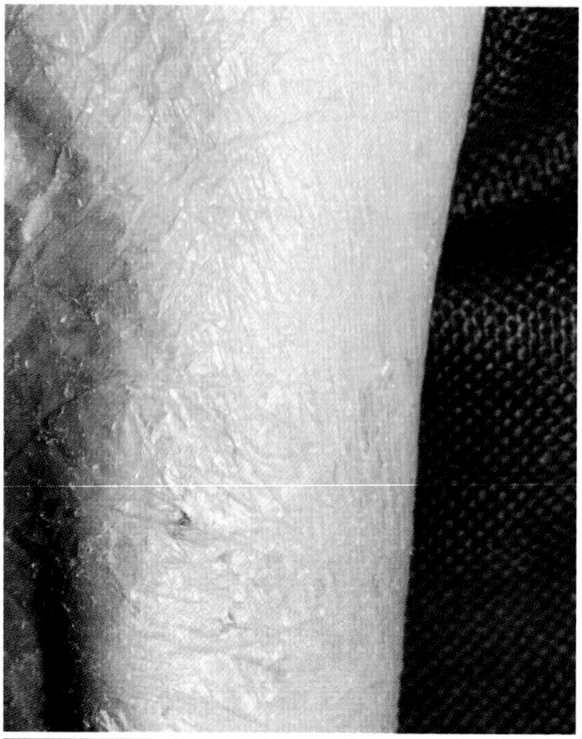

FIGURE 29–5 Acquired ichthyosis in a patient with carcinoma of the lung.

lar malignancies, as well as carcinoma of the lung, breast, and cervix, and Kaposi's sarcoma have been associated.

Other conditions associated with late-onset ichthyosis vulgaris–like changes include sarcoidosis, thyroid disease, and human immunodeficiency virus.

Trousseau's Syndrome

William R. Bell, M.D.

Trousseau's syndrome most commonly associated with carcinomas of prostate, stomach, and tail of pancreas and leukemia

The presence of multiple, migratory, superficial episodes of thrombophlebitis, especially of the upper extremities, is associated with the presence of internal malignancies. This syndrome is characterized by tender, erythematous, linear nodules occurring along superficial veins. These lesions gradually heal over a period of several weeks but are followed by the development of new lesions. Leukocytosis and fever frequently occur. Unfortunately, in as many as 50% of cases, the tumor has metastasized. In one study, three-quarters of the patients with Trousseau's syndrome had carcinoma of the prostate, stomach, or tail of the pancreas, or a hematologic malignancy.

Increased risk of the development of malignancies in patients less than 50 years of age who have a deep vein thrombosis with or without a pulmonary embolus

There is evidence that deep venous thrombosis (DVT) of the legs, with or without pulmonary emboli, are associated with the presence of occult malignancy. One study indicates a relative risk of 19.1 of an occult malignancy occurring within 2 years of a DVT in patients younger than 50 years. In another study by the same group, 13 of 88 pulmonary emboli patients (14.7%) developed malignancy within 2 years, compared with none in the control group ($p < .001$). Thus, the recurrence of DVT, with or without pulmonary emboli, especially in patients younger than 50 years, should prompt an investigation for an occult malignancy, leukemia, or the presence of the antiphospholipid syndrome. (For further discussion, see Mondor's Disease in Chapter 9, "Antiphospholipid Syndrome.")

Widespread cutaneous infarction due to thrombosis (purpura fulminans) or cutaneous hemorrhage (defibrinogenation) may be seen in association with cancer. Patients with cancer have increased levels of both coagulation and inhibitor of coagulation factors. A disturbance produced by local trauma or infections may disturb the precarious balance between coagulation and anticoagulation. Thrombosis and/or bleeding may occur.

Cancer patients have increased quantities of coagulation and inhibitors of coagulation factors.

The complexity of the balance between hemostatic mechanisms in cancer patients is illustrated by a study from our institution. Historical data of 182 cancer patients with disseminated intravascular coagulopathy indicated that 50% had migratory phlebitis; 60% had at least one episode of a DVT; 40% had hemorrhagic complications; 25% had arterial embolization; and 7% had thromboses, hemorrhagic manifestations, and arterial emboli.

Cancer patients may demonstrate thrombosis and hemorrhagic and embolization manifestations.

Annotated Bibliography

Pradoni P, Lensing WA, Buller HR, et al. Deep vein thrombosis and the incidence of subsequent symptomatic cancer. N Engl J Med 1992;37:1128–1132.

These investigators demonstrate a statistically significant increased frequency of malignancy occurring within 1 year of an episode of idiopathic DVT.

Sack GH Jr, Levin J, Bell WR. Trousseau's syndrome and other manifestations of chronic disseminated coagulopathy in patients with neoplasm: clinical, pathophysiological and therapeutic features. Medicine 1977;56:1–30.

This is a highly referenced paper demonstrating that cancer patients may have recurrent thrombophlebitis, as well as hemorrhagic complications. Embolization is also common, and a few cancer patients may have a triad of thrombophlebitis, hemorrhage, and arterial emboli.

Cryofibrinogenemia may occur in these patients and be responsible for infarctive lesions in the acral areas (digits, ears, and nose).

Miller SP, Sanchez-Alvolos J, Stefanski T, et al. Coagulation disorder in cancer I: clinical and laboratory studies. Cancer 1967;20:1452–1458.

This article categorizes the hypercoagulable state seen in some patients with malignancies. These studies demonstrated a marked elevation in plasma levels of various clotting factors, as well as an increase in the number of platelets. Coagulation studies demonstrated a shortened bleeding time and a decrease in the partial thromboplastin time.

Sproul EE. Carcinoma and venous thrombosis: the frequency of association of carcinoma in the body or tail of the pancreas with multiple venous thrombosis. Am J Cancer 1938;34:566–574.

This classic paper highlights the frequent occurrence of venous thrombosis in association with carcinoma of the body and tail of the pancreas. These thromboses were bland, lacking evidence of inflammation or tumor invasion.

Gore JM, Appelbaum JS, Greene HL, et al. Occult cancer in patients with acute pulmonary embolism. Ann Intern Med 1982;96:556–560.

Goldberg RJ, Seneff M, Gore JM. Occult malignant neoplasm in patients with deep venous thrombosis. Ann Intern Med 1987;147:251–253.

Kakkar VV, Howe CT, Nicolaides AN, et al. Deep vein thrombosis of the leg: is there a "high risk" group? Am J Surg 1970;120:527–530.

These three articles demonstrate the increased frequency of DVT and pulmonary emboli and the presence of an occult neoplasm.

Schulman S, et al. Incidence of cancer after prophylaxis with warfarin against recurrent venous thrombosis. N Engl J Med 2000;342:1953–1958.

The incidence of cancer is increased during the first year after the diagnosis of venous thromboembolism. The risk seems to be lower subsequently in those individuals treated with oral anticoagulants for 6 months than in those treated for 6 weeks.

Zeilinski CC, Hejna N. Warfarin for cancer prevention [editorial]. N Engl J Med 2000; 342:1991–1992.

The authors indicate that the incidence for cancer after a thromboembolic event are particularly high for cancers of the ovary, pancreas, liver, lung, kidney, brain, esophagus, and Hodgkin's and non–Hodgkin's lymphoma. They further note that the difference in the incidence of cancer emerged after 2 years of follow-up. This, they interpret, makes it likely that the anticoagulants were not acting on pre-existing clinically overt tumors but, rather, were preventing the development of new cancerous lesions.

Amyloidosis

Primary amyloidosis is frequently associated with multiple myeloma. Approximately 30 to 40% of these patients have cutaneous features. (For further discussion, see Chapter 24, "Leukemia, B-cell Lymphomas, and Multiple Myeloma Paraproteins.")

Vasculitis

Vasculitic lesions associated with internal malignancy can present as purpura, urticaria-like lesions, superficial ulcerations, or gangrene. The vasculitis can be associated with arthralgias, arthritis, renal involvement, as well as hepatic abnormalities. Lymphoproliferative disorders, especially hairy cell leukemia, and, to a much lesser extent, solid tumors are associated with these lesions. These lesions are the manifestations of a putative immune complex disease process.

Vasculitis caused by putative immune complexes composed of tumor-related antigens

Frequently, cryoglobulins are detected in the serum of patients with vasculitis. Most commonly, these cryoglobulins belong to type II, demonstrating both monoclonal IgM and polyclonal IgG immunoglobulins. Lymphatic leukemia, lymphoma, and hairy cell leukemia are frequently associated with these cryoglobulins. (For further discussion, see Chapter 12, "Vasculitis.")

Acrocyanosis

May be seen with a myeloproliferative disorder

Acrocyanosis is an unusual clinical picture. It is characterized by a persistent, dusky, cyanotic appearance of the hands and, to a lesser extent, the feet. The exact cause of this condition is not known. It is conceivable that an increase in blood viscosity and a concomitant decrease in the oxygen content of the blood are responsible. On unusual occasions, this disorder has been associated with a myeloproliferative disorder and, more recently, has been uncommonly associated with the presence of antibodies directed against phospholipid proteins.

Annotated Bibliography

Frankel DH, Larson RA, Lorincz AL. Acrolivedosis—a sign of myeloproliferative diseases. Arch Dermatol 1987;123:921–924.

This is the original description of acrocyanosis.

Acute Febrile Neutrophilic Dermatosis

Approximately 10 to 15% of cases seen with malignancy, most commonly myelogenous leukemia

Acute febrile neutrophilic dermatosis, also known as "Sweet's syndrome," may precede, accompany, or follow the development of an acute myelogenous or myelocytic leukemic disease process. The skin lesions, characterized as erythematous-to-violaceous papules, nodules, or plaques, usually involve the head, neck, and arms (Figure 29–6). Pustules and vesicles may occur. On unusual occasions, mucosal lesions (conjunctivitis) and arthritis are seen. The presence of oral ulcers, bullous formation, or ulcerated lesions and anemia are more suggestive of an associated malignant process. It has been estimated that approximately 10 to 15% of patients with Sweet's syndrome, especially those who are male or older, have an associated underlying malignancy. Although most of the malignancies are hematologic, several reports of solid tumors have been associated with this cutaneous presentation.

We have recently seen a 36-year-old female who developed widespread nodules and plaques (Sweet's syndrome) associated with the development of acute myelogenous leukemia.

Annotated Bibliography

Cooper PH, Innes DJ, Greer KF. Acute febrile neutrophilic dermatosis (Sweet's syndrome) and myeloproliferative disorders. Cancer 1983;51:1518–1526.

This article provides a description of Sweet's syndrome associated with leukemia and makes a comparison with Sweet's syndrome occurring in healthy individuals.

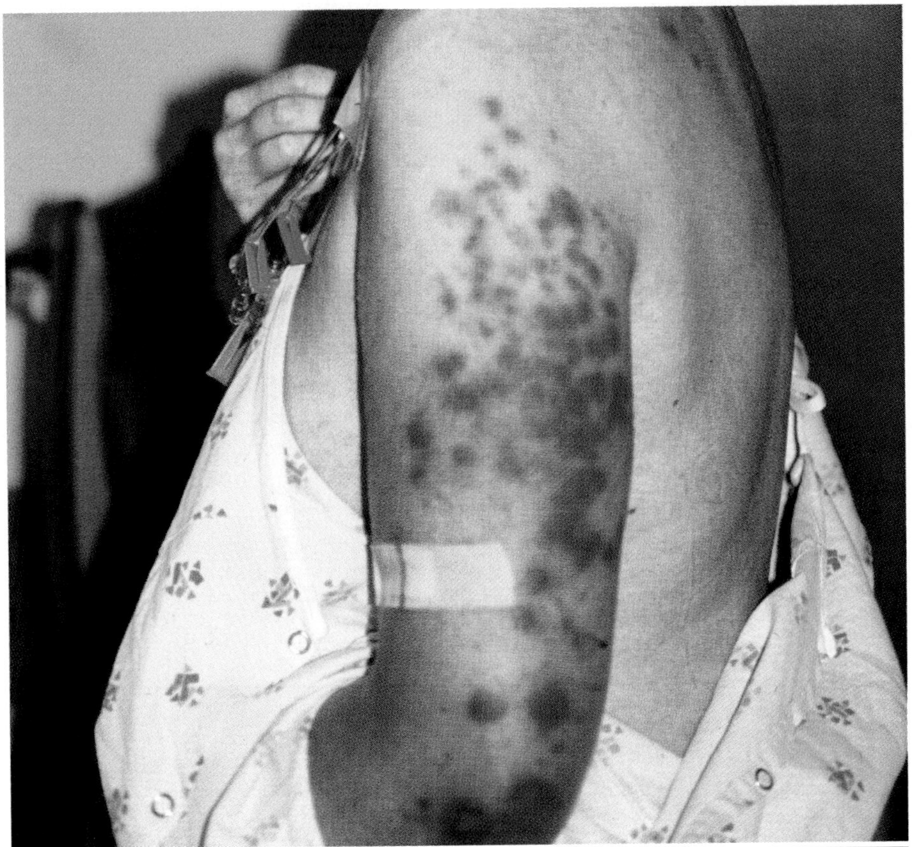

FIGURE 29–6 Sweet's syndrome occurring in a patient with acute myelogenous leukemia.

Cronkhite-Canada Syndrome

Cronkhite-Canada syndrome is an uncommon disease process characterized by the adult onset of alopecia, nail dystrophy, cutaneous hyperpigmentation, and hamartomas involving the gastrointestinal tract extending from the stomach to the rectum (Table 29–2).

Cronkhite-Canada syndrome shares many pathologic gastrointestinal features with Ménétrier's disease.

The esophagus is rarely involved. The gastrointestinal lesions are multiple, sessile, and pedunculated polyps. In addition, the gastric mucosa are thickened, showing dilated tortuous glands, some of which are cystically dilated, filled with proteinaceous material. These features resemble Ménétrier's disease, which is thought by many to share a pathologic relationship with Cronkhite-Canada syndrome.

Alopecia, ranging from localized to progressive total body hair loss, has been reported (Figure 29–7). The cutaneous pigmentation is macular, involving the upper extremities, particularly the palms. The face, neck, trunk, scalp, and soles can also be involved. The pigmentation is lentiginous. At times, patchy vitiligo may occur. Equally unusual is the presence of mucosal hyperpigmentation.

Alopecia, hyperpigmentation, and dystrophic nails

All 20 nails are involved. The nails are dystrophic and may be darkly discolored (Figure 29–8). Atrophy of the tongue and fissuring can occur. In addition, diarrhea, anorexia, weight loss, and abdominal pain are present. In general, the ectodermal changes follow the gastrointestinal symptomatology, but there are several instances in which the ectodermal changes have been reported to precede the gastrointestinal manifestations.

Excessive electrolyte loss is characterized by hypokalemia, hypocalcemia, and hypomagnesemia. Hypoalbuminemia is also present and, on occasions, occult blood loss may produce a mild to moderate anemia.

Controversial whether or not associated with gastrointestinal malignancies

Recent evidence, perhaps still controversial, suggests that the Cronkhite-Canada syndrome may be associated with an increased frequency of gastrointestinal malignancies. The overall mortality in one study was approximately 60% despite therapy. Spontaneous remissions have been reported. These remissions have been associated with a fluctuating pigmentary changes over time as well as a reversal of nail and hair changes.

Pathogenesis of ectodermal changes unknown

The pathogenesis of this disease is unknown. It is suspected that the severe malnutrition secondary to a protein-losing enteropathy and diarrhea are dominant in the pathogenesis of the diffuse ectodermal changes. However, as noted above, on occasions, the ectodermal changes may precede the gastrointestinal symptomatology. Therefore, the exact pathogenesis of this disease is unknown at present.

A total colectomy may be needed because of massive polyps.

Recommendations have been made that polyps greater than 1 cm be removed or a biopsy performed on them. Furthermore, antibiotics, especially tetracycline, ampicillin, or trimethoprim-sulfamethoxazole should be used to alleviate suspected bacterial overgrowth. Surgery is recommended for the treatment of prolapse, intussusception, and, obviously, malignancy. A total colectomy and, at times, a gastrectomy, may prove necessary to protect patients who have a massive density of polyps or a severe protein-losing enteropathy.

TABLE 29–2 Clinical Features and Recommended Evaluation of Cronkhite-Canada Patients

Clinical Features	Diagnostic Evaluation
Multiple small- and large-bowel polyps	Colonoscopic examination every 3 years
Hyperpigmentation	
Alopecia	
Nail dystrophy	

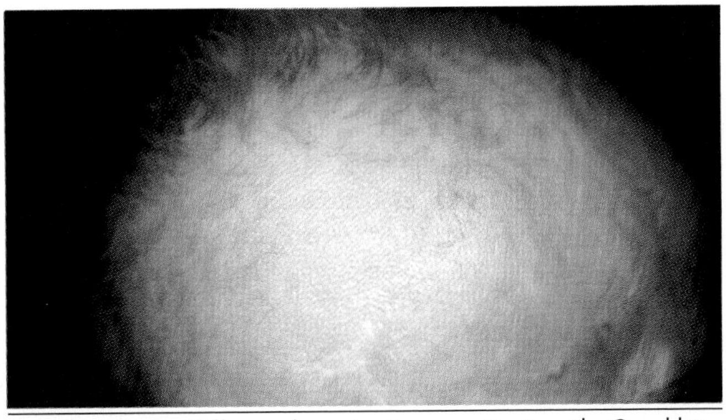

FIGURE 29-7 Diffuse alopecia in a patient with Cronkhite-Canada syndrome.

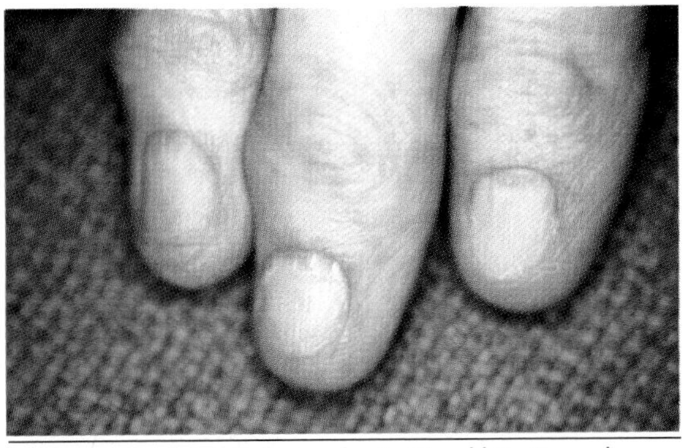

FIGURE 29-8 Nail dystrophy in Cronkhite-Canada syndrome.

Annotated Bibliography

Cronkhite LW, Canada WJ. Generalized gastrointestinal polyposis: an unusual syndrome of polyposis, pigmentation, alopecia and onychotrophia. N Engl J Med 1955;252: 1011–1015.

This is the original description of the syndrome that bears these authors' names.

Daniel ES, Ludwig SL, Lewin KJ. The Cronkhite-Canada syndrome: an analysis of clinical and pathologic features and therapy in 55 patients. Medicine 1982;61:293–309.

This is a review of a large group of patients with the Cronkhite-Canada syndrome. In this series of 55 patients, there were 30 deaths (55%). In 20 patients, the cause of death was attributable to the disease and its complications. These complications included severe cachexia, anemia, congestive heart failure, bronchopneumonia, embolism, septicemia, and shock. Surgery and postoperative complications were contributing factors in 7 patients.

These authors comment that a relationship between this syndrome and Ménétrier's disease has been emphasized by many. They point out that the morphology of the gastric mucosa is similar in both disorders, and both are associated with a protein-losing enteropathy.

Carcinoma of the gastrointestinal tract was found in 8 patients (14.5%). In 5 patients, the carcinomas occurred in the colon or rectum. In a sixth patient, it was found in the stomach.

Dermatomyositis

For discussion of the malignant associations, see Chapter 6, "Dermatomyositis."

Paraneoplastic Pemphigus

See Chapter 15, "Autoimmune Blistering Mucocutaneous Diseases," for discussion of Pemphigus.

Pyoderma Gangrenosum

Bullous and superficial lesions of pyoderma gangrenosum associated with myelogenous leukemia

Pyoderma gangrenosum is an inflammatory disease characterized by rapidly evolving, painful nodular ulcers, demonstrating a violaceous border with a necrotic base. These lesions can reach 3 to 5 cm in a relatively short period of time (2 to 3 weeks). Bullous formation may also occur. The abdomen, buttocks, and lower extremities are most commonly involved. The lesions typically heal with cribriform scarring. Biopsies demonstrate a neutrophilic infiltrate, abscess formation, and epidermal necrosis. In contradistinction to the pyoderma gangrenosum lesions associated with granulomatous bowel disease, the pyoderma gangrenosum lesions associated with myelogenous leukemia are frequently bullous and superficial, generally not extending into subcutaneous and fascial tissues. The cause of pyoderma gangrenosum is unknown. Some evidence indicates that a vasculopathy is the primary event.

It has been estimated that approximately 10% of patients with pyoderma gangrenosum have myelogenous leukemia or multiple myeloma. (For further discussion, see Chapter 34, "Pyoderma Gangrenosum.")

Annotated Bibliography

Hecker MS, Lebwohl MG. Recalcitrant pyoderma gangrenosum: treatment with thalidomide. J Am Acad Dermatol 1998;38:490–491.

This is a report of a 49-year-old man with a 27-year history of pyoderma gangrenosum. The patient's disease had been recalcitrant to all forms of therapy but was cleared when thalidomide was used. The authors cite references indicating two additional cases of pyoderma gangrenosum successfully treated with thalidomide.

Erythromelalgia

Erythromelalgia is characterized by intense burning pain associated with increased temperature and erythema over the skin of the lower extremities, especially the feet (Figure 29–9). There is no evidence for arterial insufficiency. Furthermore, the symptoms are precipitated by heat. Relief is obtained by cooling or elevation of the extremity.

Biopsy of these lesions has demonstrated thrombotic occlusion of arterials, composed of platelet aggregates.

Polycythemia vera and essential thrombocythemia detected in one-fifth of patients

Most cases of adult-onset erythromelalgia are of unknown etiology. However, approximately 20% are associated with polycythemia vera or essential thrombocythemia.

Low-dose aspirin may be effective.

In patients with either polycythemia vera or essential thrombocythemia, arterial plugging of thrombi, secondary to platelet activation, has been noted. Low-dose aspirin (500 mg/day) has been associated with dramatic improvement in at least one case.

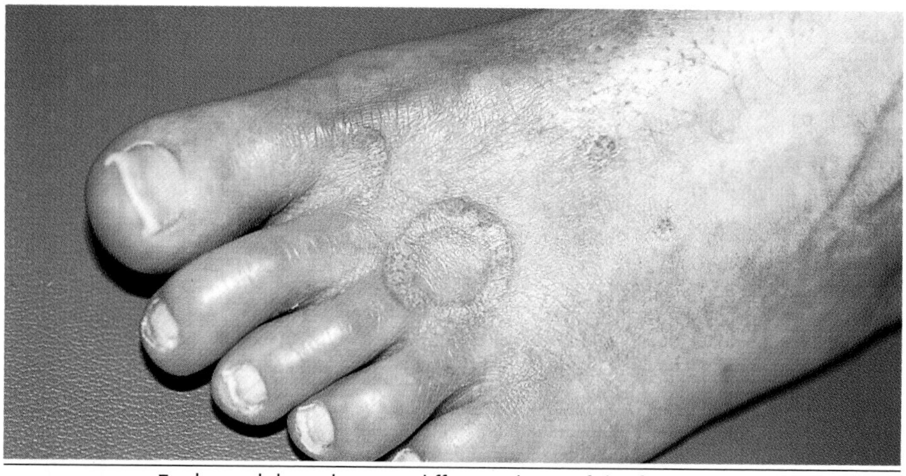

FIGURE 29–9 Erythromelalgia showing diffuse redness of the foot.

Annotated Bibliography

Babb RR, Alarcon-Segovia D, Fairbairn JF. Erythromelalgia. Circulation 1964;29:136–141.

The study reports that 9 of 51 cases had polycythemia; 30 patients had no associated disease.

Exfoliative Erythroderma

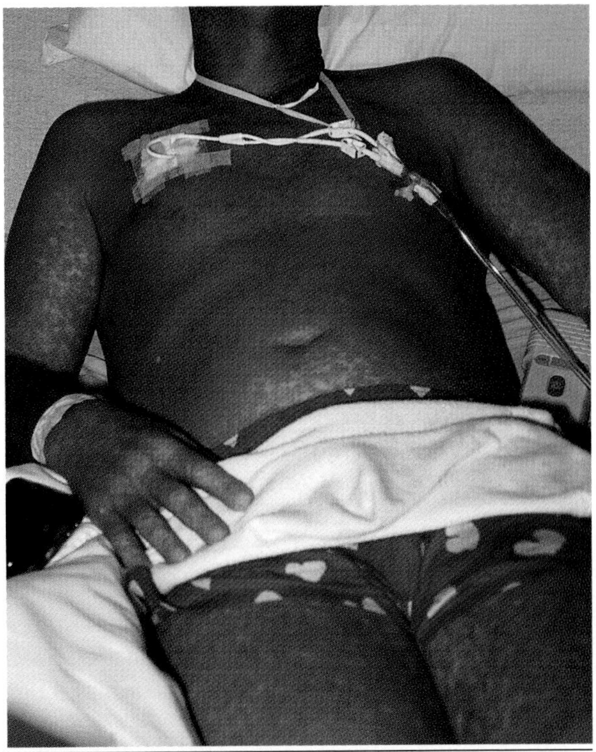

FIGURE 29–10 Generalized erythroderma.

Exfoliative erythroderma, or erythroderma, is a relatively uncommon, serious, inflammatory skin disease characterized by generalized erythema and scale formation (Figure 29–10). Keratoderma of the palms and soles, malaise, pruritus, generalized lymphadenopathy, and loss of temperature control (poikilothermy) characterize the clinical disease process. High-output cardiac failure can rarely complicate this condition. A microcytic hypochromic anemia, an elevated erythrocyte sedimentation rate, eosinophilia, low serum proteins, and electrolyte abnormalities characterize the laboratory findings.

The etiology of 602 exfoliative erythroderma patients summarized from five separate series is presented in Table 29–3.

A pre-existing skin disease (eg, atopic dermatitis, psoriasis, seborrheic dermatitis, allergic contact dermatitis) was the most common cause, occurring in approximately 40% of patients. The second most common cause is systemic drugs, which include barbiturates, phenytoin, gold, sulfonamides, chloroquine, penicillins, allopurinol, and thiazides. In the past, heavy metals including arsenicals and mercurials were frequent causes.

TABLE 29–3 Etiology of Exfoliative Erythroderma

	Patients *(N = 602)	
Etiology	Number	Percentage
Drugs	137	23
Pre-existing skin disease	236	39
Malignancy	58	10
Idiopathic	128	21
Other	43	7

*Summary of five separate studies.

Adapted from:
Nicolis GD, Helwig EB. Exfoliative dermatitis: a clinicopathology study of 135 cases. Arch Dermatol 1973;108:788–797.
Abraham I, McCarthy JT, Sanders SC. 101 cases of exfoliative dermatitis. Arch Dermatol 1963;87:136–141.
King LE, Dufresne RG, Lovett GL, et al. Erythroderma: review of 82 cases. South Med J 1986;79:1210–1215.
Sehgal VN, Srivastava G. Exfoliative dermatitis. A prospective study of 80 patients. Dermatologica 1986;173:278–284.
Thestrup-Pedersen K, Halkier-Sorensen L, Sogaard H, et al. The red man syndrome: exfoliative dermatitis of unknown etiology: a description and follow up of 38 patients. J Am Acad Dermatol 1988;18:1307–1312.

TABLE 29–4 Long-Term Follow-Up* of 38 Patients with Exfoliative Erythroderma of Unknown Etiology

	Patients (N = 38)	
Etiology	Number	Percentage
Idiopathic	18	47
Cutaneous T-cell lymphoma	13	34
Poikiloderma	1	3
Lymphoma	2	5
Other	4	11

*Median follow-up of 30 months.

Adapted from:
Thestrup-Pedersen K, Halkier-Sorensen L, Sogaard H, Zacharie H. The red man syndrome: exfoliative dermatitis of unknown etiology: a description and follow up of 38 patients. J Am Acad Dermatol 1988;18:1307–1312.

The third most common cause of exfoliative erythroderma was classified as being idiopathic and represented approximately 22% of patients. One follow-up study evaluating 38 erythroderma patients ("red man syndrome") of unknown etiology, over a 15-year period detected that 13 of 38 patients (34%) subsequently developed or were suspected of having mycosis fungoides (Table 29–4).

In addition, two cases developed a reticulosis (lymphoma), and one was diagnosed as poikiloderma. One-third of these original idiopathic exfoliative erythroderma patients experienced complete remission. A striking male to female ratio of nearly 7:1 was noted in this group of patients.

Ten percent of exfoliative erythroderma patients have a malignancy—most commonly a lymphoma.

Malignancy was initially detected in approximately 10% (58 of 602 patients). The types of malignancies associated with exfoliative erythroderma are depicted in Table 29–5.

TABLE 29–5 Exfoliative Erythroderma

	Patients (N = 58)	
Type of Malignancy	Number	Percent
Cutaneous T-cell lymphoma	28	48
Hodgkin's disease	9	16
Lymphatic leukemia	6	10
Lymphoma	4	7
Myelogenous leukemia	3	5
Prostate	2	3
Cancer of the lung	4	7
Thyroid, liver, melanoma, ovarian, rectal, and breast cancers	6	—

Adapted from:
Nicolis GD, Helwig EB. Exfoliative dermatitis: a clinicopathology study of 135 cases. Arch Dermatol 1973;108:788–797.
Abraham I, McCarthy JT, Sanders SC. 101 cases of exfoliative dermatitis. Arch Dermatol 1963;87:136–141.
King LE, Dufresne RG, Lovett GL, et al. Erythroderma: review of 82 cases. South Med J 1986;79:1210–1215.
Sehgal VN, Srivastava G. Exfoliative dermatitis. A prospective study of 80 patients. Dermatologica 1986;173:278–284.
Thestrup-Pedersen K, Halkier-Sorensen L, Sogaard H, et al. The red man syndrome: exfoliative dermatitis of unknown etiology: a description and follow up of 38 patients. J Am Acad Dermatol 1988;18:1307–1312.

At least 75% of the malignancies associated with exfoliative erythroderma are lymphatic in origin, with mycosis fungoides (cutaneous T-cell lymphoma) accounting for approximately 48%. On unusual occasions, exfoliative erythroderma is associated with myelogenous leukemia and visceral cancers, such as those of the lung and prostate.

May be precursor to development of mycosis fungoides

In general, the exfoliative erythroderma associated with pre-existing skin disease develops more slowly than the exfoliative erythroderma associated with drugs and malignancy. The single most important diagnostic tool is a biopsy. The earliest lesion should be sought; however, multiple biopsies may have to be performed. One study indicated that 43% of patients were diagnosed by biopsy; however, when mycosis fungoides (cutaneous T-cell lymphoma) was excluded, only 22% of biopsies in nonmalignant exfoliative erythroderma patients were diagnostic.

In general, routine laboratory tests as well as lymph node biopsies are not very helpful. The presence of eosinophilia suggests a drug etiology, but lymphomas can also be associated with eosinophilia. It should be noted that exfoliative erythroderma may precede the diagnosis of malignancy by years.

Exfoliative erythroderma (erythroderma) not only presents a challenge to determine the underlying etiology, but this condition produces severe, pathologic alterations in temperature regulation, cardiac hemodynamics, and fluid and electrolyte balance in patients. The alterations produced by an exfoliative erythroderma in a patient are listed in Table 29–6.

In elderly patients or in patients with cardiac disease, exfoliative erythroderma, which induces shunting of as much as 20% of the cardiac output to the skin secondary to severe vascular dilatation, may induce high-output cardiac failure.

Exfoliative erythroderma may produce severe systemic alterations.

Although treatment is directed at the underlying cause, general measures, such as placing the patient in a warm room (75 to 80°F), the use of midpotent

TABLE 29–6 Systemic Effects of an Exfoliative Erythroderma

Systemic Effect	Resulting Manifestation
Increased blood flow to skin	May exceed 50% of cardiac output and induce cardiac failure in elderly or younger patients who have compromised cardiac status
Increased capillary permeability, high oncotic pressure of tissue exudate, hypoalbuminemia, and increased central venous pressure	Edema of extremities
Dysregulation of temperature control	Poikilothermia Hypothermia Hyperpyrexia Increased metabolic rate
Increased metabolic need of skin disease (epidermal turnover)	Folate deficiency
Dermatopathic enteropathy	Folate deficiency from malabsorption
Desquamation	Iron deficiency
Dilutional effect in plasma with expansion of extravascular spaces, leaky capillaries, and increased protein loss through skin and bowel	Hypoalbuminemia
Increased water loss through skin	Dehydration Oliguria and increased thirst

Adapted from:
Shuster S. High output cardiac failure from skin disease. Lancet 1963;1:1338–1341.
Shuster S. The metabolic and haemodynamic effects of skin disease. Ann Clin Res 1971;3:135-142.

topical steroids, the frequent use of emollients, and hydration of the patient, are necessary to provide comfort.

On rare occasions, chronic exfoliation can deplete iron levels (as much as 5 mg of iron can be lost with desquamation each day) and produce a folic acid deficiency (secondary to rapid cutaneous turnover with increased DNA synthesis).

Annotated Bibliography

Abrahams I, McCarthy JT, Sanders SI. One hundred and one cases of exfoliative dermatitis. Arch Dermatol 1963;87:136–141.

Sehgal VN, Srivastava G. Exfoliative dermatitis. A perspective study of 80 patients. Dermatologica 1986;173:278–284.

Nicolis GD, Helwig EV. Exfoliative dermatitis: a clinical pathologic study of 135 cases. Arch Dermatol 1973;108:788–797.

King LE, Dufresne RG, Lovett GL, et al. Erythroderma: review of 82 cases. South Med J 1986;79:1210–1214.

These four studies document the fact that pre-existing conditions are a very common cause of exfoliative erythroderma. In the studies by Nicolis, Helwig, and King, et al., 20% of patients had lymphoreticular malignancies. By contrast, the articles by Abrahams et al. and Sehgal and Srivastava reported approximately 8% and 0%, respectively.

Thestrup-Pedersen K, Halkier L, Sorensen L, et al. The red man's syndrome exfoliative dermatitis of unknown etiology: a description and follow up of 38 patients. J Am Acad Dermatol 1988;18:1307–1312.

This highly quoted study indicates that over a 15-year period, one-third of patients diagnosed with an exfoliative dermatitis went into complete remission: 4 developed definite mycosis fungoides, and 9 were suspected of having mycosis fungoides. Thus, 13 of 38 patients (34%) developed or were suspected to have developed mycosis fungoides.

Porphyria Cutanea Tarda

Porphyria cutanea tarda is characterized by hypertrichosis, skin fragility, and blister formation. The relative risk of hepatocellular carcinoma in these patients is increased with a reported high of 61.

The increased risk of malignancy probably associated with presence of hepatitis C infection

Recent evidence has indicated that hepatitis C (non-A, non-B hepatitis) is frequently associated with the presence of sporadic cases of porphyria cutanea tarda. One large study of over 100 sporadic cases of porphyria cutanea tarda reported a very high frequency of serologic evidence for an antecedent hepatitis C infection. Hepatitis C is also associated with the development of hepatocellular carcinoma (hepatoma). Thus, it appears very likely that the association of porphyria cutanea tarda with an increased frequency of hepatocellular carcinoma is reflective of an antecedent hepatitis C infection. (For further discussion, see Chapter 39, "Porphyrias.")

Annotated Bibliography

Cauppinen R, Mustajocki P. Acute hepatic porphyria and hepatocellular carcinoma. Br J Cancer 1988;57:117–121.

This interesting article was written prior to knowledge of hepatitis C.

Acanthosis Nigricans

Acanthosis nigricans involvement of flexural areas; may also involve mucous membranes

Acanthosis nigricans is a distinctive clinical syndrome characterized by hyperpigmentation and velvety acanthosis involving the nape and sides of the neck,

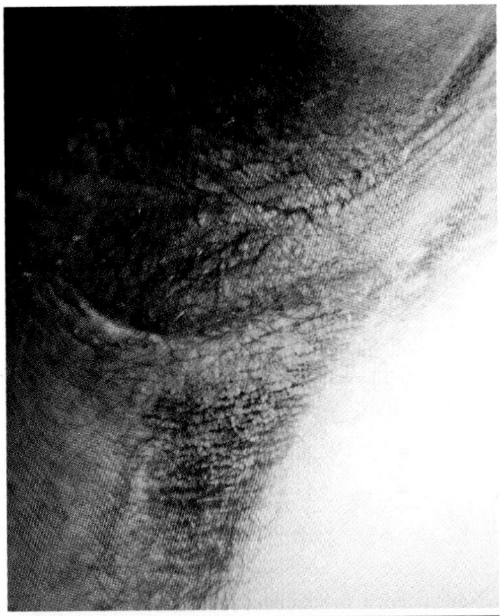

FIGURE 29–11 Acanthosis nigricans in the axillary region.

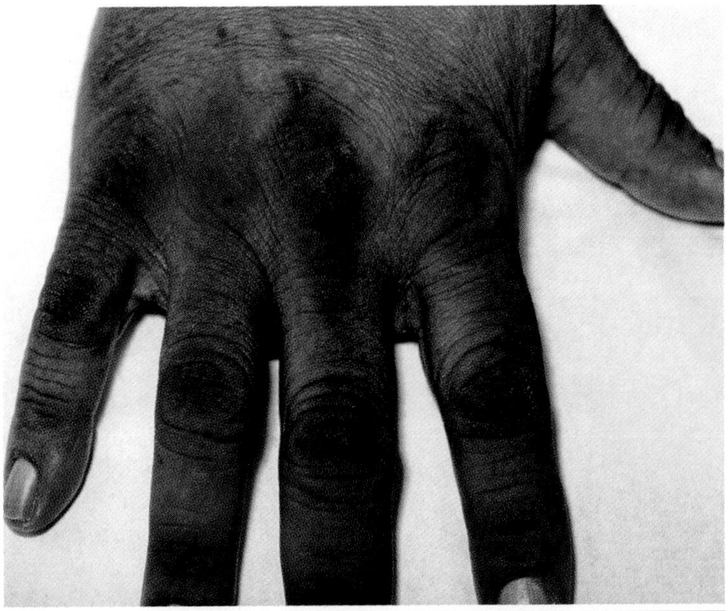

FIGURE 29–12 Acanthosis nigricans on the dorsal surface of the hands.

axilla, and groin (Figures 29–11 and 29–12). To a lesser extent, the antecubital area, the popliteal fossa, and the umbilical area may be involved. Papillomatosis involving the oral mucosa, larynx, pharynx, and esophagus, as well as the anogenital mucosa may occur. Hyperpigmentation, although present in the oral mucosa, is not as prominent as the acanthosis.

Etiology

Multiple associations with acanthosis nigricans

During the past 25 years, our understanding of acanthosis nigricans has undergone a dramatic reassessment. The early studies of Curth emphasized the relationship of acanthosis nigricans with internal malignancy, especially adenocarcinoma of the stomach. Acanthosis nigricans was also recognized to be an inherited autosomal dominant disorder and in association with several genetic syndromes, including leprechaunism and lipodystrophy. It was also seen in association with obesity.

In 1976, Kahn and Flier reported the association of acanthosis nigricans with insulin-resistant states. Two types of syndrome were recognized: type A and type B. Type A patients are predominantly African American young females who in early childhood demonstrate acanthosis nigricans associated with hirsutism, clitoromegaly, a masculine habitus, and increased growth. Polycystic ovaries have been diagnosed in many cases, as well as elevated plasma androgens.

Insulin resistance

These patients have genetic defects in the insulin receptor. This is manifested either by a quantitative decrease or a qualitative dysfunctional abnormality. High plasma insulin concentrations are characteristic.

Type B patients develop acanthosis nigricans characteristically in the fourth decade of life. These are predominantly African American females, and the disease is most commonly associated with an underlying immunologic disease—systemic lupus erythematosus. Insulin resistance is secondary to autoantibodies directed against the insulin receptor. These patients also have high plasma insulin concentrations.

Congenital syndromes of fat depletion (lipodystrophy) are characterized either by partial or total absence of body fat. These patients may develop hyperglycemia, but ketosis does not occur. Hypertriglyceridemia, with eruptive xanthomas, is common. Hepatosplenomegaly, cardiomegaly, lymphadenopathy, and muscle hypertrophy also occur, and mental retardation is common, along with hirsutism and hypertrophied external genitalia. The insulin resistance in this group of patients is secondary to a decreased quantity of the insulin receptors or a diminished affinity of the insulin receptor for insulin. Elevated plasma insulin levels are detected.

In leprechaunism, the insulin receptor is dysfunctional. This syndrome is characterized by elfin facies, the absence of subcutaneous fat, and hirsutism.

The Rabson-Mendenhall syndrome is another hereditary disorder characterized by acanthosis and insulin resistance. This syndrome consists of dental dysplasia, dystrophic nails, and premature puberty. The quantity of insulin receptors appears to be normal but dysfunctional.

A unifying hypothesis to explain all these different forms of acanthosis nigricans has been proposed by Cruz and Hud. They propose that tissue resistance to insulin results in the pancreatic islet B-cells producing increased quantities of insulin. At low concentrations, they believe, insulin preferentially binds to its classic receptor. However, at higher concentrations, insulin has a relatively greater affinity for insulin-like growth factor receptors. These receptors are thought to mediate the effects of insulin on proliferating cells (acanthosis).

The virilization that is commonly seen in the hereditary type A syndrome may result from insulin stimulation of the ovarian stroma granulosa cells. These cells, in turn, produce androgens.

The malignant acanthosis nigricans syndrome is characterized by rapidity of development and spread. It is hypothesized that tumor products, with insulin-like activity at the cell receptor level, are responsible for the development of acanthosis nigricans, associated with malignancies.

Prevalence

Most commonly associated malignancy is carcinoma of the stomach; however, other malignancies have been associated

Between 60 and 70% of the reported tumors associated with malignant acanthosis nigricans are adenocarcinomas of the stomach. There are, however, many reports of squamous cell carcinomas, sarcomas, and hematologic malignancies associated with malignant acanthosis nigricans.

Approximately 60% of acanthosis nigricans occurs before the detection of the malignancy. Frequently, the malignant acanthosis nigricans remits with excision of the tumor and may recur with the reappearance of the tumors. In many cases, however, the tumor is very aggressive.

In addition to acanthosis nigricans associated with insulin resistance and malignancy, a nevoid form of acanthosis nigricans, which is associated with unilateral clinical features, has been recognized. It is thought to be inherited as an autosomal dominant trait. Furthermore, acanthosis nigricans has been induced by drugs, most commonly nicotinic acid and estrogens, such as diethylstilbestrol.

The prevalence of acanthosis nigricans in a general adolescent population is approximately 7%. It appears to be more prevalent in Hispanics and blacks with approximate frequencies of 5 and 13%, respectively, compared with a 1% frequency in Caucasians. Hud detected a prevalence of approximately 74% in an obese adult hospital clinic, whereas Stewart detected a prevalence of approximately 28% in obese children in a primary school. Obese women with polycystic ovarian disease were found to have a 50% frequency of acanthosis nigricans, and obese women with hyperandrogenic manifestations demonstrated an approximate 5% prevalence.

The frequency of acanthosis nigricans in malignancies is rare. Andreev reported only 2 of 12,000 cancer patients to be affected with acanthosis nigricans.

Clinical Features

In addition to the hyperpigmentation and velvety acanthosis involving the axilla, nape and sides of the neck, groin, and antecubital, popliteal, and umbilical areas, extensive papillomatosis of the eyelids, lips, and vulva may be present. Oral papillomatosis, as well as papillomatosis involving the larynx, pharynx, and the esophageal and anogenital regions may be present. At times, the mucosal involvement may be great, producing a cobblestone-like surface. Diffuse papillomatosis may involve the entire esophageal mucosa. In addition, hyperkeratosis of the nipple and areola may be found.

In nondiabetic, obese, hirsute, hyperandrogenic females, prominent vulval involvement is detected. A localized or generalized pruritus is seen in approximately 30 to 40% of patients. Hyperkeratosis of the palms and soles (tylosis) also may be prominent. The epidermal thickening of the palms may produce the appearance of tripe palms.

Schwartz has proposed that acanthosis nigricans, florid cutaneous papillomatosis, hyperkeratosis of the palms and soles, and the sign of Leser-Trélat may be viewed as a continuum of similar responses to malignancy-associated factors. He further points out that these distinct cutaneous lesions may occur alone or together.

Annotated Bibliography

Cruz PDJ, Hud JAJ. Excess insulin binding to insulin-like growth factor receptors: proposed mechanism for acanthosis nigricans. J Invest Dermatol 1992;98:82S–91S.

This is a thought-provoking article.

Ellis DL, Kafka SP, Chow JC, et al. Melanoma, growth factors, acanthosis nigricans, the sign of Leser-Trélat and multiple acrochordons. A possible role for alpha-transforming growth factor in cutaneous neoplastic syndromes. N Engl J Med 1987;317: 1582–1587.

This thought-provoking paper demonstrates that there were increased quantities of epidermal growth factor receptors throughout all the nucleated keratinocyte layers and hyperproliferative lesions, compared with those found in normal epidermal tissue. Following surgical removal of the melanoma, there was a decrease in the density of epidermal growth factor receptors with the staining returning toward the normal primary basilar-cell staining. Prior to the removal of the melanoma, the patient's urine fractions demonstrated intense staining for transforming growth factor alpha (TGF-α), which could not be detected in normal urine.

These investigators hypothesize that the cutaneous paraneoplastic syndromes of acanthosis nigricans, the sign of Leser-Trélat, and multiple acrochordons were the result of the increased density of epidermal growth factor receptors and the presence of TGF-α.

Nodular Fat Necrosis

Tender, erythematous nodules involving all areas of the body, characterized as firm and tender, freely movable, and not attached to either the skin or underlying fascia, have been described in association with carcinoma of the pancreas. Fever, anorexia, weight loss, and an inflammatory arthritis may also be present.

Biopsy of these lesions demonstrates a central area of coagulation necrosis, surrounded by fat-laden macrophages and rare giant cells. Ghost-like fat cells consisting of the cellular remnants of lipocytes are seen.

This syndrome is associated with chronic pancreatitis, lipase-secreting acinar cell pancreatic adenocarcinomas. High levels of lipase and amylase are associated with this syndrome.

Annotated Bibliography

Potts DE, Mass MF, Iseman MD. Syndrome of pancreatic disease subcutaneous fat necrosis and polyserositis: case report and review of the literature. Am J Med 1975;58: 417–423.

This is an excellent review of the association of nodular fat necrosis with pancreatitis and acinar and pancreatic adenocarcinomas.

Annotated Bibliography

Ihde DC. Paraneoplastic syndromes. Hosp Prac 1987;22(8):105–112, 117–124.

Kurzrock R, Cohen PR. Cutaneous paraneoplastic syndromes in solid tumors. Am J Med 1995;99:662–671.

Poole S, Fenske NA. Cutaneous markers of internal malignancy. II. Paraneoplastic dermatosis and environmental carcinogens. J Am Acad Dermatol 1993;28:147–164.

These three very good articles describe the paraneoplastic syndromes associated with various tumors.

Poole S, Fenske NA. Cutaneous markers of internal malignancy. I. Malignant involvement of the skin and the genodermatoses. J Am Acad Dermatol 1993;28:1–13.

This well-written review, especially of genodermatoses and the associated malignancies, is well referenced, containing 141 citations.

Dunn T, Laman SD. Cutaneous manifestations of internal malignancy. In: Stein JH, ed. Internal Medicine. St. Louis: Mosby, 1998, pp 1316–1320.

Ha V, Laman SD. Cutaneous manifestations of gastrointestinal diseases. In: Stein JH, ed. Internal Medicine. St. Louis: Mosby, 1998, pp 1320–1322.

These two articles detail the cutaneous features associated with internal malignancies.

CHAPTER 30

Hereditary Paraneoplastic Syndromes

Thomas T. Provost, M.D., Susan D. Laman, M.D., Francis M. Giardiello, M.D.

There are various genodermatoses associated with the development of internal malignancies. They are listed in Table 30–1.

Muir-Torre Syndrome

Clinical Features

This autosomal dominant syndrome, initially described by Muir et al. in 1967 and Torre in 1968, is characterized by a spectrum of sebaceous growths. These yellowish papular sebaceous growths occur on the face and trunk and range pathologically from sebaceous hyperplasia, sebaceous adenoma, sebaceous epithelioma basal cell carcinoma with sebaceous differentiation to sebaceous car-

TABLE 30–1 Hereditary Cutaneous Paraneoplastic Syndromes

Cutaneous Diseases	Malignancy
Muir-Torre syndrome	Colon cancer
Gardner's syndrome	Colon cancer, duodenal, pancreatic, thyroid, brain, hepatoblastoma
Cowden disease	Breast and thyroid cancer, gynecologic malignancy
Peutz-Jeghers syndrome	Gastrointestinal, pancreatic, lung, breast, gynecologic malignancy
Nevoid basal cell carcinoma syndrome	Medulloblastoma
Neurofibromatosis type 1	Gliomas, sarcomas
Neurofibromatosis type 2	Acoustic neuroma, meningioma
Xeroderma pigmentosum	Melanoma and nonmelanoma skin cancer
Ataxia telangiectasia	Lymphomas
Multiple endocrine neoplasia syndromes	Medullary carcinoma, pheochromocytoma
Bloom's syndrome	Leukemia, lymphoma, gastrointestinal cancer
Fanconi's anemia	Leukemia, squamous cell carcinoma (oral, esophageal)
Dyskeratosis congenita	Oral, nasal, esophageal, and cervical cancer
Howell-Evans' syndrome	Esophageal cancer (see discussion on tylosis and tripe hands in "Paraneoplastic Dermatoses," Chapter 29)

cinoma. The presence of a solitary sebaceous gland tumor on the eyelid is thought to be pathognomonic.

Autosomal dominant; papular, nodular, sebaceous growths
Range pathologically from sebaceous hyperplasia to malignancy
Solitary sebaceous eyelid growth thought to be pathognomonic
Associated with gastrointestinal, genitourinary, and hematologic malignancies

Colonic cancers arising from polyps, predominantly in the proximal colon, are common. In addition, malignancies of the larynx, breast, endometrium, and urogenital tract, as well as hematologic malignancies, have been described.

Regular medical checkups with a focus on gastrointestinal endoscopic examinations are mandatory (Table 30–2).

Etiology

Genomic instability caused by hypervariability in simple repeat sequences
Suggests mutations in mismatch repair genes

Repair genes hMSH2 and hMLH1

There is evidence that the Muir-Torre syndrome is associated with microsatellite genomic instability caused by instability at simple repeat sequences. Expansion or contractions of simple repeat sequences (eg, adenine, cytosine) are seen at different chromosome locations in human colon tumors. Expression of this genetic instability may cause further mutations. Microsatellite instability in the tumor cells from hereditary nonpolyposis colon cancer correlate with mutations in mismatch repair genes (hMSH2 and hMLH1). These genes are located on chromosomes 2p22–21 and 3p21–23. Defects in this repair pathway can theoretically facilitate cancer development.

Annotated Bibliography

Housholder MS, Zeligman I. Sebaceous neoplasms associated with visceral carcinomas. Arch Dermatol 1980;116:61–64.

TABLE 30–2 Hereditary Gastrointestinal Disease Associated with Malignancy Syndromes

Disorder	Clinical Features and Associated Malignancies	Gene	Screening Tests
Muir-Torre	Colonic polyposis and malignancy Genitourinary malignancy Sebaceous tumors	Autosomal dominant Chromosome 2p22–21 Chromosome 3p21–23	Colonoscopy every 3 years Urinalysis yearly
Gardner's	Familial adenomatous polyposis with malignancies and extraintestinal manifestations Osteomas Lipomas Desmoids Pigmented ocular lesions	*APC* gene Chromosome 5q21 Autosomal dominant	First-degree relatives: evaluate for *APC* gene If positive sigmoidoscopy Ages 12–25, yearly Ages 26–35, every 2 years Ages 36-50, every 3 years Surveillance Endoscopy of retained rectum every 6 months Endoscopy every 1 to 4 years for duodenal cancer Thyroid examination yearly
Turcot's	Polyps/polyposis with malignancies and central nervous system tumors Medulloblastoma Glioblastoma Astrocytoma	*APC* gene Autosomal dominant	Colonic surveillance similar to Gardner's syndrome
Peutz-Jeghers	Small intestinal polyps with extraintestinal manifestations Melanin pigmentation Lips Buccal mucosa Hands, feet, eyelids Nongastrointestinal malignancy Breast Ovary Endometrium Pancreas	STK11 gene Chromosome 19p Autosomal dominant	Males beginning at age 25 Yearly CA 19 determination Yearly hematocrit Biannual upper and lower endoscopy Biannual small-bowel series Biannual abdominal CT Females beginning at age 15 Biannual upper and lower endoscopy Biannual small-bowel series Biannual abdominal CT Females beginning at age 18 Yearly mammography

CT = computed tomography scan.

This article provides a discussion of sebaceous growths associated with this hereditary paraneoplastic syndrome.

Weinstein IB, Carothers AM, Santella RM, et al. Molecular mechanisms of mutagenesis and multistage carcinogenesis. In: Mendelsohn J, Howley PPM, Israel MA, Liotta L, eds. The Molecular Basis of Cancer. Philadelphia: WB Saunders, 1995, 4, p 70.

This is a discussion of genomic instability, its association with the mismatch repair genes, and its correlation with hereditary nonpolyposis colonic cancer.

Gardner's Syndrome

Clinical Features

"Gardner's syndrome" is the term applied to familial adenomatous polyposis (FAP) patients with extra colonic manifestations.

Extra colonic manifestations in FAP patients

In 1953, Gardner described this autosomal dominant syndrome as characterized by epidermoid cysts of the face, scalp, and trunk (Figure 30–1); osteomas of the maxilla, mandible, and cranium (Figure 30–2); desmoids and other fibrous tumors of the skin and subcutaneous tissue; and intestinal polyposis with a high rate of malignant transformation (Figure 30–3).

Epidermoid cysts
Osteomas of flat bones of face and skull
Desmoid tumors

Frequency of occurrence is 1 per 8,000 to 14,000 births. Polyposis usually develops by the age of 15 and is unusual after age 35.

The desmoids are fibrous, locally invasive neoplasms, composed of proliferating fibroblasts. They commonly occur on the lower abdomen. The lesions are firm, irregular tumors attached to muscles or to the abdominal mesentary. Retroperitoneal desmoid formation is a severe complication of abdominal surgical procedures in these patients. Although most commonly associated with Gardner's syndrome, desmoids can occur in the absence of this syndrome. These

Locally invasive fibromas

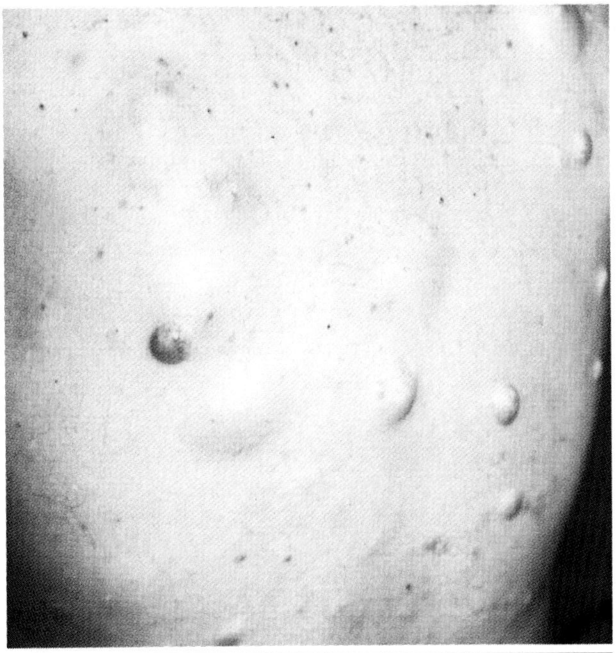

FIGURE 30–1 Multiple epidermoid cysts on the back of a patient with Gardner's syndrome.

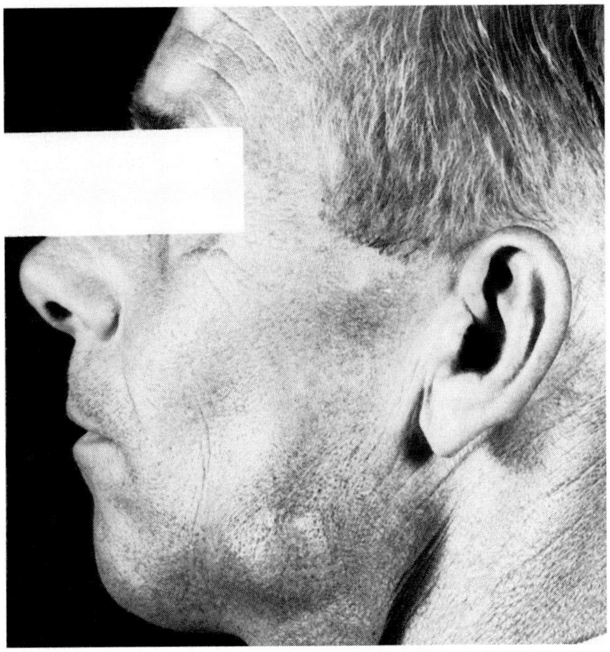

FIGURE 30–2 Gardner's syndrome/FAP patient with osteoma at angle of jaw and epidermal cyst on forehead. (Reprinted from Giardiello F. GI polyposis syndromes and HNPCC. In: Rustgi A, ed. Gasstrointestinal Cancers. Philadelphia: Lippincott-Raven, 1995.)

tumors contain estrogen receptors and may undergo increased growth during pregnancy. Preliminary data suggest tamoxifen and the nonsteroidal anti-inflammatory drug sulindac may be successful in treating some desmoids. Wide surgical excision is necessary to effect a cure.

Gardner's syndrome, FAP syndrome, and Turcot's syndrome are phenotypically different presentations of same genetic defect—5q21.

Gardner's syndrome is also related to Turcot's syndrome (a central nervous system malignancy [meduloblastoma] associated with FAP). The genetic defect in FAP, Gardner's, and Turcot's syndromes is mutation of the *APC* (adenomatous polyposis coli) gene on the fifth chromosome (5q21). Large FAP kindreds have family members with and without extracolonic manifestations, including brain tumors. The cause of the phenotypic variation is unknown.

Malignant degeneration of polyps approaches 100%.

Malignant transformation of the colonic adenomatous polyps occurs in approximately 100% of patients unless colectomy is performed. The second most common malignancy in these patients is carcinoma of the ampulla of Vater in the duodenum.

Because FAP is an autosomal dominant disorder, screening of at-risk relatives is recommended at age 10 to 12 years by *APC* gene testing or annual sigmoidoscopy. In affected patients, endoscopic evaluation of the stomach and duodenum is recommended every 1 to 4 years.

Prophylactic colectomy with either an ileorectal anastomosis or an endorectal pull-through procedure preserving the anal sphincter is recommended. If rectal mucosa is remaining, there is an increased risk for rectal carcinoma. Thus, continued endoscopic surveillance is mandatory.

Sulindac and calcium, in preliminary studies, have produced regression in size and number of polyps.

Retinal pigmentation abnormalities
Annual sigmoidoscopies
Endoscopic examination of stomach and duodenum every 3 years

In addition to colonic and small-bowel carcinomas, studies of large pedigrees have revealed thyroid and pancreatic carcinomas, hepatoblastomas, nasopharyngeal angiofibroma, dental abnormalities, and a peculiar retinal abnormality characterized by oval, pigmented lesions, together with tall, normal, retinal, pigmented epithelial cells (Figure 30–4).

(We have recently seen an anti-Ro (SS-A) antibody–positive systemic cutaneous lupus erythmatosus patient with a photosensitive malar dermatitis. A routine eye examination performed as a baseline before starting hydroxychloroquine detected this eye abnormality. Family history revealed multiple relatives succumbing to colon cancer.)

Etiology

The adenomatous polyposis coli (*APC*) gene is a relatively large gene with at least 15 exons encoding a protein of 2843 amino acids. The protein's function is

FIGURE 30–3 Colectomy specimen demonstrating diffuse polyposis, from a patient with familial adenomatous polyposis.

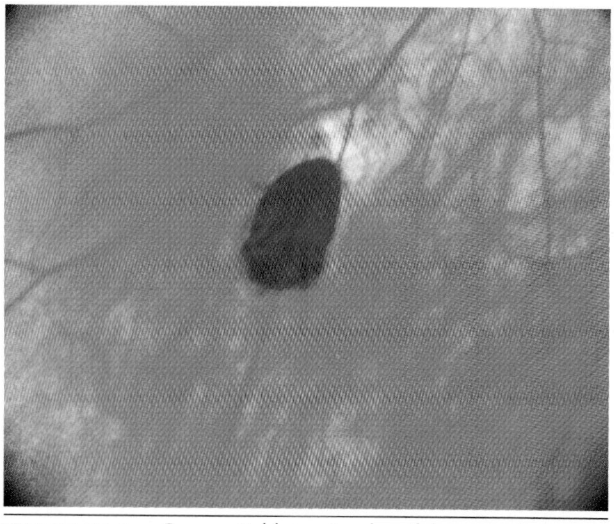

FIGURE 30–4 Congenital hypertrophy of the retinal pigment epithelium in a patient with familial adenomatous polyposis.

unknown, but it is predicted to be localized to the cytoplasm. The *APC* gene appears to be expressed in most tissues. Germline mutations have been identified in about 80% of the FAP and Gardner's syndrome families. These mutations include gross deletions of the gene and point mutations, which cause frame shifts or create stop codons or missense mutations in the gene product. Thus far, the location of germline mutations in FAP and Gardner's syndrome patients have detected no gene mutations to explain variation in phenotypic expression between the two syndromes. In some patients, the mutations identified are identical at the DNA level in patients with both Gardner's and FAP syndrome.

Various gene defects have been detected: gross deletions, frame shifts, stop codons, missense

Thus far, no gene defects have been identified to explain phenotypic variation.

The identification of the *APC* gene on chromosome 5q21 and the demonstration of germline alterations in the gene in 80% of families with FAP and Gardner's syndrome form the basis for genetic counseling for families at risk for polyposis. As noted above, those individuals who have inherited a mutant allele should be closely monitored with frequent colonoscopic examinations (see Table 30–2).

Importance of detecting gene defect in family members

Annotated Bibliography

Ristgi AK. Hereditary gastrointestinal polyposis and non polyposis syndromes. N Engl J Med 1994;331:1694–1702.

This is an excellent review of gastrointestinal polyposis. The article also provides a discussion of the clinical and genetic screenings of kindreds with familial adenomatous polyposis.

Traboulsi EI, Krush AJ, Gardner EJ, et al. Prevalence and importance of pigmented ocular fundus lesions in Gardner's syndrome. N Engl J Med 1987;316:661–667.

This study demonstrates the presence of darkish brown or black patches of pigment lying deep in the retina in patients with Gardner's syndrome. Other lesions vary from light brown to dark brown or black and are ovoid in shape. These lesions tend to be at the periphery of the retina and areas around them show evidence of diffuse disturbances of retinal pigment epithelium. Their data indicate that bilateral pigmented lesions have a specificity for Gardner's syndrome of 0.952 and a sensitivity of 0.780. It should be noted that several patients with Gardner's syndrome failed to demonstrate these lesions.

Steinbach G, et al. The effect of celecoxib, a cyclooxygenase-2 inhibitor, in familial adenomatous polyposis. N Engl J Med 2000;342:1946–1952.

This is a double-blind placebo control study which demonstrated that 6 months of twice daily treatment with 400 mg of celecoxib, a cyclooxygenase-2 inhibator, produced a 28% reduction in the mean number of colorectal polyps, and a 30.7% reduction in the polyp burden (the sum of polyp diameters). This compared to reductions of 4.5% and 4.9% respectively in the placebo group.

Cyclooxygenase-2 is upregulated in clonic neoplasms including adenomas and carcinomas. The specific cellular pathways responsible for the effects of cyclooxygenase-2 on tumorigenesis is not known at the present time. However, cyclooxygenase-2 mediates mitogenic growth factor signaling, and downregulates apoptosis, thus promoting tumor growth. The induction of apoptosis by selective inhibition of cyclooxygenase-2 is thought to be of central therapeutic importance in familial adenomatous polyposis in which apoptosis is considered to be attenuated.

Jänne PA, Mayer RJ. Chemo prevention of colorectal cancer. N Engl J Med 2000;342: 1960–1968.

This is an excellent review of the molecular events occurring in the progressive development of colon cancer. It also details the mechanism of action of non steroidal anti-inflammatory drugs, folate, calcium, and estrogens in the prevention of colon cancer. The article contains 99 references.

Winawer SJ, et al. A Comparison of colonscopy and double contrast barium enema for surveillance after polypectomy. N Engl J Med 2000;342:1766–1772.

This study indicates that colonscopic examination is a more effective method of surveillance than double contrast barium enema in high risk patients.

Tsao H. Update on familial cancer syndromes and the skin. J Am Acad Dermatol 2000; 42:939–969.

This is an excellent update article detailing the genetic basis of familial cancer syndromes involving the skin. It contains 302 references.

Cowden Disease

Autosomal dominant
Multiple trichilemmomas
Cobblestone appearance of oral mucosa

Cowden disease, also known as "multiple hamartoma syndrome" is named for the propositus. Described in 1963, this autosomal dominant disease is characterized by multiple trichilemmoma papules involving the central portion of the face and ears. Mucous membrane trichilemmomas can be prominent, giving a cobblestone appearance. Acrokeratotic lesions of the hands may resemble flat warts. Developmental abnormalities (highly arched palate, adenoid facies) may be detected.

Increased frequency of thyroid and breast malignancies

Breast cancers (often bilateral) appear to occur with increased frequency (approximately one-third of patients). Thyroid tumors, more commonly adenomas than carcinomas, occur. In addition to thyroid and breast malignancies, gastrointestinal tract polyposis (involving the entire gastrointestinal tract, but most commonly the sigmoid and rectum) are also detected. These polyps are not at increased risk for malignant transformation.

Annotated Bibliography

Gentry WC Jr, Eskritt NR, Gorlin RJ. Multiple hamartoma syndrome (Cowden disease). Arch Dermatol 1974;109:521–525.

This article provides a good description of the clinical features.

Peutz-Jeghers Syndrome

Cutaneous and mucous membrane pigmentations
Mucosal pigmentation persists, cutaneous pigmentation disappears

This autosomal dominant syndrome is characterized by hyperpigmented macules involving both the skin and mucous membrane. It occurs once in 8,300 to 29,000 births. Characteristically, at birth or early infancy grouped brownish, macular, pigmented lesions are detected around the mouth and central portion of the face. In addition, fingers, toes, palms, and soles may also be involved with this pigmented process. These lesions may disappear with puberty. The mucosal pigmented lesions, however, persist for life (Figure 30–5).

Approximate 100- fold increased frequency of pancreatic carcinoma

This syndrome is associated with hamartomatous polyps (0.1–4.0 cm in size), most commonly involving the small bowel. Malignant transformation may occur. Other tumors occurring with increased frequency include granulosa theca cells, pancreatic carcinoma, breast carcinomas, adenocarcinomas of the cervix, and testicular cancer. There is a 100-fold risk of pancreatic carcinoma and one study indicates that the overall cancer relative risk in Peutz-Jeghers syndrome approaches 18.

It is recommended that gastrointestinal polyps greater than 1.5 cm be removed. Also, cancer screening must take into consideration increased gynecologic and breast cancers. The large macular hyperpigmented lesions on the face with a histologic appearance of a freckle, have been successfully treated with lasers.

Annotated Bibliography

Giardiello FM, Welsh SB, Hamilton S, et al. Increased risk of cancer in the Peutz-Jeghers syndrome. N Engl J Med 1987;316:1511–1514.

This study demonstrated that 15 of 31 patients (48%) developed malignancies. These malignancies included adenocarcinomas involving the stomach, pancreas, colon, lung, and ovary. In addition, ductal carcinomas of the breast and multiple myeloma were detected. These data indicate that Peutz-Jeghers syndrome patients have an 18 times greater frequency of cancer than expected in the general population. P value is < .0001.

The frequency of pancreatic carcinoma observed in this patient population represents a 100-fold excess of pancreatic carcinoma in this patient population. Of special concern is that Peutz-Jeghers' patients not only have a tendency to develop gastrointestinal and nongastrointestinal malignancies, but they appear to have an increased frequency of breast and gynecologic malignancies.

Jeghers H, McKusick VA, Katz KH. Generalized intestinal polyposis and melanin spots of the oral mucosa, lips, and digits. N Engl J Med 1949;241:993–1005.

This is a classic, scholarly description of this syndrome.

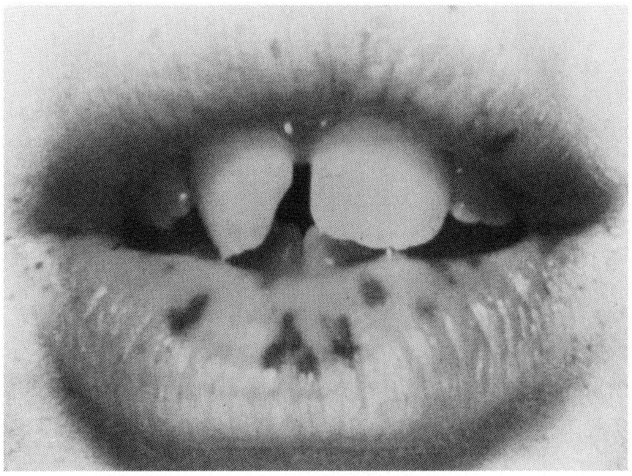

FIGURE 30-5 Patient with Peutz-Jegher syndrome demonstrating characteristic melanin pigmentation on the lips. (Reprinted from Giardiello F. GI polyposis syndromes and HNPCC. In: Rustgi A, ed. Gastrointestinal Cancers. Philadelphia: Lippincott-Raven, 1995.)

Spigelman AD, Murday V, Phillips RKS. Peutz-Jegher syndrome and cancer. Gut 1989;30:1588–1590.

This article from the United Kingdom reports 16 malignancies among 72 patients with Peutz-Jeghers syndrome (22%). There was a relative risk of 13 for death occurring from gastrointestinal malignancies, and the relative risk of dying from any malignancy was 9. The chance of dying of cancer by the age of 57 years was 48%.

Nevoid Basal Cell Carcinoma Syndrome

This syndrome consists of multiple basal cell carcinomas, palmar pitting, cystic lesions of the mandible, skeletal abnormalities, and malignancy (Figures 30–6 to 30–9).

Nevoid basal cell carcinoma syndrome:
- *pitting of palms*
- *jaw cysts*

Should avoid radiation and sun exposure

The most common malignant tumor is a medulloblastoma. Astrocytomas, meningiomas, and craniopharyngiomas can occur. On occasion, fibrosarcoma and Hodgkin's disease have been reported. These patients develop increased fre-

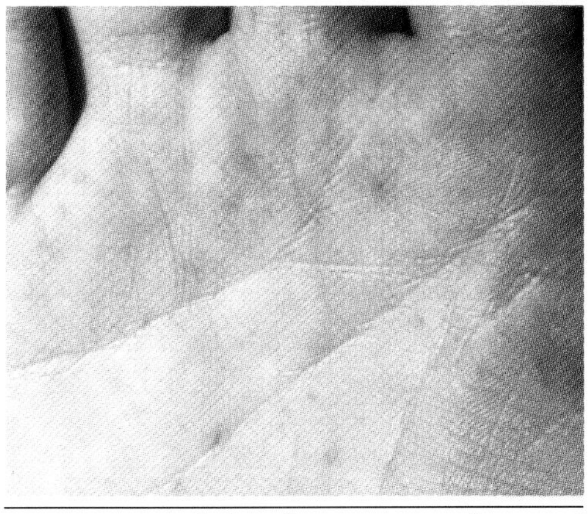

FIGURE 30-6 Palm of a patient with nevoid basal cell syndrome. Note pits.

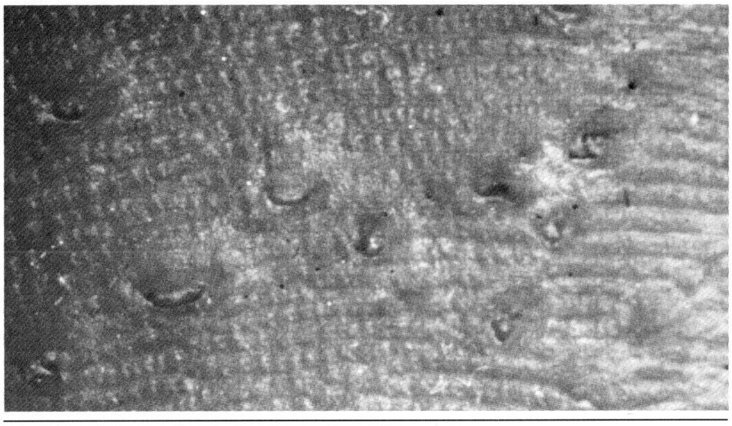

FIGURE 30-7 Close-up of palmar pits in a patient with nevoid basal cell syndrome.

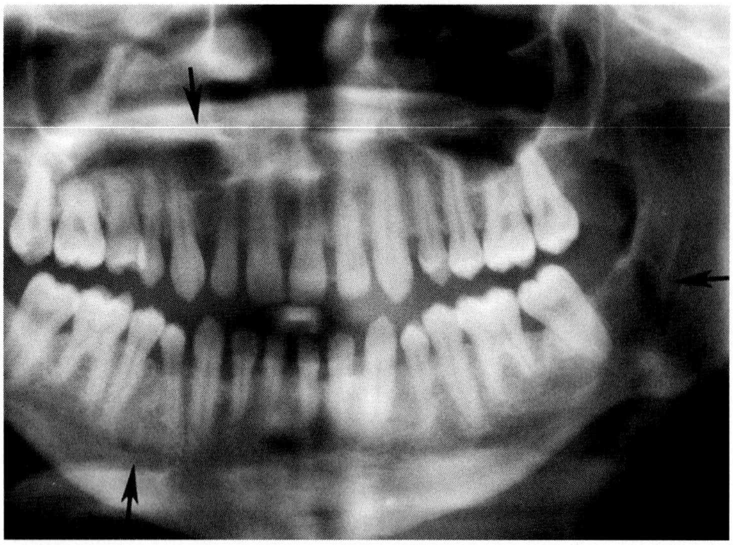

FIGURE 30–8 Radiographic image showing multiple cysts in the mandible and maxillary bones (arrows) in the jaw of a nevoid basal cell syndrome patient.

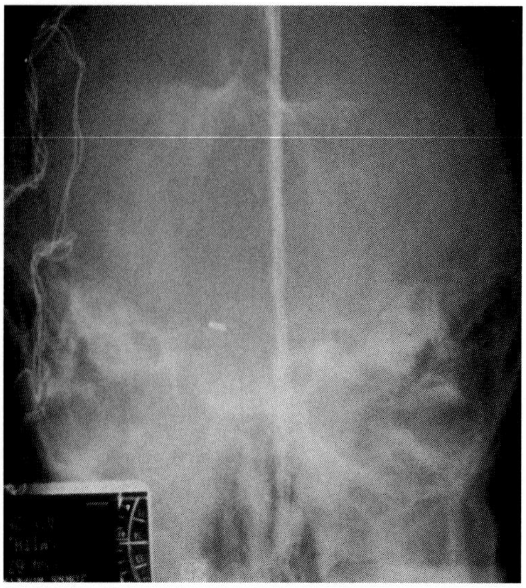

FIGURE 30–9 Calcification of falx cerebri in a nevoid basal cell syndrome patient.

quency of skin tumors on exposure to ultraviolet light and x-ray radiation. (For further discussion of *PTCH* gene mutations and clinical features, see Chapter 26, "Basal Cell and Squamous Cell Carcinomas.")

Annotated Bibliography

Gorlin RJ. Nevoid basal cell carcinoma syndrome. Medicine 1987;66:98–113.

This is an excellent review of this syndrome by a recognized leader in the field. It details findings in 53 patients and documents both the common as well as the lesser known manifestations of this disorder.

The article points out that the skin tumors, which were originally thought to be independent of sun exposure, are more frequent in sun-exposed areas and in areas subjected to radiation therapy (eg, treatment of medulloblastoma). The article also emphasizes that other forms of neoplasia exist in this syndrome: medulloblastoma, meningioma, ovarian fibroma, ovarian fibrosarcoma, and chylous cysts of the mesentery.

Neurofibromatosis

NF1 associated with proliferation of cells derived from neural crest

Neurofibromatosis, especially neurofibromatosis type 1 (NF1), has been associated with malignant tumors. Neurofibromatosis type 1 is characterized by an abnormal proliferation of neural crest-derived cells. This syndrome occurs once in every 3500 people. In mild forms of the disease, abnormal growth of melanocytes produces café-au-lait spots. In more severe forms, the disease induces proliferation of Schwann cells. Multiple types of tumors occur, including benign neural tumors (peripheral and intracranial) and malignant schwannomas and fibrosarcoma. Acute and chronic myelogenous leukemia has also been reported. (For further discussion, see Chapter 44, "Neurofibromatosis.")

NF1 gene product stimulates GTPase activity. Defect causes signaling for uncontrolled growth.

The NF1 gene encodes a protein that regulates *ras* proteins. The *ras* GTPase-activating proteins have regulating activity on cell growth. The NF1 protein binds to the P21 *ras* proto-oncogene protein and stimulates GTPase activity. In the absence of functioning NF1 protein, *ras* remains in its active (*ras* GTP) form, signaling uncontrolled growth of cells.

The inheritance pattern is autosomal dominant. Like those genetic defects observed with retinoblastoma, P53 and Wilms' tumor genes, the inheritance of one defective allele and the subsequent mutation of the second allele is associated with cancer formation.

NF2 protein interacts with cytoskeleton.

The neurofibromatosis type 2 (NF2) gene encodes a protein that is structurally related to Ezrin/Moesin/Talin family of genes. The products of these genes localize to the internal surface of the plasma membrane and appear to interact with the cytoskeleton. Mutations of this gene occur in patients with NF2. Like NF1, tumors from these patients have lost both copies of the NF2 gene. The most common tumors produced are meningioma and acoustic neuroma. (For further discussion, see Chapter 44, "Neurofibromatosis.")

Annotated Bibliography

Levine AJ. Tumor suppressor genes. In: Mendelsohn J, Howley PM, Israel MA, Liotta LA eds. The Molecular Basis of Cancer. Philadelphia: WB Saunders, 1995, pp 86–104.

This provides a good discussion of the molecular basis of NF1 disease.

Xeroderma Pigmentosum

Xeroderma pigmentosum: increased frequency of all types of skin tumors

Xeroderma pigmentosum is inherited as an autosomal recessive disorder in which children by the age of 2 to 3 demonstrate senility of the skin, basal cell carcinomas, keratoacanthomas, squamous cell carcinomas, and on occasions, malignant melanoma (Figure 30–10). These patients demonstrate abnormal reactivity to ultraviolet light (UV), most commonly in the sunburn (UVB) spectrum (290–320 nm). Both abnormal and normal skin responds with a persistence of erythema for prolonged periods of time. In addition, xeroderma pigmentosum patients have increased frequencies of internal malignancies.

De Sanctis-Cacchione variant

Neurologic abnormalities, including mental deficiency, spastic paralysis, deafness, ataxia, choreoathetosis, and hypo- to areflexia have been reported. This variant is termed "De Sanctis-Cacchione" syndrome. Microcephaly, dwarfism, and immature sexual development occur with increased frequency. These patients have defective ability to repair UV- damaged DNA. Some patients demonstrate a defective ability to excise UV-induced DNA dimers. Other patients show only partial defects in the excision of UV-damaged DNA.

Eight complementation groups

Hybridization techniques fusing fibroblast from a xeroderma pigmentosum patient with normal fibroblast corrects the defect. Fibroblast cultures from affected siblings demonstrate similar levels of defective repair. Fibroblast from one xeroderma pigmentosum patient fused with that of another was found to correct each other's defective repair of UV-damaged DNA (complementation). This observation implied that the two fibroblasts had different defects. Using these techniques, eight complementation groups (A-H) have been detected.

Defective repair of UV-damaged DNA

Based on these observations it has been hypothesized that there is a close relationship between the defective repair of UV-damaged DNA and the development of the multiple malignancies present in these children. However, other studies have demonstrated defective cell-mediated immunity in xeroderma pigmentosum patients, which also could contribute to the increased risk for malignancy.

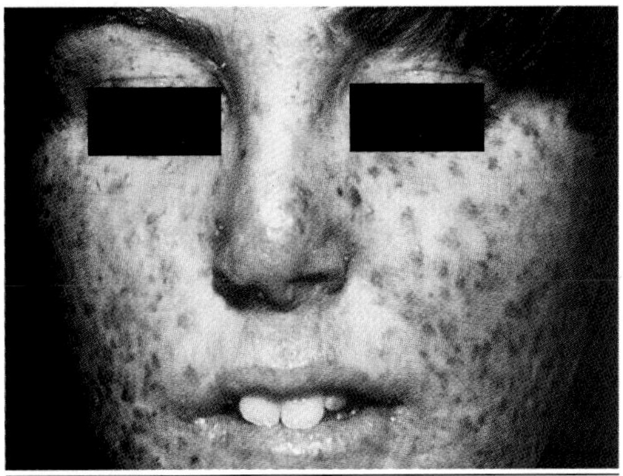

FIGURE 30–10 Multiple lentigines in a patient with xeroderma pigmentosum.

Annotated Bibliography

Kraemer KH, Lee MM, Scotto J. Xeroderma pigmentosum: cutaneous ocular and neurologic abnormalities in 830 published cases. Arch Dermatol 1987;123:241–250.

This literature review of 297 articles indicates that between the first and second year, cutaneous features of sun damage (freckling) was detected. Forty-five percent of patients had a basal cell carcinoma. The median age of the first non-melanoma skin cancer was 8 years. Melanomas were detected in 5% of patients.

Forty percent of patients had ocular abnormalities involving the lid, conjunctiva, and cornea. Neurologic abnormalities occurred in 18%.

Ataxia Telangiectasia

Progressive cerebellar ataxia and increased risk for multiple malignancies

Ataxia telangiectasia is an autosomal recessive disorder. Distinctive ocular telangiectasia occurs within the first year of life followed by the development of progressive cerebellar ataxia. Additional cutaneous telangiectasia involving the face becomes prominent as the child develops. In the second and third decade of life, these patients develop various cancers, including lymphomas, leukemias, cancer of the stomach, liver, ovaries, salivary glands, oral cavity, and pancreas. However, carcinoma of the breast is especially problematic. A heterozygous state is also associated with increased frequency of malignancy. The frequency of ataxia telangiectasia heterozygosity in the general population is 1.4%. It is estimated that 10 to 15% of all breast cancer patients are heterozygous for ataxia telangiectasia. Radiation appears to be a special risk factor in women heterozygous for ataxia telangiectasia. Fibroblasts of patients with ataxia telangiectasia have demonstrated increased sensitivity to radiography but not to UV light irradiation. Five complementation groups have been described.

Heterozygous patients at increased risk to harmful effects of radiation

α–fetoprotein

Defective cell-mediated immunity has also been detected in these patients. These patients possess in their circulation α-fetoprotein.

(For further discussion, see Chapter 20, "Cutaneous Manifestations of Primary Immunodeficiency Diseases.")

Annotated Bibliography

Swift M, Morrell B, Massey RB, et al. Incidence of cancer in 161 families affected by ataxia telangiectasia. N Engl J Med 1991;325:1831–1836.

This study indicates that the ataxia telangiectasia gene predisposes heterozygotes to cancer, especially breast cancer. The estimated risk of cancer of the breast in heterozygous women is 5.1 and for all types of cancer, 3.8 in men and 3.5 in women.

It is estimated that 1.4% of the general population are heterozygous for the ataxia telangiectasia gene. Incidental radiologic exposure from diagnostic radiographic imaging may be of etiologic significance in the development of breast cancer in these cancer-prone individuals.

Homozygous ataxia telangiectasia patients have a risk of cancer of 61 to 184 times higher than that of the general population.

Multiple Endocrine Neoplasia Syndromes

In addition to glucagonoma, ectopic adrenocorticotropic hormone, and carcinoid tumors, autosomal dominant inherited tumors of the endocrine system, termed "multiple endocrine neoplasia (MEN) syndromes" involving these cells, have been described. Two of these syndromes have cutaneous or mucous membrane features.

Cutaneous angiofibromas

The MEN type I syndrome is characterized by pituitary, pancreatic islet, adrenal cortex, and parathyroid tumors. These patients frequently demonstrate cutaneous angiofibromas histologically and clinically reminiscent of tuberous sclerosis. Café-au-lait spots, collagenomas, and lipomas also occur.

MEN-IIb syndrome:
Mucosal neuromas
Marfanoid–habitus

The MEN type IIa syndrome (Sipple's syndrome) is characterized by parathyroid adenomas, bilateral pheochromocytomas, and medullary carcinoma of the thyroid gland (C cells).

The MEN-IIb syndrome is characterized by parathyroid adenomas, bilateral pheochromocytomas, and medullary thyroid carcinoma. In addition, these patients demonstrate multiple mucosal neuromas and a marfanoid habitus. However, unlike Marfan's syndrome, aortic abnormalities and ectopia lentis are absent. (For further discussion, see Chapter 32, "Evaluation and Treatment of Endocrine Disorders.")

Bloom's Syndrome

This is a rare, autosomal recessive, hereditary paraneoplastic disease associated with a gene defect localized to chromosome 15q26.1. The gene encodes a protein that is involved in the unwinding of DNA.

Gene defect chromosome 15q26.1

These patients characteristically have a short stature, photosensitivity, prominent facial telangiectasia, and a defective immune system. Also, they frequently have upper respiratory infections.

Short stature
Facial telangiectasia
Photosensitivity

Approximately 20% of Bloom's syndrome patients develop malignancies most commonly of the skin and gastrointestinal tract and acute leukemias. Many of these malignancies occur before the third decade of life.

Malignancies of the skin and gastrointestinal tract
Acute leukemias

Annotated Bibliography

Getzula JC, et al. Bloom's syndrome. J Am Acad Dermatol 1987;17:479–484.

This article provides a review of the clinical features.

Ellis NA, German J. Molecular genetics of Bloom's syndrome. Hum Mol Genet 1996;5: 1457–1462.

This article provides a valuable discussion of the molecular basics of this disease.

Fanconi's Anemia

This is an autosomal recessive, hereditary disease characterized by progressive pancytopenia, diffuse hyperpigmentation, and musculoskeletal abnormalities.

Progressive pancytopenia
Hyperpigmentation
Musculoskeletal abnormalities

These patients have an increased frequency of chromosomal breakage. Ultraviolet light exposure and radiographic irradiation exacerbate these abnormalities. The exact cause of this hypersensitivity is unknown. The radiation-induced DNA cross-linking is thought to be either a result of defective DNA repair or exaggerated DNA damage induced by irradiation.

Increased in vitro chromosomal breakage with ultraviolet and radiographic irradiation

The bone marrow abnormalities begin in the first decade of life and consist of a hypocellular bone marrow. There is a progressive decrease in all blood elements.

The hyperpigmentation is detected in infancy and is most prominent over the neck, trunk, and joints. Café-au-lait macular and amelanotic lesions are commonly detected.

These patients frequently demonstrate musculoskeletal abnormalities (aplasia and hypoplasia of the thumbs, fingers, and forearms), short stature, hip dislocation, and scoliosis.

Aplasia of distal extremities

Fanconi's anemia patients have an increased frequency of myelogenous leukemia.

Increased frequency of myelogenous leukemia

In general, these patients have a progressive disease that is eventually fatal. In some Fanconi's anemia patients, autologous bone marrow transplantation has been beneficial.

Annotated Bibliography

Zanis-Neto J, et al. Bone marrow transplantation for patients with Fanconi anemia: a study of 24 cases from a single institution. Bone Marrow Transplant 1995;15: 293–300.

This article describes the varied success with autologous bone marrow transplantation.

Joenje H, et al. Evidence for at least eight Fanconi anemia genes. Am J Hum Genet 1997;61:940–948.

This article demonstrates the complex molecular basis of this syndrome.

Dyskeratosis Congenita

Rare X-linked disease
Gene defect localized to X q28

This is a rare, X-linked hereditary disease, characterized by dystrophic nails, photosensitivity, reticulated hyperpigmentation, and leukoplakia. The genetic defect has been localized to X q28. The gene product appears to have a function in normal cell cycle activity.

Photosensitive poikiloderma

Nail dystrophy
Leukoplakia of all mucous membranes
Squamous cell carcinoma

These patients demonstrate a photosensitivity characterized by the development in early childhood of poikilodermatous changes in sun-exposed areas. Nail dystrophy is universal. Leukoplakia involving oral, rectal, and urethral mucosal membranes and the glans penis and vagina is common. Strictures of these epithelial mucous membranes, including the esophagus, occur. Squamous cell carcinomas of the mucous membranes occur with increased frequency.

Progressive bone marrow failure

Dental caries with early loss of teeth is common. Some patients have demonstrated defective immune function. A progressive bone marrow failure, similar to Fanconi's anemia, has been described.

Allogenic bone marrow transplantation has been employed to treat some of these patients.

Annotated Bibliography

Connor JM, Teague RH. Dyskeratosis congenita. Report of a large kindred. Br J Dermatol 1981;105:321–330.

This is a good clinical description.

Heiss NS, et al. X-linked dyskeratosis congenita is caused by mutation in a highly conserved gene with putative nucleolar functions. Nat Genet 1998;19:32–36.

This article describes the molecular basis for the disease.

Kraemer KH. Hereditable diseases with increased sensitivity to cellular injury. In: Freedberg IM, Diser AZ, Wolff K, et al., eds. Fitzpatrick's Dermatology in General Medicine. 5th ed. New York: McGraw-Hill, 1999, pp 1848–1862.

This is a valuable discussion of hereditary diseases with increased sensitivity to cellular injury. The author has contributed much to this area. The chapter has an excellent bibliography.

Howell-Evans Syndrome

(For discussion of Howell-Evans syndrome, see Chapter 29, "Paraneoplastic Syndromes.")

CHAPTER 31

Hormonally Mediated Paraneoplastic Syndromes

Thomas T. Provost, M.D., Amy H. Gordon, M.D., Susan D. Laman, M.D.

Ectopic Cushing's Syndrome

Tumors may also produce cutaneous manifestations by secretion of hormones. The best described hormonally induced paraneoplastic syndromes are those in which neural endocrine derived tumors secrete polypeptides. These tumors are also referred to as "apudomas," which are tumor cells composed of APUD (amine precursor uptake and decarboxylation) properties.

The apudomas are pluripotential cells capable of secreting a variety of biologically active amines and polypeptide hormones. These neuroectodermal-derived cells include the bronchial Kulchitsky cells; the alpha, beta, and delta cells of the pancreas; the thyroid C cells; the chromaffin cells of the adrenal medulla; the intestinal enterochromaffin system cells; the corticotrophs and melanotrophs of the anterior pituitary; the autonomic nervous system cells, chemoreceptor system cells; and the hypothalamic cells producing posterior pituitary hormones.

The tumors produced by these apudoma cells with cutaneous features are listed in Table 31–1.

The most common hormonally associated paraneoplastic syndrome is ectopic Cushing's syndrome. Ectopic Cushing's syndrome is characterized by hyperglycemia, hypokalemia, muscle weakness, hypertension, edema, and weight loss. The rapid growth of the tumor generally does not allow time for the classic cushingoid features of cutaneous striae and centripetal obesity (buffalo hump, moon facies) to develop.

Ectopic Cushing's syndrome:
- *hypokalemia*
- *muscle wasting*
- *edema*
- *hypertension*

Approximately 50% of ectopic Cushing's syndrome cases are associated with carcinoma of the lung, most commonly oat cell bronchogenic carcinoma. Ectopic Cushing's syndrome is also seen with carcinoid, pancreatic islet, thymoma, medullary carcinoma of the thyroid and pheochromocytoma and neuroblastoma tumors. These are neuroendocrine-derived tumors, related embryologically and biologically and, as described above, are pluripotential and capable of secreting numerous hormonally active peptides. In addition, ectopic adrenocorticotropic

Bronchogenic carcinoma of the lung most common

TABLE 31–1 Hormonally Mediated Paraneoplastic Syndromes with Cutaneous Manifestations

Ectopic Cushing's syndrome
Carcinoid syndrome
Glucagonoma syndrome

hormone (ACTH), on occasion, is produced by leukemic cells and ovarian and parotid tumors.

Increased tumor secretion and degradation of pro-opiomelanocortin producing ACTH

Ectopic Cushing's syndrome is secondary to the increased tumor secretion of the prohormone of the ACTH hormone. This prohormone, termed "pro-opiomelanocortin," contains in addition to ACTH, melanocyte-stimulating hormone and endogenous opiate-like substances (β-lipotropin, β-endorphin, and met-enkephalin). Biologically active ACTH and other hormones are produced by the enzymatic cleavage of the prohormone by the tumor. The ACTH stimulates adrenal secretion of mineral and glucocorticoids, as well as androgens.

Hypokalemia may be sole presenting abnormality

Hyperpigmentation may be prominent.

Hypokalemic alkalosis may be the sole presenting manifestation (the cause of the hypokalemia is unknown). Prominent generalized hyperpigmentation may also be present.

In addition to ACTH, other hormonally active peptides are released.

In addition to ACTH, ectopic Cushing's syndrome is frequently associated with the secretion of numerous polypeptides, including antidiuretic hormone, thyroid-stimulating hormone, glucagon, insulin, histamine, and growth factor(s). Furthermore, gonadotropin-like polypeptides may also be secreted, producing painful gynecomastia. Indeed, adult-onset gynecomastia can precede the diagnosis of lung cancer.

Diagnosis

Plasma cortisol and urinary 17-ketosteroids are elevated. Diagnostically, it is characteristic that the ectopic ACTH-secreting-tumor patients fail to demonstrate the diurnal variation in the production of cortisol. In addition, the 48-hour dexamethasone suppression test fails to suppress ACTH production to 40% of baseline values. Exceptions, however, do exist.

Treatment

Successful surgical removal of the ectopic ACTH-secreting tumor is associated with a fall in ACTH levels. If unsuccessful, the drugs designed to inhibit adrenal steroid biosynthesis (eg, aminoglutethimide, metyrapone) are therapeutic options.

Most patients with ectopic Cushing's syndrome have far advanced disease, and palliative therapy is all that can be done.

Annotated Bibliography

Liddle GW, Givens JR, Nicholson WE, et al. The ectopic ACTH syndrome. Cancer Res 1965;25:1057–1061.

This is a classic reference for this syndrome.

Ihde DC. Paraneoplastic syndromes. Hosp Pract 1987;105–124.

This article provides a good discussion of ectopic Cushing's syndrome.

Carcinoid Syndrome

Amy H. Gordon, M.D.

Generally found in gastrointestinal tract and bronchi

The carcinoid syndrome is a complex condition frequently presenting with dramatic cutaneous and systemic manifestations resulting from excess neuroendocrine hormone secretion. Carcinoid tumors arise from enterochromaffin or gut endocrine tissue found primarily in the gastrointestinal tract and bronchial tree. Carcinoids may also rarely occur in the thymus, thyroid, ovaries, and testes.

Incidence and Prevalence

Asymptomatic carcinoid tumor is a commonly detected incidental finding in the appendix and at autopsy

The incidence of carcinoid tumors varies. For instance, carcinoid tumors are noted as an incidental finding in 1 of every 200 to 300 appendectomy specimens (the most common site for carcinoids). They are also noted incidentally in 0.5 to

0.75% of all autopsies. In comparison with other neuroendocrine tumors, carcinoid tumors are 11 times more common than insulinomas and 26 times more common than gastrinomas. Although they may occur at any age, they are more common in individuals aged 50 to 70 years.

Pathogenesis

Secrete serotonin and a variety of bioactive substances

Carcinoid tumors are easily identified by immunohistochemical staining and are characterized by the secretion of serotonin and serotonin breakdown products. Figure 31–1 depicts the synthesis and degradation of serotonin. Under normal conditions, 1% of dietary tryptophan is metabolized to serotonin, which later degrades to 5-hydroxyindoleacetic acid (5-HIAA). In individuals with the carcinoid syndrome, up to 60% of dietary tryptophan may be converted to serotonin leading to an excess of serotonin and its breakdown products.

Carcinoid tumors grow slowly, metastasize late, and secrete a variety of bioactive substances in addition to serotonin.

Classification based on site of origin:
- *foregut*
- *midgut*
- *hindgut*

These tumors can be classified by their site of origin. Some arise from the foregut, most arise from the midgut, and others arise from the hindgut. The site of origin of the tumor usually determines the secretory products and clinical features. For instance, gastric carcinoids (foregut) frequently release large quantities of 5-hydroxytryptamine because they are deficient in the enzyme acid decarboxylase. They also produce histamine. Ileocarcinoids (midgut) secrete large amounts of 5-HIAA. Hindgut carcinoids are generally nonsecretors and are asymptomatic.

Clinical Features

Despite the fact that most carcinoid tumors originate in the gastrointestinal tract, the presentation of carcinoids may be diverse.

Asymptomatic State

Frequently asymptomatic

First, as noted earlier, carcinoid tumors may be entirely asymptomatic and found only incidentally at surgery or autopsy. For example, in one study, only 4% of 3,500 carcinoid patients developed flushing.

Localized Disease

Second, carcinoid tumors may present as a consequence of localized disease, produced by local inflammation and fibrosis associated with the tumor. The presentation depends on the site and spread of the tumor. In the small bowel, for example,

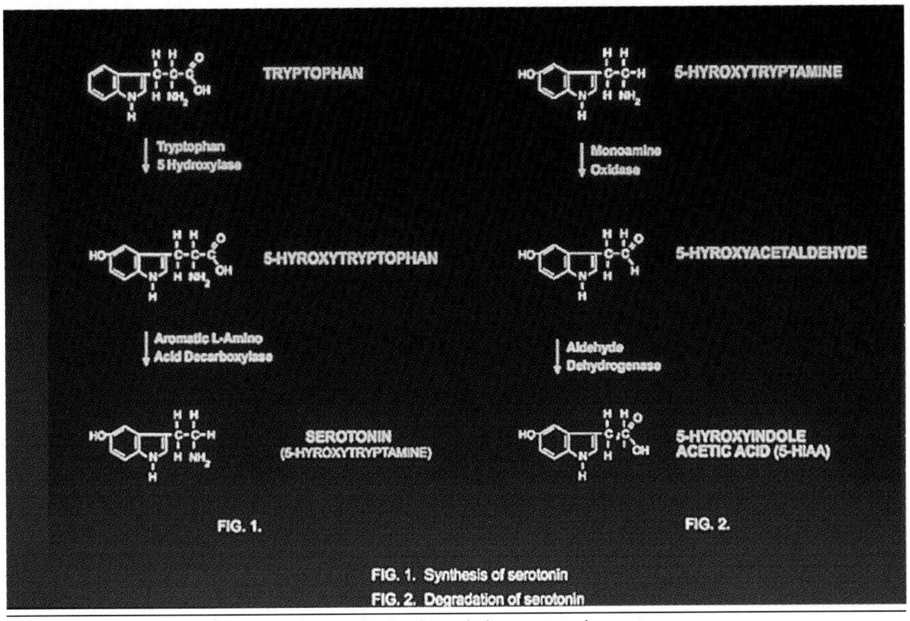

FIGURE 31–1 Serotonin and metabolic breakdown products.

Carcinoid-induced local fibrosis may produce signs and symptoms

fibrosis from a carcinoid tumor may produce mesenteric ischemia, presenting as pain or bowel obstruction. In the lungs, wheezing, coughing, or dyspnea may occur.

Carcinoid Syndrome

Bioactive products detoxified by liver

Only rarely does carcinoid syndrome occur in the absence of metastasis

Third, the tumors may present with carcinoid syndrome. Carcinoid syndrome occurs when sufficient concentrations of hormonal products released by the tumor reach the systemic circulation. In most cases of carcinoid syndrome, the tumor is located in the intestine and drains via the portal circulation, where the hormones are largely metabolized by the first-pass effect of the liver. When the hormones reach sufficient concentration to overwhelm the metabolic capacity of the liver or bypass the liver (eg, metastasis), the carcinoid syndrome becomes manifest. Only in rare cases, such as drainage directly into the systemic rather than the portal circulation as occurs in bronchial, testicular, or ovarian carcinoid, can carcinoid syndrome occur in the absence of overwhelming tumor burden or metastasis (Table 31–2).

The carcinoid flush is seen in up to 95% of patients and is produced by humoral peptides. The flushing associated with foregut tumors is brighter (salmon pink to red), compared with that associated with midgut tumors. It is also more intense and persistent and is associated with wheezing, sweating, lacrimation, and vomiting.

In contrast, midgut carcinoids are associated with a cyanotic hue, together with areas of both erythema and pallor. Bronchoconstriction and hypotension may also occur.

The hindgut carcinoids, as noted above, classically are nonsecretors and are clinically silent.

Cutaneous flush

The carcinoid flush may initially be episodic, associated with facial edema and conjunctival chemosis. The episodic flushing may be precipitated by palpation of the liver or ingestion of alcohol or cheese. With time, however, permanent flushing occurs and the patient may appear to have a recalcitrant form of acne rosacea. This acne rosacea–like picture also includes rhinophyma, facial telangiectasia, and injected sclera.

Although the exact mediator of the flush is unknown, serotonin and histamine are thought to play a role. Serotonin may be influential in producing the cyanotic component. Serotonin antagonists as well as depleters, such as methysergide and parachlorophenylaline, are effective in controlling the diarrhea but have no effect on the erythematous flush. Both H_1 and H_2 antihistamines have been reported to be effective in controlling the erythematous flush. Other drugs, such as clonidine, have also been helpful, suggesting a role for catecholamines.

Pellagra-like lesions

Dietary tryptophan is needed for the formation of protein and nicotinic acid; therefore, pellagra may result from carcinoid tumors that shunt large amounts of dietary tryptophan into the hydroxylation pathway. The pellagra-like skin lesions that occur in the carcinoid syndrome are manifested by photosensitivity, hyperkeratosis, and hyperpigmentation. Patients who develop pellagra may also demonstrate emotional and cognitive dysfunctions.

TABLE 31–2 Clinical Features of Carcinoid Syndrome

Features	Frequency (%)
Flushing	95
Diarrhea	85
Cardiac involvement	50
Bronchospasm	25
Other skin lesions (eg, scleredematous changes)	10

Other cutaneous manifestations include severe pruritus, orange blotches, acropachyderma, pachyperiostitis, and sclerodermatous changes. Cutaneous metastatic nodules are infrequent.

Chronic, watery diarrhea due to gastrointestinal hypermotility occurs in 85% of patients and is frequently the presenting complaint. The diarrhea may be so severe that it results in dehydration. The diarrhea may be induced by vasoactive intestinal peptide secreted by the carcinoid.

Diarrhea frequent and may be severe

The cardiac disease of carcinoid syndrome is manifested by a unique form of fibrosis involving the endocardium. This is primarily on the ventricular surface of the tricuspid valve and on the pulmonary artery surface of the pulmonic valve. Heart failure may develop. Diffuse, patchy, fibrotic areas may also occur in the skin, lungs, bladder, peritoneum, and retroperitoneal spaces. Serotonin and other amines have been implicated in the pathogenesis.

Cardiac fibrosis

Paroxysmal attacks of wheezing, dyspnea, and chest pain may occur in 25% of patients with carcinoid tumors and are related to the release of histamine, serotonin, and other hormones, all of which result in bronchospasm.

Wheezing a frequent occurrence

Diagnosis

The diagnosis of a carcinoid tumor is based on clinical history, documentation of elevated hormone levels, which is usually an elevated 5-HIAA, and localization of the primary tumor and metastatic disease (if present). As most tumors usually occur in the small bowel (appendix), an upper gastrointestinal (GI) examination and a small-bowel series is frequently adequate to localize a primary tumor. A computed axial tomography (CAT) scan is helpful in not only localizing the primary tumor but also determining the extent of metastatic disease, particularly in the liver.

Most tumors in small intestine are detected by routine bowel radiographic studies

Our increasing understanding of carcinoid and other neuroendocrine tumors at a cellular and molecular level has led to the development of several new radiopharmaceutical compounds for imaging. The presence of an increased number of somatostatin receptors has been documented in carcinoid and other neuroendocrine tumors. Somatostatin is a cyclic polypeptide composed of 14 linked amino acids. It commonly depresses the release of many pituitary and extrapituitary hormones and inhibits pancreatic, biliary, and gastrointestinal secretions. Somatostatin has been used to effectively reduce the classic carcinoid flush and diarrheal output in patients with carcinoid tumors. Because native somatostatin has a very short half-life of only 2 to 3 minutes, it is impractical for diagnostic or therapeutic uses. However, octreotide, an 8–amino acid analogue with a similar loop structure that binds to somatostatin binding sites, has a half-life of approximately 2 hours, making it clinically useful. By using nuclear medicine techniques and radiolabeling octreotide with indium-111, carcinoid tumors can be localized by their preferential uptake of indium-labeled octreotide.

Somatostatin receptors found on carcinoid tumors

Octreotide, a somatostatin analogue

^{131}Iodine-metaiodobenzylguanidine (^{131}I-MIBG), an analogue of a bioamine precursor taken up by chromaffin cells and stored in the neurosecretory storage granules, can also be used for scanning carcinoid and other neuroendocrine tumors.

Case Report

History of Present Illness

A 44-year-old Caucasian woman presented with a 5-year history of diarrhea and a 15-pound weight loss. Her initial evaluation included stool studies and colonoscopy with biopsy, which were unrevealing.

Past Medical History

Her past medical history was significant for what was described as "the world's worst case of acne rosacea." She had been treated with topical as well as oral antibiotics and steroid creams, which were not helpful. She had a history of migraine headaches which had been occurring for 4 years. Head CAT scan, performed 2 years previously, was normal. Her headaches had been worsening in the previous 6 months. She also had a history of anterior uterine fibroids.

Physical Examination

The patient was a thin, anxious woman in no acute distress. She was afebrile. Blood pressure was 104/70 mm Hg with a pulse of 60 beats per minute. Abdominal examination revealed a scaphoid abdomen that was nontender. There was no hepatosplenomegaly. An area of fullness in her pelvic area was consistent with her diagnosis of anterior uterine fibroids. Rectal examination was heme-negative and without masses.

Skin examination was notable for the fact that she was wearing very heavy stage makeup through which an intense red hue could be seen (Figure 31–2). After removal of the makeup, marked erythema and telangiectasias involving the forehead, nose, cheeks, chin, and chest were evident. Perioral and periorbital areas were spared. At times, the patient's face had a distinct erythema, and at other times it had a blue cyanotic hue (Figure 31–3). She also had xerotic patches on her arms and legs.

Laboratory evaluation revealed normal chemistry, electrolyte, and thyroid profile. Blood histamine levels were normal. Plasma catecholamines, as well as urinary VMA and metanephrines, were normal. Urinary 5-HIAA was markedly elevated at 91 mg every 24 hours (normal 0 to 9 mg/24 hr).

Because of her striking clinical and biochemical presentations, it was clear that this patient had a carcinoid tumor. Upper GI examination with small-bowel series was performed to locate the primary. The study revealed rapid transit time but no other abnormalities. A CAT scan of the abdomen revealed no intra-abdominal masses, liver metastasis, or adenopathy. A CAT scan of the pelvis revealed a mass just superior to the uterus and of similar density. It was interpreted as a pedunculated uterine fibroid. Ultrasonography and magnetic resonance imaging (MRI) also suggested that this mass was a pedunculated uterine polyp.

An indium-111–labeled octreotide scan, however, localized uptake in the pelvis in the area of the so-called "pedunculated uterine polyp," which suggested that this was, in fact, a carcinoid tumor (Figure 31–4). The patient was taken to the operating room where she was found to have a 8.5-cm, left ovarian mass that was adjacent to the uterus in the location of the pedunculated polyp, a uterus with several small fibroid tumors and a normal right ovary. There was no evidence of metastasis. She underwent bilateral oophorectomy and myomectomy.

Pathology revealed an ovarian carcinoid with no evidence of metastatic disease. Within days, her diarrhea and headaches resolved. Over the ensuing 3 months, she regained her usual weight. Three years postoperatively, she is disease free with a normal urinary 5-HIAA (Figure 31–5).

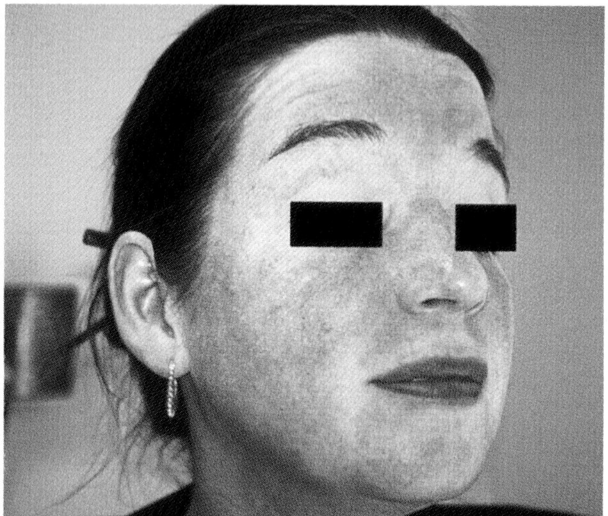

FIGURE 31–2 Bright red flush of carcinoid syndrome.

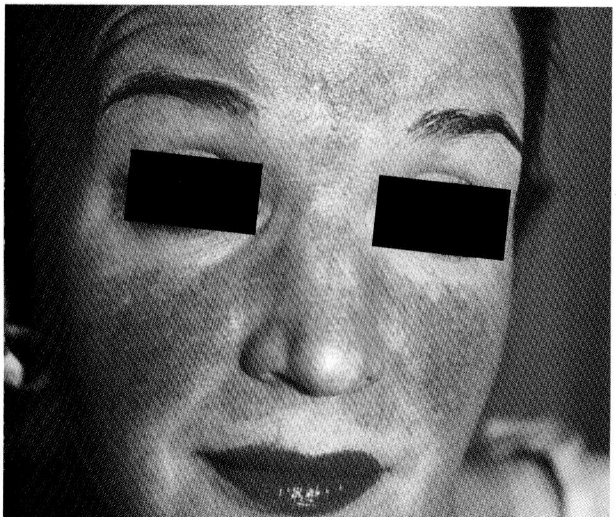

FIGURE 31–3 Dark red, blue, and brown flush of the same carcinoid patient.

Treatment

Although the clinical course is often protracted, carcinoid tumors are malignant. Therapeutic intervention is based on the principles of surgical excision or debulking, combined with other modalities, such as hepatic artery embolization and/or chemotherapy. The use of somatostatin analogues, as well as a variety of other drugs, including interferon-alpha, in combination with other antitumor agents, has controlled the often dramatic symptoms induced by the bioactive amines. Control of debilitating symptoms has also been attempted using 5-hydroxytryptamine antagonists and alpha-2 receptor agonists, such as clonidine, with variable success. (For further discussion, see annotated bibliography.)

Annotated Bibliography

Lubarsch O. Ueber den primaren Krebs des Ileum nebst Bemerkungen uber das gleichzeitige Vorkommen von Krebs und Tuberkulose. Arch Pathol Anat 1888;111: 280–317.

Oberndorfeer S. Karzinoide Tumoren des Dunndarms. Frankf Sch Pathol 1907;1: 416–430.

Masson P. Carcinoids (argentaffin-cell tumors) and nerve hyperplasia of the appendicular mucosa. Am J Pathol 1928;4:181–212.

These classic initial articles describe carcinoid tumors.

Lamberts SWJ, Van Der Lely AJ, De Herder WW, et al. Octreotide. N Engl J Med 1996; 334:246–254.

Forssell-Aronsson E, Fjalling M, Nilsson O, et al. Indium-111 activity concentration in tissue samples after intravenous injection of indium-111-DTPA-D-phea-1-octreotide. J Nucl Med 1995;36:7–12.

Taal BG, Hoefnagel CA, Valdes Olmos RA, Boot H. Combined diagnostic imaging with 131I-metaiodobenzylguanidine and 111Inpentetreotide in carcinoid tumours. Eur J Cancer 1996;32A:1924–1932.

These articles review the use of octreotide and the development of new radiopharmaceuticals for imaging of carcinoid and other neuroendocrine tumors.

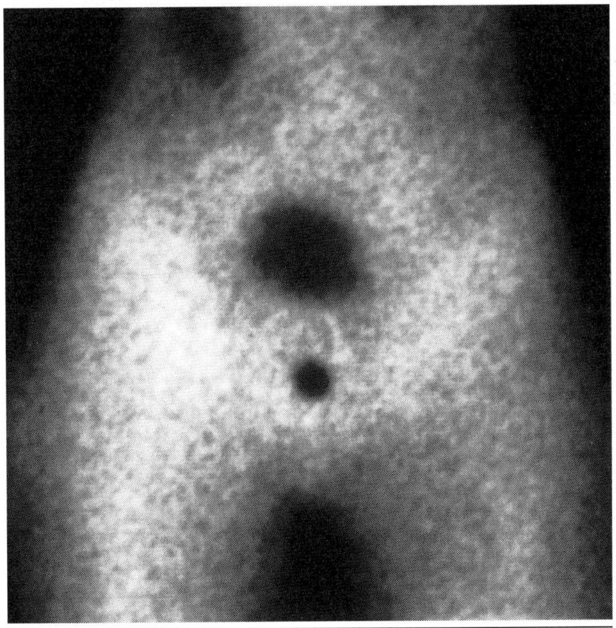

FIGURE 31–4 An indium-111 octreotide scan demonstrating localized uptake in the pelvis (large dark area); small dark collection inferiorly is uptake of radiolabel in bladder; uptake in the right upper quadrant is the liver.

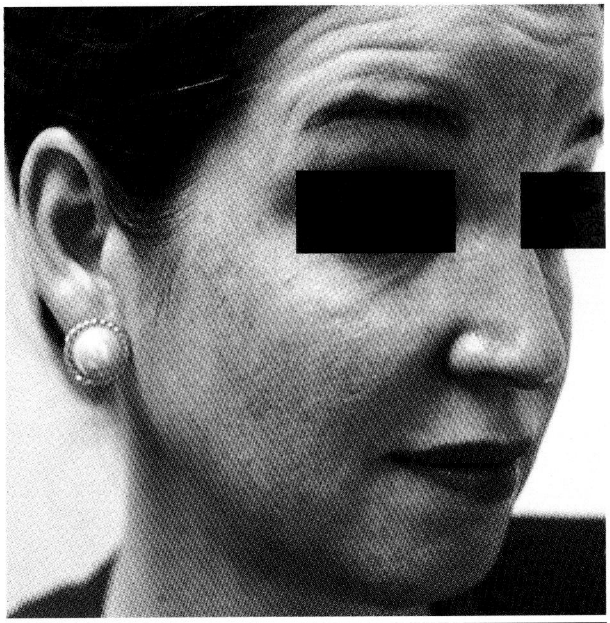

FIGURE 31–5 Picture of carcinoid patient in Figures 31–2 and 31–3, 3 years following surgical removal of the ovarian carcinoid.

Neary PC, Redmond PH, Houghton T, et al. Carcinoid disease: review of the literature. Dis Colon Rectum 1997;40:349–362.

This is an excellent review of the literature on the spectrum of carcinoid disease.

Trapanotto V, Hamper UM, Gordon A, et al. Primary ovarian carcinoid: value of octreotide scintography for diagnosis and correlation with other cross-sectional imaging modalities and pathology. J Ultrasound Med 1997;16:505–508.

This is an article demonstrating that octreotide, a somatostatin analogue, is of value in the detection of carcinoid tumors. In this case, the carcinoid tumor was ovarian in origin.

Newman CB, Melmed S, Synder PJ, et al. Safety and efficacy of long-term octreotide therapy of acromegaly: results of a multicenter trial in 103 patients—a clinical research center study. J Clin Endocrinol Metab 1995;80:2768–2775.

This study demonstrates that octreotide in doses of 100 μg subcutaneously every 8 hours and gradually increased to a maximum of 1,500 μg daily was a safe and effective form of therapy. Gastrointestinal discomfort was the most common side effect. Of interest was that approximately 24% of patients developed silent gallstones during the first year of treatment.

Quatrini M, Basilisco G, Conte D, et al. Effects of somatostatin infusion in 4 patients with malignant carcinoid. Am J Gastroenterol 1983;78:149–151.

This study demonstrates successful control of spontaneous flushes and diarrhea with the infusion of somatostatin. Urinary 5-HIAA and plasma gastrin levels were not significantly affected. This study provides evidence that serotonin and gastrin did not play a major role in the symptoms of diarrhea or the flush associated with carcinoid syndrome.

Diaco DS, Hajarizadeh H, Mueller CR, et al. Treatment of metastatic carcinoid tumors using multimodality of octreotide acetate, intraarterial chemotherapy, and hepatic arterial chemoembolization. Am J Surg 1995;169:523–528.

This study demonstrates this combination therapy effectively retards tumor growth in patients demonstrating metastatic carcinoid tumors. Sixty percent of the patients had a greater than 50% reduction of their tumor size.

Durward G, Blackford S, Roberts D, et al. Cutaneous scleroderma in association with carcinoid syndrome. Br J Dermatol 1994;123;299–300.

This is a report of a case and review of the literature. It indicates that the carcinoid tumors associated with cutaneous scleroderma features are all of midgut origin and that liver metastasis was present. All patients subsequently developed fibrotic heart disease.

Pavolic M, Saiag P, Lotz J-P, et al. Regression of sclerodermatous skin lesions in a patient with carcinoid syndrome, treated with octreotide. Arch Dermatol 1995;131: 1207–1208.

This case report indicates that octreotide (1,500 μg/d) was associated with a complete regression of the cutaneous sclerosis in this carcinoid patient.

Wilkin JK, Rountree CB. Blockade of carcinoid flush with cimetidine and clonidine. Arch Dermatol 1982;118:109–111.

This is a case report indicating that clonidine, an α-adrenergic agonist is effective in preventing the flushing of the carcinoid syndrome. In addition, cimetidine, an H_2 histamine receptor antagonist, but not chloropheneramine, was effective in blocking the flushing in carcinoid syndrome.

Glucagonoma Syndrome

Thomas T. Provost, M.D., Susan D. Laman, M.D.

Glucagonoma syndrome is rare. It is characterized by a distinctive dermatosis, glossitis, glucose intolerance, venous thrombosis, weight loss, and neuropsychiatric manifestations. The distinctive dermatosis, which most commonly involves the pelvic region, is termed "necrolytic migratory erythema" (NME).

Glucagonoma syndrome

Rare

Distinctive dermatosis

Becker, Kahn, and Rothman first described this entity in 1942. However, it was not until 1966 that McGavran et al. first described this entity in association with a glucagon-secreting alpha cell carcinoma of the pancreas.

A recent report of 21 cases (the largest series of cases from one institution) indicated that the presenting clinical features in these 21 patients were NME in 14 (67%), diabetes mellitus in 8 (38%), diarrhea in 6 (29%), and stomatitis in 6 (29%). In a small percentage, abdominal pain, nausea, neuropathy, and a history of thrombosis were detected. One individual had a psychiatric history. All 21 patients demonstrated NME at one point in their disease. Five patients developed thrombosis during the course of their disease. In 3, deep vein thrombosis of the lower extremities was detected. Ataxia, fecal and urinary incontinence, and visual difficulties developed in 3.

Dermatosis, with time, occurs in virtually all patients.

Cutaneous Manifestations

NME is a rare dermatosis. It is characterized by transient, erythematous, weeping eczematous patches with a distinctive collarette of scale. The lesions typically wax and wane over 7 to 14 days, although prolonged intervals of remission (weeks to months) may occur.

Individual lesions begin as erythematous macules and papules, centrifugally spreading with the occasional development of flaccid bullae. Extensive denudation may occur, which is exacerbated by trauma. The lesions are typically located on the perineum, abdomen, and buttocks but have been reported on the hands, feet, and extremities (Figures 31–6 to 31–9). The lesions may be either painful or pruritic. At times, the dermatosis may be confused with eczema craquelé, pemphigus foliaceus, pustular psoriasis, bacterial intertrigo, or candidiasis. NME is frequently accompanied by perioral scale and glossitis. Similar cutaneous eruptions have also been described with zinc deficiency (acrodermatitis enteropathica), biotin deficiency, and fatty acid deficiency.

Necrolytic migratory erythema is transient dermatosis, most prominent in groin and perineum

Glossitis and perioral dermatitis are characteristic.

The classic findings on skin biopsy include a perivascular lymphocytic infiltrate, dermal edema, and necrosis of the upper portion of the epidermis with or without subcorneal pustules. Multiple biopsies may be required to find these changes.

Edema and necrosis of upper portion of epidermis

Pathogenesis

Several mechanisms for NME have been proposed, including hyperglucagonemia, zinc deficiency, fatty acid deficiency, hypoaminoaciduria, and hepatic impairment.

In the past, it has been theorized that elevated glucagon levels associated with glucagonoma were directly responsible for NME. Indeed, debulking procedures, resulting in decreased glucagon levels, were frequently associated with an improvement of the NME. A zinc deficiency was also postulated, as a similar cutaneous change is noted in acrodermatitis enteropathica. This theory has been disproved, since the zinc levels are not decreased in all patients with NME. Improvement of the NME in a patient with glucagonoma has been reported with the administration of intravenous amino acids; however, this does not occur in all cases.

Skin disease similar to acrodermatitis enteropathica

Goodenberger et al. reported two patients with clinical and histologic evidence of NME. Neither had an elevated glucagon level or a pancreatic islet cell

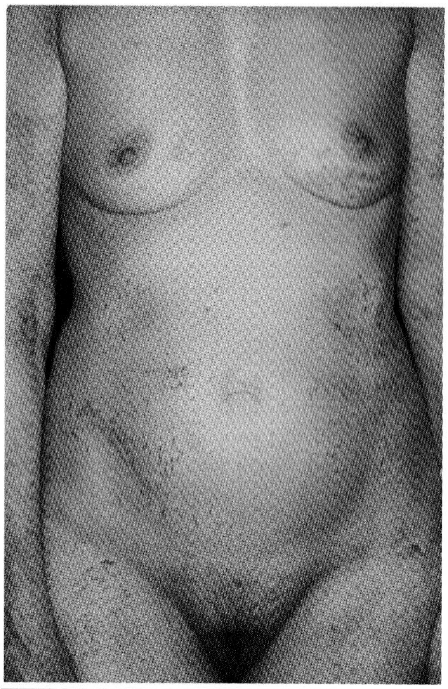

FIGURE 31-6 Widespread eczema cracquelé-like lesions on trunk, thighs, and arms of a glucagonoma syndrome patient. Reproduced with permission from: Binnick AN, et al. Glucagonoma syndrome. Arch Dermatol 1977;113:749–754.

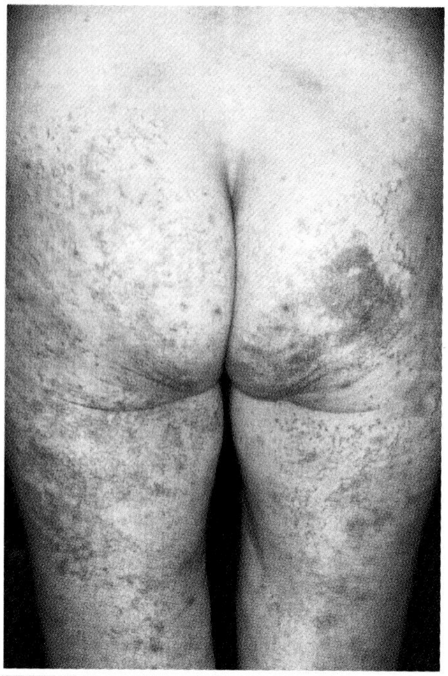

FIGURE 31-7 Widespread eczema cracquelé on buttocks of same patient. Reproduced with permission from: Binnick AN, et al. Glucagonoma syndrome. Arch Dermatol 1977;113:749–754.

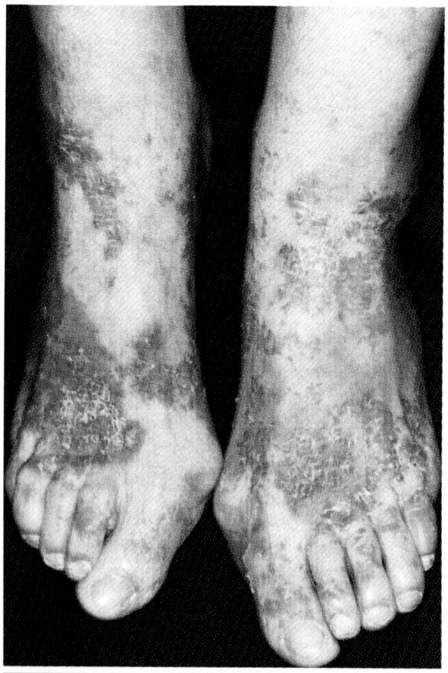

FIGURE 31-8 Acral distribution of erythematous dermatitis associated with glucagonoma syndrome. Reproduced with-permission from: Binnick AN, et al. Glucagonoma syndrome. Arch Dermatol 1977;113:749–754.

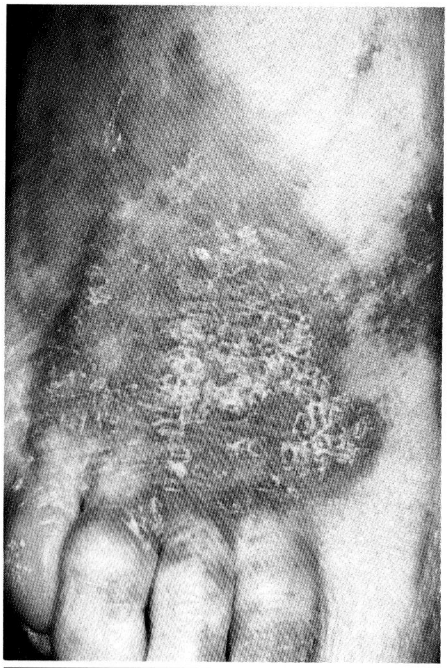

FIGURE 31-9 Close-up of dermatitis on foot of patient with glucagonoma syndrome. Reproduced with permission from: Binnick AN, et al. Glucagonoma syndrome. Arch Dermatol 1977;113:749–754.

tumor. Both, however, had villous atrophy of the small bowel. This was noted in one patient at autopsy and in the other during the workup of chronic diarrhea. In the latter patient, a 25 to 50% reduction in serum amino acid levels was also detected. This patient was treated with diiodohydroxyquin, resulting in complete clearing of the eruption within 1 week. Discontinuation of the drug therapy resulted in the prompt recurrence of the NME.

May occur in absence of elevated glucagon levels or a pancreatic islet cell tumor

Finally, there is evidence that the somatostatin analogue (SMS-209-995) has been employed successfully to treat a patient with metastatic glucagonoma. The rash rapidly disappeared. Since this somatostatin analogue inhibits peptide release from various hormonally active tumors (eg., insulinomas, carcinoids, gastrinomas), it has been theorized that the classic NME may be caused by, although as yet unrecognized, peptide secreted by the glucagonoma.

Best evidence suggests dermatosis induced by an uncharacterized peptide secreted by this islet cell tumor

Laboratory Studies

The majority of patients with NME have glucagonomas, although, as noted earlier, acrodermatitis enteropathica patients may have a dermatitis resembling NME. Also, NME may be seen in patients with low serum amino acid levels, fatty acid deficiency, and hepatic dysfunction. Thus, laboratory evaluation should include those tests to evaluate these conditions.

Patients with a glucagonoma will have an elevated glucagon level. In one series, the mean serum glucagon value was 1,400 pg per mL. The alpha cell has multiple endocrine capabilities, glucagon being only one of several hormonally active peptides that can be secreted. In one study, approximately 50% of glucagonoma patients tested demonstrated additional abnormal hormone levels. For example, vasoactive intestinal peptide was detected in 1 of 17, gastrin levels were abnormal in 4 of 19, 5-hydroxyindoleacetic acid was abnormal in 6 of 14, insulin levels (insulin resistance) were abnormal in 6 of 13, human pancreatic peptide was detected in 2 of 14, calcitonin abnormalities were noted in 2 of 4, and adrenocorticotropin was abnormal in 2 of 13. In addition, 7 of 9 patients demonstrated a significant reduction of multiple amino acid levels in both serum and urine. In contrast to this evidence indicating pancreatic endocrine hyperfunction, exocrine hypofunction detected by a secretin test, which measures bicarbonate and water output, is commonly observed.

Multiple peptides with hormonal activity are detected in glucagonoma patients.

Diagnosis

In addition to the skin biopsy and laboratory studies outlined above, computerized axial tomography (CAT) scans, nuclear magnetic resonance imaging, and arteriograms are of great value in detecting pancreatic carcinoma. In one study of 21 patients, the primary pancreatic tumor was identified in 18 by CAT scans.

Computed axial tomography is a valuable diagnostic tool

Annotated Bibliography

Altimari AF, Bhoopalam N, O'Dorsio T, et al. Use of somatostatin analog (SMS 201-995) in the glucagonoma syndrome. Surgery 1986;100:989–996.

This is a very fascinating article indicating that a somatostatin analogue, which inhibits polypeptide secretion by neuroendocrine tumors, produced a dramatic improvement in the rash associated with glucagonoma within 48 hours, with complete resolution within the first week of treatment. Discontinuance of the somatostatin analogue resulted in the rapid reappearance of the dermatitis.

Since glucagonoma syndrome has been reported in the absence of increased glucagon levels, one can reason from this finding that the somatostatin analogue, in all probability, inhibits the secretion of a polypeptide (not glucagon), which is responsible for the induction of the characteristic dermatitis (Irwin Braverman, in his recent text, has also come to the same conclusion. Braverman I. Skin Signs of Systemic Disease, 3rd ed. Philadelphia: WB Saunders Co., 1998.)

Binnick AN, Spencer SK, Dennison WL, et al. Glucagonoma syndrome: report of two cases and review of the literature. Arch Dermatol 1977;113:749–754.

Becker SW, Kahn D, Rothman S. Cutaneous manifestations of internal malignant tumors. Arch Dermatol 1942;45:1069–1075.

These articles describe the classic cutaneous features of NME.

Wermers RA, Fatourechi V, Wynne AG, et al. The glucagonoma syndrome: clinical and pathological features in 21 patients. Medicine 1996;75:53–62.

This is an excellent summary of the clinical and pathologic features of this syndrome.

Goodenberger DM, Lawley TJ, Strober W, et al. Necrolytic migratory erythema without glucagonoma. Arch Dermatol 1979;115:1429–1432.

This is a very thought-provoking paper reporting two individuals with classic features of NME, unassociated with elevated glucagon levels or pancreatic islet cell tumor. In one of the patients, diiodohydroxyquin produced a prompt and complete clearing of the eruption within 1 week. Both patients had diarrhea, malabsorption, and jejunal villous atrophy.

Black CK, Piette WW. The multi-syndrome spectrum of necrolytic migratory erythema. Curr Opin Dermatol 1995;87–93.

This thought-provoking paper indicates clinically and histologically that similar lesions to NME have been detected in a variety of conditions, especially in protein-, fatty acid–, and vitamin-deficient conditions.

CHAPTER 32

Evaluation and Treatment of Endocrine Disorders

Michael Boyne, M.D., Adrian S. Dobs, M.D., Alan S. Krasner, M.D., Thomas T. Provost M.D.

The development of endocrinology as a specialty occurred during an era when diseases presented in their most extreme and, hence, most recognizable forms. Today, many endocrine diseases are discovered earlier in their natural histories, largely due to the widespread use of objective laboratory tests. Also, physicians are being asked to prevent diseases or, at least, recognize diseases at very early stages, when it is easier to treat/cure and to offset sequelae of these diseases.

The arsenal of diagnostic tests has greatly increased over the past several decades. Consider that 60 years ago doctors had to go through the laborious exercise of measuring a patient's basal metabolic rate by indirect calorimetry to confirm a diagnosis of thyrotoxicosis, whereas it is now done by determining thyroid hormone levels through a simple phlebotomy. However, it is this wide array of complementary and overlapping diagnostic tests that has made the task so daunting for the average physician, as he/she tries to assimilate the information and wade through diagnostic algorithms. Not every test is as easy as a phlebotomy, and obviously, the more invasive testing will carry potential risk, morbidity, or discomfort for the patient. The positive and negative predictive values of each test will also play an important role in deciding which test to choose.

Physical examination of skin, nails, and hair important in evaluating endocrine diseases

The diagnosis of endocrine disorders begins with a careful history, thorough physical examination, and then confirmatory laboratory testing. In general, symptoms associated with endocrine disorders are remarkably nonspecific. Complaints such as alteration in bowel habit, weight gain or loss, anorexia, abdominal pain, changes in hair or nails, rashes, palpitations, decreased libido, anxiety, and depression are very common, and the differential diagnoses for each is enormous. Evaluating each complaint with an exhaustive battery of tests would, of course, be frequently unrewarding, expensive, and taxing on the patient and would produce a high rate of false-positive tests. Consequently, recognition of symptom patterns is very important in order to determine a reasonable pretest probability of disease. Hence, the chance of Graves' disease is more remote in a patient who reports only weight loss than it is in a patient who also reports insomnia, palpitations, and proptosis. The physical examination can be complementary to the history. Many of the signs of endocrine diseases are subtle and localized to the integumentary system, so attention to the skin, nails, and hair is important.

Once it is clinically determined that there is a reasonable chance of an endocrine disease being present, the doctor has to decide on the appropriate diagnostic test. Free hormone levels in plasma or urine at baseline can be helpful, but there is one caveat. Randomly measuring the concentrations of many hormones with short half-lives that are secreted in a pulsatile fashion gives little information about abnormalities in the production of these hormones. Random

Random measurement of hormones rarely helpful

measurements of cortisol and growth hormone, for example, are rarely of much diagnostic value.

Consideration of the existence of feedback loops important when evaluating hormone levels

Hormonal assessment is also based on the fact that most hormones exist in feedback loops, which affects the proper interpretation of the measured concentrations. For example, parathyroid hormone (PTH) is under negative feedback by calcium, and so both need to be assayed simultaneously. At times, pathology is recognized because there is an inappropriate response of the hormone caused by a perturbation. Hence, primary hyperparathyroidism may be diagnosed when there is hypercalcemia, even though the PTH level is (inappropriately) in the normal range. The same is true for the glucose/insulin, thyrotropin/thyroxine, and gonadotropins/sex steroid axes.

The concept of feedback is also exploited by performing diagnostic dynamic testing. In hypersecretory states, attempts are made to suppress hormone production and then to assay the levels of the hormone in question. For example, in Cushing's syndrome when there is chronic hypercortisolism, the doctor looks for the normal suppression of cortisol in response to the administration of exogenous dexamethasone. Conversely, in states of hormonal underproduction, efforts are made to stimulate hormonal production. An example of this is during the evaluation of adrenal insufficiency when exogenous adrenocorticotropic hormone (ACTH) is given in an effort to increase cortisol production by the adrenal glands.

Imaging studies should be performed after hormone abnormality established

Once a biochemical diagnosis is firmly established, then imaging studies of the involved gland are often used to determine the etiology of the identified disorder. Imaging should not be performed until a hormonal disorder is firmly established because as many as 5 to 20% of individuals may have benign gland abnormalities that do not cause identifiable disease states (incidentalomas). Patients with normal endocrine function have little or no reason for imaging studies, with the possible exception of an evaluation for malignancy.

Pituitary

Acromegaly

Growth hormone (somatotropin) stimulates increase in plasma insulin-like growth factor-1
Acromegaly in adults
Gigantism in children

Acromegaly is the syndrome caused by hypersecretion of the growth hormone (GH) somatotropin resulting in an increase in plasma insulin-like growth factor-1 (IGF-1). Its onset is usually insidious, and characteristic physical findings, due to the overgrowth of connective tissue and bone, are usually present by the time it is diagnosed. In children, whose epiphyses are not closed, gigantism is produced. The prevalence of acromegaly has been reported to be between 38 and 69 cases per million in European countries, with an annual incidence of approximately 3 to 4 cases per million. However, it is widely believed that these figures represent under-reporting as the diagnosis is often missed or delayed.

Adenoma or eosinophilic hyperplasia in adenohypophysis

The first description of the syndrome was made by Marie in 1886, and subsequent workers helped to establish the relationship of the syndrome to pituitary tumors. Over 95% of individuals with acromegaly have a pituitary somatotropic adenoma responsible for the syndrome. They are mostly macroadenomas (≥ 10 mm in diameter) and in many cases co-secrete prolactin. On usual occasions, acromegaly is associated with eosinophilic cell hyperplasia in the adenohypo physis. Occasionally, acromegaly is due to nonpituitary tumors giving rise to ectopic secretion of GH-releasing hormone (GH-RH) or rarely GH itself (Table 32–1).

Clinical Features

In children, increase in linear growth

The pituitary tumor can cause local symptoms, such as headaches, visual field impairment, cranial neuropathies, and obstructive hydrocephalus.

In children, GH hypersecretion produces increases in linear growth, resulting in the syndrome of gigantism (height > 2.5 standard deviations above mean height for age). Most patients, however, develop GH hypersecretion as adults when their epiphyseal growth plates are closed, thereby preventing linear growth.

TABLE 32–1 Etiology of Acromegaly

Pituitary acromegaly
Pituitary adenomas
Mixed GH cell and prolactin cell adenoma
Multiple endocrine neoplasia
Partially empty sella syndrome
Lymphocytic hypophysitis
Pituitary carcinoma
Extrapituitary acromegaly
GH-RH hypersecretion from hypothalamic hamartoma
GH-RH hypersecretion from peripheral tumors (eg, carcinoid, small cell lung cancer, pheochromocytoma)
Ectopic pituitary adenomas
McCune-Albright syndrom

GH = growth hormone; GH-RH = GH-releasing hormone.

Cutaneous Manifestations

GH and IGF-1 stimulate collagen cartilage and glycosaminoglycan formation, as well as epithelial replication, producing the phenotypic changes characteristic for this disease. Periosteal new bone formation is most prominent in the dermal membrane bones, such as the facial bones and the lateral aspects of long bones. This leads to prognathism, frontal bossing, separation and malocclusion of the teeth, overbite, and enlargement of the paranasal sinuses. Arthropathy is a common complication of long-bone changes, and nerve entrapment syndromes (eg, carpal tunnel syndrome) can occur. Hypertrophy of soft tissues in the hands and feet leads to acral enlargement. Patients also have a coarsening of facial features, resulting in a thickened lower lip, edematous thick eyelids, large ears, and a thickened nose. Cutis verticis gyrata (thickened folds of the skin on the scalp), oily leathery skin, hyperhidrosis, hirsutism, and colonic polyps may occur. Skin tags, also called "fibroma molluscum," increase in number over the trunk, neck, groin, and axillae. Acanthosis nigricans can be observed in the axillae, nape, and inguinal areas. Hyperpigmentation, due to increased melanocyte-stimulating hormone (MSH), and hirsutism may occur (Table 32–2).

Acral bone enlargement
Increased quantities of skin

Increased sebaceous gland activity
Acanthosis nigricans
Generalized hyperpigmentation

Systemic Manifestations

Visceromegaly occurs in acromegaly, with macroglossia, goiter, hepatosplenomegaly, and enlargement of the kidneys, but these are rarely clinically apparent. Left ventricular hypertrophy, which is common, along with the increased incidence of hypertension and ventricular failure, contributes to the two- to threefold excess mortality among acromegalics. Other manifestations of acromegaly include obstructive sleep apnea, narcolepsy, osteoarthritis, fatigue, proximal myopathy, reproductive disorders, glucose intolerance/insulin resistance, hypertriglyceridemia, and hypercalciuria.

Visceromegaly
Left ventricular hypertrophy
Mortality increased two- to threefold

TABLE 32–2 Cutaneous Changes in Acromegaly

Soft tissue swelling of the face, hands, and feet
Fibroma molluscum (skin tags)
Seborrhea
Acanthosis nigricans
Hyperhidrosis
Cutis verticis gyrata
Hyperpigmentation

Diagnosis

Plasma IGF-1 best screening test
Oral glucose challenge test measuring reduction of GH is definitive test
After confirming diagnosis, MRI of pituitary gland should be performed

Every patient who is suspected clinically to have acromegaly should undergo biochemical screening. GH levels fluctuate wildly and, therefore, are not useful (both low-positive and negative predictive values) in making the diagnosis. The best screening test is a plasma IGF-1 level. The effects of GH are largely mediated through the action of IGF-1, which is synthesized mostly in the liver under the stimulatory influence of GH. As IGF-1 has a long half-life, elevated levels in the plasma reflect chronic GH hypersecretion. An oral glucose challenge test is the definitive test for acromegaly. Normally, GH concentrations are suppressed to less than 2 ng/mL 2 hours after the ingestion of 100 g of glucose. If there is a failure of suppression, acromegaly is confirmed. GH-RH stimulation test and serum IGF binding protein-3 (IGF-BP3) levels can also be helpful diagnostically. After biochemical confirmation of acromegaly, magnetic resonance imaging (MRI) of the pituitary gland is the imaging procedure of choice. Of note, acromegaly has to be distinguished from pachydermoperiostosis, which is a rare familial condition characterized by coarsened facial features and osteoarthropathy (Figure 32–1). However, the GH and IGF-1 levels are normal in this condition, and there is a normal response to an oral glucose challenge.

Other ancillary tests in the management of the acromegalic patient include formal visual-field testing, a complete evaluation of pituitary function, lipid profile, screening for diabetes/glucose intolerance, echocardiographic assessment for left ventricular function, sleep studies for the assessment of sleep apnea, and colonoscopy (Table 32–3).

Management

Treatment:
- *trans-sphenoidal resection of pituitary*
- *pituitary irradiation*
- *medical treatment*
  - *-octreotide*
  - *-bromocriptine*
  - *-cabergoline*

The primary goal of treatment is to normalize GH levels so as to improve survival and decrease morbidity of the acromegalic patient. Untreated acromegalic patients have a mortality rate that is at least twice that of normal individuals, and this excess mortality is accounted for by increased cardiovascular mortality (coronary artery disease and left ventricular failure). Trans-sphenoidal surgical resection of the pituitary adenoma offers a potential for cure and should be attempted by an experienced neurosurgeon. A biochemical cure is achieved when the GH level is less than 2 ng/mL after a glucose challenge and after normalization of the IGF-1 level. If this does not occur, patients should be considered for pituitary irradiation or medical management with somatostatin analogues (eg, octreotide) or dopamine agonists (eg, bromocriptine or cabergoline). Attainment of a cure can be difficult, but it does lead to resolution of fatigue, soft tissue swelling of the feet and hands, entrapment neuropathies, and headache. Sleep apnea, hypertension, arthralgias, hyperhidrosis, cardiac function, and glucose intolerance also improve (Table 32–4).

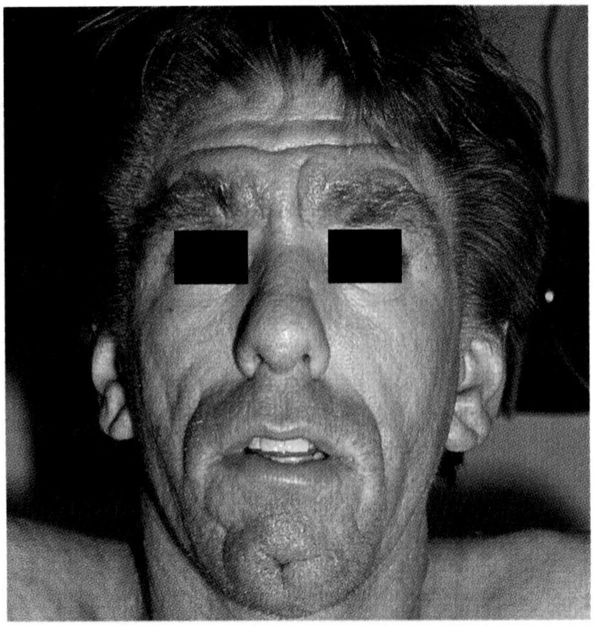

FIGURE 32–1 Patient with pachydermoperiostosis demonstrating prominent cutaneous folds over the forehead and coarse features. The lack of acral enlargement readily differentiates this condition from acromegaly.

Annotated Bibliography

Melmed S, Ho K, Klibanski A, et al. Recent advances in pathogenesis, diagnosis and management of acromegaly. J Clin Endocrinol Metab 1995;80:3395–3402.

A review outlining the molecular mechanisms of tumorigenesis and the clinical management of acromegaly, with emphasis on octreotide therapy.

Hypopituitarism

Failure of the adenohypophysis, also known as the "anterior pituitary gland," may be monotropic (deficiency of a single hormone) or multitropic (loss of several hormones). Total pituitary failure (panhypopitu-

TABLE 32–3 Diagnosis of Acromegaly

Diagnostic tests
- Serum IGF-1
- Oral glucose tolerance test for GH suppression
- GH-RH stimulation test
- IGF-BP3

Localization studies
- MRI of the pituitary
- Computed tomography (CT) scanning of chest/abdomen and octreotide nuclear scan, if extrapituitary acromegaly is suspected

Ancillary studies
- Visual-field testing
- Assessment for hypopituitarism
- Lipid profile
- Diabetes screening
- Echocardiography
- Sleep studies
- Colonoscopy

IGF-I = insulin-like growth factor-1; GH-RH = growth hormone releasing hormone; IGF-BP3 = IGF-binding protein 3; MRI = magnetic resonance imaging.

itarism) occurs when more than 75% of the gland is destroyed. Anterior pituitary failure can be due to primary pituitary dysfunction leading to deficiencies of the glycoproteins—GH, ACTH, thyroid-stimulating hormone (TSH), and the gonadotropins luteinizing hormone (LH) and follicle-stimulating hormone (FSH). Alternatively, there could be hypothalamic damage leading to the loss of hypothalamic regulatory hormones—GHRH, corticotropin-releasing hormone (CRH), thyrotropin-releasing hormone (TRH), gonadotropin-releasing hormone (Gn-RH), and dopamine. Hormonal loss can be partial or complete.

Total pituitary failure occurs with 75% destruction of gland

Hypopituitarism is an uncommon disease and the most common etiology is a pituitary adenoma causing compression atrophy of the normal pituitary tissue. Most commonly, the adenomas are nonfunctional, but many are prolactin secreting (prolactinomas). However, other space-occupying lesions and infiltrative processes can also cause the same clinical picture as shown in Table 32–2. Chronic granulomatous infections can cause hypopituitarism and these should be considered in the workup. The empty sella syndrome describes an invagination of cerebrospinal fluid (CSF) into the sella turcica. This is usually diagnosed incidentally by imaging of the brain performed for unrelated reasons. It can, however, be associated with hormonal abnormalities, most commonly hyperprolactinemia and much less often hypopituitarism. Lymphocytic hypophysitis is most commonly seen in premenopausal women, especially in the peripartum period. Patients usually present with headache or symptoms of hypopituitarism, which may be monotropic (eg, isolated ACTH deficiency). Sheehan's syndrome is ischemic pituitary necrosis that occurs in approximately 30% of women who experience hypotensive shock as a result of peripartum hemorrhage. If a patient has diabetes insipidus in association with hypopituitarism, the doctor should suspect a hypothalamic lesion leading to deficiencies of hypothalamic-releasing fac-

Pituitary adenoma most common cause

Adenomas may secrete prolactin

Chronic granulomatous infections

Sheehan's syndrome

Sarcoidosis
Histiocytosis

TABLE 32–4 Management of Acromegaly

Trans-sphenoidal resection

Pituitary irradiation

Octreotide

Bromocriptine, cabergoline

tors, as can be seen in sarcoidosis, histiocytosis X, or metastatic tumors. Other clinical features of hypothalamic disease include abnormalities of appetite, sleeping habits, memory, and sexual drive (Tables 32–5 and 32–6).

Clinical Features

Generally slow onset

Hypopituitarism usually develops slowly, but occasionally, it can present with life-threatening emergencies. In chronic presentations, depending on the etiology, the clinical features can include any combination of mass effects, hormonal hypersecretion, and hypopituitarism.

Headaches
Visual defects

Space-occupying lesions of the pituitary can present with mass effects. Such patients may complain of a headache, which is often described as dull and poorly localized. The pain is thought to be due to superior extension of the pituitary mass, causing stretching of the overlying diaphragma sellae. Not uncommonly, anterosuperior suprasellar extension of the pituitary mass causes impingement of the optic chiasm. Patients can have visual-field defects (ie, bitemporal hemianopsia, with or without scotomas). There may also be evidence of a hypothalamic syndrome, with disturbances in appetite, thirst, sleeping habits, memory, and sexual drive. Obstructive hydrocephalus and frontal lobe syndromes have also been described. Lateral extension can lead to cranial neuropathies involving cranial nerves III, IV, V, and VI and, in some cases, temporal lobe syndromes. Inferior extension can lead to CSF rhinorrhea and sinus involvement.

Prolactin secretion in females:
- *amenorrhea*
- *oligomenorrhea*
- *subfertility*
- *galactorrhea*

In males:
- *decreased libido*
- *gynecomastia*
- *subfertility*

Many tumors, such as prolactin-secreting macroadenomas, can hypersecrete one or more hormones while compressing and impairing the function of normal pituicytes. These patients have prolactin levels greater than 200 ng/mL, and in women, they cause amenorrhea/oligomenorrhea, subfertility, and galactorrhea. These effects are due to prolactin-inhibiting LH/FSH production, therefore, causing a hypogonadal state. Men have decreased libido, erectile failure, gynecomastia, and subfertility; these symptoms are due to a combination of a hypogonadal state and a presumed direct effect on the testes by prolactin. Other hormonal hypersecretion can occur resulting in acromegaly/gigantism, Cushing's disease, and thyrotoxicosis (TSH-secreting adenomas). Adenomas that secrete gonadotropins and the alpha subunit are usually clinically silent. The dermatologic changes in the hypersecretory states of acromegaly, Cushing's disease, and thyrotoxicosis are described elsewhere in this chapter.

Patients with anterior pituitary failure can present with any combination of growth failure/short stature (GH deficiency), primary amenorrhea or delayed puberty (gonadal deficiency), central hypothyroidism, adrenal insufficiency, and adult-onset hypogonadism. The secondary failure of the adrenal, thyroid, and gonads is not as severe as in the primary failure, as there may still be some endogenous production of hormones independent of the stimulatory effect of the pituitary trophic hormones.

Cutaneous Manifestations

In panhypopituitarism, the changes in the skin are dependent on the amount of the different cell lines that have been destroyed. Hence, the clinical picture is the composite of the deficiencies of each hormonal axis. In chronic, slowly progres-

TABLE 32–5 Pituitary Tumors

Usually benign
Classified as microadenomas (< 10 mm in diameter) or macroadenomas (> 10 mm)
80 to 90% are functioning (hormonally active), and 10 to 20% are nonfunctioning
Of the functioning tumors, 40 to 50% secrete prolactin, 15% GH, 15% ACTH, 5% FSH/LH, 5% TSH, and 5% alpha subunits
Described as sellar or suprasellar (if they extend beyond the sella turcica)

GH = growth hormone; ACTH = adrenocorticotropic hormone; FSH = follicle stimulating hormone; LH = luteinizing hormone; TSH = thyroid stimulating hormone.

TABLE 32–6 Causes of Hypopituitarism

Process	Causes
Primary pituitary processes	
Pituitary tumors	Adenomas, craniopharyngiomas, metastases from breast, lung, etc.
Vascular	Postpartum necrosis (Sheehan's syndrome), diabetes mellitus, sickle cell anemia, vasculitis, eclampsia, pituitary infarction (including pituitary apoplexy, internal carotid artery aneurysm, cavernous sinus thrombosis)
Inflammatory/infiltrative	Lymphocytic hypophysitis, hemochromatosis, sarcoidosis, infections (eg, tuberculosis, syphilis, fungal, pituitary abscess after meningitis)
Trauma	Surgical hypophysectomy, radiotherapy
Congenital	Idiopathic, empty sella syndrome
Secondary pituitary process (hypothalamic)	
Functional	Anorexia nervosa/bulimia, obesity, psychogenic stress, chronic systemic diseases
Neoplasms	Metastases, gliomas, craniopharyngiomas, dysgerminomas, meningiomas
Trauma	Stalk section, irradiation
Congenital	Kallmann's syndrome, hypothalamic hormone genetic defects (mostly monotropic, includes the Laron dwarfism, congenital insensitivity to ACTH)
Drugs	Glucocorticoids, thyroxine, gonadal steroids
Infiltrative	Sarcoidosis, histiocytosis X

sive cases, the dominant picture is that of hypogonadism, whereas hypothyroidism and adrenal insufficiency tend to be mild. Hence, patients have generalized loss of body hair starting in the axillae, as sex steroids are trophic to hair follicles. The hair loss eventually progresses to the pubic hair. Men will notice a reduced need to shave their facial hair. There is also thinning of scalp hair. The secretions of sweat and sebaceous glands are diminished because they are stimulated by sex steroids. Thinning of the epidermis, dermis, and subcutaneous tissues occurs, leading to fine wrinkling, especially around the mouth and eyes.

Generalized loss of hair
Thinning of the skin with fine wrinkling

Deficiency of pituitary secretion of pro-opiomelanocortin (POMC) (the precursor of ACTH) causes concurrent decreased MSH levels, resulting in decreased melanin production and generalized hypopigmentation. (The molecules responsible for regulating melanin pigmentation are ATCH, α-MSH, and β-lipotropin. These are enzymatic cleavage products of the pituitary hormone POMC. β-MSH does not exist in nature but is an artificial split product of β-lipotropin.) Hence, pallor is prominent, but the mucous membranes remain pink. There is an absence of tanning, and sensitivity to sunlight is increased. Hypogonadism also contributes to the pallor, as androgens increase melanin production, especially in sexual areas. Hence, the pallor of the nipples, areolae, and rugae of the scrotum is most noticeable. If there is concomitant hypothyroidism, there may be a yellow tinge of the skin secondary to carotenemia. Other findings include xerosis and puffiness of the face. The hair is typically dry and brittle.

Generalized hypopigmentation
Hypogonadism contributes to pallor, which is most prominent in sexual areas (i.e., nipples, scrotum)

Diagnosis

All patients with suspected hypopituitarism should have an endocrinologic evaluation before imaging of the pituitary. A prolactin concentration higher than 200 ng/mL is nearly always due to a prolactin-secreting tumor (prolactinoma). Prolactin levels less than 200 ng/mL can be caused by a prolactin-secreting tumor, pregnancy, drugs (eg, phenothiazines, metoclopramide, estrogens, α-methyldopa), primary hypothyroidism, nipple stimulation, as well as non–prolactin-secreting tumors. Hyperprolactinemia related to non–prolactin-secreting tumors is caused by compression of the pituitary stalk and inhibition of the passage of prolactin-inhibiting factor (dopamine) to the prolactin-secreting cells in the pituitary (lactotrophs).

Prolactin level

Thyroid function studies show low T_4 with normal or low TSH

Adrenal gland testing

Thyroid function tests are important, as in central hypothyroidism, where there is a low free-thyroxine (T_4) level with an inappropriately normal or low serum TSH level. Screening for adrenal insufficiency should be performed in all cases of hypopituitarism. ACTH stimulation testing is usually performed first and, if abnormal, is diagnostic of adrenal insufficiency. This test, however, can be normal in the presence of true central adrenal insufficiency. Therefore, if there is clinical evidence for adrenal insufficiency and the ACTH stimulation test is normal, the patient should proceed to a test of central adrenal axis function, such as insulin-induced hypoglycemia, metyrapone, CRH stimulation, or low-dose ACTH stimulation testing. Low testosterone levels in men and low estradiol levels in women who have inappropriately low or normal levels of LH and FSH indicate central hypogonadism. An IGF-1 level or random GH level does not accurately reflect GH deficiency, and a stimulatory test using insulin-induced hypoglycemia, clonidine, arginine, or GH-RH would be needed. Patients with diabetes insipidus will have polyuria (> 2.5 L/d) and hypo-osmolar urine and hypernatremia will result if the patient is unable to keep up with free water losses. Diabetes insipidus is confirmed by a water deprivation test.

After documentation of hormonal abnormality, an MRI or a CT scan of pituitary is performed

Once hypopituitarism has been confirmed, an MRI or a CT scan of the pituitary and hypothalamus should be performed. A full ophthalmic examination, including visual-field testing, should also be done. It may be necessary afterward to do further diagnostic workup to determine the etiology of the hypopituitarism (Table 32–7).

Management

Life-long appropriate hormonal replacement

Management involves recognition and treatment of the underlying cause of the hypopituitarism. In a few cases, treatment of the cause results in reversal of the hypopituitarism. In most cases, however, the hormonal deficits are permanent, necessitating life-long hormonal replacement. (Details on adrenal and thyroid replacement are covered elsewhere in this chapter.) T_4 accelerates the catabolism of cortisol, which can precipitate adrenal crisis in panhypopituitarism, so glucocorticoid replacement should always precede T_4 replacement. It should also be noted that in patients with central hypothyroidism, the adequacy of thyroid hormone replacement has to be monitored by the free-T_4 level and not the serum TSH. Hypogonadal female patients will need estrogen replacement (given orally or transdermally), and hypogonadal male patients will need testosterone (depot injection or transdermal). The required doses of glucocorticoid, T_4, and sex steroids for full replacement may be lower than those used in primary organ failure. Mineralocorticoid replacement is not necessary in panhypopituitarism because aldosterone production is normally controlled by the renin-angiotensin-

TABLE 32–7 Tests in Establishing the Diagnosis of Hypopituitarism

Prolactin
Free T_4, TSH
LH, FSH, sex steroids
Early morning cortisol, ACTH stimulation
Insulin-induced hypoglycemia test, CRH stimulation
Serum sodium, urine osmolality, water deprivation
IGF-1, GH stimulation
Visual field by perimetry
MRI of pituitary with contrast

TSH = thyroid-stimulating hormone; LH = luteinizing hormone; FSH = follicle stimulating hormone; ACTH = adrenocorticotropic hormone; CRH = corticotropin-releasing hormone; IGF = insulin-like growth factor; GH = growth factor; MRI = magnetic resonance imaging.

aldosterone system. Children may also require GH replacement (given subcutaneously) so as to facilitate normal growth. Some adults may have changes of mood, body composition, and energy level that are also ameliorated with GH treatment. Patients with hyperprolactinemia are treated with a dopamine agonist, such as bromocriptine, cabergoline, or pergolide, to normalize prolactin levels and shrink the tumor. Patients with impairment of their visual fields or other mass effects may require surgical resection of the mass. Diabetes insipidus is treated with nasal or oral desmopressin in doses that reduce urine output to less than 3 L per day and minimize nocturia.

Annotated Bibliography

Vance ML. Hypopituitarism. N Engl J Med 1994; 330: 1651-1662. (Erratum, N Engl J Med 1994;331:487.)

A discussion of the different diagnoses, clinical features, and general management of hypopituitarism.

Thyroid

Hyperthyroidism

Hyperthyroidism, also known as "thyrotoxicosis," refers to the clinical state caused by tissue exposure to excess thyroid hormone (T_4 and/or triiodothyronine T_3). The source of the excessive thyroid hormone can be endogenous or exogenous. Thyrotoxicosis is found in 2% of women and 0.5% of men. The causes of thyrotoxicosis are listed in Table 32–8.

Graves' disease is the most common cause of hyperthyroidism, accounting for up to 80% of cases. It is an autoimmune process caused by circulating thyroid-stimulating immunoglobulins (TSI) that act as TSH-receptor agonists (anti–TSH-receptor antibodies), stimulating both growth of the gland as well as overproduction of thyroid hormone. Nonpathogenic antithyroid peroxidase and antithyroglobulin antibodies are also frequently present. The clinical features are due to the effects of the hyperthyroxinemia and also to the distinct, but commonly associated, autoimmune processes affecting retro-orbital tissues and pretibial dermal fibroblasts. Graves' disease is diagnosed when one or more components of the diagnostic triad (hyperthyroidism, ophthalmopathy, pretibial myxedema) are present.

Graves' disease:
- *TSIs*
- *Nonpathogenic antithyroid peroxidase and antithyroglobulin antibodies frequently present*

Clinical Features

Thyrotoxic patients, regardless of the etiology, have similar symptoms and signs with the exception of ophthalmopathy and pretibial myxedema, which are spe-

TABLE 32–8 Etiology of Thyrotoxicosis

Graves' disease
Toxic multinodular goiter
Toxic adenoma (Plummer's disease)
Exogenous thyroid hormone
Thyroiditis (silent, subacute, postpartum, drug induced)
TSH-secreting pituitary adenomas
Iodine and iodine-containing drugs (eg, radiocontrast dye, amiodarone)
Endometrial human chorionic gonadotropin (eg, trophoblastic tumors)
Struma ovarii
Metastatic follicular carcinoma of the thyroid

TSH = thyroid-stimulating hormone.

Elderly patients may present with depression

Increase in β-adrenergic responsivity

cific for Graves' disease. The severity of thyrotoxicosis is directly dependent on the age of the patient, the duration of disease, and the magnitude of the hyperthyroxinemia. Elderly patients may present with depression or weight loss as their only clinical finding. This is often referred to as "apathetic hyperthyroidism." The metabolic effects of thyroid hormones are mediated by T_3, 80% of which are derived from peripheral deiodination of T_4. T_3 binds to receptors primarily in the nucleus (but plasma membrane activity is also being recognized), resulting in transcription of sections of DNA called thyroid hormone–responsive elements (TREs). One consequence of thyroid hormone exposure is an increase in β-adrenergic responsivity. This accounts for many of the adrenergic symptoms of thyrotoxicosis. The clinical and laboratory features are found in Table 32–9.

Cutaneous Manifestations

Skin changes due to increased blood flow and vasodilitation
Nail growth accelerated
Onycholysis
Pruritus
Increased frequency of dermatitis herpetiformis

The skin changes seen in thyrotoxicosis are due to peripheral vasodilatation and increased blood flow. These include warm, velvety, soft, moist skin; persistent facial flushing; and palmar erythema. Increased sweating is due to sympathetic overactivity and is pronounced on the palms and soles. Nail growth is accelerated, and there may be distal onycholysis, also called Plummer's nails. Other skin changes include diffuse thinning of scalp hair, alopecia areata, pruritus, chronic urticaria, and diffuse hyperpigmentation. There is also an increased incidence of dermatitis herpetiformis. Palmoplantar pustulosis, a pustular variant of chronic hand dermatitis, is also associated with autoimmune thyroiditis seen in patients with Graves' disease, Hashimoto's thyroiditis, or nodular goiter with high titers of antithyroid antibodies.

In Graves' disease, pretibial myxedema occurs in approximately 5% of cases, and orbitopathy is usually simultaneously present (Figures 32–2 and 32–3).

TABLE 32–9 Clinical and Laboratory Features of Thyrotoxicosis

Feature	Symptom
Constitutional	Weight loss despite preserved appetite, heat intolerance, increased basal temperature, flushing
Neuropsychiatric	Nervousness, poor ability to concentrate, fatigue, insomnia, irritability, anxiety, emotional lability, restlessness, tremor, increased reflexes; delirium and chorea may be seen rarely
Musculoskeletal	Proximal myopathy, osteopenia in chronic cases, periodic paralysis in Asians
Cardiovascular	Palpitations, congestive heart failure, exertional dyspnea, angina, tachycardia, atrial fibrillation, and flow murmurs
Reproductive	Oligomenorrhea, decreased menstrual flow, anovulation, subfertility; men may develop gynecomastia, decreased sperm count, and decreased libido
Gastrointestinal	Hyperdefecation, tongue tremor, transaminase elevations, hepatomegaly
Ocular system	Lid lag and stare due to increased sympathetic activity resulting in contraction of the levator palpebrae superior; patients with Graves' disease develop retro-orbital edema of extraocular muscles leading to extraocular palsies, proptosis (exophthalmos), chemosis, lid edema, exposure conjunctivitis, and keratitis
Hematologic	Normocytic anemia, lymphocytosis, splenomegaly (rare), thymus enlargement
Metabolic	Hypercalcemia, hypercalciuria, increased alkaline phosphatase, hypoglycemia

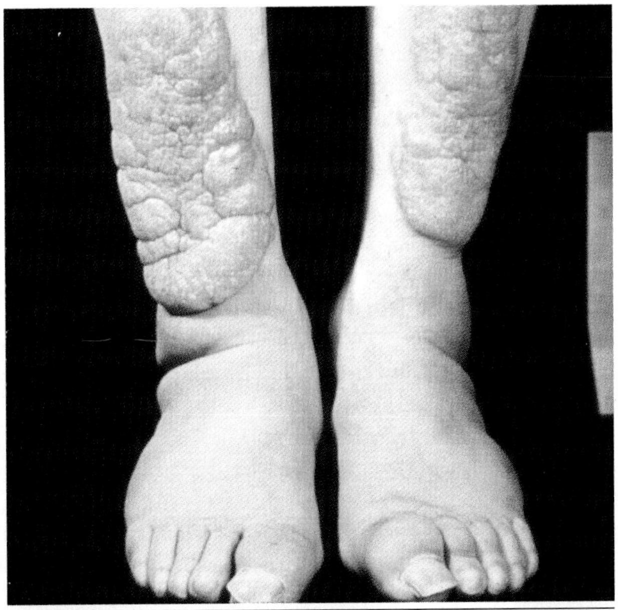

FIGURE 32–2 Pretibial myxedema in a patient with Graves' disease. This is a dramatic example of the size of plaques and nodules that can develop in this condition.

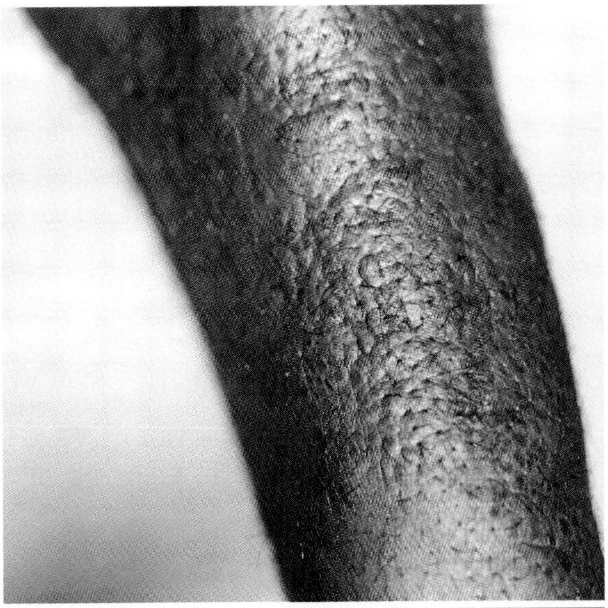

FIGURE 32–3 Pretibial myxedema showing diffuse thickness of the skin over the lower leg. Note "peau d'orange" appearance.

Pretibial myxedema occurs in approximately 5% of Graves' disease patients

Pretibial myxedema is a localized thickening of the skin of the pretibial areas. The lesions may develop at the time of hyperthyroidism or occur years after an euthyroid state has been achieved, either surgically or medically.

Increased mucin in tissue
Pathogenesis is controversial

Histopathology of pretibial myxedematous lesions demonstrates the presence of increased mucin composed of acid glycosaminoglycans (Figure 32–4). Although most patients with pretibial myxedema, treated or untreated, demonstrate elevated levels of a TSI, there is controversial evidence that an antibody against a cell-surface fibroblast receptor is causative. On the other hand, however, there is evidence for the existence of a serum factor in pretibial myxedema patients that is capable, in vitro, of inducing a two- to threefold increase of hyaluronic acid production by normal pretibial fibroblasts, but not by fibroblasts from other areas of the body. The possible role of an immunoglobulin-mediated pathogenesis has been suggested again by the observation that pretibial fibroblasts have receptors for thyrotropin (TSH).

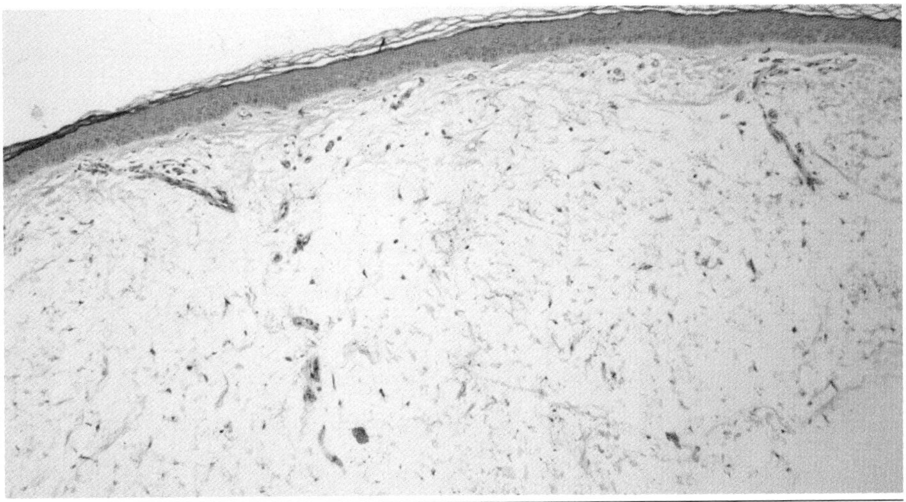

FIGURE 32–4 Pretibial myxedema histology showing separation of reticular collagen bundles with fine strands of blue-gray mucopolysaccharides.

Heterogeneous effect of anti-TSH receptor antibodies

The polyclonal immunoglobulin G (IgG) anti-TSH receptor antibodies are heterogeneous with regard to their functional effect. Some of these antibodies bind receptor epitopes, resulting in thyroid stimulation; others bind epitopes that block the action of TSH, producing myxedema.

Euthyroid Graves' disease

Approximately 15% of Hashimoto's thyroiditis patients also possess anti-TSH receptor antibodies. There are instances when these antibodies are present and the patients have euthyroid Graves' disease or euthyroid ophthalmopathy. (The exact pathogenesis of the ophthalmopathy is unknown, but evidence suggests that it may result from the stimulation of orbital fibroblasts and muscles expressing the TSH receptor or from cell-mediated and humoral immunity to retro-orbital muscle antigen.)

It is theorized that the balance between inhibition and stimulation of the TSH receptor by these antibodies determines whether there is hyper- or hypoactivity of the thyroid. However, these and possibly other antibodies reacting against TSH receptors on fibroblasts in the pretibial region and ocular muscles induce the pretibial myxedema and opthalmopathy in Graves' disease.

"Peau d'orange" appearance

The lesions of pretibial myxedema are characterized by a thickening of the skin of the lower limbs, producing a pink- or skin-colored erythematous, waxy, plaque-like lesion with prominent hair follicles, giving a "peau d'orange" appearance (see Figure 32–3). Sharply demarcated nodular lesions may occur, or the lesions may be diffuse (see Figure 32–2). (We have discovered a patient with nodular lesions of pretibial myxedema involving only one leg, which developed 14 years after treatment of Graves' disease with radioactive iodine.)

At times, edema and epidermal proliferation produce an elephantiasis-like lesion (elephantiasis verrucosa nostra). Although the lower extremities are characteristically involved, similar lesions occasionally are found elsewhere, especially on the extensor forearms.

Lesions may respond to steroids under occlusion, octreotide, or PUVA

These lesions can be treated with steroids under occlusion (Cordan tape). Octreotide, an analogue of somatostatin, and psoralen plus ultraviolet A (PUVA) are investigational therapies that have proven successful. Mild lesions may resolve spontaneously.

Thyroid acropathy very rare

Thyroid acropathy is extremely rare (Figures 32–5 and 32–6). Of patients with pretibial myxedema, only 7% develop acropathy. It is characterized by painless soft tissue swelling of the fingers and toes, along with clubbing of the digits, hyperkeratosis of the overlying skin, and periosteal new bone formation. There is no known effective therapy. (We have seen one individual who developed thyroid acropathy 7 years after becoming euthyroid following radioiodine

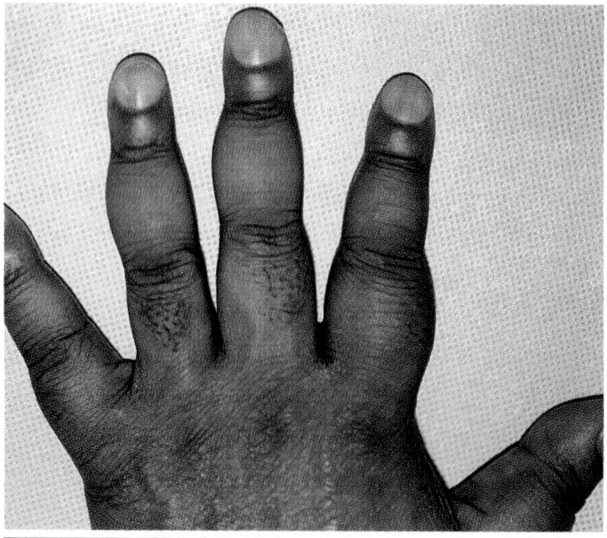

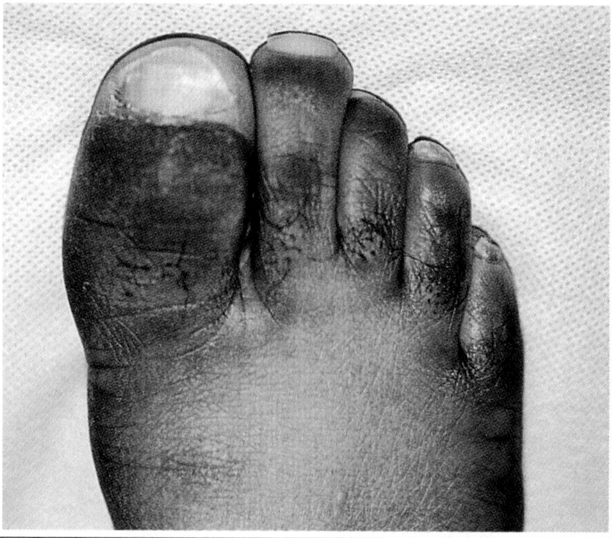

FIGURES 32–5 AND 32–6 Thyroid acropathy showing thickening of digits of hand and foot in a patient with Graves' disease.

treatment and 5 years after developing exophthalmos and pretibial myxedema.) A list of cutaneous manifestations of thyrotoxicosis is presented in Table 32–10.

Diagnosis

Reductions of TSH and increase of T_3 and/or T_4

Although the diagnosis of thyrotoxicosis is often suspected on the basis of clinical evaluation, it must be confirmed biochemically. Overt hyperthyroidism is typically associated with reductions of circulating TSH and elevations of thyroid hormones (T_4 and/or T_3). The TSH in this setting is usually undetectable by high-sensitivity assays. TSH levels fall before thyroid hormone levels rise out of the normal range. Mild or subclinical hyperthyroidism often presents with low TSH and normal T_4 and T_3. Radioisotope thyroid scans (eg, technetium pertechnetate or radioiodine) can also be useful diagnostically. They are most useful for distinguishing persistent forms of hyperthyroidism (eg, Graves' disease, toxic multinodular goiter) from transient varieties (eg, subacute thyroiditis, postpartum thyroiditis). Measuring TSI titers are rarely helpful, except in special circumstances, such as in the evaluation of patients presenting with ophthalmopathy in the absence of hyperthyroidism (euthyroid Graves' ophthalmopathy).

Management

Treatment:

- *use of β-blockers*
- *asthma and congestive heart failure are contraindications to the use of β-blockers*

Patients with symptomatic thyrotoxicosis should be treated with a β-blocker to minimize hyperadrenergic symptoms. Practically all β-blockers have been shown to be efficacious. The dose should be titrated to achieve control of symptoms without causing hypotension or bradycardia. Asthma and congestive heart failure are relative contraindications to β-blocker use.

Thionamide preparations:

- *propylthiouracil*
- *methimazole*

Hyperthyroidism caused by the overproduction of thyroid hormone (Graves' disease, toxic multinodular goiter) can be treated with thiocynamide medications (methimazole or propylthiouracil). These drugs inhibit thyroid hormone synthesis within the gland. The thionamides are well tolerated, but approximately 5% of patients develop dermatitis, nausea, elevation of serum transaminases, and arthralgia. In less than 0.5% of cases, reversible agranulocytosis can occur. The initial dose is gradually reduced until the minimally effective dose is reached that maintains normal thyroid hormone levels. However, withdrawal of medical therapy frequently results in clinical relapse (especially if there is a large goiter, ophthalmopathy, or high baseline T_3 levels), necessitating chronic administration unless a definitive therapy is undertaken)

Radioactive iodine most popular therapy
Substantial risk of hypothyroidism developing

In the United States, many patients and treating physicians opt for radioactive iodine therapy, which can permanently cure hyperthyroidism but has a 55 to 60% risk of producing hypothyroidism over 10 years, with a continuing rate of 2 to 3% per year thereafter. There is a small possibility of exacerbation of pre-

TABLE 32–10 Cutaneous Manifestations of Thyrotoxicosis

Soft velvety skin
Increased sweating of palms and soles
Fast-growing nails
Onycholysis
Alopecia
Hyperpigmentation
Facial flushing
Palmar erythema
Pruritus
Urticaria
Pretibial myxedema (Graves')
Thyroid acropathy (Graves')
Palmoplantar pustulosis

existing Graves' ophthalmopathy during radioactive iodine administration, but this can be abrogated by the use of a course of glucocorticoids. Of note, there is no increased incidence of secondary cancers after treatment. It takes weeks to months after administration of radioactive iodine for thyroid destruction to evolve, so patients should remain on a thionamide during this time, after which patients can be weaned and it can be safely discontinued.

Thyroidectomy

Thyroidectomy is also a therapeutic option, but it is usually reserved for failure of medical management and, possibly, also for patients with large goiters. The clinical course of the ophthalmopathy can be independent of hyperthyroidism. Patients with significant proptosis and diplopia should be evaluated by an ophthalmologist experienced in Graves' ophthalmopathy, as they may require retro-orbital decompression, tarsorraphy, or extraocular muscle surgery.

Toxic nodular disease can be treated with thionamides, radioactive iodine, or surgery. Antithyroid medications are a less attractive long-term therapy because this form of hyperthyroidism cannot be induced into a remission.

Thyroiditis is usually self-limited, and so treatment with only a β-blocker for symptoms is required. Anti-inflammatory drugs are useful for cases complicated by pain or severe symptomatic thyrotoxicosis.

"Thyroid storm" describes severe hyperthyroidism, usually in the setting of precipitating medical illness (eg, gastrointestinal hemorrhage, sepsis, myocardial infarction, trauma), that is also characterized by hyperpyrexia, mental status changes, and multiple organ failure. In such cases, mortality is high (10 to 75% in untreated cases). Treatment for thyroid storm includes large doses of thionamides, β-blockers, iodide (usually sodium ipodate), and glucocorticoids.

Annotated Bibliography

Singer PA, Cooper DS, Levy EG, et al. Treatment guidelines for patients with hyperthyroidism and hypothyroidism. Standards of Care Committee, American Thyroid Association. JAMA 1995;273:808–812.

This article describes standards of care devised by an expert panel from the American Thyroid Association, emphasizing cost-effective and evidence-based approaches of care.

Dabon-Almirante CL, Surks MI. Clinical and laboratory diagnosis of thyrotoxicosis. Endocrinol Metab Clin North Am 1998;25–35.

This article gives useful clinical descriptions for Graves' disease and other forms of thyrotoxicosis, with 31 relevant references.

Noppakun N, Bancheun K, Chandraprasert S. Unusual locations of localized myxedema in Graves' disease. Arch Dermatol 1986;122:85–88.

Bahn RS, Heufelder AE. Pathogenesis of Graves' ophthalmopathy. N Engl J Med 1993;329:468.

Cheung HS, Nicoloff JT, Kamiel MB, et al. Stimulation of fibroblast biosynthetic activity by serum of patients with pretibial myxedema. J Invest Dermatol 1978;71:12.

Lynch PJ, Maize JC, Sisson JC. Pretibial myxedema in nonthyrotoxic thyroid disease. Arch Dermatol 1973;107:107–111.

Hypothyroidism

May affect as many as 2% of population

Hypothyroidism, also known as "myxedema," is defined as the clinical syndrome resulting from deficiency of thyroid hormones (Table 32–11). Myxedema refers to the presence of the characteristic physical changes of the skin and muscle due to connective tissue deposition of glycosaminoglycans, as seen in chronic and severe hypothyroidism. The Whickham survey in rural England showed that the mean age of onset of hypothyroidism is 57 years. The study found evidence for hypothyroidism in 2% of the population, with a female to male ratio of 10:1.

Autoimmune thyroiditis most common cause of hypothyroidism

Autoimmune thyroiditis is the most common cause of hypothyroidism in the United States. Pathophysiologically, autoimmunized lymphocytes infiltrate and impair the functioning of the gland. Associated with the cellular response is a

TABLE 32–11 Etiology of Hypothyroidism

Primary hypothyroidism
Autoimmune thyroiditis
Hashimoto's disease (goitrous hypothyroidism)
Atrophic thyroiditis (primary myxedema)
Transient neonatal hypothyroidism
Radioactive iodine therapy (postablative hypothyroidism)
Surgical hypothyroidism
Thyroiditis—subacute, painless, postpartum
Biosynthetic defects in hormonogenesis
Iodine-induced hypothyroidism
Iodide deficiency
Goitrogens (eg, lithium, thionamides)
Congenital hypothyroidism
Infiltrative diseases (eg, sarcoidosis, amyloidosis, hemochromatosis, Riedel's thyroiditis)
Secondary/central hypothyroidism
Hypopituitarism or hypothalamic dysfunction
Generalized resistance to thyroid hormone

humoral autoimmune response. Patients with autoimmune thyroiditis are commonly found to have circulating antibodies directed against thyroid antigens including thyroglobulin and thyroid peroxidase (microsomal antibodies). Although these antibodies are not thought to directly cause thyroid destruction, they are sensitive and specific markers for autoimmune thyroiditis. On physical examination, patients are often found to have a firm, bosselated thyroid gland. Autoimmune thyroiditis is commonly associated with other autoimmune diseases, such as pernicious anemia, vitiligo, Addison's disease, rheumatoid arthritis, myasthenia gravis, Sjögren's syndrome, and type I diabetes mellitus.

Clinical Features

In the Clinical Society of London's report on myxedema in 1888, the dermatologic signs featured prominently and were described as follows:

> The features (of the face) are broad, puffy, and coarse. The eyelids are always the seat of transparent swelling, and the eyebrows are generally raised in order to help sustain the upper lid. The nostrils are swollen and broadened; the lower lip thickened, everted and livid; the mouth widened transversely. Over the cheeks and nose there is a well-defined red patch, in strong contrast with the pallid, porcelain-like orbital area. The skin is dry and scaly, and there is usually marked absence of any tendency to perspiration and of sebaceous secretion. The nails are apt to suffer, becoming stunted or brittle. The hair of the dry, scurfy scalp, in nearly all cases, is dry, ragged, and brittle, presenting a very characteristic appearance.

The dermatologic changes are due mostly to the accumulation of hyaluronic acid and chondroitin sulfate (glycosaminoglycans) in the dermis and around cutaneous appendages. There may also be a perivascular infiltration of activated lymphocytes. The hydrophilic nature of the glycosaminoglycans leads to interstitial edema. Other changes in the dermis include decreased elastic fibers, decreased turnover of collagen, and increased interstitial edema from the decreased free-water clearance that occurs in hypothyroidism; these changes all contribute to the signs and symptoms listed in Table 32–12.

Skin changes due mostly to increased accumulation of hyaluronic acid and glycosaminoglycans.

TABLE 32–12 Cutaneous Changes in Hypothyroidism

Puffy facies with blepharoptosis
Dry (xerotic), rough skin progressing to eczema craquelé in severe cases
Nonpitting edema of hands, face, and ankles (pitting can also occur)
Periorbital swelling
Pallor due to vasoconstriction, anemia, and interstitial fluid
Carotenemia leading to yellowish discoloration of the skin
Coarse brittle hair and hair loss, including the lateral aspect of the eyebrows (madarosis) (see Figure 32–7)
Dry axillae
Brittle, thickened, slow-growing, striated nails
Malar flush
Enlarged tongue

Other symptoms and signs are attributable to decreased metabolic rate and glycosaminoglycan infiltration of other organs. Virtually every organ system can be affected, as listed in Table 32–13.

Diagnosis

Elevated TSH and low free-T_4

A diagnosis of hypothyroidism should be suspected on the basis of characteristic history and physical findings. It is confirmed by a high serum TSH concentration (usually > 10 μ/mL) and a low free-T_4 level. T_3 levels are variable in hypothyroid patients and are not useful for establishing this diagnosis. TSH concentrations rise before T_4 levels fall into the subnormal range. A mildly elevated TSH (< 10 μ/mL) and normal levels of free-T_4 is defined as mild thyroid failure or subclinical hypothyroidism. Patients with mild thyroid failure can have reversible symptoms of hypothyroidism and may have a secondary hyperlipidemia. Measuring antithyroid antibody titers can help confirm the presence of autoimmune thyroiditis but are not usually necessary. If the TSH is low or low-normal, with a low free-T_4, central hypothyroidism should be suspected.

Antithyroid antibodies help confirm diagnosis of autoimmune-mediated thyroiditis

Ancillary laboratory tests may show hyponatremia; increased creatine kinase, aspartate transaminase, L-lactate dehydrogenase, cholesterol, low-density lipoprotein cholesterol and prolactin; normochromic anemia due to decreased red blood cell mass; altered LH/FSH ratio; and decreased oxygen consumption.

Management

Treatment with levothyroxine

Levothyroxine (T_4) replacement in physiologic dosages is required regardless of the etiology. Its half-life is 7 days, so it can be given once daily. The tablet is normally given in the morning to avoid possible symptoms such as insomnia. The mean replacement dose is 1.7 μg/kg/d in adults, but the dose is much higher in children and lower in the elderly. Factors affecting dosing are listed in Table 32–14. In the elderly, T_4 should be initiated at a low dose (eg, 12.5 to 50 μg/d) and advanced in 25-μg increments. This conservative dosing is less likely to precipitate coronary events in patients with underlying coronary artery disease. Clinical improvement occurs in 1 to 2 weeks, but achievement of steady state levels takes 4 to 6 weeks. After this period has elapsed, re-evaluation with a serum TSH is needed and the dose adjusted with the goal of achieving a normal TSH level. Full resolution of symptoms, including the dermatologic changes, is generally complete in 4 to 6 months. Once equilibrium is achieved, the TSH can be checked once a year. Individuals with mild thyroid failure are often treated with T_4 supplementation. Indications for treatment of mild thyroid fail-

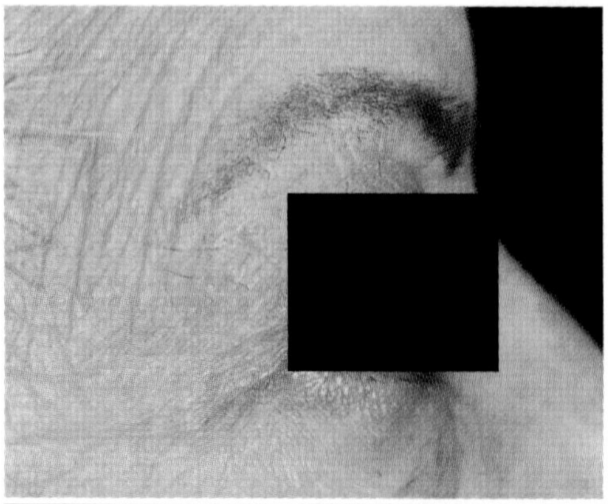

FIGURE 32–7 Patient with myxedema demonstrating loss of lateral eyebrow.

TABLE 32–13 Complications of Hypothyroidism by Organ System

Organ System	Complication
Metabolic	Cold intolerance, fatigue, mild weight gain, hypothermia
Central nervous system	Lethargy, memory deficits, poor attention span, personality change, somnolence, slow speech, decreased hearing and taste, cerebellar ataxia, psychopathology (myxedematous madness), cretinism
Neuromuscular system	Weakness, muscle cramps, arthralgia, delayed relaxation phase of deep tendon reflexes, carpal tunnel syndrome
Gastrointestinal	Constipation, macroglossia, ascites
Cardiorespiratory	Decreased exercise tolerance, hoarse voice, sleep apnea, bradycardia, mild diastolic hypertension, pericardial effusion, pleural effusion
Renal	Decreased free-water clearance, hyponatremia
Reproductive	Decreased libido, subfertility, menorrhagia, amenorrhea, galactorrhea

ure include positive antithyroid antibody titers, the presence of a goiter, symptoms of hypothyroidism, or hyperlipidemia.

Annotated Bibliography

Singer PA, Cooper DS, Levy EG, et al. Treatment guidelines for patients with hyperthyroidism and hypothyroidism. Standards of Care Committee, American Thyroid Association. JAMA 1995;273:808–812.

This article reports standards of care devised by an expert panel from the American Thyroid Association, emphasizing cost-effective and evidence-based approaches of care.

Adrenal

Hypercortisolism

Exogenous and endogenous sources of excess glucocorticosteroids

"Cushing's syndrome" refers to the clinical syndrome caused by chronic hypercortisolism. Cushing first described the syndrome in 1912, when he recognized an association of diabetes mellitus, central obesity with striae, moon facies, hirsutism, and adrenal hyperplasia in a young woman. In 1932, Cushing published 11 more cases, and he attributed the syndrome to basophilic pituitary adenomas.

The source of excess glucocorticoid in patients with Cushing's syndrome is either endogenous or exogenous (Table 32–15). Endogenous causes are classified as either ACTH-dependent or ACTH-independent. In the former, ACTH can be secreted by the pituitary gland, in which case it is formally referred to as Cushing's disease. Alternatively, an extrapituitary neoplasm may produce ectopic

TABLE 32–14 Factors Altering Dosage of T_4

Pseudomalabsorbtion (noncompliance)
Increased dose requirements
Malabsorbtion syndromes, iron sulfate, aluminum hydroxide, cholestyramine, and sucralfate decrease absorption
Phenytoin, carbamazepine, rifampin, and young age increase hepatic clearance
Pregnancy, obesity
Decreased dose requirements
Older age

TABLE 32–15 Causes of Cushing's Syndrome

Exogenous	
	Iatrogenic, factitious
ACTH-dependent	
	Pituitary adenoma (Cushing's disease, usually microadenomas)
	Ectopic ACTH syndrome (eg, bronchial carcinoids, small cell lung cancer)
	Ectopic CRH syndrome
ACTH-independent	
	Adrenal adenoma
	Adrenal carcinoma
	Micronodular hyperplasia
	Macronodular hyperplasia

ACTH = adrenocorticotropic hormone; CRC = corticotropin-releasing hormone.

ACTH or CRH. Individuals with ACTH-independent Cushing's syndrome have excess cortisol production from adrenal adenoma, carcinoma, or hyperplasia, thereby suppressing pituitary production of ACTH. Cushing's disease accounts for approximately 70% of cases of endogenous Cushing's syndrome, whereas the ectopic ACTH syndrome, adrenal adenomas, and adrenal carcinomas each represent 8 to 12% of cases.

Endogenous Cushing's syndrome is rare; its prevalence is estimated as 10 cases per million. The mortality and morbidity rates in untreated cases are high, and therefore, whenever there is clinical suspicion, screening for the syndrome is essential, although difficult, as false-positive results are not uncommon. Consequently, it is important to pay rigorous attention to ensuring a proper biochemical diagnosis.

Clinical Features

Glucocorticoids have many metabolic effects that include increasing protein catabolism (including collagen), hepatic gluconeogenesis and glycogenesis, peripheral insulin resistance, salt and water retention due to a mineralocorticoid effect, and peripheral lymphocytic destruction; inhibiting of cytokine formation; and inhibiting of fibroblastic and osteoblastic activity while promoting hypercalciuria. Consequently, the clinical signs and symptoms are legion and can range from mild to profoundly severe.

Centripetal obesity

The most common (and often the initial) symptom is the development of obesity, usually in a centripetal distribution, but it may be generalized. The fat deposition is associated with the development of a dorsocervical fat pad (buffalo hump), supraclavicular fat pads, typical moon facies, and facial plethora due to telangiectasia. Supraclavicular fat pads are more specific for Cushing's syndrome than buffalo humps. Atrophy of the epidermis from protein catabolism leads to easy bruisability and, hence, multiple ecchymoses over the limbs. The cutaneous thinning results in wrinkling over the dorsum of the hand and elbows. Thinning is less commonly seen in affected men, children, and women with concurrent androgen production. Striae develop on the abdomen and flanks but may also be seen over the breasts and axillae. These are typically wide (> 1 cm) and violaceous.

Atrophy of epidermis
Striae

Proximal myopathy
Osteoporosis

A majority of patients have muscle wasting of the limbs with proximal myopathy. Also seen are diastolic hypertension, glucose intolerance, pitting edema, and an increased susceptibility to infections. The infections may vary from the superficial, such as fungal dermatoses (eg, mucocutaneous candidiasis, tinea versicolor, tinea unguium) to life-threatening systemic infections. Osteoporosis is common and may present as vertebral collapse. There is mild hirsutism due to moderate increases in adrenal androgens. Excess hair is mostly seen as lanugo hair over the cheeks and terminal hair over the face rather than the trunk. Severe hirsutism and virilism should indicate the possibility of an adrenocortical carcinoma. Women have oligomenorrhea, amenorrhea, and subfertility, whereas men have decreased libido. These symptoms are due mostly to hypercortisolism rather than excess androgens as traditionally espoused. Depression, insomnia, emotional lability, and, occasionally, frank psychosis are seen.

Acne lesions occurring in nonacne areas
Hyperpigmentation

Acne and seborrhea are prevalent. In exogenous Cushing's syndrome, the acne-induced lesions, in contrast to acne vulgaris, are generally inflammatory papules occurring in traditionally nonacne areas. Comedones and cysts are absent. It is commonly thought that hyperpigmentation may be seen in Cushing's disease, but this is unusual, as the plasma ACTH levels are only moderately high. When it is seen, it is usually in the setting of the ectopic ACTH syndrome when the plasma ACTH levels are extremely elevated. The hyperpigmentation is thought to be due to stimulation of epidermal melanocytes by ACTH and other co-secreted peptides, such as MSHs, which are produced from their common precursor molecule (POMC).

Carny's syndrome
Anti-ACTH receptor antibodies

Rarely, pediatric patients may have an ACTH-independent form of Cushing's syndrome due to pigmented nodular adrenal disease called "Carny's syndrome." These patients have lentigines, cardiac and soft tissue myxomatous masses, and other endocrinopathies, including acromegaly. Anti-ACTH receptor antibodies are detected. Their presence stimulates adrenal growth and steroidogenesis.

No individual clinical finding is pathnognomic of Cushing's syndrome, and it is the confluence of several manifestations simultaneously that should arouse clinical suspicion. The presence of centripetal obesity, proximal myopathy, facial plethora, spontaneous ecchymoses, purple striae, and osteoporosis strongly increase the likelihood of the syndrome. Also, serial photographs of the patient may be useful for finding evidence of progressive physical changes (Table 32–16).

Diagnosis

24-hour urine cortisol level
Dexamethasone suppression test

The patient with suspected Cushing's syndrome should first be screened for evidence of hypercortisolism. This can be done in the outpatient setting by measuring 24-hour urinary free-cortisol excretion, which has a sensitivity greater than 95%. Two or three collections may be needed. Alternatively, a 1-mg overnight

TABLE 32–16 Manifestations of Cushing's Syndrome

Cutaneous Manifestations
Facial plethora
Spontaneous ecchymoses
Wide violaceous striae
Acne
Hirsutism, including lanugo hair
Fungal dermatoses (eg, tinea corporis, tinea versicolor)
Seborrhea
Keratosis pilaris (uncommon)
Verruca vulgaris (uncommon)
General and endocrine manifestations
Centripetal obesity
Proximal myopathy
Thin extremities
Hypertension
Osteoporosis
Psychiatric disorders (eg, depression, emotional lability)
Glucose intolerance
Cessation of linear growth in children and delayed bone age
Menstrual irregularities, decreased libido
Hypokalemic alkalosis
Hypercalciuria and nephrolithiasis
Leukocytosis with relative lymphopenia and eosinopenia

dexamethasone suppression test can be performed (1 mg of dexamethasone is given at 11 pm orally, plasma cortisol is measured at 8 am, and a result > 5 μg/dL indicates hypercortisolism).

Cases with equivocal or mildly elevated cortisol levels, as determined by either method, may have pseudo-Cushing's syndrome, which is seen in stressed patients, anorexia nervosa/bulimia, alcohol abuse, chronic depression, and obesity. These subjects should then undergo further testing, such as a formal two-day low-dose dexamethasone test. Difficult cases also may undergo a CRH-dexamethasone test or midnight cortisol measurement.

Low ACTH levels suggest adrenal-secreting tumor

Patients with nonsuppressible hypercortisolism are then evaluated for localization of the source of excess cortisol. A low plasma ACTH is suggestive of a cortisol-secreting adrenal tumor. Such patients should undergo adrenal CT or MRI.

Elevated ACTH may originate in pituitary or from an ectopic site

Patients with high ACTH levels are more complicated and will need an evaluation to distinguish a pituitary source from an ectopic source of ACTH. Traditionally, this is by a high-dose dexamethasone suppression test (2 mg dexamethasone given every 6 hours for 48 hours); pituitary sources will have reductions in urinary free-cortisol levels, unlike in the ectopic ACTH syndrome where there is complete resistance to glucocorticoid-negative feedback. This testing can be equivocal. Bilateral inferior petrosal sinus sampling with CRH stimulation may be necessary to distinguish pituitary from extrapituitary sources of ACTH.

Management

Cushing's disease treatment:
- *surgery*
- *irradiation*

Treatment for patients with Cushing's disease is trans-sphenoidal microadenomectomy or partial hypophysectomy, and this results in a biochemical cure in 80% of cases. The remainder of patients may need pituitary irradiation (4,000 to 5,000 cGy), which will cure an additional 10%. The remaining 10% of cases that are not cured may need bilateral adrenalectomy to remove the source of cortisol. However, approximately one-third of adrenalectomized patients develop Nelson's syndrome (aggressive, locally invasive pituitary macroadenomas that secrete ACTH) years later. The secondary pituitary tumors of Nelson's syndrome present with cranial neuropathies, chiasmal syndromes, and frontal lobe dysfunction; they are notoriously difficult to treat by surgery. Patients with the ectopic ACTH syndrome can have tumors localized by a chest scan, an abdominal CT or MRI, or a somatostatin scan. The tumor should then be surgically resected. Adrenal tumors can be resected laparoscopically or through a laparotomy. Occasionally, patients with Cushing's syndrome are not cured by surgery, or the tumors cannot be localized. In such instances, medical therapy using ketoconazole, mitotane, and/or metyrapone can reduce hypercortisolism until the source of the tumor can be located.

Nelson's syndrome

Annotated Bibliography

Carney JA. Carney complex: the complex of myxomas, spotty pigmentation, endocrine overactivity and schwannomas. Semin Dermatol 1995;14:90.

Newell-Price J, Trainer P, Besser M, et al. The diagnosis and differential diagnosis of Cushing's syndrome and pseudo-Cushing's states. Endocr Rev 1998;19:647–672.

This reference gives a detailed account of the diagnostic modalities currently available for diagnosing Cushing's syndrome. The authors include a useful algorithm that outlines a practical clinical workup for the patient with suspected Cushing's syndrome.

Hirsutism

Hirsutism, defined as "as excessive growth of coarse terminal hair" in females, is a common clinical problem. Subtle alterations in adrenal steroidogenesis is frequently causative. The exact incidence of hirsutism is unknown. Facial hair is common in some ethnic groups (Mediterranean basin) and uncommon in others (northern European) women. There is a wide range of normal, with most women having terminal hair on the upper lips and chin and around the areolae.

Hirsutism can be divided into five major types: familial, congenital, idiopathic, drug-induced, and androgen excess–induced syndromes. Hirsutism can also be seen in porphyria cutanea tarda. The mechanism is unknown.

The exact incidence of hormonal abnormalities in hirsute women is unknown. However, it has been estimated that 85% of hirsute women will demonstrate some form of hyperandrogenemia. In most cases, the cause is idiopathic and has been ascribed to an increased sensitivity of the hair follicles to normal circulating testosterone levels.

The ovary and adrenal glands are the source of all androgens and their intermediate products. Androstenedione and testosterone are produced by both the ovaries and the adrenal glands. On the other hand, dehydroepiandrosterone (DHEA) and its sulfated product, DHEA-sulfate (DHEA-S), are markers of adrenal androgens, since 80% are secreted by the adrenal glands and 20% by the ovaries.

Ovaries and adrenal glands sources of all androgens and their intermediate products
DHEA and DHEA-S markers for adrenal androgens

The androgen excess syndromes capable of inducing hirsutism are either ovarian or adrenal in origin. The ovarian conditions capable of inducing hirsutism include polycystic ovaries (hyperandrogenism syndrome), hilus cell ovarian hyperplasia, arrhenoblastoma, granular cell tumor, and Brenner tumor.

Idiopathic elevations of DHEA most common adrenal cause of hirsutism

The adrenal conditions capable of inducing hirsutism are Cushing's syndrome, congenital adrenal hyperplasia, and idiopathic elevations in serum DHEA (probably the most common cause and most likely the result of occult defective adrenal steroidogenesis). Both adenomas and carcinomas of the adrenal gland are also capable of inducing hirsutism.

The genetically determined adrenogenital syndromes involve various enzyme defects leading to reduced levels of hydrocortisone. A partial or complete absence of the enzyme responsible for hydroxylation at the C-21 position is the most common cause. Low levels of serum cortisol induces more ACTH to be secreted to provide for adequate cortisol levels. As a result of increased ACTH, large quantities of androgens are produced. Virilization of females and sexual precocity of males occur.

Adrenogenital syndrome:
- *multiple enzyme defects*
- *decreased levels of hydrocortisone*
- *increased ACTH*
- *as a result of increased ACTH, excess quantities of androgens produced*

The drugs capable of inducing hirsutism include testosterone, danazol, anabolic steroids, ACTH, metyrapone, phenothiazines, acetazolamide, progesterone, phenytoin, cyclosporine, triamterene with hydrochlorothiazide preparations, minoxidil, glucocorticosteroids, hexachlorobenzine, penicillamine, and psoralens.

Evaluation

Because hirsutism represents a large heterogenous group, patients should be carefully examined and questioned regarding their health history and family members who have increased facial and body hair. This information will generally determine whether the putative hirsutism is familial in nature. Increased libido, oligomenorrhea, deepening of the voice, acne, hair loss, enlargement of the clitoris, and increase in musculature are important physical findings. The presence of virilization usually means the presence of extremely high serum testosterone levels.

Workup:
- *careful history, especially focused on family members*
- *history of menstrual irregularities, increased libido and evidence of acne and hair loss*
- *Physical evidence of virilization*

Longstanding hirsutism, however, with or without menstrual abnormalities, is the most common presentation. These patients do not present with significant systemic manifestations, and virilization is minimal or absent.

Basic screening of adrenal, ovarian, and pituitary function is necessary to evaluate these patients. The basic screening should include free testosterone and DHEA-S tests. If an adrenal source is suspected, then 17 α-hydroxyprogesterone, progesterone, and cortisol may be indicated.

Screening tests:
- *free testosterone*
- *DHEA-S*
- *17 α-hydroxyprogesterone cortisol*

Ovarian androgen excess syndromes are characterized by the presence of elevated free testosterone and/or androstenedione. Although adrenal androgen excess syndromes can occur in which free testosterone and androstenedione levels are elevated, elevated DHEA-S levels differentiate adrenal from ovarian origins. In addition, 17 α-hydroxyprogesterone, 11-deoxycortisol, and cortisol levels are elevated in adrenal androgen excess syndromes.

Elevated DHEA-S distinguishes adrenal from ovarian origins

The pituitary origin of excess androgens can be evaluated with a prolactin level. Elevated prolactin levels have been detected in patients with adrenal hyperplasia, as well as those with polycystic ovarian disease.

Dexamethasone suppression test

The dexamethasone suppression tests, performed over a 7- to 10-day period can be used to distinguish adrenal hyperplasia from adrenal tumors. Following a 7- to 10-day dexamethasone suppression, the cortisol, 17 α-hydroxyprogesterone, and DHEA-S levels are determined. In Cushing's disease (pituitary adenoma), there is no change in all three tests. In congenital adrenal hyperplasia, all tests demonstrate suppression. In benign and malignant adrenal androgen-secreting tumors, the cortisol and 17 α-hydroxyprogesterone are depressed; however, the DHEA-S determination shows no change.

ACTH stimulation test

An ACTH stimulation test is valuable in testing hirsutism patients who have congenital adrenal hyperplasia and those patients who have subtle steroidogenesis defects with or without normal DHEA-S levels. For example, serum levels of 17 α-hydroxyprogesterone will be elevated in women in a 21-hydroxylase deficiency form of congenital adrenal hyperplasia.

Treatment

Treatment of Cushing's disease or androgen-secreting tumors of either the ovaries or adrenal glands is surgical removal.

Treatment:
- *low-dose corticosteroids*
- *spironolactone*

Hyperandrogenism, secondary to adrenal hyperplasia can be suppressed using low-dose corticosteroids. This can be accomplished using 2.5 to 5 mg of prednisone or 0.25 to 0.75 mg of dexamethasone.

Spironolactone can also be used. At doses of 200 mg per day, spironolactone suppresses secretion of adrenal androgens and also blocks androgen receptor sites on hair follicles. Mild elevations in DHEA without congenital adrenal hyperplasia are generally treated with spironolactone rather than with corticosteroids because of the latter's long-term complications.

Leuprolide

In severe cases of ovarian testosterone hypersecretion, the gonadotropin-releasing hormone inhibitor, leuprolide acetate, can be used to induce hypogonadism, then oral contraceptives, as a source of estrogen, can be added back.

Cyproterone acetate is a potent antiandrogen that has been used in Europe to successfully treat hirsutism, acne vulgaris, and seborrhea. It interferes with androgen-binding sites, having an action similar to spironolactone.

Estrogen

Estrogen cyclic therapy has also been used to treat the androgen excess syndromes associated with polycystic ovaries and the adrenal glands.

In addition to these drugs, depilatory creams containing calcium thioglycolate, waxing techniques, electrolysis, epilation, shaving, and, most recently, lasers have been used successfully in the cosmetic management of hirsutism.

Annotated Bibliography

Siegel SF, Finegold DN, Lanes R, et al. ACTH stimulation test and plasma dehydroepiandrosterone sulfate levels in women with hirsutism. N Engl J Med 1990;323:849–854.

This article identified 31 females with hirsutism who were subjected to an ACTH stimulation test and the following hormones measured: progesterone, 17-hydroxypregnenolone, 17 α-hydroxyprogesterone, DHEA, androstenedione, 11-deoxycortisol, and cortisol.

Nineteen of these patients (61%) demonstrated subtle defects in adrenal steroidogenesis; however, there was no significant correlation between basal plasma DHEA-S levels and hormonal response to ACTH. Eleven patients had elevated basal levels of DHEA-S; 5 of these patients had ACTH responses suggestive of compromise of steroidogenesis. However, 13 patients with defective steroidogenesis had normal DHEA-S levels.

These studies demonstrate that many women with hirsutism have mild, late-onset (nonclassic) congenital adrenal hyperplasia, revealed by an ACTH stimulation test. Furthermore, these studies indicate that basal levels of

DHEA-S and 17 α-hydroxyprogesterone may fail to differentiate the causes of androgen excess.

Bergfeld WF. Hirsutism. In: Provost TT, Farmer ER, eds. Current Therapy in Dermatology, 1985–1986. Hamilton, ON: BC Decker, 1985, pp 119–123.

Adrenal Insufficiency

Most common cause of exogenous adrenal insufficiency is glucocorticosteroids

Adrenal insufficiency occurs when the adrenal production of glucocorticoids falls below the requirements of the body. Primary adrenal insufficiency refers to adrenal gland destruction/dysfunction, and secondary disease is due to hypothalamus-pituitary dysfunction. The latter results in CRH or ACTH deficiency.

The most common cause of adrenal insufficiency is glucocorticoids. Individuals who have received supraphysiologic doses of glucocorticoids for other diseases (eg, inflammatory conditions, such as rheumatoid arthritis, dermatitis, systemic lupus erythematosus) may have had their production of CRH suppressed. This can lead to adrenal insufficiency when the glucocorticoids are discontinued. The probability of insufficiency has traditionally been related to the dosage and duration of therapy. A treatment period longer than 2 to 3 weeks and doses greater than 12 to 15 mg/m^2/d are more likely to induce clinically significant adrenal insufficiency. The use of such schedules does not cause adrenal insufficiency universally, so it is important that the clinician evaluate each patient with any history of glucocorticoid treatment for its presence. The other causes of secondary adrenal insufficiency include all the causes of panhypopituitarism, but these are much less common.

Most common cause of Addison's disease worldwide is tuberculosis.
Autoimmune adrenalitis most common cause in developed countries

Primary adrenal insufficiency is otherwise called "Addison's disease," after Addison who, in 1855, described 11 patients with primary adrenal insufficiency due to tuberculosis, hemorrhage, and metastatic involvement of the adrenals. The most common cause of Addison's disease worldwide is miliary tuberculosis. This occurs when more than 90% of the adrenal glands are infiltrated by caseating granulomas and inflammatory cells. In the developed nations, the most common cause is idiopathic disease, accounting for approximately 65 to 70% of cases. Idiopathic disease is probably autoimmune adrenalitis in most cases. This syndrome is characterized by atrophy/fibrous scarring of the glands and circulating antibodies to the adrenals (in 50 to 67% of patients). Multiple autoimmune diseases, such as Hashimoto's disease, pernicious anemia, and type II diabetes mellitus can coexist. This is referred to as polyglandular deficiency syndrome type 2. Adrenal insufficiency is also seen in the polyglandular deficiency syndrome type 1, which is an autosomal recessive disorder that presents with adrenal insufficiency, hypoparathyroidism, and mucocutaneous candidiasis. Other causes of Addison's disease are outlined in Table 32–17.

Clinical Features

Presenting symptoms include severe fatigue, weakness, unrefreshing sleep, anorexia, malaise, weight loss, nausea, diarrhea, and abdominal pain. Signs that indicate primary adrenal insufficiency are orthostatic hypotension from hypoaldosteronism, salt cravings, and adrenal calcifications. In secondary adrenal insufficiency, patients have pallor rather than hyperpigmentation. Other symptoms of panhypopituitarism may be evident.

Acute adrenal insufficiency can occur if there is a hemorrhage into the adrenal or pituitary glands. More commonly, it is seen when there is superimposed stress in a patient with chronic adrenal insufficiency. It is usually manifested as cardiovascular collapse that is minimally responsive to vasopressor agents and volume expansion. Delirium and abdominal pain may also be seen.

Cutaneous Manifestations

Striking hyperpigmentation due to increased secretion of ACTH

Diffuse loss of hair, especially in androgen-dependent areas, is common and is most easily appreciated in the axillae. In the primary form of the disease, there can be striking hyperpigmentation of the skin in the chronic cases. The hyperpigmentation is thought to be due to the action of elevated levels of ACTH and

TABLE 32–17 Etiology of Adrenal Insufficiency

Primary adrenal insufficiency (Addison's disease)
Tuberculosis
Idiopathic (autoimmune adrenalitis)—associated with polyglandular deficiency syndrome types 1 and 2
Adrenal hemorrhage (in the setting of trauma, sepsis, anticoagulants, and antiphospholipid antibody syndrome)
Fungal infections (eg, histoplasmosis, blastomycosis)
Infiltrative diseases (eg, sarcoidosis, amyloidosis)
Acquired immunodeficiency syndrome
Metastases, especially from lung, breast, melanoma, and gastrointestinal tract
Congenital adrenal hyperplasia
Medications (eg, ketoconazole)
Adrenoleukodystrophy, adrenomyeloneuropathy
Familial glucocorticoid deficiency
Secondary adrenal insufficiency
Withdrawal of exogenous glucocorticoids
Panhypopituitarism
After-cure of Cushing's syndrome
Isolated deficiency of ACTH

ACTH = adrenocorticotropin hormone.

Increased pigment seen in creases of palms, knuckles, axillae, and elbows

MSH secondary to the feedback loop of the hypothalamus-pituitary-adrenal axis, leading to increased melanin production by melanocytes. This increased pigment is characteristically seen in the mucous membranes of the mouth (lips, gums, hard palate, and tongue) as spots and patches but has also been described on the conjunctiva and vagina. The skin, especially in exposed areas, such as the face, become tanned and bronzed. Also, increased pigment is seen in the creases of the palms, knuckles, axillae, and elbows. Old scars, hair, the linea alba, areolae, the perineum, and nails can be involved. Approximately 15% of patients develop areas of vitiligo.

Diagnosis

Classically, a normocytic, normochromic anemia (due to cortisol and androgen deficiency) is seen with a relative eosinophilia and lymphocytosis. Biochemically, there may also be a mild metabolic acidosis, hypoglycemia, mild hypercalcemia, and signs of intravascular depletion (ie, increased serum urea nitrogen and uric acid). Patients with primary insufficiency can have hyperkalemia due to hypoaldosteronism. Hyponatremia is seen frequently in both primary and secondary insufficiency.

Morning cortisol level
Short ACTH stimulation test

Generally, random cortisol levels cannot establish the diagnosis, as these fluctuate widely even in the adrenally insufficient individual. However, patients with a morning (between 8 and 9 am) cortisol level less than 3 μg/dL can be presumed to have adrenal insufficiency. Most patients will, however, need dynamic (stimulatory) testing. The most common test used is the short ACTH stimulation test. In this test, 250 μg of synthetic corticotropin (ie, Cosyntropin) is given intravenously or intramuscularly, and cortisol is measured before and again 30 and 60 minutes after. In a normal individual, the stimulated cortisol level is greater than 18 μg/dL. This test measures the ability of the adrenal glands to respond to ACTH stimulation and, therefore, does not differentiate primary or secondary insufficiency. Normal results can be seen in acute secondary adrenal insufficiency. Patients at risk for secondary adrenal insufficiency may need one of the following tests performed if the standard ACTH stimulation test is normal: insulin-induced hypoglycemia, overnight metyrapone, CRH stimulation, or low-dose (1 μg) ACTH stimulation (Table 32–18).

TABLE 32–18 Tests Used to Evaluate Adrenal Insufficiency

Test	Method
Diagnosis	
Short ACTH stimulation testing	After 1 μg ACTH stimulated cortisol is normally > 18 mg/dL.
Early morning cortisol	Early morning cortisol is < 3 μg/dL.
Insulin hypoglycemia test	After an overnight fast, regular insulin 0.10–0.15 U/kg is given intravenously, aiming for a blood glucose < 40 mg/dL or a decrease of 50% below the fasting level; cortisol and ACTH are measured at 0 and 60 minutes and at the glucose nadir; in normal patients, ACTH levels should be > 50 pg/mL and cortisol > 20 μg/dL
Localization	
Plasma ACTH level	Generally > 100 pg/mL in primary insufficiency
Adrenal autoantibody tests	Positive in approximately 65 to 70% cases of autoimmune adrenalitis
Prolonged ACTH stimulation test	3 μg/h ACTH infused over 48 hours with 24-hour urine collection for 17 α-hydroxysteroids on the first and second days; in primary insufficiency, 17 α-hydroxysteroids are 4 mg/24 h and in secondary insufficiency it is 10 mg/24 h
Short metyrapone test	30 mg/kg of metyrapone results in a plasma 11-deoxycortisol at 8 hours of 7 μg/dL and a plasma ACTH > 150 pg/mL in primary insufficiency but minimal responses in secondary insufficiency
CRH test	1 μg/kg CRH given intravenously and cortisol/ACTH collected at intervals of -15, 0, 15, 30, 60, 90, and 120 minutes; flat response of ACTH in pituitary disease; high ACTH and low cortisol levels in primary disease
Aldosterone stimulation test	ACTH stimulation test with aldosterone levels at 0 and 60 minutes; aldosterone levels < 5 ng/dL indicate primary disease

After making the diagnosis of adrenal insufficiency, various tests can be used to localize the level of the lesion. Measurement of a random ACTH level prior to starting replacement glucocorticoids is useful, easy, and sensitive. In primary insufficiency, ACTH levels are generally elevated to greater than 100 pg/mL. Other localizing tests include a prolonged ACTH stimulation test, CRH stimulation test, and short metyrapone test (see Table 32–18). Once the level of the lesion is localized, the pituitary or adrenal gland should be imaged by MRI or CT.

Management

Symptomatic patients should be treated with glucocorticoid replacement. Practically, most adults are maintained on hydrocortisone 20 mg/d. The dose is then decreased to between 10 and 15 mg per day as tolerated. Alternatively, some physicians use cortisone acetate (20 to 37.5 mg per day) or prednisone (5 to 7.5 mg per day). Replacement with glucocorticoid will result in gradual resolution of the hyperpigmentation or pallor. Patients with primary insufficiency may also require mineralocorticoid replacement as fludrocortisone (50 to 200 μg as a single dose). They should take the minimum dose that relieves orthostasis, hyperkalemia, and secondary hyper-reninemia without inducing supine hypertension. Patients should also wear an identification bracelet so that emergency personnel will administer stress doses of glucocorticoids. Stress doses range from twice the normal maintenance dose for minor stress to 100 mg hydrocortisone intramuscularly/intravenously every 6 to 8 hours for major stresses, such as major trauma, surgery, burns, or shock.

Annotated Bibliography

Oelkers W. Adrenal insufficiency. N Engl J Med 1996;335:1206–1212.

This article discusses the clinical features and laboratory evaluation of suspected adrenal insufficiency, with 43 references.

Pancreas

Diabetes mellitus refers to a syndrome of dysmetabolism characterized by hyperglycemia and polyuria. Polyuric states were recognized by the ancient Egyptians as far back as 1550 B.C. The term "diabetes" was coined during the second century A.D. and means "to pass through," referring to the characteristic polyuria associated with the disease. The Indians in fifth to sixth century A.D. recognized that urine was characteristically sweet to taste, leading to the term "mellitus" being added by Rollo in the 18th century.

The central and defining phenotypic characteristic of diabetes mellitus is chronic and sustained hyperglycemia, which can be seen in a fasting state or after challenge by a glucose load. At present, there are two operational criteria for the diagnosis of diabetes mellitus, the 1997 American Diabetes Association (ADA) criteria and the 1985 modified World Health Organization (WHO) criteria (Tables 32–19 and 32–20).

The WHO has a consultation committee that is at present revising the criteria and is expected to produce a report in 1999, which will incorporate elements of the ADA guidelines but probably retain the old standard of the oral glucose tolerance test. Glycosylated hemoglobin is not a sensitive screen for diabetes and is not at present used to establish the diagnosis.

Common disease

Diabetes mellitus occurs in 8% of the population in the United States. The prevalence varies in other countries of the world, being much higher in Polynesia and lower in the less developed countries. The worldwide burden of disease is estimated as being over 100 million people, which is increasing and estimated to reach 239 million by 2010.

Diabetes mellitus is classified as (1) type I, characterized by beta cell destruction by autoimmune or idiopathic mechanisms; (2) type II, notable for varying degrees of insulin resistance, beta cell dysfunction, and inappropriate glucose production; (3) miscellaneous types, including those caused by genetic defects of beta cell function or insulin action, pancreatic insufficiency, or drugs or those secondary to endocrinopathies and other genetic syndromes; or (4) gestational, which is hyperglycemia with onset or first recognition during pregnancy.

TABLE 32–19 1997 ADA Criteria for the Diagnosis of Diabetes Mellitus

Symptoms of diabetes plus casual plasma glucose concentration 200 mg/dL (11.1 mmol/L), or
Fasting plasma glucose 126 mg/dL (7.0 µmol/L), or
2-hour plasma glucose 200 mg/dL during an OGTT
It was recommended to confirm values in the asymptomatic patient by repeat testing on a different day, and the OGTT was not recommended for routine clinical use.

OGTT = oral glucose tolerance test.

TABLE 32–20 1985 Modified WHO Criteria for the Diagnosis of Diabetes

Symptoms of diabetes with a casual plasma glucose 270 mg/dL (15 mmol/L), or
Fasting plasma glucose 140 mg/dL (7.8 µmol/L), or
2-hour postprandial glucose 200 mg/dL (11.1 µmol/L) in the OGTT

Regardless of the form of diabetes mellitus, it is associated with increased morbidity and mortality. The relative or absolute deficiency of insulin causes disturbed/altered intermediary metabolism, including lipolysis, dyslipidemia, protein catabolism, hepatic gluconeogenesis, and electrolyte disturbances. Sustained hyperglycemia enables the nonenzymatic covalent bonding of glucose to various proteins of the body (called "glycation"), which can result in altered function of structural proteins, enzymes, receptors, and other body proteins.

Type I Diabetes

Autoimmune destruction of pancreatic β cells

Ketoacidosis

In type I diabetes, there is autoimmune destruction of the beta cells leading to an absolute insulin deficiency (insulinopenia). The trigger for this destruction is widely presumed to be an antecedent viral infection. The mechanism is thought to be a form of molecular mimicry leading to immune cross-reactivity with an antigen of the islets of Langerhans. Environmental factors have also been suspected, including early exposure to cow's milk antigens and chemicals. There are also geographical differences in the prevalence, with the highest rates in temperate countries, and recently, it has been shown that the incidence rates are increasing, especially in the very young (< 5 years old). Patients with type I diabetes tend to be young, are prone to ketoacidosis, and have autoantibodies to the islet cell, insulin, and glutamic acid decarboxylase in the early phase of the disease.

Type II Diabetes

Most common form
Insulin resistance to ketoacidosis

Type II is the most prevalent form of diabetes, representing over 90 % of cases. It is more commonly seen in older individuals and has a stronger familial frequency. This form is due to insulin resistance in the periphery leading to compensatory hyperinsulinemia. As there is some endogenous insulin production, these patients are usually resistant to the development of ketoacidosis. The underlying insulin resistance is also associated with a constellation of other metabolic disturbances, collectively referred to as "syndrome X." These include dyslipidemia (most commonly elevated triglyceride and LDL-cholesterol levels and low HDL-cholesterol levels), hypertension, a procoagulant state, and atherosclerosis.

Clinical Features of Diabetes

Polyuria
Polydipsia

Many patients with type II diabetes are asymptomatic, and as such, it is estimated that many patients have undetected diabetes for a median of 4 to 5 years prior to clinical diagnosis. Classically, patients may complain of urinary frequency, polyuria, thirst, and weight loss despite increased hunger. Patients can develop dehydration and electrolyte disturbances from the polyuria, which is induced by the osmotic diuresis of glycosuria. In severe cases, especially if there is a superimposed illness such as sepsis, myocardial infarction, or drug abuse, there may be delirium and severe hyperglycemia. In patients with type I diabetes, this leads to diabetic ketoacidosis. Type II patients are more resistant to ketoacidosis and develop, instead, hyperosmolar nonketotic hyperglycemia.

Lazy leukocyte syndrome
Increased infections

Hyperglycemia alters leukocyte chemotaxis (lazy leukocyte syndrome) and interferes with neutrophil phagocytosis and bactericidal action. Therefore, diabetic patients have increased susceptibility to bacterial and fungal infections. Infections of the skin, respiratory tract, and urinary tract are the most common, but any area of the body can be involved.

Cutaneous Manifestations of Diabetes

Diabetic Dermopathy

Not specific

Diabetic dermopathy is characterized by oval, dull red-brown macules and papules approximately 0.5 cm in diameter occurring predominantly over the anterior lower legs but also on the thighs and forearms. These lesions evolve slowly, producing a brownish, atrophic scar. These lesions, not specific for diabetes mellitus, generally occur in diabetes mellitus patients with evidence of other microvascular abnormalities (eg, retinopathy).

Histopathologic examination demonstrates a thickened periodic acid Schiff (PAS)-positive basement membrane of involved blood vessels. Hemosiderin deposition is responsible for the pigment alteration.

Necrobiosis Lipoidica Diabeticorum

May occur in nondiabetic as well as diabetic patients

Necrobiosis lipoidica diabeticorum (NLD) is a relatively rare cutaneous manifestation of diabetes occurring in less than 0.5% of patients (Figures 32–8 to 32–10). Approximately 70% of NLD patients have overt diabetes. In general, the onset of NLD occurs after the diabetes have been established for many years. However, at times, it occurs simultaneously, and there are instances in which NLD antedates the development of overt diabetes mellitus. It has been reported that a steroid-augmented glucose tolerance test may uncover latent diabetes in NLD patients without evidence of overt diabetes mellitus. Other studies dispute this.

(It is our experience that despite the steroid-augmented glucose tolerance tests, several NLD patients have failed to demonstrate evidence of glucose metabolism dysfunction. Thus, the majority, but not all, of NLD lesions occur in diabetic individuals.)

The exact pathophysiology of NLD is unknown, although it has been assumed by some investigators that the microangiopathy associated with dia-

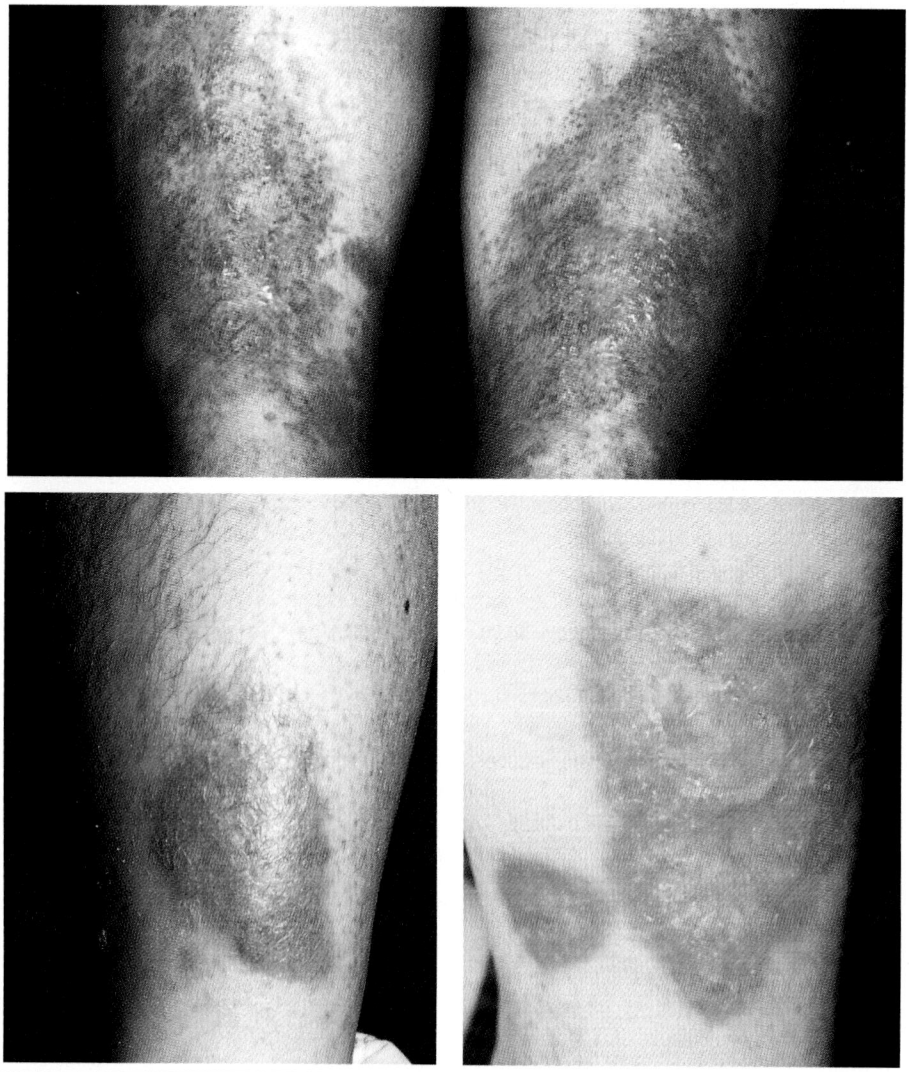

FIGURES 32–8 AND 32–10 Examples of necrobiosis lipoidica diabeticorum. Note brownish-yellow pigmentation. (Figure 32–10 Reproduced with permission from Rick Stearns, M.D., Tulsa, OK)

betes is involved in the pathogenesis. The histopathology of these lesions indicates that thickening of the blood vessels is almost a universal finding. Vascular occlusion may occur (Figures 32–11 and 32–12). This may result in necrosis. The granulomatous reaction that occurs, however, remains unexplained.

The classic lesions of NLD are indurated, annular plaques occurring predominantly over the anterior lower extremities. Induration, sclerosis, and atrophy occur in varying degrees. The individual lesions may be sharply demarcated, demonstrating a brownish-red and, at times, violaceous hue. In general, the atrophic center demonstrates a yellowish discoloration. Prominent telangiectasia may be seen.

Generally occurs on lower legs

The lesions are relatively anesthetic and may demonstrate a great deal of scale formation due to xerosis. Ulceration may occur and, at times, may be very extensive.

In addition to the anterior shins, approximately 15% of patients will demonstrate lesions at other sites, including, for example, the arms, trunk, scalp, ankles, and backs of legs.

May also occur on other areas of the body

The lesions occur predominantly in females, and diabetic retinopathy is infrequently present. The lesions may extend slowly over many years. On rare occasions, squamous cell carcinomas have been detected.

Rarely a squamous cell carcinoma may occur

The lesions of NLD may respond to local corticosteroid therapy in the form of injections or the application of a steroid-impregnated tape. PUVA therapy has been found to be effective (For further discussion on the use of ultraviolet light in the treatment of nonpsoriatic conditions, see Chapter 71, "Phototherapy and Photochemotherapy of Skin Diseases.")

Vascular Ulcers

Large and small vessel angiopathy producing atherosclerosis frequently occurs in patients with diabetes mellitus. Manifestations of atherosclerosis are intermittent claudication, pallor, and cooling of the distal extremities, as well as ulcer formation. The ulcers most commonly occur on the lateral aspect of the ankle. Healing is difficult.

Diabetic Neuropathy

Small blood vessel angiopathy involving the peripheral nerves is a complication of long standing diabetes mellitus. An indolent perforating ulcer (mal perforans)

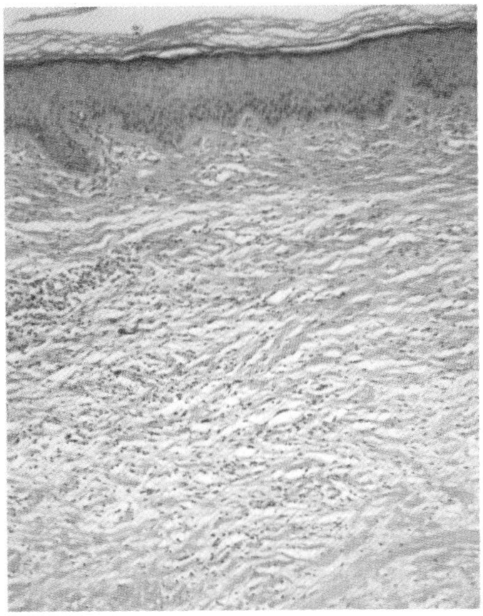

FIGURE 32–11 Necrobiosis lipoidica diabeticorum—broad bands of horizontal fibrosis alternating with layers of chronic inflammation.

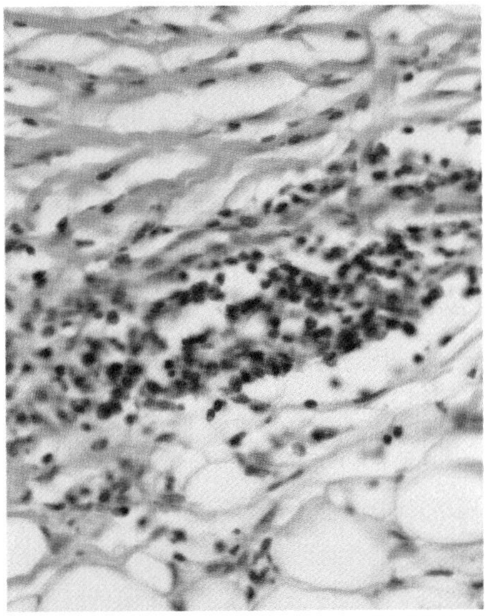

FIGURE 32–12 Necrobiosis lipoidica diabeticorum—histiocytes and lymphocytes surrounding degenerated collagen.

Ulceration on feet a common complication

may occur on all areas of the foot, most commonly on pressure areas. Penetrating ulcers slowly evolve. Secondary infection may produce an osteomyelitis. Loss of temperature and pain sensation is frequently characteristic. At times, Charcot's joint may result.

A motor neuropathy may produce subluxation of the digits, depressed metatarsal heads, and hammer toes. Sensory abnormalities of the lower extremities, including numbness, tingling, burning, or an aching sensation, may occur. An autonomic neuropathy may produce decreased or absent sweating, especially of the lower extremities, accompanied by edema, erythema, and atrophy.

Bullous Lesions

Subepidermal split through lamina lucida

Subepidermal bullae predominantly involving the lower extremities, especially the feet, are a rare complication. The subepidermal split is through the lamina lucida. Most of the patients with this complication have significant diabetic retinopathy, suggesting that weakness of the basement membrane zones, secondary to a microangiopathy, reduces the threshold for blister formation.

Scleredema Adultorum

May also be seen in children with a viral infection and rarely with multiple myeloma

Scleredema adultorum is a rare complication of adult-onset diabetes characterized by indurated skin, usually beginning on the posterior and lateral aspects of the neck. This is a painless swelling that gradually spreads to the face and upper portions of the body producing stiffness. At times, it may involve the abdomen as well as the arms and hands. There is a nonpitting induration caused by thickened collagen bundles and the deposition of glycosaminoglycans. The exact pathophysiology of this unusual complication is unknown.

Bacterial Infections

Staphylococcal infections

Staphylococcal infections, candidiasis, and dermatophyte infections have been associated with poorly controlled diabetes mellitus. Staphylococcal pyoderma, especially abscesses and furunculosis, has previously been associated with significant morbidity for diabetes mellitus patients. The frequency of these lesions, however, is not as great as it was due to better diabetic control and the use of antibiotics.

Of special significance is foot care in patients with diabetes mellitus. The presence of a low-grade fungal infection in diabetes mellitus patients of long standing who have atherosclerosis and peripheral neuropathy is problematic. Small, microabrasions in the skin are excellent portals of entry for bacteria. These bacterial infections induce poorly healing ulcerations in an already compromised skin.

Foot care very important

Compulsive foot care is mandatory. The use of topical antifungal agents, cleansing of the feet, and routine visits to a podiatrist are indicated. Aggressive treatment of the most banal of wounds with systemic antibiotics is effective.

(Provost has found that the application with a Q-tip of a 3% salicylic acid, 70% isopropyl alcohol solution to the toenails, intertriginous areas, and the soles of the feet, on a nightly basis, is an effective prophylactic measure.)

Yeast Infections

Usually seen in poorly controlled diabetics

Candida albicans vaginitis is a common complication of diabetes. In addition, *C. albicans* infections of the intertriginous areas of the groin and pendulous breasts may be reflective of poorly controlled diabetes. Control of the diabetes eliminates this problem.

Mucormycosis

Life-threatening

Mucormycosis is a rare, life-threatening, fungal infection involving the perinasal sinuses and extending into the central nervous system. It occurs in diabetics who have ketoacidosis. The fungal infection extends from the nasal mucosa to involve the eye, producing a painful, inflammatory proptosis and ophthalmoplegia. Cavernous sinus thrombosis occurs and direct invasion of the cerebral cortex is common. Saprophytic fungi belonging to the genera *Mucor*, *Rhizopus*, *Rhizomucor*, and *Absidia* have been associated.

Xanthomatosis

Manifestation of poorly controlled diabetes

Poorly controlled diabetes associated with increased quantities of blood lipids, especially chylomicrons, may induce the formation of eruptive xanthomas. These are small, reddish-yellow nodules approximately 2 to 3 mm in size, occurring in groups most commonly over the extensor surfaces and the buttocks. These eruptive xanthomas have an erythematous base and contain predominantly triglycerides. They rapidly disappear on control of the diabetes.

Pruritus

Probably not a manifestation of diabetes

Generalized pruritus has been erroneously attributed to diabetes on the basis of one report published in 1927. Diabetic patients, however, may commonly have pruritus ani and pruritus vulvae, especially if candidiasis is present.

Perforating Collagenosis

Diabetic patients in renal failure are at risk of developing perforating collagenosis (Figures 32–13 and 32–14). This is a highly pruritic, papular disease process involving the trunk and extremities. Umbilicated hyperpigmented papules containing keratotic debris are detected. Collagen fibers penetrate through the epidermis, forming the keratotic debris.

Granuloma Annulare

Probably not a manifestation of diabetes mellitus

The histologic features of granuloma annulare are quite similar to NLD and rheumatoid arthritis. In the past, it has been suggested that disseminated granuloma annulare is associated with diabetes. However, other studies have failed to confirm such findings (Provost's personal experience with two patients who had generalized granuloma annulare failed to reveal altered glucose metabolism using a steroid-augmented glucose tolerance test.) Granuloma annulare may respond to PUVA therapy. (For further discussion on ultraviolet light therapy, see Chapter 71, "Phototherapy and Photochemotherapy of Skin Diseases.")

Vitiligo

Vitiligo has been found to occur with greater frequency than expected in patients who have insulin-dependent diabetes mellitus. The exact relationship of vitiligo to diabetes is unknown, but if diabetes is indeed an autoimmune disease, an increased frequency of vitiligo putative autoimmune disease would not be unexpected.

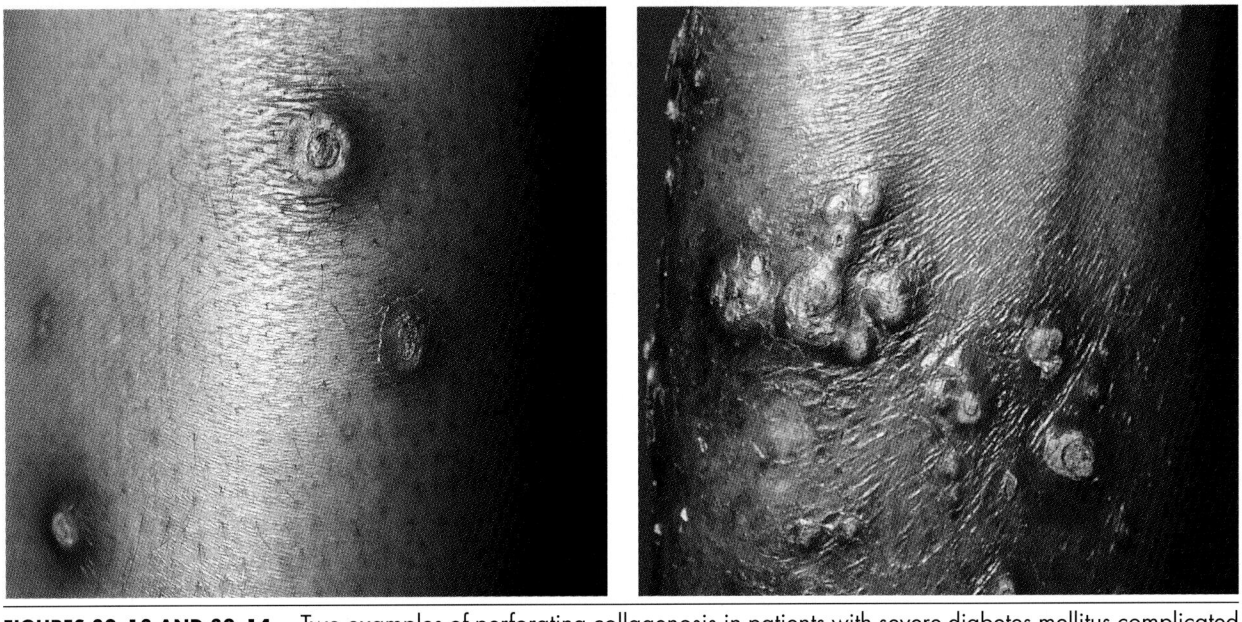

FIGURES 32–13 AND 32–14 Two examples of perforating collagenosis in patients with severe diabetes mellitus complicated by renal failure.

Acanthosis Nigricans

Indicative of insulin resistance

It is now known that acanthosis nigricans is found in association with a variety of endocrinopathies in which insulin resistance is detected. It has been proposed that the pathogenesis of acanthosis nigricans is secondary to hyperinsulinemia induced by insulin resistance. Insulin, in high concentration, then competes for growth factor receptors on keratinocytes that promote growth. (For further discussion of acanthosis nigricans, see Chapter 29, "Paraneoplastic Dermatoses.")

Other Complications

The microvascular complications of diabetes are retinopathy, neuropathy, and nephropathy. These develop after a disease period of 5 to 15 years (mean of 6 to 8 years). Approximately 25% of individuals will have complications at the time of diagnosis. Type I diabetic patients do not have microvascular complications at diagnosis as the onset of the disease is relatively abrupt and clinically apparent.

After a mean duration of 7 years of clinical diabetes, approximately 30 to 40% of diabetics have background retinopathy. These patients will have microaneurysms, hard exudates, and dot and blot hemorrhages. Although these background changes are not vision threatening, retinopathy can progress to macular edema and proliferative retinopathy. Visual loss due to these advanced forms of diabetic retinopathy can often be prevented by early recognition and laser photocoagulation.

Neuropathy is also very common in 20 to 40% of patients after 10 years. Neuropathy can present in a variety of ways as listed in Table 32–21.

Most of the neuropathies are thought to be due to neuronal ischemia created by microvascular dysfunction of the vaso nervosum, glycated end products, and abnormal metabolic products, such as polyols in the nerve.

Diabetic nephropathy occurs in approximately 20% of type II and 40 % of Type I diabetic patients. It is first evident as microalbuminuria, which progresses to overt proteinuria, falling glomerular filtration, nephrotic syndrome, and ultimately, end-stage renal failure. Diabetes is the most common cause of end-stage renal failure necessitating dialysis in the United States.

Increased mortality due to cardiovascular disease

Although microvascular complications increase the morbidity of patients with diabetes, it is the macrovascular complications that increase the mortality. Patients with diabetes have a mortality rate attributable to cardiovascular disease that is 2 to 3 times that of the normal population. There is a high prevalence of coronary artery disease, cerebrovascular disease, and peripheral vascular disease. Although hyperglycemia contributes to the development of these processes, the excess prevalence of atherosclerotic disease is due mostly to the dysmetabolism that accompanies diabetes. Hence, attention needs to be given to the concurrent dyslipidemia, hypertension, and procoagulant state.

TABLE 32–21 Presentations of Diabetic Neuropathy

Neuropathy	Presentation
Sensory polyneuropathy (the most common)	Numbness and paresthesiae in a glove-and-stocking distribution of the limbs; absent ankle jerks; decreased sensation to vibration, pressure and propioception resulting in increased risk of ulceration, Charcot's joints, and trauma
Painful neuropathy	Dysthesiae, especially of the feet
Mononeuritis multiplex	Individual sensory, motor and cranial nerves can undergo temporary paresis
Autonomic neuropathy	Diabetic gastropathy, orthostatic hypotension, diarrhea, erectile failure, and detrusor dysfunction
Diabetic amyopathy	Transient plexopathy leading to lower limb weakness, pain, and weight loss

Management of Diabetes

Strict glycemic control significantly reduces complications

The aim of therapy is to achieve normoglycemia without inducing hypoglycemia, prevent microvascular and macrovascular complications, and treat concurrent dysmetabolism. It was proven in the Diabetes Control and Complications Trial, that strict glycemic control in type I diabetes decreases microvascular complications by 34 to 76%. The United Kingdom Prospective Diabetes Study also showed that in type II diabetes, similar control reduced complications by an average of 25%. These reductions occurred irrespective of the therapy (insulin or oral hypoglycemic agents) used. Macrovascular complications slightly decreased with euglycemia, but significant decrements were seen when blood pressure and lipids were also normalized. The attainment of all these goals mandates a dedicated team of professionals providing care, including physicians, diabetic nurse educators, nutritionists, podiatrists, ophthalmologists, physical therapists, and psychologists.

Education is key to success

Maintenance of ideal weight important

All patients require education about diabetes and appropriate lifestyles with respect to diet, weight loss, exercise, smoking cessation, foot care, and home glucose monitoring. Diabetic education and alteration of lifestyles are the most important aspects of diabetes care but, sadly, are neglected by many patients and their physicians. The diet in patients with type I diabetes is calculated to provide adequate calories to maintain ideal body weight. Meals should be composed of complex carbohydrates, low cholesterol, and modest protein (to provide 10 to 20% of calories) and fat intake should be limited to 20 to 30% of the total calories. Patients with type II diabetes are frequently overweight or frankly obese, so their diet should provide modest calorie restriction to promote weight reduction. Exercise not only helps to maintain any weight loss but also serves to increase the sensitivity of peripheral tissues to insulin. Hence, this decreased insulin resistance acutely reduces blood glucose levels and reduces the need for insulin or oral agents.

Patients with type I diabetes require insulin for survival, with average requirements being 0.5 to 1.0 U per kg body weight per day. Insulin can be administered as multiple subcutaneous injections or through a continuous subcutaneous insulin infusion pump. Some type II patients have resolution of hyperglycemia as a result of lifestyle changes. However, in the majority of cases, pharmacologic therapy will also be required. The arsenal of available drugs include:

1. Sulfonylureas, such as glyburide, glipizide, chlorpropamide facilitate insulin release by the beta cells and, until recently, were the only antidiabetic agents available in the United States. Side effects are hypoglycemia, especially in the agents with long half-lives, and weight gain.
2. Metformin primarily decreases hepatic gluconeogenesis, increases peripheral insulin sensitivity, and may encourage slight weight loss. Approximately 20% of patients can suffer from nausea, cramps, and diarrhea. Metformin should not be used in the patient who has renal insufficiency (creatinine ± 1.5 mg/dL), congestive heart failure, alcoholism, and cirrhosis, where dangerous lactic acidosis can occur.
3. Troglitazone decreases peripheral insulin resistance. The mechanism is thought to be mediated by activation of the peroxisomal proliferator activator receptor gamma that regulates adipocyte differentiation and modifies insulin sensitivity. The drug has to be carefully monitored on initiation as idiosyncratic irreversible hepatic dysfunction can occur. Its efficacy in reducing the glycosylated hemoglobin (HbA1c) is similar to metformin.
4. Acarbose decreases the breakdown of oligosaccharides into absorbable monosaccharides in the intestine. This slows the absorption of carbohydrate and reduces postprandial hyperglycemia. It reduces HbA1c by only 0.5 to 1% when used as monotherapy. Common side effects include gastrointestinal discomfort, flatulence, and diarrhea.

Monotherapy is often not sufficient to maintain normoglycemia in the long term as beta cell failure is progressive necessitating combination oral therapy. Ultimately, combination therapy can fail and patients will need insulin, which can be administered along with the oral agents or as a single agent. As there is insulin resistance in type II diabetic patients, their insulin requirements are higher than those of a type I patient by up to 2.0 U per kg per day. Details of treatment with oral agents and insulin are beyond the scope of this chapter, but reviews are included in the bibliography.

All patients will also require annual eye examinations to screen for retinopathy, annual evaluation for urinary microalbumin, regular examinations of their feet, screening for neuropathy, and assessment for cardiovascular risk factors. (For a discussion on glucagonoma syndrome, see Chapter 31, "Hormonally Mediated Paraneoplastic Syndromes.")

Annotated Bibliography

Daggo-Jack S, Santiago JV. Pathophysiology of type II diabetes and the modes of action of therapeutic interventions. Arch Intern Med 1997;157:1802–1817.

This comprehensive overview of the pathophysiology of type II diabetes discusses insulin resistance, beta-cell dysfunction, and hepatic gluconeogenesis. It also describes the newly available pharmacologic options for type II diabetes.

American Diabetes Association. Standards of medical care for patients with diabetes mellitus. Diabetes Care 1998;21:S23–S31.

This article provides concise description of the standard of care for the type I or II diabetic patient.

Boulton AJM, Cutfield RG, Abouganem D, et al. Necrobiosis lipoidica diabeticorum: a clinical pathologic study. J Am Acad Dermatol 1988;18:530–537.

Danowski TS, Saben G, Sarver ME. Skin spots and diabetes mellitus. Am J Med Sci 1960;251:570.

Clegg DO, Zone JJ, Piepkorn MW. Necrobiosis lipoidica associated with jejunoileal bypass surgery. Arch Dermatol 1982;118:135–136.

Clement M, Guy R, Pembroke AC. Squamous cell carcinoma arising in longstanding necrobiosis lipoidica. Arch Dermatol 1985;121:24–25.

Gray HR, Graham JH, Johnson WC. Necrobiosis lipoidica diabeticorum: a histopathologic and histochemical study. J Invest Dermatol 1965;44:369–380.

MacKay JP. Necrobiosis lipoidica diabeticorum involving scalp and face. Br J Dermatol 1975;93:729–730.

Bernstein JE, Levine LE, Medenica MM, et al. Reduced threshold to suction-induced blister formation in insulin dependent diabetics. J Am Acad Dermatol 1983;8:790–791.

This study demonstrates that diabetics have an increased susceptibility to cutaneous blister formation. Using a suction blister machine, the mean average of 31.9 minutes was needed to induce a suction blister in diabetics, versus 68 minutes for the controls ($p < .01$*). Whether these observations are germane to a bullous eruption detected in diabetics is unknown. Subepidermal blister formation through the lamina lucida is seen in diabetics with neuropathy, retinopathy, or nephropathy. In this study, only 3 of 15 patients had such diabetic complications.*

Cohn BA, Wheeler CE, Briggaman RA. Scleredema adultorum of Buschke and diabetes mellitus. Arch Dermatol 1970;101:27–35.

This is a review of three patients with longstanding diabetes who developed changes consistent with scleredema adultorum of Buschke. In addition, these authors reviewed 10 additional cases from the literature with a similar association.

Huntley AC. The cutaneous manifestations of diabetes mellitus. J Am Acad Dermatol 1982;7:427–455.

This is an exceptionally well-written article detailing the cutaneous manifestations of diabetes mellitus. Of special interest is the discussion of the auto-

nomic as well as peripheral neuropathies associated with diabetes. References cited total 188.

Jelinek JE. The skin in diabetes mellitus: cutaneous manifestations, complications and association. In: Yearbook of Dermatology, 1970. Chicago: Yearbook Medical Publications, 1970, pp 5–35.

This is another excellent article summarizing the cutaneous manifestations of diabetes mellitus.

Rosenbloom AL, Silverstein JH, Lezotte DC, et al. Limited joint mobility in childhood diabetes mellitus indicates increased risk of microvascular disease. N Engl J Med 1981;305:191–194.

This is a very interesting paper describing limited mobility of small and large joints in 92 (30%) of 309 patients with diabetes mellitus. We feel that this limited joint mobility identifies a population at risk for the early development of microvascular complications.

Muller SA, Winkelmann RK. Necrobiosis lipoidica diabeticorum. Arch Dermatol 1966;93:272–281.

This classic paper describes the existence of NLD in association with diabetes mellitus, as well as the existence of a group of NLD patients in whom no diabetes can be demonstrated.

Joshi N, et al. Infections in patients with diabetes mellitus. N Engl J Med 1999; 341:1906–1912.

A good review of the infectious complications associated with diabetes mellitus. It contains 69 references.

Multiple Endocrine Neoplasia

Neoplastic processes involving multiple endocrine glands in predictable patterns have long been recognized. The glands most commonly involved are the pituitary, parathyroid, pancreas, adrenal, and thyroid. Erdheim, in 1903, first described a patient with an eosinophilic pituitary adenoma and four enlarged parathyroid glands. Later, in 1953, Underdahl et al. described a case series with adenomas of the pancreas, pituitary, and parathyroids. However, it was Wermer who, in 1954, recognized the genetic origin of the syndrome when he described adenomas of the parathyroid, pancreas, and pituitary glands in two consecutive generations of the same family (four sisters and their father). The pattern of inheritance is autosomal dominant, with varying degrees of penetrance and expressivity. The cell types of these tumors are thought to have the same embryonic precursor from neuroectoderm.

At present, there are three classes of multiple endocrine neoplasia (MEN): MEN-I, MEN-IIa, MEN-IIb.

MEN-I

MEN-I, also called "Wermer's syndrome," involves tumors of the pancreas islet cell, pituitary, and parathyroids. The pancreatic tumors can include gastrinomas, insulinomas, glucagonomas, somatostatinomas, and VIPomas. Pituitary tumors are mostly nonfunctional adenomas, but ACTH, GH, and prolactin-secreting adenomas have been described. Parathyroid adenomas cause hyperparathyroidism. Occasionally, carcinoids and nonfunctioning thyroid and adrenal tumors have been described. Recently, the gene causing MEN-I has been identified. It is thought that a mutation in a tumor suppressor gene causes the clinical syndrome of MEN-I when both copies of the gene are sequentially inactivated.

Multiple facial angiofibromas

MEN-I has been associated with several dermatologic abnormalities. Multiple facial angiofibromas, typical of tuberous sclerosis both clinically and histologically, were present in 88% of subjects in association with seborrheic skin and small telangiectasia. Multiple collagenomas on the upper torso were seen in 72%, multiple lipomas in 34%, and café-au-lait macules in 38%. Epidermal inclusion cysts and leiomyomas have also been described.

MEN-IIa

MEN-IIa, also called "Sipple's syndrome," comprises medullary thyroid carcinoma, pheochromocytoma, and hyperparathyroidism. Pheochromocytoma is manifested by severe and, at times, uncontrollable hypertension. There is also orthostatic hypotension, headaches, and, symptoms identical to an injection of epinephrine (ie, palpitations, diaphoresis, and anxiety). Mutations of the *RET* proto-oncogene on chromosome 10 has been identified and is used clinically for familial screening.

Patients with MEN-IIa have a normal physical appearance, although occasionally they may have cutaneous lichen amyloidosis.

MEN-IIb

MEN-IIb is characterized by medullary thyroid carcinoma and pheochromocytoma; however, hyperparathyroidism occurs in only 5% of cases.

Individuals with MEN-IIb have a distinctive physical appearance. They have ganglioneuromas in a centrofacial distribution (ie, tongue, buccal mucosa, lips) that appear as yellow or pink nodules, giving a lumpy appearance. The oral lesions are generally present before puberty and, in some cases, are present at birth. These neuromas can also be present in the eyelids causing a diffuse or nodular thickening of the tarsal plates, conjunctiva, and cornea. They are associated with thickened corneal nerve fibers easily seen with a slit lamp. The ganglioneuromas can also be seen in other mucosal surfaces, including that of the gastrointestinal tract. Patients may also have café-au-lait macules, neurofibromas, or diffuse lentigines.

Multiple ganglioneuromas on central portion of face, tongue, mucous membranes

Skeletal abnormalities and a marfanoid habitus are commonly present in the mucosal neuroma syndrome, so patients have tall, thin statures with abnormal arm-span/height ratios, high-arched palates, pectus carinatum or excavatum, and kyphosis. Patients, however, do not have aortic insufficiency or ectopia lentis.

Treatment of the MEN syndromes involves managing each individual element of the syndrome, and the workup is similar to that outlined in the relevant sections of this chapter. Generally, surgical resection of the tumors is the preferred mode of therapy. In MEN-IIa, genetic screening is offered to other family members so as to prevent or treat unrecognized subclinical medullary thyroid carcinomas and/or pheochromocytoma.

Annotated Bibliography

Darling TN, Skarulis MC, Steinberg SM, et al. Multiple facial angiofibromas and collagenomas in patients with multiple endocrine neoplasia type 1. Arch Dermatol 1997;133:853–857.

The first description of skin lesions in a series of 32 individuals with MEN-I at the National Institutes of Health, including multiple facial angiofibromas that were previously thought to be pathognomonic for tuberous sclerosis.

Disorders of Calcium Metabolism

Hypoparathyroidism

Hypoparathyroidism most commonly results from complications of neck surgery. When it occurs spontaneously, it is usually thought to result from an autoimmune process. There is an increased prevalence of associated Addison's disease, Hashimoto's disease, pernicious anemia, and vitiligo. There are also rare congenital cases that are due to abnormalities in the calcium sensor protein. Hypoparathyroidism is biochemically defined by hypocalcemia with inappropriately low PTH concentrations.

Cutaneous Manifestations

The cutaneous manifestations of hypoparathyroidism can be subtle and include dry, scaly skin. The nails are characteristically brittle. On unusual occasions, a psoriasiform and exfoliative dermatitis has been described.

Hypoparathyroidism in childhood is associated with dental abnormalities, including absence of enamel hypoplasia and, at times, the absence of permanent teeth. Dental radiographs reveal a widening of the lamina dura.

In childhood, hypoparathyroidism may be associated with candidiasis (mucocutaneous and nail involvement). This is usually accompanied by demonstrable defects in cell-mediated immunity (ie, DeGeorge syndrome).

Mucocutaneous candidiasis may be present

Treatment

Oral calcium and vitamin D therapy is effective in treating hypoparathyroidism.

Pseudohypoparathyroidism

Pseudohypoparathyroidism is a disorder caused by a mutation in the $G_{s\alpha}$ subunit of the G protein. The G protein mediates intracellular responses resulting from the binding of several hormones to their cell-surface receptors. Consequently, there is resistance to PTH, resulting in high PTH levels and hypo- or normocalcemia. There may also be associated hypothyroidism, hyperthyroidism, hypogonadism, and diabetes mellitus. There is a characteristic phenotype of short stature, brachydactyly, round facies, and heterotopic calcification of the skin. Rarely, ectopic bone formation may occur. Characteristically, the index finger is longer than the middle finger. When the patient makes a fist, there is a depression where the second metacarpal phalangeal joint is present.

Primary Hyperparathyroidism

Primary hyperparathyroidism is usually discovered by the presence of hypercalcemia with an inappropriately normal or elevated PTH level. It can occur sporadically or as part of the MEN syndromes. In 85% of cases, it is due to a single parathyroid adenoma, whereas the remainder is due to hyperplasia of up to four glands (more commonly seen in MEN). If the calcium-phosphorus product is exceeded, metastatic calcification may occur, and nodules filled with a chalk-like material may be seen.

Cutaneous Manifestations

Linear white bands on the lateral margin or cornea are frequently detected (band keratopathy). Similar lesions can be detected with other causes of hypercalcemia (eg, vitamin D intoxication, and sarcoidosis).

Metastatic calcification in the dermis and subcutaneous tissue occurs, especially in patients with chronic renal failure.

Management

The management of symptomatic patients with hyperparathyroidism involves parathyroid adenomectomy. If there is parathyroid hyperplasia, 3½ glands are resected, and the other half gland is reimplanted in the forearm.

Calciphylaxis

Calciphylaxis is a fulminating, explosive onset of calcium deposition, characterized by violaceous, hard, ulcerating nodules most commonly detected on the legs and thighs. It is associated with ischemic necrosis. There is a high mortality due to sepsis. In general, it is most commonly seen in association with abnormalities of calcium, phosphrous, and PTH (eg, hemodialysis and renal failure patients). The exact cause and pathogenesis are unknown, but the initial insult may be a

Fulminating vasculopathy associated with bland thrombi and calcium deposition

vasculopathy with "bland" thrombosis. Some patients demonstrate a functional decrease in protein C.

Although most cases occur in association with calcium, phosphorus, and PTH abnormalities, we have seen two cases in which no calcium, phosphorus, or PTH abnormalities were detected.

The first patient was a 21-year-old Caucasian female with systemic lupus erythematosus and anti-U_1RNP antibodies. She developed widespread, painful, hard, ulcerating nodules of calciphylaxis on her extremities. Her lupus disease process was characterized by Raynaud's phenomenon and pulmonary insufficiency. Unfortunately, the patient developed pulmonary hypertension and died.

The second patient, a 56-year-old African American female, while under chemotherapy treatment for carcinoma of the breast, developed tender, hard, ulcerating nodules of the legs and subsequently died of sepsis. Recent evidence suggests breast cancer patients receiving methotrexate cyclophosphamide and 5-fluorouracil may be at an increased risk.

Annotated Bibliography

Gipstein RN, Coburn JW, Adams DA. Calciphylaxis in man: a syndrome of tissue necrosis and vascular calcification in 11 patients with chronic renal failure. Arch Intern Med 1976;136:1273–1280.

This is a report of 11 patients who developed ischemic ulcers of fingers, legs, thighs, or a combination of all three. Five patients were on hemodialysis, and 6 had renal homographs. All demonstrated severe hyperphosphatemia, and 7 demonstrated radiographic evidence of subperiosteal resorption. The disease process was relentless and progressive, associated with serious morbidity and mortality.

Mehta RL, Scott G, Sloand JA, Francis CW. Skin necrosis associated with acquired protein C deficiency in patients with renal failure and calciphylaxis. Am J Med 1990;88: 252–257.

This article documents antigenic and functional decreased activity of protein C and protein S vitamin K–dependent clotting inhibitors (inhibits factor V and factor VIII) in renal disease and breast cancer patients under treatment. These studies strongly suggest deficient levels of protein C and protein S are of pathologic significance in calciphylaxis.

Roger JS, et al. Chemotherpay for breast cancer decreases plasma protein C and protein S. J Clin Oncol 1988;6:276–281.

Rella C, et al. A prothromic state in breast cancer patients treated with adjuvant chemotherapy. Breast Cancer Res Treat 1996;40:151–159.

Goyal S, Huhn KM, Provost TT. Calciphylaxis in a patient without renal failure or elevated parathyroid hormone: possible etiologic role of chemotherapy. Br J Dermatol [In press]

Three articles suggesting an etiologic role of chemotherapeutic depression of protein C and protein S in the pathogenesis of calciphylaxis.

Werner's Syndrome

Werner's syndrome describes a syndrome of premature aging (progeria), with atrophic scleroderma-like skin and cataracts. There are several endocrine manifestations, which include glucose intolerance or diabetes mellitus type II, primary hypogonadism, papillary thyroid carcinoma, dyslipidemia (lipoprotein type 2a), and early osteopenia. It is an autosomal recessive trait, and it is believed that a mutated DNA helicase is responsible, reducing the replicative life span of fibroblasts.

General Annotated Bibliography

Feingold KR, Elias PM. Endocrine-skin interactions: cutaneous manifestations of pituitary disease, thyroid disease, calcium disorders and diabetes. J Am Acad Dermatol 1987;17:921–940.

Feingold KR, Elias PM. Endocrine-skin interactions: cutaneous manifestations of adrenal disease, pheochromocytoma, carcinoid syndrome, sex hormone excess and deficiency, polyglandular autoimmune syndromes, multiple endocrine neoplasia syndromes, and other miscellaneous disorders. J Am Acad Dermatol 1988;19:1–20.

These are two excellent, well-written, well-referenced reviews of the cutaneous manifestations of endocrinologic disorders.

CHAPTER 33

Hepatitis

Adam S. Geyer, M.D., David S. Rosenburg, M.D.,
H. Franklin Herlong, M.D., Thomas T. Provost, M.D.

Manifestations of viral hepatitis vary

Viral hepatitis is the most common cause of acute hepatocellular injury and can vary in its clinical spectrum from asymptomatic aminotransferase elevations to fulminant liver failure with coagulopathy, jaundice, ascites, and encephalopathy. Patients who fail to clear the virus after the acute infection develop chronic hepatitis. In some patients, the hepatocellular injury can remain mild for prolonged periods of time, not producing clinically significant disease, whereas in others, progression to cirrhosis, with complications of portal hypertension and decreased synthetic function of the liver, occurs. For many hepatitis patients, liver transplantation may be the only effective therapy.

Five distinct hepatitis viruses have been recognized

Five distinct hepatitis viruses have been identified and characterized: hepatitis A, B, C, D [delta], and E. Other viruses (such as Epstein-Barr, cytomegalovirus, and herpes simplex) can cause systemic illnesses with hepatic involvement, but in most cases, extrahepatic manifestations dominate the clinical picture.

Immune complex–mediated features common with hepatitis B

The primary viral hepatitides may have similar clinical features, but their natural histories vary considerably. For example, patients with acute hepatitis A may be asymptomatic or experience malaise, fatigue, anorexia, nausea, vomiting, dull right upper quadrant pain, and an altered sense of taste or smell. Fewer than one-third have jaundice, which usually develops after the onset of initial symptoms. Cirrhosis almost never occurs. However, up to 50% of patients with acute hepatitis B develop arthritis and urticaria-like vasculitis (implying an immune complex pathogenesis). Cirrhosis and hepatoma are significant sequelae.

Pruritus may be problematic.

Treatment of pruritus associated with liver disease is varied

Patients with a cholestatic form of acute viral hepatitis frequently have pruritus, which may be debilitating. Elevated levels of circulating bile salts are known to have a direct association with symptoms, but no direct correlation between blood or tissue levels of bile acids and pruritus has been made. Because the pathogenesis has not been fully determined, therapy for pruritus is largely empiric. The orally administered ionic-binding resins cholestyramine and cholestipol reduce itching by sequestering potential pruritogens in the gut. Phenobarbital increases biliary clearance and may be effective in some patients. Antihistamines, however, are ineffective. Opioid-receptor antagonists, such as naloxone, can ameliorate itching, suggesting a centrally mediated process. Ultraviolet B (UVB) light and ultraviolet A (UVA) light are effective therapies for some types of pruritus. (For further discussion, see Chapter 71, "Phototherapy and Photochemotherapy of Skin Disease.")

Jaundice, which is harmless in adults, results from an accumulation of bilirubin and its metabolites in the skin and mucous membranes. Patients with long-standing cholestasis develop a patchy, diffuse, grayish pigmentation from hypermelanosis produced by an increase in the melanin content of melanosomes in the skin. Spider angioma occurs most often on the face, upper trunk, and distal upper extremities and are seen in both acute and chronic viral hepatitis. Palmar erythema with increased mottling of the hands or discrete erythematous patches, such as spider angioma on the thenar and hypothenar eminences, is caused by altered hepatic metabolism of estrogens.

Hyperestrogen state induces gynecomastia spider angioma and palmar erythema

Hepatitis A

Hepatitis A, transmitted by fecal-oral routes, occurs sporadically or in epidemics and accounts for about one-quarter of the cases of acute hepatitis in the United States. The illness, caused by a ribonucleic acid (RNA) enterovirus, is short lived and often asymptomatic. Jaundice and other cutaneous manifestations are unusual in uncomplicated hepatitis A. Urticaria occurs in less than 2% of patients and may be due to immune-complex deposition in the skin. Since the hepatitis A virus (HAV) is detectable in the blood in low quantities for only a brief period of time, mostly during the prodrome, HAV-associated urticaria-like vasculitis is usually short lived. Theoretically, the immune complexes formed tend to be in antibody-excess. Also, because of this brief period of HAV antigenemia, HAV rarely, if ever, causes post-transfusion hepatitis. The diagnosis of hepatitis A is confirmed by the detection of HAV antibody in the blood. Anti-HAV (the immunoglobulin IgM) characterizes the initial immune response and is detectable early in the prodromal period and throughout the acute phase. Its presence is diagnostic of acute hepatitis A. Anti-HAV (IgG), appearing later in the disease, often remains indefinitely and conveys immunity against re-infection.

Hepatitis A often anicteric HAV present in blood a short period of time

Anti-HAV (IgM) diagnostic Anti-HAV (IgG) conveys immunity

Hepatitis A does not produce chronic hepatitis or cirrhosis, although two variants with prolonged courses have been described: (1) a cholestatic variant, and (2) a relapsing form where cutaneous features are prominent.

In the relapsing variant, symptoms resolve, and laboratory tests improve, only to have a recurrence approximately 4 weeks after the initial remission. Anti-HAV (IgM), which had initially disappeared, is again detectable. Using anti-HAV (IgM) testing, it has been noted that the relapsing form may affect 4 to 20% of patients, many of whom are asymptomatic and anicteric. However, pruritus, often accompanied by purpura, is a common complaint in those with relapsing HAV infection. In one report of 14 patients with relapsing HAV, pruritus occurred in 3 patients and purpura in 1 during the first phase of their disease. All but 1 had an initial complete clinical remission. In the relapse phase, purpura was demonstrated in 5 patients, and 7 complained of pruritus. Rheumatoid factor activity was positive in 7 of 13 patients, and HAV RNA was detected in the blood in over one-third of those tested. Biopsies of the purpuric lesions in 2 of the patients demonstrated a leukocytoclastic angiitis. Thus, it is likely that immune complex formation plays a role in the pathogenesis of the urticaria-like lesions seen in relapsing HAV.

Relapsing form of HAV infection uncommon; frequently associated with purpura and pruritus

Urticaria associated with HAV is probably immune complex–mediated urticarial vasculitis.

Other dermatologic manifestations associated with hepatitis A are rare, although HAV has been recognized as an etiologic factor in the development of cases of septal panniculitis, scarlatiniform eruptions on the upper trunk and extremities, and a necrotizing vasculitis seen more frequently in children.

The vast majority of patients with acute hepatitis A recover uneventfully without treatment. Fulminant hepatitis occurs in less than 1 in 1,000 cases and may necessitate liver transplantation. To date, there is no specific therapy that alters the natural history of hepatitis A infection; therefore, attention is directed toward prevention. Passive immunization given to household and sexual contacts of infected individuals within 2 weeks of exposure results in a 90% protection rate. An effective vaccine for the prevention of hepatitis A is currently available and should be administered to high-risk populations.

Prognosis excellent

Annotated Bibliography

Scully LJ, Ryan AE. Urticaria and acute hepatitis A virus infection. Am J Gastroenterol 1993;88:277–278.

Glikson M, Galune E, Oren R, et al. Relapsing hepatitis A: review of 14 cases and literature survey. Medicine 1992;71:14–23.

These two articles detail the common occurrence of pruritus in HAV infections and the occasional presence of urticaria-like vasculitis.

Press J, Maslovitz S, Avinoach I. Cutaneous necrotizing vasculitis associated with hepatitis A virus infection. J Rheumatol 1997;24:965–967.

This article provides a good description of a case with a brief, clear overview of HAV-associated vasculitis.

Hepatitis B

Precore mutant of HBV produces fulminant disease

Hepatitis B is the most common cause of acute viral hepatitis in the United States, with approximately 300,000 new cases annually and about 1.5 million chronic carriers. The virus is transmitted parenterally as well as through sexual contact. The hepatitis B virus (HBV), a small DNA virus of the family Hepadnaviridae, contains a thick outer lipoprotein layer containing the hepatitis B surface antigen (HBsAg) and an electron-dense core housing the hepatitis B core antigen (HBcAg). HBV also contains an endogenous DNA polymerase and uses reverse transcriptase to replicate its DNA. The HbcAg is derived from a cleavage of the translation product of the entire precore and core regions. The process of reverse transcription has allowed a number of mutant viruses to be produced, including a precore mutant (conversion of tryptophan to a stop codon) associated with a fulminant course.

Immune complex–mediated arthritis, urticaria-like vasculitis, and glomerulonephritis

With an incubation period of 30 to 180 days, HBV replicates prolifically early in its course. High levels of HBV DNA along with HBsAg are found in the serum of patients during this period (good condition for formation of pathologic soluble immune complexes [antigen excess]). Many people with hepatitis B infection are asymptomatic and anicteric. Deposition of immune complexes and complement accounts for the prodromal symptoms of arthritis and urticaria-like vasculitis; glomerulonephritis may be seen occasionally. Later, patients develop malaise, fatigue, myalgias, anorexia, and nausea. Fever and right upper quadrant pain are frequently present.

Physical examination reveals mild tender hepatomegaly with jaundice. Laboratory investigation shows elevated serum aminotransferase (up to 10 times the upper limits of normal) and a slight rise in serum alkaline phosphatase. Prolongation of the prothrombin time by greater than 5 seconds over the control value suggests a severe hepatitis that may become fulminant.

Serum HBsAg is diagnostic Anti HbsAg antibodies are protective

Detecting HBsAg in the blood of an individual with symptoms of acute hepatitis is diagnostic of hepatitis B in most cases. However, occasionally in severe cases, anti-HBc may be cleared quickly, and anti-HBcAg may be the only serologic marker of hepatitis B infection. The HBcAg is seen only in the nucleus of infected hepatocytes and does not circulate in the patient's serum. Hepatitis B e antigen (HBeAg), a short protein cleaved during viral replication, appears transiently in the serum during acute infection. Its presence, representing active viral replication, is found in association with HBV DNA and implies an intact circulating virus. Anti-HBs (antibodies) develop late in the infection and indicate convalescence and protection from re-infection with HBV. Vaccination with purified HBsAg protein results in protective titers of anti-HBs and is recommended to adults at risk for infection and universally in children.

Health care workers are at risk

Since HBV is transmitted through sexual or parenteral routes, risk factors include intravenous drug use, blood transfusions, and sexual contact with high-risk partners. In addition, unvaccinated health care providers are at high risk. In one study, 15 to 30% of unvaccinated health care workers who had frequent contact with blood, demonstrated markers of HBV infection. This frequency was 3 to 10 times higher than that detected in health care providers without contact with blood. In a study of 584 dermatologists, 15.4% possessed serologic evidence for previous HBV infection, highlighting the absolute need for all physicians and health care providers to be vaccinated for HBV. The virus is also transmitted perinatally, particularly where the HBV carrier rate is high, such as in the Far East and sub-Saharan Africa.

Carrier state

Chronic infection develops in 5 to 10% of patients with hepatitis B. The carrier state is defined by persistent HBs antigenemia for more than 6 months after initial detection. Since HBV itself is not directly cytopathic, the outcome of infection is determined by the host's immunologic response. Factors influencing the likelihood of chronicity include (1) age at the time of infection (90% of infected neonates become chronically infected), (2) clinical expression of the acute disease (anicteric hepatitis is more likely to become chronic), (3) gender (male to female ratio is 5:1), and (4) immune status (immunocompromised patients are more likely to become carriers).

Chronic active hepatitis B patients frequently develop cirrhosis and are at risk for hepatoma

Patients who remain surface antigen positive for greater than 6 months and have elevated aminotransferase have some form of chronic hepatitis. A liver biopsy is required in these patients to determine the severity of inflammation, which is graded as mild, moderate, or severe. In addition, the degree of fibrosis can be assessed. Patients with chronic active hepatitis B frequently progress to cirrhosis and may die from complications of portal hypertension and hepatic synthetic failure. Chronic HBV infection is a potent risk factor for the development of hepatocellular carcinoma.

Therapeutic approaches to HBV infection include prevention through vaccination and eradication by the use of antiviral agents. Recombinant vaccines are available to prevent primary infection and as a postexposure prophylaxis. Hyperimmune globulin should also be administered to unvaccinated individuals exposed acutely to HBV.

Only 30% respond to interferon alpha

Interferon alpha has been evaluated extensively in the treatment of hepatitis B, but only about 30% of patients respond favorably. Patients are more likely to respond if they have low circulating levels of HBV DNA. Side effects of interferon, such as fatigue, malaise, fever, and depression, can limit its efficacy. Lamivudine (3-TC), a nucleoside analogue, has similar efficacy but with fewer side effects. Thus, lamivudine is now considered first-line therapy.

Four principal cutaneous manifestations of HBV infection have been recognized: (1) urticaria-like vasculitis, (2) polyarteritis nodosa, (3) cryoglobulinemic vasculitis, and (4) papular acrodermatitis of childhood.

Urticaria-like Vasculitis

Urticaria-like vasculitis prodromal feature
Also a recurrent feature

Urticaria is a frequent prodromal symptom of acute HBV infection. Ten to 20% of individuals develop urticaria, often associated with other prodromal symptoms, such as malaise, fatigue, and arthralgias (Figure 33–1). Biopsy of these lesions shows a leukocytoclastic angiitis. Direct immunofluorescence typically shows IgG, IgM, C3, and HBsAg in the perivascular areas of the vasculitic lesions. Patients may develop a necrotizing vasculitis that can be systemic or limited to the skin. It should be noted that the urticaria-like vasculitis associated with HBV infection is not confined to the prodromal period and frequently presents as recurrent urticaria.

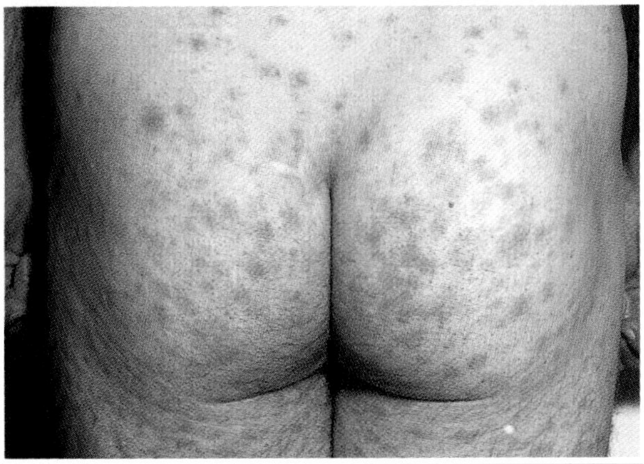

FIGURE 33–1 Urticaria-like vasculitic lesions in prodrome of hepatitis B infection.

Polyarteritis Nodosa

Chronic HBV infection associated with immune-complex formation has been detected in 15 to 20% of polyarteritis nodosa (PAN) patients. Additionally, HBV has been detected in biopsies of diseased blood vessels. Patients with PAN often have fever, malaise, arthralgias, and, less frequently, abdominal pain from mesenteric vasculitis, mononeuritis multiplex from vasculitis

15–20% of polyarteritis nodosa patients are HBV positive

of the vaso vasorum, and glomerulonephritis. The skin can show palpable purpura with nonblanching purple nodules on the lower extremities. Other dermatologic lesions include livedo reticularis, angioedema, urticaria, ulcerations, and, in its most severe form, acral gangrene (Figures 33–2 and 33–3). Treatment of hepatitis B–associated PAN is controversial and may involve immunosuppressive drugs, such as corticosteroids and cyclophosphamide, to reduce the severity of the vasculitis and antiviral agents to eradicate the underlying antigenic stimulus. (For further discussion, see Chapter 12, "Vasculitis.")

Cryoglobulinemic Vasculitis

Cryoglobulinemic vasculitis associated with HBV

The symptoms of cryoglobulinemia are similar to PAN, with purpuric skin lesions as the predominant cutaneous manifestation. In addition, patients may develop erythrocyanosis and Raynaud's phenomenon. About 15% of patients with chronic HBV infection have cryoglobulins in the blood. (For further discussion, see Chapter 12, "Vasculitis.")

Rarer dermatologic manifestations associated with HBV infection include an increased incidence of lichen planus, pyoderma gangrenosum, and erythema nodosum. Cases of a dermatomyositis-like syndrome, with a purplish heliotrope rash, malar erythema, and proximal muscle weakness, have recently been reported in association with acute HBs antigenemia.

Papular Acrodermatitis of Childhood

Gianotti-Crosti syndrome associated with a variety of viral infections, including HBV

Papular acrodermatitis of childhood, also known as Gianotti-Crosti syndrome, is frequently associated with viral infections. In addition to hepatitis B, other implicated viruses include cytomegalovirus, Coxsackie virus, and Epstein-Barr virus. This syndrome is characterized by the development of nonpruritic, erythematous papules on the buttocks, thighs, and extensor surfaces of the arms and legs. The lesions are usually discrete, 2 to 3 mm papules that do not coalesce. Generally, this is an asymptomatic disease lasting 1 to 2 months; however, lassitude, mild fever, and generalized lymphadenopathy may be present. The underlying hepatitis is usually mild and frequently anicteric. Jaundice rarely is present and is associated with a more prolonged illness up to 3 years.

Annotated Bibliography

Lee WM. Hepatitis B virus. N Engl J Med 1997;337:1733–1745.

This excellent review article has 102 references. Its discussion of the stages of hepatitis B infection is especially excellent.

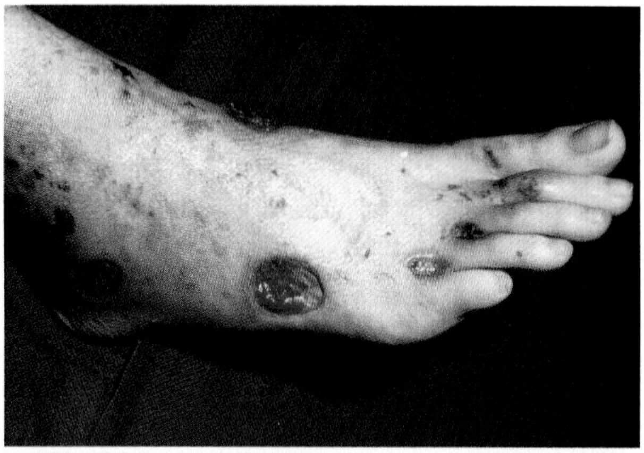

FIGURE 33–2 Multiple ulcers on the lower leg and foot of a polyarteritis nodosa patient with HBV. The depth of lesions indicates involvement of muscular arteries.

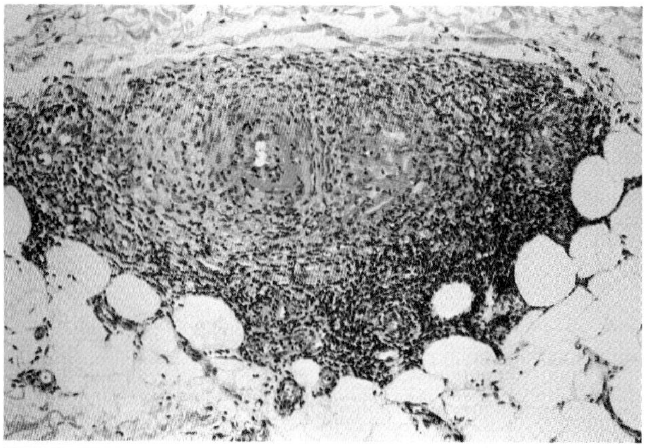

FIGURE 33–3 Pathology of polyarteritis nodosa demonstrating inflammatory involvement with fibrin deposition of the muscular artery at the dermal subcutaneous junction.

Gocke DJ, Hsu K, Morgan C, et al. Vasculitis in association with Australian antigen. J Exp Med 1971;134:330.

This classic article demonstrates the association of Australian antigen (HBV) with polyarteritis nodosa.

Parsons ME, Russo GG, Millikan LE. Dermatologic disorders associated with viral hepatitis. Int J Dermatol 1996;35:77–81.

This article provides a clear, concise overview of the cutaneous manifestations of hepatitis A to E. The section on hepatitis B is well developed.

Boeck K, Mempel M, Schmidt T, et al. Gianotti-Crosti syndrome: clinical, serologic, and therapeutic data from nine children. Cutis 1998;62: 271–274.

This article is helpful in understanding Gianotti-Crosti syndrome and its association with underlying viral infections.

Hepatitis C

Post-transfusion hepatitis

Initially called non-A, non-B hepatitis, hepatitis C has been more accurately classified as an illness caused by a small RNA virus in the Flaviviridae family. Prior to the availability of routine screening tests for the virus, it was the leading cause of post-transfusion hepatitis. Currently, the most common modes of transmission are the sharing of needles among intravenous drug users and accidental exposure of medical and dental personnel. Transmission may occur perinatally and via hemodialysis and organ transplants, but rarely through sexual contact. In approximately 40% of patients, the source of infection is not detected. It may be difficult to determine when the patient became infected, since the acute illness is virtually always asymptomatic. In addition, symptoms rarely are present in chronic infection, and as a result, most infections are identified when elevated aminotransferase are discovered during routine blood screening or with blood donation. It is estimated that approximately 150,00 new cases of hepatitis C occur annually in the United States.

Chronic hepatitis and cirrhosis common, as is hepatoma

Hepatitis C virus (HCV) infection leads to chronic hepatitis in 70% of cases, with about 50% developing cirrhosis. These patients also have a higher prevalence of hepatocellular carcinoma. Rarely, extrahepatic manifestations, such as aplastic anemia, hemolytic anemia, and agranulocytosis, may dominate the clinical picture. The diagnosis of hepatitis C is made by detecting HCV antibody in the blood. However, this antibody does not appear for up to 6 months after inoculation. During this interval, the diagnosis requires polymerase chain reaction testing to identify HCV RNA.

Interferon and ribavirin effective in 40% of patients

Combination therapy with interferon and ribavirin is now considered standard treatment for patients with chronic hepatitis C. This regimen results in a sustained response in about 40% of treated patients. Several factors affect the success of therapy, one of which is viral genotype. There are six major genotypes of HCV, with type 1 the most prevalent in the United States; it is also associated with a lower probability of a therapeutic response to antiviral treatment. Viral load is another well-recognized predictor of response to treatment, with a viral load greater than 2 million copies per mL associated with a less favorable outcome. A pretreatment liver biopsy is helpful in determining the extent of hepatic fibrosis and can be an important factor in establishing prognosis.

Side effects of antiviral therapy are due predominantly to interferon. Myalgias, arthralgias, fever, anorexia, pharyngitis, and insomnia occur with varying frequency and can usually be managed by symptomatic treatment with agents such as acetaminophen. More serious side effects, such as emotional lability and depression, may require discontinuing therapy. The addition of ribavirin to the regimen may produce significant hemolysis. Currently, no effective vaccine has been developed to prevent hepatitis C.

Three prominent cutaneous manifestations have been associated with chronic hepatitis C infection: (1) vasculitis seen in the setting of essential cryoglobulinemia, (2) porphyria cutanea tarda, and (3) lichen planus.

Vasculitis and Essential Mixed Cryoglobulinemic Syndrome

Vasculitis involving various sized vessels common; also, arthritis, glomerulonephritis, and hypocomplementemia

In patients with essential mixed cryoglobulinemia, evidence of underlying hepatitis C infection is common. The predominant cryoglobulins are type II, consisting of polyclonal IgG, and monoclonal IgM, with rheumatoid factor activity. The syndrome is characterized by cutaneous vasculitis, arthritis, and glomerulonephritis, often with hypocomplementemia. The arthritis, affecting primarily the toes, hands, ankles, and wrists, is symmetrical and nondeforming. Pulmonary involvement and peripheral neuropathy may also occur.

The manifestations of hepatitis C are listed in Table 33–1.

Ninety-five percent of patients with hepatitis C–induced mixed cryoglobulinemia have palpable and nonpalpable purpura, most often on the lower extremities, with or without ulceration (Figure 33–4). On occasion, the ulcerations are deep, involving the subcutaneous tissue, which is indicative of muscular artery involvement. Biopsy of these lesions demonstrates the presence of a leukocytoclastic angiitis with evidence of immunoglobulin and complement deposition in the affected blood vessels. In addition to classic palpable and nonpalpable purpura, erythematous papules, pustules, hemorrhagic bullae, livedo reticularis, and acrocyanosis have been detected. Pruritus is also common.

The pathogenesis of cutaneous vasculitis in HCV-associated cryoglobulinemia is presumably related to the deposition of immune complexes involving HCV in the vessels. In these complexes, the concentration of HCV and its antibody is much greater than that found in the serum.

Hepatosplenomegaly is also a common physical finding, occurring in 20 to 75% of patients, depending on the cohort reported. Renal involvement in one large series was reported in 17% of patients. Peripheral neuropathy and profound weakness appears to be common in patients with mixed cryoglobulinemic syndrome associated with HCV infections.

We have recently seen a 38-year-old Caucasian male, a former intravenous drug user with a 2-year history of recurrent, palpable purpura of the lower extremities, arthritis, arthralgia, and severe weakness. Biopsy demonstrated a leukocytoclastic vasculitis. Laboratory studies indicated an increase in the alanine aminotransferase, rheumatoid factor, cryoglobulins, and HCV antibodies.

There are three types of cryoglobulins, two of which may be seen with HCV infections:

Type I cryoglobulins consist of a monoclonal immunoglobulin. (For further discussion, see Chapter 24, "Leukemia, B-cell Lymphomas, and Multiple Myeloma and Paraproteins.")

Type II cryoglobulins consist of a polyclonal IgG and monoclonal IgM rheumatoid factors. Most of these type II cryoglobulins are classified as essential—there is no underlying disease process detected. The secondary type II cryoglobulins occur mainly in association with malignancies of the immune system.

Type III cryoglobulins consist of polyclonal IgG and polyclonal rheumatoid factors. Like type II cryoglobulins, most are classified as essential. Secondary

TABLE 33–1 Manifestations of Hepatitis C

Purpura with or without ulceration
Arthralgias/arthritis
Weakness
Peripheral neuropathy
Renal disease
Hepatosplenomegaly

type III cryoglobulins occur in infections and in autoimmune and chronic liver diseases (Table 33–2).

Data have now been obtained indicating the prevalence of HCV antibodies ranging from 30 to 98% in the sera of patients with type II and type III essential mixed cryoglobulinemia. Most recent studies of patients with type II mixed cryoglobulinemia, using quantitative polymerase chain reaction methodology, have demonstrated a high prevalence of HCV infection. These studies demonstrated an approximate 10-fold increase in the HCV antibody, and a 1,000-fold increased concentration of the HCV RNA in the essential type II cryoglobulins, compared with the sera. HCV antigens have been demonstrated in the vascular lesions of mixed cryoglobulinemia.

High frequency of HCV infection in type II and type III mixed cryoglobulinemic patients

HCV found in diseased blood vessels

We recently evaluated a patient with a 7-year history of intermittent attacks of angioneurotic edema involving her lips. Complement studies have revealed a markedly depressed total hemolytic complement (CH50) and depressed C4 and C1q levels. Cryoglobulins and anti-HCV antibodies were detected. Liver enzymes were slightly elevated.

Essential mixed cryoglobulinemia in this patient is due to HCV infection. Immune complex–mediated complement activation and, at times, a consumption of C1 esterase inhibitor (C1INH) are thought to be occurring. The relative deficiency of C1INH results in acquired angioedema. Complement activation is occurring via C1q, producing decreased quantities. (In hereditary angioneurotic edema, C1q is normal.) (For further discussion, see Acquired Angioneurotic Edema in Chapter 70, "Miscellaneous Diseases.")

Studies of the monoclonal rheumatoid factor (mRF) in type II mixed cryoglobulinemia have demonstrated that 65% contain the major cross-idiotype, WA. This is an antigen, localized to the antibody-combining site of the monoclonal IgM RF involving both heavy and light chains. This idiotype, WA, is a product of germline genes. Most WA mRF are encoded by germline Vκ3b and VH_1 genes with little or no somatic mutation. This idiotype does not occur in the polyclonal rheumatoid factor of rheumatoid arthritis patients but is frequently present in the polyclonal rheumatoid factor in primary Sjögren's syndrome.

The presence of the same idiotype mRF in type II mixed cryoglobulinemia and primary Sjögren's syndrome may indicate a broader involvement of this particular idiotype in primary Sjögren's syndrome. However, the precise frequency of occurrence or the relationship between these two entities has not been defined.

Striking presence of shared major cross-idiotype in rheumatoid factors seen in type II mixed cryoglobulinemia and Sjögren's syndrome

Porphyria Cutanea Tarda

Porphyria cutanea tarda (PCT), which is characterized by blister formation on the skin, skin fragility, and hirsutism, results from a deficiency of the hepatic uroporphyrinogen decarboxylase enzyme (Figure 33–5). (For discussion of clinical features, see Porphyria Cutanea Tarda in Chapter 29,"Paraneoplastic Syndromes.") This is the most common porphyria, existing as an acquired familial form. Alcohol, estrogens, cirrhosis, and hepatocellular carcinoma have been etiologically implicated. In recent years, evidence has accumulated indicating a strong association of sporadic cases of PCT with evidence of HCV infection. In one study of 100 consecutive PCT Spanish patients with PCT, 79% of patients with sporadic PCT demonstrated antibodies to HCV by the enzyme-linked immunosorbent assay and the recombinant immunoblot assay. In addition to HCV antibodies, polymerase chain reaction techniques have demonstrated the presence of HCV RNA in the sera of PCT patients. The familial form of PCT is not associated with an HCV infection. In general, these sporadic PCT patients demonstrate enzymatic hepatic abnormalities.

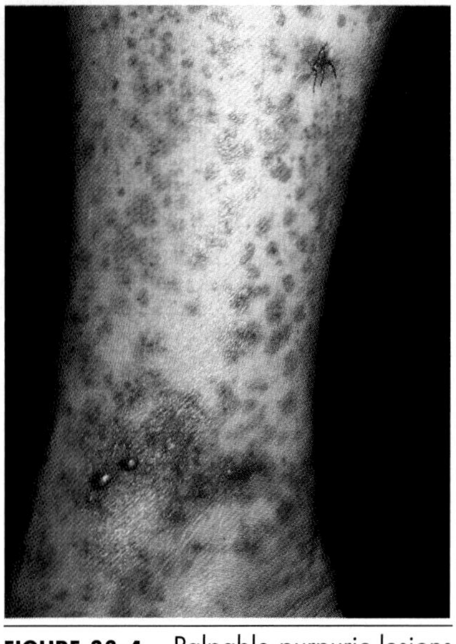

FIGURE 33–4 Palpable purpuric lesions on the lower leg in a patient with leukocytoclastic vasculitis and HCV.

The frequency of HCV in sporadic porphyria varies. For example, cohorts of PCT patients from Spain, France, and Italy have the highest frequency of an associated HCV infection (as high as 90%). A study from Germany of 106 PCT patients, however, detected that only 8

TABLE 33–2 Diseases Associated with Cryoglobulinemia

Chronic infections (ie, hepatitis, subacute bacterial endocarditis, leprosy)*
Autoimmune diseases (ie, Sjögren's syndrome, vasculitis, rheumatoid arthritis, systemic lupus erythematosus)*
Lymphoproliferative diseases (ie, multiple myeloma, lymphoma, and macroglobulinemia)†

*Chronic infections and autoimmune diseases are associated with type II and type III cryoglobulins,

†The paraproteins associated with B-cell lymphoproliferative diseases are type I cryoglobulins.

Regional variation in frequency of association of HCV with PCT

On occasions, other forms of porphyria may be associated with PCT

Not a direct association of PCT with hepatitis
Other hepatic toxic factors probably necessary

(8%) were positive for hepatitis C antibodies and had HCV RNA in their sera. Thus, it appears that HCV infection does not play a major role in the pathogenesis of PCT in Germany.

Fragmentary evidence also indicates that hepatitis B and, perhaps, human immunodeficiency virus (HIV) infection may play an etiopathologic role in some cases of PCT. Furthermore, HCV infections may be of etiopathologic significance in other forms of porphyria (ie, variegate).

The exact pathogenesis for the development of PCT in HCV-infected patients is unknown. Measurement of serum porphyrins in HCV- and HIV-infected patients indicate that a small number have elevated serum porphyrin levels. These studies suggest that these viral infections may predispose these patients to develop symptomatic PCT; however, additional hepatotoxic events are probably necessary.

Two cases illustrative of multiple hepatotoxic insults of potential etiologic significance are presented. The first involves a 42-year-old firefighter who had been followed up for approximately 15 years for recurrent episodes of PCT. These episodes, which totalled three, were successfully treated with phlebotomies. After each series, the blisters and fragility of the skin rapidly disappeared, and hirsutism slowly diminished. The hemoglobulin fell to 10 g, and the hematocrit to between 33 and 35.The serum iron stores also decreased.

The patient drank at least six bottles of beer per day, and each episode of recurrence of PCT was associated with excessive beer consumption in the previous 3 to 6 months.

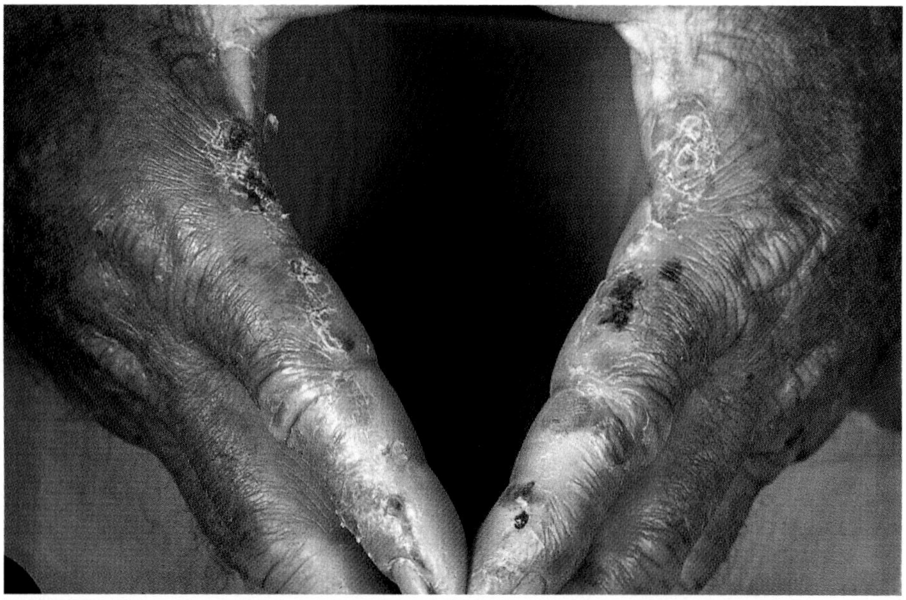

FIGURE 33–5 Hand of a patient with the sporadic form of PCT demonstrating blister formation, skin fragility, and hirsutism. (Reproduced with permission from: Dr. Richard Taylor, Miami, FL)

During his last episode of PCT, laboratory studies detected the presence of HCV antibodies. The patient has never had hepatitis nor a history of jaundice.

A 43-year-old heavily tattooed male developed fragile blistering skin of his hands and marked facial hirsutism of 4-years' duration. He had never had hepatitis and admitted to drinking 3 to 4 bottles of beer per day. His urine porphyrin level was markedly elevated and his aspartate transaminase and alanine aminotransferase were minimally elevated. His HCV antibody determination was positive.

Lichen Planus

Lichen planus lesions may represent hypersensitivity reaction associated with HCV

An association between lichen planus and liver disease has been suspected for years, but in the last decade, evidence suggests a specific link with hepatitis C. The prevalence of HCV antibodies in patients with LP varies from 4 to 38% on the basis of different studies.

Other skin disorders, such as erythema multiforme, urticaria, erythema nodosum, and salivary gland lesions, have all been described in the literature in association with HCV but have not been definitively linked to the disease. Additionally, there are extrahepatic disorders associated with HCV, such as thyroiditis and HCV-related thrombocytopenia, which may have cutaneous features.

Annotated Bibliography

Schwaber MJ, Zlotogorski A. Dermatologic manifestations of hepatitis C infection. Int J Dermatol 1997;36:251–254.

This is a good concise review of the major HCV-associated dermatoses.

Abel G, Zhang QX, Agnello V. Hepatitis C virus infection in type II mixed cryoglobulinemia. Arthritis Rheum 1993;36:1341–1349.

This is an excellent review of HCV data in essential mixed cryoglobulinemia by an investigator (Agnello) who has made significant contributions in the field.

Wener MH, Johnson RJ, Sasso EH, et al. Hepatitis C virus and rheumatic disease (editorial). J Rheumatol 1996;23:953–959.

This excellent review of rheumatic features associated with HCV infections also provides an excellent bibliography.

Levey JM, Bjornsson V, Banner B, et al. Mixed cryoglobulinemia in chronic hepatitis C infection: a clinical pathologic analysis of 10 cases and review of recent literature. Medicine 1994;73:53–67.

Ferri C, Greco F, Longobardo G, et al. Antibodies to hepatitis C virus in patients with mixed cryoglobulinemia. Arthritis Rheum 1991;34:1606–1610.

Abe Y, Tanaka Y, Tanenaka M, et al. Leucocytoclastic vasculitis associated with mixed cryoglobulinaemia and hepatitis C virus infection. Br J Dermatol 1997;136:272–274.

These three articles detail cutaneous features of HCV infection, focusing on the relationship between HCV and mixed cryoglobulinemia.

Fisher DA, Wright TL. Pruritus as a symptom of hepatitis C. J Am Acad Dermatol 1994;30:629–632.

This article details the occurrence of pruritus in HCV infections.

Herrero C, Vicente A, Bruguera M, et al. Is hepatitis C virus infection a trigger of porphyria cutanea tarda. Lancet 341:1993;788-789,1534–1535.

This study represents one of the first, if not the first study, to strongly suggest an association of HCV infection with the sporadic form of porphyria cutanea tarda.

Cribier B, Rey D, Uhl G, et al. Abnormal urinary co-proporphyrin levels in patients infected by hepatitis C virus with or without human immunodeficiency virus. A study of 177 patients. Arch Dermatol 1996;132:1448–1452.

This thought-provoking study demonstrates that the presence of a PCT urinary profile is rare among HIV- and HCV-infected patients. However, coproporphyrin excretion is increased, suggesting that hepatic damage is induced by these viruses. This study suggests that other hepatotoxic events may be necessary to induce symptomatic PCT.

Nomura N, Zolla-Pazner S, Simberkoff M, et al. Abnormal serum porphyrin levels in patients with the acquired immunodeficiency syndrome with or without hepatitis C virus infection. Arch Dermatol 1996;132:906–910.

This study indicates the lack of a direct effect of HIV and HCV infections in the pathogenesis of symptomatic PCT. It also reports that although HIV and HCV infections potentially predispose patients to the development of PCT, other hepatotoxic events are also involved.

Agnello V, Abel G. Localization of hepatitis C virus in cutaneous vasculitic lesions in patients with type II cryoglobulinemia. Arthritis Rheum 1997;40:2007–2015.

This article provides direct evidence for the participation of HCV virus in vasculitis, presumably in the form of immune complexes.

Hepatitis D

HDV is defective virus requiring the prescence of HBV for pathogenicity

Hepatitis D, also called "delta hepatitis," is caused by the hepatitis D virus (HDV), a defective hepatotropic RNA virus that requires the presence of HBV for pathogenicity. There are two modes of clinical expression: (1) co-infection when inoculation with HDV and HBV occur simultaneously, and (2) superinfection of HDV on a previous chronic HBV carrier state.

May induce a fulminant hepatitis

Since HBV and HDV have different incubation periods, co-infection is associated with a biphasic or relapsing pattern with two aminotransferase peaks. The first peak is caused by HBV and the second by HDV. Hepatitis D is often more clinically severe than hepatitis B alone, with a fulminant course in 30%. The diagnosis may be obscured in acute infection because HDV causes transient suppression of HBV replication causing a brief disappearance of HBsAg from the blood. The diagnosis of hepatitis D is confirmed by detecting anti-HDV in the blood.

Superinfection with HDV results in a carrier state in more than 90% of cases. When asymptomatic HBV carriers are superinfected with HDV, they often develop symptoms of hepatitis, and the histologic injury becomes more severe.

Mortality is significant

Mortality rates for acute hepatitis D are five times greater than those for hepatitis B alone. Transmission occurs most commonly through intravenous drug use. Successful vaccination for hepatitis B will prevent both HBV and HDV infection. The treatment of HDV is directed at eradication of the underlying HBV infection. Interferon has been used most frequently but has limited efficacy.

The dermatologic manifestations of hepatitis D are similar to those of hepatitis B.

Hepatitis E

Hepatitis E resembles hepatitis A in many respects. Symptoms are usually mild, and neither causes chronic liver disease. The hepatitis E virus (HEV) causes sporadic and epidemic hepatitis in the Indian subcontinent, Southeast Asia, North Africa, and Mexico; thus, it is considered a "traveler's disease" in the United States. Transmission is primarily enteric, occurring most often through contaminated water. A high prevalence of fulminant hepatitis occurs in pregnant women infected with HEV. Disseminated intravascular coagulation (DIC) occurs at a higher rate in HEV-infected individuals, so the clinical picture of hepatitis E may include cutaneous features of DIC. (For discussion of clinical features, see Purpura Fulminans in Chapter 47, "Septicemia.")

Mild disease generally

May be associated with DIC

There are presently no widely available tests to diagnose hepatitis E. Standard hygienic practices are the only preventive measures for hepatitis E. Immunoglobulin, even from postexposure patients, is not protective. Supportive care is the only treatment for HEV infection.

Conclusion

As an understanding of the mechanisms of hepatic disease and the spectrum of the viral hepatitides has progressed, numerous associations with dermatologic manifestations have been made. In fact, because the hepatitides are often clinically silent, the dermatoses may often be the only clinical evidence of underlying liver disease. Therefore, an appreciation of the wide spectrum of cutaneous disorders associated with viral hepatitis can result in early diagnosis with prompt institution of effective therapy, when possible.

CHAPTER 34

Pyoderma Gangrenosum

Thomas T. Provost, M.D., Mary L. Harris, M.D.

Pain is dominant symptom

Rapidly expanding ulcerative lesion with purplish-red, undermined border

Pyoderma gangrenosum is characterized by the sudden onset of painful pustules, papules, and nodules that quickly break down, producing rapidly enlarging ulcers with a characteristic purplish undermined border. These lesions are very painful. Palpation is associated with a great deal of tenderness. These lesions may be solitary or multiple and may occur over the entire body, although they appear most commonly on the lower extremities. The mucous membranes are generally spared but may be involved (pyostomatitis vegetans) (See Chapter 73, "Oral Manifestations of Systemic Disease.") These lesions may occur at any age.

Bullous variant may herald development of myelogenous leukemia

Bullous pyoderma gangrenosum is a clinical variant that may herald a myelodysplastic state or the onset of myelogenous leukemia. (See Chapter 29, "Paraneoplastic Dermatoses.")

Pyoderma gangrenosum is associated with several systemic diseases (Table 34–1).

Pyoderma gangrenosum may occur in ulcerative colitis patients unrelated to disease activity

Approximately 40 to 50% of cases of pyoderma gangrenosum are idiopathic. Depending on the series, 30 to 60% of cases are associated with ulcerative colitis. In most cases, symptoms of ulcerative colitis precede the development of pyoderma gangrenosum. On occasions, however, it may signal exacerbation of gut disease. We have however, seen several cases of pyoderma gangrenosum occurring in ulcerative colitis patients in whom no clinically active bowel disease could be demonstrated. Although pyoderma gangrenosum is frequently associated with ulcerative colitis, only approximately 1 to 5% of ulcerative colitis patients develop this complication.

Approximately 15% of pyoderma gangrenosum patients have Crohn's disease. However, only 0.1 to 1.2% of Crohn's disease patients develop pyoderma gangrenosum.

Approximately 30 to 40% of patients with pyoderma gangrenosum have arthritis. A spectrum of arthritis occurs: some patients are rheumatoid factor positive; other patients demonstrate a nondestructive oligoarthritis with or without spondylitis associated with gut disease.

Approximately 10 to 20% of pyoderma gangrenosum patients have an associated monoclonal gammopathy. Most commonly, the monoclonal gammopathy is immunoglobulin (Ig)A, but other immunoglobulin classes also may be involved. It has been noted that many of the monoclonal paraproteins do not progress to myeloma. However, pyoderma gangrenosum has been seen in patients who have subsequently developed myeloma.

Pyoderma gangrenosum associated with myelogenous leukemia may be more superficial

In approximately 10% of pyoderma gangrenosum cases, hematologic investigation reveals either myelodysplasia or the presence of acute or chronic myelogenous leukemia. Hairy cell leukemia has also been found in association with pyoderma gangrenosum.

TABLE 34–1 Frequency of Occurrence of Associated Diseases with Pyoderma Gangrenosum

Type of Disease	Percentage of Cases
Idiopathic	~ 50
Ulcerative colitis	30–60
Crohn's disease	10–15
Arthritis	25–40
Paraproteins	10–25
Myelodysplastic and myeloproliferative diseases	10

On unusual occasions, pyoderma gangrenosum may be seen in association with chronic active hepatitis, primary biliary cirrhosis, systemic lupus erythematosus, and Behçet's syndrome. There appears to be a striking association in Japan with Takayasu's disease. As many as 30% of patients with this large vessel vasculitis have pyoderma gangrenosum–like lesions.

Pyoderma gangrenosum may be found in association with other neutrophilic pustular diseases, such as subcorneal pustular dermatosis of Sneddon and Wilkinson and Sweet's and Behçet's syndromes. It may be seen in individuals who develop a generalized pustular disease in association with ulcerative colitis. These individual pustular lesions may or may not evolve into pyoderma gangrenosum.

May be seen with Sweet's syndrome, subcorneal pustulosis of Sneddon and Wilkinson, and Behçet's syndrome

Etiology

The etiology of this disease is unknown. There is no evidence for bacterial, viral, or fungal infections. The disease is seen in patients who have autoimmune diseases. In addition, approximately 20% of these patients demonstrate pathergy. This is a phenomenon in which a neutrophilic infiltrate occurs at sites of venisection or trauma, leading to pustule formation.

Defective cell-mediated immunity has been described in these patients. This is manifested by cutaneous anergy to a battery of common antigens and failure to be sensitized with dinitrochlorobenzine. Some reports have indicated defects in vitro in lymphocytic proliferation to specific and nonspecific mitogens; other studies have failed to confirm these findings. A nondialyzable, heat-stable serum factor has been found in some patients' sera that inhibits both allogenic and autologous mixed lymphocyte reactions. A defect in monocyte chemotaxis and phagocytosis has been reported. Defective neutrophil chemotaxis has also been detected.

It should be noted that these defects are present in some, but not all, patients with pyoderma gangrenosum. It is not known whether these abnormalities are an integral part of the disease process or whether they represent epiphenomena.

No evidence for an infectious etiology
Pathergy
Many immulologic aberrations have been detected
No evidence for primary immunologic deficiency as an etiologic factor

A large body of evidence suggests a possible primary vasculopathy in the etiology of this cutaneous disease: individual case reports and studies demonstrate the presence of a leukocytoclastic angiitis in association with pyoderma gangrenosum, pathology studies demonstrate the presence of vasculitis in the normal-appearing perilesional skin of pyoderma gangrenosum patients, pyoderma gangrenosum occurs in Wegner's granulomatosis patients and frequently in Japanese patients with Takayasu's disease, and laboratory studies indicate the presence of circulating immune complexes in some patients.

An underlying vasculopathy may be etiologically significant

Laboratory Findings

There are no specific laboratory findings associated with pyoderma gangrenosum. Several reports have detected the presence of circulating immune complexes.

Necrotizing vasculitis in noninvolved perilesional skin

Biopsies of pyoderma gangrenosum lesions demonstrate a heavy neutrophilic infiltrate; however, biopsies of the lesions themselves fail to reveal any specific findings. Several studies indicate biopsies of noninvolved perilesional skin may demonstrate the presence of a necrotizing vasculitis.

Clinical Features

The disease process is characterized, generally, by the explosive onset of painful hemorrhagic pustules or nodules. These lesions rapidly ulcerate and spread, reaching sizes of 5 to 10 cm within 1 to 2 weeks. The reddish-purplish, undermined borders frequently demonstrate sinus tracts (Figures 34–1 and 34–2). The base of the lesion is boggy and necrotic and may extend to the fat and fascia.

Some lesions of pyoderma gangrenosum begin as erythematous, tender nodules mimicking abscess formation.

We have recently seen a young Caucasian female, with longstanding ulcerative colitis on 50 mg azathioprine three times per day, who developed a tender, hot nodule on her right lower leg. Incision and drainage for suspected abscess failed to demonstrate any evidence of a bacterial infection. Extension of the lesion occurred following surgery (pathergy). The lesion resolved quickly following intravenous methylprednisone 500 mg infused slowly over a 4-hour period.

Although the onset is generally explosive, with much pain, fever, and toxicity, a second variant is characterized by indolence, slow growth, massive granulation tissue, and spontaneous regression and healing in one area and progression in another. Both types of pyoderma gangrenosum heal with thin, atrophic, cribriform scars.

Treatment

Topical therapy of little value

Topical steroid therapy is generally of little value in the treatment of the early lesions of pyoderma gangrenosum. Intralesional injection of triamcinolone (5 to 10 mg/cc) has proven effective in aborting early lesions of pyoderma gangrenosum.

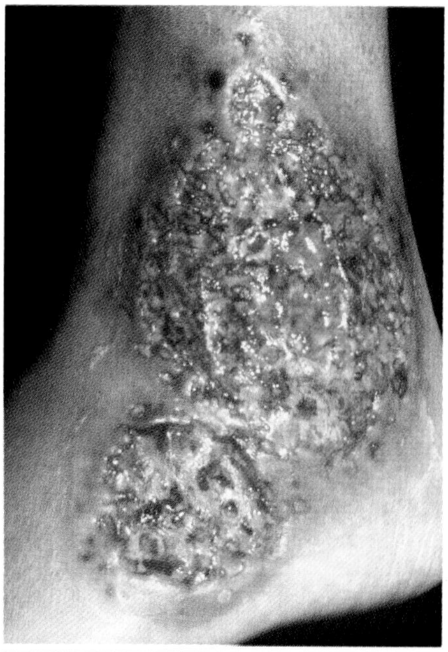

FIGURE 34–1 Pyoderma gangrenosum lesion in lateral ankle.

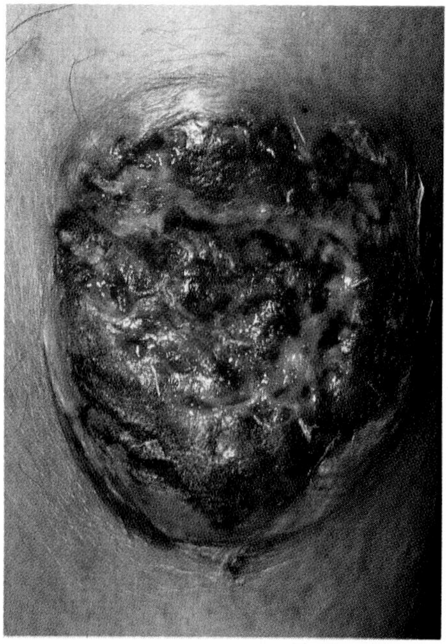

FIGURE 34–2 Pyoderma gangrenosum lesion demonstrating purplish undermined edge.

The ulcerative lesions of pyoderma gangrenosum have been treated with oral steroids (equivalent to 100 to 200 mg/d of prednisone). Unfortunately, severe side effects have developed in 50% of patients treated with this therapeutic regimen for prolonged periods.

Pulse steroids generally effective

The work of Lazarus's group has demonstrated that pulse steroids (the slow infusion of 1 g of methylprednisolone over a 4-hour period daily for 5 consecutive days) are able to stop the disease process with an immediate cessation of pain. (Patients over the age of 50 years or with heart disease should be placed on a cardiac monitor because rapid fluxes in electrolytes can occur.) This form of therapy coupled with a gradually tapered dose of oral steroids has proven to be an effective form of therapy in our experience. Cyclophosphamide, azathioprine and 6-mercaptopurine have also been reported to be successful in treating patients with pyoderma gangrenosum.

Cyclosporine is an effective form of therapy

In addition, clofazimine (200 to 300 mg per day) has been reported to be successful in some, but not all, cases. A generalized pinkish discoloration of the skin is associated with this form of therapy. Plasmapheresis and thalidomide have also been reported to be successful. In some cases, dapsone (100 to 150 mg/d) has also been reported to be efficacious. (It is interesting to note that dapsone appears to be effective in treating a number of skin diseases characterized by accumulations of neutrophils including erythema elevatum diutinum, dermatitis herpetiformis, Sneddon-Wilkinson disease, Sweet's syndrome, and pyoderma gangrenosum.)

On rare occasions, pyoderma gangrenosum may be recalcitrant to all forms of the above therapies. In these cases, cyclosporine may be effective. Renal toxicity and hypertension may be the sequelae.

We have recently seen a 30-year-old Caucasian female, with a 6-year history of ulcerative colitis, who developed a very painful, pustular, hemorrhagic nodule, which rapidly evolved into a 5-cm ulceration on the lateral aspect of the upper portion of her right lower leg. Evaluation of the status of her ulcerative colitis, using barium enema as well as a colonoscopic examination, failed to reveal any activity. Oral steroids, as much as 100 mg of prednisone per day, together with dapsone 100 mg per day, sulfasalazine 1 g four times a day, and azathioprine 150 mg per day failed to control this very painful lesion.

Cyclosporine 4 mg per kg was instituted. Within a 2-week period, the patient's pyoderma gangrenosum had healed. The most striking finding was that the pain disappeared within a 48h to 96-hour period after starting cyclosporine.

This case is illustrative of two facts: (1) Although this patient had a 6-year history of ulcerative colitis, the development of pyoderma gangrenosum was not associated with any evidence of activity of her bowel disease; and (2) although oral and pulse steroids have been effective in almost all the pyoderma gangrenosum patients that we have treated, this patient's cutaneous disease process was recalcitrant not only to these steroid regimens but also to azathioprine and diaminodiphenylsulfone. Cyclosporine proved to be very effective.

Annotated Bibliography

Wong E, Greaves MW. Pyoderma gangrenosum and leukocytoclastic vasculitis. Clin Exp Dermatol 1985;10:68–71.

English JSC, Fenton DA, Barth J, et al. Pyoderma gangrenosum and leukocytoclastic vasculitis in association with rheumatoid arthritis—a report of two cases. Clin Exp Dermatol 1984;9:270–273.

Calabrese LH. Cutaneous vasculitis, hypersensitivity vasculitis, erythema nodosum, and pyoderma gangrenosum. Curr Opin Rheumatol 1990;2:66–69.

Frances C, Boisnic S, Bletry O, et al. Cutaneous manifestations of Takayasu arteritis. A retrospective study of 80 cases. Dermatologica 1990;181: 266–272.

These four clinical articles describe the occurrence of pyoderma gangrenosum in vasculitis patients.

Powell FC, Su WPD, Perry Ho. Pyoderma gangrenosum: classification and management. J Am Acad Dermatol 1996;34:395–409.

This is an excellent review article from the Mayo Clinic, which over the years has had a great deal of experience evaluating patients with pyoderma gangrenosum. The article contains 168 references.

Curley RK, MacFarlane AW, Vickers CFH. Pyoderma gangrenosum treated with cyclosporine A. Br J Dermatol 1985;113:601–604.
Elgart G, Stover P, Larson K, et al. Treatment of pyoderma gangrenosum with cyclosporine: results in seven patients. J Am Acad Dermatol 1991;24:83–86.
O'Donnell B, Powell FC. Cyclosporine treatment of pyoderma gangrenosum. J Am Acad Dermatol 1991;24:141–143.

These three articles detail the efficacy of treatment of pyoderma gangrenosum lesions with cyclosporin A.

Brunsting LA, Gockerman WH, O'Leary PA. Pyoderma gangrenosum: clinical and experimental observations in five cases occurring in adults. Arch Dermatol 1930;22:655–680.

This is the early classic paper detailing the first description and use of the term "pyoderma gangrenosum" to describe this entity.

O'Loughlin S, Perry HO. A diffuse pustular eruption associated with ulcerative colitis. Arch Dermatol 1978;114:1061–1064.

This article demonstrates that not all painful, pustular lesions associated with ulcerative colitis evolve into classic pyoderma gangrenosum.

VanHale H, Rogers RS, Zone JJ. Pyostomatitis vegetans: a reactive mucosal marker for inflammatory disease of the gut. Arch Dermatol 1985;121:94–98.
Neville BW, Smith SE, Maize JC, et al. Pyostomatitis vegetans. Am J Dermatopathol 1985;7:67–77.

These two articles detail the clinical and histopathologic features of the variant of pyoderma gangrenosum involving the oral mucosa.

Perry HO, Winkelmann RK. Bullous pyoderma gangrenosum in leukemia. Arch Dermatol 1972;106:901–905.

This variant of pyoderma gangrenosum is less destructive and much more superficial than the typical ulcerative colitis. Approximately 40 patients have thus far been described, demonstrating the association of this superficial bullous variant with leukemia.

Johnson RB, Lazarus GS. Pulse therapy: therapeutic efficacy in the treatment of pyoderma gangrenosum. Arch Dermatol 1982;118:76–84.

This article details the efficacy of pulse, high-dose methylprednisolone therapy in the treatment of patients with pyoderma gangrenosum. This type of therapy has been excellent—rapidly controlling severe cases of pyoderma gangrenosum.

Hidano A, Watanabe K. Pyoderma gangraenosum and cardiovasculopathies, particularly Takayasu arteritis. Review of the Japanese literature. Ann Dermatol Venereol 1981;108:13–21.
Su WPD, Schroeter AL, Perry HO, et al. Histopathologic and immunopathologic study of pyoderma gangrenosum. J Cutan Pathol 1986;13: 323–330.

These two articles are of potential etiologic significance in explaining the rapid development of lesions of pyoderma gangrenosum. These reports detail the presence of pyoderma gangrenosum in association with evidence of vasculitis.

CHAPTER 35

Acrodermatitis Enteropathica

Bernard A. Cohen, M.D., Thomas T. Provost, M.D.

Clinical Features

Rare recessive disease associated with a peculiar dermatitis, alopecia, diarrhea, and stunting of growth

Acrodermatitis enteropathica is a rare autosomal recessive disease characterized by the onset of a scaly, crusted vesiculobullous dermatitis involving hands, feet, perioral region, and perineum 4 to 6 weeks after weaning (Figures 35–1, 35–2, 35–3, 35–4). Hair loss, diarrhea, and stunting of growth occur. There is also a decreased resistance to infections, and wound healing is impaired. The average age at time of recognition is 9 months with a predominance of females. A proctitis, with or without gastrointestinal candidiasis, is prominent.

Skin biopsies demonstrate intraepidermal bullae and acantholytic cells, together with hyper- and parakeratotic changes.

In the past, untreated acrodermatitis enteropathica frequently led to an early death, and long-term survival of untreated patients was associated with mental and growth retardation.

Experimental Studies

The events in our understanding of acrodermatitis enteropathica are provided in Table 35–1.

Zinc deficiency

Since the work of Moynahan in the early 1970s, zinc deficiency has been recognized as the cause of acrodermatitis enteropathica. Acquired zinc deficiencies resulting in a syndrome reminiscent of acrodermatitis enteropathica have been observed in premature infants treated with prolonged intravenous alimentation without supplemental zinc. It has also been observed in patients with Crohn's disease and cystic fibrosis and in adults receiving total hyperalimentation.

It is important to distinguish acrodermatitis enteropathica from acquired zinc deficiency states resulting from gastrointestinal malabsorption. Gastrointestinal disease can produce protein, fat, calorie, multiple vitamin, and trace element deficiencies, which are only partially corrected with zinc supplementation.

In addition, zinc deficiency has been shown to be associated with decreased numbers of T cells and impaired T-cell function, as well as monocyte and leukocyte chemotactic defects. These defects, associated with increased susceptibility to infections, are corrected by supplemental zinc.

In addition to the hereditary form of acrodermatitis enteropathica and the syndrome induced by zinc-deficient hyperalimentation, the clinical features of acrodermatitis enteropathica rarely have been detected in infants fed human milk. Human breast milk has been reported to be superior to cow's milk in providing bioavailable zinc, despite a lower absolute zinc content. Breast milk contains a

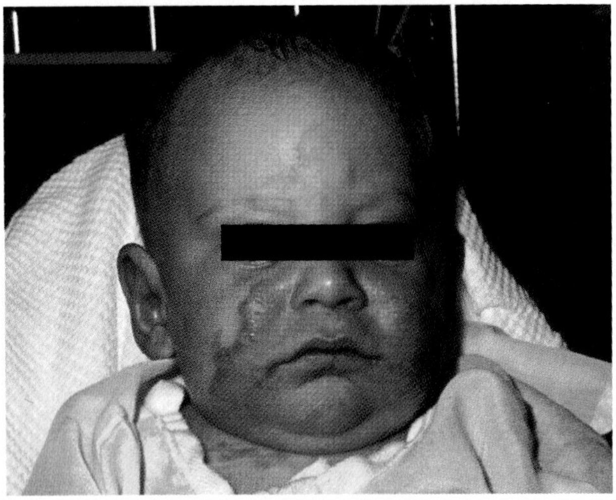

FIGURE 35-1 Perioral and hand dermatitis in an infant with acrodermatitis enteropathica.

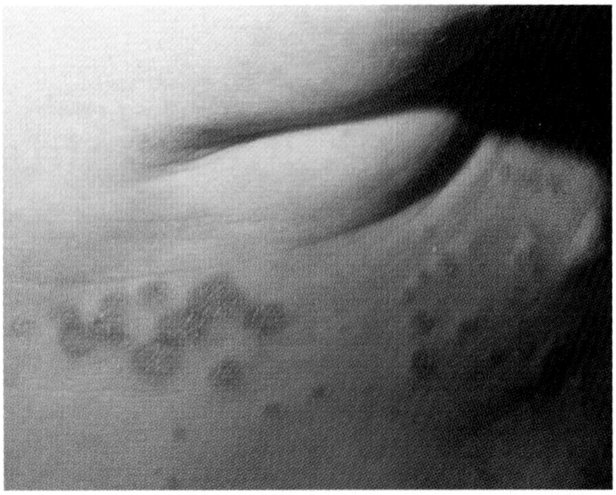

FIGURE 35-2 Individual erythematous rupture vesiculobullous dermatitis of acrodermatitis enteropathica.

A syndrome similar to acrodermatitis and all responsive to supplemental zinc has been detected in:
Zinc deficient hyperalimentation
Infants of mothers with defective zinc transport to their breast milk

"Lethal milk" syndrome in inbred mice, an autosomal recessive disease associated with low quantities of breast milk zinc, is a murine model of this disease

zinc-binding protein which potentiates zinc absorption even in infants with acrodermatitis enteropathica who lack a similar protein in their own gastrointestinal tracts. That explains why symptoms of zinc deficiency do not occur until 4 to 6 weeks after human breast-fed infants are weaned. Cases now have been reported in which acrodermatitis enteropathica occurred in breast-fed, premature and full-term infants. Investigations have demonstrated that the mother's breast milk, despite normal maternal zinc intake and serum zinc levels, was low in zinc. It is surmised that defective zinc levels in the breast milk indicate that zinc secretion into breast milk is controlled by a process independent of maternal zinc intake or serum zinc level. Roberts, Shadwick and Bergstresser, in a report of two such infants, reviewed data indicating that a mouse model for defective mammary gland zinc secretion exists. Mice born of the C57BL/6 (B/6) strain produce mammary milk with defective zinc levels, known as "lethal milk syndrome" (lm). Mice pups nursed by dams with this defect developed an acute dermatitis and alopecia, had stunted growth, and died rapidly. Genetic studies demonstrated

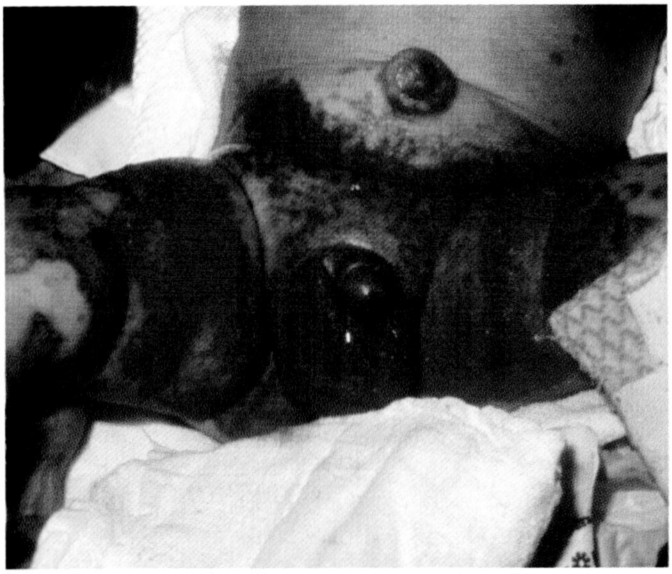

FIGURE 35-3 Severe involvement of perineum in a patient with acrodermatitis enteropathica.

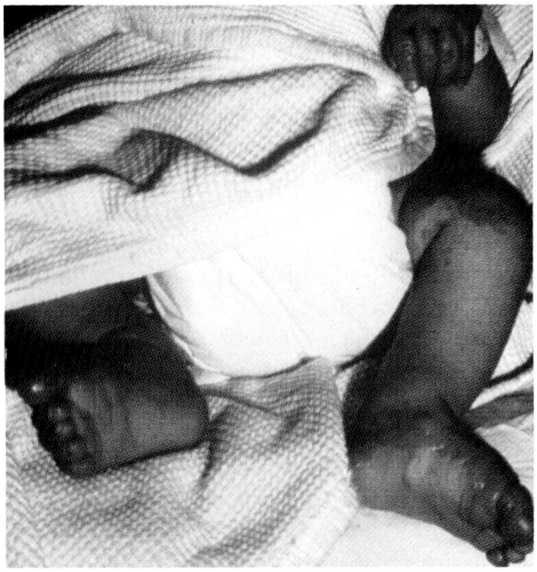

FIGURE 35-4 Hand and foot involvement in a patient with acrodermatitis.

Table 35–1 Glossary of Events in Our Understanding of Acrodermatitis Enteropathica

1936	Brandt first recognizes this entity and notes therapeutic benefits of human milk.
1942	Danbolt and Closs name the disease.
1953	Dillaha, Lorinez and Aavik successfully use iodoquinol to treat acrodermatitis enteropathica.
1973	Moynahan and Barnes describe zinc deficiency in acrodermatitis enteropathica.
1976	Zinc deficiency associated with parenteral alimentation is recognized.

that the defect existed as a recessive mutation and that the affected dams were homozygous for this defect (lm/lm). Furthermore, metabolic studies established that the inability of nursing pups to survive on milk from the homozygous mothers correlated directly with a reduced milk zinc content.

We have seen an Amish infant with this form of acrodermatitis enteropathica. This maternal breast milk zinc was low despite normal serum zinc levels. Switching the infant to bovine milk and temporary oral zinc supplementation immediately corrected the problem.

Iodoquinol enhances absorbtion of zinc from gastrointestinal tract

Prior to treatment with zinc supplements, halogenated derivatives of the 8-hydroxyquinolines, principally di-iodohydroxyquin (iodoquinol) was effective in treating acrodermatitis enteropathica. Studies have now demonstrated that this drug enhances the absorption of zinc from the gastrointestinal tract.

Laboratory Diagnosis

Diagnosis of acrodermatitis enteropathica is dependent on demonstrating a deficiency of plasma zinc (normal concentration > 55 µg per 100 mL). The concentration of zinc in breast milk during the first month of lactation is usually 300 µg per100 mL); however, by six months postpartum, the zinc level may fall below 100 µg/100 mL. Infants with acrodermatitis enteropathica have been reported as having levels that approximate 20 µg per 100 mL. One adult with acrodermatitis enteropathica had a level of 10 µg per 100 mL during one phase of treatment.

Measurement of serum zinc or urinary excretion of zinc confirms diagnosis

In addition to measuring plasma zinc, urinary zinc excretion can also be measured (normal urinary zinc excretion rate is 174–888 µg for 24 hours).

Alkaline phosphatase levels are low

Alkaline phosphatase is one of the zinc metalloenzymes. Very low serum levels of this enzyme suggest depletion of total body zinc. The normal range for serum alkaline phosphatase is 21–85 IU per L.

Care must be taken to use syringes and collection tubes free of detectable zinc, which can be accomplished by previously washing the plastic syringes and polypropylene tubes with hydrochloric acid or 10% nitric acid. Rinsing is done in double distilled deionized water.

Treatment

Treatment of acrodermatitis enteropathica and acquired forms of zinc deficiency is supplemental zinc

The treatment of the hereditary form of acrodermatitis enteropathica, as well as the acquired form, is supplemental zinc. The normal daily recommended allowance of zinc per adult is 15 mg. It has been noted that as little as 100 mg of zinc sulfate, which contains only 22 mg of elemental zinc, is effective in producing a rapid and dramatic clinical improvement in an adult with acrodermatitis enteropathica. The malaise and depression that frequently characterize this disease improves within 24 hours, and the cutaneous lesions are generally gone within 3 to 5 days.

In infants, oral zinc sulfate (5–10 mg per kg per day elemental zinc) has been successfully used. However, zinc gluconate may be better tolerated with less diarrhea.

Annotated Bibliography

Van Wouwe JP. Clinical and laboratory assessment of zinc deficiency in Dutch children, a review. Biol Trace Elem Res 1995;49:211–215.

The clinical spectrum of acrodermatitis enteropathica are compared with symptoms reported in other zinc deficiency states, including total parenteral nutrition, protein energy malnutrition, gastrointestinal disease, geophagia, and low dietary intake. The results of laboratory tests used in making the diagnosis of zinc deficiency are also reviewed. The sheer numbers of patients with each clinical disorder make this review invaluable.

Prasad AS. Zinc: an overview. Nutrition 1995;11:93–99.

This article reviews clinical aspects of zinc deficiency with a special emphasis on defects in the immune system, particularly lymphocyte dysfunction.

Krasovec M, Frenk E. Acrodermatitis enteropathica secondary to Crohn's disease. Dermatology 1996;193:361–363.

These authors discuss patients who developed zinc deficiency dermatoses that must be distinguished from primary acrodermatitis enteropathica. Cystic fibrosis in young children can be particularly challenging. Response to zinc supplementation alone in acrodermatitis enteropathica and, when available, specific gene and biochemical markers in some disorders will aid in diagnosis.

Grider A, Mouat MF. The acrodermatitis enteropathica mutation affects protein expression in human fibroblasts: analysis by two-dimensional gel electrophoresis. J Nutr 1996;126:219–224.

These investigators have identified novel proteins that may be the cause of reduced zinc uptake and abnormal zinc metabolism characteristics of fibroblasts containing the acrodermatitis enteropathica mutation.

Roberts LJ, Shadwick CF, Bergstresser PR. Zinc deficiency in two full-term breast-fed infants. J Am Acad Dermatol 1987;16:301–304.

Very interesting case reports and discussion.

CHAPTER 36

Ulcerative Colitis and Crohn's Disease

Mary L. Harris, M.D., Thomas T. Provost, M.D.

Extraintestinal complications are frequent in patients with the inflammatory bowel diseases (IBD), ulcerative colitis, and Crohn's disease. Extraintestinal manifestations of IBD include pyoderma gangrenosum and erythema nodosum, arthropathies, uveitis, sclerosing cholangitis, growth retardation, iron deficiency anemia, and nephrolithiasis (Figure 36–1).

Ulcerative Colitis

General Clinical Features

Rectal bleeding common feature in ulcerative colitis

Ulcerative colitis can have three patterns of mucosal inflammation: (1) proctitis or distal colitis, (2) left-sided ulcerative colitis, and (3) extensive pancolitis or disease extending proximally to the splenic flexure of the colon. Patients with proctitis, which is inflammation and friability of the rectal mucosa, present with rectal bleeding that often can be mistakenly attributed to hemorrhoids or fissures. With increasing inflammation, the patient develops urgency, frequency, tenesmus, or dry heaves of the rectum. If the disease extends proximally to involve the left colon or pancolitis, the patient can become dehydrated from diarrhea and develop electrolyte disorders, which can contribute to other systemic complaints.

Mucocutaneous Manifestations

The mucocutaneous manifestations of ulcerative colitis are presented in Table 36–1.

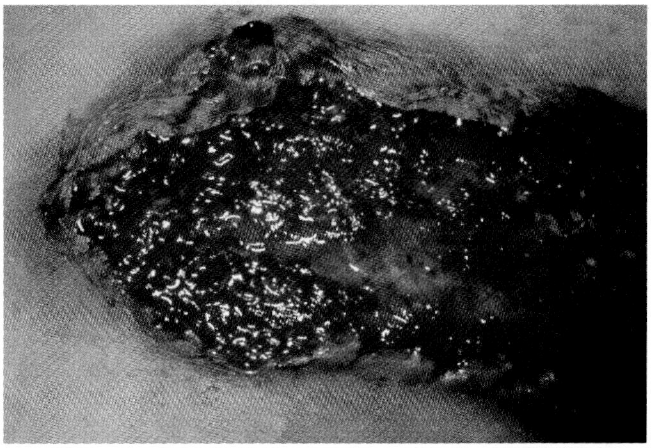

FIGURE 36–1 Pyoderma gangrenosum of the leg in a patient with ulcerative colitis. Similar lesions can be seen in Crohn's patients.

Crohn's Disease

General Clinical Features

Crohn's disease can have several subtypes or patterns of disease involvement: ileal disease, ileal-right colonic inflammation, colitis, jejunoileitis, or perirectal disease. The most common presentation of Crohn's disease is an appendicitis-like pattern with postprandial abdominal pain and obstructive symptoms. Disease activity of Crohn's disease is also classified according to inflammatory, stricturizing, or perforating. With transmural

TABLE 36–1 Mucocutaneous Manifestations of Ulcerative Colitis

Manifestation	Description
Aphthous stomatitis	Lesions generally occur with exacerbation of disease. Occurs in approximately 5% of patients. Presence of intractable lesions should lead one to investigate for occult ulcerative colitis.
Erythema nodosum	Lesions correlate with gut disease activity.
Arthritis and arthralgias	Acute onset of toxic arthritis generally involves large joints. Correlates with activity of gut disease.
Pyoderma gangrenosum	Disease affects 1–5% of patients. In general, occurs independent of gastrointestinal disease activity (Figure 36–1).
Papular, pustular lesions	Lesions are generally painful and may evolve into pyoderma gangrenosum. Generally, they heal spontaneously. May represent a forme fruste of pyoderma gangrenosum.
Pyoderma vegetans	Disease involves intertriginous areas.
Pyostomatitis vegetans	This unusual variant involves oral cavity.
Hypercoaguable state manifested predominantly by venous thrombosis	This is an uncommon event. Increased factor VIII and thrombocytosis have been described.

Fistula formation common in Crohn's disease

inflammation, fistulas can occur in other loops of the intestinal tract, the retroperitoneal cavity, the bladder, vagina, or enterocutaneous tracts. Crohn's disease in the colon causes diarrhea and may be difficult to distinguish from ulcerative colitis.

Mucocutaneous Manifestations

The mucocutaneous manifestations of Crohn's disease are presented in Table 36–2.

The following are four cases of biopsy-proven Crohn's disease, illustrative of some of the diffuse mucocutaneous manifestations of this disease:

The first patient was a 28-year-old Caucasian female referred for treatment of recalcitrant erythema nodosum lesions of the right ankle and dorsum of the foot. Biopsy demonstrated a septal panniculitis. Approximately 5 years prior, the patient had been diagnosed as having Crohn's disease. An upper gastrointestinal barium study and a small bowel follow-through demonstrated involvement of the terminal ilium.

TABLE 36–2 Mucocutaneous Manifestations of Crohn's Disease

Manifestation	Description
Pyoderma gangrenosum	Occurs in approximately 1% of patients. May or may not be reflective of gastrointestinal disease activity.
Erythema nodosum	Generally reflective of disease activity.
Aphthous stomatitis	Generally reflects active gastrointestinal disease.
Granulomas of the oral mucosa	Examples are cheilitis granulomatosa and Melkersson-Rosenthal syndrome (Figure 36–2).
Fistula and abscess formation in the perianal region	May present as inflammation of anal Morgagni's crypts. May also present as fistulas in the abdominal wall (Figures 36–3 and 36–4).
Metastatic Crohn's disease	Presents as distant granulomatous lesions with no contiguous connection with the bowel disease (Figures 36–5 and 36–6).
Arthritis	Large joints usually involved. In general, correlates with active disease.

The second patient, a 32-year-old African American female with known Crohn's disease, developed nonhealing ulcers of the perineum and inguinal folds and beneath the breasts (Figures 36–5 to 36–6). Biopsies of all sites revealed granulomatous lesions indicative of metastatic Crohn's disease.

The third patient, a 28-year-old Caucasian female, developed Melkersson-Rosenthal syndrome involving the right side of the face and the lower lip, which spontaneously resolved over several months (Figure 36–2). Two years later, she consulted an otolaryngologist for hoarseness. She was discovered to have an enlarged uvula, which upon biopsy, demonstrated granulomas. Examination of the larynx demonstrated a nodule on the epiglottis, and small-bowel endoscopy demonstrated biopsy-proven Crohn's disease involving the terminal ileum.

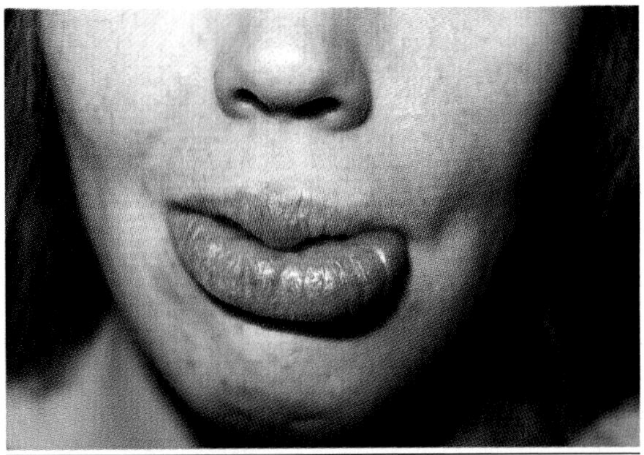

FIGURE 36–2 Granulomatous cheilitis of the lower lip. These lesions may occur in Crohn's disease.

The fourth patient, a 5-year-old Caucasian boy was seen and evaluated for a perianal swollen skin tag and swelling of the scrotum (Figures 36–3 and 36–4). One year later, the child developed gastrointestinal features of Crohn's disease.

Etiology of Inflammatory Bowel Disease

The etiology of IBD, specifically Crohn's disease and ulcerative colitis, is unknown; however, strong genetic influences are suggested by the appearance of both diseases in families, especially in individuals of Ashkenazi Jew descent. Identical twins have an 85% concordance for Crohn's disease and fraternal twins have the same concordance as patients with a family history, which is approximately 15 to 20% for families of patients with Crohn's disease and 10 to 12% for families of patients with ulcerative colitis. The immune system has also been clearly implicated in IBD. Activated T4 lymphocytes have been demonstrated in affected bowel walls. They release lymphokines, which activate and recruit monocytes, macrophages, polymorphonuclear leukocytes, and mast cells. The inflammatory response is also induced by tumor necrosis factor alpha (TNF-α) and interleukins (IL), specifically IL-10.

IBD:
More common in identical twins
Suspected to be T cell-mediated

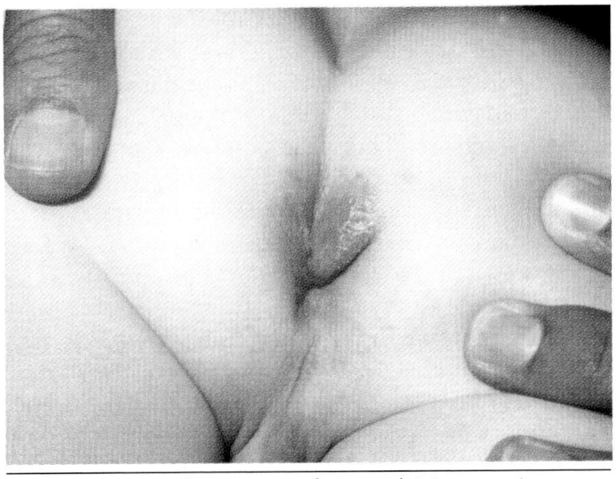

FIGURE 36–3 Inflammation of an anal (Morgagni) crypt in a child who subsequently developed Crohn's disease.

FIGURE 36–4 Scrotal edema in the same child. The lesions in Figures 36–3 and 36–4 preceded, by one year, the establishment and diagnosis of Crohn's disease.

Evaluation of Patients

Any patient with pyoderma gangrenosum should be evaluated for IBD.

A thorough history of the present illness will include an extensive review of systems for uveitis, arthritis or other musculoskeletal problems, hepatic disease, additional dermatologic lesions, oral aphthous ulcers, growth retardation, iron deficiency anemia, and nephrolithiasis. A past medical history of an appendectomy or any episodes of peritonitis reflecting an intestinal perforation are noteworthy. Family history regarding colonic polyposis, cancer, and any predisposition to other inflammatory processes is important to obtain. The physical examination must involve looking for evidence of clubbing of the digits and toes, episcleritis, oral aphthous ulcers, abdominal tenderness, rebound or guarding, hepatosplenomegaly, perirectal abscess or fistulas, and dermatologic conditions (ie, pyoderma gangrenosum, recurrent pustules, cutaneous ulcers, or rarely, cheilitis granulomatosa).

Diagnostic Studies

Laboratory studies frequently demonstrate a leukocytosis, anemia, and thrombocytosis. A mean corpuscular volume will detect iron, vitamin B_{12}, or folate deficiencies. In addition, it is important to obtain levels of a C-reactive protein, electrolytes, renal and hepatic function, vitamin B_{12}, red blood cell folate, and iron levels.

Diagnostic techniques:
- *biopsies*
- *radiographic imaging techniques*

Endoscopic surveillance includes colonoscopic examination with intubation of the terminal ileum and multiple surveillance biopsies to look for histopathologic evidence of acute and chronic inflammation. Imaging studies can include obtaining an abdominal flat and upright radiographic images to look for air fluid levels, evidence of ankylosing spondylitis or sacroiliitis, and a dedicated small-bowel series to rule out jejunoileitis. If an abdominal mass or perforation is suspected, abdominal computerized tomography is also indicated.

Treatment

Medical Management

Treatment:
- *sulfasalazine*
- *mesalamine*
- *steroid suppositories*
- *metronidazole*
- *ciprofloxacin*

Medical management of Crohn's disease and ulcerative colitis can include several routes of administration. Topical, oral, intramuscular, and intravenous therapy can provide a multiregimen approach to control the inflammatory process, diarrhea, and other systemic manifestations. Oral sulfasalazine is indicated for mild to moderate colonic disease in ulcerative colitis and Crohn's disease. Oral mesalamine is useful in treating jejunal or ileal Crohn's disease. With symptoms of frequency, urgency, and tenesmus, topical suppositories or enemas can be prescribed from the corticosteroid or mesalamine categories. Antibiotics, specifically metronidazole and ciprofloxacin, can be useful in Crohn's disease. Ciprofloxacin has also been useful in management of ulcerative colitis. For moderate-to-severe disease activity that impairs daily living activities, corticosteroid therapy is indicated. Chronic steroid use, however, can have debilitating side effects. Hypertension, diabetes, insomnia, psychosis, osteoporosis, avascular necrosis, and cataracts are among the most common adverse effects. To avoid steroid side effects, immunomodulators (ie, azathioprine, 6-mercaptopurine, methotrexate) are indicated. These medications are also used to maintain remission. Side effects of immunosuppressive drugs include bone marrow suppression, hepatitis, and pancreatitis as well as a pneumonitis, which is rarely seen with methotrexate. For patients with disease refractory to immunomodulators and for those with perianal fistulas, chimeric monoclonal antibody to TNF may be an effective alternative. Preliminary evidence suggests that more than 50% of patients receiving a single infusion will experience a clinical response, including remission. (Our preliminary experience with anti–TNF-α has been very promising. Our patient who has Crohn's disease with metastatic lesions (see Figures 36–5 and 36–6) has had a dramatic response with healing of recalcitrant fissures in the groin and submammary areas.) Drawbacks include the potential need for multiple dosing, concern for developing lymphoma, and unknown long-term consequences. Other modalities under investigation include oral budesonide (a nonabsorbed corticosteroid) and IL-10 infusion/topical therapy. Enteral nutrition, involving monomeric, oligomeric, or polymeric diets may provide short-term remission in approximately two-thirds of patients. There is no particular difference between the diets themselves. Total parenteral nutrition therapy instituted for medically refractive patients can induce remission in approximately 60% of cases, although the vast majority will eventually relapse.

Surgical Approaches

For patients with Crohn's disease refractory to previously described medical management regimens, surgical approaches can provide a fresh start. Limited small bowel or colonic resections can be accomplished via the laparoscopic route or an open laparotomy. Diversion of the fecal stream in order to allow for bowel rest and resolution of inflammation can be accomplished by a diverting ileostomy or a diverting descending colostomy. Nevertheless, inflammation will be found in any areas of intestine that are diverted from the fecal stream, as these areas are devoid of short-chained fatty acids, the nutritional substrate for colonocytes.

Another approach to patients with potential for a short-gut syndrome is strictureplasty, a form of enteroplasty. This method, which enlarges the luminal caliber of the bowel but does not remove the diseased bowel, provides symptomatic relief.

Risk of cancer from long-term therapy for ulcerative colitis: avoid by total proctocolectomy

In ulcerative colitis, a total proctocolectomy is curative for the patient and avoids the long-term complications associated with medical therapy (risk of cancer). For patients who are uncomfortable with the standard Brooke ileostomy and use of appliances, a two-to three-step ileal anal pouch anastomosis procedure can be an alternative for younger, nonobese patients. Nevertheless, pouch inflammation following reservoir procedure is common and may increase urgency and frequency of bowel movements and necessitate antibiotic therapy. Patients may also experience incontinence or nocturnal leakage with these reservoir procedures.

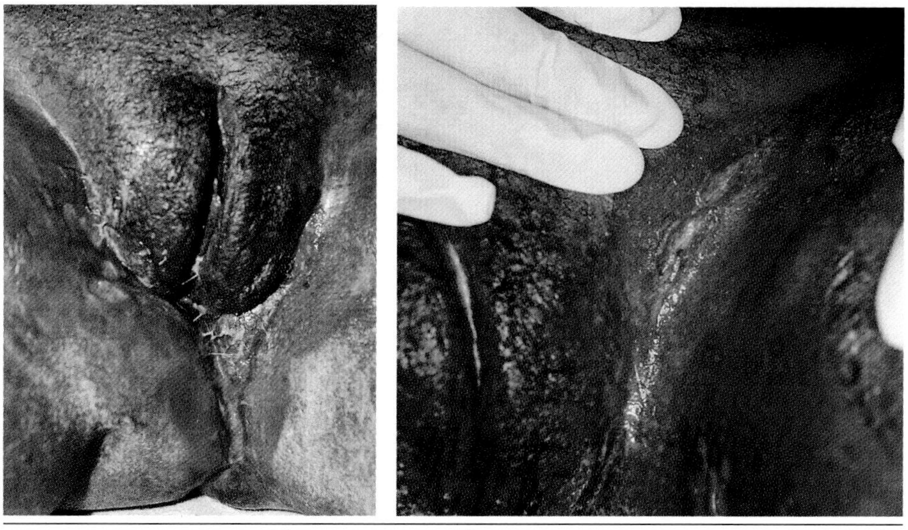

FIGURE 36–5 AND 36–6 Ulcerative inguinal lesions representing metastatic Crohn's disease. Similar lesions detected in inframammary regions. Biopsies demonstrated granulomatous disease.

Patient education is important

Patients who receive a diagnosis of Crohn's disease or ulcerative colitis may have inaccurate perceptions and mistaken beliefs because of information from family, friends, and the public. Therefore, the benefits of educating patients who have IBD cannot be underscored. Accurate communication with the physician, dealing with fears and expectations, complying with the medical regimen, and building support among family and friends are essential for the well-being of these patients. Information about mutual support or self-help groups and the role of the National Foundation for Ileitis and Colitis, now renamed the "Crohn's and Colitis Foundation of America," should be provided in all physician offices. Health-related quality of life plays an important role for patients with ulcerative colitis and Crohn's disease.

Annotated Bibliography

Sandborn WJ. A review of immune modifier therapy for inflammatory bowel disease: Azathioprine, 6-mercaptopurine, cyclosporin, and methotrexate. Am J Gastroenterol 1996;91:423–433.

This article provides a good summary of medical therapeutic options.

Targan SR, Hanauer SB, van Deventer SJ, et al. A short-term study of chimeric monoclonal antibody cA2 to tumor necrosis factor alpha for Crohn's disease. Crohn's disease cA2 Study Group. N Engl J Med 1997;337:1029–1035.

This article reports on an innovative new therapeutic approach to treating Crohn's disease using molecular technologies.

Irvine EJ. Quality of life issues in patients with inflammatory bowel disease. Am J Gastroenterol 1997;92(12Suppl):18S–24S.

This is a good article.

Das KM. Relationship of extraintestinal involvements in inflammatory bowel disease: new insights into autoimmune pathogenesis. Dig Dis Sci 1999;44:1–13.

This is a good review of extraintestinal manifestations.

CHAPTER 37

Hyperlipidemia

Simeon Margolis, M.D., Ph.D., Thomas T. Provost, M.D.

A xanthoma may indicate a disorder of lipid metabolism associated with elevated levels of blood lipids (hyperlipidemia). However, the vast majority of people with hyperlipidemia do not have xanthomas. In some instances, this cutaneous manifestation is the first clinical feature to be recognized and associated with a disorder of lipid metabolism. Thus, recognition and institution of the appropriate work-up is critical in the management of these patients. Xanthomas, however, are frequently overlooked by physicians during physical examinations.

First sign of lipid disorder may be development of xanthoma
Most patients with lipid disorders do not have xanthomas
Nondermatologists may not recognize xanthomas

Xanthomas may occur in familial hypercholesterolemia (type IIa or b), familial combined hyperlipidemia (types IV or V), and dysbetalipoproteinemia (type III hyperlipoproteinemia). The familial hyperlipidemias are inherited as dominant traits. Therefore, low-density lipoprotein (LDL) and high-density lipoprotein (HDL) cholesterol and triglyceride levels should be obtained not only in the patients but also in the children and siblings of patients with xanthomas or hyperlipidemia.

Various morphologic types of xanthoma have been recognized, including xanthelasma palpebarum, tuberous xanthomas, tendinous xanthomas, eruptive xanthomas, and plane xanthomas.

Cutaneous Manifestations

Xanthelasma Palpebarum

Xanthelasma palpebarum is characterized by bilateral macular, papular, yellowish lesions occurring predominantly on the upper eyelid, frequently extending to the inner canthus. Approximately 50% of the time this is a localized cutaneous process. In the other 50%, however, these lesions are associated with types II and III hyperlipoproteinemia. They also occur in patients with primary biliary cirrhosis.

Xanthelasma palpebarum:
50% of time localized cutaneous process
50% of time associated with elevated cholesterol

Tuberous Xanthomas

Tuberous xanthomas are firm, nodular, yellow tumors occurring on the extensor surfaces of limbs, particularly the knees and elbows. These painless lesions are seen with elevated cholesterol or triglyceride levels in types II, III, and IV hyperlipoproteinemias, hypothyroidism, and biliary cirrhosis.

Tuberous xanthomas: associated with elevated cholesterol or triglyceride levels

Tendinous Xanthomas

Tendinous xanthomas are painless, nodular lesions occurring most frequently in the extensor tendons of the hands and feet, as well as the Achilles tendons. It should be noted, however, that any tendon can be involved. Tendon xanthomas are found almost exclusively, if not exclusively, in familial hypercholesterolemia (type II).

Tendinous xanthomas:
found over extensor tendons of feet and hands
associated with familial hypercholesterolemia

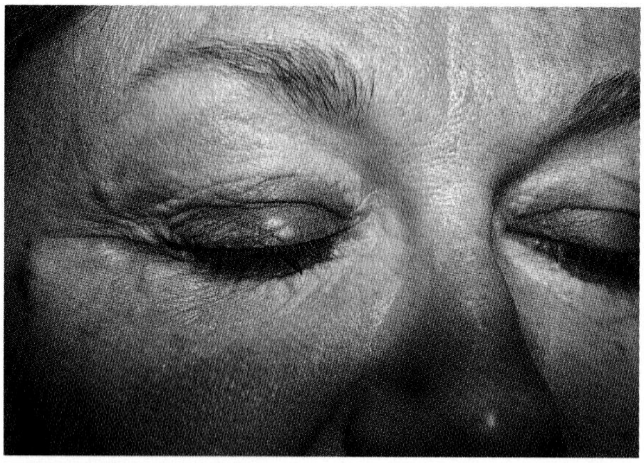

FIGURE 37–1 Xanthelasma in a patient with type II hyperlipoproteinemia.

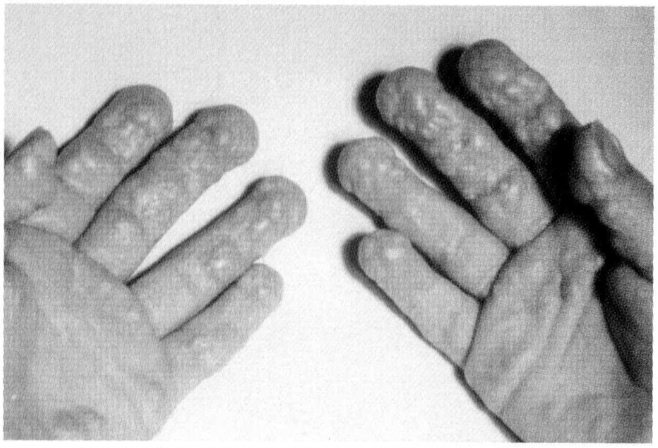

FIGURE 37–2 Tuberoxanthoma in a patient with type III hyperlipoproteinemia.

Eruptive Xanthomas

Eruptive xanthomas: associated with severe hypertriglyceridemia

Eruptive xanthomas are small, yellowish, macular, papular lesions surrounded by an erythematous halo. These lesions are associated with severe hypertriglyceridemia and are features of types I, III, and V hyperlipoproteinemia. Uncontrolled diabetes mellitus may trigger the hypertriglyceridemia that produces these lesions.

Plane Xanthomas

Plane xanthomas: creases of palms

Plane xanthomas are yellowish, macular lesions that can occur anywhere but are commonly seen in the creases of the palms. They are virtually pathognomonic for type III hyperlipoproteinemia. Plane xanthomas can also be seen in association with multiple myeloma. (See Chapter 24, "Leukemia, B-cell lymphomas, and Multiple Myeloma," subsection on multiple myeloma.)

Evaluation

All plasma lipids are carried on four lipoproteins. Very low-density lipoprotein (VLDL) is synthesized in the liver and is the major carrier of triglycerides. Removal of triglycerides from circulating VLDL produces LDL, a highly atherogenic lipoprotein and the major carrier of cholesterol. The liver also produces

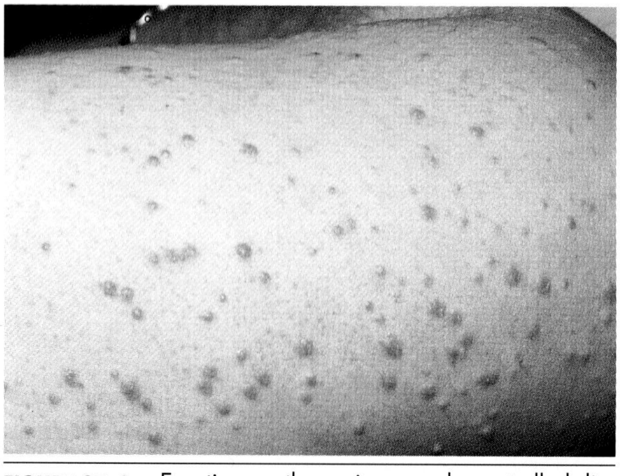

FIGURE 37–3 Eruptive xanthoma in a poorly controlled diabetic patient. Markedly elevated triglyceride levels were detected.

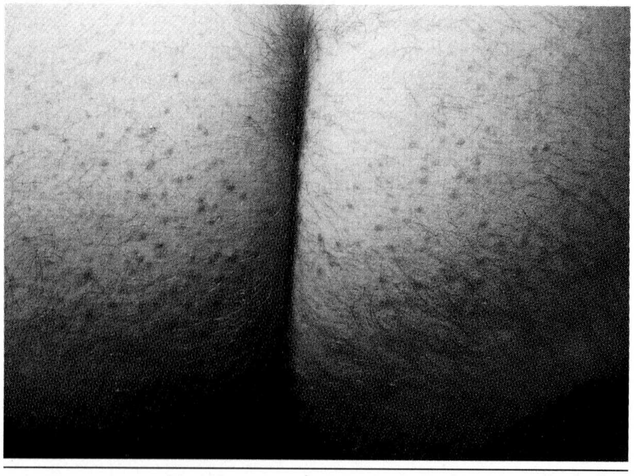

FIGURE 37–4 Eruptive xanthoma in poorly controlled diabetic. (Reproduced with permission from the slide collection of the late Dr. R. C. V. Robinson)

HDL, which protects against atherosclerosis by removing cholesterol from the arterial wall. These three lipoproteins are always present in plasma. Fat absorbed from the intestine (mostly triglycerides) is transported on chylomicrons, which are rapidly cleared from the circulation so that they are not present after an overnight fast in normal individuals.

Four classes of lipoproteins:
- *very low-density lipoproteins*
- *low-density lipoprotein*
- *high-density lipoproteins*
- *chylomicrons*

A lipid profile, consisting of cholesterol, HDL cholesterol, and triglycerides, should be obtained after an overnight fast in all patients who present with xanthomas. In addition, the plasma should be refrigerated overnight to look for the presence of chylomicrons, which appear as a white band at the top of the tube. These tests will make it possible to estimate the concentration of LDL cholesterol as well as to determine the type of lipoprotein abnormality in most cases, although ultracentrifugation in a specialized laboratory is necessary to identify type III hyperlipoproteinemia. Except for type III, the typing scheme for the hyperlipoproteinemias is based on which lipoproteins are present in excessive amounts, as follows: type I, increased chylomicrons; type IIa, increased LDL, type IIb, increased LDL and VLDL; type IV, increased VLDL; and type V, increased chylomicrons and VLDL. Type III is characterized by the presence of high concentrations of intermediates in the conversion of VLDL to LDL. The hyperlipidemias may be inherited, usually as an autosomal dominant trait, as a primary disorder or complicate some underlying disease as a secondary hyperlipidemia (Table 37–1).

Five types of hyperlipoproteinemia:
- *type I: increased chylomicrons*
- *type IIa: increased LDL*
- *type IIb: increased LDL and VLDL*
- *type III: intermediates in conversion of VLDL to LDL*
- *type IV: increased VLDL*
- *type V: increased VLDL and chylomicrons*

Treatment

The treatment of hyperlipidemia is aimed at preventing cardiovascular disease due to atherosclerosis, as well as preventing attacks of acute pancreatitis, which can result from extremely high triglyceride levels (> 1000 mg/dL). Decisions on treating hypercholesterolemia are based on the level of the LDL cholesterol and the risk status of the patient for coronary heart disease. Patients are at very high risk if they have diabetes or proven cardiovascular disease (coronary, cerebral, or peripheral vascular disease). High-risk patients have two or more risk factors, whereas those with zero or one risk factor are considered at low risk. The risk factors include a family history of premature coronary disease in first-degree relatives (before age 55 in males and before age 65 in females), age 45 or older in men, age 55 or older or premature menopause in women, cigarette smoking, hypertension, and an HDL cholesterol less than 35 mg per dL.

Risk factors:
- *family history of premature vascular disease*
- *male 45 or older*
- *female 55 or older or premature menopause*
- *cigarette smoking*
- *hypertension HDL<35 mg/dL*

Treatment of hyperlipidemias begins with lifestyle measures—diet and exercise. The initial dietary targets are a restriction of total fat intake to less than 30% of total calories and cholesterol to less than 300 mg a day. Saturated fat is reduced to less than 10% of calories. Further limitations may be prescribed if these measures do not lower total and LDL cholesterol sufficiently. Weight loss to achieve a desirable body weight, along with regular exercise, is an important goal, but they are more likely to lower triglycerides than cholesterol levels. When patients are not compliant or lifestyle changes are inadequate to reach appropriate goals, lipid-lowering drugs may be used. Most effective in lowering total and LDL cholesterol are the hydroxymethyglutaryl coenzyme A (HMGCoA) reductase

Drug treatment:
- *Cholesterol—*
- *HMGCoA reductase inhibitors or "statins"*
- *bile acid sequestrants*
- *triglycerides*
- *gemfibrozil*
- *fenofibrate*
- *niacin raises HDL may be poorly tolerated*

TABLE 37–1 Causes of Secondary Hyperlipidemia

Diabetes mellitus
Hypothyroidism
Nephrotic syndrome
Primary biliary cirrhosis
Glycogen storage diseases

inhibitors, also known as "statins" (atorvastatin, cerivastatin, fluvastatin, lovastatin, pravastatin, and simvastatin). HMGCoA reductase is the rate limiting enzyme in cholesterol synthesis. A reduction in cholesterol synthesis signals cells to increase synthesis of LDL receptors reducing LDL receptors reducing LDL serum levels. The statins also raise HDL cholesterol by about 8% and lower triglycerides by an average of 10%. The bile acid sequestrants, cholestyramine and colestipol, also reduce LDL cholesterol and can be used in combination with any of the other lipid-lowering medications. The most effective drugs for elevated triglycerides are gemfibrozil and fenofibrate. They also raise HDL cholesterol by about 10%. Niacin is the most potent agent for raising HDL cholesterol levels; it also lowers triglycerides and cholesterol but may be poorly tolerated due to side effects.

Annotated Bibliography

Downs JR, Clearfield M, Weis D, et al. Primary prevention of acute coronary events with lovastatin in men and women with average cholesterol levels. Results of AFCAPS/TexCAPS. J Am Med Assoc 1998;279: 1615–1622.

This is one of five large intervention trials that show a decrease in coronary events and strokes when LDL cholesterol levels are reduced with a statin. This study involved men and women with no history of coronary disease and only modestly elevated cholesterol levels.

Mahley RW, Weisgraber P, Farese RV Jr. Disorders of lipid metabolism. In: Wilson JD, Foster DW, Kronenberg HM, Larsen PR, eds. Williams Textbook of Endocrinology, 9th ed. Philadelphia: WB Saunders, 1998, pp 1099–1153.

This is an excellent review of lipid and lipoprotein metabolism. It also contains a description of the types of xanthomas found in association with each type of hyperlipidemia.

Summary of the second report of the National Cholesterol Education Program (NCEP) Expert Panel on Detection, Evaluation, and Treatment of High Blood Cholesterol in Adults. JAMA 1993;269:3015–3023.

This report summarizes the most commonly used guidelines for decisions on when to treat patients with elevated cholesterol levels.

Knopp RH. Dry treatment of lipid disorders. N Engl J Med 1999;341:498–511.

This is a critical, up-to-date discussion of the drugs used for the treatment of hyperlipidemia, along with a review of the results of cholesterol-lowering intervention trials.

CHAPTER 38

Ochronosis

Thomas T. Provost, M.D., John A. Flynn, M.D.

Automsomal recessive disease

Deficiency of homogentisic acid oxidase

Ochronosis is a rare inborn error of tyrosine metabolism disease caused by a deficiency of the enzyme homogentisic acid oxidase. This enzyme is localized to chromosome 3q (Figure 38–1). It is inherited as an autosomal recessive disorder and is characterized by the deposition of homogentisic acid in the skin and cartilage.

The disease is also known as "alkaptonuria," a term denoting the presence in alkaline urine of a substance that avidly binds oxygen and turns dark. The term "alkapton" was given to this substance. Subsequently, the deposition of a bluish-black pigment was noted in the cartilage of patients with alkaptonuria. The term "ochronosis" was given to the microscopic appearance of this pigment, which was yellow (ochre).

Increased frequencey in areas of world in which consaguinity is common

In the general population, the frequency is 1 in 250,000.

Phenylalanine

↓

Tyrosine

↓

p-Hydroxyphenylpyruvic acid

↓

Homogentisic acid

↓ → alkaptonuria block

(Homogentisic acid oxidase deficiency)

Maleylacetoacetic acid

FIGURE 38–1 Inborn error of homogentisic acid metabolism.

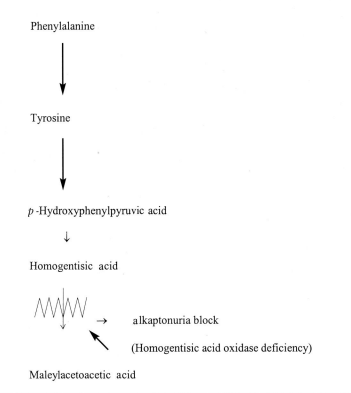

Homogentisic acid preferentially binds to connective tissue

Homogentisic acid is colorless, rapidly turning dark in alkaline urine

The excessive amounts of homogentisic acid are deposited in connective tissue, appearing to localize preferentially in the skin and cartilage. For example, rats fed a high tyrosine diet demonstrate the deposition of homogentisic acid in joint capsules, the trachea, and the sternum. There is some evidence to suggest that oxidized polymers of homogentisic acid may cross-link with collagen.

Cutaneous Manifestations

Skin manifestations are protean occurring in third or fourth decade

Staining of cerumen or axillary region

The cutaneous manifestations of ochronosis are generally not detected until the individual reaches the third or fourth decade of life. Renal disease, inhibiting the excretion of homogentisic acid, however, may result in an accelerated development of the cutaneous features. Although generally insidious, homogentisic acid pigmentation may occur around sebaceous and sweat gland orifices. A bluish-black discoloration of skin over cartilage surfaces and tendons may become prominent with time. For example, sebaceous gland secretion of homogentisic acid may produce dark cerumen or axillary staining. The cartilage of the ear and nose may show a bluish-gray tinge (Figure 38–2). Calcification may occur. The deposition of the homogentisic acid may produce a degeneration of the tympanic membrane and ossicles, resulting in tinnitus and deafness.

Pigmentation on tip of nose and ears

The cartilage deposition of homogentisic acid, with time, becomes more and more apparent. The areas of hyperpigmentation are characteristically the tip of the nose and the cartilage of the ear. The sclera may demonstrate a grayish-black pigmentation anterior to the horizontal recti muscle insertion. With time, pigment deposits may be seen adjacent to the limbus.

Systemic Manifestations

Cartilage deposition of homogentisic acid produces an accelerated degenerative articular disease process, which becomes manifest in the third and fourth decades of life. Involvement of the hips, knees, spine, and shoulder joints, associated with episodes of acute inflammation, limit motion (Figures 38–3 to 38–5). Lordosis, kyphosis, and lumbar pain are characteristic.

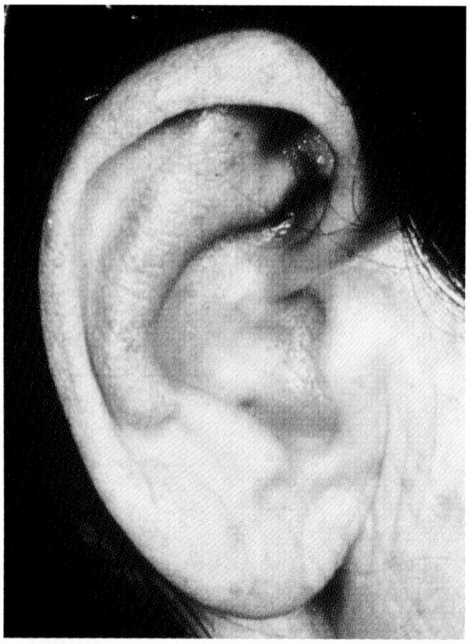

FIGURE 38–2 Extreme pigmentation in the upper ear cartilage in a patient with ochronosis. No explanation for this localization.

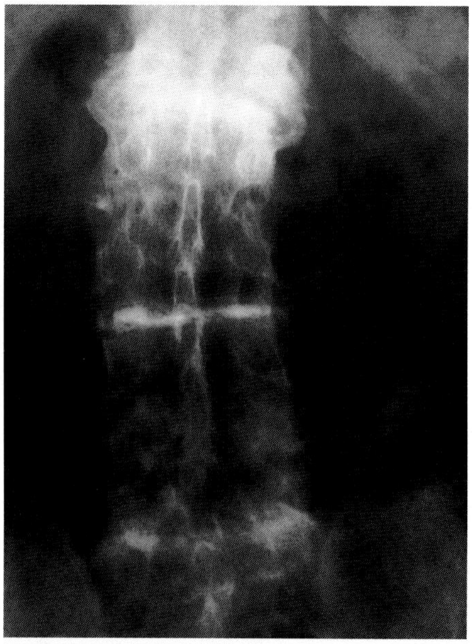

FIGURE 38–3 Intervertebral disc calcification in a patient with ochronosis.

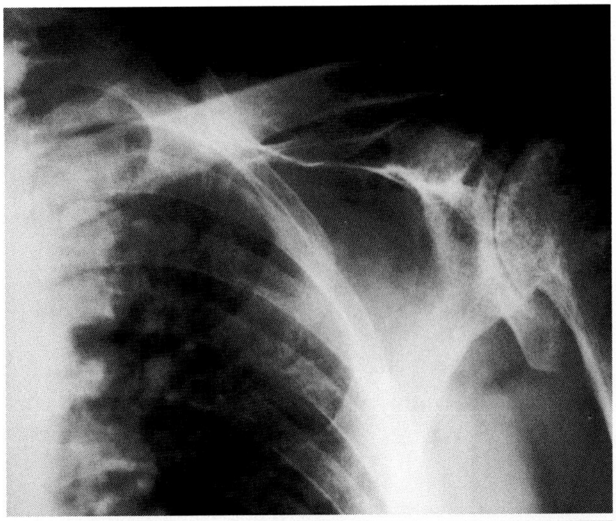

FIGURE 38–4 Severe degenerative arthritis in the right shoulder of a patient with ochronosis.

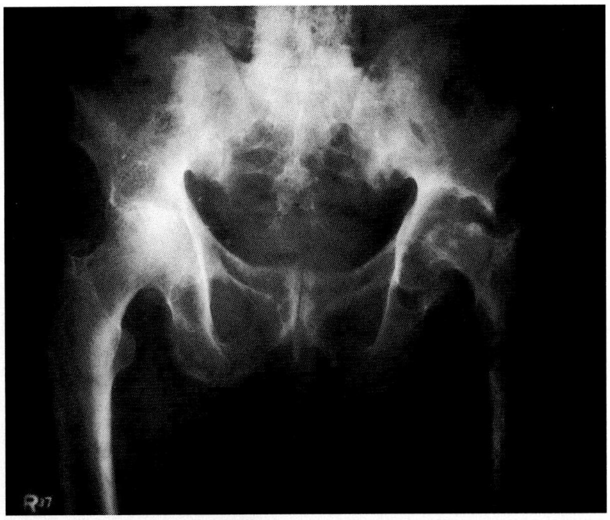

FIGURE 38–5 Bilateral hip joint degeneration in a patient with ochronosis.

Radiographic images demonstrate early calcification of the intervertebral disk with osteophyte formation. Disk collapse and loss of height frequently occur. The small joints of the hands and feet are generally spared.

Degenerative large joint disease

Degeneration and calcification of the intervertebral discs

In addition to generalized large joint progressive degenerative arthritis, autopsies have demonstrated pigmentary alterations in heart valves, sometimes leading to calcific aortic stenosis. There is also evidence that patients may produce pigmented calculi in the kidneys and prostate, which is associated with alkaline secretions.

Heart valve involvement an incidental autopsy finding

Diagnosis

Before disposable diapers, the earliest diagnosis of ochronosis was frequently made by the inadvertent detection of discoloration of diapers following washing with an alkaline soap. Diagnosis is now usually made by quantitating urine and blood homogentisic acid levels by direct spectrophotometric analysis.

First sign of disease in past was dark staining of diapers following worsening with alkaline soap

Radiographic images of the spine demonstrate the characteristic early calcification of the intervertebral disk. Subsequent radiographs may show disk collapse with marked kyphosis.

The differential diagnosis of ochronosis includes porphyria, hemoglobinuria, hyperbilirubinuria, myoglobinuria, and melanuria.

Localized Ochronosis

Among African Americans, the use of bleaching creams containing hydroquinone may result in increased dark pigmentation. Quinones inhibit homogentisic acid oxidase (Figures 38–6 and 38–7). Biopsy of these lesions demonstrates the presence of exogenous ochronosis (Figures 38–8). This localized form of ochronosis is not associated with any joint manifestations.

Localized ochronosis following use of hydroquinone bleaching cream

Treatment

No effective therapy is available for this disease. Analgesics and other rheumatologic measures to alleviate joint pain are indicated. In patients with advanced degenerative joint disease, replacement with artificial joints is a consideration.

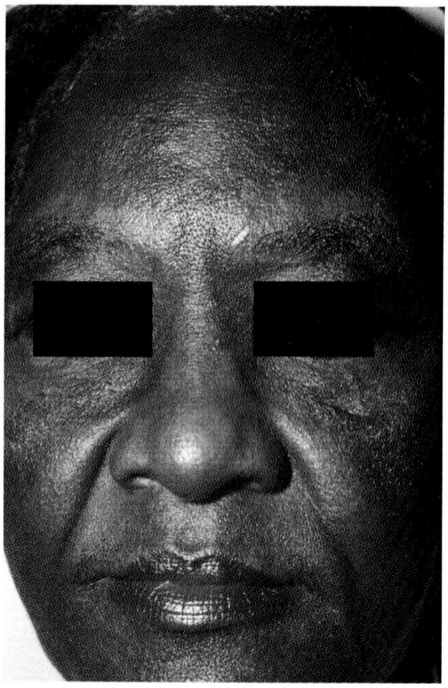

FIGURE 38-6 Localized ochronosis.

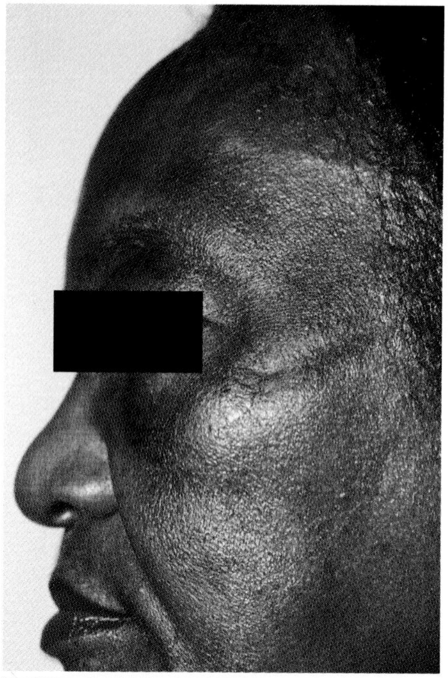

FIGURE 38-7 Side view demonstrating periorbital pigmentation.

Annotated Bibliography

LaDu BN. Alkaptonuria. In: Scriver CS, Beaudet AL, Sly WS, Valle D, eds. The Metabolic Basis of Inherited Diseases, 6th ed. New York: McGraw-Hill, 1989, p 775.

This is a classic reference.

Wyre CLW. Alkaptonuria with extensive ochronosis. Arch Dermatol 1979;115:461–463.

This dramatic case report documents the onset of severe hyperpigmentation with the onset of renal disease. The photographs are striking.

Hardwick N, et al. Exogenous ochronosis: an epidemiological study. Br J Dermatol 1989;120:229–238.

This article demonstrates that the prevalence of ochronosis among users of bleaching creams is 69%.

Hoshawr A, Zimmerman KG, Menter A. Ochronosis-like pigmentation from hydroquinone bleaching creams in American blacks. Arch Dermatol 1985;121:105–108.

This provides good photographic documentation of this entity.

Goldsmith LA. Cutaneous changes in errors of amino acid metabolism: tyrosinemia II, phenyl, ketonuria, argininosuccinic aciduria and alkaptonuria. In: Freedberg IM, Eisen AZ, Wolff K, et al., eds. Fitzpatrick's Dermatology in General Medicine, 5th ed. New York: McGraw Hill, 1999, 149, pp 145–156.

This is an excellent discussion with a large bibliography.

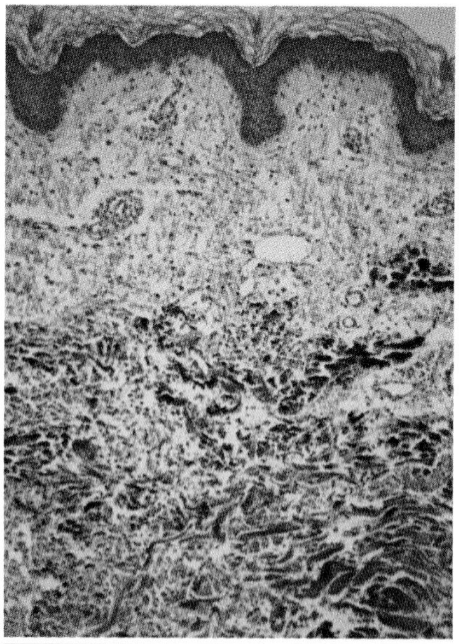

FIGURE 38-8 Biopsy of localized area of ochronosis demonstrating yellowish or ochre-colored pigment in the dermis (×10 original magnification).

CHAPTER 39

Porphyrias

Thomas T. Provost, M.D., George H. Sack Jr., M.D., Ph.D.

The term "porphyria" is derived from the Greek word *porphyreos* meaning "purple." The term refers to the prominent colors of several of the metabolites. Porphyrias comprise a group of disorders resulting from inherited or acquired defects in the biosynthetic pathway for heme and other porphyrins, and their classification is based on the site of the molecular defect, consequences for the bone marrow, and/or liver, and rarely both, and their manifestations.

Porphyrias are metabolic diseases associated with individual hereditary or acquired enzymatic defects in the porphyrin-heme pathway. Defects occur in the bone marrow, liver, and rarely, both organs.

Because the formation of heme is such a prominent end point of porphyrin metabolism, one group of porphyrias is referred to as "erythrocytic." This group involves cells of erythrocyte lineage and includes erythropoietic porphyria, erythropoietic protoporphyria (EPP) and erythropoietic coproporphyria.

Porphyrins also are essential components of other proteins, including catalase, peroxidase, and cytochromes. These are synthesized in other organs and tissues, predominantly the liver. Defects in the synthesis of these have been referred to as "hepatic" porphyrias. They include acute intermittent porphyria (in which neuropathy is a prominent feature), variegate porphyria, (VP) coproporphyria, porphyria cutanea tarda (PCT), and δ-aminolevulinic acid (δ-ALA) dehydratase porphyria. One other disorder, hepatoerythropoietic porphyria, involves both hepatic and erythrocytic pathways.

This chapter will emphasize three forms of inherited and acquired porphyria most commonly encountered by dermatologists; the inherited cutaneous porphyrias are shown in Table 39–1. Erythropoietic porphyria, hereditary coproporphyria, and erythropoietic porphyria will be mentioned only briefly; these are quite rare, although they do have prominent cutaneous manifestations. Additional details about porphyrias can be found in the bibliography under the article by Kappas et al.

Erythropoietic protoporphyria, porphyria cutanea tarda, and variegate porphyria are relatively common porphyrias with cutaneous manifestations.

Pathophysiology

The biosynthesis of heme has been well studied. It is a highly regulated, committed biochemical pathway. As shown in Figure 39–1, the only natural intermediates in heme formation are the porphyrinogens. Porphyrins corresponding to these are not biosynthetic intermediates but are the products of irreversible oxidation (usually photocatalytic).

As complex organic compounds, porphyrins differ in their solubility. Some are poorly soluble in water and, hence, cannot be detected in assays of urine. These are generally measured by assays of feces, and the discussion of laboratory diagnostic distinctions that follows emphasizes the importance of both urinary and fecal porphyrin measurements for establishing specific diagnoses. In only a few of the porphyrias can the enzymatic abnormalities be tested directly.

TABLE 39–1 Inherited Cutaneous Porphyrias

Disease	OMIM * Number	Defective Enzyme	Chromosome Position
Porphyria cutanea tarda (PCT)	176100	Uroporphyrinogen decarboxylase	1p34
Variegate porphyria (VP)	176200	Protoporphyrinogen oxidase	1q22
Erythropoietic (EPP) protoporphyria	177000	Ferrochelatase	18q21.3

*On-line Mendelian Inheritance in Man (www.ncbi.nlm.nih.gov/OMIM)

Because of their complex conjugated ring structures, porphyrins are very photoreactive. They have an absorption maximum around 400 nm. Although not completely understood, porphyrins that accumulate in the skin absorb radiation and reach an excited energy state. The latter can produce highly reactive singlet oxygen leading to oxidative tissue damage. This pathophysiology is consistent with the therapeutic effect of β-carotene, which can quench singlet oxygen.

The three common forms of porphyria with cutaneous manifestations to be discussed are usually inherited as autosomal dominant traits. Although this means that they often have passed through multiple generations, all individuals with the biochemical defect are not necessarily symptomatic. Not all of the factors that determine the clinical expression of the underlying defect are known.

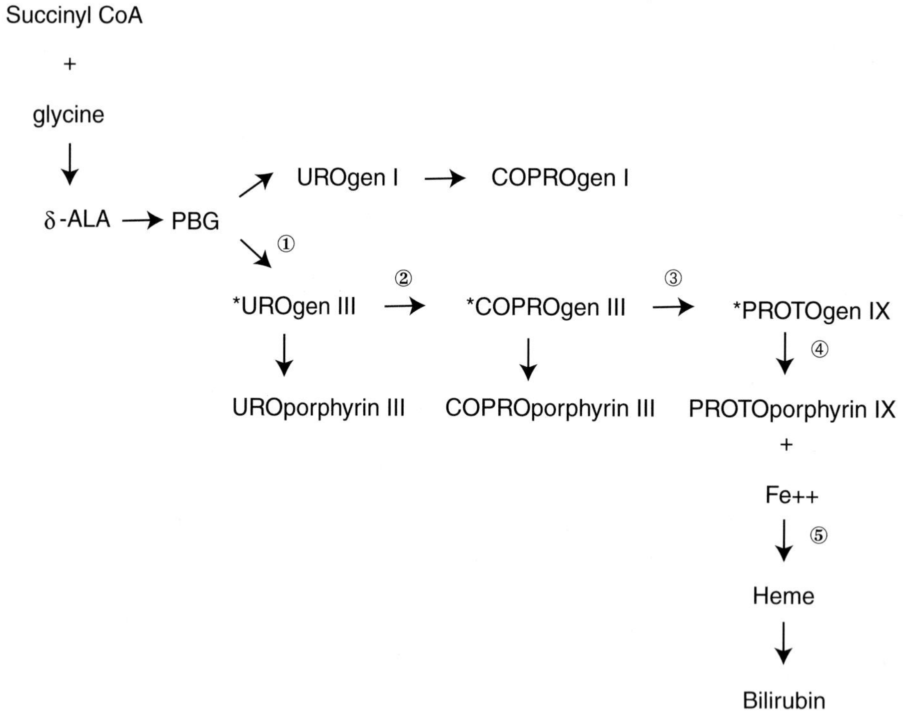

Numbers ①–⑤ designate enzymatic deficiency sites in porphyrias with prominent cutaneous lesions:

① Erythropoietic porphyria (Günther's disease) deficiency of UROporphyrinogen III cosynthetase—shifts porphyrin synthesis to type I isomer UROporphyrinogen I
② Porphyria cutanea tarda—deficiency of UROporphyrinogen III decarboxylase
③ Hereditary coproporphyria—deficiency of COPROproporphyinogen III oxidase
④ Variegate porphyria—deficiency of PROTOporphrinogen IX oxidase
⑤ Erythropoietic protoporphyria—deficiency of heme synthetase (ferrochelatase)

FIGURE 39–1 Heme biosynthetic pathway. UROgen III = uroporphyrinogen III; COPROgen III = coproporphyrinogen III; δ-ALA = δ-aminolevulinic acid; PBG = porphobilinogen; PROTOgen = protoporphyrinogen IX; Fe++ = ferrous iron.

Erythropoietic Protoporphyria

EPP (OMIM #177000) is an autosomal dominant porphyria characterized by an enzymatic deficiency of heme synthetase (ferrochelatase). Although initially described as an autosomal dominant disease, more recent studies indicate that recessive inheritance also can be found. These two different patterns appear to reflect different mutations in the ferrochelatase gene (at least 20 have been identified). Although some individuals are compound heterozygotes (having a different mutation on each of their chromosomes 18) and, thus, generally appear in families with no previous history, others have mutations that are more severe and that cause problems in those who are heterozygous for only a single mutation (hence, these latter individuals show autosomal dominant inheritance). Although the exact incidence is unknown, the disease occurs in all ethnic groups.

EPP most commonly inherited as an autosomal dominant
On unusual cases, an autosomal recessive inheritance is detected.

Cutaneous Manifestations

Classically, the onset of symptoms occurs very early in life (< 5 years of age) and is characterized by photosensitivity occuring within minutes of sun exposure. This manifests itself as a burning, stinging sensation in light-exposed areas. Erythema, petechiae, and urticaria-like lesions occur in addition to lichenoid, edematous papules. Small, ice-pick–like, atrophic scars are the residua (Figure 39–2). These are especially prominent over the bridge of the nose and cheeks. Phototoxic-induced onycholysis has been reported. In temperate climates, the disease occurs in the spring and diminishes in the fall and winter.

Symptoms of photosensitivity begin early in life

We have seen a 4-year-old female with EPP who complained of her skin stinging immediately following sun exposure during the late spring and summer, for two successive years prior to diagnosis. Her symptomatology completely disappeared during the fall and winter.

Systemic manifestations are uncommon. However, on occasions a hemolytic anemia can occur and gallstones (composed of protoporphyrins) have been reported. Periportal fibrosis, although an uncommon complication, can lead to terminal hepatic failure, as a result of the deposition of protoporphyrin in the liver.

Systemic features are uncommon
hemolytic anemia
cirrhosis
gallstones

The cutaneous manifestations of EPP must be differentiated from polymorphic light eruption, solar urticaria, and lupus erythematosus. A history of burning or stinging sensations immediately following sun exposure is characteristic, as is a family history.

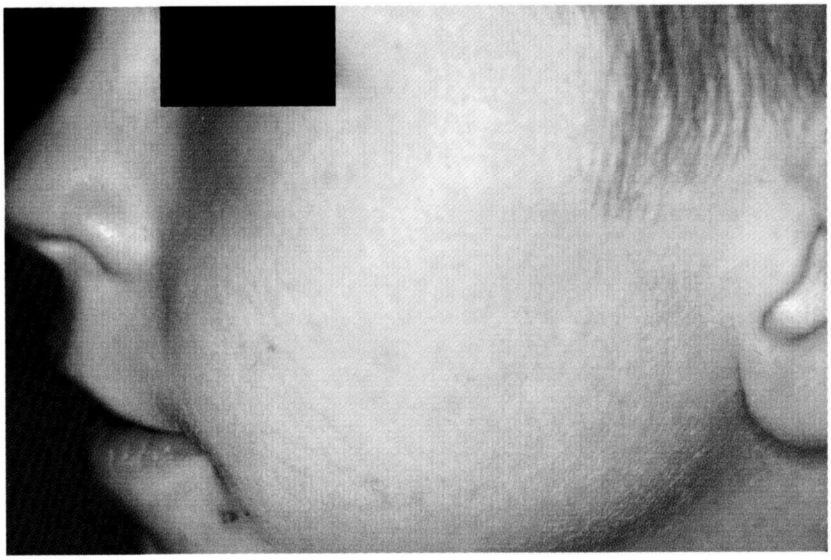

FIGURE 39–2 Eight-year-old Caucasian male with petechial, edematous, lichenoid papules of erythropoietic protoporphyria on his cheeks. The patient experienced immediate burning of skin exposed to sunlight.

Diagnosis

Transient fluorescence of 10 to 15% of peripheral red blood cells

No urinary porphyrin abnormalities

Examination of a blood smear with fluorescence microscopy reveals a transient, red fluorescence in approximately 10 to 15% of erythrocytes. In addition, there is a quantitative assay for free erythrocyte protoporphyrin levels. Elevated protoporphyrin levels also can be detected in the feces. However, the urine fails to demonstrate increased protoporphyrin levels because protoporphyrins are poorly soluble in water (Table 39–2).

Treatment

β-carotene may be effective by theoretically blocking or dampening singlet oxygen formation, free radical formation, and the photoexcited state of the protoporphyrin

The treatment of this condition is problematic. β-carotene (60 to 180 mg/d) has been reported to minimize the photosensitivity in some, but not all, patients. Theoretically, as noted earlier, β-carotene blocks the development of singlet oxygen and free radical formation after porphyrin excitation by light. Window glass, which blocks ultraviolet (UV) light less than 320 nm, does not protect these patients; thus, these patients may burn through window glass. UV wavelengths 400 to 410 nm are capable of exciting erythropoietic protoporphyria patients. Broad spectrum sunscreens and sun-protective clothing may be helpful.

Porphyria Cutanea Tarda

PCT occurs in two forms:
- *hereditary*
- *sporadic*

In contrast to the onset of EPP in childhood, the light-sensitive dermatitis of PCT generally occurs in adults (hence the term "tarda"). PCT is divided into two forms. The more common of these (80 – 90%) is sporadic or acquired. The other much less common form (10–15%), is hereditary (OMIM #176100). Both forms are due to decreased uroporphyrinogen decarboxylase activity. This enzyme defect is largely confined to the liver in the sporadic form of PCT and is generalized (involving all organs) in the hereditary form of PCT. It is inherited as an autosomal dominant trait.

Hepatotoxic Factors

PCT can be aggravated by:
- *alcohol*
- *estrogens*
- *iron overload*
- *hexachlorobenzene and related compounds*

Certain chemicals have been shown to induce PCT, notably alcohol and estrogens. The latter includes males treated with estrogens for prostatic carcinoma or females receiving birth control pills. The exact mechanism of how these drugs lead to PCT is unknown. Both drugs induce hepatic enzyme δ-aminolevulinic acid synthetase, the rate-limiting enzyme in porphyrin biosynthesis and, hence, increase flux through the porphyrin pathology. Other chemicals can induce PCT; several are considered below.

Hexachlorobenzene

Hexachlorobenzene, which was used as fungicide on wheat, induced an epidemic of PCT in Turkey during the 1950s. Hexachlorobenzene inhibits uropor-

TABLE 39–2 Urine and Stool Biochemical Abnormalities and Inheritance in the Porphyrias

Disease	Inheritance	Urine	Stool
Congenital erythropoietic porphyria (Gunther's disease)	Recessive	URO I > COPRO I	COPRO I > URO I
Porphyria cutanea tarda	Dominant	URO III > COPRO III	ISOCOPRO III; COPRO IV
Hereditary coproporphyria	Dominant	COPRO III > URO III δ-ALA, PBG	COPRO III > PROTO
Variegate porphyria	Dominant	COPRO III, δ-ALA, PBG	PROTO ≥ COPRO III
Erythropoietic* protoporphyria	Dominant	Normal	PROTO > COPRO III

*Red blood cell fluorescence is stable in congenital erythropoietic porphyria and transient in erythropoietic protoporphyria.

URO = uroporphyrin ; COPRO = coproporphyrin; ISCOPRO = isocoproporphyrin; δ-ALA = aminolevulinic acid; PBG = porphobilinogen.

phyrinogen decarboxylase, mimicking classic PCT. However, not all individuals exposed to this food contaminant developed PCT. Furthermore, this outbreak of PCT occurred among different ethnic groups, indicating that PCT could be induced in patients on a nongenetic basis.

Epidemic of PCT in Turkey Hexachlorobenzene inhibits uroporphyrinogen decarboxylase mimicking classic PCT

PCT has also developed in workers during the manufacture of two closely related hexachlorobenzene fungicides, 2,4-dichlorophenoxyacetic acid and 2,4,5-trichlorophenoxyacetic acid.

Tetrachlorodibenzo-p-*dioxin*

Tetrachlorodibenzo-*p*-dioxin can induce PCT in laboratory animals. Iron appears to be a co-factor because iron depletion of mice can abolish this effect. Iron has a deleterious effect upon the clinical expression of PCT. The exact mechanism, however, is unknown. Elevated plasma iron levels and hepatic iron overload are common in PCT and prolonged clinical remission can follow phlebotomy. In addition, the beneficial effects of phlebotomy can be reversed by the simultaneous administration of iron. These observations support a pathophysiologic role for iron in PCT.

Theoretically, iron may have multiple effects upon the porphyrin-heme biosynthetic pathway. It may facilitate the inhibitory effects of halogenated phenols on uroporphyrinogen decarboxylase and the induction of δ-aminolevulinic acid synthetase by estrogens and alcohol.

Iron may facilitate inhibitory effects of halogenated phenols and the induction of δ-aminolevulinic acid synthetase by estrogen and alcohol upon uroporphyrinogen decarboxylase.

Hepatitis C

Recent studies indicate that most cases of sporadic PCT in the United States are associated with infection by the hepatitis C virus (HCV). The effect of HCV upon the expression of PCT does not seem to be direct because only a few patients with hepatitis C demonstrate abnormal porphyrin synthesis (For further discussion on hepatitis C, see Chapter 33, "Hepatitis.")

Most sporadic cases of PCT are associated with hepatitis C virus infection.

It should also be noted that PCT has rarely been detected in patients with human immunodeficiency virus.

Cutaneous Manifestations

Skin fragility, characterized by the development of vesicles and bullae over the extensor surfaces of the hands, is characteristic. Minor trauma produces lesions that resolve, leaving crusted erosions associated with multiple, small milia (Figure 39–3).

Skin fragility subepidermal blisters, hypertrichosis and milia characterize cutaneous manifestations.

Hyper- and hypopigmentation, especially over the malar eminences, associated with hirsutism is common. The hirsutism is prominent in the periorbital areas, temples, and cheeks of the face. This is frequently a presenting complaint in women. (In the hexachlorobenzene outbreak in Turkey, hypertrichosis of the face, especially in children, was striking.) An erythematous suffusion involving the central portion of the face may also be seen.

Waxy-yellow-to-white plaques, resembling morphea or scleroderma, may be seen in 10 to 15% of patients. This is especially prominent on the neck and chest. Dystrophic calcification may occur in these lesions. The cause of these plaques is unknown. Sclerodermoid plaques may be the direct result of uroprophyrinogen and/or UV stimulation of collagen synthesis in skin fibroblasts.

Morphea-like lesions are seen on occasion.

The reported increased frequency of PCT in association with lupus erythematosus, in retrospect, may be a fortuitous association rather than a direct relationship. (If it is a direct relationship, it is rare; Provost has never personally seen this association in the evaluation of several hundred systemic lupus erythematosus patients. May be related to unmasking of PCT in lupus patients treated with antimalarials.)

Pseudoporphyria

A subepidermal blistering process reminiscent of PCT has been seen in patients taking certain drugs. These drugs include pyridoxine, naproxen, tetracycline, nalidixic acid, and furosemide. Hirsutism is not a feature (Figures 39–4 and 39–5). Biopsy and direct immunofluorescence examination of the involved skin fails to demonstrate the characteristic immunofluorescence in a perivascular distribution seen in PCT. Furthermore, porphyrin excretion is normal in these individuals

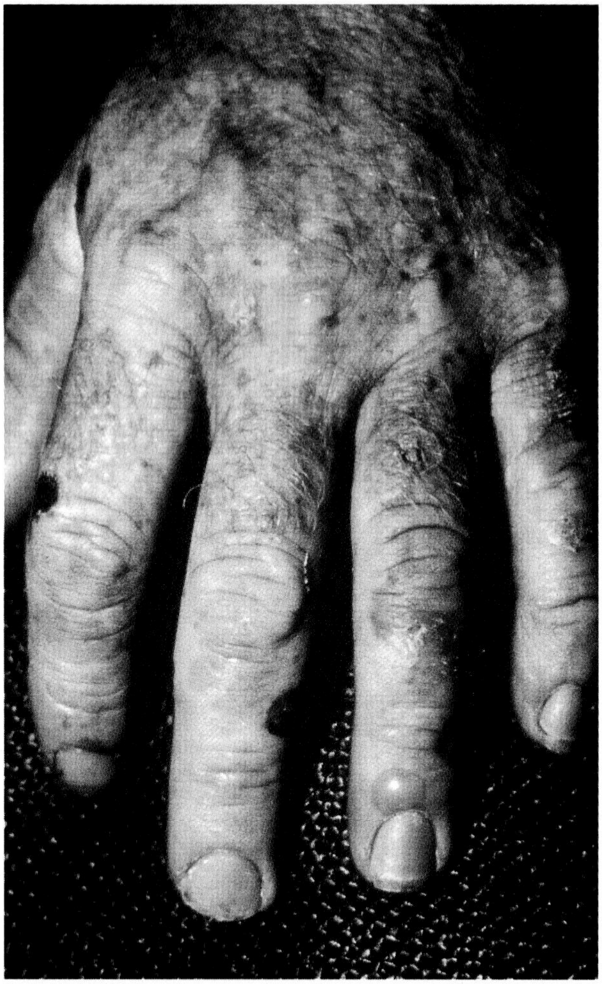

FIGURE 39–3 Hand of a patient with the sporadic form of porphyria cutanea tarda. Patient is hepatitis C–positive with a mild elevation of hepatic transaminases.

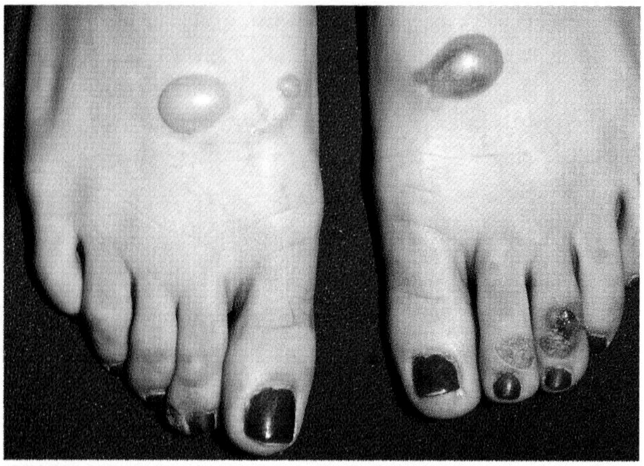

FIGURE 39–4 Feet of a patient with pseudoporphyria who was taking nalidixic acid.

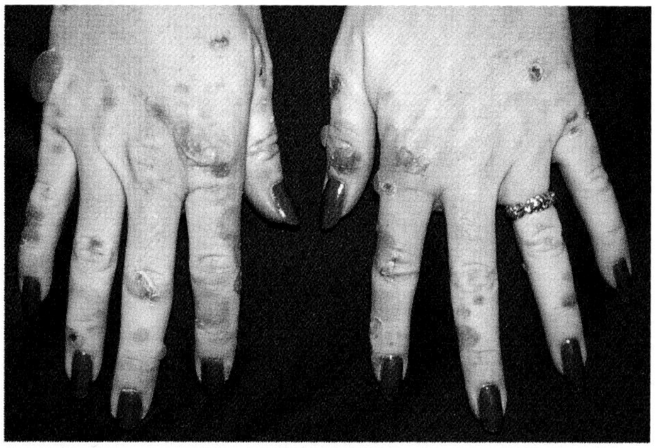

FIGURE 39–5 Hands of the same patient with pseudoporphyria.

Provost has seen two instances of pseudoporphyria associated with widespread acral blister formation and skin fragility. One was a young woman who was taking large quantities of vitamin B_6 (pyridoxine) as a supplement. The other was a middle-aged woman taking naproxen for arthritis. In addition, for years this latter patient used a tanning booth on a weekly basis. Discontinuance of the medications in both instances and stopping of the UV light treatments led to a disappearance of the blisters.

Pseudoporphyria associated with skin fragility and subepidermal blister formation occurs in association with drugs and hemodialysis
no hypertrichosis is seen in pseudoporphyria
UV therapy may produce a pseudoporphyria-like picture

A second form of pseudoporphyria has been described, uncommonly, in patients undergoing hemodialysis. The cause of this problem is presumed to be inadequate clearance of plasma porphyrins or possibly leaching of a toxic substance from the dialysis membrane, which stimulates increased porphyrin production. Increased plasma and erythrocyte porphyrin levels have been detected in 60 to 70% of asymptomatic chronic hemodialysis patients.

In addition, PCT is associated with an increased risk of hepatoma and also can be seen in hepatoma patients. (See Chapter 33, "Hepatitis," for further discussion).

Diagnosis

Increased levels of urinary porphyrins are characteristic. They may be detected in fresh urine that is left standing (burgundy wine appearance) or with the addition of a small amount of acetic acid. Red-pink fluorescence is demonstrated with a Wood's lamp (~365 nm) (Figure 39–6 and 39–7). A 24-hour urine collection for porphyrins will demonstrate a high concentration of uroporphyrins compared with coproporphyrins (URO > COPRO) (See Table 39–2).

FIGURE 39–6 Burgundy-colored urine of a patient with PCT. Urine assumes this color when left standing or with the addition of acid. Normal urine on left.

FIGURE 39–7 Fluorescence of fresh urine from a PCT patient. Normal urine on right.

Twenty-four hour fecal porphyrin excretion is variable but also can be helpful in establishing the diagnosis. The porphyrin content of the stool consists primarily of isocoproporphyrin (product of coproporphyrinogen oxidase activity on 5-carboxyldehydroisocoproporphyrin). Uroporphyrin and coproporphyrin levels are less notable.

Direct immunofluorescence of blister reveals characteristic deposition of immunoglobulins and complement in a perivascular distribution

Biopsy of the skin lesion in PCT demonstrates subepidermal bullae (Figures 39–8 and 39–9). There is little or no inflammation. Direct immunofluorescence studies reveal complement and IgG in a characteristic perivascular globular deposition, as well as a granular pattern at the dermal-epidermal junction (Figures 39–10 and 39–11).

These patients demonstrate excessive iron stores characterized by increased serum and hepatocellular iron concentrations.

Differential diagnosis includes epidermolysis bullosa acquisita, pseudoporphyria and scleroderma
Also must rule out variegate porphyria

PCT must be differentiated from variegate porphyria (VP), pseudoporphyria, scleroderma, and epidermolysis bullosa acquisita. In general, the history and physical examination, as well as appropriate screening of urinary and fecal prophyrins, will establish the diagnosis. Distinguishing variegate porphyria may be problematic because different members of some families have been shown to have PCT and others variegate porphyria. In variegate porphyria, stool protoporphyrin and coproporphyrin excretion is increased, whereas urinary porphyrin levels (COPRO > URO) are only moderately increased. As noted above,

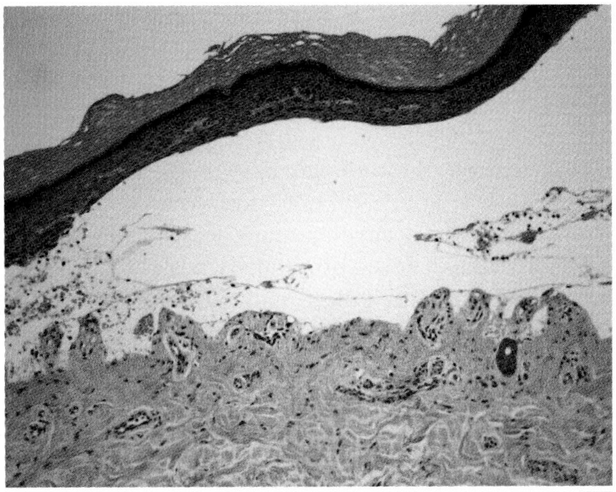

FIGURE 39–8 Subepidermal blister formation of a PCT patient.

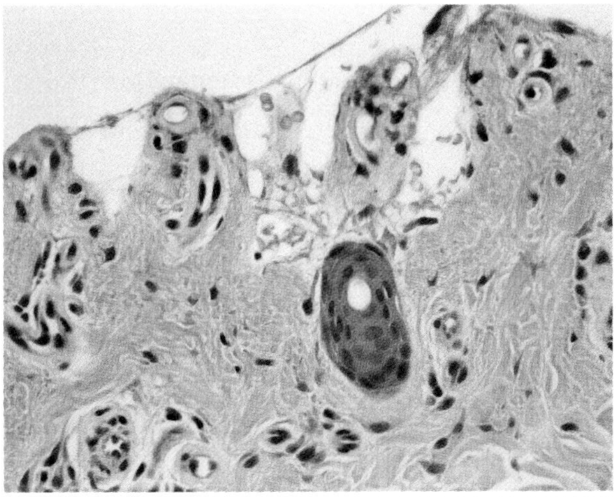

FIGURE 39–9 Close-up of the base of the blister of a PCT patient. Note relative absence of inflammatory cells.

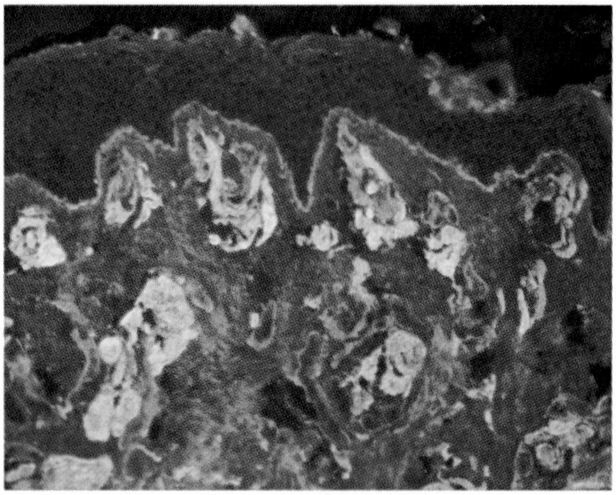

FIGURE 39–10 Direct immunofluorescence examination of a PCT patient showing perivascular IgG deposition. Similar deposits are seen in erythropoietic protoporphyrin and variegate porphyria.

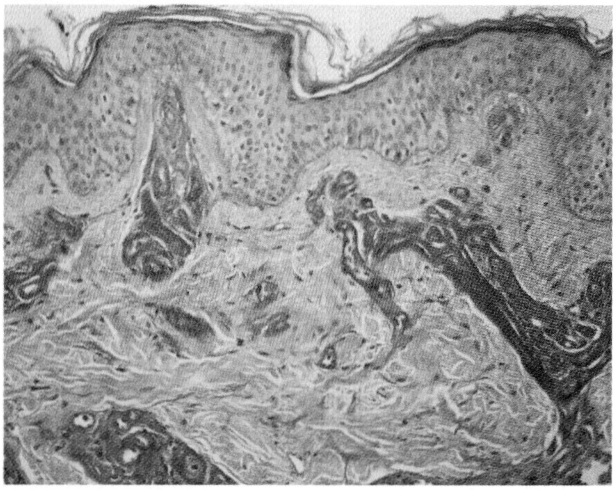

FIGURE 39–11 Periodic acid–Schiff stain shows deposition of presumed immunoglobulin corresponding to the IgG staining in Figure 39–10.

stool isocoproporphyrin is the dominant porphyrin in PCT, and the total urinary porphyrin (URO > COPRO) is much higher than seen in VP.

It is important to perform stool studies in PCT patients to eliminate the possibility of missing an occult variegate porphyria and avoid the potentially lethal attacks of acute intermittent porphyria (see below).

Therapy

Eliminate alcohol and estrogens

In addition to eliminating exposure to environmental toxins, alcohol, and estrogens, two forms of therapy, and possibly a third, have been shown to be effective in the treatment of PCT: phlebotomy, antimalarials, and interferon treatment of hepatitis C–associated PCT.

Phlebotomy

Phlebotomies are standard forms of therapy for PCT

Phlebotomy is an accepted treatment for PCT and is associated with the depletion of excessive hepatic iron stores and biochemical remission of the PCT. As noted above, iron replenishment following or during phlebotomy may induce a biochemical and clinical exacerbation of the PCT. Weekly or biweekly phlebotomies of approximately 500 mL of blood are performed until the hemoglobin reaches approximately 10 g per dL, and the serum iron approaches approximately 50 μg per dL. The length of remission is variable, and in Provost's experience, if alcohol and estrogens are avoided, remissions of 6 to 12 months are not uncommon.

Antimalarials

Antimalarials in low doses also are effective
This is a hepatotoxic form of therapy

Antimalarials (chloroquine and hydroxychloroquine) have been successful in treating PCT. However, this approach is to be used only if phlebotomy has been unsuccessful as severe hepatotoxicity may occur—alarming increases in hepatic enzymes have been reported with regular doses of antimalarials. Chloroquine, 125 mg twice weekly, is a successful form of treatment, minimizing the severity of the hepatotoxic effect. Remissions have been reported for as long as several years.

Interferon Alpha

Treatment of hepatitis C infection with interferon-alpha may be associated with clinical remission.

With the recent evidence indicating a strong association with HCV infections in PCT, preliminary data indicate that treatment of the hepatitis C infection with interferon alpha also may produce biochemical and clinical improvement in the PCT. Much more information will be needed before this form of therapy is to be accepted as a standard for the treatment of HCV–associated PCT.

Variegate Porphyria

VP (OMIM #176200), also known as "mixed porphyria," is an autosomal dominant disease associated with a 50% decrease in protoporphyrinogen oxidase activity. This form of porphyria, once thought to be limited to South Africa, is now seen worldwide and many cases of PCT described in the United States are, in fact, VP.

Variegate porphyria once thought to be isolated to South Africa is now known to be worldwide

Clinically, similar to acute intermittent porphyria

Clinically, VP is characterized by attacks similar to those of acute intermittent porphyria and is generally precipitated by drugs such as barbiturates and sulfonamides or by estrogens or pregnancy. (In addition, nutritional factors, including starvation, may precipitate the acute manifestations of this disease.) These attacks are characterized physically by abdominal pain, nausea, vomiting, and abdominal distension and neurologically by paralysis, motor neuropathy, and neurotic or psychotic behavior; in some cases, they can lead to death.

Cutaneous Manifestations

The cutaneous manifestations of VP are indistinguishable from PCT. The skin is fragile and bullae, erosions, or ulcers follow minor trauma. The skin lesions usually develop at an earlier age (second or third decade), whereas in PCT the cutaneous manifestations usually begin in the fourth and fifth decades of life.

Cutaneous features are those of PCT

Laboratory Features

During acute attacks of VP, urinary δ-ALA and porphobilogen (PBG) are elevated. Hence, the Watson-Schwartz or other tests for urinary PBG will be positive, similar to the pattern seen in attacks of acute intermittent porphyria. Increased quantities of protoporphyrin and coproporphyrin are detected in the stools between attacks. In VP, urinary uroporphyrin is moderately elevated and generally less than the quantity of coproporphyrin. In PCT, urinary uroporphyrin is much higher than coproporphyrin. Plasma obtained from patients with VP has a characteristic fluorescence emission spectral peak (626 nm) not seen in PCT (Figure 39–12).

Increased urinary δ-ALA and PBG during attacks

Plasma contains a characteristic emission spectra of 626 nm

Treatment

The treatment of VP involves administering intravenous glucose and/or hematin to suppress the flux of metabolites through the porphyrin biosynthetic pathway. These agents inhibit the induction of δ-ALA synthetase. Phlebotomy and antimalarials are not effective. Prophylaxis against future attacks is approached through patient education to avoid agents capable of inducing attacks. Because of the potential for attacks of life-threatening severity, Sack recommends that affected individuals wear a Medic-Alert® tag or bracelet.

Annotated Bibliography

Bleiberg J, Wallen M, Brodkin R, et al. Industrially acquired porphyria. Arch Dermatol 1964;89:793–797.

Dean G. The Porphyrias, A Story of Inheritance and Environment, 2nd ed. Philadelphia: JB Lippincott, 1972.

Kappas A, Sassa S, Galbraith RA, et al. The porphyrias. In: Scriver CR, Beaudet AL, Sly WS, et al., eds. The Metabolic and Molecular Basis of Inherited Disease, 7th ed. New York: McGraw-Hill; 1995; pp 2103–2159.

Grossman ME, Bickers DR, Poh-Fitzpatrick M, et al. Porphyria cutanea tarda: clinical features and laboratory findings in 40 patients. Am J Med 1979;67:277–286.

This is an important study of PCT, describing the frequency of bullae, skin fragility, facial hypertrichosis, hyperpigmentation, sclerodermoid changes, as well as a dystrophic calcification.

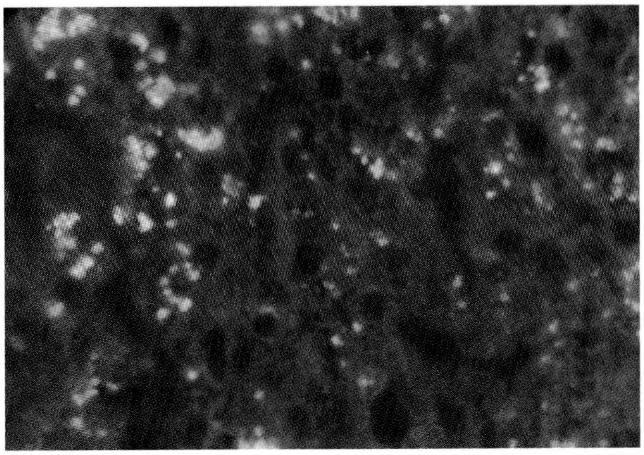

FIGURE 39–12 Fluorescence of a liver biopsy of a patient with variegate porphyria demonstrating hepatocyte fluorescence.

Day RS, Eales L, Meissner D. Coexistent variegate porphyria and porphyria cutanea tarda. N Engl J Med 1982;307:36–41.

This is an important study, demonstrating that 25 of 106 patients with VP had porphyrin excretion patterns typical of PCT. The authors emphasize that if a patient is suspected of PCT and is evaluated by employing only urinary porphyrins, the presence of dual porphyria will be missed and the possible serious consequences of VP will be unrecognized. Drugs may potentially provoke a fatal acute attack in patients with VP. These authors believe that mandatory evaluation of fecal porphyrins, as well as urinary porphyrins, will avoid this possibility.

Norris PG, Nunn AV, Hawk JLM, et al. Genetic heterogeneity in erythropoietic protoporphyria: a study of the enzymatic defect in nine affected families. J Invest Dermatol 1990;95:260–263.

This study measures the ability to use zinc as a substrate to investigate the inheritance pattern of EPP. In three families with parent-to-child transmission, the asymptomatic parent had an enzymatic activity within the normal range. In three pedigrees, where the parents were asymptomatic, enzymatic activities were below 95% in both parents. This study established the fact that EPP is a heterogenetic defined disease at the molecular level.

Todd DJ. Erythroprotoporphyria. Br J Dermatol 1994;131:751–766.

This useful review addresses the complications in inheritance patterns seen, which at the least reflect multiple mutations in the gene for ferrochelatase. The possibility of definitive gene treatment is discussed because the basic defect is at the level of bone marrow stem cells.

Kushner JP. Laboratory diagnosis of the porphyrias. N Engl J Med 1991;324:1432–1434.

This article presents a summary of laboratory methods for detecting the biochemical manifestations of enzymatic defects in the heme biosynthetic pathway. The author has made significant contributions, demonstrating defective uroporphyrinogen decarboxylase in all forms of PCT.

Mustajoki P. Variegate porphyria. Ann Intern Med 1978;89:238–244.

This useful review of VP emphasizes the possibility of having acute symptomatic attacks in addition to skin fragility and sensitivity. It emphasizes the value of fecal porphyrin determination where protoporphyrin predominates. Because the acute attacks are indistinguishable from acute intermittent porphyria, the fecal measurements are essential.

CHAPTER 40

Gout

John A. Flynn, M.D., Thomas T. Provost, M.D.

Gout is a heterogeneous metabolic disease associated with hyperuricemia. Uric acid is the end degradation product of purine metabolism. There are multiple causes of hyperuricemia. The very rare enzymatic causes of primary overproduction of uric acid include phosphoribosylpyrophosphate synthetase superactivity and hypoxanthine-guanine phosphoribosyltransferase deficiency (Lesch-Nyhan syndrome). Secondary hyperuricemia may be the result of excessive dietary purine intake or increased nucleotide turnover as seen in myeloproliferative and lymphoproliferative disorders, as well as psoriasis.

Multiple causes

Hyperuricemia may result from decreased excretion of uric acid or from enhanced tubular urate reabsorption. Certain drugs, such as cyclosporine, pyrazinamide, thiazide, diuretics, ethambutol, and low-dose salicylate induce diminished excretion of uric acid.

Associated with hyperuricemia

Pathogenesis

Gout results from the deposition of monosodium urate crystals within soft tissues. In general, there is a fine balance between the production of purines and the renal excretion of uric acid. If, however, the serum uric acid level rises above 7 mg per dL in men and 6 mg per dL in women, crystals of monosodium urate may precipitate out into tissue. (It is estimated that less than 20% of hyperuricemic individuals develop gout.) This precipitation causes an inflammatory reaction with increased numbers of polymorphonuclear cells. The exact pathogenesis of the exquisitely painful inflammation is unknown but thought to involve urate crystal activation of endothelial cell-derived prostaglandins and cleavage of complement and kinin precursors.

Clinical Features

Deposition of urate crystals in tissue, which induces an inflammatory response

Gout uncommon in women

Podagra

Gout is predominantly a disease of males; only 5% of patients are female (uniformly post menopausal). The initial onset of disease generally occurs between the fourth and fifth decades of life. Sudden onset of excruciating, throbbing pain in one of the joints of the lower extremity, most commonly the first metatarsophalangeal joint, associated with warmth, redness, and exquisite tenderness to touch (podagra) is characteristic. Patients often complain that bed clothing cannot be tolerated. An acute attack will usually subside within a 7- to 10-day period and is followed by a quiescent phase. If not treated, however, acute attacks may accelerate in frequency. Finally, a polyarticular stage is reached in which one attack

Tophus stage of gout associated with permanent damage to tissue

Tophi

blends into another, with multiple joints being involved. Large deposits of uric acid crystals (gouty tophi) occur and may produce structural damage to the bone, cartilage, and skin. This stage is much more difficult to treat.

The cutaneous presentation of the tophaceous stage of gout is characterized by a salmon-pink–colored papulonodule seen on the helix of the ear, over the bursa of the elbows, and on the fingers and first metatarsophalangeal joint (Figures 40–1 and 40–2). Gouty tophi may drain, releasing a white, chalky substance (Figure 40–3).

Treatment

Nonsteroidal anti-inflammatory drugs

An acute attack of gout will respond to therapy with nonsteroidal anti-inflammatory drugs, such as ibuprofen or indomethacin. Oral and intra-articular glucocorticosteroids have also proven to be effective. Colchicine, which has a very narrow therapeutic window, does have a limited role in treating acute attacks, if used properly.

Most gout patients undersecretors of uric acid

Allopurinol is now the favored drug

Prophylactic therapy for gout has included the use of uricosuric agents such as probenecid and sulfinpyrazone. These medications promote uric acid secretion and in the past were very popular because approximately 90% of gout patients undersecrete uric acid. In recent years, however, allopurinol has become the therapy of choice. Allopurinol blocks xanthine oxidase and inhibits the production of uric acid. The incidence of gouty arthritis has decreased substantially using allopurinol therapy. Low-dose, daily colchicine may also be used for prophylaxis against recurrent gouty attacks.

Annotated Bibliography

Cronstein BN, Molad Y, Reibman J, et al. Colchicine alters the quantitative and qualitative display of selectins on endothelial cells and neutrophils. J Clin Invest 1995;96: 994–1002.

This provocative paper explores the possible therapeutic effect of colchicine.

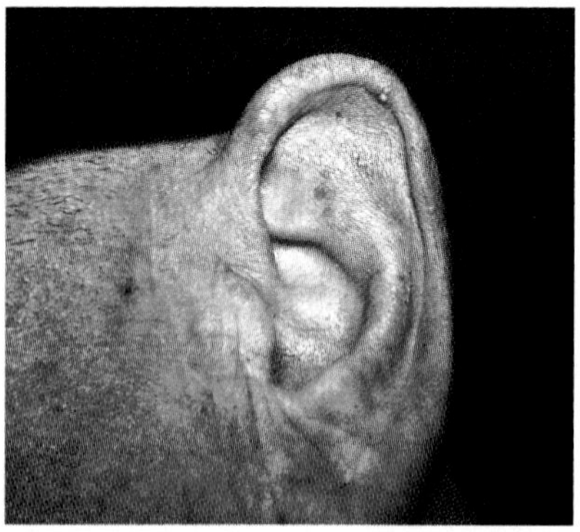

FIGURE 40–1 Patient with tophus on antihelix. Differential diagnosis is chondrodermatitis helicis chronicus, rheumatoid nodule, and basal cell carcinoma.

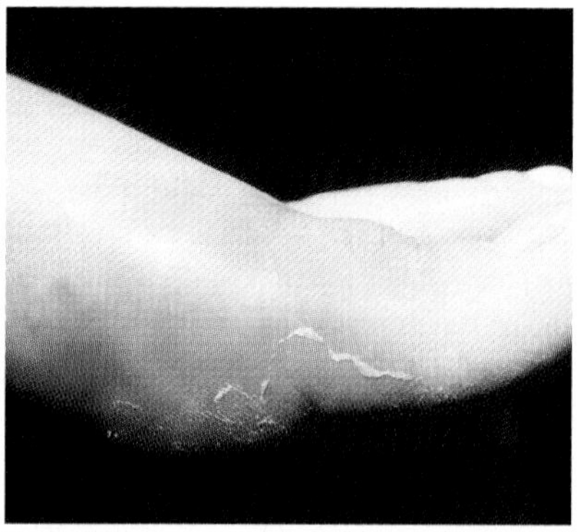

FIGURE 40–2 Acute gout attack on the first metatarsophalangeal joint (podagra). (Reproduced with permission from Rick Stearns, M.D., Tulsa, OK)

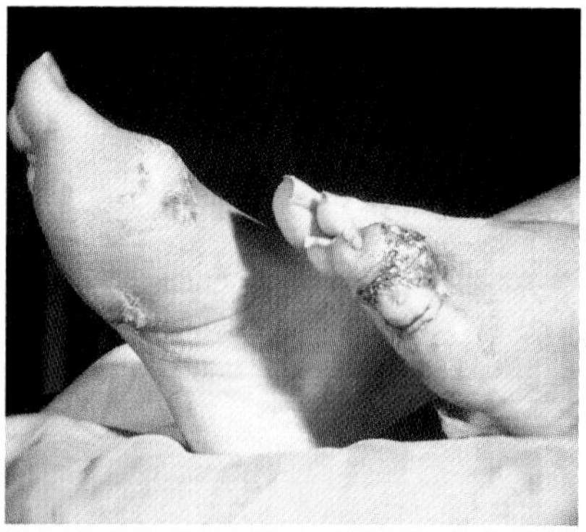

FIGURE 40–3 Chronic tophus gout demonstrating tissue deposition of monosodium urate. Note large swelling of the right first metatarsophalangeal joint area with healed ulcer. The left foot shows ulceration of tophus over the fifth metacarpophalangeal area.

CHAPTER 41

Lipoid Proteinosis (Hyalinosis Cutis et Mucosae)

Thomas T. Provost, M.D.

Lipoid proteinosis is a rare recessive disease with no sex predilection that is characterized by the deposition of hyaline material in the skin, oral pharynx, and other organs. The exact composition of the hyaline material is unknown, but the best evidence indicates that this may represent a lysosomal storage disease. There is also some evidence to suggest that lipoid proteinosis may be the result of a defect in collagen metabolism. Ultrastructure changes in fibroblasts have been detected.

Rare disease

Best evidence a lysosomal storage disease

The earliest manifestations of the disease begin in infancy with a hoarse cry. Yellowish-white infiltrates are detected in the pharynx, oral mucosa, lips and tongue. Nodules on the epiglottis and vocal cords produce hoarseness. With time, the tongue becomes enlarged and firm. Similar mucosal involvement may occur on the labia and vagina.

Hoarse cry earliest manifestation

Skin manifestations are characterized by yellow-white waxy nodules on the face and lips (Figure 41–1). The margins of the upper and lower eyelids are involved, producing typical "beaded" papules. The eyelashes may be absent. With time, the skin deposits may become hyperkeratotic. Trauma to the skin and mucous membrane may induce the formation of these lesions (Koebner's phenomenon).

Yellowish-white cutaneous nodules

Koebner's phenomenon

Visceral involvement is common but may not be symptomatic. The deposition of hyaline material in the brain is associated with intercranial calcification and epilepsy.

Systemic involvement

Histopathology

The histopathologic picture is characterized by the deposition of hyaline material around capillaries and sweat coils. With time, hyaline material is very prominent in the dermis, staining strongly with periodic acid–Schiff.

Periodic acid–Schiff–positive material prominent in dermis

Histologically, this hyaline deposition must be distinguished from erythropoietic protoporphyria. In lipoid proteinosis, the hyaline deposition is more extensive and appears around sweat coils. (The disease, histologically, must also be differentiated from xanthomatosis and amyloidosis.)

Disease Course

The disease is generally diagnosed early in childhood by the observation of hoarseness, thickening and stiffening of the tongue, and the subsequent development of characteristic yellow-white infiltrates on the lips, oral mucosa, and margins of the eyelids.

Hoarseness is an early diagnostic feature.

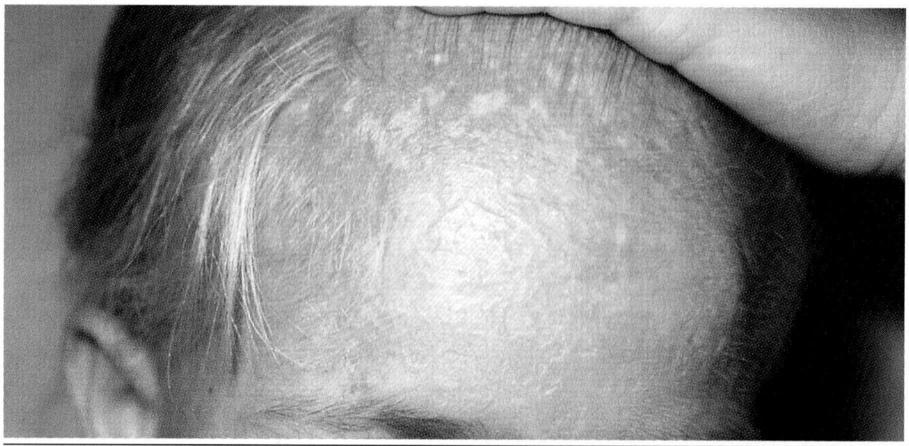

FIGURE 41–1 Skin-colored lichenoid papules on the forehead of a child with lipoid proteinosis.

The prognosis for lipoid proteinosis is good. On unusual occasions, the involvement of the larynx may necessitate a tracheotomy.

Treatment

Good prognosis

Dimethylsulfoxide and oral vitamin A derivatives may be effective.

There are individual case reports indicating the lipoid proteinosis may respond to dimethylsulphoxide. Topical steroids have also been employed with some success. Oral vitamin A derivatives may be of value. However, at present, no definitive therapy exists.

Annotated Bibliography

Caplan RM. Visceral involvement in lipoid proteinosis. Arch Dermatol 1967;95: 149–155.

This highly quoted article details the systemic features of lipoid proteinosis.

Konstantinov K, Kabakchiev P, Karchev T, et al. Lipoid proteinosis. Review. J Am Acad Dermatol 1992;27:293–297.

This is a good review.

CHAPTER 42

Anderson-Fabry's Disease

Thomas T. Provost, M.D.

Anderson-Fabry's disease, also known as "angiokeratoma corporis diffusum universale," is a rare, sex-linked, inborn error of the (lysomal storage diseases) metabolism characterized by a defective or absent α–galactosidase A enzyme. The defective gene has been localized to chromosome Xq21.33–q22. The presence of α-galactosidase A enzyme normally cleaves the terminal galactose from the trihexosylceramide galactose-galactose-glucose ceramide. The abnormal accumulation of the trihexosylceramide in the endothelium of blood vessels produces blood vessel occlusion affecting all vessels. Clinically, the most important blood vessels involved are renal, cardiac, and cerebral.

Sex-linked disease
α-galactosidase A deficiency
Abnormal accumulation of glycolipid in blood vessel walls

Clinical Features

The disease is characterized by hundreds of individual red, blue, and black keratotic punctate telangiectasia that are found over the entire body, but most commonly between the umbilicus and knees (Figure 42–1). These usually begin to appear at puberty. Incapacitating, agonizing episodes of pain, many times induced by temperature changes (ie, fever, heat, cold) or exertion occur. The pain is initially episodic but then becomes constant, generally characterized by a burning sensation and paresthesia involving the hands and feet. The pain is frequently accompanied by a low-grade fever and an elevated erythrocyte sedimentation rate.

Punctate keratotic telangiectasia around pelvic girdle

Pain and paresthesia of extremities

Corneal lesions characterized by whorled streaks extending from the center to the periphery are characteristic.

Corneal opacities

Patients usually die in their thirties of renal failure and hypertension. Others succumb to cardiac and cerebral vascular accidents.

Diagnosis

Biopsy demonstrates focal telangiectasia (Figure 42–2). The presumptive diagnosis can be made by a skin biopsy demonstrating refractile lipid blood vessel occlusions (Maltese crosses). An ophthalmologic examination that demonstrates characteristic corneal opacities is helpful in making a diagnosis as is an examination of the urine sediment that reveals birefringent material (Maltese crosses). The diagnosis is confirmed biochemically.

Maltese crosses in blood vessels and urine sediment

Similar clinical disease features are seen with other liposomal enzymatic deficiencies. These enzymatic defects include fucosidosis, β-galactosidase, and α-neuraminidase deficiencies.

Other liposomal enzymatic deficiencies produce similar diseases.

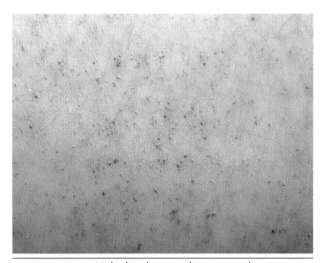

FIGURE 42–1 Multiple discrete keratotic telangiectasias over the trunk and waist of a patient with angiokeratoma corporis universale.

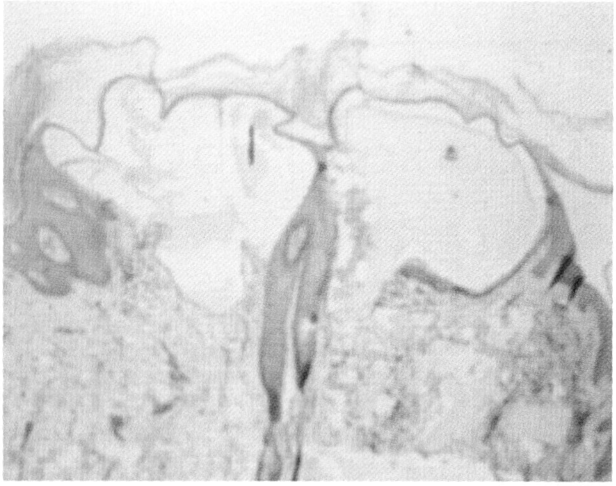

FIGURE 42–2 Histology demonstrating focal telangiectasia and thinned epidermis in a patient with Anderson-Fabry's disease (×40 original magnification).

Treatment

Renal transplantation

Renal transplantation appears to be an effective means for treating renal failure. The renal transplant also provides normal α-galactosidase A enzyme.

In the future, genetically produced α-galactosidase enzyme offers therapeutic possibilities.

Annotated Bibliography

Ioannou YA, Bishop DF, Desnick RJ, et al. Overexpression of human alpha-galactosidase A results in its intracellular aggregation, crystallization in liposomes and selective secretion. J Cell Biol 1992;119:1137–1140.

This article describes a potential new therapy.

Desnick RJ, et al. α-Galactosidase A deficiency: Fabry disease. In: Scriver CR, Beaudet AL, Sly WS, Valle D, eds., Metabolic and Molecular Basis of Inherited Disease, 7th ed. New York: McGraw-Hill, 1995, pp 2741–2784.

This is a thorough review of the subject and provides an excellent bibliography.

CHAPTER 43

Tuberous Sclerosis

Thomas T. Provost, M.D.

There are many neurologic diseases with cutaneous expression. These include acquired immunodeficiency syndrome, herpes zoster, the antiphospholipid syndrome, Fabry's disease, diabetes mellitus, leprosy, Lyme disease, Behçet's disease, sarcoidosis, rheumatoid arthritis, scleroderma, Sjögren's syndrome, vasculitis, dermatomyositis, systemic lupus erythematosus, variegate porphyria, pellagra, and xeroderma pigmentosum. These diseases, which may have a prominent central and/or peripheral nervous system and muscular manifestations, are covered in other chapters in this book. This chapter will focus on tuberous sclerosis.

Tuberous sclerosis (TS), also known as "Bourneville's disease," is an autosomal dominant disease characterized by hamartomas in various organs, including the skin, heart, central nervous system, and kidneys. The presence of adenoma sebaceum (actually, an angiofibroma), epilepsy, and mental retardation is termed "Vogt's triad." "Epiloia" is an archaic term denoting adenoma sebaceum, epilepsy, mental retardation, and tumors of the brain and other organs. This is an uncommon disease occurring once in every 6,000 to 12,000 births.

Multisystem genetic disease
Epiloia:
- *adenoma sebaceum*
- *epilepsy*
- *mental retardation*
- *tumors of brain and other organs*

Although the disease is inherited as an autosomal dominant, approximately 70% of cases represent presumable de novo mutations. The disease is heterogeneous, involving two different loci encoding two proteins: hamartin and tuberin. The hamartin gene is located on 9q34 (tuberous sclerosis complex [TSC1]) and encodes a 130-kD protein located in the nucleus.

Autosomal dominant
~70% de novo mutations
Genetic mutations present at two different loci

The tuberin gene is on chromosome 16p13.3 (TSC2) and encodes a protein that shares homologies with a guanosine triphosphatase-accelerating protein. This protein regulates entrance into the S phase of the cell cycle.

Hamartin and tuberin are proteins derived from putative tumor suppressor genes, and loss of the heterozygous state (second hit) in the various tumors of TS supports this theory.

Hamartin and tuberin thought to be products of tumor suppressor genes

The genetics of TS is further complicated by the demonstration of mosaicism. This is a phenomenon in which only a fraction of germline and somatic cells contain a mutation of TSC1 or TSC2. Unless sensitive techniques are employed, these mutations may be missed. For example, in one study, only one-third of the leukocytes from TSC1 patients whose DNA was examined, demonstrated a mutation at the TSC1 allele.

The tumors, which occur in various organs, are ectodermal and mesodermal derived. Although there is excessive proliferation, malignant degeneration is rare.

Hamartomas composed of ectodermal and mesodermal-derived components

Clinical Features

Only hypopigmented patches present at birth

The cutaneous manifestations of TS, with the exception of macular hypopigmented patches, are not present at birth.

"Ash leaf" hypopigmented patches located on all areas of body
Valuable diagnostic tool

Hypomelanotic macules, characterized by an "ash leaf" shape, are seen in approximately 90% of patients (Figure 43–1). These lesions, located on all areas of the body but generally sparing the face, range in size from several millimeters to several centimeters. Some patients have only a few of these lesions, whereas others have several dozen. These lesions are valuable diagnostically because they occur before other cutaneous lesions of the disease and can be used to detect TS during infancy. However, it must be remembered that most infants with a hypomelanotic patch do not have TS. Thus, unless the infant has multiple hypomelanotic patches, a workup for TS is not indicated.

First indication is delay in neurologic developmental milestones.

The cutaneous manifestations (adenoma sebaceum) occur around the age of 5 (Figures 43–2 and 43–3). The first indication of the disease may be a delay in achieving neurologic developmental milestones (eg, crawling, sitting, walking). Subsequently, between the second and third year of life, mental retardations and convulsions may appear.

Heterogeneous clinical presentation

The disease is very heterogeneous in expression. Some patients will have epilepsy without mental deficiency or prominent cutaneous features (Table 43–1). A few will have skin lesions without any evidence of neurologic disease. However, those individuals with mental retardation almost always have cutaneous, as well as epileptic, features.

Yellow-gray plaques occur on the retina in approximately 50% of patients. In addition, benign cardiac rhabdomyomas are also seen in approximately one-half of cases. Hamartomas occurring in other organs, including angiolipomas and cysts of the kidneys, are also frequently detected.

Adenoma sebaceum occurs in 50% of patients.

Adenoma sebaceum (angiofibromas) occur in approximately 50% of patients older than 4 years. They are typically localized to the nasolabial folds, are pink or red, smooth papules and nodules. Sparing of the upper lip is characteristic and helps differentiate this condition from trichoepitheliomas (Brooke's tumor). These lesions may also involve the cheeks and chin. At times, large plaques of these lesions may appear on the forehead.

Shagreen patch: plaques of subepidermal fibromas

The shagreen patch, found most commonly in the lumbosacral region, is another diagnostic sign of TS (Figures 43–4 to 43–6). These plaques of subepidermal fibrosis are flesh colored and range in size from 1 to 5 cm. These patches, or slightly elevated lesions, have an "orange peel" or "elephant hide" appearance.

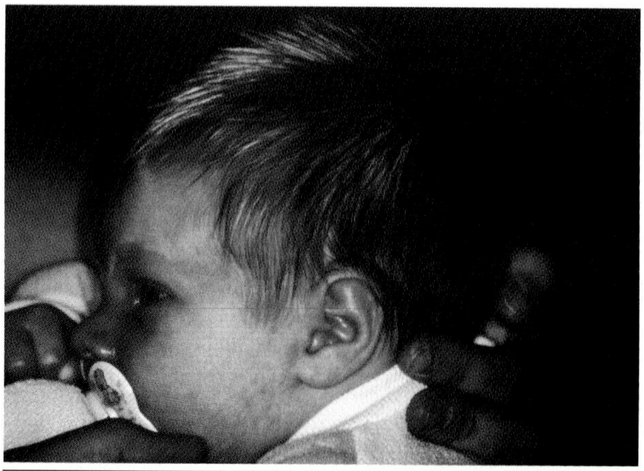

FIGURE 43–1 Hypopigmented patches on the cheek and forehead (poliosis) in a child who has motor retardation and is diagnosed with tuberous sclerosis.

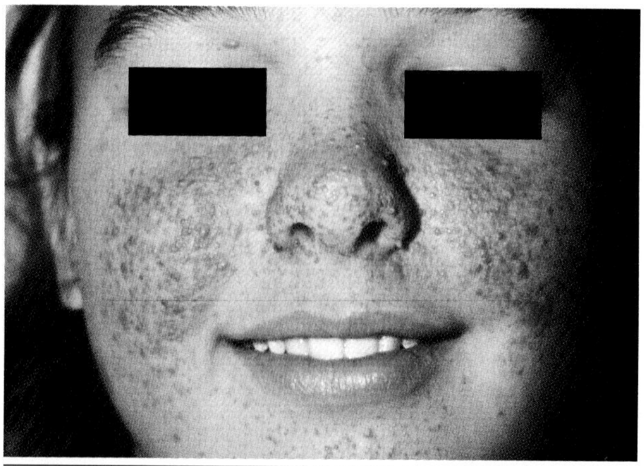

FIGURE 43–2 Young girl with adenoma sebaceum. Note sparing of the upper lip.

TABLE 43–1 Approximate Frequency of Findings in Tuberous Sclerosis

Clinical Feature	Percentage
Seizure disorder	90
Hypomelanotic patches	90
Adenoma sebaceum	80
Mental retardation	60
Phakomas	50
Brain calcification	50
Cardiac rhabdomyomas	50
Shagreen patch	20
Subungual fibroma	15

Koenen's tumors are another diagnostic cutaneous feature of TS. These peri- and subungual fibromas are characteristic.

Peri- and subungual fibromas termed "Koenen's tumors"

Pathology

The cutaneous manifestations are hamartomas composed of fibroblasts with collagen strands and blood vessels. The shagreen patch is a sclerotic mass of collagen with relatively few blood vessels. The ash leaf spots contain normal quantities of melanocytes, but these melanocytes have few melanosomes.

"Ash leaf" spots contain melanocytes with few melanosomes.

The brain lesions are composed of hamartomas that produce nodular (tubers) tumors ranging from 0.5 to 3 cm. These whitish tubers are composed of fibrous tissue and glial cells. Large distorted neurons and fibrous astrocytes are characteristic. These lesions contain flecks of calcium. On radiographic images of the skull, they produce the characteristic brain stones. The ventricles may be outlined by similar lesions. These large tubers may block the aqueduct of the fourth ventricle, producing hydrocephalus. The retinal lesions are composed of neuronal and glial components with fibrous tissue.

Brain stones:
flecks of calcium in brain hamartomas
may induce internal hydrocephalus

Diagnosis

The presence of characteristic cutaneous manifestations, plus a history of mental deficiency and convulsions, easily establish the diagnosis. However, as noted earlier, with the exception of the ash leaf patches, cutaneous manifestations frequently lag behind the development of epilepsy and mental retardation.

Diagnosis may be problematic if full-blown clinical picture not present.

The search for hypomelanotic ash leaf macules is especially valuable in infants and small children demonstrating delay in psychomotor development and epilepsy. Skull radiographic images, computed tomography scans, and magnetic resonance imaging are useful in demonstrating the various tumor deposits throughout the brain.

Ash leaf spots are valuable diagnostic features.

Prognosis

Tuberous sclerosis, unfortunately, is a slowly progressive disease. Approximately one-third die before the fifth year of age, and as many as 75% die before adulthood. The rhabdomyomas may produce potentially lethal arrhythmias or obstruct blood flow. Although unusual, malignant degeneration resulting in death may occur.

Generally a slowly progressive disease

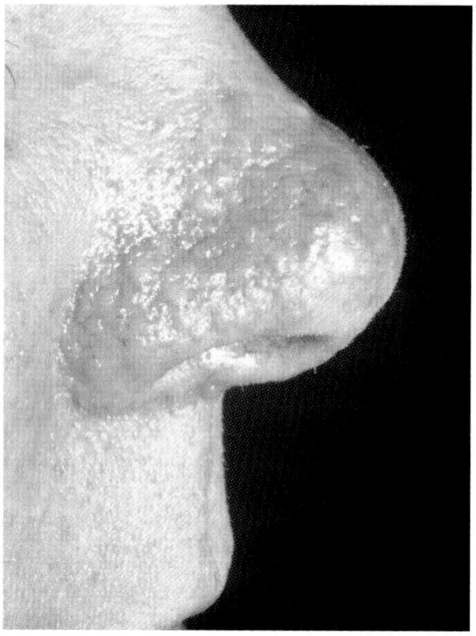

FIGURE 43-3 Multiple adenoma sebaceum of the nose. Note sparing of upper lip.

Annotated Bibliography

Kennedy JL Jr, Kalish GH. Incidence of depigmented nevi in 1000 term newborns. Pediatr Res 1972;6:411.

Most infants with hypomelanotic patch do not have tuberous sclerosis.

Hurko O, Provost TT. Neurology and the skin. In: Hughes RAC, Perkin GD, eds. Neurology and Medicine. London: BMJ Books, 1999, 11, pp 307–343.

This provides an overview of the cutaneous manifestations of neurologic diseases and has 115 references.

Jones AC, Daniells CE, Snell RG, et al. Molecular genetic and phenotypic analysis reveals differences between TSC1 and TSC2 associated familial and sporadic tuberous sclerosis. Hum Mol Genet 1997;6:2155–2161.

Mutations in the TSC1 allele are more commonly associated with mental retardation; mutations in the TSC2 allele are more commonly associated with cystic kidney lesions.

Kwiatkowska J, Wigowska-Sowenska J, Napierala D, et al. Mosaicism in tuberous sclerosis as a potential failure of molecular diagnosis. N Engl J Med 1999;340:703–707.

This interesting article demonstrates the differences in the frequency of the TSC1 allele mutation in various tissues of a patient with TS.

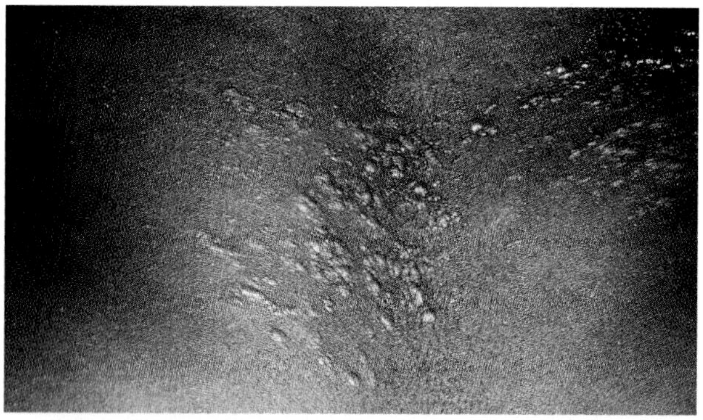

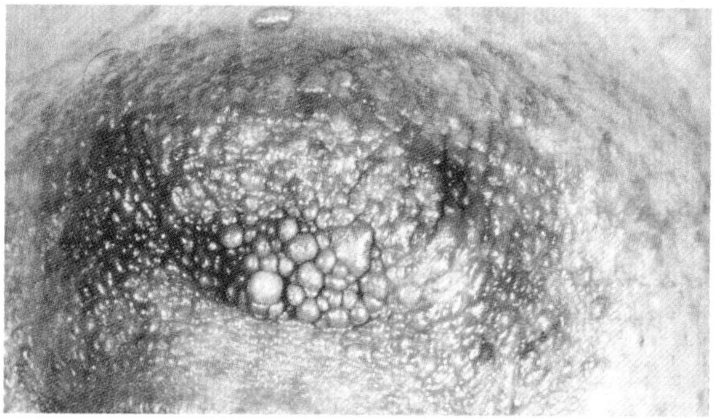

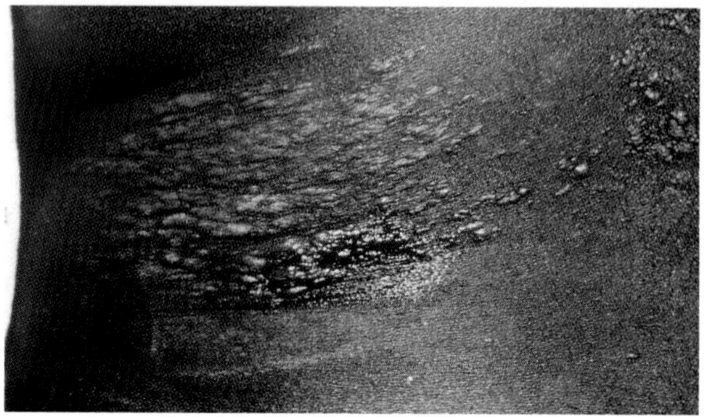

FIGURES 43-4 TO 43-6 Three examples of the variation in morphology of subepidermal fibromas (shagreen patches), all located in the lumbar region of patients with tuberous sclerosis.

CHAPTER 44

Neurofibromatosis

Thomas T. Provost, M.D.

The two forms of neurofibromatosis are designated NF1 and NF2; both are inherited as an autosomal dominant. However, at least 30% of NF1 patients do not have a family history and have occurred de novo. The incidence of NF1 is 30 to 40 per 100,000 per year, whereas NF2 occurs much less frequently with an incidence of 1 per 100,000 per year.

Two forms of neurofibromatosis:
- *NF1 and NF2*
- *NF1 common*

Autosomal dominant inherited diseases

The NF1 gene is localized to chromosome 17q11.2 and appears to be a tumor suppressor gene encoding neurofibromin. This protein inactivates the tumor suppressor proto-oncogene *ras* protein by its guanosine triphosphatase activity. Mutations in neurofibromin allow unregulated growth and proliferation.

NF1 gene localized to 17q11.2
Tumor suppressor gene

The NF2 gene is located on chromosome 22q12 and is also a putative tumor suppressor gene. The gene product, termed "MERLIN," shows a close relationship to a family of cytoskeletal associated proteins (*m*oesin-*e*zrin-*r*adixin-*l*ike prote*in*).

NF2 gene localized to 22q12
Tumor suppressor gene

Clinical Features

The cutaneous manifestations of NF1 (von Recklinghausen's disease) are extremely varied and range from a few café-au-lait spots and a few neurofibromas to scoliosis and gross deformities.

Clinical features varied

The café-au-lait spots are macular, hyperpigmented lesions occurring on all areas of the body. Axillary freckling, although less frequently observed, is characteristic. Freckling may also be prominent in the groin and inframammary regions (Figures 44–1 and 44–2).

The neurofibromas occur on all areas of the body. They increase in size and number with age and initially may demonstrate a violaceous hue, although later they become flesh colored. The application of pressure to these lesions causes them to herniate into the dermis. This phenomenon is termed "buttonholing" and is characteristic (Figures 44–3, 44–4, 44–5, and 44–6).

Neurofibromas
"Buttonholing"

Large neurofibromas can also be pedunculated and broad based; others can produce gross hypertrophies of the skin, associated with underlying bone and tissue enlargement. These changes may be accompanied by hyperpigmentation and hypertrichosis. Subcutaneous and nodular plexiform neurofibromas occur. Malignant degeneration (fibrosarcoma) occurs in approximately 5% of plexiform neurofibromas.

In addition to cutaneous neurofibromas, nodular dermal and plexiform neurofibromas occur.

Malignant degeneration in approximately 5% of plexiform neurofibromas

Lisch nodules (multiple melanocytic iris hamartomas) are present in approximately 90% of adult NF1 patients. Optic gliomas, best demonstrated by magnetic resonance imaging occur in approximately 10% of NF1 patients and may or may not be symptomatic.

Lisch nodules

FIGURE 44–1 Café-au-lait spots on the flank of a patient with NF1.

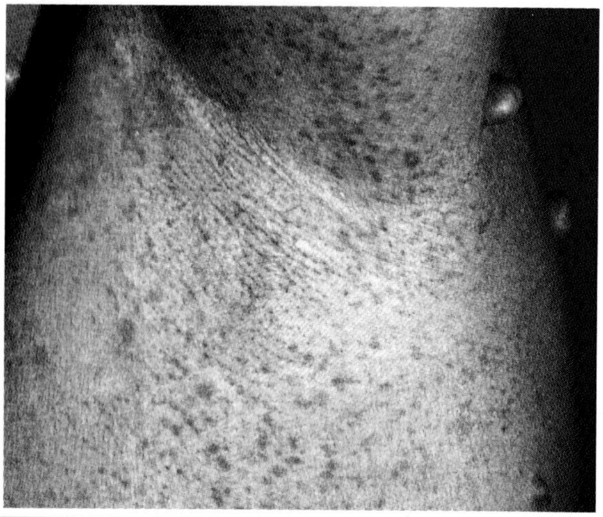

FIGURE 44–2 Axillary freckling in a patient with NF1 (Crowe's sign).

Neuropsychologic and learning disabilities are frequent.

Central nervous system manifestations include meningiomas, ependymomas, and astrocytomas. Approximately 5% of patients have mental retardation and approximately 5% have epilepsy. Neuropsychologic deficits and learning disabilities, however, are detected in at least 30 to 50% of patients.

Skeletal abnormalities (most commonly scoliosis) occur in approximately 5% of patients. As many as 20% of children with scoliosis may have NF1. The NF1 patients may also have short stature and macrocephaly. Dysplasia of the wings of the sphenoid bone occurs in approximately 5% of patients and may result in a pulsating exophthalmos.

Pheochromocytomas

Pheochromocytoma is occasionally detected. Approximately 5 to 10% of pheochromocytoma patients have NF1. Essential hypertension is more common. Also, there is an increased frequency of renal artery stenosis in children with NF1.

The National Institutes of Health consensus criteria for the diagnosis of NF1 are presented in Table 44–1.

The cutaneous manifestations of NF2 are much less prominent than those seen in NF1. The number and size of the café-au-lait spots and neurofibromas are less. Lisch nodules generally do not occur.

The NF2 patients frequently present with nerve deafness, dizziness, ataxia, headache, etc. Furthermore, neuromas involving cranial nerve VII can produce

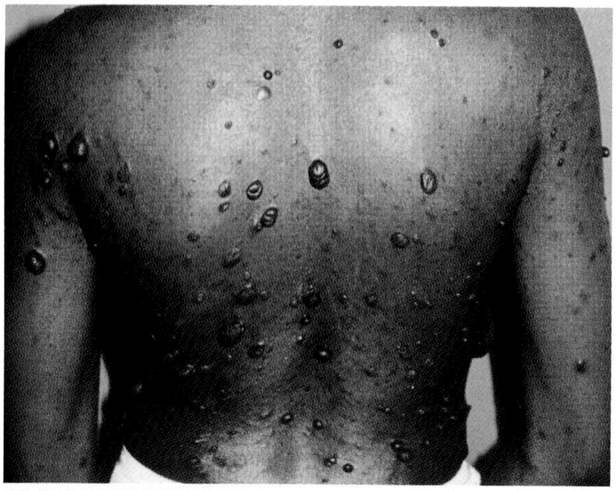

FIGURE 44–3 Neurofibroma in an African American female.

FIGURE 44–4 Closeup of the multiple neurofibromas on the patient in Figure 44–3.

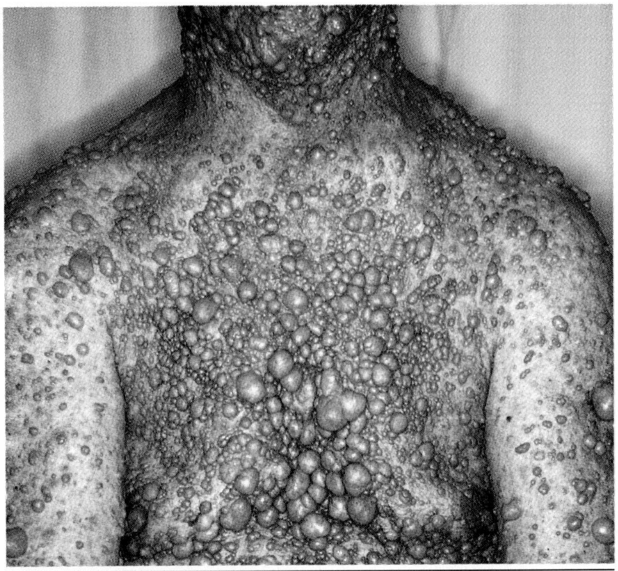

FIGURE 44–5 An NF1 patient demonstrating multiple neurofibroma tumors.

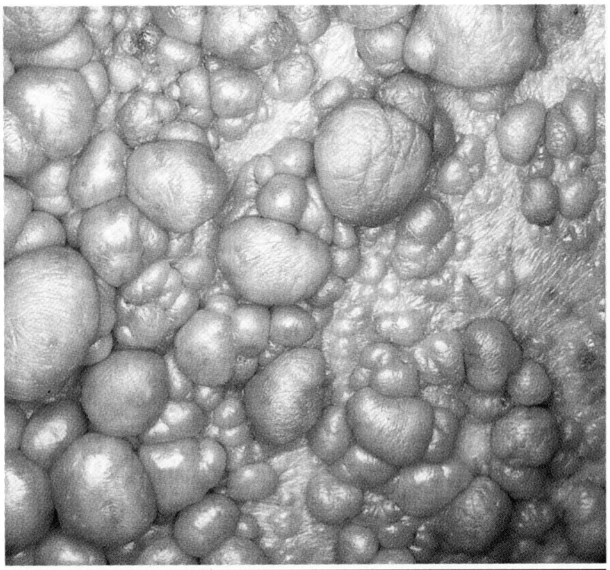

FIGURE 44–6 Closeup of the multiple tumors of neurofibromatosis.

facial pain, numbness, and neuromas involving cranial nerves IX, X, and XI, producing dysphagia, weakness, and hemiatrophy of the tongue.

The diagnostic criteria for NF2 are presented in Table 44–2.

Pathology

Giant melanosomes

The café-au-lait spots have increased quantities of melanocytes. In addition, there are giant pigment granules (melanosomes). The neurofibromas are indistinguishable from single neurofibromas detected in normal individuals.

Diagnosis

The presence of café-au-lait spots in a female child is a diagnostic problem. These lesions must be differentiated from the pigmented lesions of the McCune-Albright syndrome (polyostotic fibrous dysplasia associated with sexual precocity in females). This syndrome does occur in males, but is much more commonly detected in females. The café-au-lait lesions may be impossible to differentiate, although it is purported that the café-au-lait lesions in neurofibromatosis do not

TABLE 44–1 Criteria for Diagnosis of NF1*

Six or more café-au-lait spots > 5 mm in diameter before puberty, and > 15 mm in adulthood
Axillary and inguinal freckling
Two or more neurofibromas or one plexiform neurofibroma
Two or more Lisch nodules
Optic glioma
Sphenoid dysplasia or thinning of long bone cortex with or without pseudarthrosis
A first-degree relative exhibiting these changes

*A diagnosis of von Recklinghausen's disease (NF1) requires at least two of the above features.

Adapted from: Stumf DA, et al. National Institutes of Health Consensus Conference. Neurofibromatosis conference statement. Arch Neurol 1988;45:575–578.

TABLE 44–2 Diagnostic Criteria for NF2*

Bilateral eighth nerve acoustic neuromas
A parent, sibling, or child who has NF2 with either unilateral eighth nerve masses or any two of the following: neurofibroma, meningioma, glioma, schwannoma, or juvenile posterior subcapsular lenticular opacity

*A diagnosis of NF2 requires one of the above features.

Adapted from: Stumf DA, et al. National Institutes of Health Consensus Conference. Neurofibromatosis conference statement. Arch Neurol 1988;45:575–578.

follow normal skin lines (Blaschko's lines), whereas those of McCune-Albright syndrome do. Biopsy of café-au-lait spots in neurofibromatosis demonstrates giant melanosomes, which are said to be rare in the McCune-Albright syndrome

McCune-Albright syndrome

The McCune-Albright syndrome represents genetic mosaicism. Somatic mutations occur in the gene encoding the alpha subunit for G protein. These mutations prevent regulation of cyclic adenosine monophosphate (cAMP) allowing unregulated growth and hyperfunction of multiple glands, including the gonads, thyroid, adrenal cortex, and pituitary, and the melanocytes and osteoblasts. Some of the clinical features of the McCune-Albright syndrome are listed in Table 44–3.

TABLE 44–3 Clinical Features Associated with the McCune-Albright Syndrome

Precocious puberty
Excessive growth resulting in coarse features (acromegaly)
Hyperthyroidism
Hyperparathyroidism
Hyperprolactinemia
Cushing's syndrome
Hypophosphatemic osteomalacia

Prognosis

Progressive diseases

Patients with NF1 or NF2 have a progressive disease with many complications.

Annotated Bibliography

Gutmann DH, Collins FS. von Recklinghausen neurofibromatosis. In: Scriver CR, Beaudet AL, Sly WS, Valle D, eds. The Metabolic and Molecular Basis of Inherited Disease. New York: McGraw Hill, 1995, 14, pp 677–696.

This is a comprehensive review of the subject.

Upadhyaya M, Sheu M, Cherryson A, et al. Analysis of mutations at the neurofibromatosis 1 (NF1) locus. Hum Mol Genet 1992;38:880–885.

Jacoby LB, Jones D, Davis K, et al. Molecular analysis of the NF2 tumor-suppressor gene in schwannomatosis. Am J Hum Genet 1997;61:1293–1302.

These two articles describe genetic defects in NF1 and NF2.

Hurko O, Provost TT. Neurology and the skin. In: Hughes RAC, Perkin GD, eds. Neurology and Medicine. London: BMJ Books, 1999, 11, pp 307–343.

This chapter provides additional up-to-date references regarding molecular defects.

CHAPTER 45

Sturge-Weber and Klippel-Trénaunay-Weber Syndromes

Thomas T. Provost, M.D.

Etiology

In recent years it has been proposed that Sturge-Weber syndrome, also known as "encephalofacial or encephalotrigeminal angiomatosis," may be a genetically transmitted condition. The direct proof of this is scanty. An isolated case of the occurrence of Sturge-Weber syndrome in monozygotic twins has been reported.

Relationship of Sturge-Weber and Klippel-Trénaunay-Weber syndromes

In addition, it has been hypothesized that the Klippel-Trénaunay-Weber syndrome may be a genetically transmitted disease closely related to the Sturge-Weber syndrome. The direct proof is also scanty and includes the report by Happle of a familial aggregation of Klippel-Trénaunay-Weber syndrome and the unusual association of Sturge-Weber and the Klippel-Trénaunay-Weber syndromes in the same patient. (For photograph documentation of this association, see Happle R. Neurocutaneous diseases. In: Freedberg IM, Eisen AZ, Wolff K, et al., eds. Fitzpatrick's Dermatology in General Medicine, 5th ed. New York: McGraw-Hill, 1999, 189, pp 2143.)

Suggested to be paradominant inheritance

Happle has proposed a paradominant inheritance to explain this phenomenon, (i.e., the inheritance of a heterozygotic, phenotypically normal trait) with the subsequent somatic mutation producing phenotypically abnormal cells which are homozygous for the defect).

Clinical Features

Sturge-Weber Syndrome

Importance of port-wine stain eye involvement

In the case of Sturge-Weber syndrome, the child is born with a unilateral telangiectatic nevus ("port-wine stain") involving the ophthalmic division of the fifth cranial nerve (Figure 45–1). Those individuals with involvement of the upper and lower eyelids are at more risk to have associated neurologic features compared with those individuals with telangiectatic nevi below the eye. It must be emphasized that not all patients with a port-wine stain over the ophthalmic division of the fifth cranial nerve have the neurologic features of Sturge-Weber syndrome. These lesions are generally unilateral but bilateral lesions occur. On occasions, the oral cavity is also involved.

Leptomeningeal angiomatosis

Epilepsy and mental retardation

The neurologic abnormalities are related to ipsilateral leptomeningeal angiomatosis. Calcification of these angiomatous malformations occurs, which is detected by computer axial tomography or magnetic resonance imagery in infancy. These patients frequently have seizures and mental retardation and may develop hemiparesis. Macrocephaly may occur. In addition to the neurologic defects, ophthalmic defects, including glaucoma and occipital lobe blindness, may occur.

Klippel-Trénaunay-Weber Syndrome

Port-wine stain over extremities associated with hypertrophy and elongation of extremity

The clinical features of the Klippel-Trénaunay-Weber syndrome are characterized by a port-wine stain occurring over an extremity. On occasions, it may occur bilaterally (Figure 45–2). Soft tissue hypertrophy and bone enlargement and elongation occur. In approximately one-quarter of these patients, an arterial venous malformation can be detected in the affected limb.

Annotated Bibliography

Tallman B, Tan OT, Morelli JG, et al. Location of port-wine stains and the likelihood of ophthalmic and/or central nervous system complications. Pediatrics 1991;87:323–327.

This article described the orbital involvement with port-wine stain and the increased frequency of central nervous system involvement.

Happle R. Lethal genes surviving by mosaicism: a possible explanation for sporadic birth defects involving the skin. J Am Acad Dermatol 1987;16:899–906.

Happle R. Klippel-Trénaunay syndrome: is it a paradominant trait? Br J Dermatol 1993; 128:465–466.

These two interesting articles outline possible paradominant inheritance in Sturge-Weber and Klippel-Trénaunay-Weber syndromes.

Sujansky E, Conradi S. Outcome of Sturge-Weber syndrome in 52 adults. Am J Med Genet 1995;57:35–42.

The prevalence of glaucoma (60%), seizures (83%), and neurologic deficit (65%) indicates the serious complications associated with this syndrome. Seizures were associated with developmental delay and special educational requirements. Despite these problems, approximately 40% were financially self-sufficient.

Happle R. Loss of heterozygosity in human skin. J Am Acad Dermatol 1999;41:143–161.

This is a well written review article, giving a comprehensive review of skin disorders in which loss of gene heterozygosity in human skin has been shown to result in malignant degeneration as well as benign hamartomas. Happle has referred to this occurrence in such diseases as Sturge-Weber and Klippel-Trénaunay syndrome as a paradominant inheritance.

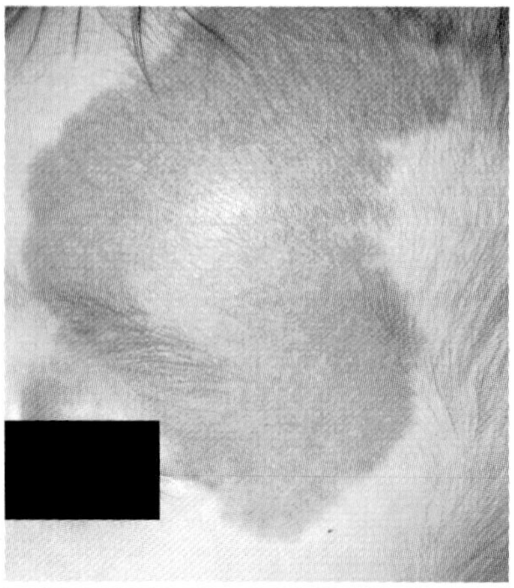

FIGURE 45–1 Port-wine stain in a patient with Sturge-Weber syndrome. (Reproduced with permission from: Bernard Cohen, M.D., Baltimore, MD)

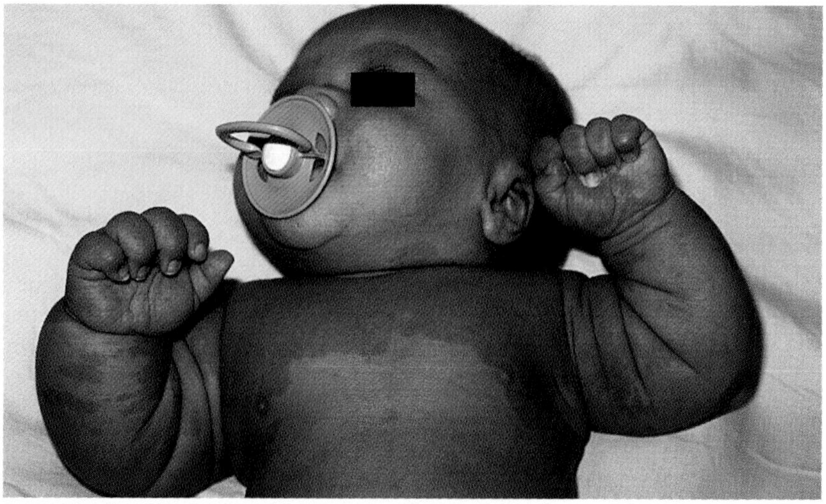

FIGURE 45–2 Bilateral port-wine stain over the shoulders in a patient with Klippel-Trénaunay-Weber syndrome.

CHAPTER 46

Sarcoidosis

Thomas T. Provost, M.D., David R. Moller, M.D., Walter Royal III, M.D.

Sarcoidosis is a multiorgan, noncaseating granulomatous disease of unknown etiology. It affects all races, occurring worldwide. Its presenting features may be protean (eg, nondescript papulonodular skin lesions or asymptomatic pulmonary lesions detected on routine chest radiographic examination). In one study of approximately 500 Scandinavian pulmonary sarcoidosis patients, only one-third of patients were detected because of clinical signs and symptoms (Table 46–1). Almost 60% were detected on routine screening chest radiography. The events important in our understanding of this disease are listed in Table 46–2.

Protean disease
In many patients, sarcoidosis is asymptomatic, detected only by radiography.

The prevalence of sarcoidosis is estimated to be between 1 and 40 cases per 100,000 worldwide. In the United States, the estimated prevalence is approximately 10 per 100,000 for Caucasians and 35 per 100,000 for African Americans. African Americans appear to be more severely affected and have a higher mortality rate. Higher frequencies also occur in Irish and Scandinavian populations

African American, Irish, and Scandinavians appear to be at increased risk.

The disease must be differentiated from hypersensitivity pneumonitis, mycobacterial and fungal infections, chronic berylliosis disease, as well as foreign-body granulomas.

Clusters of sarcoidosis have occurred that appear to be spatially and temporarily related, suggesting the presence of a common, perhaps infectious or etiologic environmental factor. Furthermore, cases have been transmitted by pul-

Fragmentary evidence suggesting common environmental factor(s)

TABLE 46–1 Sign or Symptom at Time of Presentation of Sarcoidosis*

Sign or Symptom	Total (%)
Erythema nodosum	14.1
Nonproductive cough	8.5
Joint pains	8.3
Dyspnea	6.3
Fever	5.9
Lymphadenopathy	2.6
Skin lesions	2.4
Eye involvement	1.6
Neurologic disease	0.4

*Total number of pulmonary sarcoidosis patients was 505 of which 32% were detected by presentation of signs and symptoms, 57% of patients detected by routine health screening radiography, and 10% discovered by chance on a radiograph obtained for other reasons.

Adapted from: Hillerdal G, Nöu E, Osterman K, et al. Sarcoidosis: epidemology and prognosis. Am Rev Respir Dis 1984;130:29–32.

TABLE 46–2 Glossary of Events in Development of Knowledge of Sarcoidosis

1892, 1898	Jonathan Hutchinson describes Mortimer's malady and relapsing uveitis.
1889	Besnier describes lupus pernio.
1899	Boeck describes a patient with nodules over face and back with significant lymphadenopathy. Pathologic examination revealed lesions similar to sarcoma; hence, the derivation of sarcoid (sarcoma-like).
1909	Heerfordt describes uveoparotid fever.
1914	Schaumann and Kuznitsky and Bittorf determine a correlation of skin with systemic features (pulmonary disease).
1934	The first international conference on sarcoidosis is held and sarcoidosis is recognized as a distinct entity.
1942, 1946	Kerley and, later, Löfgren describe the association of erythema nodosum with bilateral hilar lymphadenopathy.
1981	Hunninghake and Crystal demonstrate by bronchial lavage studies the dominant presence of CD4-positive T lymphocytes at sites of disease activity.

monary, cardiac, and bone marrow transplantation, supporting an infectious etiology. The Kveim-Siltzbach test (a homogenate of human sarcoid spleen) induces the formation of granulomas at the site of infection in some sarcoid patients. No definitive evidence of an infectious agent, however, has been detected. Most, but not all, recent studies using molecular biologic techniques have failed to detect evidence of mycobacterial DNA.

The interpretation of the meaning of clusters is controversial. Current data do not unequivocally provide support for person-to-person transmission. Rather, clusters may represent common environmental exposures that could be infectious (eg, *Legionella* [legionnaire's disease]) but not communicable person-to-person. Until unequivocal data support person-to-person transmission (which would have an extremely low rate of transmission), we would argue against proposing a communicable infection as a possible etiology.

Genetic factors may be important
Familial clustering

Increased frequency of HLA-A1, -B8, -DR3 phenotypes

Genetic factors may be important. For example, sarcoidosis occurs more commonly in monozygotic than dizygotic twins. Familial clusters of sarcoidosis exist. Two studies (one from Ireland, the other a study of African Americans) have demonstrated that approximately 9% of affected individuals have an affected sibling. Furthermore, approximately 2% of all siblings of affected individuals are also affected. The rate is higher in affected African American than Caucasian families. There is also evidence for an increased frequency of human leukocyte antigen (HLA)-A1, -B8, and -DR3 phenotypes among some sarcoidosis patients, although the relative risk is not as striking as that seen in autoimmune disease.

It appears likely that sarcoidosis is induced by multiple etiologies. (For an in-depth review of sarcoid etiology studies, see reference by Moller in annotated bibliography.)

Clinical Features

Fever, fatigue, night sweats, and gradual weight loss may occur with systemic sarcoidosis.

Cutaneous Manifestations

The cutaneous sarcoid lesions are characterized as nonspecific and specific. Table 46–3 outlines the specific cutaneous lesions. Approximately 25% of sarcoidosis patients have cutaneous features.

Erythema Nodosum

Erythema nodosum is a nonspecific lesion that occurs in approximately 15 to 20% of sarcoidosis cases (much less frequently seen in the United States compared with Scandinavian populations). These lesions are generally erythematous,

TABLE 46–3 Specific Cutaneous Lesions

Lesion	Description
Papules and macules	On all areas of the body but especially prominent around the eyes and nasolabial folds; frequently skin colored and may assume annular configuration in African Americans
Nodules	May be colorless or red and purple; occur on all areas of the body
Plaques	Generally violaceous in color and most prominent on the ears, nose, fingers, and toes; also termed "lupus pernio"
Patches	Scaling patches mimicking discoid lupus erythematosus; some have psoriasiform appearance, especially in African Americans
Ulcers	Unusual cutaneous manifestation most prominently seen in African Americans
Ichthyosiform	Unusual superficial form of sarcoidosis
Hypopigmented patches	Especially prominent feature in African Americans
Enlarged scars	Keloid formation
Fusiform swelling of fingers	Digititis

tender, subcutaneous nodules appearing over the extensor surface of the lower legs. Involvement of the extensor surfaces of the forearms may also occur. Erythema nodosum lesions may be accompanied by fever, fatigue, and arthralgias. Ecchymosis may occur, especially with resolution. Also, postinflammatory hyperpigmentation is commonly noted. At times, the erythema nodosum may have an atypical presentation demonstrating tender, erythematous, indurated nodular lesions around both ankles.

Erythema nodosum generally a good prognostic sign
Generally extensor surfaces of lower legs
May present as tender, indurated lesions around ankles

Löfgren's syndrome is characterized by erythema nodosum and hilar adenopathy, polyarthritis, and often uveitis. Löfgren's syndrome is benign, generally demonstrating spontaneous involution in approximately 80% of individuals during a 6-month period.

Löfgren's syndrome: erythema nodosum and bilateral hilar lymphadenopathy
A benign disease

Histologically, early in the disease, erythema nodosum lesions demonstrate a septal panniculitis characterized by an inflammatory infiltrate of predominantly neutrophils. Lymphocytes, histiocytes, occasional granulomatous lesions, and giant cells occur late in the disease.

Pathology of lesion reveals a septal panniculitis

In general, the lesions of erythema nodosum constitute a good, benign, prognostic sign in patients with sarcoidosis.

Lupus Pernio

In addition to erythema nodosum, sarcoidosis patients may demonstrate specific lesions characterized by violaceous, nodular, plaque-like lesions over the central portion of the face, nasal alae, earlobes, and eyelids. These lesions most commonly occur in women and are often associated with uveitis and involvement of the upper respiratory tract. The lupus pernio type of lesion may produce granular, polypoidal masses and ulcerations of the nasopharynx and nasal septum (Figures 46–1 to 46–3). Bronchial obstruction may also occur.

In addition, lupus pernio lesions may produce significant cutaneous scarring and are recalcitrant to therapy.

Lupus pernio:
face, nose, ears
often associated with upper airway and eye involvement
scar formation problematic
may be recalcitrant to therapy

Papular, Nodular, and Plaque Lesions

In addition to lupus pernio, many patients with sarcoidosis display erythematous, brownish papules and nodules that can involve all areas of the body (Figures 46–4 to 46–7). At times, telangiectasia may be prominent. ("Angiolupoid" is the morphologic term applied to describe these lesions.)

Angiolupoid:
brownish sarcoid lesions with telangiectasia

Small, colorless papular lesions involving the eyelids, the central portion of the face, and the external orifices of the nares are common. Nasal stuffiness is often

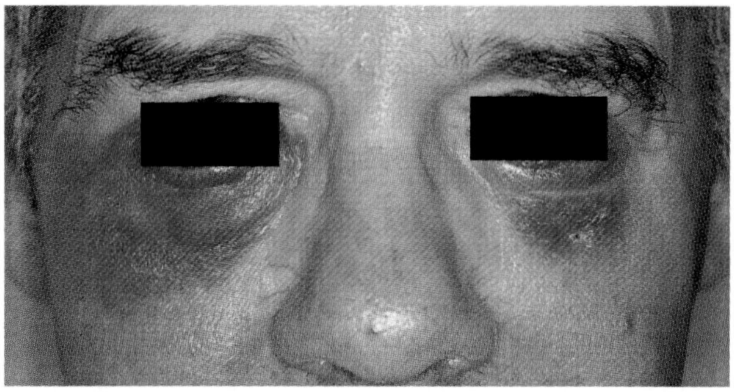

FIGURE 46–1 Lupus pernio beneath both eyes.

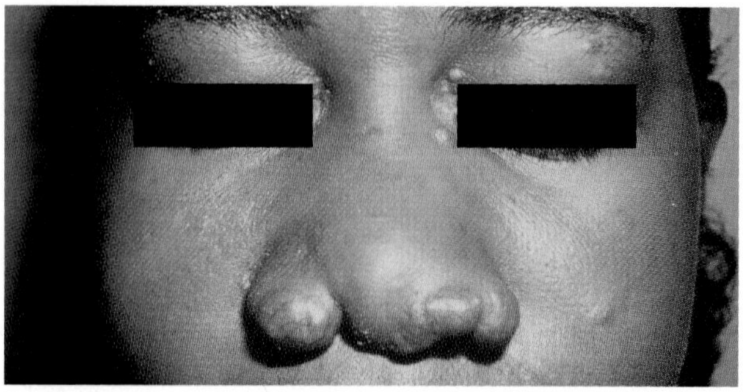

FIGURE 46–2 Lupus pernio producing nodular scarred lesions on the nose.

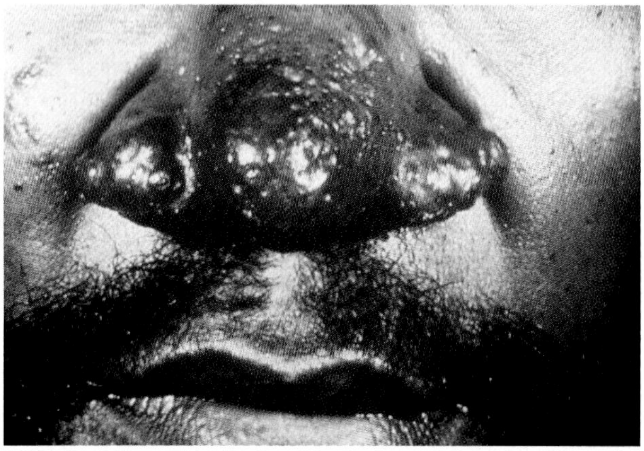

FIGURE 46–3 Lupus pernio of the nose associated with prominent postinflammatory hyperpigmentation.

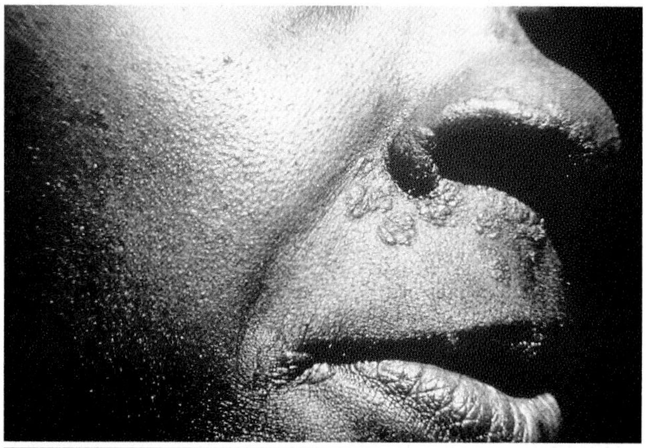

FIGURE 46–4 Skin-colored papules on the upper lip of a sarcoidosis patient. Note the involvement of the ala nasi.

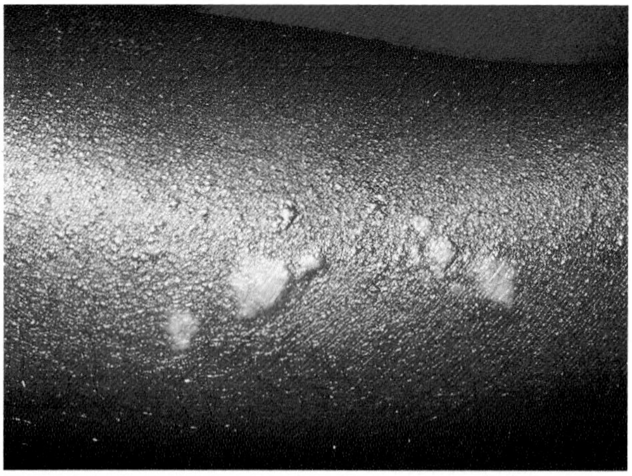

FIGURE 46–5 Papules and nodules of sarcoidosis involving the arm.

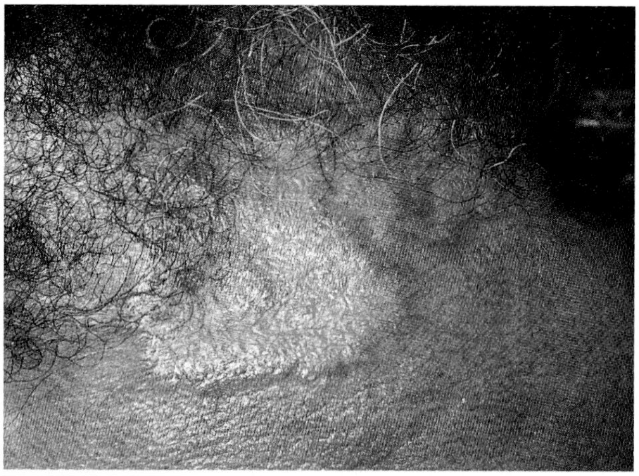

FIGURE 46–6 Annular patch of sarcoid on the forehead near the hairline.

present but generally detected only by direct questioning. Involvement of the central portion of the face with these types of sarcoid lesions is commonly, but not invariably, seen in association with uveitis.

In contradistinction to lupus pernio, these sarcoid lesions do not produce scarring and are generally responsive to therapy.

Sarcoidosis can present as skin-colored, translucent, waxy-appearing, asymptomatic, macular, papular, annular lesions, some of which demonstrate hypopigmentation. Hypopigmentation and annularity are especially prominent in African

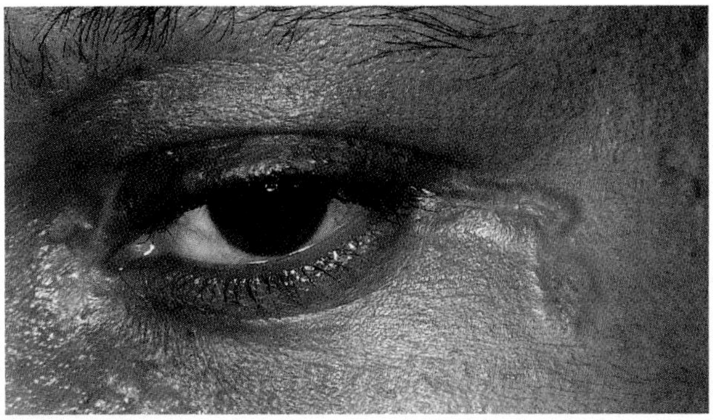

FIGURE 46–7 Periorbital papular annular lesions of sarcoidosis.

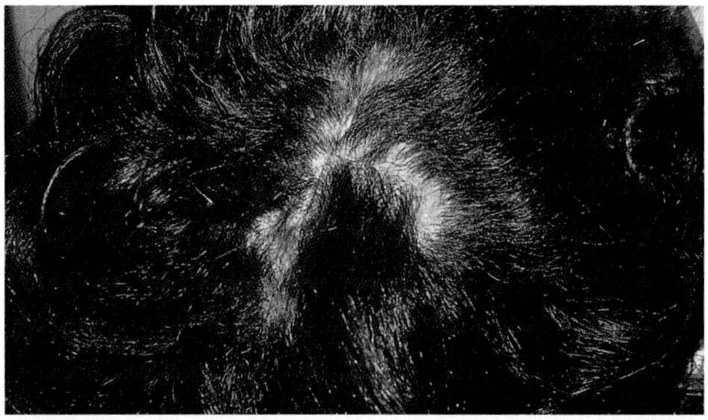

FIGURE 46–8 Sarcoid of the scalp producing a scarring alopecia.

Americans. It is only by biopsy that the true nature of the hypopigmented lesion may be determined.

On unusual occasions, ulcerations occur, and this too is seen predominantly in African Americans. On rare occasions, sarcoidosis can involve the scalp, producing a scarring alopecia (Figure 46–8). (We have seen a middle-aged Caucasian female present with a biopsy-proven scarring plaque on the vertex of the scalp as the sole cutaneous manifestation of sarcoidosis.) An ichthyosiform and an erythrodermic form of sarcoidosis has been occasionally detected. Subcutaneous sarcoidosis (Darier-Roussy sarcoidosis), characterized by painless subcutaneous nodules, is an uncommon form of sarcoidosis often recalcitrant to treatment. Sarcoid granulomas may appear in scars (Figures 46–9 and 46–10). Asymptomatic or tender swelling may be noted. On unusual occasions, sarcoid cutaneous lesions may be psoriasiform.

Eye involvement with sarcoid lesions, central portion of face problematic

Generally nonscarring, responds to treatment

Sarcoid lesions may have atypical presentations:
skin-colored papules
hypopigmented macules
scarring alopecia
annular
ulcerative
erythrodermic
ichthyosiform
subcutaneous nodules
appear in sites of previous scars
psoriasiform

Recently we evaluated a 40-year-old African American woman with a 2-year history of a generalized papulosquamous psoriasiform dermatitis involving large areas of the body. Initial biopsies of nodular lesions of the lower extremities revealed a noncaseating, granulomatous panniculitis associated with admixture of lymphocytes and plasma cells. Subsequently, the dermatitis became generalized, associated with prominent scale formation. Biopsies of these lesions demonstrated noncaseating granulomatous lesions throughout the dermis. Chest radiographs and the angiotensin-converting enzyme assay were normal. However, granulomatous liver and pericardial involvement were detected. Multiple bacteriologic and fungal cultures and serologic tests for syphilis were negative. All granulomatous lesions responded to 40 mg of prednisone.

Pulmonary Disease

Pulmonary disease in the form of hilar lymphadenopathy is commonly seen in patients with sarcoidosis. Chest pains in the retrosternal area, intensified by alcohol consumption, may occur. Cough and dyspnea occur in approximately one-third of patients.

Hilar lymphadenopathy is common in sarcoidosis.

Pulmonary disease is classified by chest radiography in four stages:

Stage 1 is defined as bilateral, hilar lymphadenopathy with no parenchymal lung involvement.

Stage 2 is characterized by the presence of bilateral, hilar lymphadenopathy and parenchymal lung involvement.

Stage 3 is characterized by parenchymal (interstitial) lung involvement without evidence of hilar lymphadenopathy.

Stage 4 is characterized by pulmonary interstitial fibrosis with fibrocystic changes or, less commonly, by "honeycomb" lung. (Honeycomb lung is actually uncommon in sarcoidosis—advanced disease has fibrocystic changes.) Pulmonary insufficiency is often found in these patients.

A large proportion of patients with stage 1 disease spontaneously resolve. For example, in one study 44.5% of the patients who were initially in stage 1 demon-

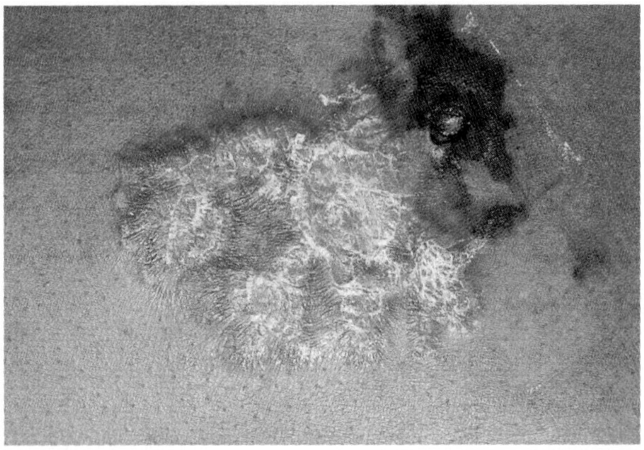

FIGURE 46–9 Sarcoidosis arising in a scar on the shoulder.

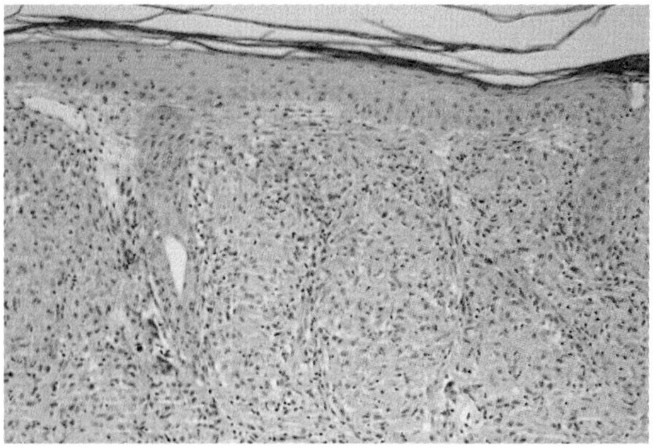

FIGURE 46–10 Biopsy of a scarred area showing sarcoid granulomas.

Four stages of pulmonary sarcoidosis:
stage 1 hilar lymph nodes
stage 2 hilar lymph nodes and parenchymal lung involvement
stage 3 lung involvement without hilar lymph nodes
stage 4 pulmonary fibrosis, fibrocystic changes, and insufficiency

Spontaneous resolution common in stages 1 and 2; less so in stage 3

strated spontaneous remission after 1 year. After 5 years, the radiographic appearance of the lungs was normal in 82.4%. Approximately 7% of patients with stage 1 chest radiographs remained in stage 1 for more than 6 years. Less than 10% of patients in stage 1 progressed to stage 2. Less than 1% progressed further to stage 3.

Of stage 2 pulmonary sarcoidosis patients, 21.7% demonstrated normal chest radiographs after 1 year. After 5 years, 68.3% of patients with stage 2 chest radiographs had spontaneously resolved.

The percentage of patients who progressed to a stage 4 chest radiograph, which is defined as "overt parenchymal destruction" (ie, shrinkage and/or emphysematous blebs) totalled 5.5%. In approximately 15% of patients, the hilar nodes were normal radiologically, but pulmonary infiltrates persisted (ie, they evolved into stage 3). Of these stage 3 patients, approximately one-half subsequently resolved spontaneously.

Of the 49 patients with stage 3 pulmonary sarcoidosis, 18 (36.7%) regained normal chest radiographs, most during the first 2 years of observation. Three patients (6.1%) developed stage 4 disease.

Pulmonary diffusion abnormalities commonly detected

Pulmonary studies characteristically reveal restrictive impairment, although an obstructive component involving large and small airways may be more common if sensitive tests are used. Pulmonary diffusion abnormalities are frequent, particularly when there is restrictive impairment.

Ocular Sarcoidosis

Ocular sarcoidosis occurs in approximately 25% of patients
Acute uveitis in approximately 80% of patients

Ocular sarcoidosis is seen in 25 to 50% of patients. Acute uveitis occurs in approximately 80% of patients with ocular sarcoidosis. It is characterized by the sudden appearance of redness of the eye, cloudy vision, photophobia, and epiphora. The pupils are irregular and keratotic precipitates termed "mutton fat" are detected in the anterior chamber.

Posterior chamber involvement is most commonly manifested by chorioretinitis. Neovascularization of the retina is associated with a bad prognosis.

Colorless sarcoid lesions involving conjunctiva are common

The conjunctiva is frequently involved with small, colorless nodules, which on biopsy demonstrate the characteristic histology. In the past, conjunctival biopsy was a favorite site because of the frequent involvement by sarcoidosis.

Heerfordt's syndrome "Uveoparotid fever"

Heerfordt's syndrome (uveoparotid fever), an uncommon presentation of sarcoidosis, is characterized by fever, uveitis, and lacrimal and parotid gland involvement. Erythema nodosum may be present.

Neurologic Sarcoidosis

Involvement of the central nervous system is present in approximately 5% of patients. In addition to eye involvement, the clinical features of central nervous system sarcoidosis include aseptic meningitis, vasculitis with central nervous system ischemia, and in some cases, stroke, focal nervous system mass lesions, cranial and peripheral neuropathies, and muscle involvement.

Aseptic Meningitis

A chronic aseptic meningitis is manifested by headache and, in some cases, by nuchal rigidity and cranial nerve and radicular signs. On rare occasions, patients may develop a communicating hydrocephalus. Analysis of the cerebral spinal fluid demonstrates a mononuclear pleocytosis. Chronic meningeal disease tends to be more severe at the base of the brain, explaining the tendency for cranial nerve, hypothalamic, and pituitary involvement. The meninges overlying the spinal cord may also be affected.

Parenchymal Disease

Space-occupying lesions are infrequent and may produce headaches, lethargy, seizures, hydrocephalus, and papilledema. Granulomatous involvement of the hypothalamic or pituitary regions is associated with hyperprolactinemia, the galactorrhea-amenorrhea syndrome, and diabetes insipidus; hypothalamic hypothyroidism rarely occurs. Involvement of the spinal cord and cerebellum are also rare. Psychiatric manifestations secondary to parenchymal brain sarcoidosis have been reported.

Central nervous system sarcoidosis
Acute and chronic meningeal involvement
Space-occupying lesions infrequent
Hypothalamic and pituitary involvement
Cerebellar involvement rare
Rarely psychiatric involvement

Cranial Nerve Involvement

Neurologic sarcoidosis occurs infrequently.
Cranial nerve involvement:
- *facial*
- *optic*
- *glossopharyngeal*

Facial nerve

Facial nerve involvement is the most common cranial nerve involvement with sarcoidosis. In approximately one-third of cases it may be bilateral. The mechanism of involvement appears to be secondary to sarcoidosis-related chronic aseptic meningitis and inflammation of the nerves.

Optic nerve

Optic nerve involvement is the second most common cranial nerve affected by sarcoidosis. In addition to uveitis and chorioretinitis, patients may develop visual field defects due to inflammation of the optic nerve, optic chiasm, and optic tract. Low vision and field defects are symptoms. Optic neuritis and optic atrophy secondary to granulomatous infiltration may occur.

We have recently evaluated a 49-year-old Caucasian woman with a presumptive diagnosis of neurosarcoidosis. She developed painful nodular lesions on the left lower leg. Biopsy demonstrated a septal panniculitis consistent with erythema nodosum. She was treated with oral prednisone, resulting in the disappearance of the erythema nodosum lesions; she was then referred to Johns Hopkins Hospital for further evaluation. The steroids were completely tapered over several months at which time the patient complained of headaches, a left visual field defect, and right leg numbness and paresthesia. She also developed painful lesions on her anterior left lower leg.

An ophthalmologic evaluation revealed evidence of mild left optic nerve atrophy and a central scotoma consistent with ischemic optic neuropathy; nerve conduction studies demonstrated a right L5 radiculopathy. Chest radiograph, brain magnetic resonance imaging (MRI), and cerebral spinal fluid studies were unremarkable.

Because of patient's clinical signs and symptoms, a presumptive diagnosis of neurosarcoidosis was made and the patient was treated with high-dose oral prednisone with resolution of cutaneous and neurologic signs.

Other cranial nerves

Hoarseness, slurred speech, and swallowing difficulties can be produced by glossopharyngeal, vagus, or hypoglossal nerve involvement. Patients with third nerve lesions complain of diplopia and blurred vision; eighth nerve involvement is characterized by deafness and vestibular complaints. Trigeminal and sixth cranial nerve involvement has also been reported.

Peripheral Neuropathy

Patients may develop peripheral nerve abnormalities in association with entrapment (eg, carpal tunnel syndrome) secondary to granulomatous involvement of cutaneous, intramuscular peripheral nerve bundles or nerve roots or due to extension of disease from spinal cord meninges into proximal nerve roots. Inflammation and granulomatous lesions may involve the epineural and neural spaces, as well as the nerve vasculature. Symptoms occur most often in association with axonal damage and, less frequently, are due to demyelination. Widespread nerve involvement may resemble Guillain-Barré syndrome. Patients may develop focal pain, paresthesias, or weakness. The diagnosis should be considered in patients with respiratory failure that is not explained by the severity of the pulmonary disease.

Neurologic Workup For Sarcoidosis

In patients with aseptic meningitis, enhancement may be seen on MRI scans with gadolinium. Lesions of the brain and spinal cord can be demonstrated on MRI and computed tomography (CT) scans. In these cases, lesion enhancement can also be seen following administration of contrast agents. In some patients with cranial nerve or proximal peripheral nerve root involvement, enhanced MRI may show enhancement along the involved segment of nerve. Patients with peripheral nerve abnormalities should be evaluated with nerve conduction velocity studies and nerve biopsy. Brain stem auditory-evoked responses frequently demonstrate brain stem abnormalities, as well as evidence of a lesion involving the eighth nerve.

Muscle Involvement

*Muscle involvement:
may be asymptomatic or symptomatic
chronic lesions with scarring are recalcitrant to therapy*

Asymptomatic muscle involvement is commonly detected in patients with sarcoidosis and is frequently an incidental finding at autopsy. Symptomatic muscle involvement is rare, characterized by the presence of nodules and an acute and chronic myopathy. Muscle enzymes are elevated and electromyogram studies (EMG) are abnormal. The chronic form of myositis is especially recalcitrant to steroid therapy. Clinically, patients frequently manifest proximal upper or lower extremity weakness that may be difficult to distinguish from steroid-induced myopathy.

Lymphatic Involvement

90% involvement of hilar lymph nodes

As noted above, hilar lymphadenopathy may occur in as many as 90% of sarcoidosis patients. Splenic involvement occurs in 10 to 25% of patients. Peripheral lymphadenopathy is common. These painless nodes are discrete, shotty, freely mobile, and commonly detected in the cervical, inguinal, and epitrochlear areas.

Hepatic Involvement

Frequent subclinical liver involvement

Subclinical liver involvement occurs frequently. Liver biopsies in one study demonstrated approximately 60% positivity.

Heart Involvement

Sudden death may be a sequela of cardiac involvement

The true incidence of involvement of the myocardium with sarcoid granulomas is unknown. One autopsy study demonstrated 27% involvement. Only about 5% of patients are clinically symptomatic. Symptomatic cardiac involvement is associated with sudden death, secondary to a ventricular tachycardia and complete heart block. Pathologic studies reveal ventricular myocardial and endocardial granulomas as well as granulomas involving the conduction system.

Bone Involvement

Bone involvement may occur in as many as 15 to 20% of patients and is generally asymptomatic. Cystic lesions, most commonly detected in the terminal phalanges of the hands and feet, are characteristic, producing a bulbous or sausage-like deformity.

An arthritis clinically reminiscent of rheumatoid arthritis may occur. Clinically, warm, tender joints with effusions may be detected, and this arthritis may be the initial manifestation and antedate the other sarcoid manifestations by years.

Bone involvement: cystic bone involvement of terminal phalanges a rheumatoid-like arthritis

Hypercalcemia

Hypercalcemia occurs in 3 to 25% of patients. It is generally transient but may be persistent, producing nephrocalcinosis and resulting in renal failure and even death. The hypercalcemia is caused by the enhanced gastrointestinal absorption of calcium. This is induced by high levels of 1,25-dihydroxyvitamin D_3. This metabolite also facilitates osteoclastic bone resorption. Pulmonary lavage studies from sarcoidosis patients have demonstrated the presence of this vitamin D metabolite. The origin of this metabolite appears to be activated macrophages at the sites of inflammation (granuloma formation).

Glucocorticosteroid and chloroquine produce reductions in the level of 1,25-dihydroxyvitamin D_3, correcting the hypercalcemia.

Hypocalcemia is variably present Secondary to metabolite of vitamin D_3, produced at least in part by pulmonary macrophages

Pathology

Noncaseating granuloma formation occurs following the aggregation and differentiation of macrophages into epithelioid and multinucleated giant cells. The CD4 T cells are abundant. Fully formed granulomas show a rim of CD4 and CD8 T lymphocytes. The B lymphocytes are present to a lesser extent. Eosinophilia is unusual and serum hypergammaglobulinemia is common.

Fibroblasts, mast cells, collagen fibers, and proteoglycans surround the granuloma. The scar formation resulting from the fibroblastic proliferation produces permanent organ damage.

Pathology: noncaseating granuloma CD4 T cells present

These studies suggest an antigen-driven T-cell immune event. The development of the sarcoidal granuloma involves a T_h1 response characterized by the presence of interferon-γ, interleukin-2, and interleukin-12. Macrophages, T lymphocytes, and possibly mast cells control the fibroblastic response.

Several studies have demonstrated an increase in oligoclonal T cells expressing specific T-cell antigen receptor genes. These studies provide evidence that sarcoidosis is an antigen-driven process, though the nature of the antigen(s) remains unknown.

May be a T-cell driven immune event responsible for the granuloma formation in sarcoidosis

There is also evidence to suggest that sarcoidosis is a disease of immune dysregulation (production of large quantities of interleukin-12, theoretically perpetuating granuloma formation).

Prognosis

Löfgren's syndrome is generally associated with the best prognosis. Approximately 80% of patients with hilar lymphadenopathy without parenchymal lesions (stage 1 disease) spontaneously remit.

Löfgren's syndrome best prognosis

Approximately 50 to 60% of patients with hilar lymphadenopathy and pulmonary infiltrates remit (stage 2 disease), but only 30% of patients with parenchymal disease without adenopathy (stage 3 patients) undergo a spontaneous remission. Those individuals who have involvement of more than three organ systems or stage 3 or 4 pulmonary disease (ie, parenchymal involvement without lymphadenopathy or fibrocystic changes) appear to have the poorest prognosis. In addition, black race origins, onset after the age of 40, and absence of erythema nodosum are associated with poor prognosis. Relapse is common in patients with stage 2 or stage 3 pulmonary disease once therapy is discontinued.

Sarcoidosis patients without erythema nodosum poorer prognosis

Evidence of serum angiotensin-converting enzyme elevation, in contradistinction to previous reports, does not aid in predicting those patients who deteriorate. The enzyme is likely derived from epithelioid cells and thus, is theoretically predictive of the granuloma load in the body. However, its value is limited because of frequent false-negative results and, to a lesser extent, false-positive results.

Serum angiotensin-converting enzyme: theoretically predicts granuloma load problematic because of false-negative and false-positive results

Gallium-67 scanning does not predict those patients who will have a deteriorating disease process and is of limited value. Measurement of the forced vital capacity is generally considered to be the best single test to follow pulmonary sarcoidosis. Carbon monoxide diffusing capacity and exercise testing may also be helpful but are not routinely needed.

Examination of bronchoalveolar lavage has not proved to be a good predictor of the disease course.

At the present time, serial clinical examination of affected organs is the best estimate of prognosis.

Therapy

At present, oral corticosteroids are the first line of treatment in patients with sarcoidosis. Corticosteroids are used to treat patients with ocular, neurologic, cardiac, and pulmonary disease. A large prospective study has confirmed that steroids improve the long-term outcome of patients with stage 2 or 3 pulmonary sarcoidosis.

Neurosarcoidosis is treated with prednisone, 40 to 80 mg per day, with a subsequent taper over 6 weeks to 6 months. Methotrexate and cyclosporine are used to treat recalcitrant disease. Anticonvulsant, antidepressant, and neuroleptic drugs may be necessary to treat seizures and psychiatric manifestations. Patients with hydrocephalus should be evaluated for the placement of a ventriculoperitoneal shunt.

Methotrexate may be effective in treating severe cutaneous sarcoidosis
Results in pulmonary sarcoidosis are controversial and unproven

Methotrexate has been effectively used in the treatment of severe cutaneous and upper respiratory tract sarcoidosis; its benefit in treating pulmonary sarcoidosis is controversial. Ten to 20 mg of oral methotrexate once weekly has been found to have steroid-sparing effects in some patients, although benefits may not be apparent for 6 months.

Cyclosporine not effective except possibly in a few patients with neuro-ocular disease

Cyclosporine has not been shown to be effective in treating pulmonary or systemic sarcoidosis. Furthermore, reports indicate that recurrent sarcoidosis has developed in some recipients of cardiac and bone marrow transplants, despite long-term cyclosporine therapy. Anecdotal case reports suggest that refractory skin lesions, as well as optic neuropathy, may respond to this treatment.

Antimalarials effective in managing cutaneous sarcoidosis

For a number of years, the antimalarials hydroxychloroquine and chloroquine have been successfully used to treat chronic disfiguring skin lesions. These drugs may also be effective in managing of mucosal disease (ie, nasal, sinus, and laryngeal sarcoidosis) and hypercalcemia of sarcoidosis. Quinolone drugs and ketoconazole may also be effective in reducing serum calcium levels.

Inhaled corticosteroids may be of value in treating patients with endobronchial sarcoidosis but are generally ineffective in parenchymal pulmonary sarcoidosis. Mechanical dilatation of bronchial stenosis may, on occasions, be needed. Systemic corticosteroids may be necessary to maintain the patency of the airways. Heart transplantation has been performed in patients with cardiac sarcoidosis who do not respond to corticosteroids, antiarrhythmic agents, implantable pacemakers, and heart failure medications. Implantable cardioverter-defibrillators may prevent sudden death in patients who have developed lethal ventricular arrhythmias associated with sarcoidosis.

Topical corticosteroids have proved effective in the treatment of ocular sarcoidosis.

Annotated Bibliography

Hillerdal G, Nou E, Osterman K, Schmekel B. Sarcoidosis: epidemiology and prognosis of 15-year European study. Am Rev Respir Dis 1984;130:29–32.

This excellent article reviews long-term prognosis of pulmonary sarcoidosis.

Newman LS, Rose CS, Maier LA. Sarcoidosis. N Engl J Med 1997;336:1224–1234.

This is an excellent review article.

Singer FR, Adams JS. Abnormal calcium homeostasis in sarcoidosis. [editorial]. N Engl J Med 1986;315:755–757.

This article reviews hypercalcemia data in sarcoidosis. There is a strong suggestion that pulmonary macrophages are the source of vitamin D metabolite that is responsible for hypercalcemia.

Shammas RL, Movahed A. Sarcoidosis of the heart. Clin Cardiol 1993;16:462–472.

This article provides a good review of the cardiac manifestations of sarcoidosis.

Delaney P. Neurologic manifestations in sarcoidosis: review of literature with a report of 23 cases. Ann Intern Med 1977;87:336–345.

Sharma OP, Sharma AM. Sarcoidosis of the nervous system: a clinical approach. Arch Intern Med 1991;151:1317–1321.

Scott TF. Neurosarcoidosis: progress and clinical aspects. Neurology 1993;43:8–12.

Luke RA, Stern BJ, Krumholz A, Johns CJ. Neurosarcoidosis: the long-term clinical course. Neurology 1987;37:461–463.

These four articles summarize the little appreciated neurologic features of sarcoidosis. The article by Luke et al. summarizes the Johns Hopkins experience.

Parkes SA, Baker SB, Bourdillon RE, et al. Epidemiology of sarcoidosis in the Isle of Man. A case controlled study. Thorax 1987;42:420–426.

Hills SE, Parkes SA, Baker SB. Epidemiology of sarcoidosis in the Isle of Man 2. Evidence for space time clustering. Thorax 1987;42:427–430.

These two articles summarize clustering studies on the Isle of Man in the United Kingdom.

Burke WMJ, Keogh A, Maloney PJ, et al. Transmission of sarcoidosis via cardiac transplantation. Lancet 1990;336:1579.

Heyll A, Meckenstock G, Aul C, et al. Possible transmission of sarcoidosis via allogeneic bone marrow transplantation. Bone Marrow Transplant 1994;14:161–164.

These are two provocative articles that question the infectious nature of sarcoidosis.

Harrington DW, Major M, Rybicki B, et al. Familial sarcoidosis: analysis of 91 families. Sarcoidosis 1994;11:240–243.

Brennan NJ, Crean P, Long JP, et al. High prevalence of familial sarcoidosis in an Irish population. Thorax 1984;39:14–18.

These two articles demonstrate the clustering of cases of sarcoidosis among siblings of affected individuals.

Moller DR. Etiology of sarcoidosis. Clin Chest Med 1997;18:695–706.

This a well-written article reviews the possible etiologies for sarcoidosis. One hundred eleven references are cited.

Johns CJ, Michele TM. The clinical management of sarcoidosis. A 50 year experience at the Johns Hopkins Hospital. Medicine (Baltimore) 1999;78:65–111.

A scholarly review of therapeutic approaches to sarcoidosis by an eminent physician.

CHAPTER 47

Septicemia

Paul G. Auwaerter, M.D., Thomas T. Provost, M.D.

Cutaneous manifestations of septicemia are the result of a disseminated intravascular coagulopathy, direct blood vessel invasion, immune complex vasculitis, septic emboli, and the toxic effects of the infectious disease process on the vascular system.

Intravascular Coagulopathy

Purpura Fulminans

Most common in children, secondary to infections caused by:
- *group A β-hemolytic streptococci*
- *varicella*
- *staphylococci*
- *pneumococci*
- *meningococci*

This is an uncommon hemorrhagic infarction of the skin, the result of a disseminated intravascular coagulopathy. The disease process is most common in children but can affect adults. In a study of 100 cases, the age range was from birth to 74 years, with a median age of 46 months. The disease appears to occur more commonly in the winter and spring. Group A β hemolytic streptococcal infection (scarlet fever) commonly preceded purpura fulminans in the past. A preceding upper respiratory infection and varicella infection has also been detected. Staphylococcal, pneumococcal, and meningococcal bacteremias have also been associated.

Cutaneous Manifestations

Hemorrhagic infarction

The cutaneous hemorrhagic infarction has a tendency to be symmetric and to most commonly involve the lower extremities (also called symmetric gangrene). The buttocks, thighs, ankles, upper extremities, and abdomen are also frequently involved, but the chest and head are unusual sites of involvement excepting the tip of the nose.

Amputations and/or extensive skin grafts commonly needed

The individual skin lesions are characterized by a localized, massive ecchymosis, sharply demarcated from normal-appearing skin. A narrow, erythematous border may be detected. Necrosis with sterile blister formation is common. Involvement of the feet, hands, and digits may produce acrocyanosis. In more severe cases, the rapid development of gangrene (symmetric, peripheral gangrene) occurs, necessitating amputation. In one review of 100 cases, 19% needed amputation. Skin grafting is also frequently required to correct the large defects created by the infarctive disease process.

Significant mortality despite heparin and antibiotic therapy

In addition to the very striking and alarming cutaneous manifestations, these patients often develop hypovolemic shock. In the past, mortality had been reported to be as high as 90%. However, with aggressive treatment of shock, antibiotic therapy, and heparin, mortality has fallen below 20%.

Hematologic Findings

A leukocytosis often greater than 20,000 per mm^3 with a shift to the left and thrombocytopenia are frequent findings along with anemia, especially following hydration. A smear of the peripheral blood usually demonstrates features of microangiopathic hemolytic anemia, characterized by the presence of schistocytes (burr and helmet cells).

Coagulation abnormalities characterized by a prolonged bleeding and clotting time may lead to hemorrhage. The prothrombin time and the partial thromboplastin time may be prolonged in approximately 80% of patients. Varying degrees of hypofibrinogenemia can be found. Coagulation factors V, VII, and VIII are depressed, and fibrin split degradation products are often observed.

Features of a disseminated intravascular coagulopathy detected

Annotated Bibliography

Spicer TE, Rau JM. Purpura fulminans. Am J Med 1976;61:566–571.

This is an excellent review.

Coumadin Necrosis

Rarely, patients given Coumadin therapy may develop lesions similar to purpura fulminans. These patients, usually women, have a deficiency of a vitamin K–dependent anticoagulant, termed "protein C." With the initiation of Coumadin therapy, a transient state of hypercoagulability occurs due to the fact that protein C anticoagulant levels decrease more rapidly than vitamin K–dependent coagulation factors, producing a transient state of relative hypercoagulability. Biopsies demonstrate thrombin clots in affected blood vessels.

Protein C deficiency

Most recent data indicate a functional deficiency of protein C may have an etiopathologic role in the thrombotic lesions of calciphylaxis. See Chapter 32, "Evaluation and Treatment of Endocrine Disorders," for further discussion.

Direct Blood Vessel Bacterial Invasion

Purpura

In contradistinction to purpura fulminans, purpuric lesions associated with septicemia often contain bacteria. An accompanying disseminated intravascular coagulopathy may be present. Biopsy of the involved area may reveal fibrin thrombi and hemorrhage, as well as bacteria (Figures 47–1 and 47–2).

Fibrin thrombi

Meningococcemia (*Neisseria meningitidis*) is the most well-recognized bacterial infection presenting with purpuric lesions. Generalized macular, papular, pruritic lesions rapidly evolve and are associated with a good deal of cutaneous pain. Hemorrhagic vesicles may also be seen. Characteristically, necrosis of individual lesions occurs. This condition may be associated with the Waterhouse-Friderichsen syndrome or adrenal crisis as the result of overwhelming sepsis precipitating bilateral hemorrhagic infarction of the adrenal glands.

Adrenal hemorrhage and necrosis

In addition to meningococcemia, *Streptococcus pneumoniae* can also cause widespread purpuric lesions associated with coagulopathy. Asplenic patients are at increased risk.

Asplenia associated with increased risk

Ecthyma Gangrenosum

Ecthyma gangrenosum is a characteristic manifestation of *Pseudomonas* septicemia (Figures 47–3 and 47–4). These cutaneous manifestations are the result of bacterial invasion of the walls of small arteries and veins. The endothelial surface of the blood vessel is rarely involved, and thrombosis is not a feature. The blood vessel walls are destroyed by the inflammatory infiltrate resulting in extravasation of red blood cells, edema, and necrosis. Ischemia due to the inter-

Pseudomonas septicemia

Black eschar

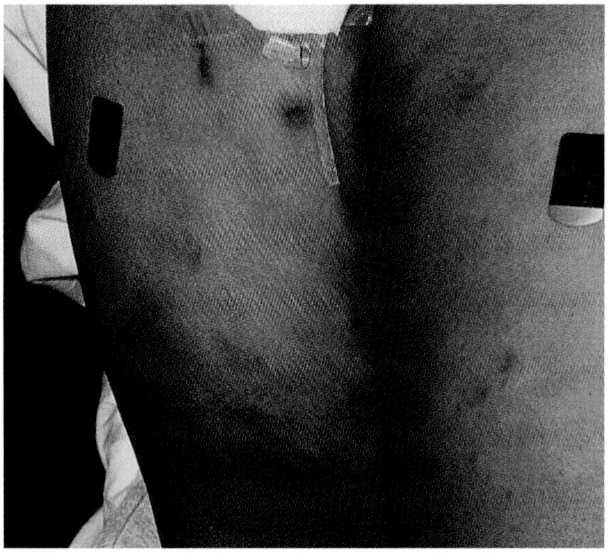

FIGURE 47–1 Purpuric lesions in the upper legs of a patient with meningococcemia.

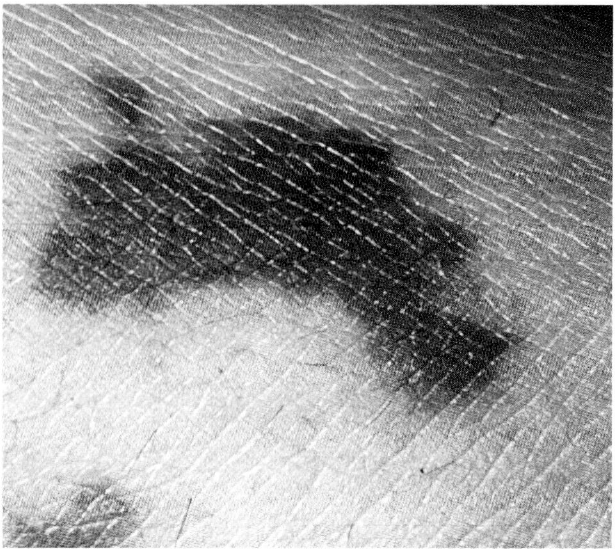

FIGURE 47–2 Hemorrhagic infarctive lesion in a patient with meningococcemia.

ruption of the blood supply to the area further complicates the situation. Bullae, hemorrhagic cellulitis, and gangrenous changes occur. The typical skin lesions evolve with erythema, edema, and nodular formation, followed by a central hemorrhagic vesicle. Ulceration occurs, producing a dense, black necrotic base.

A smear of the vesicle fluid will demonstrate prominent gram-negative rods. Granulocyte and inflammatory responses are minimal.

May also be seen with other gram-negative organisms

Although ecthyma gangrenosum lesions are most frequently observed with *Pseudomonas* infection, they also have been associated with other gram-negative organisms, as well as disseminated infections caused by *Candida*.

Disseminated Fungal Infections

Associated with immunosuppression

Candida albicans and other opportunistic fungi may produce septic embolization. These infections are increaseingly common as the use of immunosuppressive agents has become more widespread frequently recognized. It may be a lethal complication. Macronodular lesions are reported in approximately 10%

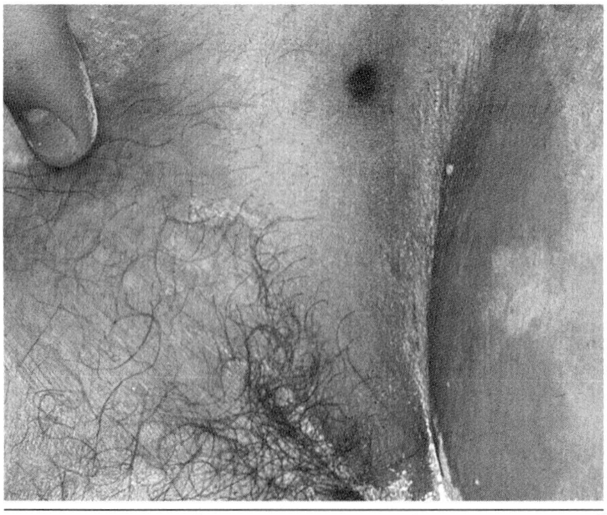

FIGURE 47–3 Ecthyma gangrenosum lesion in groin of patient with *Pseudomonas* septicemia. Note black necrotic area with surrounding erythema.

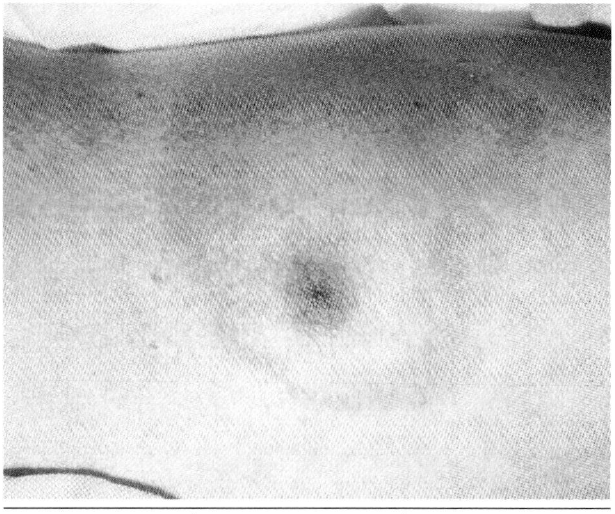

FIGURE 47–4 Ecthyma gangrenosum lesion on an extremity of patient with *Pseudomonas* infection. Note area of necrosis and surrounding erythema.

of patients with disseminated candidiasis. Nodules are firm, raised, and well-circumscribed, with pale centers that may hemorrhage rarely resembling ecthyma gangrenosum. Examination of skin biopsies demonstrate, in the mid- and lower dermis, hyphae occurring both inside and outside blood vessels. *Aspergillus* and *Mucor* species have a predilection for angioinvasion especially in immunocompromised patients. Lesions may develop a blackened eschar after an initial infarction of the skin causing little inflammation (Figure 47–5).

Biopsies demonstrate organisms

Rickettsial Infections

The most severe of the rickettsial infections is Rocky Mountain spotted fever. The disease is caused by *Rickettsia rickettsii* which is transmitted via a tick bite. In the western part of the United States, the wood tick *Dermacentor andersoni* is the vector; in the eastern United States, it is the dog tick *Dermacentor variabilis*.

The disease process usually begins with fever, chills, myalgias, arthralgias, and a severe headache. The organisms invade the blood vessel endothelial cells and multiply. Ultimately, destruction of the media and intima of the blood vessels occurs, producing thrombosis, microinfarctions, and extravasation of red blood cells.

The characteristic dermatitis usually begins on the third or fourth day of illness, initially on the ankles and feet, spreading to the wrists and hands and then to the trunk and head. Individual lesions begin as macules, evolve within hours into papules that then become purpuric. Scrotal and a vulvar involvement are characteristic.

Classic dermatitis begins on periphery and spreads centrally.

Biopsies will demonstrate, by direct immunofluorescence, the presence of coccobacillary rickettsiae in the walls of affected blood vessels.

Direct invasion of affected blood vessel walls by coccobacillary rickettsiae

Severe infections have a tendency to be more widespread and their progression is much more rapid.

Immune Complex–Mediated Vasculitis

It is conceivable that chronic infections such as chronic meningococcemia, as well as the gonococcal cutaneous arthritis syndrome, induced by *Neisseria gonorrhoeae*, are associated with immune complex formation.

Chronic Meningococcemia

Chronic meningococcemia is rare. Recurrent crops of erythematous, macular, papular lesions occur. In addition, erythema nodosum–like lesions have been detected. Petechiae with vesicular pustular lesions, as well as ulcerations, have been detected.

Biopsies, in contradistinction to acute meningococcemia, which demonstrates many organisms, generally fail to demonstrate the presence of meningococcal bacteria. A leukocytoclastic angiitis has been reported.

May be seen in association with a homozygous deficiency of a terminal complement component

Gonococcal Arthritis Syndrome

The gonococcal cutaneous arthritis syndrome is found predominantly in women who have a chronic gonococcal infection, characterized by a vaginal discharge and proctitis (secondary to the fact that lymphatic drainage from the vagina is perirectal). Frequently, these patients are asymptomatic. Dissemination occurs especially during pregnancy or menses.

Occurs during menses and pregnancy

May be associated with signs and symptoms of a proctitis

The dermatitis is characterized by tender, inflammatory macules that rapidly develop a papular vesicular component (Figure 47–6). They may become hemorrhagic and pustular. Necrosis occurs on a hemorrhagic base. These lesions usually number less than 10 and are generally seen distal to the elbows and knees. Biopsy demonstrates features consistent with a leukocytoclastic vasculitis. In general, few or no organisms are demonstrated, but immunofluorescent studies will frequently demonstrate the presence of gonococcal antigen. In addition, serum immune complexes have been demonstrated in patients with this disseminated gonococcal arthritis syndrome.

Tender, papular, pustular necrotic lesions

Septic Embolization

SBE cutaneous manifestations most probably due to immune complex formation

Studies of subacute bacterial endocarditis (SBE) have established that septic emboli and/or immune complexes involving bacterial organisms are capable of inducing purpuric, pustular, and erythematous lesions in the skin (Figures 47–5 to 47–8). In addition, Osler's nodes and Janeway lesions may develop. Furthermore, retinal hemorrhagic lesions (Roth's spots) may be observed. Petechiae are also common. Splinter hemorrhages of the fingernails, especially those involving the mid one-third of the nail, are manifestations. (In general, splinter hemorrhages, especially those on the outer one-third of the nail, are due to trauma.)

Typical Osler's nodes are characterized by transient, painful, erythematous, nodular lesions with a pale center ranging in size from several millimeters to 1 cm. They are usually localized to the finger and toe pads and, to a lesser extent, the palms and soles.

Biopsies demonstrate microemboli in adjacent arterials, as well as microabscess formation. Bacterial smears reveal gram-positive cocci. Also, a leukocytoclastic angiitis has been described.

Janeway lesions are painless, purpuric, erythematous lesions that, on biopsy, demonstrate a neutrophilic infiltrate of capillaries and tissue microabscess formation. Gram stains demonstrate gram-positive cocci.

Cutaneous manifestations associated with acute bacterial endocarditis most probably due to septic emboli

It appears likely that Osler's nodes and Janeway lesions are very closely related. Immune complex formation involving bacterial antigens is a likely explanation, at least in SBE. Septic embolization may be the etiology in acute bacterial endocarditis. The main morphologic difference is likely due to the site of cutaneous immune-complex deposition or embolization. In Janeway lesions, the site of pathology appears to involve more superficial blood vessels, resulting in purpuric lesions, whereas in Osler's nodes, the lesions may be deeper in the dermis, resulting in a nodular formation.

Toxin Effects on Vasculature

The vascular effect of toxins produces many of the cutaneous manifestations associated with the following diseases: scarlet fever (see Chapter 48, "Streptococcal Infections"), toxic shock syndrome (see Chapter 49, "Staphylococcal Infections"), scalded skin syndrome (see Chapter 49, "Staphylococcal Infections"), and Kawasaki's disease (see Chapter 12, "Vasculitis").

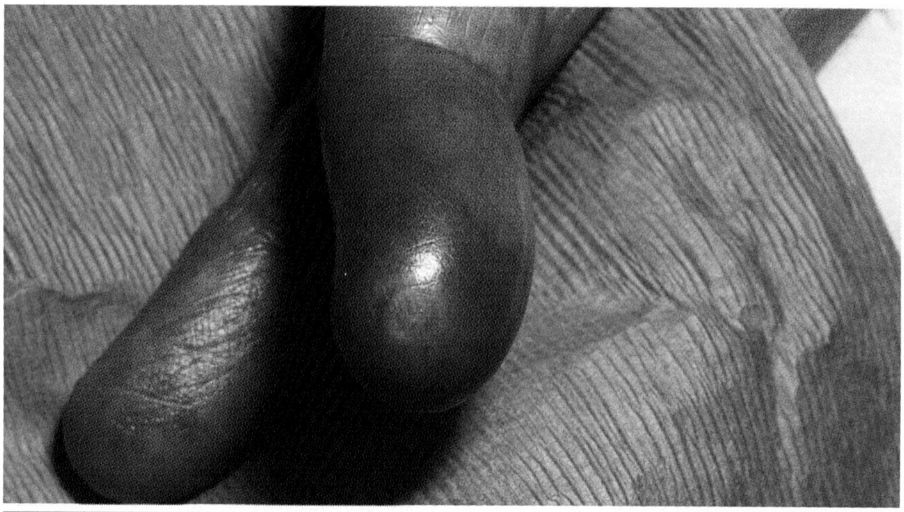

FIGURE 47–5 Septic embolization to the tip of the finger. Note pale center with surrounding erythema. The organism responsible is from the genus *Aspergillus*.

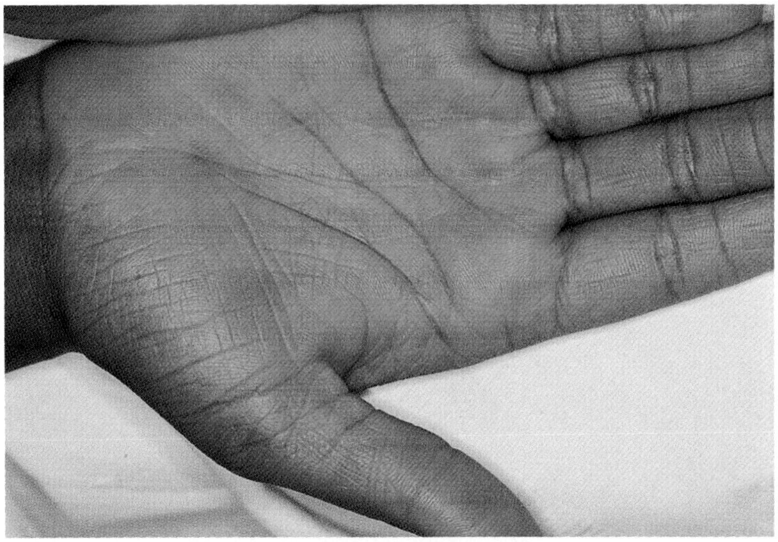

FIGURE 47–6 Macular, erythematous, tender lesions on the palmar surface in a woman with the gonococcal arthritis syndrome.

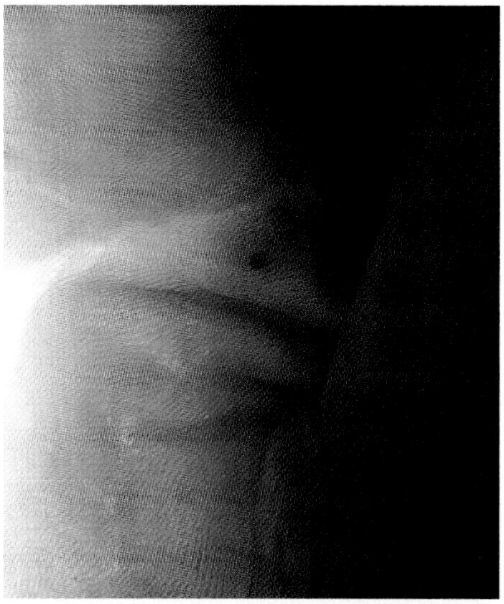

FIGURE 47–7 Septic embolic lesion on the hand of a patient with subacute bacterial endocarditis.

The toxic shock syndrome, which is due to toxins elaborated by a staphylococcal infection, was originally detected in women using tampons. This fulminant infection may cause altered mental status, and liver and renal dysfunction. However, this syndrome may be seen in the absence of either tampons or menstruation and can occur in children and men with staphylococcal or streptococcal infections. In fact, the nonmenstruating form of the disease is now the dominant form of the disease. A skin rash is almost universal and is characterized as a diffuse, macular erythroderma, fading in 3 to 4 days. A patchy desquamation with prominent peeling of the skin over the fingers, palms, and soles then occurs.

Biopsies demonstrate vascular dilatation with perivascular edema.

Annotated Bibliography

Kingston ME, Mackey D. Skin clues in the diagnosis of life-threatening infections. Rev Infect Dis 1986;8;1–11.

This valuable, readable article combines a clinical approach with pathophysiologic mechanisms to explain the cutaneous manifestations seen in septicemia.

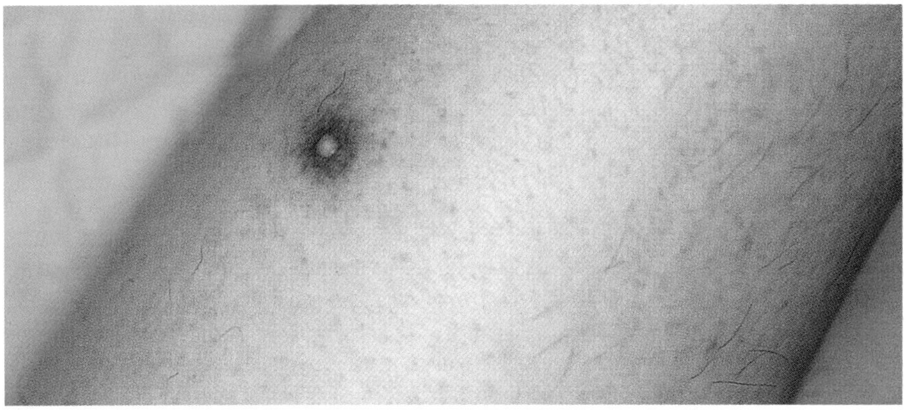

FIGURE 47–8 Embolic infarctive lesion in a woman with bowel bypass syndrome. Showers of painful embolic lesions associated with bacterial overgrowth in the gastrointestinal tract occurred.

CHAPTER 48

Streptococcal Infections

Paul G. Auwaerter, M.D., Thomas T. Provost, M.D.

Group A β-hemolytic streptococci (GAS) produce many types of infections, including impetigo, ecthyma, cellulitis, and pharyngitis. In addition, scarlet fever, glomerulonephritis (poststreptococcal glomerulonephritis [PSGN]), rheumatic fever, and toxic shock syndrome are among the serious potential sequelae.

Scarlet fever, glomerulonephritis, and rheumatic fever are serious sequelae.

Serologic groups A-T (Lancefield's classification) are based on different carbohydrate antigens in the bacterial cell wall. Almost all group A streptococci produce β-hemolysins. Group A streptococci infections are the most common, although other streptococci are also capable of producing a wide variety of infections. In this chapter, discussion will be limited to GAS.

Rheumatic Fever and Glomerulonephritis

Site of infection influences immunologic responses and sequelae.

Rheumatic fever associated with streptococcal pharyngitis

Most common site of nephrogenic streptococcal infection is the skin. Occult or neglected pyodermas problematic

Group A β-hemolytic streptococci are spread by person-to-person contact. Oral pharyngeal colonization (a carrier state) may occur in the absence of signs of infection. Furthermore, the site of infection influences the development of complications as well as the immunologic responses to streptococci. For example, acute rheumatic fever generally occurs 2 to 3 weeks following a GAS pharyngitis, whereas it does not occur following cutaneous streptococcal infections. By contrast, acute PSGN occurs after a latent period of approximately 10 days following either streptococcal infection of the skin (usual source) or a pharyngitis.

ASO titers are elevated in pharyngeal infections.

ASO titers feeble in streptococcal pyodermas; anti-DNAase B and antihyaluronidase titers are prominent.

The immunologic hallmark of streptococcal upper respiratory tract infection is the development of an antistreptolysin O (ASO) antibody titer. In contrast, the ASO titer following a streptococcal pyoderma is typically minimal, whereas the anti-DNAase B and antihyaluronidase titers are elevated. The reasons for these discordant immunologic responses are unknown. At least 90% of patients with PSGN have increased anti-DNAase B and antihyaluronidase titers (suggesting pyoderma as the source of the nephrogenic strain).

Fibrillar structures on the streptococci are the site of the antigens detected in the M subtyping of streptococci.

Subtyping of streptococcal M proteins (fibrillar structures on the surface of streptococci) demonstrate that type 12 infections of the pharynx and, to a lesser extent, types 1, 4, 25, and 49 are associated with the development of an acute nephritis. The pyoderma-associated streptococcal nephritic strains are 2, 49, 55, 57, and 60. An estimated 10% of sporadic infections with a nephrogenic strain result in acute glomerulonephritis. However, epidemics associated with a particular nephrogenic strain have been reported, and PSGN appears to occur in 6-year cycles on the Caribbean island of Trinidad.

Occult or neglected pyoderma are the dominant sites of infection antedating the development of acute glomerulonephritis. Dillon and Reeves documented, in a large study of a pediatric patient population at the University of Alabama, that 130 of 152 patients (85%) with acute glomerulonephritis had streptococcal pyoderma. Furthermore, 112 (73%) had pyoderma alone, whereas only 22 (14%) had a streptococcal upper respiratory infection.

The acute nephritis is usually self-limited, with 95% of patients demonstrating normal renal function within 2 years. Chronic progressive renal disease is very rare, and when it does occur, antecedent renal disease rather than poststreptococcal glomerulonephritis may be more responsible.

Acute post-streptococcal glomerulonephritis is a transient, self-limited disease that rarely progresses to chronic renal disease
Immune complex–mediated.

The pathophysiologic mechanism responsible for the acute glomerulonephritis is immune complex formation. Immunofluorescent and immunoelectron microscopic studies demonstrate deposition of immune complexes within the glomeruli.

See Chapter 14, "Rheumatic Fever," for discussion.

Cutaneous Manifestations of Group A β-Hemolytic Streptococci

Impetigo

Highly communicable impetigo lesions due to *Streptococcus pyogenes* are commonly overgrown with *Staphylococcus aureus* and in older lesions potentially obscure the presence of a streptococcal infection.

Crowded living conditions and neglected personal hygiene are responsible for spread of streptococcal infection in families. Furthermore, *S. pyogenes* may infect cutaneous lesions due to, for example, abrasions, eczema, and varicella.

Common form of streptococcal infection

Older lesions may be superinfected with staphylococci.

Individual impetiginous lesions begin as small vesicles surrounded by erythema. The vesicles and pustules eventually rupture producing a thin golden-yellow, stuck-on crust. These lesions, usually measuring approximately 0.5 cm in diameter, can occur on any part of the body but most commonly are found on the extremities and face. Lesions will spontaneously resolve in 2 to 3 weeks.

Gram stain of vesicular fluid will reveal gram-positive cocci, and bacterial culture will yield GAS readily.

Some strains resistant to erythromycin

The standard treatment is penicillin for 10 days. If the patient is allergic to penicillin, erythromycin 250 mg four times a day can be substituted; however, some streptococcal strains are now resistant to erythromycin.

Because of the possible sequela of acute glomerulonephritis, topical antibiotics do not have a role in the treatment of proven streptococcal impetigo. As a preventative strategy, abrasions, insect bites, and eczematous lesions may be treated with topical bacitracin, neomycin, and polymyxin B.

Ecthyma

Ecthyma is similar to impetigo but extends deeper into the dermis. Ecthyma exhibits a necrotic base, and a prominent eschar is characteristic. Acute glomerulonephritis can also be a sequela of streptococcal ecthyma (Figure 48–1).

Erysipelas

Erysipelas is due to GAS and can occur in all age groups, although diabetics, alcoholics, patients with chronic venous or lymphatic obstruction, and patients receiving immunosuppressive therapy appear to be at increased risk. In many cases, the initial portal of entry is not detected.

Occurs on face
Sharply demarcated
Raised, painful, erythematous lesion
Associated with systemic toxicity

Erysipelas is characterized by brawny induration of involved skin producing a "peau d'orange" appearance. The lesion is erythematous, sharply demarcated, and painful to touch. Constitutional symptoms, including fever, rigors, and chills are observed. Prominent petechiae and hemorrhagic bullae may develop. The most common site is the nose and malar eminence, but erysipelas may occur on all areas of the body.

Cellulitis

Cellulitis is a common form of GAS (Figure 48–2). It is characterized by erythema, edema, and tenderness. On the fingers, blisters may form (usually seen in children). Cellulitis may occur on all areas of the body but most commonly on the lower extremities. Lymphatic streaking and lymphadenitis in the regional drainage of involved skin are common. Streptococcal cellulitis may occur as a postoperative wound infection, and outbreaks have been noted in hospitals that were traced to the streptococcal carrier state in medical personnel.

Common site of infection lower extremities
Sites of chronic lymphatic obstruction (areas of lipodermal sclerosis)
Venous insufficiency
Portal of entry the feet

Venous insufficiency with chronic edema in the legs associated with dermal sclerosis is particularly predisposing to GAS infection. The sclerosis (lipodermal sclerosis) produces obstruction of normal lymphatic and venous drainage. It is theorized that streptococcal organisms then gain entry via abrasions on the soles of the feet or the toe webs. The normal clearance of these organisms is impaired by the poor lymphatic and venous drainage (locus minoris resistentiae) resulting in a range of cellulitis from low-grade to fulminant infection.

Saphenous vein donor site especially problematic for the development of streptococcal cellulitis

In our experience, this type of complication is not an uncommon postsurgical complication in patients with a total knee replacement or at donor sites for saphenous veins.

Streptococcal Gangrene

Streptococcal septicemia still associated with significant mortality.

Streptococcal gangrene is severe form of cellulitis characterized by fibrinoid necrosis and formation of fibrin thrombi in small blood vessels, producing widespread necrosis. These infections are associated with septicemia, toxemia, and hypotension. In the preantibiotic era, mortality was very high. Today, streptococcal infections with an associated septicemia still carry a significant mortality.

At times, streptococcal infections that enter systemic circulation may result in disseminated intravascular coagulopathy producing cutaneous necrosis (purpura fulminans).

Scarlet Fever

Both GAS pharyngitis and pyodermas may be associated with a generalized erythema and, at times, severe toxicity. There are three clinical types of scarlet fever:

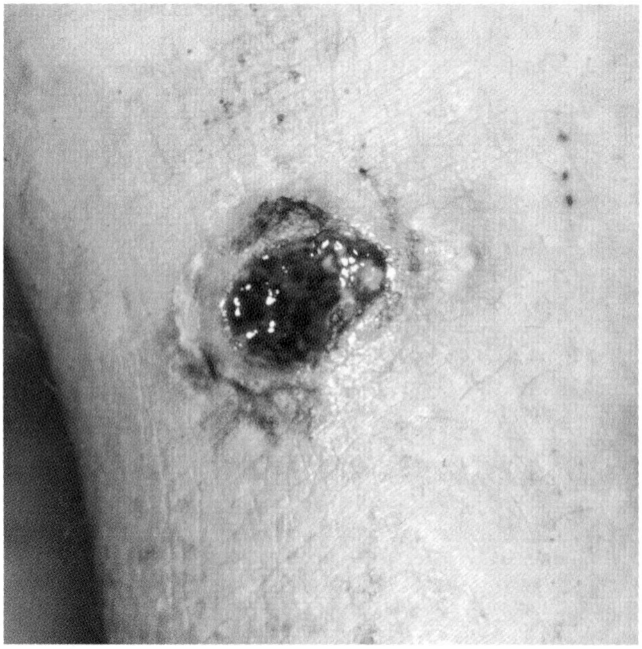

FIGURE 48–1 Ecthyma lesion in patient with acute glomerulonephritis. Group A β-hemolytic streptococci were recovered from this lesion.

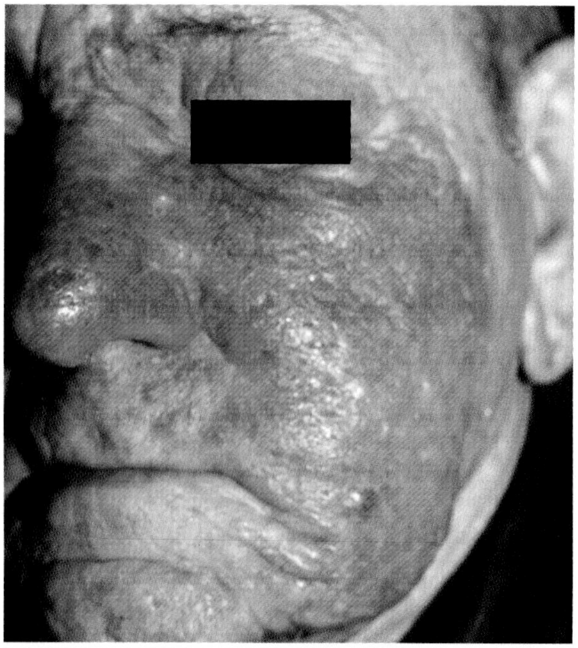

FIGURE 48–2 Streptococcal cellulitis in an alcoholic. (Reproduced with permission from: Courtesy Rick Stearns, M.D., Tulsa, OK)

a benign scarlet fever, a scarlet fever with local suppuration and invasions of the deep structures of the neck, and a malignant scarlet fever characterized by hyperpyrexia (107°F), neurologic complications, and cardiovascular collapse. Most of the deaths occur with the latter type of scarlet fever. A diffuse, erythematous eruption may be produced by certain strains of erythrogenic toxins (type A, B, C, SSA, and MF) of strains of group A streptococci. These toxins are encoded by lysogenic bacteriophages.

Scarlet fever virulent form of streptococcal infection Associated with release of erythrogenic toxins.

Scarlet fever classically occurs in children. Within 48 hours of the onset of pharyngeal symptomatology, the patient develops fever, malaise, nausea and vomiting, headache, generalized lymphadenopathy, and a widespread, erythematous, macular eruption. Examination of the pharynx demonstrates beefy red edematous tonsils, uvula, and palate. A yellowish-white exudate on the tonsils is characteristic. In the pre-antibiotic era, severe edema at the base of the tongue (quinsy) produced life-threatening airway obstruction. Tender or even fluctuant anterocervical lymphadenopathy can be noted. The tongue becomes red with prominent papillae, giving it a strawberry appearance.

Severe systemic toxicity

An erythematous, macular dermatitis generally begins on the neck and rapidly involves the entire body. Numerous small 1- to 2-mm papular, erythematous lesions have led to the description of a sandpaper-like effect. The erythema is blanchable by pressure. Linear petechial lesions are detected in the antecubital fossa and axillary folds (Pastia's lines).

Desquamation characteristically begins on the face and then spreads to the trunk and extremities following the macular, papular erythema. Large desquamating sheets typically occur on the hands and feet.

Historically, physicians used bacterial cultures and the Dick test. The latter involved an intercutaneous injection of 0.1 mL of erythrogenic toxin that was deemed positive if greater than 1.0 cm of an area of local erythema developed at 24 hours. This positive reaction indicated that the individual lacked immunity and, therefore, was at risk of developing scarlet fever. The Schultz-Charlton test was another diagnostic test used in patients with suspected scarlet fever. This test used 0.1 mL of antitoxin that was injected into the erythematous dermatitis. The subsequent occurrence of blanching within 12 to 24 hours was considered diagnostic.

Dick test
Shultz-Charlton test

Scarlet fever was a much feared illness in the 1800s and early 1900s with significant mortality (as high as 25%). For example, in one epidemic in Baltimore, Maryland, in the 1870s, over 500 patients died. Differences in the erythrogenic toxins elaborated by the offending *S. pyogenes* and their differing abilities to act as superantigens that stimulate an intense cytokine cascade by T lymphocytes may explain the decline in severity of scarlet fever in contemporary times. This hypothesis is supported by recent data indicating the association of mild scarlet fever associated with the erythrogenic toxin C, whereas erythrogenic toxin A was associated with the more virulent forms of scarlet fever in the past. The recent emergence of virulent stains of streptococci ("flesh-eating") may be due to the toxins elaborated.

Penicillin, given early in the disease, produces clearance of GAS in the oropharyngeal region or cutaneous infection, as well as in the associated toxemia.

Other Infections

On unusual occasions, streptococcal infections may be associated with a toxic shock–like syndrome, which is more commonly associated with *S. aureus* infection. The relationship of this toxin-mediated entity to the scarlet fever syndrome is unclear. A mortality rate as high as 30% has been reported despite aggressive therapy. (For discussion of toxic shock syndrome and citations of toxic shock syndrome associated with a *S. pyogenes* infection, see Chapter 49, "Staphylococcal Infections.")

Psoriasis

Erythrogenic toxins are produced by the majority of group A β-hemolytic streptococci. Once exposed, patients produce a neutralizing antibody. It is conceivable that this immune reaction in the skin involving the erythrogenic toxin and its cognant antibody could trigger the development of psoriatic lesions (Koebner's phenomenon). Another theory of the pathogenesis of psoriasis in patients with streptococcal pharyngitis involves the superantigen-induced cytokine cascade activated by the streptococci toxin.

Annotated Bibliography

Potter EV, Abidh S, Sharrett AR, et al. Clinical healing 2 to 6 years after post streptococcal glomerulonephritis in Trinidad. N Engl J Med 1978;298:767–772.

This study demonstrates that 1.8% of 760 patients with acute PSGN had persistence of urine abnormalities 2 years following their disease. This study demonstrates a low-incidence chronicity for acute PSGN.

Kurtzman D. Does acute post streptococcal glomerulonephritis lead to chronic renal disease N Engl J Med 1978;298:795–796.

This is an editorial to the article by Potter et al. reviewing all the data regarding the chronicity following acute PSGN. Kurtzman believes that most patients, both children and adults, with acute PSGN will recover completely, if they have had no pre-existing renal disease.

Dillon HC, Reeves MS, Maxted WR. Acute glomerulonephritis following skin infection due to streptococci of M-type 2. Lancet 1968;1:543–545.

One of a series of articles by Dillon and colleagues link the association of certain S. pyogenes *serologic types with the development of acute glomerulonephritis. These and other studies have demonstrated that 85 to 90% of acute PSGN are associated with a pyoderma, usually impetigo contagiosa.*

Kaplan EL, Anthony BF, Chapman B, et al. The influence of the site of infection on immune response to group A streptococci. J Clin Invest 1970;49:1405–1414.

This study is one of several demonstrating that following GAS upper respiratory tract infection, the ASO antibody response is strong, whereas in streptococcal skin infections, this antibody response is very weak.

Dillon HC, Reeves MSA. Streptococcal immune responses in the nephritis after skin infection. Am J Med 1974;56:333–346.

This is an additional study further demonstrating differences in immune responses to S. pyogenes. *In this study, anti-DNAase B titers were elevated in over 90% of patients with acute glomerulonephritis. Sequential studies demonstrated that the anti-DNAase B titer arose more often and persisted longer than the ASO titer in patients with pyoderma and acute glomerulonephritis.*

Wesselhoeft C, Weinstein L. Scarlet fever. N Engl J Med 1945;232:500–505.

This is a classic paper.

Stevens DL. Streptococcal toxic shock syndrome associated with necrotizing fascitis. Ann Rev Med 2000;51:271–288.

A current update on the syndrome by a leading investigator in the field.

Stevens DL. Rationale for the use of intravenous gamma globulin in the treatment of streptococcal toxic shock syndrome. Clin Infect Dis 1998;26(3):639–641.

Balanced discussion of why gamma globulin is one of the few active interventions that may make a difference in patient outcome.

CHAPTER 49

Staphylococcal Infections

Paul G. Auwaerter, M.D., Thomas T. Provost, M.D.

Staphylococci belong to the Micrococcaceae family. There are two genera: *Micrococcus* and the *Staphylococcus*. *Staphylococcus aureus* is clinically the most important pathogen. Its importance continues to grow due to the ever-increasing emergence of methicillin-resistant *S. aureus* (MRSA) strains. The term "aureus" was originally derived from the observation of bright, golden-yellow pigment detected in blood agar medium surrounding the colony of *S. aureus*. However, now the term is applied to all staphylococcal strains producing coagulase (an enzyme which plays an important role in the virulence of the organism). Coagulase-negative *Staphylococcus epidermidis* is a common culture contaminant but may be a significant pathogen in prosthetic valve endocarditis, cerebral fluid shunt infections, and prosthetic joint infections.

Staphylococci that are coagulase-positive are termed S. aureus.

S. aureus colonizes the skin and mucous membrane in more than 25% of adults. The organism is generally spread via hand contact and can quickly invade through minor breaks in the integument. The capsule of the staphylococci interferes with complement activation, thereby inhibiting opsonization and phagocytosis of the bacteria.

Cell capsule prevents complement-mediated opsonization and phagocytosis.

In addition to the capsule, certain extracellular enzymes secreted by *S. aureus* are part of an important virulence strategy by this bacteria. For example, there are the enterotoxins associated with food poisoning and exotoxins, such as the toxic shock syndrome toxin (TSST-1), which behaves as a superantigen, and exfoliative toxins A and B that are responsible for staphylococcal scalded skin syndrome (SSS). The exfoliative toxins were previously designated exfoliatin or epidermolysin.

Staphylococcal exotoxins are important in pathogenesis of staphylococcal scalded skin syndrome and staphylococcal toxic shock syndrome.

The Carrier State

The staphylococcal carrier state plays a significant epidemiologic role in staphylococcal infections. Normal persons may have significant numbers of staphylococci in their nose and throat. In addition, atopic eczema and hyper-IgE syndrome patients have increased *S. aureus* colonization on the skin. The factor responsible for staphylococcal colonization in the nares of some persons is unknown. However, these colonizing bacteria are of clinical importance, since the staphylococci present in the nose and throat may be identical to the staphylococci isolated from the bloodstream of septicemic patients. Individuals at increased risk for developing staphylococcal cutaneous infections are those who regularly receive injections (eg, diabetics, drug addicts) and those with indwelling intravenous lines. A staphylococcal carrier state in medical personnel also has been implicated in neonatal nursery epidemics of staphylococcal scalded skin syndrome.

The carrier state is an important source of infection not only to the carrier but also to others.

The use of needles by S. aureus carrier puts them at increased risk of cutaneous infection.

Clinical Features

Meningococcemia-like picture

The clinical features associated with *S. aureus* include impetigo as well as a variety of soft tissue infections: furuncles and carbuncles, cellulitis, lymphangitis, and lymphadenitis (Figures 49–1 and 49–2). Furthermore, extension of infections through the skin can produce bacteremia and subsequent endocarditis, osteomyelitis, or septic arthritis. *S. aureus* bacteremia/septicemia is a serious illness that may be characterized by high fevers and shock and potentially disseminated intravascular coagulation.

Staphylococcal cutaneous infections include:
- *abscess formation*
- *furuncles and carbuncles*
- *cellulitis*
- *lymphangitis*
- *lymphadenitis*

S. aureus bacteremia associated with systemic abscess formation.

Abscess Formation

In addition, one of the characteristics of *S. aureus* is its ability to hematogenously seed internal organs. Moreover, the longer the state of bacteremia, the more likely it is that an initially occult deep staphylococcal abscess may occur.

Endocarditis

Acute bacterial endocarditis

Acute staphylococcal endocarditis can be rapidly progressive and comes with a high rate of mortality (40 to 80%). In a nonparenteral drug-using population, this is generally a left-sided valvular process. Affected individuals characteristically develop heralding nonspecific flu-like symptoms followed by the rapid onset of a high fever, toxemia leading to septic shock, or disseminated intravascular coagulation. This is frequently accompanied by acute valvular dysfunction (usually mitral valve) or metastatic abscess formation. Cutaneous manifestations include Osler's nodes, Janeway lesions, petechial splinter hemorrhages of the nails, and Roth's spots (hemorrhagic spot on the retina).

Intravenous drug users

By contrast, parenteral drug abusers are at risk to develop a more indolent, right-sided staphylococcal endocarditis (tricuspid valve) characterized by fever, chills, malaise, and pleuritic chest pain from septic pulmonary emboli. The mortality in the drug users is low, but the morbidity is high. Pulmonary abscesses, with or without empyema, meningitis, glomerulonephritis, and septic arthritis, are sequelae.

Toxic Shock Syndrome

In addition to the staphylococcal cutaneous infections, there are two specific types of *S. aureus* infections associated with elaboration of toxins that produce syndromes with prominent cutaneous features. These are toxic shock syndrome (TSS) and staphylococcal SSS.

The TSS is characterized by a generalized erythematous dermatitis associated with fever, hypotension, and dysfunction of at least three organ systems. It is thought to result from the superantigen capabilities of the TSST-1 toxin causing a release of a cascade of cytokines from activated T lymphocytes. Although ini-

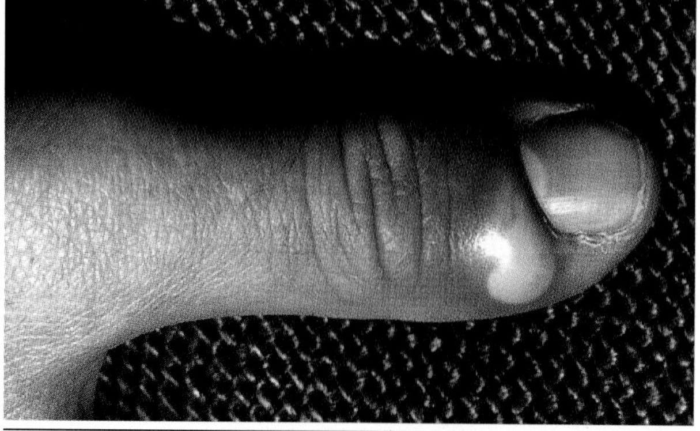

FIGURE 49–1 Periungual *S. aureus* abscess. (Reproduced with permission from: Rick Stearns, M.D., Tulsa, OK)

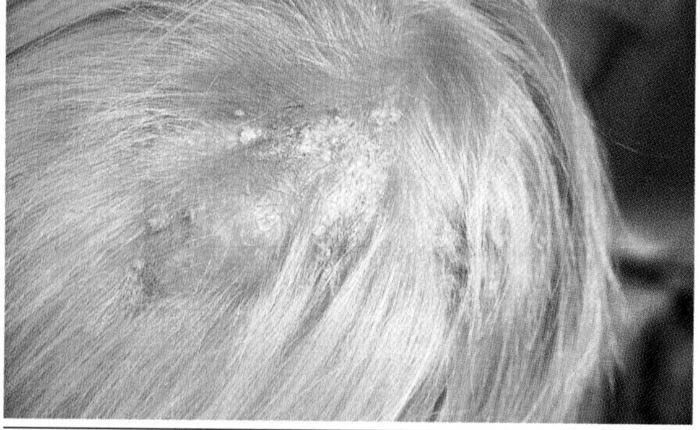

FIGURE 49–2 Cold scalp *S. aureus* abscess in a patient with hyper-IgE syndrome (Job's syndrome).

tially described in menstruating women using tampons, TSS has also been detected in association with staphylococcal infections occurring in children and men, including postsurgical-associated cases. The nonmenstrual TSS subsets are now the most frequent causes of TSS. Approximately 50% of the nonmenstrual TSS infections produce TSST-1 toxin, the remainder interotoxin B and C.

Two types of clinical toxic shock syndromes:
- *menstruating women (using tampons)*
- *nonmenstruating associated with soft tissue infections*

Cutaneous Manifestations

A scarlatiniform, erythematous, tender dermatitis associated with conjunctivitis is characteristic. Subsequently, desquamation, especially of the palms and soles, generally occurs 7 to 10 days after the onset of the disease. Hypotension, diarrhea, vomiting, rhabdomyolysis, encephalopathy, renal failure resulting in azotemia, liver enzyme abnormalities, and thrombocytopenia are often noted.

The differential diagnosis includes Kawasaki syndrome, staphylococcal SSS, and scarlet fever. The presence of hypotension in an adult differentiates TSS from other conditions. (For further discussion on Kawasaki syndrome, see Chapter 12, "Vasculitis.")

Tampon removal was previously deemed important. Today, drainage of any suspected abscess, together with an antibiotic, such as intravenous nafcillin, and aggressive fluid replacement to combat the hypotension, are critical, although the role of antibiotics remains uncertain in this toxin-based process. More recently, success has been reported in several studies using pooled gammaglobulin (IVIG) containing TSST-1 antibodies.

Erythematous, tender skin with subsequent desquamation
Hypotension
Liver enzyme abnormalities
Thrombocytopenia
Azotemia

Staphylococcal Scalded Skin Syndrome

Staphylococcal SSS is an exfoliative dermatitis generally occurring in children under the age of 5 years. It is induced by staphylococcal exfoliative toxins A and B. These toxins are produced generally, but not exclusively, by phage group II (types 55, 71) *S. aureus*. (There are five groups of staphylococci with similar characteristics detected by bacteriophage typing. Bacteriophages are viruses that bind to the cell wall of the staphylococci.) These toxins have an approximate 26-kD molecular weight. A glossary of our knowledge regarding the pathogenesis of SSS is presented in Table 49–1.

The toxins induce SSS by cleavage of squamous epithelia through the granular cell layer. The exact mechanism is unknown, but the individual cells are not killed. There is an unconfirmed abstract reporting that the toxins may bind to desmoglein-I. Other reports hypothesize toxin-based proteolytic enzymes target desmosomes.

The flaccid bullae demonstrate acantholytic cells, and bacterial cultures of these bullae are characteristically negative. Furthermore, little or no inflammation in either the dermis or the epidermis is detected. Additional evidence that the toxins alone are capable of inducing the disease is the fact that injection of the toxins into neonatal mice pups produces a similar disease. Also, the intradermal injection of the toxins into humans induces intraepidermal bullae formation.

Caused by exfoliative toxins A and B exotoxins produced by phage group II S. aureus

Acantholytic process associated with flaccid bullae formation at the level of the stratum granulosum.

The development in the host of an immune response to the toxins is presumably associated with the disappearance of the disease. It is reasoned the antibody response neutralizes the toxins. This probably explains why staphylococcal SSS is dominantly a disease of very young children, rarely occurring in adults. When it does occur in adults, it generally occurs in immunosuppressed individuals or those with renal failure who presumably cannot clear the toxins. In adults, with SSS, unlike in children, *S. aureus* is often cultured from the blood, and mortality is significant.

Cutaneous Manifestations

Staphylococcal SSS generally begins abruptly. It is usually preceded by a staphylococcal upper respiratory infection (producing pharyngitis, conjunctivitis, and/or rhinorrhea) (Figure 49–3). SSS may also be preceded by a staphylococcal skin infection. The onset of the disease is characterized by diffuse, tender, erythematous skin and by a fever. The application of shearing pressure (Nikolsky's

Upper respiratory tract or skin source of S. aureus

Tender, erythematous skin
Nikolsky's sign
Widespread desquamation

sign) produces denuding of the skin (Figure 49–4). Widespread flaccid bullae appear that easily rupture. Fluid loss may be significant but is generally transient, and temperature regulation may also be problematic. Healing is associated with exfoliation of large areas of skin. Unless complicated by a secondary infection, antibiotic and fluid replacement therapy generally produces complete resolution within 7 to 10 days.

"Neonatal pemphigus" and "Ritter's disease" (named for Ritter von Rittershain) are previous names for this condition. Isolated outbreaks of this condition have been described in newborn nurseries, traced to phage group II *S. aureus* carriers among nursing personnel and physicians. This condition was much more prevalent before modern hygienic techniques (eg, frequent washing of hands with antiseptic soap) were developed.

(For a discussion on the differentiation of toxic epidermal necrolysis from scalded skin syndrome, see Chapter 67, "Toxic Epidermal Necrolysis.")

Presumed Cutaneous Manifestations

Bullous impetigo. Bullous impetigo is a flaccid, localized bullous disease occurring most commonly in infants and, to a much lesser extent, in older children and adults (Figure 49–5). The bullae generally arise in normal-appearing skin. The bullous lesion is presumably due to local production of exfoliative toxins because rupture reveals a clear yellow fluid, and culture of this fluid demonstrates the presence of phage group II *S. aureus.*

Staphylococcal scarlet fever. This condition, which is identical to the streptococcal-induced variant, is produced by a phage group II *S. aureus* organism. Diffuse, erythematous, tender skin with a roughened texture characterizes this condition. Unlike streptococcal-induced scarlet fever, strawberry tongue and palatal erythema are absent, although Pastia's lines are present.

The site of infection can be variable and include external otitis, abscess formation, as well as conjunctivitis. In general, healing occurs within 2 to 5 days and is associated with generalized desquamation.

Staphylococcal scarlet fever an abortive form of staphylococcal scalded skin syndrome

This condition appears to be an abortive form of the staphylococcal SSS. Indeed, Mellish and Glasgow noted that in the murine model, the condition may halt spontaneously at the scarlatina stage, without development of exfoliation (Table 49–1).

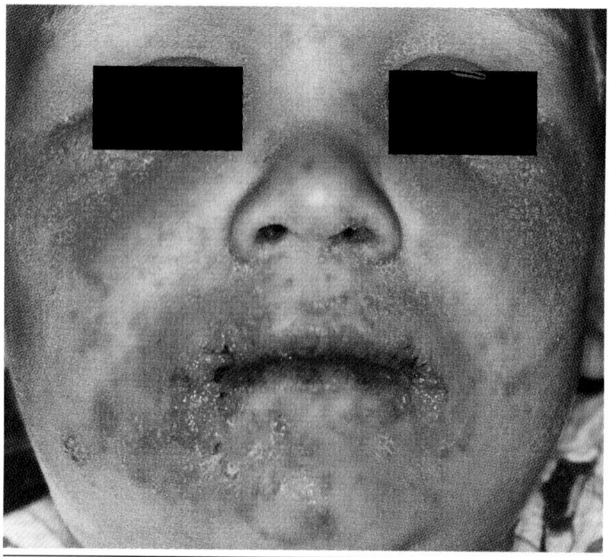

FIGURE 49–3 Coryza and patchy erythema on the face of a 3-year-old with the scalded skin syndrome. (Reproduced with permission from : Bernard Cohen, M.D., Baltimore, MD)

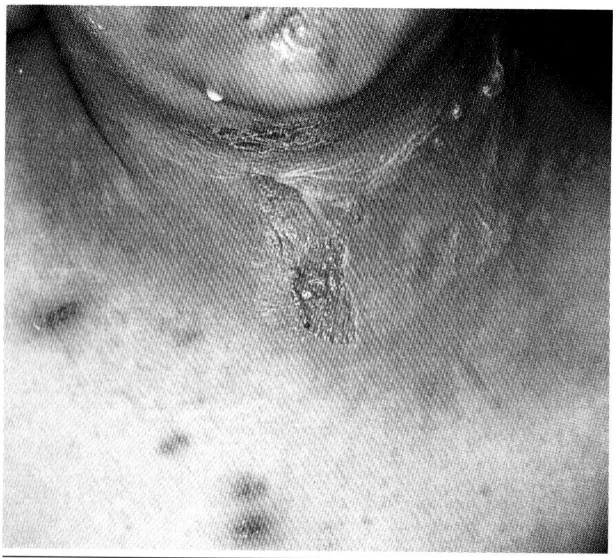

FIGURE 49–4 Erythema and denuding of the skin around the neck of a patient with the scalded skin syndrome. (Reproduced with permission from: Bernard Cohen, M.D., Baltimore, MD)

Treatment of Cutaneous Lesions

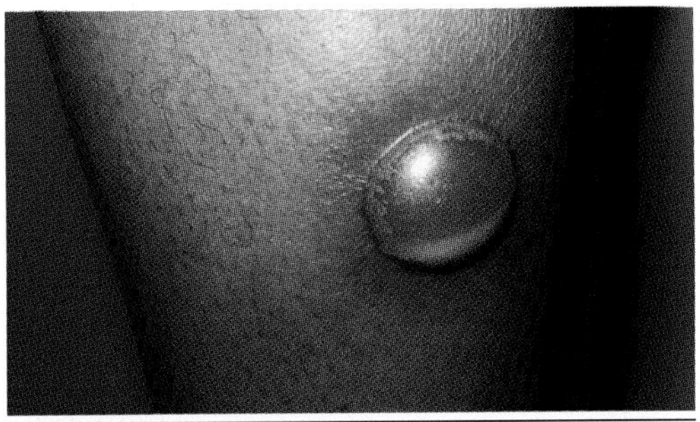

FIGURE 49-5 Acute blister formation at the site of cellulitis. Culture yielded growth of *S. aureus*.

Although not every cutaneous staphylococcal infection requires antibiotic treatment, in selected patients with chronic conditions, such as diabetes, renal disease, or immune suppression, even pedestrian infections, such as the nasal carrier state, may require treatment and close follow-up.

Importance of treating for staphylococcal skin infections

Generally, all suspected *S. aureus* pyodermas, abscesses, and furuncles and carbuncles should be treated with a 48- to 72-hour course of either an oral or parenteral penicillinase-resistant penicillin (eg, intravenous nafcillin or oxacillin, oral cloxacillin or dicloxacillin) prior to drainage. Bacterial culture may be important in patients who are otherwise not completely healthy, not only to determine whether the *S. aureus* is penicillin sensitive or resistant but also to discern whether there is an alternative microbial explanation, such as a group A streptococci.

Evaluation of Recurrent Infections

Patients with recurrent S. aureus infections deserve special attention.

For those individuals with recurrent staphylococcal infections, a complete history and physical examination should be performed to detect the following predisposing factors: (1) the use of immunosuppressive agents (eg, corticosteroids, azathioprine); (2) the presence of immunodeficiency syndromes involving immunoglobulins, complement components, or neutrophil chemotactic or phagocytic defects; (3) the presence of atopic eczema, perhaps indicating the hyper-IgE (Job's) syndrome; (4) the presence of diabetes mellitus; (5) drug addiction (intravenous or skin popping).

Treatment of carrier state

In patients with recurrent *S. aureus* infections, nares, or sites of suspected cutaneous infection (eg, umbilicus) should be cultured for *S. aureus*. If these organisms are found in the nares, the internasal application of a 2% mupirocin ointment (most effective) or bacitracin ointment (less effective) is indicated.

Rifampin therapy should be combined with another systemic antibiotic to prevent the emergence of resistance.

For individuals failing topical therapy, rifampin 600 mg daily for 10 days is recommended. The addition of a second drug, such as a sulfonamide, quinoline or minocycline, together with rifampin has been recommended in order to prevent the emergence of a rifampin-resistant strain of *S. aureus*.

Annotated Bibliography

Elias PM, Fritsch P, Epstein EH. Staphylococcal scalded skin syndrome. Arch Dermatol 1977;113:207–219.

This is an excellent, well-written summary of the pathophysiologic mechanisms of exfoliatin in the production of staphylococcal SSS.

TABLE 49–1 Glossary of Knowledge Regarding Staphylococcal Scalded Skin Syndrome

1885	A description of the epidemics of Ritter's disease (SSS) is provided.
1956	Lang and Walker rediscover this disease. Lyell describes the disease as part of toxic epidermal necrolysis designation.
1970	Mellish and Glasgow describe an animal model.
1973	Mellish et al., Abuthnott et al., and Kapral and Miller establish an etiologic role of exfoliatin.
1977	Elias et al. demonstrate remarkable species and tissue specificity of exfoliatin.

Lyell A. Toxic epidermal necrolysis (the scalded skin syndrome): a reappraisal. Br J Dermatol 1979;100:69–86.

This is a candid article by a dermatologist who played a great role in calling attention to what is now known as staphylococcal SSS. He originally described toxic epidermal necrolysis syndrome. Subsequent work stimulated by these observations led to the realization that the original toxic epidermal necrolysis description was composed of two distinct diseases: (1) staphylococcal SSS occurring predominantly in children, and (2) immunologically mediated toxic epidermal necrolysis syndrome occurring in adults. The latter is associated with significant mortality, the former is not.

Mellish ME, Glasgow LA. The staphylococcal scalded skin syndrome: development of an experimental model. N Engl J Med 1970;282:1114–1119.

This classic paper demonstrates the pathogenic roles of exotoxins elaborated by phage group II staphylococcal organisms.

Gribier B, Piemont Y, Grosshans E. Staphylococcal scalded skin syndrome in adults. J Am Acad Dermatol 1994;30:319–324.

This is a case report of adult-onset staphylococcal SSS in an "immunocompetent" octogenarian. Most adult cases occur in the presence of renal insufficiency and in immunocompromised individuals. Mortality is significant and staphylococcal bacteremia/septicemia is frequently detected.

Stevens DL, Tanner MH, Winship J, et al. Severe group A streptococcal infections associated with a toxic shock-like syndrome and scarlet fever toxin A. N Engl J Med 1989;321:1–7.

Cone LA, Woodard DR, Schlievert PM, et al. Clinical and bacteriological observations of a toxic shock-like syndrome due to *Streptococcus pyogenes*. N Engl J Med 1987;317:146–149.

These two articles describe toxic shock–like syndrome associated with Streptococcus pyogenes.

Kac G, et al. Methicillin-resistant *Staphylococcus aureus* nosocomial acquisition and carrier state in a wound care center. Arch Dermatol 2000;136:735–739.

This study demonstrates an approximate 20% frequency of methicillin-resistant Staphylococcus aureus *carriers in a wound center population.*

Stevens DL. The toxic shock syndrome. Infect Dis Clin North Am 1996;10(4):727–746.

Excellent review of history, diagnosis, and management.

Dinges MM, Orwin PM, Schlievert PM. Exotoxins of *Staphylococcus aureus*. Clin Microbiol Rev 2000;13(1):16–34, table of contents.

CHAPTER 50

Meningococcal Infections

Thomas T. Provost, M.D., Paul G. Auwaerter, M.D.

Neisseria meningitidis, an aerobic, gram-negative coccus, is a normal inhabitant of the nasal or oropharyngeal mucosa. It is spread from person to person by aerosol droplets. For successful colonization, it needs to attach to the columnar epithelium of the nasopharynx, which is facilitated by filiform structures, termed "pili," on the cell surface of the organisms along with other outer membrane proteins (actual mucosal penetration is poorly understood); it may secrete a protease capable of digesting the immunoglobulin IgA and other epithelial protective host cell proteins to promote its survival; and it must be encapsulated to resist phagocytosis.

Normal inhabitant of upper respiratory tract. Pathogenesis enhanced by: filiform pili, IgA proteases, capsule which resists phagocytosis

Multiple factors are likely involved in the transition from colonization to invasive disease, but it appears most commonly in newly infected hosts who do not have IgM or IgG-neutralizing antimeningococcal antibodies against the specific strain of *N. meningitidis*. Antecedent viral infection has also been suggested as a cofactor in producing invasive disease. Tropism for the shin, joints, meninges, and adrenal glands is prominent. Fulminant cases may be facilitated by a cell wall polysaccharide endotoxin.

With intercurrent upper respiratory viral infection or a new strain, N. Meningitides may proliferate; may be aspirated or gain entrance to the systemic circulation, produce pneumonia, meningitis, or endocarditis

These organisms can be cultured on chocolate agar (blood enriched) in the presence of 5 to 10% carbon dioxide. In addition, enriched (Mueller-Hinton) and Thayer Martin selective media are effective substrates.

Cultured on chocolate agar in presence of 5–10% CO_2. Also Thayer Martin agar

Patients possessing a homozygous deficiency of the late complement (C5-C9) and alternative complement pathway components are at special risk to develop recurrent meningococcal infections. For reasons not well understood, these patients generally have a mild disease. (Homozygous complement component deficiency can be detected by a total hemolytic complement assay CH50 or CH100. A reading of zero is diagnostic. Individual complement components are assayed). By contrast, asplenia individuals are at increased risk of developing a fulminant infection with high mortality.

Late complement component deficiency (homozygous) and asplenia patients associated with increased risk

Once gaining entrance into the bloodstream, the *N. meningitidis* organisms invade and damage endothelial cells, producing thrombosis and necrosis. The overlying skin may demonstrate petechiae, echymosis, purpura, and/or infarction (pupura fulminans).

Cutaneous Manifestations

Chronic Meningococcemia

Chronic meningococcemia a rare disease
May evolve into classic acute meningococcemia, meningitis, or endocarditis

Chronic meningococcemia is a rare disease characterized by low-grade fever, intense polyarthralgia or polyarthritis, and a nondescript rash that may last months. The infection may evolve into classic acute meningococcemia, meningitis, or endocarditis.

Rose-colored, macular eruption, which may become petachial

Individual cutaneous lesions are characterized by small, rose-colored, macular, papular lesions of varying sizes. Tender erythema nodosum–like lesions with a special predilection for the lower extremities may occur, and individual lesions may develop petechiae.

Biopsies may demonstrate a leukocytoclastic angiitis. In general, however, no bacterial or meningococcal antigens can be recognized microscopically or with direct immunofluorescent techniques. Differential diagnosis of this disease falls within the arthritis-dermatitis syndromes, including disseminated gonococcal infection, rheumatic fever, subacute bacterial endocarditis, Henoch-Schönlein purpura, and erythema multiforme.

Diagnosis made by blood culture

The diagnosis is established by blood cultures that can be enhanced if obtained with charcoal-resin bottles. The charcoal resin inactivates human complement components that may inhibit the *Neisseria* groups.

Acute Meningococcemia

Acute meningococcemia, in contradistinction to chronic meningococcemia, is a rapidly progressive disease process associated with significant morbidity and mortality. The meningeal form begins as an upper respiratory–like infection with the rapid onset of fever, followed by obtundation and meningismis.

Acute meningococcemia rapid onset. Meningeal signs and symptoms may occur within hours. Fulminant disease. Death may ensue. Petechial rash characteristic

Hypotension and disseminated intravascular coagulopathy may occur: Waterhouse-Friderichsen syndrome

Acute infection can also occur without meningitis (acute meningococcemia); it may not be linked with a sepsis syndrome (simple bacteremia), or it may be associated with sepsis. At times, the meningitis occurs in the absence of meningoccemia. Petechiae and transient urticaria, as well as nondescript macular, papular, erythematous lesions (some of which associated with petechiae) may be found over the entire body. A petechial rash is almost always detected. Skin can be painful to the touch. In severe cases, gangrene with hemorrhagic bullae and purpura fulminans can develop as a consequence of disseminated intravascular coagulopathy, often with adrenal glands causing acute insufficiency–induced hypotension (Waterhouse-Friderichsen syndrome). Other acute forms of *N. meningitidis* include pneumonia and urethritis.

The differential diagnosis of acute meningococcemia includes acute bacterial endocarditis, vasculitis, Rocky Mountain spotted fever, purpura fulminans due to other bacteria, and toxic shock syndrome. (For further discussion on meningococcus, see section Purpura in Chapter 47, "Septicemia.")

With meningeal presentations, the cerebrospinal fluid will display a polymorphonuclear pleocytosis with a gram stain showing characteristic gram-negative diplococci in more than approximately 50% of cases. A latex agglutination technique can be performed for rapid detection of meningococcal-specific antigens. Aspiration of individual cutaneous lesions will frequently demonstrate gram-negative cocci on gram staining.

Disease of youth

Although infection can occur at any age, chronic meningococcemia and fulminant meningococcemia occur with highest frequency during infancy and the teen/young adult years. A protective humoral immunity to *Neisseria* tends to develop with increasing age. It is theorized that this immunity occurs following subclinical infection with and colonization by *N. meningitidis* or as a result of the production of cross-reactive antibodies induced by exposure to antigenically related bacteria as one ages.

The major pathologic strains of *N. meningitidis*-induced meningitis belong to the A, B, C, and W-135 serogroups, identified by serogrouping of capsular polysaccharide. A vaccine has been developed against the A, C, Y, and W-135 serogroups and is currently used in the military and by travelers to endemic regions, such as sub-Saharan Africa. University health administrators have just recently advocated consideration of immunization for all entering freshmen.

The Findley Institute in Cuba has developed an effective vaccine against group B (a significant cause of disease), but it is not available in the United States.

Treatment

The treatment of choice for adults is 10 to 24 million units of penicillin given intravenously for 7 to 10 days or 2 g ceftriaxone given everyday. For penicillin-allergic patients, 1 g of chloramphenicol every 6 hours is recommended.

For prophylaxis of family members, rifampin remains the designated drug of choice (600 mg/12 h for 2 days). For children, rifampin (10 mg per kg per 12 hours for 2 days) is effective. However, increasing resistance and prophylaxis failure have prompted many experts to recommend use of ciprofloxacin (500 mg single dose) or ceftriaxone (250 mg intramuscularly single dose for adults, 125 mg intramuscularly for children).

Annotated Bibliography

Adams EM, et al. Absence of the seventh component of complement in a patient with chronic meningococcemia presenting as vasculitis. Ann Intern Med 1983;99:35–39.

Densen P. Familial properdin deficiency and fatal bacteremia. Correction of the bacterial defect by vaccination. N Engl J Med 1987;316:922–926.

These two articles demonstrate the absence of late complement components and properdin associated with meningococcemia.

Ross SC, Densen P. Complement deficiency and infection. Medicine (Baltimore) 1984;63:243.

This is an excellent review article.

Fass RJ, Saslaw S. Chronic meningococcemia: possible pathogenic role of IgM deficiency. Arch Intern Med 1972;130:943–946.

Apicella MA. *Neisseria meningitidis*. In: Mandell GL, Douglas RG Jr, Bennett JE, eds. Principles and Practice of Infectious Diseases, 5th ed. New York: Wiley, 2000, pp 2228–2241.

This is an excellent review by a leading researcher.

CHAPTER 51

Rickettsial Infections

Thomas T. Provost, M.D., Paul G. Auwaerter, M.D.

Rocky Mountain spotted fever is a tick-borne disease.

The most prevalent rickettsial infection in the United States is Rocky Mountain spotted fever (RMSF). This serious disease is caused by *Rickettsia rickettsii.* It is transmitted via a tick bite. The most common vector is the wood tick (*Dermacentor andersoni*) in the western part of the United States and the dog tick (*Dermacentor variabilis*) in the eastern United States.

Other vector-borne rickettsial diseases include boutonneuse fever, African tick typhus, epidemic typhus, murine typhus, scrub typhus, Q fever, and ehrlichiosis, all which can be associated with skin lesions. In this chapter, discussion will be limited to RMSF.

Pathophysiology

Invasion of endothelial cells

RMSF is a serious systemic infection with a significant mortality in untreated patients. It is usually heralded by the sudden onset of fever, chills, myalgias, and arthralgias, with a severe headache. The organisms invade the vascular endothelial cells, especially of the arterial system, and multiply. Ultimately, destruction of the media and intima of the blood vessels occurs, producing edema, thrombosis, and microinfarctions, as well as focal extravasation of red blood cells. The blood vessels of all organs, including the heart, gastrointestinal tract, and brain, may be involved.

Cutaneous Manifestations

Rash initially around ankles, then on wrists and hands

Scrotal and vulvar involvement

The characteristic dermatitis usually begins on the third or fourth day of illness, initially appearing on the ankles and feet, then spreading to the wrists and hands and finally to the trunk and head (Figures 51–1 to 51–3). Individual lesions begin as macules, evolving within hours into papules that become petechial and purpuric. Cuatneous infarcts and gangrene may occur. An accompanying disseminated intravascular coagulopathy may occur in severe disease producing thrombosis of small- and medim-sized arteries (Figure 51–4). Scrotal and vulvar involvement is characteristic.

The differential diagnosis includes Henoch-Schöenlein purpura, meningococcemia, enteroviral infections, hepatitis, and typhoid fever.

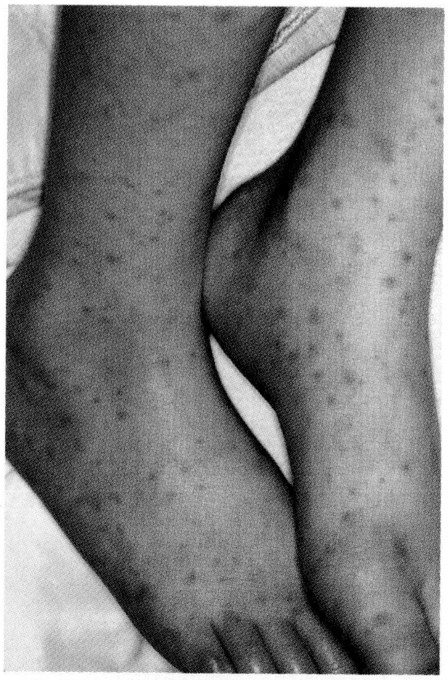

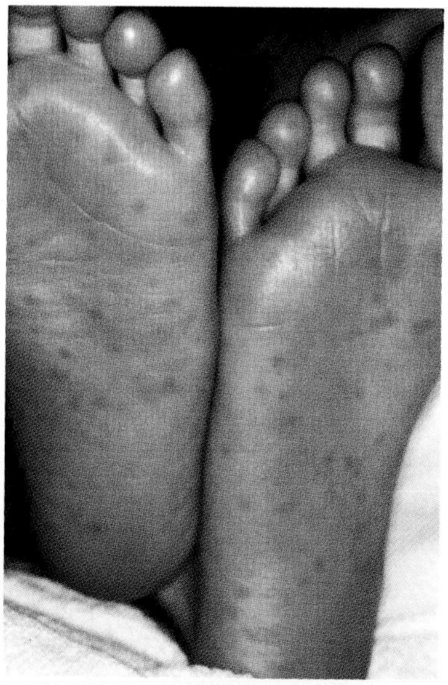

FIGURES 51-1 AND 51-2 Early petechial lesions over the lower extremities and plantar surfaces in a patient with Rocky Mountain spotted fever. (Reproduced with permission from: Bernard Cohen, M.D., Baltimore, MD)

Laboratory Diagnosis

Characteristically, these patients demonstrate normal or low white counts. Thrombocytopenia may be seen. Hyponatremia, hypoalbuminemia, and elevated serum transaminase, alkaline phosphatase, and bilirubin may occur.

The Weil-Felix test, a hemagglutination technique using cross-reacting *Proteus* Ox19, Ox2, and OxK antigens, was the main serologic testing for rick-

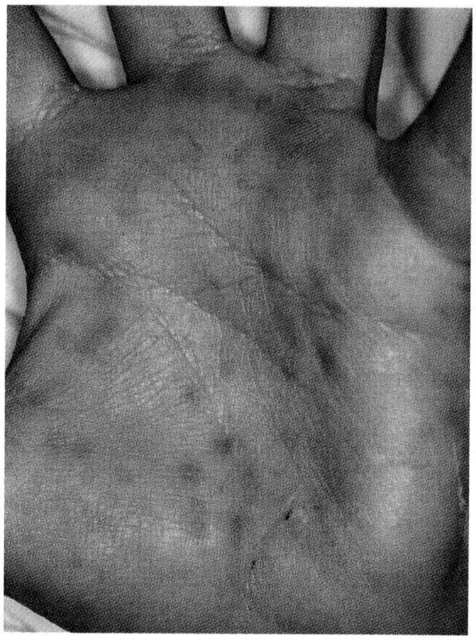

FIGURE 51-3 Petechial lesions on the palms of a patient with Rocky Mountain spotted fever. (Reproduced with permission from: Bernard Cohen, M.D., Baltimore, MD)

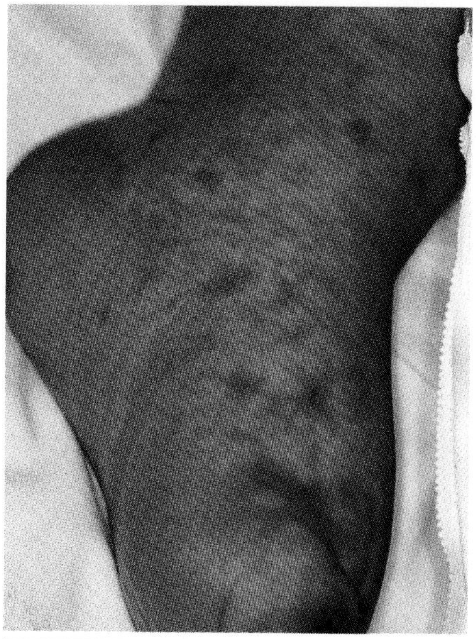

FIGURE 51-4 Extensive petechial lesions with an associated disseminated intravascular coagulopathy in a patient with Rocky Mountain spotted fever. (Reproduced with permission from: Bernard Cohen, M.D., Baltimore, MD)

ettsial infections for decades. Because of low specificity and sensitivity, they have now been replaced with indirect fluorescent antibody and latex agglutination techniques. Rapid diagnosis is now best accomplished by obtaining a biopsy of the skin. Biopsies will demonstrate, by direct immunofluorescence or immunoperoxidase techniques, the presence of coccobacillary rickettsiae in the walls of affected blood vessels.

Treatment

Rapid diagnosis is performed by direct immunofluorescence or immunoperoxidase staining of biopsy from neck or elsewhere.

Early treatment with doxycycline ore chloramphenicol is effective.

Doxycycline (100 mg/bid) is the treatment of choice. Chloramphenicol (50 to 75 mg per kg in four divided doses) is an alternative. These drugs are highly effective and should be given at the earliest possible time when the diagnosis is suspected. Early drug administration best correlates with low mortality. The drugs should be continued for 2 to 3 days after the fever resolves.

Annotated Bibliography

Helmick GG, Bernard KW, D'Angelo LJ. Rocky Mountain spotted fever: clinical, laboratory and epidemiologic features of 262 cases. J Infect Dis 1984;150:480–489.

Burnett JW. Rickettsiosis: a review for the dermatologist. J Am Acad Dermatol 1980;2:359–373.

These provide two excellent reviews of Rocky Mountain spotted fever.

Li H, Walker DH. rOmpA is a critical protein for the adhesion of *Rickettsia rickettsii* to host cells. Microb Pathol 1998;24:289–298.

Article provides insight into the pathogenesis of RMSF.

Dalton MJ, Clarke MJ, Holman RC, et al. National surveillance for Rocky Mountain spotted fever, 1981-1992: epidemeilogic summary and evaluation of risk factors for fatal outcome. Am J Trop Med Hyg 1995;52:405–413.

McDade JE, Newhouse VF. Natural history of *Rickettsia rickettsii*. Ann Rev Microbiol 1986;40:287–309.

Raoult D, Drancourt M. Antimicrobial therapy of rickettsial diseases. Antimicrob Agents Chemother 1991;35:2457–2462.

Walker DH. Pathology and pathogenesis of the vasculotropic rickettsioses. In: Walker DH, ed. Biology of Rickettsial Diseases, Vol. 1. Boca Raton, FL: CRC Press, 1988, pp. 115–138.

CHAPTER 52

Hemophilus influenzae

Paul G. Auwaerter, M.D., Thomas T. Provost, M.D.

Clinical Features

Hemophilus influenzae is a gram-negative diplococcus that causes meningitis, epiglottitis, bronchitis, and cellulitis. Children can develop a peculiar rash involving the cheek, characterized by blue, violaceous, edematous, erythematous cellulitis (Figure 52–1). This distinctive cellulitis (caused by *H. influenzae* type B) is usually only seen in children between the ages of 3 months and 3 years and is often associated with high fever and an upper respiratory infection. Bacteremia is extremely common, and children often concurrently develop other infections, such as meningitis.

Diffuse, edematous, erythematous, tender cellulitis of the face

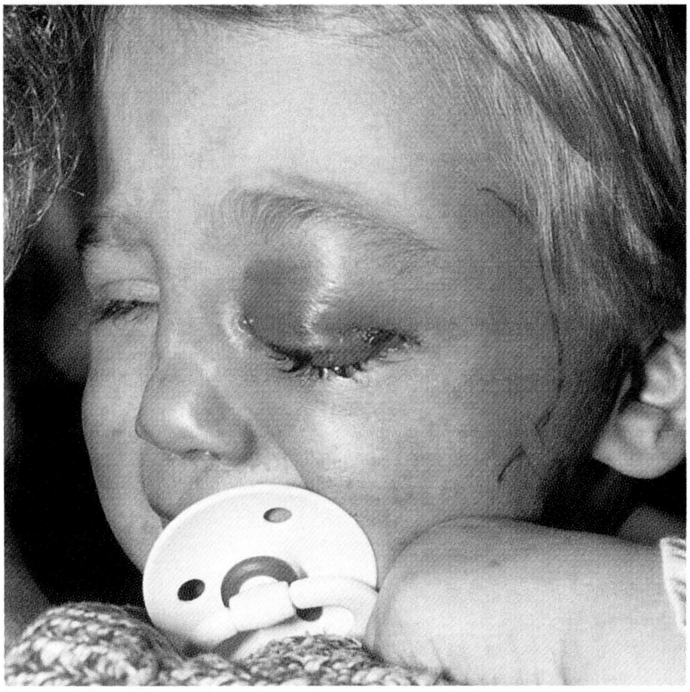

FIGURE 52–1 Characteristic *Hemophilus influenzae* cellulitis of the face demonstrating reddish-blue discoloration in the periorbital region. (Reproduced with permission from: Bernard Cohen, M.D., Baltimore, MD)

At increased risk are infants from poor socioeconomic groups and those with complement or antibody deficiencies and asplenia.

Treatment

The emergence of β-lactamase producing *H. influenzae* has made third-generation cephalosporins (ceftriaxone or cefotaxime) the drugs of choice for empirical therapy.

Immunization with *H. influenzae* B strain, capsular polysaccharide increases circulating antibodies and provides protection, making *H. influenzae* cellulitis now quite rare in children.

Annotated Bibliography

Eskola J, et al. A randomized prospective trial of a conjugate vaccine in the protection of infants and young children against invasive *Haemophilus influenzae* type B disease. N Engl J Med 1990;20: 1381–1388.

This informative article indicates the protective effect of vaccine.

CHAPTER 53

Tuberculosis

Thomas T. Provost, M.D., Paul G. Auwaerter, M.D.

Mycobacterium tuberculosis and *Mycobacterium bovis*, the causative species of tuberculosis, are human pathogens that in prior times have been the scourge of the human race. Today, with modern hygiene, tuberculosis control programs, and effective antibiotics, the frequency of tuberculosis in North America and Europe has dramatically decreased over the past 40 years. However, the disease is still prevalent in the developing countries and of increasing importance among acquired immunodeficiency syndrome (AIDS) patients. A multiple drug-resistant strain has recently emerged. Tuberculosis is responsible for approximately 3 million deaths worldwide per year.

Mycobacterium tuberculosis and Mycobacterium bovis continue to cause significant infections.

The immunology of tuberculosis is complex, involving a balance between cell-mediated immunity and delayed hypersensitivity. For an excellent discussion, see the review by Dannenburg.

Briefly, the macrophage is key to the development of resistance to tuberculosis. Normal or inactivated macrophages ingest but cannot kill *M. tuberculosis*. The bacilli multiply and the host responds with a hypersensitivity reaction (delayed hypersensitivity). The macrophages and tissue are destroyed, leading to caseation necrosis. The tubercular bacilli cannot replicate readily in this environment and most die. Some survive, remain dormant for years, and then, in later years, reactivate. Liquefaction of the caseation necrosis provides a favorable milieu for the bacilli to replicate. Caseation necrosis is a destructive process with the potential to produce widespread scarring and damage to the host tissue. In contradistinction, caseous granulomata are composed of epitheloid cells and Langerhans' giant cells, which are highly activated macrophages that secrete lytic enzymes and cytokines. These activated macrophages (part of cell-mediated immunity) are capable of ingesting and killing *M. tuberculosis* in the absence of tissue destruction (delayed hypersensitivity) in the host.

The balance between cellular immunity and delayed-type hypersensitivity determines the clinical (and cutaneous) manifestations of tuberculosis.

Cutaneous Manifestations

Tuberculous Chancre

Primary cutaneous tuberculosis

Painless ulcer and Ghon's complex

Tuberculous chancre is caused by a primary cutaneous exposure to tuberculosis. Inoculation of *M. tuberculosis* into an individual never exposed to tuberculosis produces a painless, ulcerating lesion (Figure 53–1). Approximately 2 to 4 weeks after the inoculation, a small papule, which quickly ulcerates, occurs at the site of inoculation. Regional lymphadenopathy quickly follows (primary Ghon's complex). The lymphadenopathy, generally painless, slowly enlarges over a period

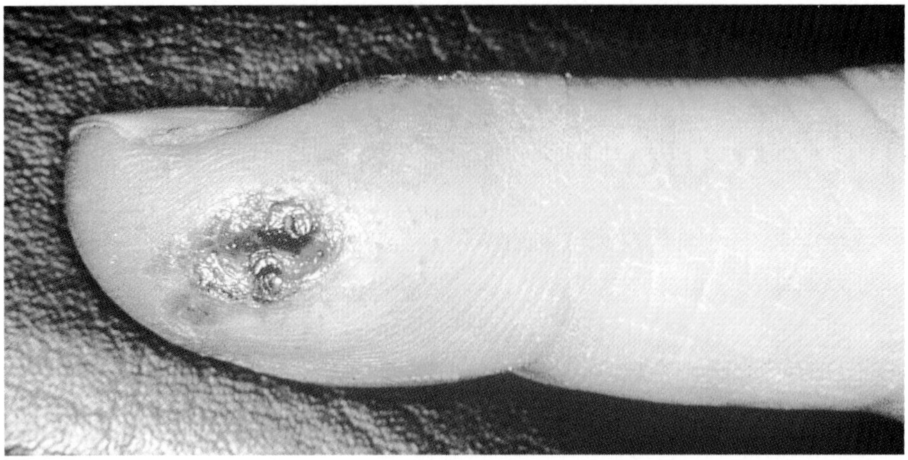

FIGURE 53–1 Primary inoculation tuberculosis in a pathologist. Epitrochlear lymphadenopathy also occurred (Ghon's complex).

Impairment of host resistance may lead to miliary spread.

of months. The primary tuberculous chancre and the lymphadenopathy gradually resolve and may calcify. The regional lymph nodes, however, may occasionally break down, and sinus tracts to the skin form. However, this is the exception—most primary tuberculosis complexes produce a state of hypersensitivity and immunity. Erythema nodosum lesions may occur (for unknown reasons, more commonly reported in European cases). If, however, host resistance is inadequate, primary inoculation may produce an hematogenous spread to other organs (miliary tuberculosis).

The histopathology demonstrates the early presence of organisms, followed by the development of epithelioid and antigen-driven giant cell formation and the disappearance of organisms.

The primary painless tuberculous ulcer must be differentiated from a syphilitic chancre, an atypical mycobacterium, and a sporotrichosis infection.

Tuberculosis verrucosa cutis: lesion produced by inoculation of tuberculosis organisms into skin of individual with both delayed hypersensitivity and cell-mediated immunity to M. tuberculosis

Occupational health hazard for medical personnel

Prosector's wart

Slowly progressive disease over years

Tuberculosis Verrucosa Cutis

The inoculation of *M. tuberculosis* into the skin of an individual who has acquired specific cell-mediated immunity and delayed hypersensitivity to the organism produces a different cutaneous reaction than that described with tuberculous chancre. This cutaneous inoculation was a common problem years ago among medical personnel and was commonly known as a "prosector's wart," since pathologists during postmortem examination of tuberculous patients would inadvertently inoculate themselves.

A traumatized site, usually on the hands, is the site of inoculation (Figure 53–2). This lesion may begin as a small papular pustule that becomes hyperkeratotic and warty. The lesion slowly grows with peripheral expansion. Usually, the lesion is solitary but, on occasion, may be multiple. As the lesion expands, the center becomes soft. In contradistinction to primary inoculation tuberculosis, the regional lymph nodes are generally uninvolved. Untreated, the lesion slowly progresses over years and may spontaneously involute, leaving an atrophic scar.

The histopathology of this lesion is characterized by pseudocarcinomatous epithelial hyperplasia, and Langerhans' giant cells. Mycobacteria are occasionally detected.

This lesion must be differentiated from the common wart, hypertrophic lupus erythematosus, hypertrophic lichen planus, atypical mycobacteria, tertiary syphilis (nodular ulcerative), and sporotrichosis.

Verrucous Vulgaris

Verrucous vulgaris, also known as "lupus vulgaris," is a type of tuberculosis that occurs in individuals with a high degree of delayed sensitivity and a moderate

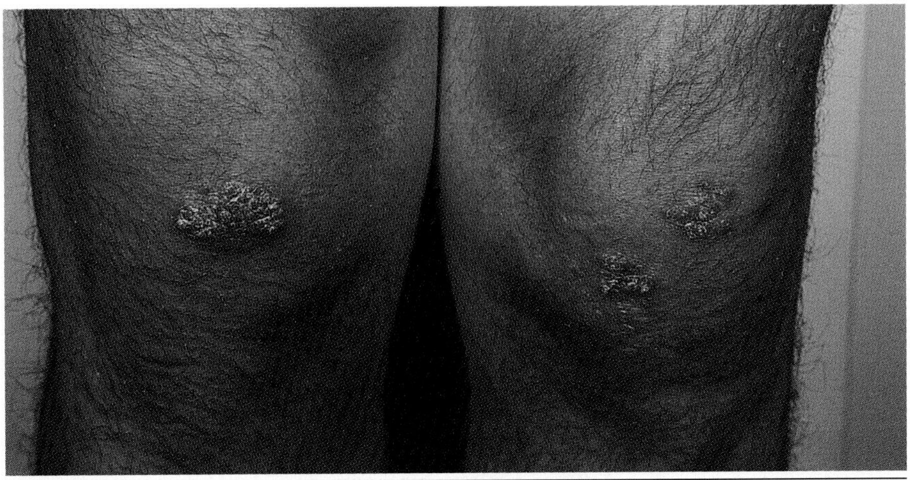

FIGURE 53–2 Tuberculosis verrucosa cutis on the knees of a child. In adults, the most common location is the dorsal surface of hands; in children, it is the lower extremities. (Reproduced from the slide collection of the late R.C.V. Robinson, M.D.)

Verrucous vulgaris: cutaneous tuberculosis occurring in individual with prominent delayed hypersensitivity and moderate cell-mediated immunity to M. tuberculosis

Brownish-red papules with apple-colored nodules on diascopy

Involution and growth occur simultaneously in the same lesion.

Activation of cutaneous tuberculosis lesions and systemic tuberculosis was commonly seen during measles epidemics in the past.

cell-mediated immunity. These patients frequently have pulmonary tuberculosis. An inoculation of *M. tuberculosis* in their skin produces a lesion that continues to expand over many years (Figure 53–3). The lesion, generally asymptomatic and solitary, occurs primarily on the head and neck. It is characterized by brownish-red papules that, on diascopy, demonstrate soft, apple-colored, jellied nodules. The lesion, slowly expands centrifically and may become scaly and elevated. Healing characteristically occurs in one area and expansion in another area. Ulceration and scarring are frequent. Squamous cell and basal cell carcinomas can occur. In the past, these lesions flared and expanded during the temporary immune suppression produced by a measles infection.

Individual lesions may be produced from the breakdown of an underlying lymph node with a sinus tract extending to the skin (scrofuloderma). These lesions may also develop on the mucous membranes. Rarely, these lesions may evolve from a primary inoculation or from hematogenous spread (miliary tuberculosis).

The histopathology of these lesions demonstrate typical tubercles with giant cells. Organisms may be cultured from the lesion.

Scrofuloderma

Breakdown of tuberculosus lymph node in patient with increased delayed-type hypersensitivity to tuberculosis

Usually unilateral

Usually on the neck

Scrofuloderma is also called "tuberculosis colliquativa cutis." It is caused by the breakdown of tuberculous lymphadenitis or the development of tuberculosis of the bones, which frequently produces a cold abscess beneath the skin that subsequently breaks down (Figure 53–4). Scrofuloderma most often involves the cervical lymph nodes and is generally unilateral. The lesions frequently discharge a purulent material. Individuals with this type of cutaneous tuberculosis demonstrate increased tuberculin sensitivity and low cell-mediated immunity.

Characteristically, the lesions demonstrate necrosis with some granuloma formation. *M. tuberculosis* organisms are few in number.

These lesions must be differentiated from a syphilitic gumma and deep fungal infections, such as nocardiosis, actinomycosis, and sporotrichosis.

Tuberculous Abscess

Tuberculous abscess generally from hematogenous spread in person with depressed tuberculosis-specific delayed hypersensitivity and low cell-mediated immunity

A tuberculous abscess on the skin is the result of hematogenous spread in a patient with low cell-mediated immunity and low-delayed hypersensitivity. Biopsies of these lesions demonstrate many organisms.

Orificial Tuberculosis

This is a rare, painful form of tuberculosis generally occurring on the oral mucosa. It is caused by the seeding of the mucous membranes by tuberculous

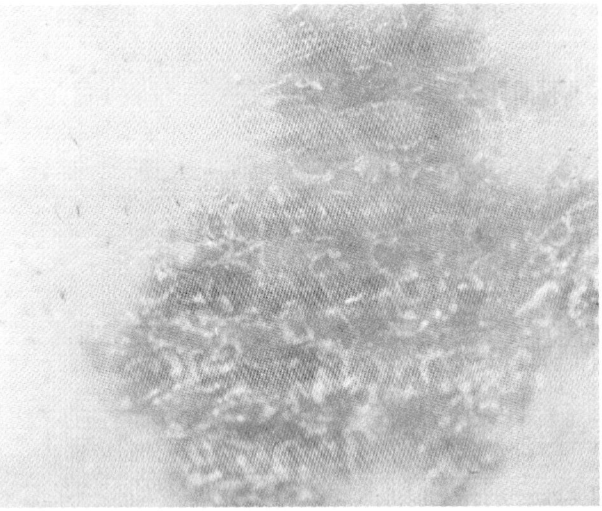

FIGURE 53–3 Lupus vulgaris characterized by a brownish, erythematous, scaling lesion. Chronic indolent lesion simultaneously showing areas of healing and extension. Untreated, malignant degeneration may occur. (Reproduced with permission from: Matt Katz, M.D., Bethesda, MD)

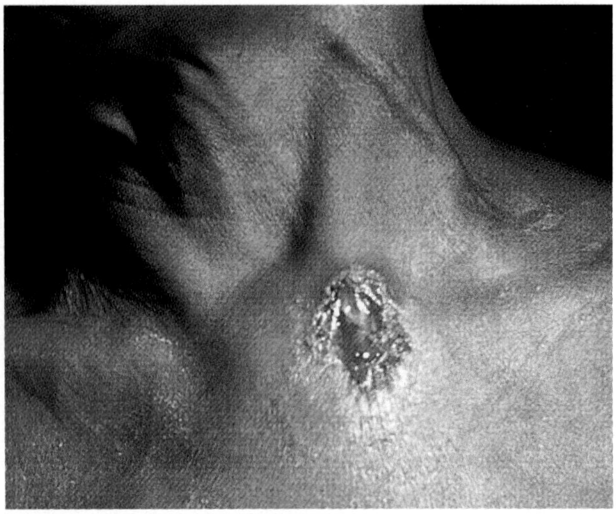

FIGURE 53–4 Scrofuloderma. Cold abscess formation in the anterior cervical region lymph nodes. (Reproduced from the slide collection of the late R.C.V. Robinson, M.D.)

Rare form of mucous membrane tuberculosis

May occur in oral, anal, and vulvar mucosa

Poor prognostic sign

bacilli resulting from a systemic infection, usually originating in the lungs. However, similar lesions may also be seen on the perineum in women with tuberculosis of the genitourinary tract and in the anal region of individuals with gastrointestinal tuberculosis. This is a sign of advanced disease and organisms are easily detected on biopsy.

These patients have weak delayed hypersensitivity to *M. tuberculosis* and low cell-mediated immunity.

Acute Miliary Tuberculosis of the Skin

Acute cutaneous miliary tuberculosis

Usually seen in infants

This is a rare cutaneous manifestation of tuberculosis, generally seen in infants. However, it can be seen in adults. Small erythematous macules and papules, as well as purpuric lesions, are detected. Biopsy demonstrates nonspecific inflammatory changes. Mycobacteria are easily detected. Tuberculin sensitivity is usually absent, and cell-mediated immunity is low or absent.

The patient usually has meningeal or pulmonary involvement, or this condition may follow measles infection, which induces transient immunosuppression. The prognosis in these patients is extremely guarded.

Treatment

The treatment of tuberculosis has been standardized to include (1) isoniazid and pyridoxine, 2) rifampicin, 3) pyrazinamide, and (4) ethambutol. Please consult standard infectious disease texts for dosage, side effects, time course, and treatment of resistant strains.

Tuberculosis of the Skin Secondary to Bacille Calmette-Guérin Vaccination

Bacille Calmette-Guérin (BCG) is a vaccination that has been used extensively in countries other than the United States in an effort to control tuberculosis. It originated as an attenuated strain of *Mycobacterium bovis*. This form of therapy may be effective in reducing the incidence and severity of childhood tuberculosis; however, more recent data suggest there is little overall benefit.

In recent years, BCG vaccination has been used as adjuvant immunotherapy, especially in the treatment of bladder cancer. Following inoculation with BCG, an inflammatory papule develops that slowly grows, ulcerates, then heals, leaving a scar. Regional lymphadenopathy may occur, especially in those individuals who have not previously been exposed to tuberculosis, and dissemination of BCG occurs rarely.

On occasion, BCG vaccination is complicated by the development of tuberculous skin lesions. Specific lesions appear to be determined by the immunologic status of the host toward the tuberculosis bacillus. For example, lupus vulgaris may also develop at the site of vaccination. Cutaneous necrosis and ulceration may occur in association with regional lymphadenitis and constitutional symptoms. In addition, subcutaneous abscess formation and scrofuloderma have been reported.

Use of BCG vaccination therapy in cancer patient may produce various cutaneous forms of tuberculosis depending on the degree of tuberculosis, delayed hypersensitivity, and host cellular immune status.

In the setting of severe combined immune deficiency syndrome or other profound immune suppression, a number of fatal BCG reactions have been reported. These immune-deficient patients develop a generalized BCG infection termed "BCGosis."

BCGosis

Fatal disease occurring in severe combined immune-deficient patients undergoing BCG vaccination for prevention of tuberculosis.

Annotated Bibliography

Aungst CW, Sokal JE, Jager BV. Complications of BCG vaccination in neoplastic disease. Ann Intern Med 1975;82:666–669.

The use of BCG to enhance the immune response in neoplastic diseases resulted in the reporting of a series of complications. Persistent acid-fast infections could be established with BCG vaccination. Some of these infections could disseminate widely. In other instances, a previously dormant acid-fast infection would be activated. Finally, a group of reactions characterized by exaggerated hypersensitivity were reported. This latter complication most commonly is characterized by a febrile reaction lasting 1 to 2 days. On rare occasions, fatal reactions following intralesional injection of BCG in highly sensitized patients have been reported. Fever and chills associated with hypotension and pancytopenia, with evidence of a disseminated intravascular coagulopathy, have been described.

Dostrovsky A, Sagher F. Dermatological complications of BCG vaccination. Br J Dermatol 1963;75:181–192.

This article documents the complications detected in approximately 200,000 patients and children vaccinated with BCG in Israel between 1949 and 1950. Scrofuloderma-like lesions were detected in 5, lupus vulgaris–like lesions in 2, excessive specific lymphadenitis in 10, papular tuberculosis–like and lichen scrofulosorum–like lesions in 4, and at the vaccination site in 5.

Curtis HM, Leck I, Bamford FN. Incidence of childhood tuberculosis after neonatal BCG vaccination. Lancet 1984;1:145–148.

This is a highly quoted study demonstrating a significant reduction in the incidence of tuberculosis among children who received BCG vaccination in the neonatal period. Although the data collection may be open to question, the authors present arguments that "tuberculosis was generally several times less common in the children vaccinated." They estimated that BCG neonatal vaccination provided a level of protection for greater than 75% of the infants.

Izumi AK, Matsunaga J. BCG vaccine-induced lupus vulgaris. Arch Dermatol 1982;118: 171–172.

This is a case report of a lupus-like tuberculosis cutis progressing over 30 years following intradermal BCG vaccination. Fatal BCG-disseminated disease has previously been reported in 17 cases between the years of 1953 and 1974. All of these patients had a predisposing immunodeficient state. Lupus vulgaris following a single BCG vaccination is rare; however, multiple BCG vaccinations markedly increase the incidence of lupus vulgaris.

Bloom BR, Small PM. Evolving relation between humans and *Mycobacterium tuberculosis.* N Engl J Med 1998;338:677–678.

This is an excellent editorial discussing the emergence of virulent strains of Mycobacterium *and genetic susceptibility.*

Dannenberg AM. Immunopathogenesis of pulmonary tuberculosis. Hosp Pract 1993;51–58.

This is a well-written review of host defense mechanisms against tuberculosis by a well-respected investigator in the field.

Bellamy R, Ruwende C, Corrah T, et al. Variations in the NRAMP1 gene and susceptibility to tuberculosis in West Africans. N Engl J Med 1998;338:640–644.

The natural resistance–associated macrophage protein 1 gene (NRAMP1) is expressed only on reticuloendothelial cells. In inbred mice, natural resistance to tuberculous infection is controlled by a single, dominant gene designated BCG. The NRAMP1 and BCG genes are identical. In addition to susceptibility and resistance to early stage infection with M. bovis *(BCG), this locus also controls resistance and susceptibility to* Mycobacterium avium-intracellurare, Mycobacterium lepraemurium, Leishmania donovani, *and* Salmonella typhimurium.

The human homologue designated NRAMP1 has been cloned and mapped to human chromosome 2q35. This study demonstrated that four NRAMP1 polymorphisms were each significantly associated with tuberculosis. The 3' UTR variant allele associated with increased susceptibility to tuberculosis in Africans is uncommon in Europeans. It was present in approximately one-quarter of the West African black population.

The protein encoded by the NRAMP1 locus is localized to the late endocytic compartment of resting macrophages. After phagocytosis, this protein is recruited to the membrane of the phagosome. These data suggest that this protein may restrict the replication of intercellular pathogens by altering the phagolysomal environment. The authors further point out that the unlinked but related gene NRAMP2 *has been shown to encode an iron transporter. Therefore, it is conceivable that this protein may be a regulator of interphagosomal manganese/iron or other divalent cations.*

It will be fascinating to know if other ethnic groups with increased frequencies of tuberculosis demonstrate the same polymorphism at the NRAMP1 loci.

Valway SE, Sanchez MPC, Shinnick TF, et al. An outbreak involving extensive transmission of a virulent strain of *Mycobacterium tuberculosis.* N Engl J Med 1998;338:6433–6439.

This fascinating study demonstrates individual variation in virulence among strains of tuberculosis. The study resulted from an outbreak of tuberculosis that was caused by a highly virulent strain of M. tuberculosis. *The spread of this infection was due to the virulence of the strain rather than to environmental factors or patient characteristics.*

This article highlights the important roles that strain virulence of M. tuberculosis *and host susceptibility play in the transmission and development of clinical tuberculosis.*

Atypical Mycobacterial Infections

Mycobacterium marinum

Mycobacterium marinum has been found in both fresh and salt water. It is also frequently isolated from fish tanks and poorly chlorinated swimming pools. Violaceous plaques occur generally in 2 to 3 weeks at the sites of trauma (most ofter hands, knees) (Figures 53–5 to 53–7). They are usually solitary but can be multiple. On occasion, they may have a linear, lymphatic distribution suggestive of sporotrichosis. In unusual circumstances, ulcerations may occur in contradistinction to a primary inoculation with *M. tuberculosis*. Regional lymphadenopathy is rare.

Not an uncommon infection in patients living near fresh or salt water

Generally solitary lesion on extremities

The differential diagnosis of this infection includes verruca vulgaris, tuberculosis verrucosa cutis, and sporotrichosis. Minocycline, tetracycline, trimethoprim sulfamethoxazole, rifampin, and ethambutol maybe effective forms of therapy; however, antimicrobial sensitivities should lend further guidance.

Mycobacterium kansasii

This is an atypical mycobacterium usually causing disease in immunocompromised individuals. The cutaneous manifestations generally follow trauma and are reminiscent of a sporotrichosis infection. Ulceration and metastatic lesions may develop. Pulmonary disease resembling tuberculosis is the most common presentation. The organism is susceptible to most antituberculous drugs, and minocycline has been reported to be effective.

Atypical mycobacterial infection most common in immunocompromised patients

Mycobacterium avium-intracellulare

Mycobacterium avium-intracellulare, also referred to as "*Mycobacterium avium* complex," is an atypical mycobacterial infection generally only producing pulmonary disease, although dissemination is commonplace in human immunodeficiency virus infection. Skin disease with this organism is most unusual. Yellowish crusted plaques have been reported in immunosuppressed patients, and the skin lesions may be secondary to dissemination. The organism may be susceptible to carithromycin, ethambutol, rifampin, and clofazimine.

Most commonly seen in immunocompromised patients Human immunodeficiency virus

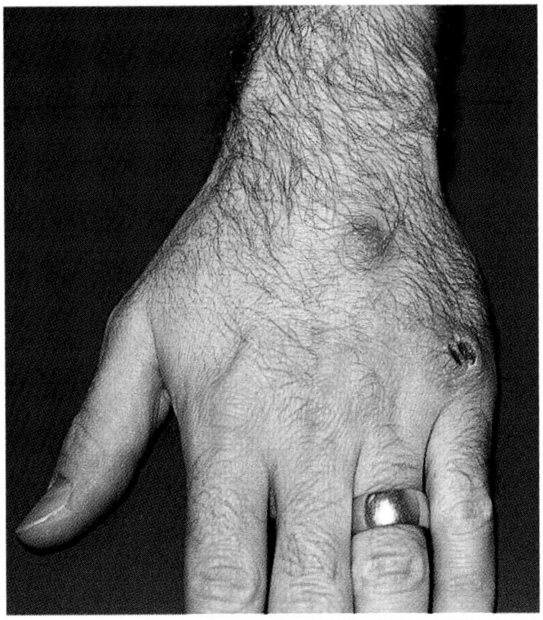

FIGURE 53–5 *M. marinum* infection on dorsal surface of the hand. (Reproduced with permmission from the slide collection of the late R.C.V. Robinson, M.D.)

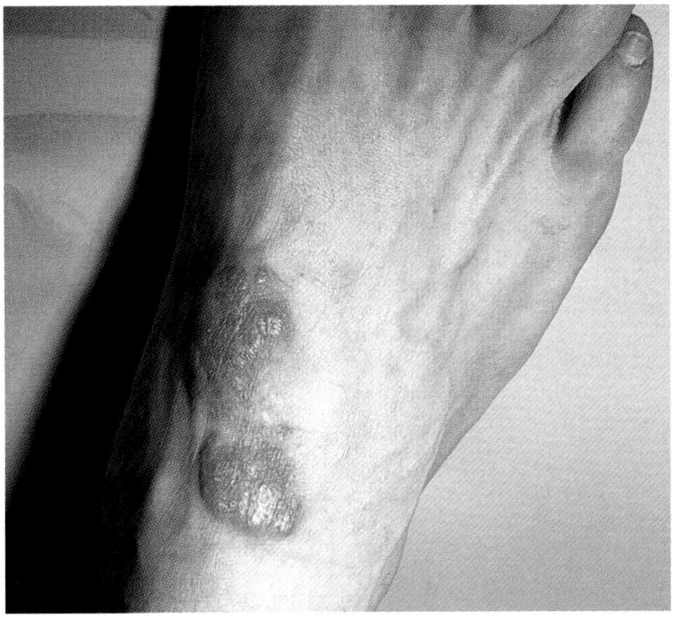

FIGURE 53–6 *M. marinum* on dorsal surface of the foot.

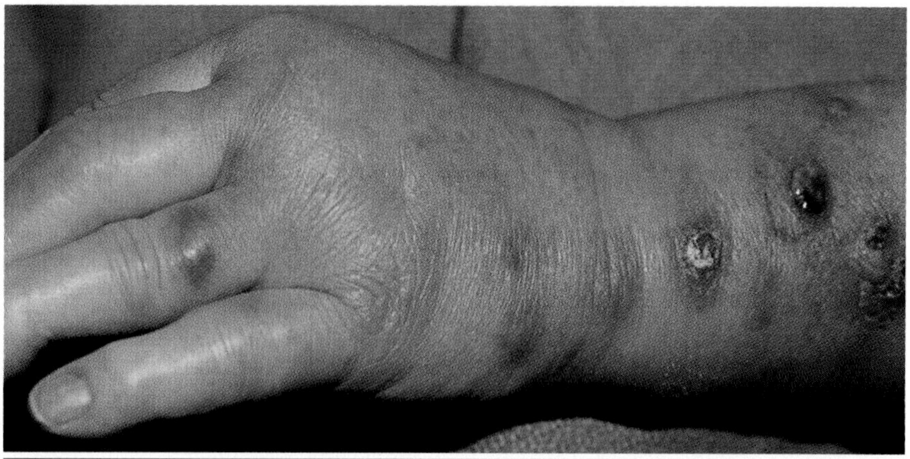

FIGURE 53–7 *M. chelonei* infection. This is a rapid growing atypical mycobacterium. This patient, who was receiving immunosuppressive therapy, developed these widespread pustular lesions. This atypical mycobacterial infection has a lymphocutaneous presentation resembling sporotrichosis.

May occur in immunocompetent patients

Recently, Provost saw a case of *M. avium-intracellulare* infection occurring in the skin, reported at the Montreal Dermatology Society. Three years after acupuncture, multiple yellow crusted lesions in areas of previous acupuncture sites developed. Histologically, noncaseating tuberculoid granulomas were detected. Acid-fast bacilli cultures demonstrated *M. avium-intercellulare*. Radiographs revealed a severe osteomyelitis of the humerus on the ipsilateral site of previous acupuncture. This patient did not demonstrate any evidence of immune deficiency.

Myobacterium fortuitum, Myobacterium chelonai, Myobacterial abscesses

These rapidly growing, atypical bacterial organisms, previously grouped under the *Mycobacterium fortuitium* complex, are now classified as individual species. Cutaneous infection, the result of trauma or injections, is characterized by inflammatory nodules and pustules (see Figure 53–7). Widespread dissemination can occur in immunosuppressed individuals.

Annotated Bibliography

Wolinsky E. Mycobacterial diseases other than tuberculosis. Clin Infect Dis 1992;15:1–20.

This is an excellent survey of atypical mycobacterial infections.

CHAPTER 54

Leprosy

Thomas T. Provost, M.D., Paul G. Auwaerter, M.D.

Mycobacterium leprae causes the chronic, deforming infectious disease, leprosy, known to medicine from biblical times. Once, the disease was endemic in Europe and Scandinavia. Today, despite effective drug therapy, leprosy remains a major worldwide health problem, predominantly occurring in tropical and subtropical regions.

Previously endemic in Scandinavia and Europe; now found predominantly in tropical and subtropical countries

Humans are the principal but not the sole reservoir for the disease. Armadillos in the Southern United States also carry the bacteria and the organism has also recently been found in soil. Transmission of the disease occurs after an extended period of close contact.

A glossary of events leading to our understanding of leprosy is presented in Table 54–1.

The major virulence of *M. leprae* is due to its tropism for peripheral nerves as well as its ability to survive in endothelial and phagocytic cells. Nerve involvement is universal and occurs early in the disease. Antibodies are not protective, and cell-mediated immunity produces severe neurologic sequelae (see below).

Nerve involvement a constant feature in all forms of leprosy

The cutaneous manifestations of leprosy, analogous to tuberculosis, are the result of the host's level of immunity toward *M. leprae*. The immune status of the patient toward lepromatous bacilli may change, producing dynamic alterations in the cutaneous expression of this disease. Five distinct cutaneous lesions are recognized: tuberculoid leprosy (TL), borderline tuberculoid (BT) leprosy, borderline (BB) leprosy, borderline lepromatous (BL) leprosy, and lepromatous leprosy (LL) (Figure 54–1).

Five distinct types of skin lesions detected

Features determined, in large part, by immunologic reactive status of patient toward M. leprae

TABLE 54–1 Glossary of Events Leading to Our Understanding of Leprosy

1873	Hansen describes *M. leprae* as the cause of leprosy.
1919	Mitsuda describes a test to detect host resistance to *M. leprae*.
1943	Sulfones are introduced.
1961	*M. leprae* are detected to have limited growth in mouse foot pad.
1970	Rifampin is introduced.
1971	Leprosy is detected in nine-banded armadillo providing a large source of *M. leprae* to the study.
1985	Molecular techniques provide *M. leprae* proteins for immunologic studies.
1991	Studies demonstrate host immune response to *M. leprae*.

	Tuberculoid Leprosy	Borderline Tuberculoid Leprosy	Borderline Leprosy	Borderline Lepromatous Leprosy	Lepromatous Leprosy
Immune response	4+ cell-mediated response ←——→				4+ antibody response
Reversal reactions	←——				Type I
	Type II ——→				

FIGURE 54–1 Spectrum of cutaneous lesions detected in leprosy. Diagram shows relationship of distinctive cutaneous lesions with immunologic reactive state of the host towards *M. leprae*. The type I reversal reaction is associated with an immunologic change in host reactivity toward a relative increased cellular immunity. The type II reversal reaction is associated with change in host immunity toward a relative increase in antibody reactivity.

Cutaneous Manifestations

Tuberculoid Leprosy

Tuberculoid leprosy: strong cell-mediated immune response to M. leprae

TL often presents as a single or at most a few lesions with sharply defined, erythematous, elevated borders. The center of the lesion tends to be hypopigmented or contain coppery-colored macules (Figure 54–2). The lesion is dry (nonsweating). There is loss of sensation, alopecia, and the presence of spatially associated, thickened peripheral nerves. Scale formation may be prominent. Biopsy demonstrates tuberculoid granulomas with nerve involvement. A slit skin examination fails to reveal organisms; however, the lepromin test is strongly positive (the intradermal injection of *M. leprae* antigens resulting in a granulomatous lesion at the site 3 to 4 weeks later). Tuberculoid leprosy is associated with a T_h1-cytokine profile (interferon alpha and interleukin [IL]-2).

Borderline Tuberculoid Leprosy

Borderline tuberculoid leprosy: weakly to moderately positive cell-mediated response to M. leprae

BT leprosy may be characterized by a single lesion or by a few lesions of varying sizes that are annular and plaque-like with clear centers (Figure 54–3). The lesions are dry, and sensation is moderately diminished. Hair growth is minimal. The borders are less distinct and the lesions are less erythematous than tuberculoid lesions. Multiple peripheral nerves are involved. The slit skin examination demonstrates no organisms or only a few organisms. The lepromin test is weakly to moderately positive.

Borderline Leprosy

Borderline leprosy lesions are transient

The BB leprosy lesions, which are generally early indeterminate lesions, are polymorphic with poorly defined edges. A few of the lesions will demonstrate symmetry. They are hypopigmented or slightly erythematous and have a tendency for clearing at the center (Figure 54–4). Sensation appears to be slightly diminished and nerve damage is variable. The patient may complain of numbness. Hair growth is moderately diminished and the skin appears shiny, indicative of sweating. These lesions are transient, either rapidly upgrading to BT leprosy or downgrading to BL leprosy. Skin slits reveal a small number of bacilli, and the lepromin test is negative. Biopsy demonstrates a mononuclear infiltrate involving the nerves. Epithelioid granulomas without giant cells are present.

Borderline Lepromatous Leprosy

BL leprosy is characterized by many lesions of variable sizes and shiny skin with a slight decrease in sensation and hair growth (Figures 54–5 and 54–6). The lesions are macular and plaque-like with a tendency to become papular and nodular with "punched-out" areas of normal-appearing skin. Individual lesions demonstrate indistinct outer borders and distinct inner borders around a central

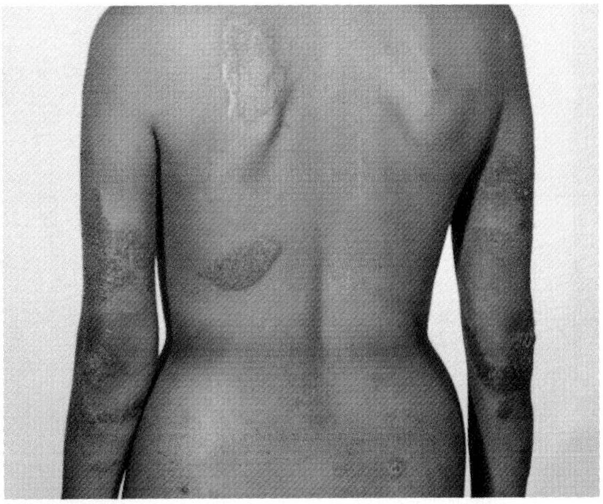

FIGURE 54–2 Sharply demarcated, anesthetic, erythematous lesion of TL on the back. (Reproduced from the slide collection of the late R. C. V. Robinson, M.D., Assistant Professor of Dermatology, The Johns Hopkins Medical Institutions.)

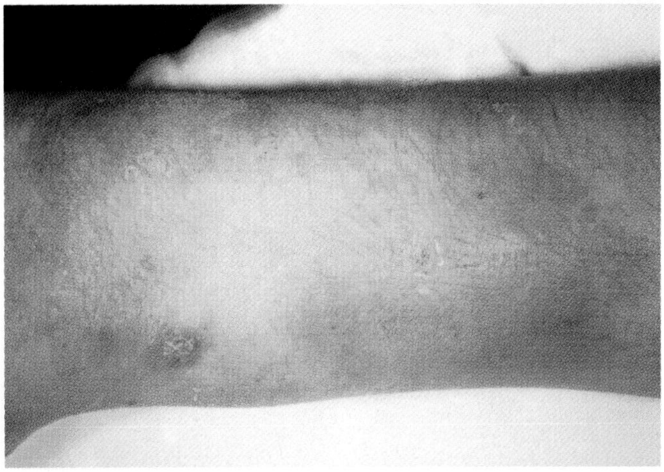

FIGURE 54–3 BT leprosy. Note slightly erythematous lesions with clearing of center. (Reproduced from the slide collection of the late R. C. V. Robinson, M.D., Assistant Professor of Dermatology, The Johns Hopkins Medical Institutions, with permission.)

hypopigmented area (classic dimorphic lesion). A slit skin examination demonstrates many *M. leprae* bacilli. Nerve damage may be widespread and symmetrical. Biopsy demonstrates a lymphocytic, foamy macrophage involving the nerves, which features lamination of the perineurium.

Antibody response to M. leprae; *many bacilli in lesion*

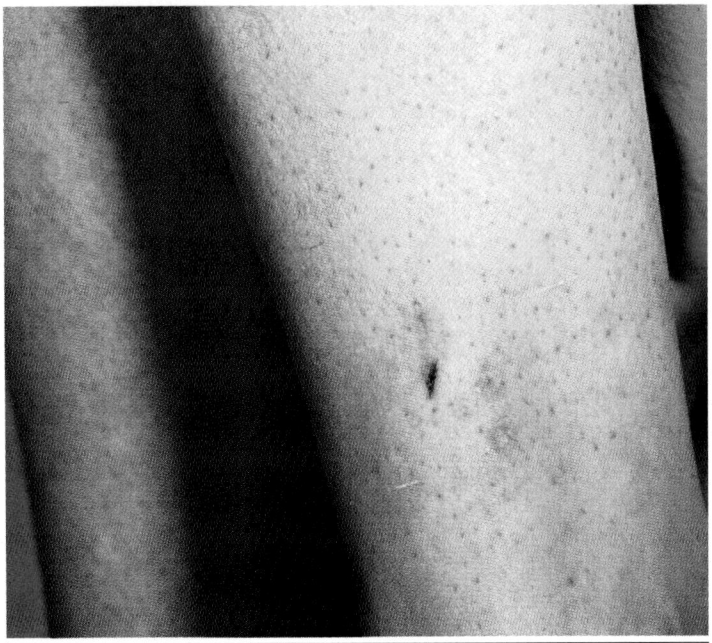

FIGURE 54–4 BB leprosy. In this case, an early lesion of leprosy on the lower leg characterized by a hypopigmented area of decreased sensation with indistinct borders. (Note mark from the slit skin examination.) (Reproduced from the slide collection of the late R. C. V. Robinson, M.D., Assistant Professor of Dermatology, The Johns Hopkins Medical Institutions.)

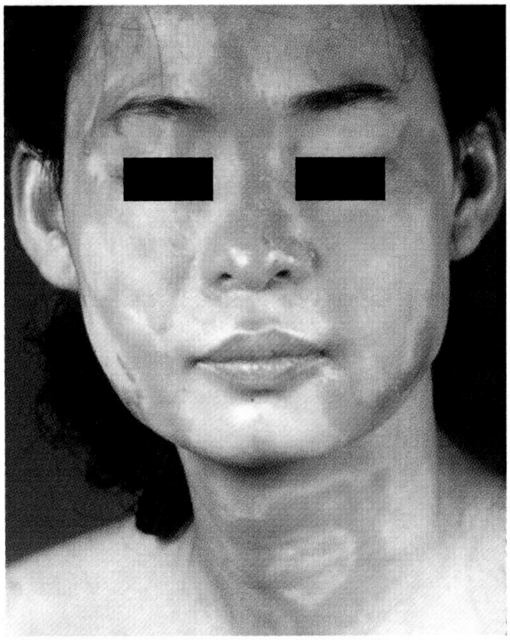

FIGURE 54–5 Woman with BL leprosy. Note widespread, shiny, asymmetric lesions with punched-out central clearing. The inner border is more sharply demarcated than the outer border (a classic dimorphic feature). (Reproduced from the slide collection of the late R. C. V. Robinson, M.D., Assistant Professor of Dermatology, The Johns Hopkins Medical Institutions.)

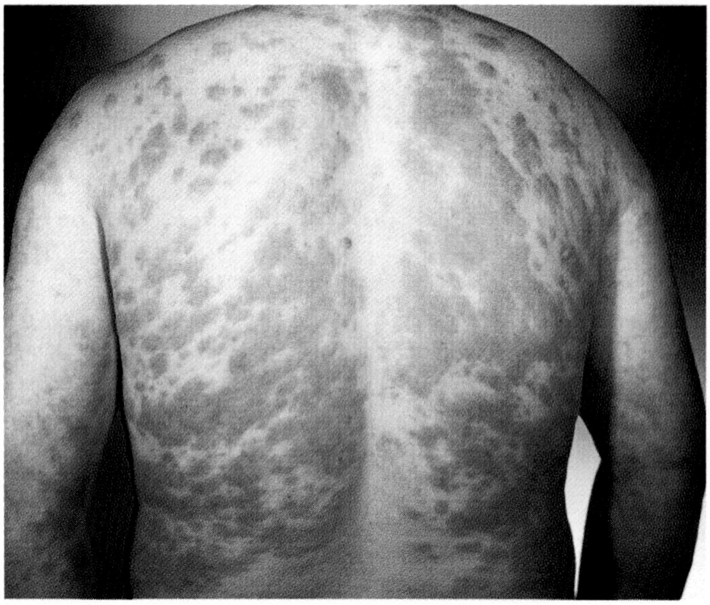

FIGURE 54–6 BL leprosy on the back. (Reproduced from the slide collection of the late R. C. V. Robinson, M.D., Assistant Professor of Dermatology, The Johns Hopkins Medical Institutions.)

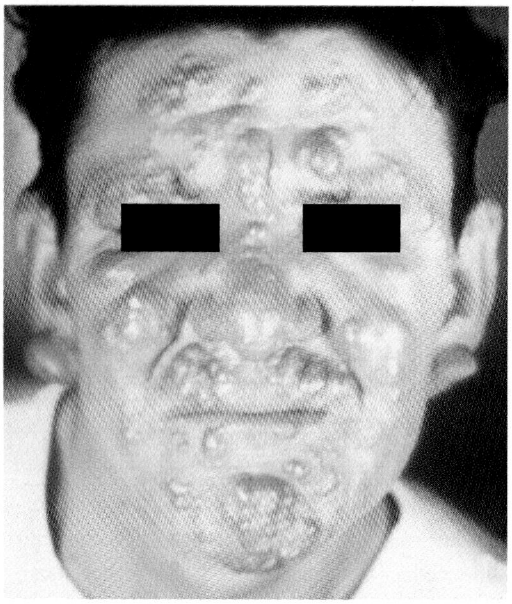

FIGURE 54–7 Leonine facies of LL. Note skin-colored nodular lesions and loss of lateral eyebrows. (Reproduced from the slide collection of the late R. C. V. Robinson, M.D., Assistant Professor of Dermatology, The Johns Hopkins Medical Institutions.)

Lepromatous leprosy

Lepromatous leprosy: lepromin test negative; antibody response-immune complex formation huge amount of bacilli in lesions

M. leprae *survives in cooler temperatures (reason for general lack of lesions in intertrigenous areas and scalp)*

LL is characterized by widespread, numerous skin-colored lesions with the involvement of multiple organs.The individual lesions are macular with poorly defined borders. *M. leprae* survive in cooler temperatures and can involve the entire body except the scalp and areas of increased warmth, such as the axilla, groin, and perineum. The lesions are shiny, and there is no alteration in sensation. These macular lesions with time become papular and nodular with the development of leonine facies (Figure 54–7). The lepromin test is negative, and a slit skin examination reveals a heavy load of organisms. Biopsy demonstrates a dermal infiltrate with foamy macrophages involving the nerves.

Systemic involvement probably immune complex–mediated to a large extent

These lesions are most prominent over the extensor surface of the arms and the backs of the hands (Figures 54–8 to 54–11) In the earlier stages, no nerve involvement may be perceived. Later, firm enlargement of many nerves can be detected with sensory and autonomic nerve loss. In addition to skin, eye, nose, testicular, and kidney damage, LL may cause damage to other organs. Immune complex mechanism may be responsible.

Lepromatous leprosy is associated with a T_h2-cytokine profile (IL-4, IL-6, IL-10).

Reversal Reactions

Type I reversal reaction characterized by increased cell-mediated immune response

Reversal reactions are common manifestations of a changed immunologic state with shifts in histologic and clinical features. There are two types: type I and type II. A type I reversal reaction is associated with an increase in the host's cell-mediated immunity with a progressively robust T_h-1-cytokine profile. Individual lesions suddenly become red, shiny, or swollen, and ulcerations may occur. In addition, nerves swell and become tender, and there is increased loss of sensation. Motor paralysis may also occur.

A type II reaction is characterized by an increase in antibody response and subsequent development of immune complexes. A general decrease in cell-mediated

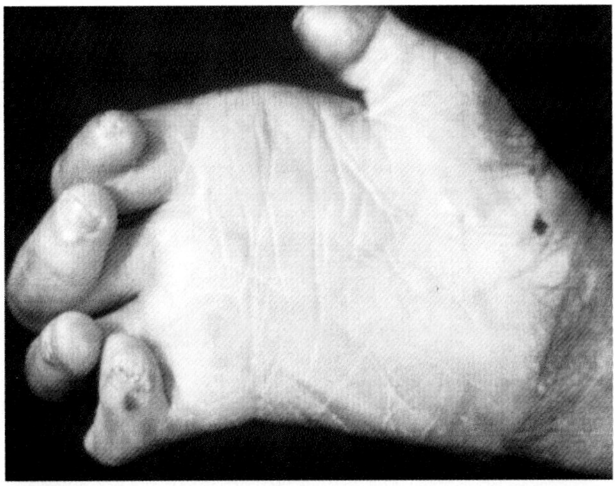

FIGURE 54-8 Deformed hand of an LL patient. Note shortening of the fingers. Reproduced from the slide collection of the late R. C. V. Robinson, M.D., Assistant Professor of Dermatology, The Johns Hopkins Medical Institutions.

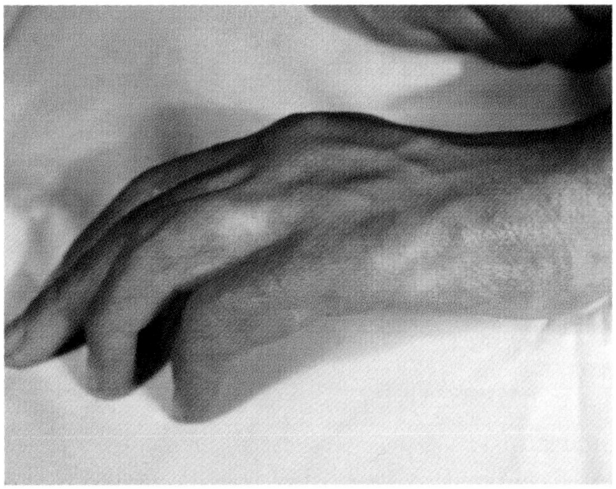

FIGURE 54-9 Early hand deformity in a leprosy patient. Note thickened ulnar nerve. Reproduced from the slide collection of the late R. C. V. Robinson, M.D., Assistant Professor of Dermatology, The Johns Hopkins Medical Institutions.

immunity to *M. leprae* occurs. On the face, arms, and legs, tender red nodules develop (Figure 54–12). Individual lesions may also become vesicular, bullous, and ulcerated (Figure 54–13). This type of reaction, termed "erythema nodosum leprosum," is frequently characterized by the presence of iritis, arthritis, nephritis, and neuritis. It involves an acute vasculitis or panniculitis occurring in over one-half of patients with LL; 90% of cases occur after the initiation of antibiotic therapy.

Type II reversal reaction characterized by increased antibody response to M. leprae

Lucio's Phenomenon

Lucio's phenomenon in untreated lepromatous leprosy

This cutaneous manifestation of LL was described in Mexico and occurs in untreated patients. Painful, red patches develop on the extremities, often with

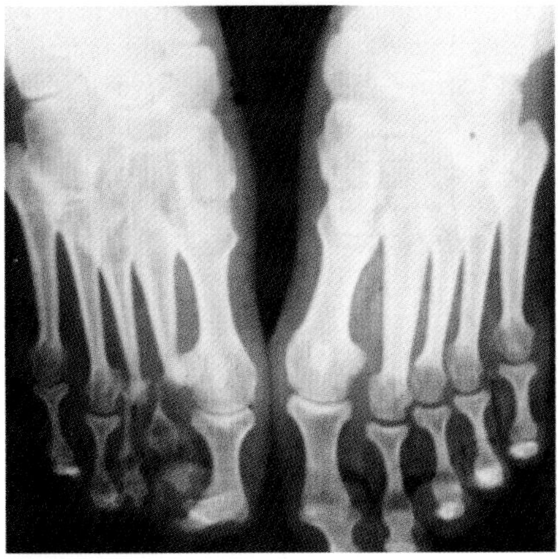

FIGURE 54-10 Radiograph of the feet of a patient with LL showing osteoporosis of the phalanges. (Reproduced from the slide collection of the late R. C. V. Robinson, M.D., Assistant Professor of Dermatology, The Johns Hopkins Medical Institutions.)

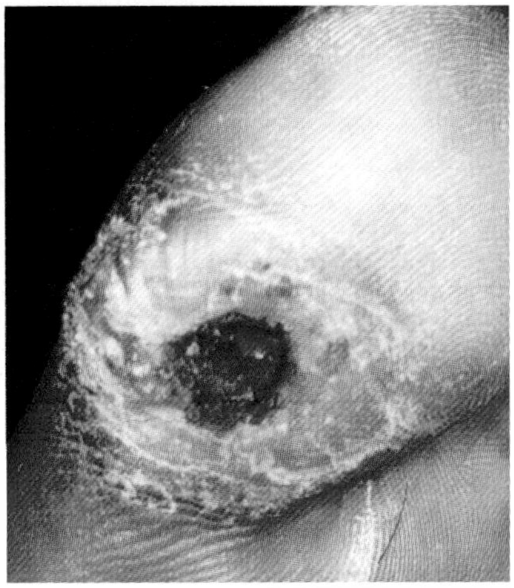

FIGURE 54-11 Mal perforans ulcer of great toe in a leprosy patient. (Reproduced from the slide collection of the late R. C. V. Robinson, M.D., Assistant Professor of Dermatology, The Johns Hopkins Medical Institutions.)

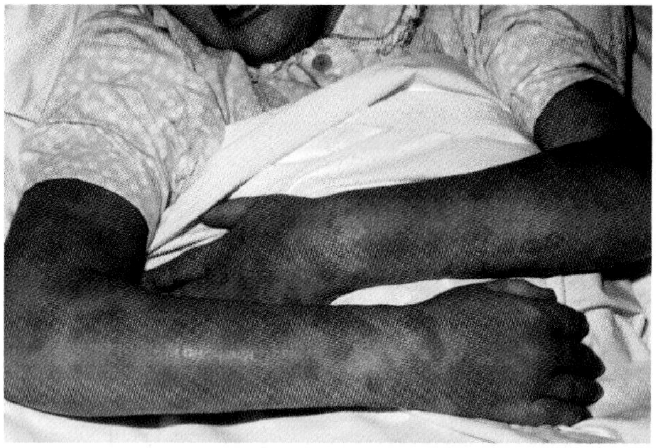

FIGURE 54–12 Erythema nodosum leprosum lesions characterized by the acute onset of painful, red lesions in a patient with LL. (Reproduced from the slide collection of the late R. C. V. Robinson, M.D., Assistant Professor of Dermatology, The Johns Hopkins Medical Institutions.)

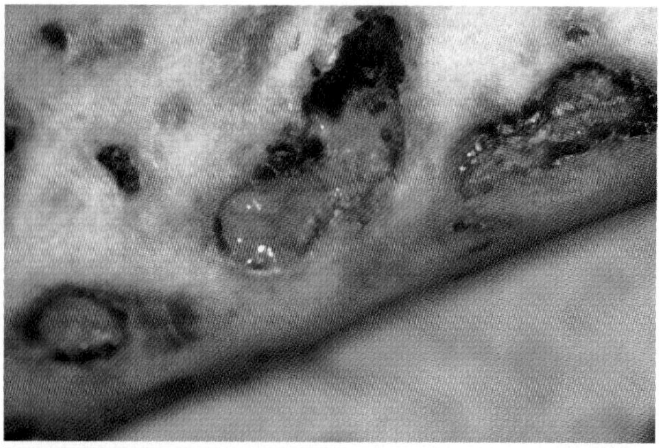

FIGURE 54–13 Ulcerations following an erythema nodosum leprosum reaction. (Reproduced from the slide collection of the late R. C. V. Robinson, M.D., Assistant Professor of Dermatology, The Johns Hopkins Medical Institutions.)

Immune complex-mediated vasculitis

ulceration. A biopsy will demonstrate a necrotizing vasculopathy with large numbers of organisms in the endothelial cells. This type of reaction may respond to prednisone, but severe cases in the developing countries have been managed by exchange transfusion (theoretically to remove immune complexes).

Diagnosis

Biopsy

A biopsy is key diagnostic technique

Careful examination of nerves

The diagnosis of leprosy is made by performing a biopsy at an involved site. The biopsy should contain subcutaneous tissue and nerve. The acid-fast organisms are detected by carbol fuchsin staining, using the Fite-Farrow modification of the Ziehl-Neelson method.

Lepromin Test

The lepromin test is used only to gauge the resistance of the host. An extract of *M. leprae* is injected intradermally. After 3 to 4 weeks, a granulomatous reaction may occur (Mitsuda reaction). A positive reaction (> 5 mm) is indicative of resistance and occurs in TL and BT leprosy. BB leprosy, BL leprosy, and LL fail to give a positive reaction.

The pilocarpine test measures sweat production, and the histamine test detects axonal flare in individual lesions. These tests are of limited value and are more of interest from an academic viewpoint.

Slit Skin Examinations

Slit skin examination used to monitor patient progress

The slit skin examinations are of value in monitoring the progress of a patient. A bacterial index measuring log-fold changes in the quantity of *M. leprae* bacilli has been established. Slit skin examinations are made from both earlobes and two active sites (Figure 54–14). A bacterial index of zero indicates that no organisms are seen in 100 oil immersion fields, 1+ indicates 1 to 10 organisms in 100 oil immersion fields, 2+ indicates 1 to 10 organisms in 10 fields, 3+ indicates 1 to 10 organisms in 1 oil immersion field, 4+ indicates 10 to 100 organisms in 1 oil immersion field, 5+ indicates 100 to 1,000 organisms in an average oil immersion field, and 6+ indicates greater than 1,000 organisms in an average oil immersion field.

Effective treatment produces granular or beaded changes in the *M. leprae* bacilli.

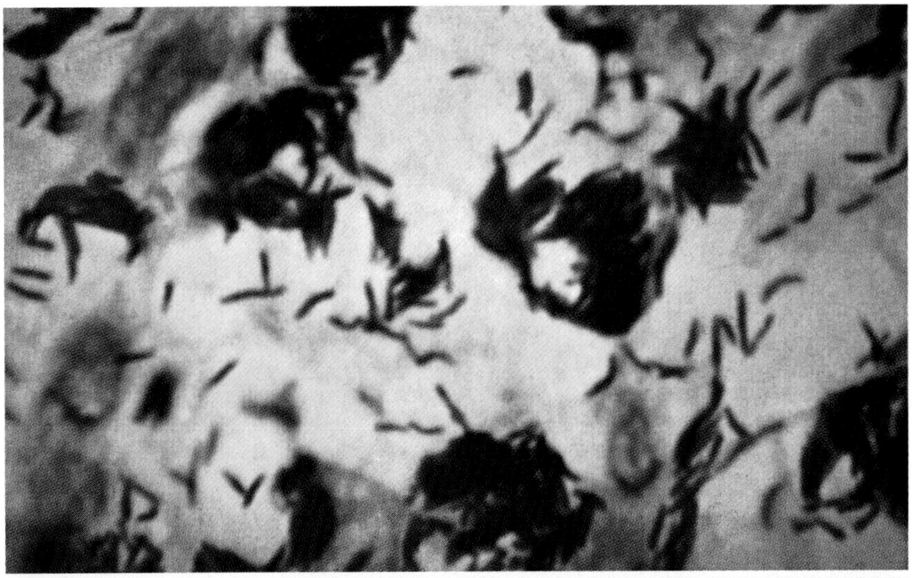

FIGURE 54–14 Slit skin examination showing single bacillus and clusters of acid-fast bacilli. Some clusters of bacilli (globi) are located in the macrophage. (Reproduced from the slide collection of the late R. C. V. Robinson, M.D., Assistant Professor of Dermatology, The Johns Hopkins Medical Institutions.)

Treatment

Treatment of LL, BL leprosy, and BB leprosy requires rifampin 600 mg and clofazimine 300 mg administered monthly, with dapsone 100 mg and clofazimine 50 mg given daily. The patients are then monitored using slit skin examinations.

Clofazimine, rifampin, and dapsone are used to treat lepromatous leprosy.

TL and BT leprosy are treated with rifampin 600 mg monthly and dapsone 100 mg daily.

Rifampin and dapsone are used to treat tuberculoid leprosy.

The duration of treatment for LL, BL leprosy, and BB leprosy is a minimum of 2 years or until the slit-skin smears are negative. The patients are usually followed up for a minimum of 5 years with a clinical and bacteriologic examination every 12 months.

The lepromatous and indeterminate stages of leprosy monitored for at least 5 years

TL and BT leprosy patients are treated for 6 months, and then all treatment stops. The patients are followed up for a minimum of 2 years with a clinical examination at least every 12 months.

Tuberculoid and borderline tuberculoid leprosy patients followed up for at least 2 years.

The treatment of type I reversal reactions is variable. Chloroquine, antimonials, aspirin, and in severe cases, oral steroids have been used. In addition, clofazimine has also been found to be useful, but thalidomide is not effective.

Type I reversal reaction may require steroids to control; thalidomide is not effective.

In type II reversal reactions, steroids have been found to be effective and should be used if there is any clinical evidence of neuritis. Thalidomide, however, is the drug of choice in the control of type II reactions; the vast majority of patients demonstrate a dramatic response. Clofazimine is also effective.

Type II reversal reactions

Thalidomide drug of choice

Annotated Bibliography

Turk JL, Bryceson ADM. Immunological phenomena in leprosy and related diseases. Adv Immunol 1971;13:209–216.

This is a classic reference for immunologic abnormalities associated with various clinical presentations of leprosy.

Ridley DS. Histological classification and the immunological spectrum of leprosy. Bull World Health Org 1974;51:451–465.

This is a good paper discussing the correlation of histologic and immunologic features of various forms of leprosy.

Rea TH, Modlin RL. Leprosy. In: Freedberg IM, Eisen AZ, Wolff K, eds. Fitzpatrick's Dermatology in General Medicine, 5th ed. New York: McGraw-Hill, 1999, pp. 2306–2318.

This is an excellent discussion by the two leading American dermatolog experts in leprosy. The bibliography is excellent.

Russ S, et al. Armadillo exposure in Hansen's disease: an epidemiologic survey in southern Texas. J Am Dermatol 2000;43:223–228.

This is an interesting survey, evaluating exposure of non-Asian versus Asian leprosy patients to armadillos in Southern Texas. Seventy-one percent of the non-Asian leprosy patients had either direct or indirect armadillo exposure, compared with none of the Asian patients. At the very least, the authors indicate that the armadillo acts as a reservoir for human disease. There is no direct evidence at the present time for transmission of leprosy from the armadillo to humans.

CHAPTER 55

Syphilis

Thomas T. Provost, M.D., Paul G. Auwaerter, M.D.

Syphilis continues to be a significant disease that has had a tremendous impact on the human race over the centuries. It is caused by *Treponema pallidum*, a cylindrical, corkscrew, prokaryotic spirochete. The organism undulates, or bends, at right angles. The treponemes normally infect only humans, but experimental infections have been induced in monkeys, rabbits, and llamas. The organism may live as a commensal in rats, mice, and guinea pigs.

A scourge of the human race

Caused by Treponema pallidum

Normally a disease limited to humans

The virulent *T. pallidum* has not been cultured by routine techniques. Successful culture of virulent *T. pallidum* has only been accomplished by inoculation of rabbit testes. An orchitis occurs in 6 to 10 days, readily demonstrating the organism. The Nichols strain of *T. pallidum* was isolated over 60 years ago from human cerebral spinal fluid and has been preserved by repeated passage in rabbits. The Reiter strain is an avirulent cultured treponema.

T. Pallidum *has not been cultured with routine techniques*

Injection into rabbit testes produces orchitis in 6 to 10 days that readily demonstrates organisms

T. pallidum rapidly dies outside the body. It is killed by drying (desiccation), and soap and water. It may survive in tissue and blood up to 4 days. It can be killed by high temperature, but it is unlikely to be killed by temperatures tolerated by humans (this was the erroneous theoretical basis for the treatment of neurosyphilis with malaria).

Nichols strain a virulent strain of T. Pallidum

Reiter strain a nonvirulent strain

The organism is not detected in tissues with routine staining but can be detected by silver impregnation techniques (Levaditi's method and Fontana's stain).

T. Pallidum *detected in tissues with silver stains*

Syphilis was first described in Europe in 1495. This fact has given rise to the Columbian theory, which postulates that syphilis was brought to Europe by Columbus' sailors after they had contracted syphilis from New World natives. However, this theory is in doubt because there is evidence that prehistoric fossils found in Africa and Australia demonstrate syphilitic changes.

Columbian theory of origin of syphilis

The term "syphilis" is taken from a Latin poem by Fracastorius entitled *Syphilus Sive Morbis Gallicus*, which was published in 1530. The shepherd hero, Syphilus, was infected. The name Syphilus may have been derived from the Greek *syn,* meaning "together," and *philein,* meaning "to love." The term *lues* comes from Latin, meaning "plague" or "pestilence."

Syphilus: shepherd in 1530 poem

Lues means plague

Natural History

Early Syphilis

The mode of infection is usually a direct inoculation of the organism into the skin or a mucous membrane. Rarely, the organism can be transmitted by infected mucous or serous secretions (the common mode of infection among dentists, physicians, and laboratory workers). Within 24 hours after inoculation, the treponemes disseminate throughout the body. This early asymptomatic phase of

Mode of infection direct penetration into skin or mucous membrane

Medical workers can become infected via contact with bodily secretions.

Chancre generally occurs 3 to 4 weeks after inoculation.

Secondary lesions may occur 8 to 16 weeks following inoculation.

syphilis corresponds to the incubation period for the development of a chancre. In males, the chancre appears 3 to 4 weeks after inoculation, although it may occur as early as 10 days or as late as 90 days after inoculation. (The rapidity of onset of the chancre appears to be inversely related to the size of the inoculum.) In the female, the chancre may not be observed in as many as 50% of patients, and the first sign of disease may be secondary lesions. These secondary lesions almost never appear before 6 weeks and usually occur 8 to 16 weeks following inoculation. It has been estimated that in 15 to 30% of patients, neither the primary and secondary stages are recognized.

VDRL and RPR rarely positive before 4 weeks. FTA-positive 2½ weeks following inoculation

Serologic tests such as the Venereal Disease Research Laboratory test (VDRL) test and rapid plasma reagin (RPR) test are rarely positive less than 4 weeks following infection. However, the fluorescent treponemal antibody test (FTA) is usually positive 2½ weeks after infection. Thus, if a physician suspects a chancre, the physician should order an FTA because the VDRL or RPR may or may not be positive at the time of onset of the primary chancre.

Primary syphilis and secondary lesions are highly infectious.

In secondary syphilis, serologies are always positive.

Abundant treponemes in the blood make the patient highly infectious when the chancre appears. However, the spirochetes soon disappear from the blood and localize to specific tissues. The secondary lesions of syphilis usually, but not always, develop before the chancre disappears. Therefore, primary and secondary stages may overlap. The secondary stage of syphilis represents the initial reaction to *T. pallidum*. The individual lesions are loaded with treponemes, but the blood only intermittently demonstrates the presence of treponemes. In general, the secondary stage of syphilis develops 2 to 6 months after infection. Serologic tests are always positive. The lesions are most prominent on the skin and mucous membranes. A darkfield examination shows many treponemes. The lesions heal over a period of weeks to months but may last more than 1 year. The lesions are nondestructive and heal without scarring.

Secondary syphilis clinically terminates when the lesions disappear. Early syphilis (encompassing the clinical stages of primary and secondary syphilis) terminates immunologically when the host immune response has reached a permanent refractory state toward the development of additional early infectious lesions. For example, within 2 years after infection with untreated syphilis, permanent host changes occur making it impossible for the tissue to react to a subsequent syphilitic inoculation; patients do not develop primary or secondary syphilitic lesions. However, if the patient is treated before the refractory state is established, re-infection or relapse usually is followed by the development of new, early syphilitic lesions.

Immunologically early syphilis terminates when permanent refractory state occurs toward the development of early syphilitic lesions with re-infection.

Other studies indicate that inoculation of human subjects with treated late syphilis may develop gummas at the site of inoculation.

Infectious Relapse

Infectious relapse occurs in 25% of untreated patients.

Infectious relapse is defined as the reappearance of early, darkfield-positive lesions weeks to months after all previous early lesions have healed. It has been estimated that 25% of untreated syphilitic patients will experience a relapse. The manifestations include atypical chancre and/or the lesions of secondary syphilis. Infectious relapse also occurs in inadequately treated patients. With inadequate treatment, it is theorized that many treponemes are destroyed, retarding the development of tissue resistance. A few treponemes survive, multiply, and reproduce the early lesions. The term "chancre redux" or "monorecidive chancre" is given to the appearance of a new chancre at the site of the original chancre.

In relapsing syphilis, a serologic relapse has also been noted. This is defined as negative serology turning to a positive serology or reversal in a downward trend in the titer without clinical lesions. This may precede the infectious relapse. In the past, it was most frequently seen after unsuccessful therapy.

Histologic Features

Plasma cell "cuffing" of small blood vessels

The histologic features of a chancre are characterized by mild acanthosis at the periphery of the ulcer and a dermal infiltrate composed predominantly of lymphocytes and plasma cells. Endothelial proliferation and swelling are prominent. Silver impregnation stains demonstrate numerous spirochetes, particularly around the capillaries.

The histopathology of secondary syphilis is more variable. If the characteristic vascular changes and plasma cells are not seen, the diagnosis is problematic. Therefore, if a diagnosis of syphilis is clinically considered, the pathologist should be alerted because silver impregnation stains will demonstrate treponemes.

Value of silver impregnation stains

Immunologic techniques, either using immunoperoxidase or fluorescent antibody techniques, also have been employed successfully to demonstrate organisms in tissues. The fluorescent techniques use frozen tissue sections, whereas the immunoperoxidase technique uses formalin-fixed, paraffin-embedded tissue.

Immunofluorescent and immunoperoxidase techniques

Late Syphilis

Early Latent Syphilis

Early latent syphilis is defined as an asymptomatic stage diagnosed by a positive serology (positive VDRL or FTA) and a history of prior syphilis. By definition, these patients have a normal physical examination, a normal cardiac fluoroscopy, and a negative cerebral spinal fluid examination, although they demonstrate a positive serology. Clinically, this stage begins after the early lesions disappear and immunity to formation of early lesions is established. As noted above, this is usually 2 years after an untreated infection. There may be an active inflammatory site at this time, but usually these patients are not infectious, although the blood may contain treponemes at times. Thus, it is possible, but not common, for a pregnant woman with latent syphilis to infect her fetus.

Early latent syphilis is characterized by:
- *normal physical examination*
- *no relevant clinical disease*
- *normal cardiac fluoroscopy*
- *negative cerebral spinal fluid examination*
- *positive RPR and FTA*

The outcome of this latent syphilis is persistence as such for many decades, as the development of symptomatic late syphilis occurs in approximately 25 to 40% of cases, although spontaneous cure occurs in nearly a quarter.

Asymptomatic Neurosyphilis

Asymptomatic neurosyphilis is a diagnosis established when a patient has evidence of cerebral spinal fluid findings in the absence of clinical disease. In untreated cases, asymptomatic neurosyphilis will occur within 2 years or not at all. In inadequately treated syphilitic patients, it may occur within 4 years. The presence of a normal cerebral spinal fluid 4 years after infection, however, means permanent immunity to the development of neurosyphilis except in the setting of HIV infection. The asymptomatic neurosyphilitic state may last for decades.

Asymptomatic neurosyphilis is characterized by:
- *positive cerebral spinal fluid findings*
- *absence of clinical signs*

Late Symptomatic Syphilis

Late symptomatic syphilitic lesions are destructive and chronic. There are two types: one is characterized by an explosive allergic reaction (gumma); the second is characterized by foci of chronic, diffuse, granulomatous inflammation.

These lesions generally occur 10 to 30 years after infection and, for reasons not well understood, are rarely seen now. The gummas are characterized by discrete ulcerated swellings of the skin, nose, throat, esophagus, stomach, and bladder. Small or large tumors may occur in the liver, testes, bone, and other parenchymal organs. It is theorized that gummas represent a vigorous sensitivity reaction of tissue exposed to a few treponemes reaching the tissue from the bloodstream or lymphatics. Gummas are characterized by coagulation necrosis surrounded by mononuclear cells. Giant cells are rare.

Gummas represent exuberant immune responses within tissue containing a few treponemes.

Cell-mediated reaction

The granulomatous infiltrate in the skin is characterized by multiple giant cells and mononuclear cells. In both the gummas and the granulomatous, nodular, ulcerative syphilitic lesions, treponemes are rare.

Granulomatous reaction is a less intense chronic tissue reaction to treponemes.

Cardiovascular involvement. Cardiovascular involvement in late syphilis is characterized predominantly by involvement of the aorta. Treponemes invade the aorta during the first few weeks of infection. An inflammatory reaction (endarteritis) involving small blood vessels in the aortic wall begins soon after the secondary stage but is rarely diagnosed before 10 years. A dissecting

Ascending aorta characteristically involved in late cardiovascular syphilis

aneurysm of the ascending portion of the aorta with aortic valve incompetence is characteristic. Involvement of the coronary artery ostia may result in ischemia and myocardial infarction.

Late central nervous system involvement may be secondary to inadequate immune responses.

Central nervous system involvement. The central nervous system manifestations of late syphilis are secondary to inadequate immune responses. Cerebral spinal fluid findings indicate that inflammation of the central nervous system begins in the early phases of a syphilitic infection. There is then a slow, chronic course. This contrasts with gumma formation, which is an explosive reaction of highly sensitized tissue to the presence of treponemes.

In contrast to primary and secondary syphilis, the tissue and blood of patients with late cardiovascular and central nervous system syphilis are rarely infectious.

Immunologic Aspects

Immunologic information very incomplete

In recent years, the immunologic aspects of syphilis have received a good deal of attention. However, our information regarding the immunology of syphilis is very incomplete.

Early lesions associated with both a T-cell and B-cell response

The initial inflammatory infiltrate of the early syphilitic lesion is neutrophilic. Neutrophils in the early skin lesions are replaced by T lymphocytes (Th-1 cytokine profile). In addition, *Treponemal*-specific antibodies are detected at the time of chancre formation. This indicates that the early phase of treponemal infection in the skin is associated with both cell-mediated and humoral responses. However, at the stage when most of the organisms appear to have been eliminated, generalized *Treponema*-positive skin lesions develop (secondary stage of syphilis).

Secondary syphilis associated with transient decrease in T-cell responses and with prominent B-cell responses.

In secondary syphilis, an immune complex–mediated glomerulonephritis may occur.

During the secondary stage, cell immune responses measured by blastogenic responses of lymphocytes to syphilitic spirochetes are depressed. The mechanism for this depressed cell-mediated immune response is unknown. (Recent studies suggest that macrophages temporarily recreate increased quantities of prostaglandin E_2 suppressing IL-2 production.) During this phase of the disease, proliferation of the spirochete occurs and antitreponemal antibody titers rise. Pathologic immune complex formation may occur. On unusual occasions, glomerulonephritis occurs. Furthermore, immunologic studies have demonstrated immune complex deposition in the affected kidneys, and acid elution studies have demonstrated the presence of enhanced concentrations of treponema antibodies. These excellent data suggest a pathologic role for immune complexes composed of treponemal antigens and treponemal antibodies in the pathogenesis of the glomerulonephritis of secondary syphilis.

The tertiary stage of syphilis (late syphilis) is thought to represent predominantly T cell–mediated response.

Following the secondary stage of syphilis, delayed hypersensitivity responses to the treponemal antigens are present. This latency phase can last for prolonged periods. The gumma and the nodular, ulcerative syphilis lesions each contain a histologic picture that is thought to be indicative of a T cell–mediated immune response.

Despite this information, little is known regarding the immune mechanisms that produce protective immunity.

Clinical Features

Primary Syphilis

Primary syphilis is characterized by chancres that are indurated, rubbery, firm, nontender papules. They are associated with nonfluctuant, firm, regional lymph nodes that are bilateral with genital lesions and unilateral with extragenital lesions (Figure 55–1). Atypical sites of involvement include the anus, lips, throat, nipples, tonsils, and fingers. Extagenital lesions may be warty or modular and nonulcerated (Figures 55–2 and 55–3). Although the chancre is generally solitary, multiple chancres may occur.

The chancre is painless, although it may become painful with secondary infection. It may coexist with chancroid, scabies, and herpes genitalis producing a confusing picture. In women, the cervix is most commonly involved.

A painless rubbery ulcer on genitalia may be associated with bilateral firm, nontender inguinal lymph nodes.
May be painful if secondarily infected

A darkfield examination is the most reliable diagnostic technique for early primary syphilis. Nonpathogenic spirochetes may produce a confusing picture in darkfield preparations from the mouth or anus. If the darkfield examination is negative, the recommendation is to repeat it on three consecutive days. With the availability of the FTA test, however, early diagnosis of syphilis is facilitated. Both the VDRL and RPR tests are cost-effective slide agglutination tests. The RPR and VDRL tests, however, may be negative at a time when the FTA test is positive. With repeat testing, however, a rapidly rising titer occurs with all syphilitic tests. (A false-positive FTA examination characterized by a beaded fluorescent pattern on the treponemes is detected in some systemic lupus erythematosus patients. This may represent antinuclear antibodies reacting with nuclear material that is exposed by disruption of the walls of the treponemes.) Systemic lupus erythematosus patients possessing antiphospholipid antibodies are generally VDRL positive.

In early syphilitic infections, the VDRL and RPR tests may be negative.

In some systemic lupus erythematosus patients, a false-positive FTA may occur.

Systemic lupus erythematosus patients with antiphospholipid antibodies may be RPR positive.

Secondary Syphilis

The skin eruptions may be widespread or localized. They are usually asymptomatic. (In general, these lesions are nonpruritic; on unusual occasions, pruritus has been noted, more commonly among African American patients.) These lesions are characterized early by an exanthematous macular roseola. They may become papular, papulosquamous (psoriasiform), or follicular (Figure 55–4). Later lesions may be annular, corymbose, or pustular. They are never vesiculobullous, except, on occasions, in infants. Copper-colored, dry, macular or papular, keratotic, inflammatory lesions may be seen on the palms and soles (lues cornu) (Figures 55–5 and 55–6). Split papular formation may be detected at the corners of the mouth. Kissing lesions may also occur in the folds of the skin of the genitalia. In patients of African descent, annular, bizarre, sometimes hyperpigmented, lesions may be detected.

Skin lesions are generally classifiable as papulosquamous lesions.

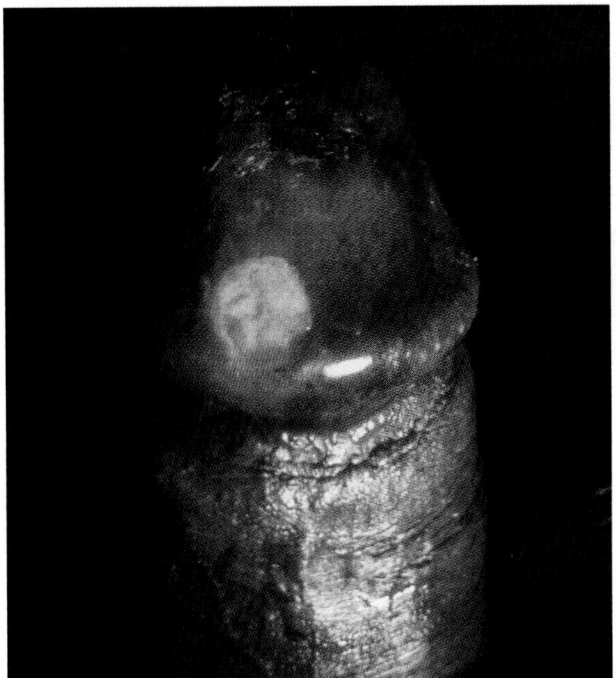

FIGURE 55–1 Primary chancre of the glans penis.

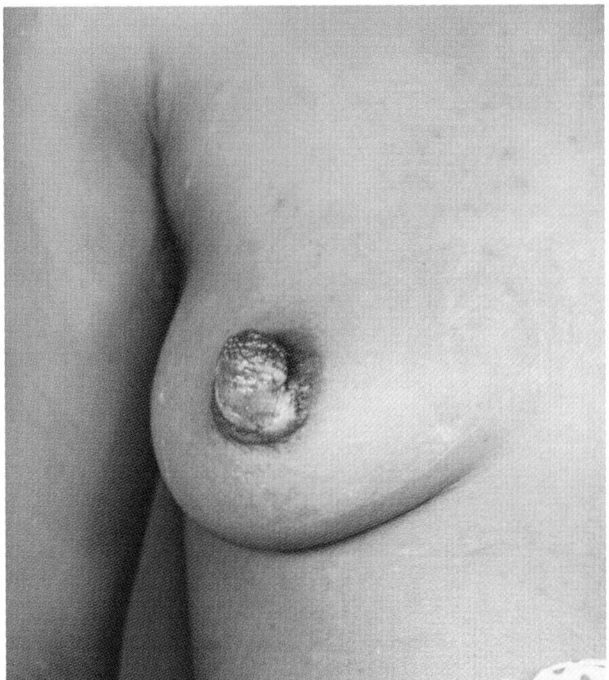

FIGURE 55–2 Primary chancre of the nipple.

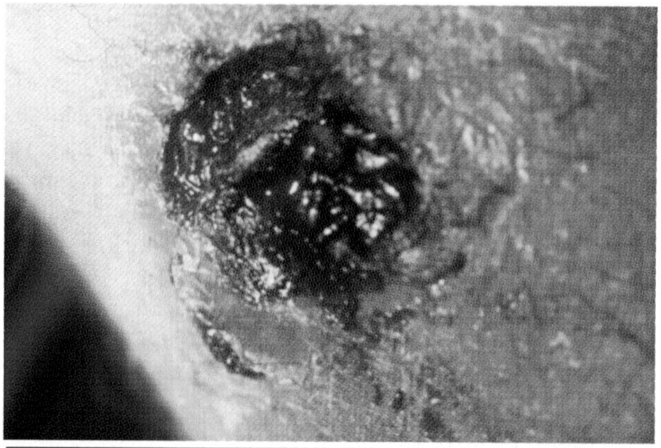

FIGURE 55-3 Atypical lesion of primary chancre on leg.

Painless mucous patch lesions may occur on the lips, mouth, tonsils, genitalia, and anus. The lesions may macerate, producing a flat, grayish, soggy erosion. The lesions of condyloma latum are hypertrophic and oozing, involving the genitalia, rectum, and between the toes. These lesions are very infectious.

Postinflammatory hyperpigmentation, as well as hypopigmentation, may occur. A peculiar, persistent macular hypopigmentation on the sides of the neck that is superimposed on reticulated hyperpigmented linear patches occurs frequently in women (Venus necklace).

Features of secondary syphilis:
- *lues cornu on hands*
- *split papules at the corners of the mouth*
- *annular lesions in African Americans*
- *mucous patches of the mouth*
- *venus necklace*

All lesions of secondary syphilis, except transient roseola-like macular dermatitis, loaded with treponemes.

Syphilis serologies always positive

Diagnosis of secondary syphilis can be made by darkfield examination. The treponemes are readily demonstrated in all secondary infections, especially in mucous membrane lesions. They are not easily demonstrated, however, in transient roseola-like macular lesions. Standard serologic testing is positive in 100% of patients.

In addition, alopecia (transient involvement of the scalp and eyebrows), iritis, neuroretinitis, and arthralgias are common. Rarely, periostitis, hepatitis, nephrosis, vasculitis, and acute meningitis occur. These manifestations may be accompanied by malaise, fever, and a generalized, mild lymphadenopathy.

Malignant syphilis (lues maligna, lues maligna praecox) is a rare, dramatic-appearing form of syphilis, demonstrating severely destructive, ulcerative lesions during the secondary stage of syphilis. Patients with this form of syphilis develop bizarre, grotesque facies with disseminated, destructive ulceration. The differential diagnosis includes deep fungal infections, leishmaniasis, verrucous sarcoidosis, bartonellosis, leprosy, yaws, and mycosis fungoides.

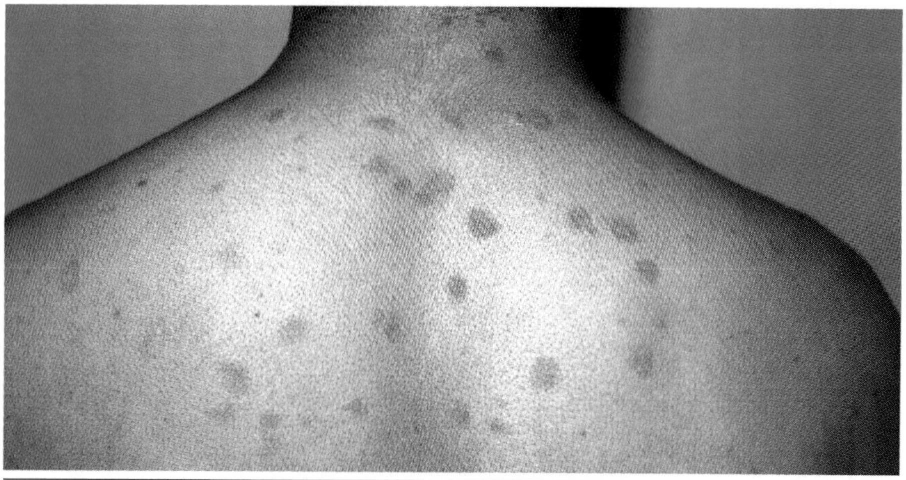

FIGURE 55-4 Papulosquamous lesions of secondary syphilis.

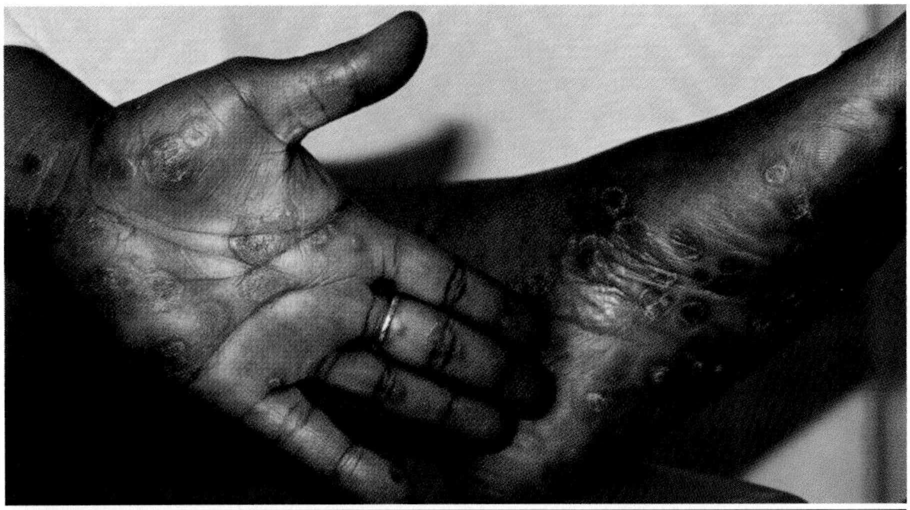

FIGURE 55-5 Lesions of secondary syphilis on palms and soles.

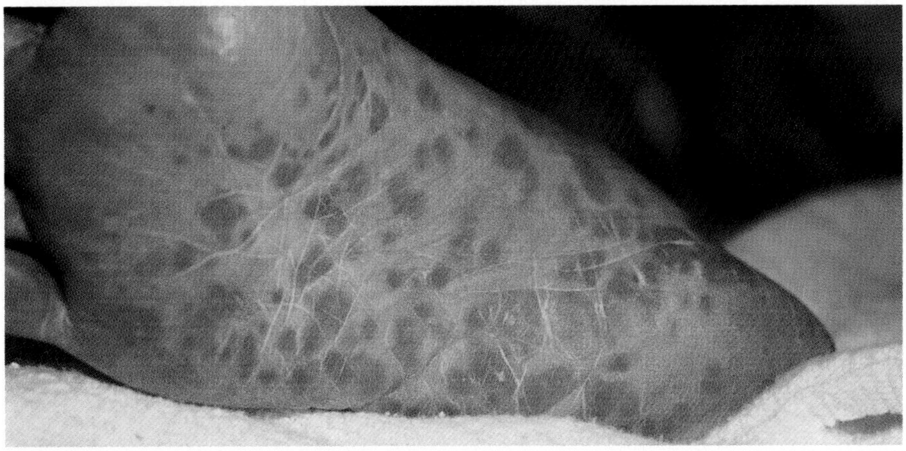

FIGURE 55-6 Copper-brown characteristic plantar lesions of secondary syphilis.

Malignant syphilis a severe form characterized by destructive lesions.

Thought to be a form of secondary syphilis

This form of syphilis may be heralded by a prodrome of fever, headache, and muscle pains. The skin lesions are widespread and start as papulopustules that soon become necrotic. Sharp, marginated ulcers covered by a thick, rupioid crust are characteristic. The face and scalp are most frequently involved, but the dermatitis is generalized. In one series, approximately one-third of patients demonstrated mucous membrane involvement. Early in the disease, the RPR test may be negative. However, late in this form of syphilis, the RPR test has been reported to be positive.

Skin biopsies demonstrate dense infiltrates of plasma cells and histiocytes. An obliterative vasculitis of medium-sized vessels at the dermal-subcutaneous junction, resulting in thrombosis with subsequent necrosis of the overlying skin, has been postulated as the pathophysiologic mechanism for the development of ulceration.

Unlike other cutaneous lesions in secondary syphilis, darkfield examinations in two studies and a histopathologic examination in one study of malignant syphilis failed to demonstrate spirochetes in the tissue. (In general, all other forms of secondary syphilis demonstrate large quantities of spirochetes in individual lesions.)

No evidence for immune complex–mediated vasculitis has been detected. The histology of individual ulcerative skin lesions demonstrates thrombosis of medium-sized vessels. Also, thromboses of smaller-sized vessels in the heart, thyroid, pancreas, and urinary bladder have been detected in at least one case.

The mechanism of ulceration in this form of syphilis is unknown. (From a conceptual viewpoint, Provost believes that the specificity of the anticardiolipin antibody in this rare form of syphilis should be investigated. In general, a positive VDRL test and anticardiolipin antibodies in syphilis are not associated with a hypercoagulable state, whereas the anticardiolipin antibody found in patients with systemic lupus erythematosus and the antiphospholipid syndrome are associated with a hypercoagulable state. In syphilis, the anticardiolipin antibody is directed at the cardiolipin, whereas in hypercoagulable states associated with lupus erythematous and the primary antiphospholipid syndrome, the antibody specificity is directed against epitopes created by the binding of β_2-glycoprotein 1 with cardiolipin. In other cases, the anticardiolipin antibody binds to the β_2-glycoprotein 1.)

Belief that malignant syphilis was the form of syphilis that swept through Europe in the 16th century.

In Europe in the 1500s, syphilis was associated with widespread cutaneous ulcerations. It has been proposed that this form of syphilis is identical to lues maligna. However, Derek Cripps and Arthur Curtis, who reviewed a number of treatises on syphilis since the year 1494, have rejected this possibility.

Late Benign Syphilis

Two types of lesions are associated with late syphilis: nodular, ulcerative lesions and gummas.

Skin Lesions

Late syphilitic lesions:
- *nodular, ulcerative*
- *gummas of the skin*

The features of nodular, ulcerative syphilis are characterized by arciform, polycyclic lesions that may be solitary or few in number (Figures 55–7 and 55–8). They are asymmetric and indolent. The borders are sharply marginated, and "punched-out" ulcers may occur. Central clearing may simultaneously occur with peripheral extension of an individual lesion. Atrophic scarring and persistent peripheral hyperpigmentation of an individual lesion may be present.

Gummas, as noted above, are violent tissue reactions to a few treponemes delivered possibly by hematogenous spread to the resistant tissue (Figure 55–9). They can occur anywhere on the skin.

Mucous Membrane Lesions

Mucous membrane involvement may occur in late syphilis. A superficial glossitis, which may ulcerate producing smooth atrophy, may also be seen along with scarring macroglossia associated with leukoplakia.

Glossitis of the tongue

Gummas of the tongue, soft and hard palate

A solitary gumma, which readily ulcerates, may be found on the tongue. A gumma of the hard or soft palate may produce perforation. There appears to be a high rate of malignant degeneration with these types of lesions.

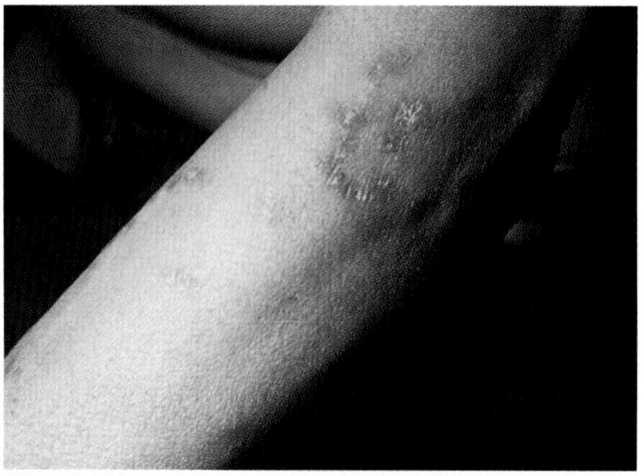

FIGURE 55–7 Nodular, serpiginous lesions of tertiary syphilis.

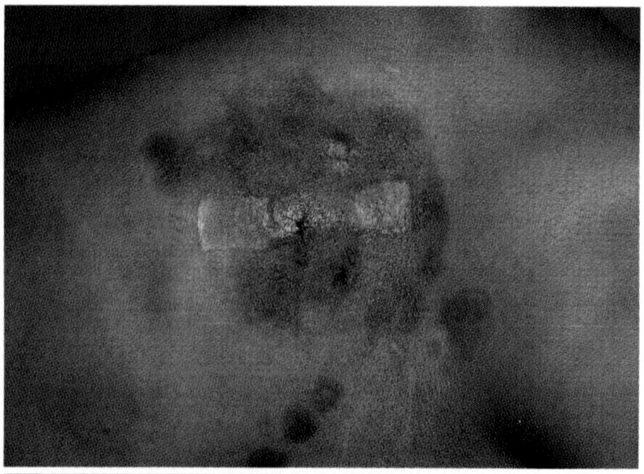

FIGURE 55–8 Plaque lesion with sharply demarcated borders of tertiary syphilis.

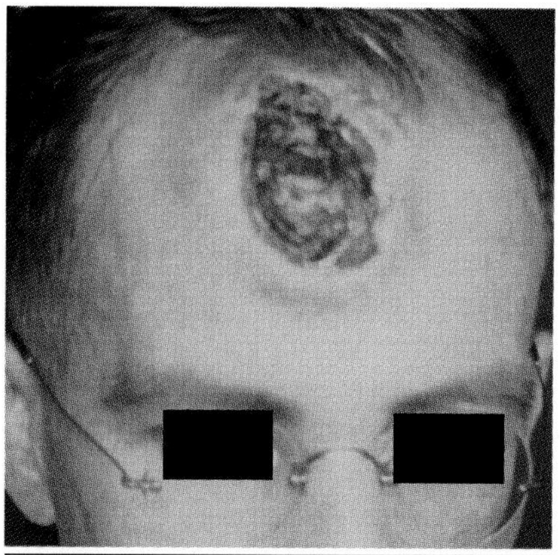

FIGURE 55-9 Gumma on forehead. (Reproduced from the slide collection of the late R. C. V. Robinson, M.D.)

Eye Lesions

Chorioretinitis of the eye

Late syphilis affecting the eyes generally produces a chorioretinitis.

Bone Lesions

Periostitis, ostitis, and gummas of bones

Involvement of the bone can produce a diffuse osteitis and periostitis. This is more common than osteolysis. Gumma formation, which usually occurs in the diaphysis of long bones, may be seen. Joint pain from an adjacent periostitis may also occur.

A Charcot joint, most commonly found in tabes dorsalis, is characterized by a swollen, painless joint secondary to multiple fractures of the joint and cartilage that are thought to be related to decreased proprioception.

Gastrointestinal Lesions

Linitis plastica

Hepar lobatum

The stomach may be involved with a gumma or diffuse inflammation (linitis plastica). Liver involvement may be secondary to gumma formation, producing scarring and lobulation (hepar lobatum). Scarring of the hilum, especially during treatment, may produce jaundice and portal hypertension.

Genitourinary Tract Lesions

The genitourinary tract may be affected. The ovaries, fallopian tubes, and the body of the uterus are rarely involved. Endocrine gland involvement is rare, except for the testes.

Hematologic Abnormalities

Paroxysymal cold hemoglobinuria

Paroxysmal cold hemoglobinuria (PCH) is an acute hemolytic anemia associated with chills, fever, malaise, myalgias, abdominal pain, and the production of brown urine. This is an autoimmune hemolytic anemia in which an antibody binds to the red blood cells following cold exposure. Once the body temperature returns to normal, complement activation and hemolysis occur. The Coomb's test is positive, and the diagnosis of PCH can be made by the Donath-Landsteiner test. This is usually seen in congenital syphilis. Antisyphilitic therapy results in a cure.

Late Malignant Syphilis

Late syphilitic lesions affecting the cardiovascular and central nervous systems frequently are lethal.

Cardiovascular Syphilis

Life-threatening late syphilitic lesions, a saccular aneurysm of aorta

Cardiovascular syphilis seems to be more common in men and in African Americans. It usually appears in the second or third decade after infection. The fundamental lesion is an aortitis that destroys the media with dilatation, producing aortic insufficiency and a saccular aneurysm of the arch of the aorta. Linear calcification with aortic dilatation demonstrated on a radiograph and increased aortic pulsation demonstrated on a cardiac angiogram are diagnostic. Aortic intimal thickening with occlusion of coronary orifices may produce coronary insufficiency. Gumma formation is rare.

Neurosyphilis

Spirochetes invade the central nervous system early in the infection, but only 10 to 15% of untreated patients develop late central nervous system symptoms. Meningeal and vascular symptoms develop relatively early, are inflammatory, and are often reversible. Parenchymous involvement (general paresis and tabes) devel-

Central nervous system

ops late (10 to 20 years after infection). It is degenerative and often irreversible. Gummas of the brain and spinal cord produce symptoms similar to tumors.

Although neurosyphilis is viewed as a late manifestation, neurologic involvement may occur at all stages of syphilis. The neurologic stages of syphilis are acute syphilitic meningitis, general paresis, tabes dorsalis, and primary optic atrophy.

Erb's spastic paraplegia

Acute syphilitic meningitis. Acute syphilitic meningitis usually occurs within the first 2 years. Meningovascular syphilis is characterized by thrombosis of the branches of the cerebral and spinal arteries with leptomeningitis. Strokes are common. Hemiplegia, cranial nerve palsies, as well as a transverse myelitis, may occur. Eighth nerve deafness is also common. Spastic spinal paraplegia (extrapyramidal tract involvement termed "Erb's spastic paraplegia") may occur. Spinal paraplegia due to spinal artery infarction may also be seen.

Argyll Robertson pupil

Pupillary changes, characterized by miosis, poor light reactions, irregular outline, poor response to atropine, and absent ciliospinal reaction may be present. The Argyll Robertson pupil is more common in tabes dorsalis. It is characterized by miosis and poor light reaction but good convergence.

In meningovascular syphilis, the cerebral spinal fluid will show a pleiocytosis, elevated protein, but usually normal glucose level.

General paresis

General paresis. Extensive spirochetal invasion of the brain produces atrophy of the parenchyma, which is progressive and fatal. Psychoses, dementia, euphoria, paranoia, and depression may result. A fine tremor, slurred speech, pupillary changes, and increased deep tendon reflexes occur. The patients may have repeated cerebral vascular accidents.

The cerebral spinal fluid has a positive VDRL in 100% of cases.

Tabes dorsalis

Charcot's joints

Tabes dorsalis. Tabes dorsalis is a selective degeneration of the posterior columns of the spinal cord characterized by demyelinization and an associated leptomeningitis. Spirochetes are rarely found in these lesions. The disease process arrests spontaneously. It usually occurs 20 to 30 years after infection and is more frequent in men. It is characterized by lightning pains and paresthesias. Gastric crisis can occur, characterized by abdominal pain, nausea, and vomiting. A broad-based ataxia is characteristic. Loss of position sense and sluggish reflexes are common. Trophic changes are manifested by Charcot's joints and mal perforans ulcers (painless ulcers of the feet). An atonic cord bladder is also commonly noted. Postural hypotension and paroxysmal hypertension, secondary to autonomic nervous involvement, may be seen. Ocular nerve paralysis, producing diplopia and ptosis, and an Argyll Robertson pupil are frequent.

Cerebral spinal fluid findings are positive early; however, with longstanding tabes dorsalis cases, cerebral spinal fluid may be normal in 20%, and the serologic tests for syphilis of the blood may be negative in 30 to 50%. The pathogenesis is unknown.

Optic atrophy

Primary optic atrophy. Primary optic atrophy is most commonly seen in patients with tabes dorsalis. It occurs in 10 to 15% of these patients. It is characterized by a gradual diminution of vision, progressing to blindness.

Syphilis in Pregnancy

Fetus infected after 16th week of gestation

Mothers giving birth to syphilitic infants acquired syphilis within the first 7 months of pregnancy.

The fetus is infected only after the 16th week. This occurs via an infection of the placenta and is usually a complication of early untreated syphilis. More rarely, it may also occur in late syphilis. Approximately 100% of women giving birth to an infant with congenital syphilis become infected during the first 7 months of pregnancy.

With succeeding pregnancies, the chance of a fetus being infected decreases. Potential outcomes of subsequent pregnancies are late abortion (after the fourth month), stillbirth, congenital infection or the infant may develop syphilis, and the infant may be uninfected.

Congenital Syphilis

Early congenital syphilis corresponds roughly to adult secondary syphilis. Late congenital syphilis corresponds roughly to adult tertiary syphilis. The time when clinical signs first appear depends on the time the fetus is infected in utero. Manifestations at birth indicate severe infection. The infant, however, is usually healthy at birth, with onset of symptoms within the second day and sixth week of life. In late congenital syphilis, the early symptoms may be absent, or the infection may remain permanently latent.

Early Congenital Syphilis

Manifestations of early congenital syphilis:
- *snuffles*
- *rhagades*
- *destructive cutaneous lesions*
- *condyloma latum*
- *bone abnormalities*
- *Parrot's pseudoparalysis*

Early congenital syphilis occurring within the first 2 years is generally more severe than adult secondary syphilis. There may be central nervous system involvement and evidence of significant septicemia. Some infants are very ill, malnourished, and dehydrated; some are marasmic; others are well. The cutaneous manifestations are similar to secondary syphilis, but unlike secondary syphilis, they may be destructive, eczematous, and bullous. Alopecia of the eyebrows ("moth-eaten") and eyelashes may be present. Rhinitis ("snuffles") is usually the first sign. The mucopurulent discharge is very infectious. Upper lip ulceration with scarring may occur. Destructive lesions at the corners of the mouth may produce radiating scars (rhagades). In addition, moist papules and erosive lesions of the mouth, throat, genitalia, and anus can occur. These are analogous to condyloma latum. Bone and cartilage involvement may be evident at birth, with flattening of the bridge of the nose due to destruction of the cartilage. An osteochondritis and periostitis of the long bones, face, and skull may be diagnosed by radiograph. Parrot's pseudoparalysis, due to a periostitis of the arms and legs, produces pain on passive motion. Severe osteitis of the phalanges (syphilitic dactylitis) may occur.

Jaundice

Meningitis

Other features of early congenital syphilis include hepatosplenomegaly, associated with jaundice and edema, as well as anemia. The presence of jaundice, anemia, edema, and postdermatitis hyperpigmentation may produce a dirty, whitish-brown café-au-lait appearance. Meningitis may occur in 40 to 50% of infants.

Lesions are dark field-positive

Serologic testing for syphilis in a newborn is problematic because of possible contamination from mother. A cord blood immunoglobulin IgM FTA circumvents the problem of passive transfer of antibodies from the mother. However, the infant may not have had time to develop antibodies of its own. A darkfield examination of the syphilitic lesion will be positive.

Late Congenital Syphilis

Higouménaki's sign
Hutchinson's teeth

The cutaneous stigmata of congenital syphilis, occurring after the age of 2 years are due to scars of early lesions and developmental changes caused by early infection, include frontal bossing (Parrot's nodes). This is a bulging of the upper half of the frontal bones. Saddle nose, overgrowth of maxilla and mandible, rhagades, thickening of the proximal clavicle (Higouménaki's sign), winged scapula, sabre shin (thickening and anterior bowing of the tibia), and dental dystrophies may also occur (Figures 55–10 to 55–12). The first teeth are normal. However, the buds of permanent teeth are injured during the fifth to seventh months of gestation. This may manifest as poorly formed teeth, which are spaced far apart, have poor enamel, and quickly decay, known as Hutchinson's teeth (peg-shaped incisors with a notch) and mulberry (Moon's) molars (poorly formed cusp).

Late congenital syphilis may not be associated with cutaneous stigmata. Cardiovascular involvement is very rare. Interstitial keratitis, characterized by vascularization of the cornea producing scarring and opacity, usually occurs between the ages of 10 and 20 years. It may involve one or both eyes. Although the exact etiology is unknown, it is theorized that it may develop as a consequence of early infection that produces an increased susceptibility to vascularization. It

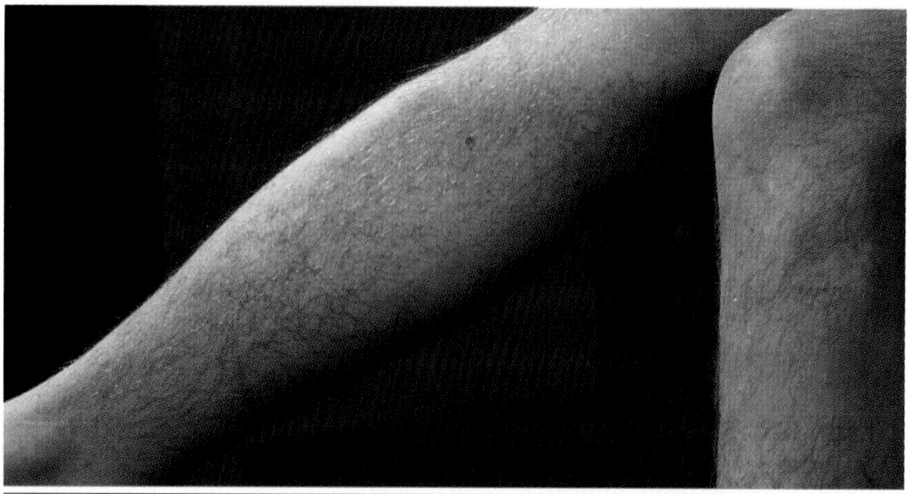

FIGURE 55-10 Sabre shin of congenital syphilis. Note anterior bowing of the tibia. (Reproduced from the slide collection of the late R. C. V. Robinson, M.D.)

Manifestations of late congenital syphilis:
- *Clutton's joints*
- *eighth nerve deafness*
- *interstitial keratitis*
- *Hutchinson's triad*

may also arise as a local disturbance in the tissue immune reaction (hypersensitivity reaction). However, it is not due to corneal invasion by the spirochete.

A painless syphilitic synovitis (Clutton's joints), producing a great deal of swelling, mainly of large joints, has been described in late congenital syphilis.

The manifestations of late congenital neurosyphilis are similar to acquired neurosyphilis. Meningovascular disease is most common and may lead to an eighth nerve deafness. Juvenile paresis usually occurs in the teens. Hutchinson's triad, characterized by Hutchinson's teeth, interstitial keratitis, and eighth nerve deafness. Paroxysmal hemoglobinuria is a feature, but gummas and gummatous infiltrations are unusual.

(For a discussion of syphilis and human immunodeficiency virus infection, see Chapter 64, "Human Immunodeficiency Virus.")

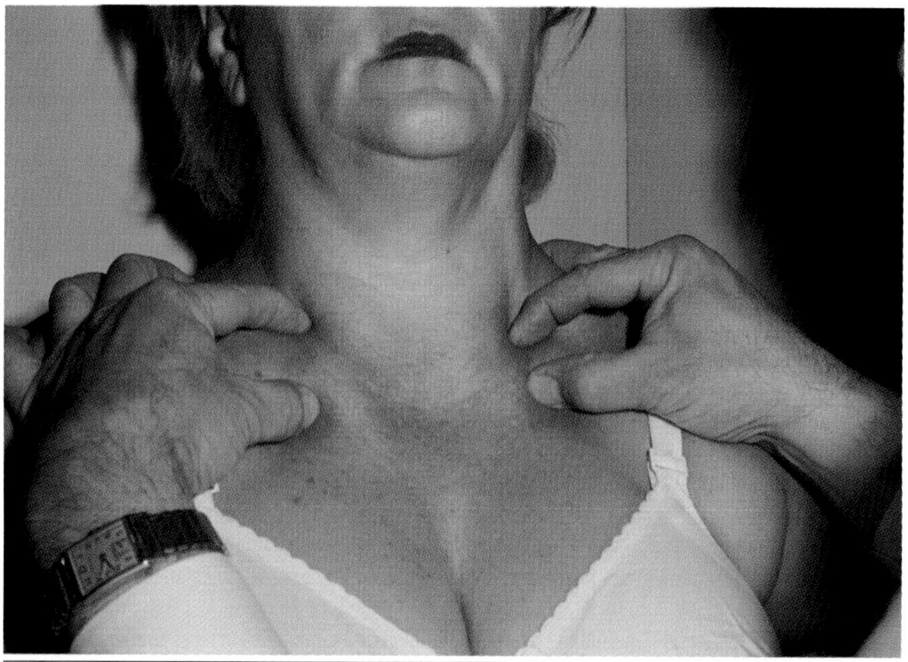

FIGURE 55-11 Higouménakis' sign of congenital syphilis. Note thickness of the proximal clavicles. (Reproduced from the slide collection of the late R. C. V. Robinson, M.D.)

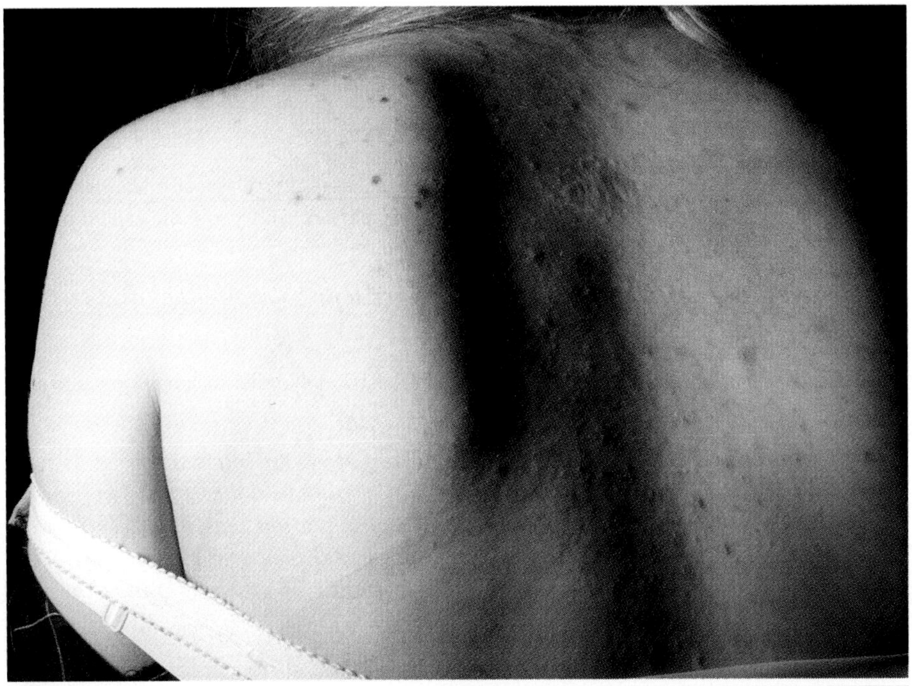

FIGURE 55–12 Winged or scaphoid scapula of congenital syphilis. (Reproduced from the slide collection of the late R. C. V. Robinson, M.D.)

Jarisch-Herxheimer Reaction

Jarisch-Herxheimer reaction usually occurs in early syphilis. Within 12 hours of injection of penicillin, patients may develop a temperature as high as 105°F, systemic toxic symptoms, and a flare of skin lesions. This usually subsides within a few hours with no residual damage. This is thought to be due to the rapid release of breakdown products of killed spirochetes and may represent an acute immune complex reaction. It is estimated to occur in 50% of patients.

In late syphilis, a similar reaction occurs in approximately 10% of patients. It generally develops within the first 24 hours. There may be a transient flare of systemic signs and symptoms. These signs and symptoms are usually milder than in early syphilis. It may produce a temporary psychotic agitation in patients with neurosyphilis. It may rarely be disastrous in cardiovascular and central nervous system syphilis. For example, if there are spirochetes in the coronary ostia, the wall of an aneurysm, or the brain, the Jarisch-Herxheimer reaction may result in anatomic damage with rapid healing of late syphilitic lesions with scar formation. This is termed a "therapeutic paradox."

Jarisch-Herxheimer reaction:
- *generalized toxic reaction with high fever following penicillin therapy*
- *occurs in approximately 50% of early syphilitic patients*
- *occurs in approximately 10% of late syphilitic patients*
- *believed to be immune complex-mediated*

Annotated Bibliography

Sell S, Norris SJ. The biology, pathology and immunology of syphilis. Int Rev Exp Pathol 1983;24:203.

Baughn RE, Musher DM. Syphilis immunology is very like an elephant. Prog Dermatol 1983;17(2):1–11.

These two excellent articles summarize the immunology of syphilis.

Cripps DJ, Curtis AC. Syphilis maligna praecox. Syphilis of the great epidemic? A historical review. Arch Intern Med 1967;119:411–418.

This is an interesting paper regarding malignant syphilis during the 1500s.

Tomecki KJ, Tomecki EC. Neglect of syphilis in hospitalized patients. South Med J 1984;77:1118–1120.

Tomecki KJ, Plaut ME. Syphilis surveillance. Failure to screen in the university hospital. J Am Med Assoc 1976;236:2641–2642.

These two papers demonstrate the failure of physicians to screen for syphilis among hospitalized patients from two different university medical centers.

Kraus SJ, Haserick JR, Lantz MA. Fluorescent treponema antibody absorption test reactions in lupus erythematosus. Atypical beading pattern and probable false positive reactions. N Engl J Med 1970;282:1287–1290.

This interesting paper details the experience with false-positive FTA tests in systemic lupus erythematosus patients.

Magnuson JH, Thomas EW, Olansky S, et al. Inoculation syphilis in human volunteers. Medicine 1956;35:33–82.

This is an excellent study demonstrating the effect of inoculation of T. pallidum *into nonsyphilitic, as well as syphilitic, human volunteers. This study, in general, demonstrated that the size of the inoculum was inversely related to the length of incubation time before the appearance of a primary chancre. As few as 10* T. pallidum *organisms were capable of infecting a human.*

This study also provided excellent evidence indicating that the development of resistance to superinfection occurred in patients with untreated syphilis for at least 2 years. Furthermore, early treated syphilis failed to develop resistance. Finally, evidence was presented that late latent syphilis patients, on re-inoculation, were at risk to develop gummas.

CHAPTER 56

Other Sexually Transmitted Diseases

Thomas T. Provost, M.D., Paul G. Auwaerter, M.D.

Chancroid

Chancroid (soft chancre) is a sexually transmitted disease characterized by the development of an ulcerated, nonindurated lesion on the genitalia that is usually associated with painful inguinal adenitis. The causative agent is *Haemophilus ducreyi*, a gram-negative bacillus. This sexually transmitted disease is commonly found in the developing countries, especially Africa, and tropical countries, most often in lower socioeconomic groups. Poor personal hygiene is also etiologically important. Like other sexually transmitted diseases, chancroid has been recognized as a risk factor for the heterosexual transmission of the human immunodeficiency virus (HIV).

A fastidious organism, *H. ducreyi* is a facultative anaerobe requiring blood (factor X) for growth on laboratory media. Advances in isolation techniques have led to better recognition of the disease, which is more common than previously described and is worldwide in distribution.

Common in tropics and subtropics

Painful, nonindurating chancre

Soft chancre caused by Haemophilus ducreyi

Extragenital sites of infection are rare.

Painful unilateral inguinal lymphadenitis

Clinical Features

Pain and tenderness characterize the chancroid, in contrast to the painless chancre of syphilis. Moreover, the ulcer has ragged and indeterminate edges. These ulcers usually measure 2 to 3 mm but can be as large as 2 cm. The typical incubation period is 2 to 5 days following exposure. The most common location in men for the ulcer is the prepuce of the glans and shaft of the penis. In women, the labia as well as the vaginal vestibule are characteristic sites of involvement (Figure 56–1). Extragenital sites of infection rarely occur and include the mouth, breast, and fingers from local inoculation.

A transient unilateral and painful inguinal adenitis is characteristic. The lymph nodes often suppurate and break down causing a bubo.

Differential Diagnosis

Differential diagnosis of the painful genital ulceration of the *H. ducreyi* includes primary or recurrent herpes simplex ulcers, a primary chancre of syphilis, and lymphogranuloma venereum (LGV). Chancroid is commonly diagnosed on clinical grounds, but swabbing of the base of the ulcer should be attempted for culture. A quick diagnosis can be obtained by the demonstration of gram-negative coccobacilli (school of fish pattern). Syphilis must be ruled out in any case of chancroid because of the overlapping features of the diagnoses. Recommendations are to perform a darkfield examination of the ulcer or to follow up with sequential syphilis serologies.

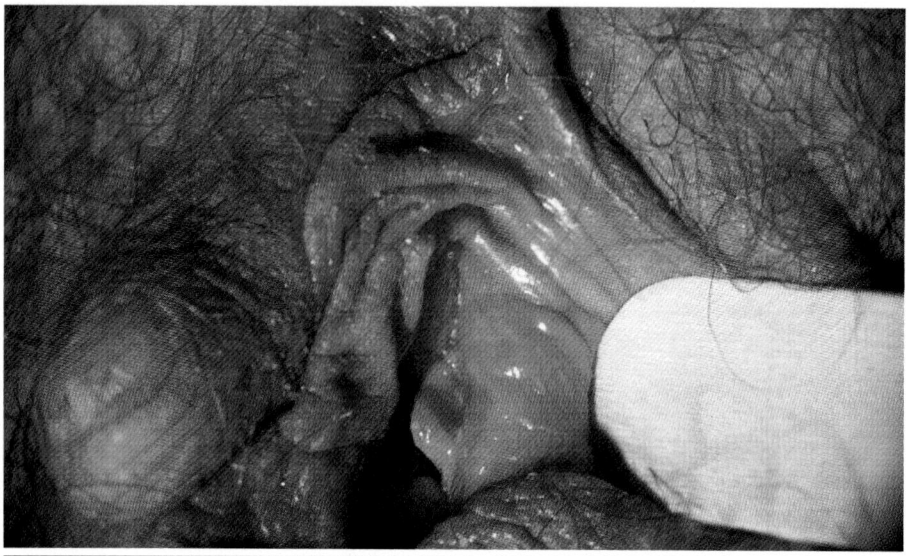

FIGURE 56–1 Painful ulcer of chancroid labia minora (Reproduced from the slide collection of the late R.C.V. Robinson, M.D.)

Treatment

Resistance to certain antibiotics

Plasmid-mediated resistance to ampicillin, sulfonamides, chloramphenicol, tetracycline, and kanamycin all have been described in *H. Ducreyi*. The oral treatments of choice include either azithromycin (1 g in a single dose) or ceftriaxone (250 mg intramuscularly in a single dose). Ceftriaxone has a high faiure rate in HIV-positive men. Erythromycin (500 mg qid for a 7-day period), amoxicillin plus clavulanate potassium (Augmentin) (500/125 mg orally tid for 7 days), and ciprofloxacin (500 mg bid for 3 days) are also effective.

The organism is now often resistant to sulfa drugs or tetracyclines, and single-dose azithromycin treatment failure has been reported.

Identification of sexual partners is imperative. Contacts must be treated because an asymptomatic carrier state is difficult to ascertain.

Annotated Bibliography

Morse SA, Trees DL, Htun Y, et al. Comparison of clinical diagnosis and standard laboratory and molecular methods for the diagnosis of genital ulcer disease. J Infect Dis 1997;175:583–589.

This is an excellent investigation regarding state-of-the-art detection of genital ulcers.

Schmid GP, Sanders LL Jr, Blount JH, et al. Chancroid in the United States. Reestablishment of an old disease. JAMA 1987;258:3265–3268.

Once thought uncommon, chancroid is increasingly recognized in the United States.

Lymphogranuloma Venereum

Chlamydia trachomatis *serovars L1, L2, and L3*

Lymphogranuloma venereum is a sexually transmitted disease most commonly found in tropical and subtropical countries. It is spread by direct inoculation and is caused by *Chlamydia trachomatis* serovars L1, L2, and L3.

Clinical Features

Three well-described stages of LGV occur. The first is characterized by a soft, erythematous, painless erosion generally occurring on the genitalia, but which may also occur in the perirectal or pharyngeal regions. These erosions heal within a few days and are frequently not recognized by the patient or physician.

"Groove" sign

The second stage occurs days to weeks later in lymph nodes draining the ulcer site. Lymphadenopathy occurs above and below Poupart's ligament in the inguinal region. The ligament characteristically produces a "groove" sign through the matted mass of inflamed lymph nodes. The lymph nodes may rupture producing chronic sinus formation. Systemic symptoms are common during the secondary stage (see below).

Prominent lymphadenopathy above and below Poupart's ligament

The third stage involves healing with scar formation but may include the complication of esthiomene (from Greek, meaning "eating away") in women, referring to the hypertrophic granulomas and the swelling and ulceration of external granulomas.

Elephantiasis a sequela

Systemic manifestations occur, including fever, arthralgias, and headache. Hepatosplenomegaly, light sensitivity in Caucasians, and rarely meningitis and encephalitis may occur. Elephantiasis of the penis and scrotum are late sequelae due to scarring of involved lymphatics. Rectal stricture occurs in homosexual men due to anal infection but may also occur in women as the result of perirectal lymphatic drainage from the vagina. Elephantiasis of the perineum may occur in women.

The lymph nodes histologically demonstrate characteristic stellate abscess formation with a cellular infiltrate composed of polymorphonuclear leukocytes and macrophages surrounded by epithelioid and plasma cells.

Like chancroid, LGV genital infection is a risk factor for the spread of HIV infection.

Diagnosis

The differential diagnosis of inguinal adenopathy in sexually active patients includes syphilis, herpes simplex virus, chancroid, granuloma inguinale, and rarely, lymphoma or cat-scratch disease.

Frei's test no longer used

In the past, the Frei test was used for diagnosis. It consisted of interdermal inoculation of killed LGV organisms. The test is no longer used, having been replaced by the isolation and detection of organisms from tissue or body fluids, although this is only positive in 30% of cases. In addition to direct culture techniques, complement fixation and microimmunofluorescent assays are available for serologic diagnosis. These tests, unfortunately, are not specific because all members of the genus *Chlamydia* are detected. The radioimmunoassay and enzyme-linked immunoabsorbent assay (ELISA) have from lack of specificity.

Treatment

Responds to doxycycline and sulfisoxazole

Lymphogranuloma venereum responds to doxycycline (100 mg bid for 21 days) with erythromycin (500 mg orally qid). Sulfisoxazole (1 g qid for 3 weeks) is also effective but is not the treatment of choice.

Rectal LGV may require re-treatment. Late stage scarring responds variably to antibiotic treatment.

The suppurative nodes, like those of chancroid, should not be excised but should be drained using a large syringe. The fluctuant buboes should be aspirated from a lateral approach through normal skin, preventing sinus tract formation.

Annotated Bibliography

Becker LE. Lymphogranuloma venereum. Int J Dermatol 1976;15:26–33.

This is a dated but good review of the subject.

1998 guidelines for treatment of sexually transmitted diseases. Centers for Disease Control and Prevention MMWR Morb Mortal Wkly Rep 1998;47(RR-1):1–111.

This report provides current antibiotic recommendations.

Granuloma Inguinale

Common in tropics and subtropics

Granuloma inguinale, also termed "donovanosis," is a chronic, progressive, ulcerative disease caused by *Calymmatobacterium granulomatis*, a gram-negative bacillus. Rare in the United States, it is a major cause of genital ulceration in Southeast Asia, Africa, the Caribbean, and South America. The organism has been detected in the gastrointestinal tract, and Goldberg postulates that *C. granulomatis* is a commensal that then autoinfects the genital tract. Poor hygiene, lower socioeconomic status, and the practice of rectal intercourse appear to be etiologically significant. Homosexuals have an increased frequency of this disease. This disease of the genitalia is a risk factor for the spread of HIV infections.

Clinical Features

Indolent granulomatous ulceration

Lymphadenopathy very rare

Granuloma inguinale usually begins as a firm, papulonodule or subcutaneous nodule. These papules and nodules quickly break down producing a characteristic, sharply demarcated nonpainful ulcer with no regional lymphadenopathy. The lesions occur on all areas of the genitalia. The ulcer, untreated, is indolent and continues to spread. True lymphadenopathy is very rare, but pseudobuboes occur because of intense granulomatous inflammation from subcutaneous spread. Rarely, the disease may produce elephantiasis of the penis, scrotum, or vulva. On unusual occasions, metastatic involvement of the liver, spleen, and bones may occur.

Diagnosis

The diagnosis is commonly made on clinical presentation, but confusion with other ulcerative processes, such as LGV, syphilis, and squamous cell carcinoma, is common. Diagnosis is often confirmed by histopathologic examination of ulcer scrapings demonstrating gram-negative, bipolar "safety pin–shaped" rods in the cytoplasm of macrophages. These rods, termed "Donovan bodies," in the cytoplasm of macrophages can be detected using Wright's or Giemsa stain of a touch preparation from the lesion. The silver impregnation stain (Warthin-Starry) is also valuable for detecting these organisms.

Calymmatobacterium granulomatis recently has been successfully grown in tissue culture systems using monocytes or HEp-2 cells.

Treatment

Tetracycline most common treatment

The most common treatment for granuloma inguinale is tetracycline (500 mg qid) or doxycycline (100 mg bid for 3 to 4 weeks or until complete re-epithelization has occurred, whichever is later). The disease also responds to sulfisoxazole, ampicillin, and the quinolones, but treatment failures have been reported with each of these drugs. Recent studies using azithromycin show great promise.

Annotated Bibliography

Davis CM. Granuloma inguinale: a clinical, histological and ultrastructural study. JAMA 1970;211:632–639.

Rosen T, Tschen JA, Ramsdell W, et al. Granuloma inguinale. J Am Acad Dermatol 1984;11:433–438.

These are two review articles of value.

Goldberg J. Studies on granuloma inguinale VII. Some epidemiological consideration of the disease. Br J Vener Dis 1967;40:140.

This article postulates that the natural reservoir of C. granulomatis *is in the gastrointestinal tract.*

Gonorrhea

Gram-negative diplococcus

Cervicitis in women frequently asymptomatic

Gonorrhea (GC) is a sexually transmitted disease caused by the gram-negative diplococcus *Neisseria gonorrhoeae*. The disease is spread almost exclusively by sexual contact and most commonly presents as an acute urethritis in men and cervicitis in females. Rectal and pharyngeal lesions may also occur. Newborns may be infected by passage through a contaminated birth canal, presenting with eye involvement (ophthalmia neonatorum). The infection in women, unfortunately, may be asymptomatic in as many as 70%.

Gonorrhea has been declining as a sexually transmitted disease since the mid-1970s in many developed countries, including the United States, and has been virtually eradicated, for example, in Sweden. The highest incidence is now found in the developing countries, with an estimated prevalence of 10% in pregnant women in Africa.

Clinical Features

Urethritis in men

As noted earlier, urethritis characterized by a painful, purulent discharge is the most common presentation in males after a 2- to 5-day typical incubation period. As many as 15% of GC-infected men may have minimal symptoms and may not seek treatment. These untreated males may go on to develop an epididymitis or prostatitis and remain infectious.

Asymptomatic State

In females, it has been estimated that as many as 30 to 60% of infected women are asymptomatic. These asymptomatic, long-term carriers, like their male counterparts, are capable of spreading the disease.

In women:

- *proctitis*
- *endometritis*
- *peritonitis*

The disease in women may spread via the lymphatics to the perirectal region, producing a proctitis. The ascending spread of the infection from the endocervix can produce endometritis, salpingitis, and pelvic peritonitis.

Pelvic Inflammatory Disease

An ascending genital infection, resulting in pelvic inflammatory disease (PID), occurs in 10 to 20% of GC-infected women and may produce combinations of endometritis, cervicitis, ovarian abscess, and peritonitis. In addition to chronic pain, PID may result in subsequent infertility and ectopic pregnancy. An usual complication of GC–PID is acute gonococcal perihepatitis with peritonitis, fibrosis, and adhesions occurring on the capsule of the liver surface (Fitz-Hugh-Curtis syndrome). This condition manifests itself as abdominal wall pain in the right upper quadrant and may be mistaken for acute cholecystitis or viral hepatitis. Most cases occur in the setting of clear-cut PID, but some women may lack pelvic signs. Though this syndrome is classically associated with GC, *Chlamydia trachomatis* is the most common cause.

Gonococcal arthritis syndrome

On unusual occasions, women may develop an arthritis dermatitis syndrome as a manifestation of disseminated gonococcal infection (DGI). (See Chapter 21, "Nonimmunologic and Reactive Arthritides.") DGI occurs in 0.5 to 3% of infected patients and presents with a syndrome of septic arthritis, polyarthritis, tenosynovitis, and/or dermatitis.

Diagnosis

In men, a gram stain of the urethral discharge will demonstrate gram-negative diplococci in the cytoplasm of neutrophils and, using trained technicians, has near equivalent sensitivity to culture. The organism also can be cultured using chocolate agar and is considered the definitive test with a sensitivity of 95% in men and 80 to 90% in women.

The selective medium (a modified Thayer-Martin medium) is commonly employed. Another selective medium, Transgrow, contains CO_2 and is good for transport.

A DNA probe now increasingly used to identify organism.

More recent advances in the field have included a DNA probe assay (Gen-Probe). This genetic tool, detecting GC-specific DNA, is now commonly used in many laboratories directly on swabbed specimens. It avoids the problem of rapid and careful transport of *N. gonorrhoeae* to the laboratory. A variety of polymerase chain reaction–based tests have been developed and are pending approval by the US Food and Drug Administration.

Treatment

Tetracycline and penicillin drug resistance has recently emerged.

In recent years, *N. gonorrhoeae* drug resistance has become problematic. Penicillinase-producing *N. gonorrhoeae* was first detected in the late 1980s. Now, approximately one-third of islets of *N. gonorrhoeae* show penicillin or tetracycline resistance. Even resistance to quinolones is problematic, especially in Southeast Asia.

The current 1998 recommendation of the U.S. Public Health Service for uncomplicated GC is ceftriaxone (125 mg intramuscularly), azithromycin (1 g orally [PO]), ciprofloxacin (500 mg PO), cefixime (400 g PO), and ofloxacin (400 mg PO). These medications are given in a single dosage with the additional dose of either azithromycin (1 g PO) or doxycycline (PO bid for 7 days) to treat chlamydia, even if it is not detected.

Annotated Bibliography

Handsfield HH, Lipman TO, Harnisch JP, et al. Asymptomatic gonorrhea in men–diagnosis, natural course, prevalence and significance. N Engl J Med 1974;290:117–122.

This is an excellent article.

Kleine EJ, Fisher LS, Chow AW, et al. Anorectal gonococcal infection. Ann Intern Med 1977;86:340–346.

This article describes women developing proctitis from the lymphatic spread of a vaginal infection via the perirectal lymphatics draining the vagina.

Petersen BH, Graham JA, Brooks GF, et al. Human deficiency of the eighth component of complement. J Clin Invest 1976;57;283–287.

This article explains the increased susceptibility of patients who are homozygous deficient of the late complement components to neisserial infections.

Vlaspolder F, Mutsaers JA, Blog F, et al. Value of a DNA probe assay (Gen-Probe) compared with that of culture for diagnosis of gonococcal infection. J Clin Microbiol 1993;31:107–111.

This article describes a genetic tool for diagnosing gonococcal infections.

Hook EW, Holmes KK. Gonococcal infections. Ann Intern Med 1985;102:229–243.

This is an excellent review.

O'Brien JB, Goldenberg DL, Rice PA. Disseminated gonococcal infection: a prospective analysis of 49 patients and a review of pathophysiology and immune mechanisms. Medicine 1983;62:395–405.

This is a classic paper.

CHAPTER 57

Lyme Disease

Paul G. Auwaerter, M.D., Thomas T. Provost, M.D.

In the last 25 years *Borrelia burgdorferi* has been recognized as the spirochete responsible for an infectious disorder that may include a spectrum of clinical findings, such as erythema chronicum migrans (ECM), neurologic disease, arthritis, and cardiac conduction abnormalities. The term "Lyme disease" has been applied to this disease because of the extensive epidemiologic studies performed near Old Lyme, Connecticut, a town where the disease was initially described in the 1970s.

Lyme disease (named for a town in Connecticut where disease is endemic) caused by the spirochete Borrelia burgdorferi.

Though three phases of the disease are frequently described in the literature, there may be considerable overlap of symptoms, and by no means are each of these stages present chronologically. These phases are as follows:

1. A cutaneous phase in which ECM dominates the clinical picture. Approximately 85% of patients demonstrate ECM. Minor constitutional symptoms including fever, headache, and local lymphadenopathy may also be present.
2. An early disseminated phase in which multiple ECM lesions occur associated with neurologic disease, arthralgia or arthritis, carditis, and other organ involvement.
3. A late phase, which is characterized by neurologic, rheumatic, and other organ involvement persisting or remitting for at least 12 months.

Cutaneous phase

Early disseminated phase

Late phase

The vector for this disease is a small deer tick belonging to the genus *Ixodes*. The principle reservoirs for *B. burgdorferi* appear to be rodents and deer. A deer tick feeding on a diseased animal becomes infected. When feeding on humans, the infected tick successfully transmits the disease, usually only after more than 48 hours of attachment. The spring through autumn months are the most prevalent times of transmission.

Vector is a deer tick belonging to Ixodes genus.

Cutaneous Manifestations

Approximately 1 to 3 weeks following a tick bite, an erythematous, macular lesion occurs at the site of the tick bite (Figures 57–1). The lesion spreads centrifugally, creating an annular erythematous lesion with central fading of the erythema. However, at the site of the tick bite, a reddish macule may persist. The borders of the ECM lesions may be 10 to 20 cm in diameter, and the individual lesions may persist for several months. The lesions are most commonly detected on the lower extremity but can be seen anywhere on the body. A slight pruritus has been noted. Minor constitutional symptoms such as headache, a low-grade fever, and malaise may be accompanied by regional lymphadenopathy. At times, the presentation may be atypical, demonstrating urticaria-like, hemorrhagic blisters, or erythema nodosum–like lesions.

Erythema chronicum migrans:
- *develops at site of tick bite*
- *rapidly expands*
- *generally asymptomatic*
- *minor constitutional features*

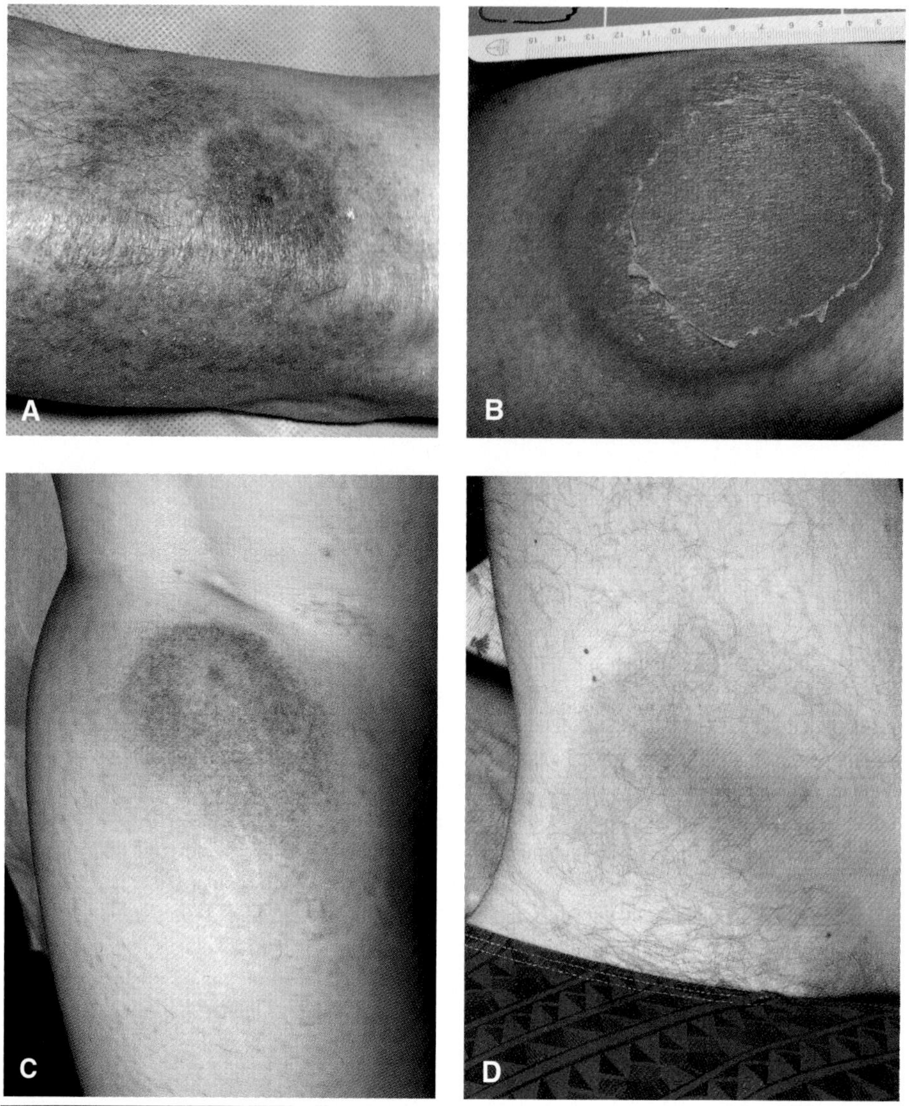

FIGURES 57–1 Four examples of erythema chronicum migrans. In Figures A and C, note a prominent central erythema at the site of bite. In Figure B, note the erythema annulare centrifugum pattern.

Borrelia *lymphocytoma*

Significantly more common in Europe than in the United States, *Borrelia* lymphocytoma may be most commonly found on the earlobes of children and on the anterior chest in adults. The scrotum and nose may also be sites of involvement. These lesions are characterized as bluish-red papular nodules.

Acrodermatitis chronica atrophicans

In addition, acrodermatitis chronica atrophicans is another cutaneous feature of borreliosis that is almost only observed in Europe. This is a chronic inflammatory disease process involving most commonly the lower extremities. It is initially characterized by a bluish, erythematous swelling and edema. Fibrous thickening with indurated linear bands and nodules producing sclerodermoid-like features occur in a minority of cases. The end result of the inflammatory process is extensive dermal atrophy associated with a prominent venous pattern.

Early Disseminated Phase

Early disseminated phase represents hematogenous spread.

The early disseminated phase of borreliosis is potentially characterized by the development of multiple ECM lesions. This feature heralds the hematogenous dissemination of the organism and may be associated with neurologic, arthritic, and cardiac manifestations. A radiculopathy may occur near the sites of the ECM. Another neurologic feature of early neuroborreliosis is a facial palsy.

A radiculopathy occurs characterized by sharp, radiating nerve pain at site of cutaneous involvement.

A mono- or oligoarthritis, most commonly involving the large joints, characterizes the arthritic component of borreliosis and is seen in early or late disease. Painless swelling dominates the clinical picture with joints that appear cool. It has been estimated that approximately 10% of patients with Lyme disease develop chronic arthritis.

Large joint mono- or oligoarthritis

Prominent joint swelling

The most striking arthritis that Provost has seen in association with Lyme disease occurred in a 61-year-old Caucasian male. Approximately 6 months prior, the patient had been evaluated for asymptomatic urticarial-like lesions, which spontaneously resolved. Subsequently, the patient developed an oligoarthritis characterized by prominent joint effusions in his knees. Lyme antibody titers were positive and the arthritis gradually subsided and disappeared after treatment for 2 weeks with intravenous ceftriaxone.

Ocular lesions may be characterized by motor palsies, iritis, iridocyclitis, keratitis, retinal hemorrhage, and optic neuritis. The cardiac manifestations are characterized by a myocarditis that can produce congestive heart failure or, more commonly, heart block, causing palpitation or syncope. First degree atrioventricular (AV) block is clinically silent, although it may herald development of second- and third-degree block, which are less frequently observed.

Ocular features:
- *iritis*
- *keratitis*
- *optic neuritis*

Heart block

Late Phase

In the late form of the disease, cutaneous manifestations are absent. Neurologic involvement may be characterized by a myriad of neurologic problems, including peripheral nerve disease, radiculopathy, a progressive multiple sclerosis–like disease pattern, depression, and dementia.

Late neurologic disease:
- *peripheral nerve disease*
- *multiple sclerosis–like picture*
- *depression, dementia*

It has been estimated that 10% of untreated borreliosis patients will develop neurologic features, 5% will develop cardiac manifestations, and up to 50% will develop arthritis.

Our personal experience with potential neuroborreliosis has been limited to two cases.

One case involved a female physician who observed the cutaneous lesion of ECM and treated herself for 2 weeks with tetracycline. Six months later she developed a mild hemiparesis. The Lyme antibody titer was positive. Intravenous therapy with ceftriaxone was given. Gradual improvement occurred; the patient has minimal residual right side upper extremity weakness.

In the second case, the patient developed an alarming 50% decrease in her hearing acuity and was detected to have a positive Lyme test. The patient, who lived in a suburb with a large deer population, had not had the ECM dermatitis. Intravenous therapy with ceftriaxone resulted in stabilization of her hearing defect.

Diagnosis

Laboratory diagnosis of Lyme disease is difficult. The spirochete has fastidious growth requirements including cultivation at temperatures of 33 to 37°C using a modified Kelly medium. The cultivation period takes 1 to 4 weeks and is not performed routinely except in reference laboratories.

Currently available serologic tests for Lyme are likewise problematic. Both false-negative and false-positive results are common. An estimated 10 to 15% of uninfected individuals living in endemic areas are seropositive by enzyme-linked immunosorbent assay (ELISA), thereby limiting the diagnostic value. ELISA positivity should be confirmed by Western blot analysis. An IgM Western blot should only be ordered in suspected early Lyme disease of less than 1 month's duration because false-positive Lyme IgM Western blots frequently occur. An IgG Western blot is a necessary second step for analysis of any positive Lyme ELISA. Five

Serologic diagnosis unreliable

Treat if high index of suspicion

bands must be present, but even this test can be falsely positive and rarely falsely negative. Because of these testing problems, Lyme disease remains a clinical diagnosis with the laboratory only serving to help affirm or disallow the diagnosis. Additionally, Lyme serologies are often negative early in disease, so the presence of ECM alone is enough to secure the diagnosis. Lyme infection of the central nervous system may be supported by observing intrathecal production of Lyme antibodies or positive Lyme polymerase chain reaction (PCR) analysis. Lyme arthritis frequently yields a Lyme-specific PCR test from joint fluid.

Treatment

Organism is sensitive to β-lactam and tetracycline-based antibiotics.

Uncomplicated ECM can be treated with a variety of antibiotics including penicillin, tetracycline, amoxicillin, and doxycycline. Doxycycline (100 mg bid for a 2- to 3-week period) is a favored recommendation since other tick-borne diseases such as Rocky Mountain spotted fever are also covered.

The treatment of neuroborreliosis requires penicillin G (3 g intravenously [IV] 3 to 4 times a day) or ceftriaxone (2 g IV for 14 to 28 days). However, the radiculopathies and facial palsies usually respond to an oral doxycycline regimen.

Doxycycline is most commonly used to treat erythema chronicum migrans in U.S.A.

Most cardiac abnormalities and Lyme arthritis can be treated with doxycycline (100 mg bid for 28 days) or, if symptoms appear refractory to oral therapy, penicillin G (3 g IV 3 to 4 times a day) or ceftriaxone (1–2 g IV/d) for 28 days. Permanent pacemakers are not required for advanced AV block as antibiotics alone resolve the delay.

Annotated Bibliography

Steere AC, et al. The clinical evolution of Lyme arthritis. Ann Intern Med 1987;107:725–731.

Steere AC, et al. The early clinical manifestations of Lyme disease. Ann Intern Med 1983;99:76–82.

These classic articles describe cutaneous and other manifestations of Lyme disease. The author has contributed much to our understanding of this disease.

Berglund J, Itrem R, Ornstein K, et al. An epidemiologic study of Lyme disease in southern Sweden. N Engl J Med 1995;333:1319–1324.

The overall incidence was 69 cases per 100,000 inhabitants per year, although this varied considerably among different regions. In lower Saxony, in Germany, the estimated annual incidence was 22 per 100,000 inhabitants, whereas in Connecticut the incidence was 41 per 100,000. The highest incidence in the United States is 1,198 cases per 100,000 inhabitants in Nantucket, MA. The overall incidence in the United States has been reported at 3.3 per 100,000.

The anatomical location of the tick bite was found to be related to the clinical manifestation of the disease. In children, tick bites of the head and neck were more frequent, as was the incidence of neuroborreliosis.

Steere AC, Batsford WP, Weinberg M, et al. Lyme carditis: cardiac abnormalities of Lyme disease. Am J Med 1980;93:8–16.

These investigators reported 20 patients with cardiac abnormalities associated with Lyme disease. The onset of the cardiac manifestations was a median of 21 days after the onset of ECM (range 4 to 83 days). Three-quarters of the patients still had skin lesions with the onset of cardiac manifestations. Seven had meningoencephalitis. Syncope, dizziness, shortness of breath, and palpitations were common manifestations. Electrocardiographic abnormalities demonstrated that half of the patients had high-degree atrioventricular block (complete in 8 and Wenckebach in 2).

In one study by the same group, cardiac manifestations were an uncommon manifestation of Lyme disease, detected in 8% of patients.

Gerber MA, Shapiro ED, Burke GS, et al. Lyme disease in children in southeastern Connecticut. N Engl J Med 1996;335:1270–1274.

This is an excellent study of approximately 200 children with the median age of 7 years (range 1 to 21). A single, erythematous chronicum migrans lesion was the most common initial presentation, occurring in 66% of patients. The ECM lesion in 90% of these patients was at least 5 cm in diameter. Twenty-six percent of these patients had lesions on the head and neck, 25% on the extremities, 24% on the back, and 9% on the abdomen. Younger children tended to have head and neck lesions, whereas older children had arm and leg lesions.

In 6% of the cases arthritis was the presentation, in 3% facial nerve palsy, in 2% aseptic meningitis, and in 0.5% myocarditis.

All patients responded promptly to antimicrobial therapy. A follow-up study 2 years later revealed that none of the patients had evidence of either chronic or recurrent Lyme disease.

CHAPTER 58

Diphtheria

Thomas T. Provost, M.D.

Diphtheria is caused by the gram-positive bacillus *Corynebacterium diphtheriae*. The only known reservoir is humans. *Corynebacterium diphtheriae* occurs as a carrier state in the nasopharynx of asymptomatic individuals. Spread between individuals occurs via aerosolized droplets. The organism is fastidious, surviving for months in the dust around infected individuals. The serious sequelae (myocarditis and neuritis) are due to a 62-kD exotoxin that penetrates cells, inhibiting polypeptide chain elongation by inactivating elongation factor 2. All cells are affected but myocardial and nerve cells are especially susceptible. Only strains of *C. diphtheriae* infected with a lysogenic bacteriophage produce this toxin.

The ability of this organism to produce disease is related to the immunologic status of the host. For example, since the introduction of vaccination with diphtheria toxoid in the 1920s, the incidence of this reportable disease has dramatically decreased in the United States. When diphtheria occurs in immunized individuals, it is generally mild. Diphtheria is, however, a significant problem in developing countries.

Classic diphtheria is a nasopharyngeal infection with an exudative web.

Toxemia out of proportion to clinical picture

Classic diphtheria produces a nasopharyngeal infection characterized by fever and a sore throat. An exudative gray, thick web may occur in the nasal passage, pharynx, or hypopharynx. Swelling and pain in the neck are common, and toxemia is out of proportion to the clinical picture.

Cutaneous diphtheria seen in unvaccinated migrant workers and derelict alcoholics.

Diphtheria can produce skin disease. This occurs commonly in the tropics. Because of widespread vaccination here in the United States, this form of diphtheria is rare. Cutaneous diphtheria, however, has been reported among nonimmunized migrant workers and homeless alcoholics. In these cases, poor hygiene, skin trauma, and prior skin disease are of etiologic importance.

Cutaneous Manifestations

Cranial and peripheral nerves affected by diphtheria neurotoxin.

Cutaneous disease may occur alone or accompany pharyngeal involvement. Frequently, the same strain of *C. diphtheriae* is present in the asymptomatic nasopharynx and in the cutaneous lesion. The cutaneous lesions are indolent, tender ulcers with a leathery membrane. Cranial nerve and peripheral nerve involvement may occur. For example, paralysis of oculomotor and ciliary nerves produces blurred vision and diplopia. Paralysis of cranial nerves IX and X is problematic, resulting in aspiration. Long tract sensory and motor involvement may occur. The Guillain-Barré syndrome occurs in a few patients. Myocarditis infrequently occurs but is more common with nasopharyngeal diphtheria.

Characteristically, cutaneous diphtheria is generally a secondary infection of a pre-existing wound, such as a laceration, abrasion, or an eczematous lesion. For example, *Streptococcus pyogenes* in one study was cultured from approximately 75% of *C. diphtheriae* lesions. After a latent period of approximately 3 weeks, the infected wound became painful and erythematous with a gray membrane.

Oval, "punched-out" lesions ("jungle sores") demonstrating a rolled, bluish border were commonly reported as manifestations of cutaneous diphtheria in soldiers and prisoners of war serving in the China-Burma Theater during World War II. Pain, tenderness, and membrane formation were characteristic. This type of cutaneous infection is rare in those cutaneous diphtheria cases reported in the United States. (The late Clarence Livingood, who served as a medical officer in this theater, believed that the lesions seen in Southeast Asia were due to *C. diphtheriae*-infected insect bites [personal communication, December 1997].)

Cutaneous diphtheria commonly a contaminating infection of traumatized skin characterized by:
- *gray membrane formation*
- *pain and tenderness*

Treatment

The disease responds to penicillin or erythromycin and intravenous horse antidiphtheria toxin (20,000–40,000 units).

Annotated Bibliography

Belsey MA, et al. *Corynebacterium diphtheriae* skin infections in Alabama and Louisiana, a factor in the epidemiology of diphtheria. N Engl J Med 1969;280:135–138.

Harnish JP, et al. Diphtheria among alcoholic urban adults. A decade of experience in Seattle. Ann Intern Med 1989;111:71–75.

These two articles detail the epidemiology of cutaneous diphtheria.

CHAPTER 59

Erysipeloid

Thomas T. Provost, M.D., Paul G. Auwaerter, M.D.

This cutaneous infectious disease caused by *Erysipelothrix insipidosa* (previously termed *"Erysipelothrix rhusiopathiae"*), occurs primarily in people handling raw fish, poultry, and meat products (eg, fishermen, hunters, farmers, cooks, and butchers). It is caused by a pleiomorphic, gram-positive, slender, curved bacillus. Outbreaks usually occur during summer months and the hands are the most common site of infection. Infection is especially common among fishermen. Crab fishermen refer to it as "crab dermatitis."

Cutaneous Manifestations

Localized skin disease

Adjacent joint arthritis and rarely bacteremia

Erythematous, violaceous, raised, sharply demarcated lesions usually on the hands

The lesions are usually localized and solitary; however, they may be multiple predominantly on the hands.

The disease is termed "erysipeloid" to distinguish this infection from the superficial cellulitis induced by group A streptococci. Cutaneous lesions are characterized by burning pain at the site of trauma inoculation, such as through an abrasion. The dermatitis then develops within 72 hours in subacute fashion, characterized by a violaceous, raised lesion that may be associated with low-grade fever and malaise. Lymphadenitis and regional lymphadenopathy may also occur in as many as one-third of cases. Bacteremia may rarely be associated with endocarditis and pleura and brain involvement.

An arthritis of the joints adjacent to the involved skin may occur, although distal joint involvement also may occur, signaling hematogenous spread. The individual lesions, which usually involve the hands, are warm, tender, erythematous, violaceous, and sharply demarcated. As the lesions enlarge centrifugally, central clearing occurs with brownish postinflammatory hyperpigmentation.

Culture from a biopsy of the border will occasionally demonstrate the organism. Gram stains of biopsy material variably demonstrate the organism.

Treatment

These lesions respond to high doses of penicillin, although other antibiotics (eg, erythromycin, tetracycline) are also effective.

Annotated Bibliography

Barnett JH, Estes SA, Wisman JA, et al. Erysipeloid. J Am Acad Dermatol 1983;9:116–123.

Gorby GL, Peacock JE Jr. *Erysipelothrix rhusiopathiae* endocarditis: microbiologic, epidemiologic, and clinical features of an occupational disease. Rev Infect Dis 1988;10:317–325.

These two excellent articles describe this unusual infection.

CHAPTER 60

Pseudomonas aeruginosa

Thomas T. Provost, M.D., Paul G. Auwaerter, M.D.

Pseudomonas aeruginosa is a small gram-negative bacillus found widely in the environment, especially in areas of high humidity.

Clinical Features

May produce greenish discoloration of nails

Greenish toe-web infection

Tender folliculitis on sides of trunk of patients using contaminated hot tub

Pseudomonas aeruginosa may cause a number of cutaneous conditions, including painful paronychial infections associated with either a green-blue or green-yellow discoloration of the nail. This nail infection is usually found in individuals who have had their hands in a good deal of water. *P. aeruginosa* may also produce a greenish toe-web infection, which is especially common following prolonged use of wet footwear. Hot tub folliculitis is an eruptive, diffuse, erythematous, painful maculopapular or vesiculopapular rash that develops on the sides of the trunk of patients following exposure to contaminated whirlpool tubs, spas, and swimming pools. External otitis media, due to *P. aeruginosa*, is found in diabetics and acquired immunodeficiency syndrome patients and requires immediate attention (malignant otitis externa). Often a serious contaminating infection of burn wounds, *P. aeruginosa* is associated with a significant mortality. Simple *Pseudomonas* cellulitis can develop in diabetics or neutropenic patients and frequently causes septicemia in chronically debilitated patients.

When the organism gains entrance into tissue, perivascular and adventitial edema are characteristic. This swelling can curtail blood supply to the tissue, producing bullae, hemorrhagic bullae, infarction, and subsequent gangrenous changes. In addition, *P. aeruginosa* elaborates various enzymes and exotoxins which contribute to its virulence.

Ecthyma gangrenosum

Ecthyma gangrenosum is a characteristic lesion caused by *P. aeruginosa* that may be a primary or metastatic infection occurring in the presence or absence of detectable bacteremia (Figure 60–1). Ecthyma gangrenosum tends to occur in immunocompromised patients, especially those with neutropenia or a hematologic malignancy. These lesions are characterized by a "gun-metal" gray, painless, indurated ulcer most frequently occurring in the anogenital region. (For further discussion, see Chapter 47, "Septicemia.")

In infants, *Pseudomonas* septicemia may manifest with vesicles and bullae that become hemorrhagic and are associated with surrounding erythema. *Pseudomonal* septicemia may be associated with macular, papular, nodular, erythematous, nondescript lesions in adults and children. Gangrenous cellulitis, appearing like a decubitus lesion but occurring in nonpressure-bearing areas, has been described with *Pseudomonas* septicemia.

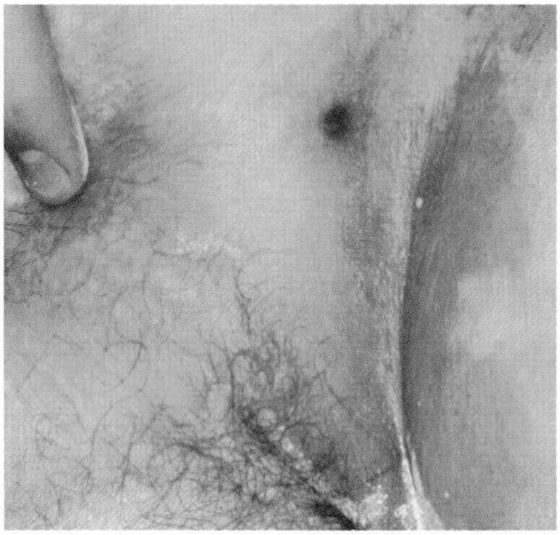

FIGURE 60–1 Classic "gun-metal" gray lesion of ecthyma gangrenosum in inguinal region caused by *Pseudomonas aeruginosa* septicemia.

Treatment

Superficial wounds respond to 1% acetic acid wet dressings or silver sulfadiazine cream. Systemic infections carry a guarded prognosis. Aminoglycosides (eg, gentamicin or amikacin) in combination with an extended spectrum penicillin, ceftazidime, or ciprofloxacin may be necessary to treat severe systemic infections.

Annotated Bibliography

Greene SL, Su WP, Muller SA. Ecthyma gangrenosum: report of clinical, histopathologic and bacteriologic aspects of eight cases. J Am Acad Dermatol 1984;11:781–786.

Huminer D, Siegman-Ingra Y, Morduchowicz G, et al. Ecthyma gangrenosum without bacteremia. Report of six cases and review of the literature. Arch Intern Med 1987;147:299–303.

These two excellent articles describe the cutaneous and bacteriologic features of ecthyma gangrenosum.

CHAPTER 61

Herpes Simplex

Gina V. Hanna, M.D., Thomas T. Provost, M.D.

Herpes simplex infections are caused by two deoxyribonucleic acid (DNA) viruses, herpes simplex virus types 1 and 2 (HSV-1 and HSV-2), which share 50% DNA nucleotide sequence homology. The clinical expression of a herpes simplex infection is determined by the host's previous exposure to the virus. A primary infection tends to be more severe, the recurrent disease milder (Figures 61–1 and 61–2). The recurrent disease is caused by reactivation of a dormant HSV, which travels from a regional sensory ganglion along nerve fibers to create an infection on the skin.

HSV-1 and HSV-2 are DNA viruses.

Host's previous experience with virus determines clinical expression.

Cutaneous Manifestations

Primary Infection

A primary herpes simplex infection most commonly occurs in children under 5 years of age. In most cases, it is subclinical. Children generally develop mucous membrane infections, most commonly in the mouth and pharynx. On unusual occasions, the initial infection occurs in adults.

The oral pharyngeal disease is generally characterized by a sore throat and/or the development of painful vesicles and erosions on the lips, tongue, palate, or buccal mucosa. It may be mild or severe and can be associated with high fevers. In the severe form, inability to eat and regional lymphadenopathy are noted. The diagnosis is suspected by a Tzanck smear and confirmed by culture (Figure 61–3).

Primary infection more severe

Usually in children under 5 years of age; frequently subclinical

May uncommonly occur in adults

Oral mucosa generally site of infection

In adults, may be mild or severe and associated with high fever.

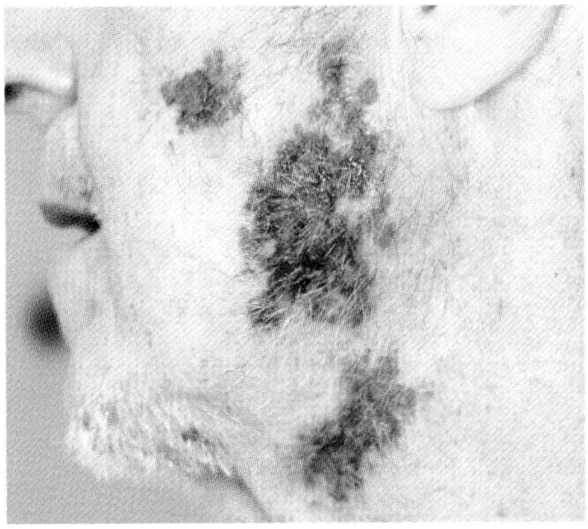

FIGURE 61–1 Atypical recurrent herpes simplex infection in an adult.

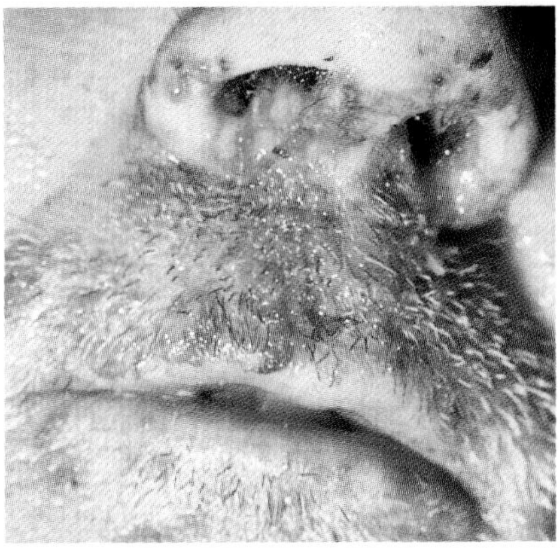

FIGURE 61–2 Recurrent HSV-1 infection involving the perioral region and nose.

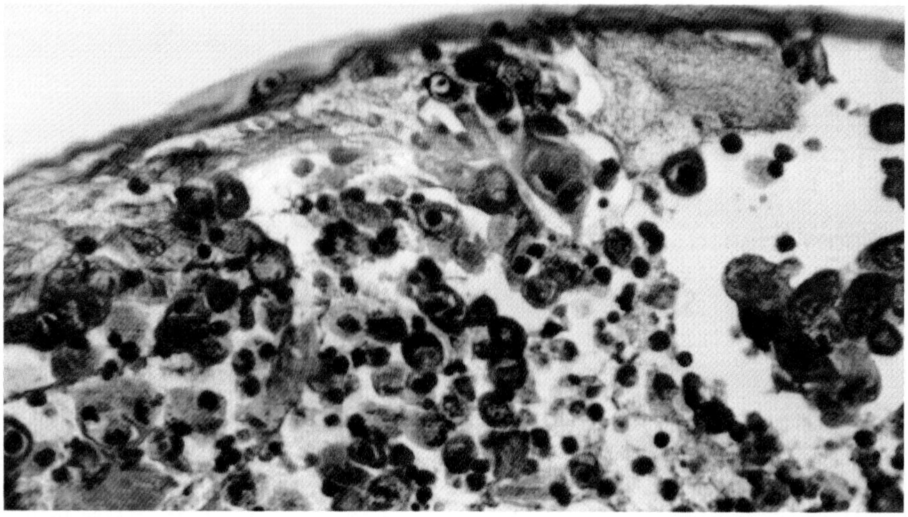

FIGURE 61–3 Biopsy of a herpes simplex lesion. Note the giant cells in the blister cavity. (×40 original magnification)

The differential diagnosis includes streptococcal or Coxsackie infections, erythema multiforme, recurrent aphthous stomatitis, or Behçet's disease. In adults, bullous pemphigoid and pemphigus vulgaris should also be considered.

Recurrent Infection

Approximately one-third of Americans have recurrent HSV-1 infections.

Trauma, sun exposure, fatigue, and stress are etiologically significant.

Recurrent HSV-1 infections occur in as many as one-third of Americans. The onset of the disease usually involves the perioral region (most commonly the lips) and is a mild disease characterized by a pruritic, burning sensation with the rapid development of papulovesicular lesions that readily ulcerate. Sun exposure, trauma (dental procedures), and debilitating diseases are thought to be of etiologic importance. The presence of grouped vesicles and the recurrence of lesions on the same part of the outer lip differentiates this infection from recurrent aphthous stomatitis. At times, recurrent grouped vesicular lesions on an erythematous base may occur on the cheek or other parts of the face. On unusual occasions, recurrent herpes simplex may occur on other parts of the upper body (see Figures 61–1, 61–2, 61–4, and 61–5).

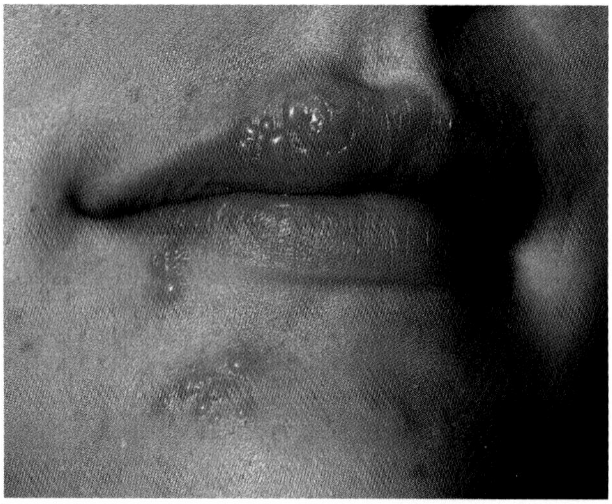

FIGURE 61–4 Recurrent HSV-1 infection manifested as typical "cold sore" involving the right upper lip and the lower right lip and chin. This is a typical infection. (Reproduced from the slide collection of the late R.C.V. Robinson, M.D.)

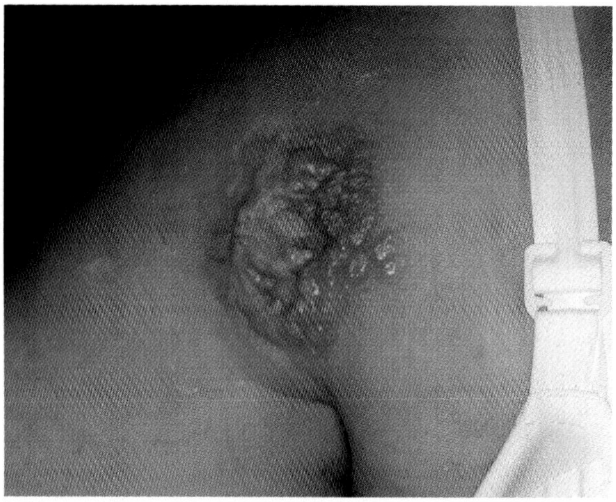

FIGURE 61–5 Recurrent herpes simplex on the shoulder.

Primary Genital Herpes

Primary genital herpes is a sexually transmitted disease caused by HSV-2 (80% of the time) and HSV-1 (20% of the time). Primary genital herpes generally occurs usually within 2 weeks of sexual exposure. There has been a marked increase in the frequency of genital herpes during the past three decades due to changes in sexual practices.

Primary genital herpes simplex infections most commonly involve HSV-2 infections.

The primary genital lesions are characterized by tender, grouped vesicles occurring on an erythematous base. These rapidly ulcerate. Painful, tender lymphadenopathy is characteristic. Dysuria and a vaginal discharge may occur. Acute urinary retention is uncommon. Headache, fever, and meningeal signs (signifying an aseptic meningitis, which is more common in women) may also occur. Cerebral spinal fluid examination will demonstrate a mild lymphocytosis.

Aseptic meningitis may occur.

More common in women

The differential diagnosis includes Behçet's syndrome, chancroid, and lymphogranuloma venereum.

In women, cervical lesions are frequently asymptomatic, and exposure is only determined by serologic studies (see below).

Cervical herpes simplex may be asymptomatic.

Recurrent Herpes Genitalis

Recurrent genital herpes simplex is almost always caused by HSV-2 infection. It generally begins with a burning, painful, tingling sensation (Figures 61–6 to 61–8). The patient may note a pain in the buttocks or down the thighs. The individual is infectious until the ulcers crust over. Recurrences may be as infrequent as once a year or as frequent as once a month.

Recurrent genital herpes simplex infection almost always due to HSV-2.

Relationship with Human Immunodeficiency Virus

The relationship of recurrent herpes simplex infection and human immunodeficiency virus (HIV) disease is intriguing. Before the readily available HIV testing, persistent herpes simplex anogenital ulcerations was a common initial feature of acquired immunodeficiency syndrome (AIDS). Indeed, the first AIDS patient detected at our institution presented with a persistent herpes simplex genital ulceration, which led to testing and the diagnosis of AIDS.

In all immunocompromised individuals, irrespective of cause (eg, HIV infection, steroids, immunosuppressive agents, Hodgkin's disease, etc), recurrent herpes

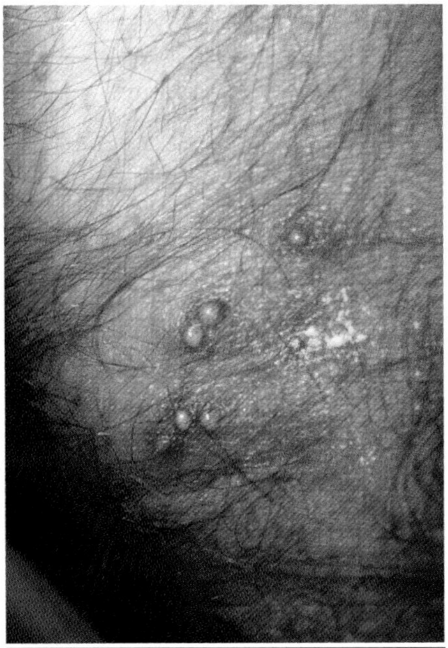

FIGURE 61–6 Recurrent herpes simplex on the inner thigh.

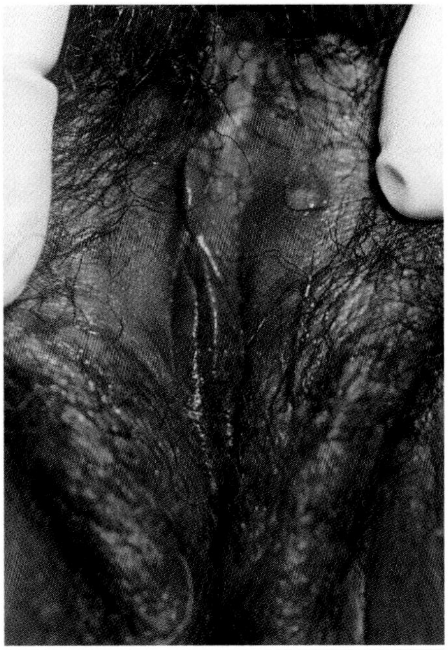

FIGURE 61–7 Recurrent HSV-2 infection. Note multiple lesions on the labia minora.

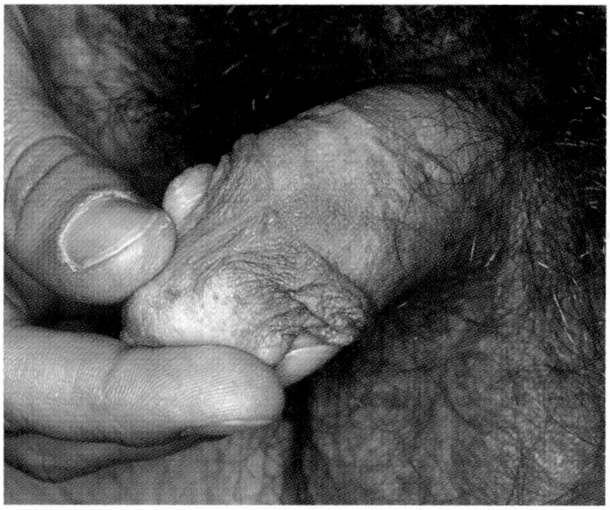

FIGURE 61–8 Recurrent herpes simplex infection on the shaft of the penis.

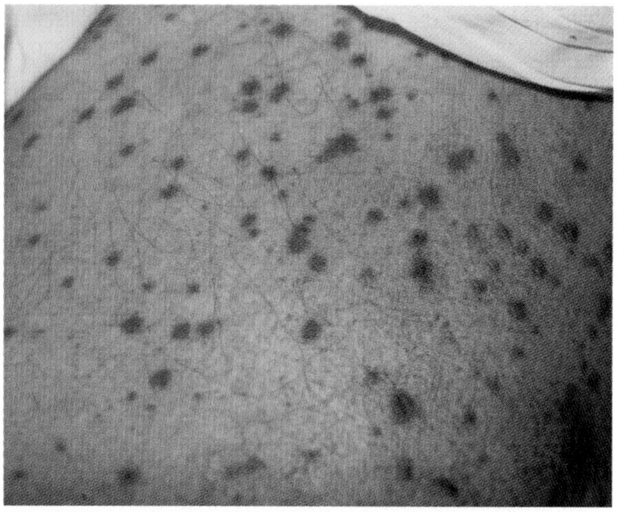

FIGURE 61–9 Disseminated herpes simplex infection in a patient with Hodgkin's disease.

simplex may be more frequent, more severe, and more prolonged (Figures 61–9 and 61–10). Herpes simplex infections also occur with increased frequency in atopic eczema patients (eg, eczema herpeticum, Kaposi's varicelliform eruption).

Indolent herpes simplex ulcers a feature of the immunocompromised host

Open genital HSV ulcers may play etiopathogenic role in sexually transmitted HIV.

In addition to being the first indicator of AIDS, recurrent herpes genital ulcerations like chancroid lymphogranuloma venereum and granuloma inguinale could conceivably be a factor in the sexual transmission of HIV due to the open genital wounds these infections produce.

Distinctive Cutaneous Presentations

Herpes simplex virus infections may present with unique cutaneous presentations. These include herpetic whitlows, herpes gladiatorum, herpes keratoconjunctivitis, recurrent lumbosacral infections in association with erythema multiforme (minor), and a Kaposi's varicelliform eruption.

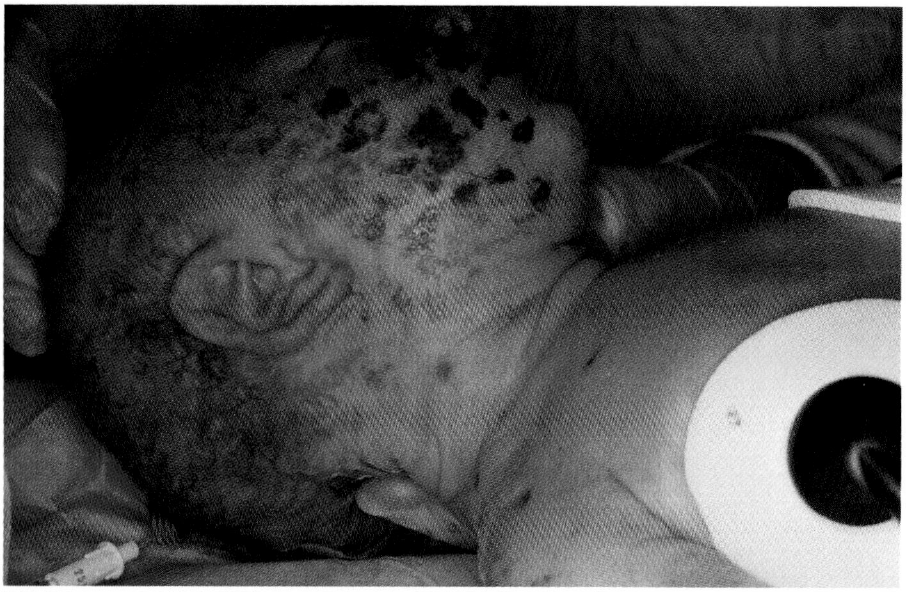

FIGURE 61–10 Neonatal herpes simplex infection. (Reproduced from the slide collection of the late R.C.V. Robinson, M.D.)

Herpetic Whitlow

The herpetic whitlow is commonly seen in medical workers (eg, ungloved dentists, physicians, dental technicians) (Figure 61–11). It exists either as a primary infection, characterized by painful, grouped vesicles on an erythematous base on a finger with associated tender epitrochlear and axillary lymphadenopathy, or as a milder recurrent form associated with minimal finger tenderness and ulceration.

Herpetic whitlow occupational hazard for medical workers

Herpes Gladiatorum

Herpes gladiatorum is a very peculiar form of herpes simplex in which transmission occurs via skin-to-skin contact, predominantly among high school and college Greco-Roman wrestlers. Painful, grouped erythematous vesicles occur over the side of the face. This form of herpes has been reported in epidemic form.

Herpes gladiatorum has occurred in epidemic proportions among Greco-Roman style wrestlers.

Herpes Keratoconjunctivitis

Herpes keratoconjunctivitis is especially problematic, producing scarring opacity of the cornea and blindness.

Keratoconjunctivitis can cause blindness.

Recurrent Lumbosacral Infection

Recurrent lumbosacral herpes simplex infection consists of grouped vesicles on an erythematous base occurring over the buttocks and lumbosacral areas. A deep pelvic ache or radiating leg pain, simulating sciatica, may be prodromal. These lesions may be triggered by the onset of the menstrual cycle.

Kaposi's Varicelliform Eruption

Kaposi's varicelliform eruption is a potentially serious infection in a relatively cell-mediated immune-deficient, atopic eczema patient. The disease can either be primary or secondary and can be associated with fever, malaise, and lymphadenopathy. Similar eruptions are also found in patients with Darier's disease.

We have also seen this complication in a pemphigus vulgaris patient receiving high-dose oral steroids (> 100 mg prednisone).

Kaposi's varicelliform eruption is a serious infection occurring in atopic eczema and Darier's disease patients.

Recurrent Erythema Multiforme

The work of the Colorado group has established that recurrent erythema multiforme minor (the Hebra type) is frequently (> 70%) associated with the presence of recurrent herpes simplex infections, most commonly of the lips. Erythema multiforme lesions frequently demonstrate the classic targetoid features and are found, most prominently, on the palms and soles.

Recurrent erythema multiforme minor associated with recurrent HSV infections most commonly on the lips.

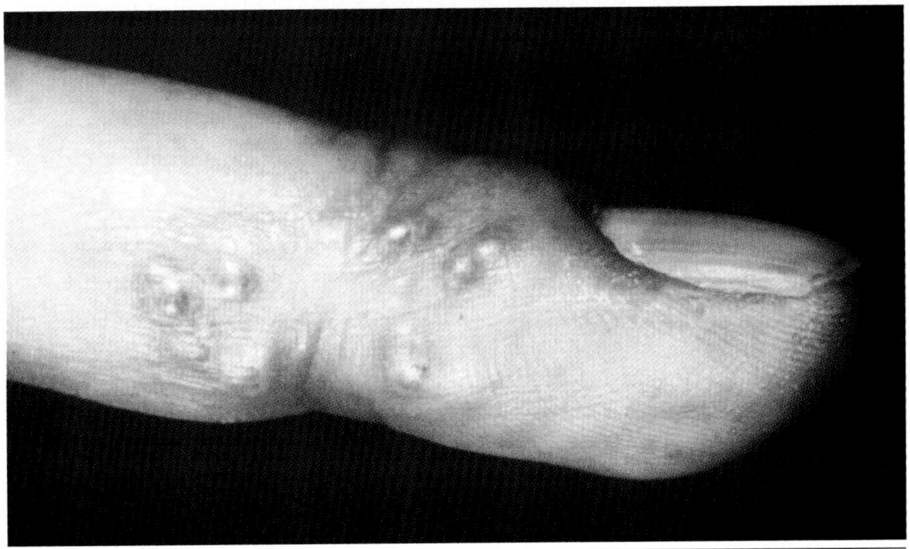

FIGURE 61–11 Recurrent herpetic whitlow as grouped vesicles on the distal portion of the finger. Medical personnel are at increased risk.

Pregnancy-Associated Infections

Herpes simplex virus type 2 is the cause of most cases of genital herpes. A recent study revealed a 2.6% prevalence of infection and 3.7% seroconversion rate of 7,000 pregnant women followed to term.

None of the infants of women who seroconverted just prior to delivery developed neonatal sequelae. However, there were 9 women who had active lesions, but no anti-HSV antibodies. Four of their babies developed neonatal HSV infection. Additionally, 60% of women who seroconverted had subclinical infections, but no cases of neonatal HSV infection occurred in this group. Several studies have documented the occurrence of serologic evidence of HSV exposure in the absence of symptoms in women.

Maternal effects of a herpes simplex infection include an increased incidence of transmission of other sexually transmitted diseases (STDs) presumably due to the disruption of skin barriers and the subsequent easy exchange of body fluids. Earlier studies indicated an increase in prematurity, pregnancy loss, and recurrent abortion. However, more recent data show no strong association with these conditions. Fetal effects, although rare, include microcephaly, periventricular calcifications, chorioretinitis, and intrauterine growth restriction—all of which can be associated with severe neurologic defects.

Herpes simplex infections in small infants can produce a fatal encephalitis.

Can be transmitted by an open "cold sore"

Most commonly occurs following exposure to HSV ulcer in birth canal during birthing

For women who develop HSV-related antibodies prior to delivery, the fetus is relatively well protected from sequelae. Otherwise, the risk is 40% that severe neonatal consequences will develop (overwhelming encephalitis, meningitis, and death). This is likely due to the immunocompromised status of the neonate.

In addition to exposure to HSV ulcer during birth, infants can be infected by an open cold sore.

It may be the presence of maternal antibodies that maintains the low (1 to 2%) rate of neonatal infection in women with recurrent herpes simplex infection at the time of delivery. However, among those 1 to 2% who gain passive immunity via their mothers, there is a 50% risk of severe infant disease or death.

Current management strategies are not 100% successful due to the lack of efficacy in diagnosis, treatment, and prevention. There remains no cure for HSV infection; treatment is palliative only. Due to asymptomatic shedding, there is no fail-safe method of preventing transmission at delivery.

In order to decrease the risk of neonatal infection, current strategies include maternal questioning for a history of STDs, counseling regarding neonatal risk when a history of HSV is elicited, and a recommendation for cesarean section (C/S) in the presence of active genital herpes at the time of delivery. Unfortunately, the baseline risks of C/S-related morbidity in the presence of genital infection adds more risk. Neonates delivered by C/S have an increased risk of transient tachypnea, respiratory distress, intensive care admission, and mother-infant separation problems leading to decreased bonding and difficulties with breastfeeding.

The question of elective cesarean delivery in patients with only a positive serology or history has yet to be answered. For example, there is a case report involving a parturient who was having twins. She ultimately had a cesarean delivery, although she had no active HSV lesions. The report describes the use of a fetal scalp electrode on the first twin. That twin developed HSV scalp lesions, whereas the second twin, who was delivered by C/S with intact membranes, developed HSV encephalitis. On the contrary, a large study of 217 pregnancies resulted in a 0% transmission of HSV when caesarean deliveries were performed only in the presence of active HSV lesions.

Prevention of recurrent herpes outbreaks appears to be the key to eliminating neonatal infection. Acyclovir, long a mainstay in the therapy for HSV, has poor oral bioavailability and requires multiple dosing (200 mg 5 times/d for treatment or 400 mg bid for suppression). It is a pregnancy category C drug. However, there are no well-documented reports of adverse effects in human pregnancy. Any neonate that is thought to be at risk of HSV infection will receive intravenous acyclovir in the nursery. There are numerous conflicting clinical trial reports regarding the efficacy of acyclovir. Comparison among these reports is difficult due to differing primary outcome measures. For example, most studies were initiated as a means of decreasing the cesarean delivery rate with varying results—either a decrease or no change in the C/S rate is most frequently observed. Few studies have been designed to investigate the incidence of neonatal herpes. Due to the low transmission rate of recurrent HSV, studies designed to investigate C/S rates lack statistical power.

Valacyclovir is a prodrug form of acyclovir with a 3 to 5 times greater oral bioavailability and can be administered once or twice per day. A phase 1 clinical trial completed revealed that valacyclovir (500 mg bid) was superior to acyclovir (400 mg tid) in that higher serum plasma levels were obtained and maintained for greater duration in pregnancy. Thus, it has an advantage over acyclovir due to its availability for once-daily dosing for suppression and resulting patient compliance.

Because 85% of cases of neonatal herpes simplex infection occur in deliveries to asymptomatic women, a more effective method of prophylaxis is sought. Nonoxynol-9 has been shown to be effective in preventing neonatal HSV in vaginally delivered mouse pups. However, the required doses can lead to breakdown of mucosal barriers in humans, paradoxically increasing the risk of transmission. Interest is growing in the use of either valacyclovir or acyclovir in pregnancy in order to decrease both the C/S rate and the neonatal infant risk. Due to the lack of large, randomized studies, it is still premature to make a broad recommendation for the use of chemoprophylaxis for the prevention of maternal recurrent herpes simplex infection and neonatal herpes simplex infection, and to decrease the HSV-related cesarean delivery rate. Important questions remain concerning the optimal time of initiation of therapy and the exact dosing regimen.

At this time, C/S remains the most useful tool to decrease the risk of neonatal HSV infection in the presence of active genital herpes at the time of delivery.

Presence of herpes simplex ulcer on genitalia of woman in labor is an indication for a cesarean section.

Encephalitis

Herpes simplex encephalitis can occur in children and adults irrespective of whether they have had a previous infection. It is the most common cause of sporadic encephalitis. The HSV most often causes a hemorrhagic temporal lobe encephalitis. Cerebral spinal fluid analysis, electroencephalogram, computerized axial tomography, and magnetic resonance imaging are important investigative tools. Brain biopsy with cultures is diagnostic.

Diagnosis

The diagnosis of herpes simplex is made with assurance by culture. The Tzanck smear performed on characteristic clinical lesions is an excellent outpatient test. Both HSV and the varicella-zoster virus produce multinucleated giant cells. Differentiation of these two entities is impossible on a Tzanck smear but is accomplished by culture.

Tzanck smear is good clinical tool to detect a herpes infection.

Diagnosis proven with culture

The diagnosis of genital herpes simplex infection in women is problematic. In the past, the diagnosis has relied upon the clinical findings and selective use of viral cultures. In a recent study of 779 randomly selected women attending an STD clinic, evidence of HSV-2 infection was detected in 363 women (47%). Nine additional patients (1%) had positive cultures, indicative of urogenital or anal infection with HSV-1. Of these 372 women, only 82 (22%) had symptoms and 216 (58%) had antibodies to HSV-2 without a history of clinical episodes. Furthermore, only two-thirds of 66 women with positive HSV cultures had characteristic ulcerations on the external genitalia. The others had atypical genital lesions or asymptomatic viral shedding.

Diagnosis of genital herpes in females problematic

Serologic testing for HSV-2 in women detects occult or silent genital infections.

Treatment

The treatment of choice of all forms of herpes simplex infection is acyclovir or one of its derivatives. They are well tolerated. Prophylactic oral treatment has been used successfully to treat debilitating, recurrent oral and genital herpes simplex. The topical preparation of acyclovir may or may not be effective in modifying the clinical course of recurring herpetic lesions.

The herpes simplex viral enzyme thymidine kinase (TK), but not human cellular kinases, induces phosphorylation of acyclovir, creating acyclovir triphosphate. Acyclovir triphosphate is a potent inhibitor of viral DNA polymerase. Herpes simplex resistant strains have been detected. These resistant strains are TK enzyme–deficient mutants. In resistant strains of HSV, foscarnet (phosphonoformic acid), a drug that directly inhibits viral DNA polymerase, has been successfully substituted.

Annotated Bibliography

Prober CG, Sullender WM, Yasukawa LL, et al. Low risk of herpes simplex virus infection in neonates exposed to virus at the time of vaginal delivery to mothers with recurrent genital herpes simplex virus infections. N Engl J Med 1987;316:240–244.

This excellent article demonstrates the potential devastating effects of neonatal herpes simplex central nervous system infections, which can infrequently occur in infants exposed to HSV in a mother with recurrent genital HSV infections at the time of birth.

Straus SE, Takiff HE, Seidlin M, et al. Suppression of frequently recurring genital herpes. A placebo-controlled double-blind trial of oral acyclovir. N Engl J Med 1984;310: 1545–1550.

This is one of the first articles demonstrating the efficacy of oral acyclovir in the suppression of genital herpes in patients with frequent recurrences.

Crumpacker CS, Schnipper LE, Marlowe SI, et al. Resistance to antiviral drugs of herpes simplex virus isolated from a patient treated with acyclovir. N Engl J Med 1982;306: 343–346.

This is the description of the emergence of a strain of HSV resistant to acyclovir. This article demonstrates a mutation of the TK-enzyme system.

Reeves WC, Corey L, Adams HG, et al. Risk of recurrence after first episodes of genital herpes: relation to HSV type and antibody response. N Engl J Med 1981; 305:315–319.

This article demonstrates that the risk of recurrence of genital herpes is much more prevalent in HSV-2 infections. Furthermore, patients with a high titer of neutralizing antibody to HSV-2 were more likely to have recurrences than those without HSV-2–neutralizing antibodies. It is theorized that the presence of neutralizing antibodies to HSV-2 may represent a serologic marker for the presence of latent ganglionic infection.

Whitley RJ. Viral encephalitis. N Engl J Med 1990;323:242–250.

This is an excellent review of herpes simplex and other virally induced encephalitides in the United States.

Koutsky LA, Stevens CE, Holmes KK, et al. Underdiagnosis of genital herpes by current clinical and viral-isolation procedures. N Engl J Med 1992;326:1533–1539.

This study demonstrates the superiority of serologic testing for HSV-2 in detecting asymptomatic infection.

CHAPTER 62

Herpes Zoster

Michael R. Clark, M.D., M.P.H., Thomas T. Provost, M.D.

The varicella-zoster virus (VZV) is responsible for two clinical diseases: varicella (chickenpox) and herpes zoster (shingles), which is a unilateral reactivation of a latent VZV infection. Varicella is generally a contagious disease of childhood spread by airborne droplets. It is induced by a deoxyribonucleic acid (DNA) virus. Varicella in adulthood is uncommon and is a much more severe infection. The varicella infection generally confers lifelong immunity.

Varicella-zoster virus is a DNA virus causing two distinct clinical diseases:
- *chickenpox*
- *shingles*

Following a primary infection, reactivation of latent varicella (herpes zoster) occurs in the total absence of exogenous exposure to the VZV. Instead, evidence indicates that during the primary varicella infection, the VZV is transmitted up sensory fibers to the regional sensory ganglia. There, a latent infection occurs. The VZV, however, may be reactivated, but reactivation occurs only sporadically.

VZV produces a latent infection in sensory ganglia.

A number of conditions favor reactivation, including local trauma and immunosuppression of all types (eg, human immunodeficiency infection, Hodgkin's disease, immunosuppressive drugs, and corticosteroids). Activation also occurs following irradiation or surgical manipulation of the spinal cord.

Immunosuppressed patients are at increased risk.

The most important predisposing factor, however, is advanced age, which decreases immunity. Most VZV patients are over the age of 50 years. It is theorized that when the host resistance falls below a critical level, the patient becomes at risk for the development of herpes zoster. The virus migrates down the sensory nerve causing a painful neuritis and spreads into the skin. On the skin, characteristic clusters of zoster vesicles surmounted on an erythematous base are produced. Although the infection is generally dermatomal, a few distal vesicles can be seen. In immunosuppressed patients, widespread generalized zoster can occur. Furthermore, the routine zoster infections are frequently associated with evidence of a leptomeningitis, characterized by headache, inability to concentrate, and sensitivity to bright lights or loud sounds. Cerebral spinal fluid examination frequently reveals the presence of increased protein and mononuclear cells.

With increased age there is decreasing immunity and increased risk to develop zoster.

Pantropic disease with involvement of peripheral and central nervous systems

During a herpes zoster infection, an anamnestic immune response occurs restoring the immunity of the host. Second and third attacks of herpes zoster are uncommon but do occur. Those patients who are either on immunosuppressive agents or who have an immune suppression disease generally have a more severe and prolonged course.

Cutaneous Manifestations

Varicella Infection

The primary varicella infection is characterized by an incubation period of approximately 2 weeks. The rash is frequently accompanied by low-grade fever, chills, and headache. The rash begins on the face and scalp, is highly pruritic, and spreads caudalward. New lesions appear in crops (Figure 62–1). The prescence of vesicles at all stages of development is characteristic. Vesicles in the scalp and the oral mucosa are also characteristic.

Individual vesicles are surmounted on an erythematous base.

Pruritus is a major feature of varicella.

Individual varicella lesions rapidly develop from rose-colored macules producing a very superficial vesicle surmounted upon an erythematous base (Figure 62–2). These clear, dome-shaped vesicles appear as "water drops." The vesicles quickly become cloudy and rupture, producing an umbilicated pustule, which then crusts. The lesions heal within 1 to 3 weeks. Although the varicella lesions generally do not scar, scarring can occur in those lesions secondarily infected. Pruritus is a major feature of the disease.

Varicella in older children and adults is a severe disease.

Severity of primary varicella infection in childhood is usually minimal. However, in older children and young adults varicella produces a great deal of morbidity and, on occasions, mortality. High fever, headaches, and myalgias are prominent features of severe varicella infections.

Varicella pneumonia is a serious problem.

Varicella pneumonia (Hecht's pneumonia) is uncommon in childhood varicella but is frequently detected in older children and young adults. High fever, cough, dyspnea, cyanosis, and hemoptysis can occur. Varicella pneumonia in the past has been associated with a significant mortality. It still is problematic in immunocompromised individuals.

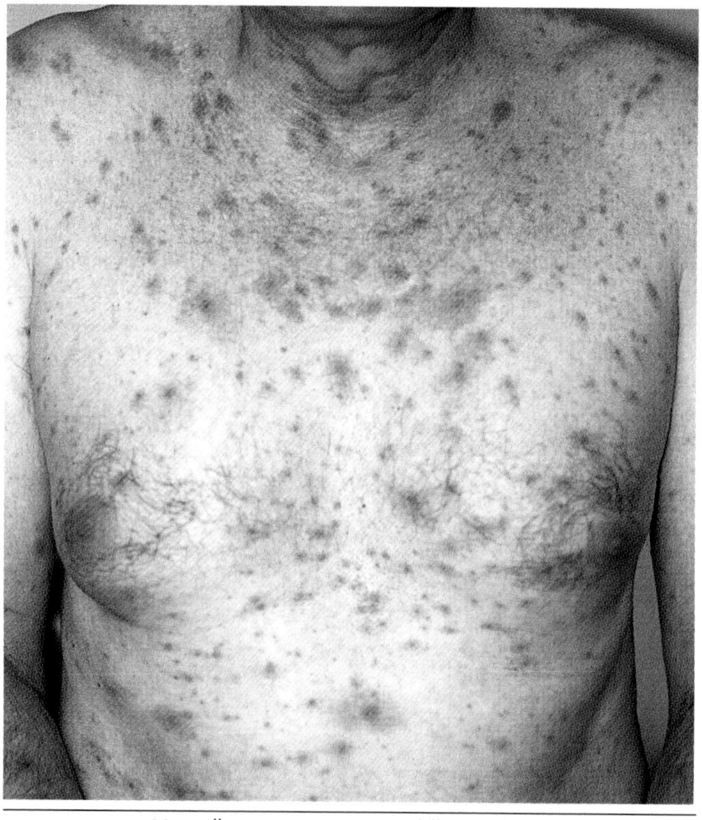

FIGURE 62–1 Varicella occurring in a middle-aged male. Note lesions are at various stages of development. This patient became very ill despite early treatment with famciclovir.

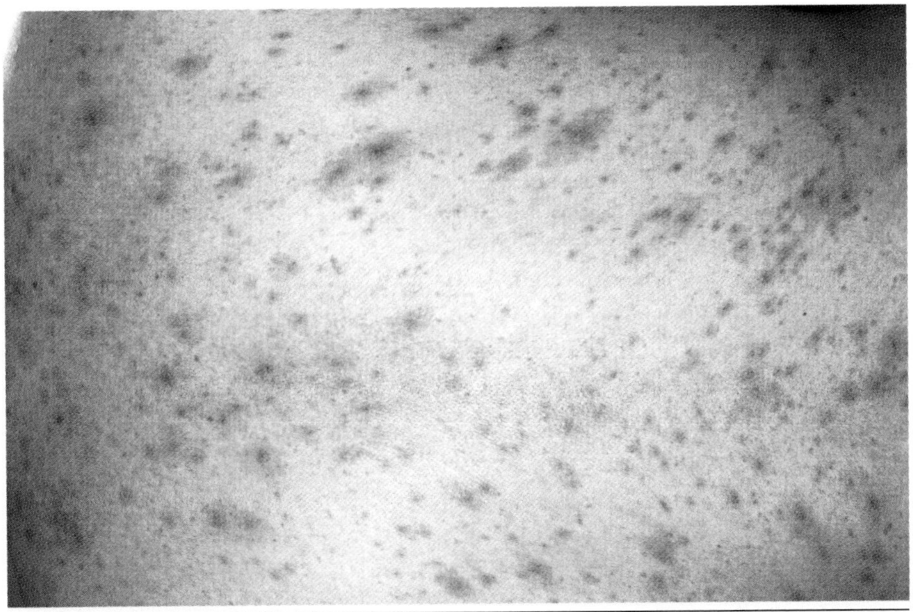

FIGURE 62–2 Close-up of varicella lesions demonstrating vesicles arising on erythematous macules.

In days prior to the advent of effective anti-VZV therapy, the inadvertent exposure of immune-deficient and immune-suppressed individuals was problematic. Provost is familiar with one epidemic in a children's hospital setting in which several lymphoma patients, as well as a patient with severe combined immune deficiency, succumbed to widespread VZV following the inadvertent exposure of these patients to a child with chickenpox.

Varicella and zoster lesions may become infected with streptococci or staphylococci.

In addition to extensive varicella or zoster associated with immune deficiency and immune suppression, individual lesions of varicella and zoster can be complicated by secondary streptococcal and staphylococcal infections. This complication frequently produces scarring.

On rare occasions, central nervous system complications may occur. These include Reye's syndrome and Guillain-Barré syndrome. A meningoencephalitis and an encephalitis probably occur frequently, but are generally subclinical.

Varicella in Pregnancy

Maternal varicella infection in early pregnancy can result in various congenital defects in infants.

The onset of varicella in pregnancy is problematic. The mother is at risk for varicella pneumonia. Congenital VZV infection follows a varicella infection in the mother during the earliest stages of pregnancy. A variety of congenital abnormalities are detected. These abnormalities include hypoplasia of an extremity, cortical atrophy, and ocular abnormalities including coloboma. Children, however, may be born without any visible evidence of a varicella infection. These infants, however, are at risk to develop herpes zoster at a very early age (< 10 years of age).

Varicella maternal infection near term can produce widespread disease in infant.

Varicella occurring within 10 days of birth is especially problematic because the infant has not had time to receive from the mother sufficient quantities of passively transferred VZV antibodies to modify the infection. Widespread dissemination and increased mortality can occur.

Herpes Zoster

The dominant feature of herpes zoster is the development of pain or hyperpathia. This generally occurs 1 to 4 days prior to the onset of the dermatitis. The patients also may experience sensations such as pruritus, tingling, or burning. Young adults and children may not experience any pain.

Pain is dominant feature of herpes zoster.

The dermatitis of herpes zoster usually begins as a unilateral erythematous plaque or urticarial-like lesion involving several dermatomes upon which vesicles rapidly develop. The vesicles may become purulent, hemorrhagic, or necrotic (Figures 62–3 and 62–4). With the onset of the dermatitis, the pain may become severe and have a marked detrimental impact upon the quality of life. On unusual occasions, herpes zoster without skin involvement may occur, manifest by dermatomal pain in the absence of lesions. This is known as "zoster sine herpete."

Trunkal involvement is most common.

Herpes zoster most frequently occurs on the trunk (approximately 50% of the time). The ophthalmic division of the trigeminal nerve is the second most commonly affected area (approximately 20% of the time). Cervical and lumbar involvement occur with approximate equal frequency (approximately 10%), and the sacral involvement occurs in 1 to 2% of patients. It is thought that the rash of herpes zoster occurs in dermatomes previously demonstrating heaviest varicella involvement.

Vesicles occurring outside of the involved dermatome is common.
Widespread dissemination indicative of low host immunity to VZV

Although herpes zoster is most commonly described as a unilateral disease process, on unusual occasions, bilateral zoster or zoster occurring simultaneously in multiple areas has been described. It should be noted, however, that although herpes zoster is most commonly a localized disease process, it is not uncommon for several vesicles to be found outside of the predominant involved dermatomes. Widespread dissemination, indicative of low host immunity, however, is uncommon, occurring most commonly in elderly patients and immunocompromised patients.

Subclinical central nervous system disease

Although patients with classic herpes zoster are not systemically ill, they may on occasions have fever, myalgias, and fatigue. Tender, local lymphadenopathy may occur. Patients may also complain of headaches and stiffness of the neck and frequently of difficulty concentrating. A lumbar puncture frequently demonstrates increased protein and a mild pleocytosis composed of a few mononuclear cells. Thus although localized, there is subtle clinical as well as laboratory evidence to indicate that the herpes zoster infection is a pantropic disease process affecting sensory and, on occasions, motor peripheral nerves, as well as the central nervous system.

Immunosuppressed patients have widespread and prolonged disease.
Is an AIDS-defining illness

In general, the eruption of herpes zoster resolves within 2 weeks. Complications are related to the localization of the herpes zoster and to the immunologic status of the host. For example, as noted earlier, herpes zoster occurring in immunocompromised patients (eg, patients who have Hodgkin's disease, lymphoma, or leukemia or who are receiving cytotoxic and immunosuppressive

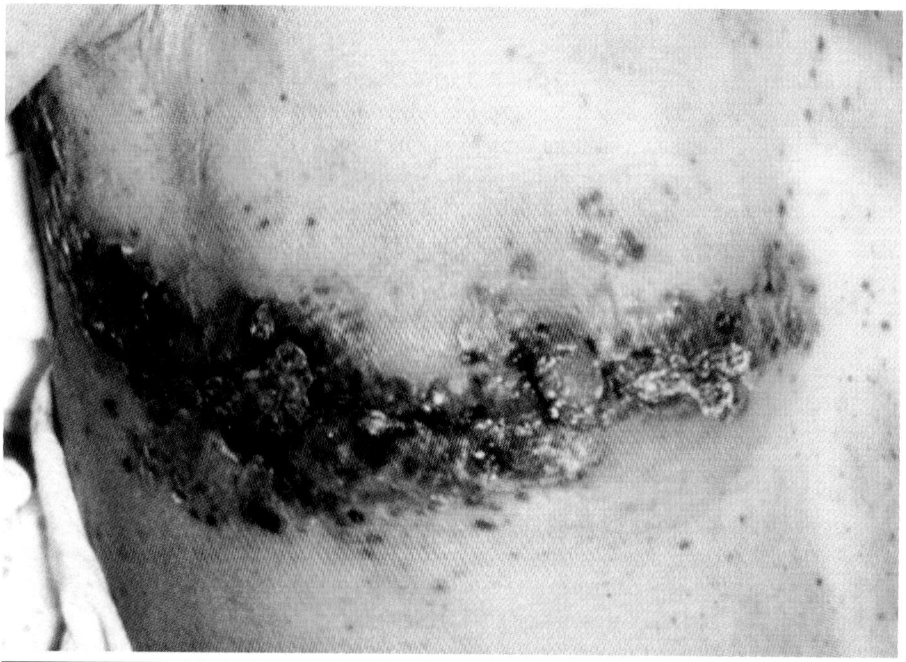

FIGURE 62–3 Necrotic lesions of herpes zoster in a zonal distribution on the chest.

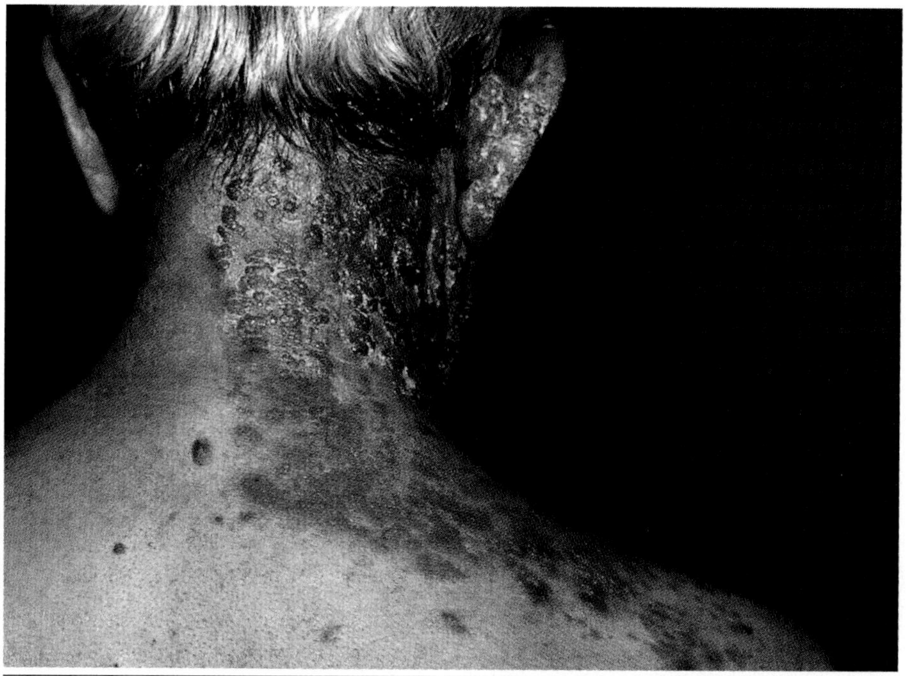

FIGURE 62–4 Herpes zoster involving the right side of posterior neck and shoulder.

drugs) frequently demonstrates cutaneous dissemination and a prolonged disease course. Herpes zoster in recent years has been recognized as an acquired immunodeficiency syndrome (AIDS)-defining illness (Figure 62–5).

Herpes zoster generally occurs as a complication in cancer patients with advanced disease.

Although herpes zoster occurs with increased frequency in patients with immunologic suppressive diseases, clinical experience indicates that it is not cost effective to evaluate isolated herpes zoster patients for the presence of an underlying malignancy. It should be noted that in cancer patients, herpes zoster generally occurs with advanced disease or in association with cytotoxic or irradiation therapy. It is not an early sign of an underlying malignancy.

Post-herpetic neuralgia can be very debilitating.

In addition to widespread cutaneous dissemination, post-herpetic neuralgia (PHN) is a very life-debilitating complication, generally occurring in patients over the age of 50 years. In general, spontaneous resolution of pain usually occurs 4 weeks after the onset of the disease. Post-herpetic neuralgia is a frequent complication in elderly individuals. One study indicates that approximately 75% of patients over the age of 70 years had pain beyond 1 month. It is not possible to predict which individual will develop PHN; however, those individuals with ophthalmic zoster appear to have an increased frequency of PHN.

Depression and suicide ideation can occur.

The pain of PHN is variable. Some patients describe a burning, itching, or aching sensation. Others describe lancinating pain or pain aggravated by the application of light touch or temperature changes to the skin. Sleep deprivation is a prominent clinical problem. Depression and even suicide has resulted. (See discussion on treatment of PHN.)

Motor nerve involvement can occur.

Although sensory nerve involvement is the most dominant clinical problem of herpes zoster, motor nerve involvement can occur. Diaphragmatic paralysis and weakness has been associated with phrenic nerve involvement, and lumbar sacral zoster may produce dysfunction of the bowel and bladder, as well as weakness in the leg or foot drop.

Bell's palsy
Ramsay Hunt syndrome

The most commonly recognized motor involvement is a facial palsy (Bell's palsy). This may occur with herpes zoster involvement of the ear, the ear canal, or postauricular areas and is known as "Ramsay Hunt syndrome." (It is theorized that in the Ramsay Hunt syndrome, herpes zoster involving the geniculate ganglion occurs with subsequent spreading to the facial nerves [cranial nerve VII] producing Bell's palsy.) Damage to the ocular muscle nerves (cranial nerves III, IV, and VI) and the auditory nerve may occur.

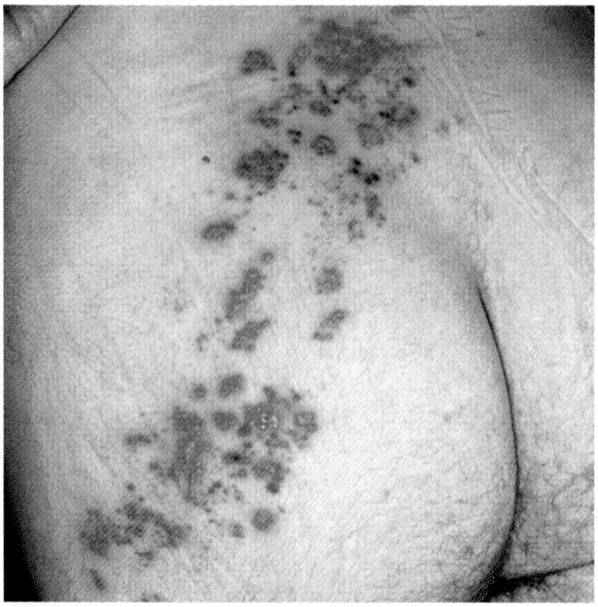

FIGURE 62–5 Herpes zoster in left lumbar sacral region in a human immunodeficiency–positive patient.

Lesion on tip of nose may indicate involvement of nasociliary branch of ophthalmic nerve.

Ophthalmic complications develop in nearly two-thirds of patients with herpes zoster of the ophthalmic division of cranial nerve V. In many cases, the presence of vesicles on the tip of the nose heralds the involvement of the nasociliary branch of the ophthalmic nerve. A subsequent dendritic keratopathy, corneal scarring, or anterior uveitis may lead to serious visual impairment.

Herpes zoster patients are contagious. Susceptible individuals in contact with herpes zoster patients can develop varicella.

Diagnosis

Tzanck smear

A presumptive diagnosis of herpes zoster can be made by a Tzanck preparation of clinically characteristic, localized group vesicles on an erythematous base. This preparation will show giant cells and acantholytic epidermal cells with swollen nuclei.

Diagnosis confirmed with viral culture.

Confirmation of the diagnosis is achieved by viral culture. The VZV produces typical cytopathic effects in 5 to 10 days compared with the herpes simplex virus which produces typical cytopathic effects within 24 to 48 hours.

Treatment

Acyclovir phosphorylated by viral and not human thymidine kinase

In recent years, acyclovir and derivative antiviral agents (ie, famciclovir, valacyclovir) have become the drugs of choice in the treatment of patients at risk to develop complications. Acyclovir is activated by its phosphorylation induced by viral thymidine kinase producing acyclovir triphosphate. This compound directly inhibits viral DNA polymerase. The drug is activated by viral thymidine kinase and not by the thymidine kinases of human cells. The derivative compounds of acyclovir (famciclovir, valacyclovir) appear to achieve antiviral blood levels much faster, and there is some evidence to suggest that the use of these drugs within 24 to 48 hours may inhibit the development of PHN.

Glucocorticosteroid Therapy

Use of prednisone may decrease acute pain of herpes zoster.

High-dose systemic steroid therapy has been proposed in the treatment of patients at risk for PHN. Some studies have shown a statistically significant decrease in pain at 4 weeks in patients treated with steroid therapy versus controls. Other studies, however, have failed to show an effect. Prednisone may help relieve the acute pain of zoster, but the evidence to suggest that it prevents PHN is still lacking.

Treatment of Immunosuppressed Patients

Intravenous antiviral therapy has been shown to be effective in the treatment of immunosuppressed patients with herpes zoster. Regression of disease, inhibition of cutaneous dissemination, and prevention of pneumonia have all been shown to occur with this therapy. Few complications occur with intravenous therapy. Crystalluria is easily averted with good hydration.

Treatment of Post-herpetic Neuralgia

PHN
Pain persisting for 1 to 3 months after resolution of shingles
50% of PHN patients have persistence for 2 years.

Post-herpetic neuralgia, a debilitating, chronic, neuropathic pain disease, is a common sequela to an episode of herpes zoster in elderly patients. Post-herpetic neuralgia is defined as pain persisting or recurring at the site of shingles 1 to 3 months after resolution of the varicella zoster rash. Sensory deficits, mechanical allodynia, thermal hyperalgesia, and ongoing pain all occur in varying degrees. The most common clinical picture consists of ongoing pain associated with mechanical allodynia but not with thermal hyperalgesia. A subset of patients have both mechanical allodynia and thermal hyperalgesia, and even fewer have ongoing pain with no mechanical allodynia or thermal hyperalgesia. The intensity and quality of the pain in PHN are frequently reported as being "severe, excruciating, debilitating, or incapacitating." Post-herpetic neuralgia occurs in 10 to 34% of individuals affected by herpes zoster. The incidence of PHN increases with age; the average age of patients is between 67 and 70 years, and women are affected twice as often as men. Patients with cancer, diabetes mellitus, and immunosuppression are more likely to develop PHN. Epidemiologic studies reveal that the duration of PHN is less than 1 year in 78% of patients with PHN; however, it can persist for years or indefinitely in others. For example, in one long-term follow-up study of 157 patients, 53% were still in severe pain after a median duration of 2 years. Approximately 15% of referrals to pain clinics are for the treatment of PHN. Post-herpetic neuralgia is often refractory to treatment and, as a result, associated with significant morbidity, depression, and health care utilization.

Exact pathogenesis is complex.

Although PHN has a single well-defined etiology, the underlying pathophysiology may vary from patient to patient with the duration of PHN representing a complex interplay of peripheral and central mechanisms. Degeneration and destruction of motor and sensory fibers of the mixed dorsal root ganglion characterize acute varicella zoster, but other forms of neurologic damage have been described. These include inflammation of the spinal cord, myelin disruption, axonal damage, and decreases in the number of nerve endings in the affected skin. Studies have suggested the role of both peripheral and central mechanisms probably resulting from the loss of large-caliber neurons and subsequent central sensitization, but adrenergic receptor activation and alterations in C-fiber activity have also been reported. Early in the disease, the predominant mechanism for pain may be a peripheral nociceptor drive from cutaneous sites that results in central sensitization. In a more long-standing disease, a central generator may be responsible for the ongoing pain, and anatomical reorganization in the spinal dorsal horn may be responsible for the allodynia. The presence of mechanical allodynia without thermal hyperalgesia in a subset of patients with PHN is similar to the presence of sensory changes characteristic of the zone of secondary hyperalgesia that surrounds cutaneous injury or inflammation. Central changes are thought to cause secondary hyperalgesia, whereas sensitization of nociceptors is considered to be responsible for primary hyperalgesia at the site of injury.

Three categories of post-herpetic neuralgia

It has been proposed that PHN patients be classified into three categories based on the presence or absence of mechanical allodynia and cutaneous sensory deficits and on the response to topical therapies with local anesthetic agents and capsaicin application.

The patients with cutaneous allodynia from both thermal and mechanical stimuli are thought to have irritable or sensitized cutaneous nociceptors. Cutaneous sensitivity to thermal stimuli is intact or minimally affected in this subset of PHN patients. Evidence for the presence of peripheral pain generators was provided by reports of pain relief after topical application of local anesthetics to the PHN site.

A second subset of patients present with spontaneous pain, mechanical allodynia, and thermal sensory deficits as evidenced by elevated thresholds for warmth and heat pain. The mechanical allodynia in this subset of patients is considered to be secondary to synaptic plasticity in the central nervous system and the development of aberrant connections in the dorsal horn of the spinal cord due to partial deafferentation.

A third category is patients with severe, spontaneous pain without cutaneous hyperalgesia or allodynia. These patients presumably have lost both large-myelinated and small-unmyelinated fibers. It is hypothesized that their pain is due to spontaneous activity in central neurons as a result of either release of inhibition or hyperactivity of central pain transmission neurons in the presence of marked sensory deafferentation.

Understanding the different pathophysiologic mechanisms that might contribute to the pain of PHN may help to develop clinical strategies to assess and treat patients with PHN. For example, in patients with irritable nociceptors, topical local anesthetics may be beneficial. Topical capsaicin might be contraindicated in these patients as the activation of nociceptors enhances the central sensitization process. Treatment of varicella zoster with low-dose amitriptyline reduced the prevalence of pain at 6 months by 50%. However, both central and peripheral mechanisms may present in a given patient.

Several classes of medications are under investigation for the treatment of PHN, but the following are considered to possess the best efficacy: antidepressants, anticonvulsants, and opioids.

Antidepressants

Tricyclic antidepressants

In 1960, the first report of imipramine used to treat trigeminal neuralgia was published. Since then, the antidepressants and, in particular, the tricyclic agents have been commonly prescribed for the treatment of many chronic pain syndromes, especially neuropathic pain such as PHN. Current research suggests antidepressant effects on pain are mediated by the blockade of norepinephrine and serotonin reuptake that increases the levels of these neurotransmitters and enhances the activation of descending inhibitory neurons. Tricyclic antidepressants (TCAs) may reduce hyperalgesia but not tactile allodynia because different neuronal mechanisms underlie different manifestations of neuropathic pain. Generally, amitriptyline or TCAs with a similar pharmacologic profile are considered most effective, but randomized controlled trials have not demonstrated consistent differences between the TCAs.

In a review of 39 placebo-controlled studies, 80% found antidepressants superior to placebo for the treatment of neuropathic pain. A recent systematic review of randomized controlled trials and meta-analysis concluded that TCAs are the only agents proven to benefit PHN. Tricyclic antidepressants have been most effective in relieving neuropathic pain and headache syndromes, with the analgesic activity independent of effects on mood. A variety of treatment studies of PHN and painful diabetic peripheral neuropathy have used TCAs with mean daily doses ranging from 100 to 250 mg. Over 60% of patients reported improvement usually beginning in the third week of treatment, with serum levels in the low end of the therapeutic range for the treatment of depression. The results of investigations of drug concentrations needed for pain relief remain contradictory and no clear guidelines have been established.

The role of biogenic amines in the descending inhibition of pain suggests a potential efficacy for all antidepressants in the treatment of chronic pain, despite their different pharmacologic actions. For example, venlafaxine inhibits the reuptake of both serotonin and norepinephrine with fewer side effects than TCAs. In an animal model of neuropathic pain, venlafaxine reversed hyperalgesia as well as preventing its development. The serotonin reuptake inhibitors (SRIs) have not been found to be as effective as the TCAs for many chronic pain conditions. One study of patients with diabetic neuropathy did find beneficial effects with paroxetine. Other studies indicate that fluoxetine significantly reduces pain in patients with rheumatoid arthritis and is comparable to amitriptyline. Recently, the SRIs have demonstrated effectiveness in the treatment of headache, especially migraine, and were well tolerated by patients. Until the results with SRIs are more consistent, they are not recommended as first-choice medications unless a specific contraindication exists for TCAs.

Anticonvulsants

Anticonvulsants are considered most effective in the treatment of trigeminal neuralgia, diabetic neuropathy, and migraine recurrence. Most anticonvulsants block the activity of use-dependent sodium channels. This property stabilizes the presynaptic neuronal membrane, preventing the release of excitatory neurotransmitters, and decreases the spontaneous firing rate in damaged and regenerating nociceptive fibers. Subsequently, the activation of secondary spinal nociceptive neurons via *N*-methyl-D-aspartate (NMDA) receptors is prevented. Therapeutic serum levels have not been clearly established; some evidence suggests levels lower than those recommended for the treatment of epilepsy may be effective in decreasing pain.

Consequently, phenytoin and carbamazepine have been considered logical choices for the treatment of neuropathic pain syndromes. Phenytoin was first reported as a successful treatment for trigeminal neuralgia in 1942. Carbamazepine is the most widely studied anticonvulsant in the treatment of neuropathic pain, with documented efficacy for a variety of conditions including PHN. Unfortunately, the use of carbamazepine can be limited by intolerable side effects, such as sedation, ataxia, and aplastic anemia.

Newer classes of anticonvulsants represent novel pharmacologic actions that could potentially produce analgesia. Valproic acid is the most commonly used prophylaxis of migraine but is also effective in treating neuropathy pain. The mechanism of action of valproate is probably related to increased γ-aminobutyric acid (GABA) levels by the inhibition of GABA transaminase and enhanced GABA synthesis. Gabapentin has been reported in open trials to reduce the pain of neuropathic states, such as multiple sclerosis, migraine, PHN, and reflex sympathetic dystrophy. The mechanism of action of gabapentin includes selectively interacting with the α-2-delta subunit of voltage-dependent calcium channels.

Lamotrigine may be effective in reducing the pain of phantom limbs, neuroma hypersensitivity, trigeminal neuralgia, causalgia, central post-stroke pain, and PHN. The mechanism of action of lamotrigine may be due to its ability to decrease long-term excitatory effects of nociceptive glutaminergic transmission mediated by NMDA receptors, but it also blocks use-dependent voltage-gated sodium channels. Topiramate, tiagapine, vigabatrin, and zonisamide are new anticonvulsants with a spectrum of pharmacologic actions that include enhancing neuronal inhibition, decreasing neuronal excitability, and protecting neurons from free radical damage.

Opioids

The use of opioids in nonmalignant chronic pain remains a subject of considerable debate. Until recently, opioids were reserved for use only in the treatment of acute and cancer pain syndromes. Nonmalignant chronic pain was considered to be unresponsive to opioids, which were associated with too many risks. Recently, several controlled trials have examined the effectiveness of opioids in treating chronic nonmalignant pain including PHN. They support the use of opioids to provide direct analgesic actions, not just to counteract the unpleasantness of pain. Other studies have documented the presence of opioid receptors in the peripheral tissues that become activated by inflammation.

Post-herpetic pain may require long-term use of opioids.

Fears of regulatory pressure, medication abuse, and the development of tolerance create reluctance to prescribe opioids, and many studies have documented this "underutilization." Fortunately, recent studies of physicians specializing in pain, as well as those who do not, have shown that prescription of long-term opioids is increasingly common. Surveys and open label clinical trials support the safety and effectiveness of opioids in patients with chronic nonmalignant pain.

Annotated Bibliography

Huff JA. Herpes zoster. Curr Probl Dermatol 1988;1:1–40.

This is an excellent, well-written review article with 227 references.

Hope-Simpson RE. The nature of herpes zoster: a long-term study and a new hypothesis. Proc R Soc Med 1965;58:9–20.

This is a remarkable, well-conceived and well-written study by a general practitioner who observed all cases of herpes zoster in his general practice during a 16-year period and then formed a hypothesis of the etiology of herpes zoster that today is well accepted. His observations led to the conclusion that following a primary chicken pox infection, the varicella virus becomes latent in the sensory ganglia. There, after many years, it is reactivated, producing herpes zoster.

Kost RG, Straus SE. Post herpetic neuralgia—pathogenesis, treatment, and prevention. N Engl J Med 1996;335:32–42.

This is a well-written article summarizing the pathogenesis, treatment, and prevention of PHN. It contains 110 references.

These authors recommend, for prevention of PHN, the institution of famciclovir, valacyclovir, or acyclovir within 72 hours of the appearance of the dermatitis. These agents reduce the acute pain of herpes zoster. Whether they affect PHN is unclear. Famciclovir and valacyclovir have better bioavailability and appear to shorten the duration of zoster-associated pain. These authors believe, however, there is no reason to recommend one drug over the other.

They further point out that five control studies have evaluated the use of oral corticosteroids. The drug was beneficial in two trials and not beneficial in two others. In the fifth study, the acute neuritis resolved significantly earlier in the prednisone-treated group than in the controls, and there was a shorter period of analgesic treatment. The prednisone-treated patients resumed, more quickly, a normal sleep and activity pattern. Because of these observations, these authors recommend consideration of the use of corticosteroids in high-risk patients over the age of 50 years, who have moderate to severe pain, in whom corticosteroids are not contraindicated.

These authors also strongly recommend the use of adequate, around-the-clock analgesics to provide comfort for the acute pain of herpes zoster.

The treatment of PHN is problematic. Topical lidocaine-prilocaine cream or 5% lidocaine gel is recommended as initial therapy. They do not recommend topical capsaicin because of the burning sensation that it induces. Narcotics should be given, but the risk of sedation and dependence needs to be recognized.

Amitriptyline or desipramine may be given in small doses—12.5 to 25 mg at bedtime. These medications may be increased weekly until the pain subsides or the side effects become unacceptable. Maprotiline or nortriptyline may be substituted. If these antidepressant drugs produce only partial control, an anticonvulsant drug should be tried. Anticonvulsants (phenytoin, valproate, sodium carbamazepine) are especially effective in reducing the lancinating component of the neuropathic pain.

Counter irritation, in the form of ethyl chloride spray and transcutaneous electrical nerve stimulation, has been effective, but one trial of acupuncture was not.

Hayward A,Villaneuba E, Cosyns M, Levin M. Varicella zoster virus (VZV) specific cytotoxicity after immunization of nonimmune adults with Oka strain attenuated VZV vaccine. J Infect Dis 1992;166:260–264.

Preliminary studies indicate that vaccination with Oka strain may provide protection to patients older than 50 years of age. (This vaccine has recently been approved by the United States Food and Drug Administration.)

Tyring S, et al. Famciclovir for the treatment of acute herpes zoster: effects on acute disease and post herpetic neuralgia. Ann Intern Med 1995;123:89–96.

This is a randomized, double-blind, placebo-controlled study of the effects of herpes zoster involving 419 immunocompetent adults. This study, in which there was active participation by Smith, Kline, Beecham Pharmaceuticals, demonstrated that famciclovir (500–750 mg tid) was effective in controlling herpes zoster and produced a faster resolution of PHN in patients 50 years of age and older. There was a 3½-month reduction in the median duration of PHN.

Goffinet DR, Glatstein J, Merigan TC. Herpes zoster–varicella infections in lymphoma. Ann Intern Med 1972;76:235–240.

This article demonstrates an increased frequency of herpes zoster in lymphoma and Hodgkin's disease patients.

Jellinek EH, Tulloch WS. Herpes zoster with dysfunctional bladder and anus. Lancet 1976;2:1219–1222.

This is an article demonstrating the rare motor involvement that can occur with lumbar herpes zoster, producing transient bladder and anal dysfunction.

McCary ML, Severson J, Tyring SK. Varicella zoster virus. J Am Acad Dermatol 1999;41:1–14.

Good review with excellent bibliography.

CHAPTER 63

Deep Fungal Infections

Thomas T. Provost, M.D.

Candidiasis

Candida albicans is most important pathogen.

Candida albicans is the most important pathogen of the *Candida* species and is responsible for approximately 90% of mucous membrane and systemic cases occurring, generally, in the setting of diabetes mellitus, immunosuppression (eg, acquired immunodeficiency syndrome [AIDS]), chronic intravenous drug therapy, or intravenous drug abuse. Approximately 10% of cases of candidiasis are caused by other members of the *Candida* species, such as *Candida tropicalis*, *Candida stellatoidea*, and *Candida parapsilosis*. In this chapter, the discussion will be limited to *C. albicans*.

C. albicans is a normal saprophyte in the mouth, gastrointestinal tract, and vagina.

Candida albicans is a common saprophyte detected in the oral, gastrointestinal tract, and vaginal mucosa of approximately 70% of individuals. *Candida albicans* is a dimorphic fungus exhibiting a yeast form (blastospore) in its saprophytic state and a mycelial phase (pseudohyphae) in its pathologic state.

Rarely detected on the skin unless skin is warm and moist.

Candida albicans is rarely detected on normal skin but readily colonizes warm, moist, macerated areas (eg, inframammary region, groin, and between third and fourth fingers [erosio interdigitalis blastomycetica]) in patients who frequently have their hands in water.

Mannan, a cell wall polysaccharide, has endotoxin-like properties.

The pathogenicity of *C. albicans* is related to the endotoxin-like activity of mannan, a cell wall polysaccharide capable of activating the alternative complement pathway. Other *C. albicans* toxins may interfere with neutrophil and T-cell functions. Furthermore, *C. albicans* has the ability to adhere to vaginal and oral mucosa by elaborating various enzymes to invade.

Among various host defense mechanisms, cell-mediated immunity most important

The host defense mechanisms protective against *C. albicans* include phagocytosis by polymorphonuclear leukocytes and macrophages; transferrin and lactoferrin, which compete with *C. albicans* for iron; and immunoglobulin and cell-mediated immune responses. Cell-mediated immune responses appear to be the most important host defense. In infants, most but not all cases of mucocutaneous candidiasis are seen in association with hereditary defects in T-cell–mediated responses. (For further discussion, see Chapter 20, "Cutaneous Manifestations of Primary Immunodeficiency Diseases.")

Clinical Features

Cutaneous Manifestations

The cutaneous manifestations of candidiasis include candidal paronychia, erythematous cutaneous papules and nodules, erythematous erosions, vulvovaginal candidiasis, balanitis, and chronic mucocutaneous candidiasis.

Candidal paronychia. Candidal paronychia is characterized by redness and swelling of the involved fingers associated with nail dystrophy. Chronic candidal nail dystrophy is commonly detected in infants with mucocutaneous candidiasis reflecting an oral source of *C. albicans* infection (thumb or finger sucking).

Pus beneath the cuticle of the nail fold or a scraping of the nail will demonstrate the organism.

Nail dystrophies, especially thumb nail dystrophy, reflective of oral contamination

Erythematous cutaneous papules and nodules. Patients with *Candida* septicemia develop erythematous cutaneous papules and nodules, which may become hemorrhagic, on all areas of the body, but most commonly on the extremities (Figure 63–1). Some lesions may become necrotic. Biopsy and culture of the lesions will establish the diagnosis.

These lesions are commonly detected in patients who are treated with immunosuppressive agents, are on chronic intravenous therapy, or are intravenous drug abusers.

Papules and nodules associated with systemic candidiasis.

Erythematous erosions. *Candida* can cause erythematous and at times, painful erosions with characteristic satellite lesions in wet, moist, macerated areas (eg, diaper dermatitis localized to the area in contact with the diaper area, beneath pendulous breasts, and the area of the groin) (Figure 63–2).

Satellite lesions characteristic of intertriginous candidal infections

Vulvovaginal candidiasis. Vulvovaginal candidiasis occurs most frequently in women who are pregnant, using birth control pills, or are on chronic antibiotic or immunosuppressive therapy. In women with a heavy *C. albicans* vaginal infection, sexual partners may note, 3 to 4 hours following intercourse, a burning and transient erythema of the shaft of the penis (Figure 63–3).

Vaginal candidiasis detected with increased frequency in women on the "pill" or who are receiving chronic antibiotic or immunosuppressive therapy.

Balanitis. Balanitis is characterized by erythema in the coronal sulcus, with or without a whitish scale. This form of *Candida* is detected in uncircumcised males and in patients with diabetes. As noted earlier, it also can be detected in patients following intercourse with a partner with significant vaginal candidiasis. A urethritis, characterized by a transient burning with the initial voiding in the morning, may be an important diagnostic clue explaining the source of recurrent *C. albicans* vulvovaginitis and balanitis in couples.

Balanitis seen in uncircumsized males and diabetics.

Chronic mucocutaneous candidiasis. Chronic mucocutaneous candidiasis, with or without granuloma formation, is most commonly detected in children

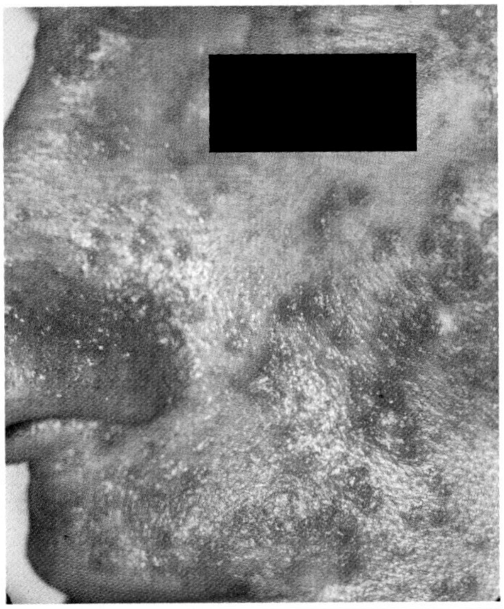

FIGURE 63–1 Inflammatory papules and nodules in an acquired immunodeficiency syndrome patient with systemic candidiasis.

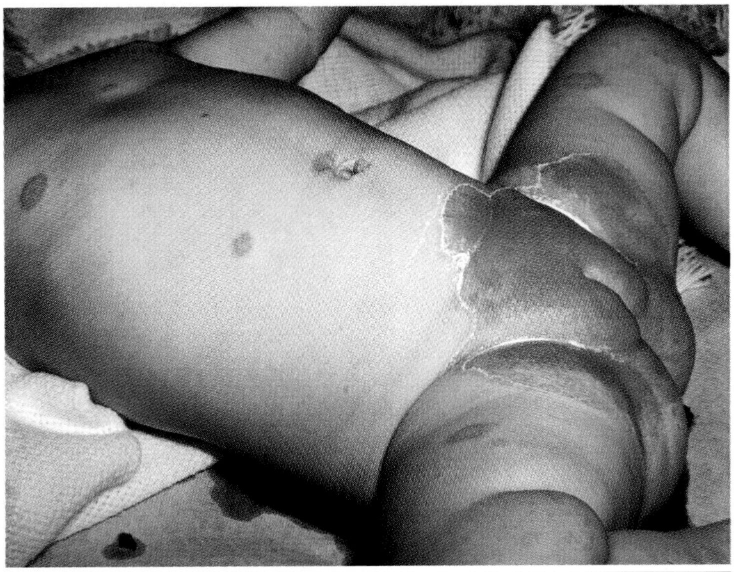

FIGURE 63–2 Diaper dermatitis secondary to *C. albicans.* This infant also has axillary involvement.

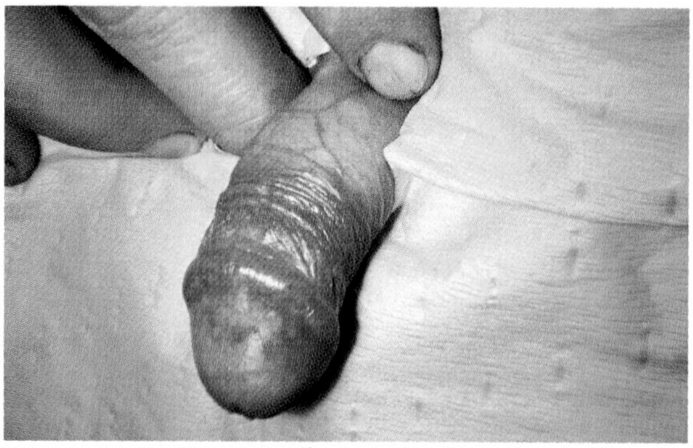

FIGURE 63–3 Irritant reaction on shaft of penis following intercourse with sexual partner who has vaginal candidiasis. Characteristically, this irritant reaction is KOH-negative and culture-negative, presumably, secondary to the endotoxin-like action of mannan and other candidal products.

Also seen in children with a hereditary polyendocrinopathy

(Figure 63–4). These children commonly demonstrate an associated polyendocrinopathy (hypoparathyroidism, hypothyroidism, hypoadrenalism, vitiligo, alopecia totalis, pernicious anemia, diabetes mellitus, and malabsorption). The cutaneous lesions are characterized by involvement of the oropharynx, nails, and skin of the face.

Chronic mucocutaneous candidiasis frequently detected in children with gross or subtle defects in T-cell immunity.

Chronic mucocutaneous candidiasis in children may also be associated with various T-cell immune deficiencies, including severe combined immune deficiency and DiGeorge syndrome. These children may demonstrate isolated defects in cell-mediated immunity, including defective lymphocyte transformation, defective T-cell lymphokine production, defective T-cell suppression, and defective T helper cell function.

Defects in macrophage, polymorphonuclear leukocyte function

Defects have also been described in macrophage and polymorphonuclear cells, as well as complement functions. Finally, some of these children have been detected to have serum factors inhibiting neutrophil and T-cell functions.

In adults, cutaneous candidiasis may be initial presentation of a thymoma.

In adults and adolescents, chronic mucocutaneous candidiasis is frequently an initial presentation with a thymoma with or without myasthenia gravis. Unexplained oral thrush in an adult should also make one suspect AIDS.

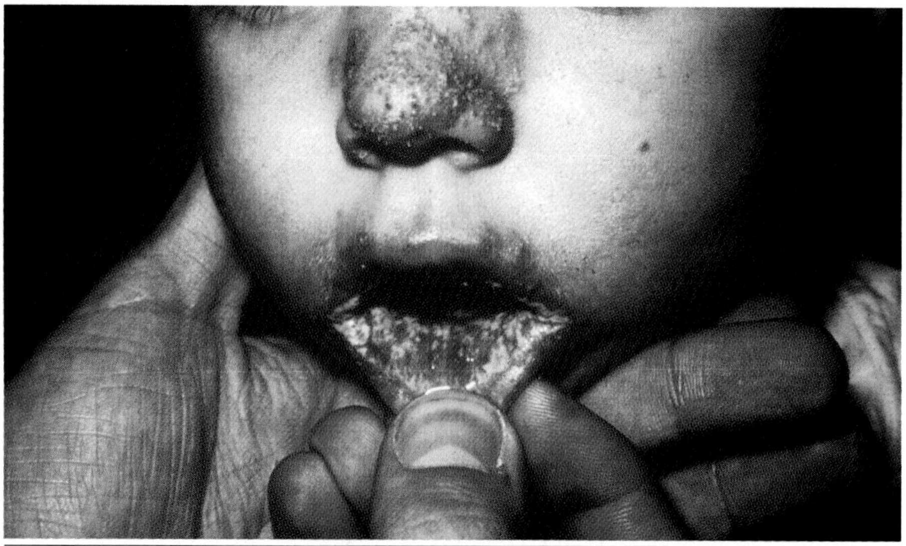

FIGURE 63–4 Child with mucocutaneous candidiasis and profound T-cell effect involving both defective cell-mediated immunity and antibody responses.

One of this author's first patients during dermatology residency was a middle-aged Caucasian female with widespread cutaneous lesions of *C. albicans*. Radiographs demonstrated a mediastinal mass that, on thoracic exploration, revealed a thymoma. Removal of the tumor and topical nystatin cream "cured" the mucocutaneous candidiasis (Figures 63–5 and 63–6).

In general, mucocutaneous candidiasis is a disease without systemic features.

Oral Manifestations

Oral candidiasis is frequently a complication of the use of systemic antibiotics and/or immunosuppressive therapy. It may also be a complication of an oral disease that may have been treated with corticosteroids or immunosuppressive drugs (Figures 63–7 and 63–8).

Oral candidiasis may be secondary to antibiotic and/or immunosuppressive therapy; complication of oral diseases.

The morphologic features of oral candidiasis are presented in Chapter 73, "Oral Manifestations of Systemic Disease." These diseases include erosive lichen planus, pemphigus vulgaris, benign mucous membrane pemphigoid, and Sjögren's syndrome.

Oral candidiasis frequent complication of oral disease, especially in those individuals who have dentures

In the author's experience, oral candidiasis manifesting itself as a burning erythematous tongue and buccal mucosa (acute atrophic candidiasis) is a common complication of Sjögren's syndrome, especially in patients with an upper denture.

Treatment

There are now several effective drugs for the treatment of various forms of candidiasis.

Cutaneous candidiasis can be effectively treated with nystatin powder or cream. The powder vehicle is especially effective for groin and inframammary infections during the heat of summer. Other successful therapies include miconazole powder and cream and ketoconazole and clotrimazole cream preparations.

Cutaneous candidiasis: nystatin, miconazole, clotrimazole

Oral candidiasis can be successfully treated with nystatin oral suspension (1 tsp. tid, swish, and swallow) or clotrimazole troches. For resistant cases, oral ketoconazole, itraconazole, and fluconazole have proved effective. Because of ketoconazole hepatotoxicity, itraconazole and fluconazole are preferred. Typical dose for fluconazole is 200 mg the first day and 100 mg daily for 2 weeks.

Oral candidiasis: nystatin oral suspension, clotrimazole troches; for resistant cases, oral ketoconazole, itraconazole, and fluconazole effective

Dentures should be cleaned nightly. Scouring the mucosal surface using nystatin powder and a toothbrush has proved effective.

Denture cleaning important

Vaginal candidiasis can be effectively treated with fluconazole 150 mg in a single dose. Nystatin vaginal clotrimazole suppositories and clotrimazole cream are effective.

Fluconazole effective in single dose to treat vaginal candidiasis

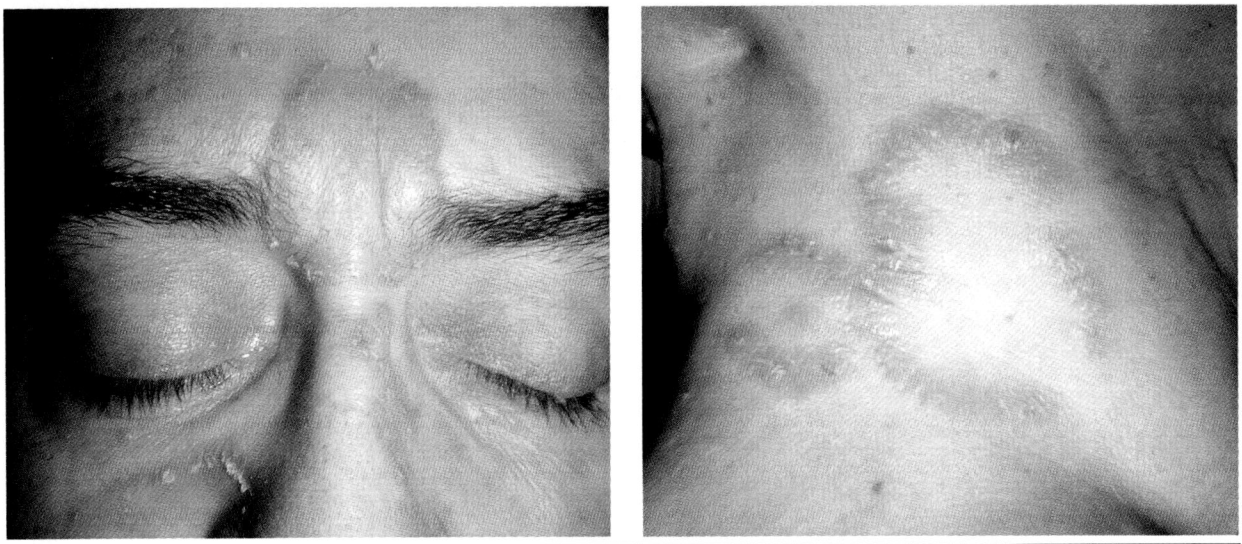

FIGURES 63–5 AND 63–6 Cutaneous *C. albicans* infections of face and shoulder in a T-cell deficient patient with a thymoma. (Reproduced with permission from Richard Baughman, M.D., Hanover, NH)

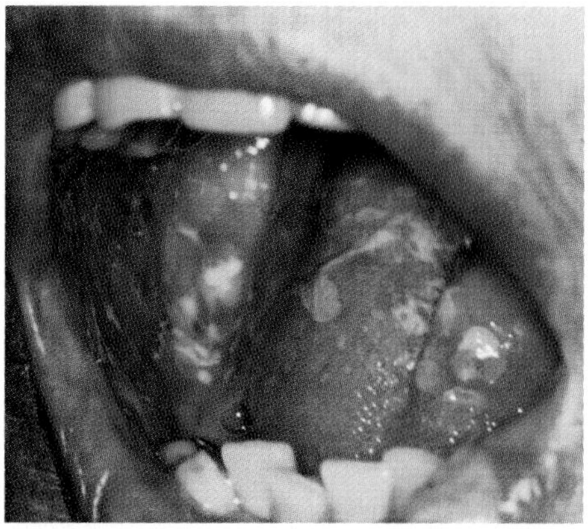

FIGURE 63-7 Pseudomembranous candidiasis (thrush) involving buccal mucosa and tongue.

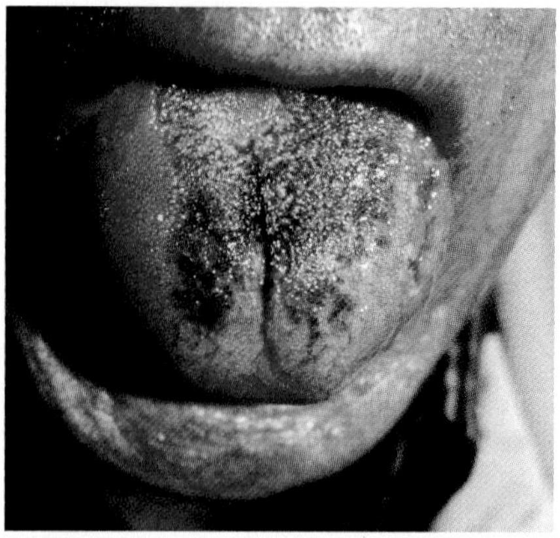

FIGURE 63-8 Black, hairy tongue due to *C. albicans* in a patient on chronic antibiotic therapy. (Reproduced with permission from Rick Stearns, M.D., Tulsa, OK)

Urethral meatus may be occult site of C. albicans *infection.*

Candidal balanitis is especially problematic, requiring treatment of the male and his sexual partner at the same time. Topical nystatin or miconazole powder is valuable in uncircumcised males. The application of nystatin cream to the male urethral meatus may prove valuable in eliminating a reservoir for *C. albicans.*

Disseminated candidiasis treatment is beyond the scope of this book. Amphotericin B, 5-flucytosine, ketoconazole, and itraconazole have been employed.

Annotated Bibliography

Provost TT, Garretson LK, Zeschke R, et al. Combined immune deficiency, autoantibody formation and mucocutaneous candidiasis. Clin Immunol Immunopathol 1973;1:429–438.

This article provides a description of a child with mucocutaneous candidiasis and defective antibody and cell-mediated immune responses. In retrospect, this was probably a patient with defective T helper cell function.

Kirkpatrick CH. Chronic mucocutaneous candidiasis. J Am Acad Dermatol 1994;31:14–17.

This is an excellent review by a noted authority in the field.

Hay RJ. Antifungal therapy of yeast infections. J Am Acad Dermatol 1994;31:6–9.

This is a good overview of therapeutic options.

Maiboch HI, Klegman AM. The biology of experimental human cutaneous moniliasis (*Candida albicans*). Arch Dermatol 1962;85:233–238.

Ray TL, Wuepper KD. Experimental cutaneous candidiasis in rodents. II. Role of the stratum corneum barrier and serum complement as a mediator of a protective inflammatory response. Arch Dermatol 1978;114:539–544.

Two articles demonstrating pathogenesis of Candida albicans *infections.*

Histoplasmosis

Endemic along Ohio and Mississippi valleys

Organism found in excreta of birds.

Histoplasmosis is a chronic fungal disease caused by the dimorphic (yeast at 37°C, mycelial form at room temperature) fungus *Histoplasma capsulatum.* This fungal disease is endemic along the Ohio and Mississippi river basins with isolated pockets in North Carolina, Wisconsin, and Minnesota. The organism (spore) is found in excreta of birds and bats and also in the soil, particularly in areas frequented by large numbers of birds. The disease is acquired by inhalation of spores. Epidemics of histoplasmosis are frequently associated with human contact with heavily contaminated ground (eg, demolition of gazebos, pigeon coops).

Epidemics have been reported with human contact with heavily contaminated structures.

Although the disease is endemic in many areas, it is generally clinically silent and only detected by the use of delayed hypersensitivity skin reactions to histoplasmin. In endemic areas, as many as 80% of the population are histoplasmin test–positive. Individuals with decreased cell-mediated resistance, such as those with lymphoma, Hodgkin's disease, and AIDS, and those receiving immunosuppressive agents, appear to be at increased risk. It is an AIDS-defining illness in human immunodeficiency virus (HIV)-positive patients.

As many as 80% of individuals in endemic areas infected with self-limited disease. Those individuals with cell-mediated immune deficiency at increased risk.

Clinical Features

The organism invades the host through the mucous membranes of the mouth and upper respiratory tract. The acute form of this disease is characterized by the onset of fever and malaise. Cough and dyspnea are frequently noted. A chest radiograph will generally demonstrate nodular densities. The lesions may heal with a characteristic "eggshell" calcification. This form of the disease is self-limited.

Upper respiratory infection
"Egg shell" calcification

On occasions, however, a disseminated form of histoplasmosis may occur. This generally occurs in immunosuppressed individuals. It is frequently characterized by the presence of ulceration of the oral mucous membranes and subcutaneous nodules. Liver and bone marrow involvement are common, and on occasions, adrenal insufficiency (Addison's disease) may occur. A markedly elevated serum lactate dehydrogenase is characteristic.

Dissemination in immune-suppressed individuals
Addison's disease
Elevated serum lactate Dehydrogenase

With the exception of erythema nodosum, glabrous skin involvement is very unusual. Among health care workers, primary cutaneous infections may occur from accidental inoculation of *H. capsulatum* into the skin.

Erythema nodosum

Diagnosis

The histoplasmin test is an epidemiologic research tool and is of little clinical value. Sputum, urine, lymph node, and bone marrow cultures are of value.

Serologic tests include a complement fixation assay and a precipitin antibody test to H and M antigens. In recent years, a radioimmunoassay has been successfully employed to detect polysaccharide antigens of *H. capsulatum* in urine and blood. It is a highly sensitive, excellent diagnostic test and is useful in monitoring drug therapy. A decreasing titer indicates drug effectiveness; a rising titer indicates drug failure.

Precipitin antibody test for H and M antigens
Radioimmunoassay to detect antigen I blood and urine
Diagnostic test also monitors drug effectiveness

Treatment

Previously, amphotericin B therapy was the mainstay of therapy. Today, itraconazole 400 mg per day for at least 3 months is effective and commonly employed.

Annotated Bibliography

Wheat LJ, et al. Disseminated histoplasmosis in AIDS: clinical findings, diagnosis and treatment and review of the literature. Medicine 1990;69:361–374.

This is an excellent review.

North American Blastomycosis

North American blastomycosis is a chronic fungal disease caused by the dimorphic fungus *Blastomyces dermatitidis*. It occurs in the southeastern United States and is found in the soil. The disease was co-discovered in 1894 by Gilchrist and Stokes, the former a physician at Johns Hopkins. Individuals are infected by inhalation of the fungi, and dissemination occurs from a primary focus in the lungs.

Found in southeastern U.S.A.

Clinical Features

Cutaneous manifestations are commonly detected in disseminated disease and are characterized by verrucous, annular-like, crusted lesions with central clearing and a peripheral border displaying multiple small pustules. Face, hands, and

Annular, crusted lesions with pustules

Bone involvement

Erythema nodosum

arms are most frequently involved. Bone involvement is also common (lumbar, thoracic, and sacral vertebrae).

Erythema nodosum occurs but is less frequent than in other deep fungal infections. Health care workers may develop a primary skin infection at the site of accidental inoculation. Multiple or single cavitary pulmonary lesions and subcutaneous abscess formation may occur. Oral and nasomucosal involvement occurs but not as frequently as in histoplasmosis. The prostate, testes, and epididymis may be involved.

Pathologic examination of tissue reveals pseudoepitheliomatous hyperplasia and a chronic granulomatous disease process characterized by giant cells and the presence of budding yeast.

Diagnosis

Diagnosis is established by culture. Urine culture and prostatic secretions may be positive, even in the absence of symptoms.

Treatment

Itraconazole 400 mg daily for 6 months is a common therapy.

Annotated Bibliography

Bradsher RW. Blastomycosis. Clin Infect Dis 1994;14(1);S82–90.

This is a good review.

Coccidioidomycosis

Found in southwestern U.S.A.

Over 90% of individuals in affected area have had a subclinical infection.

Coccidioidomycosis is a deep fungal disease caused by the geophilic dimorphic fungus *Coccidioides immitis*. This disease is endemic in the southwestern United States, especially the San Joaquin Valley of California, and in northern Mexico. It is also found in Venezuela, Paraguay, and northern Argentina. African Americans, Mexican Indians, and Filipinos are at increased risk to develop a severe disseminated disease; however, the reason is unknown. Pregnancy also appears to be another risk factor for the development of disseminated disease. Infection is common as judged by the delayed hypersensitivity skin reaction to coccidioidin. As many as 95% of individuals in endemic areas are skin test–positive to coccidioidin.

Clinical Features

"Valley fever"

People are infected by the inhalation of airborne spores. The primary site of infection is the lungs. An acute coccidioidomycosis may occur, characterized by fever, chills, and malaise ("Valley fever"). Pleuritic chest pain and a cough may be present and erythema nodosum may occur. The disease usually resolves spontaneously.

Dissemination may occur in immune-suppressed individuals, pregnant women, African Americans, and Filipinos.

Approximately 1% of patients may develop a disseminated form of the disease. Immunosuppressed and HIV patients living in the endemic area are at risk to develop a disseminated disease. Dissemination is secondary to a hematogenous spread. Osteomyelitis, with adjoining tissue abscess formation, may occur. Meningitis is frequently detected, characterized by fever, chills, weight loss, malaise, and anorexia.

On unusual occasions, a chronic pulmonary form of the disease may develop, characterized by solitary or multiple cavities, pulmonary fibrosis, and bronchiectasis.

The cutaneous manifestations of disseminated coccidioidomycosis are characterized by nodular, papular lesions that may ulcerate. A papular, nodular primary skin infection with regional lymphadenopathy may occur in health care workers accidentally inoculated.

Characteristically, the pathology demonstrates granulomas surrounding sporangia. Foreign body giant cells, lymphocytes, and histiocytes are commonly detected. Hyphal elements may be seen.

Diagnosis

Diagnosis is suspected by the demonstration of large spores in KOH examination of sputum, pus, or cerebral spinal fluid. Diagnosis is confirmed by culture. Precipitin antibody tests are available. However, complement fixation tests are more commonly used.

Precipitin and complement fixation antibody tests are available.

Treatment

No treatment is necessary for the limited disease. In the disseminated form of the disease, amphotericin B, itraconazole, and fluconazole are effective. Relapse is common; thus patients must be monitored closely.

Annotated Bibliography

Galgiani JN, Ampel NM. Coccidioidomycosis in HIV-infected patients. J Infect Dis 1990;162:1165–1168.

This article describes the difficulty in treating coccidioidomycosis in an immune-suppressed population.

Cryptococcosis

Cryptococcosis is a deep fungal disease caused by the yeast *Cryptococcus neoformans*. The organism is ubiquitous; it is found in the soil and in pigeon droppings. The disease appears to be acquired by inhalation of the organisms. Those patients with defective cell-mediated immunity, especially lymphoma, Hodgkin's disease, sarcoidosis, and AIDS patients, are at increased risk. In addition, patients with chronic debilitating diseases who are receiving low-dose steroids and/or immunosuppressive agents also appear to be at risk.

Geophilic fungus commonly infects individuals who work with the soil.

Clinical Features

The skin lesions of cryptococcosis are purpuric, papular, nodular, and plaque-like and may ulcerate. They are the result of hematogenous spread from a primary focus in the lungs and may resemble molluscum contagiosum (Figure 63–9). Subcutaneous swelling may also occur. At times, cutaneous cryptococcosis may be an AIDS-defining illness in HIV-positive patients.

Rarely pulmonary disease

(The author has seen several HIV-positive patients with papular, nodular lesions that on biopsy demonstrated cryptococcosis. The lesions were noninflammatory, and the patients were totally asymptomatic.)

In the recent past, an epidemic of cryptococcosis was detected by biopsy of asymptomatic nodular lesions occurring in chronic rheumatic disease patients receiving low-dose prednisone. These patients frequented a park-like area

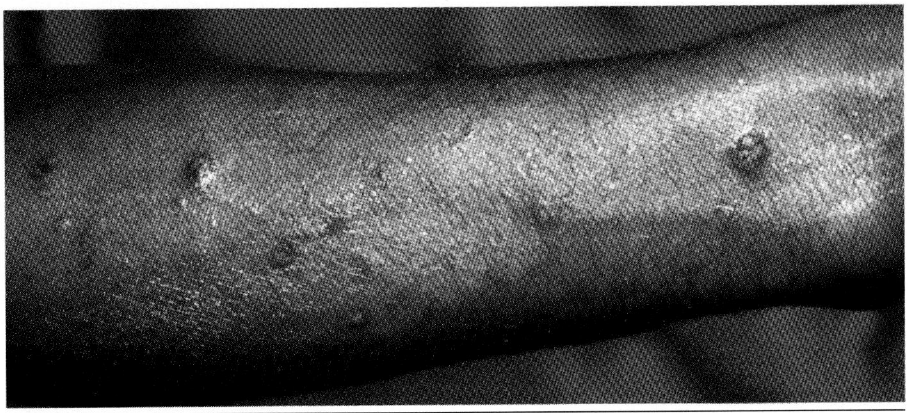

FIGURE 63–9 Nodular lesions of cutaneous cryptococcosis in a patient with AIDS. Some appeared as large molluscum contagiosum lesions.

exposed to many pigeons. Culture of pigeon droppings revealed *C. neoformans*. Elimination of the pigeon population was associated with a complete disappearance of the epidemic.

An asymptomatic pulmonary infection frequently occurs with cryptococcosis. This may be totally asymptomatic or associated with a productive cough. It is commonly detected in AIDS patients.

Meningitis is the most frequent systemic finding. The onset may be insidious or associated with a headache. An altered mental status may be the only finding. A pleocytosis (predominantly lymphocytes), an elevated protein, and a decreased glucose level are characteristic.

A primary cutaneous cryptococcosis infection, characterized by an isolated nodule that frequently ulcerates, is the result of inadvertent inoculation of *C. neoformans* into the skin. The ulcerated nodule is frequently accompanied by regional lymphadenopathy. Such lesions are frequently the result of laboratory accidents.

Diagnosis

Biopsy of the cutaneous lesions frequently demonstrates a minimal inflammatory response. Yeast forms are detected, but the diagnosis is established by culture.

An India ink preparation, an antigen agglutination test, and an enzyme-linked immunosorbent assay, are especially valuable in examining the cerebral spinal fluid and serum of AIDS patients.

Treatment

In the past, amphotericin B was the treatment. Now, fluconazole with or without flucytosine, is commonly used. Itraconazole has also been used successfully.

Annotated Bibliography

Perfect JD. Cryptococcus. Infect Dis Clin North Am 1989;3:77–102.

This is a good review.

Van der Horst CM, et al. Treatment of cryptococcal associated with the acquired immunodeficiency syndrome. N Engl J Med 1997;337:15–21.

This article describes the difficulty in treating cryptococcal meningitis in AIDS patients.

Sporotrichosis

Geophilic fungus commonly infects individuals who work with the soil.

Sporotrichosis is primarily a cutaneous fungal disease that may, on unusual occasions, become systemic. It is caused, in most cases, by the accidental inoculation into the skin of the dimorphic fungus *Sporothrix schenckii*. First described in 1898 by Schenck, a Johns Hopkins physician, this is a geophilic fungus, commonly cultured from the soil, sphagnum moss, and the surface of rose thorns. Most affected individuals are workers with frequent contact with soil (ie, farmers, gardeners).

Clinical Features

The initial lesion, most commonly occurring on the extremities, is a dermal, erythematous nodule occurring within 2 to 3 weeks at the site of inoculation, which ulcerates. The draining lymphatics characteristically develop satellite lesions along their course. These also may ulcerate (Figure 63–10).

Rarely pulmonary disease

Rarely, pulmonary disease, osteomyelitis, arthritis, and meningitis may develop. An epidemic of pulmonary sporotrichosis occurred in South Africa among gold-mine workers who inhaled *S. schenckii* spores from infested timbers used to support mine shafts.

Diagnosis

The organism is difficult to detect in biopsy specimens but is readily cultured. The differential diagnosis includes atypical *Mycobacterium* lesions (caused by

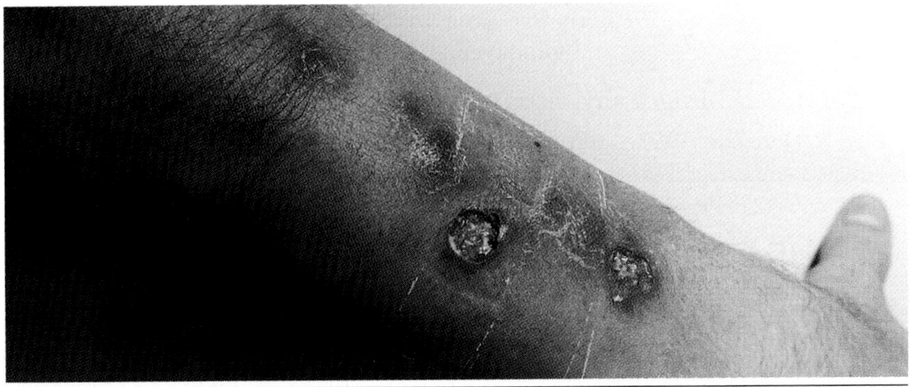

FIGURE 63–10 Ulceration and nodular lesions in a linear fashion along lymphatics on the arm of a patient with sporotrichosis. (Reproduced from the slide collection of the late R.C.V. Robinson, M.D.)

Mycobacterium marinum, *Mycobacterium chelonai,* and *Mycobacterium fortuitum*), actinomycosis, and nocardiosis.

Treatment

A saturated solution of potassium iodide, 5 drops three times a day gradually increased to a maximum of 120 drops per day, should be continued for 3 to 4 weeks.

Itraconazole, terbinafine, and fluconazole are also effective.

Annotated Bibliograpy

Winn RE. Sporotrichosis. Infect Dis Clin North Am 1988;2:899–911.

This is a good review.

Nocardiosis

Gram-positive, acid-fast organism

Nocardiosis is most commonly caused by the aerobic, acid-fast actinomycete *Nocardia asteroides*. Other members of the *Nocardia* species also may cause disease. The organism is branched, filamentous, Gram stain–positive, and slow growing. This organism is found in the soil.

Clinical Features

Skin lesions, which are very unusual, are generally the manifestation of a hematogenous spread from a primary pulmonary focus. The cutaneous lesions are nondescript, papular nodules. Biopsy will frequently demonstrate abscess formation.

Pulmonary disease

Dyspnea, chest pain, and a bloody sputum characterize the pulmonary involvement. Radiographs demonstrate cavitary disease. The brain is frequently involved and abscesses of other internal organs, such as the kidney and liver, occur but are less frequent.

Acquired immunodeficiency syndrome and other immunocompromised patients are at increased risk.

Diagnosis

Biopsy will frequently demonstrate abscess formation. Branching hyphae are easily detected with a Gram stain. Differentiation from actinomycosis is done by demonstrating acid-fast features of *Nocardia.*

Treatment

Sulfonamides (sulfadiazine) are most commonly used to treat nocardiosis and should be given for at least 6 months. Trimethoprim-sulfamethoxazole has also been successfully used. Alternative drugs for sulfonamide-allergic patients are erythromycin, ampicillin, and minocycline.

Annotated Bibliography

Tavaly K, Horowitz HW, Wormser GP. Nocardiosis in patients with human immune deficiency virus: report of 2 cases and review of the literature. Medicine (Baltimore) 1992;71:128–138.

This article reviews the increased risk of nocardiosis in AIDS patients.

Actinomycosis

Actinomycosis is a chronic disease caused by *Actinomyces israelii*, a gram-positive, human commensal bacteria most commonly found in the oral mucosa.

Clinical Features

Lumpy jaw

Three forms of the disease are recognized: cervicofacial, thoracic, and abdominal.

A "lumpy jaw" or a wooden, hard, indurated lesion over the lower portion of the face or upper portion of the neck characterizes the cervicofacial form of actinomycosis. Sinus tract formation is common. In general, patients with this form of actinomycosis have had predisposing trauma (eg, dental procedure).

Thoracic abscess or draining sinus

A draining sinus tract or an abscess in the thoracic area characterizes the thoracic form of actinomycosis. It generally results from an aspiration pneumonia but can be caused by an extension from a neck or an abdominal actinomycosis. Rarely, it results from hematogenous spread.

Abdominal draining abscesses

In the abdominal form of actinomycosis, a draining sinus tract and/or a subcutaneous abscess formation in the groin may be present. Fever, chills, night sweats, weight loss, and fatigue may occur.

Diagnosis

Sulfur granules

Biopsy demonstrates multiple abscess formations with communicating sinuses. Multiple, small hyphal forms may be recognized. Sulfur granules (yellowish) are frequently detected. A Gram stain of these crushed granules will demonstrate gram-positive, club-shaped structures composed of tiny hyphae.

Culture of actinomycetes may be problematic if anaerobic cultures are not obtained.

Treatment

Most cases respond to intravenous penicillin given for 4 to 6 weeks. Oral penicillin should then be given for at least 3 months after the intravenous therapy.

Surgery to remove chronic sinus tracts may be necessary.

Annotated Bibliography

Burden P. Actinomycosis. J Infect Dis 1989;19:95.

This is a good review article.

Chatwani A, Amin-Hanjani S. Incidence of actinomycosis associated with intrauterine devices. J Reprod Med 1994;39:585–587.

This article provides evidence that intrauterine devices predispose to colonization with and development of pelvic actinomycosis.

CHAPTER 64

Human Immunodeficiency Virus

Ciro R. Martins, M.D., Jihad Al-Hariri, M.D.

The skin is commonly affected in individuals infected with the human immunodeficiency virus (HIV), and it is not an overstatement to say that virtually 100% of the HIV-infected individuals will develop some form of cutaneous disease during their lifetime. It is, therefore, very important for every health care provider to be familiar with the different typical and atypical cutaneous manifestations of common skin diseases that affect this patient population.

The cutaneous changes can be seen from the early stages of HIV infection, and the manifestations may vary from minimal and barely noticeable to severe, exuberant, and widespread. It is also important to keep in mind that apparently simple cutaneous diseases may be the first sign of a severe systemic problem, such as generalized infectious processes.

Cutaneous disease occurs in virtually 100% of HIV-infected patients.

The earliest cutaneous manifestation is seen during the acute retroviral syndrome, which is characterized by a mononucleosis-like syndrome, with fever, malaise, myalgias, and lymphadenopathy. This acute syndrome is seen in 50 to 90% of individuals, of whom approximately 50 to 75% will develop a rash. The most common presentation for this rash is that of a morbiliform exanthem (measles-like). This acute seroconversion exanthem is rarely diagnosed as associated with HIV infection; rather it is diagnosed as a drug eruption or a nonspecific viral exanthem.

Morbiliform rash associated with seroconversion to HIV-positivity.

The severity and the extent of HIV-related skin diseases is correlated with reductions in the peripheral CD4 T-cell counts. Early on in the infection, the manifestations may be mild, and they usually do not differ significantly from skin conditions such as seborrheic dermatitis, molluscum contagiosum, viral warts, and psoriasis that are commonly seen in HIV-negative, healthy individuals. As the CD4 counts drop to significantly low levels, these conditions tend to be more chronic, severe, and resistant to the usual therapies. Also as the CD4 counts drop even further, the more unusual skin manifestations, such as generalized cutaneous cryptococcosis, Kaposi's sarcoma, and bacillary angiomatosis, start to occur.

In past, cutaneous manifestations could be correlated with CD4 counts

Attempts have been made to classify and categorize the different cutaneous diseases by looking at their incidence in relation to the absolute CD4 T-cell counts. After the advent of antiretroviral therapy and, more specifically, after *h*ighly *a*ctive *a*nti*r*etroviral *t*herapy (HAART) started being used, the course of the HIV infection under treatment changed significantly and so did the course of cutaneous diseases, making these classifications less reliable.

The incidence of specific skin conditions also varies according to the patient population. Cutaneous problems seen in the pediatric HIV population are somewhat different than those seen in adults. Even among the adult subgroups there is considerable variation depending on the gender, sexual orientation, and ethnicity.

Even though cutaneous diseases are rarely life threatening, it is very important to consider the psychosocial aspects involved. Successful treatment can greatly improve the patient's quality of life and provide them with a sense of control over the most visible aspect of their HIV disease.

The cutaneous manifestations of HIV infection commonly have been divided into four broad categories: (1) inflammatory/hyperproliferative diseases, (2) infectious processes, (3) infestations, and (4) neoplasias. This chapter will cover the most commonly encountered conditions in each one of these categories.

Inflammatory/Hyperproliferative Conditions

Pruritus and Prurigo

Pruritus very common

Pruritus is the most common cutaneous complaint of patients with HIV. It may occur relatively early during the course of the HIV infection, and very often no primary cutaneous lesions are seen. The pruritus may be so intense that it becomes incapacitating, and not infrequently patients with severe pruritus have suicidal ideation. The cause of such severe pruritus remains unknown, but xerosis is still the most common identifiable and correctable cause of pruritus, especially in the fall and winter months. Another possible explanation is based on the immune dysregulation that takes place after HIV infection with the shift between the two cytokine profiles (T helper cells T_h1 versus T_h2). Also, HIV itself in the form of high viral load may induce pruritus by unknown mechanisms. It is imperative to rule out other possible cutaneous and noncutaneous causes of pruritus. Systemic diseases that can cause generalized pruritus include uremia, liver failure, polycythemia vera, lymphomas, and thyroid dysfunctions, all of which can be seen in association with HIV.

Antihistamine medications, skin lubrication, and topical antipruritic lotions may provide some relief, but the most severe and resistant cases require therapy with ultraviolet light. Thalidomide has also been described as being effective in controlling intractable pruritus.

Prurigo nodularis

Excoriations are extremely common in these patients, and the excoriated skin is even more pruritic than the surrounding intact epithelium (Figure 64–1). This starts a cycle of scratching, itching, excoriation, and pruritus. This vicious cycle perpetuates the excoriations, and with time, the individual lesions become hypertrophic, hyperkeratotic, and hyperpigmented. Later on they will become nodular and progressively more pruritic representing the condition known as "prurigo nodularis" (Figure 64–2). Treatment can be very difficult and the first and most important step is discontinuing the habit of traumatizing the individual lesions. High-potency (class 1 or 2) topical corticosteroid preparations can be used in an attempt to induce atrophy of the hypertrophic lesions. Intralesional injections of triamcinolone at the concentration of 40 mg per cubic centimeter can also be very helpful. Surgical excision of individual nodules and cryotherapy with liquid nitrogen can also be performed as a last resort.

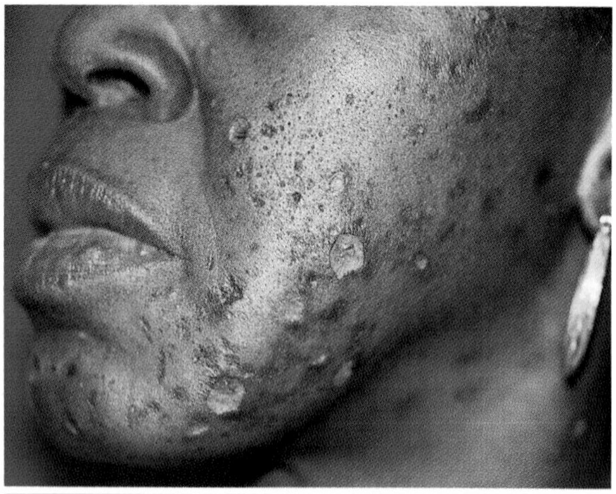

FIGURE 64–1 Prurigo simplex. Severe pruritus caused self-induced excoriation and the development of these lesions, characterized by "punched-out" shallow ulcers, and hyperpigmented macules and scars. The lack of primary skin lesions suggests the traumatic nature of this process.

Seborrheic Dermatitis

Seborrheic dermatitis is a very common eczematous process that occurs in approximately 1 to 3% of the general population but may occur in up to 80% of HIV-infected people. Even though it may appear early on, the extent and the severity of the skin lesions

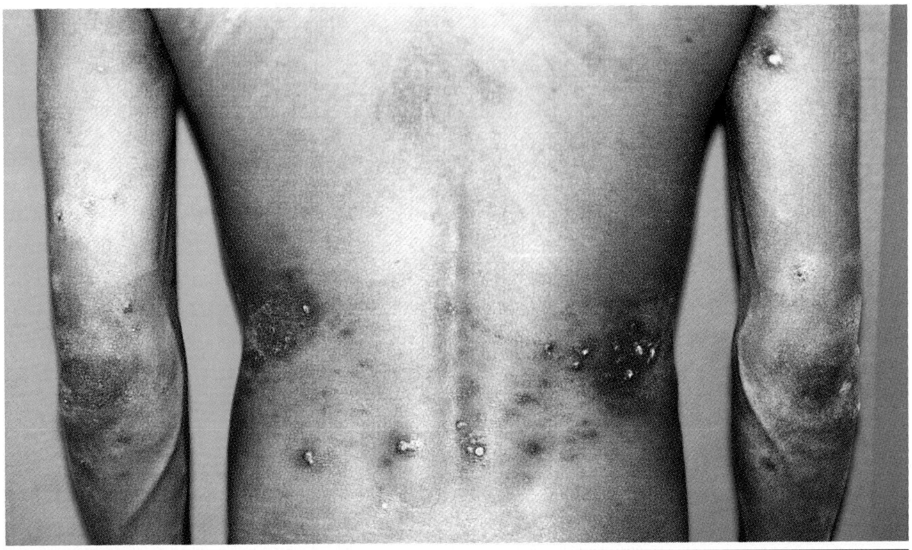

FIGURE 64–2 Prurigo nodularis. Chronic trauma, such as scratching and picking, to individual pruritic lesions causes the development of papules and nodules characterized by hyperkeratosis and hyperpigmentation. Note the sparing of the mid- to upper portions of the back where access is more difficult.

increase as the HIV disease progresses to more advanced stages. Clinically, it is manifested by erythema and scaling either diffusely or in fairly well-circumscribed plaques affecting the scalp area, including the anterior and posterior auricular areas and the external ear canal, and the central portion of the face, especially the eyebrows, nasolabial folds, and chin area. Less commonly, it can affect other areas of the body, such as the genitals, groin, axilla, and presternal and pubic areas. In severly immunocompromised patients, the eczematous lesions may generalize into an erythrodermic state.

Seborrheic dermatitis *is a very common disease; may be extensive.*

The cause of seborrheic dermatitis remains undetermined even though it is well known that there is some relationship with increased activity of the sebaceous glands, neurologic disorders, emotional stress, and *Pityrosporum ovale*, a yeast present in the normal cutaneous flora. Standard treatment for this condition includes topical applications of mild-to-medium potency corticosteroid preparations, as well as topical antifungal creams that have good activity against yeasts such as the imidazole derivatives. For the scalp, shampoos that contain coal tar, selenium sulfide, salicylic acid, and zinc pyrithione, as well as ketoconazole, are also very effective.

Xerosis Cutis and Asteatotic Eczema

Xerosis associated with pruritus and asteatotic eczema.

Xerosis cutis, or pronounced skin dryness, is a very common problem seen in the early stages of HIV infection and is more prevalent during the fall and winter months when the humidity is very low. This condition is often associated with intense pruritus and invariably, if not corrected, will progress to fissuring and development of eczematous patches and plaques known as "asteatotic eczema" (Figure 64–3). Eczematization increases the pruritus and trauma, and rubbing and scratching predisposes the affected areas to secondary bacterial infection. The acute and subacute eczematous changes frequently progress to the chronic stages of eczema, characterized by lichenification with skin thickening, hyperpigmentation, and accentuation of the skin markings. Patient education regarding the importance of avoiding excessive use of soaps, limiting exposure to hot water, and using emollients daily may significantly reduce the incidence of possible complications. Oral antihistamines should also be used to alleviate pruritus.

Acquired ichthyosis vulgaris can also be a manifestation of HIV infection. This is clinically characterized by large polygonal fishnet-like scales affecting, most commonly, the extensor surfaces of the lower extremities, but which may

Acquired ichthyosis manifestation of HIV infection

progress to a more generalized eruption. In previously healthy patients, with no prior history of this condition or atopy, who develop ichthyosis vulgaris later in life, the possibility of HIV infection must be considered. Treatment with α-hydroxy acids or urea-based moisturizers can be effective.

Psoriasis

No increased incidence of psoriasis, but increased severity

Psoriasis is a papulosquamous disease that affects approximately 1 to 2% of the general population, and even though it is frequently a problem for individuals with HIV, the incidence of psoriasis itself is not increased in this population. The clinical presentation of psoriasis changes as the HIV disease progresses. It is not uncommon to see new onset of explosive and very aggressive psoriasis in a patient previously undiagnosed as having this disease (Figure 64–4). It is also common to see more extensive and more atypical exacerbations of previously stable and chronic plaque-type psoriasis. Atypical variants, such as pustular psoriasis, erythrodermic psoriasis, explosive guttate psoriasis, deforming psoriatic arthritis, and extensive nail disease, are all more commonly seen in these patients. There is also an increased prevalence of human leukocyte antigen (HLA)-B27–positivity in HIV-infected patients with psoriatic arthritis.

Topical treatment consists of regular application of emollients, coal-tar preparations, vitamin A (retinoic acid) and vitamin D derivatives, or anthralin. Salicylic acid products can be used as keratolytics. Systemic treatment is somewhat restricted since methotrexate and other immunosuppresive agents, such as

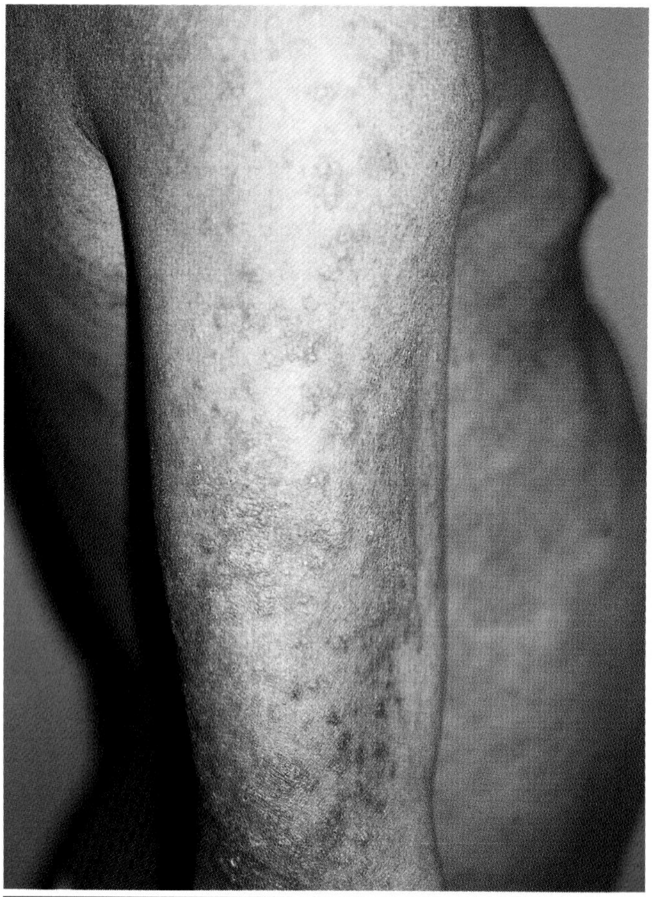

FIGURE 64–3 Asteatotic eczema. This patient developed multiple, widespread patches and plaques of subacute eczema due to excessive skin dryness. HIV-positive patients are prone to developing different types of eczema, and asteatotic eczema is very common in the winter months.

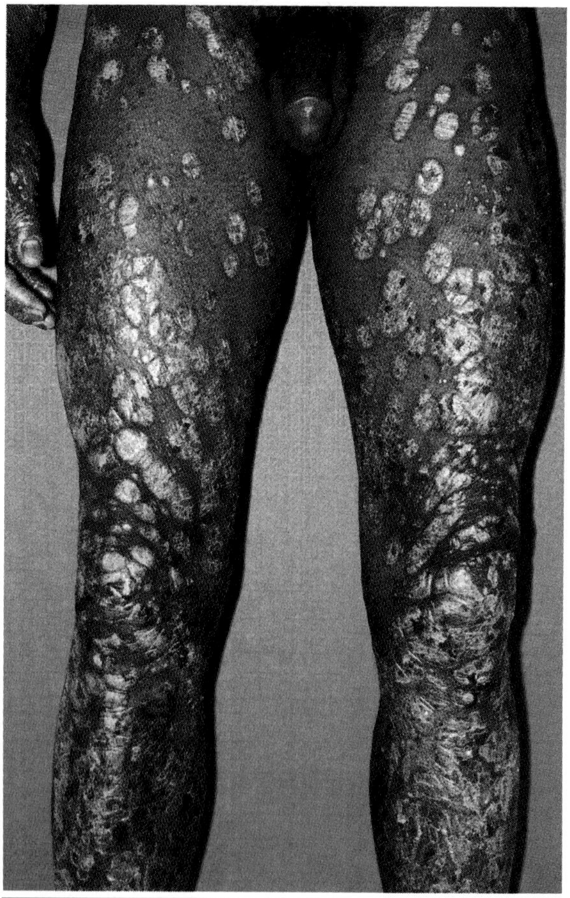

FIGURE 64–4 Generalized plaque-type psoriasis. This HIV-positive man with no previous history of psoriasis developed, over a short period of time, widespread skin-colored to slightly erythematous plaques with thick, easily detachable, silvery scales.

cyclosporine and prednisone, should be avoided in these patients. Oral acitretin can be very effective alone or in combination with phototherapy. Even though the issue of phototherapy safety for HIV-infected patients has been the subject of several controversial studies, clinical practice shows this therapy to be very effective and safe for treating numerous skin conditions that commonly affect these individuals, including generalized psoriasis. Psoralen plus ultraviolet A (PUVA) or ultra violet B (UVB) alone can be used in these patients with good success.

Reiter's Syndrome

Reiter's syndrome is characterized classically by the triad of severe arthritis, urethritis, and conjunctivitis. It is associated with positivity of the HLA-B27 antigen in 80 to 90% of individuals, and the arthritis is considered to be reactive to several different infectious agents.

Reiter's syndrome appears to be triggered by HIV infection.

The diagnosis of Reiter's syndrome is often hard to establish; therefore, the cutaneous lesions seen can be a very helpful clinical tool. The typical cutaneous manifestations of Reiter's syndrome are represented by keratoderma blennorrhagicum, which is characterized by hyperkeratotic, yellowish papules and plaques over an erythematous base with intact and ruptured vesicles or pustules. It most commonly affects the soles but can also affect the periungual tissue and dorsal surfaces of both the hands and feet. These lesions may resemble pustular psoriasis. Another cutaneous manifestation of Reiter's is balanitis circinata, characterized by shallow erosions of the glans penis which coalesce to form larger areas of erosion with scalloped borders. This is usually seen in patients who are uncircumcised and resembles lesions of psoriasis. The clinicopathologic features as well as the genetic markers for psoriasis and Reiter's syndrome in HIV patients frequently overlap, and many consider these two entities to represent different poles in the same spectrum of disease.

Drug Reactions

Difficult management problem

Sulfamethoxazole/ trimethoprim, amoxicillin, phenytoin, and antituberculosis drugs commonly cause rashes.

Drug reactions can be one of the most challenging problems for health care providers following patients with HIV. Not uncommonly, HIV-infected patients, take more than ten different types of medications daily, including antiretroviral medications, multiple drug regimens for prophylaxis of opportunistic infections, and medications for controlling the side effects caused by these treatments. Any medication can potentially produce a cutaneous drug eruption, but the most commonly involved medications are sulfamethoxazole/trimethoprim, amoxicillin, and other antibiotics, phenytoin, and antituberculosis medications, all of which are widely used in these patients.

The most common drug eruption is a morbiliform exanthem characterized by erthematous macules and papules isolated and coalescent into larger patches and plaques affecting the trunk and extremities. The skin lesions usually start 7 to 10 days after initiation of therapy with a new drug, and as a general rule, whenever a patient develops a drug reaction, the most suspicious drugs are those in close temporal relationship with the onset of the reaction.

Other types of drug reactions seen are erythema multiforme with a clinical spectrum ranging from erythema multiforme minor, to erythema multiforme major. The former is typically characterized by the presence of target or bull's eye lesions with dusky, violaceous centers. These can be localized, with only a few lesions on the palms and soles, but can also be generalized with widespread cutaneous lesions and blister formation (Figure 64–5). Erythema multiforme major or Stevens-Johnson syndrome is the more severe and life-threatening end of the spectrum where the cutaneous lesions are associated with mucosal involvement and manifest as oral ulcerations, conjunctival erosions, and widespread blistering and sloughing off of large areas of the skin. Systemic symptoms are prominent.

The practical use of desensitization techniques is very limited.

Treatment should be established based not only on the extent and the severity of the reaction itself, but also on the symptoms associated with the reaction. Mild reactions may run their course and resolve spontaneously. If more severe and more symptomatic reactions are seen, then a chemically unrelated drug should be

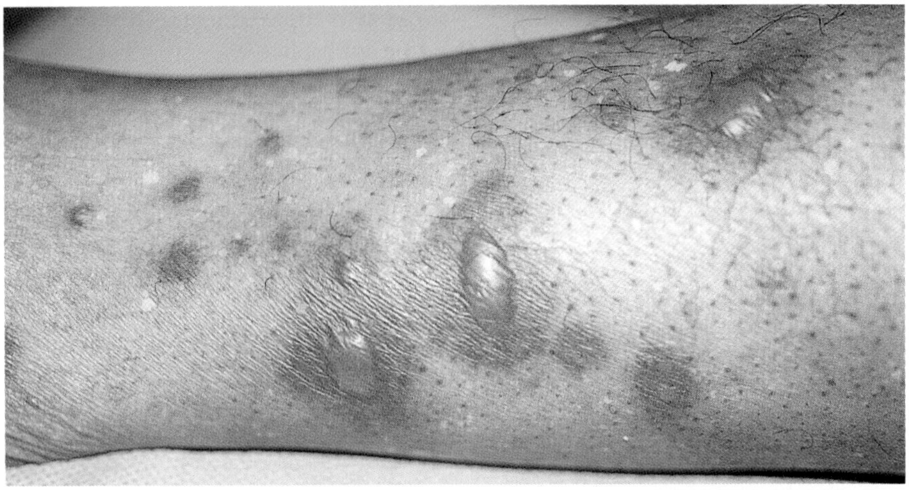

FIGURE 64–5 Erythema multiforme. This 38-year-old HIV-positive female developed round-to oval-shaped erythematous macules and plaques with hyperpigmented and somewhat dusky centers that progressed to blister formation on her arms, legs, hands, and feet. These lesions started 2 weeks after she was started on trimethoprim/sulfamethoxazole. Mucosal surfaces were not involved and she had no systemic symptoms.

substituted for the culprit medication. If such a drug cannot be identified, then all of the medications that are not absolutely necessary should be discontinued and the vital medications should be replaced by chemically unrelated ones with the same functions. Desensitization techniques have been described for drugs such as trimethoprim/sulfamethoxazole, but their practical clinical use is very limited.

Severe drug reactions such as Stevens-Johnson syndrome or toxic epidermal necrolysis should be managed in an intensive care setting, such as a burn unit, for the prevention of secondary infection and the control of electrolytes and fluid imbalances. Drug reactions may persist long after the therapy has been discontinued, and it is very likely that the same type of reaction will recur if the patient is rechallenged with the same medication.

Protease Inhibitor-Associated Lipodystrophy

Although insulin resistance is commonly detected, overt diabetes is unusual.

It is now well known that patients receiving HIV protease inhibitors can develop a syndrome characterized by lipodystrophy, which consists of fat wasting that affects the face, upper and lower extremities, and upper part of the trunk and causes hyperlipidemia and insulin resistance. This was initially described in patients receiving indinavir but has subsequently been described in patients with other protease inhibitors such as ritonavir, saquinavir and a combination of these drugs. Clinically, lipodystrophy is characterized by the loss of subcutaneous fat, which is more noticeable on the face but also can occur on the arms and legs where it makes the muscles and veins more visible. There is also relative sparing and possibly accumulation of abdominal fat both on the abdominal wall and intra-abdominally, causing a relative central obesity (Figures 64–6A and 64–6B). There are also descriptions of redistribution of fat to the upper part of the posterior aspect of the neck causing the appearance of a "buffalo hump" such as that seen in Cushingoid patients. When compared with patients who do not develop lipodystrophy and with HIV-negative individuals, these patients have an overall similar body weight and fat-free mass, although they do have a significantly lower total fat mass. Recent studies show that the minimum time for developing lipodystrophy appears to be 10 months. Protease inhibitor–associated lipodystrophy should not be confused with acquired immunodeficiency syndrome (AIDS) wasting observed in patients in the late stages of HIV infection when there is significant loss of total body mass due to a loss of lean body mass in addition to total subcutaneous fat. The studies also show that lipodystrophy is more common and more severe in patients receiving a combination of ritonavir and saquinavir as compared with those individuals receiving indinavir alone. Even though insulin resistance can be associated with the syndrome, overt type II diabetes mellitus is not commonly observed. The associated hyperlipidemia is characterized by significantly higher levels of triglyceride and cholesterol, and this may be caused by the mobilization of fat during the fat redistribution process that leads to lipodystrophy. The pathogenesis of this syndrome remains unclear at this point as further data on the metabolic effects of the different HIV protease inhibitors are needed.

Treatment is not available, and some patients benefit from switching from the combination of protease inhibitors to a single protease inhibitor associated with other classes of antiretroviral medications. The cosmetic aspects of the lipodystrophy affecting the face can be devastating, and unpublished data are available describing cosmetic procedures, such as collagen injections and autologous fat transplant to the sunken areas of the face, to improve the overall appearance of these patients.

Photosensitivity Reactions

Some patients infected with HIV become very sensitive to UV radiation. This type of sensitivity is more commonly seen in African American patients and other patients with a dark complexion. The exact etiology of this reaction remains unclear. These patients are usually taking multiple medications, and treatment regimens often include medications such as acyclovir, captopril, ethambutol, chloroquine, interferon, β-blockers, thiazide diuretics, and some nonsteroidal anti-inflammatory drugs that can predispose them to photosensitivity. The HIV itself, other infectious agents, or the immune disregulation caused by the HIV infection can all be possible causes for this hypersensitivity reaction as well.

The mechanism of photosensitivity in HIV is unknown.

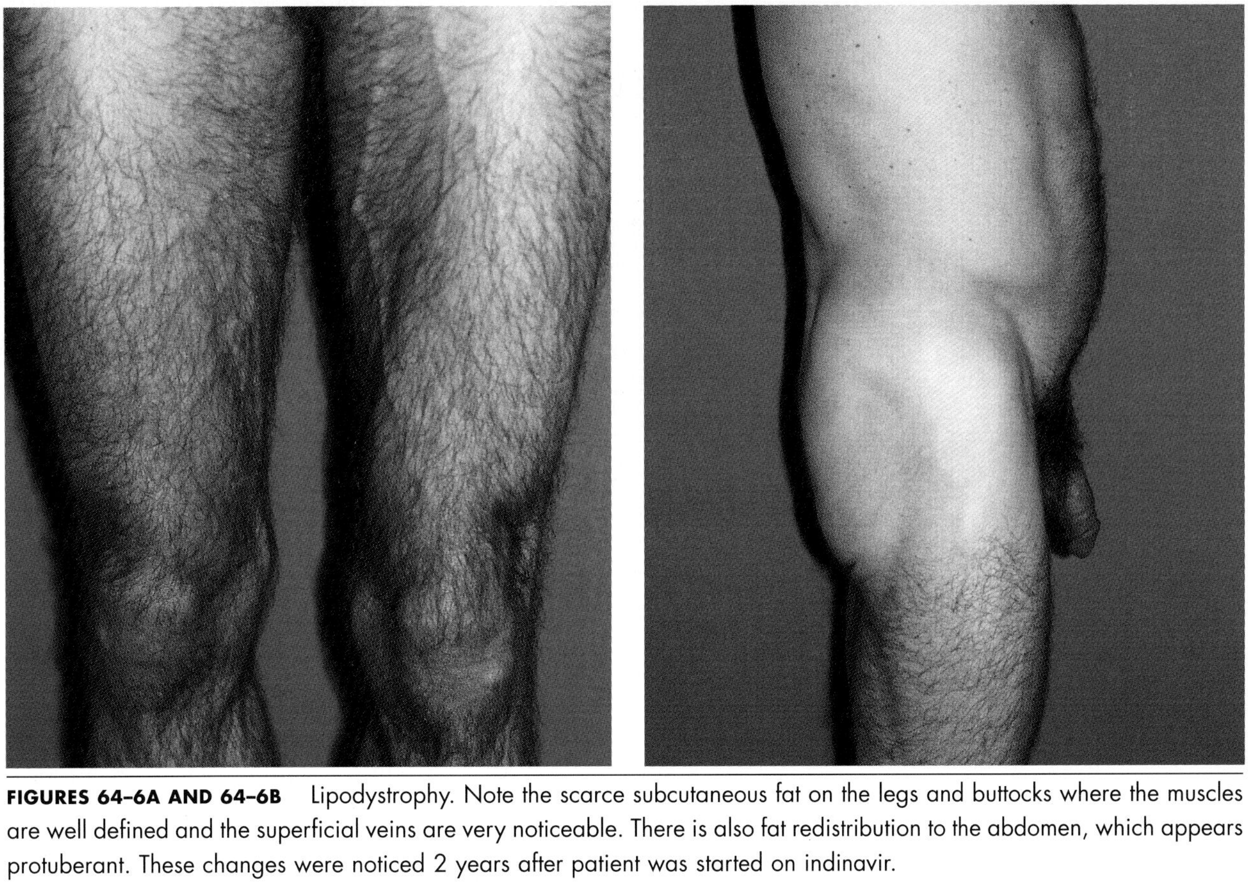

FIGURES 64–6A AND 64–6B Lipodystrophy. Note the scarce subcutaneous fat on the legs and buttocks where the muscles are well defined and the superficial veins are very noticeable. There is also fat redistribution to the abdomen, which appears protuberant. These changes were noticed 2 years after patient was started on indinavir.

Different clinical diseases have been described in patients with HIV that are characterized by hypersensitivity to UV radiation. Examples of these diseases include porphyria cutanea tarda (PCT) of the acquired type; chronic actinic dermatitis, which is a chronic eczematous eruption triggered by and maintained by UV exposure; bullous photosensitivity (pseudo-PCT); photodistributed granuloma annulare; lichenoid dermatitis; and hyperpigmentation of sun-exposed areas (Figure 64–7).

PCT occurs in a few HIV patients.

Acquired PCT seen in HIV infection is characterized by an acquired deficiency of the enzyme uroporphyrinogen decarboxylase. This enzyme deficiency causes a disorder in the metabolism of heme, and it manifests clinically by increased skin fragility and the development of blisters and erosions on exposed areas of the face, forearms, and dorsum of the hands. Associated findings include hyperpigmentation and hypertrichosis of the face. After the blisters and the erosions heal, scars and milia can be seen in addition to skin thickening resembling scleroderma in the sun-exposed areas.

Chronic actinic dermatitis is another form of photosensitivity reaction that has been described in HIV-positive people. Clinically it is characterized by subacute to chronic eczematous changes with lichenification, crusting, mild erythema, and severe pruritus on sun-exposed areas of the body.

Lichenoid eruption in advanced stages of HIV disease

Lichenoid eruption of HIV is an inflammatory cutaneous eruption. It also is most commonly seen in African American and dark-skinned individuals in the advanced stages of HIV disease, when the CD4 counts fall below 50 cells per cubic millimeter. It usually affects sun-exposed areas of the skin, but it can also affect protected areas of the body. Clinically, it is characterized by multiple hyperpigmented to violaceous, flat papules and plaques with accentuation of the skin markings and a shiny surface. Scaling and subacute eczematous changes may also be present simultaneously. Even though drugs are likely to be involved in this type of photosensitivity, the exact etiology of this eruption remains to be determined.

There is ongoing controversy and debate regarding the effects of UV light in promoting viral gene expression and the possible activation of HIV in vivo. In vitro studies have demonstrated that sunlight, UVB, and PUVA can activate HIV. In vivo studies, however, are contradictory and controversial, and clinical practice shows that the benefits obtained from phototherapy using UV radiation far exceed the theoretic risk of HIV activation. Further investigation is underway to settle this matter.

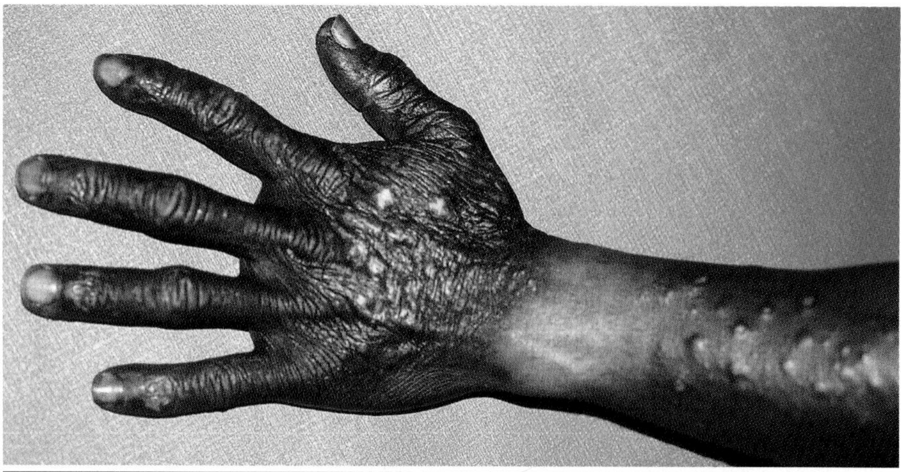

FIGURE 64–7 Lichenoid photoeruption of HIV. This is a photosensitivity reaction of unknown etiology commonly seen in African Americans with HIV. Note the sparing of the area protected by the wristwatch. The sun-exposed skin is hyperpigmented and thickened and the skin surface markings are accentuated, characterizing the lichenoid appearance. Due to the intense pruritus, lesions of prurigo nodularis and excoriations are often seen concomitantly.

Vasculitis

Immune complex-mediated vasculitis

Several case reports are available in the world literature describing the various types of vasculitis that affect both adults and children at all stages of HIV infection. Circulating immune complexes are commonly detected in the serum of HIV-infected patients, and these are associated with the HIV itself or are secondary to opportunistic infections such as by varicella-zoster virus, parvovirus, herpes simplex virus, and *Toxoplasma gondii.* It is conceivable that vascular deposition of these circulating immune complexes initiates the immunologic cascade that culminates in the development of vasculitis. The HIV antigenic determinants have been identified in immune complexes in vascular lesions of infected patients. It is also possible that local replication of HIV plays a direct role in the development of vasculitis.

Polyarteritis nodosa-like vasculitis associated with HIV infection is very well described. Patients present with digital ischemic changes and gangrene, along with peripheral neuropathy and other systemic manifestations. Histologically, necrotizing vasculitic lesions of medium-sized vessels are present. Other necrotizing vasculitides, such as Churg-Strauss and polyangiitis, have also been reported. Henoch-Schönlein purpura and hypersensitivity vasculitis are characterized by universal involvement of the skin with the most characteristic cutaneous manifestation being palpable purpura. The pathology is that of leukocytoclastic vasculitis affecting the small vessels. Leukocytoclastic vasculitis can be caused by a variety of infections, autoimmune diseases, and medications, and careful investigation is required to determine the exact etiologic agent before assuming that the development of vasculitis is due to the underlying HIV infection itself.

Folliculitis

Folliculitis is characterized clinically by the presence of multiple follicular, erythematous, inflammatory papules and pustules most commonly affecting the upper trunk, face, neck, and proximal upper extremities. Due to the intense pruritus, it is not uncommon to find several excoriated papules and superficial ulcers and hyperpigmentation due to postinflammatory phenomenon. It usually becomes a significant clinical problem when the CD4 counts fall below 250 cells per cubic millimeter. Folliculitis can commonly be caused by known infectious agents such as *Staphylococcus aureus*, *P. ovale*, or the saprophytic mite *Demodex folliculorum* (Figure 64–8). Etiologic diagnosis can be obtained by gram stain and culture of the pustules, direct potassium hydroxide (KOH) examination of the follicular contents, or skin biopsy.

Very frequently an infectious etiology cannot be identified. Histopathology of the follicular papule shows perifollicular admixed inflammatory infiltrate abundant in eosinophils and destruction of the follicular wall by eosinophilic infiltrate forming small eosinophilic abscesses in the follicular lumen. Special stains for fungus and bacteria fail to reveal any specific infectious agent. These histologic features are very similar to the eosinophilic pustular folliculitis described by Ofuji, but clinically and epidemiologically this folliculitis does not have any correlation with the originally described syndrome. Eosinophilic folliculitis of HIV is characterized by very pruritic follicular papules and sometimes perifollicular, urticarial lesions. The course is usually characerized by recurrences and resistance to therapy.

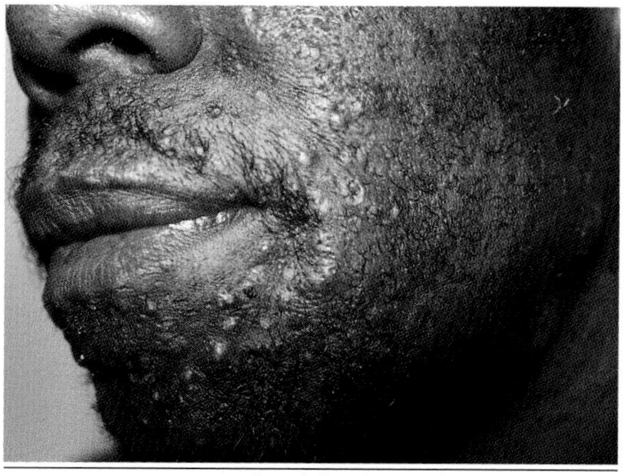

FIGURE 64–8 *Demodex* folliculitis. Multiple follicular erythematous, edematous papules with few pustules and multiple excoriated lesions are suggestive of *Demodex folliculorum* as the etiology in this case of folliculitis.

Regardless of the etiology, folliculitis in HIV disease tends to be a chronic and recurring process. Treatment aimed at specific infectious agents may be beneficial in some patients. In cases of eosinophilic folliculitis, phototherapy seems to be the only modality capable of inducing prolonged symptomatic relief and clinical remission. Other therapeutic approaches include anti-

Eosinophilic folliculitis generally resistant to all therapies except UV light

histamines; antifungal agents, such as itraconazole and metronidazole; vitamin A derivatives, such as acitretin; and even dapsone. Several topical treatments have been described, but most of them cause only temporary relief of symptoms.

Reactivation of acne can also be seen relatively early in the course of HIV infection and affects mainly younger men.

Infectious Conditions

As a general rule, the organisms that usually infect the skin of HIV-negative individuals are also the most common pathogens found in HIV-positive patients. In patients in late stages of HIV disease, the cutaneous infections tend to be more severe, more resistant to common therapies, and recurrent. The most common infectious agents causing cutaneous disease in these patients are *S. aureus,* herpes simplex virus (HSV), varicella-zoster virus (VZV), poxvirus (molluscum contagiosum), *Candida* spp, and dermatophytes.

As a general rule of thumb, lesions that are behaving in an unusual way and are not responding to the usual antimicrobial agents need to be biopsied, and the tissue must be sent for histologic examination, using special stains for organisms and cultures. As the HIV disease progresses and the CD4 counts drop, one must be more aware of unusual infectious agents, such as atypical mycobacteria, protozoal infections, and unusual fungi.

Viral Infections

Of all the viruses that can cause disease in humans, eight specific viruses can cause significant morbidity in individuals affected by HIV. Six of those viruses are represented by herpes viruses: HSV type 1 (HSV-1) and HSV type 2 (HSV-2), VZV, Epstein-Barr virus (EBV), human herpesvirus type 8 (HHV-8), Kaposi's sarcoma-associated herpesvirus (KSHV), and cytomegalovirus (CMV). In addition, human papillomaviruses (HPV) produce different kinds of warts, and the poxvirus causes molluscum contagiosum. All of these viruses can cause cutaneous disease, and the severity of the cutaneous involvement varies according to the state of deterioration of the host's immune system. Other viruses such as the JC virus and the human parvovirus B19 are also responsible for opportunistic infections in patients with AIDS but generally do not cause cutaneous disease.

Herpes Simplex Virus Types 1 and 2

The HSV-1 and HSV-2 infections are very common in the general, non–HIV-infected population, and the same is true in patients infected by HIV. The vast majority of the population shows serologic evidence of HSV-1 infection and approximately 25% of the general population of the United States is also seropositive for HSV-2. The HSV-1 seems to be acquired early in life or in adulthood through direct contact. The HSV-2 is acquired between the teen years and the fourth decade of life and is considered a sexually transmitted pathogen. Although the rate of HSV-1 infection does not vary in HIV-positive individuals as compared with the HIV-negative population, the incidence of HSV-2 infection is significantly increased in patients with HIV. The risk of contracting and transmitting HIV infection does increase with the presence of active lesions of HSV-2 infections and, more rarely, with HSV-1 infections.

Increased frequency of HSV-2 infections and HSV-1 infections increases risk of contracting HIV.

In persons with asymptomatic HIV infection and absolute CD4 counts greater than 100 cells per cubic millimeter, HSV-1 and HSV-2 are usually manifested clinically by recurrent, self-limited clusters of vesicles and papulovesicles on the oral mucosa or genital area. There is also an increased incidence of perianal ulcers and perianal vesicles, but the appearance of the individual lesions and the overall clinical presentation does not vary compared with individuals without HIV infection. In more advanced HIV disease, however, there is increased severity of the lesions, higher frequency of reactivation, and a more chronic course for both HSV-2 and HSV-1 mucocutaneous lesions.

In patients with advanced HIV disease with CD4 counts lower than 100 per cubic millimeter, the clinical presentation may be very atypical. The ulcers are usually larger, as well as deeper, and heal much more slowly. The HSV can also be disseminated to other cutaneous sites and become generalized on the skin with both papulovesicles or unusual-looking lesions, such as chronic shallow ulcers, crust-covered erosions, or verrucous papules and plaques (Figure 64–9).

The virus can also disseminate to other internal organs, especially along the gastrointestinal tract, with significant symptomatic HSV esophagitis. Other organs involved are the lungs and central nervous system, and usually when systemic disease ensues, the patient is very ill with pronounced constitutional symptoms. Other unusual presentations of HSV in the severely immunocompromised patient include herpetic glossitis, characterized by flat-topped papules on the tongue, and herpetic whitlow, characterized by edema and erythema of the periungual tissues of one or more fingers. This latter condition is usually acquired through sexual practices and can be easily confused with a bacterial or a candidal periungual infection.

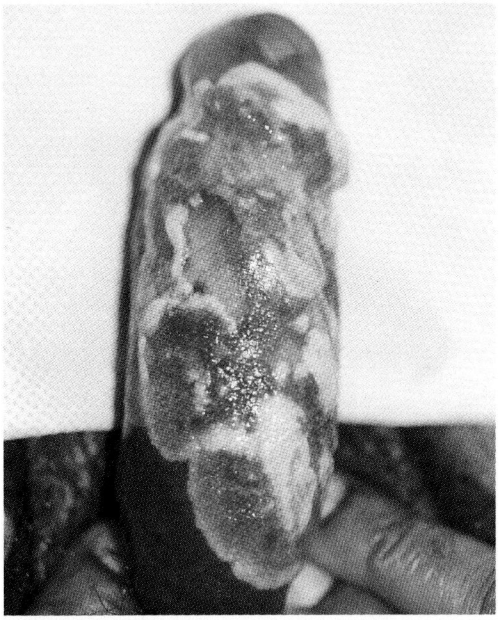

FIGURE 64–9 Chronic HSV-2 infection. This patient was infected with an acyclovir-resistant strain of HSV-2, which resulted in these vegetating plaques on the penile shaft. This clinical presentation of chronic HSV is known as pyoderma vegetans or blastomycosis-like pyoderma.

The diagnosis of HSV infections can, in most cases, be established based on clinical features alone, but in unusual presentations, this is often not possible. Diagnostic tests include a Tzanck smear performed on scrapings obtained from the base of an intact vesicle and a direct immunofluorescent antibody stain. These tests are fast and easily obtained. A more sensitive and specific diagnostic test is the viral culture, which takes several days before results can be obtained. Since the incidence of acyclovir resistance is significantly increased in this population, a viral culture with in vitro susceptibility testing is always recommended when the lesions are not responding to therapy.

Increased risk of drug-resistant strains in HIV patients

The treatment of choice is acyclovir, valacyclovir, or famciclovir. These are given orally for uncomplicated HSV infections, 3 to 5 times per day depending on the drug used. Intravenous therapy is recommended in cases of disseminated disease with significant systemic symptoms or central nervous system involvement. Cases resistant to acyclovir therapy should be treated with foscarnet given intravenously. Patients who do not respond to foscarnet alone may respond to a combination of foscarnet and acyclovir or one of the other two similar drugs. Cidofovir is also given intravenously, and it has proven activity against acyclovir-resistant HSV; therefore, it may become a suitable alternative treatment to foscarnet in cases of acyclovir resistance. The main goal of topical treatment is to facilitate healing and to prevent secondary bacterial infection. Topical antiviral medications, such as penciclovir, have also recently been shown to be effective in controlling lesions.

Herpes Zoster

Herpes zoster (shingles) is caused by reactivation of the VZV. It is primarily a disease of the elderly population, occurring predominantly in the sixth and seventh decades of life. Herpes zoster is also associated with immune suppression and immunodeficiency, occasionally affecting healthy, young adults. In the early stages of the AIDS epidemic, it was thought that an episode of herpes zoster was an early sign of immune suppression in the HIV-positive individual. The precise relationship between shingles and the natural history of HIV infection remains unclear. The prognostic significance of the recurrence of VZV infection in the progression of HIV disease has also been controversial. Recent studies suggest that the incidence of shingles is increased in the later stages of HIV infection, but the occurrence of shingles itself is not associated with a more rapid progression to end-stage HIV disease and death.

Increased incidence in later stages of HIV infection

Herpes zoster tend to disseminate and be severe in later stages of HIV.

The clinical presentation of shingles is usually a cluster of erythematous papules and papulovesicles with significant inflammation following a dermatomal pattern identical to that seen in the immune-competent host. Depending on the degree of immunosuppression, dissemination of cutaneous disease can occur, characterized by more than 10 lesions affecting a dermatome that is noncontiguous to the originally affected dermatome. In addition to disseminated cutaneous disease, patients can have an unusual clinical course with prolonged and chronic lesions of VZV. These chronic lesions tend to present an unusual morphology, such as chronic shallow erosions covered by crusting or even verrucous lesions resembling North American blastomycosis (Figure 64–10). Disseminated secondary disease as well as primary varicella infection may evolve into varicella pneumonia.

Uncomplicated VZV infection in asymptomatic HIV infection responds well to oral treatment with acyclovir, valacyclovir, or famciclovir for a course of 7 to 14 days. The dosage required for treatment of VZV is higher than that required for treatment of recurrences of HSV infection. Intravenous therapy with high-dose acyclovir is indicated in symptomatic systemic involvement or in special types of shingles involving the cranial nerves with certain complications, such as zoster ophthalmicus; Ramsey Hunt syndrome; and cutaneous, disseminated, chronic or extremely severe lesions affecting patients with end-stage HIV disease. Patients with more indolent lesions who do not respond to oral and intravenous acyclovir should be suspected of having a resistant strain of VZV. These cases should be treated with intravenous foscarnet.

Human Papillomavirus

Warts are very common in HIV patients.

Human papillomaviruses are the etiologic agents of common warts, plantar warts, flat warts, perianal and genital warts (condyloma acuminatum), oral mucosal papillomas, and certain types of carcinomas mainly affecting the anogenital area. Anogenital warts are usually acquired through sexual intercourse, and HPV infection is the most prevalent sexually transmitted disease in North America. The incidence of anogenital warts is increased in the HIV-positive population.

Bowenoid papulosis

The clinical presentation of common warts is that of a typical hyperkeratotic, yellowish-colored, inelastic, hard papule affecting mainly the hands and feet, although it also can be seen on other areas of the body. When affecting the mucosal areas and the mucocutaneous transitional areas, the clinical appearance of these lesions is somewhat different (Figure 64–11). These lesions appear as soft, multilobulated, often pedunculated papules and plaques, often resembling

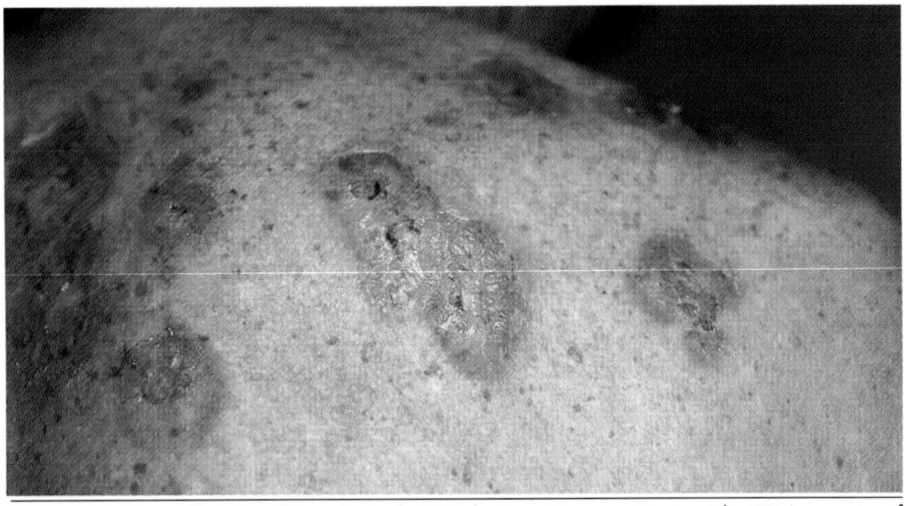

FIGURE 64–10 Chronic disseminated VZV lesions in a patient with CD4 counts of 14/mm^3. Note the multiple shallow, crust-covered erosions on the trunk.

a cauliflower. Unusual clinical presentations in the HIV-infected population include bowenoid papulosis, characterized by multiple flat, hyperpigmented, hyperkeratotic papules with a chronic course. Skin biopsy of these lesions reveals full thickness cytologic atypia within the epithelium, characterizing in situ squamous cell carcinoma (Figure 64–12). Unlike other squamous cell carcinomas in situ of the anogenital area, bowenoid papulosis lacks metastatic potential.

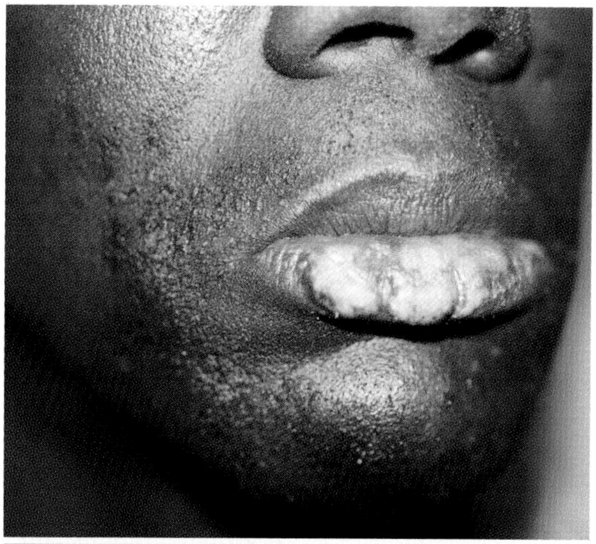

FIGURE 64–11 Oral mucosal warts in a patient with HIV. HPV infection of the oral mucosa is unusual in immunocompetent individuals, and their presence should raise the suspicion of an immunodefficiency state.

The HPV infections are hard to control in the immune-competent individual, and this is even more true in the immune-compromised host. Very often, treatment is aimed at reducing the bulk of the lesions, therefore making the patient more comfortable, and improving their physiologic functions and overall quality of life. Even though the risk of developing HPV-induced neoplasia is increased in HIV-positive individuals, the treatment of warts does not prevent this from occurring. Therefore, close surveillance with Papanicolaou smears and frequent rectal and perianal examinations in patients with HIV is recommended to detect early malignant changes. As previously mentioned, the treatment of warts for most patients is palliative. The goal is to keep the size and distribution of the lesions somewhat limited. Several therapeutic modalities are available, and the treatment goal is to destroy the affected tissue. Several chemical and physical therapeutic modalities are used for that purpose, including cryotherapy with liquid nitrogen, electrocauterization, laser ablation, chemical cauterization using trichloroacetic acid, podophyllum resin, nonspecific immunologic stimulants such as cantharidin (beetle juice extract), dinitrochlorobenzene, imiquimod, and intralesional injections of drugs such as chemotherapeutic agents (bleomycin, 5-fluorouracil) and interferon. Perianal condylomata are particularly recalcitrant, and rectal lesions must be treated concomitantly by a proctologist if the goal is to completely clear the patient of clinical lesions.

In immune-compromised patients, warts are very hard to control.

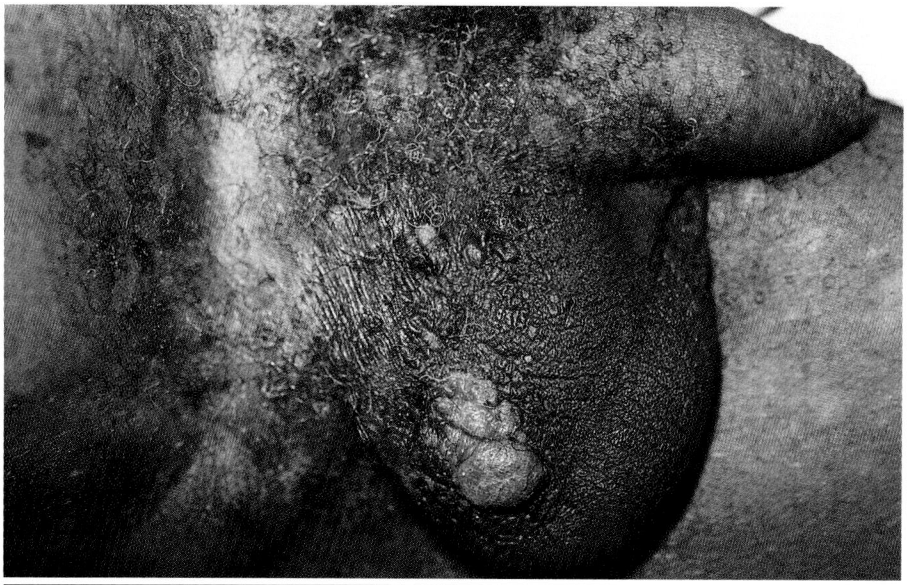

FIGURE 64–12 Bowenoid papulosis. Multiple hyperpigmented flat papules on the scrotum and groin of this male with advanced HIV disease. A biopsy of the erythematous plaque observed in the photograph revealed invasive squamous cell carcinoma.

Molluscum Contagiosum

Cutaneous lesions of molluscum can be widespread in HIV patients.

Molluscum contagiosum is caused by a poxvirus, which is frequently seen infecting children; however, since the beginning of the AIDS epidemic, it is seen in HIV-positive adults as well. The typical morphology of a lesion is that of a small, light-colored, dome-shaped, firm papule, often with a small, central depression (umbilication). It most frequently affects the face, neck, and genitalia. In patients with advanced HIV disease, the individual lesions can reach several centimeters in diameter, forming nodules and tumor masses. These are referred to as giant mollusca (Figure 64–13). Even though this infection is not associated with any serious health risks, it can cause devastating psychologic problems for the patient, leading to social isolation and significantly decreased quality of life. Progression to extensive involvement and frequent recurrences is the usual course, despite repeated treatments in patients with poorly controlled HIV disease. Cutaneous lesions of disseminated fungal infections, such as disseminated cryptococcosis and disseminated histoplasmosis, can mimic generalized molluscum, and in patients with acute onset of these lesions, very low CD4 counts, and the systemic symptoms of malaise, fatigue, and fever, a skin biopsy is recommended to establish the diagnosis.

Treatment is recommended as early as possible in order to prevent self-inoculation and widespread disease. It includes chemical or physical destruction of the individual papules and nonspecific immunologic stimulants as previously described for the treatment of warts. In addition, simple curettage of individual lesions is very effective. Since HIV-positive men are frequently affected and most commonly on the face and neck, they should be advised to avoid shaving.

Oral Hairy Leukoplakia

Very common condition in HIV patients
No evidence for malignant transformation

Oral hairy leukoplakia (OHL) is caused by the herpes virus EBV. Clinically, it is characterized by a thick white plaque usually affecting the lateral aspect of the tongue giving it a corrugated surface (corduroy appearance) or, in more advanced lesions, a hairy appearance. Oral hairy leukoplakia can also occur on the buccal mucosa and floor of the mouth, but it does not affect other epithelia of mucosal origin, such as the vaginal or perianal mucosa. This condition was initially described in HIV-positive individuals, and the current reported frequency of this condition is approximately 20%, affecting those with asympto-

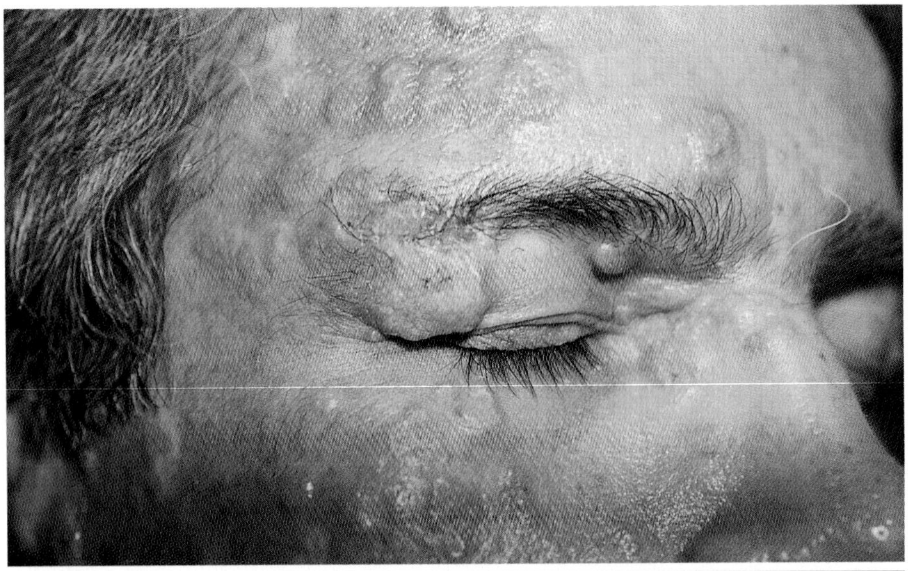

FIGURE 64–13 Giant mollusca. These multiple pink-colored, lobulated plaques and tumors are almost impossible to treat or conceal, causing significant compromise in the quality of life of these patients.

matic HIV infection. The frequency increases as the CD4 count drops and the HIV disease progresses. Oral hairy leukoplakia is not only seen in HIV-infected individuals, but also among immune-suppressed transplant recipients. Very few cases have been reported in immunocompetent individuals. These lesions are easily differentiated from oral candidiasis since they are not easily scraped off from the oral mucosa. In addition, the KOH preparation is negative. Malignant transformation has not been seen in association with OHL. These lesions are usually asymptomatic, and no treatment is required unless the thickening and cosmetic appearance of the tongue are bothersome to the patient. There have been reports of complete, but temporary, responses to acyclovir or gancyclovir. Also, topical treatment with podophyllum resin and retinoic acid derivatives have been reported to be effective. Oral hairy leukoplakia can be a clinical marker of a previously undetected HIV infection, or as some studies suggest, it may herald a more rapid progression to full-blown AIDS and end-stage HIV disease.

Other Viral Infections

Although CMV infections are a major source of morbidity and mortality in immune-deficient patients, this virus is rarely associated with specific cutaneous lesions. There have been reports of concomitant infection of chronic perianal ulcers with both CMV and HSV-2. There have been fewer than 30 cases of cutaneous CMV infection reported in the world literature. The clinical appearance of cutaneous CMV is highly variable and includes cutaneous ulcers, nodules, morbilliform exanthems, verrucous plaques, and leukocytoclastic vasculitis. Genital/perianal ulcerations are the most common, having been described in approximately 30% of the reported cases. The significance of the incidental discovery of CMV inclusions and skin biopsy specimens of nonspecific cutaneous lesions in immune-compromised hosts is controversial.

Infections by HHV-8 or KSHV cause the most common AIDS-associated neoplasms. This clinical entity will be discussed further in the section of this chapter describing neoplasms.

Fungal Infections

Fungal infections are typically divided into superficial mycoses and deep fungal infections.

Superficial Mycoses

Superficial mycoses comprise dermatophyte infections and yeast infections of the skin and mucosal surfaces caused by *Candida* spp and *P. ovale*. The dermatophytes cause the different tineas, represented by tinea corporis, tinea cruris, tinea pedis, tinea manuum, tinea faciei, and onychomycosis. These superficial mycoses are among the most common infections seen in HIV-infected patients. As a rule, the dermatophyte infections remain on the skin surface and do not cause systemic disease. The typical presentation is characterized by a well-circumscribed, erythematous, scaly patch with elevated active borders that may assume an annular to polycyclic shape, often with central clearing. Again, in HIV-infected individuals, the presentation can be atypical with diffuse scaling without any circumscribed limits. At times, the dermatophytes can cause eczematous plaques resembling nummular eczema, follicular papules resembling folliculitis, and psoriasiform plaques mimicking psoriasis vulgaris. The assessment and diagnosis of scaly lesions is even very important in patients with HIV; in the search for fungal organisims every lesion that has a scaly surface must be scraped and analyzed by microscopy using a KOH preparation. Very often, simple and typical dermatophyte infections are morphologically altered by inadequate therapy with different topical steroids, and diagnosis is even more challenging. Fungal cultures can be very helpful when clinical suspicion is not confirmed by a positive KOH preparation, and also for the diagnosis of hair and nail infections.

Atypical presentations are common.
Any scaling lesion should be scraped and a KOH preparation performed.

Candidiasis is the most common fungal infection observed in HIV-infected patients. *Candida* species are ubiquitous yeasts that colonize the mucosal surfaces in all individuals and *Candida albicans* is the most common species responsible for mucocutaneous lesions in HIV-positive individuals. Disease of the mucous membranes occur in more than 90% of patients at some point during the course of their HIV disease, and oral candidiasis may occur in up to 70% of patients as one of the initial manifestations of HIV disease. The incidence of candidal infections increases as the immune defficiency progresses, and it becomes a common problem when CD4 counts fall below 200 to 300 per cubic millimeter.

Oral candidiasis

The most trivial presentation is that of oral candidiasis, or thrush. This is easily recognizable by examination of the oral cavity where whitish plaques, which are easily scraped off from the mucosal surface, are seen covering the buccal mucosa, tongue, palate, and oral pharynx. Oral candidiasis can be completely asymptomatic or the patient may report changes in taste, a burning sensation, or a dry mouth. There are several clinically distinct forms of oral candidiasis and the pseudomembranous form described above is the most common clinical variant. Atrophic and hypertrophic candidiasis follow in terms of frequency (Figure 64–14). Occasionally, more subtle atypical presentations are seen, such as atrophic and hypertrophic glossitis (represented clinically by atrophic and hypertrophic patches on the surface of the tongue respectively), angular cheilitis (characterized by fissuring and maceration of the corners of the mouth), extensive candidal intertrigo (characterized by extensive areas of erythema and maceration with malodorous exudation in bodyfold areas), and candidal balanitis (where eroded, beefy-red patches of the penile glands cause significant discomfort, especially in uncircumcised males). Candidal infection of the oral mucosa can extend down into the gastrointestinal tract, and esophageal candidiasis is a very common complication. This usually happens when the CD4 counts drop to below 100 per cubic millimeter. Also, due to the varying symptoms, it can significantly compromise the patient's nutrition. *Candida* can also infect the nail and periungual tissue, causing a fungal paronychia. The diagnosis of candidal infection is done by the clinical morphology as well as by assessment of a KOH preparation performed on scrapings obtained from the inflammatory or macerated areas. The identification of spores or pseudohyphae is diagnostic.

Very pruritic folliculitis

Pityrosporum ovale is a yeast that is also part of the normal cutaneous flora found in the stratum corneum and inside the hair follicles of most individuals. This yeast multiplies under aerobic, microaerophilic, or anaerobic conditions and it has lipase activity. *Pityrosporum ovale* can cause the very commonly seen tinea versicolor, but in the HIV-infected population it commonly causes a very pruritic type of folliculitis, characterized clinically by small, discrete, follicular, erythematous papules and follicular pustules mainly on the upper portion of the back, the anterior chest, and to a lesser extent, the shoulders, and proximal arms. Clinical diagnosis can be aided by scraping one of the pustules and performing a KOH preparation, or a periodic acid–Schiff (PAS) staining for visualization of the fungus. Most often, it is extremely difficult to differentiate this condition from the other types of folliculitis, such as bacterial, parasitic, or even eosinophilic/inflammatory folliculitis.

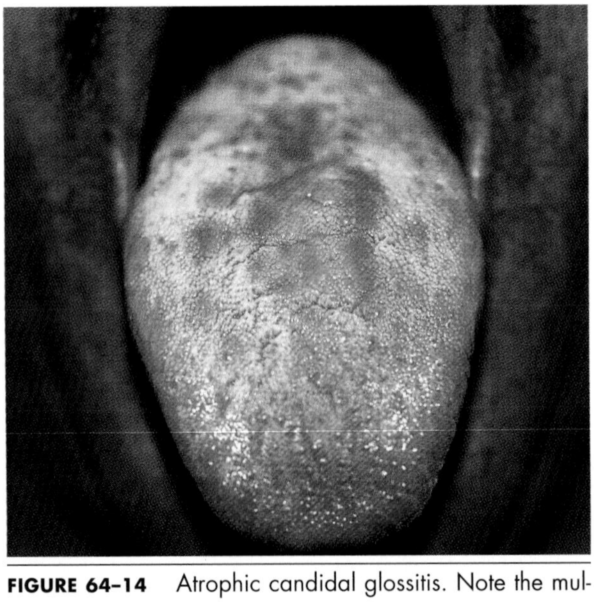

FIGURE 64–14 Atrophic candidal glossitis. Note the multiple "bare" patches with a shiny surface on the dorsum of the tongue. This form of candidiasis is often accompanied by angular cheilitis, another clinical variant of *Candida* infection.

The treatment of dermatophyte infections (tineas) can be done with topical medications when the disease is localized or limited to one or very few body surface areas. The drugs available include several imidazole derivatives, such as ketoconazole, miconazole, oxiconazole, and alilamines, such as terbinafine. Infections of the nail and hair follicles and more extensive cutaneous infections must be treated with systemic medications. These include ketaconazole, fluconazole, itraconazole, griseofulvin (rarely used), and terbinafine. Candidal infections, if localized, are treated with topical medications such as nystatin, clotrimazole, and other imidazole derivatives. More severe or internal organ involvement should be treated with oral fluconazole; in cases of the more extreme disseminated candidiasis, treatment with intravenous amphotericin B is recommended.

Deep Fungal Infections

The most common fungi to cause disseminated disease with cutaneous involvement in patients who have advanced HIV disease are *Histoplasma capsulatum* and *Cryptococcus neoformans.* Other systemic fungal infections that can disseminate to the skin include coccidioidomycosis caused by the soil fungus *Coccidioides immitis*, found only in the western hemisphere; sporotrichosis, caused by *Sporothrix schenckii*; blastomycosis caused by *Blastomyces dermatitidis*; and even more rarely, penicilliosis caused by different species of *Penicillium—Penicillium marneffei* being recognized as the most significant of these pathogens in southeast Asia.

May resemble molluscum

Histoplasmosis is the most common endemic mycosis in patients with AIDS. *Histoplasma capsulatum* is found along the major river valleys in the temperate zone of North America. The route of entry is aspiration of infective spores and establishment of pulmonary disease, which can be asymptomatic. Histoplasmosis disseminates in 95% of cases among patients with AIDS. Often, it disseminates to the skin, and cutaneous lesions can be observed in up to 17% of cases. Clinical manifestations include erythematous papules; pustular folliculitis; widespread ulcers; ulcerative plaques; papular, necrotic lesions; eczematous papules and plaques; erythema multiforme; and rosacea-like lesions. One very common presentation that deserves special mention is that of dome-shaped, skin-colored to hypopigmented papules with central umbilication resembling molluscum contagiosum (Figure 64–15). As previously mentioned, any patient with such lesions and evidence of systemic disease and late stage HIV infection needs to have a biopsy performed on one of the lesions for diagnosis.

Leading cause of morbidity and mortality caused by a fungal infection in HIV patients

Cryptococcosis is the leading cause of morbidity and mortality attributed to fungal infections in patients with HIV and AIDS. *Cryptococcus neoformans* is an encapsulated yeast that is found worldwide but most commonly in the excreta of pigeons and other birds. The portal of entry of the organism is assumed to be the respiratory tract, and meningitis is the most common initial manifestation of the

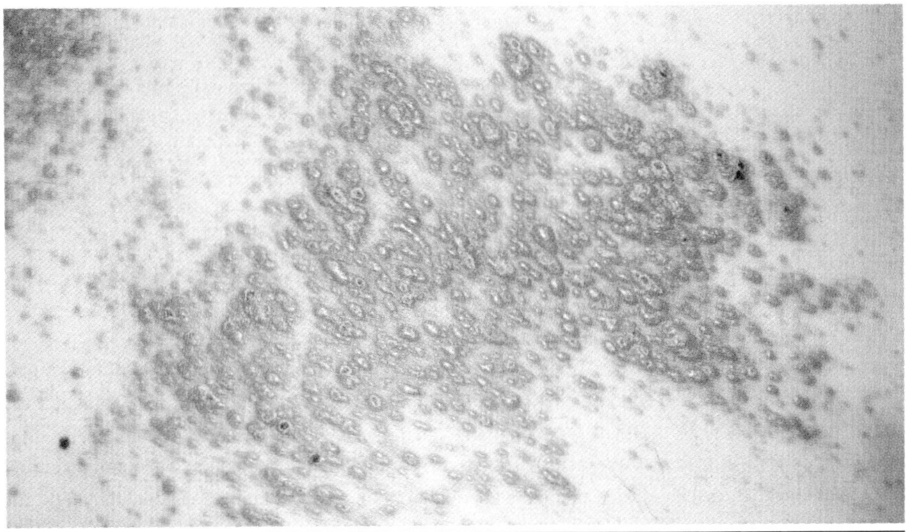

FIGURE 64–15 Disseminated histoplasmosis with generalized cutaneous involvement. The morphology of the individual lesions mimics molluscum contagiosum. The distribution and relatively acute history, as well as the associated systemic symptoms, suggest a more severe systemic infection.

infection, affecting 72 to 90% of individuals. Skin lesions may occur in at least 10% of patients with disseminated cryptococcosis, and it may be the first manifestation of the disease. Several morphologic types of lesions have been described, the most common being erythematous papules. Less commonly pustules and umbilicated papules resembling molluscum contagiosum are also seen. The most usual locations of cutaneous lesions are the upper body, face, neck, and scalp. If left untreated, cryptococcosis is invariably fatal.

Treatment depends on the organs involved and on the immune status of the infected individual. For treatment of cryptococcal meningitis, the drug of choice is amphotericin B with or without concomitant use of flucytosine. As an alternative, fluconazole alone or in combination with flucytosine are also shown to be effective. Extra neurologic cryptococcal infections can be treated with fluconazole alone. Treatment of histoplasmosis should be initiated with a course of intravenous amphotericin B followed by the oral administration of itraconazole. Lifelong maintenance therapy after the initial treatment is necessary to prevent relapse. This maintenance involves using smaller doses of amphotericin B weekly or biweekly or oral itraconazole daily for a prolonged period.

Bacterial Infections

Common problem

Bacterial infections due to the common pathogens *S. aureus* or *Streptococcus pyogenes* are also the most common cutaneous bacterial infections associated with HIV disease. The most common presentations are folliculitis, which was described earlier, impetigo simplex, and abscesses. These are characterized by the development of deep-seated inflammatory nodules that are extremely tender to the touch and may progress to fully developed furuncles with central fluctuation and subsequent drainage of abundant purulent material. Since the incidence of chronic carrier state for *S. aureus* is increased in patients infected with HIV, they are prone to developing recurrent lesions. These patients are also prone to developing a secondary bacterial infection of previously existing noninfectious cutaneous lesions, a process known as impetiginization.

Treatment is with systemic antibiotics that cover penicillinase-producing organisms. If the infection is recurrent or not responding to the usual therapies, it is very helpful to obtain a culture of the purulent secretion or the lesion bed and to perform appropriate antibiotic sensitivity testing. In addition to antibiotic therapy, abscesses, furuncles, and any other lesions with central fluctuation need to be incised and drained. Treatment of frequent recurrences may require prolonged courses of systemic antibiotics associated with topical medications applied to the *Staphylococcus*-carrying areas of the body such as the nares, navel, and the interdigital spaces of the toe webs.

Cellulitis is also a common infection and can be a complication of other cutaneous lesions that form a port of entry for bacteria, such as inflammatory tinea pedis with fissuring or lesions of Kaposi's sarcoma. Drug users as well as patients with indwelling catheters are also at higher risk for developing bacterial infections. Other common bacterial agents that are described as causing infections in this patient population are *Haemophilus influenzae*, causing cellulitis, and *Pseudomonas aeruginosa*, causing folliculitis and ulcers.

The cutaneous manifestations of bacterial sexually transmitted diseases (STDs) such as syphilis, are described elsewhere in this book, but some important aspects are worth mentioning because they are unique to patients infected with HIV. It is important to realize that the presence of an ulcerating STD facilitates transmission as well as acquisition of HIV infection. Also, the incidence of STDs is significantly increased in patients with HIV. Several reports are available about the unusual behavior of these STDs and different stages of the HIV infection. In the case of syphilis, there have been reports showing a more rapid progression to later stages of syphilitic infection in patients with HIV. Serologic testing has been found to be less reliable in these patients, with a higher incidence of false-negative tests. For syphilis, as well as for the other bacterial STDs, the clinical presentation may be atypical and the course of the disease can be dramatic. The response to therapy can also be different in these patients. For this reason, biopsies should be performed on genital ulcers that have an unusual clinical course or an unusual response to therapy, and the tissue should be sent for multiple cultures, including special media as directed by the clinical suspicion. Last, but not least, it is important for physicians to realize that the prevention and adequate treatment of STDs significantly reduces the incidence of new cases of HIV infection.

Presence of ulcerating syphilitic lesion facilitates transmission of HIV.

Mycobacterial Infections

Mycobacterial infections primarily involving the skin are rare. This is especially remarkable considering the high incidence of disseminated *Mycobacterium avium-intracellulare* infections in patients with HIV. Disseminated miliary cutaneous tuberculosis, as well as scrofuloderma affecting the skin adjacent to the lymph nodes, has been reported in HIV-positive individuals. Mycobacteria other than tuberculosis referred to as "atypical" mycobacteria, are also reported to cause cutaneous ulcerations and other cutaneous lesions in these patients. These include *Mycobacterium haemophilum*, *Mycobacterium chelonei*, *Mycobacterium fortuitum,* and *Mycobacterium kansasii.* Cutaneous lesions reported vary greatly from disseminated inflammatory papules, lymphangitic-spreading nodules, ulcers, folliculitis, and cellulitis (Figure 64–16). Recurrences with these infections are very common, and antibiotic therapy using a multidrug regimen may be beneficial on a long-term basis.

Mycobacterial skin infections are rare.

Bacillary Angiomatosis

Bacillary angiomatosis was first reported in 1982 and is now known to be caused by a gram-negative coccobacillus belonging to the genus *Bartonella*, more specifically *Bartonella quintana* and *Bartonella henselae*. The disease affects individuals with advanced stages of HIV infection with an average CD4 count of 57 per cubic millimeter. The majority of the affected patients are men, and the lesions are characterized by red to purple-colored angiomatous papules or nodules resembling pyogenic granuloma (Figure 64–17). These skin lesions can be solitary or multiple, reaching hundreds in the same patient. They can be small in size, but lesions as large as 10 centimeters in diameter have been noted. Other clinical presentations include subcutaneous nodules with or without ulceration and indurated, hyperpigmented plaques with poorly defined borders and hyperkeratotic centers resembling lesions of Kaposi's sarcoma. A skin biopsy with

Bacillary angiomatosis caused by a gram-negative coccobacillus.

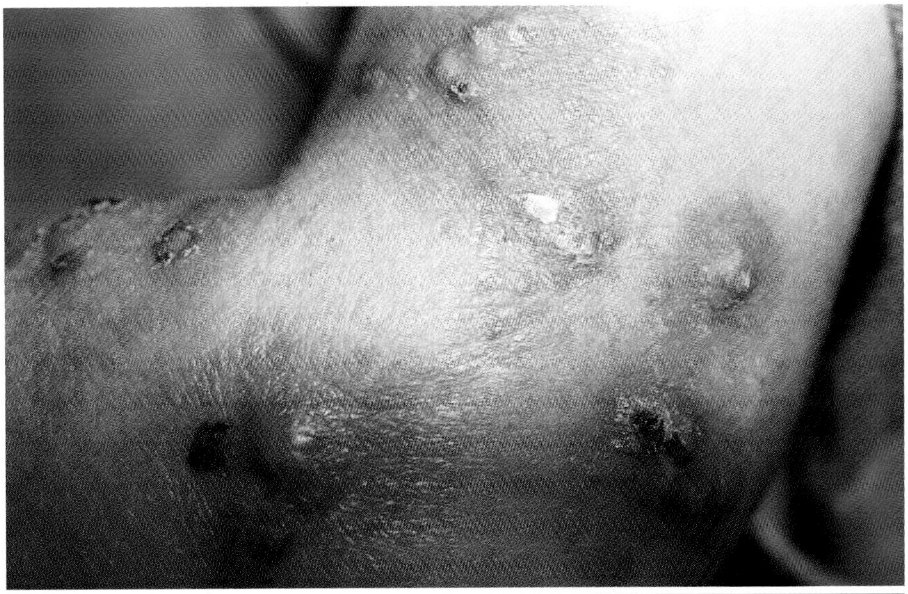

FIGURE 64–16 Multiple inflammatory papules, nodules, and plaques are seen on the arm of this HIV-positive male. Multiple cultures revealed *M. chelonei*.

special stains that help determine the infectious agent is necessary to establish the final diagnosis. The infection most commonly affects the skin but, extracutaneous manifestations can also be seen.

Biopsy using Warthin-Starry stain is best way to detect organism.

Extracutaneous general manifestations include fever, chills, night sweats, poor appetite, and weight loss. Other organ systems involved include the respiratory tract with the development of endobronchial lesions that may progress to obstructive disease, cardiovascular involvement with development of endocarditis, bone marrow and lymph node infection, keratitis, necrotizing splenitis, and central nervous system involvement, which may present as new-onset seizures. Peliosis hepatis can present as an isolated condition or concomitantly with cutaneous or extracutaneous bacillary angiomatosis. This is characterized by blood-filled cystic spaces in the liver accompanied by other signs of gastrointestinal disease, such as nausea, vomiting, diarrhea, abdominal distention, and hepatosplenomegaly. The diagnosis of bacillary angiomatosis is best made with a biopsy and histopathologic studies including Warthin-Starry stain since the organism is very difficult to culture. Early diagnostic tools include detection of antibodies to the organism using the enzyme-linked immunosorbent assay technique.

The treatment of choice is with erythromycin or doxycycline for a prolonged period of time (weeks to months). Other treatment options are minocycline, tetracycline, chloramphenicol, azithromycin, and trimethoprim/sulfamethoxazole.

Infestations

Demodicidosis

Folliculitis

The follicular mites *Demodex folliculorum* and *Demodex brevis* are common mites inhabiting the hair follicle and are considered part of the normal flora in the healthy, non–HIV-infected population. In patients infected with HIV, the presence of the mite inside the hair follicle can trigger an inflammatory reaction characterized by abundant eosinophils and clinically by the development of erythematous, edematous follicular papules that are usually extremely pruritic. The commonly affected areas are the face and neck and occasionally the anterior chest area. This form of folliculitis does not represent a true infestation since there appears to be no increased numbers of mites in the affected patients, and it is not a contagious process; however, it does appear to be a hyperreactive process in a patient with an immunologic dysfunction.

Treatment of *Demodex* folliculitis can be done with topical application of a metronidazole-based creams and gels every night at bedtime until there is improvement of the symptoms. Alternatively, permethrin creams can be applied to the affected areas every night at bedtime for seven days.

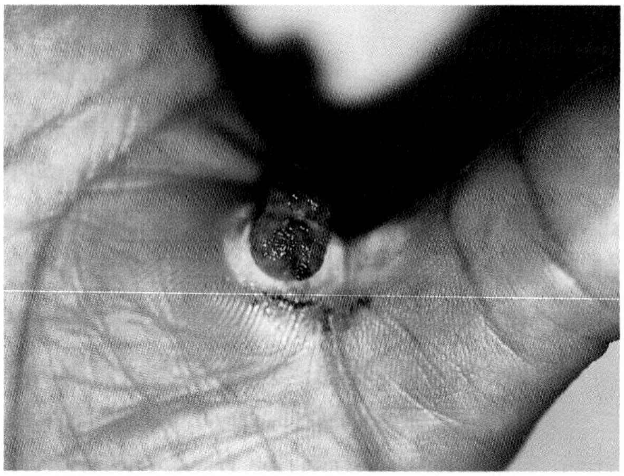

FIGURE 64–17 Bacillary angiomatosis. This vascular, exophytic, wet papule surrounded by a collarette of hyperkeratosis at the base resembles a common pyogenic granuloma.

Scabies

Pruritus is the most common cutaneous complaint of patients infected with HIV, and as previously mentioned, there are several different possible causes for this symptom. Scabetic infestation is one that is usually underdiagnosed and can be a difficult problem not only for the patients but for family members and for health care providers as well. Scabies usually presents with the classic eruption characterized by pinpoint to pinhead-sized papules with excoriations and occasional burrows involving the finger webs, wrists, anterior axillary folds, periareolar areas in females, and periumbilical areas in a belt-like distribution along the waistline. Patients with advanced HIV disease, however, may develop an overwhelming infestation characterized by widespread lesions and generalized pruritus. Not uncommonly, they develop a clinical form of the infestation known as "Norwegian" or "crusted" scabies. This clinical variant is characterized by thick, crusted, hyperkeratotic, scaly plaques involving larger areas of the body, typically the scalp, beard area, palms, soles, and extensor surfaces of the arms and legs (Figure 64–18). These can mimic other cutaneous diseases and one must always keep a high level of suspicion when dealing with patients who complain of severe pruritus associated with what appears to be a papulosquamous disease such as psoriasis or chronic eczematous processes. Patients with crusted scabies are usually infested with thousands of mites, and the diagnosis is easily made by scraping off some scales from the plaques and papules, covering the scales with mineral oil, and looking under a microscope in order to identify the adult mites, the eggs, or the stools known as "sciballae."

Norwegian scabies in advanced AIDS

Treatment of regular scabies is done with permethrin cream applied to the whole body, from the neck down, at night and washed off in the morning. The patients must wash all personal clothing and linens, and the treatment should be repeated after 7 to 10 days. All household members and close contacts must be treated simultaneously. Other alternative treatments are lindane creams and lotions which have the potential of being absorbed and may cause neurotoxicity in small children and infants. Lindane should also be used on the entire body in a single application and repeated after 7 to 10 days. Other topical medications used for treating scabies include crotamiton oil, benzyl benzoate, and precipitated sulfur. Patients with the crusted form of scabies should be treated for a longer time with the same medications described above, and these are usually applied on a daily basis for 7 days. Keratolytic agents, such as urea-based creams or salicylic acid preparations, can also be used concomitantly to rid the patient of the crusts and hyperkeratotic debris that are filled with mites.

All household members and close contacts must be treated simultaneously.

Systemic treatment for scabies is now approved and is done with oral ivermectin given in a single dose. When this treatment is chosen, the patient must be made aware of the need to treat their personal belongings and clothing, and topical treatment should be prescribed to all of the patient's contacts. Patients treated with ivermectin also benefit greatly from topical application of keratolytic and moisturizing agents as previously mentioned.

Ivermectin

Neoplasms

Several malignant and benign neoplasms have been associated with HIV infection. Some of them, such as Kaposi's sarcoma, primary central nervous system lymphoma, non-Hodgkin's lymphoma, and cervical carcinoma, represent AIDS-defining illnesses. In the setting of HIV infection, they can be characterized by more aggressive clinical behavior and by higher-grade lesions with a more advanced stage and shortened survival when compared with similar neoplasms affecting HIV seronegative individuals. It is possible that the progressive loss of CD4 lymphocytes could decrease immune surveillance and, therefore, facilitate the development of different types of malignancies.

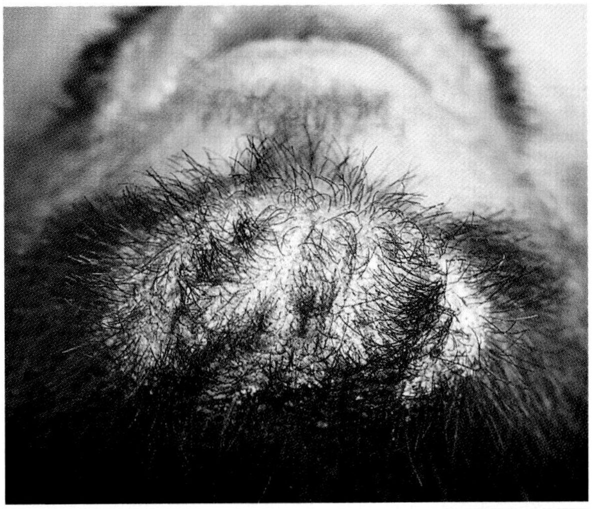

FIGURE 64–18 Crusted (Norwegian) scabies. This hyperkeratotic scaly plaque on the beard area was moderately pruritic and had been treated for months as seborrheic dermatitis. Crusted scabies can also mimic psoriasis.

Kaposi's Sarcoma

Kaposi's sarcoma (KS) was the first tumor described as a specific manifestation of HIV infection and full-blown AIDS. Four different forms of KS have been characterized to date based on differences in age of onset, geographic distribution, and course of the disease: the classic type seen in males of Mediterranean origin; the endemic type seen in sub-Saharan African countries; the iatrogenic type caused by immunosuppressive medications, which is seen in transplant patients; and the AIDS-related KS seen almost exclusively in homosexual and bisexual men. The histopathology of the skin lesions in the four types of KS is identical.

Human herpesvirus type 8

The pathogenesis of KS is multifactorial, and the exact mechanisms involved in the development of cutaneous and extracutaneous lesions remain unknown. A new human herpesvirus, HHV-8, or KSHV, has been identified in all lesions of all the four types of KS, and it is definitely associated with the pathogenesis of this disease. There is considerable debate whether the presence of HHV-8 alone can trigger the development of KS lesions, and the possible mechanisms by which this herpesvirus can induce neoplastic changes in the skin are being extensively investigated. The presence of HHV-8 infections as detected by HHV-8 seropositivity is high among homosexual and bisexual men and correlates with the number of sexual partners. The prevalence of HHV-8 seropositivity among HIV-infected women was 7 to 9 times lower than among HIV-infected homosexual men. The overall seroprevalence of HHV-8 in asymptomatic homosexual males who are HIV-positive is 56%. The HHV-8-positivity precedes the development of KS by many years (average 6.8 years). The HHV-8 is a sexually transmitted virus, and it is completely absent in children with HIV infection and AIDS. Growth factors, such as the fibroblast growth factors and hepatocyte growth factor; certain glycoproteins, such as oncostatin M; inflammatory cytokines; and protein gene products, such as the TAT protein, a product of the HIV-transactivating gene *TAT*, can all induce proliferation and angiogenic differentiation of normal vascular cells and can potentially be involved in the pathogenesis of KS.

The clinical presentation is characterized more commonly by pink-, red- to violet-, or brown-colored macules or papules ranging in size from several millimeters to several centimeters in diameter. The most typical shape is round to oval, and plaque-type lesions are especially common on the feet and thighs. Occasionally, there are exophytic nodules and tumors developing into fungating masses of large proportions (Figure 64–19). The lesions can be single, but they are usually multiple and have a tendency to be symmetrically distributed. Lymphedema is a common finding, particularly affecting the face, genitalia, and lower extremities. This edema may be out of proportion to the extent of the cutaneous disease. The clinical course may vary from minimal involvement, where one or two cutaneous lesions are an incidental finding, to a more explosive and aggressive growth resulting in significant morbidity and mortality. The most common extracutaneous form of KS is in the oral cavity, an area which is affected in one-third of the patients; it can be the initial presenting site in approximately 15% of the individuals affected. The palate is the most commonly involved intraoral site, and oral lesions are commonly associated with involvement of other areas of the gastrointestinal tract. Gastrointestinal involvement is seen in approximately 40% of the patients with cutaneous KS when it is initially diagnosed, and the incidence is as high as 80% as an autopsy finding. The clinical presentation may vary from asymptomatic to significant nausea and vomiting, upper gastrointestinal bleeds, and abdominal pain and distention. Pulmonary involvement is relatively common, and it can range from an asymptomatic finding on chest radiograph to severe dyspnea, cough, hemoptysis, and chest pain. Lymph node involvement may be present even in the absence of mucocutaneous disease.

Oral cavity and gastrointestinal involvement common

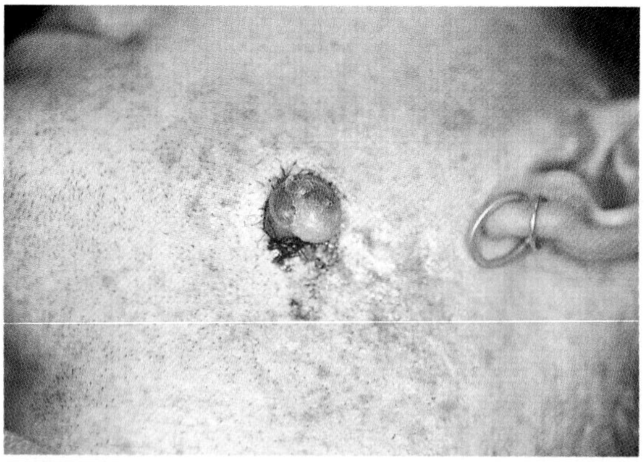

FIGURE 64–19 Nodular Kaposi's sarcoma. Single, pedunculated nodule on the beard area of this otherwise healthy male with AIDS. This was the only cutaneous lesion present and it was easily treated by surgical excision and cauterization of the base.

Treatment is determined for the most part by the presence of symptomatic systemic involvement or of cutaneous disease extensive enough to significantly impair the patient's quality of life. Successful treatment of the HIV-infection with protease inhibitors may stabilize or even reduce the size and the severity of the KS lesions. It is a well-known fact that some patients show complete resolution of the KS after they are started on protease inhibitors, their CD4 counts increase and the HIV viral load is significantly reduced. Small, individual lesions can be treated for cosmetic purposes with different therapeutic modalities: cryotherapy, where liquid nitrogen is applied to selected lesions repeatedly over a period of 1 to 2 months; simple surgical excision of individual nodules with suturing of the skin; and laser ablation using a carbon dioxide or argon laser. These lesions can also be treated with intralesional injections of chemotherapeutic agents, such as vinblastine; interferon alpha; and sodium tetradecyl sulfate, which is used for sclerotherapy of vascular lesions. Recently, a noninvasive therapeutic option was made available, and it consists of topical applications of alitretinoin gel, a retinoic acid derivative. Even though this medication has a relatively low efficacy rate (35%), it is still a very good option since it is essentially noninvasive.

For larger multifocal lesions or for extracutaneous involvement with significant systemic symptoms, systemic treatment is recommended (Figure 64–20). Treatments available include radiation therapy, which is usually effective in reducing the edema and decreasing the tumor mass; single-agent and combination chemotherapy regimens using doxorubicin, bleomycin, vinblastine, and vincristine; and systemic interferon therapy. Several pathogenesis-targeted therapies have been described using angiogenesis inhibitors, granulocyte-macrophage colony–stimulating factor (GM-CSF), β-human chorionic gonadotropin and other growth factors, and cytokine inhibitors.

Lymphomas

The most common types of lymphoma affecting HIV-infected patients are non-Hodgkin's lymphomas, usually of the intermediate-grade or high-grade B-cell type. Four major components are thought to be relevant in the pathogenesis of these neoplasms including disrupted immunosurveillance, chronic antigenic stimulation, cytokine dysregulation, and concomitant viral infections (eg, EBV). These tumors have very aggressive behavior and very frequently involve extranodal sites (approximately 90% of the cases), such as the bone marrow, the gastrointestinal system, the central nervous system, and the skin. The typical cutaneous lesions are purple- or plum-colored erythematous nodules and plaques isolated or coalescent to form larger tumor masses. Occasionally, fungating tumors are also seen (Figure 64–21). The HIV-infected patients with persistent generalized lymphadenopathy are at higher risk for developing these lymphomas. Treatment is with combination chemotherapy; however, it may exacer-

Lymphomas tend to involve extranodal sites and are aggressive.

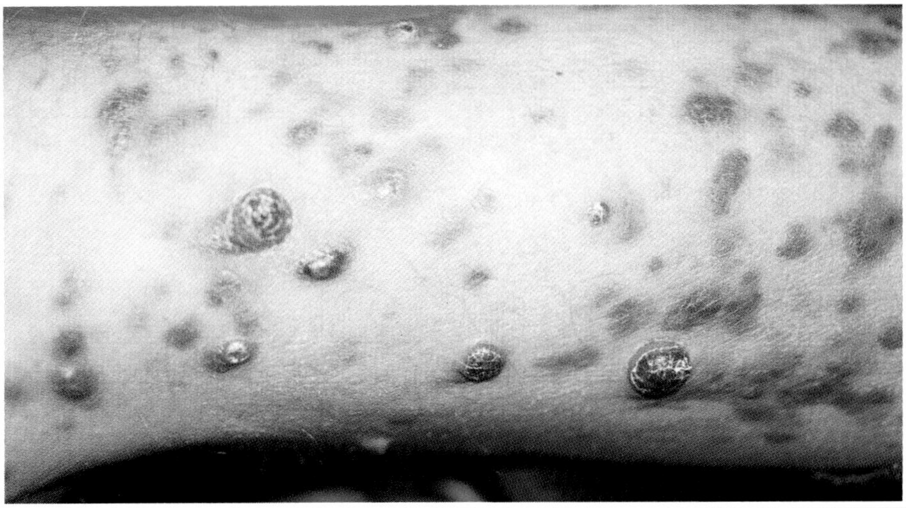

FIGURE 64–20 Generalized cutaneous Kaposi's sarcoma. This patient with late stages of HIV infection developed generalized purple-colored papules, nodules, and tumors, but lesions were more pronounced on the thighs. Systemic treatment is the only option.

bate the immune deficiency state, resulting in an increased incidence of opportunistic infections and a shortening of survival.

Primary central nervous system lymphomas represent a very severe complication that usually affects people who have an advanced HIV disease and an average CD4 count of 34 per cubic millimeter. The prognosis is very poor, and the mean survival time is 3 months even if the lymphoma is treated. Radiation therapy can improve the quality of life but does not improve the length of survival.

Cutaneous T-cell lymphoma

Cutaneous T-cell lymphomas (CTCLs) are only occasionally seen in these patients, and the typical cutaneous lesions are usually the same as those seen in HIV-negative individuals—erythematous patches and plaques that may progress to the development of tumors on the skin. There is, however, a slight predominance of erythrodermic forms in HIV-positive persons. Immunophenotyping shows a predominance of CD8-positive (supressor-cytotoxic) CTCLs in HIV-positive individuals as opposed to the general population with CTCL, which usually expresses a helper-inducer (CD4+) phenotype. The reason for this remains unknown.

Cervical and Anal Neoplasias

The incidence of cervical neoplasia is increased in HIV-positive women, especially those with a history of HPV infection, multiple sexual partners, and very low CD4 counts. The disease is usually more aggressive than that seen in HIV-negative women, and it is less likely to be successfully treated by standard therapies.

HPV-associated cervical cancer and HPV-associated anal cancer are significantly increased in HIV-positive individuals.

The rates of both invasive anal squamous cell carcinoma and anal intraepithelial neoplasias are much higher in HIV-infected men. The incidence is significantly increased in men who practice receptive anal intercourse, with the incidence among homosexual and bisexual men with AIDS being 40% higher than the general population. These patients also usually have a prior history of HPV infection or active condyloma acuminatum. The HIV-positive males who have receptive anal intercourse and a previous history of perianal HPV must have anal Papanicolaou smears done on a regular basis for screening purposes.

Skin Cancers

Basal cell carcinoma can be aggressive.

Basal cell carcinomas are seen more frequently in HIV-infected individuals, and they can be extremely aggressive and recurrent after standard therapeutic modalities, such as electrodesiccation and curettage, cryotherapy, or simple surgical excision.

Squamous cell carcinomas are also reported to affect HIV-positive individuals more frequently. The incidence is particularly increased for squamous cell

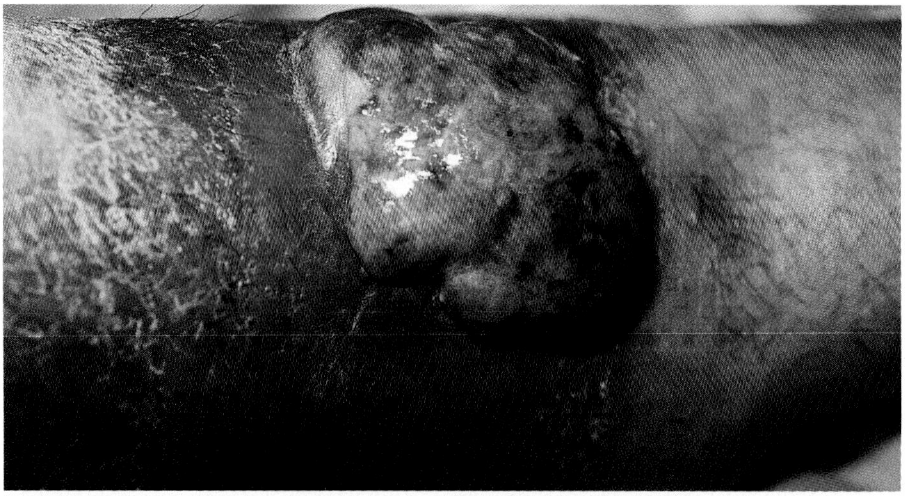

FIGURE 64–21 Cutaneous B-cell lymphoma. This wet, lobulated tumor mass could be easily misdiagnosed as tumor-stage Kaposi's sarcoma or bacillary angiomatosis. Skin biopsy with cultures and special stains is mandatory in all cutaneous tumors developing in HIV-positive individuals.

carcinoma affecting the oral mucosa, the conjunctiva, and the head/neck region. Just like basal cell carcinomas, squamous cell carcinomas recur in to up to 20% of the cases after standard treatment.

Squamous cell carcinomas more aggressive

There are reports of eruptive dysplastic nevi in HIV-infected individuals concomitantly with the onset of other HIV-related symptoms. A few reports on the clinical behavior of malignant melanomas in HIV-positive patients suggest a very poor prognosis and early dissemination, and there also appears to be an inverse correlation between the absolute CD4 counts and the tumor thickness.

Melanomas tend to be more aggressive.

Just like in the non–HIV-infected population, patients with HIV with a history of significant sun exposure in the past and very light complexion, such as skin types I and II, are at increased risk for developing basal cell and squamous cell carcinomas and melanoma.

Annotated Bibliography

Quinn TA. Acute primary HIV infection. JAMA 1997;278:58–62.

This article contains a good review of the clinical spectrum of the acute retroviral syndrome.

Myskowski PL, Ahkami R. Dermatologic complications of HIV infection. Med Clin North Am 1996;80:1415–1435.

This is a good review with a good bibliography.

Uthayakumar S, Nandwani R, Drinkwater T, et al. The prevalence of skin disease in HIV infection and its relationship to the degree of immunosuppression. Br J Dermatol 1997;137:595–598.

Reinhard Brodt H, Kamps BS, Gute P, et al. Changing incidence of AIDS-defining illnesses in the era of antiretroviral combination therapy. AIDS 1997;11:1731–1738.

Arnett FC, Reveille JD, Duvic M. Psoriasis and psoriatic arthritis associated with human immunodeficiency virus. Rheum Dis Clin North Am 1991;17:59–77.

Romani J, Puig L, Baselga E, et al. Reiter's syndrome-like pattern in AIDS-associated psoriasiform dermatitis. Int J Dermatol 1996;35:484–488.

Smith KJ, Skelton HG III, James WD, et al. Papular eruption of human immunodeficiency virus disease. Am J Dermatopathol 1991;13:445–451.

Magro CMJ, Crowson AN. Eosinophilic pustular follicular reaction: a paradigm of immune dysregulation. Int J Dermatol 1994;33:172–178.

Sadick NS, McNutt NS. Cutaneous hypersensitivity reactions in patients with AIDS. Int J Dermatol 1993;32:621–627.

Coopman SA, Johnson RA, Platt R, et al. Cutaneous disease and drug reaction in HIV infection. N Engl J Med 1993;328:1670–1674.

Carr A, Samaras K, Burton S. A syndrome of peripheral lipodystrophy, hyperlipidaemia and insulin resistance in patients receiving HIV protease inhibitors. AIDS 1998;12(7): F51–F58

Berger TG, Dahr A. Lichenoid photoeruptions in human immunodeficiency virus infection. Arch Dermatol 1994;130:609–613.

Pappert A, Gossman N, DeLeo V. Photosensitivity as the presenting illness in four patients with human immunodeficiency virus infection. Arch Dermatol 1994;130:618–623.

Gherardi R, Belec L, Mhiri C. The spectrum of vasculitis in human immunodeficiency virus-infected patients. Arthritis Rheum 1996;36:1164–1174.

Cavert W. Viral infections in human immunodeficiency virus disease. Med Clin North Am 1997;81:411–423.

Balfour HH, Benson C, Braun J, et al. Management of acyclovir-resistant herpes simplex and varicella-zoster virus infections. J Acquir Immune Defic Syndr Hum Retrovirol 1994;7(3):254–260.

A symposium: Human papillomavirus infection. Am J Med 1997;102(5A):1–37.

Gottlieb SL, Myskowski PL. Molluscum contagiosum. Int J Dermatol 1994;33:453–459.

Triantos D, Porter SR, Scully C. Oral hairy leukoplakia: clinicopathologic features, pathogenesis, diagnosis and clinical significance. Clin Infect Dis 1997;25:1392–1396.

Minamoto GY, Rosenberg AS. Fungal infections in patients with acquired immunodeficiency syndrome. Med Clin North Am 1997;81:381–407.

Cohen PR, Grossman ME. Recognizing skin lesions of systemic fungal infections in patients with AIDS. Am Fam Phys 1994;49(7):1627–1634.

Cockerell CJ. Bacillary angiomatosis and related diseases caused by *Rochalimaea*. J Am Acad Dermatol 1995;5:783–790.

Wasserheit JN. Epidemiological synergy—interrelationships between human immunodeficiency virus infection and other sexually transmitted diseases. Sex Transm Dis 1992;19:61–76.

Grosskurth H, Mosha F, Todd J, et al. Impact of improved treatment of sexually transmitted diseases on HIV infection in rural Tanzania: randomized controlled trial. Lancet 1997;346:530–536.

Martin JN, Ganem DE, Osmond DH, et al. Sexual transmission and the natural history of human herpesvirus 8 infection. N Engl J Med 1998;338:948–954.

Greenblatt RM. Kaposi's sarcoma and human herpesvirus-8. Infect Dis Clin North Am 1998;12:63–81.

Straus DJ. Human immunodeficiency virus-associated lymphomas. Med Clin North Am 1997;81:495–508.

Northfelt DW, Swift PS, Palefsky JM. Anal neoplasias. Hematol Oncol Clin North Am 1996;10:1177–1187.

Wang C, Brodland DG, Daniel Su WP. Skin cancers associated with acquired immunodeficiency syndrome. Mayo Clin Proc 1995;70:766–772.

These are a series of articles describing various cutaneous features of AIDS. All have excellent bibliographies.

CHAPTER 65

Graft-versus-Host Disease

Evan F. Farmer, M.D.

Graft-versus-host disease (GVHD) is a clinical syndrome characterized by cutaneous lesions, diarrhea, and liver dysfunction. Graft-versus-host disease is the primary complication of allogeneic bone marrow transplantation. Graft-versus-host disease also occurs as a complication of autologous or syngeneic bone marrow transplantation, blood transfusion, maternal-fetal transfusion, and, rarely, solid organ transplantation. The phenomenon of lymphocyte recovery shares histologic and clinical features with GVHD and probably represents an alternative pathway, analogous to autologous bone marrow transplantation, of developing GVHD. Our understanding of the pathogenesis, prevention, and treatment of GVHD has evolved over the past 50 years, from the early animal experiments to the routine use of stem cell infusions in outpatient settings.

Eruption of lymphocyte recovery shares features with GVHD.

Incidence

Graft-versus-host disease occurs in up to 50% of optimally matched and chemoprophylaxed sibling allogeneic bone marrow transplantations. In the autologous or syngeneic bone marrow transplantations, GVHD occurs in up to 10% of patients. Following stem cell infusions, GVHD occurs in 7 to 50% of patients. Graft-versus-host disease is a rare phenomenon as a complication of blood transfusion, maternal-fetal transfusion, and solid organ transplantation. The incidence of GVHD following blood transfusion is increased in populations that are more genetically heterogeneous. Graft-versus-host disease occurring in solid organ transplantation is due to the presence of passenger lymphocytes.

GVHD occurs with stem cell infusions.

Pathogenesis

In 1966, Billingham proposed three requirements for the development of GVHD: (1) transfer of viable immunocompetent cells to the host, (2) incompetence of the host to reject the transferred cells, and (3) antigenic disparity between the host and the transferred immunocompetent cells. The recognition of GVHD occurring after autologous or syngeneic bone marrow transplantation, as well as the phenomenon of lymphocyte recovery, suggested that antigen disparity between the host and the transferred immunocompetent cells was not an absolute requirement. Autologous and syngeneic GVHD and the phenomenon of lymphocyte recovery appear to be mediated by autoreactive immune cells that evade the normal negative selection process during immunologic reconstitution. (This appears to be a defect in peripheral suppression; for further discussion, see Chapter 4, “Theories of Autoimmune Disease Mechanisms.”) In acute GVHD, foreign or

CD4+ and CD8+ lymphocytes and TNF-α play roles.

autoreactive T lymphocytes appear to be the prime mediators of GVHD. Both CD4+ and CD8+ lymphocytes have been identified in the infiltrate. B lymphocytes do not appear to play a role, while the role of natural killer cells is unknown. Cytokines such as tumor necrosis factor alpha (TNF-α) and interleukin (IL)-1α play a significant role and probably function as the chemical mediators and sustainers of the disease. In chronic GVHD, CD8+ lymphocytes predominate in the infiltrate over CD4+ lymphocytes, suggesting that suppressor/cytotoxic T cells are playing a major role in the pathogenesis.

Clinical Features

Multiple different presentations of GVHD exist

Graft-versus-host disease clinically presents in three distinct but, at times, overlapping phases. The phases are generally related to the time elapsed after marrow or white blood cell infusion and have been labeled acute, chronic lichenoid, and chronic sclerodermoid. Two additional, relatively unusual phases have been recognized and labeled explosive and progressive. All of these phases are depicted on a timeline in Figure 65–1. The clinical features of the GVHD are similar, irrespective of the source of the lymphocytes, whether from marrow infusions, peripheral white cell infusions, or as passenger lymphocytes in solid organ transplantations.

Acute Graft-versus-Host Disease

Periungual erythema is characteristic.

Acute GVHD targets the epithelia of the skin, gastrointestinal tract, and the small intrahepatic bile ducts. The skin lesions are relatively characteristic in their appearance, symptoms, and distribution. Therefore, a clinical diagnosis can be made with a high degree of probability. The skin lesions almost always precede the systemic manifestations of GVHD but may develop simultaneously. It is unusual to have systemic manifestations of GVHD in the absence of skin involvement. The skin lesions of acute GVHD usually present as pruritic or burning erythematous macules or papules that involve the palms, soles, ears, neck, and upper back 15 to 40 days after marrow infusion. Periungual erythema is a characteristic finding (Figure 65–2). The timing of the skin eruption correlates with marrow recovery. The individual skin lesions may be localized to the hair follicle ostia or become widespread, resulting in the erythroderma. Severe cases may develop bullae, or large areas of skin may slough, resembling toxic epidermal necrolysis. Mild cases of acute GVHD tend to regress spontaneously, while severe cases have a poor prognosis. The clinical grading system of acute cutaneous GVHD is presented in Table 65–1. The differential diagnosis of acute cutaneous GVHD is predominantly limited to adverse drug reactions or viral exanthemas. The associated clinical features, chronologic timing of drug administration, and skin biopsy find-

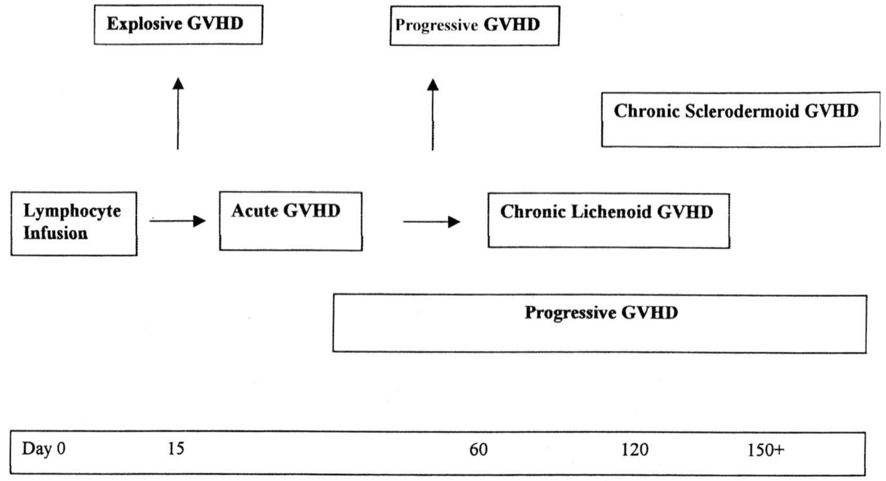

FIGURE 65–1 Clinical sequence of graft-versus-host disease.

ings help establish the most likely correct diagnosis. The timing of the skin eruption, the appearance of the lesions, the distribution of the lesions, and the relationship to marrow recovery are all very helpful factors favoring the diagnosis of acute GVHD over a drug reaction or a viral exanthema.

In acute GVHD, systemic manifestations predominantly involve the gastrointestinal tract and liver. Nausea, vomiting, abdominal pain, ileus, and diarrhea indicate gastrointestinal tract involvement. The volume of diarrhea may be several liters per day and often is bloody. Liver involvement is manifested by right upper abdominal pain and jaundice. Bilirubin and liver enzyme levels are elevated. Oral and ocular mucous membranes may be involved with erythema, pain, and ulcerations.

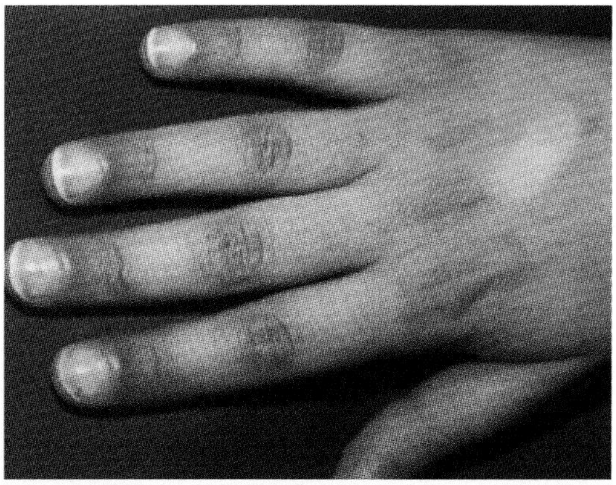

FIGURE 65–2 Acute graft-versus-host disease. This hand demonstrates the typical periungual erythema and erythema over the proximal interphalangeal joint.

Chronic Graft-versus-Host Disease

Chronic GVHD may occur as early as 40 days following marrow infusion but usually initially occurs between 60 and the 100 days. The first phase of chronic GVHD resembles lichen planus and has been labeled chronic lichenoid GVHD. The second phase of chronic GVHD usually but not necessarily, follows chronic lichenoid GVHD, and this phase resembles idiopathic scleroderma. This phase usually begins approximately 6 months following marrow infusion and is labeled chronic sclerodermoid GVHD.

Resembles lichen planus

Chronic Lichenoid Graft-versus-Host Disease

Chronic lichenoid GVHD is characterized by pruritic, violaceous, lichen planus–like papules often presenting on the palms, soles, and face and later becoming generalized (Figure 65–3). These lesions are indistinguishable from idiopathic lichen planus. (For further discussion of immunologic features, see Lichen Planus in Chapter 70, "Other Diseases.") Mucosal lesions involving the oral cavity are frequent, but these lichenoid lesions may also occur on the genitalia (Figure 65–4). Follicular lesions resulting in alopecia and lesions involving the nail with subsequent destruction of the nails also occur. Rarely, lichenoid lesions occur in a dermatomal distribution, suggesting a relationship to a prior herpes zoster infection. The skin lesions may persist for a long period of time or progress to chronic sclerodermoid GVHD. The lichenoid lesions resolve, leaving areas of hyperpigmentation and, sometimes, hypopigmentation or even depigmentation. Cutaneous scarring is an unusual sequelae.

Chronic Sclerodermoid Graft-versus-Host Disease

Chronic sclerodermoid GVHD is characterized by sclerosis of the skin, resembling scleroderma. The lesions may be localized or widespread (Figures 65–5 and 65–6). When widespread, the lesions tend to be quite symmetrical, and the color may vary from white to dark brown. The shoulders, antecubital fossae, hips, and thighs are frequent areas of involvement. When the sclerosis occurs over a joint,

Resembles localized and systemic sclerosis

Difficult to treat with a high mortality

TABLE 65–1 Clinical Grading of Acute Cutaneous Graft-versus-Host Disease

Grade	Clinical Lesions
1	Erythematous, macular, and papular rash involving < 25% of the body surface
2	Erythematous, macular, and papular rash involving 25–50% of the body surface
3	Erythroderma—defined as > 50% of the body surface involved
4	Blister formation spontaneous, usually with positive Nikolsky sign

Adapted from:
Glucksberg H, Storb R, Fefer A, et al. Clinical manifestations of graft-versus-host disease in human recipients of marrow from HLA-matched sibling donors. Transplantation 1974;18:295–304.

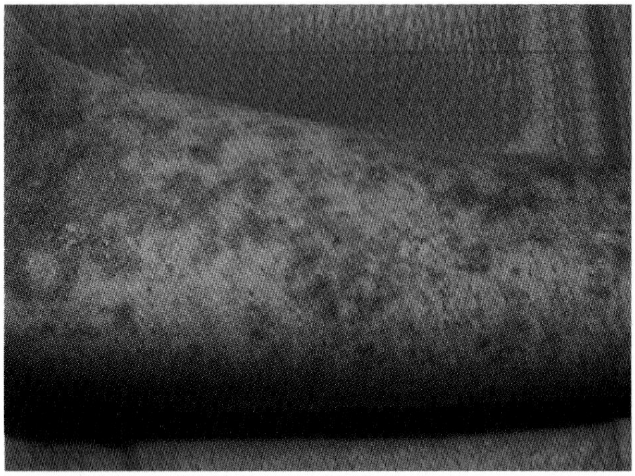

FIGURE 65–3 Chronic, lichenoid graft-versus-host disease. This forearm has discrete and confluent violaceous macules and papules.

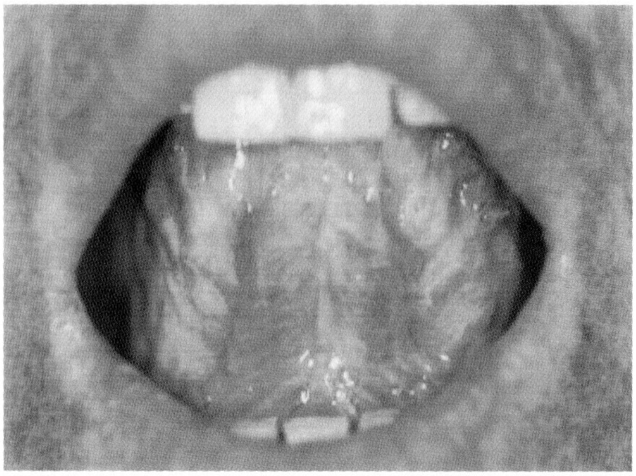

FIGURE 65–4 Chronic, lichenoid graft-versus-host disease. The under surface of the tongue shows leukoplakia on a violaceous background.

there is a high probability of decreased range of motion or even fixation of the joint. The sclerotic areas may break down to form ulcers or become secondarily infected. Chronic sclerodermoid GVHD resembles scleroderma but differs by the absence of Raynaud's phenomenon and the lack of acrosclerosis especially involving the fingertips. In severe chronic GVHD, mortality approaches 50%, and the survivors may experience severe disability. In some cases, the sclerosis tends to resolve spontaneously, but this may require months to years. Death is usually the sequela of infection or liver dysfunction.

Extracutaneous Involvement

In either chronic lichenoid or chronic sclerodermoid GVHD, systemic involvement may occur. The involved organs include the gastrointestinal tract, liver, lungs, lymphoid tissue, and musculoskeletal system. Involvement of the lymphoid system may result in lymphoid atrophy, with lymphopenia and increased risk of infection. At times, the manifestations of chronic GVHD resemble connective tissue diseases, especially systemic lupus erythematosus, scleroderma, and dermatomyositis.

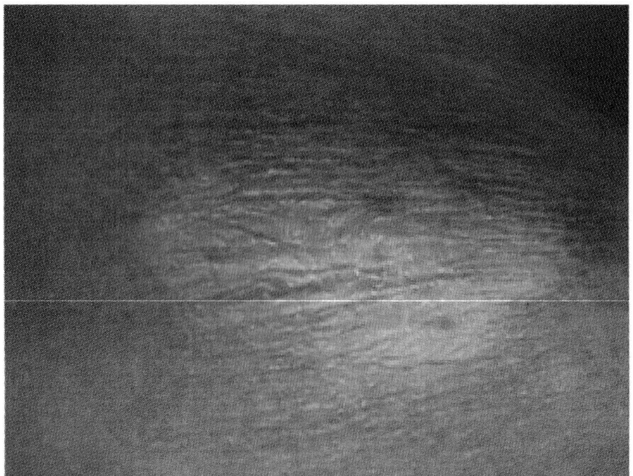

FIGURE 65–5 Chronic, sclerodermoid graft-versus-host disease. There is a solitary sclerotic plaque on the hip.

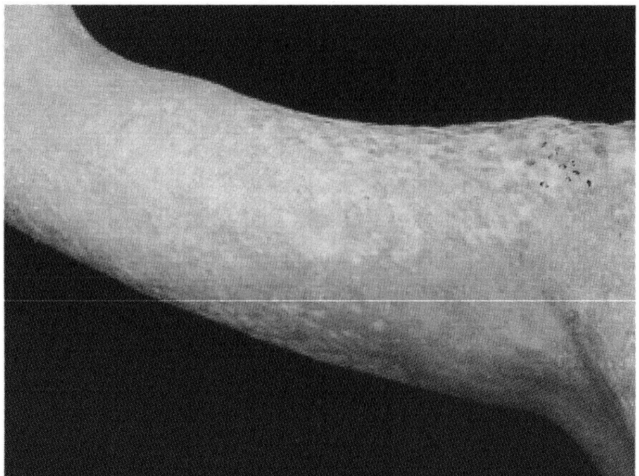

FIGURE 65–6 Chronic, sclerodermoid graft-versus-host disease. There is diffuse sclerosis with hypopigmentation involving the arm and shoulder.

Progressive Graft-versus-Host Disease

Patients with acute GVHD, instead of resolving their lesions, may progress directly to chronic lichenoid GVHD or erythroderma (Figure 65–7). These patients tend to have a more severe disease with a worse prognosis. These patients are also highly likely to subsequently develop chronic sclerodermoid GVHD.

Explosive Graft-versus-Host Disease

Occurs in three scenarios

Explosive or hyperacute GVHD may occur in three different scenarios. The first scenario occurs shortly after marrow infusion, usually within 1 week, and is characterized by severe generalized inflammation, fever, liver involvement, fluid retention, vascular leakage, and shock. These patients usually would have had infusion of non–HLA-identical marrow and would not have sufficient immunosuppression. However, hyperacute GVHD, in the first week after marrow infusion, has occurred in settings without these risk factors. The second scenario is precipitated by the abrupt withdrawal of immunosuppressive therapy in patients with severe acute GVHD, progressive GVHD, or lichenoid GVHD (Figure 65–8). In these settings, the clinical presentation is similar to that occurring 1 week after marrow infusion. The third scenario occurs with infusion of donor lymphocytes for treatment of relapsed leukemia. In any of these situations, the prognosis is grave, with a high probability of mortality.

Treatment

Prevention by donor marrow T-lymphocyte depletion or post-transplantation cyclosporine and methotrexate

Multiple strategies have been devised to prevent or attenuate the development of GVHD. These include T-cell depletion of the donor marrow, the use of marrow or peripheral blood stem cells rather than active lymphocytes as the infusion, pretransplantation irradiation of lymphoid tissue in the recipient, and post-transplantation immunosuppression with cyclosporine and methotrexate. These strategies have been moderately successful, but a balance is required to prevent GVHD while also preventing a relapse of the underlying leukemia.

Acute Graft-versus-Host Disease

The treatment of acute GVHD depends on the degree of severity. This chapter focuses only on the treatment of skin disease. A grading system has been developed on the basis of the extent of body surface area involved and the presence or absence of blister formation or denudation of the skin. See Table 65–1 for the grading system of skin disease.

For skin disease involving less than 25% of the body surface area, no treatment may be necessary, as in most cases, these lesions spontaneously resolve. The decision to withhold medication assumes that no gastrointestinal tract or liver involvement is occurring simultaneously. In patients with greater than 25% of the body surface area involved, with blister formation, or with denudation of the skin, therapy should be initiated as soon as possible. Consideration for therapy should be given for all grades greater than 1. In general, it is better to start with high-dose immunosuppression and then taper, rather than starting with a lower or medium dose and then increasing the dose because of lack of response. Most therapies are more effective in mild or moderate than in severe disease. Systemic glucocorticoids are considered to be the most effective and most rapidly acting agents. The initial

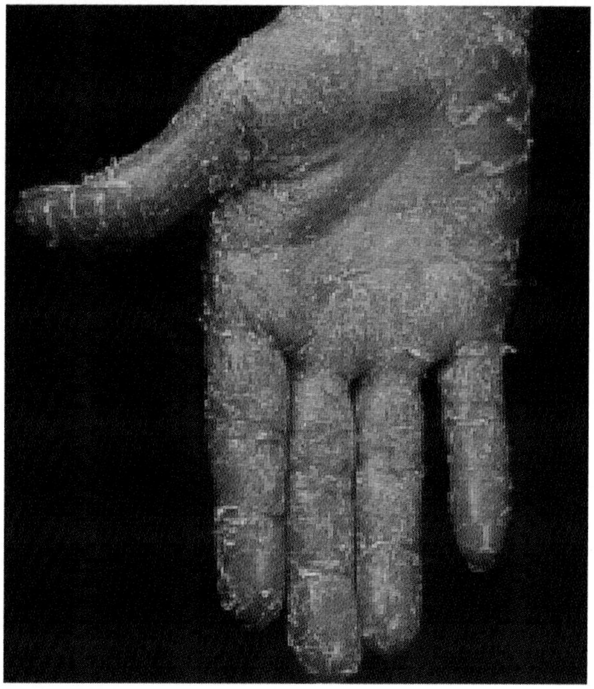

FIGURE 65–7 Progressive graft-versus-host disease. This patient has exfoliative dermatitis involving most of the body.

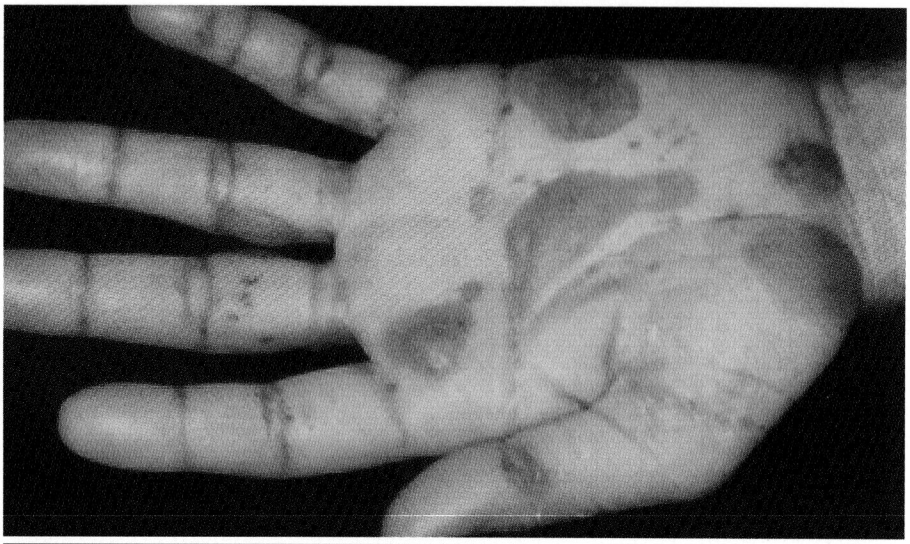

FIGURE 65–8 Explosive graft-versus-host disease. This patient abruptly stopped his medications while being treated for graft-versus-host disease and 7 days later developed widespread subepidermal blisters.

Prednisolone and cyclosporine are primary medications.

dose of methylprednisolone is commonly 2 mg per kg intravenously daily. The patient should respond within 96 hours by a decrease in symptoms and a cessation of new lesions. If the patient is responding, a taper can be started at this point and is usually a 25% dose reduction every 4 days as long as the patient continues to respond. If the patient does not respond, the dose can be held at that level for an additional 4 days. Switching the route of administration from intravenous to oral may be done at any time, depending on patient tolerance. If the dose of methylprednisolone cannot be reduced or the patient continues to worsen, other medications should be considered. The primary second drug is cyclosporine. Cyclosporine is usually given intravenously at a dose of 3 to 5 mg per kg per day. Other medications include antithymocyte globulin, FK 506, and mycophenolate mofetil. Phototherapy, especially psoralen and ultraviolet A (PUVA), has been used in some cases.

Chronic Graft-versus-Host Disease

Chronic Lichenoid Graft-versus-Host Disease

Prednisone and cyclosporine are primary medications. PUVA is a second choice.

Patients with limited disease may not require treatment, but close monitoring should be maintained to evaluate for extension of disease, the development of mucosal lesions, especially sicca syndrome, and progression to chronic sclerodermoid GVHD. Treatment of extensive chronic lichenoid GVHD decreases the chance of progression to widespread disease and to chronic sclerodermoid GVHD. Chronic GVHD generally does not require as high a dose of immunosuppression as acute GVHD but does require more prolonged therapy. Oral prednisolone is the most commonly used agent and generally is initiated at an oral dose of 1 mg per kg per day. The dose may be tapered after achieving a response, which usually takes 4 to 8 weeks. At this point, prednisolone may be given on an alternate-day basis and is usually continued for 6 to 9 months. Localized lichenoid lesions involving the skin or oral mucosa may be treated with a class I topical corticosteroid. Patients who do not respond to oral corticosteroids may require the addition of cyclosporine. Refractory chronic lichenoid GVHD has been successfully treated with PUVA or thalidomide.

Chronic Sclerodermoid Graft-versus-Host Disease

Prednisone and cyclosporine are primary medications.

Chronic sclerodermoid GVHD may respond to oral prednisolone. Cyclosporine has also been successfully given for chronic lichenoid GVHD. However, it does not respond as rapidly or as well. Thalidomide and mycophenolate mofetil have been successful in some refractory cases. Etretinate has been successful in diminishing the sclerosis in one uncontrolled series of refractory patients. The dose of etretinate varied between 0.5 and 1.0 mg per kg per day, depending on tolerance and response. The duration of treatment requires several months, and there may be a relapse once the etretinate is discontinued. Psoralen and ultraviolet A has been used successfully in some cases but has not been consistently effective. The degree of effectiveness of extracorporeal photochemotherapy remains to be established. In addition to medical therapy for chronic sclerodermoid GVHD, physical therapy to maintain mobility of joints is important. Ulceration and secondary infection are frequent complications and require good wound care, antibiotic therapy, minimizing of immunosuppression, and maintenance of immunoglobulin levels.

Thalidomide and etretinate are alternative choices.

Progressive Graft-versus-Host Disease

Since progressive GVHD shares features of acute and chronic GVHD, the treatment of progressive GVHD is initially the same as for acute GVHD. As the disease progresses, therapy is modified to a more chronic GVHD regimen.

Prednisolone and cyclosporine are primary medications.

Explosive Graft-versus-Host Disease

Since explosive GVHD is in reality hyperacute acute GVHD, the treatment of explosive GVHD is the same as for acute GVHD.

Prednisolone and cyclosporine are primary medications.

Annotated Bibliography

Aractingi S, Chosidow O. Cutaneous graft-versus-host disease. Arch Dermatol 1998;134: 602–612.

This review article discusses the clinical and histopathologic aspects, pathogenesis, and therapy of cutaneous graft-versus-host disease and incorporates 75 references.

Basara N, Blau WI, Romer E. Mycophenolate mofetil for the treatment of acute and chronic GVHD in bone marrow transplant patients. Bone Marrow Transplant 1998; 22:61–65.

This article presents the results from a single-center open trial of 24 patients with GVHD (acute = 17; chronic = 7) treated with 2 g daily of mycophenolate mofetil, in addition to variable doses of cyclosporine and prednisolone. Eleven of 17 patients with acute GVHD improved, while 3 of 7 patients with chronic GVHD improved.

Billingham RE. The biology of graft-versus-host reactions. Harvey Lect 1966;62:21–78.

This is Billingham's classic article.

Burdick JF, Vogelsang GB, Smith WJ, et al. Severe graft-versus-host disease in a liver-transplant recipient. N Engl J Med 1988;318:689–691.

This is a case report of graft-versus-host disease developing from passenger lymphocytes in the transplanted liver.

Darmstadt GL, Donnenberg AD, Vogelsang GB, et al. Clinical, laboratory, and histopathologic indicators of the development of progressive acute graft-versus-host disease. J Invest Dermatol 1992;99:397–402.

This article presents a retrospective study of 69 patients with cyclosporine-treated, allogeneic bone marrow transplants. The study demonstrated that monitoring of total bilirubin, stool output, extent of rash, and overall clinical stage of GVHD were the most useful prognostic indicators.

Fernandez-Herrera J, Valks R, Feal C, et al. Induction of hyperacute graft-vs-host disease after donor leukocyte infusions. Arch Dermatol 1999;135:304–308.

This is a case report of two patients who developed severe, hyperacute, fatal GVHD after treatment with donor leukocyte infusions and interferon alpha for relapse of leukemia.

Freemer CS, Farmer ER, Corio RL, et al. Lichenoid chronic graft-vs-host disease occurring in a dermatomal distribution. Arch Dermatol 1994;130:70–72.

This is a case report of two patients who developed linear chronic lichenoid GVHD. The potential role of varicella-zoster virus infection is discussed.

Friedman KJ, LeBoit PE, Farmer ER. Acute follicular graft-vs-host reaction. A distinct clinicopathologic presentation. Arch Dermatol 1988;124:688–691.

This is a case report of three patients who developed acute GVHD primarily affecting the hair follicles.

Gilliam AC, Whitaker-Menezes D, Korngold R, et al. Apoptosis is the predominant form of epithelial target cell injury in acute experimental graft-versus-host disease. J Invest Dermatol 1996;107:377–383.

In a murine model of acute GVHD, the authors demonstrated a bimodal appearance of apoptosis: one preceding the appearance of lymphocyte infiltration in the tissue, and the other correlating with the appearance of lymphocytes. This study establishes a central role for apoptosis in the pathogenesis of GVHD.

Glucksberg H, Storb R, Fefer A, et al. Clinical manifestations of graft-versus-host disease in human recipients of marrow from HLA-matched sibling donors. Transplantation 1974;18:295–304.

This is a classic article describing the Seattle experience with bone marrow transplantation.

Herrera C, Torres A, Garcia-Castellano JM, et al. Prevention of graft-versus-host disease in high risk patients by depletion of CD4+ and reduction of CD8+ lymphocytes in the marrow graft. Bone Marrow Transplant 1999;23:443–450.

This article presents a retrospective study of 30 patients with various hematologic malignancies treated with depletion of CD4+ lymphocytes and partial depletion of CD8+ lymphocytes in an attempt to prevent GVHD. Six of 30 patients developed acute GVHD, and no patients had severe GVHD. Post-transplantation cyclosporine and methotrexate were also used in the protocol.

Hood AF, Vogelsang GB, Black LP, et al. Acute graft-vs-host disease. Development following autologous and syngeneic bone marrow transplantation. Arch Dermatol 1987;123:745–750.

This article presents a retrospective study of 96 autologous and 19 syngeneic bone marrow transplant patients from one institution. Seven of the autologous transplant patients and 2 of the syngeneic transplant patients developed acute GVHD.

Jampel RM, Farmer ER, Vogelsang G, et al. PUVA therapy for chronic cutaneous graft-vs-host disease. Arch Dermatol 1991;127:1673–1678.

This article presents a retrospective study of 6 patients treated with PUVA for chronic GVHD (lichenoid = 5; sclerodermoid = 1). Five of the 6 patients with chronic lichenoid GVHD showed improvement, and there was complete clearance in 3. The one patient with chronic sclerodermoid GVHD did not improve.

Johnson ML, Farmer ER. Graft-versus-host reactions in dermatology. J Am Acad Dermatol 1998;38:369–392.

This review article discusses the clinical and histopathologic aspects, pathogenesis, and therapy of cutaneous graft-versus-host disease and incorporates 272 references.

Kennedy MS, Deeg HJ, Storb R, et al. Treatment of acute graft-versus-host disease after allogeneic marrow transplantation. Randomized study comparing corticosteroids and cyclosporine. Am J Med 1985;78:978–983.

This article presents the results of a two-arm, randomly assigned study comparing cyclosporine (12–15 mg/kg/d orally or 3–5 mg/kg/d intravenously) versus methylprednisolone (2 mg/kg/d intravenously) in the treatment of acute GVHD. The results indicated cyclosporine was comparable in efficacy with methylprednisolone.

Leskinen R, Taskinen E, Volin L, et al. Immunohistology of skin and rectum biopsies in bone marrow transplant recipients. APMIS 1992;100:1115–1122.

This article presents a retrospective study of 39 skin biopsies and 30 rectal biopsies from bone marrow transplant recipients, with the biopsies having been obtained before transplantation, after transplantation without GVHD, during acute GVHD, and during chronic GVHD. CD4+ and CD8+ lymphocytes were found in both acute and chronic cutaneous GVHD. Natural killer cells were also seen in most biopsies of acute GVHD.

Mahmoud H, Fahmy O, Kamel A, et al. Peripheral blood vs bone marrow as a source for allogeneic hematopoietic stem cell transplantation. Bone Marrow Transplant 1999;24:355–358.

The authors compared 15 patients treated with peripheral blood stem cell infusion with 15 patients treated with allogeneic bone marrow transplantation for various hematologic malignancies. The patients treated with peripheral blood stem cell infusion had a faster hematopoietic recovery and a decreased incidence of acute GVHD (6.7% versus 46.7%).

Marcellus DC, Altomonte VL, Farmer ER, et al. Etretinate therapy for refractory sclerodermatous chronic graft-versus-host disease. Blood 1999;93:66–70.

This article presents a retrospective study of 27 patients with chronic sclerodermoid GVHD refractory to standard therapy who were subsequently treated with etretinate. Twenty showed improvement, including softening of the skin, flattening of cutaneous lesions, increased range of motion, and improved performance status.

Martin PJ, Schoch G, Fisher L, et al. A retrospective analysis of therapy for acute graft-versus-host disease: initial treatment. Blood 1990;76:1464–1472.

This article presents results of therapy in 740 patients with grades II-IV acute GVHD after allogeneic marrow transplantation. Graft-versus-host disease prophylaxis using cyclosporine combined with methotrexate was associated with favorable GVHD treatment outcome, compared with prophylaxis with either agent alone, and treatment with glucocorticoids or cyclosporine was more successful than treatment with antithymocyte globulin. Results of this analysis indicate that glucocorticoids represent the best initial therapy available for treatment of acute GVHD.

Martin PJ, Schoch G, Fisher L, et al. A retrospective analysis of therapy for acute graft-versus-host disease: secondary treatment. Blood 1991;77:1821–1828.

This article presents the results of secondary therapy in 427 patients with acute GVHD who did not have a durable satisfactory response after primary treatment. The highest complete response rate with secondary therapy (23%) was seen when GVHD recurred during the taper phase of primary glucocorticoid treatment and was managed by increasing the dose of glucocorticoids.

Severe dysfunction in the skin, liver, and gut at the beginning of treatment was associated both with a decreased likelihood of complete response and an increased treatment failure rate.

Martin RW III, Farmer ER, Altomonte VL, et al. Lichenoid graft-vs-host disease in an autologous bone marrow transplant recipient. Arch Dermatol 1995;131:333–335.

This is a case report of chronic lichenoid GVHD involving the skin and oral mucosa developing in an autologous bone marrow transplant patient.

Owsianowski M, Gollnick H, Siegert W, et al. Successful treatment of chronic graft-versus-host disease with extracorporeal photopheresis. Bone Marrow Transplant 1994;14:845–848.

This is a case report of a patient with chronic sclerodermoid GVHD successfully treated with extracorporeal photopheresis.

Ratanatharathorn V, Nash RA, Przepiorka D, et al. Phase III study comparing methotrexate and tacrolimus (Prograf, FK506) with methotrexate and cyclosporine for graft-versus-host disease prophylaxis after HLA-identical sibling bone marrow transplantation. Blood 1998;92:2303–2314.

This article presents the results of a phase III open-label, randomized, multicenter trial comparing tacrolimus/methotrexate with cyclosporine/methotrexate for GVHD prophylaxis after HLA-identical sibling marrow transplantation in patients with hematologic malignancy. These results show the superiority of tacrolimus/methotrexate over cyclosporine/methotrexate in the prevention of grade II–IV acute GVHD, with no difference in disease-free or overall survival in patients with nonadvanced disease. The survival disadvantage in patients with advanced disease receiving tacrolimus warrants further investigation.

Schmitz N, Bacigalupo A, Hasenclever D, et al. Allogeneic bone marrow transplantation vs filgrastim-mobilised peripheral blood progenitor cell transplantation in patients with early leukaemia: first results of a randomised multicentre trial of the European Group for Blood and Marrow Transplantation. Bone Marrow Transplant 1998;21: 995–1003.

This article presents the results from a multicenter trial involving 20 transplantation centers from 10 countries. Hematopoietic stem cells were obtained either from the bone marrow of 33 sibling donors or from the peripheral blood of 33 such donors after administration of filgrastim. Sixteen patients (48%) transplanted with bone marrow and 18 patients (54%) transplanted with PBPC developed acute GVHD of grades II to IV; acute GVHD of grades III or IV developed in 6 (18%) and 7 (21%) patients, respectively. The incidence of moderate to severe acute GVHD, transplant-related mortality, and leukemia-free survival did not show striking differences.

Takeda H, Mitsuhashi Y, Kondo S, et al. Toxic epidermal necrolysis possibly linked to hyperacute graft-versus-host disease after allogeneic bone marrow transplantation. J Dermatol 1997;24:635–641.

This is a case report of toxic epidermal necrolysis developing 8 days after bone marrow transplantation.

Vigorito AC, Azevedo WM, Marques JF, et al. A randomised, prospective comparison of peripheral blood progenitor cell transplantation and allogeneic bone marrow and in the treatment of haematological malignancies. Bone Marrow Transplant 1998;22: 1145–1151.

This article presents the results of a prospective, randomized study comparing peripheral blood progenitor cell transplantation and allogeneic bone marrow in the treatment of 37 patients with hematologic malignancies. The inci-

dence of acute and chronic GVHD was similar in both groups, but the severity of chronic GVHD was higher with peripheral blood progenitor cell transplantation.

Vogelsang GB, Farmer ER, Hess AD, et al. Thalidomide for the treatment of chronic graft-versus-host disease. N Engl J Med 1992;326:1055–1058.

This article presents the results of a retrospective study of 23 patients with chronic GVHD refractory to conventional treatment and 21 patients with "high-risk" chronic GVHD. A complete response was observed in 14 patients, a partial response in 12 patients, and no response in 18. Side effects were minor, most notably sedation in almost all patients.

Vogelsang GB, Wolff D, Altomonte V, et al. Treatment of chronic graft-versus-host disease with ultraviolet irradiation and psoralen (PUVA). Bone Marrow Transplant 1996;17: 1061–1067.

This article presents a retrospective study of treatment of 35 patients with refractory chronic GVHD and 5 patients presenting with high-risk chronic GVHD. Overall, 31 of 40 patients improved on PUVA treatment. Sixteen patients achieved a complete response to PUVA added to their GVHD regimen. Four of the 15 partial responders had complete resolution of cutaneous GVHD but persistence of other systemic manifestations. The remaining partial responders had at least a 50% improvement in GVHD.

Wingard JR, Piantadosi S, Vogelsang GB, et al. Predictors of death from chronic graft-versus-host disease after bone marrow transplantation. Blood 1989;74:1428–1435.

This article presents a retrospective study of 85 patients with chronic GVHD to determine risk factors for death. In a multivariate proportional hazard analysis, three baseline factors emerged as independent predictors of death: progressive presentation (chronic GVHD following acute GVHD without resolution of acute GVHD [hazard ratio of 4.1, 95% Cl = 2.1 to 7.8]); lichenoid changes on skin histology (hazard ratio of 2.2, 95% Cl = 1.1 to 4.3), and elevation of serum bilirubin greater than 1.2 mg per dL (hazard ratio = 2.1, 95% Cl = 1.1 to 4.1).

CHAPTER 66

Cutaneous Manifestations of Drug Reactions: Drug Eruptions

Antoinette F. Hood, M.D.

Drugs are ubiquitous in our North American society. In a society focused on health and wellness, it is rare to encounter a person who is not taking a prescription medication, over-the-counter drug, or alternative/herbal preparation for treatment of a disease process or symptom, replacement therapy, or prophylaxis. In the United States, millions of people regularly ingest aspirin and other anti-inflammatory drugs, antibiotics, hormones, cardiovascular drugs, and psychopharmacologic drugs, to mention just a few. A recent interest in vitamin supplementation and herbal therapies, so-called alternative medicines, has added another dimension to the already complex issue.

Incidence and Prevalence

60,000 to 90,000 inpatients/year develop cutaneous drug reactions.

The number of outpatients developing cutaneous drug reactions is probably much higher.

The exact incidence of adverse reactions to these and other medications is unknown. According to the Boston Collaborative Drug Surveillance Program, 30% of medical service inpatients had one or more complications as a result of drugs administered during hospitalization; 2 to 3% of the patients developed a "skin rash." Among hospitalized patients, the incidence of cutaneous reactions per course of therapy has been reported to be 3 per 1,000. It has been estimated that 60,000 to 90,000 inpatients develop cutaneous drug reactions each year. Fortunately, these reactions are rarely life threatening; nonetheless, they may produce significant morbidity and expense, especially in the form of prolonged hospitalization.

The Boston Collaborative Drug Surveillance Program reflects the incidence of drug reactions on an inpatient medical service. These figures may not accurately reflect the problem in other units of the hospital, such as surgery, pediatrics, and oncology. We surveyed an oncology ward in the Johns Hopkins Medical Institutions for a 2-month period and discovered that 50% of the patients developed one or more cutaneous eruptions that were clinically consistent with drug eruptions. These reactions often resulted in great discomfort to the patient and necessitated complex therapy manipulations on the part of the attending physicians.

Even less is known about the frequency of cutaneous reactions occurring in an outpatient setting. Attempts to monitor drug reactions are obviously fraught with difficulties. However, at one time, the American Academy of Dermatology made an important effort to do this by sponsoring the Adverse Drug Reaction Reporting System. This system permitted dermatologists to share their experience with adverse cutaneous reactions to drugs and to obtain information about such reactions as contained in the registry and in the medical literature.

Definition

An adverse cutaneous reaction produced by a drug is any unintended or undesired change in the structure or function of the skin, mucous membranes, or adnexae following the administration of a medication for any purpose.

Classification

Adverse drug reactions can be divided simplistically into two major categories: type A reactions, which are normal but augmented responses; and type B reactions, which are totally abnormal or bizarre responses. Type A reactions are pharmacologically predictable and dose dependent. They generally are of high incidence and morbidity but low mortality. Examples of type A reactions in the skin include aspirin-induced purpura, mucositis, and alopecia caused by antimitotic chemotherapeutic drugs, striae associated with corticosteroid administration, and perhaps demeclocycline-induced phytotoxicity. Type B (bizarre or idiosyncratic) reactions are less common, are pharmacologically unpredictable, and are not dose dependent. They may be produced by a variety of chemicals, including the active constituent in the medication, decomposition or byproducts of the active ingredient, or the various additives, solubilizers, stabilizers, and colorizers in a preparation. Most of the cutaneous reactions that we consider to be induced by drugs, whether they are immunologically or nonimmunologically mediated, fall into this category.

Type A reactions:
- *normal but augmented*
- *predictable*
- *dose dependent*

Type B reactions:
- *abnormal or bizarre*
- *pharmacologically unpredictable*
- *ot dose dependent*

Few controlled or stringent studies have been done on drug reactions, and for practical purposes, it is not convenient to categorize them by etiology. Traditionally, drug reactions are classified morphologically. In terms of the frequency of types of drug rashes, the morbilliform pattern is seen most commonly, followed by urticarial eruptions, fixed drug eruptions, erythema multiforme, and others. There is a clinical dictum that states that any drug may produce any reaction, and although this may be true, it is also accepted that certain drugs are more likely to produce particular morphologic cutaneous reactions than are others. Table 66–1 lists the various types of drug reactions and some of the more common drugs responsible for the eruptions.

Drug eruptions are classified by morphologic pattern.

Pathogenesis

The pathobiology of most cutaneous drug reactions is not well understood; the overused terms "hypersensitivity" and "allergic" should be limited to describing reactions that are immunologically mediated or those that can reasonably be presumed to be immunologically mediated. True allergic reactions usually affect a small percentage of the population receiving the drug, require a prior exposure or latent period for the development of an immune response, can occur at subtherapeutic or very low doses, and usually simulate other known hypersensitivity reactions. Examples of cutaneous allergic drug reactions are listed in Table 66–2.

The term "allergic" drug eruption should be restricted to reactions with known immunologic mechanisms.

There is increasing evidence that many drug reactions, including erythema multiforme, toxic epidermal necrolysis, lichenoid reactions, systemic lupus erythematosus (SLE)-like reactions, and some morbilliform reactions, involve T-lymphocyte reactions against altered self.

Rashes of unknown etiology but which are presumed to be immune mediated include morbilliform-exanthematous eruptions, fixed drug eruptions, erythema multiforme, toxic epidermal necrolysis, exfoliative erythroderma, and erythema nodosum.

TABLE 66–1 Drug-Induced Cutaneous Reactions

- Acneiform eruptions
  - Cyanocobalamin (vitamin B_{12})
  - Dactinomycin
  - Halogens (bromides, iodides)
  - Hormones (ACTH, androgens, corticosteroids, oral contraceptives)
  - Isoniazid (INH)
  - Lithium
  - Phenytoin
- Alopecia
  - Allopurinol
  - Amphetamines
  - Anticoagulants (coumarin, heparin)
  - Antithyroid drugs
  - Chemotherapeutic agents
  - Heavy metals
  - Hormones (androgens, oral contraceptives)
  - Hypocholesterolemic drugs
  - Retinoids
- Eczematous eruptions
  - Ampicillin
  - Chlorabutanol, chloral hydrate
  - Diphenhydramine (Caladryl, Benadryl)
  - Disulfiram (Antabuse)
  - Ethylenediamine, aminophylline, antihistamines
  - Iodine, iodides
  - Neomycin sulfate, streptomycin, kanamycin
  - Para-amino aromatic benzenes, para-aminobenzoic acid, sulfonamides, tolbutamide
  - Penicillin
- Erythema multiforme
  - Allopurinol
  - Barbiturates
  - Chlorpropamide
  - Griseofulvin
  - Hydantoins
  - Nonsteroidal anti-inflammatory agents
  - Penicillin
  - Phenothiazines
  - Sulfonamides
  - Thiazides
- Erythema nodosum
  - All-*trans*-retinoic acid
  - Codeine
  - Halogens (bromides, iodides)
  - Oral contraceptives
  - Penicillin
  - Salicylates
  - Sulfonamides
- Exfoliative
  - Allopurinol
  - Carbamazepine
  - Gold salts
  - Hydantoins
  - Para-aminosalicylic acid
  - Phenylbutazone
  - Streptomycin
  - Sulfonamides
- Fixed drug eruptions
  - Allopurinol
  - Barbiturates
  - Chlordiazepoxide
  - Naproxen
  - Nonsteroidal anti-inflammatory agents
  - Phenolphthalein
  - Phenacetin
  - Sulindac
  - Sulfonamides
  - Tetracyclines
- Lichenoid and lichen planus–eruptions
  - Antimalarials
  - Captopril
  - Chlordiazepoxide
  - Gold salts
  - Hydroxyurea
  - Para-aminosalicylic acid
  - Penicillamine
  - Phenothiazine
  - Quinidine
  - Tetracycline
  - Thiazides
- Photosensitivity eruptions
  - Amiodarone
  - Griseofulvin
  - Nonsteroidal anti-inflammatory agents
  - Phenothiazine
  - Sulfonamides
  - Sulfonylureas
  - Tetracyclines
  - Thiazides
- Morbilliform/exanthematous
  - Allopurinol
  - Antibiotics
  - Anticonvulsants
  - Barbiturates
  - Benzodiazepines
  - Captopril
  - Chlorpropamide
  - Gold salts
  - Isoniazid
  - Nonsteroidal anti-inflammatory agents
  - Para-aminosalicylic acid
  - Penicillamine
  - Phenothiazine
  - Quinidine
  - Thiazide diuretics
- Urticaria
  - Dextran
  - Enzymes (L-asparaginase)
  - Indomethacin
  - Nonsteroidal anti-inflammatory agents
  - Opiates
  - Penicillin and related antibiotics
  - Polymyxin
  - Salicylates
  - Sulfonamides
  - Radiocontrast media
- Vasculitis
  - Allopurinol
  - Cimetidine
  - Gold salts
  - Hydantoins
  - Nonsteroidal anti-inflammatory agents
  - Penicillin
  - Phenothiazine
  - Sulfonamides
  - Thiazides
  - Thiouracils

ACTH = adrenocorticotropic hormone.

Clinical Features

deShazo and Kemp have divided the clinical features of adverse drug reactions into three main categories: multiple organ system patterns, patterns of cutaneous reactions, and other patterns.

Multiple Organ System Patterns

Anaphylaxis

Anaphylaxis is a life-threatening immunologic reaction (immunoglobulin E [IgE] mediated) manifesting as pruritus, urticaria, angioedema, and respiratory, gastrointestinal, and cardiovascular symptoms. This systemic reaction usually

TABLE 66–2 Allergic (Immunologically Mediated) Drug Eruptions*

Type	Immunologic Mechanisms	Clinical Expression in Skin	Laboratory Testing
Type I: anaphylactic	IgE-mediated reactions to allergic haptens; involve mast cell activation and subsequent release of histamine, leukotrienes, and eosinophil-chemotactic factors of anaphylaxis; neutrophil chemotactic factors, platelet-activating factor, serotonin, and kinins may be involved.	Urticaria Angioedema Transient cold urticaria Generalized pruritus	Radioallergoabsorbent test (RAST) Enzyme-linked immunosorbent assay (ELISA)
Type II: antibody-mediated (cytotoxic) injury	IgG or IgM antibodies activate complement through the classic pathway; under certain conditions antigens and antibodies localized on circulating erythrocytes, leukocytes, or platelets cause drug-induced, antibody-dependent lysis of these cells.	Thrombocytopenic reactions	Skin testing
Type III: antigen-antibody immune complex	IgG or IgM antibodies form circulating immune complexes with antigen and complement, activating complement-derived chemotactic factors and producing localized tissue inflammation.	Serum sickness Leukocytoclastic vasculitis Drug-induced systemic lupus erythematosus	Direct immunofluorescence performed on biopsy specimen
Type IV: cell-mediated injury	Sensitized T lymphocytes react with allergen and thereby generate lymphokines.	Allergic contact dermatitis Photoallergic reactions Granuloma formation following topical use of zirconium	Lymphocyte transformation Patch test

*Based on the C'oombs and Gell classification.
Ig = immunoglobin.

begins minutes to hours after administration of a drug. The most common causes of fatal drug-induced anaphylactic shock are radiocontrast media, antibiotics, and extracts of allergens. Anaphylaxis is unlikely to occur with a medication that is given continuously over a long period of time; intermittent administration, on the other hand, may predispose to anaphylaxis. The principal causes of anaphylaxis are antibiotics (particularly penicillin) and radiocontrast media.

Drug Reactions due to Histamine Release

Mast cell release by vancomycin may produce a red-man syndrome.

Drugs such as opiates, radiocontrast media, and thiamine pharmacologically induce release of mast cell products that produce reactions indistinguishable from IgE-mediated allergic reactions. Other drugs such as vancomycin can directly stimulate the mast cell to release histamine. This can produce a dose-dependent "red-man syndrome" with generalized pruritus, diffuse erythema, and a deep burning sensation. Altering the infusion rate of vancomycin may reduce or eliminate the reaction completely.

Erythema Multiforme/Stevens-Johnson Syndrome

Erythema mutliforme minor
Erythema multiforme major (Stevens-Johnson syndrome)

It has been estimated that drugs cause 10 to 20% of cases of erythema multiforme. Cutaneous lesions of erythema multiforme minor include macular, papular, and urticarial lesions as well as the pathognomonic target, or iris, lesions (Figure 66–1). The eruption is symmetrical and has a predilection for the distal extremities. Lesions may involve the palms or trunk. When the oral or genital mucous membranes are involved, the disorder is called erythema multiforme major or Stevens-Johnson syndrome (Figure 66–2). Mucosal erosions and ulcerations may produce considerable morbidity. Attempts at clinically and histologically differentiating erythema multiforme major/Stevens-Johnson syndrome and toxic epidermal necrolysis have not been uniformly successful. The list of drugs implicated in the cause of erythema multiforme is long and includes antibiotics, antifungals, nonsteroidal anti-inflammatory drugs (NSAIDs), anticonvulsants, psychotropics, and antihypertensive agents.

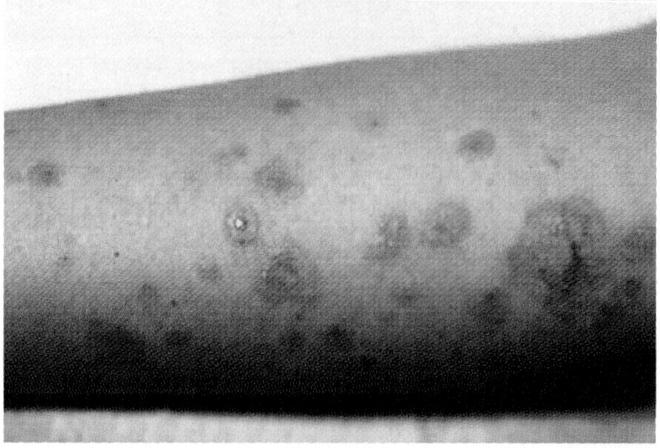

FIGURE 66–1 Erythema multiforme minor. Classic target lesions on the arm. (Courtesy of Tsu-Yi Chuang, M.D., M.P.H.)

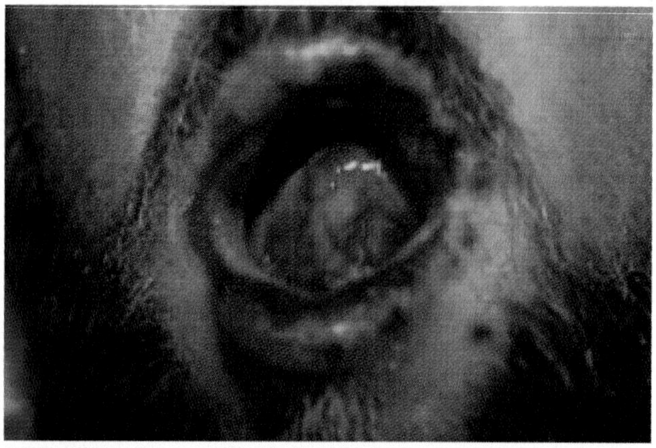

FIGURE 66–2 Erythema multiforme major/Stevens-Johnson syndrome with mucosal involvement. (Courtesy of Tsu-Yi Chuang, M.D., M.P.H.)

Toxic Epidermal Necrolysis

This important, life-threatening disorder is discussed in detail in Chapter 67, "Toxic Epidermal Necrolysis."

Hypersensitivity Syndromes

Hypersensitivity reaction to anticonvulsants:
- *rash*
- *fever*
- *lymphadenopathy*
- *hepatitis, nephritis*
- *leukocytosis*

Hypersensivity reactions to anticonvulsant therapy are distinctive and potentially life threatening. Estimated to occur as frequently as 1 per 1,000 patients treated with phenytoin, carbamazepine, or phenobarbital, these reactions typically begin within 1 to 3 weeks of initiation of therapy. Clinical manifestations include fever, an erythematous papular eruption, generalized lymphadenopathy, hepatitis, nephritis, and leukocytosis with atypical circulating lymphocytes. The reaction results from an inherited deficiency of epoxide hydroxylase, an enzyme required for the metabolism of intermediates formed by cytochrome p450. Allopurinol and sulfasalazine may cause a similar reaction.

Patterns of Cutaneous Drug Reactions

Some of the more common cutaneous patterns associated with drug reactions will be discussed here. It should be noted that the morphology of the cutaneous reaction does not usually identify the drug causing the particular reaction; widely disparate drugs may cause similar-appearing skin eruptions. Secondly, although repeated administration of a particular drug usually provokes the same reaction in an individual patient, this is not entirely predictable, and occasionally different reactions may be produced. And last, one drug may produce markedly different reactions in different individuals.

Morbilliform/Macular-Papular/Exanthematous Eruptions

Morbilliform eruptions are most common.

Eruption may occur up to 2 weeks after medicine is initiated.

This is the most frequently encountered form of drug rash. Individual lesions are bright-red blanchable macules or papules that may coalesce to form large confluent patches or plaques. The lesions are widely distributed and generally symmetrical and usually involve the trunk, extremities, and often the palms and soles (Figure 66–3). Purpuric lesions may occur, especially on the legs; an erosive stomatitis may develop. Fever and eosinophilia are often present; pruritus is common but not invariable. The eruption typically begins 2 to 3 days after the offending medication is begun; however, some antibiotics and allopurinol may induce eruptions that do not appear until 2 weeks after administration of the agent. Continued administration of the offending medication may result in a generalized eruption and exfoliative erythroderma, although occasionally the eruption subsides despite continuation of the medication. It is not possible to identify the offending agent by the appearance of the eruption. Common causes of morbilliform eruptions include β-lactam antibiotics, sulfonamides, anticonvulsants, allopurinol, and NSAIDs. Morbilliform eruptions occur more frequently with ampicillin than with other penicillins. Exanthematous eruptions occur more commonly in certain populations: women have a higher incidence of this type of reaction than men; 50 to 80% of patients with Epstein-Barr virus infection who receive ampicillin develop a morbilliform rash; human immunodeficiency virus (HIV)-infected individuals taking sulfonamides, particularly trimethoprim-sulfamethoxazole, have an unusually high reaction rate.

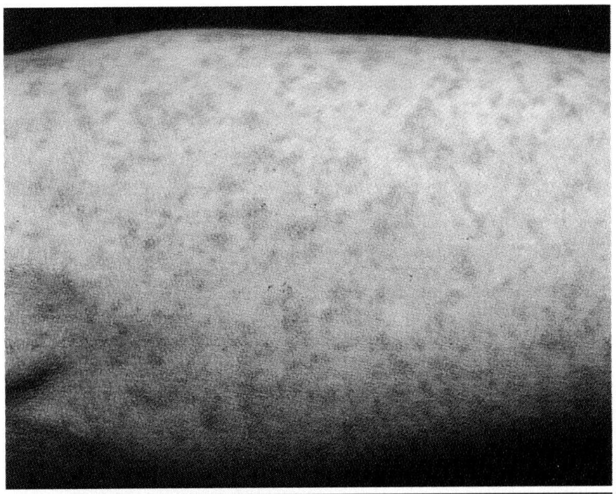

FIGURE 66–3 Morbilliform eruption on the arm due to trimethoprim-sulfamethoxazole.

Urticaria and Angioedema

The second most common drug-induced reaction after morbilliform eruptions is urticaria. Immunoglobin E–mediated urticaria occurs within minutes to hours of administration of the drug; urticarial lesions associated with serum sickness (actually urticaria-like vasculitis) occur 7 to 10 days after administration of the offending agent. Individual lesions are blanchable, last less than 24 hours, and are pruritic (Figure 66–4). The lesions resolve rapidly when the drug is discontinued. Angioedema involves the deeper dermis and subcutis and is seen less frequently than urticaria. Agents most frequently implicated as a cause of urticaria are antibiotics (particularly penicillin), radiocontrast media, NSAIDs, and opiates. Opiates, radiocontrast media, dextran, and polymyxin may produce urticaria through either complement activation or by direct stimulation of mast cells and basophils.

Urticaria occurs minutes to hours after administration of drug.

Vasculitis

Drug-induced leukocytoclastic vasculitis (LCV) presents as palpable and nonpalpable purpura that is clinically indistinguishable from idiopathic LCV or that produced by infection or systemic disease (Figure 66–5). The reaction may also involve internal organs, particularly the heart, liver, and kidneys. The lesions usually resolve when the medicine is discontinued. The presumed mechanism is an immune complex–mediated reaction. Drugs most frequently implicated are the penicillins, sulfonamides, and allopurinol.

Vasculitis may involve internal organs.

Exfoliative Dermatitis

Exfoliative dermatitis or erythroderma caused by drugs is indistinguishable from exfoliative dermatitis caused by primary skin disorders. The eruption begins with localized erythema that gradually spreads to involve the entire body (Figure

Exfoliative dermatitis may result in:
- *temperature fluctuation*
- *fluid and electrolyte imbalance*
- *right ventricular failure*

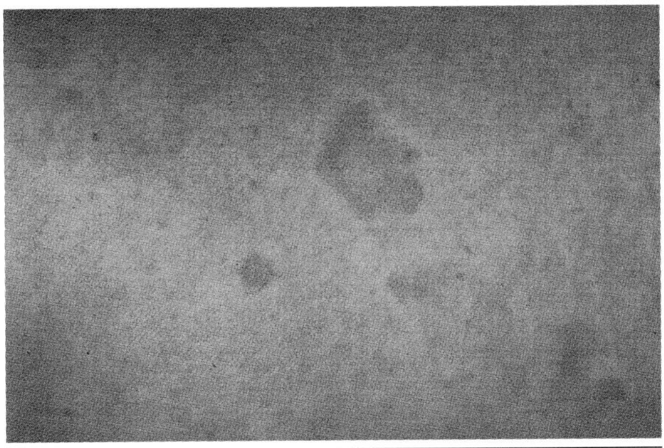

FIGURE 66–4 Urticarial lesions due to penicillin.

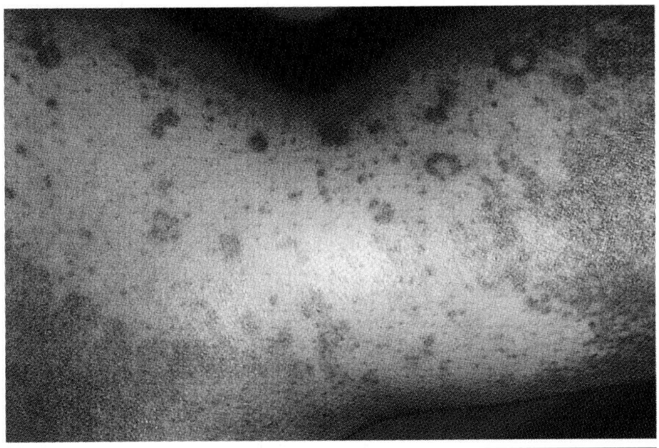

FIGURE 66–5 Palpable purpuric lesions which on biopsy showed leukocytoclastic vasculitis. Drug-induced and idiopathic lesions are clinically and histologically indistinguishable.

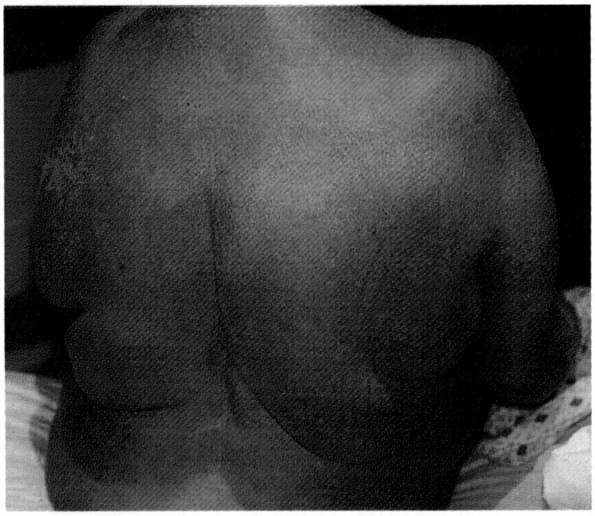

FIGURE 66–6 Exfoliative erythroderma. At the time this eruption began, the patient was taking allopurinol and a thiazide diuretic.

66–6). Abnormal temperature regulation, fluid imbalance, and right ventricular failure may result from extreme and persistent vasodilatation. The erythematous eruption is followed by diffuse desquamation. The drugs most frequently implicated in this form of cutaneous reaction pattern are gold salts and sulfonamides.

Fixed Drug Eruption

This uncommon reaction has very distinctive clinical and histologic presentations. Skin lesions characteristically recur at the same site or sites each time the drug is administered. The eruption begins as a sharply marginated erythematous round or oval macule that evolves into an edematous plaque that becomes violaceous or brown (Figure 66–7). Vesicles and bullae may occur on the surface of the plaque. Resolution is characterized by intense postinflammatory hyperpigmentation. Lesions may be solitary initially, but with repeated episodes, new lesions appear. Lesions are more common on the extremities than on the trunk; the feet, genitalia, and perianal areas are favored. Drugs implicated in causing fixed drug eruption include phenolphthalein, tetracycline, and oxyphenbutazone.

Eczematous Eruptions

Many drugs are used both topically and systemically. An eczematous type of eruption resembles contact dermatitis and develops in individuals who are already sensitized by topical exposure to a class of drugs. Subsequent systemic administration results in an acute erythematous papular or papular-vesicular eruption. This reaction typically occurs within 2 days of administration of the systemic drug and tends to be localized to the site of the previous allergic contact dermatitis initially but may subsequently become generalized. Agents present in topical preparations that often are associated with allergic contact dermatitis include neomycin, benzocaine, ethylenediamine, diphenhydramine, and parabens.

Lichenoid and Lichen Planus–Like Eruptions

There are drug eruptions clinically and histologically indistinguishable from lichen planus; however, lichenoid drug eruptions tend to be more scaly, psoriasiform, or eczematous in appearance (Figure 66–8). They also may occur in a different distribution than idiopathic lichen planus, with sparing of the flexor sur-

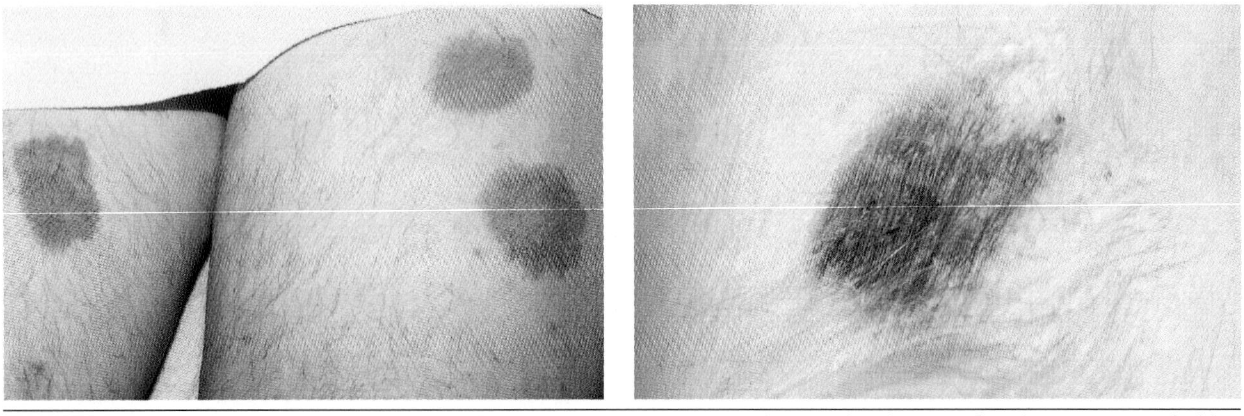

FIGURE 66–7 Fixed drug eruption. On the left, there are erythematous plaques that began after the ingestion of chlordiazepoxide. (Courtesy of Tsu-Yi Chuang, M.D., M.P.H.) On the right, there is an older lesion in the axilla with prominent hyperpigmentation. (Courtesy of Robert Hurwitz, M.D.)

faces of the skin and the mucous membranes. Pruritus is often intense. The eruption may develop weeks to months after initiation of a medication. Progression to an exfoliative erythroderma may occur. Resolution is often slow, and postinflammatory hyperpigmentation may be extensive and disfiguring. Drugs implicated include gold salts, antimalarials, penicillamine, and diuretics.

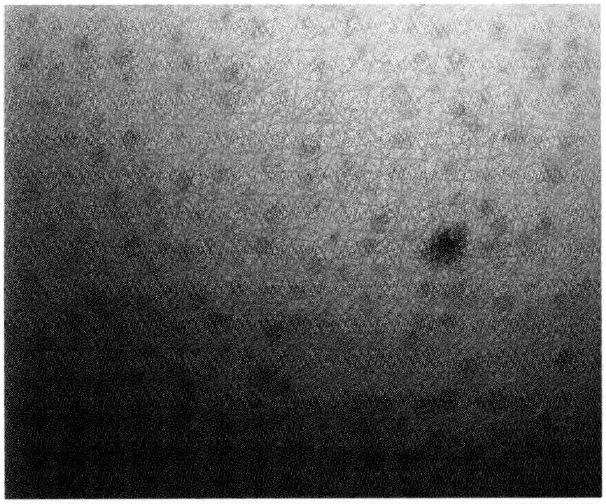

FIGURE 66–8 Lichenoid eruption attributed to a sulfa medication. (Courtesy of Tsu-Yi Chuang, M.D., M.P.H.)

Photosensitivity

Reactions between drugs and light which cause eruptions on exposed areas may be either phototoxic or photoallergic in nature. These reactions cannot always be distinguished clinically, and some drugs may produce cutaneous involvement by both mechanisms. Phototoxic reactions can be produced in any individual receiving enough drug and enough light. Lesions, which occur 5 to 20 hours after exposure, resemble a sunburn with confluent erythema, edema, and occasionally vesiculation. The eruption is restricted to the area of ultraviolet light exposure (Figure 66–9). Recognized causes of phototoxicity are tetracycline (particularly demeclocycline), sulfonamides, phenothiazines, amiodarone, and nalidixic acid. Photoallergic reactions are immunologically mediated and require re-exposure to drug and light in a previously sensitized individual. Photoallergic reactions may result from a photocontact dermatitis to a topical photoallergen or may occur as a result of systemically administered drugs. Photoallergic reactions may spread beyond areas of light exposure.

Phototoxicity
Photoallergic reactions

Practical Approach to the Diagnosis of a Suspected Drug Eruption

As physicians, we are well aware that there are undoubtedly many more adverse reactions to drugs than are suspected, and that conversely, many cutaneous reactions suspected of being drug induced actually may have other etiologies. In eval-

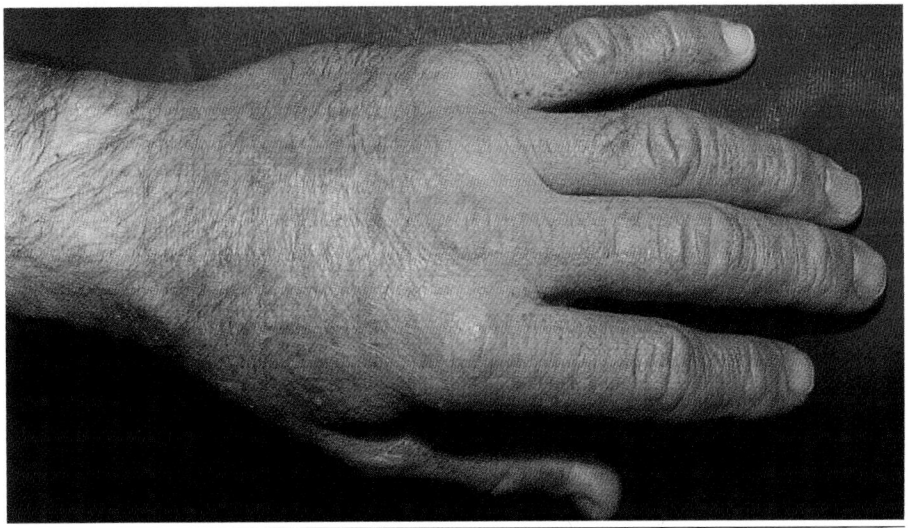

FIGURE 66–9 Phototoxic reaction associated with piroxicam. Note sharp demarcation at the wrist.

uating a suspected drug reaction, every effort should be directed toward diagnosis, discovery, and discontinuation.

Diagnosis requires:
- *index of suspicion*
- *detailed history*
- *careful examination*

Diagnosis requires a high index of suspicion, a detailed and directed history, careful examination, classification of the eruption by morphologic characteristics, evaluation of accompanying signs and symptoms, collection of adjuvant laboratory test results, and elimination of other causes of similar eruptions. Important historical information includes the onset and evolution of the eruption, any history of drug eruptions, and detailed descriptions of all medications being taken, including proprietary products, vitamins, and herbal supplements. If a true allergic reaction is suspected, a history of similar medications taken systemically or applied topically may be important. Note any accompanying symptomatology, such as pruritus (favors a drug reaction), sore throat (against drug eruption), fever, and malaise (neither pro nor con). Categorizing the eruption by the morphologic appearance of the lesions is helpful in determining the type of reaction (allergic versus nonallergic) and in limiting the possible etiologic agents responsible for the eruption (see Table 66–2). Other physical findings, such as mucosal involvement, lymphadenopathy, and temperature elevation, are important.

Adjuvant tests may be helpful by pointing either toward or away from the diagnosis of drug-induced eruption (Table 66–3). Routine studies should include a complete blood cell count, a differential count urinalysis, and a multiphasic screening panel; other tests such as skin biopsy and patch and light testing are also important in categorizing the type and sometimes the cause of the reaction. Realistically, although not necessarily practically, challenge by re-introduction of the suspected drug is still the most useful means of definitively diagnosing a drug eruption.

Treatment

Discontinue most likely agent

The treatment of a drug reaction depends on the type of reaction, the severity of the reaction, and the presumed etiologic mechanism. With few exceptions, use of the suspected offender should be discontinued and the eruption treated symptomatically with antihistamines or antipruritics, compresses, and soothing lotions, as needed. If the patient is taking multiple medications that are important to his or her health and well being, it is reasonable to select the most likely causative drug and stop its administration first. If the eruption persists or progresses over the next 48 hours, the next most likely medication is discontinued, and so on. Another approach is to discontinue all medications until the rash fades or clears completely and then re-institute the medications one at a time at 48- to 72-hour intervals. This approach is not recommended in the treatment of IgE-mediated urticaria or angioedema (since the challenging might induce a life-threatening anaphylactic reaction) or multisystem drug reactions which concomitantly involve the liver or kidneys.

TABLE 66–3 Diagnostic Procedures

History
Physical examination
Laboratory tests
Complete blood cell count with differential count
Multiphasic screening panel
Serum IgE RAST
Skin biopsy
Patch tests
Ultraviolet light testing

RAST = radioallergoabsorbent test.

Severe widespread or extremely symptomatic drug eruptions may require a short course of prednisone therapy to reduce inflammation and shorten the natural course of the reaction. Assuming that there are no medical contraindications, prednisone can be administered orally, at a dose of 0.5 to 1 mg per kg per day, in divided doses. As soon as it is apparent that the eruption is resolving, the dosage may be rapidly tapered to 5 to 10 mg per day.

A short course of prednisone may hasten resolution.

TABLE 66–4 Mucocutaneous Complications of Chemotherapeutic Agents

- Alopecia
  - Amsacrine
  - Bleomycin
  - Busulfan
  - Cyclosporine
  - Cytarabine
  - Dactinomycin
  - Daunorubicin
  - Doxorubicin
  - Etoposide
  - Fluorouracil
  - Hydroxyurea
  - Idarubicin
  - Ifosfamide
  - Interleukin-2
  - Mechlorethamine
  - Methotrexate
  - Nitrosoureas
  - Paclitaxel
  - Procarbazine
  - Vinblastine
  - Vincristine
- Stomatitis
  - Bleomycin
  - Cyclophosphamide
  - Dactinomycin
  - Daunorubicin
  - Docetaxel
  - Doxorubicin
  - Fluorouracil
  - Interleukin-2
  - Mercaptopurine
  - Methotrexate
  - Mithramycin
  - Nitrosoureas
  - Procarbazine
  - Vinblastine
  - Vincristine
- Tissue injury
  - Phlebitis
    - Amsacrine
    - Carmustine
    - Dacarbazine
    - Dactinomycin
    - Daunorubicin
    - Mechlorethamine
    - Mitomycin
    - Vinblastine
  - Chemical cellulitis and/or ulceration
    - Bleomycin
    - Cisplatin
    - Dactinomycin
    - Dacarbazine
    - Daunorubicin
    - Doxorubicin
    - Fluorouracil
    - Mechlorethamine
    - Methotrexate
    - Mithramycin
    - Mitomycin
    - Mitoxantrone
    - Streptozotocin
    - Taxol
    - Vinblastine
    - Vincristine
    - VP-16
- Hypersensitivity reactions (Type I)
  - Amsacrine
  - Asparaginase
  - Bleomycin
  - Carboplatin
  - Chlorambucil
  - Cisplatin
  - Cyclophosphamide
  - Daunorubicin
  - Docetaxel
  - Doxorubicin
  - Etoposide
  - Mechlorethamine
  - Melphalan
  - Methotrexate
  - Mitoxantrone
  - Paclitaxel
  - Pentostatin
  - Procarbazine
  - Teniposide
  - Thiotepa
- Hyperpigmentation
  - Localized
    - Bleomycin
    - Cisplatin
    - Cyclophosphamide
    - Doxorubicin
    - Fluorouracil
    - Ifosfamide
    - Thiotepa
  - Diffuse
    - Cyclophosphamide
    - Hydroxyurea
    - Methotrexate
  - Mucous membranes
    - Busulfan
    - Cisplatin
    - Cyclophosphamide
    - Daunorubicin
    - Doxorubicin
    - Fluorouracil
    - Hydroxyurea
  - Hair
    - Cisplatin
    - Cyclophosphamide
    - Methotrexate
  - Teeth
    - Cyclophosphamide
- Interactions with radiation
  - Radiation enhancement
    - Bleomycin
    - Dactinomycin
    - Doxorubicin
    - Etoposide
    - Fluorouracil
    - Hydroxyurea
    - Interferons
    - Methotrexate
  - Radiation recall
    - Dactinomycin
    - Doxorubicin
  - Photosensitivity/phototoxicity
    - Dacarbazine
    - Fluorouracil
    - Methotrexate
    - Mitomycin
    - Tegafur
    - Vinblastine
  - Reactivation of UV-induced erythema
    - Methotrexate
- Miscellaneous reactions
  - Acral erythema/erythrodysesthesia
    - Bleomycin
    - Cytarabine
    - Doxorubicin
    - Fluorouracil
    - Methotrexate
    - Thiotepa
  - Raynaud's phenomenon and scleroderma-like changes
    - Bleomycin
    - Busulfan
    - Vincristine
    - Vinblastine
  - Hypertrichosis
    - Cyclosporine
  - Folliculitis
    - Cyclosporine
    - Dactinomycin
    - Methotrexate
  - Inflammation of seborrheic or actinic keratoses
    - Cisplatin
    - Cytarabine
    - Dacarbazine
    - Dactinomycin
    - Doxorubicin
    - Fluorouracil
    - Pentostatin
  - Neutrophilic eccrine hidradenitis
    - Bleomycin
    - Chlorambucil
    - Cyclophosphamide
    - Cytarabine
    - Doxorubicin
    - Lomustine
    - Mitoxantrone
  - Vasculitis
    - Cytarabine
    - Hydroxyurea
    - Methotrexate

Patient education regarding drug use

Rarely, it may be necessary to continue treatment in spite of a drug-induced eruption. This may occur when the suspected medication is absolutely necessary and there are no unrelated drug substitutes of similar efficacy. We have occasion to do this on the oncology ward or when treating other immunocompromised patients for life-threatening infections. (For drug reactions associated with chemotherapeutic agents, see Table 66–4.) In these situations, the severity of the reaction may be diminished by switching modes of administration from intermittent to continuous intravenous administration of drugs (ticarcillin) or from daily administration to treatment three times a week (trimethoprim-sulfamethoxazole). Once a drug has been implicated in a drug reaction, the patient should be given the name of the drug and a list of similar chemical compounds to avoid in the future. The front of the chart should be clearly labeled, other physicians caring for the patient should be informed, and ideally the manufacturer of the medication should be notified of the reaction.

Annotated Bibliography

Roujeau JC, Stern RS. Severe adverse cutaneous reactions to drugs. N Engl J Med 1994;19:1272–1285.

This is an excellent review article discussing the clinical features, epidemiology, pathophysiology, differential diagnosis, and management of several of the more serious cutaneous reactions to drugs.

deShazo RD, Kemp SF. Allergic reactions to drugs and biologic agents. JAMA 1997;278:1895–1906.

This is a review article written by allergists and contains several excellent tables, including organ-specific patterns of drug reactions, and practical algorithms for evaluating drug reactions.

Naranjo CA, Shear NH, Lanctot KL. Advances in the diagnosis of adverse drug reactions. J Clin Pharmacol 1992;32:897–904.

This paper discusses the advances made in the diagnosis of adverse drug reactions. One of these is the lymphocyte toxicity assay (LTA), used to evaluate hypersensitivity reactions based on the hypothesis that they are associated with a defect in the detoxification of toxic drug metabolites. Another is the Bayesian Adverse Reaction Diagnostic Instrument (BARDI), which combines previous and current knowledge of adverse drug reactions with information about a specific case to assess the likelihood that a particular drug produced a particular reaction.

CHAPTER 67

Cutaneous Manifestations of Drug Reactions: Toxic Epidermal Necrolysis

Andrew M. Munster, M.D., Ken Nagamoto, M.D., Thomas T. Provost, M.D.

Toxic epidermal necrolysis (TEN) is a rare dermatosis characterized by widespread sloughing of the skin and mucous membranes. It is almost invariably associated with the use of a medication and has a high mortality rate.

Rare disease
Skin and mucous membrane sloughing

The onset of disease is heralded by prodromal influenza-like symptoms, usually occurring 1 to 3 days before the onset of the cutaneous changes. The skin becomes dusky, erythematous, and generally painful with the development of flaccid bullae. A shearing force applied to the skin produces epidermal-dermal dyshesion and separation (Nikolsky's sign), revealing a red, oozing dermis.

Nikolsky's sign
Associated with medication
High mortality

Mucous membrane involvement of eyes, mouth, and vagina may be extensive, with widespread sloughing, exposing raw dermis. Severe pain is common.

As a result of widespread denuding of the mucous membranes and skin, there is loss of fluid, protein, and electrolyte. Unlike a second-degree burn, which this cutaneous disease resembles, hepatic, hematologic, and pulmonary involvement are frequently present.

Resembles second-degree burn

The overall mortality rate varies. Generally, a 20 to 60% mortality rate is quoted. In one large retrospective French study of 253 well-documented cases, between the years 1981 and 1985, 76 deaths occurred (30% mortality). The

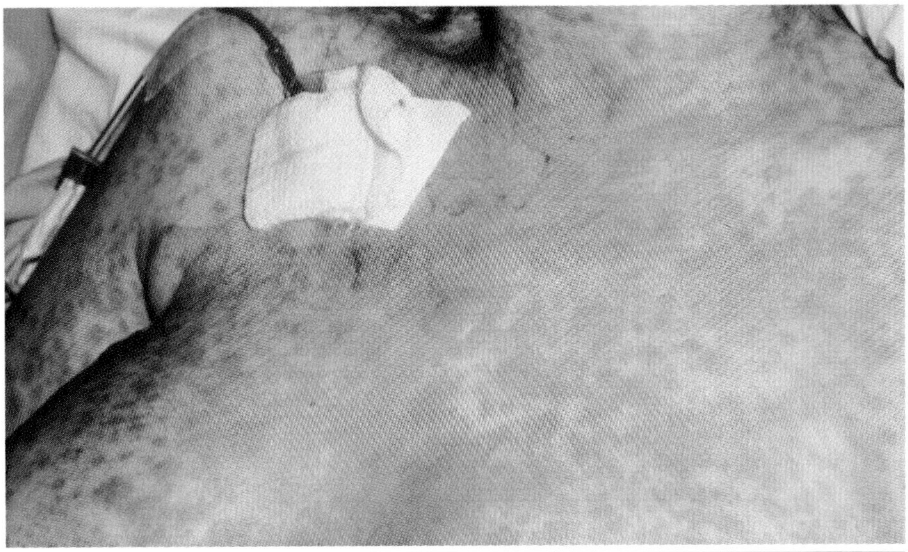

FIGURE 67–1 Dusky erythematous generalized TEN eruption as a manifestation of a drug eruption.

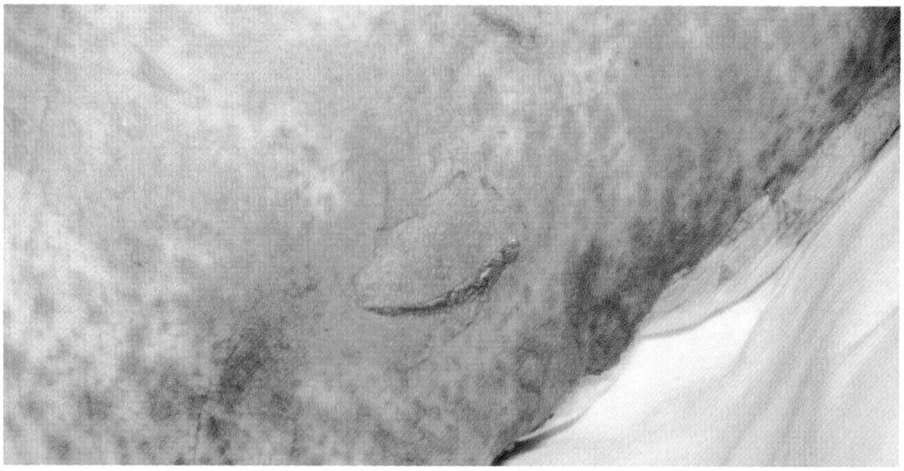

FIGURE 67–2 Sloughing of skin of back of same patient (Nikolsky's sign).

The drugs most commonly associated are:
- *sulfonamides*
- *penicillin*
- *phenobarbitol*
- *phenytoin*
- *nonsteroidal anti-inflammatory drugs*

cause of death is frequently sepsis. This is especially true in patients who have been initially treated with high doses of corticosteroids (see below).

This is a rare disease! In a Swedish study performed between 1964 and 1969 as well as in the French study performed between 1981 and 1985, an incidence of 1.2 per million was established. In one study, almost all patients were suspected to have had a drug-induced disease process. For example, only 15 of 253 cases (6%) had clinical or serologic evidence of an intercurrent infection; the remainder (94%) were drug associated. While the exact frequency of individual drug associations varies, depending on local medical practices, the most commonly implicated drugs appear to be sulfonamides, penicillin, anticonvulsants (phenobarbitol and phenytoin), and nonsteroidal anti-inflammatory drugs (NSAIDs).

On unusual occasions, infections are associated

Other cases of TEN have been associated with recent vaccinations and varicella zoster virus, herpes simplex virus, human immunodeficiency virus (HIV), cytomegalovirus, and Epstein-Barr virus infections. *Mycoplasma pneumoniae* also has been detected. Finally, a severe form of acute graft-versus-host disease (GVHD) may evolve into a TEN-like picture.

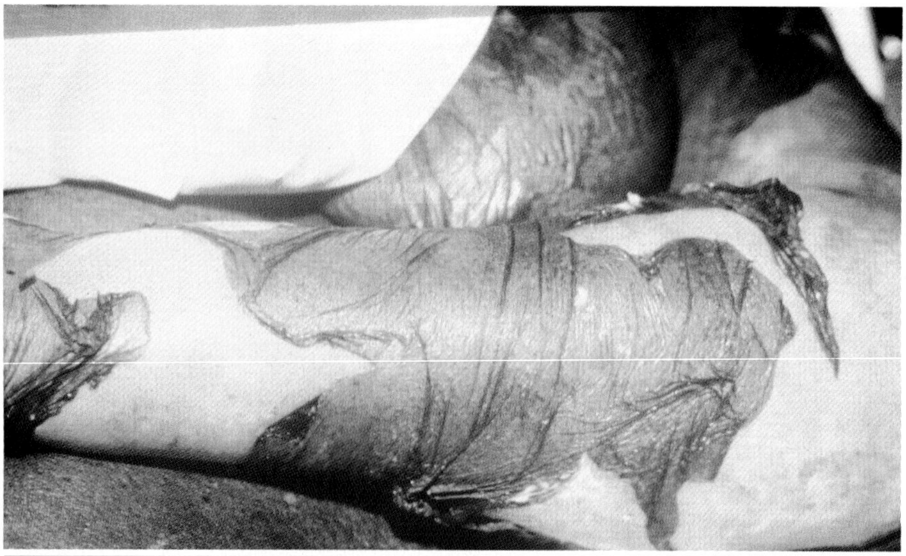

FIGURE 67–3 Severe sloughing of the skin on the arm of an African American female. Note wrinkling of the skin of the breast and the absence of disease on the thigh. (Courtesy of Rick Stearns, M.D., Tulsa, OK)

The association with drugs, as well as with GVHD, suggests that immunologic mechanisms may be operative, but this has not been proven. The disease predominates in women. The ratio in one study was 1.6 females to 1.0 males.

Immunologically mediated

Most recent data indicate that keratinocyte apoptotic Fas receptors are activated, stimulated by large quantities of Fas ligand (FasL), some of which is released from affected keratinocytes. This produces massive death of keratinocytes. Preliminary clinical experimental evidence indicates intravenous pooled human immunoglobulin, which contains anti–Fas receptor antibodies, may be a potentially therapeutically important modality, theoretically blocking the ability of FasL to bind to the Fas receptor on the keratinocyte.

Clinical Features

As noted above, the disease process is usually associated with a prodromal phase lasting 1 to 3 days. Fever, sore throat, conjunctivitis, difficulty voiding, and in some cases skin tenderness and pain, together with dusky erythema occur rapidly (within 48 hours). Urticaria-like plaques associated with flaccid bullae may develop. The palms and soles may be entirely denuded. The scalp, for some unknown reason, is usually spared. Nikolsky's sign is present in the dusky, erythematous areas.

3-day prodrome
Skin erythema and tenderness

Denuding of the conjunctival, buccal, tracheal, bronchial, pharyngeal, esophageal, anal, nasal, vaginal, and perianal areas occurs frequently. Urethritis and urinary retention are common. Severe oral pain is characteristic, and food and fluid intake is difficult, if not impossible.

Extensive denuding of mucous membranes

This acute phase lasts 8 to 12 days and is followed by a recovery phase lasting 1 to 2 weeks. Necrolysis rarely recurs in areas which have begun to heal. In general, healing appears to be faster than in comparable second-degree burns. However, the skin of the glans penis may take several months to heal.

Generally heals faster than second-degree burns
Persistence of glans penis involvement

The cutaneous complications of TEN syndrome are prominent hypo- and hyperpigmentation, nail loss and dystrophy, hypohidrosis, hypertrophic scars with contractures, and, if the scalp is involved, scarring alopecia.

Pigment and nail alterations are common sequelae

Mucosal involvement may be complicated by the development of esophageal strictures, xerostomia, and chronic oral ulcerations. Vaginal dryness and ulcerations may occur. Inflammation of the glans penis may produce phimosis.

The ocular complications are potentially very serious. With acute conjunctivitis, ulcers occur and may become secondarily infected. Corneal abrasions and ulcers may be associated with neovascularization and corneal opacities. Lacrimal duct destruction may occur, producing dry eyes. Severe conjunctival inflammation can result in symblepharon formation. Blindness, as a result of corneal scarring, has been reported in approximately 5% of individuals.

Ocular complications may be serious.

Photophobia can be an especially annoying complication. Inflammation of the conjunctiva over the posterior upper eyelid results in scar formation. Repeated closure of the eye produces corneal abrasions resulting in photophobia.

Photophobia

In one such patient, a young boy, a vitamin A cream produced, presumably, a dramatic alteration in the conjunctival surface on the posterior upper eyelid resulting in a marked improvement in his condition.

Pulmonary complications occur in a significant percentage of these patients. It has been estimated that approximately 30% will develop pneumonia. Aspiration of thick, mucous secretions and the mucosal debris from the upper airway produces atelectasis and pneumonia.

Aspiration especially problematic
Pneumonia is frequent.

In addition to pneumonia, septicemia is another lethal complication and may be associated with the development of a disseminated intravascular coagulopathy. The widespread skin damage provides an excellent portal of entry for such organisms as *Staphylococcus aureus* and *Pseudomonas aeruginosa*. It has been estimated in one study that 50% of deaths were the result of sepsis.

Septicemia may be responsible for 50% of deaths.

Recently, a fulminating TEN syndrome has been described associated with a systemic inflammatory response similar to that seen following major trauma or burns. It is characterized by a rapid onset of multisystem organ failure, adult respiratory distress syndrome, and, in some cases, severe, acute pancreatitis. This is an extremely rare but, to date, uniformly fatal form of TEN syndrome.

Stevens-Johnson syndrome may be a similar disease process in which mucous membrane involvement dominates. Less total body surface is involved.

The relationship between this entity and Stevens-Johnson syndrome is debatable. Indeed, one classification of TEN indicates that those individuals with type 1 disease have Stevens-Johnson syndrome; those with type 2 disease have a Stevens-Johnson/TEN syndrome characterized by approximately 60% total body surface involvement. Type 3 patients have TEN and have greater than 70% total body surface involvement.

Biopsy shows full-thickness epidermal slough.

Histologically, biopsies of patients with TEN demonstrate subepidermal blister formation, with necrosis of the blister roof and sparse lymphocytic infiltrate in the dermis.

Differential Diagnosis

Differential diagnosis:
- *staphylococcal scalded skin syndrome*
- *Stevens-Johnson syndrome*
- *toxic shock syndrome*
- *Kawasaki syndrome*

The differential diagnosis of TEN is the staphylococcal scalded skin syndrome induced generally by group II phage 71 *Staphylococcus aureus*. See Chapter 48, "Staphylococcal Infections" for further discussion. In addition, as noted above, Stevens-Johnson syndrome has to be considered. This disease process, unlike TEN, is associated with far less body surface involvement. The toxic shock syndrome, as well as Kawasaki syndrome, must also be considered.

Prognosis guarded

The prognosis is very guarded. A review of the literature indicates that individuals at highest risk are (1) those patients who have been treated with high doses of corticosteroids; (2) those patients with leukopenia; (3) those patients with extensive total body surface involvement; and (4) elderly patients.

Management of TEN Patients in a Burn Center

Burn center therapy:
- *no steroids*
- *débridement and topical therapy*
- *nutritional support*
- *specialized wound care*
- *monitoring and control of septic complications*

Over the last 10 years, there has been a national trend toward referring TEN patients to burn centers for care. There is some evidence that the cytokine cascade may be activated in these patients, as in burn patients, leading to increased metabolic demands and the need for nutritional support. Because of the similarity of the syndrome to an extensive second-degree burn, the significant requirement for nursing care of the wounds and the need for expertise on topical care,

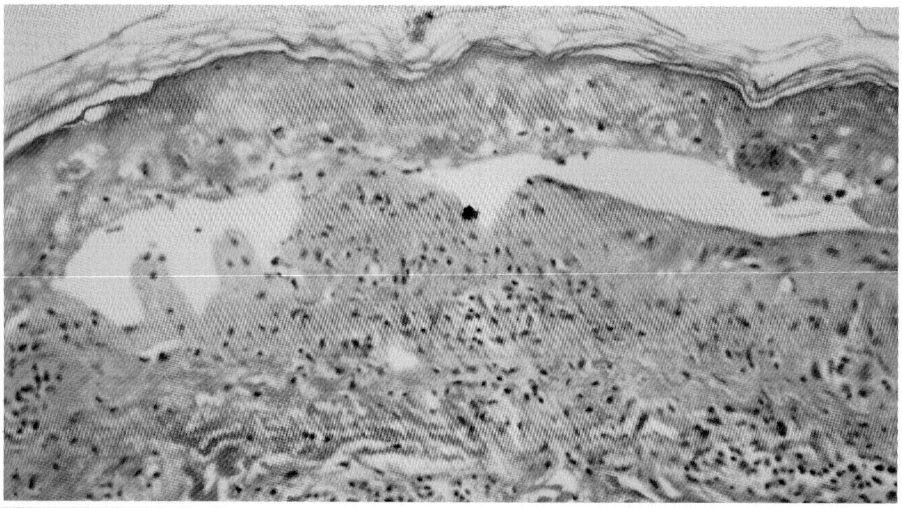

FIGURE 67–4 Histopathology demonstrating subepidermal cell–poor blister with necrosis of the blister roof and relative absence of a dermal inflammatory infiltrate.

as well as the ready availability of various types of special care beds, a burn center is probably most conducive to caring for patients with severe TEN.

From the point of view of the burn center, little attention is paid to the semantic differences among Stevens-Johnson syndrome, TEN, and other nomenclatures. In early stages, the disease may only be essentially erythema multiforme with a positive Nikolsky's sign. Because there is evidence that early referral improves the outcome and reduces mortality, most burn centers would much prefer to accept such patients earlier rather than later.

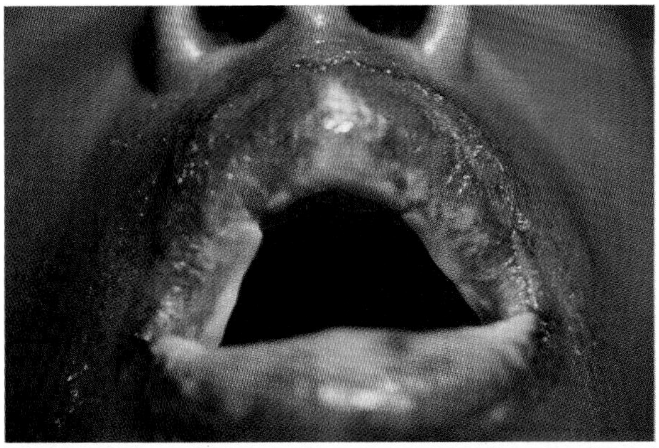

FIGURE 67–5 Severe oral ulceration in a patient with Stevens-Johnson syndrome.

The topical management of wounds varies widely. The use of sulfonamide-containing creams (silver sulfadiazine, mafenide) should be avoided even if TEN was not caused by sulfa drugs. These creams are fairly adherent, and in the process of wound care, washing, and débridement of the old cream prior to the application of new cream, delicate epithelial surfaces can be denuded which otherwise may re-adhere as the disease runs its course. If the patient is received early enough (3 to 4 days from the onset of the disease), then it is appropriate to débride the blisters, clean the wound surface under light general anesthesia, apply a biologic dressing, and leave the wound undisturbed for several days. If, however, the patient is referred late, then the blister fluid must be considered contaminated by the resident flora of the skin, which can become pathogenic. Topical antibacterial protection must be provided. Currently, the best way to do this is the application of 5% silver nitrate solution, with changes of wound dressings every second day. If the patient is clinically septic, then the dressings must be changed more frequently.

Studies have shown that the resting energy expenditure in patients with this disease is as high as in patients with equivalent-sized burns. Therefore, nutritional

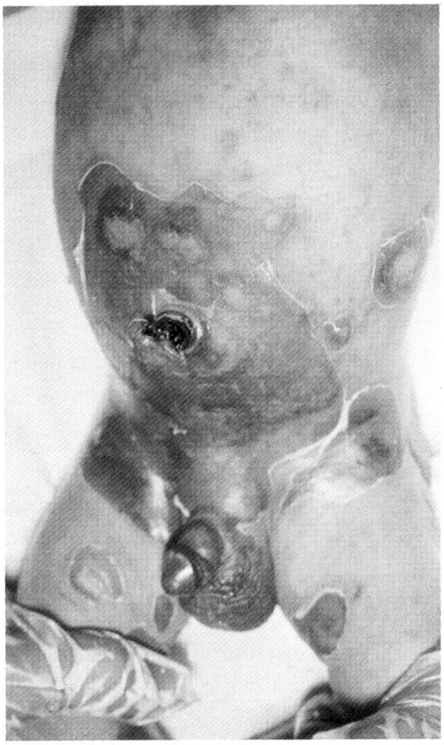

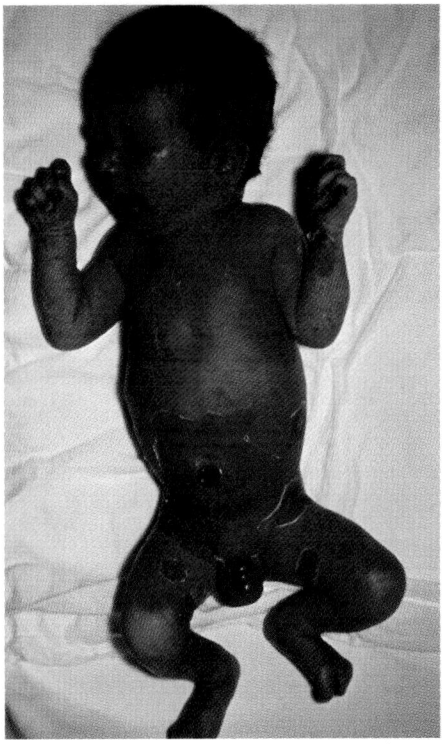

FIGURES 67–6 AND 67–7 Superficial sloughing of skin in "scalded skin" syndrome induced by a toxin discharged during group II *Staphylococcus aureus* phage infections.

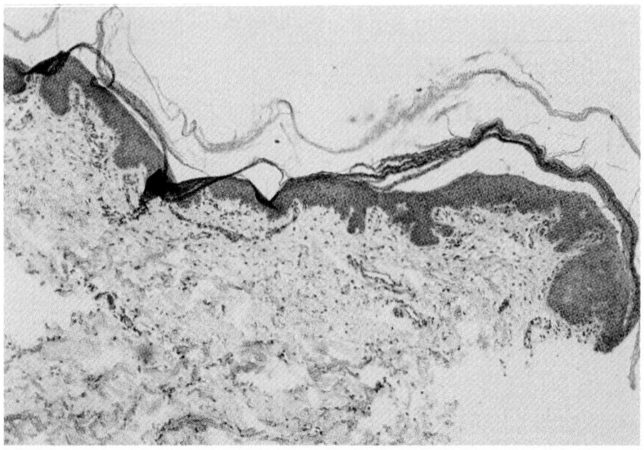

FIGURE 67–8 Scalded skin syndrome: superficial denuding of the skin induced by cleavage through the granular cell layer of the epidermis. Compare this histopathologic picture with the histopathology presented in Figure 67–4.

support must be provided at a level calculated for an equivalent-sized burn, for which the Curreri formula may be used (daily calories to be provided = 40 cal/kg × total percentage of body surface area involved). If this support cannot be provided orally or enterally, then it needs to be provided parenterally. Most patients with lesions covering more than 50% of total body surface area should be placed on an air-fluidized bed system to minimize shearing pressure to the back.

In the Johns Hopkins Burn Center experience, which has treated more than 70 TEN patients during the last 13 years, the mortality rate approaches 30%. In our experience, the prognosis is worse in patients with advanced neoplasms, advanced age, and renal failure or if the inciting factor is associated with HIV or HIV therapy. There is a statistically significant difference in mortality rate according to whether the patient was referred to the burn center early or later than 7 days following initial onset of lesions.

Annotated Bibliography

Roujeau JC, Guillaume JC, Fabre JP, et al. Toxic epidermal necrolysis (Lyell's syndrome). Arch Dermatol 1990;126:37–42.

This is a retrospective study of 253 validated cases of TEN. The suspected incidence was 1.2 cases per million per year. The study indicates that sulfonamides and nonsteroidal drugs were most commonly implicated in the etiology.

Avakian R, Flowers FP, Araujo O, et al. Toxic epidermal necrolysis: a review. J Am Acad Dermatol 1991;25:69–79.

This is an excellent review of TEN. It is well written, covering the clinical phases and summarizing arguments regarding the use and nonuse of steroids in the treatment of TEN. These authors are proponents of burn center management of TEN patients. The article contains 40 citations.

Kim PS, Goldfarb MD, Garsford MD, et al. Stevens-Johnson syndrome and toxic epidermal necrolysis: a pathophysiologic review with recommendations for a treatment protocol. J Burn Care Rehabil 1983;4:91–100.

The first article (a small series) demonstrates that steroid therapy may be detrimental to patients treated for TEN. The article also demonstrates that leukopenia frequently occurs in TEN patients, whether or not treatment with steroids has occurred.

Halebian PH, Corder VJ, Madden MR, et al. Improved burn center survival of patients with toxic epidermal necrolysis managed without corticosteroids. Ann Surg 1986;204:503–512.

This is a highly quoted study demonstrating a 33% survival rate in a 15-patient steroid-treated TEN cohort, compared with a 66% survival rate in a 15-patient TEN cohort treated without steroids. In the steroid-treated group, mortality was related to total body surface involvement; in the non–steroid-treated group, mortality was related to advanced age and associated illnesses.

Viard I, Wehrli P, Bullani R, et al. Inhibition of toxic epidermal necrolysis by blockade of CD95 with human intravenous immunoglobulin. Science 1998;282:490–493.

This is a potential breakthrough article about not only our understanding of the pathogenesis of the severe epidermal cell death, the characteristic hall-

mark of TEN, but also about a new therapeutic modality to treat this potentially lethal disease. The death receptor Fas (CD95) is normally expressed on keratinocytes. Toxic epidermal necrolysis patients also express, on their keratinocytes, lytically active Fas ligand (FasL). This study also indicated that keratinocyte FasL from patients with TEN could induce Fas-mediated cell death in "normal" keratinocytes. Frozen skin sections of TEN patients were overlaid with Fas-sensitive Jurkat (tissue culture cell line). Jurkat cell apoptosis was induced by the TEN frozen skin sections, but not from healthy controls or from patients with a widespread drug-induced macular papular rash.

Intravenous immunoglobulin (IVIG) infused into TEN patients produced a dramatic improvement within 24 to 48 hours in 10 consecutive patients. Further analysis revealed that the Fas inhibitory activity of IVIG was due to the presence of naturally occurring anti–Fas receptor antibodies.

On the basis of these data, it is tempting to speculate that TEN occurs in individuals lacking sufficient natural anti–Fas receptor antibodies. The drug reaction produces detectable quantities of FasL in the circulation (source probably activated lymphocytes). The FasL diffuses across the dermal-epidermal junction binding Fas receptors on keratinocytes, inducing apoptosis and the release of FasL from keratinocytes. This domino effect induces widespread keratinocyte death. Hepatocytes and other organs possessing Fas receptors may also be involved.

The quantity of naturally occurring anti–Fas receptor antibodies may be the critical factor determining whether or not a drug reaction induces a TEN response.

Paul C, Wolkenstein P, Adle H, et al. Apoptosis as a mechanism of keratinocyte death in toxic epidermal necrolysis. Br J Dermatol 1996;134:710–714.

Skin biopsies from three toxic TEN patients were examined by electron microscopy, DNA nick end labeling, and internucleosomal degradation of DNA. Extensive apoptotic keratinocytes were found throughout the epidermis.

McGee T, Munster AM. Toxic epidermal necrolysis syndrome: mortality rate reduced with early referral to regional burn center. Plast Reconstr Surg 1998;102(4):1018–1022.

Thirty-six patients are reviewed in this article. The age and total body surface area involvement, as a percentage of body surface area, did not correlate with mortality or survival. However, there was a statistically highly significant improvement in survival if the patients were referred within 7 days of onset.

Khoo AK, Foo CL. Toxic epidermal necrolysis in a burn center: a six-year review. Burns 1996;22(4):275–278.

In this review of 23 patients from Singapore, the authors achieved 90% survival with a group of patients whose mean surface area of involvement was 57.2%. Patients were managed in the burn center with collaborative effort by an internist, a dermatologist, and an infectious disease specialist.

Cheriyan S, Patterson R, Greenberger PA, et al. The outcome of Stevens-Johnson syndrome treated with steroids. Allergy Proc 1995;4:151–155.

This is an article demonstrating that 13 patients with Stevens-Johnson syndrome, treated with methylprednisolone, and in one case, prednisone, dosage ranging from 240 mg to 750 mg per day, that all 13 patients responded to therapy with a full recovery. These authors also summarize their experience with 54 patients with Stevens-Johnson syndrome, seen over a 15- to 20-year period of time. All 54 patients have survived. There have been no deaths. The authors conclude that corticosteroids hasten recovery and have no major side effects for the period of time required to treat Stevens-Johnson syndrome.

This group is a leading proponent of the continued use of steroids in the treatment of Stevens-Johnson syndrome. None of their patients was referred to a burn center.

It should be noted that the number of days before corticosteroid therapy was begun ranges from 0 to14 days, with a mean of 7.1 days in the series. Thus, many of these patients did not represent fulminating Steven-Johnson syndrome but probably had a more stable disease, and only two of them had developed bullae formation.

This article is highlighted here to indicate that the use of steroids in the treatment of patients with severe Stevens-Johnson syndrome and TEN still is somewhat controversial. However, with time, more and more articles are appearing, indicating that treatment in a burn center appears to be the treatment of choice.

CHAPTER 68

Mastocytosis

Lisa A. Beck, M.D., Thomas T. Provost, M.D.

Mastocytosis is a disease characterized by increased number of mast cells in various organs, including the skin. The mast cell contains a variety of biologically active substances which, when released, produce systemic manifestations (Table 68–1).

Mastocytosis term to designate increased quantity of mast cells in various tissues
Mast cells contain various pharmacologic substances.

The National Institutes of Health (NIH) consensus classification emphasizing systemic features of mastocytosis is presented in Table 68–2.

Mast Cell Ontogeny

Mast cells are derived from the bone marrow pluripotential stem cell (CD34+). Their differentiation is mediated by stem cell factor (SCF, also known as mast cell growth factor, and c-kit ligand) and interleukin (IL)-3, although several other cytokines have been shown to induce their proliferation (IL-4, IL-9, IL-10, and nerve growth factor [NGF]). Evidence suggests that mast cell growth factor is the most potent mast cell mediator. Its receptor is a mast cell surface molecule, c-kit.

Derived from bone marrow pluripotential stem cell

Under normal conditions, mast cells circulate through the blood in small numbers. They home to tissue sites, where they localize around blood and lymphatic vessels, nerves, and appendageal structures, such as glands and hair follicles. Tissue localization is thought to be mediated by the adhesion of integrins on the mast cell surface to components of the extracellular matrix (eg, laminin, vitronectin, or fibronectin).

More recent studies indicate that the atypical response of mast cells to various cytokines, including the c-kit ligand (mast cell growth factor) induces mast cell proliferation. It appears that most cases of mastocytosis are either a local or

TABLE 68–1 Mast Cell–Derived Mediators

Histamine
Heparin
Serine proteinases (tryptase, chymase, carboxypeptidase)
Leukotrienes (LTC_4, LTD_4, LTE_4)
Prostaglandin D_2
Platelet activating factor
TGF-β
IL-3, IL-5, stem cell factor

TGF = transforming growth factor; IL = interleukin.

TABLE 68–2 Classification of Mastocytosis

Indolent
Syncope
Cutaneous disease
Ulcerative disease
Malabsorption
Bone marrow mast cell aggregates
Skeletal disease
Hepatosplenomegaly
Lymphadenopathy
Hematologic disorder
Myeloproliferative disorder
Myelodysplastic disorder
Aggressive
Lymphadenopathic mastocytosis with eosinophilia
Mast cell leukemia

a systemic reactive proliferative process and only rarely a malignant disease (Figures 68–1 to 68–3).

Tryptase-chymase (TC) mast cells predominate in the skin.

Tryptase (T) mast cells detected along gastrointestinal tract.

Two distinct mast cell populations exist. These are designated tryptase-chymase (TC) mast cells and tryptase (T) mast cells. The TC mast cells predominate in the skin, whereas the T mast cells are found along the gastrointestinal mucosa and lungs.

The inflammatory mediators present in the TC mast cells are listed in Table 68–3.

Immunologic and nonimmunologic activation of mast cells

Both immunologic and nonimmunologic stimuli induce mast cell degranulation. The immunologic release of mast cell mediators is facilitated by the presence of mast cell membrane-bound immunoglobulin E (IgE) antibodies. The binding of specific antigen to these IgE antibodies and subsequent cross-linking of the IgE induces mast cell degranulation. Nonimmunologic mediators of mast cell degranulation are listed in Table 68–4.

Cutaneous Mastocytosis

At least 10% of patients with cutaneous mastocytosis have systemic manifestations.

In general, mastocytosis is localized to the skin. However, at the very least, approximately 10% of patients demonstrate some systemic involvement. The lymph nodes, liver, spleen, bone marrow, and bones are systemic sites of increased quantities of mast cells. The clinical features of mastocytosis are secondary to the mediators released from the excessive number of mast cells.

Urticaria Pigmentosam

Urticaria pigmentosa is most common form of mastocytosis.

The most common form of cutaneous mastocytosis is urticaria pigmentosa. Cutaneous lesions of urticaria pigmentosa are small, reddish-brown, yellowish-tan macules or papules, which vary in number from a very few to hundreds of lesions. They may occur over the entire body. They most commonly occur in children and, in general, spontaneously disappear over time.

Darier's sign
In infants, rubbing of lesion may produce a blister.

Gentle rubbing of the individual urticaria pigmentosa lesion will induce redness, swelling, and pruritus (Darier's sign). This reaction is due to histamine release. The characteristic hyperpigmentation is due to increased melanin in the basal cells of the epidermis. This is thought to result from stimulation of melanocytes by soluble SCF, inducing increased production of melanin. In infants, degranulation of an individual urticaria pigmentosa lesion may even produce a subepidermal blister.

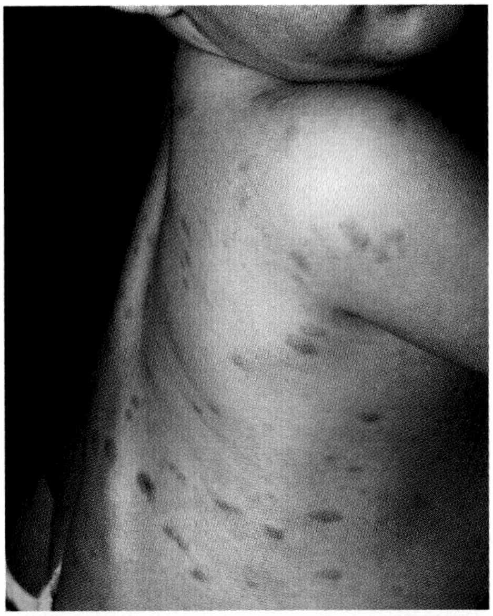

FIGURE 68–1 Brownish-red macular lesions of urticaria pigmentosa. (Courtesy of Rick Stearns, M.D., Tulsa, OK)

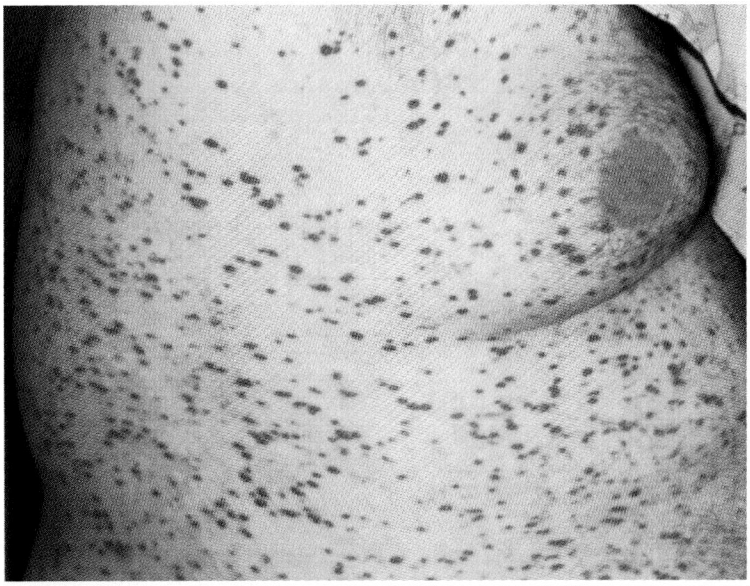

FIGURE 68–2 Widespread urticaria pigmentosa of at least 10 years duration in an adult. No evidence of systemic involvement detected.

Diffuse Cutaneous Mastocytosis

Diffuse cutaneous mastocytosis is a rare disorder. The entire skin surface is thickened (leather-like) and yellowish in color. The cutaneous folds may be exaggerated, especially in the axilla and groin. Nodules and small dermal lesions can occur, and pruritus may be intense. Blister formation, following minor trauma, is characteristic. Systemic involvement is frequently present.

Diffuse cutaneous mastocytosis is rare—yellowish thickened skin.

Telangiectasia Macularis Eruptiva Perstans

Another unusual cutaneous variant of mastocytosis is telangiectasia macularis eruptiva perstans. This condition presents in adults as red telangiectatic macules with little pigmentation and is generally very recalcitrant to therapy.

Telangiectasia macularis eruptiva perstans is another unusual form of urticaria pigmentosa.

On occasion, cutaneous lesions of mastocytosis may bleed, which is thought to be secondary to the release of heparin from mast cells (see Figures 68–3 and 68–4).

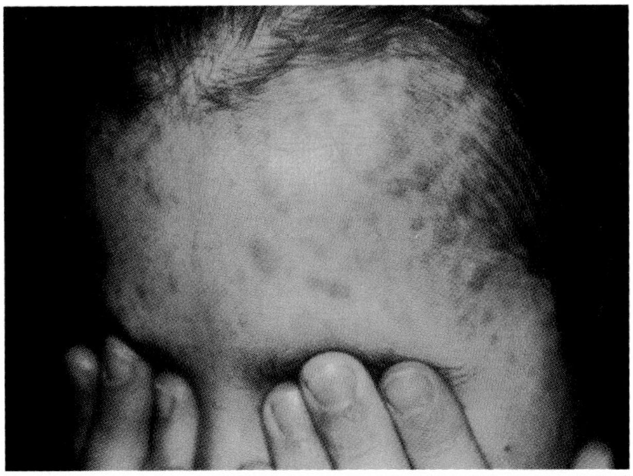

FIGURE 68–3 Brownish-red macular lesions of urticaria pigmentosa on the forehead.

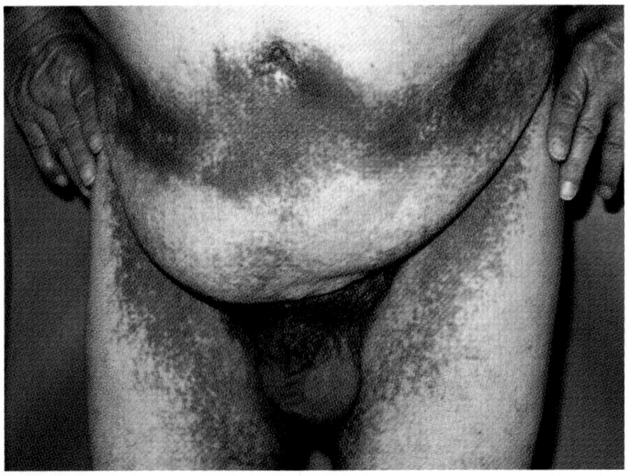

FIGURE 68–4 Hemorrhagic extensive brown macular lesions of urticaria pigmentosa. Episodic flushing noted, controlled by antihistamines.

TABLE 68–3 Preformed Mediators Found in Mast Cells (TC)

Histamine, heparin, chymase, tryptase, carboxypeptidase, LTD_4, LTC_4, PGD_2, TNF-α, PAF

LT = leukotriene; PG = prostaglandin; TNF-α = tumor necrosis factor alpha; PAF = platelet activating factor.

TABLE 68–4 Agents Capable of Inducing Mast Cell Degranulation in a Non–IgE-Dependent Fashion

Morphine, codeine, aspirin, polymyxin B, alcohol, compound 48/80, IV contrast dyes, neuropeptides, chemokines (IL-8), cytokines (IL-1, IL-3, GM-CSF), complement fragments (C3a and C5a)

IV = intravenous; IL = interleukin; GM-CSF = granulocyte-macrophage colony–stimulating factor.

Solitary Mastocytoma

Solitary mastocytosis may be symptomatic.

A solitary mastocytoma occurs in approximately 15% of patients. The response to minor trauma may range from nothing to urticaria to blister formation, or to generalized flushing (Figures 68–5 and 68–6).

Pathology

Biopsy of the individual lesion demonstrates increased numbers of normal-appearing mast cells (Figures 68–7 and 68–8). These mast cells usually stain metachromatically with toluidine blue or Giemsa stains. In some cases of mastocytosis, mast cells will be missed if not stained for tryptase. Mast cells are located predominantly perivascularly but may also accumulate as dermal nodules. Eosinophils are occasionally present.

Systemic Mastocytosis

Systemic mastocytosis may occur with or without skin lesions
In general, systemic mastocytosis occurs in patients who have had urticaria pigmentosa for years.
Malignant transformation is rare.

Histamine-induced gastric hypersecretion and peptic ulcer disease problematic
Diarrhea and abdominal pain

Some cases of mastocytosis may be associated with a wide variety of systemic features (Table 68–5).

Approximately 50% of systemic mastocytosis patients have urticaria pigmentosa, which has gradually evolved into systemic disease. Various gastrointestinal manifestations have been detected, ranging from peptic ulcer disease to malabsorption. Mast cell invasion of the mucosa of the gastrointestinal tract may produce, on radiography, abnormal mucosal patterns, induced by edema and/or the presence of multiple, nodular mast cell lesions.

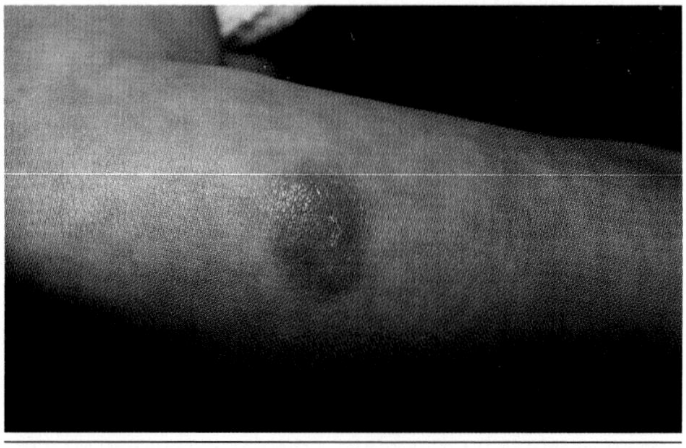

FIGURE 68–5 Single red nodular lesion of solitary mastocytosis. No systemic features.

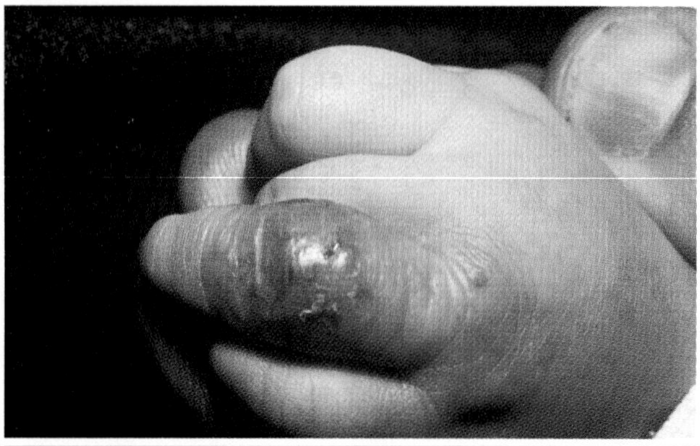

FIGURE 68–6 Single lesion of solitary mastocytosis of finger.

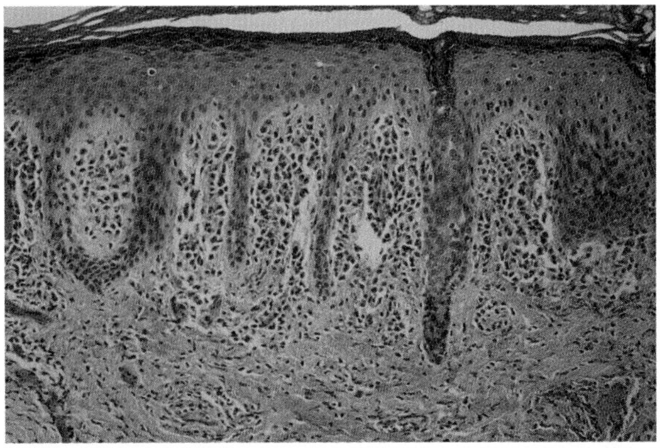

FIGURE 68–7 Biopsy of mastocytoma revealing spindle-shaped mast cells in the papillary and upper reticular dermis.

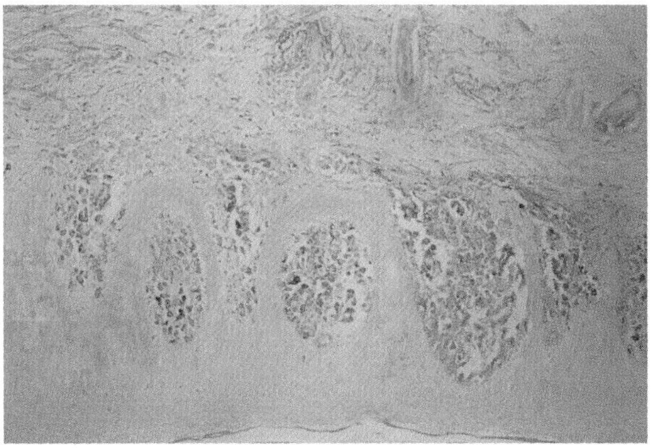

FIGURE 68–8 Toluidine blue stain of mastocytoma demonstrating metachromatically staining granules to the mast cells.

Flushing attacks, accompanied by headache, dyspnea, and wheezing, may occur. These flushing attacks are reminiscent of the flushing attacks seen in carcinoid syndrome, especially of the foregut variety. (See section on carcinoids.) The flushing and the accompanying vasodilatation may produce vascular collapse (anaphylaxis). This may be induced by exercise, infections, aspirin, or alcohol. Also, there are reports of *Hymenoptera stings* inducing anaphylaxis in mastocytosis patients.

Flushing attacks may be associated with headache and wheezing.

In addition to skin and gut involvement, liver involvement may infrequently occur. An elevated alkaline phosphatase, which needs to be differentiated from bone-derived alkaline phosphatase, is a characteristic finding. Spleen involvement may produce splenomegaly.

Increased liver alkaline phosphatase

Bone lesions (osteosclerosis or osteoporosis) may occur, although rarely, in children and may produce pain. Characteristic bone involvement occurs in the proximal long bones as well as the ribs, skull, and pelvis. A bone scan is more sensitive than a radiographic survey in detecting active lesions.

Bone lesions associated with pain

Central nervous system involvement, characterized by difficulty concentrating, cognitive dysfunction, and depression, have been noted.

Pathogenesis

Although the pathogenesis of systemic mastocytosis remains unclear, there are at least two possible mechanisms. Longley et al. have identified that the skin of

TABLE 68–5 Systemic Features of Mastocytosis

Gastrointestinal disturbances
Gastritis, peptic ulcer, crampy abdominal pain, diarrhea, and malabsorption
Liver involvement (alkaline phosphatase elevated)
Splenic enlargement
Bone marrow involvement
Rare in children
Thrombocytopenia and anemia with systemic disease
Bone involvement
Occurs in approximately 20 to 25% of patients with systemic disease
Bone pain
Neuropsychiatric manifestations
Cognitive impairment
Depression

patients with mastocytosis produces increased amounts of soluble SCF, leading to mast cell proliferation. Other groups have identified a somatic point mutation in codon 816 of the c-kit mast cell receptor. This mutation results in autoactivation or signaling through this receptor inducing proliferation and has been found primarily in adults with severe indolent disease or those with associated hematologic disorders. This mutation is rarely found in childhood cases.

The suggested work-up of systemic mastocytosis is listed in Table 68–6.

Mast Cell Leukemia

Mast cell leukemia rare but fatal disease

Mast cell leukemia is a rare, but fatal, form of mastocytosis. There appears to be a high incidence of peptic ulceration. Rarely do urticaria pigmentosa lesions occur in this form of mastocytosis.

Differential Diagnosis

Differential diagnosis include sarcoidosis, syphilis, and histiocytosis.

Bullous lesions in infants must be distinguished from bullous form of incontinentia pigmenti.

Lesions of urticaria pigmentosa must be differentiated from secondary syphilis, sarcoidosis, and histiocytosis. Darier's sign, when present, distinguishes urticaria pigmentosa from these lesions.

The bullous form of urticaria pigmentosa, detected in childhood, must be differentiated from the bullae accompanying incontinentia pigmenti and erythema multiforme, as well as the autoimmune and hereditary blistering diseases of childhood.

Prognosis

Generally, an excellent prognosis

Urticaria pigmentosa carries an excellent prognosis. Systemic mastocytosis is treated symptomatically, achieving moderate control in most patients. Patients with hematologic abnormalities have a significantly reduced survival. Mast cell leukemia is often fatal.

Treatment

Avoid mast cell–activating substances, such as alcohol, codeine, and morphine

H_1 and H_2 combination antihistamines effective in controlling peptic ulcer disease and flushes

The treatment of the systemic manifestations of mastocytosis involves avoidance of mast cell degranulating agents, such as alcohol, codeine, and morphine.

A combination of an H_1-antihistamine (eg, hydroxyzine) and an H_2-antihistamine (eg, cimetidine) may be effective in reducing the histamine-induced gastric hyperacidity. In addition, this combination of H_1 and H_2 antihistamines may control many of the cutaneous flushing episodes.

TABLE 68–6 Diagnostic Work-Up for Systemic Mastocytosis

Bone marrow biopsy and aspiration
24-hour urine for mediators
Histamine
Methyl imidazole acetic acid
Serum tryptase
Bone scan
Upper GI series, small bowel radiography, abdominal CT scan, endoscopy
EEG, neuropsychiatric evaluation

GI = gastrointestinal; CT = computed tomography; EEG = electroencephalogram.

Gastrointestinal manifestations may be treated with disodium cromoglycate.

Disodium cromoglycate effective in controlling gastrointestinal manifestations

Psoralen and ultraviolet A therapy has been shown to be effective in producing symptomatic relief of the cutaneous lesions of urticaria pigmentosa. (See Chapter 71, "Phototherapy and Photochemotherapy of Skin Diseases," for a discussion of ultraviolet light therapy for nonpsoriatic conditions.)

PUVA therapy is effective in controlling urticaria pigmentosa.

Aspirin has been successfully employed to presumably interfere with the metabolite of cyclo-oxygenase (prostaglandin D_2) in mastocytosis. It must be stated, however, that aspirin is capable of inducing a flare of systemic symptoms of mastocytosis. Therefore, use of aspirin should always be accompanied by the use of antihistamines, and close observation or hospitalization should be considered.

Aspirin therapy problematic Is capable of producing systemic flare.

Finally, it should be noted that the prolonged topical application (6 weeks) of potent corticosteroids, under occlusion, has also been effective in controlling urticaria pigmentosa. Recent evidence indicates that steroids inhibit synthesis of c-kit ligand (SCF) by resident fibroblasts.

Fluorinated steroids under occlusion effective in suppressing urticaria pigmentosa

Annotated Bibliography

Soter NA, Austen KF, Wasserman SI. Oral disodium cromoglycate in the treatment of systemic mastocytosis. N Engl J Med 1979;301:465–469.

Czarnetzki BM, Behrendt H. Urticaria pigmentosa: clinical picture and response to oral disodium cromoglycate. Br J Dermatol 1981;105:563–567.

These two articles detail the efficacy of disodium cromoglycate in the treatment of gastrointestinal mastocytosis.

Caplan RM. The natural course of urticaria pigmentosa. Analysis and follow up of 112 cases. Arch Dermatol 1963;87:146–157.

This is a classic, highly referenced article.

Christophers E, Hönigsmann K, Wolff K, et al. PUVA treatment of urticaria pigmentosa. Br J Dermatol 1978;98:701–702.

This article discusses the efficacy of PUVA in the treatment of urticaria pigmentosa.

Guillet GY, Dove N, Maleville J. Heparin liberation in urticaria pigmentosa. Arch Dermatol 1982;118:532–533.

This article presents a description of bleeding in urticaria pigmentosa lesions.

Kendall ME, Fields JP, King LE Jr. Cutaneous mastocytosis without clinically obvious skin lesions. J Am Acad Dermatol 1984;10:903–905.

This is an interesting article on an unusual form of cutaneous mastocytosis.

Travis WD, Li CY, Bergstrach EJ, et al. Systemic mast cell disease analysis of 58 cases and review of the literature. Medicine 1988;67:345.

This report indicates the following are features found in patients with systemic mastocytosis: urticaria pigmentosa (53%); anaphylactic episodes (14%); bone manifestations (28%); gastrointestinal manifestations (35%); hepatic manifestations (41%); neurologic manifestations (19%); myelodysplastic syndromes (15%); and myeloproliferative disorders (9%).

Travis WD, Li CY, Yam LT, et al. Significance of systemic mast cell disease associated with hematologic disorders. Cancer 1988;62:965–972.

This article presents a detailed description of hematologic abnormalities in mastocytosis in the Mayo Clinic experience.

Webb TA, Li CY, Yam LT. Systemic mast cell disease. A clinical and hemopathologic study of 26 cases. Cancer 1982;49:927–938.

This is a very informative article indicating that approximately 50% of patients with systemic mast cell disease fail to demonstrate cutaneous manifestations. The remaining 50% are generally those who have had urticaria pigmentosa for many years which has gradually evolved into a systemic disease. Interestingly, one of the patients had telangiectasia macularis eruptiva perstans.

Myelodysplastic features are highlighted by these authors.

Finolto S, Mekori YA, Metcalfe DD. Glucocorticoid decreases tissue mast cell number by reducing the production of the c-kit ligand, stem cell factor by resident cells. J Clin Invest 1997;99:1721–1728.

This article demonstrates the therapeutic effect of steroids in the treatment of cutaneous mast cell disease.

Longley BJ, Morganroth GS, Tyrrell L, et al. Altered metabolism of mast cell growth factor (c-kit ligand) in cutaneous mastocytosis. N Engl J Med 1993;328;1302–1307.

This article demonstrates that the abnormal concentration of soluble mast cell stem factor in the skin of patients with cutaneous mastocytosis abnormality is probably due to increased proteolytic processing and not due to splicing or sequence of mast cell stem factor mRNA.

Metcalfe DD. Classification and diagnosis of mastocytosis: current status and conclusions. J Invest Dermatol 1991;96:2S-4S, 64S–70S.

This is an excellent overview of the various features of mastocytosis.

Longley BJ, Tyrrell L, Lu SZ, et al. Somatic c-kit activating mutation in urticaria pigmentosa and aggressive mastocytosis: establishment of clonality in a human mast cell neoplasm. Nat Genet 1996;12:312–316.

This article demonstrates that a defective c-kit ligand receptor presumably leads to increased stimulation of mast cells.

CHAPTER 69

Langerhans' Cell Histiocytosis

Bernard A. Cohen, M.D., Thomas T. Provost, M.D.

In 1953, Lichtenstein proposed the unifying term "histiocytosis X" to encompass related disorders known by the previous eponyms eosinophilic granuloma, Letterer-Siwe disease, and Hand-Schüller-Christian disease. In 1987, the Histiocyte Society introduced the term Langerhans' cell histiocytosis (LCH) to reflect the importance of the Langerhans' cell in the pathogenesis of these disorders.

Rare disease previously divided into three clinical forms:

- *Letterer-Siwe disease*
- *Hand-Schüller-Christian syndrome*
- *eosinophilic granuloma*

Despite the protean clinical features, all cases demonstrate dendritic epidermal Langerhans' cells in the inflammatory infiltrates of involved organs. In addition to histiocytes, the infiltrates contain eosinophils, lymphocytes, and fibroblasts.

Epidermal Langerhans' cells found in all forms

? reactive versus malignant process—this is controversial

The presence of aberrant immunophenotypes and proliferative markers suggests that LCH is more likely to be a clonal neoplastic process than a reactive one. However, this is controversial, for there is no evidence of clonal T-cell receptor gene rearrangements, and other environmental and genetic factors may be required for the disorder to progress. Definite proof of a neoplastic etiology undoubtedly awaits further study by new cytogenetic and molecular techniques.

Ontogeny of Langerhans' Cells

Bone marrow origin of Langerhans' cells

Derived from CD34+ colony-forming unit–neutrophil/macrophage (CFU-NM) cell

The Langerhans' cell is a bone marrow–derived histiocytic cell. The development of the Langerhans' cell is unknown, but it is speculated that these cells develop from a CD34+ common bone marrow progenitor cell, the colony-forming unit–neutrophil/macrophage (CFU-NM) cell.

Langerhans' cell may give rise to veiled cell in lymphatics and interdigitating cell in paracortical areas of lymph nodes.

The details of the migration of these cells to the epidermis and the fate of the epidermal Langerhans' cells is an area of active investigation. The development and migration of the Langerhans' cell to and from the epidermis are regulated by cytokines in the microenvironment of the bone marrow and epidermis. (See reference by Stengl et al. for an excellent discussion.) Some investigators believe that the Langerhans' cell migrates from the skin in lymphatics as a veiled cell, populating the paracortical zone of the regional lymph nodes. There, these cells are theorized to evolve into interdigitating reticulum cells.

Langerhans' cells have characteristic cell surface markers (CD1a, MHC class II, FcIgG receptors, C3b receptors, CD4 and CD25 molecules).

The epidermal Langerhans' cells express a number of characteristic cell surface molecules, which identifies them. These include CD1a, major histocompatibility complex (MHC) class II molecules, Fc immunoglobulin G (IgG) receptors, C3b receptors, and CD4 and CD25 molecules.

Birbeck granule

Langerhans' cells, on electron microscopic examination, demonstrate the trilaminate cytoplasmic organelle—the Birbeck granule. These rod-shaped structures have a central lamella and a terminal vesicular dilatation, giving the characteristic "tennis racket" appearance. The function(s) of these granules is (are) unknown.

Histiocytic cells have two potential functions:
- *phagocytosis*
- *antigen processing*

Antigen-processing cells produce IL-1 and IL-2

Histiocytic cells, including Langerhans' cells, possess phagocytic capabilities. All these histiocytic cells express specific complement cell surface receptors (CR1 and CR3). These receptors bind C3b and C3bi, and FcIgG receptors bind the Fc fragment of Ig.

The blood dendritic cell, epidermal Langerhans' cells, the interdigitating reticulum cell of the lymph node paracortex, and the veil cell of the efferent lymph, also have antigen-presenting capabilities. These cells phagocytize, internalize, and process the antigen. The antigen is then re-expressed on the cell surface in association with MHC class II molecules. There is also some evidence for antigen presentation in association with MHC class I molecules. These cells also elaborate the cytokines needed for the induction of an immune response.

Clinical Presentation

Variation with Age

Peak incidence between 1 to 3 years of age

Although LCH can present at any age, peak incidence occurs in children between ages 1 and 3 years. In congenital cases, disease is often restricted to the skin and regresses spontaneously (congenital self-healing reticulohistiocytosis, Hashimoto-Pritzker disease). However, these patients, on rare occasions, return months or years later with limited or widespread visceral involvement, which can be life threatening.

Organ involvement characteristically occurs in older infants and toddlers.

In older infants and toddlers, multiorgan involvement is typical and can be associated with severe constitutional symptoms, including weight loss, fever, rash, lymphadenopathy, ear discharge, tachypnea, dyspnea, anemia, polydipsia, jaundice, anemia, and hepatosplenomegaly. Organ failure can occur because of direct infiltration of Langerhans' cells. The course tends to fluctuate, and aggressive systemic therapy may be required. Although lesions may gradually regress, there is a high risk of morbidity and mortality from organ failure and complications of therapy.

In older children and adults, lesions generally confined to a single organ

In older children and adults, lesions may be asymptomatic and are usually confined to a single organ. Although significant morbidity or mortality occasionally occur, most lesions resolve without therapy.

Specific Organ Involvement

Cutaneous Involvement

Cutaneous involvement occurs in at least 50% of patients and may be the first diagnostic clue. Lesions can affect any area of the skin and may be transient or persistent and limited or widespread. Disease can be restricted to the skin for years before visceral involvement develops.

Hemorrhagic or petechial eczema-like lesions are characteristic.

The scalp is the most common site in both children and adults (Figure 69–1). Diffuse symmetric scaly red patches typically become crusted, hemorrhagic, and erosive. Lesions often spread from the postauricular area and are usually asymptomatic or somewhat tender. Diffuse alopecia may develop but resolves as the disease regresses.

Seborrheia-like dermatitis

The flexures, including the groin, perianal area, inframammary area in women, neck, and axillae, are also commonly affected (Figure 69–2). Red macules evolve to crusted erosive patches, which early on may simulate seborrheic dermatitis. Ulcerations can be persistent and resistant to therapy.

Widespread disease commonly involves perineum in elderly women.

Seborrheic dermatitis–like scaling and papules can appear around the nose and, less commonly, diffusely over the trunk and proximal extremities (Figure 69–3). These lesions can also become crusted and hemorrhagic. Involvement of the external genitals is also common, particularly in older women, in whom it presents with chronic tender infiltration of the labia, perineum, and suprapubic area. Induration and erythema of the skin and draining sinuses may develop over bony or lymph node lesions most commonly on the neck and axillae.

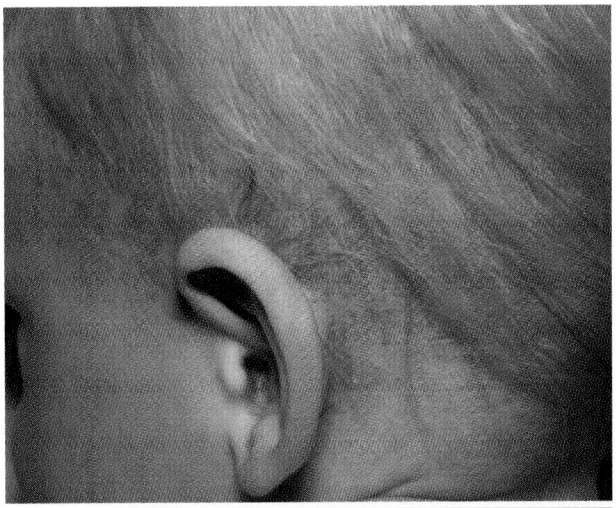

FIGURE 69–1 This 3-year-old boy developed hemorrhagic crusted patches in the scalp, behind the ears, and in the groin creases. A skin biopsy from the scalp showed histiocytic infiltrates typical of LCH.

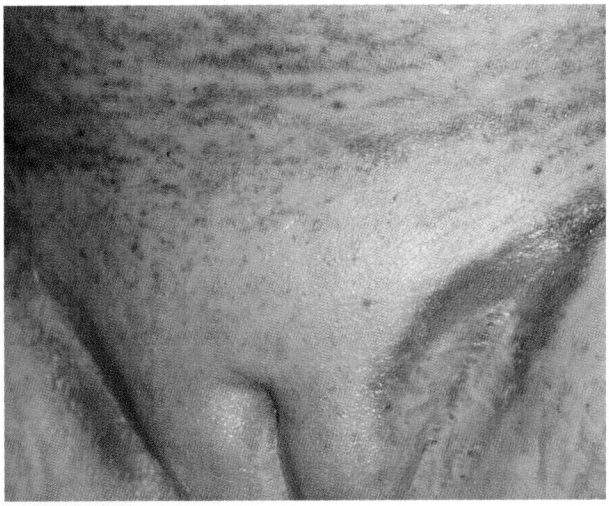

FIGURE 69–2 Violaceous indurated abdominal plaques and macerated eczematous patches in the groin creases waxed and waned in this 9-month-old girl with pancytopenia and LCH.

Bony Skeleton Involvement

Bony involvement occurs in a third of patients. Osteolytic lesions in the skull can be appreciated clinically because of associated deep soft tissue nodules and plaques and palpable bony defects. Although the skull is most commonly affected, lesions in the long bones and flat bones can also appear. The hands and feet are usually spared.

Osteolytic lesions most commonly involving scalp.

Symptoms vary with the area of involvement. Isolated or multiple lesions in the scalp may be asymptomatic or somewhat tender. Osteolytic lesions around the ear can mimic mastoiditis or chronic otitis media. Periorbital involvement can lead to proptosis, vertebral lesions are frequently associated with bony collapse, and mandibular involvement may produce loose teeth.

Proptosis
Loose teeth

Visceral Involvement

Lymphadenopathy occurs in 10% of patients and most commonly involves the neck, where massive enlargement can develop. At other sites, adenopathy usually occurs in association with contiguous bone or skin disease.

Cervical lymphadenopathy may be very prominent.

Although pancytopenia is common in disseminated disease, marrow infiltration is usually limited or absent. Hepatic and splenic enlargements also occur commonly, but significant organ dysfunction is usually limited to patients with severe disseminated disease. Diffuse interstitial infiltrates in the lungs can be associated with tachypnea, dyspnea, and, rarely, respiratory failure. Rare infiltration of the gastrointestinal tract in young children can be associated with poor weight gain, intestinal malabsorption, and protein-losing enteropathy.

Hepatosplenomegaly commonly occurs
Pancytopenia
Bone marrow involvement unusual
Interstitial lung disease

The most common cause of diabetes insipidus in children is probably infiltration of the pituitary in LCH. The diagnosis should be considered in any child who presents with polyuria and polydipsia. Other endocrinologic manifestations include growth hormone and thyroid hormone deficiencies.

Diabetes insipidus in children

Pathology

Histologic examination reveals Langerhans' cells, characterized by homogeneous pink cytoplasm and lobulated, coffee bean–like nuclei. The epidermis contains macrophages, whereas lymphocytes and eosinophils are prominent in the dermis. There is no correlation between the perceived aggressiveness of the infiltrate and the extent of disease.

No correlation between histologic features and extent of disease

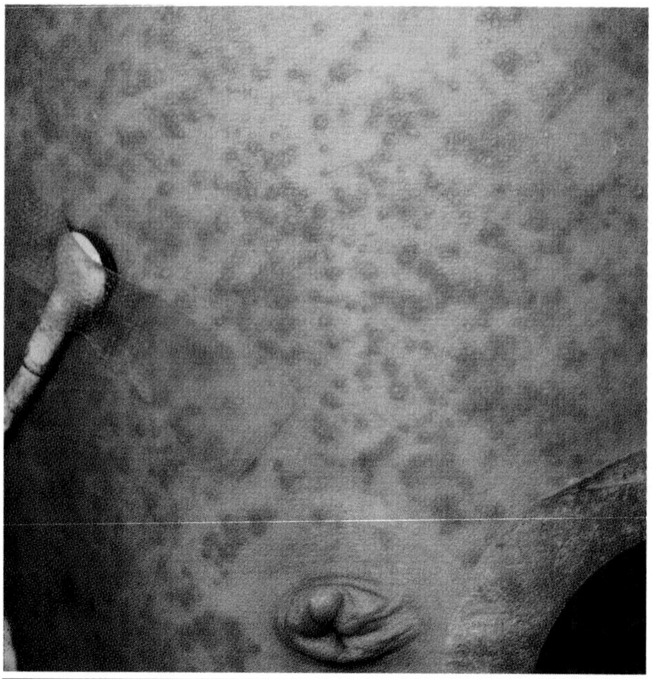

FIGURE 69–3 Widely disseminated red papules and plaques shown here on the chest and abdomen of this toddler with LCH were associated with hepatosplenomegaly, generalized lymphadenopathy, and pneumonitis.

The histologic differential diagnosis includes seborrheic dermatitis, atopic dermatitis, juvenile xanthogranuloma, and xanthoma disseminatum.

Diagnosis established by demonstrating Birbeck granules on EM or CD1 positivity by immunofluorescence.

The diagnosis can be established by the detection of Birbeck granules by electron microscopy, or the demonstration of CD1a positivity on the cell surface of the Langerhans' cells. Positive staining for adenosinetriphosphatase, S-100 protein, alpha d-mannosidase, or the peanut lectin may also help establish the diagnosis.

Treatment

Isolated lesions frequently spontaneously resolve

Treatment of LCH is still problematic and should be restricted to disease associated with organ dysfunction or disfigurement. Isolated cutaneous lesions may resolve without therapy.

Cutaneous lesions may respond quickly to moderate-potency topical steroids. Topical nitrogen mustard and psoralen ultraviolet A (PUVA) have also been used with some success.

Cytotoxic agents

With systemic involvement or recalcitrant cutaneous disease, therapy with oral steroids and/or vinblastine is recommended. Other cytotoxic agents, including cyclophosphamide, chlorambucil, and etoposide (VP-16), may be useful. Other experimental therapies, including cyclosporine, thalidomide, transplantation, and monoclonal antibodies, are being studied.

Prognosis

Prognosis guarded for children under 2 years of age and adults over 60 years of age

The severity and extent of organ dysfunction correlate best with prognosis. Newborns and older patients without organ dysfunction fare the best, with spontaneous resolution being the rule. Children under 2 years old and adults over the age of 60 years, with organ dysfunction, have the worst outcome with survival less than 50%. The prognosis is particularly poor in patients with symptomatic multiorgan involvement.

Morbidity in survivors depends largely on late sequelae of the healed lesions and their sites. Complications from endocrinologic dysfunction can be minimized by monitoring for diabetes insipidus and growth hormone and thyroid failure. Late reactivations of LCH may also occur even in patients with minimal early disease.

Annotated Bibliography

Arico M, Egeler RM. Clinical aspects of Langerhans' cell histiocytosis. Hematol Oncol Clin North Am 1998;12:246–258.

Lam K. Langerhans' cell histiocytosis. Postgrad Med J 1997;73:391–394.

These articles succinctly review the classification of the histiocytoses as well as the pathogenesis, clinical presentation, treatment, and prognosis of LCH. Pathology and immunohistochemical markers are also discussed.

Munn S, Chu AC. LCH of the skin. Hematol Oncol Clin North Am 1998;12:269–286.

The clinical findings, treatment, and histopathology of cutaneous LCH are reviewed. Good-quality clinical photographs, photomicrographs, and electron microscopy are also included.

Mejia R, Dano JA, Roberts R, et al. LCH in adults. J Am Acad Dermatol 1997;37:314–317.

Several unusual cases of LCH in adults are presented. The authors demonstrate the difficulties in making the diagnosis, particularly when the dermatopathology is not initially diagnostic and the primary cutaneous lesions are obscured by secondary infection.

Willman CL, McClain KL. An update on clonality, cytokines, and viral etiology in LCH. Hematol Oncol Clin North Am 1998;12:407–416.

The latest scientific research on molecular assessment of clonality in LCH is presented. The role of cytokines and viruses in the pathogenesis of disease is also reviewed. The authors propose that LCH is a clonal neoplastic disease with highly variable biologic behavior and clinical severity.

Stengl G, Maurer D, Hauser C, et al. The epidermis: an immunologic microenvironment. In: Freedberg IM, Eisen AZ, Wolff K, et al., eds. Fitzpatrick's Dermatology in General Medicine, 5th ed. New York: McGraw-Hill, 1999, pp 346–349.

This article presents a very informative discussion by the leading group of Langerhans' cell investigators on the origin and migration of the epidermal Langerhans' cell to and from the epidermis. It also contains an excellent bibliography.

CHAPTER 70

Miscellaneous Diseases

René Genadry, M.D., Thomas T. Provost, M.D.

Lichen Planus

Best evidence is that lichen planus is an immunologically mediated disease.

This is an inflammatory disease of unknown etiology, generally characterized by flat-top, erythematous, highly pruritic papules. These lesions demonstrate, histopathologically, a band-like mononuclear inflammatory cell infiltrate, hugging the epidermis. The best evidence indicates that this is an autoimmune T cell–mediated disease. This evidence is summarized as follows:

T cell mediated

- The inflammatory infiltrate consists predominantly of HLA-DR–positive, activated T cells (both CD4 and CD8); in young lesions, CD4 lymphocytes predominate; in older established lesions, the majority of lymphocytes are CD8+ (cytotoxic).
- There are increased numbers of Langerhans' cells and human leukocyte antigen (HLA)-DR–positive keratinocytes in the involved areas.
- There is evidence for a familial occurrence of lichen planus and increased frequencies of specific HLA phenotypes in familial lichen planus patients.
- The frequency of lichen planus is increased in women, although formal studies are lacking.

Associated with other autoimmune diseases

- Lichen planus has been seen in association with autoimmune diseases, including ulcerative colitis, alopecia areata, and vitiligo. It also has been seen in association with primary biliary cirrhosis, Sjögren's syndrome, and as an allergic reaction to drugs and photographic chemicals.

A lichen planus–like eruption occurs in graft-versus-host disease

- A lichenoid dermatitis that is similar, if not identical, to lichen planus occurs in chronic graft-versus-host disease (GVHD). (See Chapter 65, "Graft-versus-Host Disease," for further discussion.)

Histopathology

Max Joseph clefts

"Saw tooth" acanthosis

The histopathology of lichen planus is characterized, in addition to a band-like mononuclear infiltrate at the dermal-epidermal junction, by "colloid or civatte bodies" representing degenerating epidermal basal cells (apoptosis). The epidermal changes consist of irregular acanthosis producing a characteristic "saw tooth" histologic picture. Orthokeratotic hyperkeratosis is present. Cleft formation (Max Joseph cleft formation), representing a focal separation of the epidermis from the dermis, is a frequent occurrence. Melanin pigmentary incontinence is characteristically seen.

Fibrin deposition on direct immunoflouorescence

Direct immunofluorescent examination of lichen planus reveal dermal globular deposits of immunoglobulin M (IgM), and, occasionally, IgA and IgG. Fibrin deposition is usually heavy at the dermal-epidermal junction. (This fibrin deposition is an especially helpful diagnostic finding in direct immunofluorescent examination of erosive lichen planus mucosal lesions.)

Clinical Features

Wickham's striae

Clinically, lichen planus is characterized by shiny, flat-top, erythematous, violaceous papules (Figure 70–1). White lines (Wickham's striae) occur on the epidermal surface. Linear lesions, occurring along scratch marks (Koebner's phenomena), are also characteristic. Postinflammatory hyperpigmentation, especially in African Americans, is problematic (Figure 70–2).

Lichen planus lesions may demonstrate varying morphologies, including: (1) hypertrophic; (2) linear; (3) annular; (4) vesiculobullous; (5) follicular; (6) ulcerative; (7) zosteriform lesions; and (8) solitary lesion.

The lesions may be focal or widespread. There is no significant malignant degeneration of cutaneous lichen planus lesions.

Mucous Membrane Involvement

Oral

Mucous membrane involvement in lichen planus is frequent (occurs in approximately two-thirds of patients). The lesions may demonstrate a characteristic lace-like pattern of white streaks on the buccal mucosa (Figures 70–3 and 70–4). Many of these lesions ulcerate, producing erosive, painful lesions (Figure 70–5). Oral lesions are frequently complicated by oral candidiasis, producing a burning or painful mouth (Figure 70–6). Malignant degeneration (squamous cell carcinoma) infrequently occurs.

Perineal Involvement

Frequency of genital involvement is unknown.

Genital lichen planus was infrequently reported in the early part of the 20th century, and its prevalence today continues to be underestimated. There are multiple reasons for this statement. For example, most skin and oral lichen planus lesions are treated without adequate evaluation of the vulva. Furthermore, on the vulva, the most commonly involved area is the vestibule, which may be overlooked. In addition, vaginal lichen planus lesions are frequently detected but are not recognized as lichen planus because they mimic desquamative vaginitis.

One additional reason that the true frequency of genital lichen planus is unknown is, historically, lichen planus and lichen sclerosis were considered by some gynecologists, to be a spectrum of the same disease, with the latter considered a sclerotic form of lichen planus.

Pathology. The histopathology of lichen planus varies depending on the perineal site of involvement. On the keratinized vulvar skin, irregular thickening of the epidermis with hyperkeratosis and/or parakeratosis is common. There is

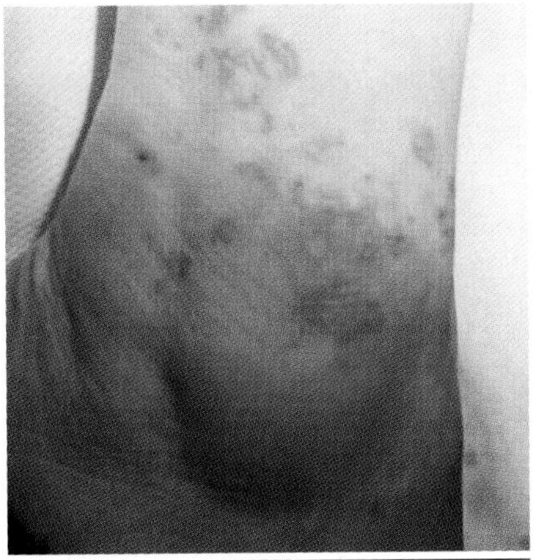

FIGURE 70–1 Violaceous flat-top polygonal lesions of lichen planus.

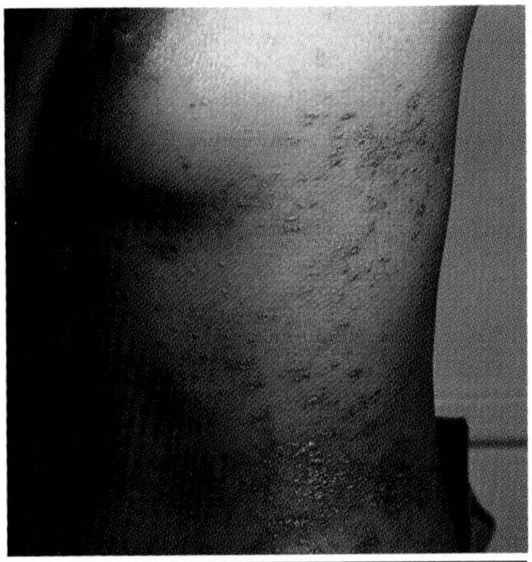

FIGURE 70–2 Extensive postinflammatory hyperpigmentation of lichen planus lesions in an African American female.

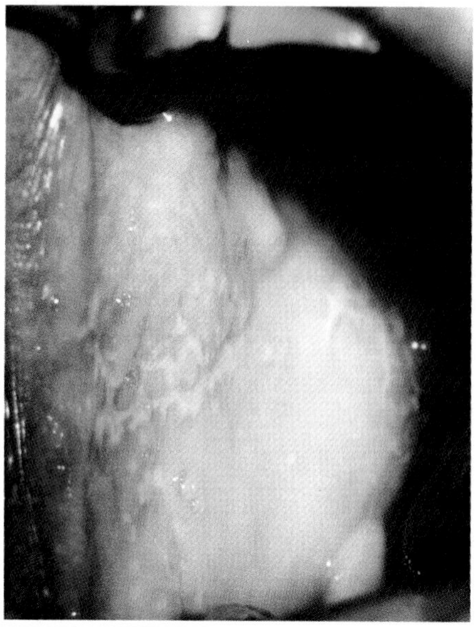

FIGURE 70–3 Wickham's striae buccal mucosa of a patient with lichen planus.

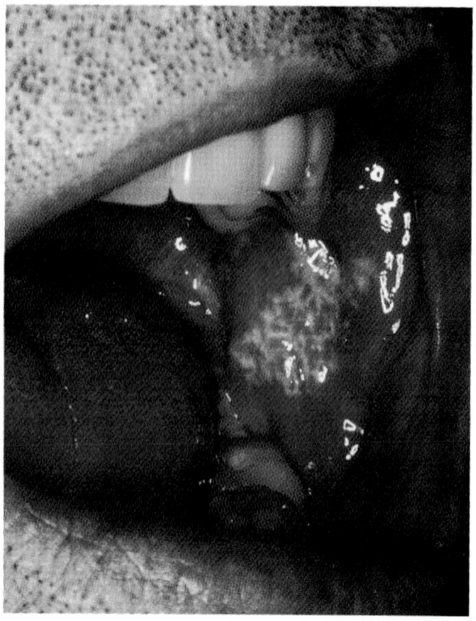

FIGURE 70–4 Wichham's striae buccal mucosa.

often thinning of the epidermis with a mononuclear infiltrate at the basal layer of the epidermis associated with individual keratinocyte necrosis.

On the mucous membrane portion of the perineum, parakeratosis and epidermal necrosis are more common. Occasionally, subepidermal blistering may occur in association with erosions.

Although rare, the risk of malignant transformation exists in chronic erosive and hyperplastic lichen planus lesions on the perineum.

Pain and dyspareunia

Clinical Features. At times, vulvar lichen planus is asymptomatic and discovered only following a directed gynecologic examination after the detection of oral or cutaneous lesions. Other types of perineal lichen planus present with soreness, rawness, or burning. Itching can be present but is an infrequent complaint. Dyspareunia, however, is a common complaint. Persistent vulvovaginal irritation and discharge, occasionally blood tinged, which are resistant to common topical therapies is frequent. Vulvar lichen planus is more common in middle-aged women and in later life (sixth decade). The clinical presentation is variable and may be nonerosive, erosive, or hypertrophic.

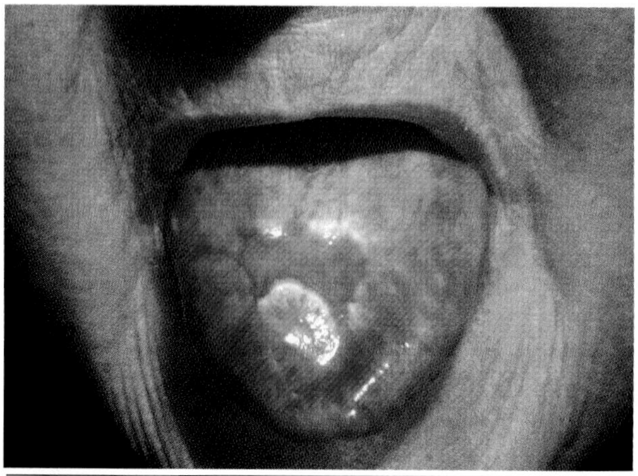

FIGURE 70–5 Ulcerative lichen planus on the tongue.

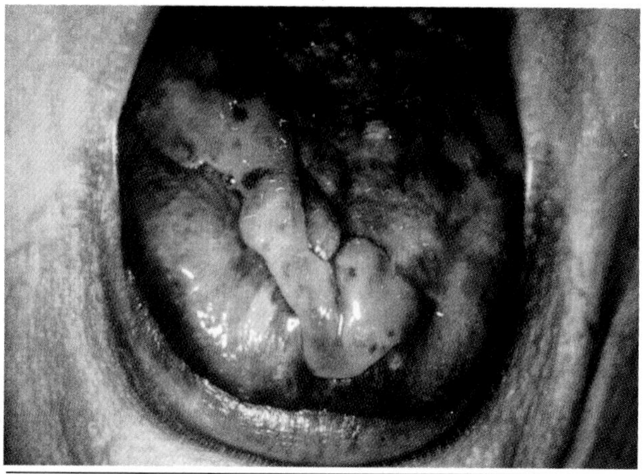

FIGURE 70–6 Ulcerative lichen planus of the tongue complicated by candidiasis.

Nonerosive Lesions. Nonerosive mucous membrane lesions are whitish, poorly marginated plaques or papules with a linear or reticular shape. The vestibule and the vagina are most frequently involved. The vestibule demonstrates a reticular pattern (Wickham's striae).

Erosive Lesions. The erosive form of lichen planus is a chronic recalcitrant condition, resulting in scarring and associated with pain, pruritus, and dyspareunia. The erosive lesions are primarily noted in the vestibule and in the vagina, which is usually markedly erythematous. At times, the vagina may be involved in the absence of vulvar disease (Figure 70–7). A serosanguinous discharge is common and can be a presenting complaint. With disease progression, the walls of the vagina may adhere to one another resulting in stenosis, shortening of the vagina, and dyspareunia. A superimposed infection may be present. The normal vulvar architecture may be obliterated due to scarring, atrophy, and resorption of the labia minora and clitoral hood resulting in phimosis.

Vaginal stenosis

Vulvar architecture scarred

Vulvo-vaginal-gingival syndrome represents a variant of erosive lichen planus. Originally described by Pelisse, it involves the vulva, vagina, and gingiva. It has been estimated that 65% of lichen planus patients with cutaneous lesions suffer oral involvement, while 50% of oral lesions are associated with genital disease. Erosive lichen planus is a chronic recalcitrant disease characterized by exacerbations and remissions with scarring, irritation, and pain.

Vulvo-vaginal-gingival syndrome, a variant of erosive lichen planus

Hypertrophic Perineal Lichen Planus. Hypertrophic lichen planus is the least common type seen on the vulva. Itching is the most common symptom, and these lesions may have a warty appearance. It may involve the perineal and perianal regions. Cervical involvement has also been described.

Gynecologic Management. The management of lichen planus of the vulva is difficult. No single therapy is predictably effective. In nonerosive lesions, a cream-based midpotency steroid is well tolerated.

Erosive lichen planus is less responsive to topical therapy and frequently requires systemic steroid therapy. Limited areas can be treated with intralesional steroids. Triamcinolone injections can often result in healing of the affected areas. Oral and topical retinoids, as well as cyclosporin, griseofulvin, and dapsone, have been shown to be inconsistently beneficial. The use of regular vaginal

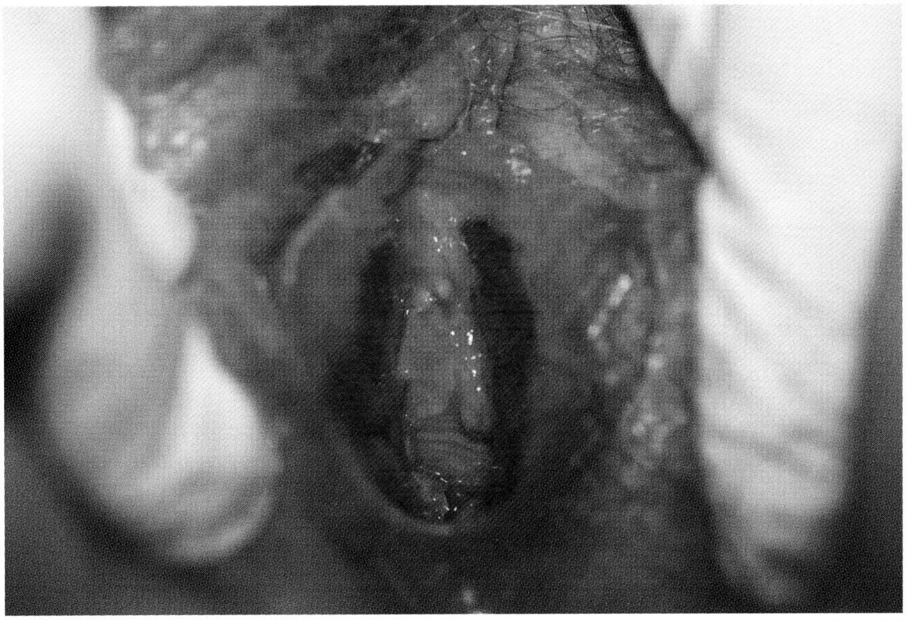

FIGURE 70–7 Erosive lesions of lichen planus. Intralabial and vestibule erosive lesions. Only mucosal lesions; skin is normal.

dilators may be helpful in maintaining vaginal depth and integrity. In late-stage disease, surgery may be required. It should be limited to circumstances where active disease has been controlled. Medical treatment should be continued in order to avoid the flare-ups (Koebner's phenomenon).

Patients with vulvar lichen planus usually require supportive therapy, counseling, and education. Liberal use of antidepressant therapy should be prescribed to allow severely depressed patients to handle this most distressing period of time.

We have become impressed with the severe debility associated with erosive lichen planus of the vagina in some patients. In order to provide a better quality of life in selected patients, we have successfully employed immunosuppressive agents. An example of one of these patients is given below.

A 73-year-old Caucasian female with a 20-year history of erosive vaginal lesions was found to have mild erosive lichen planus of the oral gingiva associated with Wickham's striae. The vaginal erosive lichen planus had produced ablation of the sulcus between the labia and the clitoris and narrowing of the vaginal introitus with scar formation. The erosive lesions around the urethral meatus made voiding very painful. The patient designed an apparatus to prevent the urine from contacting the eroded tissue. Hydroxychloroquine 200 mg twice daily had no success, and the patient could not tolerate azathioprine. Methotrexate 5.0 mg, once weekly, however, controlled her symptoms, and examination revealed that the vaginal ulcerations and erosions had healed.

Lichen Planopilaris

In addition to the glabrous and mucous membrane lichen planus, involvement of hair follicles, especially of the scalp, producing a patchy scarring alopecia may be noted (lichen planopilaris) (Figure 70–8).

Lichen Planus Pemphigoides

This entity most likely represents the occurrence of lichen planus and bullous pemphigoid in the same patient and must be differentiated from bullous lichen planus. Direct and indirect immunofluorescence studies will differentiate the two conditions.

Lichen Planus–Lupus Erythematosus Overlap

This is a very rare association and most likely represents the coexistence of lichen planus and lupus erythematosus in same patient. Serologic and immunofluorescence studies will help differentiate. One of the authors (TTP) has only seen this occurrence once. The patient was anti–Ro (SSA) antibody positive.

Lichen Planus Drug Eruptions and Contact Dermatitis

Lichen planus–like eruptions have been detected in association with use of antimalarials, gold, thiazide diuretics, streptomycin, propranolol, and lithium carbonate.

Lichenoid reactions to photographic color developers, resembling lichen planus, have been reported. The active ingredients in the developers are substituted paraphenylene diamines.

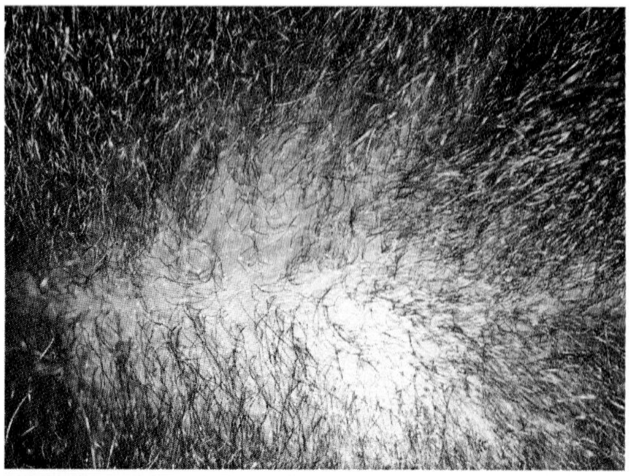

FIGURE 70–8 Patchy scarring alopecia of lichen planopilaris in an African American female.

Lichen Planus Nail Involvement

Lichen planus can involve the nails, producing loss of nail (anonychia) and characteristic pterygium formation (Figure 70–9). All nails can be involved, with or without cutaneous involvement.

Treatment

Glabrous skin lichen planus responds to topical steroids, ultraviolet light, and hydroxychloroquine therapy. Oral mucous membrane lichen planus, in our experience, has been found to be generally very responsive to hydroxychloroquine 200 mg twice daily. We have found lichen planopilaris also may respond to hydroxychloroquine 200 mg twice daily.

As noted above, vaginal lichen planus is a recalcitrant disease; the response to hydroxychloroquine has been disappointing. We have found azathioprine 50 to 150 mg daily to be effective. Methotrexate, 5.0 to 7.5 mg once weekly, is also an effective form of therapy (Table 70–1).

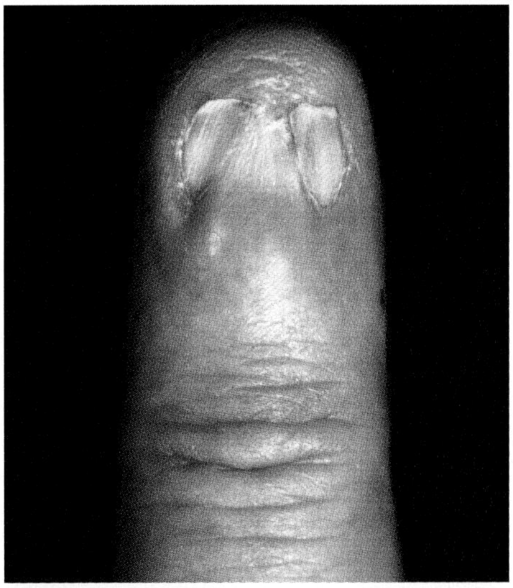

FIGURE 70–9 Lichen planus of the nail producing loss of nail and characteristic ptergium (extension of cuticle nailfold skin over the nail bed).

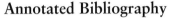

TABLE 70–1 Treatment of Lichen Planus

- Hydroxychloroquine 200 mg twice daily, effective in glabrous and oral, but generally not vaginal, lichen planus
- Azathioprine 100 to 150 mg per day, effective for erosive lichen planus on the perineum
- Methotrexate, 5.0 to 7.5 mg once weekly, effective for erosive lichen planus on the perineum

Annotated Bibliography

Edwards L. Vulvar lichen planus. Arch Dermatol 1989;125:1677–1680.

This is a report of seven cases demonstrating the fact that erosive lichen planus can produce severe discomfort and scarring, resulting in a complete ablation of the normal vulvar architecture.

In most instances, involvement of the buccal mucosa and gingiva was also detected.

Buckley WR. Lichenoid eruptions following contact dermatitis. Arch Dermatol 1958;78:454–457.

Liden C. Lichen planus in relation to occupational and nonoccupational exposure to chemicals. Br J Dermatol 1986;115:23–31.

These two articles highlight the occurrence of lichen planus–like lesions as an allergic reaction to various chemicals.

Graham-Brown RAC, Sarkany I, Sherlock S. Lichen planus and primary biliary cirrhosis. Br J Dermatol 1982;106;699–703.

This is an interesting paper reporting the association of lichen planus and primary biliary cirrhosis in five patients. The authors believe that the coexistence of these two diseases is probably more than coincidental.

Lewis FM. Vulvar lichen planus. Br J Dermatol 1998;138:569–575.

This is a good review of vulvar lichen planus and highlights management strategies.

Fung MA, LeBoit PE. Light microscopic criteria for the diagnosis of early vulvar lichen sclerosus: a comparison with lichen planus. Am J Surg Pathol 1998;22(4):473–478.

On the basis of a review of nine cases of early lichen sclerosus compared with six cases of lichen planus, the authors propose microscopic criteria for early lichen sclerosus et atrophicus (LS and A) and differentiate this entity from lichen planus.

Holmes SC, Burden AD. Lichen sclerosus and lichen planus: a spectrum of disease? Clin Exp Dermatol 1998;23:129–131.

This is a report of two cases and review of the literature.

Lichen Sclerosus et Atrophicus

Uncommon inflammatory disease of unknown etiology

Most commonly occurring in women

Perineum involvement

In men, balanitis xerotica obliterans

Lichen sclerosus et atrophicus is an uncommon inflammatory disease. It is characterized, most commonly, by white atrophic lesions, producing an hour-glass appearance, surrounding the anus and vagina. It also can occur on other areas of the body, producing white, atrophic, macular lesions with central delling (Figures 70–10 to 70–12). Females outnumber males by 10:1. Balanitis xerotica obliterans of the penis is the same disease in males.

May be familial and associated with autoimmune diseases

On unusual occasions, the disease has been detected in monozygotic and dizygotic female twins. It has also been described in mother-daughter, mother-son, brother-sister, and father-son combinations. There also appears to be an increased frequency of autoimmune diseases and autoantibodies in patients and first-degree relatives. These observations suggest a genetic predisposition and an autoimmune etiology.

The possible relationship of LS and A with scleroderma is intriguing. The coexistence of these conditions in the same patient, in one of the author's (TTP) experience, is an occasional occurrence.

Pathology

The pathology of LS and A demonstrates hyalinization and edema of dermal collagen. The epidermis may show variable acanthosis, hyperkeratosis, and follicular plugging. Beneath the hyalinized collagen is a band of lymphocytes.

At present, the authors are unaware of any phenotypic studies characterizing the types of lymphocytes in the infiltrate. (It is tempting to speculate that they are T cells secreting lymphokines which induce dermal fibroblasts to secrete various nonfibrous connective tissue proteins [eg, hyaluronic acid] and, to a lesser extent, collagen. These fibroblast secretory products may induce many of the clinical features recognized as being LS and A.)

Cutaneous Manifestations

Vulvar Lichen Sclerosis

Common gynecologic condition

In women, LS and A is more frequent and extensive on the vulva and is one of the most common conditions evaluated in vulvar clinics. The LS and A is more common in Caucasians and Hispanics and rare in Africans. It has been described in all age groups (as early as 4 weeks to 6 months of age) but occurs more frequently in the perimenopausal and postmenopausal age groups.

Figure-eight configuration involving the perineum and perianal regions

Initially asymptomatic, the lesion of LS and A begins as a yellowish-blue papule that progressively involves, by coalescence, the anogenital area surrounding the vulva and perianal areas in a figure-eight pattern. Progressively, the

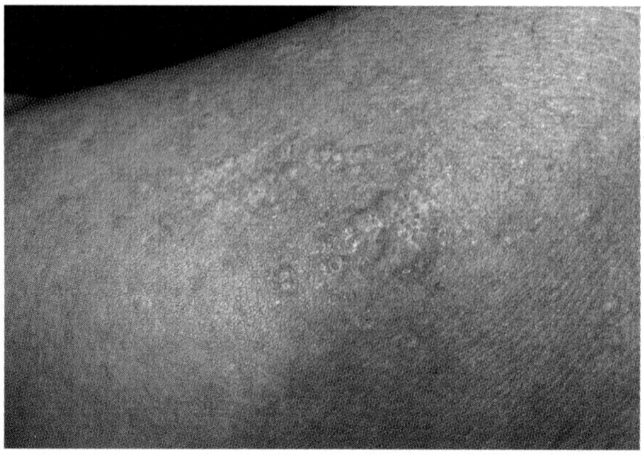

FIGURE 70–10 Macular atrophic white lesions with central delling of lichen sclerosis et atrophicus.

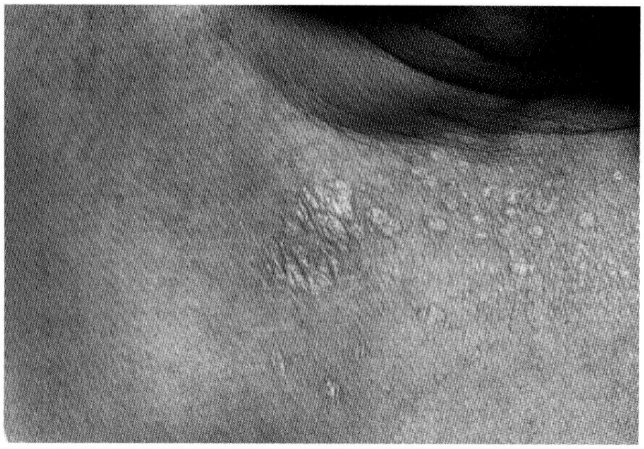

FIGURE 70–11 Similar lesions as depicted in Figure 70–10.

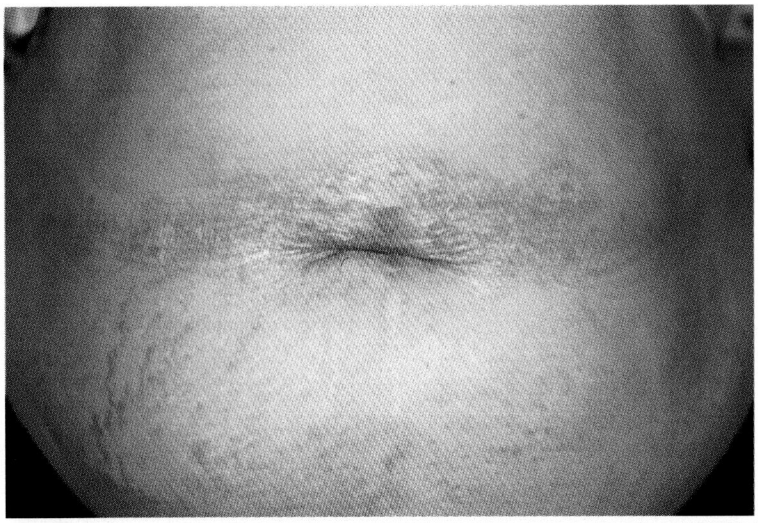

FIGURE 70-12 Atrophic patches of lichen sclerosis around the waist and in the periumbilical region.

skin becomes hypopigmented, takes on a parchment-like appearance, and becomes sharply demarcated from the normal adjacent skin (Figure 70–13). These areas are easily irritated, especially in the postmenopausal state, producing the dominant presenting symptom, pruritus. The epidermal thinning makes LS and A prone to trauma, although hemorrhagic and bullous lesions are uncommon. Excoriation and hyperplasia may develop. In the younger premenarchal age group, such traumatic irritation can lead to changes commonly seen in sexually abused children, often leading to investigation and false accusations. Malignant degeneration may occur. The progression of LS and A produces shrinkage of the vulva, resulting in a constricted outlet. The skin easily splits. This condition has been termed kraurosis vulvae.

LS and A varies in severity

May be asymptomatic

May be pruritic

May produce vaginal scarring and dyspareunia

Clinical Features. Clinically, the initial lesions in some patients are asymptomatic and noted only on close examination as a thinning or atrophy of the vulvar skin. It is unusual to note any vaginal mucosal abnormality. On occasion, the patient experiences mild pruritus. With increasing age, however, pruritus becomes more prominent and progressive scarring occurs, producing vaginal introitus stenosis and fissuring. This leads to burning and slight bleeding with sexual activity. A chronic state of dyspareunia frequently becomes established even in the absence of progression of the underlying skin disorder.

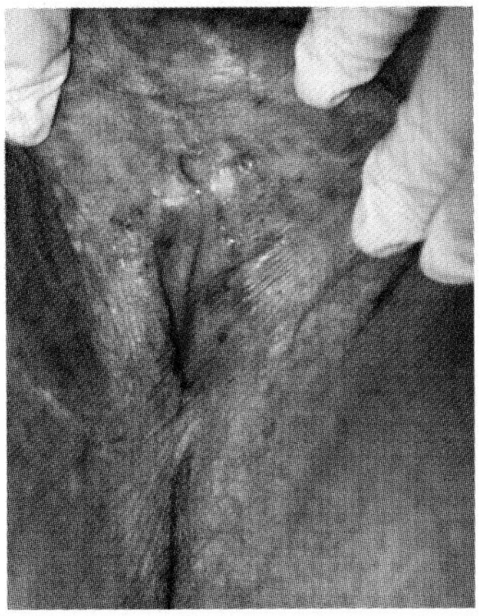

FIGURE 70-13 LS and A of vulva. Severe atropic changes of the perineum. Note normal architecture in clitoris, labia majora and labia minora have been obliterated (agglutinated) by the disease processl

In other instances, pruritus is the presenting and dominant symptom. The irritated skin lesions are further aggravated by constant scratching. These patients may demonstrate varied clinical features (atrophic, old, sclerotic, and thinned skin to hyperplastic, hyperkeratotic, white, leukoplakic lesions). Other patients may demonstrate ulcerated, eroded lesions.

LS and A may interfere with urination and defecation

Late in the process, scarring becomes the dominant feature responsible for the stenosis that interferes with comfortable urination, defecation, and sexual enjoyment. This scarring is associated with loss of the normal vulvar architecture. Phimosis and agglutination of the clitoral hood occurs. Atrophy of the labia minora is frequent, and the vaginal introitus narrows as agglutination of the labia majora occurs. The posterior fourchette becomes fragile and bleeds easily.

Treatment. Treatment of lichen sclerosis aims at altering its progression and preventing the devastating effect of scarring. Maintenance of normal anatomy as well as restoration of normal function is the rationale for treatment. Thus, the main goal of therapy, depending on the stage of the disease, includes symptomatic relief, preservation of anatomy and function, arrest of progression, and early detection and prevention of neoplasia in those patients who are at increased risk.

In patients who are asymptomatic, monitoring of the anatomic changes remains the main purpose of observation. Any change, particularly, thickened hyperplastic changes and nonhealing ulcerative changes should be biopsied.

In those patients complaining of itching, burning, soreness, or rawness, local steroid therapy is effective in alleviating symptoms. In patients with hyperplastic changes not responsive to topical steroids, injections of steroids may be necessary. In rare circumstances and in those situations resistant to topical therapies, systemic steroid therapy has provided some relief.

Testosterone cream

In an attempt to alter the progression of the disease and overcome what was previously perceived as poor nutrition of the underlying skin, testosterone therapy has been used and continues to be used with some effectiveness. Whether such therapy is effective through its hormonal or emollient effect is unclear. Two percent testosterone propionate in petrolatum, employed two to three times a day up to 6 months, has provided relief in situations unresponsive to steroid therapy. After this intense therapy, the frequency of application can be reduced to a maintenance level of once a day depending on the response and the side effects. These side effects have been variable but, when present, have included clitoromegaly and mild hirsutism. Since testosterone therapy does not address the pruritus, patients should also be continued on a steroid cream or given systemic antipruritic agents (antihistamines).

Progesterone cream

In the premenarchal patient, in order to avoid the masculinizing effect of testosterone, progesterone has been used effectively. Four hundred milligrams of progesterone in oil, mixed with four ounces of Aquaphor, may be applied twice a day to the affected area for up to 6 months. At that time, applications can be reduced, depending on response. Oral and topical retinoids have been used at times with some benefit and might be considered in individual patients.

In hyperplastic, poorly healed or poorly responsive lesions, local excision may be entertained. The surgical treatment of lichen sclerosis of the vulva has also included vulvectomy, cryotherapy, and laser ablation. These procedures are associated with a high recurrence rate and are suitable only for patients who have failed medical therapy. It should be noted that lichen sclerosis has developed in the grafted skin following vulvectomy in as many as 50% of patients.

Risk of malignancy

The most important aspect of the gynecologic management of patients with lichen sclerosis is close follow-up, as the risk of malignant transformation is approximately 10%. Malignant degeneration occurs most commonly in areas of hyperplastic or chronically eroded skin.

The severe debilitating nature of LS and A are illustrated by three patients in whom immunosuppressive therapy was employed.

Treatment is difficult

Preliminary evidence indicates that hydroxychloroquine, azathioprine, or methotrexate have proven beneficial in recalcitrant cases.

Recently, we saw a woman in her 40s with severe, symptomatic LS and A involving the vulva, producing narrowing of the vaginal introitus. She had had LS and A since her teenage years. Her sister also had LS and A. Dyspareunia was a prominent feature. High potency steroid creams, topical estrogen, topical testosterone preparations, as well as adrenocorticotropic hormone (ACTH) injections and steroid injections provided the patient only partial relief of her symptomatology. Finally, in order to improve her quality of life, immunosuppression was tried in the form of azathioprine 50 mg twice daily. She could not tolerate this medication, but methotrexate 5.0 mg once weekly provided the patient almost total relief of her symptomatology.

A second patient with identical complaints was also successfully treated with methotrexate 7.5 mg once weekly.

We also have been successful using hydroxychloroquine 200 mg twice daily in providing symptomatic relief for a woman with LS and A with severe dyspareunia.

These preliminary studies indicate that hydroxychloroquine and immunosuppressive agents, in low doses, may be effective in treating some severe forms of LS and A, in which the quality of life is greatly compromised.

Balanitis Xerotica Obliterans

In the male, balanitis xerotica obliterans, involving the glans penis, produces pruritus and soreness (Figure 70–14). With scarring, the prepuce becomes sclerotic and retraction impossible. Narrowing of the urethral meatus may occur, necessitating surgical correction. As in women, carcinoma may develop, but the frequency is unknown. Treatment with corticosteroid creams is only marginally successful. We have, thus far, no experience with the use of hydroxychloroquine or immunosuppressive agents in this group of patients.

Annotated Bibliography

Harrington CI, Dunsmore IR. Investigation into the incidence of autoimmune disorders in patients with lichen sclerosis et atrophicus. Br J Dermatol 1981;104:563–566.

Meryrick-Thomas RH, Ridley CM, Black MM. The association of lichen sclerosis et atrophicus and autoimmune related disease in males. Br J Dermatol 1983;109: 661–664.

Meryrick-Thomas RH, Ridley CM, McGibbon DH, et al. Lichen sclerosis et atrophicus and autoimmunity—a study of 350 women. Br J Dermatol 1988;118:41–46.

These are three fascinating articles, demonstrating the increased frequency in LS and A patients of autoimmune diseases (such as pernicious anemia, thyroid disease, vitiligo, and alopecia areata) and the increased frequency of various tissue autoantibodies (such as antithyroid, antinuclear, and antiparietal cell antibodies). Furthermore, there are data to suggest an increased frequency of autoimmune diseases and autoantibodies in first-degree relatives.

Connelly MG, Winkelmann RK. Coexistence of lichen sclerosis, morphea, and lichen planus. J Am Acad Dermatol 1985;12:844–851.

This is a very fascinating paper describing the coexistence of lichen planus, lichen sclerosis, and generalized morphea in four patients, as well as a review of eight cases reported in the literature. A review of the cases in the literature indicate that two had systemic scleroderma, three had vitiligo, and one patient with vitiligo also had alopecia areata. A positive rheumatoid factor and a biologic false-positive serologic test for syphilis was detected in one patient each. One patient also had autoimmune thyroid disease.

This striking aggregation of these unusual inflammatory cutaneous diseases and associated autoimmune phenomena suggest an immunologic-mediated disease etiology for lichen sclerosis.

Meryrick-Thomas RH, Kennedy CTC. The development of lichen sclerosis et atrophicus in monozygotic twin girls. Br J Dermatol 1986;114:377–379.

Cox NH, Mitchell JNS, Morley WN. Lichen sclerosis et atrophicus in nonidentical female twins. Br J Dermatol 1986;115:743–746.

These two articles, describing the rare occurrence of LS and A in twin girls, provide further evidence that genetic factors may be important in the etiology of this disorder. The article by Meryrick-Thomas reviews information on 15 previous instances of familial lichen sclerosis et atrophicus.

Abramov Y, et al. Surgical treatment of vulvar lichen sclerosis. Obstet Gynecol Surv 1996;51:193–199.

This is a good review of the topic, including indications and limitations.

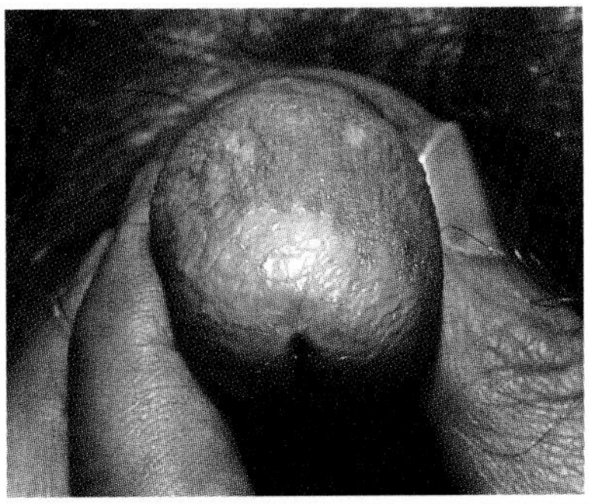

FIGURE 70–14 Atrophic white scarring lesion of balanitis xerotica obliterans on the tip of the glans penis.

Thomas RH, et al. Anogenital lichen sclerosis in women. J R Soc Med 1996;89:694–698.

Reports of a study of 357 women with biopsy-proven lichen sclerosis of the anogenital region showing a wide age range, an association with scleroderma and lichen planus as well as the occurrence of squamous cell carcinoma in some cases. This article suggests that inappropriate surgery continues to be carried out for this benign disease.

Carlson JA, et al. Vulvar lichen sclerosis and squamous cell carcinoma: a cohort, case control, and investigational study with historical perspective; implications for chronic inflammation and sclerosis in the development of neoplasia. Hum Pathol 1998;29:932–948.

As a chronic scarring inflammatory dermatosis, a case is made for LS and A to act as an initiator and a promotor of carcinogenesis. A genetic cause is suggested involving the p53 gene.

Ulmer A, et al. Amelanotic malignant melanoma of the vulva. Case report and review of the literature. Arch Gynecol Obstet 1996;259:45–50.

This article describes a case of mistaken identity of LS and A. Indicates the value of biopsy of atypical perineal lesions.

Pellagra

Pellagra is a rare nutritional disease caused by an inadequate ingestion of niacin and tryptophan. In the past, it was a severe medicosocial problem in the United States. For example, in the United States alone, there were over 6,000 deaths in 1928. In 1930, there were 30,000 pellagra patients in the state of Georgia.

Niacin is an essential component of coenzyme I (NAD) and coenzyme II (NADP). These enzymes are ubiquitous, donating or accepting hydrogen in many biochemical reactions. Tryptophan is an essential amino acid which can be converted to niacin.

Pellagra seen in:
- *alcoholics*
- *patients with gastrointestinal diseases*
- *carcinoid syndrome*

In the past, pellagra was generally detected in individuals with an unbalanced diet consisting primarily of maize. Today, it is still endemic in regions (such as in India) where maize or jowal (sorghum vulgare) are basic foods (maize has a normal content of niacin but is bound in a form humans' digestion cannot process). The disease is rarely seen today in developed countries, but when it does occur, it is usually associated with chronic alcoholism or severe gastrointestinal diseases (eg, short bowel syndrome). Pellagra may be seen in the carcinoid syndrome, in which tryptophan is shunted to produce serotonin.

Cutaneous Manifestations

Photosensitive dermatosis

Casal's necklace

A photodermatosis, characterized by redness and scaling, is the dominant feature (without sun exposure, no dermatitis). Dusky, brown-red postinflammatory hyperpigmentation follows sun exposure, producing a butterfly-like eruption, a well-demarcated dermatosis involving the neck (Casal's necklace) and dorsal surface of the hands (gauntlet pellagra) (Figures 70–15 to 70–17).

Four D's of pellagra:
- *Dermatitis*
- *Diarrhea*
- *Dementia*
- *Death is seldom seen today*

In addition to the dermatitis, gastrointestinal symptomatology (pain and diarrhea) occur in at least one-half of the patients. Neurologic manifestations, including disorientation, peripheral neuritis, and dementia, are also commonly detected. Death is rare.

Annotated Bibliography

Stratigos JD, Katsambas A. Pellagra: a still existing disease. Br J Dermatol 1977;96: 99–106.

This is an excellent article. Pellagra now occurs in the following settings: (1) chronic alcoholics, and aged widowers living alone (poor dietary intake of proteins); (2) malabsorption (Crohn's disease, gastroenterostomy patients);

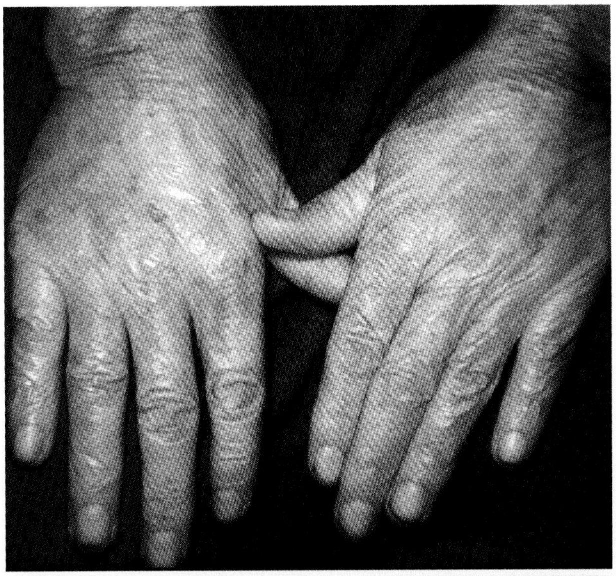

FIGURE 70-15 Phototoxic dermatitis on dorsal surface of hands of a patient with pellagra. (Courtesy of William MacEachern, M.D., Waterloo, Ontario.)

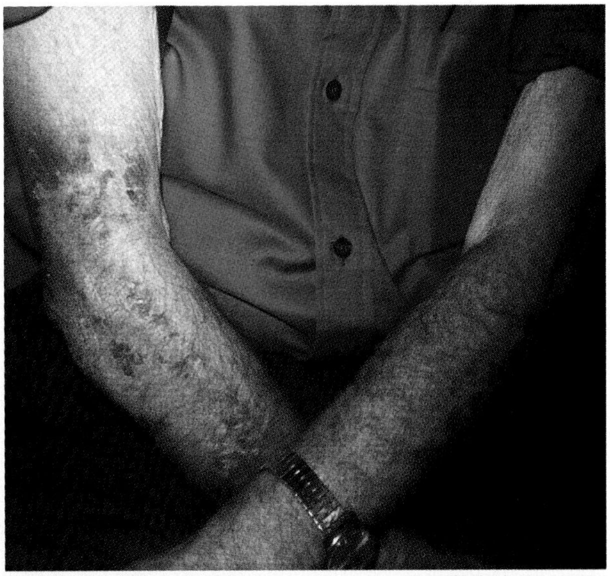

FIGURE 70-16 Phototoxic reaction with postinflammatory hyperpigmentation over extensor surface of forearms. (Note: normal skin, lower portion right upper arm.) (Courtesy of William MacEachern, M.D., Waterloo, Ontario.)

(3) deviation of tryptophan metabolism (carcinoid syndrome, Hartnup disease); and (4) chemotherapy (6-mercaptopurine; 5-fluorouracil) and isoniazid therapy.

Vitamin C Deficiency

Vitamin C deficiency (scurvy) is rare today. Ascorbic acid (vitamin C) is heat labile and plays a key role in the metabolism of collagen, ground substance, aromatic amino acids, and folic acid. It is a strong reducing agent and is easily oxidized. This vitamin is found in green vegetables and fruits.

Absence of vitamin C from the diet is a serious problem. It most commonly occurs in association with alcoholism, but food fads are also responsible. The senior author once detected an outbreak of scurvy among elderly women, who passed their time playing bridge, drinking hot tea, and eating cookies.

Vitamin C deficiency seen in alcoholic patients

Also may be seen associated with food fads

Cutaneous Manifestations

The initial cutaneous feature of scurvy is follicular keratosis with coiled hairs (corkscrewed hairs), most commonly detected on the lower abdomen but also occurring on the upper arms, back, buttocks, as well as the lower extremities. Lower leg swelling and perifollicular petechiae and ecchymosis occur, simulating cutaneous vasculitis. Swollen bleeding gums and epistaxis also occur. Sudden death has been reported.

In a controlled study, patients deprived of vitamin C developed prominent fatigue as the initial manifestation. The cutaneous manifestations appear later, after patients have been deprived of dietary vitamin C for at least 180 days. Anemia and mental depression are also noted. The anemia is a macrocytic anemia, probably related to a concomitant folic acid deficiency.

Perifollicular petechiae

"Corkscrewed" hairs

Fatigue is a major symptom and may antedate the development of petechiae.

Annotated Bibliography

Reuler JB, Broudy VC, Cooney TC. Adult scurvy. J Am Med Assoc 1968;253:805–807.

This article emphasizes the importance of lower extremity swelling and cutaneous bleeding with follicular disease in vitamin C deficiency. Epidemiologic

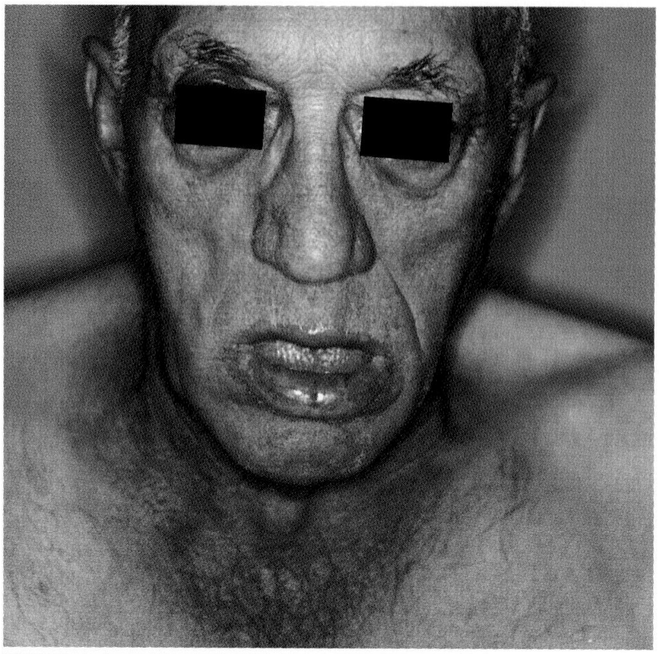

FIGURE 70–17 Phototoxic reaction with postinflammatory hyperpigmentation around neck (Casal's necklace). (Courtesy of Richard Baughman, M.D., Hanover, NH.)

studies suggest that elderly patients (especially men living alone), those individuals avoiding "acid-containing" foods because of esophageal reflux, and peritoneal and hemodialysis patients are at risk.

Hirschman JV, Raugi SJ. Scurvy. J Am Acad Dermatol 1999;4:895–906.

This is an intresting review article detailing the historic impact of scurvy on maritime nations. It also details clinical features and highlights the fact that sudden death is a complication of scurvy.

Erythema Nodosum

Erythema nodosum: inflammatory disease most commonly of the lower legs ? Immunologically mediated

This is an inflammatory disease process characterized by tender, nodular lesions, occurring over the extensor surfaces, predominantly, but not exclusively, of the lower legs (Figure 70–18). This disease process may be recurrent.

Erythema nodosum occurs more frequently in females during the third and fourth decades of life. The disease process occurs in association with a variety of systemic diseases, and a hypersensitivity reaction is thought to be the etiology.

May involve forearms

Although recurrent, tender, erythematous nodules, occurring over the tibia are characteristic, these lesions may extend to the lateral aspect of the lower legs as well as the extensor forearms. As the lesions resolve, postinflammatory hyperpigmentation may appear.

Constitutional symptoms may be present

Erythema nodosum migrans an unusual variant

Constitutional symptoms (fever and malaise) frequently are present. Myalgias and arthralgias are also commonly, but not invariably, present.

Erythema nodosum migrans, characterized by erythematous nodular lesions which extend peripherally, assuming annular or arciform patterns, is an unusual variant.

Pathology

Erythema nodosum, histologically, is characterized by a septal panniculitis in which the inflammatory infiltrate is composed predominantly of neutrophils.

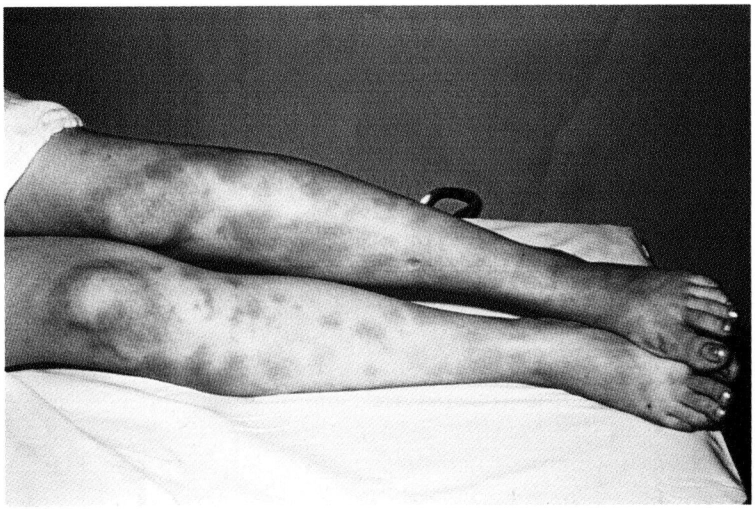

FIGURE 70–18 Erythema nodosum lesions of lower legs.

Vascular swelling and edema may be present, but no vasculitis is seen. With progression of the disease, a mononuclear and histiocytic giant cell infiltrate develops. Lobular portions of the subcutaneous tissue become involved, and fibrosis may occur. In the dermis, a perivascular mononuclear inflammatory infiltrate is frequently detected.

Pathology:
- *septal panniculitis*
- *neutrophilic infiltrate early*
- *mononuclear infiltrate late*

Clinical Associations

Erythema nodosum is a hypersensitivity reaction occurring in various clinical settings (Table 70–2).

In the United States, the most common association is a poststreptococcal infection. The antistreptolysin-O (ASO), and the antistreptococcal DNAase titers are commonly elevated.

Disease associations: streptococcal infections

The second most common cause of erythema nodosum is the use of oral contraceptives. On occasion, erythema nodosum is seen in pregnancy. In addition to oral contraceptives, sulfonamides have been associated with erythema nodosum.

Drug reaction

Oral contraceptives

The third most common cause of erythema nodosum is sarcoidosis. In many instances, the erythema nodosum is noted in association with bilateral hilar adenopathy, and frequently, this is the presenting sign of sarcoidosis (Löfgren's syndrome).

Sarcoidosis

In addition to these common associations, erythema nodosum has been associated with tuberculosis. This is most commonly reported, for some unknown reason, from Europe, in particular, the United Kingdom. In addition,

Tuberculosis, especially prominent in the UK

TABLE 70–2 Diseases Commonly Associated with Erythema Nodosum

- Group A beta hemolytic streptococcal infection
- Drug sensitivity (eg, oral contraceptives, sulfonamides)
- Pregnancy
- Sarcoidosis (Löfgren's syndrome, generally, but not always, associated with benign self-limited sarcoidosis; see Chapter 46 on Sarcoidosis)
- Deep fungal infections (eg, histoplasmosis, North American blastomycosis, coccidioidomycosis)
- Tuberculosis (frequently reported from the United Kingdom in the past)
- Inflammatory bowel diseases (Crohn's disease and ulcerative colitis)

Mycoplasma pneumoniae

Deep fungal infections

erythema nodosum has been associated with other infections, including leptospirosis, tularemia, *Yersinia*, enterocolitica, and *Mycoplasma pneumoniae*. Erythema nodosum is also associated with systemic fungal infections, such as North American blastomycosis, histoplasmosis, and coccidioidomycosis. Viral infections, including paravaccinia, infectious mononucleosis, lymphogranuloma venereum, cat scratch disease, and hepatitis B, have also been associated with erythema nodosum.

Inflammatory bowel disease

Inflammatory bowel disease (ulcerative colitis and Crohn's disease) have been associated with erythema nodosum. There is evidence to indicate that the presence of erythema nodosum reflects bowel disease activity.

Malignancies

Following radiation therapy

Malignant diseases, including leukemia and Hodgkin's disease, have been associated with erythema nodosum. In addition, radiation therapy appears to correlate with the onset of erythema nodosum in some patients with malignancies. The author believes that the erythema nodosum–like reactions associated with irradiation of lymphoma patients may, in fact, represent nodular vasculitis secondary to immune complex formation.

Behçet's disease

Finally, Behçet's disease is frequently associated with erythema nodosum lesions.

Annotated Bibliography

Braverman I. Erythema nodosum. In: Braverman I. Skin Signs of Systemic diseases, 3rd ed. Philadelphia, PA: WB Saunders, 1998, pp 349–353.

This is a well written discussion, with a good bibliography. Author has reviewed the world literature.

Ryan TJ. Erythema nodosum. In: Champion RH, Burton JL, Ebling FJG, eds. Textbook on Dermatology, 5th ed. London: Blackwell Scientific Publications, 1992, pp 1931–1939.

This article presents an excellent bibliography.

Erythema Multiforme

Erythema multiforme

Two variants:
- *macular-urticarial*
- *vesicobullous*

This is a hypersensitivity reaction characterized by an erythematous eruption of varying morphology—erythematous, macular, targetoid to bullous lesions. The classic targetoid, or minor variant, is also referred to as the Hebra form (Figures 70–19 and 70–20).

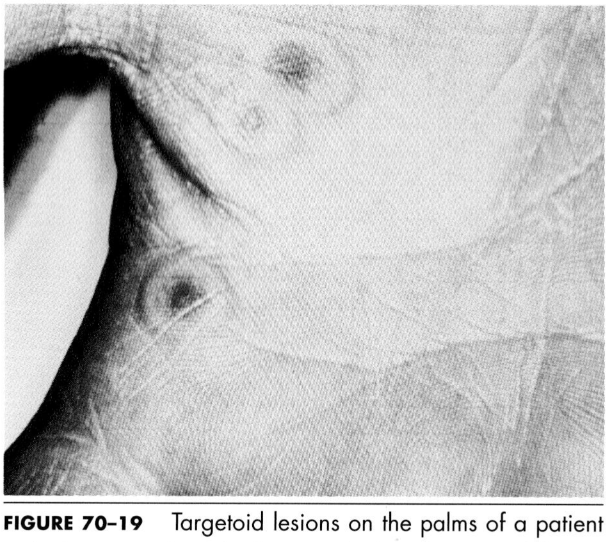

FIGURE 70–19 Targetoid lesions on the palms of a patient with the minor form (Hebra type) of erythema multiforme. This was associated with recurrent herpes simplex.

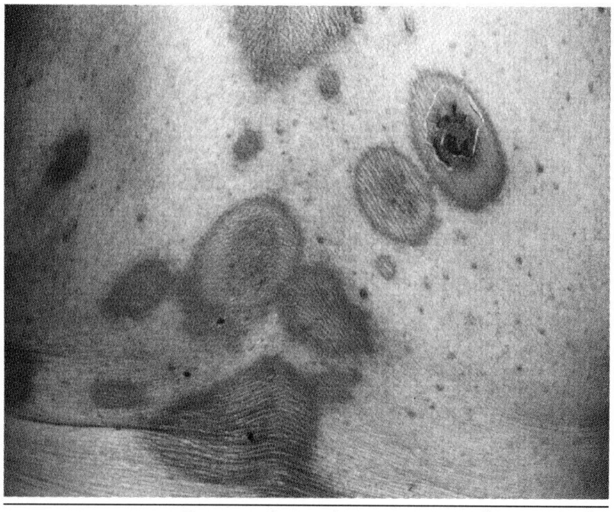

FIGURE 70–20 Targetoid erythematous erythema multiforme lesions on the back of a patient with an allergic drug reaction.

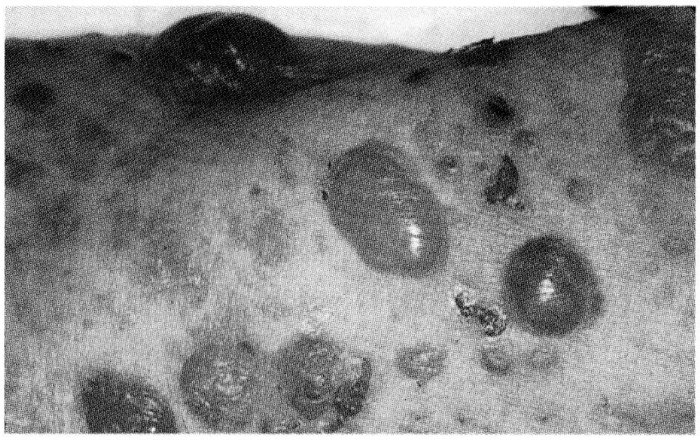

FIGURE 70-21 Bullous form of erythema multiforme.

In addition to the minor variant, a bullous form of erythema multiforme, characterized by widespread subepidermal bullae, has been reported (Figure 70–21). Mucous membrane involvement may or may not be present. Widespread mucosal erosions, involving the oral pharynx, conjunctiva, urethra, and vaginal mucosa, may occur (Stevens-Johnson syndrome). Infrequently, recurrent oral lesions may occur in the absence of skin lesions.

Stevens-Johnson variant

In addition, some classifications include toxic epidermal necrolysis (TEN) as part of the spectrum of bullous erythema multiforme. Recent data suggest that TEN is probably a separate disease entity. For further discussion, see Chapter 66, "Toxic Epidermal Necrolysis."

Relationship with TEN

Clinical Associations

Erythema multiforme occurs in association with various diseases. In general, the bullous forms and Stevens-Johnson variants are usually a manifestation of a drug hypersensitivity reaction (Table 70–3).

TABLE 70–3 Causes of Erythema Multiforme

- Herpes simplex infections (This is the most common cause of the Hebra form of erythema multiforme. Generally, these lesions occur within a week or 10 days following a herpes simplex infection. These lesions are most commonly detected on the palmar surface of the hands and contain classic targetoid lesions. Herpes antigen has been demonstrated in epidermal keratinocytes in the involved areas.)
- *Mycoplasma pneumoniae* infections
- Viral infections, such as Coxsackie and influenza type A
- Following vaccination
- Drug hypersensitivities (eg, penicillin, sulfonamides, barbiturates)
- Following irradiation of tumors
- Rarely, it can be an indicator of activity of ulcerative colitis or Crohn's disease

Annotated Bibliography

Huff JC, Weston WL, Tonnesen MG. Erythema multiforme: a critical review of characteristics, diagnostic criteria and other causes. J Am Acad Dermatol 1983;8:763–775.

Huff JC, Weston WL. Recurrent erythema multiforme. Medicine 1989;63:763–775.

These are two excellent articles.

Idiopathic Lobular Panniculitis (Weber-Christian Disease)

This is a rare inflammatory disease, producing a lobular panniculitis. On the basis of individual reports of Weber and Christian, the term "relapsing febrile nodular panniculitis," or Weber-Christian disease, has been applied to a lobular panniculitis of unknown etiology, with systemic manifestations.

Weber-Christian disease: rare inflammatory lobular panniculitis

It is highly likely that Weber-Christian disease encompassed, in the past, such entities as lupus panniculitis, histiocytic cytophagic panniculitis (subcutaneous T-cell lymphoma), $alpha_1$-antitrypsin deficiency panniculitis, and possibly, panniculitis associated with pancreatic disease.

Probably encompasses many diseases:
?lupus panniculitis
?subcutaneous T-cell lymphoma
$alpha_1$-antitrypsin deficiency
panniculitis associated with pancreatic disease

Weber-Christian disease is diagnosed very rarely today, which is probably indicative of our increased knowledge of the many etiologies capable of producing a lobular panniculitis. Furthermore, in patients with systemic lupus erythematosus

(SLE), the routine employment of steroids and immunosuppressive agents to treat the SLE effectively treats and prevents the nodular, septal vasculitis which could produce a syndrome identical to relapsing febrile nodular panniculitis.

In the author's experience, spanning a clinical career of over 30 years, the diagnosis of Weber-Christian disease has been entertained only twice. In both instances, a histiocytic cytophagic panniculitis (subcutaneous T-cell lymphoma) diagnosis was established, and both these cases were fatal.

Clinical Features

Recurrent waves of tender nodules

Weber-Christian disease is characterized by recurrent erythematous, tender, subcutaneous nodules which can grow to several centimeters in size and ulcerate. They are most commonly detected on the thighs and lower legs but can occur on all areas of the body. Ulceration of the overlying skin and necrosis of the fat occurs, discharging an oily yellow-brown liquid. Involution occurs over a few weeks, producing depressed atrophic scars with postinflammatory hyperpigmentation.

Constitutional symptoms

In addition to fever, these patients may complain of malaise and fatigue. Fat necrosis may also be detected in the liver, spleen, and adrenal glands. In addition, the perivisceral fat may be involved (ie, pericardium, pleura, mesenteric, and omental fat).

Diagnosis

Weber-Christian disease is to be differentiated from subcutaneous T-cell lymphoma, the panniculitis associated with pancreatic disease, and alpha$_1$-antitrypsin deficiency. (See section on cutaneous malignancy in Chapter 23 for a discussion on subcutaneous T-cell lymphoma; see below for discussion on panniculitis associated with pancreatic diseases and alpha$_1$-antitrypsin deficiency.)

Annotated Bibliography

Weber FP. A case of relapsing nonsuppurative nodular panniculitis. Br J Dermatol 1925;37:301–305.

Christian HA. Relapsing febrile nodular nonsuppurative panniculitis. Arch Intern Med 1928;41:338–342.

These two articles are the classic references for this entity.

Lupus Panniculitis

Lupus panniculitis
Inflammatory infiltrate extending down from SLE lesion

Lupus panniculitis, an inflammatory panniculitis, is an uncommon cutaneous manifestation of SLE. It can occur in the presence of classic lupus lesions, representing an extension of the inflammatory infiltrate, down through the dermis, into the subcutaneous level (lupus profundus). In addition, the subcutaneous inflammatory infiltrate can occur in the absence of a cutaneous lupus lesion (lupus panniculitis) (Figures 70–22 and 70–23).

Biopsy of these lesions demonstrates a lobular panniculitis with an inflammatory infiltrate composed predominantly of lymphocytes, associated with fat necrosis. Scar formation frequently results in a depressed scar. Dystrophic calcification may be detected.

In the author's and other investigators' experience, this type of cutaneous lesion can be detected in benign cutaneous as well as systemic lupus erythematosus. Antimalarials (chloroquine and hydroxychloroquine) are effective therapy.

Annotated Bibliography

Weber EP. A case of relapsing nonsuppurative nodular panniculitis. Br J Dermatol 1925;37:301.

Christian HA. Relapsing febrile nodular nonsuppurative panniculitis. Arch Intern Med 1928;41:338.

These two articles are the classic references for this entity.

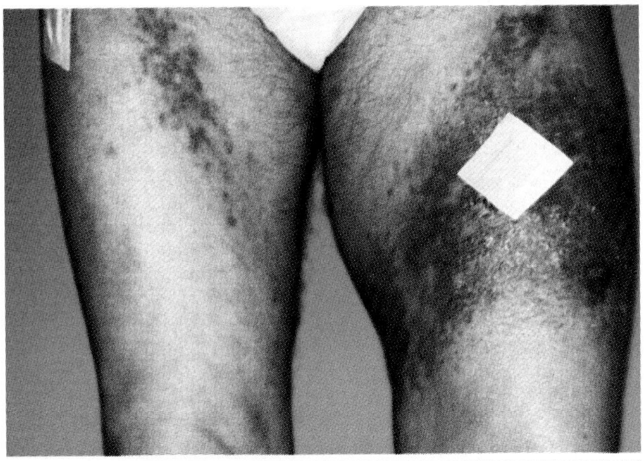

FIGURE 70–22 Lupus panniculitis on left thigh.

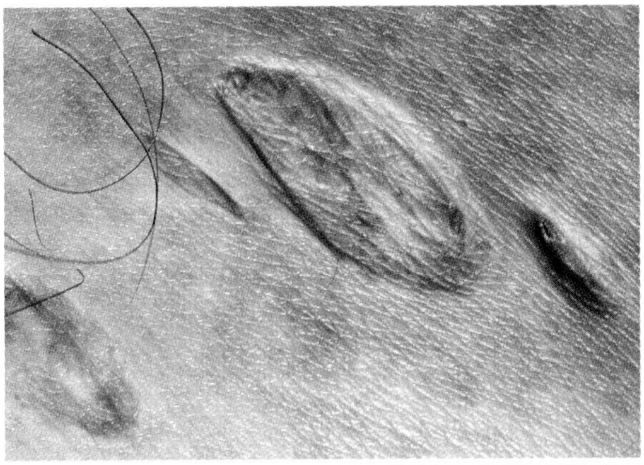

FIGURE 70–23 Atrophic depressed scar, the result of lupus panniculitis.

Smith KC, Su WPD, Pittekow MR, et al. Clinical and pathologic correlations in 96 patients with panniculitis. J Am Acad Dermatol 1989;21:1192.

This is a highly quoted article. Fifteen of these patients were alpha$_1$-antitrypsin deficient.

Tuffanelli DL. Lupus panniculitis (profundus). Semin Dermatol 1985;4:49–82.

Excellent review!

Pancreatic Panniculitis

Panniculitis associated with pancreatitis and rarely pancreatic carcinoma

Since the mid-1960s, it has been recognized that a form of lobular panniculitis, mimicking the original description by Weber-Christian disease, can be found in association with pancreatic disease (pancreatitis, and more rarely, pancreatic carcinoma).

Polyserositis and pleural pericardial involvement may occur.

Patients with this syndrome have recurrent crops of painful, erythematous nodules that are most commonly, but not invariably, detected in the pretibial regions. Polyserositis, characterized by pleuritis, pericarditis, or synovitis, may occur in as many as 60% of these patients.

Among patients with pancreatic carcinoma, acinar carcinomas, rather than the more common adenocarcinomas, are much more frequently associated with this form of panniculitis.

The lesions are thought to be caused by the release of the pancreatic enzymes lipase and amylase.

Laboratory Studies

Elevated serum and urinary lipase levels

The most sensitive test appears to be an elevated serum and urinary lipase determination. This can occur in the presence of normal serum amylase. A skin biopsy, deep enough to include the subcutaneous tissue, will demonstrate ghost-like fat cells with thick walls, and no nuclei. Dystrophic calcification may occur. The inflammatory infiltrate surrounding areas of fat necrosis is usually polymorphic. Adjacent fatty lobules may be absolutely normal.

Annotated Bibliography

Potts DE, Mass MF, Iseman MD. Syndrome of pancreatic disease, subcutaneous fat necrosis and polyserositis. Am J Med 1975;58:417–423.

This is an excellent review of the clinical features and emphasizes the occurrence of the syndrome with both pancreatitis and pancreatic carcinoma. Pleural effusions may be a clinical feature.

Alpha$_1$-Antitrypsin Deficiency

Rare, hereditary deficiency disease

Liver disease

Emphysema

Relapsing, febrile, nonsuppurative nodular panniculitis

Alpha$_1$ (α_1)-antitrypsin deficiency (a rare disease) is associated with chronic liver disease, emphysema, and a nodular panniculitis in many respects reminiscent of the description of Weber-Christian disease (relapsing, febrile, nonsuppurative nodular panniculitis). The hepatic disease occurs in newborns and is characterized by the deposition of periodic acid–Schiff (PAS) diastase-resistant vesicular deposits leading to the development of cirrhosis. The chronic obstructive pulmonary disease and panniculitis occurs in adulthood. On occasion, patients may develop a rheumatoid arthritic-like condition.

α_1-Antitrypsin, an important inhibitor of various proteolytic enzymes

Composes ~90% of protein content of α_1-region on serum electrophoresis

Alpha$_1$-antitrypsin and antichymotrypsin are protease inhibitors, which block or modify the activity of proteolytic enzymes. The most important protease inhibitor in the blood is α_1-antitrypsin. Antitrypsin composes at least 90 to 95% of the protein content in the α_1 region on serum electrophoresis. This enzyme is capable of inactivating various enzymes including trypsin, serine enzymes, elastase, and leukocyte enzymes.

Homozygous deficiency associated with disease; heterozygous state is generally not

Alpha$_1$-antitrypsin is encoded by multiple alleles at a loci given the designation Pi. The quantity of α_1-antitrypsin is inherited as a co-dominant, thus, the combination of two alleles determines the α_1-antitrypsin phenotype. The most common allele associated with normal quantities of α_1-antitrypsin is the M allele (the normal concentration is 2 to 4 g/L); on the other hand, the Z allele, is associated with reduction in plasma α_1-antitrypsin. The homozygotic individual (PiZZ) is associated with a marked decrease in plasma α_1-antitrypsin activity (approximately 5 to 10% of normal). In the heterozygotic state (ie, PiMZ) there may be only a moderate reduction in plasma α_1-antitrypsin levels and generally no disease.

The homozygotic or the PiZZ state is rare; the frequency is approximately 1:100 cases.

Phenotyping of the different alleles is performed by electrophoretic techniques. The plasma content of α_1-antitrypsin is unreliable in differentiating the various phenotypes.

Cutaneous Manifestations

In general, individuals who develop the panniculitis are in their third and fourth decades of life. However, all ages can be affected. Only a small percentage of α_1-antitrypsin deficient individuals develop panniculitis. The pathogenesis is unknown.

Painful subcutaneous nodules induced by trauma

Yellowish, nonpurulent discharge

A history of erythematous, painful, subcutaneous nodules arising on all areas of the body, but most commonly localized to the lower extremities at sites of previous trauma, is common. Ulceration may occur, discharging a yellowish serous material. Cultures and biopsy specimens fail to detect microbial organisms. In addition, the amylase content of the drainage fluid is normal. Not all lesions ulcerate, some resolve uneventfully in 7 to 10 days. Approximately 15% of cases of panniculitis are estimated to be due to α_1-antitrypsin deficiency.

Characteristically, the panniculitis is unresponsive to oral steroids, colchicine, and nonsteroidal anti-inflammatory drugs (NSAIDs).

Pathologic Features

Examination of an established nodule demonstrates a mixed cellular infiltrate composed of mononuclear, neutrophil, and histiocytic cells in the subcutaneous tissue. These cells are localized inside the fat lobule. Fat degeneration is evident. Lipophages are prominent.

Systemic Manifestations

Multiple areas of fat necrosis detected at autopsy

Systemic manifestations are frequent. Clinically, patients may demonstrate fever and malaise and may present with an acute abdomen manifesting as paralytic ileus, necessitating exploratory laparotomy.

At autopsy, in addition to multiple subcutaneous areas of panniculitis, emphysema, and microscopic evidence of PAS-positive diastase-resistant vesicles in the liver, there is frequently evidence of acute pancreatitis and panniculitis involving the retrosternum, epicardium, and mesentery. Multiple pulmonary emboli may occur.

Pulmonary emboli may be detected

Diagnosis

As part of a history and physical examination of patients with recurrent panniculitis, especially induced by trauma, one should inquire regarding a family history of emphysema, hepatitis, and cirrhosis, as well as similar subcutaneous nodular lesions in siblings. A routine serum electrophoretic pattern will demonstrate a flat α_1-region indicative of α_1-antitrypsin deficiency.

Treatment

The infusion of human α_1-proteinase inhibitor has been reported to be successful. Dapsone has been reported to be effective, but these are isolated case reports.

Annotated Bibliography

Smith KC, Su WPD, Pittekow MR, et al. Clinical and pathologic correlations in 96 patients with panniculitis. J Am Acad Dermatol 1989;21:1191–1196.

This is a highly quoted article. Fifteen of these panniculitis were patients α_1-antitrypsin deficient.

Smith KC, Pittelkow MR, Su WPD. Panniculitis associated with severe α_1-antitrypsin deficiency. Treatment and review of the literature. Arch Dermatol 1987;123: 1655–1661.

This is a valuable article.

Rubinstein HM, Jaffer AM, Kudrna JC, et al. Alpha$_1$-antitrypsin deficiency with severe panniculitis. Ann Intern Med 1977;86:742–744.

Bleumink E, Klokke HA. Protease inhibitor deficiencies in a patient with Weber-Christian panniculitis. Arch Dermatol 1984;120:936–940.

Breit SN, Clark P, Robinson JP, et al. Familial occurrence of α_1-antitrypsin deficiency in Weber-Christian disease. Arch Dermatol 1983;119:198–202.

The above three articles detail cutaneous features of α_1-antitrypsin deficiency.

Yellow Nail Syndrome

This is a very rare condition, affecting all nails and characterized by the development of pale yellow to greenish-yellow nails. The nails are hard, with a smooth surface, and characteristically, the cuticles are lost (Figure 70–24).

Chronic disease associated with nail bed lymphatic obstruction

Biopsy of the nail bed demonstrates dense, fibrous tissue with ectatic vessels. In many cases, lymphatic obstruction is thought to be the cause. On occasion, recurrent pleural effusions have been detected. Edema, secondary to lymphatic atresia, or varicosities, has been detected in some cases. There appears to be an increased incidence of pulmonary malignancy. The condition can also be seen in association with nephrotic syndrome, hypothyroidism, and acquired immune deficiency syndrome (AIDS).

May be associated with various pulmonary diseases, including malignancy

In general, the disease process is permanent, but spontaneous remissions have been reported.

Annotated Bibliography

DeCoste SD, Imber MJ, Baden HP. Yellow nail syndrome. J Am Acad Dermatol 1990;22:608–611.

This article presents a description of nail bed pathology.

Miller E, Rosenow EC, Olsen AM. Pulmonary manifestations of the yellow nail syndrome. Chest 1972;61:452–458.

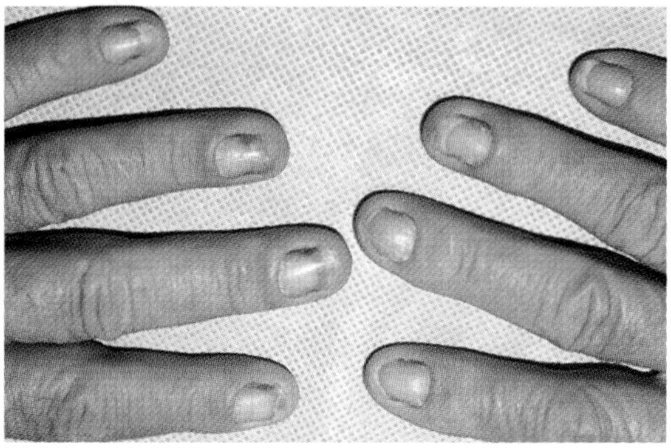

FIGURE 70–24 Yellow nail syndrome characterized by smooth yellowish discolored nails. Note absent cuticle nail folds.

This article describes the presence of pleural effusions in approximately 50% of patients. Also, in the study, bronchiectasis was detected in several patients.

Polymorphic Light Eruption

The polymorphic light eruption (PMLE) is a common condition affecting approximately 10% of the population. It is characterized by the development of erythematous, pruritic papules, plaques, or vesicles, on exposure to ultraviolet light. It occurs predominantly in women in the spring and improves during the summer. Both ultraviolet (UV)B and UVA exposure are capable of inducing the disease, although evidence suggests that most of the cases are secondary to UVA exposure.

Polymorphic light eruption:
- *most commonly affects women*
- *springtime occurrence*
- *predominantly induced by UVA*
- *T-cell-mediated disease*

The disease process is postulated to be induced by a delayed hypersensitivity immunologic mechanism. The lesions are characterized by epidermal spongiosis and a perivascular lymphocytic infiltrate. Biopsies of early lesions demonstrate, predominantly, a perivascular CD4+ T-cell inflammatory infiltrate, followed by an influx of CD8+ T lymphocytes. Upregulation of keratinocyte expression of intercellular adhesion molecule-1 (ICAM-1) has also been detected.

Clinical Features

Recurrent light-induced lesions occurring in spring

Gets better during summer months

Papules, nodules, and plaques

Women under the age of 30 years are most commonly affected. All ethnic groups are affected. The disease process, as noted above, most commonly begins in the spring and improves during the summer months. The disease process, unlike solar urticaria and erythropoetic protoporphyria, is delayed several hours in onset, lasting days or, rarely, weeks. The lesions occur on light-exposed areas, most commonly the face, sides of the neck, and dorsal surface of the hands. The disease may involve only the helix of the ears and, at times, can be associated only with pruritus.

Approximately 5% of anti-Ro (SS-A)-antibody–positive SLE patients may present with PMLE

It is recognized that approximately 5% of patients with this light-induced delayed type of urticaria-like reaction possess in their serum anti-Ro (SS-A) antibodies. Thus, determination of this antibody is recommended in evaluating these patients. As noted above, unlike erythropoietic protoporphyria and solar urticaria, which have immediate symptomatology on exposure to the sun, these lesions may be delayed for several hours following exposure to the sun.

Treatment of these lesions involves sun protection, or graded low doses of UVB or psoralen plus ultraviolet A (PUVA) therapy prior to heavy sunlight exposure may be effective in inducing tolerance. Antimalarials (hydroxychloroquine or chloroquine) may be deemed necessary. For severe cases, a short burst of steroids and, rarely, azathioprine, may be needed.

The disease process is chronic, but with time, sun sensitivity generally diminishes.

Annotated Bibliography

Jansen CT, Carvonen J. Polymorphous light eruption. A seven year follow up evaluation of 114 patients. Arch Dermatol 1984;120:862–865.

This study demonstrates that sunlight sensitivity diminishes over time.

Norris PG, Morris J, McGibbon DM, et al. Polymorphic light eruption: an immunopathologic study of evolving lesions. Br J Dermatol 1989;120:173–183.

This is a highly quoted study. Early lesions demonstrate CD4+ T cells and late lesions CD8+ T cells.

Ortel B, Tanew H, Wolff K, et al. Polymorphous light eruption: action spectrum and photoprotection. J Am Acad Dermatol 1986;14:748–753.

Of 142 PMLE patients tested, 49% developed lesions following artificial ultraviolet light exposure. In 56%, lesions were induced with UVA spectrum; 17% were induced with UVB and 25% with both UVB and UVA.

Adiposis Dolorosa

This is a rare disease, characterized by painful subcutaneous nodules and plaques. It is histologically associated with a local overgrowth of normal-appearing fat. The etiology is not known. The disease is most common among postmenopausal women. Obesity is almost universally present. All areas of the body can be involved. Weakness and fatigue are also common complaints. On palpation of involved areas, pain is present. The involved areas may feel like a "bag of worms." Initially, the disease may be only mildly discomforting, but with time, the pain may become acute. These patients may also have psychiatric disturbances.

Frequently, the involved areas of the skin may demonstrate ecchymosis. Lidocaine has been found to be effective in at least some cases. In the author's experience, topical lidocaine patches have been successful. Weight loss is recommended.

Annotated Bibliography

Juhlin L. Long standing pain relief of adiposis dolorosa (Dercum's disease) after intravenous infusion of lidocaine. J Am Acad Dermatol 1986;15:383–385.

Blue Rubber Bleb Nevus Syndrome

Rare congenital disease

Skin and internal organ hemangiomas

The blue rubber bleb nevus syndrome is rare, characterized by asymptomatic, soft, cavernous, subcutaneous hemangiomas associated with submucosal gastrointestinal angiomas. In addition, angiomas may be detected in other organs, including the lungs, liver, and brain. These lesions may occur sporadically or be inherited as an autosomal dominant. The hemangiomas may be detected at birth and vary greatly in size, ranging from small, punctate, macular lesions to those of several centimeters. Pain may or may not be present, and there may be increased sweating over the lesions.

Gastrointestinal bleeding

Gastrointestinal involvement is common, generally detected with endoscopy and CT scans. The large and small intestines are most commonly involved, but submucosal lesions are detected throughout the gastrointestinal tract. Gastrointestinal bleeding and intussusception may occur.

Annotated Bibliography

Bean WB. Vascular spiders and related lesions of the skin. Springfield, IL; Charles C. Thomas, 1958.

This is a very informative monograph.

Requena L, Sanguez OP. Cutaneous vascular abnormalities. Part 1: hamartomas, malformations and dilation of preexisting vessels. J Am Acad Dermatol 1997;37:523.

This is an excellent review.

Maffucci's Syndrome

Rare congenital disease

Venous malformations in extremities associated with enchondromas

This is a rare syndrome characterized by venous malformations in the extremities, frequently associated with enchondromas at the metaphysis of the fingers, toes, and long bones. Cavernous lymphangiomas may also be present.

Malignant degeneration problematic

Growth abnormalities resulting in deformities of the bones are common. Malignant degeneration, most commonly chondrosarcoma, occurs. Other mesodermal malignant tumors have been associated. (CH70BOX 64)

The cutaneous manifestations generally begin in infancy, characterized by soft, bluish, nodular, subcutaneous lesions. They may or may not be tender and continue to grow in size.

Annotated Bibliography

Bean WB. Dyschondroplasia and hemangiomata (Maffucci's syndrome). Arch Intern Med 1958;102:544–550.

This is a classic article describing clinical features.

Kasabach-Merritt Syndrome

This is an uncommon coagulopathy occurring in infants or during the first year of life. A consumptive coagulopathy occurs, caused by intervascular clotting within a large kaposiform hemangioendothelioma. This tumor rapidly grows, caused by local hemorrhage, is violaceous red, and occurs on the limbs or in the cervical-facial region. These lesions also occur in the retroperitoneal area and are associated with significant mortality, commonly due to compression of adjacent vital structures (eg, airway obstruction). There is depletion of clotting factors, as well as thrombocytopenia. Petechiae, ecchymosis, and hemorrhage at sites distant from hemangioendothelioma can occur. Irradiation, corticosteroid therapy, and, recently, interleukin alpha-2a therapy, have been employed successfully to treat these lesions. Heparin, aspirin, and dipyridamole may be beneficial.

Annotated Bibliography

Sarkar M, et al. Thrombocytopenic coagulopathy (Kasabach-Merritt phenomenon) is associated with kaposiform hemangioendothelioma and not with common infantile hemangioma. Plast Reconstr Surg 1997;100:1377–1382.

This is a very informative article regarding the true nature of the hemangioma and the fact that at least 50% of tumors do not occur on the skin.

Esterly NB, Margileth AM, Kahn G, et al. Management of disseminated eruptive hemangiomata in infants. Pediatr Dermatol 1984;1:312–317.

This is an informative therapeutic article.

Clemmensen O. A case of multiple neonatal hemangiomatosis successfully treated with systemic steroids. Dermatologica 1979;159:495–499.

This is a good article demonstrating the efficacy of systemic steroids in some of these patients.

Acquired Complement Deficiencies

Acquired Angioneurotic Edema

In addition to hereditary angioneurotic edema, it has been recognized in recent years that angioedema can occur, on unusual occasions, in association with lymphoproliferative disorders. These patients have the same clinical manifestations as those with the hereditary type of angioneurotic edema. Upper airway and gastrointestinal tract involvement, producing impaired breathing and abdominal pain, are serious complications. In addition, these patients will frequently have nonpruritic edema involving the face and hands. The lymphoproliferative disorders associated with acquired C1 inhibitor (C1/INH) deficiency include IgA myeloma,

Waldenstrom's macroglobulinemia, chronic lymphocytic leukemia, non–Hodgkin's B-cell lymphoma, lymphocytic lymphoma, and lymphosarcoma. An acquired C1 inhibitor deficiency also has been associated with the presence of autoantibodies directed against C1 INH.

Acquired angioneurotic edema

Serious disease

Seen in patients with lymphoproliferative disorders

In hereditary angioneurotic edema, 85% of patients demonstrate an absence of the protein. In 15%, the protein is present but defective. The complement profile associated with hereditary angioneurotic edema demonstrates a normal C1 concentration. The C4 is always reduced, and C2 is reduced during acute episodes. In contrast, the acquired C1 inhibitor deficiency is associated with decreased levels of C1, C2, and C4. This consumption of C1 distinguishes the acquired C1 inhibitor deficiency from classic hereditary angioneurotic edema.

Unlike hereditary form of angioneurotic edema, C1 is decreased

Most cases of acquired angioneurotic edema are associated with a monoclonal gammopathy. Evidence indicates that immune complexes, composed of these monoclonal proteins and anti-idiotype antibodies, fix complement, consuming the C1 inhibitor and producing acquired angioneurotic edema syndrome. Other paraproteins contain antibody directed against C1 INH.

Etiology:
immune complexes associated with anti-idiotypic antibodies
C1 INH antibodies

Annotated bibliography

Geha RS, et al. Acquired C1-inhibitor deficiency associated with antiidiotypic antibody to monoclonal immunoglobulins. N Engl J Med 1985;312:534–539.

This is an excellent article demonstrating the presence of anti-idiotypic antibodies in monoclonal proliferative disorders associated with acquired C1 INH deficiency.

Cicardi M, et al. Relevance of lymphoproliferative disorders and of anti C1-inhibitor autoantibodies in acquired angioedema. Clin Exp Immunol 1996;106:475–478.

This article discusses a second mechanism of acquired C1 INH deficiency; that is the presence of paraproteins with anti-C1 inhibitor activity.

Partial Lipodystrophy

This is another example of an acquired complement deficiency syndrome inducing cutaneous disease. In general, patients note gradual loss of subcutaneous fat, most commonly beginning on the face and spreading downward. In most instances, the area below the thighs is not involved, but exceptions have been reported. The disease most commonly occurs in females and begins around puberty.

Partial lipodystrophy

Loss of fat generally from upper part of body

In a few cases, prominent fat loss from below thighs (this is unusual)

Clinical Findings

Clinically, most patients have a cachectic appearance, with loss of fat from the face. Examination of the upper extremities reveals a muscular-appearing individual with prominent veins.

Laboratory Findings

In addition to the lipodystrophy, many of these patients have diabetes as well as hypertriglyceridemia. Characteristically, C3 is diminished. These patients also demonstrate the C3 nephritic factor in their serum. This is an IgG directed against the alternative pathway C3 convertase (C3bBb). This antibody stabilizes this convertase, preventing its decay and inactivation and resulting in continued consumption of the third component of complement. Many of these patients will develop membranoproliferative glomerulonephritis (approximately 30%). The relationship between the consumption of the third component of complement and the pathogenesis of the glomerulonephritis and the lipodystrophy is unknown at the present time. A few patients with partial lipodystrophy syndrome have also been detected to have increased infections.

May also have diabetes and hypertriglyceridemia

An antibody directed against alternative complement pathway C3 convertase (C3bBb)

Consumption of C3

Many but not all of these patients have membranoproliferative glomerulonephritis

In addition to acquired angioneurotic edema and partial lipodystrophy, recurrent neisserial infections (gonococcal, meningococcal) are associated with hereditary deficiencies of individual late components of the classic and alternative complement pathways. Furthermore, systemic lupus erythematosus and, on

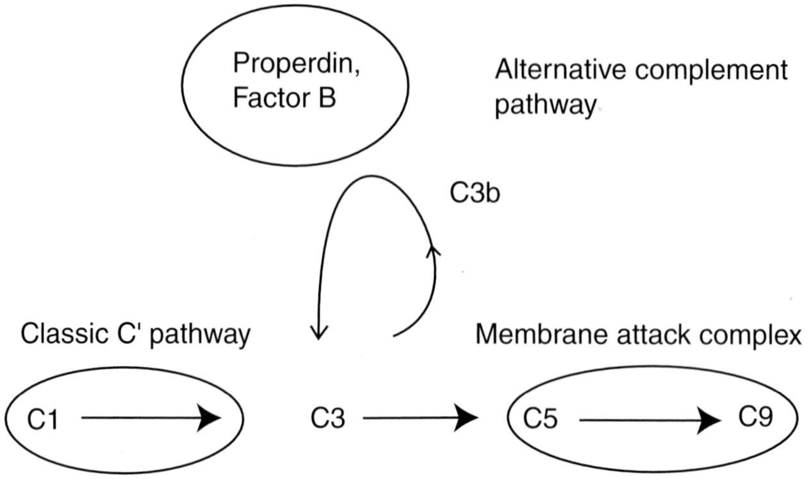

Complement Activation Pathway Deficiencies and Associated Diseases

Complement Activation Pathway Deficiency	Associated Diseases
Classic pathway	Immune complex disease (SLE)
Alternative pathway	Neisserial infections Pyogenic infections
Membrane attack complex	Neisserial infections

FIGURE 70–25 Complement pathways.

occasion, vasculitis have been associated predominantly with hereditary deficiencies of the early components of the classic complement pathway. These associations are presented in Figure 70–25 and Tables 70–4 and 70–5.

For further information, consult chapters on systemic lupus erythematosus (Chapter 5), immune deficiency syndromes (Chapter 20), and meningococcal (Chapter 50) and gonococcal infections (Chapter 56).

TABLE 70–4 Complement Deficiencies and Associated Diseases

Component	Associated Disease
C1q	Systemic lupus erythematosus
Clr/ls	Systemic lupus erythematosus
C4	Systemic lupus erythematosus (anti-Ro (SS-A) antibody positive)
C2	Systemic lupus erythematosus (anti-Ro (SS-A) antibody positive); pyogenic infections; at least 25% normal
C3	Pyogenic infections; glomerulonephritis; systemic lupus erythematosus
C5	Neisserial infections (gonococcal and meningococcal infections); rarely systemic lupus erythematosus
C6	Neisserial infections (gonococcal and meningococcal infections); rarely systemic lupus erythematosus
C7	Neisserial infections (gonococcal and meningococcal infections); rarely systemic lupus erythematosus
C8	Neisserial infections; rarely systemic lupus erythematosus
C9	Neisserial infections (Caucasians); ? a Japanese association with neisserial infections

TABLE 70–5 Deficiencies of Alternative Complement Components and Disease Associations

Component	Disease Association
Properdin	Neisserial infections
Factor D	Neisserial infections
Factor I	Results in unregulated C3bBb (C3 convertase activation), producing C3 deficiency. Pyogenic infections and glomerulonephritis

Annotated Bibliography

Sissons JGP, West RJ, Fallows J, et al. Complement abnormalities of lipodystrophy. N Engl J Med 1976;294;461–465.

This is a classic, highly quoted paper, demonstrating that 17 of 21 patients with partial lipodystrophy had low serum C3 levels. In 14, a serum C3 convertase (C3 nephritic factor) was present. In 10 of these patients, no clinically overt renal disease was detected. However, 7 patients had clinically overt nephritis, and in 6 of the biopsies of the kidneys, membranoproliferative glomerulonephritis was demonstrated.

In contrast, in three patients with a total body lipodystrophy and in one with limb lipodystrophy, no complement abnormalities were detected.

CHAPTER 71

Phototherapy and Photochemotherapy of Skin Diseases

Warwick L. Morison, M.D.

Four types of UV therapy now used

Therapy with ultraviolet (UV) radiation has a long history in dermatology, but only in recent years has there been a clear scientific basis for its use. For example, acne was commonly treated with UV radiation, although there are no studies documenting its efficacy, and it probably provides only the camouflage effect of a tan. The Goeckerman therapy for psoriasis was considered to be a form of photochemotherapy based on the phototoxic interaction of tar and UV radiation, but it is now known that the mechanism is the additive combination of the anti-psoriatic effect of tar plus the anti-psoriatic effect of UV radiation. The changed approach started in 1974 with the publication of a controlled study demonstrating oral psoralen photochemotherapy. Psoralen plus ultraviolet A (PUVA) is an effective treatment for psoriasis. For the first time, precise dosimetry, using a light source selected on the basis of an action spectrum, was used in treatment. Since then, there have been many studies aimed at defining the spectrum of diseases that respond to UV radiation, documenting the long-term adverse effects of treatment, and exploring the mechanisms of action of treatment. In addition, new treatments have been developed on the basis of therapeutic action spectra so that now there are four clearly defined forms of therapy.

PUVA Therapy

Psoralen plus ultraviolet A therapy is a form of photochemotherapy, since it is based on the photochemical interaction between a psoralen, most commonly methoxsalen, and UVA (320–400 nm) radiation. This interaction produces several photo-products, but from a therapeutic and safety viewpoint, adducts and cross-links in deoxyribonucleic acid (DNA) are probably most important.

PUVA therapy effective in 90% of psoriatics

Psoralen plus ultraviolet A therapy has provided a new standard for the treatment of psoriasis. The treatment is effective, clearing chronic plaque psoriasis within 30 exposures in over 90% of patients. It is also convenient, since it is an outpatient treatment requiring two, three, or four exposures a week, each lasting less than 30 minutes. For the first time in UV therapy, a maintenance phase was included so that a patient can be kept largely free of disease over long periods, using a treatment weekly or even as infrequently as once a month.

Indications

More than 30 skin diseases respond.

Diseases successfully treated with PUVA are listed in Table 71–1. After psoriasis, eczema is the most commonly treated disease, and most types, with the notable exception of allergic contact dermatitis, are responsive. Limited maintenance for 6 to 12 months is usually followed by a long-term remission. Mycosis fungoides in the patch-and-plaque stage is usually responsive, and with our current knowl-

TABLE 71–1 Diseases Responsive to PUVA Therapy

Psoriasis
  Vulgaris
  Pustular
  Erythrodermic
	Alopecia areata

Palms and soles
  Psoriasis
  Pustulosis
  Eczema
	Dermatitis herpetiformis

Mycosis fungoides	Chronic urticaria
	  Physical
	  Dermographism
	  Idiopathic

Parapsoriasis en plaque	Pruritus
	  Polycythemia vera
	  Aquagenic

Pityriasis lichenoides, acute and chronic	Scleroderma, linear and morphea
Lymphomatoid papulosis	Pansclerotic morphea of childhood
Vitiligo	Scleromyxedema
Pityriasis alba	Erythema multiforme
Atopic eczema	Transient acantholytic dermatosis
Other endogenous eczemas	Wells' syndrome

Photodermatoses
  PMLE
  Solar urticaria
  Chronic actinic dermatitis
  Erythropoietic protoporphyria
	Pigmented purpuric dermatoses

Lichen planus and nitidus	Papular erythroderma
Graft-versus-host disease	Subacute prurigo
Urticaria pigmentosa	Histiocytosis X
Granuloma annulare	Reticulohistiocytosis
	Ichthyosis linearis circumflexa
	Erythrokeratodermia
	Keratosis lichenoides chronica
	Hypereosinophilic syndrome

edge, maintenance treatment for this condition should be continued for life, since a recurrence will occur in over 50% of patients if treatment is suspended. The tumor stage of this disease does not respond to PUVA therapy although, if few in number, local irradiation of the tumors can be combined with PUVA therapy.

Some of the recent additions to the list of indications are linear and generalized morphea, granuloma annulare, acute and chronic graft-versus-host disease (GVHD), and pigmented purpuric dermatoses. These are important additions, since alternative treatments are either unavailable or markedly toxic.

Technique

Psoralen plus ultraviolet A therapy usually consists of oral administration of methoxsalen and subsequent exposure to a fluorescent source of UVA radiation. In attempts to limit adverse effects, alternative approaches have been used. In Europe, 5-methoxypsoralen is frequently used because of a lower frequency of erythema and gastrointestinal side effects. This is probably due to lower available blood levels resulting from poorer absorption and greater protein-binding of this compound. Topical PUVA therapy is also widely used in the form of bath PUVA therapy. The patient soaks in a dilute solution of psoralen, dries, and is then exposed to a low dose of UVA radiation. A variation of this treatment, the so-called "soak" PUVA therapy, is used for local treatment of hands and feet. Topical PUVA therapy eliminates the systemic symptoms resulting from ingestion of psoralen and probably removes the risk of cataracts. It has also been claimed to be less carcinogenic, but long-term studies of patients receiving large numbers of exposures to this treatment are not available.

Combination therapy increases clearance and reduces exposure dose.

The long-term risks of PUVA therapy are clearly dose related, and consequently, exposure to the treatment should be kept as low as possible. This particularly applies to patients at greatest risk due to fair skin or previous excessive exposure to sunlight; conversely, there is less concern in the elderly and in patients with dark skin. Combination therapy with methotrexate or a retinoid is a useful approach in patients with psoriasis, as it permits rapid clearance at a low dose of PUVA therapy.

Adverse Effects

Erythema occurs in 10% of patients.

The main short-term problem of PUVA therapy is erythema, which occurs in a symptomatic form in about 10% of patients during a clearance course of treatment. There is no specific treatment and supportive measures are required. Gastrointestinal symptoms, mainly nausea, and central nervous system symptoms, such as headache, dizziness, and insomnia, are common, due to a central mechanism induced by high blood levels of psoralen. These can be relieved in most patients by reducing the dose of the drug.

SCC is main long-term risk

The long-term problems of PUVA therapy have been defined in a unique study of 1,400 patients first treated in 1975 to 1976 and followed up since that time at yearly intervals. Nonmelanoma skin cancer, mainly squamous cell carcinoma and to a lesser extent basal cell carcinoma, has been a significant problem, with over 25% of the cohort developing these lesions. Photoaging of the skin, monitored by freckling, is also increased. Most recently, a small increase in the frequency of melanomas has been detected beginning 15 years after first exposure.

Broadband UVB Phototherapy

Probably the most widely used form of UV treatment is broadband UVB phototherapy, utilizing a bank of fluorescent bulbs emitting some UVC radiation, all wavelengths of UVB, a substantial amount of UVA radiation, and some visible light. The treatment is simple and inexpensive to provide, which probably explains its popularity.

Indications

UVB therapy is effective in about 60% of psoriatics.

Indications are listed in Table 71–2. Psoriasis is the main indication, and this treatment clears psoriasis vulgaris within 30 exposures in about 60% of patients. Broadband UVB phototherapy is also effective in mild and moderate eczema but not in severe eczema, for which PUVA is the preferred treatment. A limitation on the use of UVB phototherapy is its restricted penetration into skin. Thus, it is effective in patients with thin plaques of psoriasis but not in patients with thick plaques, and it is probably completely ineffective in the treatment of disease on the palms and soles.

Technique

Erythemogenic doses are most effective.

Various regimens have been used with different starting doses of UVB radiation, increments in dose, and frequency of treatment. An erythemogenic protocol involves determination of the minimal erythema dose (MED), starting at 70% × MED, increments of 20% per treatment, and three to five exposures each week.

TABLE 71–2 Diseases Responsive to Broadband UVB Phototherapy

Psoriasis vulgaris	Graft-versus-host disease

Subcorneal pustular dermatosis	Chronic urticaria
	  Cholinergic
	  Physical
	  Dermographism
	  Idiopathic

Atopic eczema	Eosinophilic pustular folliculitis
Prurigo nodularis	Erythropoietic protoporphyria

Photodermatoses
  PMLE
  Solar urticaria
	Mycosis fungoides

Pityriasis rosea	Histiocytosis X
Pityriasis lichenoides chronica	Pressure sores
Subacute prurigo	

Pruritus
  Renal failure
  Primary biliary cirrhosis
  Macular amyloidosis
  Human immunodeficiency virus infection	

An erythema will occur after about half way into the treatment; if mild, the dose is held, or if symptomatic, treatment is suspended until it settles; this protocol clears the psoriasis in about 60% of unselected patients. Other protocols, usually termed suberythemogenic, have been used, and the effectiveness of the treatment declines progressively as doses are reduced below the threshold for erythema. There are no studies evaluating twice-weekly treatments for clearance of psoriasis, but it is likely that exposures need to be at least three times weekly to be therapeutic.

Combination treatments are commonly used.

The effectiveness of broadband UVB phototherapy is enhanced in diseases with scaling by prior application of a moisturizer, which produces optical index matching of the various layers of the epidermis, increasing penetration of radiation through decreased scattering and reflectance. Other treatments are frequently combined with UVB therapy for psoriasis to enhance clearing. Topical agents are anthralin, calcipotriol, and corticosteroids, although it must be noted that the latter agents appear to gain little and may reduce the duration of a remission. Systemic agents, such as methotrexate and acitretin, have also been found to improve the effectiveness of treatment. A maintenance phase of treatment has become more widely used with UVB phototherapy, and it is effective in delaying recurrence of psoriasis. However, while the disease can be controlled by one treatment a week in about 30% of patients, the remainder require two or three treatments a week, and this is too onerous a burden for most patients.

Adverse Effects

Long-term adverse effects not clearly documented

Erythema is the only short-term adverse effect and usually poses no problem if patients are warned of its inevitability and its similarity to a sunburn. Erythema is associated with accelerated clearance of disease, and this positive aspect should be emphasized. The long-term adverse effects of high-dose UVB phototherapy with maintenance treatment have not been clearly documented. Photoaging in the form of freckling does occur. Retrospective studies of patients given intermittent low-dose courses of therapy have not found an increased risk of skin cancer. However, an analysis based on epidemiologic studies and likely exposure doses suggests that patients treated with high-dose UVB phototherapy with maintenance treatment have a 2.5 to 7.5 times increased risk of nonmelanoma skin cancer, compared with outdoor workers.

Narrowband UVB Phototherapy

Wavelengths > 300 nm are most effective.

Determination of an action spectrum for the therapy of psoriasis using monochromatic radiation found wavelengths greater than 300 nm most therapeutic, while wavelengths less than 300 nm were more erythemogenic and less therapeutic. The peak of the action spectrum was around 313 nm, and this led to the development of a fluorescent bulb (Philips, TL01 lamps) with a narrow emission spectrum centered on 311 nm. Units equipped with these fluorescent bulbs are now commercially available. The lamps are expensive and have a short life, so the cost of delivery of treatment is much higher than for broadband UVB phototherapy.

Indications

Therapy is almost as effective as PUVA therapy.

The main indication is psoriasis, but some other diseases have been reported to respond (Table 71–3). It is therefore likely that the original action spectrum study simply determined the therapeutic spectrum for UVB radiation of any disease, but this possibility has not been explored. Narrowband UVB phototherapy is clearly more effective for treating psoriasis, compared with broadband therapy, both in terms of the percentage of patients cured and the number of treatments required for clearance. One preliminary study suggested that narrowband phototherapy had similar efficacy to PUVA therapy, but this has not been confirmed. The treatment is also more effective than broadband UVB phototherapy in clearing eczema, and even severe cases have responded, thus providing an alternative to PUVA therapy. One limitation is that narrowband UVB therapy is

TABLE 71–3 Diseases Responsive to Narrowband UVB Phototherapy

Psoriasis vulgaris
Subcorneal pustular dermatosis
Atopic eczema
Vitiligo
Photodermatoses

probably not effective in treating disease of the palms and soles, due to lack of penetration at those sites.

Technique

Treatment is required tiw.

Various protocols have been used, all involving an initial determination of the MED. A starting dose of 70% × MED and 10 to 20% dose increments each treatment give good results. Treatments are required three times each week on alternate days, since consecutive daily treatments are associated with an increased risk of erythema. Maintenance treatment prolongs remission, but as with broadband UVB therapy, most patients require one or two treatments each week. In fair-skinned patients, tolerance to narrowband therapy is quickly lost, so it is not possible to use treatment less often than weekly without reduction in the exposure dose.

Adverse Effects

Nonmelanoma skin cancer: a potential risk

Erythema is less common than with broadband UVB therapy, but a typical patient has at least one episode of symptomatic erythema during a clearance course of treatment; again, the time-course and the nature of the erythema resemble those of sunburn. The long-term adverse effects are unknown, as there are no published studies in humans. Photoaging is anticipated in patients receiving prolonged treatment. On the basis of action spectra for carcinoma in mice, the risk of skin cancer might be expected to be lower than with broadband UVB therapy. However, when equierythemogenic doses are used, the incidence of skin cancer is 2 to 3 times higher in mice treated with narrowband bulbs. Since the cumulative dose in MEDs of narrowband radiation required to clear psoriasis is several times lower than with broadband UVB therapy, it has been suggested that narrowband therapy may be less carcinogenic. A prospective human study is required before this can be concluded.

UVA-1 Phototherapy

The UVA spectrum has been recently divided into UVA-1 (340–400 nm) and UVA-2 (320–340 nm). The division is based on a change in the slope of the action spectrum for erythema, which occurs around 340 nm, and is due to differences in the type of photochemistry produced by the two wavebands. Ultraviolet A-1 radiation induces photochemistry via the formation of activated oxygen species, while UVA-2 produces photochemistry through direct absorption of photons by target chromophores, such as DNA and proteins. Investigation of the therapeutic effects of UVA-1 has led to the development of two types of therapy: low-dose (6–20 J/cm^2) therapy and high-dose (130 J/cm^2) treatment.

Indications

SLE and eczema are main indications.

The indications for low-dose and high-dose UVA-1 therapy are listed in Table 71–4. One center has produced all the reports of use of low-dose UVA-1 therapy in systemic lupus erythematosus, but after a series of uncontrolled studies, a controlled cross-over study comparing visible light (> 430 nm) and UVA-1 treatment found no therapeutic effect from visible light and similar beneficial results from UVA-1 as previously reported. The treatment is most effective in

TABLE 71–4 Diseases Responsive to UVA-1 Phototherapy

Low-dose	
	Systemic lupus erythematosus
	Rheumatoid arthritis
	Localized scleroderma
	Morphea
	Pansclerotic morphea
High-dose	
	Atopic eczema
	Scleroderma
	Urticaria pigmentosa
	Granuloma annulare

Ro antibody–positive patients with reduction in systemic symptoms, clearance of skin lesions, and serologic improvement. A beneficial effect has also been reported in rheumatoid arthritis, localized scleroderma, and morphea.

High-dose UVA-1 phototherapy has been used mainly in atopic eczema, with rapid improvement in as few as 10 treatments. A partial dose-finding study found high-dose treatment to be more effective than low-dose treatment in this condition. Urticaria pigmentosa and disseminated granuloma annulare are other conditions found to respond to brief courses of high-dose UVA-1 phototherapy.

Technique

Devices for delivering UVA-1 phototherapy are not commercially available in the United States. For low-dose treatment, fluorescent bulbs with a cut-off filter are suitable, since an irradiance of 20 to 30 mW per square centimeter is adequate. For high-dose treatment, a metal halide system is necessary, since irradiances around 100 mW per square centimeter are required to keep exposure times at reasonable levels.

Adverse Effects

There are no short-term adverse effects from UVA-1 phototherapy and no visible changes are seen in the skin. This waveband has produced squamous cell carcinomas in mice in one study, so this is a potential risk in humans. High-dose treatment has only been used in brief courses, but low-dose treatment has been used for several years in some patients.

Annotated Bibliography

Parrish JA, Fitzpatrick TB, Tanenbaum L, et al. Photochemotherapy of psoriasis with oral methoxsalen and longwave ultraviolet light. N Engl J Med 1974;291:1207–1211.

This is the first report of oral PUVA therapy for the treatment of psoriasis. A bilateral comparison study of PUVA therapy versus broadband UVB phototherapy in 16 patients demonstrated that PUVA therapy was a superior treatment and produced complete clearing of disease in all patients.

Melski JW, Tanenbaum L, Parrish JA, et al. Oral methoxsalen photochemotherapy for the treatment of psoriasis: a cooperative clinical trial. J Invest Dermatol 1977;68: 328–335.

This article presents a multicenter study of 1,308 patients treated with oral PUVA therapy, reporting clearance of psoriasis in 88% of patients within 30 treatments.

Honig B, Morison WL, Karp D. Photochemotherapy beyond psoriasis. J Am Acad Dermatol 1994;31:775–790.

This article presents a review of treatment of more than 30 skin diseases reported to respond to PUVA therapy and a discussion of possible mechanisms underlying these responses.

LeVine MJ, Parrish JA. Outpatient phototherapy of psoriasis. Arch Dermatol 1980;116:552–554.

This is a report of 26 patients with psoriasis treated with erythemogenic doses of broadband UVB radiation, resulting in clearance of disease in an average of 27 treatments. Topical white petrolatum was applied immediately before treatment to enhance the therapeutic effect.

Parrish JA, Jaenicke KF. Action spectrum for phototherapy of psoriasis. J Invest Dermatol 1981;76:359–362.

This article presents a determination of the action spectrum for the treatment of psoriasis. Using a monochromator, authors found wavelengths longer than 300 nm to be most effective.

Coven TR, Burack LH, Gilleaudeau P, et al. Narrowband UV-B produces superior clinical and histopathological resolution of moderate-to-severe psoriasis in patients, compared with broadband UV-B. Arch Dermatol 1997;133:1514–1522.

This bilateral comparison study found that narrowband UVB phototherapy produced faster clearing and more complete resolution of disease.

McGrath H. Ultraviolet-A1 irradiation decreases clinical disease activity and autoantibodies in patients with systemic lupus erythematosus. Clin Exp Rheum 1994;12: 129–135.

This article presents an uncontrollable study which found about 40 to 70% improvement in disease activity in 10 patients. Patients treated for prolonged periods up to 8 months had the greatest improvement, and serum autoantibodies decreased or disappeared in most patients.

Krutmann J, Czech W, Diepgen T, et al. High-dose UVA1 therapy in the treatment of patients with atopic dermatitis. J Am Acad Dermatol 1992;26:225–230.

This article demonstrates that high-dose UVA1 (130 J/cm^2) was found to be superior to UVA-UVB phototherapy for control of atopic eczema.

CHAPTER 72

Immunosuppressive Therapy

John A. Flynn, M.D., Thomas T. Provost, M.D.

Corticosteroids

Corticosteroid hormones were identified and synthesized over 50 years ago, leading to a Nobel prize in 1949. Cortisol is the principal corticosteroid hormone that is manufactured in the adrenal cortex. This has potent anti-inflammatory effects as well as extensive side effects. While corticosteroids remain the mainstay of therapy in the acute suppression of inflammatory disease, their use requires expertise in providing optimal clinical benefit and minimizing side effects.

Most important anti-inflammatory drug

Pharmacology

Corticosteroids are 21-carbon steroid molecules that are commercially synthesized in many forms (Table 72–1).

Depending on their structures, these medications have both glucocorticoid and mineralocorticoid activity. Normal plasma levels are maintained by the hypothalamic-pituitary-adrenal (HPA) axis. The average basal secretion for cortisol is roughly 20 mg per day, with typical serum levels between 5 and 20 mcg per mL. These molecules bind with corticosteroid receptors to initiate a series of events which impact on the host's ability to mount an inflammatory response. For example, corticosteroids inhibit ribonucleic acid (RNA) transcription for many proinflammatory cytokines, including interleukin (IL)-1, IL-2, tumor necrosis factor (TNF), and interferon-alpha (IFN-α). They also inhibit regulation of adhesion molecules and cyclo-oxygenase-2 formation. In addition, specific cells are modified in number and function. These include neutrophils and eosinophils, whose numbers are decreased at sites of inflammation, and macrophages and lymphocytes, whose numbers and function are also depressed by corticosteroids.

Inhibits RNA transcription for inflammatory cytokines

Clinical Efficacy

Corticosteroids are employed in multiple conditions to suppress inflammation. For example, experience in the treatment of rheumatoid arthritis shows that they can effectively suppress acute synovial inflammation. Frequently, however, higher doses are needed to maintain control of disease at the risk of significant side effects, including suppression of the HPA axis.

Effective in suppressing acute and chronic infections

Toxicity

Severe adverse effects are produced by short and prolonged exposure to high doses of corticosteroids. Acute side effects include the development of psychosis and hypertension. The latter is the result of the mineralocorticoid activity and fluid retention. Carbohydrate metabolism alterations may produce insulin resistance, glucose intolerance, and overt diabetes. Weight gain from stimulated

Side effects are many.

TABLE 72–1 Various Preparations of Corticosteroids Employed in Clinical Practice

Cortisone
Prednisolone
Methylprednisolone
Prednisone
Dexamethasone
Triamcinolone

appetite and fat redistribution produces truncal obesity, the typical "buffalo hump," and Cushingoid facies.

Suppresses immune responses

In chronic therapy of moderate duration (months), corticosteroids also produce depression of the immune responses and increase susceptibility to infection, especially in doses greater than 20 mg per day. Also, the steroids will frequently mask common symptoms associated with infection, such as fever and the development of inflammation at the site of infection.

Osteoporosis, avascular necrosis, accelerated atherosclerosis

The side effects from chronic long-time therapy (years) of corticosteroids include osteoporosis, development of glaucoma, cataract formation, avascular necrosis, and corticosteroid-induced myopathies. Cutaneous manifestations include skin thinning, with fragility and ecchymoses, as well as striae, hirsutism, and acne formation. Prolonged steroid therapy also induces accelerated atherosclerosis, especially in women treated for years with corticosteroids.

Use in Dermatology

Corticosteroids widely employed to treat inflammatory and immunologically mediated disease: acute therapy, prolonged daily therapy, steroid-sparing drugs

Corticosteroids are widely employed in dermatology to treat acute inflammatory diseases, such as poison ivy and other forms of allergic contact dermatitis (ie, nickel, chromate). Prednisone or methylprednisolone is commonly given in a short burst (ie, initially 40 to 60 mg for 4 days and totally tapered over a 2- to 3-week period of time).

Treatment of autoimmune bullous diseases and connective tissue diseases requires daily dosing, slowly tapered to the least amount of steroid to suppress the clinical features or in the case of systemic lupus erythematosus (SLE) complicated by lupus nephritis to normalize complement levels. Steroid-sparing agents, such as azathioprine and cyclophosphamide, are employed together with corticosteroids to permit a lower dose of daily steroids, minimizing corticosteroid side effects but, at the same time, suppressing the inflammatory disease.

Pulse steroid therapy

Pulse steroid therapy (ie, 1 g of intravenous methylprednisolone infused slowly over a 4-hour period, to avoid fluxes in electrolytes, for 3 successive days) has proved effective in rapidly treating such inflammatory diseases as pyoderma gangrenosum, dermatomyositis, and various forms of vasculitis.

Intralesional therapy

Intralesional steroids are commonly employed to treat individual lesions of cutaneous sarcoidosis and SLE. Use of intralesional injections can produce transient lipoatrophy at the site of injection. This is especially problematic on the face.

Prevention of Osteoporosis

Calcitonin and bisphosphonates

In recent years, prevention of osteoporosis in patients on long-term corticosteroids has become a major effort, made possible by the availability of a number of agents that inhibit bone resorption, such as calcitonin and bisphosphonates (alendronate, ethidronate, and pamidronate).

Supplemental calcium and vitamin D_2 therapy

Premenopausal women, as well as and men on long-term steroid therapy, should be considered for supplemental daily calcium and vitamin D_2 therapy.

Postmenopausal women on long-term steroid therapy should receive calcium daily plus vitamin D_2.

Hormone replacement therapy

Hormone replacement therapy should also be provided to women, preferably prescribed in collaboration with a gynecologist.

Annotated Bibliography

Hall GM, Daniels M, Doyle DV, Spector TD. Effect of hormone replacement therapy on bone mass in rheumatoid arthritis patients treated with or without steroids. Arthritis Rheum 1994;37:1499–1504.

Recommendations for the prevention and treatment of glucocorticoid induced osteoporosis. Arthritis Rheum 1996;39:1791–1793.

Saag KG, Emkey R, Schnitzer TJ, et al. Alendronate for the prevention and treatment of glucocorticoid-induced osteoporosis. Glucocorticoid-Induced Osteoporosis Intervention Study Group. N Engl J Med 1998 Jul 30;339:292–299.

These are three excellent articles outlining current therapy to prevent osteoporosis in patients on prolonged corticosteroid therapy.

Azathioprine

Analogue of 6-mercaptopurine

Azathioprine was originally synthesized in an effort to develop a purine antimetabolite of nucleic acid bases for cancer chemotherapy. This was developed as a prodrug of 6-mercaptopurine and was used in the early 1960s in combination with steroids for immunosuppression following renal transplantation.

Pharmacology

Metabolized to 6-mercaptopurine

Azathioprine is metabolized to 6-mercaptopurine. Subsequent breakdown products include thioinosinic acid, which inhibits a number of enzymes involved in the purine salvage pathway. The result of this is to reduce the availability of cellular purines, which leads to decreased deoxyribonucleic acid (DNA) and RNA syntheses. This effect primarily occurs in actively dividing lymphocytes and is not altered by renal insufficiency. Azathioprine is oxidized directly by xanthine oxidase; thus, xanthine oxidase inhibitors (such as allopurinol) can potentiate the effects and toxicity of this medication.

Clinical Efficacy

Effective immunosuppressive agent in renal transplantation

Steroid-sparing agent

Azathioprine, when used in combination with prednisone, was found to be effective in preventing the rejection of newly transplanted kidneys. It was also shown to allow for the use of a lower dose of prednisone than would have otherwise been possible without it (steroid sparing). Within the past two decades, it has been mostly replaced by the use of cyclosporine. It is now primarily reserved for patients who do not respond to prednisone and cyclosporine.

It has been shown to be effective in refractory rheumatoid arthritis at dosages from 1.0 to 2.0 mg per kg daily. Its greatest role in rheumatoid arthritis has been in maintaining disease control, as opposed to inducing remission. Azathioprine is also used, in addition to prednisone, in patients with lupus nephritis. It is felt that combination therapy reduces adverse renal outcomes more significantly than would be seen with prednisone alone.

Use in Dermatology

In dermatology, used to treat connective tissue and bullous diseases

Azathioprine has been successfully employed, generally in combination with prednisone, to treat SLE and dermatomyositis. It has also been found to be effective in treating bullous pemphigoid, pemphigus vulgaris, benign mucous membrane pemphigoid, and vasculitis.

In elderly diabetic patients with bullous pemphigoid, one of the authors (TTP) has successfully employed azathioprine as monotherapy to treat bullous pemphigoid. In bullous pemphigoid, the therapeutic effect occurs within days, indicating that the beneficial effect of azathioprine is predominantly as an anti-inflammatory and not as an immunosuppressive agent.

Toxicity

Bone marrow toxicity related to thiopurine methyltransferase polymorphism

The most common side effects are nausea and vomiting after dose administration. There is also a dose-related hepatotoxicity with cholestasis, which typically occurs at greater than 2.0 mg per kg per day. This is more frequently seen in people with underlying hepatitis. An azathioprine hypersensitivity syndrome has been described, which is manifested by spiking fevers, arthralgias, myalgias, and diarrhea. There have been cases reported with peripheral eosinophilia as well as eosinophilic colitis. Patients may also develop leukopenia, and there is an increased risk of infection from immunosuppression. The toxic side effects are related to polymorphism of the enzyme thiopurine methyltransferase.

Annotated Bibliography

Snow JL, Gibson LE. The role of genetic variation in thiopure methyltransferase activity and the efficacy and/or side effects of azathioprine therapy in dermatologic patients. Arch Dermatol 1995;131:193–197.

This article provides an important consideration in the employment of azathioprine.

Mycophenolate Mofetil

Inhibits purine synthesis

Mycophenolate mofetil was developed in the early 1970s in an attempt to find an immunosuppressive agent with fewer side effects. It acts by inhibiting the end stages of purine synthesis, with depletion of guanosine and deoxyguanosine nucleotides. This is achieved through the potent inhibition of inosine monophosphate dehydrogenase.

Pharmacology

Suppresses lymphocyte proliferation and antibody synthesis

Inosine monophosphate dehydrogenase is an essential enzyme for the synthesis of purines and is the prime purine pathway used in T and B lymphocytes. As a result of this inhibition, there is a suppression of lymphocyte proliferation and antibody formation. This does not produce chromosomal breakage nor does it inhibit repair of DNA. It is rapidly absorbed after oral administration and bound to albumin.

Clinical Efficacy

Used in transplantation and treatment of autoimmune and vasculitis patients

This medication has been employed in combination with cyclosporine and prednisone for the prevention of transplant rejection. The dose of 1.0 g by mouth twice daily, in combination with the above medications, is recommended in the treatment of transplant rejection. There has been no demonstrated increase in therapeutic efficacy with higher dosages. Its dose should be decreased in people with severe renal insufficiency. It has been employed in the treatment of immune-mediated diseases. In rheumatoid arthritis, there has been a documented 15% response rate in patients refractory to methotrexate. It has also been successfully used in Takayasu's arteritis.

Uses in Dermatology

Mycophenolate mofetil has been successfully employed in combination with steroids and other immunosuppressive agents to treat recalcitrant cutaneous lupus erythematosus, dermatomyositis, bullous pemphigoid, and pemphigus vulgaris patients. Mycophenolic acid has also been employed to treat psoriasis.

Toxicity

Less toxicity than azathioprine

The most common side effect is gastrointestinal toxicity, characterized by nausea, vomiting, abdominal cramping, and diarrhea. This can be addressed by decreasing the dosage. There appears to be no hepatotoxicity, and bone marrow suppression is much less common, compared with azathioprine or cyclophosphamide. There are no long-term data on secondary infections or malignancies.

Annotated Bibliography

Plaltz KP, et al. RS-61443 (mycophenolate mofetil): a new potent immunosuppressive agent. Transplantation 1991;51:27–33.

This is a standard reference.

Gelber AC, Nousari HC, Wigley FM. Mycophenolate mofetil in the treatment of severe skin manifestations of dermatomyositis: a series of 4 cases. J Rheumatol 2000 June; 27:1542–1545.

Cyclophosphamide

Cyclophosphamide (Cytoxan) is a cyclic phosphatide mustard cytotoxic acylating agent, first introduced for the treatment of malignancies over 40 years ago. It is used to treat a variety of autoimmune disorders and malignancies. The drug induces cell death throughout the cell cycle and can be given orally or parenterally. Recent work using high-dose parenteral Cytoxan ("immunablation therapy") has produced exciting results in the treatment of severe autoimmune diseases (see below).

Introduced 40 years ago to treat malignancies

Pharmacology

Cyclophosphamide is a cyclic phosphoamide analogue of nitrogen mustard. It is largely inactive in its native state. However, when metabolized by the liver, a highly reactive phosphoramide mustard is produced along with acrolein. It is the phosphoramide mustard, which is the active alkylating and phosphorylating agent, that causes cell death, especially in rapidly proliferating cells. Through alkylation and cross-linking of the cellular molecules, particularly DNA and RNA, these biochemical reactions produce rapid cell death, presumably through apoptosis. This cytotoxic action is greatest during the S-phase of the cell cycle, when DNA synthesis occurs.

Analogue of nitrogen mustard

Produces alkylation and cross-linking of DNA and RNA molecules producing apoptosis

The other major metabolic byproduct of cyclophosphamide metabolism is acrolein. This substance produces bladder toxicity and hemorrhagic cystitis.

Acrolein produces bladder toxicity

In addition to cell death, continuously administered cyclophosphamide produces a decrease in circulating lymphocytes by inhibition of both B cells and T cells and suppression of cell-mediated immunity.

Clinical Efficacy

The method and timing of administration impact the clinical effects of cyclophosphamide. Chronic daily therapy is effective in suppressing cell-mediated immunity for long periods of time, with the risk of more frequent side effects. Parenteral bolus ("pulse cyclophosphamide") therapy is effective for antibody-mediated conditions and produces fewer side effects (ie, infection and malignancy). When provided continually on an oral basis, a typical regimen is 1.5 to 3.0 mg per kg per day. With the intermittent intravenous bolus regimen, patients typically receive between 500 and 1,500 mg per square meter every 4 weeks for a set period of time. With this regimen, hematology studies must be monitored closely to evaluate for leukopenia, which will occur in a dose-dependent fashion between the first and second weeks of dose administration. The metabolites of cyclophosphamide are renally cleared; therefore, it is important to reduce the dosage in patients with renal insufficiency. It is also important to maintain a high urine volume to minimize bladder toxicity.

Chronic daily doses

Pulse cyclophosphamide therapy

Use in Dermatology

Cyclophosphamide is extremely effective in the treatment of Wegener's granulomatosis at a continuous daily dose of 2.0 to 4.0 mg per kg, with concomitant steroid administration. Remission rates are reported to be as high as 90% with a 5-year survival rate greater than 80%. Polyarteritis nodosa patients also have a dramatic increased survival when treated with cyclophosphamide. (For further discussion, see Chapter 12, "Vasculitis," section on Wegener's granulomatosis and polyarteritis nodosa.)

Cyclophosphamide is also used in the treatment of SLE when there is serious disease with end-organ involvement, such as glomerulonephritis or vasculitis. It has also been significantly used to treat patients with polymyositis and dermatomyositis, refractory to corticosteroids and methotrexate. Cyclophosphamide, in a continuous daily-dose regimen, has been successfully employed with steroids to treat patients with pemphigus vulgaris. Some of these patients have had a total clinical and serologic remission lasting for years on no therapy.

Used to treat various forms of vasculitis, connective tissue and bullous diseases

Recently, there has been exciting evidence on the use of high-dose immunablative cyclophosphamide to treat several refractory severe autoimmune diseases, including SLE, rheumatoid arthritis with Felty's syndrome, and autoimmune hemolytic anemia. In these studies, patients received intravenous Cytoxan (as much as 50 mg per kg of body weight for 4 consecutive days), with subsequent complete remission. Due to very high levels of aldehyde dehydrogenase, hemopoietic stem cells are resistant to the cytotoxic effects of cyclophosphamide. This avoids the need for stem cell rescue.

Toxicity

Bladder toxicity

MESNA therapy

Bladder toxicity is due to the effects of acrolein on the transitional epithelium of the bladder, leading to a hemorrhagic cystitis. In mild cases, this may produce only microscopic hematuria. In severe cases, patients may have life-threatening hemorrhage. This can occur at any time after Cytoxan administration and appears to be dose dependent. Increased fluid intake to maintain a large urine output needs to be encouraged in all patients taking this medication. The introduction of *N*-acetylcysteine or MESNA (2-mercaptoethanesodiumsulfonate) has reduced the incidence of hemorrhagic cystitis with high-dose intravenous Cytoxan.

Leukopenia

Nearly all patients treated with Cytoxan develop some evidence of bone marrow suppression. This is most commonly seen as a leukopenia. Typically, this occurs 10 to 15 days after receiving intravenous bolus therapy. Ideally, the white blood cell count should not fall below 1,000 mm^3 during this nadir. For continuous oral therapy, the white blood cell count should be maintained above 3,000 mm^3. Thrombocytopenia rarely occurs. Patients may develop a macrocytic anemia, though this is generally mild. In patients who do develop severe neutropenia, human granulocyte colony-stimulating factor may be used to stimulate neutrophil production and function.

Infection

In those taking Cytoxan, the risk of infection increases in patients who are leukopenic. There is also an increased risk of infection in patients who are not leukopenic. This is most commonly detected in those patients taking concomitant prednisone therapy (30 mg/day or higher). Oral candidiasis and candidal esophagitis are common infectious complications. Patients are also at higher risk of developing herpes zoster. In addition, *Pneumocystis carinii* pneumonia has been well described. In many cases when Cytoxan is being used on a long-term basis, prophylactic antibiotics (such as trimethoprim-sulfamethoxazole or dapsone) are prescribed to prevent this infection.

Lymphomas and leukemias

Carcinogen: bladder cancer

Of great concern is the carcinogenicity associated with cyclophosphamide, primarily in the form of secondary leukemias, lymphomas, and bladder cancer. This appears to be associated with a higher cumulative dose of the medication. In some studies, there has been as high as a 14-fold increase in the development of leukemias and lymphomas, compared with disease-matched controls not treated with cyclophosphamide. Bladder cancer is more frequently seen in patients taking orally administered cyclophosphamide. Bladder cancer can occur in 6 to 16% of patients who take oral cyclophosphamide for more than 1 year. This risk is reduced by proper bladder care with vigorous hydration during administration. It also requires careful follow-up with cystoscopy, if any hematuria is evident on urinalysis.

Teratogenic, infertility

Cyclophosphamide is clearly teratogenic, though there have been case reports of normal offspring in patients taking this medication. It also is capable of causing gonadal failure and subsequent infertility in both males and females. This, too, is dose dependent and is seen with greater probability in older patients.

Annotated Bibliography

O'Loughlin S, Goldman GC, Provost TT. Pemphigus: fate of antibody following successful therapy. Arch Dermatol 1978;114:1769–1772.

This article describes a small series of pemphigus patients demonstrating that one-third were clinically and serologically free of disease for prolonged periods of time (years) following cyclophosphamide therapy.

Brodsky RA, Petri M, Smith DB, et al. Immunoablative high-dose cyclophosphamide without stem-cell rescue for refractory, severe autoimmune disease. Ann Intern Med 1998;129:1031–1035.

Immunoablative high-dose Cytoxan was successful in 7 of 8 patients with refractory, severe autoimmune disease. Stem-cell rescue is not necessary in these patients because hematopoietic stem cells express high levels of aldehyde dehydrogenase, an enzyme responsible for cellular resistance to cyclophosphamide. With the re-emergence of bone marrow function, there is no increased risk or evidence of recurrence of autoimmune lymphocytes.

Fauci AS, Haynes BF, Katz P, Wolff SM. Wegener's granulomatosis: prospective clinical and therapeutic experience with 85 patients for 21 years. Ann Intern Med 1983; 98:76–85.

This is a classic article that details the successful employment of cyclophosphamide.

Methotrexate

Methotrexate, a folic acid antagonist, has been used for 50 years in various forms to treat different medical conditions. Originally, aminopterin was employed to treat leukemias. This compound was also successfully used to treat psoriasis, psoriatic arthritis, and rheumatoid arthritis. Subsequently, in the early 1970s, methotrexate was synthesized and initially used to treat malignancies. In 1988, the United States Food and Drug Administration (FDA) approved the use of weekly methotrexate for the treatment of rheumatoid arthritis.

Used in American medicine for over 50 years

Pharmacology

At high dosages, methotrexate inhibits dihydrofolate reductase which is responsible for the reduction of folic acid to its metabolic byproducts. It is effective in inhibiting DNA synthesis, as well as IL-6 and IL-1β activity. There is no effect on lymphocytic or monocytic white blood cell production. There is, however, no firm consensus on the mechanism of action when employed in low doses for the treatment of chronic inflammatory conditions, although there may be increased adenosine (an immunosuppressive) release at the site of inflammation (see Annotated Bibliography).

High doses of methotrexate inhibit dihydrofolate reductase and DNA synthesis

Methotrexate can be administered orally or parenterally. At low doses (up to 20 mg/week), there is adequate oral absorption with bioavailability occurring in the range of 40 to 90%. This medication is excreted primarily by the kidneys and, thus, is contraindicated in patients with renal insufficiency or failure. When higher doses are required or when gastrointestinal absorption is in question (ie, inflammatory bowel disease), parenteral methotrexate may be given as a subcutaneous injection.

Mechanism of action of low-dose methotrexate is unknown.

Clinical Efficacy

In placebo-controlled trials on the use of methotrexate to treat rheumatoid arthritis, methotrexate was found to induce a 50% reduction in joint pain and swelling within a 6- to 12-week period of time. Methotrexate is superior to oral gold and azathioprine. Clinical outcomes are similar when compared with parenteral gold; however, toxicity with gold appears to be higher.

Methotrexate superior to gold and azathioprine in treatment of rheumatoid arthritis

Methotrexate is given on a weekly basis, either orally or parenterally. The typical initial dose is 7.5 mg per week. If there has not been a significant response within 6 weeks, this dosage is increased over time to a maximum dose of 20 mg per week or until a satisfactory response is obtained. Dosages greater than 20 mg per week should be given parenterally due to lack of oral bioavailability at these high doses.

Toxicity

More than half the patients who take low-dose methotrexate for rheumatoid arthritis will experience some side effects. However, in many cases, these side effects can be managed with supportive care and do not require methotrexate discontinuation. An approximate 15% drop-out rate due to toxicity occurs within 5 years.

Gastrointestinal toxicity

The most common side effects are related to the gastrointestinal tract and include nausea, anorexia, vomiting, diarrhea, and stomatitis. These typically occur early in therapy and frequently will improve over time. The concomitant use of folic acid has been shown to reduce some of the gastrointestinal toxicities. If severe gastrointestinal symptoms persist, then methotrexate may be given by subcutaneous or intramuscular injection with subsequent reduction of these symptoms.

With oral methotrexate (5 out of 7 days), occult cirrhosis developed in the treatment of psoriasis

When methotrexate was first used in the early 1980s, fear of hepatotoxicity constrained its widespread use. This was, in great part, due to earlier findings of the use of this medication in the treatment of patients with psoriasis, where rates of hepatic cirrhosis were 20% after 5 years of treatment. In patients with rheumatoid arthritis receiving methotrexate, the estimated risk of developing serious liver disease after 5 years of treatment is less than 1 per 1,000 patients treated. (It has been recognized that the previous dosing of methotrexate for 5 out of 7 days was associated with significant toxicity. Now, once-weekly dosing is rarely associated with toxicity.) The risk of toxicity is greater in people who use alcohol heavily (more than 100 g/wk) or who have underlying liver disease (ie, chronic viral hepatitis). Baseline liver biopsies are no longer recommended prior to starting methotrexate for rheumatoid arthritis. This procedure should be considered, however, in those patients who have a significant history of heavy alcohol consumption who agree to abstain, as well as in patients with evidence of chronic hepatitis B or C or other chronic liver disease. The present recommendations are to monitor serum transaminases (AST and ALT) and albumin levels every 4 to 8 weeks. A liver biopsy should be considered if there is persistent elevation of liver function tests (LFTs).

Bone marrow suppression

Bone marrow suppression develops in less than 5% of patients who take methotrexate. This can occur in the form of megaloblastic anemia, leukopenia, thrombocytopenia, or pancytopenia. Most commonly, we see a mild leukopenia which typically occurs in the setting of some other event that may suppress the bone marrow (ie, infection, folate deficiency, and use of folate antagonists, such as trimethoprim-sulfamethoxazole). These are usually reversible after the methotrexate is stopped.

"Methotrexate lung"

Acute pulmonary inflammation is an important but rare and poorly understood manifestation of methotrexate toxicity. This occurs in less than 2% of people and is sometimes referred to as "methotrexate lung." This appears to be an idiosyncratic reaction that can occur at any dose. Pre-existing pulmonary disease and concomitant tobacco use may be risk factors. This syndrome will present with flu-like symptoms of fever and a nonproductive cough, with rapid development of hypoxemia. The chest radiograph may be initially normal but will quickly demonstrate a diffuse bilateral interstitial inflammatory infiltrative pattern. Bronchoscopic biopsy findings are nonspecific, sometimes demonstrating a hypersensitivity pneumonitis with lymphocytic infiltrates. Treatment requires prompt recognition, thorough evaluation for possible infections and discontinuation of the methotrexate. Parenteral administration of high-dose corticosteroids may produce rapid clinical improvement. Respiratory failure has been described.

There is no current epidemiologic evidence proving that methotrexate is carcinogenic. However, there have been isolated reports of lymphoproliferative malignancies in patients treated with methotrexate for rheumatoid arthritis and dermatomyositis. In some of these settings, the lymphoma resolved after discontinuation of methotrexate, underscoring the necessity to be vigilant.

No evidence for increased malignancy associated with methotrexate therapy

Various central nervous system side effects have been reported and include headache, dizziness, and, less often, memory impairments. These side effects are reversible when the drug is discontinued.

Also, several opportunistic infections have been reported in patients taking low-dose methotrexate. In many of these situations, patients were also taking corticosteroids. The most common infection appears to be herpes zoster, though there have also been reports of *Pneumocystis carinii* infection and a number of fungal infections. These infections, though rare, point out the importance of diligently seeking the source of infection in patients on methotrexate who present with constitutional symptoms.

Herpes zoster

Use of Methotrexate in Dermatology

Methotrexate has been successfully employed to treat severe forms of psoriasis with or without psoriatic arthritis. In general, methotrexate is given in three doses (2.5 to 7.5 mg) 12 hours apart, once weekly. This dosage regimen is very successful, and long-term toxicity is markedly reduced, compared with the previous therapeutic regimen of 2.5 mg, 5 out of 7 days.

Today, methotrexate also has been successfully employed in the treatment of various autoimmune diseases. The senior author has observed successful treatment of benign mucous membrane pemphigoid, cutaneous lupus lesions, dermatomyositis, erosive lichen planus, and lichen sclerosis et atrophicus. These autoimmune diseases respond to the once-weekly dosing (7.5 to 20 mg).

Annotated Bibliography

Flynn JA, Hellmann DB. Methotrexate in rheumatoid arthritis when NSAIDs fail. Cleveland J Med 1995;62:351–359.

This article presents a concise overview of the use of methotrexate in rheumatoid arthritis and its associated toxicities.

Cronstein DN, Naime D, Ostad E. The antiinflammatory mechanism of methotrexate. J Clin Invest 1993;92:2675–2682.

This paper reports the potential role of methotrexate in increasing levels of adenosine release within inflamed sites, leading to suppression of inflammation, when the drug is employed at low levels.

Whiting-O'Keefe QE, Fye KH, Sack KD. Methotrexate and histologic hepatic abnormalities: a meta-analysis. Am J Med 1991;90:711–716.

This paper reviews 636 patients from 15 studies of methotrexate use in rheumatoid or psoriatic arthritis. It points out that the risk of liver toxicity with long-term low-dose methotrexate is increased in people with heavy alcohol consumption and underlying liver disease.

Cyclosporine/Tacrolimus

Cyclosporine is an effective immunosuppressive agent, employed for the treatment of organ transplant rejection and graft-versus-host disease (GVHD). In addition, cyclosporine has been used for a variety of dermatologic conditions, including psoriasis, lichen planus, Behçet's disease, atopic dermatitis, pyoderma gangrenosum, urticaria, alopecia areata, scleroderma, photodermatosis, lupus erythematosus, and dermatomyositis/polymyositis.

Cyclosporine employed to treat a variety of inflammatory conditions

Mechanism of Action

Inhibits IL-2 gene transcription

Cyclosporine interferes with the early events in the activation of T cells. It inhibits the transcription of the IL-2 gene following antigen exposure. This effectively inhibits the generation of antigen-specific T cells.

Inhibits calcineurin

Cyclosporine binds to a family of protein receptors, specific for cyclosporine, termed immunophillins. This complex subsequently inhibits calcineurin. Calcineurin is a serine-threonine phosphatase. Calcineurin is activated after T-cell antigen receptor (CD3) occupation. The substrate for the activated phosphatase is a cytoplasmic subunit of the nuclear factor of activated T cells (NF-AT). The NF-AT is a lymphocyte-specific transcription factor. With dephosphorylation of the cytoplasmic NF-AT, the protein is translocated to the nucleus and associates with a nuclear subunit to generate the functional NF-AT complex. This NF-AT factor plays a central role in the transcription of the IL-2 gene. The binding of the cyclosporine to the immunophillin prevents this nuclear translocation, blocking the stimulation of IL-2 gene transcription.

Tacrolimus also inhibits calcineurin.

Tacrolimus (FK-506, Prograf) is another immunosuppressive agent that binds to a distinct family of immunophillins, termed the FK-binding protein or FK-506–binding protein. Tacrolimus, on binding to its cognate protein, inhibits calcineurin phosphatase activity, identical to cyclosporine. Again, nuclear translocation of the cytoplasmic unit of NF-AT is inhibited.

Side Effects

Hypertension and renal toxicity problematic

Cyclosporine, in contradistinction to other immunosuppressive agents, does not have prominent myelotoxicity; however, nephrotoxicity and hypertension are common side effects. Renal vascular injury, producing renal dysfunction, vascular damage, and hypertension, are common sequelae of cyclosporine therapy. The presence of an increased serum creatinine is a risk factor for persistent renal dysfunction, following cyclosporine therapy.

There is evidence to indicate that the nephropathy is dose dependent. Doses of cyclosporine (less than 5 mg/kg/day) are generally not associated with severe renal toxicity. However, sophisticated tests, measuring the glomerulofiltration rate (iothalamate clearance) have indicated that "low-dose" cyclosporine therapy can induce nephrotoxicity, manifested predominantly by a decrease in the glomerulofiltration rate.

Hypertension is a common side effect. It may respond to dose reduction, but there is evidence to indicate that some patients appear to be prone to developing hypertension.

Isolated hyperbilirubinemia

In addition to the nephrotoxicity and hypertension associated with cyclosporine, the drug may also induce nausea, vomiting, diarrhea, and increased transaminase as well as alkaline phosphatase. It may also induce isolated hyperbilirubinemia.

One of the authors has seen one patient with an exfoliated erythroderma secondary to atopic dermatitis, who developed mild jaundice and a bilirubin level of 3.5 when treated with cyclosporine. Discontinuation of the drug was associated with the disappearance of the jaundice, and return of the bilirubin level to normal.

Gingival hyperplasia

Patients may also develop hyperkalemia, hyperuricemia, and hypomagnesemia. Hyperlipidemia may also be detected. From a cutaneous point of view, hypertrichosis is the most common complication, although patients can develop keratosis pilaris acneiform eruptions and sebaceous hyperplasia. Gingival hyperplasia is a common problem, and if the patients are on calcium channel blockers, this may occur rapidly.

Increased risk of infections

As noted above, hematologic abnormalities are very unusual, although patients may develop a mild normochromic, normocytic anemia. Like other immunosuppressive agents, patients receiving cyclosporine are at increased risk to develop infections, including Epstein-Barr virus, cytomegalovirus, and *Pneumocystis carinii* infections. These patients also may have an increased risk of non–Hodgkin's lymphoma and skin cancer. There appears to be an increase in Kaposi's sarcoma in transplant recipients.

Finally, these patients may experience constitutional symptomatology, such as altered sensations of hot and cold temperatures, headache, weakness, fatigue, and mild tingling sensations.

Drug Interactions

Cyclosporine is metabolized in the liver by cytochrome P-450-IIIA isoform. Drugs that inhibit P-450-IIIA increase cyclosporine levels. These include corticosteroids, oral contraceptives, androgenic corticosteroids, cimetidine, erythromycin, ketoconazole, and calcium channel blockers.

Drug interactions

Drugs that induce cytochrome P-450-IIIA produce decreased levels of cyclosporine. These include phenobarbital, phenytoin, dexamethasone, rifampicin. In addition, cyclosporine, together with the following drugs, may induce a synergistic nephrotoxicity: diuretics, nonsteroidal anti-inflammatory drugs, amphotericin B, and aminoglycosides and trimethoprim-sulfamethoxazole.

Administration

The drug, because of its costliness and potential toxicity, should be reserved for those individuals with severe dermatologic diseases, recalcitrant to standard forms of therapy. The drug is contraindicated in patients with uncontrolled hypertension, liver toxicity, and renal insufficiency. In addition, it should not be used in patients who have immunodeficiencies and during pregnancy.

In general, the dosage of cyclosporine should not exceed 2.5 to 5.0 mg per kg per day. Some investigators recommend that if the patients have no improvement within a 2- to 4-week period of time, the dosage can be temporarily increased, from 0.5 mg to 1 mg per kg per day to a maximum dose of 8 to 10 mg per kg. Following control of the disease, discontinuation of therapy should be attempted.

Patients on cyclosporine therapy should be closely monitored for alterations in blood pressure and liver and renal functions. Whole blood trough level concentrations should be detected by radioimmunoassay or liquid chromatography and should not exceed 200 to 250 ng per nL.

Uses in Dermatology

Psoriasis

Cyclosporine has been reported to be effective in the treatment of recalcitrant, severe psoriasis, including psoriatic erythroderma, psoriatic arthritis, and pustular psoriasis.

Atopic Dermatitis

Severe atopic dermatitis has responded to cyclosporine therapy. We have effectively treated several patients with exfoliated erythroderma secondary to atopic dermatitis.

Pyoderma Gangrenosum

Effective in the treatment of pyoderma gangrenosum

Pyoderma gangrenosum has been reported to respond to cyclosporine therapy. We have had experience with three patients with recalcitrant forms of pyoderma gangrenosum who demonstrated within a 2- to 3-week period of time a dramatic response to cyclosporine therapy. Recurrences may occur with discontinuation of the drug, but in general, our experience and that of the literature indicate that many of these patients remain in prolonged remission following cyclosporine therapy.

Lichen Planus

Oral as well as cutaneous lichen planus has been reported to respond to cyclosporine therapy. Topical cyclosporine has been reported to be effective in the treatment of oral lichen planus; however, it is very expensive.

Behçet's Disease

Cyclosporine has been effectively employed to treat the mucocutaneous, including ocular, complications of Behçet's disease.

Urticaria

Effective in some chronic urticaria patients

Patients with chronic urticaria have been successfully treated with cyclosporine. We have had experience with one patient, with incapacitating urticaria over 1 year's duration, who responded dramatically to cyclosporine therapy.

Blistering Diseases

In general, our experience has failed to indicate that cyclosporine is effective in the treatment of various blistering diseases. There are, however, reports in the literature that epidermolysis bullosa acquisita has responded to cyclosporine therapy.

Connective Tissue Diseases

Cyclosporine has been reported to be effective in the treatment of patients with lupus erythematosus and dermatomyositis. There are also isolated reports that it may be effective in the treatment of scleroderma.

Annotated Bibliography

Lim AK, Su WPD, Schroeter A, et al. Cyclosporine in the treatment of dermatologic disease: an update. Mayo Clin Proc 1996;71:1182–1191.

This is a good review article detailing the use of cyclosporine in such dermatologic diseases as psoriasis, lichen planus, Behçet's disease, atopic dermatitis, pyoderma gangrenosum, as well as epidermolysis bullosa acquisita. The review article contains an excellent bibliography.

Barlow RJ, Black AK, Greaves MW. Treatment of severe chronic urticaria with cyclosporin A. Eur J Dermatol 1993;3:273–275.

This article details experience with the use of cyclosporin A in the treatment of urticaria.

Nousari HC, Anhalt GJ. Immunosuppressive and immunomodulatory drugs. In: Freedberg IM, Eisen AZ, Wolff K, et al. eds. Fitzpatrick's Dermatology in General Medicine, 5th ed. New York, NY: McGraw Hill, 1999, pp 2853–2864.

This book chapter provides an up-to-date bibliography.

Antimalarials (Aminoquinolines)

Introduced over 50 years ago

Chloroquine, hydroxychloroquine, and quinacrine are commonly employed by dermatologists. All were introduced into American medicine 50 years ago, primarily for the treatment of malaria. All have been successfully employed as anti-inflammatory agents in the treatment of a variety of connective tissue diseases, including rheumatoid arthritis, the cutaneous lesions of dermatomyositis, and lupus erythematosus.

Pharmacology

Lysosomal stabilization

Inhibits lymphocyte transformation and complement-mediated antigen-antibody reactions

May interfere with antigen processing

The antimalarials have diverse modes of action, including lysosomal stabilization. These drugs also bind to DNA, inhibiting replication and transcriptional activity and inhibiting immunologic reactions, such as lymphocyte "blast" transformation, and complement-mediated antigen-antibody reactions.

These drugs are preferentially concentrated in the epidermis and absorb ultraviolet light. This may explain, at least in part, their photoprotective properties.

Finally, Fox has hypothesized that the antimalarials inhibit antigen presentation by altering intercellular antigen processing (see Annotated Bibliography).

Clinical Uses

The antimalarials have been successfully employed to treat the following dermatologic conditions: sarcoidosis, porphyria cutanea tarda, lichen planus, lupus erythematosus, and dermatomyositis. Further information may be obtained in the respective chapter.

Discoid and subacute cutaneous lupus lesions

One of the authors has had a great deal of experience using antimalarials in the treatment of cutaneous lupus lesions. Although no double-blind studies exist, it is the clinical experience of many dermatologists and rheumatologists that various forms of cutaneous lupus erythematosus, including hypertrophic and subacute cutaneous lupus erythematosus (SCLE) lesions, generally respond to chloroquine 250 mg per day, hydroxychloroquine 200 mg twice a day, or a combination of chloroquine or hydroxychloroquine with quinacrine 100 mg daily.

In general, the full effects of the antimalarials occur 4 to 6 weeks after the initiation of therapy.

Lichen planus

The lesions of lichen planopilaris and erosive lichen planus generally respond. However, the treatment of lichen planus involvement of the perineum has, in one of the author's experience, produced mixed results.

Dermatomyositis

The photosensitive cutaneous lesions of dermatomyositis may or may not respond to antimalarial therapy. In general, the cutaneous lesions of dermatomyositis are recalcitrant.

Sarcoidosis

Cutaneous sarcoidosis lesions generally respond. However, if they have become fibrotic, they are recalcitrant to all forms of therapy.

Polymorphic light eruption

Antimalarials have been effectively employed to treat polymorphic light eruptions. Although "hardening of the skin" using gradations of ultraviolet light exposure, most commonly PUVA, is commonly employed, antimalarials are an effective alternative.

Porphyria cutanea tarda

Low-dose antimalarials (ie, 125 mg of chloroquine twice a week for several months) is an effective form of therapy to treat porphyria cutanea tarda. In contradistinction, a daily dose of chloroquine may produce massive excretion of porphyrins associated with elevated hepatic enzymes, fever, nausea, and headache.

Antimalarials have also been employed with some success in treating lichen sclerosis et atrophicus on the vulva and reticulated erythematous mucinosis (REM).

Side Effects

Reversible

The most serious side effect of hydroxychloroquine and chloroquine is retinopathy, which appears to be related to total dosage (ie, 200 g of chloroquine). Chloroquine appears to be more problematic than hydroxychloroquine in the induction of retinopathy. The retinopathy can be easily detected by use of an Amsler chart. Patients treated with long-term hydroxychloroquine and chloroquine should have 6-monthly examinations to detect earliest features of retinopathy, before they become symptomatic.

In addition to the retinopathy, corneal deposits have been detected with hydroxychloroquine and chloroquine therapy. Headache, psychosis, leukopenia, and aplastic anemia are unusual-to-rare occurrences.

Alteration in pigment

Pigment alteration is a common complication of antimalarial therapy. Quinacrine (Atabrine) regularly produces a yellowish tint of the skin and conjunctiva reminiscent of jaundice.

Blackish-purple discoloration on shins and brown-grey pigmentation on light exposed areas are frequently detected after prolonged therapy with chloroquine and hydroxychloroquine. Diffuse and transverse blue-black bands occur in the nail beds and similar diffuse hyperpigmentation is detected on the hard palate.

Depigmentation of hair

Blond and red-haired individuals may experience depigmentation.

Lichenoid dermatitis

A lichenoid dermatitis may occur with these drugs.

The antimalarials are teratogenic and should be avoided in pregnancy.

Flare of existing psoriatic lesions or precipitation of a flare of psoriasis may occur with antimalarial therapy. This observation was initially reported in the 1950s and also has been the author's experience.

Annotated Bibliography

Jones SK. Ocular toxicity and hydroxychloroquine: guidelines for screening. Br J Dermatol 1999;140:3–7.

This article presents a British study and recommendations, reflective of the infrequent occurrence of serious retinal problems with antimalarial therapy.

Tanenbaum L, Tuffanelli DL. Antimalarial agents: chloroquine, hydroxychloroquine and quinacrine. Arch Dermatol 1980;116:587–591.

This is an excellent review article of the history, pharmacokinetics, and toxicity associated with antimalarial drugs. The discussion on ocular abnormalities associated with these drugs is especially valuable.

Fox RI, Kang HL. Mechanism of action of antimalarial drugs: inhibition of antigen processing and presentation. Lupus 1993;2:S9–S12.

This article, based on recent studies, elucidating the steps involved in the association of antigenic peptides with a major histocompatibility complex and proteins in antigen-presenting cells, proposes that antimalarials, which can diffuse across cell membranes and raise the Ph within cell vesicles, may interfere with the processing of antigenic peptides and interfere with the efficient movement of these peptides to the correct location within the cell cytoplasm or the cell surface. It is proposed that decreased presentation of autoantigenic peptides by the macrophages would then lead to downregulation of autoimmune CD4+ T cells, diminishing the clinical and laboratory signs of the autoimmune disease.

Sulfones: Dapsone (Diaminodiphenylsulfone)

Dapsone: effective in treating cutaneous disorders associated with neutrophilic infiltrates; effective in treating diseases associated with IgA

Dapsone (diaminodiphenylsulfone) is an anti-inflammatory drug, which has been found to be very effective in treating various cutaneous inflammatory diseases. These diseases include dermatitis herpetiformis, Sweet's syndrome, subcorneal pustulosis of Sneddon and Wilkinson, relapsing polychondritis, SCLE, erythema elevatum diutinum, and other forms of vasculitis, including urticarial vasculitis. It has also been found effective in the treatment of one of the bullous eruptions of SLE, bullous pemphigoid, linear immunoglobulin A (IgA) dermatosis, intraepidermal neutrophilic IgA dermatosis, and bullous disease of childhood.

Effective in treating leprosy and Pneumoncystis carinii *pneumonia*

In addition to use in the treatment of leprosy, it has efficacy as a prophylactic treatment for *Pneumocystis carinii* pneumonia.

Mechanism of Action

Inhibition of neutrophil chemotaxis

The exact antiinflammatory mechanism of action of dapsone is not known, although there is evidence to suggest that its therapeutic effect may be related to its ability to interfere with neutrophil chemotaxis. For example, Harvath et al. have demonstrated that the chemotactic responses of human neutrophils to *N*-formyl-methionyl-leucyl-phenylalanine (F-met-leu-phe) are inhibited with therapeutic concentrations of sulfones. The chemotactic effects of C5a or leukocyte-derived chemotactic factor (LDCF), however, were not affected.

Appears to interfere with chemotaxis involving participation of integrins

Other studies indicate that dapsone interferes with integrin-mediated neutrophil adherence function. These studies employed an assay to determine neutrophil chemotaxis under agarose. In this technique, neutrophils migrate radially into a space between the albumin-coated surface of a culture dish and the agarose gel. This migration is dependent on the neutrophils adhering to the protein-coated plastic dish and is mediated by the MAC-1 family of integrins. These studies demonstrated that dapsone and sulfapyridine inhibit integrin-mediated binding of neutrophils to the albumin-coated plates. These studies suggest that dapsone may interfere with adherence of neutrophils to vascular endothelium. (It is interesting to note that previous studies have demonstrated that neutrophil chemotaxis, using a millipore filter, failed to demonstrate inhibition of neutrophil chemotaxis by dapsone [one of the author's personal experience]. In this assay, the MAC-1 family of receptors are not required for neutrophil chemotaxis.)

An additional mechanism, whereby sulfones may be therapeutically effective in the treatment of IgA dermatosis, is the work reported by Thuong-Nguyen et al. These investigators, using an in vitro neutrophil adherence assay, demonstrated that neutrophils attach to basement membrane zone–bound antibody in linear IgA bullous dermatosis and bullous pemphigoid. Dapsone, added directly to the neutrophils or to the antibody source in pharmacologic doses, resulted in incremental inhibition of neutrophil adherence, strongly suggesting that dapsone inhibits adherence of neutrophils to the basement membrane IgA antibody.

Blocks adherence of neutrophils to IgA

Dapsone's bacteriostatic effect is most likely related to its inhibition of folate metabolism.

Inhibits folate metabolism

Therapeutic Considerations

Dapsone in a dosage of 50 to 150 mg per day appears to be effective in the treatment of the diseases noted above. However, doses higher than 200 mg per day may be associated with a mononucleosis-like syndrome. Furthermore, experience with dapsone as a drug employed in malaria prophylaxis in Vietnam indicated that, on occasions, agranulocytosis and aplastic anemia could occur. For this reason, it is recommended that routine complete blood counts be performed every 2 to 3 weeks for the first 6 months of therapy and periodically thereafter.

In doses greater than 200 mg, a mononucleosis-like syndrome may occur.

Agranulocytosis and aplastic anemia

In addition, a glucose-6-phosphate dehydrogenase (G6PD) determination should be determined prior to starting therapy. The absence of this enzyme in the red blood cells of the patient (generally of Mediterranean origin) can result in a very severe hemolysis.

Hemolysis of glucose-6-phosphate dehydrogenase deficient red blood cells

Dapsone regularly produces a compensated hemolytic anemia (10 to 12 g hemoglobin) as older red blood cells, relatively deficient in glucose G6PD are lysed. Also, methemoglobulinemia is commonly detected.

High-dose dapsone therapy may be associated with a peripheral neuropathy, primarily motor.

Methemoglobulinemia; motor peripheral neuropathy

Annotated Bibliography

McCormack LS, Elgart ML, Turner MLC. Annular subacute cutaneous lupus erythematosus responsive to dapsone. J Am Acad Dermatol 1984;11:397–401.

This article indicates that dapsone is effective in some patients with subacute cutaneous lupus lesions. Our experience indicates that approximately 50% of patients with recalcitrant SCLE lesions respond to dapsone.

Hornsten P, Keisu M, Bengt-Erik W. The incidence of agranulomacytosis during treatment of dermatitis herpetiformis with dapsone as reported in Sweden, 1972 through 1988. Arch Dermatol 1990;126:919–922.

This article describes that agranulocytosis occurs in 0.2 to 0.4% of dapsone-treated patients.

Harvath L, Yancey KM, Katz SI. Selective inhibition of human neutrophil chemotaxis to N-formyl-methionyl-leucyl-phenylalanine by sulfones. J Immunol 1986;137:1305–1311.

Booth SA, Moody CE, Dahl MV, et al. Dapsone suppresses integrin-mediated neutrophil adherence function. J Invest Dermatol 1992;98:135–140.

Thuong-Nguyen V, Kadunce DP, Hendrix JD, et al. Inhibition of neutrophil adherence to antibody by dapsone: a possible therapeutic mechanism of dapsone in the treatment of IgA dermatosis. J Invest Dermatol 1993;100:349–355.

These three articles demonstrate the possible roles of dapsone in the inhibition of neutrophil chemotaxis.

Beutler B. Glucose-6 phosphate dehydrogenase deficiency. N Engl J Med 1991;324: 169–174.

This is an excellent review.

Mier PD, VanDenHurk JJMA. Inhibition of lysosomal enzymes by dapsone. Br J Dermatol 1975;93:471–472.

This article presents another potential therapeutic mechanism of dapsone action.

Thalidomide

Thalidomide induces phocomelia and amelia in the fetus.

Thalidomide was initially marketed during the late 1950s as a sedative and antiemetic medication. Because of its antiemetic properties, it was employed to treat pregnant women. Subsequently, in the early 1960s, it was recognized that the drug was responsible for an embryopathy characterized by malformation of extremities, including phocomelia and amelia, as well as cardiac and renal malformations. The drug was removed from the market and has only recently been approved by the FDA in the United States for treatment of erythema nodosum leprosum. Data has indicated that lesions of erythema nodosum leprosum (type II leprosy reaction) invariably respond to thalidomide within a 24- to 48-hour period of time.

Other investigators have employed this drug successfully in the treatment of a wide variety of inflammatory conditions, including the cutaneous lesions of subacute and chronic lupus erythematosus, aphthous stomatitis of acquired immunodeficiency syndrome (AIDS), as well as Behçet's disease. It has also been employed in the treatment of pyoderma gangrenosum, GVHD, inflammatory bowel disease, and erythema multiforme.

Mode of Action

The anti-inflammatory effects of thalidomide are probably related to its ability to inhibit the various cytokine production and to downregulate the expression of adhesion molecules. Thalidomide is a potent inhibitor of IL-12 production. This results in inhibition of interferon-γ production and enhanced IL-4 and IL-5 synthesis.

Thalidomide inhibits IL-12; TNF-α; downregulates β_2- and β_1-integrins; angiogenesis

Thalidomide inhibits the synthesis of TNF-α by reducing the half-life of TNF-α messenger RNA. In addition to these effects on cytokine production, thalidomide has been shown to downregulate β_2-integrin and β_1-integrin. Furthermore, there is evidence in selected animal models to indicate that the drug administered to pregnant mice may selectively depress β_1- and α_4-integrins, preferentially in the limb buds (perhaps the mechanism for phocomelia and amelia). There is also evidence to indicate that thalidomide inhibits angiogenesis.

Clinical Uses

Clinical uses: ENL; aphthous stomatitis-AIDS, Behçet's, SCLE, DLE, GVHD

As noted above, thalidomide is now considered the standard therapy for erythema nodosum leprosum. Painful aphthous stomatitis occurring in the presence or absence of AIDS also frequently responds to thalidomide. It should be noted that not all patients respond, and many patients, following discontinuation of therapy, have recurrences. However, in many instances, the recurrences are milder than the previous disease.

Beginning in the 1980s, a series of reports emanating predominantly from western Europe, appeared in the literature, indicating the efficacy of thalidomide in the treatment of patients with cutaneous lupus erythematosus. Although there is variability in the recorded responses, it appears that at least 50% of cutaneous lupus patients respond to thalidomide therapy. Surprisingly, although thalidomide is effective in treating cutaneous lupus lesions, there is no apparent benefit to systemic manifestations.

Our experience with this drug is limited, since it has only been available in the United States for the past 18 months. We have successfully treated sex-recalcitrant anti-Ro (SS-A) antibody–positive patients with widespread, photosensitive cutaneous lesions. Prior therapy with oral steroids and hydroxychloroquine had failed to control these patients' disease. Within a 6-week period of time, these patients' disease processes had dramatically cleared on 50 mg of thalidomide twice daily.

We have also seen a patient with severe, disfiguring hypertrophic lupus erythematosus involving the face and scalp, who also responded to 50 mg of thalidomide twice daily.

These preliminary studies, plus review of the literature, indicate that low-dose (ie, 100 mg/day) thalidomide is effective in treating some patients with widespread cutaneous lupus erythematosus. Furthermore, thalidomide is effective where other drugs have totally failed.

Our institution has also had a good deal of experience using thalidomide successfully to treat chronic GVHD. Surprisingly, thalidomide is not effective for the prophylaxis of chronic GVHD.

Recent studies indicate that Langerhans' cell histiocytosis, a disease process in which TNF-α induces Langerhans' cell proliferation, has been found to be responsive to thalidomide therapy.

In all the cases discussed above, a significant percentage of patients respond to thalidomide therapy. In general, relapse may occur with discontinuation of the drug; however, there are instances in which relapse has not occurred.

The successful use of thalidomide in some patients with cutaneous lupus erythematosus and GVHD, especially those individuals unresponsive to conventional therapy, provides the dermatologist with an alternative for the treatment of these difficult conditions. Although the authors have not had personal experience with the use of thalidomide in the treatment of the recalcitrant form of cutaneous disease in dermatomyositis, with or without muscle involvement (dermatomyositis sine myositis), the experience with lupus erythematosus and GVHD indicates that thalidomide may be therapeutically effective.

Side Effects

Teratogenic effects

The teratogenic side effects of thalidomide are well recorded. The fetus between the third and fifth weeks, during the development of the limb buds, appears to be at greatest risk. Women of childbearing age must be repeatedly educated about the teratogenic side effects and must be educated regarding the use of contraceptives, both by themselves and their sexual partners. An elaborate monitoring system, termed the System for Thalidomide Education and Prescribing Safety (STEPS), is now in effect for all patients receiving thalidomide in the United States.

Thalidomide side effects

The other important side effect of thalidomide therapy is peripheral neuropathy. Both sensory and peripheral motor neuropathies have been detected, but the exact incidence of this complication is unknown. Patients receiving thalidomide should have a neurologic evaluation to rule out a pre-existing neuropathy prior to the institution of thalidomide therapy. They also should be monitored frequently for the development of peripheral neuropathy.

Annotated Bibliography

Thomas L, Ducros B, Secchi T, et al. Successful treatment of adult's Langerhans' cell histiocytosis with thalidomide. Report of two cases and literature review. Arch Dermatol 1993;129:1261–1264.

This article presents a new successful treatment.

Vogelsang GB, Farmer ER, Hess AD, et al. Thalidomide for the treatment of chronic graft-versus-host disease. N Engl J Med 1992;326:1055–1058.

This article describes the experience at our institution, including that of three members of the dermatopathology division of our department, with thalidomide in the treatment of GVHD.

Jacobson JM, Greenspan JS, Spritzler J, et al. Thalidomide for the treatment of oral aphthous stomatitis ulcers in patients with human immunodeficiency virus infection. N Engl J Med 1997;336:1487–1493.

This article presents a study in which 16 of 29 patients (55%) had complete healing of oral ulcers after 4 weeks of therapy.

Knop J, Bonsmann G, Happle R, et al. Thalidomide in the treatment of sixty cases of chronic discoid lupus erythematosus. Br J Dermatol 1983;108:461–466.

This article presents a study in which 90% of patients had marked regression or complete disappearance of discoid lupus erythematosus lesions. Twenty-five percent of patients may have had evidence of peripheral neuropathy.

Duong DJ, Spigel GT, Moxley RT III, et al. American experience with low dose thalidomide therapy for severe cutaneous lupus erythematosus. Arch Dermatol 1999 Sept; 135:109–1087.

This small study of 7 patients indicates that low-dose thalidomide, 100 mg daily in the evening, was very effective. All patients showed marked improvement. In 3 patients, the thalidomide was tapered to an alternate-day, or every-third-day dosing of 100 mg of thalidomide. Complete discontinuation of thalidomide therapy was not possible.

Pisetsky DS. Tumor necrosis factor blockers in rheumatoid arthritis. N Engl J Med 2000;342:810–811.

This is a brief review of clinical efficacy of infleximab, a chimeric anti-TNF antibody and a soluble TNF receptor, etanercept, in the treatment of rheumatoid arthritis. Since a major effect, if not the most important anti-inflammatory effect, of thalidomide is decreased synthesis of TNF-α production, it seems reasonable to hypothesize that TNF blockers may also prove valuable in the treatment of some inflammatory cutaneous diseases.

Colchicine

Time-honored therapy for gout

Colchicine is a time-honored drug in the therapy of gout. It is quite effective to treat acute attacks of gout when used appropriately and has limited effectiveness as a prophylactic anti-gout therapy. In recent years, investigators have also employed colchicine to successfully retard the development of amyloidosis of the kidney in familial Mediterranean fever. Furthermore, it has been empirically employed in the treatment of various inflammatory conditions including cutaneous vasculitis.

Mode of Action

Colchicine inhibits cell division in metaphase by interfering with mitotic spindle formation. It also produces dissolution of microtubules.

Interferes with selectin expression on vascular endothelial cells

Perhaps the mode of action most important for understanding the possible benefit of colchicine in gout and other inflammatory diseases is its capability to interfere with the expression of selectins on the surface of vascular endothelial cells. It is hypothesized that this action interferes with the migration of polymorphonuclear cells across blood vessel walls and, thus, blunts the inflammatory response.

Uses in Dermatology

Colchicine has been used empirically to treat Sweet's syndrome, pyoderma gangrenosum, aphthous stomatitis, Behçet's disease, and necrotizing venulitis.

In general, colchicine is given 0.6 mg orally two to three times daily.

Adverse Effects

Gastrointestinal toxicity

Colchicine has a narrow therapeutic window, especially in the elderly and in patients with hepatic or renal insufficiency. Colchicine produces gastrointestinal effects, characterized by nausea, vomiting, and diarrhea. In these settings, colchicine should be stopped and re-introduced at a lower dose where this gastrointestinal toxicity does not occur. Alopecia is detected frequently.

With chronic usage, bone marrow suppression, peripheral neuritis, and myopathy can occur. On occasions, renal damage, manifested by hematuria, is detected.

Bone marrow suppression, myopathy, peripheral neuritis

Colchicine is teratogenic in mice and hamsters. Its use in pregnancy should be avoided.

Annotated Bibliography

Springer TA. Traffic signals for lymphocyte recirculation and leukocyte emigration: the multistep paradigm. Cell 1994;76:301–314.

Cronstein BN, Molad Y, Reibman J, et al. Colchicine alters the quantitative and qualitative display of selectins on endothelial cells and neutrophils. J Clin Invest 1995;96:994–1002.

These are two excellent articles.

Zemer D, Pras M, Sohar E, et al. Colchicine in the prevention and treatment of the amyloidosis of familial Mediterranean fever. N Engl J Med 1986;314:1001–1005.

This is a classic article.

Kuncl RW, Duncan G, Watson D, et al. Colchicine myopathy and neuropathy. N Engl J Med 1987;316:1562–1568.

This article describes myopathy in gout patients treated with normal doses of colchicine. Because of altered renal function, elevated plasma drug levels occurred. Proximal muscle weakness and creatine phosphokinase (CPK) elevations were detected. With discontinuance of colchicine, both abnormalities disappeared within 3 to 4 weeks. The polyneuropathy is mild and also resolves spontaneously with drug discontinuance.

Biopsy demonstrates disruption of the microtubule-dependent cytoskeletal network which is interactive with lysosomes.

Intravenous IgG Therapy

Within the past several years, intravenous IgG (IVIG) therapy has been increasingly successfully employed in the treatment of a variety of autoimmune and other inflammatory diseases. In several instances, the results have been very dramatic and evidence suggests that this form of therapy, despite its cost, may be increasingly employed in the treatment of recalcitrant autoimmune diseases.

Employed to treat autoimmune and putative autoimmune diseases

Mode of Action

The exact mode of action of IVIG therapy is unknown. A variety of mechanisms, however, have been proposed. Therapeutic concentrations of IgG block Fc receptors on phagocytes and cellular factors of antibody-dependent cytotoxicity. Intravenous IgG may have immunomodullary properties due to its ability to affect anti-idiotypic antibodies and cytokine synthesis and to block receptors for cytokines and complement.

Mode of action: blocks Fc and other receptors

Recent evidence indicates that the therapeutic benefits of IgG may also be due to the ability of increased concentrations of plasma IgG to directly determine the fractional catabolic rate of IgG. Immunoglobulin G enters cells through a process of pinocytosis. This ingested IgG is protected from catabolism by binding to a transport receptor for IgG, termed FcRn. Beta2-microglobulin is a critical subunit of this receptor. It is hypothesized that the ingested IgG binds to this protective receptor (FcRn), and without this protective mechanism, the IgG would pass to the lysosome and be degraded. Instead, the IgG returns intact to the circulation.

Increases catabolism of IgG

It also should be noted that glucocorticoids downregulate the expression of FcRn messenger RNA, suggesting that corticosteroids and IVIG therapy may share a similar mechanism.

Clinical Uses

Intravenous IgG therapy has been successfully employed to treat a variety of diseases. These diseases include Kawasaki's disease, toxic epidermal necrolysis,

Successfully employed to treat toxic epidermal necrolysis and Kawasaki's disease

autoimmune hemolytic anemia, pure red cell aplasia, immune-mediated neutropenia, post-transfusion purpura, neonatal alloimmune thrombocytopenia, thrombocytopenia refractory to platelet transfusions, high-risk hypogammaglobulinemic neonates, pediatric intractable epilepsy, Guillain-Barré syndrome, myasthenia gravis, chronic inflammatory demyelinating polyneuropathy, dermatomyositis, polymyositis, systemic lupus erythematosus, and systemic vasculitic syndromes.

Employed to treat autoimmune blistering diseases

Recent evidence indicates that IVIG therapy has been successfully employed in the treatment of patients with recalcitrant pemphigus vulgaris. In addition, other forms of autoimmune blistering disease have been successfully treated. These include bullous pemphigoid, cicatricial pemphigoid, and IgA bullous disease.

A consensus statement of The University Hospital Consortium expert panel for off-label use of polyvalent intravenous administered immunoglobulin preparations, composed of representatives of 68 academic health centers, has stated that with the exception of post-transfusion purpura and Guillain-Barré syndrome, evidence does not support the routine use of IVIG therapy. However, it may be considered in patients recalcitrant to other standard forms of therapy.

Complications

Complications may be induced by osmolarity, glucose content, acid pH of IVIG preparation

The osmolarity of the IVIG must be taken into consideration when treating patients. For example, the range of osmolarity among various commercial preparations of intravenous gammaglobulin varies substantially (192 to 1,250 mOsm/L). This is due to the differences in electrolyte and sugar (glucose or sucrose) content of the various preparations. Diabetic patients may not tolerate large quantities of glucose in some of the preparations. Also, patients with congestive heart failure or chronic obstructive pulmonary disease may not be able to tolerate the fluid volume that accompanies the infusion of less concentrated IVIG solutions.

Finally, the Consensus Committee noted that the pH of the various commercial products ranges between 4.0 and 7.0. Thus, patients, such as neonates or those with renal insufficiency, may not be able to tolerate the acidic load.

Low risk of bacterial and viral transmission to recipients

Although a risk of transmission of bacterial and viral contamination to patients exists, the Consensus Committee noted the transmission of human immunodeficiency virus (HIV) infection, or hepatitis B via licensed IVIG products has not been reported in the United States as of 1994. There is evidence, however, that some patients have developed hepatitis C following IVIG. These patients most likely received the virus via the administration of the suspected IVIG products. New techniques, using a solvent detergent treatment to inactivate lipid-enveloped viral contaminants, have been incorporated into the production program. While this does not completely eliminate the risk, it does diminish the possibility of viral transmission by high-dose IVIG therapy.

Anaphylaxis

The treatment is contraindicated in patients who have a selective IgA deficiency (anaphylactoid reaction) or who have had an anaphylactoid episode to previous IVIG therapy.

Cost is problematic

Perhaps the greatest detraction to the employment of IVIG therapy is its cost. In 1994, the wholesale price of IVIG per gram varied between 42 and 104 US dollars. To treat a patient with a primary humoral immunodeficiency, the cost could range between 7,100 to 17,600 dollars per year. However, because therapy is administered intravenously, the total cost may be substantially higher.

Annotated Bibliography

Ratko TA, Burnett DA, Foulke GE, et al. Recommendations for off label use of intravenously administered immunoglobulin preparation. JAMA 1995;273:1865–1870.

This article contains a valuable synopsis of the status of IVIG therapy.

Yu Z, Lennon VA. Mechanism of intravenous immune globulin therapy in antibody mediated autoimmune diseases. N Engl J Med 1999;340:227–228.

This article presents a theoretical molecular basis for the therapeutic effect of IVIG.

CHAPTER 73

Oral Manifestations of Systemic Disease

Russell L. Corio, D.D.S., M.S.D., M.A., Thomas T. Provost, M.D.

The following is an atlas of some of the oral manifestations of systemic diseases, or diseases in which systemic therapy with steroids, immunosuppressive agents, and antimalarials may be indicated.

Oral Manifestations of Vasculitis

Figures 73–1A and 73–1B show mucous membrane involvement with vasculitis. (For further discussion, see Chapter 12, "Vasculitis.")

Hereditary Hemorrhagic Telangiectasia

Hereditary hemorrhagic telangiectasia (HHT) or Rendu-Osler-Weber disease is an autosomal dominant disease. The gene is located on chromosome 9q3. This gene defect results in a mutation of endoglin, a protein on the cell surface of endothelial cells.

Mutations in endothelial cell surface protein, endoglin

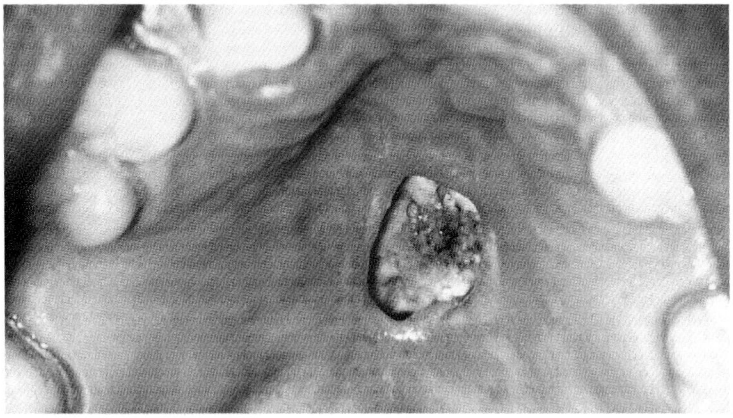

FIGURE 73–1A Wegener's granulomatosis. Necrotizing granulomatous vasculitis involving small- and medium-sized vessels. Perforation of hard palate. Septal perforations and saddle nose deformities are common. (For further discussion, see Chapter 12, "Vasculitis.")

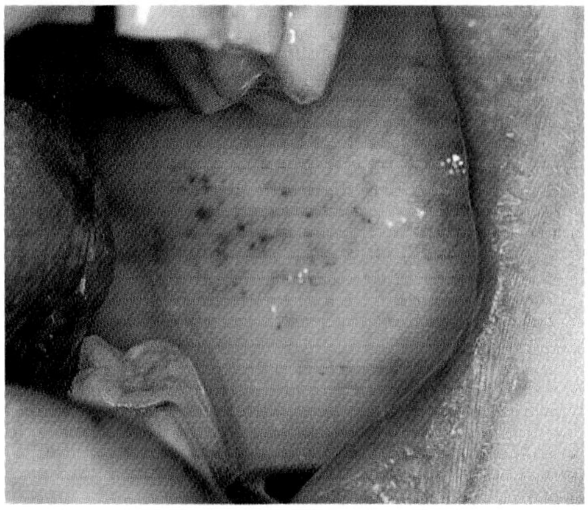

FIGURE 73–1B Small petechial lesions in the buccal mucosa of a child with Henoch-Schönlein purpura. This child developed initially cutaneous vasculitis lesions followed by arthritis and abdominal involvement. (For further discussion, see Chapter 12, "Vasculitis.")

Widespread telangiectasia which may or may not become clinically significant

This disease is characterized by vascular lesions occurring on the lips, naso-mucosa, throughout the gastrointestinal tract, as well as in the lung. Recurrent nosebleeds frequently occur. Gastrointestinal bleeding (melena) is frequent in middle age (Figures 73–2A, 73–2B).

Pulmonary arteriovenous malformations occur. On unusual occasions, clubbing, cyanosis, and polycythemia can occur. Cerebral arteriovenous malformations may occur associated with migraine-like headaches.

The disease manifests usually in the second or third decade of life, and the first and most common clinical sign is persistent nosebleeds. Small red macules and papules (1 to 3 mm in size) are seen about the mouth, face, ears, and hands and blanch readily on diascopy.

Oral lesions generally most prominent

The lesions that are the most dramatic and easily identified are telangiectatic vessels on the vermilion of the lips, tongue, and buccal mucosa, although any oral site may be affected. These telangiectasia must be differentiated from the multiple telangiectases associated with connective tissue disorders, especially *c*alcinosis, *R*aynaud's phenomenon, *e*sophageal involvement, *s*clerodactyly, and *t*elangiectasia (CREST) syndrome.

Generally, there is no treatment required for mild cases of HHT. Cryosurgery or electrocautery has been used to stop local hemorrhage. Occasionally, blood transfusions and iron supplementation may be necessary to compensate for blood loss.

Annotated Bibliography

Reilly PG, Nostrant TT. Clinical manifestations of hereditary hemorrhagic telangiectasia. Am J Gastroenterol 1984;79:363–367.

This article details the fact that significant gastrointestinal blood loss can occur.

Guttmacher AE, Marchuk DA, White RJ. Hereditary hemorrhagic telangiectasia. N Engl J Med 1995;333:918–924.

Excellent review article of clinical and molecular features of this hereditary disease.

Mager JJ, Westermann CJJ. Value of capillary microscopy in the diagnosis of hereditary hemorrhagic telangiectasia. Arch Dermatol 2000;136:732–734.

This article demonstrates that capillary microscopy may be a valuable diagnostic tool in evaluating patients suspected of having hereditary hemorrhagic telangiectasia.

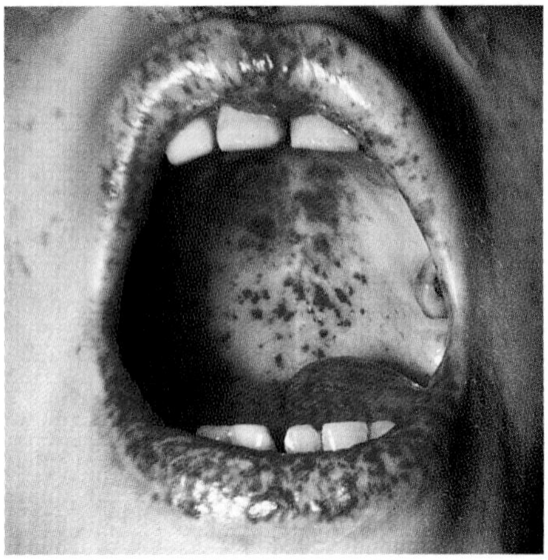

FIGURE 73–2A Rendu-Osler-Weber disease. Note telangiectatic lesions on palate.

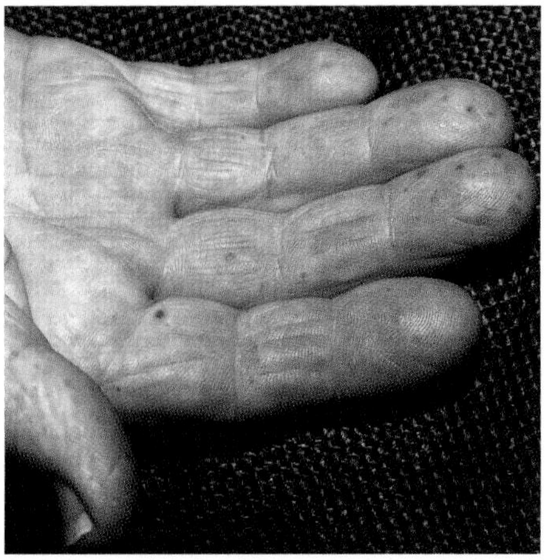

FIGURE 73–2B Lesions of hereditary hemorrhagic telangiectasia involving the fingers. (Courtesy of Rick Stearns, M.D., Tulsa, OK)

TABLE 73–1 Classification of Gingival Swelling

Fibrous gingival hyperplasia
Hereditary gingival fibromatosis
Drug-associated hyperplasia
Predominantly vascular or inflammatory
Chronic gingivitis
Associated with vitamin C deficiency
Associated with endocrine imbalance
Associated with leukemia
Orofacial angiomatosis
Orofacial granulomatosis
Wegener's granulomatosis
Idiopathic gingival hyperplasia

Bartolucci EG, Swan RH, Hurt WC. Oral manifestations of hereditary hemorrhagic telangiectasia (Osler-Weber-Rendu disease). J Periodontol 1982;53:163–167.

This article describes in detail oral manifestations.

Gingival Hyperplasia

Gingival enlargement represents an overexuberant response to a variety of local and systemic conditions; however, some may be idiopathic or genetically transmitted. The most common cause of gingival hyperplasia is a result of chronic inflammation associated with local factors; in some cases, there can be grossly increased vascularity or cellular infiltration. A suggested classification of gingival swelling is given in Table 73–1.

Drug-Associated Gingival Hyperplasia

Drug-associated gingival hyperplasia:
- *phenytoin*
- *calcium channel blockers*
- *cyclosporine*

While phenytoin is considered to be the most common cause of drug-related gingival overgrowth, many other medications can produce the same effect, including numerous calcium channel blockers and the immunosuppressant drug cyclosporine (Figure 73–3). Changes typically start after 1 to 3 months in the interdental papillae and later involve the marginal and attached gingiva and, in severe cases, may involve the crowns of associated teeth. Drug-related gingival hyperplasia appears to be aggravated by secondary bacterial infections and poor oral hygiene. Generally, the proliferative tissue will show some regression, once the medication is stopped. In those cases where drug use is mandatory, the main therapy is directed toward maintaining good oral hygiene, scaling and plaque control, and gingivectomy.

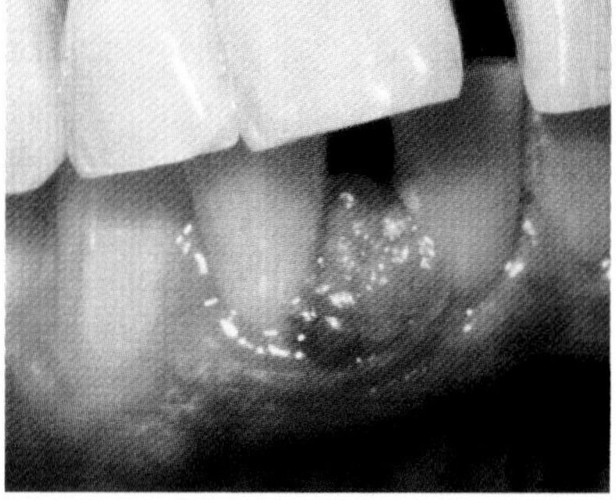

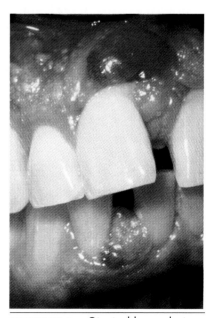

FIGURE 73–3 Gingival hyperplasia.

Annotated Bibliography

Dongari A, McDonnell HT, Langlais RP. Drug-induced gingival overgrowth. Oral Surg Oral Med Oral Pathol 1993;76:543–548.

Barclay S, Thomason JM, Seymour RA. The incidence and severity of nifedipine-induced gingival overgrowth. J Clin Periodontal 1992;19:311–314.

Thomason JM, Seymour RA, Rice N. The prevalence and severity of cyclosporin and nifedipine-induced gingival overgrowth. J Clin Periodontal 1993;20: 37–40.

Brown RS, Sein P, Corio R, Bottomley WK. Nitrendipine-induced gingival hyperplasia. Oral Surg Oral Med Oral Pathol 1990;70:593–596.

These four articles detail the fact that calcium channel blockers and cyclosporine are of etiologic significance in gingival hyperplasia.

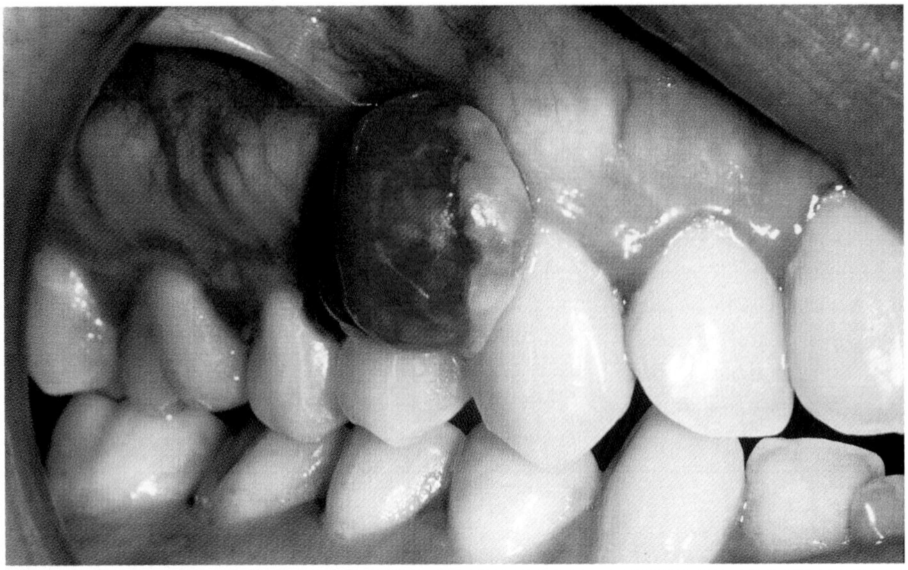

FIGURE 73–4 Oral mucosal malignant melanoma.

Oral Mucosal Malignant Melanoma

Most oral melanoma lesions are amelanotic.

Most studies demonstrate that this rare neoplasm occurs mainly in males, with a mean age in the sixth decade. Lesions involving the oral mucosa usually manifest as an asymptomatic swelling and bleeding or are associated with symptoms of discomfort. Most occur in the palate and upper gingiva. In clinical appearance, most are described as nonpigmented (case presented), making diagnosis difficult, inasmuch as most clinicians may consider melanoma only when confronted with a pigmented lesion. The primary mode of treatment of mucosal melanoma is wide surgical resection and the prognosis is poor (Figure 73–4).

Annotated Bibliography

Gorsky M, Epstein JB. Melanoma arising from the mucosal surfaces of the head and neck. Oral Surg Oral Med Oral Pathol Oral Radiol Endod 1998;86:715–719.

Berthelsen A, Andersen AP, Jensen TS, et al. Melanomas of the mucosa in the oral cavity and upper respiratory passages. Cancer 1984;54:907–912.

Conley JJ. Melanomas of the mucous membrane of the head and neck. Laryngoscope 1999;12:1248–1254.

Rapini RP, Golitz LE, Greer RO, et al. Primary malignant melanoma of the oral cavity: a review of 177 cases. Cancer 1985;55:1543–1545.

These four articles provide an excellent review.

Leukemia

The oral cavity is frequently a site of problems for patients with all forms of leukemia. All acute leukemias may present with oral findings, which include gingival enlargement, spontaneous gingival bleeding, petechial hemorrhage, oral ulcerations, and infection.

Monocytic myelomonocytic leukemia

Dense gingival leukemic infiltrates are most commonly seen in monocytic myelomonocytic leukemia (Figure 73–5).

Secondary complications may include a broad range of viral, bacterial, and yeast infections.

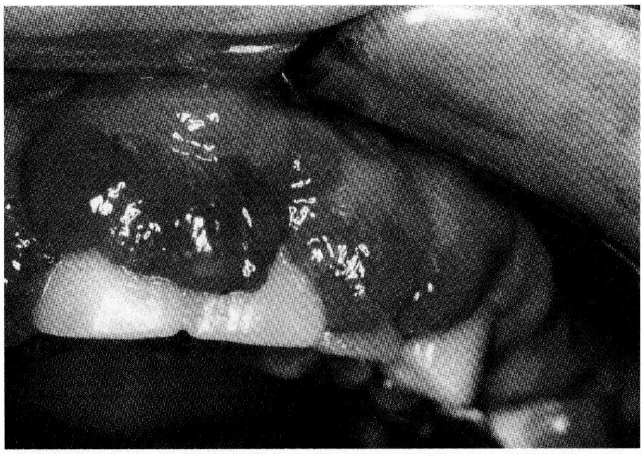

FIGURE 73-5 Leukemic infiltrates along upper gingiva. Most commonly seen in monocytic leukemia.

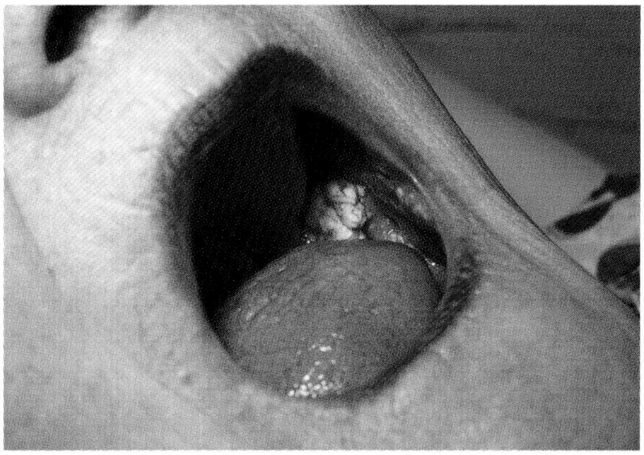

FIGURE 73-6 Example of localized papilloma (oral florid papillomatosis) in an elderly female. A premalignant lesion or verrucous carcinoma was considered. Responded to oral methotrexate.

Annotated Bibliography

Dreizen S, McCredie KB, Keating MJ, et al. Malignant gingival and skin "infiltrates" in adult leukemia. Oral Surg Oral Med Oral Pathol 1983;55:572–579.

Stafford R, Sonis S, Lockhart P, et al. Oral pathoses as diagnostic indicators in leukemia. Oral Surg Oral Med Oral Pathol 1980;50:134–139.

These are two highly quoted articles.

Dreizen S, McCredie KB, Bodey GP, et al. Microbial mucocutaneous infections in acute adult leukaemia. Postgrad Med 1986;79:107–118.

Oral Manifestations of Autoimmune Blistering Diseases

Figures 73–7A, 73–7B, 73–8A, and 73–8B show mucous membrane involvement with pemphigus vulgaris and benign mucous membrane pemphigoid. (For further discussion, see Chapter 15, "Autoimmune Bullous Diseases.")

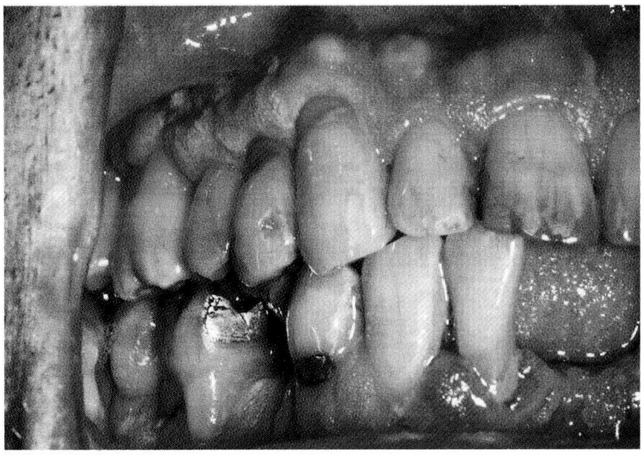

FIGURE 73-7A Abnormal-appearing gingiva in a patient with pemphigus vulgaris.

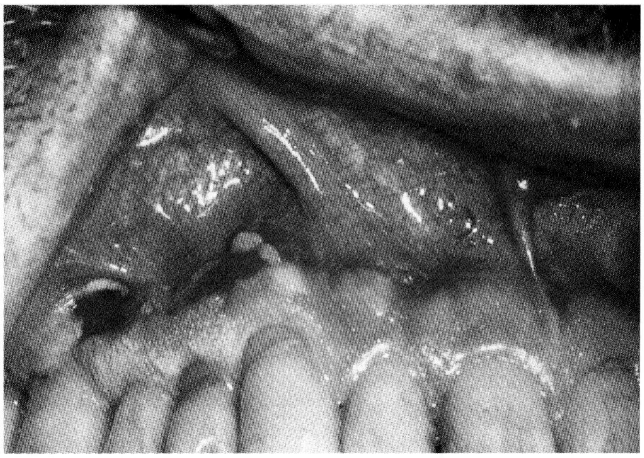

FIGURE 73-7B Erosive area following trauma. Oral lesions occur in the overwhelming majority of pemphigus vulgaris patients. Not seen in pemphigus foliaceus patients. (See Chapter 15, "Autoimmune Bullous Diseases," for further discussion.)

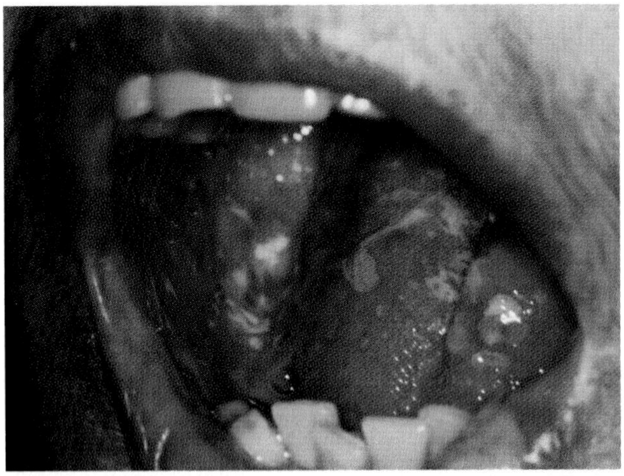

FIGURE 73–8A Benign mucous membrane pemphigoid. Oral erosive lesions of bullous pemphigoid. (See Chapter 15, "Autoimmune Bullous Diseases," for further discussion.)

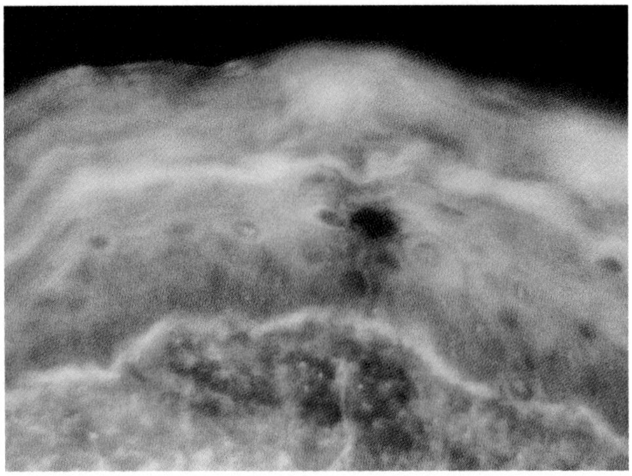

FIGURE 73–8B Direct immunofluorescent examination of biopsy of lesion of mucous membrane pemphigoid showing IgG linear deposition along dermal-epidermal junction. Only approximately 10 to 15% of these patients demonstrate circulating anti–basement membrane zone antibodies.

Exfoliative Cheilitis (Factitious Cheilitis)

At times, crusting on lips may be dramatic.

Most cases of exfoliative cheilitis represent factitious injuries, although other causes such as cheilitis glandularis, actinic cheilitis, infection, and contact dermatitis should be ruled out. Evidence suggests that there may be an association between thyroid dysfunction and some psychiatric disturbances. Most cases occur in women younger than 30 years. In severe cases, as depicted, the vermilion of both lips may be covered with a thickened, yellowish hyperkeratotic crust with fissuring. Most diffuse cases represent a secondary candidal infection in areas of low-grade trauma (cheilocandidiasis). In most cases, however, there is no underlying physical, infectious, or allergic cause. Treatment modalities include psychotherapy, often combined with mild tranquilization, moisturizing ointments, topical antifungal agents, and antibiotics (Figures 73–9A, 73–9B, and 73–9C).

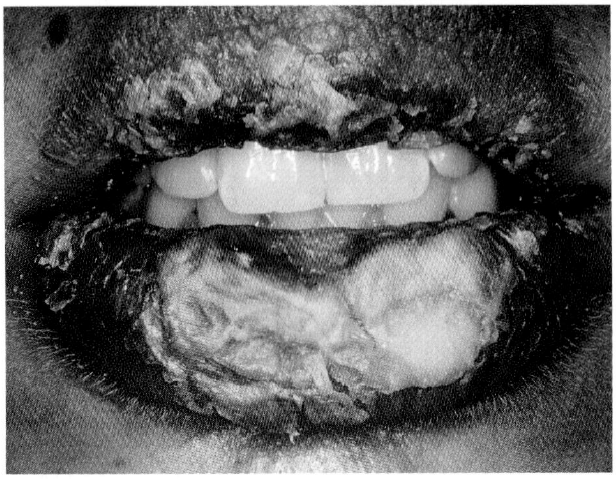

FIGURE 73–9A Exfoliative cheilitis (factitious cheilitis).

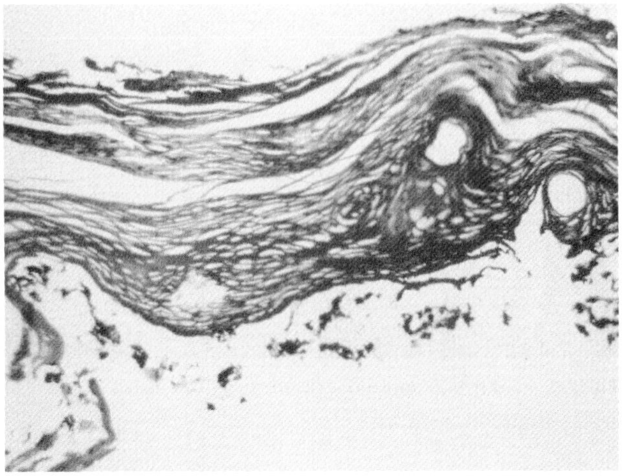

FIGURE 73–9B Histopathology of exfoliative cheilitis.

Annotated Bibliography

Reade PC, Sim R. Exfoliative cheilitis—a factitious disorder? Int J Oral Maxillofac Surg 1986;15:313–317.

Thomas JR, Greene SL, Dicken CH. Factitious cheilitis. J Am Acad Dermatol 1983;8:368–372.

Crotty CP, Dicken CH. Factitious lip crusting. Arch Dermatol 1981;117:338–340.

These three articles provide a spectrum of clinical presentations.

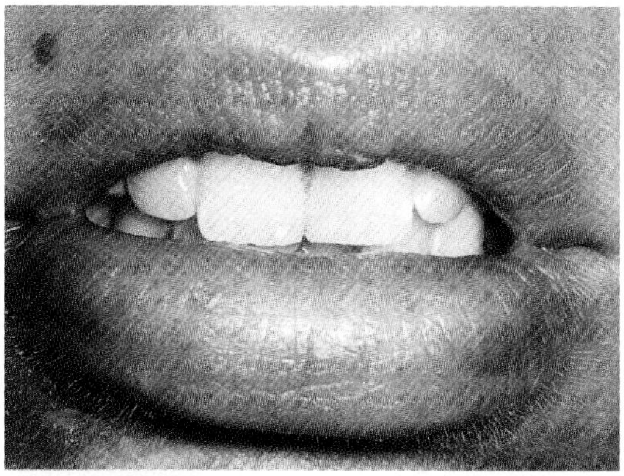

FIGURE 73–9C Resolution of exfoliative cheilitis.

Granulomatous Cheilitis (Melkersson-Rosenthal Syndrome: Miescher's Cheilitis)

This disease process, in its most localized form, is characterized by granulomatous changes confined to the lips (Meischer's cheilitis). Facial palsy and a swollen tongue have also been described with labial edema. The term "Melkersson-Rosenthal syndrome" refers to this full-blown syndrome (Figure 73–10).

The cause of this disease is unknown. In some individuals, it may represent a localized form of sarcoidosis. There is evidence to indicate that some patients with granulomatous cheilitis may have, or subsequently develop, Crohn's disease. The pathology reveals a perivascular lymphocytic infiltrate with small focal granulomas, which are indistinguishable from sarcoidosis or Crohn's disease.

May be associated with Crohn's disease or sarcoidosis

Cutaneous Manifestations

The earliest features of the disease are characterized by swelling involving the lips. On unusual occasions, swelling can occur on the cheeks and forehead. Fever, malaise, headaches, and visual disturbances may occur. With time, the swelling may become rubbery hard. There may be regional lymphadenopathy.

In approximately one-third of patients, a scrotal tongue or facial palsy occur. The recurrent attacks may occur for months or years. They may be unilateral or bilateral. On unusual occasions, the olfactory, auditory, glossal, pharyngeal, and hypoglossal nerves may be involved.

Various cranial nerve palsies have been described.

We recently evaluated a 28-year-old Caucasian female who 18 months ago had developed right-sided facial swelling associated with right lower lip edema and intermittent fever, which gradually resolved. She consulted an otolaryngologist for voice changes. He noted a large edematous uvula. Biopsy revealed a "sarcoid-like" granulomatous lesion.

Subsequent endoscopic examination revealed inflammation of the terminal ilium which, on biopsy, demonstrated granuloma consistent with Crohn's disease.

The cutaneous manifestations of Crohn's disease also include erythema nodosum, anal and perianal lesions, spreading ulceration of perineum and buttocks (metastatic Crohn's disease), skin changes around ileostomies and colostomies, sarcoid-type lesions, pyostomatitis, pyoderma gangrenosum, epidermolysis bullosa acquisita, and nonspecific changes due to malabsorption (Figure 73–11). (See Chapter 36, "Ulcerative Colitis and Crohn's Disease," for discussion.)

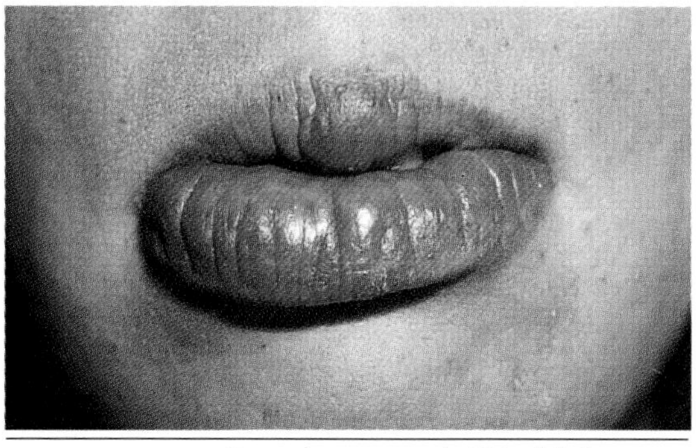

FIGURE 73–10 Granulomatous cheilitis (Melkersson-Rosenthal syndrome: Miescher's cheilitis).

Annotated Bibliography

Talbot T, Jewell L, Schloss E, et al. Cheilitis antedating Crohn's disease. Case report and literature review. J Clin Gastroenterol 1984;6:349–354.

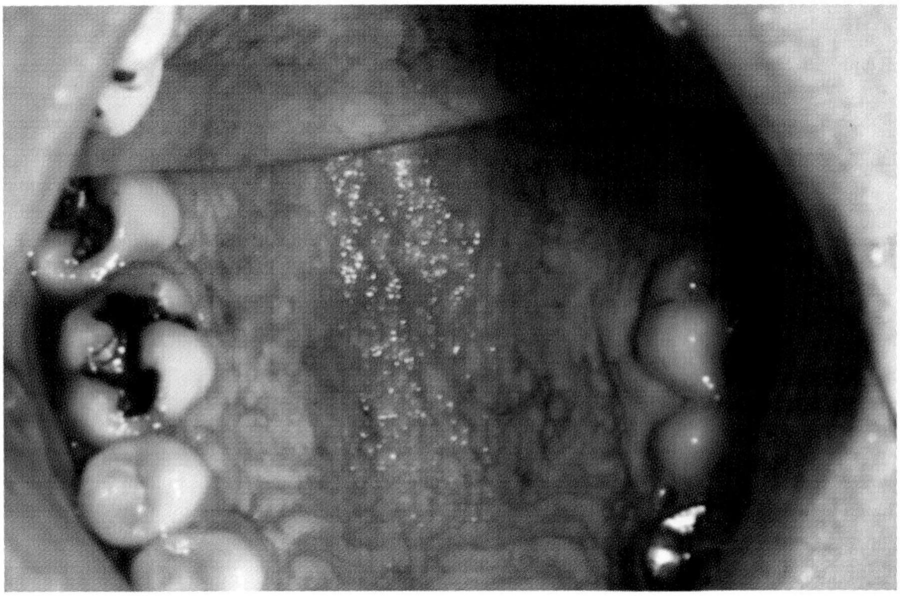

FIGURE 73-11 Pyostomatitis vegetans characterized by acanthotic hyperplastic erosive lesions on the hard palate in a patient with ulcerative colitis. Similar lesions of this rare entity may be seen in Crohn's disease. (Courtesy of Roy Rogers, M.D., Rochester, MN; Van Hale H, Rogers RS, Zone JJ. Pyostomatitis vegetans: a reactive mucosal marker for inflammatory disease of the gut. Arch Dermatol 1985;121:94–98, with permission.)

Tatnall FM, Dodd HJ, Sarkany I. Crohn's disease with metastatic cutaneous involvement and granulomatous cheilitis. J R Soc Med 1987;80:49–50.

Carr D. Granulomatous cheilitis in Crohn's disease. Br Med J 1974;IV:636.

These three articles indicate association with Crohn's disease.

Hornstein OP. Melkersson-Rosenthal syndrome. A neural mucocutaneous disease of complex origin. Recurr Prob Dermatol 1973;5:117–156.

Erythema Migrans (Geographic Tongue, Stomatitis Areata Migrans)

Common condition

Absolutely benign

Erythema migrans is considered to be one of the most common conditions of the oral mucosa that primarily affects the tongue. About 2% of the population is estimated to have the disorder and it may be found in up to 15% of teenagers and young adults. Females are affected more frequently than males, and the condition may start in early childhood.

Dynamic clinical presentation

Generally asymptomatic

Lesions characteristically occur on the anterior two-thirds of the dorsal tongue as well-demarcated zones of erythema, due to atrophy of the filiform papillae, and are surrounded by a slightly elevated, yellowish-white border. Lesions develop quickly in one area, heal within a few days or weeks, then develop in other different areas. When the same condition involves other parts of the oral mucosa, it is known as "erythema migrans" or "stomatitis areata migrans."

The histopathologic features of erythema migrans are reminiscent of psoriasis and designated "psoriasiform mucositis." Some studies indicate a higher incidence of erythema migrans in psoriatic patients, especially during a flare or when pustular psoriasis is present.

Generally, no treatment is indicated for patients with erythema migrans. Most patients are relieved to know that the condition is completely benign and not a sign of any serious internal problem. Occasionally, patients may complain of tenderness or a burning sensation. In such cases, application of topical corticosteroids may provide relief (Figure 73–12).

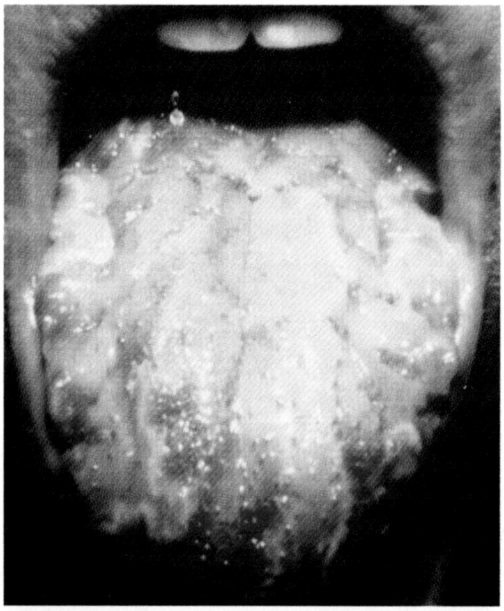

FIGURE 73–12 Erythema migrans (geographic tongue, stomatitis areata migrans). The cause of this disease is unknown.

Annotated Bibliography

Weathers DR, Baker G, Archard HO, et al. Psoriasiform lesions of the oral mucosa (with emphasis on "ectopic geographic tongue"). Oral Surg Oral Med Oral Pathol 1974;37: 872–888.

Cataldo E, McCarthy P, Yaffee H. Psoriasis with oral manifestations. Cutis 1977;20: 705–708.

Hume WJ. Geographic stomatitis: a critical review. J Dent 1975; 3:25–43.

Espelid M, et al. Geographic stomatitis. Report of 6 cases. J Oral Pathol Med 1991;20: 425–428.

Candidiasis

Candida albicans is part of the normal flora of the mouth and can be cultured in 30 to 50% of healthy persons. At the same time, it is, by far, the most common oral fungal infection in humans, manifesting itself in a variety of clinical presentations depending on the immune status of the host, the oral environment, and the strain of *C. albicans*. The clinical forms of oral candidiasis are summarized in Table 73–2 (Figures 73–13A, 73–13B, and 73–13C).

Most common oral fungal disease

Oral candidiasis presenting as a "burning mouth" is commonly detected as a complication of oral erosive lichen planus, benign mucous membrane pemphigoid, and oral pemphigus vulgaris. Corticosteroids, immunosuppressive agents, and the presence of dentures are additional risk factors for the development of oral candidiasis.

Annotated Bibliography

Allen CM. Diagnosing and managing oral candidiasis. J Am Dent Assoc 1992;123:77–82.

Fotos PG, Vincent SD, Hellstein JW. Oral candidosis: clinical, historical and therapeutic features of 100 cases. Oral Surg Oral Med Oral Pathol 1992;74:41–49.

Holmstrup T, Axell T. Classification and clinical manifestations of oral yeast infections. Acta Odontol Scand 1990;48:57–79.

Rothberg MS, Eisenbud L, Griboff S. Chronic mucocutaneous candidiasis-thymoma syndrome. Oral Surg Oral Med Oral Pathol 1989;68:411–413.

These four excellent articles detail clinical presentation, associations, and therapy.

Neurofibromatosis (von Recklinghausen's Disease of the Skin)

Neurofibromatosis (NF) is considered to be one of the most common hereditary diseases, estimated to occur in approximately 1 in every 3,000 births. Neurofibromatosis type 1 (von Recklinghausen's disease of the skin) constitutes about 90% of all cases. It is inherited as an autosomal dominant trait with variable penetrance and expressivity. Approximately one-half of all patients have no family history of the disease and apparently represent de novo mutations.

TABLE 73–2 Clinical Forms of Oral Candidiasis

Acute candidiasis
Pseudomembranous (thrush)
Atrophic (erythematous)
Chronic multifocal
Angular cheilitis (perlèche)
Chronic candidiasis
Atrophic candidiasis (denture stomatitis; denture sore mouth)
Hyperplastic (candidal leukoplakia)
Mucocutaneous candidiasis
Localized type
Familial type
Endocrine-candidiasis syndrome type

Mucosal neuromas on lips, tongue, and buccal mucosa

Some studies suggest that with thorough clinical and radiographic examination, over 90% of patients with NF type 1 may have oral manifestations. Lesions vary from small papules to larger nodules and pendulous masses. The tongue is the most common site for neurofibromas and may lead to macroglossia. About 50% of patients have enlarged fungiform papillae. Lesions, including oral pigmented macules, may also occur on the buccal and labial mucosa.

Individual lesions can be surgically removed when they interfere with function or for cosmetic purposes. Rarely, malignant transformation may occur, especially in the larger plexiform neurofibromas which are considered pathognomonic for the syndrome (Figures 73–14A and 73–14B).

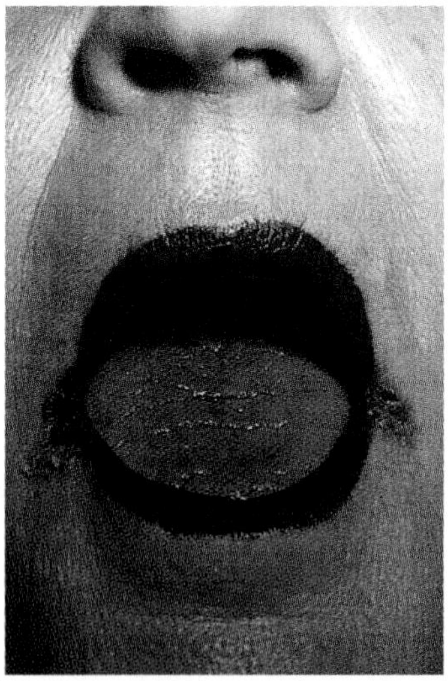

FIGURE 73–13A Classic perlèche involving the corners of the mouth. Commonly seen in elderly people with relaxation of tissue of upper lip creating fold of skin at the angle of the mouth. Also seen in patients on antibiotics and in individuals with candidiasis involving mucosal surface of upper denture.

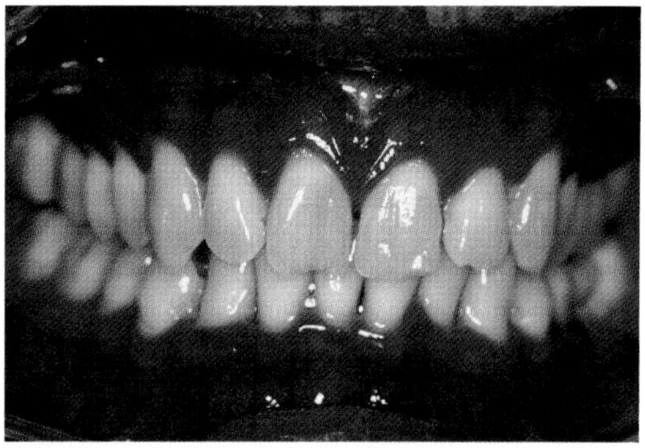

FIGURE 73–13B Acute candidiasis (atrophic) of gingiva.

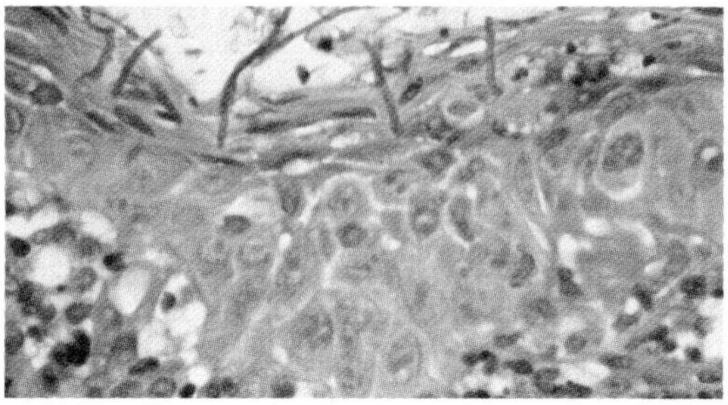

FIGURE 73–13C Biopsy of buccal mucosa showing PAS-positive *C. albicans* hyphae.

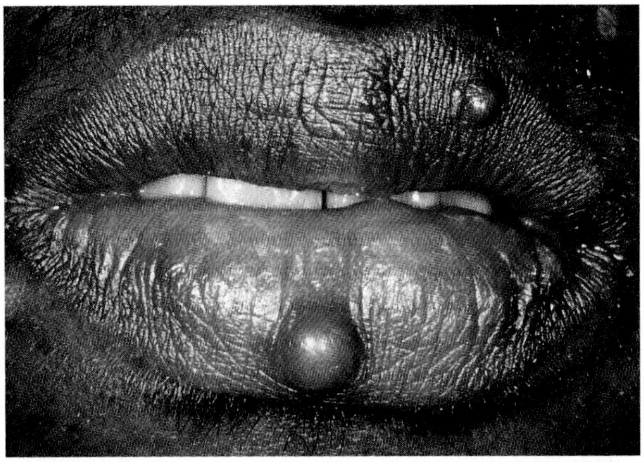

FIGURE 73–14A Nodule of neurofibromatosis on lower lip.

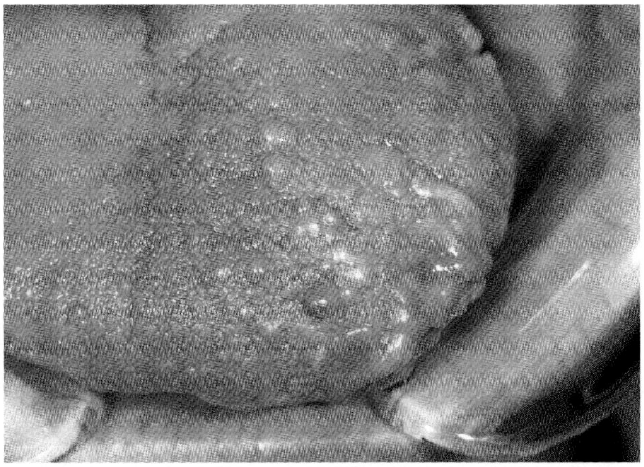

FIGURE 73–14B Papulonodular lesions of neurofibromas on tongue.

Annotated Bibliography

D'Ambrosio JA, Langlais RP, Young RS. Jaw and skull changes in neurofibromatosis. Oral Surg Oral Med Oral Pathol 1988;66:391–396.

Neville BW, Hann J, Narang R, Garen P. Oral neurofibrosarcoma associated with neurofibromatosis type 1. Oral Surg Oral Med Oral Pathol 1991;72:456–461.

Riccardi VN, Eichner JE. Neurofibromatosis: Phenotype, Natural History, and Pathogenesis. Baltimore, MD: Johns Hopkins University Press, 1986.

Geist JR, Gander DL, Stefanac SJ. Oral manifestations of neurofibromatosis types I and II. Oral Surg Oral Med Oral Pathol 1992;73:376–382.

Multiple Endocrine Neoplasia Type 2b (Multiple Mucosal Neuroma Syndrome)

Multiple endocrine neoplasia (MEN) type 2b is a component of the multiple endocrine neoplasia syndromes, which are a group of related disorders presenting with numerous endocrine neoplasms. Multiple endocrine neoplasia type 2b is inherited as an autosomal dominant disorder and patients usually present with a marfanoid appearance, thick protuberant lips, eversion of the upper eyelid, and neuromas on the conjunctiva, eyelid, or cornea.

Medullary carcinoma

Oral mucosal neuromas are usually noted on the lips, anterior tongue, buccal mucosa, gingiva, and palate and generally represent the first sign of the syndrome, appearing in childhood. About 50% of patients develop pheochromocytomas of the adrenal glands; however, the development of medullary carcinoma of the thyroid gland, which occurs in more than 90% of cases, represents the most significant aspect of this syndrome (Figures 73–15A and 73–15B).

Annotated Bibliography

Gorlin RJ, Cohen MM Jr, Levin LS. Multiple endocrine neoplasia, type 2B (multiple mucosal neuroma syndrome). In: Syndromes of the Head and Neck, 3rd ed. New York, NY: Oxford University Press, 1990, pp 385–392.

Schenberg ME, Zajac JD, Lim-Tio, et al. Multiple endocrine neoplasia syndrome - type 2B: case report and review. Int J Oral Maxillofac Surg 1992;21:110–114.

Sciubba JJ, D'Amico E, Attie JN. The occurrence of multiple endocrine neoplasia type IIb, in two children of an affected mother. J Oral Pathol 1987;16:310–316.

These are three excellent articles.

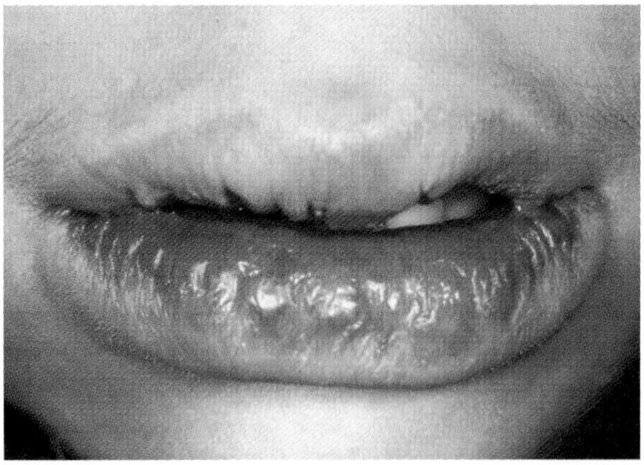

FIGURE 73–15A Protuberant lower lip in child with MEN type 2b.

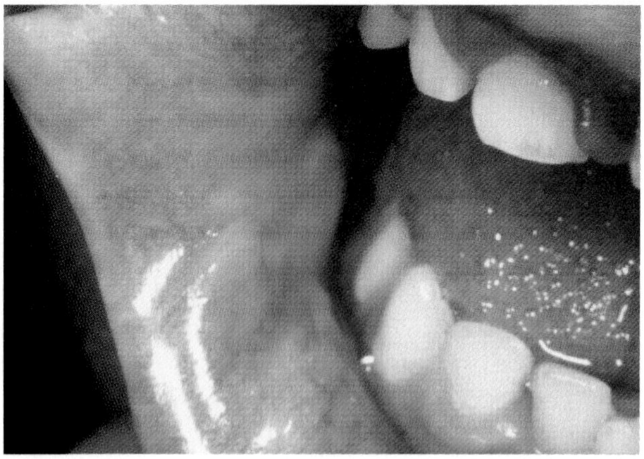

FIGURE 73–15B Small neuromas on lower lip mucosa of child with MEN type 2b.

Oral Manifestations of Dental Sinus

Figures 73–16A and 73–16B demonstrate dental sinus resulting from an abscessed tooth.

Herpes Simplex

There are two subtypes of herpes simplex virus (HSV): HSV type 1, which is responsible for most oral and extragenital disease, and HSV type 2, which is found in genital herpes.

Most initial infections subclinical

Clinically, there are two major manifestations of oral HSV-1. The initial (primary) infection occurs in individuals without antibodies to the virus, and in 95% of these individuals, the initial infection is subclinical. Approximately 5% of patients will develop a severe or, less frequently, a mild primary herpetic gingivostomatitis with general symptoms.

Secondary or recurrent HSV-1 infection occurs with reactivation of the virus and may occur either at the site of primary inoculation or in areas of surface epithelium supplied by the involved ganglion. The most common site of recur-

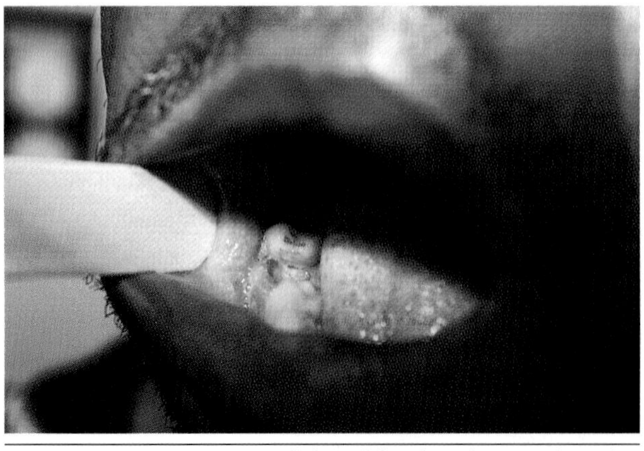

FIGURE 73–16A Origin of dental fistula: abscessed tooth.

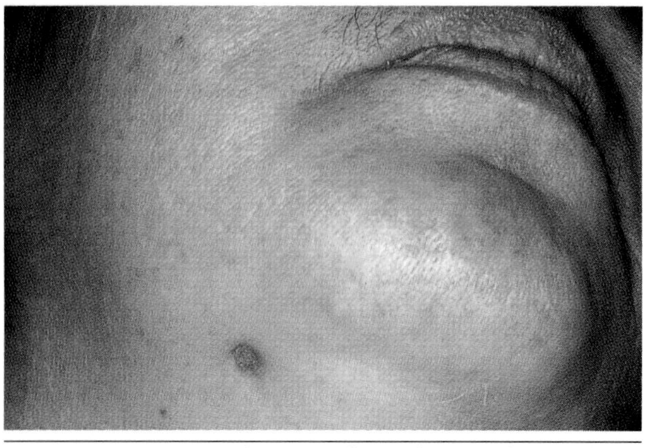

FIGURE 73–16B Fistulous tract from abscessed tooth draining to submental region. (Courtesy of slide collection of the late R.C.V. Robinson, M.D.)

rence for HSV-1 is the junction of the vermilion border and facial skin. These lesions are known of as "herpes labialis" ("cold sore" or "fever blister"). Typically, these lesions occur as multiple grouped vesicles with crusting.

Typical cold sore

Recurrent HSV-1 can also affect the oral mucosa which, in immunocompetent patients, most often is limited to the keratinized mucosa (attached gingiva and hard palate) (Figures 73–17A and 73–17B).

Annotated Bibliography

Scully C. Orofacial herpes simplex virus infections: current concepts in the epidemiology, pathogenesis, and treatment, and disorders in which the virus may be implicated. Oral Surg Oral Med Oral Pathol 1989;68:701–710.

This is an excellent review.

Weathers DR, Griffin JW. Intraoral ulcerations of recurrent herpes simplex and recurrent aphthae: two distinct clinical entities. J Am Dent Assoc 1970;81:81–88.

Griffin JW. Recurrent intraoral herpes simplex virus infection. Oral Surg Oral Med Oral Pathol 1965;19:209–213.

Varicella (Chickenpox)

Chickenpox represents the primary infection with the varicella-zoster virus (VZV:HHV-3); latency ensues, and recurrence is possible as herpes zoster. It is presumed that the virus is spread through air droplets or direct contact with active lesions. Most cases are symptomatic and occur between the ages of 5 and 9 years. The average incubation period is 15 days.

Oral lesions may precede cutaneous lesions.

Oral lesions are common and may precede the skin lesions. They begin as 3- to 4-mm white opaque vesicles, mainly on the palate and buccal mucosa, that rupture to form painful ulcers. The cytologic alterations are identical to those described for herpes simplex virus (HSV). Before current antiviral medications became available, the treatment of varicella was primarily symptomatic. Varicella-zoster immune globulin (VZIG) is used in immunocompromised patients to modify the clinical manifestations of the infection (Figure 73–18).

Annotated Bibliography

NIH Conference, Strauss SE, Ostrova JM, Inchauspa G, et al. Varicella-zoster virus infections. Biology, natural history, treatment and prevention. Ann Intern Med 1988; 108:221–237.

This is an excellent review.

Badger GR. Oral signs of chickenpox (varicella): report of two cases. J Dent Child 1980;47:349–351.

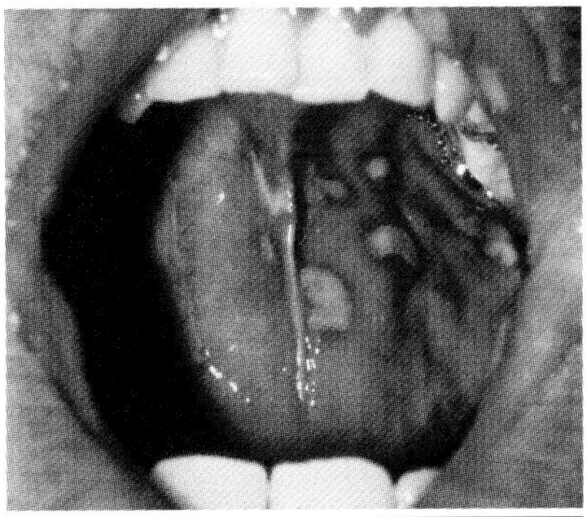

FIGURE 73–17A Primary herpes simplex of the mouth; frequently associated with severe pain, fever, cervical lymphadenopathy, and headaches.

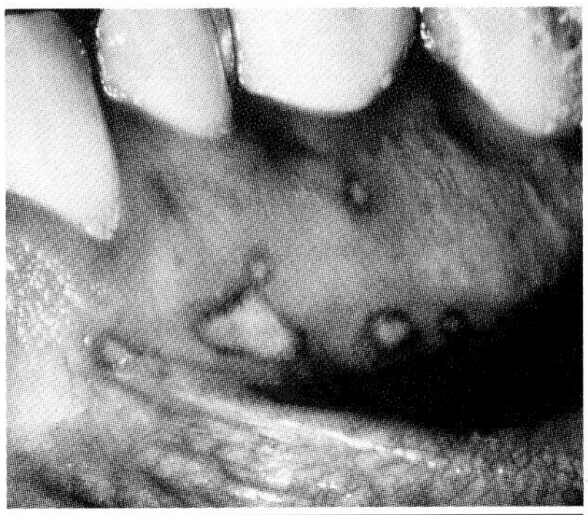

FIGURE 73–17B Relatively asymptomatic recurrent herpes simplex.

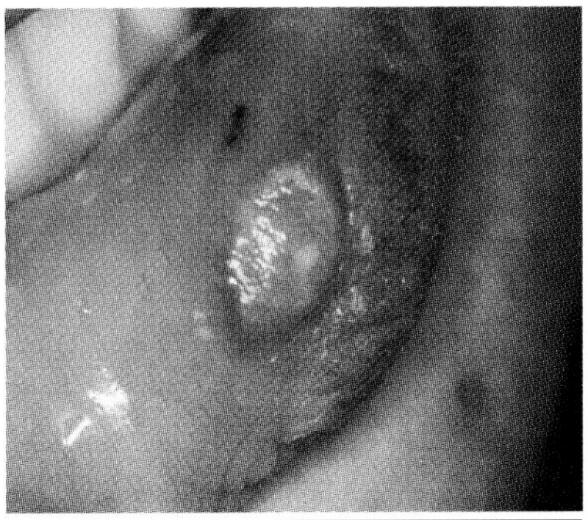

FIGURE 73–18 Varicella. This lesion may precede cutaneous lesions.

Recurrent Aphthous Stomatitis (Recurrent Aphthous Ulcerations; Canker Sores)

Common disease

Aphthous stomatitis is considered to be one of the most common diseases of the oral mucosa and affects, to some degree, 10 to 20% of the population. The exact etiology of this lesion is unknown and may be induced by various etiologic factors, which appear to fall into three general categories: primary immunodysregulation, decrease of the mucosal barrier, and increase in antigenic exposure (Figure 73–19).

Three main clinical types of aphthae can be distinguished. They are listed in Table 73–3.

Annotated Bibliography

Bagán JV, Sanchis JM, Milian MA, et al. Recurrent aphthous stomatitis. A study of the clinical characteristics of lesions in 93 cases. J Oral Pathol Med 1991;20:395–397.

Brice SL, Jester JD, Huff JC. Recurrent aphthous stomatitis. Curr Probl Dermatol 1991;3:107–127.

This is an excellent review.

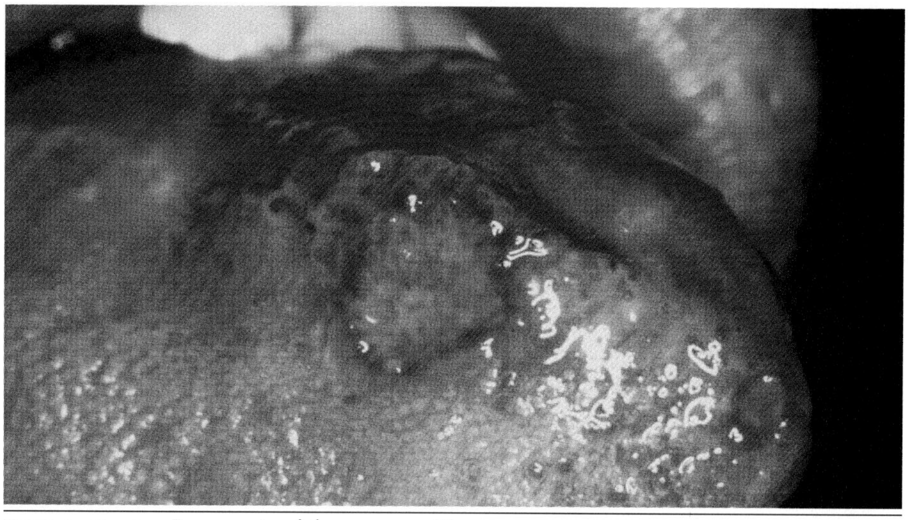

FIGURE 73–19 Recurrent aphthous stomatitis on tongue.

TABLE 73–3 Clinical Types of Aphthae

Minor aphthous ulcerations	The most common and typically one to five shallow rounded ulcers about 2 to 10 mm in diameter occurring mainly on nonmasticatory mucosa and heal without scarring in 7 to 14 days. These painful ulcers usually begin in childhood or adolescence, and the recurrence rate is highly variable.
Major aphthous ulcerations	Sutton's disease, periadenitis mucosa necrotica recurrens (PMNR), the most serious form, comprise about 10% of cases. Ulcerations may occur up to 3 cm in diameter and may persist for a month or more before slowly healing with fibrosis. Any oral surface may be affected, and recurrent episodes may continue for many years.
Herpetiform aphthous	Numerous minute (2-mm) ulcers which may coalesce into larger irregular ulcers in a field of bright erythema. Any mucosal surface may be affected.

Graft-versus-Host Disease

Graft-versus-host disease (GVHD) is a rare, complex multisystem disorder that develops in immunocompromised patients who have received histoincompatible lymphocytes from immunocompetent donors and who are incapable of rejecting them. Oral complications can be a major source of morbidity in patients receiving bone marrow transplants.

Acute GVHD

Acute GVHD affects about 50% of bone marrow transplant patients and is typically observed within the first 100 days after the transplantation procedure. The oral manifestations of acute GVHD have generally been described as painful desquamation and ulceration of the labial, buccal, lingual, palatal, and/or gingival mucosa and/or cheilitis and the presence of striae, lichenoid keratoses, white plaque-like patches, and erythema.

Painful desquamation and lichenoid striae

Chronic GVHD

Chronic GVHD develops in 25 to 45% of bone marrow transplant recipients and may evolve directly from acute GVHD, occur after resolution of acute GVHD, or occur de novo without a history of acute GVHD. Clinically and histologically, two different forms of chronic GVHD can be identified: (1) lichenoid GVHD, which appears as a fine, reticular network of white striae that resemble oral lichen planus, or in a more diffuse pattern of pinpoint white papules; (2) sclerodermoid GVHD, which frequently evolves from lichenoid chronic GVHD and is characterized by large confluent atrophic sclerotic areas analogous to scleroderma.

Lichen planus-like eruption

Sjögren-like syndrome

Sjögren-like syndrome is an important clinical feature which is seen in approximately 85% of patients with chronic GVHD and characterized by oral symptoms, including mucositis and xerostomia.

The histologic findings in oral tissues corresponding to the clinical manifestations of mucosal and salivary gland dysfunction are reported to provide reasonable high sensitivity and specificity. A histologic grading scheme for mucosal epithelium and salivary gland changes using a four-level grade (Table 73–4) is used at Johns Hopkins (Figure 73–20).

Annotated Bibliography

Kolbinson DA, Schubert MM, Flournoy N, et al. Early oral changes following bone marrow transplantation. Oral Surg Oral Med Oral Pathol 1988;66:130–138.

TABLE 73–4 Histologic Grading Scheme for Mucosal Epithelium and Salivary Gland Changes in Graft-versus-Host Disease

Grade	Feature
1	Mucosal epithelium: basal vacuolization, mild lymphocytic infiltration, mild exocytosis of lymphocytes into the epithelium
	Salivary gland: mild interstitial inflammation
2	Mucosal epithelium: basal vacuolization, dyskeratotic epithelial cells, satellite cell necrosis, moderately intense band of lymphocytes in submucosa, moderate exocytosis of lymphocytes into epithelium
	Salivary gland: mild acinar destruction, ductal dilatation, squamous metaplasia, mucus pooling, mild fibrosis, duct cell proliferation, periductal lymphocytic infiltrate
3	Mucosal epithelium: focal separation of epithelium from submucosa, heavy submucosal band of lymphocytes, dyskeratotic epithelial cells, exocytosis of lymphocytes into epithelium
	Salivary gland: marked interstitial lymphocytic infiltrate, diffuse destruction of ducts and acini
4	Mucosal epithelium: separation of epithelium from submucosa
	Salivary gland: nearly complete loss of acini, markedly dilated ducts, interstitial fibrosis with or without inflammation

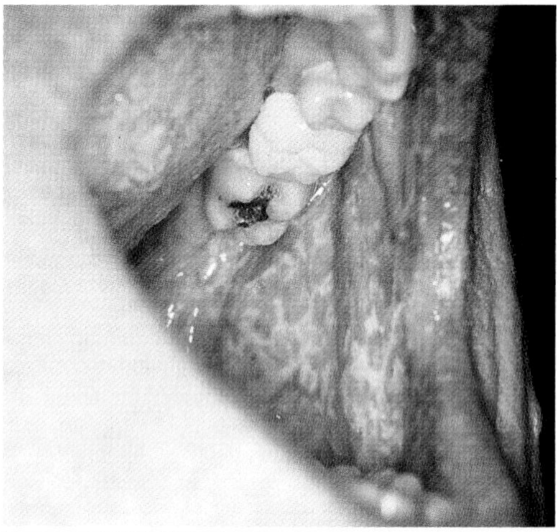

FIGURE 73–20 Graft-versus-host disease (chronic). Note lace-like lichenoid buccal mucosa involvement.

Sale GE, Shulman HM, et al. Oral and ophthalmologic pathology of graft versus host disease in man: predictive value of the lip biopsy. Hum Pathol 1981;12:1002–1030.

Horn TD, Rest EB, Mirowsky Y, et al. The significance of oral mucosal and salivary gland pathology after allogeneic bone marrow transplantation. Arch Dermatol 1995;131:964.

This is an excellent article reviewing our experience with this entity.

Erythema Multiforme

A blistering, ulcerative mucocutaneous disorder that appears to be a hypersensitivity response to certain infections and drugs (Figure 73–21). Approximately 50% of the cases are associated with a previous herpes simplex or *Mycoplasma pneumoniae* infection or exposure to any one of a variety of drugs, including antibiotics or analgesics.

Oral lesions generally occur on the anterior part of the mouth, mainly on the lips and labial mucosa. Lesions begin as erythematous patches which undergo epithelial necrosis, erosion, and ulcerations with irregular borders. Eventually, the buccal mucosa, tongue, and hard and soft palates can be involved.

Stevens-Johnson syndrome (erythema multiforme major) is an extensive and symptomatic febrile form of the disease (more common in children) and is usually triggered by drug rather than infection. Patients present with erosions and hemorrhagic crusts involving the lips and oral mucosa, although the conjunctiva, urethra, and genital and perianal areas may be affected (Figures 73–22A and 73–22B).

Toxic epidermal necrolysis is considered to be the most severe form of erythema multiforme and is characterized clinically by diffuse sloughing of a significant proportion of the skin and mucosal surfaces, producing a clinical situation analogous to an extensive burn. (See Chapter 67, "Toxic Epidermal Necrolysis," for further discussion.)

Annotated Bibliography

Lozada-Nur F, Gorsky M, Silverman S. Oral erythema multiforme: clinical observations and treatment of 95 patients. Oral Surg Oral Med Oral Pathol 1989;67:36–40.

Bastuji-Garin S, Rzany B, Stern RS, et al. Clinical classification of cases of toxic epidermal necrolysis, Stevens-Johnson syndrome, and erythema multiforme. Arch Dermatol 1993;129:92–95.

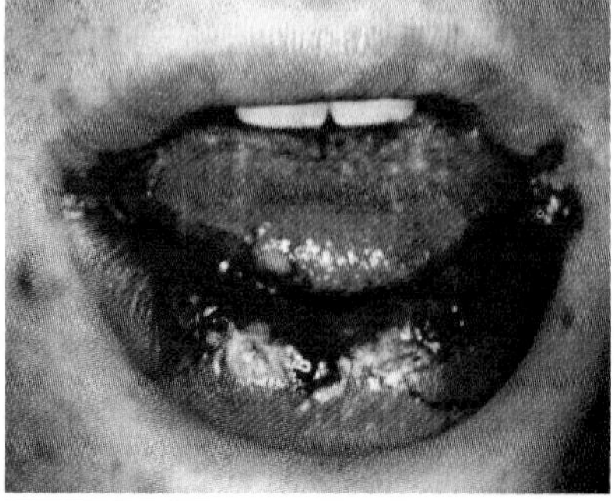

FIGURE 73–21 Erythema multiforme.

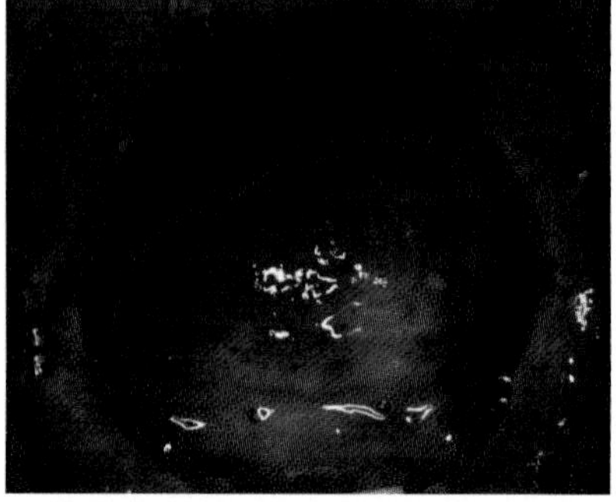

FIGURE 73–22A Oral lesions in toxic epidermal necrolysis. (See Chapter 67, "Toxic Epidermal Necrolysis," for further discussion.)

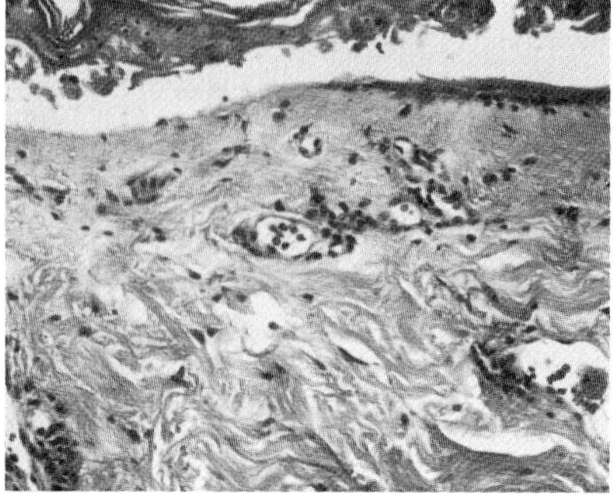

FIGURE 73–22B Biopsy showing epidermal necrosis of oral mucosa in toxic epidermal necrolysis.

Schofield JK, Tatnall FM, Leigh IM. Recurrent erythema multiforme: clinical features and treatment in a large series of patients. Br J Dermatol 1993;128:542–545.

These three articles provide excellent descriptions and treatment of the oral features of these hypersensitivity reactions.

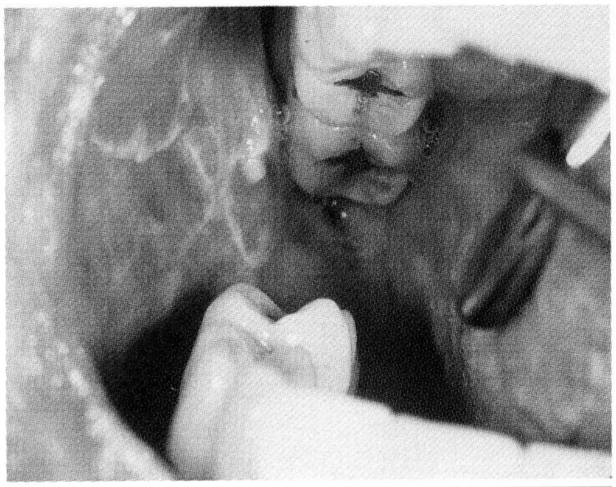

FIGURE 73–23 Lichen planus.

Lichen Planus

Lichen planus is a common disorder of oral mucous membranes of unknown etiology. Most cases occur in middle-aged adults, occurring mainly in women. Most patients with skin involvement have oral involvement; however, many patients present with only oral lichen planus. Oral lesions present mainly in two clinical forms, including a common reticular form and a less common erosive form. Lesions occur mainly in the buccal mucosa and lateral border of the tongue, although any intraoral site may be affected (Figure 73–23).

Reticular lichen planus presents in a characteristic pattern of interlacing white lines (Wickham's striae). This form of lichen planus usually causes no symptoms and generally involves the buccal mucosa bilaterally.

Erosive lichen planus is usually symptomatic and presents as large erosions with an irregular outline. When only the gingival mucosa is involved, the reaction pattern produced is designated "desquamative gingivitis." (See Lichen Planus in Chapter 70, "Miscellaneous Diseases," for discussion.)

Annotated Bibliography

Thorn JJ, et al. Course of various clinical forms of oral lichen planus. A prospective follow-up study of 611 patients. J Oral Pathol 1988;17:213–218.

Silverman S. Lichen planus. Curr Opin Dent 1991;1:769–772.

Jungell P. Oral lichen planus: a review. Int J Oral Maxillofac Surg 1991;20:129–135.

Oral Hairy Leukoplakia

Oral hairy leukoplakia (OHL) is considered to be the most common and specific oral manifestation of acquired immunodeficiency syndrome (AIDS). Studies have shown that over 80% of patients with OHL develop AIDS within 31 months (Figure 73–24). Oral hairy leukoplakia can occasionally be seen in immunocompetent patients; however, most cases occur in immunocompromised patients. The Epstein-Barr virus (EBV) is thought to be the cause of this lesion, which occurs mainly on the lateral border of the tongue; however, other mucosal sites can be involved. Clinically, the lesions vary from soft white plaques to thickened and furrowed areas of leukoplakia exhibiting a "hairy" surface.

Histologically, the lesions show parakeratosis, acanthosis, and areas of vacuolated keratinocytes in the upper spinous layer. The parakeratin layer may contain a candidal infestation with only a scarce inflammatory reaction in the lamina propria. See Chapter 64, "Human Immunodeficiency Virus," for discussion.)

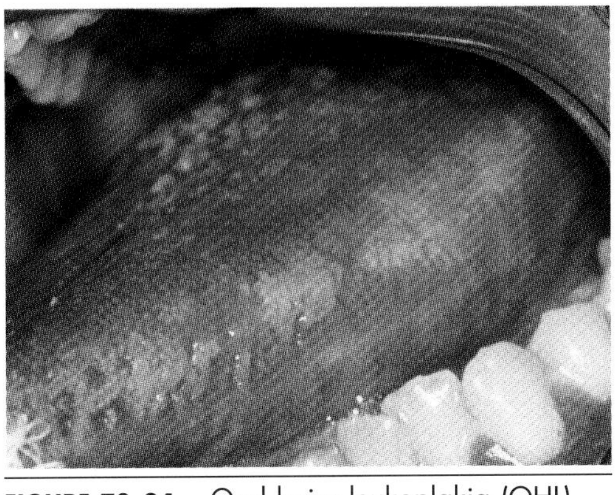

FIGURE 73–24 Oral hairy leukoplakia (OHL).

Annotated Bibliography

Greenspan D, Conant M, Silverman S, et al. Oral "hairy" leukoplakia, in male homosexuals: evidence of association with both papillomavirus and a herpes group virus. Lancet 1984;2:831–834.

Greenspan D, Greenspan JS, Hears NG. Relation of hairy leukoplakia to infection with human immunodeficiency virus and risk of developing AIDS. J Invest Dis 1987;155:475–481.

Greenspan D, Greenspan JS. Significance of oral hairy leukoplakia. Oral Surg Oral Med Oral Pathol 1992;73:151–154.

Syphilis

Figure 73–25 shows primary syphilitic chancres. (See Chapter 55, "Syphilis," for discussion).

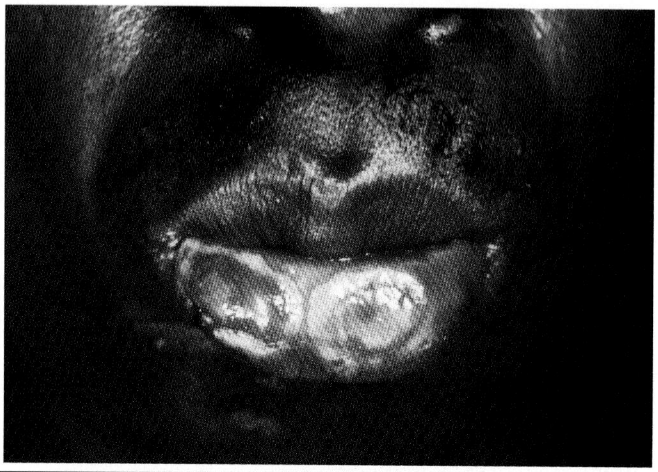

FIGURE 73–25 Primary syphilitic chancres of the lower lip. (For further discussion, see Chapter 55, "Syphilis.")

Index

B

C

D

F

G

H

I

M

N

V

W

X

Y

Z